S0-CPC-251

INTERACTIVE CASEBOOK SERIES[SM]

CRIMINAL LAW

A Contemporary Approach

FOURTH EDITION

Russell L. Weaver
PROFESSOR OF LAW AND DISTINGUISHED UNIVERSITY SCHOLAR
UNIVERSITY OF LOUISVILLE, LOUIS D. BRANDEIS SCHOOL OF LAW

John M. Burkoff
PROFESSOR OF LAW EMERITUS
UNIVERSITY OF PITTSBURGH SCHOOL OF LAW

Catherine Hancock
GEOFFREY C. BIBLE & MURRAY H. BRING PROFESSOR OF CONSTITUTIONAL LAW
TULANE UNIVERSITY SCHOOL OF LAW

The publisher is not engaged in rendering legal or other professional advice and this publication is not a substitute for the advice of an attorney. If you require legal or other expert advice, you should seek the services of a competent attorney or other professional.

Interactive Casebook Series is a servicemark registered in the U.S. Patent and Trademark Office.

444 Cedar Street, Suite 700
St. Paul, MN 55101
1-877-888-1330

Printed in the United States of America

ISBN: 978-1-68467-902-7

To Ben, Kate and Laurence, with love, ***RLW***

To Nancy, Amy & Sean, David & Emmy, Emma, Molly, Hannah, and Cyrus, with love, ***JMB***

To Peter, Elizabeth, Caitlin, and Margaret, with love, ***CH***

Preface to the Fourth Edition

This interactive criminal law casebook continues the tradition of our prior criminal law casebook (which went through four editions), but enhanced that tradition by moving to an interactive format.

As with the prior books, our primary goal was to create a "teacher's book"—a book that contains thought provoking problems (referred to as "hypos" in the Interactive Casebook Series) designed to stimulate thought and produce interesting classroom discussion. The hypos are woven throughout the chapters and are designed to help students learn doctrine, illuminate trends in the law, and ultimately produce better learning. A secondary goal was to include a focus on teaching "skills." Some of the problems place students in practical situations that they are likely to encounter in practice, and therefore encourage students to think about how they might handle those situations in real-life.

As with any book, tradeoffs are necessary. In order to prevent the book from being unduly voluminous and unwieldy, we have chosen not to include encyclopedic notes and references like those found in other books. The inclusion of too many notes impedes learning. Moreover, in the criminal law area, students have numerous high-quality secondary sources available to them, and students can consult those sources for expanded scholarly discussions of the law. By limiting the scope of notes, we were able to include more hypotheticals and to provide greater opportunity for critical thinking.

By shifting to the Interactive Casebook format, we were able to provide students with live hyperlinks and the ability to access the material interactively. In addition, we were able to provide students will find a variety of call-out boxes in the text of the principal cases, many of which provide "food for thought" questions that will help them to understand how to address the more complex questions that arise in the "points for discussion" material and in the hypotheticals. The call-out boxes also provide information about topics such as the attorneys' strategies and links to online sources that illustrate various facets of the litigation.

We welcome input and feedback on this book.

RLW, JMB & CH

Features of This Casebook

Throughout the book you will find various text boxes on either side of the page. These boxes provide information that will help you to understand a case or cause you to think more deeply about an issue.

For More Information These boxes point you to resources to consult for more information on a subject.

What's That? These boxes explain the meaning of special legal terms that appear in the main text. Black's Law Dictionary definitions may be accessed by clicking on the hyperlinked term in the text.

Take Note Here you will be prompted to take special notice of something that deserves further thought or attention.

See It These boxes point you to visual information that is relevant to the material in the text.

It's Latin to Me The law is fond of Latin terms and phrases; when you encounter these for the first time, this box will explain their meaning.

Food for Thought These boxes pose questions that prompt you to think about issues raised by the material.

Practice Pointer Here you will find advice relevant to legal practice typically inspired by the actions (or inactions) of legal counsel in the cases or simply prompted by an important issue being discussed.

FYI A self-explanatory category that shares useful or simply interesting information relevant to material in the text.

Hear It These boxes point you to an audio file that is relevant to the material in the text.

Go Online If there are relevant online resources that are worth consulting in relation to any matter being discussed, these boxes will direct you to them.

Test Your Knowledge These boxes contain hyperlinks to online assessment questions that will help you test your understanding of the material in each chapter.

Major Themes A discussion of some of the deeper themes and issues pertaining to the topic covered in that chapter.

Make the Connection When concepts or discussions that pertain to information covered in other law school courses appear in a case or elsewhere in this text, often you will find this text box to indicate the course in which you can study those topics. Here you may also be prompted to connect information in the current case to material that you have covered elsewhere in this course.

Table of Contents

Chapter 6 *Attempt* 209

Chapter 7 *Conspiracy* 247

Chapter 13 *Excuses* 577

Table of Cases

The principal cases are in **bold** type. Cases cited or discussed in the text are in roman type. References are to pages. Cases cited in principal cases and within other quoted materials are not included.

CRIMINAL LAW

A Contemporary Approach

FOURTH EDITION

Chapter 1

The Purposes of the Criminal Law

The criminal law is unique because it is premised on the idea of punishing those who violate legal norms. Permissible punishments can include fines, imprisonment, or, in extreme cases, capital punishment. In this chapter, we explore the underlying justifications for imposing punitive sanctions, and the appropriateness (and defensibility) of such sanctions. What function does the penalty of punishment serve? How does that function differ from the purposes served by the law of tort?

A. Case Study

Regina v. Dudley & Stephens

14 Q.B.D. 273 [1884].

Lord Coleridge, C.J. The two prisoners, Thomas Dudley and Edwin Stephens, were indicted for the murder of Richard Parker on the high seas. They were tried before my brother Huddleston at Exeter, and the jury returned a special verdict, the legal effect of which we are now to pronounce judgment.

On July 5, 1884, the prisoners, Thomas Dudley and Edward Stephens, with one Brooks, all able-bodied English seamen, and the deceased an English boy, between seventeen and eighteen years of age, the crew of an English yacht, were cast away in a storm on the high seas 16,000 miles from the Cape of Good Hope, and were compelled to put into an open boat. They had no water and no food, except two 1 lb. tins of turnips, and for three days they had nothing else to subsist upon. On the fourth day they caught a small turtle, upon which they subsisted for a few days, and this was the only food they had up to the twentieth day when the act now in question was committed. On the twelfth day the remains of the turtle were entirely consumed, and for the next eight days they had nothing to eat. They had no fresh water, except such rain as they from time to time caught in their oilskin capes. The boat was drifting on the ocean, and was probably more than 1,000 miles away from land. On the eighteenth day, when they had been seven days without food and five without water, the prisoners spoke to Brooks as to what should be done if no succor came, and suggested that someone should be sacrificed to save the rest, but Brooks dissented, and the boy, to whom they were understood to refer, was not consulted. On the 24th of July, the day before the act now in question, the prisoner Dudley proposed to Stephens and Brooks that lots should be cast to determine who should be put to death to save the rest, but Brooks refused to consent, and it was not put to the boy, and there was no drawing of lots. The prisoners spoke of their families, and suggested it would be better to kill the boy that their lives should be saved, and Dudley proposed that if there was no vessel in sight by the morrow morning, the boy should be killed. Next day, the 25th of July, no vessel appearing, Dudley told Brooks that he had better go and have a sleep, and made signs to Stephens and Brooks that the boy had better be killed. The prisoner Stephens agreed to the act, but Brooks dissented. The boy was then lying at the bottom of the boat quite helpless and extremely weakened by famine and by drinking sea water, and unable to make any resistance, nor did he assent to being killed. The prisoner Dudley offered a prayer asking forgiveness for them all if either of them should be tempted to commit a rash act, and that their souls might be saved. Dudley, with the assent of Stephens, went to the boy, and telling him that his time was come, put a knife unto his throat and killed him then and there; the three men fed upon the body and blood of the boy for four days; On the fourth day after the act had been committed the boat was picked up by a passing vessel, and the prisoners were rescued, still alive, but in the lowest state of prostration. They were carried to the port of Falmouth, and committed for trial at Exeter. If the men had not fed upon the body of the boy they would probably not have survived to be so picked up and rescued, but would within the four days have died of famine. The boy, being in a much weaker condition, was likely to have died before them. At the time of the act in question there was no sail in sight, nor any reasonable prospect of relief. Under these circumstances there appeared to the prisoners every probability that unless they then fed or very soon fed upon the boy or one of themselves they would die of starvation. There was no appreciable chance of saving life except by killing someone for the others to eat. Assuming any necessity to kill anybody, there was no greater necessity for killing the boy than any of the other three men. But whether upon the whole matter by the jurors found the killing of Richard Parker by Dudley and Stephens be felony and murder the jurors are ignorant, and pray the advice of the Court thereupon, and if upon the whole matter the Court shall be of opinion that the killing of Richard Parker be felony and murder, then the jurors say that Dudley and Stephens were each guilty of felony and murder as alleged on the indictment."

From these facts, it appears that the prisoners were subject to terrible temptation, to sufferings which might break down the bodily power of the strongest man, and try the conscience of the best. Other details yet more harrowing, facts still more loathsome and appalling, were presented to the jury, and are recorded in my learned Brother's notes. But nevertheless the prisoners put to death a weak and unoffending boy upon the chance of preserving their own lives by feeding upon his flesh and blood after he was killed, and with the certainty of depriving him of any possible chance of survival. The verdict finds that "if the men had not fed upon the body of the boy they would *probably* not have survived," and that "the boy being in a much weaker condition was *likely* to have died before them." They might possibly have been picked up next day by a passing ship; they might possibly not have been picked up at all; in either case it is obvious that the killing of the boy would have been an unnecessary and profitless act. It is found that the boy was incapable of resistance, and made none; and it is not even suggested that his death was due to any violence on his part attempted against, or even so much as feared by, those who killed him. Under these circumstances the jury say that they are ignorant whether those who killed him were guilty of murder, and have referred it to this Court to determine what is the legal consequence which follows from the facts which they have found.

The question is whether killing under the circumstances set forth in the verdict be or not be murder. The contention that it could be anything else was, to the minds of us all, both new and strange, and we stopped the Attorney General in his negative argument in order that we might hear what could be said in support of a proposition which appeared to us to be at once dangerous, immoral, and opposed to all legal principle and analogy. It is said that in order to save your own life you may lawfully take away the life of another, when that other is neither attempting nor threatening yours, nor is guilty of any illegal act whatever towards you or anyone else. But if these definitions be looked at they will not be found to sustain this contention. The doctrine receives no support from the great authority of Lord Hale. In his view the necessity which justified homicide is that only which has always been and is now considered a justification. Lord Hale regarded the private necessity which justified, and alone justified, the taking the life of another for the safeguard of one's own to be, what is commonly called "self-defence."

Make the Connection

In Chapters 8 and 12, we shall see that self-defense can provide a "justification" defense to various crimes, including homicide. However, we will also study the requirements for the invocation of this defense.

We are dealing with a case of private homicide, not one imposed upon men in the service of their Sovereign and in the defence of their country. The deliberate killing of this unoffending and unresisting boy was clearly murder, unless the killing can be justified by some well-recognised excuse admitted by the law. There was no such excuse, unless the killing was justified by what has been called "necessity." But the temptation to the act which existed here was not what the law has ever called necessity. Nor is this to be regretted. Though law and morality are not the same, and many things may be immoral which are not necessarily illegal, yet the absolute divorce of law from morality would be of fatal consequence; and such divorce would follow if the temptation to murder in this case were to be held by law and absolute defence of it. It is not so. To preserve one's life is generally speaking a duty, but it may be the plainest and the highest duty to sacrifice it. War is full of instances in which it is a man's duty not to live, but to die. The duty, in case of shipwreck, of a captain to his crew, of the crew to the passengers, of soldiers to women and children, as in the noble case of the *Birkenhead*; these duties impose on men the moral necessity, not of the preservation, but of the sacrifice of their lives for others, for which there is no country, least of all, it is to be hoped, in England, will men ever shrink, as indeed, they have not shrunk. It is not correct, therefore, to say that there is any absolute or unqualified necessity to preserve one's life. "Necesse est ut eam, non ut vivam," is a saying of a Roman office quoted by Lord Bacon. It would be a very easy and cheap display of commonplace learning to quote from Cicero, from Euripides, passage after passage, in which the duty of dying for others has been laid down in glowing and emphatic language

Food for Thought

Note the court's discussion of "morality" and its relationship to the criminal law. Is morality the basis on which punishment is imposed on those convicted of crime? Can you define the term "morality?" What is the basis for saying that something is "moral" or "immoral?" Religion? Societal norms? Is morality "absolute" or "relative?"

as resulting from the principles of heathen ethics; it is enough in a Christian country to remind ourselves of the Great Example whom we profess to follow. It is not needful to point out the awful danger of admitting the principle which has been contended for. Who is to be the judge of this sort of necessity? By what measure is the comparative value of lives to be measured? Is it to be strength, or intellect, or what? It is plain that the principle leaves to him who is to profit by it to determine the necessity which will justify him in deliberately taking another's life to save his own. In this case the weakest, the youngest, the most unresisting, was chosen. Was it more necessary to kill him than one of the grown men? The answer must be "No"—

So spake the Fiend, and with necessity The Tyrant's plea, excused his devilish deeds.

It is not suggested that in this particular case the deeds were "devilish," but it is quite plain that such a principle once admitted might be made the legal cloak for unbridled passion and atrocious crime. There is no safe path for judges to tread but to ascertain the law to the best of their ability and to declare it according to their judgment; and if in any case the law appears to be too severe on individuals, to leave it to the Sovereign to exercise that prerogative of mercy which the Constitution has intrusted to the hands fittest to dispense it.

It must not be supposed that in refusing to admit temptation to be an excuse for crime it is forgotten how terrible the temptation was; how awful the suffering; how hard in such trials to keep the judgment straight and the conduct pure. We are often compelled to set up standards we cannot reach ourselves, and to lay down rules which we could not ourselves satisfy. But a man has no right to declare temptation to be an excuse, though he might have yielded to it, nor allow compassion for the criminal to change or weaken in any manner the legal definition of the crime. It is therefore our duty to declare that the prisoners' act in this case was willful murder, that the facts as stated in the verdict are no legal justification of the homicide; and to say that in our unanimous opinion the prisoners are upon this special verdict guilty of murder.

FYI

The death sentence was later commuted to six months in prison. Stephens and Brooks remained in England where they died poor. Dudley emigrated to Sydney, Australia where he died of the plague in 1900. For an extensive discussion of this case, and other similar cases, *see* A.W. BRIAN SIMPSON, CANNIBALISM AND THE COMMON LAW: THE STORY OF THE TRAGIC LAST VOYAGE OF THE MIGNONETTE AND THE STRANGE LEGAL PROCEEDINGS TO WHICH IT GAVE RISE 288–89, 296–98 (1984).

[The Court then proceeded to pass sentence of death upon the prisoners].

Points for Discussion

a. Imposing Punishment

Given the circumstances that they were facing, should Dudley & Stephens have been subjected to punishment at all? Why? Why not? If punishment was appropriate, given the circumstances, what punishment should have been imposed? Was the capital punishment sentence (that the House of Lords purported to impose, but which was not ultimately imposed) appropriate? Was it appropriate to later commute the sentence to six months in prison?

b. Customs & Public Opinion

> **FYI**
>
> The public was so accepting of cannibalism that "public sympathy in the sailing ports was unquestionably behind Dudley and Stephens," and Parker's older brother came by the jail to shake hands with Dudley and Stephens "in a symbolic gesture of understanding." *See* Berring at 256–57.

Should a court consider customs, practices, and public opinion, when deciding upon a criminal sentence? Historical evidence suggests that there was widespread acceptance of maritime cannibalism at the time this case was decided: In most instances, when a ship floundered, the crew drowned. J.R. Spencer, *Book Review*, CANNIBALISM AND THE COMMON LAW, 51 U. CHI. L. REV. 1265 (1984). Those who were fortunate enough to make it into a life boat were likely to die of hunger and thirst, and it was not uncommon for them to resort to cannibalism in order to survive. *Id.* Indeed, there were "were a number of well-authenticated instances of survivors actually killing one of their number in order to eat him." *Id.* By and large, the public was oblivious to the plight of seaman. *Id.* Indeed, public acceptance of cannibalism was so widespread that Dudley "frankly described the whole ordeal to his rescuers and, on arriving in England, to government officials. Clearly, Captain Dudley's attitude was that such things happen." Robert C. Berring, *Book Review*, CANNIBALISM AND THE COMMON LAW, 73 CALIF. L. REV. 252 (1985). Should the public's acceptance of cannibalism, and the public's opinion of the case, have had any bearing on the result?

c. Selection of Victim

Should it matter how Parker was chosen as the victim? Although cannibalism was accepted at the time of the case, it was generally agreed that the stranded sailors should draw straws to determine who would be put to death rather than simply choosing a victim. John Friedl, *Book Review*, A.W. BRIAN SIMPSON, CANNIBALISM AND THE COMMON LAW: THE STORY OF THE TRAGIC LAST VOYAGE OF THE MIGNONETTE AND THE STRANGE LEGAL PROCEEDINGS TO WHICH IT GAVE RISE, 83 MICH. L. REV. 702 (1985). However, in the actual case, the evidence showed that Parker was near death anyway, and the decision to kill him was made in order "to save as much blood as possible to drink." *Id.* Indeed, Dudley actually suggested that the stranded sailors draw straws, but abandoned that idea since they believed that Parker would die anyway, as well as because two of the others were "family men whose death would condemn their wives and children to a lifetime of destitution." *Id.* Even if the law accepts the defense of necessity, should Dudley and Stephens have been condemned for deciding to kill Parker rather than drawing straws to determine who should die?

d. *Holmes* Case

In an American case, *United States v. Holmes*, 26 F. Cas. 360 (C.C.E.D.Pa. 1842), a ship struck an iceberg off Newfoundland and immediately foundered. The first mate, 8 seamen, of whom the prisoner was one (these 9 being the entire remainder of the crew), and 32 passengers, in all 41 persons, scrambled indiscriminately into the long-boat. The remaining 31 passengers were left behind to drown. When the long-boat began to leak, and the passengers were deemed to be in great jeopardy, the crew decided to throw 14 passengers overboard. The court held that:

> The passenger stands in a position different from that of the officers and seamen. It is the sailor who must encounter the hardships and perils of the voyage. Nor can this relation be changed when the ship is lost by tempest or other danger of the sea, and all on board have betaken themselves, for safety, to the small boats; for imminence of danger can not absolve from duty. The sailor is bound, as before, to undergo whatever hazard is necessary to preserve the boat and the passengers. Should the emergency become so extreme as to call for the sacrifice of life, there can be no reason why the law does not still remain the same. The passenger, not being bound either to labour or to incur the risk of life, cannot be bound to sacrifice his existence to preserve the sailor's. If the source of the danger has been obvious, and destruction ascertained to be certainly about to arrive, though at a future time, there should be consultation, and some mode of selection fixed, by which those in equal relations may have equal chance for their life. When the selection has been made by lots, the victim yields of course to his fate, or, if he resist, force may be employed to coerce submission.

The convicted crew member was sentenced to imprisonment at hard labour for six months, and ordered to pay a fine of $20. The appellate court affirmed the conviction noting that: "Considerable sympathy having been excited in favour of Holmes, by the popular press, an effort was made by several persons, and particularly by the Seamen's Friend Society, to obtain a pardon from the executive. President Tyler refused, however, to grant any pardon. The penalty was subsequently remitted."

Food for Thought

Was the punishment in *Holmes* proportionate to the crime, and would it be adequate to prevent future sailors from making similar decisions? In other words, faced with the possibility of death (if some passengers are not thrown overboard), or a prison sentence of six months, is the threat of the sentence sufficiently severe to prevent the sailors from throwing the passengers overboard?

B. Purposes of Punishment

Food for Thought

If the criminal law provides a means of social control, enforced through the medium of punishment, how does society decide which actions need to be controlled?

Individuals who violate the norms established by the criminal law can be subjected to fines, imprisonment and possibly capital punishment. In addition, a criminal conviction carries a moral stigma that can have a variety of other damaging effects upon the convicted person. In this respect, the criminal law differs from tort law. Although tort law can also impose consequences for the purpose of punishment (*e.g.*, sometimes, it imposes punitive damages), and criminal law can be like tort law in requiring compensation to those who have been injured (*e.g.*, some laws require the payment of restitution), criminal law differs from tort because it generally imposes punishment rather than compensation to achieve its objectives.

In imposing punishment, a rational system of criminal justice might attempt to accomplish a number of different objectives, including retribution, deterrence (which includes both "specific deterrence" and "general deterrence"), restraint (or "incapacitation") and rehabilitation. In this section, we think about these objectives and consider whether they provide sufficient justification for imposing punishment.

United States v. Bergman

416 F.Supp. 496, 499 (S.D.N.Y.1976).

FRANKEL, DISTRICT JUDGE. Defendant is being sentenced upon his plea of guilty to two counts of an 11-count indictment. Defendant appeared until the last couple of years to be a man of unimpeachably high character, attainments, and distinction. A doctor of divinity and an ordained rabbi, he has been acclaimed by people around the world for his works of public philanthropy, private charity, and leadership in educational enterprises. Scores of letters have come to the court from across this and other countries reporting debts of personal gratitude to him for numerous acts of extraordinary generosity. (The court has also received a petition, with fifty-odd signatures, in which the signers, based upon learning acquired as newspaper readers, denounce the defendant and urge a severe sentence.) In addition to his good works, defendant has managed to amass considerable wealth in the ownership and operation of nursing homes, in real estate ventures, and in a course of substantial investments. Beginning about two years ago, investigations of nursing homes in this area, including questions of fraudulent claims for Medicaid funds, drew to a focus upon this defendant among several others. The results that concern us were the present indictment and two state indictments. After extensive pretrial proceedings, defendant embarked upon elaborate plea negotiations with prosecutors. As part of the plea arrangements, it is expected that the prison sentence imposed by this court will comprise the total covering the state as well as the federal convictions.

The plea on Count One (carrying a maximum of five years in prison and a $10,000 fine) confesses defendant's knowing and willful participation in a scheme to defraud the United States in various ways, including the presentation of wrongfully padded claims for payments under the Medicaid program to defendant's nursing homes. Count Three, for which the guilty plea carries a theoretical maximum of three more years in prison and another $5,000 fine, is a somewhat more "technical" charge. Here, defendant admits to having participated in the filing of a partnership return which was false and fraudulent in failing to list people who had bought partnership interests from him in one of his nursing homes, had paid for such interests, and had made certain capital withdrawals. The conspiracy to defraud is by no means the worst of its kind; it is by no means as flagrant or extensive as has been portrayed in the press; it is evidently less grave than other nursing-home wrongs for which others have been convicted or publicized. At the same time, the sentence is imposed for two federal felonies including, as the more important, a knowing and purposeful conspiracy to mislead and defraud the Federal Government.

This court agrees that this defendant should not be sent to prison for "rehabilitation." Imprisonment is punishment. If someone must be imprisoned for other, valid reasons we should seek to make rehabilitative resources available to him or her. But the goal of rehabilitation cannot fairly serve in itself as grounds for the sentence to confinement.

Equally clearly, this defendant should not be confined to incapacitate him. He is not dangerous. It is most improbable that he will commit similar, or any, offenses in the future. There is no need for "specific deterrence."

Two sentencing considerations demand a prison sentence in this case: First, the aim of general deterrence, the effort to discourage similar wrongdoing by others through a reminder that the law's warnings are real and that the grim consequence of imprisonment is likely to follow from crimes of deception for gain like those defendant has admitted. Second, the related, but not identical, concern that any lesser penalty would, in the words of the Model Penal Code, s 7.01(1)(c), "depreciate the seriousness of the defendant's crime."

Resisting the first of these propositions, defense counsel invoke Immanuel Kant's axiom that "one man ought never to be dealt with merely as a means subservient to the purposes of another."[4] In a more novel effort, counsel urge that a sentence for general deterrence "would violate the Eighth Amendment proscription against cruel and unusual punishment." If general deterrence as a sentencing purpose were to be outlawed, as against a near unanimity of views among state and federal jurists, the bolt would have to come from a place higher than this. As for Dr. Kant, a criminal punished in the interest of general deterrence is not being employed "merely as a means." Reading Kant to mean that every man must be deemed more than the instrument of others, and must "always be treated as an end in himself," the humane principle is not offended here. Each of us is served by the enforcement of the law not least a person like the defendant in this case, whose wealth and privileges, so long enjoyed, are so much founded

4 Quoting from I. KANT, PHILOSOPHY OF LAW 1986 (Hastie Trans. 1887).

upon law. More broadly, we are driven regularly in our ultimate interests as members of the community to use ourselves and each other, in war and in peace, for social ends. One who has transgressed against the criminal laws is certainly among the more fitting candidates for a role of this nature. This is no arbitrary selection. Warned in advance of the prospect, the transgressor has chosen, in the law's premises, "between keeping the law required for society's protection or paying the penalty."

But the whole business, defendant argues is guesswork; we are by no means certain that deterrence "works." The position is somewhat overstated; there is, in fact, some reasonably "scientific" evidence for the efficacy of criminal sanctions as deterrents, at least as against some kinds of crimes.[9] Moreover, the time is not yet here when all we can "know" must be quantifiable and digestible by computers. The shared wisdom of generations teaches meaningfully, if somewhat amorphously, that the utilitarians have a point; we do, indeed, lapse often into rationality and act to seek pleasure and avoid pain. It would be better, to be sure, if we had more certainty and precision. Lacking these comforts, we continue to include among our working hypotheses a belief (with some concrete evidence in its support) that crimes like those in this case deliberate, purposeful, continuing, non-impulsive, and committed for profit are among those most likely to be generally deterrable by sanctions most shunned by those exposed to temptation.[11]

The idea of avoiding depreciation of the seriousness of the offense implicates two or three thoughts, not always perfectly clear or universally agreed upon, beyond the idea of deterrence. It should be proclaimed by the court's judgment that the offenses are grave, not minor or purely technical. Some attention must be paid to the demand for equal justice; it will not do to leave the penalty of imprisonment a dead letter as against "privileged" violators while it is employed regularly, and with vigor, against others. There probably is in these conceptions an element of retributiveness. Retribution, so denominated, is in some disfavor as a reason for punishment. It remains a factor, however, as Holmes perceived,[12] and as is known to anyone who talks to judges, lawyers, defendants, or people generally. It may become more palatable, and probably more humanely understood, under the rubric of "deserts" or "just deserts."[13] However the concept is formulated, we have not yet reached a state, supposing we ever should, in which the infliction of punishments for crime may be divorced generally from ideas of blameworthiness, recompense, and proportionality.

Resisting prison, defense counsel make proposals for what they call a "constructive," and therefore a "preferable" form of "behavioral sanction." One is a plan for Dr. Bergman to create and run a program of Jewish vocational and religious high school training. The other is for him to take charge of a "Committee on Holocaust Studies," concerned with education at the secondary school level. A third suggestion was that Dr. Bergman might be ordered to work as

---

9 See, e. g., F. ZIMRING AND G. HAWKINS, DETERRENCE 168–71, 282 (1973).

11 For some supporting evidence that "white-collar" offenses are somewhat specially deterrable, see Chambliss, Types of Deviance and the Effectiveness of Legal Sanctions, 1967 WIS.L.REV. 703, 708–10.

12 See O. HOLMES, COMMON LAW 41–42, 45 (1881).

13 See A. VON HIRSCH, DOING JUSTICE 45–55 (1976); see also N. MORRIS, THE FUTURE OF IMPRISONMENT 73–77 (1974).

a volunteer in some agency as a visitor and aide to the sick and the otherwise incapacitated. The proposal was that he could read, provide various forms of physical assistance, and otherwise give comfort to afflicted people.

No one can doubt either the worthiness of these proposals or Dr. Bergman's ability to make successes of them. But both of the carefully formulated "sanctions" involve work of an honorific nature, not unlike that done in other projects to which the defendant has devoted himself in the past. It is difficult to conceive of them as "punishments" at all. The more recent proposal is somewhat more suitable in character, but it is still an insufficient penalty. The seriousness of the crimes demand something more than "requiring" him to lend his talents and efforts to further philanthropic enterprises. It remains open to him to pursue the interesting suggestions later on as a matter of unforced personal choice.

In cases like this, the decision of greatest moment is whether to imprison or not. As reflected in the submissions for defendant, the prospect of the closing prison doors is the most appalling concern; the feeling is that the length of the sojourn is a lesser question once that threshold is passed. Nevertheless, the setting of a term remains to be accomplished. In some respects it is a subject even more perplexing, unregulated, and unprincipled. Days and months and years are countable with a sound of exactitude. But there can be no exactitude in the deliberations from which a number emerges. Without pretending to a nonexistent precision, the court notes at least the major factors.

The criminal behavior is blatant in character and unmitigated by any suggestion of necessitous circumstance or other pressures difficult to resist. However metaphysicians may conjure with issues about free will, it is a fundamental premise of our efforts to do criminal justice that competent people, possessed of their faculties, make choices and are accountable for them. In this sometimes harsh light, the case of this defendant is among the clearest and least relieved. Viewed against the maxima Congress ordained, and against the run of sentences in other federal criminal cases, it calls for more than a token sentence.[14]

Defendant's illustrious public life and works are in his favor, though diminished, of course, by what this case discloses. This is a first, probably a last, conviction. Defendant is 64 years old and in imperfect health, though by no means so ill, that he could be expected to suffer inordinately more than many others of advanced years who go to prison.

Defendant says others involved in recent nursing home fraud cases have received relatively light sentences for behavior more culpable than his. He lays special emphasis upon one defendant whose frauds appear indeed to have involved larger amounts and who was sentenced to a maximum of six months' incarceration, to be confined for that time only on week nights, not on week days or weekends. This court has examined the minutes of that sentencing proceeding and finds the case distinguishable in material respects. But even if there were a threat of such disparity as defendant warns against, it could not be a major weight on the scales. Our

14 Despite Biblical teachings concerning what is expected from those to whom much is given, the court has not, as his counsel feared might happen, held Dr. Bergman to a higher standard of responsibility because of his position in the community. But he has not been judged under a lower standard either.

sentencing system, deeply flawed, is characterized by disparity. We are to seek to "individualize" sentences, but no clear or clearly agreed standards govern the individualization. The lack of meaningful criteria does indeed leave sentencing judges far too much at large. But the result, with its nagging burdens on conscience, cannot be meaningfully alleviated by allowing any handful of sentences in a short series to fetter later judgments. The point is easy where Sentence No. 1 or Sentences 1–5 are notably harsh. It cannot be that a later judge, disposed to more leniency, should feel in any degree "bound." The converse is not totally different. This court has considered and given some weight to the trend of the cited sentences (though strict logic might call for none), but without treating them as forceful "precedents."

The case calls for a sentence that is more than nominal. Given the other circumstances, including that this is a first offense, by a man no longer young and not perfectly well, where danger of recidivism is not a concern it verges on cruelty to think of confinement for a term of years. We sit in a nation where prison sentences of extravagant length are more common than they are almost anywhere else. By that light, the term imposed today is not notably long. For this sentencing court, however, for a nonviolent first offense involving no direct assaults or invasions of others' security (as in bank robbery, narcotics, etc.), it is a stern sentence. For people like Dr. Bergman, who might be disposed to engage in similar wrongdoing, it should be sufficiently frightening to serve the major end of general deterrence. For all but the profoundly vengeful, it should not depreciate the seriousness of his offenses.

Much of defendant's sentencing memorandum is devoted to the extensive barrage of hostile publicity to which he has been subjected during the years before and since his indictment. He argues that the media (and people desiring to be featured in the media) have vilified him for many kinds of evildoing of which he has in fact been innocent. First, counsel express the concern that the court may be pressured toward severity by the force of the seeming public outcry. That the court should not allow itself to be affected in this way is clear beyond discussion. Whatever our ideals and mixed images about judges, it would be naive to doubt that judges have sometimes been swept by a sense of popular demand toward draconian sentencing decisions. It cannot hurt for the sentencing judge to be reminded of this and cautioned about it. There can be no guarantees. The sentencer must confront and regulate himself. But it bears reaffirmance that the court must seek to discount utterly the fact of notoriety in passing its judgment upon the defendant. Defendant's second point about his public humiliation is the frequently heard contention that he should not be incarcerated because he "has been punished enough." The thought is not without appeal. If punishment were wholly or mainly retributive, it might be a weighty factor. In the end, it must be a matter of little or no force. Defendant's notoriety should not lighten, any more than it may be permitted to aggravate, his sentence. The fact that he has been pilloried by journalists is a consequence of the prestige and privileges he enjoyed before he was exposed as a wrongdoer. The long fall from grace was possible only because of the height he had reached. The suffering from loss of public esteem reflects a body of opinion that the esteem had been, in at least some measure, wrongly bestowed and enjoyed. It is not possible to justify the notion that this mode of nonjudicial punishment should be an occasion for leniency not given to a defendant who never basked in such an admiring light. The appearance and the substance of equal justice prompts the court to discount the thought that public humiliation serves the function of imprisonment.

Writing about a particular sentence concentrates the mind with possibly special force upon the experience of the sentencer as well as the person sentenced. Consigning someone to prison, this defendant or any other, "is a sad necessity." There are impulses of avoidance from time to time toward a personally gratifying leniency or toward an opposite extreme. But there is, obviously, no place for private impulse in the judgment of the court. The course of justice must be sought with such objective rationality as we can muster, tempered with mercy, but obedient to the law, which, we do well to remember, is all that empowers a judge to make other people suffer.

Food for Thought

Bergman ultimately received a sentence of four months imprisonment. After reading the court's discussion would you have expected a sentence of that length?

The motion to postpone surrender is granted. Defendant will surrender to begin service of his sentence at 10:30 a. m. on July 7, 1976.

It is so ordered.

Points for Discussion

a. Social Condemnation

There is debate regarding the role of "social condemnation" in the criminal law. For example, Henry M. Hart, Jr., in *The Aims of the Criminal Law*, 23 LAW & CONTEMP. PROBS. 401, 405 (1958), argues that criminal conviction brings with it the "moral condemnation of the community." While society may also impose other punishments (*e.g.*, imprisonment, fines or deprivation of life), he believes that these other punishments "take their character as punishment from the condemnation which precedes them and serves as the warrant for their infliction." Louis Michael Seidman, in *Soldiers, Martyrs, and Criminals: Utilitarian Theory and the Problem of Crime Control*, 94 YALE L.J. 315, 337–38 (1984), argues that moral condemnation imposes a unique type of penalty and provides "a kind of deterrence that other punishment cannot achieve," and may deter even criminals who attach particular value to the prohibited conduct: "the condemnation is moral in character precisely because we are blaming an individual for preferring pleasure to pain in a situation where he should be obeying a categorical imperative."

b. Retribution

Many regard "retribution" as one of the principal justifications for imposing punishment. The concept of retribution is revealed in such sayings as ""an eye for an eye and a tooth for a tooth." Those who endorse this theory believe that society is morally justified in taking retribution against individuals who violate societal norms, especially when they commit heinous crimes. But

Food for Thought

As you think about a case like *Dudley & Stephens*, are those two individuals deserving of moral condemnation for killing the cabin boy? Is there a stigma associated with killing someone under such circumstances?

is retribution a justifiable objective? Herbert Wechsler, in *The Challenge of a Model Penal Code*, 65 HARV. L. REV. 1097 (1952), argues that the focus of the criminal law should be on deterrence: "while invocation of a penal sanction necessarily depends on past behavior, the object is control of harmful conduct in the future." Do you agree that deterrence principles are preferable to retribution principles?

Food for Thought

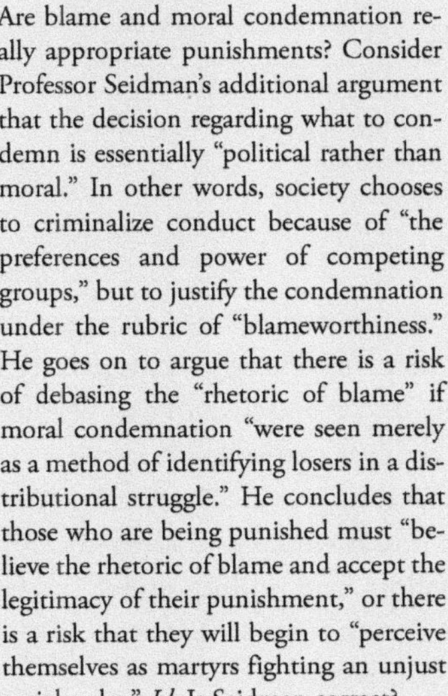

Are blame and moral condemnation really appropriate punishments? Consider Professor Seidman's additional argument that the decision regarding what to condemn is essentially "political rather than moral." In other words, society chooses to criminalize conduct because of "the preferences and power of competing groups," but to justify the condemnation under the rubric of "blameworthiness." He goes on to argue that there is a risk of debasing the "rhetoric of blame" if moral condemnation "were seen merely as a method of identifying losers in a distributional struggle." He concludes that those who are being punished must "believe the rhetoric of blame and accept the legitimacy of their punishment," or there is a risk that they will begin to "perceive themselves as martyrs fighting an unjust social order." *Id.* Is Seidman correct?

c. Rehabilitation

Should punishment focus on rehabilitation? The concept of "rehabilitiation" is particularly appealing in the criminal context. Of course, we have all heard about extraordinary cases in which criminals have rehabilitated themselves and gone on to live useful and productive lives. For example, there is the story of a former bank robber who became a "jailhouse" lawyer during his time in prison, and achieved the extraordinary feat of having two petitions for certiorari granted by the U.S. Supreme Court. He graduated from law school, and accepted a clerkship with the D.C. Circuit of the U.S. Court of Appeals. *See* Mark Memmott, *The Incredible Case of the Bank Robber Who's Now a Law Clerk*, National Public Radio, All Things Considered (Sept. 5, 2013). To the extent that society can work similar magic with other criminals, is it better for these individual, their families and (ultimately) for society to pursue rehabilitiation?

Food for Thought

Joshua Dressler, in *Hating Criminals: How Can Something that Feels so Good be Wrong?*, 88 U. MICH. L. REV. 1448–49 (1990), argues that society generally values "warm and soft emotions, such as compassion, mercy, and forgiveness," and is generally critical of "cold, hard feelings, such as resentment, revenge, and hatred." As a result, he finds it difficult to explain why some will taunt criminals or cheer the execution of a murderer. He asks whether it could be that "hatred is not as bad as we say it is, and that forgiveness and mercy are not so good?" And he raises the question of whether those involved in sentencing and punishing offenders should "keep their sentimentality to themselves for use in their private lives with their families and pets"). What do you think?

Henry M. Hart, Jr., in *The Aims of the Criminal Law*, 23 LAW & CONTEMP. PROBS. 401 (1958), asks whether "people who behave badly should simply be treated as sick people to be cured," and questions whether it is good for society to return individuals to society (following punishment) with the "negative vacuum of punishment-induced fear." Would it not be better to return them with the "affirmative and constructive equipment—physical, mental and morality—for law-abidingness"? Would the latter approach not provide a better way to protect society against anti-social conduct?

Food for Thought

As you think about the concept of retribution, consider the case of *Dudley & Stephens*. Given the circumstances under which they killed the cabin boy, do they deserve retribution?

d. Deterrence

"Deterrence" is often regarded as one of the primary justifications for imposing criminal punishment. Deterrence is often divided into "specific deterrence" and "general deterrence." With specific deterrence, the goal is to deter this particular defendant from committing future similar crimes. With general deterrence, the goal is to deter others from committing similar crimes. In theory, the concept of deterrence might help explain the outcome in *Dudley & Stephens*. While there may be no specific deterrent in that case (what is the likelihood that either of them will ever find themselves in a similar situation, and be faced with the choice of killing someone else or dying?), the judges might have hoped to provide a general deterrent that would discourage other sailors from killing under similar circumstances. However, is the deterrent likely to be a strong one? Faced with similar circumstances, is a sailor likely to be deterred from killing for fear of eventual conviction and a death sentence in England?

Food for Thought

Are we confident regarding society's ability to cure and rehabilitate criminals? Does society know how to rehabilitate individuals? Is there a concern regarding the monetary costs of rehabilitiation? Is there a fear that some individuals are mentally defective or are simply sociopaths and therefore beyond rehabilitiation? As you think about the case of *Dudley & Stephens*, do you believe that they need rehabilitation? Is there a rehabilitative purpose to be served by incarcerating them?

Food for Thought

Should deterrence govern the imposition of criminal sanctions? Henry M. Hart, Jr., in *The Aims of the Criminal Law*, 23 LAW & CONTEMP. PROBS. 401, 409–10 (1958), argues that deterrence should not be regarded as "the overriding and ultimate purpose of the criminal law" because deterrence is negative, as well as because he regards many crimes as "undeterrable." In that regard, consider whether it would have been possible to deter Dudley and Stephens from killing and eating Parker? Consider the following comments penned by Dudley in prison: "I can assure you I shall never forget the sight of my two unfortunate companions over that gastly [sic] meal we all was like mad wolfs who should get the most and for men fathers of children to commit such a deed we could not have our right reason." Book Review, *Cannibalism and the Common Law*, 98 HARV. L. REV. 1100, 1101 (1985). Is it possible to deter individuals in such circumstances?

e. Restraint

Another justification for punishment is the concept of "restraint." When individuals have committed particularly heinous crimes, there is a desire to "restrain" those individuals (e.g. put them in prison) and separate them from society for some period of time so that they cannot commit similar crimes in the future. For example, there was a recent case in Cleveland involving an individual who had held several women captive for a decade and repeatedly raped them during their detention. Likewise, there have been individuals who have committed particularly heinous crimes, or serial murders. With such individuals, there are often clamors to "lock them up" and "throw away the key" in order to ensure that they never do such things again. The Cleveland man was given life plus 1,000 years in order to ensure that he would never re-enter society (and, as a matter of fact, he ended up committing suicide shortly after sentencing). Of course, capital punishment is the ultimate form of restraint. However, even shorter detentions can serve a restraint function by removing criminals from society. One would hope that restraint also includes rehabilitation for those who will re-enter society, especially for those that have the potential to become productive members of society and avoid return to their former criminal ways.

Food for Thought

As we think about Dudley and Stephens, do they need to be restrained? Are they a threat to kill others if they are released from jail?

FYI

The criminal law might also be used to give a victim restitution for his/her loss. For example, if defendant destroys the victim's car out of malice, the trial court might require defendant (if possible) to compensate the victim for his/her loss.

f. Economic Efficiency

Should the Criminal Law be based on economic efficiency? Richard A. Posner, in *An Economic Theory of the Criminal Law*, 85 COLUM. L. REV. 1193 (1985), argues that many criminal law doctrines "can be given an economic meaning and can indeed be shown to promote efficiency," and he regards markets as the "the most efficient method of allocating resources." For example, he explains that if A wishes to own B's car, it is more efficient to force A to bargain with B regarding the price, instead of allowing A to take the car and then face judicial action to compel A's payment. A coerced transfer cannot improve the allocation of resources since "value is a function of willingness to pay." Since a coerced transfer would force A to spend resources trying to take the vehicle, and would encourage B to spend money to prevent A from doing so, these expenditures would "yield no social product." Therefore, the sanction for such a coerced transfer should be higher than B's loss to reflect the possibility "that the thief may place a higher subjective value on the object than does the victim." Likewise, for violent crimes, since it is not easy to place an economic value on such crimes (given that the damages for some violent crimes (*e.g.*, death) will be quite high), it may be beyond the ability of some individuals to pay for such damages. As a result, Posner argues that criminal sanctions are generally reserved for individuals who suffer from solvency issues because the "affluent are kept in line, for the most part, by tort law." The possibility of moral condemnation and imprisonment may deter even the impecunious. Even when the criminal law imposes only fines, the criminal penalty bears a social stigma. Heavy prison terms often help deter crime when there are "low probabilities of apprehension and conviction."

A contrasting view is provided by Louis Michael Seidman, in *Soldiers, Martyrs, and Criminals: Utilitarian Theory and the Problem of Crime Control*, 94 YALE L.J. 315 (1984). He indicates that law and economics literature suggests that society could have as little crime as it desires to have if it is willing to spend sufficient resources on "police, court, jails and so on to make probabilities of arrest very, very high for most crimes." Under this view, the present level of crime is regarded as "optimal" or society would spend more resources to reduce crime: "If one truly believes that we can have as little crime as we want, it follows that we want as much crime as we have." If the people are dissatisfied with the present level of crime, then the officials who create "our crime control strategy are either not utilitarians or are inept at performing utilitarian calculations." Although optimal deterrence requires higher sanctions for more serious crimes, than for less serious ones, it might be appropriate to raise the penalties for all crimes. Of course, all of this ignores the problem of "blameworthiness" as a basis for the criminal law. He argues that a utilitarian would contend that blame should be imposed when "doing so will maximize utility—*i.e.*, when the suffering imposed upon those who are blamed is counterbalanced by the social benefit resulting from the change in behavior." But, if blame is being imposed simply to maximize utility, that fact might "undercut the deterrent effect that justifies the distribution."

g. Reconciling the Justifications

Paul H. Robinson, in *Hybrid Principles for the Distribution of Criminal Sanctions*, 82 NW. U. L. REV. 19 (1988), argues that the justifications for punishment conflict, and that judges and legislators do not always have clear guidance about how to resolve the justifications for punishment: Is it possible to reconcile them? Consider the Model Penal Code § 1.02, Explanatory Note:

> The major goal of the criminal law is to forbid and prevent conduct that threatens substantial harm to individual or public interests and that at the same time is both unjustifiable and inexcusable. Subsidiary themes are to subject those who are disposed to commit crimes to public control, to prevent the condemnation of conduct that is without fault, to give fair warning of the conduct declared to be criminal, and to differentiate between serious and minor offenses on reasonable grounds. Subsidiary goals are to promote the correction and rehabilitation of offenders, within a scheme that safeguards them against excessive, disproportionate or arbitrary punishment, to give fair warning of the possible dispositions for criminal offenses, and to differentiate among offenders with a view to just individualization of treatment.
>
> Within a framework in which the dominant theme is the prevention of offenses, a number of specific factors are articulated which are believed to be the principle objectives of the process. The major goal is to forbid and prevent conduct that threatens substantial harm to individual or public interests and that at the same time is both unjustifiable and inexcusable. Subsidiary themes are to subject those who are disposed to commit crimes to public control, to prevent the condemnation of conduct that is without fault, to

Take Note

In this chapter, we focus only on the justifications for imposing punishment. In Chapter 14, we will examine other sentencing issues such as who is the decision maker (judge or jury), guilty pleas, sentencing factors, capital punishment and proportionality.

give fair warning of the conduct declared to be criminal, and to differentiate between serious and minor offenses on reasonable grounds.

Subsection (2) states the general purposes of the provisions governing the sentencing and treatment of offenders, again within the general framework of a preventive scheme. Subsidiary goals in this case are to promote the correction and rehabilitation of offenders, within a scheme that safeguards them against excessive, disproportionate or arbitrary punishment, to give fair warning of the possible dispositions for criminal offenses, and to differentiate among offenders with a view to just individualization of treatment.

Practice Pointer

As a practicing lawyer, if you do criminal work, you will confront (either as a prosecutor or defense attorney), situations in which a defendant is convicted, and the focus shifts to the "penalty" or "punishment" phase of the case. At that point, you will have the opportunity to argue for a greater or lesser punishment. The justifications for punishment can help you frame your arguments and can help persuade a court to impose the punishment you seek.

Now, let's think about how the justifications for punishment might apply in particular contexts, and the results that they might suggest or dictate in a particular case. Although this can be done with any type of crime, for convenience let's focus on homicide. Given the purposes of the criminal law, should different homicides be treated differently for purposes of punishment? Do the principal justifications for punishment (retribution, restraint, rehabilitation, general deterrence and special deterrence) justify different sentences based on factual differences? Think about these issues as you consider the following hypotheticals.

Hypo 1: *Brutal Murder*

Defendant brutally tortures and murders an elderly lady during a robbery and rape. In killing her, he is motivated by a desire to eliminate a potential witness. What punishment should be imposed on defendant? How do the possible justifications for punishment (e.g., retribution, restraint, deterrence and rehabilitation) affect your conclusions?

Hypo 2: *The Motorist and the Child*

Defendant is driving down a residential street, at the speed limit when a little child unexpectedly darts out in front of him. Although defendant makes a valiant effort to stop, he is unable do so and kills the child. Is punishment appropriate under these circumstances? If so, what punishment should be imposed? Would you treat defendant differently for purposes of punishment if he were proceeding at a speed that was 25 mph over the speed limit? 35 mph? 50 mph? How do the justifications for punishment affect your analysis?

Hypo 3: *The Cheating Spouse*

Defendant, who is feeling sick, comes home early from work to find his or her spouse in bed with another person. In a fit of rage, defendant kills the other person. Is punishment appropriate under such circumstances? If so, what punishment should be imposed?

Hypo 4: *Compassionate Euthanasia*

Defendant's husband is suffering from a severe, painful, debilitating fatal disease. Day-after-day, the husband begs the wife to help him end his life and thereby end his suffering. The wife repeatedly refuses. Finally, unable to deal with her husband's desperate plight, she administers poison to him. Is punishment appropriate under these circumstances? If so, what punishment should be imposed?

Hypo 5: *Culture and Murder*

Defendant drowns her infant daughter and 4-year-old son in the ocean after she learns that her husband has a mistress. She attempts to drown herself, too, but fails. Defendant, an immigrant from Japan who has lived in the United States for fourteen years, had no malicious intent, but wanted only to save her children from the shame that their father's infidelity brought on the family. There is an ancient practice in Japan of a parent committing suicide with her children in such circumstances (*oyaku shinju*). *See People v. Fumiko Kimura*, No. A–091133 (Cal. Super. Ct. L.A. County Nov. 21, 1985). Is punishment appropriate under such circumstances? If so, what punishment should be imposed?

Hypo 6: *Absent-Minded Father*

On a hot day in mid-summer, a father is supposed to take his infant child to day care on the way to work. The father, being absent-minded, forgets about the child and leaves the child in the rear car seat (buckled into his seat). Since no one happens to notice, the baby dies of suffocation. The father, who truly loved the child despite his appalling level of absent-mindedness, is devastated by the child's death and falls into a deep depression. The mother, unable to forgive the father, divorces him. Suppose that you are the prosecutor, and must decide how to handle the case. Of course, the father can be prosecuted for manslaughter. Is a criminal prosecution appropriate? If so, what purpose(s) would it serve? If you decide to prosecute, what punishment would you seek?

Hypo 7: *Loan Shark's Threat*

Defendant is charged with illegally selling narcotics. The facts reveal that defendant was not regularly engaged in the sale of narcotics. However, he borrowed money from a loan shark at an exorbitant interest rate. When defendant was unable to repay the money, the loan shark ordered defendant to "handle" a narcotic transaction for him. With a gun lying on his lap, the loan shark threatened to harm the defendant and his family. Because of this threat, defendant agreed to "handle" the drug transaction. Unfortunately for defendant, the police "got wind" of the transaction and arrested him. Given the purposes of the criminal law, does it make sense to punish defendant? Explain.

Hypo 8: *Reconsidering* Dudley & Stephens

Now, reconsider the facts in *Regina v. Dudley & Stephens*. What punishment did the defendants deserve? What is the function of the punishment? Did they need rehabilitation? Was there a risk that they or others would commit similar acts in the future, and can society hope to deter them or others by imposing punishment on them? Did they need to be "restrained" or "incapacitated" lest they run around killing others? Did they need to be punished in order for society to exact retribution for the death of Parker?

Executive Summary

Necessity Defense. Rejection of the necessity defense in *Dudley & Stephens* embodied the principle that the criminal law must enforce the moral duty to refrain from killing another, even when necessary to save lives. Even so, the sentence of six months for the crime of murder illustrated how the British used their sentencing discretion to give weight to the same mitigating circumstances that might have justified an acquittal on grounds of necessity.

Deterrence. Although general deterrence is accepted as a purpose for imposing punishment, the existence of a deterrent effect for particular punishments may be contested. Such an effect may be difficult to demonstrate empirically, especially for particular types of crimes. Similarly, the expectation that punishment will achieve "specific deterrence" of individual wrongdoers, with regard to their criminal conduct in the future, may be defeated for many reasons. Yet crime prevention is viewed as the "major goal" or "dominant theme" of modern criminal law, according to the Model Penal Code.

Restraint. The function of punishment as a form of restraint, through the incapacitation of wrongdoers achieved through confinement, may be viewed as a necessity for serious offenses. But the discretion of sentencing and corrections authorities, as well as the dictates

Major Themes

a. Morality vs. Custom—The treatment of the *Dudley & Stephens* defendants illustrates the operation of competing punishment goals. Their conviction and sentence upheld the value of life against the custom of the sea, whereas the commutation of their sentence illustrated a compassionate judgment regarding their failure to live up to an "unreachable standard" of conduct.

b. Multiple Punishment Purposes—The varied justifications for punishment sometimes produce conflicting results when applied in particular cases. Both legislatures and courts are vested with the responsibility of choosing among such justifications, when establishing or interpreting the elements of crimes and the criminal defenses.

of the legislature, will influence the terms and conditions of such confinement. The economic costs of modern systems of restraint have created incentives for experimentation with alternative punishment methods.

Rehabilitation. The rehabilitative function of punishment has been a longstanding ideal in the criminal law, but support for that ideal has waxed and waned during the decades after the Model Penal Code was proposed. Although concerns about the inherent difficulties of achieving rehabilitative goals has led to the abandonment of those goals in some contexts, the achievement of rehabilitative goals in other context remains a priority with regard to some defendants and some crimes.

Retribution. Support for the retributive function of punishment is deeply rooted in history. This perspective on punishment may be viewed as a source of such modern concerns as the avoidance of disproportionate or arbitrary sentences, and the effort to make distinctions among offenders with regard to the "grading" of their crimes and their punishments.

For More Information

- JOHN M. BURKOFF & RUSSELL L. WEAVER, INSIDE CRIMINAL LAW: WHAT MATTERS AND WHY 1–16 (2d ed. 2011).
- Lon L. Fuller, *The Case of the Speluncean Explorers*, 62 HARV. L. REV. 616 (1949).
- WAYNE R. LAFAVE, CRIMINAL LAW §§ 1.2–1.3, 1.5 (6th ed. 2017).

Test Your Knowledge

To assess your understanding of the material in this chapter, click here to take a quiz.

Chapter 2

The Requirement of a "Voluntary Act"

An essential element of just punishment is the requirement of a voluntary "act" or an "omission" to act when an appropriate duty to act exists (the "*actus reus*" requirement). If the alleged act was involuntary, there may be no justification for imposing punishment. For example, if "one person physically forces another person into bodily movement, as where A by force causes B's body to strike C; under these circumstances, there is no voluntary act by B." Wayne R. LaFave & Austin W. Scott, Jr., Criminal Law § 6.1(c), at 324 (5th ed. 2010).

It's Latin to Me

The term "*actus reus*" refers to the "act" that is forbidden by a criminal law.

A. The Act Requirement

Martin v. State

17 So.2d 427 (Ala. App. 1944).

Simpson, Judge.

Make the Connection

In Chapter 1, we examined the justifications for imposing punishment under the criminal law: retribution; restraint; deterrence (both specific and general); & rehabilitation. If the defendant commits what would otherwise be a criminal act, but lacks voluntariness, none of the justifications for imposing punishment are served by imposing criminal sanctions. Of course, the critical issue to be determined is which acts are truly involuntary.

Appellant was convicted of being drunk on a public highway, and appeals. Officers of the law arrested him at his home and took him onto the highway, where he allegedly committed the proscribed acts, viz., manifested a drunken condition by using loud and profane language.

The pertinent provisions of our statute are: "Any person who, while intoxicated or drunk, appears in any public place where one or more persons are present, and manifests a drunken condition by boisterous or indecent conduct, or loud and profane discourse, shall, on conviction, be fined." Under the plain terms of this statute, a voluntary appearance is presupposed. The rule has been declared, and we think it sound, that an accusation of drunkenness in a designated public place cannot be established by proof that the accused, while in an intoxicated condition, was involuntarily and forcibly carried to that place by the arresting officer.

Conviction of appellant was contrary to this announced principle and, in our view, erroneous. It appears that no legal conviction can be sustained under the evidence, so the judgment of the trial court is reversed and one here rendered discharging appellant.

Reversed and rendered.

FYI

As we shall see, some crimes (e.g., murder) are "result" crimes in that a conviction requires proof that defendant "caused" a particular result (with the required *mens rea*). Other crimes are "conduct" crimes in that conviction requires proof that defendant engaged in prohibited conduct with the required *mens rea*. In most instances, there must be "concurrence" between the *actus reus* and the *mens rea* when defendant engages in the conduct (as well as when defendant causes a particular result). The notions of *mens rea*, concurrence, causation and result will be explored in later chapters.

Points for Discussion

a. Model Penal Code

The MPC Commentary for § 2.01 states: "The law cannot hope to deter involuntary movement or to stimulate action that cannot physically be performed; the sense of personal security would be undermined in a society where such movement or inactivity could lead to formal social condemnation of the sort that a conviction necessarily entails." These ideas are codified as follows:

§ 2.01. Requirement of Voluntary Act; Omission as Basis of Liability; Possession as an Act.

(1) A person is not guilty of an offense unless his liability is based on conduct that includes a voluntary act or the omission to perform an act of which he is physically capable.

(2) The following are not voluntary acts within the meaning of this Section: (a) a reflex or convulsion; (b) a bodily movement during unconsciousness or sleep; (c) conduct during hypnosis or resulting from hypnotic suggestion; (d) a bodily movement that otherwise is not a product of the effort or determination of the actor, either conscious or habitual.

Take Note

Model Penal Code § 2.01 is important because it offers examples of situations when an individual's actions would be regarded as "involuntary" and therefore as inappropriate for the imposition of criminal sanctions.

b. Carried Away

In *State v. Boleyn*, 328 So.2d 95 (La. 1976), a prisoner was subjected to a sodomous rape. Afterwards, he voluntarily intoxicated himself with pills and beer. While in an unconscious drugged condition, defendant was "carried away" from the prison by another prisoner. The court concluded that "evidence of the state of consciousness of defendant and of his intoxicated or drugged condition should have been submitted to the jury." Likewise, in *People v. Shaughnessy*, 319 N.Y.S.2d 626 (1971), defendant was found not guilty of violating an ordinance prohibiting entry upon private property. The state's evidence failed to show an overt voluntary act by the defendant who was merely a passenger in a trespassing car.

Food for Thought

As a general rule, individuals cannot be prosecuted merely for "evil thoughts." Thus, an individual is free to "think about" robbing a bank, or the different ways that he might murder his arch-enemy, and cannot be prosecuted merely for "thinking bad thoughts." Why not? Suppose that it is possible to reliably ascertain an individual's inner thoughts? Why shouldn't the government be allowed to prosecute and convict individuals who have the desire, or who have formed the intent, to commit heinous acts or terroristic acts? Are there valid policy reasons for exempting such individuals from prosecution?

Take Note

Even thought individuals cannot be prosecuted merely for having "evil thoughts," as we shall see in later chapters, an individual might be subject to prosecution for soliciting someone else to commit the crime, for conspiring with others to commit it, or for taking sufficient steps to "attempt" to commit the offense.

c. When Brakes Fail

In *State v. Kremer*, 114 N.W.2d 88 (1962), the court held that a defendant could not be guilty of violating a city ordinance requiring all traffic to stop at a flashing red light when the evidence showed that his brakes failed with no prior warning. However, in *Kettering v. Greene*, 222 N.E.2d 638 (1966), the Ohio Supreme Court reached the opposite result even though defendant had no prior warning of any defect in the brakes. The court concluded that the statutory requirement to stop at a stop sign is mandatory and brake failure is not a legal excuse.

d. Possession as Voluntary Act

A voluntary act can include "possession" of an item. MPC § 2.01(4) provides: "Possession is an act, within the meaning of this Section, if the possessor knowingly procured or received the thing possessed or was aware of his control thereof for a sufficient period to have been able to terminate his possession."

Hypo 1: *Reconsidering* Martin

Was *Martin* correctly decided? Although Martin was involuntarily placed in the street, did he commit the act of being loud and boisterous? Under the circumstances, is that "act" sufficient for conviction under the relevant statute?

Hypo 2: *Cruise Control Systems and Involuntariness*

In virtually every state, speeding is a strict liability offense which requires no *mens rea*. It does require the "*actus reus*" of speeding. Suppose that defendant is charged with travelling seventy-seven miles per hour in a fifty-five miles per hour zone. Defendant testifies that he desired to travel at the speed limit, and was trying to do so, but his cruise control stuck in the "accelerate" position causing the car to exceed the posted speed limit. Defendant attempted to deactivate the cruise control by pushing the "off" and "coast" buttons, and by tapping the brakes. None of these actions was successful. Eventually, defendant switched the car's ignition to the "off" position and the car came to a stop. Subsequently, defendant had the defective cruise control repaired. Did defendant commit the *actus reus* of speeding? How would you argue this case for the defendant? *See State v. Baker*, 571 P.2d 65 (1977).

Fulcher v. State

633 P.2d 142 (Wyo. 1981).

BROWN, JUSTICE.

Appellant consumed seven or eight shots of whiskey over a period of four hours in a Torrington bar, and had previously had a drink at home. Appellant claims he got in a fight in the bar restroom, then left the bar to find a friend. The last thing he remembers until awakening in jail is going out of the door at the bar.

Appellant and his friend were found lying in the alley behind the bar by a police officer who noted abrasions on their fists and faces. Appellant and his friend swore, were uncooperative, and combative. They were subsequently booked for public intoxication and disturbing the peace. During booking appellant continued to swear, and said he and his friend were jumped by a "bunch of Mexicans." Although his speech was slurred, he was able to verbally count his money, roughly $500 to $600 in increments of $20, and was able to walk to his cell without assistance. Appellant was placed in a cell with one Martin Hernandez who was lying unconscious on the floor of the cell. After the jailer left the cell, he heard something that sounded like someone being kicked. He ran back to the cell and saw appellant standing by

Hernandez. When the jailer started to leave again, the kicking sound resumed, and he observed appellant kicking and stomping on Hernandez's head. Appellant told the officer Hernandez had fallen out of bed. Hernandez was bleeding profusely and was taken to the hospital for some 52 stitches in his head and mouth. He had lost two or three teeth as a result of the kicking.

Appellant entered a plea of not guilty. In preparation for trial, appellant was examined by Dr. Breck LeBegue, a forensic psychiatrist. The doctor reviewed the police report and conducted a number of tests. At the trial Dr. LeBegue testified that in his expert medical opinion appellant suffered brain injury and was in a state of traumatic automatism at the time of his attack on Hernandez. Dr. LeBegue defined traumatic automatism as the state of mind in which a person does not have conscious and willful control over his actions, and lacks the ability to be aware of and to perceive his external environment. Dr. LeBegue further testified that another possible symptom is an inability to remember what occurred while in a state of traumatic automatism. Dr. LeBegue was unable to state positively whether or not appellant had the requisite mental state for aggravated assault and battery, but thought appellant did not because of his altered state of mind. He could not state, however, that the character of an act is devoid of criminal intent because of mind alteration.

What's That?

The term "automatism" is defined by Black's Law Dictionary as an "action or conduct occurring without will, purpose, or reasoned intention, such as sleepwalking; behavior carried out in a state of unconsciousness or mental dissociation without full awareness."

The trial court properly received and considered evidence of unconsciousness absent a plea of "not guilty by reason of mental illness or deficiency." The defense of unconsciousness perhaps should be more precisely denominated as the defense of automatism. Automatism is the state of a person who, though capable of action, is not conscious of what he is doing. While in an automatistic state, an individual performs complex actions without an exercise of will. Because these actions are performed in a state of unconsciousness, they are involuntary. Automatistic behavior may be followed by complete or partial inability to recall the actions performed while unconscious. Thus, a person who acts automatically does so without intent, exercise of free will, or knowledge of the act.

Automatism may be caused by an abnormal condition of the mind capable of being designated a mental illness or deficiency. Automatism may also be manifest in a person with a perfectly healthy mind. In this opinion we are concerned with the defense of automatism occurring in a person with a healthy mind. In this case, we are concerned with alleged automatism caused by concussion.

The defense of automatism, while not an entirely new development in the criminal law, has been discussed in relatively few decisions by American appellate courts, most of these being in California where the defense is statutory. Some courts have held that insanity and automatism are separate and distinct defenses, and that evidence of automatism may be presented under a plea of not guilty. Some states have made this distinction by statute. In other states the distinction is made by case law.

> "A defense related to but different from the defense of insanity is that of unconsciousness, often referred to as automatism: one who engages in what would otherwise be criminal conduct is not guilty of a crime if he does so in a state of unconsciousness or semi-consciousness." LAFAVE & SCOTT, CRIMINAL LAW, § 44, p. 337 (1972).
>
> "The defenses of insanity and unconsciousness are not the same in nature, for unconsciousness at the time of the alleged criminal act need not be the result of a disease or defect of the mind. As a consequence, the two defenses are not the same in effect, for a defendant found not guilty by reason of unconsciousness, as distinct from insanity, is not subject to commitment to a hospital for the mentally ill." *State v. Caddell*, 287 N.C. 266, 215 S.E.2d 348, 360 (1975).

The principal reason for making a distinction between the defense of unconsciousness and insanity is that the consequences which follow an acquittal, will differ. The defense of unconsciousness is usually a complete defense. That is, there are no follow-up consequences after an acquittal; all action against a defendant is concluded. In the case of a finding of not guilty by reason of insanity, the defendant is ordinarily committed to a mental institution. The mental illness or deficiency plea does not adequately cover automatic behavior. Unless the plea of automatism is allowed, certain anomalies will result. For example, if the court determines that the automatistic defendant is sane, but refuses to recognize automatism, the defendant has no defense to the crime with which he is charged. If found guilty, he faces a prison term. The rehabilitative value of imprisonment for the automatistic offender who has committed the offense unconsciously is nonexistent. The cause of the act was an uncontrollable physical disorder that may never recur and is not a moral deficiency. If, however, the court treats automatism as insanity and then determines that the defendant is insane, he will be found not guilty. He then will be committed to a mental institution for an indefinite period. The commitment of an automatistic individual to a mental institution for rehabilitation has absolutely no value. Mental hospitals generally treat people with psychiatric or psychological problems. This form of treatment is not suited to unconscious behavior resulting from a bump on the head.

Make the Connection

When we study insanity in Chapter 13, we will see that courts have struggled to define the legal concept of "insanity" using several different standards.

It may be argued that evidence of unconsciousness cannot be received unless a plea of not guilty by reason of mental illness or deficiency is made pursuant to Rule 15, W.R.Cr.P. We believe this approach to be illogical. It does not seem that the definition of "mental deficiency" in § 7–11–301(a) (iii), which includes "brain damage," encompasses simple brain trauma with no permanent after effects. The "brain damage" contemplated in the statute is some serious and irreversible condition having an impact upon the ability of the person to function. It is undoubtedly something far more significant than a temporary and transitory condition. The two defenses are merged, in effect, if a plea of "not guilty by reason of mental illness or deficiency" is a prerequisite for using the defense of unconsciousness.

The committee that drafted Wyoming Pattern Jury Instructions Criminal, apparently recognized mental illness or deficiency and unconsciousness as separate and distinct defenses. Admittedly the instructions in Wyo. P.J.I.Cr. are not authoritative, because they were not approved by the Wyoming Supreme Court, and this was a matter of design. Still they are the product of a distinguished group of legal scholars, including judges, attorneys and teachers of the law. The comment to this pattern jury instruction notes that it is limited to persons of sound mind, and the comment distinguishes persons suffering from "mental deficiency or illness." In this respect, it tracks the case law from other jurisdictions, which authorities hold that unconsciousness and insanity are completely separate grounds of exemption from criminal responsibility.

Although courts hold that unconsciousness and insanity are separate and distinct defenses, there has been some uncertainty concerning the burden of proof. We believe the better rule to be that stated in *State v. Caddell*, 215 S.E.2d 348: "Unconsciousness, or automatism, is a complete defense to the criminal charge, separate and apart from the defense of insanity; that it is an affirmative defense; and that the burden rests upon the defendant to establish this defense, unless it arises out of the State's own evidence, to the satisfaction of the jury." The rationale for this rule is that the defendant is the only person who knows his actual state of consciousness.

Our ruling on the facts of this case is that the defense of unconsciousness resulting from a concussion with no permanent brain damage is an affirmative defense and is a defense separate from the defense of not guilty by reason of mental illness or deficiency. Appellant's conviction must, nevertheless, be affirmed. Dr. LeBegue was unable to state positively whether or not appellant had the requisite mental state for aggravated assault. He could not state that the character of the act was devoid of criminal intent because of the mind alteration. The presumption of mental competency was never overcome by appellant and the evidence presented formed a reasonable basis on which the trial judge could find and did find that the State had met the required burden of proof. Further, the trial judge was not bound to follow Dr. LeBegue's opinion. The trier of the facts is not bound to accept expert opinion evidence in the face of other substantial and credible evidence to the contrary. There was an abundance of other credible evidence that appellant was not unconscious at the time of the assault and battery for which he was convicted.

Affirmed.

RAPER, JUSTICE, specially concurring, with whom ROONEY, JUSTICE, joins.

The majority has taken the mistaken view that a little old bump on the head is not serious. We do not know from the record how much of a blow on the head causing concussion and brain damage was received by appellant. Wyoming did not adopt that part of the ALI Model Penal Code which would consider automatism as a separate defense:

> Section 2.01.
>
> "(1) A person is not guilty of an offense unless his liability is based on conduct which includes a voluntary act or the omission to perform an act of which he is physically capable."

Wyoming adopted language which embraced the alternative suggested in the comments to § 2.01, supra:

> Any definition must exclude a reflex or convulsion. The case of unconsciousness is equally clear when unconsciousness implies collapse or coma, as perhaps it does in ordinary usage of the term. There are, however, states of physical activity where self-awareness is grossly impaired or even absent, as in epileptic fugue, amnesia, extreme confusion and equivalent conditions. How far these active states of automatism should be assimilated to coma for this legal purpose presents a difficult issue. There is judicial authority supporting the assimilation. An alternative approach, however, is to view these cases as appropriate for exculpation on the ground of mental disease or defect excluding responsibility. This view has also had support in the decisions. It offers the advantage that it may facilitate commitment when the individual is dangerous to the community because the condition is recurrent. By the same token, however, it bears more harshly on the individual whose condition is non-recurrent, as in the case where an extraordinary reaction follows the administration of a therapeutic drug. And there may be a difficulty in regarding some of these conditions as " 'mental disease or defect,' within the meaning of section 4.01 of the draft or as 'insanity' under prevailing law, although cognition is sufficiently impaired to satisfy that aspect of the test." (Emphasis added.)

The Wyoming legislature clearly defined "mental deficiency" to unquestionably include appellant's alleged condition (brain damage).

Points for Discussion

a. Traumatic Amnesia

In *People v. Cox*, 153 P.2d 362 (1944), defendant was charged with homicide. He claimed that he was hit on the head with a bottle and was unconscious when he committed the crime. The evidence showed that he suffered from traumatic amnesia. Defendant had cuts on his forehead, had bled from the right ear, and had suffered superficial bruises on his abdomen, and suffered some type of brain injury. One witness testified that defendant had suffered a "loss of memory or traumatic amnesia caused by a blow on the head." The Court held that, because there was evidence suggesting that defendant's " conscious mind has ceased to operate and his actions are controlled by the subconscious or subjective mind," it was error not to instruct the jury regarding the legal effect of unconsciousness. *See also State v. Mercer*, 165 S.E.2d 328 (1969).

b. Reflex Shock Reaction

In accord is *People v. Newton*, 87 Cal. Rptr. 394 (1970), in which defendant was shot by a police officer, and later shot and killed the officer. At trial, defendant claimed that he was unconscious during the killing. Defense witnesses testified that "defendant's recollections were 'compatible' with the gunshot wound he had received; and that 'a gunshot wound which penetrates a body cavity, the abdominal cavity or the thoracic cavity is very likely to produce a profound reflex shock reaction, that is quite different than a gunshot wound which penetrates only skin and muscle and it is not at all uncommon for a person shot in the abdomen to lose consciousness and go into this reflex shock condition for short periods of time up to half an hour or so.' " The court concluded that defendant was entitled to an instruction on unconsciousness, and discussed the distinction between "diminished capacity" and "unconsciousness: "A trial court is under a duty to instruct upon diminished capacity, in the absence of a request and upon its own motion, where the evidence so indicates. The difference between the two states—of diminished capacity and unconsciousness—is one of degree only: where the former provides a 'partial defense' by negating a specific mental state essential to a particular crime, the latter is a "complete defense" because it negates capacity to commit any crime at all. Moreover, evidence of both states is not antithetical; jury instructions on the effect of both will be required where the evidence supports a finding of either. We hold, therefore, that the trial court should have given appropriate unconsciousness instructions upon its own motion in the present case, and that its omission to do so was prejudicial error."

What's That?

The term "diminished capacity" refers to an "impaired mental condition—short of insanity—that is caused by intoxication, trauma, or disease and that prevents a person from having the mental state necessary to be held responsible for a crime." Diminished capacity can also affect the degree of the offense or the severity of the punishment.

Hypo 1: *Sleeping Driver*

Defendant, a shuttle operator, was dispatched to pick up passengers at the local airport. On the way, she became drowsy, opened the windows for a breeze to combat the feeling, and drove on. At some point, she fell asleep, ran off the road, and killed a pedestrian. She is charged with involuntary manslaughter. Since the driver was asleep when she killed the pedestrian, did she commit a voluntary act? *See State v. Olsen*, 160 P.2d 427 (1945).

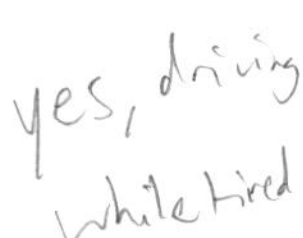

Hypo 2: *Voluntariness and Epilepsy*

James "Rambo" Royster is driving to work when he has an epileptic seizure which causes him to completely black out and lose control of his car. Rambo's car runs off the road, strikes and kills a pedestrian. In killing the pedestrian, has Rambo committed a voluntary act? Would it matter whether Rambo had suffered seizures in the past? Suppose that he had suffered several epileptic seizures a year for some years? How would you argue that Rambo has committed a voluntary act? How might the state respond? *See People v. Decina*, 157 N.Y.S.2d 558 (1956).

Hypo 3: *Control of Vehicle*

A police officer is patrolling in a squad car when he sees a car stuck in a snow-filled ditch. The headlights are on, but the motor is off. Starfield is sitting in the driver's seat. From the odor of alcohol and bloodshot eyes, the officer believes that Starfield is intoxicated. Defendant refuses to submit to a blood alcohol test. While in the squad car, when asked if she was operating the car, she replies, "Nope," but does not elaborate. At the jail, the police find a set of car keys in her pocket. While being booked, defendant states that she was not driving the car, but was waiting for her son (the driver) who had gone for help after the car went into the ditch. Defendant is charged with "driving, operating, or being in physical control of any motor vehicle while under the influence of alcohol." Under the circumstances, was Starfield in "physical control" of the vehicle? If you are the prosecutor, what evidence would you use to establish "control?" If you represent the defendant, how would you rebut this evidence? *See State v. Starfield*, 481 N.W.2d 834 (Minn. 1992); *Williams v. City of Petersburg*, 217 S.E.2d 893 (1975); *State v. Bugger*, 483 P.2d 442 (1971).

Hypo 4: *Hypnosis and Mind Control*

Defendant, 18 years old, shot and almost killed two U.S. Marshals in an attempt to help her husband (Buster) escape from custody. The shooting occurred as the marshals brought Buster into the federal building for trial on a bank robbery charge. As they did, defendant drew a revolver from her purse, and stood there indecisively. When Buster yelled "shoot 'em, baby, shoot 'em," defendant opened fire. After the shootings, defendant stood on the steps of the courthouse. At that point Buster gave up the struggle and commanded defendant, "run, baby, run." Defendant fled down the street and was captured without a struggle about a block away a few minutes later. At defendant's trial, Buster portrayed himself as a "Svengali" who had induced defendant to commit the offense under hypnosis. Buster had been hypnotizing defendant since she was 15 years old, and made her believe that he was her mother and father, and her Lord and God. He implanted in her mind a "memory" of his having held her immediately after her birth, and of his having rescued her from drowning when she was nine years old (a time before he met her). She claimed to have seen him crucified, die, and rise again, and believed he was her savior and redeemer. His testimony was that, since defendant believed he was God, she was unable to distinguish right from wrong, since "if God tells you to do something, you think it's right." He had instructed her (during her visits while he was held in the local jail) how to manage the escape. He had, he claimed, implanted in her mind the compulsion to meet him and the marshals as he was brought in for trial, to have a gun ready, and to respond to his commands as to when to use it. If Buster's claims are true, did defendant commit a voluntary act when she fired on the officers? Suppose that you represent the prosecution, what types of evidence would you use to rebut defendant's claims of involuntariness? How might the defense respond? *See United States v. Phillips*, 515 F. Supp. 758 (E.D.Ky. 1981).

Hypo 5: *More on Hypnosis and Mind Control*

Defendant McCollum entered a bank, approached a bank teller, and handed him an envelope without comment. The teller asked defendant about the envelope, and defendant simply replied "Open it. I was told to bring it here. I don't know what is in it." The teller opened the note and found that it contained a demand for $100,000, and stated that the person who had delivered it was under a hypnotic spell. The teller asked McCollum to sit down. McCollum complied, and remained seated while the bank was evacuated and police officers entered to apprehend him. McCollum failed to respond to the officers' initial questions and commands, but accompanied them to a police car. Later, while seated in the car, McCollum shook violently for a period of ten to fifteen seconds and then asked one of the officers, "What are you doing? Why am I here?" Assuming that defendant really was under hypnosis, can he be convicted of attempted bank robbery? In other words, did he commit a voluntary act? Could the person who hypnotized defendant and gave him the note be convicted of attempted bank robbery? *See United States v. McCollum*, 732 F.2d 1419 (9th Cir. 1984).

Hypo 6: *Voluntariness and Multiple Personalities*

Defendant was charged with driving under the influence of alcohol. At the time of the offense, she was dissociated from her primary personality (Robin) and in the state of consciousness of a secondary personality (Jennifer). She claims that she was suffering from psychological trauma (report of a lump on her breast) which caused her to dissociate into the personality of Jennifer who is impulsive, angry, fearful and anxious. Jennifer has a drinking problem. Defendant contends that when she is Jennifer, Robin is unaware of what is going on, has no control over Jennifer's actions, and has no memory of what Jennifer did later on when she is restored to the primary personality of Robin. As a result, Robin argues that "she" did not commit the "act" of driving under the influence. Do you agree with defendant? Are the actions of a person with a multiple personality disorder voluntary when she is dissociated from her primary personality and in the state of consciousness of a secondary personality? *State v. Grimsley*, 444 N.E.2d 1071 (1982).

Hypo 7: *Somnambulism*

Defendant was living in adultery with the deceased, Ada Jenkins. Lawrence Williams was an enemy, and had made threats against defendant. After retiring on the night of the homicide, the deceased and defendant discussed Williams, and deceased gave appellant information which alarmed him, and put him in fear of a secret attack by Williams. During the conversation and thereafter, defendant became more and more alarmed, and, as he stated, he felt "jubious and jubiouser," and removed a pistol from a table near his bed, and placed it under his pillow. Then, the following happened: "I goes off to sleep. I never waked up any more till I was disturbed by a noise in the house. I went to sleep with that on my mind. The last I remembered was that the door was not fastened. After the noise disturbed me, I was nervous, and I was not reconciled to the noise in the house. I was scared. I just jumped up with my gun and commenced shooting. I made two shots or three. And then, when I found myself and got reconciled I was standing. Then I turned to the library table at the head of the bed where I slept and lit the lamp. I found her laying there dead. She was laying at the foot of the bed next to the partition wall. As to knowing whether I killed her or not, well, I was shooting; I couldn't say I killed her because I didn't know what I was doing. When I lit the lamp she was there dead. As to my intentionally killing Ada Jenkins, or knowing I did so, I was shooting is all I can say. I was not trying to kill her; no, sir. I would not have killed her if I had known it was her for nothing in the world." Defendant was diagnosed with somnambulism. Under the circumstances, can we say that the homicide he committed was a voluntary act? *See Bradley v. State*, 277 S.W. 147 (1925).

Hypo 8: *More on Automatism*

Defendant went to the "Watering Place" where he consumed four whisky drinks during a 2.5 hour period. Defendant then witnessed an altercation between a patron and the tavern owner. The police were called to the scene and they forcibly escorted the other patron outside where he continued to resist arrest. A hostile crowd accompanied the police as they exited the tavern. Suddenly, defendant burst through the crowd, leapt into the air and struck one of the officers twice in the face. Thereafter, the officer placed defendant under arrest for aggravated battery. Defendant was very upset, excited and agitated, and great force was required to place defendant in the officer's automobile. Later, while in his jail cell, one of the jailers discovered defendant lying on his cot gasping for breath. Defendant's eyes were fixed and his back formed a rigid reversed arch, symptomatic of a grand mal convulsive seizure. The evidence shows that defendant suffers from an illness known as psychomotor epilepsy which has resulted in a number of violent attacks on other persons. In some of these attacks, physical assistance from others was required to subdue defendant. One, a knife assault in a hospital, was so violent that a police officer was forced to shoot defendant. Defendant's past history is replete with emotional outbursts and he has been convicted on several occasions of involuntary manslaughter and aggravated assault. Defendant claims that he suffered from "automatism" defined as the state of a person who, though capable of action, is not conscious of what he is doing. Did he act voluntarily when he attacked the police officer with the parking meter? *See People v. Grant*, 377 N.E.2d 4 (1978); *People v. Grant*, 360 N.E.2d 809 (1977); *see also United States v. Phillips*, 515 F. Supp. 758 (E.D.Ky. 1981).

Hypo 9: *Proving Involuntariness*

Defendant was indicted for kidnapping and raping Catherine Sutton, and there was indisputable proof that he committed the crime. However, defendant claimed that he is unable to remember anything about the events surrounding the crime. In addition, defendant stated "I never did a degrading thing like this before. I have been charged with nothing like this. I don't believe it. And if I did this, there is something wrong." However, defendant admitted that photographs of the automobile in which Ms. Sutton was carried away from her home and assaulted were pictures of his car. Because he cannot remember what happened, defendant claims that he was unconscious during the assault and therefore that his acts were involuntary. If you are hired to represent defendant, what proof might you use to show that he acted involuntarily? If you are asked to represent the state, how would you prove that he acted voluntarily? *See State v. Caddell*, 215 S.E.2d 348 (1975).

Hypo 10: *Drowsy Driver Statute*

New Jersey adopts a law prohibiting drivers from operating automobiles while drowsy. The law authorizes a conviction of vehicular homicide, punishable by up to 10 years in jail and a $100,000 fine, for anyone who causes a deadly car accident due to sleepiness. Was the new law needed? Would it have been possible to convict a motorist who grew drowsy and fell asleep of homicide without the law?

People v. Gory

28 Cal.2d 450, 170 P.2d 433 (1946).

SPENCE, JUSTICE.

Defendant was accused of (1) violating section 4573 of the Penal Code by unlawfully bringing marijuana into a prison farm; and (2) violating section 11160 of the Health and Safety Code in that he did, on or about June 2, 1944, 'willfully, unlawfully and feloniously have in his possession flowering tops and leaves of Indian Hemp (cannabis sativa),' commonly called marijuana. Defendant pleaded not guilty to the two offenses charged. The cause proceeded to trial before a jury; Count I of the information was dismissed upon motion of defendant; and defendant was found guilty on Count II as charged. From the judgment of conviction, defendant prosecutes this appeal. He contends that the evidence was insufficient to support the verdict and he specifies error in the matter of the instructions. We are convinced that the failure of the court to instruct the jury fully and clearly resulted in such prejudice as to require a reversal.

Defendant was a prisoner at the Los Angeles County Honor Farm. He shared living quarters with some thirty odd prisoners in one of the camp's bunkhouses. As part of the equipment issued to each prisoner, defendant received a metal box 18 inches long, 12 inches wide, 8 inches deep in which he kept his toilet articles and small personal effects. There was no way of locking these boxes. Each prisoner's box was placed on the floor near the head of his bed. During the day when the prisoners were engaged in duties on the farm, one man was left in charge of the bunkhouse to 'keep the inmates from monkeying with other people's property.' On June 2, 1944, several officers entered the bunkhouse. While his associates searched the boxes of other prisoners, Officer Gunderson went to defendant's bed on which defendant was lying picked up the metal box bearing the number of defendant's bed, opened the box and found marijuana. The officer examined defendant's clothes, turning the pockets 'wrong side out,' but found no marijuana either on his person or in his clothes. Deputy Sheriff Huber testified that he asked defendant what he knew about this marijuana, stating: 'This is your marijuana; where did you get it?' Defendant admitted that the marijuana was taken from his box, but stated that he had never seen it before the officers removed it from the box.

Defendant challenges the trial Court's action in withdrawing from the jury's consideration the following instructions:

> *Instruction 12:* 'In order for defendant to have in his possession the objects charged in the information, you must be convinced by the evidence and beyond a reasonable doubt that he knowingly had such objects in his possession. The meaning of the word 'possession' includes the exercise of dominion and control over the thing possessed.'
>
> *Instruction 13:* 'Even if you find from the evidence beyond a reasonable doubt that the defendant had in his possession, flowering tops of Indian Hemp or locoweed, before you can find the defendant guilty of possessing the same, you must also be

> convinced beyond a reasonable doubt that the defendant had a guilty knowledge of the character of said flowering tops of Indian Hemp and possessed a guilty intent. If you find that the defendant was innocent of the knowledge of the character of the flowering tops of Indian Hemp or did not have a guilty knowledge of possessing said flowering tops of Indian Hemp, then you will find the defendant not guilty and must acquit him.'

Section 20 of the Penal Code provides that 'In every crime or public offense there must exist a union, or joint operation of act and intent.' But this does not mean that a positive, willful intent to violate the law is an essential ingredient of every offense. Sometimes an act is expressly prohibited by statute, in which case the intentional doing of the act, regardless of good motive or ignorance of its criminal character, constitutes the offense denounced by law. Instances illustrating this principle may be found in statutes enacted for the protection of public morals, public health, and the public peace and safety. *People v. McClennegen*, 234 P. 91. If a specific intent is not made an ingredient of the statutory offense, it is not necessary to prove such specific intent in order to justify a conviction. *People v. Dillon*, 248 P. 230. Although in a prosecution for the unlawful possession of narcotics it has been said that 'Guilty knowledge and intent to violate the law may be shown by the facts and circumstances of the case, including the conduct of the defendant and any false or misleading statements which he may make to the arresting officers or others with relation to the material facts' *People v. Gibson*, 149 P.2d 25, such observation was made in a case where defendant sought to justify or explain his admitted possession of the drugs with full knowledge of their character. It was not intended to indicate that 'guilty knowledge and intent to violate the law' were essential elements requiring proof in every prosecution for possession.

While it thus appears that 'mere possession, except as authorized' is sufficient to constitute the statutory offense in question, without regard for scienter or specific intent to violate the law as would follow from evidence establishing defendant's knowledge of the contraband character of the property, the law makes the matter of knowledge in relation to defendant's awareness of the presence of the object a basic element of the offense of possession. Thus it was said in *People v. Noland*, 143 P.2d 86, 87: 'A person has 'possession' of a chattel who has physical control with the intent to exercise such control, or, having had such physical control, has not abandoned it and no other person has obtained possession. (Restatement Torts, section 216.)' But knowledge of the existence of the object is essential to 'physical control thereof with the intent to exercise such control' and such knowledge must necessarily precede the intent to exercise, or the exercise of, such control. *People v. Gallagher*, 55 P.2d 889. The distinction which must be drawn is the distinction between (1) knowledge of the character of the object and the unlawfulness of possession thereof as embraced within the concept of a specific intent to violate the law, and (2) knowledge of the presence of the object as embraced within the concept of 'physical control with the intent to exercise such control,' which constitutes the 'possession' denounced by the statute. It is 'knowledge' in the first sense which is mentioned in the authorities as being immaterial but 'knowledge' in the second sense is the essence of the offense.

Instruction 13, in requiring the finding of a 'guilty knowledge' and a 'guilty intent' on the part of defendant to sustain his conviction, was properly withdrawn from the jury as an improper matter for consideration. But instruction 12, in its predication of a finding of guilt upon defendant's 'knowingly' having 'in his possession the objects charged in the information,' should have been given to the jury. 'The word 'knowingly' imports only a knowledge that the facts exist which bring the act or omission within the provisions of this code. It does not require any knowledge of the unlawfulness of such act or omission.' Pen.Code, s 7, subd. 5. Thus instruction 12 invoked the element of knowledge in the sense of defendant's awareness of the presence of the marijuana in the box given him for the storage of his personal effects at the prison farm and so presented to the jury an issue of fact determinative of defendant's guilt or innocence of the possession prohibited by statute.

Matters tending to establish defendant's guilt are the fact that the marijuana was found in his box and the circumstance of his silence in the face of Officer Huber's accusation in the camp's bunkhouse. Matters tending to establish defendant's innocence are the fact that the box was unlocked, showing that the marijuana conceivably could have been placed there by someone other than defendant, and defendant's denial that he had ever seen the 'stuff' prior to its discovery by the officers. This may be a 'close case.' It is readily distinguishable from cases where the evidence includes express admissions and statements by defendant with respect to the possession of narcotics, which supplied the final link in the chain of circumstances connecting defendant with the offense charged against him. Likewise distinguishable are cases where the required possession of drugs was shown by testimony that the defendant threw the drug out of the window, or otherwise disposed of it upon the approach of the arresting officers, and that it was later returned and identified as having been in the custody and under the control of defendant prior to his arrest. *People v. Belli*, 15 P.2d 809. Here the principal fact relied upon by the prosecution is the finding of marijuana in defendant's unlocked box and because of the denial by defendant of knowledge of its presence there, it was the duty of the trial court, on proper instructions, to submit to the jury the question as to whether defendant had knowledge of the presence of the marijuana. *People v. Gin Shue*, 137 P.2d 742. To fail to instruct on that point might have misled the jury into believing either that knowledge was not essential or that any object found among defendant's personal effects was conclusively presumed to be there of his own knowledge. The error which would be involved in an express declaration to that effect is obvious, for knowledge is essential and though the finding of an object among defendant's effects would support an inference, it would not give rise to a conclusive presumption that the object was there with defendant's knowledge.

Our code provides that 'the word 'willfully,' when applied to the intent with which an act is done or omitted, implies simply a purpose or willingness to commit the act, or make the omission referred to. It does not require any intent to violate law' Pen.Code, s 7, subd. 1. While thus the word 'willfully' invokes the element of knowledge in the sense here required, the word was not defined in the instructions to the jury. This fact is material in view of the court's withdrawal of instruction 12, directed to the same element of knowledge in requiring that defendant must 'knowingly' have had 'in his possession the objects charged in the information' in order to be found guilty. Pen.Code, s 7, subd. 5. In this confusion in the submission of the essential issue of fact to the jury for consideration in the determination of defendant's guilt, it is doubtful whether the jury would infer from the word 'willfully' the element of knowledge in the required sense. It may be possible to argue that taking the instructions as a whole, they were sufficient to have informed the jury in a general roundabout way that before defendant could be convicted of the statutory offense of the possession of marijuana, the evidence must show his knowledge of the presence of said property in his box; but since knowledge, in that limited sense, is an essential element of the offense, he was entitled under the circumstances to a specific instruction, such as the requested instruction 12, to clarify the situation.

The judgment and the order denying defendant's motion for a new trial are reversed.

Robinson v. State of California

370 U.S. 660 (1962).

MR. JUSTICE STEWART delivered the opinion of the Court.

A California statute makes it a criminal offense for a person to "be addicted to the use of narcotics." Appellant was convicted after a jury trial in the Municipal Court of Los Angeles. The evidence against him was given by two Los Angeles police officers. Officer Brown testified that he had occasion to examine the appellant's arms one evening on a street in Los Angeles, and he observed "scar tissue and discoloration on the inside" of the appellant's right arm, and "what appeared to be numerous needle marks and a scab which was approximately three inches below the crook of the elbow" on appellant's left arm. The officer also testified that the appellant had admitted to the occasional use of narcotics. Officer Lindquist testified that he examined appellant the following morning in the Central Jail in Los Angeles. At that time he observed discolorations and scabs on appellant's arms, and he identified photographs which had been taken of appellant's arms shortly after his arrest the night before. Based upon more than ten years of experience as a member of the Narcotic Division, the witness gave his opinion that "these marks and the discoloration were the result of the injection of hypodermic needles into the tissue into the vein that was not sterile." He stated that the scabs were several days old at the time of his examination, and that appellant was neither under the influence of narcotics nor suffering withdrawal symptoms at the time he saw him. This witness also testified that appellant admitted using narcotics in the past.

The trial judge instructed the jury that the statute made it a misdemeanor for a person "either to use narcotics, or to be addicted to the use of narcotics." That portion of the statute referring to the 'use' of narcotics is based upon the 'act' of using. That portion of the statute referring to 'addicted to the use' of narcotics is based upon a condition or status. They are not identical. To be addicted to the use of narcotics is said to be a status or condition and not an act. It is a continuing offense and differs from most other offenses in the fact that it is chronic rather than acute; that it continues after it is complete and subjects the offender to arrest at any time before he reforms. The existence of such a chronic condition may be ascertained from a single examination, if the characteristic reactions of that condition be found present." The

Take Note

Note the Court's distinction between "status" crimes (e.g., being a drug addict) and crimes involving the performance of criminal acts (taking illegal drugs). This point will determine the limits of *Robinson*'s application in future cases.

judge further instructed the jury that appellant could be convicted under a general verdict if the jury agreed either that he was of the "status" or had committed the "act" denounced by the statute. "All that the People must show is either that the defendant did use a narcotic in Los Angeles County, or that while in the City of Los Angeles he was addicted to the use of narcotics." The jury returned a verdict finding the appellant "guilty of the offense charged."

It would be possible to construe the statute under which appellant was convicted as one which is operative only upon proof of the actual use of narcotics within the State's jurisdiction. But the California courts have not so construed this law. Although there was evidence that appellant had used narcotics in Los Angeles, the jury were instructed that they could convict him if they found simply that the appellant's "status" or "chronic condition" was that of being "addicted to the use of narcotics." It is impossible to know from the jury's verdict that defendant was not convicted upon precisely such a finding. This statute, therefore, is not one which punishes a person for the use of narcotics, for their purchase, sale or possession, or for antisocial or disorderly behavior resulting from their administration. It is not a law which even purports to provide or require medical treatment. Rather, we deal with a statute which makes the "status" of narcotic addiction a criminal offense, for which the offender may be prosecuted "at any time before he reforms." California has said that a person can be continuously guilty of this offense, whether or not he has ever used or possessed any narcotics within the State, and whether or not he has been guilty of any antisocial behavior there.

It is unlikely that any State at this moment in history would attempt to make it a criminal offense for a person to be mentally ill, or a leper, or to be afflicted with a venereal disease. A State might determine that the general health and welfare require that the victims of these and other human afflictions be dealt with by compulsory treatment, involving quarantine, confinement, or sequestration. But, in the light of contemporary human knowledge, a law which made a criminal offense of such a disease would doubtless be universally thought to be an infliction of cruel and unusual punishment in violation of the Eighth and Fourteenth Amendments.

We cannot but consider the statute before us as of the same category. In this Court counsel for the State recognized that narcotic addiction is an illness. Indeed, it is apparently an illness which may be contracted innocently or involuntarily.[9] We hold that a state law which imprisons a person thus afflicted as a criminal, even though he has never touched any narcotic drug within the State or been guilty of any irregular behavior there, inflicts a cruel and unusual punishment in violation of the Fourteenth Amendment. To be sure, imprisonment" for ninety days is not, in the abstract, a punishment which is either cruel or unusual. But the question

9 Not only may addiction innocently result from the use of medically prescribed narcotics, but a person may even be a narcotics addict from the moment of his birth.

cannot be considered in the abstract. Even one day in prison would be a cruel and unusual punishment for the "crime" of having a common cold.

We are not unmindful that the vicious evils of the narcotics traffic have occasioned the grave concern of government. There are countless fronts on which those evils may be legitimately attacked. We deal in this case only with an individual provision of a particularized local law as it has so far been interpreted by the California courts.

Reversed.

MR. JUSTICE DOUGLAS, concurring.

The first step toward drug addiction may be as innocent as a boy's puff on a cigarette in an alleyway. It may come from medical prescriptions. Addiction may even be present at birth. Earl Ubell recently wrote: "In Bellevue Hospital's nurseries, Dr. Saul Krugman, head of pediatrics, has been discovering babies minutes old who are heroin addicts. More than 100 such infants have turned up in the last two years, and they show all the signs of drug withdrawal: irritability, jitters, loss of appetite, vomiting, diarrhea, sometimes convulsions and death. Of course, they get the drug while in the womb from their mothers who are addicts.'"

The addict is under compulsions not capable of management without outside help. Some say the addict has a disease. Others say addiction is not a disease but "a symptom of a mental or psychiatric disorder." Some States punish addiction, though most do not. Nor does the Uniform Narcotic Drug Act, first approved in 1932 and now in effect in most of the States. We know that there is "a hard core" of "chronic and incurable drug addicts who, in reality, have lost their power of self-control." The impact that an addict has on a community causes alarm and often leads to punitive measures. Those measures are justified when they relate to acts of transgression. But I do not see how under our system being an addict can be punished as a crime. If addicts can be punished for their addiction, then the insane can also be punished for their insanity. Each has a disease and each must be treated as a sick person.

The command of the Eighth Amendment, banning "cruel and unusual punishments," stems from the Bill of Rights of 1688. And it is applicable to the States by reason of the Due Process Clause of the Fourteenth Amendment. The historic punishments that were cruel and unusual included "burning at the stake, crucifixion, breaking on the wheel", quartering, the rack and thumbscrew, and in some circumstances even solitary confinement.

The Eighth Amendment expresses the revulsion of civilized man against barbarous acts—the "cry of horror" against man's inhumanity to his fellow man. By the time of Coke, enlightenment was coming as respects the insane. Coke said that the execution of a madman "should be a miserable spectacle, both against law, and of extreme inhumanity and cruelty, and can be no example to others." Blackstone endorsed this view of Coke.

We should show the same discernment respecting drug addiction. The addict is a sick person. He may, of course, be confined for treatment or for the protection of society. Cruel and unusual punishment results not from confinement, but from convicting the addict of a crime. The purpose of § 11721 is not to cure, but to penalize. Were the purpose to cure, there would be no need for a mandatory jail term of not less than 90 days. A prosecution for addiction, with its resulting stigma and irreparable damage to the good name of the accused, cannot be justified as a means of protecting society, where a civil commitment would do as well. This age of enlightenment cannot tolerate such barbarous action.

MR. JUSTICE HARLAN, concurring.

Insofar as addiction may be identified with the use or possession of narcotics within the State, in violation of local statutes prohibiting such acts, it may surely be reached by the State's criminal law. But in this case the trial court's instructions permitted the jury to find the appellant guilty on no more proof than that he was present in California while he was addicted to narcotics. Since addiction alone cannot reasonably be thought to amount to more than a compelling propensity to use narcotics, the effect of this instruction was to authorize criminal punishment for a bare desire to commit a criminal act. The statute is an arbitrary imposition which exceeds the power that a State may exercise in enacting its criminal law. Accordingly, I agree that the application of the California statute was unconstitutional in this case.

MR. JUSTICE CLARK, dissenting.

The majority acknowledges that a State can punish persons who purchase, possess or use narcotics. Although none of these acts are harmful to society in themselves, the State constitutionally may attempt to deter and prevent them through punishment because of the grave threat of future harmful conduct which they pose. Narcotics addiction—including the incipient, volitional addiction to which this provision speaks—is no different. California courts have taken judicial notice that "the inordinate use of a narcotic drug tends to create an irresistible craving and forms a habit for its continued use until one becomes an addict, and he respects no convention or obligation and will lie, steal, or use any other base means to gratify his passion for the drug, being lost to all considerations of duty or social position." Can this Court deny the legislative and judicial judgment of California that incipient, volitional narcotic addiction poses a threat of serious crime similar to the threat inherent in the purchase or possession of narcotics? If such a threat is inherent in addiction, can this Court say that California is powerless to deter it by punishment?

It is no answer to suggest that we are dealing with an involuntary status and thus penal sanctions will be ineffective and unfair. The section at issue applies only to persons who use narcotics often or even daily but not to the point of losing self-control. When dealing with involuntary addicts California moves only through § 5355 of its Welfare Institutions Code which clearly is not penal. Even if it could be argued that § 11721 may not be limited to volitional addicts, petitioner undeniably retained the power of self-control and thus to him the statute would be constitutional. Nor is the conjecture relevant that petitioner may have acquired his habit under lawful circumstances. There was no suggestion by him to this effect at trial, and surely the State need not rebut all possible lawful sources of addiction as part of its *prima facie* case.

Properly construed, the statute provides a treatment rather than a punishment. But even if interpreted as penal, the sanction of incarceration for 3 to 12 months is not unreasonable when applied to a person who has voluntarily placed himself in a condition posing a serious threat to the State. Under either theory, its provisions for 3 to 12 months' confinement can hardly be deemed unreasonable when compared to the provisions for 3 to 24 months' confinement under § 5355 which the majority approves. I would affirm.

MR. JUSTICE WHITE, dissenting.

I do not consider appellant's conviction to be a punishment for having an illness or for simply being in some status or condition, but rather a conviction for the regular, repeated or habitual use of narcotics immediately prior to his arrest and in violation of California law. Addiction is the regular use of narcotics and can be proved only by evidence of such use. To find addiction in this case the jury had to believe that appellant had frequently used narcotics in the recent past. Nor do I find any indications that California would apply § 11721 to the case of the helpless addict. I agree that there was no evidence at all that appellant had lost the power to control his acts.

The Court does not rest its decision upon the narrow ground that the jury was not expressly instructed not to convict if it believed appellant's use of narcotics was beyond his control. The Court recognizes no degrees of addiction. The Fourteenth Amendment is today held to bar any prosecution for addiction regardless of the degree or frequency of use, and the Court's opinion bristles with indications of further consequences. If it is "cruel and unusual punishment" to convict appellant for addiction, it is difficult to understand why it would be any less offensive to the Fourteenth Amendment to convict him for use on the same evidence of use which proved he was an addict. The Court has not merely tidied up California's law by removing some irritating vestige of an outmoded approach to the control of narcotics. It has effectively removed California's power to deal effectively with the recurring case under the statute where there is ample evidence of use but no evidence of the precise location of use. Beyond this it has cast serious doubt upon the power of any State to forbid the use of narcotics under threat of criminal punishment.

Points for Discussion

a. Being Drunk in Public

What if a chronic alcoholic is convicted of the crime of "being found in a state of intoxication in a public place"? In *Powell v. Texas*, 392 U.S. 514 (1968), appellant contended that he was "afflicted with the disease of chronic alcoholism," that "his appearance in public while drunk was not of his own volition," and therefore "that to punish him criminally for that conduct would be cruel and unusual, in violation of the Eighth and Fourteenth Amendments to the United States Constitution." The Court disagreed:

> The present case does not fall within *Robinson*'s holding, since appellant was convicted, not for being a chronic alcoholic, but for being in public while drunk on a particular occasion. The State of Texas thus has not sought to punish a mere

> status, nor has it attempted to regulate appellant's behavior in the privacy of his own home. Rather, it has imposed upon appellant a criminal sanction for public behavior which may create substantial health and safety hazards, both for appellant and for members of the general public, and which offends the moral and esthetic sensibilities of a large segment of the community. This seems a far cry from convicting one for being an addict, being a chronic alcoholic, being "mentally ill, or a leper."
>
> It is suggested in dissent that *Robinson* stands for the "simple" but "subtle" principle that "criminal penalties may not be inflicted upon a person for being in a condition he is powerless to change." The thrust of *Robinson*'s interpretation of the Cruel and Unusual Punishment Clause is that criminal penalties may be inflicted only if the accused has committed some act, has engaged in some behavior, which society has an interest in preventing, or perhaps in historical common law terms, has committed some *actus reus*. It thus does not deal with the question of whether certain conduct cannot constitutionally be punished because it is, in some sense, "involuntary" or "occasioned by a compulsion." We are unable to conclude that chronic alcoholics in general, and Leroy Powell in particular, suffer from such an irresistible compulsion to drink and to get drunk in public that they are utterly unable to control their performance of either or both of these acts and thus cannot be deterred at all from public intoxication.

Mr. Justice Black concurred: "Punishment of such a defendant can clearly be justified in terms of deterrence, isolation, and treatment. Even if we were to limit any holding in this field to 'compulsions' that are 'symptomatic' of a 'disease,' the sweep of that holding would still be startling. Such a ruling would make it clear beyond any doubt that a narcotics addict could not be punished for 'being' in possession of drugs or, for that matter, for 'being' guilty of using them. A wide variety of sex offenders would be immune from punishment if they could show that their conduct was not voluntary but part of the pattern of a disease." Mr. Justice White also concurred: "Powell's conviction was for the different crime of being drunk in a public place. Many chronic alcoholics drink at home and are never seen drunk in public. The alcoholic is like a person with smallpox, who could be convicted for being on the street but not for being ill, or, like the epileptic, who would be punished for driving a car but not for his disease." Mr. Justice Fortas dissented:

> This case does not raise any question as to the right of the police to stop and detain those who are intoxicated in public, whether as a result of the disease or otherwise; or as to the State's power to commit chronic alcoholics for treatment. Nor does it concern the responsibility of an alcoholic for criminal acts. We deal here with the mere condition of being intoxicated in public. The essential constitutional defect here is the same as in *Robinson*, for in both cases the particular defendant was accused of being in a condition which he had no capacity to change or avoid. Powell is a "chronic alcoholic" which is "a disease which destroys the afflicted person's will power to resist the constant, excessive consumption of alcohol," and, therefore, "a chronic alcoholic does not appear in public by his own volition but under a

> compulsion symptomatic of the disease of chronic alcoholism." I read these findings to mean that appellant was powerless to avoid drinking; that having taken his first drink, he had "an uncontrollable compulsion to drink" to the point of intoxication; and that, once intoxicated, he could not prevent himself from appearing in public places. The findings of the trial judge call into play the principle that a person may not be punished if the condition essential to constitute the defined crime is part of the pattern of his disease and is occasioned by a compulsion symptomatic of the disease. This principle, narrow in scope and applicability, is implemented by the Eighth Amendment's prohibition of "cruel and unusual punishment," as we construed that command in *Robinson*.

b. Felon Registration Statutes

In *Lambert v. People*, 355 U.S. 225 (1957), a Los Angeles ordinance required "any convicted person" to register with the police within five days of arriving in the city. Defendant failed to register and was charged for her failure. The Court overturned her conviction because the ordinance punished passive behavior (the "mere failure to register") and there was nothing that would alert the felon to the obligation to register. Although the Court recognized the importance of the rule that "ignorance of the law will not excuse," the Court held that notice of the obligation is required under these circumstances:

> The present ordinance is entirely different. Violation of its provisions is unaccompanied by any activity whatever, mere presence in the city being the test. Moreover, circumstances which might move one to inquire as to the necessity of registration are completely lacking. At most the ordinance is but a law enforcement technique designed for the convenience of law enforcement agencies through which a list of the names and addresses of felons then residing in a given community is compiled. Appellant on first becoming aware of her duty to register was given no opportunity to comply with the law and avoid its penalty, even though her default was entirely innocent. She could but suffer the consequences of the ordinance, namely, conviction with the imposition of heavy criminal penalties there under. We believe that actual knowledge of the duty to register or proof of the probability of such knowledge and subsequent failure to comply are necessary before a conviction under the ordinance can stand.

Mr. Justice Frankfurter dissented: "The laws of the United States and of the forty-eight States are thick with provisions that command that some things not be done and others be done, although persons convicted under such provisions may have had no awareness of what the law required or that what they did was wrongdoing."

Hypo 1: *Analyzing* Robinson

How far does *Robinson*'s logic extend? Suppose that Robinson was convicted of using narcotics in the State of California and is now on probation. Following his release, a narcotics detective notices that Robinson has extensive needle marks on his arms (indicative of drug use). Rather than charging Robinson with "being addicted to the use of narcotics" (as Robinson was charged), the officer charges Robinson with actually using narcotics in California. The officer seeks to use Robinson's past history, and the recent needle marks, to infer the recent drug use. Is a conviction appropriate under these circumstances?

Food for Thought

Would it be constitutional to punish a homeless chronic alcoholic (who is destitute and unable to afford housing) for being drunk in a public place?

Hypo 2: *Drug Addicts and Drug Use*

Can the state make it a crime for a drug addict to use illegal narcotics? If the state cannot make it a crime to be "addicted to drugs," how can it punish the addict for using them? If it is permissible to punish the use of drugs, is it also permissible to punish the addict for prior acts of drug use that led to the addiction (assuming, of course, that the prior acts took place within the state)? *See State v. Bridges*, 360 S.W.2d 648 (Mo. 1962).

Hypo 3: *The Anti-Camping Ordinance and the Homeless*

The City of Santa Ana, California, passes a law banning "camping" and storage of personal property, including camping equipment, in designated public areas. The ordinance is designed to preserve public streets and public areas in a clean and accessible condition. Plaintiffs contend that the ordinance is unconstitutional as applied to homeless persons. There is some history between the city and the homeless. Previously, the City had tried to expel "vagrants" by creating early park closing times, disposing of sleeping bags and accessories, confiscating abandoned shopping carts, monitoring providers of free food, and turning on sprinklers frequently in city parks. This effort led to a lawsuit which the city settled. At that point, the City

FYI

Some statutes and ordinances punish the crime of "possession" of various items, including such things as illegal drugs or burglar's tools.

adopted the anti-camping ordinance even though the city has 3,000 homeless persons and its shelter can hold only 330 people. If enforced, the ordinance might be applied to Wilfred J., a 58-year-old who became homeless when the truck he used for hauling jobs was stolen. He lives by the railroad tracks, and sleeps on what he refers to as "God's Land," a ramp at a church. The law would also be applied to Mildred B., a 35-year-old homeless person who suffers from schizophrenia, and who sleeps near the Civic Center and in a parking garage during inclement weather. In the past, the police have seized her belongings when she left them in a public place. Does the anti-camping ordinance unfairly punish indigents for their homeless status? *See Tobe v. City of Santa Ana*, 27 Cal. Rptr. 2d 386 (Cal. App. 1994) & *Tobe v. City of Santa Ana*, 892 P.2d 1145 (1995).

B. Omissions

Even though criminal liability must be based on a voluntary act, the term "act" is defined broadly enough to include an "omission" to act when an individual is under a duty to act. For example, MPC § 2.01 provides that liability can be based on an "omission to perform an act of which he is physically capable."

Jones v. United States

308 F.2d 307 (D.C.Cir. 1962).

WRIGHT, CIRCUIT JUDGE.

Appellant, together with Shirley Green, was tried on an indictment charging them jointly with involuntary manslaughter through failure to perform their legal duty of care for Anthony Lee Green, which failure resulted in his death. Appellant was also convicted of involuntary manslaughter. Shirley Green was found not guilty. Appellant argues that there was insufficient evidence as a matter of law to warrant a jury finding of breach of duty in the care she rendered Anthony Lee. Alternatively, she argues that the trial court committed plain error in failing to instruct the jury that it must first find that appellant was under a legal obligation to provide food and necessities to Anthony Lee before finding her guilty of manslaughter in failing to provide them. The first argument is without merit. Upon the latter we reverse.

In late 1957, Shirley Green became pregnant, out of wedlock, with a child, Robert Lee, subsequently born August 17, 1958. Apparently to avoid the embarrassment of the presence of the child in the Green home, it was arranged that appellant, a family friend, would take the child to her home after birth. Appellant did so, and the child remained there continuously until removed by the police on August 5, 1960. Initially appellant made some motions toward the adoption of Robert Lee, but these came to naught, and shortly thereafter it was agreed that

Shirley Green was to pay appellant $72 a month for his care. These payments were made for only five months up to July, 1960.

Early in 1959 Shirley Green again became pregnant, this time with the child Anthony Lee, whose death is the basis of appellant's conviction. Soon after birth, Anthony Lee developed a mild jaundice condition, attributed to a blood income with his mother. The jaundice resulted in his retention in the hospital for three days beyond the usual time, when Anthony Lee was released to appellant's custody. Shirley Green, after a two or three day stay in the hospital, also lived with appellant for three weeks, after which she returned to her parents' home, leaving the children with appellant. She testified she did not see them again, except for one visit in March, until August 5, 1960. Though there does not seem to have been any specific monetary agreement with Shirley Green covering Anthony Lee's support,[5] appellant had complete custody of both children until they were rescued by the police.

With regard to medical care, the evidence is undisputed. In March, 1960, appellant called a Dr. Turner to her home to treat Anthony Lee for a bronchial condition. Appellant also telephoned the doctor at various times to consult with him concerning Anthony Lee's diet and health. In early July, 1960, appellant took Anthony Lee to Dr. Turner's office where he was treated for "simple diarrhea." At this time the doctor noted the "wizened" appearance of the child and told appellant to tell the mother of the child that he should be taken to a hospital. This was not done.

On August 2, 1960, two collectors for the local gas company had occasion to go to the basement of appellant's home, and there saw the two children. Robert Lee and Anthony Lee at this time were age two years and ten months respectively. Robert Lee was in a "crib" consisting of a framework of wood, covered with a fine wire screening, including the top which was hinged. The "crib" was lined with newspaper, which was stained, apparently with feces, and crawling with roaches. Anthony Lee was lying in a bassinet and was described as having the appearance of a "small baby monkey." One collector testified to seeing roaches on Anthony Lee. Three days later, the collectors returned to appellant's home in the company of several police officers and personnel of the Women's Bureau. At this time, Anthony Lee was upstairs in the dining room in the bassinet, but Robert Lee was still downstairs in his "crib." The officers removed the children to the D.C. General Hospital where Anthony Lee was diagnosed as suffering from severe malnutrition and lesions over large portions of his body, apparently caused by severe diaper rash. Following admission, he was fed repeatedly, apparently with no difficulty, and was described as being very hungry. His death, 34 hours after admission, was attributed without dispute to malnutrition. At birth, Anthony Lee weighed six pounds, fifteen ounces—at death at age ten months, he weighed seven pounds, thirteen ounces. Normal weight at this age would have been approximately 14 pounds.

Appellant argues that nothing in the evidence establishes that she failed to provide food to Anthony Lee. She cites her own testimony and the testimony of a lodger, Mr. Wills, that

5 During the entire period the children were in appellant's home, appellant had ample means to provide food and medical care.

she did in fact feed the baby regularly. At trial, the defense made repeated attempts to extract from the medical witnesses opinions that the jaundice, or the condition which caused it, might have prevented the baby from assimilating food. The doctors conceded this was possible but not probable since the autopsy revealed no condition which would support the defense theory. It was also shown by disinterested medical witnesses that the child had no difficulty in ingesting food immediately after birth, and that Anthony Lee, in the last hours before his death, was able to take several bottles, apparently without difficulty, and seemed very hungry. This evidence, combined with the absence of any physical cause for nonassimilation, taken in the context of the condition in which these children were kept, presents a jury question on the feeding issue.

Take Note

Note the four situations in which this court is willing to impose criminal liability for a failure to act. These four situations are fairly typical contexts in which liability is imposed.

There is substantial evidence from which the jury could have found that appellant failed to obtain proper medical care for the child. Appellant relies upon evidence showing that on one occasion she summoned a doctor for the child, on another took the child to the doctor's office, and that she telephoned the doctor on several occasions about the baby's formula. However, the last time a doctor saw the child was a month before his death, and appellant admitted that on that occasion the doctor recommended hospitalization. Appellant did not hospitalize the child, nor did she take any other steps to obtain medical care in the last crucial month. Thus there was sufficient evidence to go to the jury on the issue of medical care, as well as failure to feed.

Appellant also takes exception to the failure of the trial court to charge that the jury must find beyond a reasonable doubt, as an element of the crime, that appellant was under a legal duty to supply food and necessities to Anthony Lee. The problem of establishing the duty to take action which would preserve the life of another has not often arisen in the case law of this country. The most commonly cited statement of the rule is found in *People v. Beardsley*, 113 N.W. 1128, 1129: "The law recognizes that under some circumstances the omission of a duty owed by one individual to another, where such omission results in the death of the one to whom the duty is owing, will make the other chargeable with manslaughter. This rule of law is always based upon the proposition that the duty neglected must be a legal duty, and not a mere moral obligation. It must be a duty imposed by law or by contract, and the omission to perform the duty must be the immediate and direct cause of death."

Take Note

Consider the MPC provision relating to omission:

§ 2.01 [Omission as Basis of Liability]

* * *

(3) Liability for the commission of an offense may not be based on an omission unaccompanied by action unless:

(a) the omission is expressly made sufficient by the law defining the offense; or

(b) a duty to perform the omitted act is otherwise imposed by law.

There are at least four situations in which the failure to act may constitute breach of a legal duty. One can be held criminally liable: first, where a statute imposes a duty to care for another; second, where one stands in a certain status relationship to another; third, where one has assumed a contractual duty to care for another; and fourth, where one has voluntarily assumed the care of another and so secluded the helpless person as to prevent others from rendering aid.

It is the contention of the Government that either the third or the fourth ground is applicable here. However, the instructions given in the case failed even to suggest the necessity for finding a legal duty of care. The only reference to duty in the instructions was the reading of the indictment which charged, inter alia, that the defendants "failed to perform their legal duty." A finding of legal duty is the critical element of the crime charged and failure to instruct the jury concerning it was plain error.

Reversed and remanded.

Food for Thought

What other situations might give rise to a duty on the part of one person to assist another? Suppose that two individuals are hiking together in a remote wilderness area. One falls into a hole and breaks his leg. Does the fellow hiker have an obligation to come to his assistance?

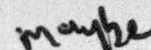

Point for Discussion

Taking Responsibility

In *Commonwealth v. Pestinikas*, 617 A.2d 1339 (1992), Joseph Kly was hospitalized with a serious illness, and subsequently chose to live with the Pestinikas in their home. When the Pestinikas took Kly from the hospital to their home, medical personnel instructed them regarding his care and gave them a prescription to fill. The prescription was never filled. Instead of giving Kly a room in their home, appellants placed him in a rural house which had no insulation, no refrigeration, no bathroom, no sink and no telephone. The walls contained cracks which exposed the room to outside weather conditions. Kly's predicament was compounded by defendants' affirmative efforts to conceal his whereabouts. They gave misleading information in response to inquiries, telling members of Kly's family that they did not know where he had gone and others that he was living in their home. At some point, appellants had their names added to Kly's savings account, and they subsequently withdrew $300 dollars per month which Kly had agreed to pay for his care. After a while, the Pestinikas withdrew much larger sums (amounting to a total of $30,000) so that only $55 dollars remained

Make the Connection

Even if defendant has a duty to act, and fails to act, criminal responsibility is not automatic. In Chapter 3, we will examine the *mens rea* (or mental state) requirement. The failure to act must have been committed with the required *mens rea*.

when Kly died. When Kly died, emergency personnel found that he was emaciated and that his ribs and sternum were greatly pronounced. Mrs. Pestinikas told police that she had given him cookies and orange juice on the morning of his death. A subsequent autopsy, however, revealed that Kly was dead at that time and may have been dead for as many as thirty-nine (39) hours before his body was found. The cause of death was determined to be starvation and dehydration. The Court affirmed the Pestinikas' conviction for murder, concluding that there was evidence suggesting that they failed to provide him with food and medical care: "The jury was required to find that appellants, by virtue of contract, had undertaken responsibility for providing necessary care for Kly to the exclusion of the members of Kly's family. This would impose upon them a legal duty to act to preserve Kly's life. If they maliciously set upon a course of withholding food and medicine and thereby caused Kly's death, appellants could be found guilty of murder." *See also People v. Montecino*, 66 Cal. App. 2d 85, 152 P.2d 5 (1944).

Hypo 1: *Applying* Jones

In the *Jones* case, if Jones had a duty to care for the child, when did that duty arise? When did she violate that duty? Did Anthony's mother likewise have a duty towards him? Did she violate that duty? Was it permissible for the mother to leave the child with Jones, or did she violate her duty simply by leaving the boy with Jones? If there was no breach of duty simply by leaving the child with Jones, when did a breach of duty occur?

Food for Thought

Every year, in every major city, people die of cold and starvation. If we impose a legal duty on all citizens to help others in distress, would that mean that a well-heeled citizen could be criminally prosecuted for refusing to help a beggar in need if the beggar dies from starvation?

Hypo 2: *Should the Law Impose a "Duty" to Rescue Others?*

Rhode Island requires those present at the scene of an emergency to render assistance to those exposed to "grave physical harm" if he/she can do so "without danger or peril to himself or herself or to others."[1] Vermont has a similar law.

1 R.I. Gen. Law § 11–56–1:

Any person at the scene of an emergency who knows that another person is exposed to, or has suffered, grave physical harm shall, to the extent that he or she can do so without danger or peril to himself or herself or to others, give reasonable assistance to the exposed person. Any person violating the provisions of this section shall be guilty of a petty misdemeanor and shall be subject to imprisonment for a term not exceeding six (6) months or by a fine of not more than five hundred dollars ($500), or both.

12 V.S.A. § 519. Emergency Medical Care

(a) A person who knows that another is exposed to grave physical harm shall, to the extent that the same can be rendered without danger or peril to himself or without interference with important duties owed to others, give reasonable assistance to the exposed person unless that assistance or care is being provided by others.

(b) A person who provides reasonable assistance in compliance with subsection (a) of this section shall not be liable in civil damages unless his acts constitute gross negligence or unless he will receive or expects to receive remuneration. Nothing contained in this subsection shall alter existing law with respect to tort liability of a practitioner of the healing arts for acts committed in the ordinary course of his practice.

(c) A person who willfully violates subsection (a) of this section shall be fined not more than $100.00.

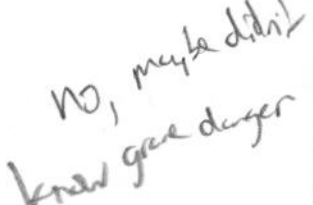

Other states have comparable laws including Wisconsin[2] and California.[3] In the *Jones* case, should appellant be responsible without regard to the existence of a "duty?" Do these laws go far enough in imposing a duty to help? Do they go too far?

---

2 W.S.A. 940.34. **Duty to aid victim or report crime:**

(1) (a) Whoever violates sub. (2)(a) is guilty of a Class C misdemeanor.

(b) Whoever violates sub. (2)(b) is guilty of a Class C misdemeanor and is subject to discipline under § 440.26(6).

(c) Whoever violates sub. (2)(c) is guilty of a Class C misdemeanor.

(2)(a) Any person who knows that a crime is being committed and that a victim is exposed to bodily harm shall summon law enforcement officers or other assistance or shall provide assistance to the victim.

(b) Any person licensed as a private detective or granted a private security permit under § 440.26 who has reasonable grounds to believe that a crime is being committed or has been committed shall notify promptly an appropriate law enforcement agency of the facts which form the basis for this belief.

* * *

(d) A person need not comply with this subsection if any of the following apply:

1. Compliance would place him or her in danger.
2. Compliance would interfere with duties the person owes to others.
3. In the circumstances described under par. (a), assistance is being summoned or provided by others.
4. In the circumstances described under par. (b) or (c), the crime or alleged crime has been reported to an appropriate law enforcement agency by others.

(2m) If a person is subject to sub. (2)(b) or (c), the person need not comply with sub. (2)(b) or (c) until after he or she has summoned or provided assistance to a victim.

(3) If a person renders emergency care for a victim, § 895.48(1) applies. Any person who provides other reasonable assistance under this section is immune from civil liability for his or her acts or omissions in providing the assistance. This immunity does not apply if the person receives or expects to receive compensation for providing the assistance.

3 **California's law provides as follows:**

Cal. Penal Code § 368. **Elder or dependent adults; infliction of pain or mental suffering or endangering health; theft or embezzlement of property; penalties; definitions**

Hypo 3: *The Kitty Genovese Case*

Consider the murder of Kitty Genovese which was described in *Moseley v. Scully*, 908 F. Supp. 1120 (E.D.N.Y. 1995), as follows:

> This case involves one of the most infamous and brutal murders committed this century, which shocked the nation when it was committed in 1964, and continues to trouble the public today. The 1964 murder of Katherine "Kitty" Genovese ("Genovese") in Queens, New York "symbolized urban apathy since 38 people heard her screams but did nothing." Defendant left his house in the early morning hours with a hunting knife for the purpose of "finding a woman and killing her." About 3:00 a.m., he spotted a red car, driven by Genovese, which he followed for approximately ten blocks. When Genovese exited her car, Moseley "stabbed her twice in the back." Because someone had called out from an open window, Moseley returned to his car and moved it, but he "could see that Genovese had gotten up and that she wasn't dead." Since he "did not think that the person that called would come down to help Genovese regardless of the fact that she had screamed, he came back and looked for her in the Long Island railroad station." Not finding her there, Moseley looked in some nearby apartment buildings, where he found her in a hallway. "As soon as she saw me, she started screaming, so I stabbed her a few times to stop her from screaming, and I stabbed her once in the neck. She only moaned after that." During this brutal attack, Moseley could hear that he had awakened residents of the apartment building. He heard a door open "at least twice, maybe three times, but when he looked up, there was nobody up there." Since he "didn't feel that these people were coming down the stairs," he decided to rape Genovese and left Genovese dead.

Can the state bring homicide prosecutions against those who overheard the incident, but who did nothing to help? If not, should the law be changed to allow prosecution of those who overheard? If so, how would you formulate the new law?

---

* * *

(b) A person who knows or reasonably should know that a person is an elder or dependent adult and who, under circumstances or conditions likely to produce great bodily harm or death, willfully causes or permits any elder or dependent adult to suffer, or inflicts thereon unjustifiable physical pain or mental suffering, or having the care or custody of any elder or dependent adult, willfully causes or permits the person or health of the elder or dependent adult to be injured, or willfully causes or permits the elder or dependent adult to be placed in a situation in which his or her person or health is endangered, is punishable by imprisonment in a county jail not exceeding one year, or by a fine not to exceed six thousand dollars ($6,000), or by both that fine and imprisonment, or by imprisonment in the state prison for two, three, or four years.

Food for Thought

Yates met defendant on the evening before her death at a party in defendant's apartment. Marijuana was in use, and defendant was flirting with the victim. Yates spent the night in defendant's apartment and the two of them shared some cocaine. Defendant then went out. When he returned, he found Yates on his bed, naked from the waist up, and in severe convulsions from the cocaine. She was hemorrhaging from her nose and mouth, and hemorrhaging blocked the passage of air to her lungs. Does defendant have a "legal duty" to seek assistance for Yates so that, if he provides no aid and she dies, he can be charged with homicide? *See Herman v. State*, 472 So.2d 770 (Fla. App.1985).

Hypo 4: *Overdose Reprise*

Defendant, a married man, worked as a bartender at a hotel. While his wife was away, defendant had an affair with a woman named Blanche Burns. The two had been acquainted for some time and had had affairs in the past. Both went to defendant's house where they drank steadily for two days. At some point, defendant helped Burns purchase morphine tablets. Defendant saw Burns consume the morphine. Before defendant's wife returned, he moved her to another apartment in the house. At the time, the victim was passed out. Burns later died from lack of medical assistance. Under the circumstances, did defendant have a "duty" to assist Burns? *See People v. Beardsley*, 113 N.W. 1128 (1907).

Food for Thought

Due to no fault of his own, defendant's building caught fire. Since defendant wanted to collect insurance on the building, he made no effort to put the fire out. In addition, he failed to report the fire to the fire department. Can defendant be convicted of burning a building with the intention of collecting the insurance proceeds? *See Commonwealth v. Cali*, 247 Mass. 20, 141 N.E. 510 (1923).

Hypo 5: *The Rapist and His Victim*

Defendant attacked and raped Edith Barton. Immediately afterwards, as she was in great distress of mind and body, she fell into a stream called Sugar Creek. Defendant made no attempt to rescue her even though he could have done so easily with no risk to himself. Edith Barton drowned. Did defendant have a legal obligation to rescue Barton? *See Jones v. State*, 220 Ind. 384, 43 N.E.2d 1017 (1942).

Hypo 6: *The Gateman*

Defendant was employed by a railroad company as a crossing gateman. Although a train was approaching, defendant failed to lower the crossing gate. Dan Goble, not realizing that a train was coming, drove across the tracks in his automobile and was hit by the train. Goble was killed. Did defendant have a legal duty to lower the gate so that he can be prosecuted criminally for his failure to do so? *See State v. Harrison*, 107 N.J.L. 213, 152 A. 867 (1931).

Hypo 7: *The Spouse and the Diabetic Husband*

Reverend Flaherty was a teacher, counselor, and chaplain at United Wesleyan College. Flaherty a thirty-four year old diabetic was taking daily doses of insulin. After hearing a visiting evangelist speaker, Flaherty proclaimed his desire to discontinue insulin treatment in reliance on the belief that God would heal his diabetic condition. When Flaherty fell ill and requested insulin, his wife discouraged him from taking it. As the day progressed, Reverend Flaherty became more ill, and vomited intermittently. The next day he remained in bed all day except for trips to the bathroom. As the Reverend's condition worsened, his wife and a friend administered cracked ice but did not summon medical aid. When the couple's eleven year old daughter inquired why a doctor had not been summoned, Mrs. Flaherty responded that her husband was "going to get better." The next morning at approximately 6 a.m., while the others were still asleep, Reverend Flaherty died of diabetic ketoacidosis. Under the circumstances, did Mrs. Flaherty have a legal obligation to summon medical assistance for her husband? *See Commonwealth v. Konz*, 498 Pa. 639, 450 A.2d 638 (1982).

Food for Thought

As a general rule, a child is under no duty to care for an ailing parent. What facts might trigger such a duty? Would it matter that the parent was senile and living with the adult child? What if the child was named as the parent's authorized representative for the purpose of receiving food stamps and social security checks? *See Davis v. Commonwealth*, 230 Va. 201, 335 S.E.2d 375 (1985).

Hypo 8: *The Father and the Psychotic Mother*

A stay-at-home mother called 911 just after midnight and stated "I've just killed my boys." She also stated that God ordered her to do it. When police arrived at the scene, they found 6 year-old and 8 year-old boys in the front yard with their skulls smashed. They also found an alive 14 month old baby in his crib with a fractured skull. The mother suffered from delusional psychotic disorder and had been through three major psychotic episodes over the prior three years. The father was aware of the psychotic episodes, but nonetheless left the children with the mother. On the night of the murders, the father was asleep and heard nothing. Did the father have a duty to protect the children against the mother? Did he breach that duty?

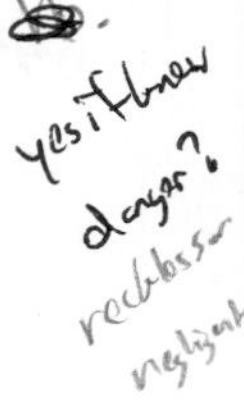

State v. Williquette

129 Wis. 2d 239, 385 N.W.2d 145 (1986).

STEINMETZ, JUSTICE.

Terri Williquette, defendant, was charged with two counts of child abuse. Count one was based on defendant's alleged failure to take action to prevent her husband, Bert Williquette, from repeatedly "sexually abusing, beating, and otherwise mistreating" her seven year old son, B.W. Count two was based on defendant's alleged failure to take any action to prevent her husband from committing similar acts against defendant's eight year old daughter, C.P.

B.W. reported being forced by his father to stand on one foot and one hand in an unbalanced position. In that position, his father would strike him. B.W. told his mother on many occasions that he had been beaten with the metal stick by Bert Williquette, but defendant never did anything about it. He also reported telling his mother about the incident on November 10, 1983, when he had been struck on the foot with the metal stick. At that time, his mother told him "not to worry about it." Dr. Ferrin Holmes, a pediatrician at the Door County Medical Center, examined B.W. and observed numerous bruises on the child's feet, upper and lower legs, lower and upper back, left arm and the side of his chest. Dr. Holmes stated that, in his professional opinion, B.W. had been beaten on at least four separate occasions in the fairly recent past, and that the beatings were inflicted with a metal stick or instrument.

C.P., defendant's daughter, stated that Bert Williquette regularly beat her and her brother at their home in Door county, on occasion using a metal stick with a hook on its end. C.P. stated that Bert Williquette would beat her and B.W. so hard that the children would wet their pants. He allegedly would also make the children balance on one hand and one leg, and then he would take the hook end of the metal stick and trip them, causing them to fall down. C.P. told Sergeant Bies that some time after Halloween in 1983, Bert Williquette hit her on the top of the head with the metal stick so hard that she bled. Sergeant Bies examined the area of C.P.'s head where she claimed Bert Williquette had struck her, and he could still feel a lump there. C.P. indicated that she had told the defendant about the incident, and that the defendant had given her an ice pack for her head. Williquette also sexually abused both children.

C.P. said that she had told defendant about all of the sexual abuse incidents involving her and B.W. but that her mother did not do anything about it. She also indicated to a social worker that she had told her mother on many occasions about the times she and B.W. were beaten by Bert Williquette. Her mother allegedly told C.P. that she would do something about it, but she never did.

The parties disagree as to whether the statute requires a person to directly inflict child abuse in order to violate the statute. Defendant contends that the legislature intended the statute to apply only to persons who directly abuse children. She maintains that the statute does not impose a duty on her to protect her own children from abuse. The state, however, argues that the statute is susceptible to an interpretation which includes persons having a special relationship to children who expose them to abuse. The state relies on the statutory language "subjects a child to cruel maltreatment." The state urges the court to construe this language to cover situations in which a parent knowingly exposes a child to abuse by placing the child in a situation where abuse has occurred and is likely to recur.

A person exposes a child to abuse when he or she causes the child to come within the influence of a foreseeable risk of cruel maltreatment. Causation in this context means that a person's conduct is a substantial factor in exposing the child to risk, and there may be more than one substantial causative factor in any given case. In this case, Bert Williquette's conduct obviously was a direct cause of the abuse his children suffered. However, defendant's alleged conduct, as the mother of the children, also was a contributing cause of risk to the children. She allegedly knew that the father abused the children in her absence, but she continued to leave the children and to entrust them to his exclusive care, and she allegedly did nothing else to prevent the abuse, such as notifying proper authorities or providing alternative child care in her absence. We conclude that defendant's conduct constituted a substantial factor which increased the risk of further abuse.

Defendant disputes that an omission to act may constitute a crime. Although the court disagrees, the alleged conduct in this case involves more than an omission to act. Defendant regularly left the children in the father's exclusive care and control despite allegedly knowing that he abused the children in her absence.

We consider leaving the children in these circumstances to be overt conduct. Therefore, even assuming that an overt act is necessary for the commission of a crime, the allegations support the charges in this case.

The court also expressly rejects defendant's claim that an act of commission, rather than omission, is a necessary element of a crime. The essence of criminal conduct is the requirement of a wrongful "act." This element, however, is satisfied by overt acts, as well as omissions to act where there is a legal duty to act. LAFAVE AND SCOTT, CRIMINAL LAW sec. 26 at 182, states the general rule applicable to omissions: "Some statutory crimes are specifically defined in terms of omission to act. With other common law and statutory crimes which are defined in terms of conduct producing a specified result, a person may be criminally liable when his omission to act produces that result, but only if (1) he has, under the circumstances, a legal duty to act, and (2) he can physically perform the act. The trend of the law has been toward enlarging the scope of duty to act." The comments to this section then state the traditional rule that a person generally has no duty to rescue or protect an endangered person unless a special relationship exists between the persons which imposes a legal duty to protect:

> For criminal liability to be based upon a failure to act it must first be found that there is a duty to act—a legal duty and not simply a moral duty. Some criminal statutes impose the legal duty to act, as with the tax statute and the hit-and-run statute. With other crimes the duty must be found outside the definition of the crime itself—perhaps in another statute, or in the common law, or in a contract.
>
> Generally, one has no legal duty to aid another person in peril, even when that aid can be rendered without danger or inconvenience to himself. He need not shout a warning to a blind man headed for a precipice or to an absent-minded one walking into a gunpowder room with a lighted candle in hand. He need not pull a neighbor's baby out of a pool of water or rescue an unconscious person stretched across the railroad tracks, though the baby is drowning or the whistle of an approaching train is heard in the distance. A doctor is not legally bound to answer a desperate call from the frantic parents of a sick child, at least if it is not one of his regular patients. A moral duty to take affirmative action is not enough to impose a legal duty to do so. But there are situations which do give rise to a duty to act:
>
> > (1) Duty based upon relationship. The common law imposes affirmative duties upon persons standing in certain personal relationships to other persons—upon parents to aid their small children, upon husbands to aid their wives, upon ship captains to aid their crews, upon masters to aid their servants. Thus a parent may be guilty of criminal homicide for failure to call a doctor for his sick child, a mother for failure to prevent the fatal beating of her baby by her lover, a husband for failure to aid his imperiled wife, a ship captain for failure to pick up a seaman or passenger fallen overboard, and an employer for failure to aid his endangered employee. Action may be required to thwart the threatened perils of nature (e.g., to combat sickness, to ward off starvation or the elements); or it may be required to protect against threatened acts by third persons. LAFAVE AND SCOTT, CRIMINAL LAW at 183–84.

The requirement of a legal duty to act is a policy limitation which prevents most omissions from being considered the proximate cause of a prohibited consequence. In a technical sense, a person's omission, i.e., whether the person fails to protect, warn or rescue, may be a substantial factor in exposing another person to harm. The concept of causation, however, is not solely a question of mechanical connection between events, but also a question of policy. A particular legal cause must be one of which the law will take cognizance. The rule that persons do not have a general duty to protect represents a public policy choice to limit criminal liability.

The requirement of an overt act, therefore, is not inherently necessary for criminal liability. Criminal liability depends on conduct which is a substantial factor in producing consequences. Omissions are as capable of producing consequences as overt acts. Thus, the common law rule that there is no general duty to protect limits criminal liability where it would otherwise exist. The special relationship exception to the "no duty to act" rule represents a choice to retain liability for some omissions, which are considered morally unacceptable.

Like most jurisdictions, Wisconsin generally does not require a person to protect others from hazardous situations. When a special relationship exists between persons, however, social policy may impose a duty to protect. The relationship between a parent and a child exemplifies a special relationship where the duty to protect is imposed. We stated the rule applicable to the parent and child relationship in *Cole v. Sears Roebuck & Co.*, 177 N.W.2d 866 (1970): "It is the right and duty of parents under the law of nature as well as the common law and the statutes of many states to protect their children, to care for them in sickness and in health, and to do whatever may be necessary for their care, maintenance, and preservation, including medical attendance, if necessary. An omission to do this is a public wrong which the state, under its police powers, may prevent. The child has the right to call upon the parent for the discharge of this duty, and public policy for the good of society will not permit or allow the parent to divest himself irrevocably of his obligations in this regard or to abandon them at his mere will or pleasure."

We conclude that a parent who fails to take any action to stop instances of child abuse can be prosecuted as a principal for exposing the child to the abuse. When liability depends on a breach of the parent's duty to protect, the parent must knowingly act in disregard of the facts giving rise to a duty to act.

Finally, we reject defendant's claim that sec. 940.201, Stats., is unconstitutionally vague if it is construed to apply to a parent's knowing failure to protect a child from abuse. A parent who knowingly exposes a child to the risk of such abhorrent conduct violates the statute. This construction of sec. 940.201 gives defendant notice that she has an affirmative duty to protect her children from a foreseeable risk of cruel maltreatment. The statute is not unconstitutionally vague.

The decision of the court of appeals is *affirmed*.

HEFFERNAN, CHIEF JUSTICE (dissenting).

The question for a court is whether the legislature has made criminal the action with which Terri Williquette has been charged. Although it points to no legislative intent contemporaneous with the passage of the law that would make Terri Williquette's conduct a felony, the majority finds that the statute means that conduct which occurred almost three years ago is now to be definitively declared criminal. The best that can be said of the law which the majority now promulgates, assuming it is otherwise appropriate, is that it is unconstitutional as *ex post facto*. I dissent.

Points for Discussion

a. Termination of Life Support

In *Barber v. Superior Court*, 195 Cal. Rptr. 484 (1983), a doctor was charged with murder for terminating life support to a patient in a persistent vegetative state. The court treated the act as an "omission," but concluded that the doctor acted permissibly:

> There is no criminal liability for failure to act unless there is a legal duty to act. Thus the critical issue becomes one of determining the duties owed by a physician to a patient who has been reliably diagnosed as in a comatose state from which any meaningful recovery of cognitive brain function is exceedingly unlikely. A physician has no duty to continue treatment, once it has proved to be ineffective. Although there may be a duty to provide life-sustaining machinery in the immediate aftermath of a cardio-respiratory arrest, there is no duty to continue its use once it has become futile in the opinion of qualified medical personnel. If it is not possible to ascertain the choice the patient would have made, the surrogate ought to be guided in his decision by the patient's best interests. Under this standard, such factors as the relief of suffering, the preservation or restoration of functioning and the quality as well as the extent of life sustained may be considered. Finally, since most people are concerned about the well-being of their loved ones, the surrogate may take into account the impact of the decision on those people closest to the patient.

b. Prayer Without Medical Care

In *Walker v. Superior Court*, 222 Cal. Rptr. 87 (Cal. App. 1986), defendant's daughter died of acute purulent meningitis which had been present in her body for at least two weeks at the time of death. Defendant knew that her daughter was ill, but chose to treat her daughter by spiritual healing rather than the use of medical specialists or practitioners. The court upheld a conviction for manslaughter: "The point at which parents may incur liability for substituting prayer treatment for medical care for their child is clear—when the lack of medical attention places the child in a situation endangering its person or health."

Hypo 1: *When Does the Duty to Act Arise?*

Defendants, husband and wife, had a 14 month old son. The father was a laborer with only a sixth-grade education. The mother had an 11th grade education. Both parents professed to love and care for the boy. However, when the boy developed an abscessed tooth that developed into a gangrenous infection of the mouth and cheeks, neither parent took the boy to the doctor even though they had the means to do so. This condition, accompanied by the child's inability to eat, brought about malnutrition, lowering the child's resistance and eventually producing pneumonia, causing death. The infection had lasted for approximately 2 weeks, and the odor generally associated with gangrene would have been present for approximately 10 days before death. Had medical care been first obtained in the last week before the baby's death, such care would have been obtained too late to have saved the baby's life. Defendant husband testified that he noticed the baby was sick about 2 weeks before the baby died. Defendant wife testified that she noticed the baby was ill about a week and a half or 2 weeks before the baby died. The evidence showed that, when the baby could still have been saved, the baby was fussy; that he could not keep his food down; and that his cheek started swelling up. The swelling went up and down, but did not disappear. In that same period, the cheek turned "a bluish color." Defendants, not realizing that the baby was as ill or that the baby was in danger of dying, attempted to provide some relief through baby aspirin and continued to do so until the night before the baby died. Defendants thought the swelling would go down and were waiting for it to do so; and defendant husband testified that he had heard that neither doctors nor dentists would extract a tooth "when it's all swollen up like that." Both parents also testified that "the way the cheek looked, and that stuff on his hair," they feared that the authorities "would think we were neglecting the child and take him away from us and not give him back." Defendant wife testified that she "was scared of losing him." Defendant husband's cousin lost a child that way. The evidence showed that the defendants did not understand the significance or seriousness of the baby's symptoms. Under the circumstances, have defendants committed a criminal violation of their duty to act? *See State v. Williams*, 484 P.2d 1167 (1971); *People v. Sealy*, 356 N.W.2d 614 (1984).

Hypo 2: *The Engineer and the Locomotive*

The engineer of a locomotive moved to the side track of a railroad yard, and was returning the locomotive to the roundhouse when he realized that the incoming track was "spiked" (in other words, it had been nailed up and put out of service). In violation of company rules, the engineer continued inward on the outgoing track. The locomotive had gone a little over a quarter of a mile on the wrong track when it collided with an oncoming train. Two railroad employees were killed. Under company rules, the locomotive's foreman is responsible for insuring that the train is on the right track. Can the foreman be convicted of manslaughter if he failed to realize that the engineer had the train on the wrong track? *See State v. Irvine*, 52 So. 567 (1910).

Executive Summary

Voluntary Act Requirement. The requirement of a voluntary act is a prerequisite for criminal liability. The MPC recognizes particular acts as involuntary, including reflexes or convulsions, a bodily movement during unconsciousness or sleep, and conduct during hypnosis or resulting from hypnotic suggestion. The MPC also endorses an all-purpose definition to

Major Themes

a. Voluntary Act—The common law and the MPC take the position that unless a defendant's act was voluntary, there is no justification for imposing punishment. In some cases, the "involuntary act" defense may be successful when the evidence shows that the bodily movement of the defendant was not the product of his or her will.

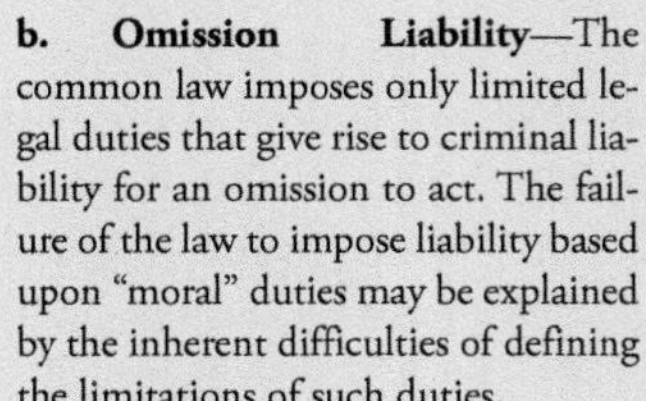

b. Omission Liability—The common law imposes only limited legal duties that give rise to criminal liability for an omission to act. The failure of the law to impose liability based upon "moral" duties may be explained by the inherent difficulties of defining the limitations of such duties.

provide recognition for other involuntary acts, namely those bodily movements that are not "a product of the effort or determination of the actor, either conscious or habitual." However, if defendant foresaw the danger (e.g., she became drowsy while driving, but kept driving), unconsciousness or sleep may not provide a defense.

Unconsciousness Defense. Courts have recognized the availability of the unconsciousness defense in cases in which a concussion or gunshot wound caused symptoms of unconscious behavior that could be diagnosed by expert witnesses and supported with sufficient evidence.

Other Involuntary Act Defenses. Some other types of conduct have been recognized as justifying an instruction on the involuntary act defense, such as conduct during an epileptic seizure or an episode of somnambulism. When such conduct allegedly occurs during a hypnotic state, however, courts have been reluctant to grant a jury instruction.

Status Crime. The U.S. Supreme Court relied on the Eighth Amendment to invalidate a statute that made it a crime "to be addicted to the use of narcotics." This law created a "status crime" because it punished an illness and required no proof of an act, such as the use or possession of drugs. This ruling provided some constitutional recognition of the fundamental nature of the voluntary act requirement. However, the Court limited the scope of this ruling by later upholding a statute that made it a crime to be "found in a state of intoxication in a public place," reasoning that this statute did not penalize a "status crime" because it required an act.

Omissions to Act. Even though criminal liability must be based on a voluntary act, the term "act" is defined broadly enough to include an "omission" to act. For example, the Model Penal Code provides that liability may be based on an "omission to perform an act of which a person is physically capable."

Legal Duty to Act. Courts have established a narrow set of legal duties to act, so that the failure to act in accordance with that duty may lead to criminal liability based on omission. Such legal duties arise in these contexts: 1) when a statute imposes a duty to care for another; 2) when a person has a particular status relationship with another that gives rise to the duty of care; 3) when a person has assumed a contractual duty to care for another; and 4) when a person voluntarily assumed the care of another and then secluded the other person in a way that prevented others from rendering aid.

Duty to Rescue. Although not recognized at common law, the duty to provide assistance at the scene of an emergency has been imposed by statute in some states.

For More Information

- AMERICAN LAW INSTITUTE, MODEL PENAL CODE AND COMMENTARIES, Part I, § 2.01, Comments at 214–225 (1980).
- JOHN M. BURKOFF & RUSSELL L. WEAVER, INSIDE CRIMINAL LAW: WHAT MATTERS AND WHY 17–34 (2d ed. 2011).
- WAYNE R. LAFAVE, CRIMINAL LAW §§ 6.1–6.2 (5th ed. 2010).

Test Your Knowledge

To assess your understanding of the material in this chapter, click here to take a quiz.

Chapter 3

Mens Rea

Traditionally, the criminal law looked to a person's mental state (his or her "*mens rea*") and the associated notion of that person's presumed "blameworthiness" in assessing the existence or absence of criminal culpability. From this perspective, intentional criminal conduct has classically been viewed as more serious—more wicked, more immoral, more blameworthy—than unintentional criminal conduct. Indeed, Oliver Wendell Holmes made this same point more than a century ago when he observed that "even a dog distinguishes between being stumbled over and being kicked." Oliver Wendell Holmes, Jr., The Common Law 3 (1881).

A. Levels of Criminal Intention

At common law, a number of different mental states were used as elements of different crimes. In addition to the mental state used in the following case ("maliciously"), courts often referred to other types of criminal intentions, such as "fraudulently," "corruptly," "willfully," "feloniously" and "intent to steal."

Regina v. Faulkner

13 Cox Crim. Cas. 550 (1877).

[The prisoner was indicted for setting fire to the ship Zemindar, on the high seas, on June 26, 1876. The indictment charged that he "feloniously, unlawfully, and maliciously" burned a ship with the intent "to prejudice the owner of the ship and the owners of certain goods and chattels then laden, and being on board said ship." The ship was carrying a cargo of rum, sugar, and cotton, worth £50,000. The facts showed that the prisoner, a seaman on the ship, went into the bulk head, and forecastle hold, opened the sliding door in the bulk head, to steal rum. The facts further showed that he bored a hole in the cask with a gimlet, that the rum ran out, that when trying to put a spile in the hole out of which the rum was running, he had a lighted match in his hand; that the rum caught fire; that he was burned on the arms and neck; and that the ship caught fire and was completely destroyed. At the close of the Crown's case, counsel for the prisoner asked for a direction of an acquittal on the ground that on the facts proved the indictment was not sustained, nor the allegation that the prisoner had unlawfully and maliciously set fire to the ship proved. The Crown contended that inasmuch as the prisoner was at the time engaged in the commission of a felony, the indictment was sustained, and the allegation of intent was immaterial].

At the second hearing of the case before the Court for Crown Cases Reserved, the learned judge made the addition of the following paragraph to the case stated by him for the court.

"It was conceded that the prisoner had no actual intention of burning the vessel, and I was not asked to leave any question as to the jury as to the prisoner's knowing the probable consequences his act, or as to his reckless conduct."

The learned judge told the jury that although the prisoner had no actual intention of burning the vessel, still if they found he was engaged in stealing the rum, and that the fire took place in the manner above stated, they ought to find him guilty. The jury found the prisoner guilty on both counts, and he was sentenced to seven years penal servitude. The question for the court was whether the direction of the learned judge was right, if not, the conviction should be quashed.

Dowse, B., gave judgment to the effect that the conviction should be quashed.

BARRY, J.—A very broad proposition has been contended for by the Crown, namely, that if, while a person is engaged in committing a felony, or, having committed it, is endeavouring to conceal his act, or prevent or spoil waste consequent on that act, he accidently does some collateral act which if done wilfully would be another felony either at common law or by statute, he is guilty of the latter felony. I am by no means anxious to throw any doubt upon, or limit in any way, the legal responsibility of those who engage in the commission of felony, or acts *mala in se*; but I am not prepared without more consideration to give my assent to so wide a proposition. No express authority either by way of decision or dictum from judge or text writer has been cited in support of it. I consider myself bound by the authority of *Reg. v. Pembliton* (12 Cox C. C. 607). That case must be taken as deciding that to constitute an offence under the Malicious Injuries to Property Act, sect. 51, the act done must be in fact intentional and wilful, although the intention and will may (perhaps) be held to exist in, or be proved by, the fact that the accused knew that the injury would be the probable result of his unlawful act, and yet did the act reckless of such consequences. The present indictment charges the offence to be under the 42nd section of the same Act, and it is not disputed that the same construction must be applied to both sections. The jury was directed to give a verdict of guilty upon the simple ground that the firing of the ship, though accidental, was caused by an act

> Non constat jus civile a posteriori
>
> **It's Latin to Me**
>
> *Malum in se*. A crime or an act that is inherently immoral, such as murder, arson, or rape.

> **Take Note**
>
> Do you agree? Whatever the law is, simply as a matter of sound policy, why *shouldn't* someone who commits a bad act simply be responsible for any harm that follows, whatever his or her intent was?

done in the course of, or immediately consequent upon, a felonious operation, and no question of the prisoner's malice, constructive or otherwise, was left to the jury. I am of opinion that, according to *Reg. v. Pembliton*, that direction was erroneous, and that the conviction should be quashed.

FITZGERALD, J.—I concur in opinion with my brother Barry, and for the reasons he has given, that the direction of the learned judge cannot be sustained in law, and that therefore the conviction should be quashed. [In] order to establish the charge of felony under sect. 42, the intention of the accused forms an element in the crime to the extent that it should appear that the defendant intended to do the very act with which he is charged, or that it was the necessary consequence of some other felonious or criminal act in which he was engaged, or that having a probable result which the defendant foresaw, or ought to have foreseen, he, nevertheless, persevered in such other felonious or criminal act. The prisoner did not intend to set fire to the ship; the fire was not the necessary result of the felony he was attempting; and if it was a probable result, which he ought to have foreseen, of the felonious transaction on which he was engaged, and from which a malicious design to commit the injurious act with which he is charged might have been fairly imputed to him, that view of the case was not submitted to the jury. Counsel for the prosecution in effect insisted that the defendant, being engaged in the commission of, or in an attempt to commit a felony, was criminally responsible for every result that was occasioned thereby, even though it was not a probable consequence of his act or such as he could have reasonably foreseen or intended. No authority has been cited for a proposition so extensive, and I am of opinion that it is not warranted by law.

Food for Thought

If the jury had been properly charged that a showing of recklessness would have sufficed here to establish Faulkner's culpability for this offense, do you agree that recklessness was made out on these facts?

O'BRIEN, J.—I am also [of the] opinion that the conviction should be quashed. At the trial, the Crown's counsel conceded that the prisoner had no intention of burning the vessel, or of igniting the rum; and raised no questions as to prisoner's imagining or having any ground for supposing that the fire would be the result or consequence of his act in stealing the rum. The reasonable inference from the evidence is that the prisoner lighted the match for the purpose of putting the spile in the hole to stop the further running of the rum, and that while he was attempting to do so the rum came in contact with the lighted match and took fire.

KEOGH, J.—I have the misfortune to differ from the other members of the Court. I am of the opinion, that the conviction should stand, as I consider all questions of intention and malice are closed by the finding of the jury, that the prisoner committed the act with which he was charged whilst engaged in the commission of a substantive felony.

PALLES, C.B.—I concur in the opinion of the majority of the Court. The Lord Chief Justice of the Common Pleas, who, in consequence of illness, has been unable to preside to-day, has authorized me to state that he considers that the case before us is concluded by *Reg. v. Pembliton*.

DEASY, B., and LAWSON, J., concurred.

Conviction quashed.

Points for Discussion

a. Model Penal Code

The drafters of the Model Penal Code chose to abandon most of the common law mental states, and to focus upon only four standard *mens rea* terms:

§ 2.02. General Requirements of Culpability.

(1) **Minimum Requirements of Culpability.** Except as provided in Section 2.05, a person is not guilty of an offense unless he acted purposely, knowingly, recklessly or negligently, as the law may require, with respect to each material element of the offense.

(2) Kinds of Culpability Defined.

(a) **Purposely.** A person acts purposely with respect to a material element of an offense when:

(i) if the element involves the nature of his conduct or a result thereof, it is his conscious object to engage in conduct of that nature or to cause such a result; and

(ii) if the element involves the attendant circumstances, he is aware of the existence of such circumstances or he believes or hopes that they exist.

(b) **Knowingly.** A person acts knowingly with respect to a material element of an offense when:

(i) if the element involves the nature of his conduct or the attendant circumstances, he is aware that his conduct is of that nature or that such circumstances exist; and

(ii) if the element involves a result of his conduct, he is aware that it is practically certain that his conduct will cause such a result.

(c) **Recklessly.** A person acts recklessly with respect to a material element of an offense when he consciously disregards a substantial and unjustifiable risk that the material element exists or will result from his conduct. The risk must be of such a nature and degree that, considering the nature and purpose of the actor's conduct and the circumstances known to him, its disregard involves a gross deviation from the standard of conduct that a law-abiding person would observe in the actor's situation.

(d) **Negligently.** A person acts negligently with respect to a material element of an offense when he should be aware of a substantial and unjustifiable risk that the material element exists or will result from his conduct. The risk must be of such a nature and degree that the actor's failure to perceive it, considering the nature and purpose of his conduct and the circumstances known to him, involves a gross deviation from the standard of care that a reasonable person would observe in the actor's situation.

(3) **Culpability Required Unless Otherwise Provided.** When the culpability sufficient to establish a material element of an offense is not prescribed by law, such element is established if a person acts purposely, knowingly or recklessly with respect thereto.

(4) **Prescribed Culpability Requirement Applies to All Material Elements.** When the law defining an offense prescribes the kind of culpability that is sufficient for the commission of an offense, without distinguishing among the material elements thereof, such provision shall apply to all the material elements of the offense, unless a contrary purpose plainly appears.

(5) **Substitutes for Negligence, Recklessness and Knowledge.** When the law provides that negligence suffices to establish an element of an offense, such element also is established if a person acts purposely, knowingly or recklessly. When recklessness suffices to establish an element, such element also is established if a person acts purposely or knowingly. When acting knowingly suffices to establish an element, such element also is established if a person acts purposely.

(6) **Requirement of Purpose Satisfied if Purpose Is Conditional.** When a particular purpose is an element of an offense, the element is established although such purpose is conditional, unless the condition negatives the harm or evil sought to be prevented by the law defining the offense.

(7) **Requirement of Knowledge Satisfied by Knowledge of High Probability.** When knowledge of the existence of a particular fact is an element of an offense, such knowledge is established if a person is aware of a high probability of its existence, unless he actually believes that it does not exist.

(8) **Requirement of Wilfulness Satisfied by Acting Knowingly.** A requirement that an offense be committed wilfully is satisfied if a person acts knowingly with respect to the material elements of the offense, unless a purpose to impose further requirements appears.

(9) **Culpability as to Illegality of Conduct.** Neither knowledge nor recklessness or negligence as to whether conduct constitutes an offense or as to the existence, meaning or application of the law determining the elements of an offense is an element of such offense, unless the definition of the offense or the Code so provides.

(10) **Culpability as Determinant of Grade of Offense.** When the grade or degree of an offense depends on whether the offense is committed purposely, knowingly, recklessly or negligently, its grade or degree shall be the lowest for which the

determinative kind of culpability is established with respect to any material element of the offense.

b. Jurisdictional Variation in *Mens Rea* Definitions

Although there are often similarities between the definitions of various *mens rea* terms in different jurisdictions and, sometimes these terms were taken (at least initially) from the Model Penal Code, it is nonetheless important for criminal law practitioners to discern the precise meaning—and judicial interpretation—of each *mens rea* term for each criminal offense in the Crimes Code in his or her jurisdiction. There is great—and often significant—variation in the definition of the same *mens rea* term of art in different jurisdictions. *See, e.g.*, Jerome Hall, General Principles of Criminal Law 142 (2d ed. 1960) ("there must be as many mentes reae as there are crimes").

State v. Jackowski

181 Vt. 73, 915 A.2d 767 (2006).

JOHNSON, J.

Defendant Rosemarie Jackowski appeals her conviction for disorderly conduct. Defendant argues that the trial court improperly instructed the jury to consider whether defendant was "practically certain" that her conduct would cause public inconvenience or annoyance, when she was charged with intentionally causing public inconvenience or annoyance. We reverse and remand.

Defendant was arrested on March 20, 2003, during an anti-war demonstration at the intersection of Routes 7 and 9 in Bennington. During the demonstration, protesters blocked traffic at the intersection for approximately fifteen minutes. Defendant stood in the intersection, praying and holding a sign bearing anti-war slogans and newspaper clippings, including an article accompanied by a photograph of a wounded Iraqi child. Police officers repeatedly asked defendant to leave the intersection, and when she refused, she was arrested, along with eleven other protesters. The State charged them with disorderly conduct, alleging that defendant and the other protesters, "with intent to cause public inconvenience and annoyance, obstructed vehicular traffic, in violation of 13 V.S.A. § 1026(5)."

Defendant's intent was the only issue contested during her one-day jury trial. After several police officers testified for the State, defendant took the stand, admitting to blocking traffic, but stating that her only intention in doing so was to protest the war in Iraq, not to cause public inconvenience or annoyance. At the conclusion of the trial, the court instructed the jury on the issue of intent. The court first instructed the jury that the State could establish defendant's intent to cause public inconvenience or annoyance by proving beyond a reasonable doubt that she acted "with the conscious object of bothering, disturbing, irritating, or harassing some other person or persons." The court then added, "This intent may also be shown if the State proves beyond a reasonable doubt that the defendant was practically certain that another person or persons would be bothered, disturbed, irritated, or harassed." The jury convicted defendant of disorderly conduct. Defendant appeals.

Defendant argues that the jury charge was improper because the trial court failed to instruct the jury to consider whether defendant acted with the requisite criminal intent. Defendant relies on *State v. Trombley* to draw a distinction between offenses that require purposeful or intentional misconduct and those that require only knowing misconduct. 174 Vt. 459, 462, 807 A.2d 400, 404–05 (2002). In *Trombley*, we held that it was error for the trial court to instruct the jury to consider whether the defendant in an aggravated assault case acted "knowingly" or "purposely," when he was charged with "purposely" causing serious bodily injury. The aggravated assault statute in *Trombley* had been amended in 1972 to adopt the Model Penal Code's approach to mens rea, which distinguishes among crimes that are committed "purposely," "knowingly," and "recklessly." Under this approach, a person acts "purposely" when "it is his conscious object to engage in conduct of that nature or to cause such a result." A person acts "knowingly" when "he is aware that it is practically certain that his conduct will cause such a result." Thus, the trial court in *Trombley* erred in instructing the jury that it could find that the defendant acted "purposely" if "he was practically certain that his conduct would cause serious bodily injury."

Defendant argues that *Trombley* controls here, as the trial court used a similarly worded jury charge, and the disorderly conduct statute was amended at the same time, and for the same reasons, as the aggravated assault statute in *Trombley*. The State attempts to distinguish *Trombley* based on differences in the language of the aggravated assault and disorderly conduct statutes. Unlike the aggravated assault statute, the disorderly conduct statute contains the words "with intent" and not "purposely." This is a purely semantic distinction, and it does not indicate a departure from the Code's approach to mens rea, the adoption of which was "the major statutory change" accomplished by the Legislature's 1972 amendments. The Code does not differentiate between "with intent" and "purposely"; instead, it uses the two terms interchangeably, explaining in its definitions that " 'intentionally' or 'with intent' means purposely." There is no indication that the Legislature used the phrase "with intent" to register disagreement with the Code's approach to disorderly conduct, and such disagreement seems unlikely in the context of an otherwise unqualified adoption of the Code's approach.

The State cites several cases supporting the proposition that both "purposely" and "knowingly" causing harm involve some element of "intent," and thus, that *Trombley*'s distinction between " purposely" and "knowingly" is illusory. Each of these cases predates our decision in *Trombley*, however, and each adheres to an outmoded distinction between "specific intent" and "general intent" crimes-the distinction that the Legislature rejected in adopting the Code's approach to mens rea. At common law, crimes committed "purposely" and those committed "knowingly" would both have been specific intent offenses. These cases provide no basis for distinguishing or limiting *Trombley* here. It was therefore error for the trial court to charge the jury to consider whether defendant was "practically certain" that her actions would cause public annoyance or inconvenience.

Food for Thought

Where a *mens rea* requirement contains a subjective element, how does the prosecution prove the existence of such an element, particularly when the accused testifies that he or she did not actually hold the prescribed intent? What type of evidence might the prosecution introduce to make such a showing? Should a jury be able to infer a particular *mens rea* from circumstantial evidence even where the accused has testified to the contrary?

Intent was the only issue defendant contested at trial. Defendant claimed that she intended only to protest the war in Iraq, not to cause public annoyance or inconvenience. The State is correct that defendant could have had multiple intents, and a jury could certainly have convicted defendant based on the evidence presented at trial. The law makes a distinction between intentional and knowing acts, however, and defendant was entitled to have a jury decide whether causing public annoyance or inconvenience was her conscious object. The trial court's instruction prevented the jury from considering that question, effectively removing the element of intent from the crime, if not directing a guilty verdict. We cannot say that this error was harmless beyond a reasonable doubt, so we must reverse defendant's conviction.

Reversed.

BURGESS, J., dissenting.

Confident that the trial court's misdescription of the intent element in this particular case was harmless beyond a reasonable doubt, I respectfully dissent. The majority is correct that the trial court erred in allowing the jury the option to find defendant guilty of disorderly conduct by acting either "with the conscious object," that is "with intent," to cause public inconvenience or annoyance, or by acting with "practical certainty," or "knowingly," that public inconvenience or annoyance would result from her actions. The majority is also correct that the element of "intentional" action in a criminal statute derived from the Model Penal Code, such as the disorderly conduct statute, means to act not "knowingly," but " purposely." The State was required to prove, as it expressly charged, that defendant obstructed traffic "with intent to cause," rather than "knowingly" cause, public inconvenience and annoyance. Nevertheless, given the overwhelming evidence of defendant's actual intent to cause public inconvenience by obstructing traffic, the error was harmless because "we can say beyond a reasonable doubt that the result would have been the same in the absence of the error."

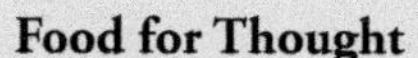

Food for Thought

Was Jackowski's claim that it was not her conscious object to block traffic so ridiculous that it shouldn't matter if the jury was misinstructed about *mens rea*?

Defendant's testimony proved the elements of disorderly conduct as charged: that she obstructed vehicular traffic "with intent to cause public inconvenience or annoyance, in violation of 13 V.S.A. § 1026(5)," and did so "purposely" under the Model Penal Code applied in Trombley. The Code states that a person acts "purposely" when: "if the element involves the nature of his conduct or a result thereof, it is his conscious object to engage in conduct of that nature or to cause such a result."

Defendant's intentional obstruction of traffic was not disputed. That defendant was also motivated by a noncriminal urge to communicate and show political opposition does not mutually exclude a contemporaneous and, in this case, manifest criminal intent to cause public inconvenience and annoyance.

Accordingly, I would affirm the conviction.

Hypo 1: *Tire Blow Out*

Amanda was driving on a city street when the left front tire of her car blew out. Despite her best efforts, the car swerved off the road and killed a pedestrian. If she is charged with a homicide offense which uses a MPC *mens rea*—purpose, knowledge, recklessness or negligence—would she be found guilty in any of the following circumstances:

- if she was driving at or near the speed limit (35 mph) on new tires and had no reason to believe that there were any problems with the tires?
- if she was driving at or near the speed limit but her tires were old and bald?
- if she was driving at a speed of 65 mph in a 35 mph zone when the blow out occurred?

Hypo 2: *The Epileptic Driver*

Amir is an epileptic who periodically has seizures. One day, while he was driving his car on an interstate highway, he had a seizure and ran into another car killing the passenger. If Amir is charged with homicide, can a jury conclude that he acted with purpose, knowledge, recklessness or negligence?

Hypo 3: *Russian Roulette*

Two teenage boys are playing Russian Roulette. They place one bullet in the chamber of a gun, spin it, hold it to one of their heads, and pull the trigger. The gun discharges, killing one of the boys instantly. Can it be said that the surviving boy acted purposely, knowingly, recklessly or negligently in causing the death of the other boy?

Hypo 4: *Running over "Leaves"*

Cinthya was driving home when she decided to run over a pile of leaves on the side of the road, just for fun. She felt a bump when the passenger-side tire ran over the leaves, later saying that it felt "like if I went over a pothole." Tragically, Cinthya had run over and killed a little girl who had been playing in the leaf pile. Do you think that Cinthya acted purposely, knowingly, recklessly, or negligently in causing the death of the little girl? *Cf. State v. Garcia-Cisneros*, 285 Or. App. 252, 397 P.3d 49 (2017).

State v. Ducker

1999 WL 160981 (Tenn. Crim.App. 1999), *aff'd*, 27 S.W.3d 889 (Tenn. 2000).

HAYES.

The appellant, Jennie Bain Ducker, was indicted on two counts of first degree murder resulting from the aggravated child abuse of her two children, ages 13 months and 23 months. A jury found the appellant guilty of two counts of the lesser charged offense of aggravated child abuse. Concurrent sentences of eighteen years were imposed for each of the class A felony convictions. We affirm.

The events leading to the tragic deaths of thirteen month old Dustin Ducker and twenty-three month old Devin Ducker began in the early evening hours of June 5, 1995. At approximately 3:45 a.m., the appellant arrived at Room 222 of the Holiday Inn in McMinnville. This was the temporary residence of Micah Majors, another boyfriend of the appellant. With [her] children securely strapped in their car seats, the appellant closed the windows and locked the doors. Others were already in the room with Micah when the appellant arrived. The four men were playing a Sega video golf game and drinking alcoholic beverages. The men continued to play their video game, paying little or no attention to the appellant. They did notice, however, that the appellant poured herself a glass of wine. Additionally, they observed her leave the room on two occasions, once to get ice and once to get BC powders from Micah's car. The appellant never mentioned that her children were in her car or that she needed to check on the children. All four men testified that, despite her usual "dingy" attitude, the appellant did not appear intoxicated. The others left Micah's room around 5:00 a.m. The appellant followed the three men to the parking lot, but never checked on her children. As they were pulling out of the parking lot, Pepper noticed that the appellant was already back on the second floor balcony near Micah's room.

Micah had changed into boxer shorts and gotten into bed. The appellant knocked on his door and he let her back in the room. Micah testified that he was trying to go to sleep, but the appellant sat next to him on the bed trying to talk to him about a "commitment" in their relationship. Micah then fell asleep. When his alarm went off the next afternoon around twelve or one o'clock, the appellant was still there. She patted Micah on the side of the leg and said, "I have to go." She never mentioned her children.

At 1:03 p.m., the appellant arrived at the emergency room of the River Park Hospital in McMinnville. While she was attempting to get one child out of the car, David Smith, a bystander, heard her say, "Somebody help me. My babies have been in the car for four hours." He responded to her plea for assistance. When he reached the appellant, he observed that the child she was carrying appeared lifeless. The appellant told Fults that the children had been left in a car for three hours with the windows closed. She explained that she had fallen asleep at a friend's house on Lucky Road. At this point, the appellant became frantic, "she was pacing the floor," "wringing her hands," "running her hands through her hair."

The appellant testified that she did not see any danger in leaving her thirteen month old and twenty-three month old sons in her locked car for over nine hours while she visited with Micah in his motel room. Appellant claimed that "she checked on the kids four to five times." However, she could not explain why she did not tell the others that her children were in her car or that she needed to check on them. Based upon this evidence, the jury returned guilty verdicts as to two counts of aggravated child abuse.

Appellant contends that the evidence is insufficient to support her convictions for aggravated child abuse because the State failed to prove "knowing conduct" beyond a reasonable doubt, i.e., that she "was actually aware that her conduct was reasonably certain to cause the resulting injury to her children." Specifically, the appellant challenges the trial court's instructions to the jury as they relate to the requisite mental state of "knowing" as the definition of this term applies to the offense of aggravated child abuse. She argues that the erroneous charge altered the State's burden of proving the elements of the offense beyond a reasonable doubt.

Central to the concept of criminal liability is that, before there can be a crime, there must be an act, or *actus reus*, which must be accompanied by a criminal mind, or mens rea. The early concept of mens rea meant little more than a "general notion of blameworthiness," or an "evil meaning mind." Over time, this general concept shifted from this vague notion of wickedness to a more definite requirement of a specific state of mind to do that which is prohibited by the criminal law. Thus, no longer could the requirement of "wickedness" suffice. Rather, a different state of mind was required for each crime. This development in the common law culminated in the creation of eighty or so culpability terms.

The plethora of *mentes reae* originating from the common law created much confusion and ambiguity. Thus, in 1955, the drafters of the Model Penal Code sought to eliminate this confusion and narrowed the multitude of existing culpability terms to four: purpose, knowledge, recklessness, and negligence. In furtherance of this concept, the Model Penal Code and, subsequently the Tennessee Criminal Code, provide that, with the exception of strict liability offenses, some mental culpability "must be faced separately with respect to each material element of the crime,"

> Non constat jus civile a posteriori
>
> **It's Latin to Me**
>
> *Mentes reae* is simply the plural form of *mens rea.*

otherwise, no valid conviction may be obtained. Moreover, the Model Penal Code and the Tennessee Criminal Code both require that one of four levels of culpability must be proven with respect to each "material element" of the offense which may involve "(1) the nature of the forbidden conduct; (2) the attendant circumstances; or (3) the result of the conduct."

The first element, conduct, involves the nature of the proscribed act or the manner in which the defendant acts, e.g., the physical act of committing an assault, or the physical restraint of another person (kidnapping). The second element, circumstances surrounding the conduct, refers to a situation which relates to the actor's culpability, e.g., lack of victim's consent or stolen status of property. The result of the defendant's conduct constitutes the final element, in other words, the accused's conduct must at least be a physical cause of the harmful result, e.g., causing the death of another.

Many crimes are made up of not only one, but of several "conduct elements," including not only an act or omission, but also some specific result of that act or omission, or some prescribed attendant circumstances, or perhaps both result and circumstances. In other words, an offense may contain one or more of these conduct elements which, alone or in combination with the others, form the overall behavior which the Legislature has intended to criminalize, and it is those essential conduct elements to which a culpable mental state must apply. Correspondingly, each culpability term is defined with respect to each of the three kinds of "conduct elements": conduct, circumstances, and result. For example, where a specific act is criminalized because of its very nature, a culpable mental state must apply to committing the act itself, i.e., awareness of conduct. On the other hand, unspecified conduct which is criminalized because of the result requires culpability as to that result, i.e., result of conduct. Finally, where otherwise innocent behavior is criminalized due to the circumstances under which it occurs, a culpable mental state is required as to those surrounding circumstances, i.e., awareness of circumstances. In other words, the analysis of the applicable mens rea varies according to the conduct elements of the offense.

In the present offense, the applicable mens rea is "knowingly." Tenn.Code Ann. § 39–11–302(b) defines "knowing" as:

> A person who acts knowingly with respect to the conduct or to circumstances surrounding the conduct when the person is aware of the nature of the conduct or that the circumstances exist. A person acts knowingly with respect to a result of the persons conduct when the person is aware that the conduct is reasonably certain to cause the result.

When a criminal statute requires a mens rea of knowingly, it may speak to conduct, or to circumstances, or to result, or to any combination thereof, but not necessarily to all three. In essence, three theories of "knowingly" exist, i.e., (1) conduct; (2) circumstances; and (3) result of conduct, to correspond to the three conduct elements of a criminal offense. Since a crime may consist of more than one "conduct element," there may be different mens rea requirements as to the different "conduct elements" that constitute the crime, even if the required culpability is the same, e.g. "knowingly."

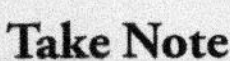

Take Note

Note that the *mens rea* for a criminal offense may be different for each separate element of the same criminal offense.

Because the applicable definition of "knowing" is element specific, a blanket instruction as to each theory, generally, will invite error. In other words, the court cannot instruct the jury that it could employ either (1) conduct or (2) circumstances; or (3) result of conduct. To do so would effectively alter the State's burden of proving each element of the offense beyond a reasonable doubt. For example, the offense of second degree murder is a result of conduct offense, that is, the intent of the legislature is to punish a person for the killing of another. The trial court may only instruct the jury as to the result of conduct theory of knowingly. If the court instructed the jury as to "awareness of conduct" or "awareness of circumstances," the jury could find a defendant guilty on less proof than that needed to show that the defendant engaged in conduct with knowledge that his conduct is reasonably certain to cause the result.

Appellant relies upon the decision of the Texas Court of Criminal Appeals in *Alvarado* which held that the trial court, in instructing the jury, must limit its charge of the applicable mental state to the "conduct element" or elements of the offense charged, because to provide a blanket charge as to the applicable culpability requirement would effectively alter the State's burden of proof. While we acknowledge that Tennessee is now at the same crossroads previously confronted by the Texas court, we decline to adopt the explicit holding in *Alvarado* as this holding may be distinguished under the circumstances of the case *sub judice*.

Take Note

The trial court must make sure that the charge it gives the jury reflects precisely the requisite *mens rea* for each element of the offense.

We agree with the appellant that to provide the jury with the option that the appellant was aware of her conduct, aware of the circumstances, or was reasonably aware that her conduct was reasonably certain to cause the result, is to relieve the State of their burden of proof. To prove that a defendant is aware of her conduct is one thing; to prove that the defendant's conduct is reasonably certain to produce a certain result is, although subtle, another. The court cannot give the jury the choice of which definition to apply to the crime charged, rather the statute defining the crime dictates which definition of "knowingly" is appropriate as to each element.

The appellant asserts that the offense of "aggravated child abuse," as charged in the present case, only contains the element of "result of conduct," as was determined in *Alvarado*. We do not agree. Upon analysis of our statutory provision, a purview into the legislative intent behind the enactment of the offense leads us to conclude that the offense, as charged in the case presently before this court, contains the elements of (1) awareness of conduct, (2) awareness of circumstances; and (3) result of conduct.

> The trial court provided the jury with the following instruction:
>
> Any person who commits the offense of aggravated child abuse is guilty of a felony. For you to find the Defendant guilty of this offense, the State must have proven beyond a reasonable doubt the existence of the following essential elements:
>
> (1) The Defendant acted knowingly; AND
>
> (2) That the Defendant did:
>
> (a) Other than by accidental means, treat a child in such a manner as to inflict injury; OR
>
> (b) Other than by accidental means, neglect a child so as to adversely affect the child's health and welfare; AND
>
> (3)(a) The Defendant used a deadly weapon to accomplish the act of abuse; OR
>
> (b) The act of abuse resulted in serious bodily injury to the child
>
> The requirement of "knowingly" is also satisfied if it is shown that the Defendant acted intentionally.
>
> A person acts "knowingly" if that person acts with an awareness either:
>
> (1) That his or her conduct is of a particular nature; or
>
> (2) That a particular circumstance exists.
>
> A person acts knowingly with respect to a result of the person's conduct when the person is aware that the conduct is reasonably certain to cause a result.

A reading of this instruction implies that, for a jury to find that the defendant acted knowingly, the jury must find that the defendant was (1) aware of her conduct or aware of the circumstances and (2) aware that the conduct was reasonably certain to cause a certain result as to each material element of the offense. Although this instruction is erroneous in that it did not charge the specific mens rea definition applicable to each "conduct element," we conclude that any such error is harmless.

Practice Pointer

No trial is ever perfect. A prosecutor need not win every issue on appeal in order to have a trial court conviction affirmed. Where the prosecutor is able to establish that whatever errors that may have existed at trial were "harmless," i.e. they did not affect the result, they are not grounds for reversal.

The prejudice in not providing a "conduct element" specific definition of the applicable mens rea is the alteration of the State's burden of proof. The instruction in the present case did not relieve the State's burden of proof. The jury was instructed that it must find each element of the offense beyond a reasonable doubt. The definition of "knowingly" provided by the court supplied a two-prong definition of the term, resulting in an added burden of proof upon the State, for which the appellant cannot now complain. Although the preferred instruction would be one that is "conduct element" specific, we conclude that the instruction provided in the present case did not prejudice the appellant. Accordingly, any such error in the instruction is harmless.

Because we have determined that the jury instruction constitutes harmless error, we must determine whether the evidence is sufficient to sustain the conviction. It is the appellate court's duty to affirm the conviction if the evidence viewed under these standards was sufficient for any rational trier of fact to have found the essential elements of the offense beyond a reasonable doubt. On appeal, the State is entitled to the strongest legitimate view of the evidence and all legitimate or reasonable inferences which may be drawn therefrom.

Before a jury can find a defendant guilty of aggravated child abuse as charged in the present case, the State must prove beyond a reasonable doubt that the defendant "knowingly, other than by accidental means, treats a child under eighteen (18) years of age in such a manner as to inflict injury or neglects such a child so as to adversely affect the child's health and welfare" and such abuse results in serious bodily injury. "Knowing" is applicable to the situations in which the accused, while not having the actual intent to accomplish a specific wrongful purpose, is consciously aware of the existence of facts which makes his conduct unlawful. "Knowing" is ordinarily established by circumstantial evidence rather than by direct proof. The undisputed proof reveals that the appellant strapped her two children, Dustin and Devin, into their car seats, secured the windows and doors, and left her children alone in the car for over nine hours, never returning to check on them. The children died as a result of systemic hyperthermia triggered by being locked in the hot vehicle. Obviously, by returning a guilty verdict, the jury did not accredit the appellant's theory of the case that the deaths of her children were an accident. Nor did the jury accredit defense testimony of the appellant's psychological problems. We conclude that a rational trier of fact could find that the appellant knew the ages of her children (circumstances), knowingly strapped her children in the car (conduct), knowingly neglected them over the next nine hours (conduct), and was aware that her conduct was reasonably certain to cause harm or injury to her children (result of conduct). Thus, the facts are sufficient to support a conviction for aggravated child abuse on each count. This issue is without merit.

Finding no reversible error committed by the trial court, we affirm the appellant's convictions and sentences imposed for two counts of aggravated child abuse.

Points for Discussion

a. Homicide with a Different *Mens Rea*: As Charges Change, Results May Change

Ducker was acquitted on two counts of *first-degree* murder. Under Tenn. Code § 39–13–210(1), it is the offense of *second-degree* murder for an individual to commit "a knowing killing of another." Similarly, if Ducker had been charged and convicted by a jury of second-degree murder on the facts set out above, would the jury verdict have been upheld? What would have happened if the prosecutor had charged her with manslaughter (which you can assume is defined to require either "recklessness" or "negligence"). Did she have the requisite mental state for that crime?

b. As Facts Change, Results May Change

Do you think that the result in this case would have been different if Ducker had in fact returned to her car four or five times in the night (as she claimed) to check on her children and found that they were asleep and in good health? What if she had checked only once?

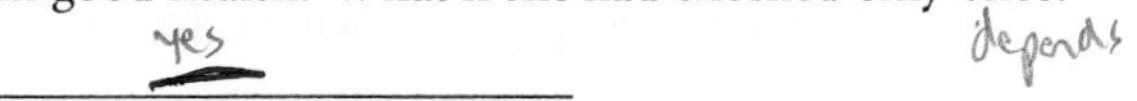

Hypo 1: *Bad Dad*

Ralph was supposed to drive his daughter to day care on his way to work. Obviously very absent minded, he forgot to drop her off and left her in the car all day in the parking lot next door to his office. The day was very hot and the child suffocated to death. Can it be said that Ralph purposely, knowingly, recklessly or negligently caused her death?

Hypo 2: *Real or Virtual Porn*

Orlando was prosecuted under a state statute that criminalizes possession of images of children other than that person's own children in "a state of nudity including a lewd exhibition or a graphic focus on the genitals." Orlando claims that he thought that the graphic images of naked children engaging in sexual activity that were found on his computer were not images of real children, but rather were images of virtual children. If a jury believes Orlando's claim, can he be found guilty of purposely, knowingly, recklessly, or negligently possessing such images in violation of this statute? *Cf. State v. Videen*, 990 N.E. 2d 173 (Ohio Ct. App. 2 Dist. 2013).

State v. Coleman

944 N.W.2d 469 (Minn. Ct. App. 2020).

COCHRAN, JUDGE

A jury found appellant Eric Joseph Coleman guilty of third-degree murder, two counts of criminal vehicular homicide, two counts of criminal vehicular operation, and two counts of driving while impaired. The district court entered convictions for all seven offenses. On appeal from his convictions, Coleman argues that the district court plainly erred in instructing the jury on the mens rea element of third-degree murder.

On the night of January 26, 2018, Coleman drove his snowmobile at a speed of 58 miles per hour (mph) on a lake where people were ice fishing. Coleman did so after drinking several alcoholic beverages. Coleman struck an eight-year-old child with his snowmobile and then struck the child's father, injuring both father and son. The child later died.

At trial, evidence was presented that on January 26, 2018, a father (father) and mother, one of their daughters, and their eight-year-old son (hereinafter "son" or "the child") went to Chisago Lake to ice fish. It had been a "warm," 40-degree day and there were a number of people on the lake. The family drove their pickup truck onto the lake and arrived at their ice-fishing spot at about 7:30 p.m. The spot they picked was in an area of the lake just south of where "there's a lot of other fish houses and different stuff on the lake." Although it was "exceptionally bright" on the lake that night, the sun had set and it was "dark enough where you would have to turn your lights on." But not all of the fish houses and vehicles on the lake had lights on.

After arriving at their spot, father began to set up the family's portable ice-fishing house. According to father, the fish house is over six feet tall when set up, and has reflectors on all four corners. As father was inside the fish house setting it up, the family heard a snowmobile start "a little ways" from their pickup truck. Mother and son were outside near the truck. The child was "very interested" in snowmobiles, and "walked down to the end of the truck to watch the snowmobile go by." Mother then observed the snowmobile "coming right towards" them, and "tried to yell for her son to get out of the way." But "as soon as [mother] could tell him to get out of the way," the "snowmobile . . . hit the truck and hit [the child] and went straight through the [fish] house." Both father and his son were injured. The child was airlifted to a hospital and died several days later from his injuries.

The jury found Coleman guilty of all seven charged offenses. The district court then sentenced Coleman to 150 months in prison for third-degree murder and 365 days in jail for one count of gross misdemeanor criminal vehicular operation, to be served concurrently. Coleman was also convicted of, but not sentenced for, the remaining offenses.

Coleman argues that the district court erred in instructing the jury on the mens rea element of third-degree murder. Jury instructions, reviewed in their entirety, must fairly and adequately explain the law. A district court has "considerable latitude" in selecting jury instructions. A jury instruction is erroneous if it materially misstates the law.

Because Coleman did not object to the jury instructions at trial, he has forfeited appellate review of the jury-instruction issue. But, under the plain-error doctrine, an appellate court has the discretion to consider a forfeited issue if the defendant establishes (1) an error, (2) that was plain, and (3) that affected his substantial rights. If the first three prongs are satisfied, the appellate court considers whether reversal is required to ensure the fairness, integrity, or public reputation of judicial proceedings. As explained below, we conclude that Coleman has established an error but the error was not plain.

We begin by examining whether the district court properly instructed the jury on the mens rea element for third-degree murder. A person commits third-degree murder when he "without intent to effect the death of any person, causes the death of another by perpetrating an act eminently dangerous to others and evincing a depraved mind, without regard for human life." Minn. Stat. § 609.195(a). Thus, the third-degree murder statute required the state to prove that Coleman: (1) caused the death of another, (2) committed an act that was eminently dangerous to others, and (3) evinced a depraved mind without regard for human life.

The district court instructed the jury with regard to the required mens rea or mental state as follows:

> [Coleman's] intentional act which caused the death of [the child] was eminently dangerous to human beings and was performed without regard for human life. Such an act may not be specifically intended to cause death and may not be specifically directed at [the child], but it was committed in a reckless or wanton manner with the knowledge that someone may be killed and with a heedless disregard of that happening.

The district court did not define any of the terms included in this instruction.

Coleman argues that this instruction was erroneous because it misstated the law. Coleman contends that to prove the existence of a "depraved mind" for third-degree murder, the evidence must establish that the defendant acted in knowing disregard of a substantial and unjustifiable risk that someone may be killed by the defendant's act. Because the third-degree murder jury instruction did not communicate "to the jury that it needed to determine that [Coleman] knew his conduct presented a substantial and unjustifiable risk of causing the death of another," Coleman contends the instruction was erroneous. Coleman emphasizes that the district court's instruction "required only that the jury find [Coleman] acted 'with knowledge that someone may be killed.' " And Coleman argues that the district court's use of the word "may" "allowed the jury to convict [him] of murder so long as it found [that Coleman] knew of and disregarded some or any level of risk of causing death," rather than requiring that the jury find that Coleman knew that his conduct presented a "substantial and unjustifiable risk of causing death." In support of his argument, Coleman points to caselaw equating the "depraved mind" mental state included in the third-degree murder statute with the mental state of recklessness.

We agree with Coleman that the district court erred when it failed to instruct the jury that it could find Coleman guilty only if it found that Coleman was aware that his conduct presented a substantial and unjustifiable risk of causing the death of another and he consciously disregarded that risk.

As both parties recognize, the supreme court has held that the mental state required for third-degree depraved-mind murder is "equivalent to a reckless standard." While there is no precedent defining the reckless standard in the context of third-degree murder, the reckless standard was examined in detail by the supreme court in State v. Engle, a case involving the reckless-discharge-of-a-firearm offense set forth in Minn. Stat. § 609.66, subd. 1a(a)(3); 743 N.W.2d 592, 593–95 (Minn. 2008). In Engle, the supreme court held that "for purposes of [the reckless-discharge-of-a-firearm offense], one acts recklessly by creating a substantial and unjustifiable risk that one is aware of and disregards."

Because the "depraved mind" mental state required for third-degree murder is the equivalent of a reckless standard, we conclude that the third-degree murder statute requires a showing of recklessness consistent with the definition adopted in Engle. Accordingly, we hold that the "depraved mind" element of the third-degree murder statute requires proof that the defendant was aware that his conduct created a substantial and unjustifiable risk of death to another person and consciously disregarded that risk. This definition of recklessness comports with most common legal usage of the term. And there is no indication that the legislature intended that a different standard apply to the third-degree murder statute.

Applying that definition of "recklessness," we conclude that the jury instruction in this case failed to correctly explain the mens rea element for third-degree murder. Because the district court did not provide a definition of the term "reckless," we conclude that a reasonable jury would not necessarily understand that before it could find Coleman guilty of third-degree murder, it had to find that Coleman was aware that his conduct created a substantial and unjustifiable risk to human life and that Coleman consciously disregarded that risk. Instead, under the instruction provided, the jury would have been allowed to find Coleman guilty if it found that Coleman acted in a careless manner, and knew only that his conduct may result in someone being killed. Accordingly, the district court's instruction did not adequately explain the law concerning the mens rea element of third-degree murder.

Next, we consider whether the district court's error in instructing the jury was plain. An error is plain if it is clear or obvious, which is typically established if the error contravenes case law, a rule, or a standard of conduct. In determining whether an error is plain, we consider the law in existence at the time of appellate review. The supreme court has previously held that the district court's failure to provide a specific explanation of an element was not plain error because it had not yet clearly required courts to explain the element in question with the specificity sought by the defendant on appeal.

Here, the instruction provided by the district court was essentially a verbatim rendering of the model jury instruction for third-degree murder. And the model instruction, in its current form, does not define "reckless" or incorporate the definition of "recklessly." Moreover, the instruction given by the district court did not contravene existing caselaw. Neither the supreme court, nor this court, has ever, in the context of a third-degree murder case under Minn. Stat. § 609.195(a), required that "recklessly" be defined as a conscious disregard of a substantial and unjustifiable risk. Although the supreme court in Engle applied that definition in a reckless-discharge-of-a-firearm case, that reasoning was applied only to that specific offense. Accordingly, the error in the jury instruction in this case was not plain. Because Coleman has not established an error

Food for Thought

Does this result make sense to you? Coleman was convicted of murder on the basis of an incorrect instruction. Shouldn't that be enough to establish "plain error," especially where the accused was convicted of murder on the basis of that error? What policy justifications can you think of for treating an instructional error as serious as this one as essentially irrelevant?

that was plain, the error in the jury instructions does not require reversal of the third-degree murder conviction.

The district court erred when it instructed the jury on third-degree murder under Minn. Stat. § 609.195(a) because it failed to properly explain a required element of the charged offense. But Coleman is unable to show that the jury-instruction error is plain, or that he is otherwise entitled to a new trial.

Flores-Figueroa v. United States

556 U.S. 646 (2009).

JUSTICE BREYER delivered the opinion of the Court.

A federal criminal statute forbidding "[a]ggravated identity theft" imposes a mandatory consecutive 2-year prison term upon individuals convicted of certain other crimes *if*, during (or in relation to) the commission of those other crimes, the offender "*knowingly* transfers, possesses, or uses, without lawful authority, *a means of identification of another person*." The question is whether the statute requires the Government to show that the defendant knew that the "means of identification" he or she unlawfully transferred, possessed, or used, in fact, belonged to "another person." We conclude that it does.

Go Online

The Department of Justice's Bureau of Justice Statistics has reported that in 2016, an estimated 10% of persons age 16 or older reported that they had been victims of identity theft during the prior 12 months. The portion of the population that experienced identity theft increased from 7% in 2014 to 10% in 2016. For 85% of identity-theft victims, the most recent incident involved the misuse or attempted misuse of only one type of existing account, such as a credit card or bank account. An estimated 12% of identity-theft victims had out-of-pocket losses of $1 or more; 88% either had no out-of-pocket losses or losses of less than $1. According to the 17.7 million persons age 16 or older who experienced one or more incidents of identity theft with known losses of $1 or more, total losses across all incidents of identity theft totaled $17.5 billion in 2016.

https://www.bjs.gov/content/pub/pdf/vit16_sum.pdf

The statutory provision in question references a set of predicate crimes, including, for example, theft of government property, fraud, or engaging in various unlawful activities related to passports, visas, and immigration. It then provides that if any person who commits any of those other crimes (in doing so) "knowingly transfers, possesses, or uses, without lawful authority, a means of identification of another person," the judge must add two years' imprisonment to the offender's underlying sentence. All parties agree that the provision applies only where the offender knows that he is transferring, possessing, or using something. And the Government reluctantly concedes that the offender likely must know that he is transferring, possessing, or using that something without lawful authority. But they do not agree whether the provision requires that a defendant also know that the something he has unlawfully transferred is, for example, a real ID belonging to another person rather than, say, a fake ID (i.e., a group of numbers that does not correspond to any real Social Security number).

Petitioner Ignacio Flores-Figueroa argues that the statute requires that the Government prove that he knew that the "means of identification" belonged to someone else, i.e., was "a means of identification of another person." The Government argues that the statute does not impose this particular knowledge requirement. The Government concedes that the statute uses the word "knowingly," but that word, the Government claims, does not modify the statute's last phrase ("a means of identification of another person") or, at the least, it does not modify the last three words of that phrase ("of another person").

The facts of this case illustrate the legal problem. Ignacio Flores-Figueroa is a citizen of Mexico. In 2000, to secure employment, Flores gave his employer a false name, birth date, and Social Security number, along with a counterfeit alien registration card. The Social Security number and the number on the alien registration card were not those of a real person. In 2006, Flores presented his employer with new counterfeit Social Security and alien registration cards; these cards (unlike Flores' old alien registration card) used his real name. But this time the numbers on both cards were in fact numbers assigned to other people.

Flores' employer reported his request to U.S. Immigration and Customs Enforcement. Customs discovered that the numbers on Flores' new documents belonged to other people. The United States then charged Flores with two predicate crimes, namely, entering the United States without inspection and misusing immigration documents. And it charged him with aggravated identity theft, the crime at issue here.

Flores moved for a judgment of acquittal on the "aggravated identity theft" counts. He claimed that the Government could not prove that he knew that the numbers on the counterfeit documents were numbers assigned to other people. The Government replied that it need not prove that knowledge, and the District Court accepted the Government's argument. After a bench trial, the court found Flores guilty of the predicate crimes and aggravated identity theft. The Court of Appeals upheld the District Court's determination.

There are strong textual reasons for rejecting the Government's position. As a matter of ordinary English grammar, it seems natural to read the statute's word "knowingly" as applying to all the subsequently listed elements of the crime. The Government cannot easily claim that the word "knowingly" applies only to the statute's first four words, or even its first seven. It makes little sense to read the provision's language as heavily penalizing a person who "transfers, possesses, or uses, without lawful authority" a something, but does not know, at the very least, that the "something" (perhaps inside a box) is a "means of identification." Would we apply a statute that makes it unlawful "knowingly to possess drugs" to a person who steals a passenger's bag without knowing that the bag has drugs inside?

The Government claims more forcefully that the word "knowingly" applies to all but the statute's last three words, i.e., "of another person." The statute, the Government says, does not require a prosecutor to show that the defendant knows that the means of identification the defendant has unlawfully used in fact belongs to another person. But how are we to square this reading with the statute's language?

In ordinary English, where a transitive verb has an object, listeners in most contexts assume that an adverb (such as knowingly) that modifies the transitive verb tells the listener how the subject performed the entire action, including the object as set forth in the sentence. Thus, if a bank official says, "Smith knowingly transferred the funds to his brother's account," we would normally understand the bank official's statement as telling us that Smith knew the account was his brother's. Nor would it matter if the bank official said "Smith knowingly transferred the funds to the account of his brother." In either instance, if the bank official later told us that Smith did not know the account belonged to Smith's brother, we should be surprised.

Of course, a statement that does not use the word "knowingly" may be unclear about just what Smith knows. Suppose Smith mails his bank draft to Tegucigalpa, which (perhaps unbeknownst to Smith) is the capital of Honduras. If the bank official says, "Smith sent a bank draft to the capital of Honduras," he has expressed next to nothing about Smith's knowledge of that geographic identity. But if the official were to say, "Smith knowingly sent a bank draft to the capital of Honduras," then the official has suggested that Smith knows his geography.

Similar examples abound. If a child knowingly takes a toy that belongs to his sibling, we assume that the child not only knows that he is taking something, but that he also knows that what he is taking is a toy and that the toy belongs to his sibling. If we say that someone knowingly ate a sandwich with cheese, we normally assume that the person knew both that he was eating a sandwich and that it contained cheese. Or consider the Government's own example, " 'John knowingly discarded the homework of his sister.' " The Government rightly points out that this sentence "does not necessarily" imply that John knew whom the homework belonged to. But that is what the sentence, as ordinarily used, does imply.

At the same time, dissimilar examples are not easy to find. The Government says that "knowingly" modifies only the verbs in the statute, while remaining indifferent to the subject's knowledge of at least part of the transitive verb's object. In certain contexts, a listener might understand the word "knowingly" to be used in that way. But the Government has not provided us with a single example of a sentence that, when used in typical fashion, would lead the hearer to believe that the word "knowingly" modifies only a transitive verb without the full object, i.e., that it leaves the hearer gravely uncertain about the subject's state of mind in respect to the full object of the transitive verb in the sentence. The likely reason is that such sentences typically involve special contexts or themselves provide a more detailed explanation of background circumstances that call for such a reading. As Justice Alito notes, the inquiry into a sentence's meaning is a contextual one. No special context is present here.

The manner in which the courts ordinarily interpret criminal statutes is fully consistent with this ordinary English usage. That is to say courts ordinarily read a phrase in a criminal statute that introduces the elements of a crime with the word "knowingly" as applying that word to each element.

The Government also considers the statute's purpose to be a circumstance showing that the linguistic context here is special. It describes that purpose as "provid[ing] enhanced protection for individuals whose identifying information is used to facilitate the commission of crimes." And it points out that without the knowledge requirement, potential offenders will take great care to avoid wrongly using IDs that belong to others, thereby enhancing the protection that the statute offers.

The question, however, is whether Congress intended to achieve this enhanced protection by permitting conviction of those who do not know the ID they unlawfully use refers to a real person, i.e., those who do not intend to cause this further harm. And, in respect to this latter point, the statute's history (outside of the statute's language) is inconclusive.

Finally, and perhaps of greatest practical importance, there is the difficulty in many circumstances of proving beyond a reasonable doubt that a defendant has the necessary knowledge. Take an instance in which an alien who unlawfully entered the United States gives an employer identification documents that in fact belong to others. How is the Government to prove that the defendant knew that this was so? The Government may be able to show that such a defendant knew the papers were not his. But perhaps the defendant did not care whether the papers (1) were real papers belonging to another person or (2) were simply counterfeit papers. The difficulties of proof along with the defendant's necessary guilt of a predicate crime and the defendant's necessary knowledge that he has acted "without lawful authority," make it reasonable, in the Government's view, to read the statute's language as dispensing with the knowledge requirement.

We do not find this argument sufficient, however, to turn the tide in the Government's favor. For one thing, in the classic case of identity theft, intent is generally not difficult to prove. For example, where a defendant has used another person's identification information to get access to that person's bank account, the Government can prove knowledge with little difficulty. The same is true when the defendant has gone through someone else's trash to find discarded credit card and bank statements, or pretends to be from the victim's bank and requests personal identifying information. Indeed, the examples of identity theft in the legislative history (dumpster diving, computer hacking, and the like) are all examples of the types of classic identity theft where intent should be relatively easy to prove, and there will be no practical enforcement problem. For another thing, to the extent that Congress may have been concerned about criminalizing the conduct of a broader class of individuals, the concerns about practical enforceability are insufficient to outweigh the clarity of the text. But had Congress placed conclusive weight upon practical enforcement, the statute would likely not read the way it now reads. Instead, Congress used the word "knowingly" followed by a list of offense elements. And we cannot find indications in statements of its purpose or in the practical problems of enforcement sufficient to overcome the ordinary meaning, in English or through ordinary interpretive practice, of the words that it wrote.

We conclude that the aggravated identity theft statute requires the Government to show that the defendant knew that the means of identification at issue belonged to another person.

JUSTICE SCALIA, with whom JUSTICE THOMAS joins, concurring in part and concurring in the judgment.

I agree with the Court that to convict petitioner for "knowingly transfer[ring], possess[ing], or us[ing], without lawful authority, a means of identification of another person," the Government must prove that he "knew that the 'means of identification' he unlawfully transferred, possessed, or used, in fact, belonged to 'another person.' " "Knowingly" is not limited to the statute's verbs. Even the Government must concede that. But once it is understood to modify the object of those verbs, there is no reason to believe it does not extend to the phrase which limits that object ("of another person"). Ordinary English usage supports this reading, as the Court's numerous sample sentences amply demonstrate.

But the Court is not content to stop at the statute's text, and I do not join that further portion of the Court's opinion. The statute's text is clear, and I would reverse the judgment of the Court of Appeals on that ground alone.

JUSTICE ALITO, concurring in part and concurring in the judgment.

I think that the Court's point about ordinary English usage is overstated. Examples of sentences that do not conform to the Court's rule are not hard to imagine. For example: "The mugger knowingly assaulted two people in the park-an employee of company X and a jogger from town Y." A person hearing this sentence would not likely assume that the mugger knew about the first victim's employer or the second victim's home town. What matters in this example, and the Court's, is context. In interpreting a criminal statute such as the one before us, I think it is fair to begin with a general presumption that the specified mens rea applies to all the elements of an offense, but it must be recognized that there are instances in which context may well rebut that presumption.

Indeed, the Government's interpretation leads to exceedingly odd results. Under that interpretation, if a defendant uses a made-up Social Security number without having any reason to know whether it belongs to a real person, the defendant's liability under this statute depends on chance: If it turns out that the number belongs to a real person, two years will be added to the defendant's sentence, but if the defendant is lucky and the number does not belong to another person, the statute is not violated.

I therefore concur in the judgment and join the opinion of the Court except insofar as it may be read to adopt an inflexible rule of construction that can rarely be overcome by contextual features pointing to a contrary reading.

Point for Discussion

Congress Gets the Last Word

If Congress disagrees with the *Flores-Figueroa* majority's holding, it is not difficult for that body to effectively "reverse" that ruling. All Congress would need to do is to enact an amendment to the federal aggravated identity theft statute that would make it absolutely, expressly clear that someone may be convicted under it who did not know that the "means of identification" he or she "transfer[red], possesse[d], or use[d]" actually belonged to "another person." Is that what Congress *should* do in your opinion?

Parenthetically, that's not what Congress *has* done. As of 2020, this statute, 18 U.S.C.A. § 1028A, has not been amended.

B. Strict Liability

Rehaif v. United States

139 S. Ct. 2191 (2019).

JUSTICE BREYER delivered the opinion of the Court.

A federal statute, 18 U.S.C. § 922(g), provides that "[i]t shall be unlawful" for certain individuals to possess firearms. The provision lists nine categories of individuals subject to the prohibition, including felons and aliens who are "illegally or unlawfully in the United States." A separate provision, § 924(a)(2), adds that anyone who "*knowingly* violates" the first provision shall be fined or imprisoned for up to 10 years.

The question here concerns the scope of the word "knowingly." Does it mean that the Government must prove that a defendant knew both that he engaged in the relevant conduct (that he possessed a firearm) and also that he fell within the relevant status (that he was a felon, an alien unlawfully in this country, or the like)? We hold that the word "knowingly" applies both to the defendant's conduct and to the defendant's status. To convict a defendant, the Government therefore must show that the defendant knew he possessed a firearm and also that he knew he had the relevant status when he possessed it.

Petitioner Hamid Rehaif entered the United States on a nonimmigrant student visa to attend university. After he received poor grades, the university dismissed him and told him that his " 'immigration status' " would be terminated unless he transferred to a different university or left the country. Rehaif did neither.

Rehaif subsequently visited a firing range, where he shot two firearms. The Government learned about his target practice and prosecuted him for possessing firearms as an alien unlawfully in the United States, in violation of § 922(g) and § 924(a)(2). At the close of Rehaif's trial, the judge instructed the jury (over Rehaif's objection) that the "United States is not required to prove" that Rehaif "knew that he was illegally or unlawfully in the United States." The jury returned a guilty verdict, and Rehaif was sentenced to 18 months' imprisonment.

Rehaif appealed. He argued that the judge erred in instructing the jury that it did not need to find that he knew he was in the country unlawfully. The Court of Appeals for the Eleventh Circuit, however, concluded that the jury instruction was correct, and it affirmed Rehaif's conviction. The Court of Appeals believed that the criminal law generally does not require a defendant to know his own status, and further observed that no court of appeals had required the Government to establish a defendant's knowledge of his status in the analogous context of felon-in-possession prosecutions.

We granted certiorari to consider whether, in prosecutions under § 922(g) and § 924(a)(2), the Government must prove that a defendant knows of his status as a person barred from possessing a firearm. We now reverse.

Whether a criminal statute requires the Government to prove that the defendant acted knowingly is a question of congressional intent. *See Staples v. United States*, 511 U.S. 600, 605, 114 S.Ct. 1793, 128 L.Ed.2d 608 (1994). In determining Congress' intent, we start from a longstanding presumption, traceable to the common law, that Congress intends to require a defendant to possess a culpable mental state regarding "each of the statutory elements that criminalize otherwise innocent conduct." We normally characterize this interpretive maxim as a presumption in favor of "scienter," by which we mean a presumption that criminal statutes require the degree of knowledge sufficient to "mak[e] a person legally responsible for the consequences of his or her act or omission."

Take Note

This is an important point. All of the justices agree that the fact that a criminal statute does not contain an explicit *mens rea* element does not necessarily mean that it is a strict liability statute. Indeed, there is a presumption precisely to the contrary. Keep reading!

We apply the presumption in favor of scienter even when Congress does not specify any scienter in the statutory text. But the presumption applies with equal or greater force when Congress includes a general scienter provision in the statute itself. *See* ALI, Model Penal Code § 2.02(4) (when a statute "prescribes the kind of culpability that is sufficient for the commission of an offense, without distinguishing among the material elements thereof, such provision shall apply to all the material elements of the offense, unless a contrary purpose plainly appears").

Here we can find no convincing reason to depart from the ordinary presumption in favor of scienter. The statutory text supports the presumption. The text of § 924(a)(2) says that "[w]hoever knowingly violates" certain subsections of § 922, including § 922(g), "shall be" subject to penalties of up to 10 years' imprisonment. The text of § 922(g) in turn provides that it "shall be unlawful for any person . . ., being an alien . . . illegally or unlawfully in the United States," to "possess in or affecting commerce, any firearm or ammunition."

The term "knowingly" in § 924(a)(2) modifies the verb "violates" and its direct object, which in this case is § 922(g). The proper interpretation of the statute thus turns on what it means for a defendant to know that he has "violate[d]" § 922(g). With some here-irrelevant omissions, § 922(g) makes possession of a firearm or ammunition unlawful when the following elements are satisfied: (1) a status element (in this case, "being an alien . . . illegally or unlawfully in the United States"); (2) a possession element (to "possess"); (3) a jurisdictional element ("in or affecting commerce"); and (4) a firearm element (a "firearm or ammunition").

No one here claims that the word "knowingly" modifies the statute's jurisdictional element. Jurisdictional elements do not describe the "evil Congress seeks to prevent," but instead simply ensure that the Federal Government has the constitutional authority to regulate the defendant's conduct (normally, as here, through its Commerce Clause power). Because jurisdictional elements normally have nothing to do with the wrongfulness of the defendant's conduct, such elements are not subject to the presumption in favor of scienter.

Jurisdictional element aside, however, the text of § 922(g) simply lists the elements that make a defendant's behavior criminal. As "a matter of ordinary English grammar," we normally read the statutory term " 'knowingly' as applying to all the subsequently listed elements of the crime." This is notably not a case where the modifier "knowingly" introduces a long statutory phrase, such that questions may reasonably arise about how far into the statute the modifier extends. And everyone agrees that the word "knowingly" applies to § 922(g)'s possession element, which is situated after the status element. We see no basis to interpret "knowingly" as applying to the second § 922(g) element but not the first. To the contrary, we think that by specifying that a defendant may be convicted only if he "knowingly violates" § 922(g), Congress intended to require the Government to establish that the defendant knew he violated the material elements of § 922(g).

Beyond the text, our reading of § 922(g) and § 924(a)(2) is consistent with a basic principle that underlies the criminal law, namely, the importance of showing what Blackstone called "a vicious will." 4 W. Blackstone, Commentaries on the Laws of England 21 (1769). As this Court has explained, the understanding that an injury is criminal only if inflicted knowingly "is as universal and persistent in mature systems of law as belief in freedom of the human will and a consequent ability and duty of the normal individual to choose between good and evil." Scienter requirements advance this basic principle of criminal law by helping to "separate those who understand the wrongful nature of their act from those who do not."

The cases in which we have emphasized scienter's importance in separating wrongful from innocent acts are legion. We have interpreted statutes to include a scienter requirement even where the statutory text is silent on the question. *See Staples*, 511 U.S. at 605, 114 S.Ct. 1793. And we have interpreted statutes to include a scienter requirement even where "the most grammatical reading of the statute" does not support one.

Applying the word "knowingly" to the defendant's status in § 922(g) helps advance the purpose of scienter, for it helps to separate wrongful from innocent acts. Assuming compliance with ordinary licensing requirements, the possession of a gun can be entirely innocent. It is therefore the defendant's status, and not his conduct alone, that makes the difference. Without knowledge of that status, the defendant may well lack the intent needed to make his behavior wrongful. His behavior may instead be an innocent mistake to which criminal sanctions normally do not attach. *Cf.* O. Holmes, The Common Law 3 (1881) ("even a dog distinguishes between being stumbled over and being kicked").

We have sometimes declined to read a scienter requirement into criminal statutes. But we have typically declined to apply the presumption in favor of scienter in cases involving statutory provisions that form part of a "regulatory" or "public welfare" program and carry only minor penalties. The firearms provisions before us are not part of a regulatory or public welfare program, and they carry a potential penalty of 10 years in prison that we have previously described as "harsh." Hence, this exception to the presumption in favor of scienter does not apply.

Food for Thought

Do you agree that this statute is not part of a "regulatory" or "public welfare" program? Why is that? And does it or should it make a difference that despite the fact that there is a theoretical ten-year maximum penalty, defendant only received an eighteen-month sentence? Is that "harsh?"

The Government's arguments to the contrary do not convince us that Congress sought to depart from the normal presumption in favor of scienter.

The Government argues that Congress does not normally require defendants to know their own status. But the Government supports this claim primarily by referring to statutes that differ significantly from the provisions at issue here. One of these statutes prohibits "an officer, employee, contractor, or consultant of the United States" from misappropriating classified information. 18 U.S.C. § 1924(a). Another statute applies to anyone "at least eighteen years of age" who solicits a minor to help avoid detection for certain federal crimes. 21 U.S.C. § 861(a)(2). A third applies to a "parent [or] legal guardian" who allows his child to be used for child pornography. 18 U.S.C. § 2251(b).

We need not decide whether we agree or disagree with the Government's interpretation of these statutes. In the provisions at issue here, the defendant's status is the "crucial element" separating innocent from wrongful conduct. But in the statutes cited by the Government, the conduct prohibited—misappropriating classified information, seeking to evade detection for certain federal crimes, and facilitating child pornography—would be wrongful irrespective of the defendant's status. This difference assures us that the presumption in favor of scienter applies here even assuming the Government is right that these other statutes do not require knowledge of status.

Nor do we believe that Congress would have expected defendants under § 922(g) and § 924(a)(2) to know their own statuses. If the provisions before us were construed to require no knowledge of status, they might well apply to an alien who was brought into the United States unlawfully as a small child and was therefore unaware of his unlawful status. Or these provisions might apply to a person who was convicted of a prior crime but sentenced only to probation, who does not know that the crime is "punishable by imprisonment for a term exceeding one year." As we have said, we normally presume that Congress did not intend to impose criminal liability on persons who, due to lack of knowledge, did not have a wrongful mental state. And we doubt that the obligation to prove a defendant's knowledge of his status will be as burdensome as the Government suggests.

The Government finally turns for support to the statutory and legislative history. Congress first enacted a criminal statute prohibiting particular categories of persons from possessing firearms in 1938. In 1968, Congress added new categories of persons subject to the prohibition. Then, in 1986, Congress passed the statute at issue here, the Firearms Owners' Protection Act, which reorganized the prohibition on firearm possession and added the language providing that only those who violate the prohibition "knowingly" may be held criminally liable.

The Government says that, prior to 1986, the courts had reached a consensus that the law did not require the Government to prove scienter regarding a defendant's status. And the Government relies on the interpretive canon providing that when particular statutory language has received a settled judicial construction, and Congress subsequently reenacts that "same language," courts should presume that Congress intended to ratify the judicial consensus.

Prior to 1986, however, there was no definitive judicial consensus that knowledge of status was not needed. This Court had not considered the matter. As the Government says, most lower courts had concluded that the statute did not require knowledge of status. But any pre-1986 consensus involved the statute as it read prior to 1986—without any explicit scienter provision. But Congress in 1986 added a provision clarifying that a defendant could be convicted only if he violated the prohibition on firearm possession "knowingly." This addition, which would serve no apparent purpose under the Government's view, makes it all but impossible to draw any inference that Congress intended to ratify a pre-existing consensus when, in 1986, it amended the statute.

We conclude that in a prosecution under 18 U.S.C. § 922(g) and § 924(a)(2), the Government must prove both that the defendant knew he possessed a firearm and that he knew he belonged to the relevant category of persons barred from possessing a firearm. We accordingly reverse the judgment of the Court of Appeals and remand the case for further proceedings consistent with this opinion.

It is so ordered.

JUSTICE ALITO, with whom JUSTICE THOMAS joins, dissenting.

The Court casually overturns the long-established interpretation of an important criminal statute, 18 U.S.C. § 922(g), an interpretation that has been adopted by every single Court of Appeals to address the question. That interpretation has been used in thousands of cases for more than 30 years. According to the majority, every one of those cases was flawed. So today's decision is no minor matter. And § 922(g) is no minor provision. It probably does more to combat gun violence than any other federal law. It prohibits the possession of firearms by, among others, convicted felons, mentally ill persons found by a court to present a danger to the community, stalkers, harassers, perpetrators of domestic violence, and illegal aliens.

Today's decision will make it significantly harder to convict persons falling into some of these categories, and the decision will create a mountain of problems with respect to the thousands of prisoners currently serving terms for § 922(g) convictions. Applications for relief by federal prisoners sentenced under § 922(g) will swamp the lower courts. A great many convictions will be subject to challenge, threatening the release or retrial of dangerous individuals whose cases fall outside the bounds of harmless-error review.

If today's decision were compelled by the text of § 922(g) or by some other clear indication of congressional intent, what the majority has done would be understandable. We must enforce the laws enacted by Congress even if we think that doing so will bring about unfortunate results. But that is not the situation in this case. There is no sound basis for today's decision.

Petitioner argues that, when § 924(a)(2) and § 922(g) are put together, they unambiguously show that a defendant must actually know that he falls into one of the nine enumerated categories. But this purportedly textual argument requires some moves that cannot be justified on the basis of the statutory text. Petitioner's argument tries to hide those moves in the manner of a sleight-of-hand artist at a carnival.

Petitioner begins by extracting the term "knowingly" from § 924(a)(2). He then transplants it into the beginning of § 922(g), ignores the extraordinarily awkward prose that this surgery produces, and proclaims that because "knowingly" appears at the beginning of the enumeration of the elements of the § 922(g) offense, we must assume that it modifies the first of those elements, i.e., being a convicted felon, illegal alien, etc. To conclude otherwise, he contends, is to commit the sin of having the term "knowingly" leap over that element and then land conveniently in front of the second.

The most natural reading is that the defendant must know only that he is an alien, not that his presence in the country is illegal or unlawful. And under this version, it is not even clear that the alien's possession of the firearm or ammunition must be knowing—even though everyone agrees that this is required.

In no prior case have we inferred that Congress intended to impose a mens rea requirement on an element that concerns the defendant's own status. Nor has petitioner pointed to any statute with text that plainly evinces such a congressional intent. Instead, in instances in which Congress has expressly incorporated a mens rea requirement into a provision with an element involving the defendant's status, it has placed the mens rea requirement after the status element.

There are sound reasons for treating § 922(g)'s status element like its jurisdictional element. The parties agree that federal criminal statutes presumptively do not require proof that an accused knew that his conduct satisfied a jurisdictional element, and our cases support this proposition. Whether or not conduct satisfies that requirement involves a complicated legal question; requiring proof of such knowledge would threaten to effectively exempt almost everyone but students of constitutional law from the statute's reach; and that would obviously defeat the statute's objectives.

Since a legislative body may enact a valid criminal statute with a strict-liability element, the dispositive question is whether it has done so or, in other words, whether the presumption that petitioner invokes is rebutted. This rebuttal can be done by the statutory text or other persuasive factors. And here, § 922(g) is best interpreted not to require proof that a defendant knew that he fell within one of the covered categories.

The majority today opens the gates to a flood of litigation that is sure to burden the lower courts with claims for relief in a host of cases where there is no basis for doubting the defendant's knowledge. The majority's interpretation of § 922(g) is not required by the statutory text, and there is no reason to suppose that it represents what Congress intended.

I respectfully dissent.

Food for Thought

Note that all of the justices agree that legislatures have the authority to enact strict liability statutes. The question is whether a statute not explicitly containing a *mens rea* term is such a statute or not.

Points for Discussion

a. Model Penal Code

Consider the MPC's approach to strict liability:

§ 2.05. When Culpability Requirements Are Inapplicable to Violations and to Offenses Defined by Other Statutes; Effect of Absolute Liability in Reducing Grade of Offense to Violation.

(1) The requirements of culpability prescribed by Sections 2.01 and 2.02 do not apply to:

(a) offenses that constitute violations, unless the requirement involved is included in the definition of the offense or the Court determines that its application is consistent with effective enforcement of the law defining the offense; or

(b) offenses defined by statutes other than the Code, insofar as a legislative purpose to impose absolute liability for such offenses or with respect to any material element thereof plainly appears.

(2) Notwithstanding any other provision of existing law and unless a subsequent statute otherwise provides:

(a) when absolute liability is imposed with respect to any material element of an offense defined by a statute other than the Code and a conviction is based upon such liability, the offense constitutes a violation; and

(b) although absolute liability is imposed by law with respect to one or more of the material elements of an offense defined by a statute other than the Code, the culpable commission of the offense may be charged and proved, in which event negligence with respect to such elements constitutes sufficient culpability and the classification of the offense and the sentence that may be imposed therefor upon conviction are determined by Section 1.04 and Article 6 of the Code.

b. Possession of Automatic Weapons: *Staples* & State Variations

In *Rehaif*, the Supreme Court referred repeatedly to its prior decision in *Staples v. United States*, 511 U.S. 600 (1994). In *Staples*, a majority of the Court ruled that in a prosecution under Section 5861(d) of the National Firearms Act, 26 U.S.C. §§ 5801–5872, the Government was required to establish that an accused knew of the characteristics of his or her weapon that made it a fully automatic weapon, a "firearm" that needed to be properly registered. The majority reached this conclusion despite the fact that the statute, violation of which could be punished by up to ten years in prison, contained no explicit *mens rea* element. The majority ruled, *inter alia*, that

> where, as here, dispensing with *mens rea* would require the defendant to have knowledge only of traditionally lawful conduct, a severe penalty is a further factor tending to suggest that Congress did not intend to eliminate a *mens rea* requirement. In such a case, the usual presumption that a defendant must know the facts that make his conduct illegal should apply.
>
> In short, we conclude that the background rule of the common law favoring *mens rea* should govern interpretation of § 5861(d) in this case. Silence does not suggest that Congress dispensed with *mens rea* for the element of § 5861(d) at issue here. Thus, to obtain a conviction, the Government should have been required to prove that petitioner knew of the features of his AR-15 that brought it within the scope of the Act.
>
> We emphasize that our holding is a narrow one. We note that our holding depends critically on our view that if Congress had intended to make outlaws of gun owners who were wholly ignorant of the offending characteristics of their weapons, and to subject them to lengthy prison terms, it would have spoken more clearly to that effect.

Similar state statutes have not always been interpreted the same way by state courts. See, e.g., *People v. May*, 47 Cal.App.5th 1001, 261 Cal. Rptr.3d 365 (2020):

> Cal. Penal Code § 32625(a) provides: "Any person . . . who within this state possesses or knowingly transports a machinegun . . . is guilty of a public offense . . . ." A machine gun is any weapon that shoots "automatically more than one shot, without manual reloading, by a single function of the trigger."
>
> In 1994, the United States Supreme Court concluded the federal law prohibiting possession of a machine gun was not a strict liability offense despite the fact the statute was silent regarding mens rea. (*Staples v. United States.*) It started with the language of the statute read in light of common law principles favoring mens rea. The Supreme Court questioned whether the presumption of a mens rea was rebutted by express or implied congressional intent to the contrary. It concluded

it was not because the statute was silent in that regard. It then analyzed whether the presumption could be rebutted because the statute defined a public welfare offense, concluding it did not.

Staples concluded the statute at issue there required some form of knowledge because the statute was silent. Here, that is not the case—the statute mentions knowledge in relation to transportation and not in relation to possession. Because the statute contains a knowledge requirement, it is not like the silent statute in *Staples*, and we can imply a legislative intent through the plain meaning of the statute. The Legislature's selective use of the word knowing in the statute should not be ignored by California courts. The failure to specify scienter for possession of a machine gun, when one was specified for transportation, indicates the Legislature intended the crime of possession to be accomplished without knowledge.

We are cognizant that times have changed, and possession of a machine gun is not always obvious. Given modern advances in weapon technology, it is possible the Legislature never envisioned a situation where formally-legal firearms could be internally modified without external clues to the modifications. Still, the language of the statute combined with its history, persuade us the offense remains strict liability.

c. Exxon Valdez

Captain Joseph Hazelwood ran his ship, the Exxon Valdez, aground off Bligh Reef off the coast of Alaska and reported he was "leaking some oil." In fact, eleven million gallons eventually poured into Prince William Sound as a result of this accident. Hazelwood was charged under an Alaska statute that provided as follows:

> **Go Online**
>
> Want to learn more about this massive oil spill? See, e.g., https://www.theatlantic.com/photo/2014/03/the-exxon-valdez-oil-spill-25-years-ago-today/100703/.

> A person may not discharge, cause to be discharged, or permit the discharge of petroleum [into], or upon the waters or land of the state except in quantities, and at times and locations or under circumstances and conditions as the department may by regulation permit.

Using the logic of *Rehaif*, should this statute be construed to impose strict liability? *See Alaska v. Hazelwood*, 946 P.2d 875 (Alaska 1997).

d. Demonstrating at the White House

Political activist Cindy Sheehan was arrested in September 2005 for demonstrating without a permit on the White House sidewalk during an antiwar protest involving more than 200 people. She was charged with violating 36 C.F.R. § 7.96(g)(2), a National Park Service regulation governing demonstrations in all park areas in the National Capital Region, including the White House sidewalk. Following a bench trial, Sheehan was convicted and assessed a $50 fine and a $25 administrative fee.

36 C.F.R. § 7.96(g)(2) provides that "demonstrations and special events may be held only pursuant to a permit issued in accordance with the provisions of this section." Under applicable regulations, demonstrations involving more than 25 people may be held only pursuant to a permit. The term "demonstrations" is defined as "including demonstrations, picketing, speechmaking, marching, holding vigils or religious services and all other like forms of conduct which involve the communication or expression of views or grievances, engaged in by one or more persons, the conduct of which has the effect, intent or propensity to draw a crowd or onlookers. This term does not include casual park use by visitors or tourists which does not have an intent or propensity to attract a crowd or onlookers."

At trial, the judge allowed the Government to prosecute the case against Ms. Sheehan on the premise that the disputed regulations imposed strict liability for her alleged expressive activity, and sustained the prosecutor's objections when defense counsel for Sheehan sought to advance a defense based on her knowledge and intent. On appeal, Sheehan argued that she was entitled to a new trial because the Government was required to prove a culpable *mens rea* on Sheehan's part and the judge's rulings and instructions eliminated the prosecutor's burden to prove this *mens rea* and barred her from presenting a defense on that issue. Should Sheehan's conviction be reversed on this ground? What arguments—if any—can she make based on the *Staples* opinion to support her contention? *See United States v. Sheehan*, 512 F.3d 621, 379 U.S. App. D.C. 187 (2008).

Hypo: *A Minor Mistake*

A Pennsylvania criminal statute provided that "a person who lures a child into a motor vehicle without the consent, express or implied, of the child's parent or guardian, unless the circumstances reasonably indicate that the child is in need of assistance, commits a misdemeanor of the first degree." 18 Pa.C.S. § 2910. Defendant Gallagher, charged under that statute, argues that he is not guilty of this crime because he did not know that 17-year-old M.N., who he invited into his car to drink and then to engage in oral sex, was only seventeen years old, i.e. he was a minor. Is this a good defense? *See Pennsylvania v. Gallagher*, 592 Pa. 262, 924 A.2d 636 (2007).

C. Intoxication & Drugged Condition

Criminals often commit criminal acts while they are "high" on alcohol and/or drugs. Where a criminal offense is *not* a strict liability offense, it is easy to imagine situations where such a defendant does not (sometimes, virtually cannot) possess the *mens rea* required for the criminal offense in question. Nonetheless, courts have been extremely reluctant to acquit on this basis. Common law jurisdictions have traditionally taken the position that an intoxication or drugged condition can negative the *mens rea* for a "specific intent" crime, but it does not negative the *mens rea* of a "general intent" crime. Just what general and specific intent mean in this setting has been the subject of considerable controversy.

People v. Atkins

25 Cal. 4th 76, 18 P.3d 660, 104 Cal. Rptr. 2d 738 (2001).

CHIN, J.

Is evidence of voluntary intoxication admissible on the issue of whether defendant formed the required mental state for arson? We conclude that such evidence is not admissible because arson is a general intent crime. Accordingly, we reverse the judgment of the Court of Appeal.

On September 26, 1997, defendant told his friends that he hated Orville Figgs and was going to burn down Figgs's house.

On the afternoon of September 27, defendant and his brother David drove by Figgs's home on the Ponderosa Sky Ranch. Defendant "flipped the bird" at Figgs as they passed by.

Later that day, around 5:00 p.m., a neighbor saw David drive a white pickup truck into the Ponderosa Sky Ranch canyon, but could not tell if he had a passenger. Around 9:00 p.m., the same neighbor saw the pickup truck drive out of the canyon at a high rate of speed. A half-hour later, a fire was reported. Shortly after 10:00 p.m., Figgs was awakened by a neighbor. Because the fire was rapidly approaching his house, Figgs set up a fire line. The fire came within 150 feet of his house.

At 9:00 or 9:30 p.m., one of defendant's friends saw defendant at David's apartment. He was angrily throwing things around. When asked if defendant was heavily intoxicated, the friend replied, "Yes. Agitated, very agitated."

The county fire marshall, Alan Carlson, responded to the fire around 1:30 a.m. and saw a large fire rapidly spreading in the canyon below the ranch. He described fire conditions on that night as "extreme." Both the weather and the vegetation were particularly dry. The wind was blowing from 12 to 27 miles per hour, with gusts up to 50 miles per hour. The canyon had heavy brush, trees, grass, and steep sloping grades. The fire could not be controlled for three days and burned an area from 2.5 to 2.8 miles long.

The fire marshall traced the origin of the fire to an approximately 10 foot-square area that was completely burned and smelled of "chainsaw mix," a combination of oil and gasoline. A soil sample taken from that area tested positive for gasoline. About 40 feet away, the marshall found defendant's wallet, which was near a recently opened beer can, and tire tracks. He also found a disposable lighter nearby and two more beer cans in other parts of the canyon. All the cans had the same expiration date.

Several days later, defendant spoke with the fire marshall. After waiving his Miranda rights, defendant told the marshall that he and his brother had spent much of the day drinking.

They then drove in David's white pickup to the Ponderosa Sky Ranch canyon, where they drank some more and stayed between three and one-half to five hours. Defendant saw that the area was in poor condition and decided to burn some of the weeds. His family had once lived there. He pulled out the weeds, placed them in a small pile in a cleared area, retrieved a plastic gasoline jug from David's truck, and from the jug poured "chainsaw mix" on the pile of weeds. Defendant put the jug down a few feet away and lit the pile of weeds with a disposable lighter. The fire quickly spread to the jug and got out of hand. He and David tried to put the fire out, unsuccessfully. They panicked and fled while the jug was still burning. Defendant told the marshal that he meant no harm, claimed the fire was an accident, but admitted that he and his family had hard feelings with the Figgs family.

The marshall testified that the fire had not been started in a cleared area. The area was covered with vegetation, and there was no evidence that the fire started accidentally during a debris burn or that someone had tried to put it out. The marshall opined that the fire was intentionally set.

An information charged defendant with arson of forest land. The trial court instructed on arson and on the lesser offenses of arson to property, unlawfully causing a fire of forest land, and misdemeanor unlawfully causing a fire of property. It described arson and all lesser offenses as general intent crimes and further instructed that voluntary intoxication is not a defense to arson and the lesser crimes and does not relieve defendant of responsibility for the crime. The jury found defendant guilty as charged.

Defendant appealed, arguing that evidence of voluntary intoxication was admissible to show that he lacked the requisite mental state for arson. The Court of Appeal agreed. It reasoned that [the] mens rea for arson is the intent to set fire to or burn or cause to be burned forest land, a specific mental state, as to which voluntary intoxication evidence is admissible under section 22, subdivision (b). The court reversed because the instruction that voluntary intoxication was not a defense to arson "denied defendant the opportunity to prove he lacked the required mental state."

Section 22 provides, as relevant:

> "(a) No act committed by a person while in a state of voluntary intoxication is less criminal by reason of his or her having been in that condition. Evidence of voluntary intoxication shall not be admitted to negate the capacity to form any mental states for the crimes charged, including, but not limited to, purpose, intent, knowledge, premeditation, deliberation, or malice aforethought, with which the accused committed the act.
>
> "(b) Evidence of voluntary intoxication is admissible solely on the issue of whether or not the defendant actually formed a required specific intent, or, when charged with murder, whether the defendant premeditated, deliberated, or harbored express malice aforethought."

Evidence of voluntary intoxication is inadmissible to negate the existence of general criminal intent. In *People v. Hood* (1969) 1 Cal. 3d 444, 82 Cal. Rptr. 618, 462 P.2d 370, we first addressed the question whether to designate a mental state as a general intent, to prohibit consideration of voluntary intoxication or a specific intent, to permit such consideration. There, we held that intoxication was relevant to negate the existence of a specific intent, but not a general intent, and that assault is a general intent crime for this purpose. We stated:

> "The distinction between specific and general intent crimes evolved as a judicial response to the problem of the intoxicated offender. That problem is to reconcile two competing theories of what is just in the treatment of those who commit crimes while intoxicated. On the one hand, the moral culpability of a drunken criminal is frequently less than that of a sober person effecting a like injury. On the other hand, it is commonly felt that a person who voluntarily gets drunk and while in that state commits a crime should not escape the consequences.
>
> "Before the nineteenth century, the common law refused to give any effect to the fact that an accused committed a crime while intoxicated. The judges were apparently troubled by this rigid traditional rule, however, for there were a number of attempts during the early part of the nineteenth century to arrive at a more humane, yet workable, doctrine. The theory that these judges explored was that evidence of intoxication could be considered to negate intent, whenever intent was an element of the crime charged. As Professor Hall notes, however, such an exculpatory doctrine could eventually have undermined the traditional rule entirely, since some form of mens rea is a requisite of all but strict liability offenses. To limit the operation of the doctrine and achieve a compromise between the conflicting feelings of sympathy and reprobation for the intoxicated offender, later courts both in England and this country drew a distinction between so-called specific intent and general intent crimes."

Although we noted in *Hood* that specific and general intent have been notoriously difficult terms to define and apply, we set forth a general definition distinguishing the two intents: "When the definition of a crime consists of only the description of a particular act, without reference to intent to do a further act or achieve a future consequence, we ask whether the defendant intended to do the proscribed act. This intention is deemed to be a general criminal intent. When the definition refers to defendant's intent to do some further act or achieve some additional consequence, the crime is deemed to be one of specific intent." The basic framework that *Hood* established in designating a criminal intent as either specific or general for purposes of determining the admissibility of evidence of voluntary intoxication has survived.

Food for Thought

Does this distinction between general and specific intent crimes make sense to you?

Defendant argues that arson requires the specific intent to burn the relevant structure or forest land, a mental state that may be negated by evidence of voluntary intoxication. The People argue that arson is a general intent crime with a mental state that cannot be negated by such evidence. The Courts of Appeal have disagreed on the intent requirement for arson.

In this case, the Court of Appeal held that the mens rea for arson, the intent to set fire to or burn or cause to be burned forest land—is a "required specific intent" for which evidence of voluntary intoxication is admissible under section 22, subdivision (b).

We agree with the People that arson requires only a general criminal intent and that the specific intent to set fire to or burn or cause to be burned the relevant structure or forest land is not an element of arson.

As relevant here, the proscribed acts within the statutory definition of arson are to: (1) set fire to; (2) burn; or (3) cause to be burned, any structure, forest land, or property. Language that typically denotes specific intent crimes, such as "with the intent" to achieve or "for the purpose of" achieving some further act, is absent. "A crime is characterized as a 'general intent' crime when the required mental state entails only an intent to do the act that causes the harm; a crime is characterized as a 'specific intent' crime when the required mental state entails an intent to cause the resulting harm." The statute does not require an additional specific intent to burn a "structure, forest land, or property," but rather requires only an intent to do the act that causes the harm. This interpretation is manifest from the fact that the statute is implicated if a person "causes to be burned any structure, forest land, or property." Thus, the intent requirement for arson fits within the *Hood* definition of general intent, i.e., the description of the proscribed act fails to refer to an intent to do a further act or achieve a future consequence.

Defendant reasons that, since arson is the more serious crime, it should have a more culpable mental state than the recklessness requirement of the lesser offense of recklessly causing a fire. From that premise, he infers that the more culpable mental state of arson must be a specific intent. However, the lesser offense requires mere recklessness; arson requires the general intent to perform the criminal act. This is a continuum that does not support specific intent. The fact that a crime requires a greater mental state than recklessness does not mean that it is a specific intent crime, rather than a general intent crime. The fact that reckless burning is a lesser offense of arson is also not dispositive.

In arson, as with assault, there is generally no complex mental state, but only relatively simple impulsive behavior. A typical arson is almost never the product of pyromania, it often is an angry impulsive act, requiring no tools other than a match or lighter, and possibly a container of gasoline. "Arson is one of the easiest crimes to commit on the spur of the moment it takes only seconds to light a match to a pile of clothes or a curtain."

The apparent legislative policy concerns are consistent with studies that have shown the following: that revenge and vindictiveness are principal motives for; that there is a strong relationship between alcohol intoxication and arson; and that recidivist arsonists committing chronic or repetitive arson have high levels of alcohol. Thus, the motivations for most arsons, the ease of its commission, and the strong connection with alcohol reflect the crime's impulsiveness. "It would therefore be anomalous to allow evidence of intoxication to relieve a man of responsibility for the crime of arson, which is so frequently committed in just such a manner."

We reverse the judgment of the Court of Appeal and remand the cause to the Court of Appeal for further proceedings consistent with this opinion.

Concurring Opinion by MOSK, J.

Although they apparently recognize that "general intent" should be affixed to the crime of arson because arson is itself closely linked to voluntary intoxication in its commission, the majority deny that the mental state required could readily be deemed to be one of specific intent. Their denial is inexplicable. It is also incorrect. They seem to rest on the premise that the perpetrator's intent must be inceptive, aiming to start a fire, and apparently need not be resultative, aiming to burn down an indicated object. Even if their premise is sound, it gives them no aid. For, even if the perpetrator's intent must be inceptive rather than resultative, the required mental state could readily be deemed to be one of specific intent—again, an intent to engage in proscribed conduct involving setting fire to an indicated object, burning it, or causing it to be burned, for the purpose of bringing about, or allowing, a proscribed result involving any other wrong, including vexation, fraud, annoyance, or injury to another person. At the end of the day, all that the majority have to justify their denial seems to be an assumption that the perpetrator's intent must be resultative rather than inceptive. *Hood* itself is plain: "When" a crime "refers to" the perpetrator's "intent to do some further act or achieve some additional consequence" beyond the "description of a particular act," the "crime is deemed to be one of specific intent." The majority's assumption is that, beyond referring to the perpetrator's setting fire to an indicated object, burning it, or causing it to be burned, arson must refer to an intent on his part to achieve a particular additional consequence, that is, to burn the object down, as opposed to doing any other wrong, including vexation, fraud, annoyance, or injury to another person. Their assumption is unsupported. Hence, it falls of its own weight.

Points for Discussion

a. Eliminating Intoxication Defense

Some jurisdictions have eliminated (or virtually eliminated) intoxication or drugged condition as a defense. See, e.g., 18 Pa. C.S. A. § 308 ("Neither voluntary intoxication nor voluntary drugged condition is a defense to a criminal charge, nor may evidence of such conditions be introduced to negative the element of intent of the offense, except that evidence of such intoxication or drugged condition of the defendant may be offered by the defendant whenever it is relevant to reduce murder from a higher degree to a lower degree of murder."). Is this a sensible approach? Doesn't this approach mean that some defendants who truly do not possess the *mens rea* specified for the offense with which they are charged will be convicted in any event? If so, is this a problem?

b. Model Penal Code

Consider the MPC's approach to the problem of intoxication and drugged condition:

§ 2.08. Intoxication.

(1) Except as provided in Subsection (4) of this Section, intoxication of the actor is not a defense unless it negatives an element of the offense.

(2) When recklessness establishes an element of the offense, if the actor, due to self-induced intoxication, is unaware of a risk of which he would have been aware had he been sober, such unawareness is immaterial.

(3) Intoxication does not, in itself, constitute mental disease within the meaning of Section 4.01.

(4) Intoxication that (a) is not self-induced or (b) is pathological is an affirmative defense if by reason of such intoxication the actor at the time of his conduct lacks substantial capacity either to appreciate its criminality [wrongfulness] or to conform his conduct to the requirements of law.

(5) **Definitions.** In this Section unless a different meaning plainly is required:

(a) "intoxication" means a disturbance of mental or physical capacities resulting from the introduction of substances into the body;

(b) "self-induced intoxication" means intoxication caused by substances that the actor knowingly introduces into his body, the tendency of which to cause intoxication he knows or ought to know, unless he introduces them pursuant to medical advice or under such circumstances as would afford a defense to a charge of crime;

(c) "pathological intoxication" means intoxication grossly excessive in degree, given the amount of the intoxicant, to which the actor does not know he is susceptible.

c. Involuntary Intoxication

Unlike voluntary intoxication or drugged condition, *involuntary* intoxication or drugged condition is typically considered a viable and complete defense. Generally, this defense is treated as an involuntary act rather than as a matter relating to a defendant's mental state.

d. Degree of Intoxication

In jurisdictions where an intoxication or drugged condition defense exists, it is *not* sufficient simply to demonstrate the use of alcohol or drugs or even the fact that a defendant was demonstrably "high." Rather, to be able to successfully use this defense, the defendant must be so intoxicated and/or drugged that he or she is not capable of possessing the specific intent at issue. On this point, consider the next case.

Tennessee v. Hatcher

310 S.W.3d 788 (Tenn. 2010).

CORNELIA A. CLARK, J.

This case arises from Shawn Hatcher's participation in the shooting death of Marcel Mackey and the gunshot injuries to Anitra Flowers and Randall White/Moore ("Red") on April 3, 2001, in Memphis, Shelby County, Tennessee. Shawn Hatcher ("Defendant") was charged with alternative counts of first degree premeditated murder and first degree felony murder, and two counts of attempted first degree premeditated murder. Also charged were Defendant's older brother, Christopher Hatcher ("Chris"), and Defendant's friend, Cornelius Jefferson ("Cornelius").

The proof at trial established that Defendant, seventeen years old at the time, was released from juvenile custody on the afternoon of April 3, 2001. That evening, Defendant, Cornelius, and a man named Dan Smith accompanied Chris to an apartment at 756 East Raines. There, the men opened fire with multiple guns, killing Mackey and injuring Flowers and Red. Defendant was arrested, and he subsequently gave a statement in December 2001. He admitted to being present at the shooting and when asked to describe the events surrounding the shooting, Defendant responded as follows:

> I came home that day and came in the house and that's when my brother told me that he got into it with Red. He said that Red tried to kill him, then he pulled out the .38 and said "I got this for him, if he decides to come to the house looking for me." I went to sleep, woke up, helped my mom bring groceries in the house. Cornelius came over, we drunk and they smoked, whatever, sit in the backyard. I stepped in the house for a minute talking to my mom and my brother came in the house and told me to come here.
>
> So I went back to the backyard, I seen Chris' rifle laying on the ground. I asked him what was it for and he said protection. So I told him I was going back in the house for a minute to talk to my mom. Then after I got through talking to her, I left. I went to the backyard, my brother was gone. I asked Cornelius where he was, he said he was gone to the Raintree to meet Dan. After that me and Cornelius walked to the store, on the way we seen my brother and Dan in the shortcut with the guns. I asked him "what's up"; he asked me "what's up". He said he was about to take care of some business. I said I was going to the store, so as we walked to the store he talked to some females, they said they were walking up to Black Store so we walked to the Black Store.
>
> We departed from them. Went back to my house, finished drinking, smoking or whatever. We wanted some more weed so we went and got my brother to get some weed from him. But instead of getting some weed from him, he didn't give us no weed. He was like he was fixing to go take some of some business. At that time he wanted us to go with him so we walked towards Randle's house. On the way we

> ran across three kids, I guess he thought one of the kids was Randle. So he walked up to him and asked who he was and the boy replied that he knew my brother then my brother pulled his rifle up on him.
>
> Then the boy ran behind me and I told my brother no. I don't know if he intended to shoot the boy or not but after I told him no, the boy ran. Chris continued to walk towards Randle's house. He and Dan walked to the door, knocked on the door and began to open fire. Chris ran and I assumed Dan ran in the house because I could hear a change in the shots fired. So I guess Dan realized he was by himself, so he ran.
>
> Cornelius shot in the air as other shots were being fired. After that all of us ran together through the shortcut. Dan caught up with us and ran through the shortcut and then we went our separate ways. Me and Cornelius paid someone $10.00 to take us to a hotel on Third. We stayed there a couple of night and he left and went home. I stayed in the motel.

Co-defendant Cornelius, also seventeen years old in April 2001, testified at trial. He explained that he and Defendant had been at Defendant's house before the shootings, "smoking weed and drinking a little liquor." Chris came over with some "long rifles" and had Cornelius and Defendant "go with him" to some nearby apartments.

The jury convicted Defendant of the first degree premeditated murder of Marcel Mackey, the alternative count of first degree felony murder, and the attempted first degree premeditated murders of Anitra Flowers and Randall White/Moore. He was sentenced to life imprisonment on the murder conviction, and 15 years on each of the attempted first degree murder convictions.

Food for Thought

If intoxication negatives one of the elements of the crime, how can the court say that it is not a defense? Does this make sense?

The defense complains about the trial court's failure to instruct the jury about voluntary intoxication. As provided by our criminal code, "voluntary intoxication itself is not a defense to prosecution for an offense. However, intoxication, whether voluntary or involuntary, is admissible in evidence, if it is relevant to negate a culpable mental state." Proof of voluntary intoxication is therefore akin to proof of a mental disease or defect that prevents a defendant from forming the culpable mental state required for the offense under consideration. However,

> proof of intoxication alone is not a defense to a charge of committing a specific intent crime nor does it entitle an accused to jury instructions; there must be evidence that the intoxication deprived the accused of the mental capacity to form specific intent.[16] The determinative question is not whether the accused was intoxicated, but what was his mental capacity.

16 This Court has recognized that our legislature has "abandoned the 'confusing distinction between general and specific intent.' " Thus, the current statute regarding proof of intoxication for defense purposes refers to "cul-

The only proof in the instant case concerning Defendant's intoxication came from Cornelius, Aja Brown, and Defendant's statement to the police. Cornelius testified that, on the afternoon of the crimes, he and Defendant smoked "weed" and drank "a little liquor." Aja Brown was of the opinion that Defendant appeared "drunk" when she saw him at the store that evening several hours before the shootings. Defendant told the police that he and Cornelius had consumed liquor that afternoon and also intimated that he had smoked some "weed."

None of this evidence demonstrated that Defendant's alleged intoxication was such that, hours later, it deprived him of the mental capacity to form the culpable mental state required for premeditated murder or attempted premeditated murder. Moreover, Defendant's statement to the police reflects that Defendant had clear memories about his actions both preceding and during the shootings, belying any claim that he was so intoxicated as to be unable to form the culpable mens rea of intent and premeditation. Accordingly, we hold that Defendant has failed to demonstrate that the trial court breached a clear and unequivocal rule of law when it failed to instruct the jury about Defendant's alleged voluntary intoxication. Defendant is not entitled to relief on this issue.

Affirmed.

Hypo 1: *The Drunken Umbrella Thief*

Upon leaving a bar, defendant picks up another customer's umbrella. Defendant is so intoxicated that she does not realize that she has an umbrella, much less that it is not her own. Defendant is charged with theft of movable property which state law defines in the following way: "A person is guilty of theft if he unlawfully takes, or exercises unlawful control over, movable property of another with purpose to deprive him thereof." Can defendant be convicted of this crime? How does her intoxication affect her culpability?

Hypo 2: *Intoxicated Partygoers*

In the following situations, is intoxication a defense to criminal charges brought in these circumstances:

- Where defendant, a heavy drinker, drank excessively in a bar, staggered out, climbed into his car, and attempted unsuccessfully to drive home. Defen-

---

pable mental state." The point remains that a jury instruction about a defendant's alleged voluntary intoxication at the time he or she committed the offense under consideration is required only if the intoxication was such that it compromised the defendant's capacity for whatever culpable mental state the offense required.

dant was so drunk that he did not realize that his intoxicated state presented a risk to the lives of others.

- Where defendant attended a party at which she consumed only non-alcoholic beverages, but where another person slipped drugs into her drink, putting her into a hallucinatory state. Oblivious to that fact, thinking she was ill rather than drugged, she got in her car and drove away.

- Where defendant who had never consumed alcoholic beverages before, drank a gin and tonic at a party and became so drunk that, getting into her car to drive home, she did not realize that her intoxicated state presented a risk to the lives of others.

Hypo 3: *Seeing Bears*

Ormond, heavily intoxicated, shot two people with his high-powered rifle. The evidence reveals that he was so drunk that he thought the two victims were bears rather than people. Is his intoxication a good defense to homicide charges?

D. Mistake of Fact

Hopson v. Texas

2009 WL 1124389 (Tex. App.-Hous. (14 Dist.) 2009).

KENT C. SULLIVAN, JUSTICE.

Appellant, Karissa Lou Hopson, was arrested at a house in Lufkin on July 7, 2007 and was charged with two offenses: (1) burglary, by entering a habitation without the owners' consent and with the intent to commit theft; and (2) criminal mischief, by intentionally or knowingly damaging or destroying tangible property without the owners' consent. A jury convicted appellant of both offenses.

On appeal of her burglary conviction, appellant insists that the evidence raised a fact issue as to whether she mistakenly believed she was preventing, not committing, a theft. She contends that this evidence required the trial court to submit a mistake-of-fact instruction to the jury, and that she was harmed by the trial court's refusal to do so. Because we hold that the requested instruction was not necessary, the trial court's judgment is affirmed.

On July 7, 2007, police officers were summoned to a residence to investigate a suspected burglary in progress. Upon arrival, the officers saw appellant standing on the front porch of the house, holding a large television. Appellant set the television on the porch and approached the officers, claiming that she knew the house owners and that she had their permission to be on the property. However, the officers noticed that several of the house windows had been broken and that appellant had blood on her shirt and hand. The officers also saw that portions of the interior of the house, including furniture, had been damaged.

Appellant was arrested at the scene. The owners of the house arrived at the scene roughly thirty minutes later. Both owners indicated that they did not know appellant, and they denied giving her permission to enter the premises or to remove their television from the house.

The State charged appellant with burglary and criminal mischief. Appellant pleaded "not guilty" to both offenses, and a jury trial ensued. Appellant testified on her own behalf and, although she acknowledged that she had entered the residence and that she was carrying the owners' television when the police arrived, she offered a different interpretation of these undisputed facts. That is, she contended that she believed that, through her actions, she was actually thwarting a burglary that was being committed by another man, Cayetano Padierna.

In support of this contention, appellant testified that she had stopped at the house to visit the owners, who were her friends. When she arrived, both owners were gone. In their place was Padierna, whom she did not know, who was removing items from the house. Thinking that Padierna was stealing from the owners, appellant confronted him and he left.[2] Appellant then walked to the side of the porch, where she found the television. She picked the television up, claiming that she meant to return it to the house, when the police-who had been summoned by Padierna-arrived and arrested her.

Based on her testimony, appellant contended that she reasonably, but mistakenly, believed Padierna was stealing from the owners and that, by picking up the owners' television, she was acting with the intent to prevent, not commit, a theft. Appellant asked the trial court to submit the following mistake-of-fact instruction to the jury:

> A defendant who thought she was performing activity may lack the necessary criminal intent where she reasonably believes she acted to prevent a crime. If you believe that at the time of the offense charged, appellant reasonably believed that she acted to prevent a theft, then you must find her not guilty.

The trial judge refused the requested instruction.

The jury found appellant guilty of burglary and Class A misdemeanor criminal mischief. The trial court assessed punishment as follows: (1) for burglary, twelve years' incarceration in the Texas Department of Criminal Justice, Institutional Division; and (2) for criminal mischief, confinement in the Angelina County jail for one year, with both sentences to run concurrently.

---

2 In his testimony, Padierna explained that he had the owners' permission to enter the house and pick up coolers that he used to sell drinks and refreshments at a nearby soccer field.

Take Note

Note that the Texas mistake-of-fact defense statute contains an objective element, i.e. the accused's mistaken belief must be reasonable. MPC § 2.04 (Ignorance or Mistake) does not contain such an objective, reasonableness element. Would it make a difference in this case if Texas followed the Model Penal Code approach?

Generally, a defendant is entitled to submission of an affirmative defensive instruction on every issue raised by the evidence even if the trial court thinks that the testimony could not be believed. In this case, appellant contends that she raised a fact issue as to the mistake-of-fact defense, which is set forth by section 8.02 of the Texas Penal Code: "It is a defense to prosecution that the actor through mistake formed a reasonable belief about a matter of fact if his mistaken belief negated the kind of culpability required for commission of the offense." Appellant contends her testimony, if believed, would negate a finding that she acted with the intent to commit theft, that is, the degree of culpability required to convict her of burglary. Therefore, she argues that the trial court erred by refusing to submit a mistake-of-fact instruction. However, we hold that the requested instruction was not necessary because appellant's defense-that she lacked the requisite intent to commit theft because of a mistaken belief-was adequately covered by the charge submitted to the jury. Therefore, we conclude the trial court did not err by refusing to submit a defensive issue that merely denied the existence of an essential element of the State's case.

To support her argument, appellant directs us to *Bang v. State*, in which the Thirteenth Court of Appeals held that a mistake-of-fact instruction should be submitted whenever raised by the evidence. 815 S.W.2d 838, 841 (Tex. App.-Corpus Christi 1991). However, *Bang* was closely followed by *Bruno v. State*, in which the Texas Court of Criminal Appeals indicated that a trial court is not always required to submit an unnecessary mistake-of-fact instruction if the defense is adequately covered by the charge as given. 845 S.W.2d 910, 913 (Tex. Crim. App. 1993).

In *Bruno*, the defendant was accused of unauthorized use of a motor vehicle but testified that he believed he had the owner's permission to drive the car. The Court of Criminal Appeals noted that, in some unauthorized-use cases, the defendant alleges that he was given permission to operate the vehicle by a third party he mistakenly believed to be the vehicle's owner. Under those facts, a mistake-of-fact instruction becomes necessary because the jury could find that (1) the defendant believed he had the consent of the third party to use the vehicle, and (2) the true owner of the vehicle had not given him permission. However, in the absence of such a third party, the Court of Criminal Appeals determined that a mistake-of-fact instruction was unnecessary:

> In the absence of this third party, the jury could not believe both the testimony of the true owner of the vehicle and the testimony of appellant. Only one of the incompatible stories could be believed.
>
> The jury heard both stories. As they would have necessarily been required to disbelieve appellant's story before they could find sufficient evidence to convict, the

> instruction need not have been given in the instant case. Simply because appellant testified that he had the consent of the owner of the vehicle does not entitle him to a mistake of fact instruction.

Here, the jury heard appellant's story. The effect of her testimony, and the thrust of her requested instruction, amounted to an attempt to convince the jury that her intent was something other than the criminal intent-that is, the intent to commit theft-that was necessary for the commission of a burglary. However, to convict her of that offense, the State was already required to prove beyond a reasonable doubt that appellant entered the house, without the effective consent of the owners, with the intent to commit theft. To that end, the jury received the following instruction:

> If you believe from the evidence beyond a reasonable doubt, that the defendant, on or about the 7th day of July, 2007, in the County of Angelina, and State of Texas, as alleged in the indictment, did then and there, *with intent to commit theft*, enter a habitation, without the effective consent of Gregorio Cartagena or Cayetano Ramirez, the owner thereof, you will find the defendant guilty of the offense of Burglary of a Habitation and so say by your verdict, but if you do not so believe, or if you have a reasonable doubt thereof, you will acquit the defendant and say by your verdict "Not Guilty."

The jury was also specifically instructed that it had to acquit the appellant if the State failed to prove, beyond a reasonable doubt, each and every element of the charged offense. Thus, unless the jury found that appellant intended to commit theft, it was required to acquit her of burglary.

Therefore, under these facts, the trial court was not required to submit a defensive issue that, in the context of this case, did no more than recast the required element of criminal intent as a defensive issue. As in *Bruno*, appellant could not have been convicted under the charge given had the jury believed her story that she lacked the intent to commit theft. Apparently, they did not.

The facts of this case may be contrasted with *Bang*, in which the defendant acted on a mistaken belief that his friend, Jesse Mouton, the principal actor in the burglary, actually owned the property in question. In that case, Jerry Bang agreed to drive Mouton, a minor, to a particular location and pick him up later. When Bang returned, Mouton had an amplifier, a guitar case, and other items which Mouton claimed he owned. The items were placed in the trunk of Bang's vehicle and driven to another location. Ultimately, it was determined that the property had been stolen from a church, and Bang was charged with burglary.

Bang admitted that he intentionally performed certain acts that resulted in a burglary and theft of property. However, he claimed not to know that, through his conduct, he was participating in a burglary and theft. Specifically, not knowing that the church was the true owner of the stolen items, Jerry Bang intended to appropriate property in a manner that deprived the actual owner-the church-of its property, and such appropriation was unlawful because it was done without the owner's consent. Under those facts, as in the unauthorized-use cases highlighted in *Bruno*, a mistake-of-fact instruction was necessary in *Bang* because the jury could have convicted him of the elements of the crime, while still believing that he lacked the requisite culpable mental state.

Food for Thought

Does this distinction that the court makes between the facts in *Bruno* and in *Bang* make sense to you?

Here, by contrast, the jury was squarely required to decide whether appellant acted with either the intent to commit theft or, under her version of the facts, with the intent to prevent a theft. The absence of a mistake-of-fact instruction did not deprive appellant of the right to have the jury consider her defense. Therefore, we hold that the trial court was not required to submit a separate mistake-of-fact instruction to the jury. We overrule appellant's only issue on appeal.

Accordingly, we affirm the judgment of the trial court.

Hypo 1: *The Gambling Ex-Girlfriend*

Charles Anderson was convicted of false imprisonment by means of violence after he dragged his intoxicated former girlfriend, Sylvia Olsen, out of the Chicken Ranch Casino while she was fighting and resisting him because she did not want to leave. Olsen later explained that she wanted the charges dropped against Anderson because they had just broken up over her gambling problem the day before and she and Anderson had made an agreement a month earlier that "[i]f he caught me in the casino, he was to take me home." Anderson knew Olsen had a limited amount of money that she was to use for her son's birthday, and that she was gambling it away. Although Olsen was clearly not consenting to being dragged out of the casino at the time that act occurred, Anderson argues that he was entitled to a mistake of fact instruction on the issue whether or not he reasonably believed Olsen was consenting to his actions based on their earlier agreement. Was he entitled to such an instruction? *See People v. Anderson*, 2008 WL 570798 (Cal.App. 5 Dist. 2008).

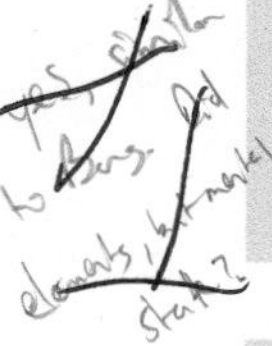

Hypo 2: *The Homicidal Clown*

As part of a circus act, a clown is supposed to point a gun loaded with blanks at another clown and pull the trigger. One day, unbeknownst to the clown who pulled the trigger, the gun was loaded with real bullets. When he pulled the trigger, he shot and killed the other clown. Does this clown have a good defense to potential homicide charges? Why?

Iowa v. Freeman

450 N.W.2d 826 (Iowa 1990).

McGIVERIN, CHIEF JUSTICE.

The facts of this case are not disputed. The defendant, Robert Eric Freeman, agreed to sell a controlled substance, cocaine, to Keith Hatcher. Unfortunately for Freeman, Hatcher was cooperating with the government. Hatcher gave Freeman $200, and Freeman gave Hatcher approximately two grams of what was supposed to be cocaine. To everyone's surprise, the "cocaine" turned out to be acetaminophen. Acetaminophen is not a controlled substance.

Freeman was convicted at a bench trial of delivering a simulated controlled substance with respect to a substance represented to be cocaine. The sole question presented by Freeman's appeal is whether he can be convicted of delivering a simulated controlled substance when, in fact, he believed he was delivering and intended to deliver cocaine.

Our review is to determine whether any error of law occurred. Finding no error, we affirm the conviction.

Iowa Code section 204.401(2) provides, in relevant part:

> It is unlawful for a person to create, deliver, or possess with intent to deliver a simulated controlled substance.

The term "simulated controlled substance" is defined by Iowa Code section 204.101(27):

> "Simulated controlled substance" means a substance which is not a controlled substance but which is expressly represented to be a controlled substance, or a substance which is not a controlled substance but which is impliedly represented to be a controlled substance and which because of its nature, packaging, or appearance would lead a reasonable person to believe it to be a controlled substance.

Our cases indicate that knowledge of the nature of the substance delivered is an imputed element of section 204.401(1) offenses[, offenses involving real, non-simulated controlled substances]. Proof of such knowledge has been required to separate those persons who innocently commit the overt acts of the offense from those persons who commit the overt acts of the offense with *scienter*, or criminal intent. In general, only the latter are criminally responsible for their acts.

Seizing upon the similarity of the statutory prohibitions, Freeman argues that he cannot be convicted of delivering a simulated controlled substance because he mistakenly believed he was delivering and intended to deliver an actual controlled substance.

We disagree. Freeman's construction of section 204.401(2) would convert the offense of delivery of a simulated controlled substance into one requiring knowing misrepresentation of the nature of the substance delivered. The statute clearly does not require knowing misrepresentation of the nature of the substance delivered.

The gist of [the 204.401(2)] offense is knowing representation of a substance to be a controlled substance and delivery of a noncontrolled substance, rather than knowing misrepresentation and delivery.

Freeman's mistaken belief regarding the substance he delivered cannot save him from conviction. Mistake of fact is a defense to a crime of *scienter* or criminal intent only where the mistake precludes the existence of the mental state necessary to commit the crime. In this case, Freeman would not be innocent of wrongdoing had the situation been as he supposed; rather, he would be guilty of delivering a controlled substance. His mistake is no defense. The *scienter* required to hold him criminally responsible for committing the overt acts of the charged offense is present regardless of the mistake. Freeman knowingly represented to Hatcher that the substance he delivered was cocaine.

Food for Thought

A mistake-of-fact defense is inapplicable to strict liability offenses as no *mens rea* is required, hence, a mistaken intention is simply irrelevant. Did the *Freeman* court interpret the simulated controlled substances statute as strict liability?

In conclusion, we hold that a person who delivers a substance that is not a controlled substance, but who knowingly represents the substance to be a controlled substance, commits the offense of delivery of a simulated controlled substance regardless of whether the person believed that the substance was controlled or not controlled.

Freeman attempted and intended to sell cocaine. The fact that Freeman was fooled as much as his customer is no defense to the charge in this case.

AFFIRMED.

Points for Discussion

a. Sale of Controlled Substances

After this decision in *Freeman*, can a mistake-of-fact defense be presented where an accused is charged with sale of controlled substances (not *simulated* controlled substances)?

b. Attempted Sale of Controlled Substances

Could Freeman have been convicted of *attempted* sale of a controlled substance? If so, why did the prosecutor not charge that offense?

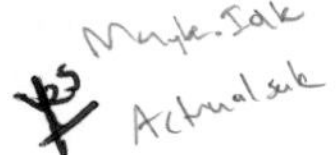

North Carolina v. Breathette

690 S.E.2d 1 (N.C. 2010).

ROBERT C. HUNTER, JUDGE.

Defendant Yasmin Pecolia Breathette appeals her convictions for taking indecent liberties with a minor. Defendant argues on appeal that the trial court erred by not giving the jury her requested instruction that mistake of age is a valid defense to the offense of indecent liberties. We conclude that mistake of age is not a defense applicable to the charge, and, therefore, the trial court properly refused to instruct the jury on the defense. Consequently, we find no error.

The State presented evidence at trial tending to establish the following facts: B.W. ("Beth") was born in March 1995 and lived in Taylors, South Carolina with her mother. When Beth was 13 years old she met defendant, who was 19 at the time, on the social networking website MySpace and the two began messaging. Beth's MySpace page indicated that she was 99 years old because she did not "want people to know her real age." When defendant asked how old Beth was, Beth told her that she was 17. The two discussed "chilling" together at defendant's apartment, exchanged cell phone numbers, and began texting and calling each other on a daily basis. Defendant, whose MySpace page indicated that she was a lesbian, asked Beth whether she was a lesbian, and Beth told her that she was gay. When texting or talking, they would sometimes discuss "sexual stuff." Sometimes Beth would initiate the sexual conversations and sometimes it was defendant.

Defendant and Beth decided that they wanted to meet in person, so defendant drove from her apartment in Winston-Salem, North Carolina on 4 June 2008, picked up Beth at a designated spot, and drove back to Winston-Salem for the weekend. When defendant and Beth got back to defendant's apartment, they watched TV together and "tongue kissed."

The next day, 5 June 2008, defendant took Beth over to her friend Francesca's house, where they stayed most of the day. While watching TV, defendant and Beth "made out" on the couch and kissed. Later that night, defendant and Beth went back to defendant's apartment, where they ordered pizza and watched TV and movies. Defendant and Beth later got into defendant's bed, where Beth gave defendant a "hickey" on her neck. Defendant kissed Beth's breast, digitally penetrated her vagina, and performed oral sex on her. After about 10 minutes, they went to sleep.

Defendant and Beth got into an argument on Friday, 6 June 2008, because Beth was "acting childish" and "getting on defendant's nerves." Although defendant told Beth that she could not spend the night at defendant's apartment, Beth ultimately spent the night there. Defendant left for work on Saturday morning before Beth woke up and Beth texted and called defendant several times during the day, asking for a ride home. Defendant did not want to drive Beth home and the two fought over the phone while defendant was at work. When defendant's supervisor overheard her yelling loudly on the phone at work, she was fired from her job. Defendant came home, yelling at Beth that she made her lose her job. Defendant collected Beth's things, threw them out into the front yard, and locked her out of the apartment.

Beth contacted Amanda, one of defendant's friends that she had met during the weekend, and Amanda let Beth spend Saturday night at her house.

The next day, 8 June 2008, Amanda dropped Beth off at Francesca's house, where Beth told Francesca's mother about her fight with defendant and that they had done "sexual stuff." Francesca's mother called the police, who came to get Beth. While there, the police interviewed Beth and she told them that she was 17. Officers took Beth to the police station, where she told them that nothing had happened. Beth's mother arrived in Winston-Salem that evening and drove her home.

Officer J.A. Sheets interviewed defendant on 9 June 2008, at her apartment. Defendant told him that she met Beth on MySpace and that they had met in person because they were interested in dating each other. Defendant also told Officer Sheets that Beth's MySpace page had been changed to indicate that she was 18, although it had originally indicated that she was 21. Defendant told Officer Sheets that they had "fingered" each other, but that only she had performed oral sex. Defendant later texted Beth, asking her why she did not tell defendant her "real age." When Beth responded that she did not know why, defendant texted back that "Beth was wrong."

Defendant was charged with two counts of taking indecent liberties with a minor and one count each of first degree kidnapping, first degree sexual offense, and attempted second degree sexual offense. Defendant pled not guilty and a jury trial was conducted 13–15 April 2009. At the close of the State's evidence, defendant moved to dismiss all five charges. The trial court dismissed the charges of kidnapping, first degree sexual offense, and attempted second degree sexual offense, but denied the motion as to the two counts of taking indecent liberties. Defendant then testified that she first came into contact with Beth through MySpace in May 2008. Defendant also found Beth on "downylink.com," a "straight, gay, lesbian, and bisexual Website for people over the age of eighteen." Defendant explained that when she saw Beth on downylink.com, she believed that Beth was over 18 because the website requires all users to verify that they are 18 years old or over. The jury convicted defendant of both charges and the trial court sentenced defendant to two consecutive presumptive-range sentences of 14 to 17 months imprisonment, but suspended the second sentence and imposed 36 months of supervised probation. Defendant timely appealed to this Court.

In a written request, defendant asked the trial court to instruct the jury that

> if you do find that the defendant was both acting under a belief that the alleged victim was older than 15 years old and that such belief was reasonable, albeit mistaken, then it would be your duty to render a verdict of not guilty to the charges of taking indecent liberties with a child as the defendant lacked the requisite guilty mind to formulate the specific intent to commit the crime.

Defendant argues that the trial court committed reversible error by not instructing the jury that mistake of age is a defense to the charge of taking indecent liberties with a minor.

If a request is made for an instruction that is a correct statement of the law and is supported by the evidence, the trial court must give the instruction, at least in substance. Failure to instruct on a substantive or material feature of the evidence and the applicable law generally results in reversible error.

Defendant is correct that "this is a case of first impression," as North Carolina's courts have not specifically addressed whether mistake of age is a recognized defense to a charge of taking indecent liberties with a minor. Generally, "ignorance or mistake as to a matter of fact is a defense if it negatives a mental state required to establish a material element of the crime" In turn, "whether a criminal intent is a necessary element of a statutory offense is a matter of construction to be determined from the language of the statute in view of its manifest purpose and design."

N.C. Gen.Stat. § 14–202.1 defines the offense of taking indecent liberties with a minor:

> A person is guilty of taking indecent liberties with children if, being 16 years of age or more and at least five years older than the child in question, he either:
>
> (1) Willfully takes or attempts to take any immoral, improper, or indecent liberties with any child of either sex under the age of 16 years for the purpose of arousing or gratifying sexual desire; or
>
> (2) Willfully commits or attempts to commit any lewd or lascivious act upon or with the body or any part or member of the body of any child of either sex under the age of 16 years.

The statute is unambiguous as to the elements of the crime: the State must prove that (1) the defendant was at least 16; (2) the defendant was five years older than the complainant; (3) the defendant willfully took or attempted to take an indecent liberty with the complainant; (4) the complainant was under 16 at the time the alleged act or attempted act occurred; and (5) the defendant's conduct was for the purpose of arousing or gratifying sexual desire.

Defendant argues that a defendant's knowledge of the complainant's age is an element of taking indecent liberties with a minor, making mistake of age a valid defense to the crime. The plain language of N.C. Gen.Stat. § 14–202.1, however, does not support defendant's contention. The statute only requires that the complainant be "under the age of 16 years" at the time of defendant's conduct constituting the offense. There is no explicit mens rea requirement in N.C. Gen.Stat. § 14–202.1 as to the complainant's age.

"When conduct is made criminal because the victim is under a certain age, it is no defense that the defendant was ignorant of or mistaken as to the victim's age; and it matters not that the defendant's mistaken belief was reasonable." 1 Charles E. Torcia, Wharton's Criminal Law § 78, at 563–64 (15th ed. 1996); accord Rollin M. Perkins & Ronald N. Boyce, Criminal Law

Food for Thought

Should this North Carolina court be relying to any degree at all upon general statements in criminal law treatises like these when they may reflect case law holdings interpreting very different—and much older—statutes?

§ 7, at 919 (3rd ed. 1982) (explaining that " 'crimes such as carnal knowledge, seduction, and the like, where the offense depends upon the victim's being below a designated age do require a mens rea,' although a reasonable mistake of fact as to the victim's age is no defense.").

In *People v. Olsen*, 36 Cal. 3d 638, 685 P.2d 52, 205 Cal. Rptr. 492 (1984), the California Supreme Court confronted a virtually identical issue of legislative intent to the one presented in this case, holding that a good faith, reasonable mistake of age was not a defense to a charge of "willfully" committing "lewd or lascivious acts involving children." The California statute at issue in Olsen, similar to our indecent liberties statute, provides:

> Any person who willfully and lewdly commits any lewd or lascivious act upon or with the body, or any part or member thereof, of a child who is under the age of 14 years, with the intent of arousing, appealing to, or gratifying the lust, passions, or sexual desires of that person or the child, is guilty of a felony.

Recognizing the "existence of a strong public policy to protect children of tender years," the *Olsen* Court concluded that a mistake of age defense was "untenable," and that "one who commits lewd or lascivious acts with a child, even with a good faith belief that the child is [over the designated age], does so at his or her peril."

This Court has similarly noted "the legislative policy, inherent in N.C. Gen.Stat. § 14–202.1, to provide broad protection to children from the sexual conduct of older persons, especially adults." Our Supreme Court has also recognized "the great breadth of protection against sexual contact the statute seeks to afford children and the reasons for it":

> Undoubtedly N.C. Gen.Stat. § 14–202.1's breadth is in recognition of the significantly greater risk of psychological damage to an impressionable child from overt sexual acts. We also bear in mind the enhanced power and control that adults, even strangers, may exercise over children who are outside the protection of home or school.

We conclude, therefore, that a defendant's mistake as to the complainant's age is not a valid defense to a charge of taking indecent liberties with a minor under N.C. Gen.Stat. § 14–202.1. As the defense is inapplicable, the trial court properly refused to give defendant's proffered instruction on the defense.

No Error.

Point for Discussion

Amending Statute

The *Breathette* Court was simply trying to ascertain the legislative intent behind the language in N.C. Gen.Stat. § 14–202.1. The North Carolina legislature could, of course, decide that it wanted to take a different approach with this statute and amend it in light of the

Breathette decision to provide for some form of mistake-of-age defense. *Should* the legislature do that? What do you think?

Hypo 1: *Mistake and the Babysitter*

Andre Knap was in bed, asleep in a darkened bedroom, when he felt someone massaging his genitals. Assuming that this person was his girlfriend, Knap began engaging in sexual relations with her. At some point, however, he realized that the person with whom he was having sex was not his girlfriend, but was instead the 13 year-old babysitter, who had come into his bed naked while he was sleeping. As soon as Knap realized this fact, he desisted. Is Knap guilty of statutory rape? *Commonwealth v. Knap*, 412 Mass. 712, 592 N.E.2d 747 (1992).

Hypo 2: *He Looked 18*

Defendant William Saponaro, Jr., 49 years old, had consensual sex with a 13 year-old boy that he met on an online site, GrindrX. Subsequently charged with sexual assault and endangering the welfare of a child, he argues that he was reasonably mistaken as to the age of the boy because: the boy told defendant that he was 18 years old; he actually appeared to be 18; and he had used a website that required him to pay with a credit card. Are any of these facts distinguishable from *Breathette*? Do you think that, if all of these averments are true, Saponaro might have a good defense to these charges? *New Jersey v. Sapanaro*, 2017 WL 2348869 (N.J. App. Div. 2017).

E. Mistake of Law

United States v. Scarmazzo

554 F. Supp. 2d 1102 (E.D.Cal. 2008).

OLIVER W. WANGER, DISTRICT JUDGE.

The following orders on motions in limine and for clarification of and addressing supplemental motions in limine have been heard and decided. The following rulings are set forth for the benefit of and as guidance to the parties.

What's That?

A *motion in limine* is a pretrial request that certain inadmissible evidence not be referred to or offered at trial.

Defendants are ordered not to introduce any evidence, questioning, or testimony, either expert or lay opinion testimony, or to argue in the presence of the jury, to suggest: Defendants' "good faith" belief that marijuana is of medical value.

Erroneous Belief Conduct Was Lawful (Irrelevant).

It is unlawful for an individual knowingly or intentionally to manufacture, distribute, dispense, or possess with intent to manufacture, distribute, or dispense a controlled substance.

Knowledge of, or intent to violate the law is not an element of this offense. A good faith defense does not apply where the law does not require as part of its mens rea element, proof of a Defendant's knowledge of the legal duty. A mistake of law element does not apply because ignorance or mistake of law is not a defense to a crime that does not require a showing the Defendant knew the illegality of conduct of which he is charged.

Where the crime requires only knowledge, not willfulness, the government need only prove the Defendants knew they were performing an act, not that they knew the act was unlawful or criminalized by statute.

Food for Thought

Should it matter that the defendants, who owned a medical marijuana dispensary that was organized lawfully under California law, believed that they were acting lawfully in possessing and distributing marijuana in reliance relying upon a California law which permits medicinal marijuana use? Why or why not?

Ignorance of the law is no defense, as statutes relating to the use and possession of drugs do not require proof of intent to violate the law. There is no requirement of knowledge of the unlawfulness of Defendant's acts under the crimes charged. The general rule, "deeply rooted in the American legal system" is "that ignorance of the law or a mistake of law is no defense to criminal prosecution."

The government is not required to prove that Defendant was aware of or intended to violate the law. A mistaken belief regarding what the law allows is a mistake of law, not a mistake of fact, and is not a defense to a criminal charge.

Good faith reliance on the advice of a counsel is not relevant because such advice can only be shown to negate a specific intent to violate the law. Here, neither good faith nor mistake as to the enforceability of the law is a defense. An attorney's advice about what the law is, medical necessity, the benefits of marijuana would only be confusing, misleading, time consuming, and prejudicial. Fundamentally, advice of counsel is irrelevant.

Food for Thought

Why do you think that the *Scarmazzo* Court concluded that a person is not entitled to rely on the advice of his or her attorney as a defense to criminal charges? Does that make sense? If a person can't rely on an attorney to figure out what the law requires, how are people supposed to find out what the law is? Research it on their own?

For the reasons stated above, the government's motions in limine are GRANTED.

Hawaii v. DeCastro

81 Haw. 147, 913 P.2d 558 (Ct.App. 1996).

BURNS, CHIEF JUDGE.

Defendant Robert DeCastro (DeCastro) appeals the October 7, 1992 Judgment entered by the District Court of the First Circuit convicting him of Resisting an Order to Stop a Motor Vehicle, Hawai'i Revised Statutes (HRS) § 710–1027(1) (1985), which states as follows:

> (1) A person commits the offense of resisting an order to stop a motor vehicle if he intentionally fails to obey a direction of a peace officer, acting under color of his official authority, to stop his vehicle.

The district court sentenced DeCastro to probation for one year and ordered him to contribute $100 to the State General Fund.

We affirm.

DeCastro owns Town and Country Moving headquartered in Kalihi. On Wednesday, December 18, 1991 at about 12:30 p.m., while returning to his warehouse from a delivery in Wahiawa, DeCastro drove his van (Van) in the Koko Head (southeasterly) direction on the H-2 freeway. DeCastro's employee, Westley Damas (Damas), was a passenger in DeCastro's Van. Near the Mililani exit, DeCastro and Damas observed police officer Derek Rodrigues (Officer Rodrigues) in a Honolulu Police Department blue and white vehicle nearly cause a "four car accident" while pursuing a speeding motorist later identified as George Hernandez (Hernandez). Hernandez had no passenger in his vehicle. After Officer Rodrigues had stopped Hernandez to issue him a citation for speeding, Officer Rodrigues noticed a white van stop about four car lengths behind his patrol car. Officer Rodrigues saw DeCastro in the driver's seat and Damas in the passenger's seat of the Van.

DeCastro testified that he stopped because he believed Officer Rodrigues had driven his police car in a reckless manner. DeCastro remained in the Van and noted the license plate numbers of Officer Rodrigues' and Hernandez' vehicles.

The Van's presence aroused Officer Rodrigues' suspicions that its occupants were friends of Hernandez. This prompted Officer Rodrigues to approach the driver's side of the Van and ask, "Oh. You with those guys up there?" DeCastro replied, "No. Do we look like we're with those guys?"

At this point, the State and DeCastro dispute what happened. DeCastro and Damas testified that, while holding his baton or nightstick in his hand, Officer Rodrigues made the following statement: "Oh, you getting pretty cocky, aren't you? You want to get cocky Eh, you fucker, you like beef? You like beef, you fucker? Step out. Both of you. Come on, step out." DeCastro admitted that at no point did Officer Rodrigues strike DeCastro or the Van with his baton. Nor did Officer Rodrigues wave his baton in the air or swing it at DeCastro. DeCastro testified that upon hearing Officer Rodrigues' statement, both he and Damas chuckled.

Nevertheless, DeCastro contends Officer Rodrigues' statement led him to be concerned for his and Damas' safety. Thereafter, Officer Rodrigues demanded DeCastro's license, and vehicle registration and insurance card, which DeCastro willingly provided. Officer Rodrigues then ordered DeCastro to "wait" while Officer Rodrigues returned to his patrol car.

Immediately after Officer Rodrigues walked away, DeCastro dialed 911 on his cellular phone. The transcript of the "911" conversation between the 911 operator and DeCastro discloses the following:

OPERATOR: You need a police?

DeCASTRO: No, I no need a police. I'm being harassed by a policeman.

OPERATOR: Hah?

DeCASTRO: I'm being harassed by a policeman.

OPERATOR: Where is the policeman?

DeCASTRO: Where are we in between?

OTHER: Waipi'o and Mililani.

DeCASTRO: Waipi'o and Mililani, and he's—I hope someone comes fast. He went ask us if, uh, we like fight with him.

OPERATOR: You have his license number?

DeCASTRO: H-P-D 734. He was reckless driving. We went go pull off on the side of the road—

OPERATOR: What's his number?

DeCASTRO:—to get his, uh, license plate.

OPERATOR: What is it?

DeCASTRO: And now he's out here with his nightstick.

OPERATOR: What is it?

DeCASTRO: You know what, I just—I should just go to my warehouse already.

OPERATOR: What's the license number?

DeCASTRO: His—his number is H-P-D—

OPERATOR: "D?"

DeCASTRO: H-P-D 734. This guy wants to fight us.

OPERATOR: You want the police right now?

DeCASTRO: Uh, well, I like just go to my warehouse, and you can send a policeman over there.

OPERATOR: Okay. When you get to the warehouse, call back.

DeCASTRO: You know what, he's gonna chase me once I leave.

OPERATOR: No, go ahead and just, uh, we got the license.

DeCASTRO: You got 'um?

OPERATOR: Yeah. Just go to the warehouse, and then call back.

DeCASTRO: Okay.

OPERATOR: Okay.

DeCASTRO: Now he's in back of me, and he wants to pull me over. And this guy wants to fight with me.

OPERATOR: Is he—is—is—well, do you wanna stay on the line?

DeCASTRO: Yeah, I wanna stay on the line. I want another policeman. I want another policeman at my warehouse 'cause I'm not gonna pull over. I'm afraid if I pull over, he's—he's gonna arrest me, or what do you want me to do?

OPERATOR: I don't know. Is he in a blue-and-white?

DeCASTRO: He's in a blue-and-white. I want a policeman at 94-478 Ukee 'Uke'e Street.

OPERATOR: But are you there now?

DeCASTRO: No, I'm on the freeway.

SUPERVISOR: This is the 911 Supervisor. May I help you?

DeCASTRO: Yeah, about an officer who I pulled over on the side of the road. I pulled him on the side of the road to take his license-plate number down. He asked me if I wanted to fight, and he came out with his nightstick.

SUPERVISOR: He couldn't be an officer.

DeCASTRO: Now there's three of 'um.

DeCASTRO: Now, now they're all coming out with their clubs. All of them have their clubs.

DeCASTRO: Now they're arresting me. Get—get the—get the chief—get the chief over here.

The State's evidence showed that before Officer Rodrigues returned to the Van, DeCastro drove it off in the same direction he was heading before he had stopped. Officer Rodrigues gave chase, using his automobile's horn, siren, and flashing lights, while maintaining a distance of about two car lengths behind DeCastro. Officer Rodrigues simultaneously called dispatch to inform them that he was pursuing DeCastro and asked for a backup unit to assist him. During the chase, Officer Rodrigues observed DeCastro "look in his rearview mirror at least ten times."

Upon stopping DeCastro, Officer Rodrigues and Sergeant Dow approached the driver's side and Officer Grilho approached the passenger's side. DeCastro refused to open the door, the window remained locked, and he continued talking on his cellular phone. Officer Rodrigues kept knocking on the window telling DeCastro to open the door. DeCastro eventually did step out of his Van. Officer Rodrigues testified that the first remark that DeCastro made was "the chief told" him "not to stop." While being handcuffed, DeCastro put up a slight struggle.

DeCastro contends that he lacked the requisite specific intent to commit the crime because he consulted with and relied on the 911 telephone operator's permission to leave the scene.

HRS § 702–220 (1985) states in relevant part as follows:

> Ignorance or mistake of law; belief that conduct not legally prohibited. In any prosecution, it shall be an affirmative defense that the defendant engaged in the conduct or caused the result alleged under the belief that the conduct or result was not legally prohibited when he acts in reasonable reliance upon an official statement of the law, afterward determined to be invalid or erroneous, contained in:
>
> (3) An administrative grant of permission; or
>
> (4) An official interpretation of the public officer or body charged by law with responsibility for the interpretation, administration, or enforcement of the law defining the offense.

Clearly, a 911 telephone operator is not "the public officer or body charged by law with responsibility for the interpretation, administration, or enforcement of the law defining the offense" of Resisting an Order to Stop a Motor Vehicle. Therefore, the HRS § 702–220(4) affirmative defense is not applicable.

The district court found that "the Court does not see anything in the information that could lead a reasonable person to conclude that somehow he was being given permission to leave the scene;" and "DeCastro's attempt to make a phone call via 911 was a rather calculating act, and, actually, an attempt to bootstrap some sort of defense." In contrast, DeCastro asserts, as an HRS § 702–220(3) affirmative defense, that the 911 telephone operator authorized him to proceed to his warehouse and he acted on the belief that he was legally authorized to leave.

Assuming DeCastro's assertion is true, the dispositive question is whether DeCastro has introduced evidence in satisfaction of his burden of proving that a 911 telephone operator's authorization is an "official statement of the law, contained in: an administrative grant of permission." Our answer is no.

The affirmative defense stated in HRS § 702–220 is a relatively recent limited exception to the following very old general rule.

> A defendant's error as to his authority to engage in particular activity, if based upon a mistaken view of legal requirements (or ignorance thereof), is a mistake of law. Typically, the fact that he relied upon the erroneous advice of another is not an exculpatory circumstance. He is still deemed to have acted with a culpable state of mind.
>
> *United States v. Barker*, 546 F.2d 940, 946–47 (D.C.Cir. 1976).

In his concurring opinion in *Barker*, District Judge Merhige explained the rationale of the rule in relevant part as follows:

> The district judge advised the jury that a mistake of law is no excuse, and, therefore, that a mistake as to the legality of the search in issue was not a defense to the charges contained in the indictment. In that regard, the district judge was applying the general rule on mistake of law that has long been an integral part of our system of jurisprudence. The most commonly asserted rationale for the continuing vitality of the rule is that its absence would encourage and reward public ignorance of the law to the detriment of our organized legal system, and would encourage universal pleas of ignorance of the law that would constantly pose confusing and, to a great extent, insolvable issues of fact to juries and judges, thereby bogging down our adjudicative system.

FYI

The *Barker* decision, cited in *DeCastro,* related to the Watergate scandal that ultimately led to the resignation of President Richard Nixon. Two of the Watergate burglars, including Bernard Barker, claimed that they mistakenly believed that the burglary they were asked to commit was lawful as a matter of national security. Although Barker's conviction was reversed, there was no binding opinion of the court in *Barker*; each of the three judges issued separate opinions. *For an interesting, discussion of the Watergate affair and the role of lawyers in it, see* http://www.abajournal.com/magazine/article/the_lawyers_of_watergate_how_a_3rd-rate_burglary_provoked_new_standards/.

Assuming a 911 telephone operator's authorization is a "statement of the law contained in an administrative grant of permission," there is nothing on the record or in the law that supports a conclusion that it is an "official statement of the law." There is nothing on the record or in the law that supports the conclusion that a 911 telephone operator is officially authorized to permit a motor vehicle operator to fail to obey a police officer's order. Thus, we do not reach the question of whether a 911 telephone operator's authorization is an "administrative grant of permission."

Food for Thought

Do you think that the result in *DeCastro* would have—or *should have*—been different if the 911 operator was, as is true in some states, a deputized police officer? What if DeCastro had actually talked to the Chief of Police, and he or she told him to continue on to his warehouse?

Accordingly, we affirm the District Court's October 7, 1992 Judgment convicting DeCastro of Resisting an Order to Stop a Motor Vehicle.

Points for Discussion

a. Ignorance of the Law Is No Excuse

In general, the old maxim, "ignorance of the law is no excuse" ("*ignorantia legis neminem excusat*"), is a perfectly accurate statement of the prevailing law, unless the criminal statute in question expressly prescribes that knowledge of the unlawfulness of one's conduct is an element of the offense.

b. Mistake of Law Exceptions

The Hawaii mistake-of-law statute, H.R.S. § 702–220, also contains provisions, not at issue in *DeCastro*, taken from the Model Penal Code, that provide a further mistake-of-law defense where an individual acts in reasonable reliance upon an official (albeit erroneous) statement of the law contained in "(1) a statute or other enactment; or (2) a judicial decision, opinion, or judgment."

Kipp v. Delaware

704 A.2d 839 (Del. 1998).

HOLLAND, JUSTICE:

This is an appeal following a bench trial in the Superior Court. The defendant-appellant, Hugh A. Kipp, Jr. ("Kipp"), was convicted of three counts of Possession of a Deadly Weapon by a Person Prohibited. The State has confessed error on appeal and submits that Kipp's judgments of conviction should be reversed.

On the morning of September 17, 1995, several police officers went to Kipp's home in Wilmington. They were investigating a "man with a gun" complaint from Kipp's girlfriend, Lisa Zeszut ("Zeszut"). At first, Kipp refused to come out of his house, but eventually surrendered to the police.

The police searched the house for other weapons. The police found a handgun and two unloaded shotguns. The police discovered ammunition for those weapons scattered on the bedroom floor. The police also found two hunting bows, with arrows. Upon checking Kipp's criminal record, police ascertained that he was a person prohibited from possessing deadly weapons.

Kipp was charged with five counts of Possession of a Deadly Weapon by a Person Prohibited.

The only defense offered by Kipp at trial was that he was unaware of his status as a "person prohibited." Kipp was a "person prohibited" as a result of his guilty plea to Assault in the Third Degree in 1990. Kipp testified he was told that he would not be prohibited from possessing weapons as a result of the plea.

The 1990 guilty plea form, which was submitted into evidence, has a space which provides that a guilty plea will result in loss of the right to possess deadly weapons. That portion of the form was marked "N/A." Kipp testified that "N/A" meant the provision did not apply to him. The completed guilty plea form was provided to the judge during the 1990 plea colloquy. Neither the prosecutor nor the judge, however, brought the error on the guilty plea form to Kipp's attention.

After hearing all of the evidence, the Superior Court concluded that the two hunting bows were not deadly weapons. The Superior Court found Kipp guilty of three counts of Possession of a Deadly Weapon by a Person Prohibited in connection with his possession of the three firearms.

Under 11 Del.C. § 1448(b), "any prohibited person who knowingly possesses, purchases, owns or controls a deadly weapon while so prohibited shall be guilty of possession of a deadly weapon by a person prohibited." A person is a "prohibited person" for purposes of § 1448(b) when, inter alia, he or she has "been convicted in this State or elsewhere of a felony or a crime of violence involving physical injury to another." Assault in the Third Degree is a misdemeanor crime of violence involving physical injury to another. A person who has been convicted of a violent misdemeanor is prohibited from possessing a deadly weapon for the five-year period from the date of conviction.

The State has confessed error in Kipp's case on appeal. Under the facts presented, the State concedes that Kipp presented a valid mistake of law defense. This Court has held that, in very narrow circumstances, mistake of law can be a defense to a criminal charge. That defense is cognizable when the defendant: (1) erroneously concludes in good faith that his particular conduct is not subject to the operation of the criminal law; (2) makes a "bona fide, diligent effort, adopting a course and resorting to sources and means at least as appropriate as any afforded or under our legal system, to ascertain and abide by the law;" (3) "acts in good faith reliance upon the results of such effort;" and (4) the conduct constituting the offense is "neither immoral nor anti-social."

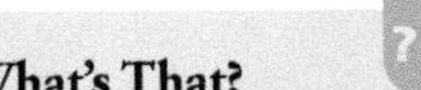

What's That?

When the State is "confessing error," it is admitting to an appellate court that it was wrong in an earlier argument. As you can see in this case, that does not always end the appellate court's independent inquiry into the issue.

Kipp presented evidence that he was misled in connection with his plea to Assault in the Third Degree. His 1990 guilty plea form, which was introduced at trial, and his testimony indicated he was told that the prohibition against possession of a deadly weapon which would result from a guilty plea was "not applicable" to the plea which he was entering. Kipp testified that he was told that prohibition was not applicable to him because he was pleading to a misdemeanor.

Kipp's plea agreement and truth-in-sentencing guilty plea form were submitted to the judge in 1990 at the plea colloquy before his guilty plea to Assault in the Third Degree was accepted. Apparently, the prosecutor and the judge who accepted his guilty plea failed to notice the "not applicable" notation on the guilty plea form. The judge referred to the plea agreement in the plea colloquy, but never informed Kipp that the "not applicable" notation was incorrect with respect to the prohibition against future possession of a deadly weapon which would result from the plea.

Under 11 Del.C. § 1448, a person is guilty of possession of a deadly weapon by a person prohibited when he is: (a) a person prohibited; and (b) knowingly possesses a deadly weapon. Thus, to be guilty of the offense, the defendant need only know that he or she possessed the weapon. Section 1448 does not require the defendant to know that it was criminal to do so.

Ignorance of the law is not a defense to crime. But "a defendant is not charged with knowledge of a penal statute if he is misled concerning whether the statute is not being applied." A mistake of law defense is appropriately recognized where the defendant demonstrates that he has been misled by information received from the State.

Under the unique circumstances of this case, the State concedes on appeal that Kipp presented a proper and complete mistake of law defense. In relying on the advice of counsel, memorialized in an official guilty plea document presented to and not corrected by either the prosecutor or the judge, Kipp had "made a bona fide, diligent effort, adopting a course and resorting to sources and means at least as appropriate as any afforded under our legal system, to ascertain and abide by the law." The State submits that Kipp's three convictions for possession of a deadly weapon by a person prohibited should be reversed.

The mistake of law defense is based upon principles of fundamental fairness. A review of the record and the applicable law supports the State's confession of error. The State's confession of error "is in accordance with the highest tradition of the Delaware Bar and the prosecutor's unique role and duty to seek justice within an adversary system."

The judgments of conviction are reversed.

FYI

On November 5, 1872, Susan B. Anthony and thirteen other women voted in an election in Rochester, New York. A federal statute made it a crime for any person to vote "without the lawful right to vote." Although the state of New York did not permit women to vote at that time (the XIX Amendment to the U.S. Constitution did not go into effect until 1920), Anthony argued that she had a lawful right to vote under the Fourteenth Amendment. The courts rejected her claim. Assuming that Anthony honestly believed that she was morally entitled to vote, did she have a tenable mistake of law claim? *See United States v. Anthony*, 24 Fed. Cas. 829 (C.C.N.D.N.Y. 1873).

See It

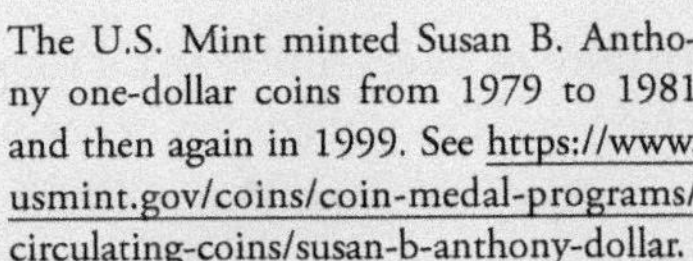

The U.S. Mint minted Susan B. Anthony one-dollar coins from 1979 to 1981 and then again in 1999. See https://www.usmint.gov/coins/coin-medal-programs/circulating-coins/susan-b-anthony-dollar.

Executive Summary

Proof of Specific *Mens Rea*. The prosecution must prove the specific *mens rea* elements of crimes beyond a reasonable doubt. A showing of general wickedness is never enough to satisfy the *mens rea* requirement.

Model Penal Code. The Model Penal Code established four levels of intentionality to be used as standard *mens rea* elements: purpose; knowledge; recklessness; and negligence. Many jurisdictions have followed all or part of this MPC approach, although there is still great variation between jurisdictions with respect to *mens rea* terms used, and their definitions.

***Mens Rea* Application.** The key to determining to which other elements of a crime a particular *mens rea* term applies is the intention of the legislature.

Strict Liability. Where a criminal statute does not contain an explicit *mens rea* element, it is still not necessarily a strict liability statute. A felonious criminal offense with common law roots is presumed to have an implicit *mens rea* element, unless there is a clear legislative intent to the contrary. The legislature has the power to decide whether a particular crime is or is not strict liability. Courts are only to interpret the legislature's intent.

Intoxication Defense. Intoxication or drugged condition is a good defense in most jurisdictions if crime is a specific intent crime only. It is not a good defense if the crime is a general intent or strict liability crime. Where intoxication is recognized as a tenable defense,

Major Themes

a. *Mens Rea* Generally Required—Most serious criminal offenses require proof of a specific criminal intention ("*mens rea*"), reflecting the view that no one should be found guilty of a serious criminal offense unless he or she was shown to have been blameworthy because he or she actually intended to commit that crime. Legislatures have the power, however, to enact strict liability criminal offenses, and they often to so with respect to minor, public welfare offenses.

b. Mistakes & *Mens Rea*—One way for the defense to establish that a *mens rea* element did not exist is to demonstrate that the accused did not think that he or she was acting with that required intent because he or she had a mistaken belief about relevant factual circumstances ("mistake of fact"). But an accused person's mistaken belief about applicable law rather than relevant facts ("mistake of law") is *not* a good defense to criminal charges.

it must be proved to have been so profound that the accused did not possess the required *mens rea*.

Mistake of Fact. A defendant's honest but mistaken belief that factual circumstances existed that would have made his or her actions *not* criminal due to the absence of the required *mens rea* is a good defense to a criminal charge. But often jurisdictions require that such an honest belief (subjective focus) also be a reasonable belief (objective focus) in order to make out a good defense to some specified crimes. Mistake of fact is never, however, a defense to strict liability crimes as it is a *mens rea* defense only.

Mistake of Law. A defendant's mistaken belief in the lawfulness of his or her otherwise criminal conduct is not a good defense unless the accused was told—officially—that such conduct was not criminal or where the criminal statute specifically makes knowledge of illegality an element of the crime.

For More Information

- AMERICAN LAW INSTITUTE, MODEL PENAL CODE AND COMMENTARIES, Part I, §§ 2.02 & 2.04 (1980).
- Darryl K. Brown, *Criminal Law Reform and the Persistence of Strict Liability*, 62 DUKE L. J. 285 (2012).
- Darryl K. Brown, *Federal Mens Rea Interpretation and the Limits of Culpability's Relevance*, 75 LAW & CONTEMP. PROBS. 109 (2012).
- JOHN M. BURKOFF & RUSSELL L. WEAVER, INSIDE CRIMINAL LAW: WHAT MATTERS AND WHY 35–62 (2d ed. 2011).
- Deborah W. Denno, *Criminal Law in a Post-Freudian World*, 2005 UNIV. ILL. L. REV. 601.
- Deborah W. Denno, "*Concocting Criminal Intent*," 105 GEO. L.J. 323 (2017).
- Eric A. Johnson, *Rethinking the Presumption of Mens Rea*, 47 WAKE FOREST L. REV. 769 (2012).
- Edwin R. Keedy, *Ignorance and Mistake in Criminal Law*, 22 HARV. L. REV. 75 (1908).
- Benjamin Levin, *Mens Rea Reform and Its Discontents*, 109 J. CRIM, LAW & CRIMINOLOGY 491 (2019).
- Gabriel S. Mendlow, *Thoughts, Crimes, and Thought Crimes*, 118 MICH. L. REV. (2020).
- Stephen J. Morse, "Lost in Translation?: An Essay on Law and Neuroscience," in Michael Freeman (ed.), Law and Neuroscience: Current Legal Issues Volume 13 (Oxford and New York: Oxford University Press, 2011).
- Gerhard O.W. Mueller, *On Common Law Mens Rea*, 42 MINN. L. REV. 1043 (1957–1958).
- Paul H. Robinson, *Mens Rea*, in 3 ENCYCLOPEDIA OF CRIME & JUSTICE 995 (Joshua Dressler *et al.* eds., 2d ed. 2002).
- Francis Bowes Sayre, *Mens Rea*, 45 HARV. L. REV. 974 (1932).
- Francis Bowes Sayre, *Public Welfare Offenses*, 33 COLUM. L. REV. 55 (1933).

- Findlay Stark, *The Reasonableness in Recklessness*, 14 CRIM. LAW & PHILOSOPHY 9 (2020).
- Herbert Wechsler, *The Challenge of a Model Penal Code*, 65 HARV. L. REV. 1097 (1952).
- Gideon Yaffe, *Intoxication, Recklessness, and Negligence*, 9 OHIO ST. J. CRIM. L. 545 (2012).
- Gerald Leonard, *Towards a Legal History of American Criminal Theory: Culture and Doctrine from Blackstone to the Model Penal Code*, 6 BUFF. CRIM. L. REV. 691 (2002).

Test Your Knowledge

To assess your understanding of the material in this chapter, click here to take a quiz.

Chapter 4

Causation

Some crimes require only an *actus reus* committed with the required *mens rea* in order to gain a conviction. Other crimes are "result" crimes which require that defendant "cause" some result. Homicide is necessarily a "result" crime because defendant must "cause" the death of another. In some instances, it is not difficult to determine that a defendant caused a particular result, as when a defendant fires bullets into a victim who falls over dead. In other instances, the "cause" of death may be less clear, as when "intervening factors" intrude between the act and the death.

Make the Connection

In Chapter 1, we examined some of the justifications for imposing punishment under the criminal law—retribution, restraint, deterrence (both general and specific) and rehabilitation. In this chapter, we learn that the fact that defendant "caused" a prohibited "result" is a factor to be taken into account in deciding on the appropriate level of punishment. In other words, a defendant might be regarded as causing greater harm, and therefore as more deserving of punishment, when defendant actually commits murder (as opposed to attempting to commit murder).

Stephenson v. State

205 Ind. 141, 179 N.E. 633 (1932).

Per Curiam.

The victim of this homicide is Miss Madge Oberholtzer who was a resident of the city of Indianapolis and lived with her father and mother. She was twenty-eight years of age, weighed about 140 pounds, and had always been in good health; was educated in the public primary and high school and Butler College. Just prior to the alleged acts, she was employed as manager of the Young People's Reading Circle.

Appellant Stephenson kidnapped Miss Oberholtzer, forced her to drink liquor, and then took her to Chicago by train. On the way, appellant pulled [her dress] over her head, against her wishes, and she tried to fight, but was weak and unsteady. Then Stephenson took hold of her hands and she did not have strength to get away because what she had drunk was affecting her. Then Stephenson took off all her clothes and pushed her into the lower berth. After the train started, Stephenson got into the berth and attacked her. He chewed all over her body; bit her neck and face; chewed her tongue; chewed her breasts until they bled and chewed her back, her legs, and her ankles, and mutilated her all. At Hammond, Indiana, Stephenson, flourishing a revolver, took her to a hotel.

Appellant argues that the evidence does not show appellant guilty of murder. After they reached the hotel, Oberholtzer left and purchased a hat and poison, voluntarily returned to his room, and at in an adjoining room to him, she swallowed the poison without his knowledge at a time when he was not present. He contends that she took her life by committing suicide; that her own act in taking the poison was an intervening responsible agent which broke the causal connection between his acts and the death; that his acts were not the proximate cause of her death, but the taking of the poison was the proximate cause of death. Appellant is charged with having caused the death of Oberholtzer while engaged in the crime of attempted rape. Appellant's control and dominion over the deceased was absolute and complete. The evidence further shows that the deceased asked for money with which to purchase a hat, and it was supplied her by "Shorty," at the direction of appellant, and that she did leave the room and was taken by Shorty to a shop and purchased a hat and then, at her request, to a drug store where she purchased the bichloride of mercury tablets, and then she was taken back to the hotel where she swallowed the poison. Appellant argues that the deceased was a free agent on this trip to purchase a hat, etc., and that she voluntarily returned to the room. This was a question for the jury, and the evidence would justify them in reaching a contrary conclusion. Appellant's chauffeur accompanied her on this trip, and the deceased had, before she left appellant's home in Indianapolis, attempted to get away, and also made two unsuccessful attempts to use the telephone to call for help. She was justified in concluding that any attempt she might make, while purchasing a hat or while in the drug store to escape or secure assistance, would be no more successful than it was in Indianapolis. Deceased was at all times from the time she was entrapped by the appellant at his home in the custody and absolute control of appellant. Neither do we think the fact that the deceased took the poison some four hours after they left the drawing-room on the train or after the crime of attempted rape had been committed necessarily prevents it from being a part of the attempted rape. Suppose they had not left the drawing-room on the train, and, instead of the deceased taking poison, she had secured possession of appellant's revolver and shot herself or thrown herself out of the window of the car and died from the fall. We see no vital difference. At the very moment Oberholtzer swallowed the poison she was subject to the passion, desire, and will of appellant. She knew not what moment she would be subjected to the same demands that she was while on the train. What would have prevented appellant from compelling her to submit to him at any moment? The same forces, the same impulses, that would impel her to shoot herself during the actual attack or throw herself out of the car window after the attack had ceased, was pressing and overwhelming her at the time she swallowed the poison. She was so weak that she staggered as she left the elevator to go to the room in the hotel, and was assisted by appellant and Gentry. She was very ill, so much so that she could not eat, all of which was the direct and proximate result of the treatment accorded her by appellant. To say that there is no causal connection between the acts of appellant and the death of Oberholtzer, and that the treatment accorded her by appellant had no causal connection with the death of Oberholtzer would be a travesty of justice. The whole criminal program was so closely connected that it should be treated as one transaction. We conclude that the evidence was sufficient and justified the jury in finding that appellant by his acts and conduct rendered the deceased distracted and mentally irresponsible, and that such was the natural and probable consequence of such unlawful and criminal treatment, and that the appellant was guilty of murder in the second degree as charged in the first count of the indictment.

The evidence justified the court in submitting the question to the jury as there was evidence that the deceased died from the joint effect of the injuries inflicted on her, which, through natural cause and effect, contributed mediately to the death. The proposition of law stated in this instruction is well supported by authority. "The general rule, both of law and reason, is, that whenever a man contributes to a particular result, brought about, either by sole volition of another, or by such volition added to his own, he is to be held responsible for the result, the same as if his own unaided hand had produced it. The contribution, however, must be of such magnitude and so near the result that sustaining to it the relation of cause and effect, the law takes it within its cognizance. These propositions conduct us to the doctrine, that whenever a blow is inflicted under circumstances to render the party inflicting it criminally responsible, if death follows, he will be holden for murder or manslaughter, though the person beaten would have died from other causes, or would not have died from this one, had not others operated with it; provided, that the blow really contributed mediately or immediately to the death as it actually took place in a degree sufficient for the law's notice." BISHOP ON CRIMINAL LAW, § 653.

We have examined all of appellant's alleged errors, and find none that would justify a reversal.

Judgment affirmed.

MARTIN, J. (dissenting in part, concurring in part, dissenting in the conclusion).

Where a wound is not dangerous and death results from cause subsequently arising (not at the direction of the one inflicting the first wound) the supervening cause is the proximate cause of death. Where a wound is inflicted by one person on another, which is not in itself dangerous or necessarily fatal, and death results, not from such wound directly, nor from such wound indirectly "through a chain of natural effects and causes, unchanged by human action," but death results from some cause subsequently arising not at the direction or connivance of the one inflicting the first wound, and but for such subsequently arising cause death would not have resulted, the infliction of the first wound is not the proximate cause of death, but the supervening cause is the proximate cause and the one responsible for the death. Where, upon deliberation, one commits suicide because of shame, humiliation, or remorse, the one who caused such mental state, although he may be morally responsible for the death in the sight of God, is not guilty of murder under the law, unless he in some way procured, advised, compelled, assisted, or exercised control over the person performing the act.

Points for Discussion

Take Note

Even though a defendant could not be charged with homicide, if the victim failed to die within a year-and-a-day, defendant could be convicted of other crimes such as attempted murder, assault or battery.

a. Year and a Day Rule

At common law, defendant's conduct could not be deemed to be the "cause" of a homicide unless the victim died within a year and a day following the defendant's acts.

b. Model Penal Code

§ 2.03 Causation.

Causal Relationship Between Conduct and Result; Divergence Between Result Designed or Contemplated and Actual Result or Between Probable and Actual Result

(1) Conduct is the cause of a result when:

(a) it is an antecedent but for which the result in question would not have occurred; and

(b) the relationship between the conduct and result satisfies any additional causal requirements imposed by the Code or by the law defining the offense.

(2) When purposely or knowingly causing a particular result is an element of an offense, the element is not established if the actual result is not within the purpose or the contemplation of the actor unless:

(a) the actual result differs from that designed or contemplated, as the case may be, only in the respect that a different person or different property is injured or affected or that the injury or harm designed or contemplated would have been more serious or more extensive than that caused; or

(b) the actual result involves the same kind of injury or harm as that designed or contemplated and is not too remote or accidental in its occurrence to have a [just] bearing on the actor's liability or on the gravity of his offense.

(3) When recklessly or negligently causing a particular result is an element of an offense, the element is not established if the actual result is not within the risk of which the actor is aware or, in the case of negligence, of which he should have been aware unless:

(a) the actual result differs from the probable result only in the respect that a different person or different property is injured or affected or that the probable injury would have been more serious or more extensive than that caused; or

(b) the actual result involves the same kind of injury or harm as the probable result and is not too remote or accidental in its occurrence to have a [just] bearing on the actor's liability or on the gravity of his offense.

(4) When causing a particular result is a material element for which absolute liability is imposed by law, the element is not established unless the actual result is a probable consequence of the actor's conduct.

c. "But for" Test

Defendant's act may be the "cause" of death even though absent his or her conduct, the death would have occurred anyway. For example, two independent actors simultaneously shoot revolvers at a single victim and each inflicts a wound which would be fatal in and of itself. Neither actor can be the "but for" cause of death because, absent the conduct of either actor, the victim would have died anyway. Nevertheless, both actors are responsible for the victim's death. Otherwise, both defendants would be able to escape liability. *See, e.g., Jones v. Commonwealth*, 281 S.W.2d 920 (Ky. App.1955): "The law will not stop, in such a case, to measure which wound is the more serious, and to speculate upon which actually caused the death."

d. Causation & Participation

In *Commonwealth v. Atencio*, 189 N.E.2d 223 (Mass. 1963), defendants and deceased decided to play a game of "Russian roulette." The deceased was the third to play. The cartridge exploded and he fell over dead. The court concluded that defendants "caused" the death: defendants' participation "in the game of Russian roulette could be found to be a cause and not a mere condition of death. The testimony does not require a ruling that when the deceased took the gun from Atencio it was an independent or intervening act not standing in any relation to the defendants' acts which would render what he did imputable to them. It is an oversimplification to contend that each participated in something that only one could do at a time. There could be found to be a mutual encouragement in a joint enterprise."

Food for Thought

Johnson is sitting in a horse-drawn carriage which is sitting still. Defendant slaps the horse in a very hard manner that startles the horse and causes it to run away wildly. Johnson, unable to gain control of the horse, is killed when the carriage turns over. Did defendant cause Johnson's death?

Hypo 1: *The Detouring Victim*

Wyman is on his way home from work when defendant fires three shots at him. Defendant's shots miss and Wyman escapes unharmed. Wyman, afraid to go home because defendant might be lying in wait for him, decides to spend the night at a friend's house. Changing his route (since he is no longer going home), Wyman is killed on the way to the friend's house. Consider the following scenarios and decide whether defendant "caused" the victim's death: A) The death resulted from lightning which struck and killed Wyman; B) The death resulted from an automobile accident, totally the fault of another driver, and Wyman just "happened" to be in the wrong place at the wrong time; C) The death resulted because Wyman was very upset by defendant's conduct and was paying insufficient attention to his driving. In each instance, argue the case for the state. How might defendant respond? How would you rule?

Food for Thought

Defendant throws a stone at a house breaking a window. The noise is heard by only one member of the household (a son). He informs his mother (who did not hear the stone hit the house) about what has happened. On hearing the news, the mother has a heart attack, collapses and dies. Did defendant "cause" the mother's death? What arguments can be made on the State's behalf? How might defendant respond? *See Commonwealth v. Colvin*, 489 A.2d 1378 (Pa. Super. 1985).

Food for Thought

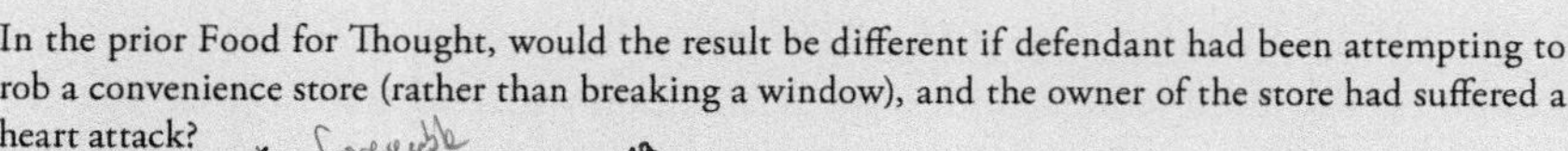

In the prior Food for Thought, would the result be different if defendant had been attempting to rob a convenience store (rather than breaking a window), and the owner of the store had suffered a heart attack?

Hypo 2: *The Doubleparked Truck Driver*

Defendant, a truck driver, double parked his truck blocking a sidewalk in violation of a local ordinance. Because of the double parking, a minor girl was forced to walk in the street to get past the truck. The girl was struck by a car and killed. Did the truck driver cause the girl's death? *See Marchl v. Dowling & Co.*, 41 A.2d 427 (Pa. Super. 1945).

Food for Thought

Suppose that a wife is forced out into freezing weather by her husband. The wife decides to go to her father's home which is safe and warm. However, for unknown reasons, after she arrives, she decides not to enter the house. She freezes to death outside the house. Has the husband "caused" the wife's death? Argue the case for the husband? How might the state respond? *See State v. Preslar*, 48 N.C. 421 (1856).

Hypo 3: *The Fatally Wounded Victim*

Defendant 1 and John Taylor fought, and defendant fatally wounded Taylor. The wound severed the mesenteric artery, was necessarily mortal, and death would have ensued within the hour. Internal hemorrhaging occurred and Taylor was suffering intense pain. While he lay dying, defendant 2 (a long-time enemy) inflicted a knife wound on Taylor. This wound was severe enough that it killed Taylor within five minutes. Medical witnesses testified that, even though death was inevitable from the initial wound, it was accelerated by the knife wound. Which defendant is responsible for the death? *See Henderson v. State*, 65 So. 721 (Ala. App. 1914); *People v. Lewis*, 57 P. 470 (Cal. 1899).

Hypo 4: *The Driver and the Jogger*

John, a jogger, is trying to cross a busy street when he is struck by defendant's vehicle. John survives the impact, but is thrown into the middle of the northbound lane of traffic with his head pointing toward the curb, and his feet pointing toward the road. A second car is fast approaching. A witness tries to flag the second car down, but is unable to do so. The second car drives over John causing severe internal injuries. John dies two hours later. Expert testimony indicates that both sets of injuries were severe and independently could have resulted in John's death. Who is responsible for his death? *See People v. Tims*, 534 N.W.2d 675 (Mich. 1995).

Food for Thought

Defendant broke into a house with intent to rob. The deceased ran out of the house and jumped into a well and remained there until he died from exposure. Did defendant "cause" the death? *See Gipe v. State*, 165 Ind. 433, 75 N.E. 881 (1905).

Hypo 5: *The Failure to Rescue*

Defendants went to the home of Pepper armed with revolvers, forcibly took possession of Pepper, bound his arms so as to render him helpless, and in the presence of Pepper avowed their purpose to kill him. Defendants placed Pepper in an automobile and started to drive away. When the car reached the banks of a river, Pepper leaped from the car into the water and drowned. Defendants stood by and made no effort to rescue Pepper. Are defendants responsible for Pepper's death? *See State v. Shelledy*, 8 Iowa 477 (1859).

Hypo 6: *The Burglary and the Suicidal Jump*

Jane Munson, the village nurse, lived alone. Late one night, defendant broke into Munson's house. He went upstairs and found the bedroom door locked. Defendant threatened to break the door down if Munson did not let him in. Munson refused. As defendant tried to break-in, Munson jumped out the window falling to her death. Is defendant criminally responsible for Munson's death? *See State v. Lassiter*, 484 A.2d 13 (N.J. Super. 1984); *Rex v. Beech* [23 Cox Cr. Law Cas. 181 (1912)].

Food for Thought

Defendants "intentionally made threats, statements and accusations against deceased for the purpose of harassing, embarrassing, and humiliating him in the presence of friends, relatives and business associates." Because of these threats, deceased became physically and mentally disturbed and committed suicide. Defendants' counsel argues that deceased's suicide is an independent intervening cause that breaks the chain of legal causation and absolves defendants from criminal responsibility. Is he right? *See Tate v. Canonica*, 180 Cal. App. 2d 898 (1960).

People v. Acosta

284 Cal. Rptr. 117 (Cal. App.1991).

WALLIN, ASSOCIATE JUSTICE.

Officers Salceda and Francis of the Santa Ana Police Department's automobile theft detail saw Acosta in Elvira Salazar's stolen Nissan Pulsar parked on the street. The officers approached Acosta and identified themselves. Acosta inched the Pulsar forward, then accelerated rapidly. He led Salceda, Francis and officers from other agencies on a 48-mile chase along numerous surface streets and freeways throughout Orange County. The chase ended near Acosta's residence in Anaheim.

During the chase, Acosta engaged in some of the most egregious driving tactics imaginable. He ran stop signs and red lights, and drove on the wrong side of streets, causing oncoming traffic to scatter or swerve to avoid colliding with him. Once, when all traffic lanes were blocked by vehicles stopped for a red light, he used a dirt shoulder to circumvent stationary vehicles and pass through the intersection. When leaving the freeway in Anaheim, he drove over a cement shoulder. Throughout the pursuit, Acosta weaved in and out of traffic, cutting in front of other cars and causing them to brake suddenly. At one point on the freeway, he crossed three lanes of traffic, struck another car, jumped the divider between the freeway and a transition lane, and passed a tanker truck, forcing it to swerve suddenly to avoid a collision. Acosta generally drove at speeds between 60 and 90 miles per hour, slowing only when necessary. During several turns, his wheels lost traction. When an officer was able to drive parallel to the Pulsar for a short distance, Acosta looked in his direction and smiled. Near the end of the chase, one of the Pulsar's front tires blew out, but Acosta continued to drive at 55 to 60 miles per hour, crossing freeway traffic lanes.

Police helicopters from Anaheim, Costa Mesa, Huntington Beach, and Newport Beach assisted in the chase by tracking Acosta. During the early part of the pursuit, the Costa Mesa and Newport Beach craft were used, pinpointing Acosta's location with their high beam spotlights. The Costa Mesa helicopter was leading the pursuit, in front of and below the Newport Beach helicopter. As they flew into Newport Beach, the pilots agreed the Newport Beach craft should take the lead. The normal procedure for such a maneuver is for the lead helicopter to move to the right and swing around clockwise behind the other craft while climbing to an altitude of 1,000 feet. At the same time, the trailing helicopter descends to 500 feet while maintaining a straight course. At the direction of the Costa Mesa pilot, the Newport Beach helicopter moved forward and descended while the Costa Mesa helicopter banked to the right. Shortly after commencing this procedure, the Costa Mesa helicopter, having terminated radio communication, came up under the Newport Beach helicopter from the right rear and collided with it. Both helicopters fell to the ground. Three occupants in the Costa Mesa helicopter died as a result of the crash.

Menzies Turner, a retired Federal Aviation Administration (FAA) investigator, testified as an expert and concluded the accident occurred because the Costa Mesa helicopter, the faster of the two aircraft, made a 360-degree turn and closed too rapidly on the Newport Beach helicopter. He opined the Costa Mesa helicopter's pilot violated an FAA regulation prohibiting careless and reckless operation of an aircraft by failing to properly clear the area, not maintaining communication with the Newport Beach helicopter, failing to keep the other aircraft in view at all times, and not changing his altitude. He also testified the Costa Mesa pilot violated another FAA regulation prohibiting operation of one aircraft so close to another as to create a collision hazard. Turner could not think of any reason for the Costa Mesa helicopter's erratic movement. The maneuver was not a difficult one, and was not affected by the ground activity at the time. He had never heard of a midair collision between two police helicopters involved in tracking a ground pursuit, and had never investigated a midair collision involving helicopters.

After his arrest Acosta told the police he knew the Pulsar was stolen and he fled the police to avoid arrest. He also saw two helicopters with spotlights, and turned off the Pulsar's lights to evade them. Acosta knew that his flight was dangerous "to the bone," but he tried to warn other cars by flashing the car lights and by otherwise being "as safe as possible."

Acosta claims there was insufficient evidence that he proximately caused the deaths of the victims. He argues that although a collision between ground vehicles was a foreseeable result of his conduct, one between airborne helicopters was not, noting his expert had never heard of a similar incident. He also contends the Costa Mesa helicopter pilot's violation of FAA regulations was a superseding cause. Because the deaths here were unusual, to say the least, the issue deserves special scrutiny.

Proximate cause in criminal cases is determined by ordinary principles of causation. It is initially a question of fact for the jury to decide. To determine whether Acosta's conduct was not, as a matter of law, a proximate cause of death of the Costa Mesa helicopter's occupants, I enter a legal realm not routinely considered in published California cases.

"Proximate cause" is the term historically used[6] to separate those results for which an actor will be held responsible from those not carrying such responsibility. The term is, in a sense,

6 The American Law Institute has urged the use of "legal cause" instead. I abide with the traditional term, "proximate cause."

artificial, serving matters of policy surrounding tort and criminal law and based partly on expediency and partly on concerns of fairness and justice. Because such concerns are sometimes more a matter of "common sense" than pure logic, the line of demarcation is flexible, and attempts to lay down uniform tests which apply evenly in all situations have failed. That does not mean general guidelines and approaches to analysis cannot be constructed.

The threshold question in examining causation is whether the defendant's act was an "actual cause" of the victim's injury. It is a *sine qua non* test: But for the defendant's act would the injury have occurred? Unless an act is an actual cause of the injury, it will not be considered a proximate cause.

The next inquiry is whether the defendant's act was a "substantial factor" in the injury. This test excludes those actual causes which, although direct, play only an insignificant role in the ultimate injury.[8] Although there is no strict definition, the RESTATEMENT SECOND OF TORTS, *supra*, section 433, lists considerations in determining whether a factor is "substantial": (1) the number and extent of other factors contributing to the harm; (2) whether the forces created by the actor are continuous in producing the harm or merely create a condition upon which independent forces act; and (3) any lapse of time between the act and the harm.

In California, the substantial factor issue has arisen most often where multiple causes act concurrently, but independently,[9] to produce the harm. The test is one of exclusion only. Unless a cause is a substantial factor in the harm it will not be considered a proximate cause, but some substantial factor causes may not be deemed proximate causes. A related concept which may lead to a refusal to treat an actual cause as a proximate cause is where a force set in motion by the defendant has "come to rest in a position of apparent safety. "Perkins and Boyce give the example of the actor who dislodges a rock which comes to rest against a tree. If the tree bends or breaks six months later, releasing the rock, the original action is not considered the proximate cause of any resulting harm.

To this point I have spoken only of direct causes, "causes which produce a result without the aid of any intervening cause." Because it is tautological, the definition is of little value in identifying a cause in the absence of a working definition of an indirect cause. However, Perkins and Boyce list several examples of direct causation, headed by the observation that, "If sequences follow one another in such a customary order that no other cause would commonly be thought of as intervening, the causal connection is spoken of as direct for juridical purposes even though many intervening causes might be recognized by a physicist."

The critical concept is that a direct cause which is a substantial factor in the ensuing injury is almost always a proximate cause of it. This is so even if the result is exacerbated by a

---

8 An independent intervening cause could be explained by saying it rendered the defendant's act "insubstantial." However, the traditional approach has been to determine only whether the defendant's act is substantial in the abstract or in comparison with a contributory or concurrent cause. If it is not, the analysis goes no further. If it is, the question becomes whether there is an intervening cause which should relieve the defendant of responsibility.

9 If the actors are acting in concert, both would be culpable using an aiding and abetting theory, even if only one directly caused the death.

latent condition in the victim or caused by a third party. *People v. Stamp* (1969) 2 Cal. App. 3d 203, 210 (defendant triggered heart attack in store clerk during armed robbery). The only exception is where the result is "highly extraordinary" in view of its cause.

However, the defendant is not always the direct cause of the harm. Sometimes forces arise between the act of the defendant and the harm, called "intervening causes." They are of two types, dependent and independent, and include acts of God. An intervening cause is dependent if it is a normal or involuntary response to, or result of, the defendant's act. These include flight and other voluntary or involuntary responses of victims, as well as defense, rescue and medical treatment by third parties. Even where such responses constitute negligent conduct, they do not supersede the defendant's act; *i.e.*, they are nevertheless considered proximate causes of the harm. *People v. Armitage, supra*, 194 Cal. App. 3d at p. 420 (victim foolishly chose to attempt to swim to shore after defendant capsized the boat).[15] Conversely, when the defendant's conduct merely places the eventual victim in a position which allows some other action to cause the harm, the other action is termed an independent intervening cause. It usually supersedes the defendant's act; *i.e.*, precludes a finding of proximate cause. 1 LAFAVE & SCOTT, *supra*, at pp. 406–407 (distinguishing matters of "response" from matters of "coincidence"). The issue usually arises when the victim has been subjected to the independent harm after being disabled by the defendant, or is somehow impacted by the defendant's flight. *See People v. Pike, supra*, 197 Cal. App. 3d at 747 (one police officer killed when struck by another while pursuing defendant).

An independent intervening variable will not be superseding in three instances: (1) where it is merely a contributing cause to the defendant's direct cause; (2) where the result was intended; or (3) where the resultant harm was reasonably foreseeable when the act was done. As to the third exception, "the consequence need not have been a strong probability; a possible consequence which might reasonably have been contemplated is enough. The precise consequence need not have been foreseen; it is enough that the defendant should have foreseen the possibility of some harm of the kind which might result from his act."

As Perkins and Boyce put it, " 'Foreseeability' is not a 'test' which can be applied without the use of common sense; it presents one of those problems in which 'we must rely on the common sense of the common man as to common things.' It is employed in the sense of 'appreciable probability.' It does not require such a degree of probability that the intervention was more likely to occur than not; and on the other hand it implies more than that someone might have imagined it as a theoretical possibility. It does not require that the defendant himself

15 The refusal to allow "contributory negligence" to be a bar to a proximate cause finding need not be the product of any mechanical policy rule. It can be grounded in the notion that it is not "abnormal" for people to react less "reasonably" under stress than if the stress were not present. For purposes of ascribing causal responsibility it may be said that a negligent or foolish response is "normal." To the extent that a dependent intervening cause is thought to "directly" carry through the act of the defendant to a harmful result, this analysis comports well with the rule that a defendant's act is the proximate cause of any harm caused directly by his act unless the result is "highly extraordinary." It also allows the court to find that a negligent, but highly extraordinary response precludes a finding of proximate cause, while a reckless but predictable response does not. The focus is properly on the objective conditions present at the time the defendant perpetrated the causal act and the predictable, albeit sometimes unreasonable, responses of human beings to them.

actually thought of it. For the purposes of proximate cause 'an appreciable probability is one which a reasonable man in ordering his conduct in view of his situation and his knowledge and means of knowledge, should, either consciously or unconsciously, take into account in connection with the other facts and probabilities then apparent.' "

Prosser and Keeton conclude that although it is desirable to exclude extremely remarkable and unusual results from the purview of proximate cause, it is virtually impossible to express a logical verbal formula which will produce uniform results. The standard should be simply stated, exclude extraordinary results, and allow the trier of fact to determine the issue on the particular facts of the case using "the common sense of the common man as to common things. "As with other ultimate issues, appellate courts must review that determination, giving due deference to the trier of fact.

The "highly extraordinary result" standard serves that purpose. It is consistent with the definition of foreseeability used in California. It does not involve the defendant's state of mind, but focuses upon the objective conditions present when he acts.[19] Like numerous other legal definitions, what it means in practice will be determined as case law develops. Limitations arising from the mental state of the actor can be left to concepts like malice, recklessness and negligence.

Because the highly extraordinary result standard is consistent with the limitation on direct causes, it simplifies the proximate cause inquiry. The analysis is: (1) was the defendant's conduct the actual cause of the harm (but for his actions would it have occurred as it did)? (2) was the result an intended consequence of the act? (3) was the defendant's action a substantial factor in the harm? and (4) was the result highly extraordinary in light of the circumstances? If the first question is answered no, proximate cause is lacking. If answered yes, the next question must be examined. If the second question is answered yes, proximate cause is established. If answered no, the next question must be examined. If the third question is answered no, proximate cause is lacking. If answered yes, proximate cause is established unless the fourth question is answered yes, in which case it is lacking. The analysis does away with the need to consider the distinction between direct, concurrent, contributory, and dependent and independent intervening causes. It focuses, as it should, upon the role the defendant's act played in the harm, limiting culpability only where the conduct was *de minimis* or the result highly extraordinary.

Here, but for Acosta's conduct of fleeing the police, the helicopters would never have been in position for the crash. However, there was no evidence he intended the harm, so I must examine questions three and four. Although an extremely close question, Acosta's conduct was a substantial factor in causing the crash. He was fleeing when the accident occurred, and there was no lapse of time between his flight and the crash—his action had not "come to rest." The only other factor operating at the time was the improper flight pattern of the Costa Mesa pilot.

---

19 The Model Penal Code takes a similar approach, focusing on whether the result is "too remote or accidental in its occurrence to have a just bearing on the actor's liability or on the gravity of his offense." Model Pen.Code, § 2.03(2)(b). LaFave and Scott also appear to look to the extraordinary nature of the result in determining causal responsibility, although they discuss it in terms of foreseeability.

Although Acosta's horrendous driving did not cause the helicopter's improper maneuver, his flight undoubtedly infused excitement and tension into the situation, which can be considered to be a substantial factor. No similar case has held otherwise, although the third party collisions all have involved accidents on the ground. The result was not highly extraordinary. Although a two-helicopter collision was unknown to expert witness Turner and no reported cases describe one, it was "a possible consequence which reasonably might have been contemplated." Given the emotional dynamics of any police pursuit, there is an appreciable probability that one of the pursuers, in the heat of the chase, may act negligently or recklessly to catch the quarry. That no pursuits have ever before resulted in a helicopter crash or midair collision is more a comment on police flying skill and technology than upon the innate probabilities involved.

Justice Crosby's opinion parts company with this analysis, reasoning that "neither the intervening negligent conduct nor the risk of harm was foreseeable." He justifies this conclusion by reference to the well-traveled opinion of Justice Cardozo in *Palsgraf v. Long Island R. Co.* 162 N.E. 99, 100 (N.Y. 1928). Reliance on *Palsgraf* reveals the error in the analysis. Justice Cardozo approached the problem from the perspective of duty, concluding that the defendant owed no duty of care to an unforeseeable plaintiff. Although the interesting facts and novel analysis of *Palsgraf*[24] have made it a favorite in law school texts, the decision is not the gospel on proximate cause. Because of its confusion between foreseeability as it relates to negligence and as it relates to causation, I have eliminated it from the proximate cause analysis.

Doing so avoids the undesirable risk of completely absolving a defendant of all liability on causation grounds when morally he should suffer some punishment for the consequences. When a defendant is the actual and substantial cause of the harm, the consequences of the act should depend upon the *mens rea* involved.

Food for Thought

Note the Acosta Court's reference to the *Palsgraf* decision which was a tort decision, but which also dealt with the issue of proximate cause. In the criminal law, the same term (proximate cause) is used. Is it being used in the same way?

NO

The undisputed facts of this case mandate the result. Contrary to Justice Moore's assertion, I do not find the result extraordinary, but almost so. I presume he does not dispute that it was extremely unusual. In fact, he cites no similar instances of aircraft colliding during police pursuits. But neither does Justice Crosby cite any case to support his claim the result was highly extraordinary. Neither concurring opinion offers case law "on all fours," suggesting this case is unique and presents a close question. Partly because this is so, it is appropriate to rely on two compelling factors: the jury found proximate cause based on proper instructions, and the dearth of case law to support a rejection of that finding. Given these circumstances, a finding of proximate cause is appropriate.

---

24 The defendant's railway attendants accidentally knocked a package of fireworks from a passenger's arms while boarding a train, causing a concussive explosion which overturned scales on the platform which struck the plaintiff.

The judgment is reversed on the murder counts and is affirmed in all other respects.

MOORE, ACTING PRESIDING JUSTICE, concurring in part and dissenting.

The events leading to the helicopter collision were set in motion by appellant's decision to flee from the police. It was predictable that the police would pursue appellant and use whatever means available to them to locate and capture him. The possibility that during the chase the pursuing police vehicles might be operated in a negligent manner thereby causing a collision was sufficiently foreseeable to establish appellant's conduct as the proximate cause of the accident. The evidence is sufficient to support the jury's finding of proximate cause. The judgment should be affirmed.

CROSBY, ASSOCIATE JUSTICE, concurring and dissenting.

To be sure, defendant represented a threat to everyone traveling the same roads and would have been responsible for any injury directly or indirectly caused by his actions in those environs; but to extend that responsibility to persons in the air, whose role was merely to observe his movements, a simple enough task in far speedier helicopters, defies common sense. It was perfectly foreseeable that someone would be hurt on the ground via some sort of causal chain connecting to defendant's conduct; the opposite is true of the airborne observers. They were not in the zone of danger by any stretch of the imagination, and the manner and circumstances of the collision could hardly have reasonably been foreseen. Although less remote than a dispatcher suffering a coronary, this was a "highly extraordinary result" by any measure and beyond the long arm of the criminal law.

Food for Thought

In the Howard Beach case, several white teenagers assaulted and threatened three black men. In the course of the assault, which was "motivated solely by the color of the victims' skin", several youths relentlessly chased Michael Griffith who was forced to retreat by jumping a barricade and attempting to cross a well-traveled six-lane highway. A passing motorist collided with Griffith, killing him. Defendants argued that the motorist's intervention rendered their conduct too remote a cause of death to warrant criminal liability. Do you agree? *See People v. Kern*, 545 N.Y.S.2d 4, 20 (1989).

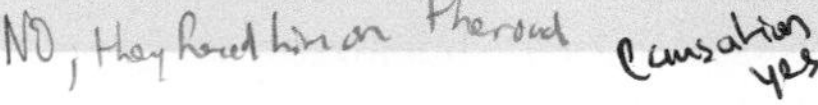

Hypo 1: *The KKK Rally*

Defendant, a Ku Klux Klan member, gave a racist speech on a city square. Throughout the speech, defendant was confronted by a large and hostile crowd. As the crowd became more hostile and potentially violent, defendant randomly fired his gun towards the crowd. Although defendant did not hit anyone, Harriett Burnett was killed when a crowd member (Joe Howard) unknown to defendant accidentally discharged his own gun while seeking refuge from defendant's gunfire. Ironically, the victim was Howard's close friend and there was no evidence of any animosity between the two. Upon seeing

Harriett on the ground, Howard immediately tried to revive her. When his efforts proved unsuccessful, Howard fired four shots in defendant's direction. Who caused the victim's death? Defendant? Howard? Both? *See Hodges v. State*, 661 So.2d 107 (Fla.App. 1995).

Hypo 2: *Sterno and the Skid Row Addicts*

Defendant operated a cigar store in the "skid-row" section of the city. One of the products he sold was Sterno, a jelly-like substance composed primarily of methanol and ethanol, which was designed for cooking and heating purposes. Sterno was manufactured and sold in two types of containers, one for home use and one for industrial use. Previously, both types of Sterno contained approximately 3.75% Methanol, or wood alcohol, and 71% Ethanol, or grain alcohol; of the two types of alcohols, methanol is far more toxic if consumed internally. Beginning a few months ago, the Sterno company began manufacturing a new type of industrial Sterno which was 54% Methanol. The cans containing the new industrial Sterno were identical to the cans containing the old industrial Sterno except that the lids of the new 54% Methanol Sterno were imprinted with the words "Institutional Sterno. Danger. Poison. For use only as a Fuel. Not for consumer use. For industrial and commercial use. Not for home use." A skull and crossbones were also lithographed on the lid. The carton in which the new Sterno was packaged and shipped did not indicate that the contents differed in any respect from the old industrial Sterno. The Sterno Corporation sent only one shipment of the new Sterno to the city; that shipment went to a company that made only one sale of the new industrial Sterno, to defendant. Defendant sold approximately 400 cans of the new industrial Sterno. Thirty-one persons died in the skid-row area as a result of methanol poisoning. The source of the methanol was traced to the new industrial Sterno. Since defendant was the only retail outlet of this type of Sterno in the area, he was arrested and indicted on thirty-one counts of involuntary manslaughter. Assuming that defendant had the necessary *mens rea* for manslaughter, can it be said that he "caused" the death of skid row residents who used the Sterno? *See Commonwealth v. Feinberg*, 253 A.2d 636 (Pa. 1969).

Hypo 3: *The Malicious Neighbor*

Defendant and Murdock, who lived close to each other, cursed and threatened each other repeatedly over their citizen's band radios. On the night in question, Murdock was legally intoxicated and defendant knew that Murdock had a problem with night vision. Defendant also knew that Murdock owned a handgun, had boasted "about how he would shoot it to scare people off," that Murdock was easily agitated and that he became especially angry if anyone disparaged his war hero, General George S. Patton. During a conversation over the radio, defendant implied that General Patton and Murdock were both homosexuals. Also, defendant persistently demanded that Murdock arm himself with his handgun and wait on his front porch for defendant to come and kill him. Murdock responded that he would be waiting on his front porch, and he told defendant to "kiss his wife and children good-bye because he would never go back home." Defendant then made an anonymous telephone call to the police department, identified Murdock by name, told the dispatcher that Murdock had "a gun on the porch," had "threatened to shoot up the neighborhood," and was "talking about shooting anything that moves." Three officers were dispatched to Murdock's home. None of the officers knew that Murdock was intoxicated or that he was in an agitated state of mind. The officers observed Murdock come out of his house with "something shiny in his hand." Murdock sat down on the top step of the porch and placed the shiny object beside him. One officer approached Murdock from the side of the porch and told him to "leave the gun alone and walk down the stairs." Murdock reached for the gun, stood up, advanced in the officer's direction, and opened fire. The officer retreated and was not struck. All three officers returned fire, and Murdock was struck. Lying wounded on the porch, he said several times, "I didn't know you was the police." He died from "a gunshot wound to the left side of his chest." Was defendant the legal "cause" of Murdock's death? *See Bailey v. Commonwealth*, 329 S.E.2d 37 (Va. 1985).

Food for Thought

Defendant, who runs a firearms business, illegally sold several gun cartridges to a minor (under the age of 16 years old) in violation of state law. The minor used the cartridge to kill someone else. Can the business owner be said to have "caused" the death so that he can be charged with negligent homicide or manslaughter? *See Mautino v. Piercedale Supply Co.*, 13 A.2d 51 (Pa. 1940).

Hypo 4: *The Firefighter*

Defendant intentionally set fire to a couch causing a serious fire on the fifth floor of an abandoned building. The fire department, responding to the conflagration, found the rear portion of the fifth and sixth floors burning. The firemen attempted to bring the situation under control, but were unable to do so and decided to withdraw. Before they could, the firemen were enveloped by a dense smoke, which arose from an independent fire that had broken out on the second floor. Although this fire was also determined to have originated in arson, there is no evidence implicating defendant. However, the combination of the thick smoke and the fifth floor fire made evacuation from the premises extremely hazardous, and one fireman sustained injuries from which he subsequently died. Did defendant "cause" the death of the fireman? *See People v. Arzon*, 401 N.Y.S.2d 156 (1978).

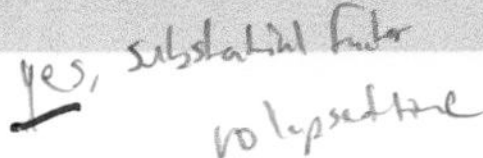

Food for Thought

Defendant, who owned a bar, continued serving drinks to a customer who was in a visibly intoxicated condition. An hour or so later, after consuming several more drinks, the customer left the bar, attacked, and killed someone on the street. Is defendant, the bar owner, the "cause" of the death? *See Schelin v. Goldberg*, 146 A.2d 648 (1958). Would your answer change if, instead of attacking someone, the customer had left the bar in his car and crashed into another car killing the victim?

Commonwealth v. Root

403 Pa. 571, 170 A.2d 310 (1961).

CHARLES ALVIN JONES, CHIEF JUSTICE.

Appellant was found guilty of involuntary manslaughter for the death of his competitor in the course of an automobile race between them on a highway. We accepted this appeal to decide the important whether defendant's unlawful and reckless conduct was a sufficiently direct cause of the death to warrant his being charged with criminal homicide.

The testimony, discloses that the defendant accepted the deceased's challenge to engage in an automobile race; that the racing took place on a rural 3-lane highway; that the night was clear and dry, and traffic light; that the speed limit on the highway was 50 miles per hour; that, immediately prior to the accident, the two automobiles were being operated at speeds from 70 to 90 miles per hour; that the accident occurred in a no-passing zone on the approach to a bridge where the highway narrowed to two directionally-opposite lanes; that, at the time of the accident, defendant was in the lead and was proceeding in his right hand lane of travel; that the deceased, in an attempt to pass the defendant's automobile, when a truck was closely approaching from the opposite direction, swerved his car to the left, crossed the highway's white dividing line and drove his automobile on the wrong side of the highway head-on into the oncoming truck with fatal effect to himself.

This evidence would support a conviction of the defendant for speeding, reckless driving and, other violations of The Vehicle Code. In fact, a recent Act makes automobile racing on a highway an independent crime punishable by fine or imprisonment or both up to $500 and three years in jail. In any event, unlawful or reckless conduct is only one ingredient of the crime of involuntary manslaughter. Another essential and distinctly separate element of the crime is that the unlawful or reckless conduct charged to the defendant was the direct cause of the death in issue. The first ingredient is obviously present in this case but the second is not.

While precedent is to be found for application of the tort law concept of "proximate cause" in fixing responsibility for criminal homicide, the want of any rational basis for its use in determining criminal liability can no longer be properly disregarded. When proximate cause was first borrowed from the field of tort law and applied to homicide prosecutions in

Pennsylvania, the concept connoted a much more direct causal relation in producing the alleged culpable result than it does today. Proximate cause, as an essential element of a tort founded in negligence, has undergone in recent times a marked extension. This area of civil law has been progressively liberalized in favor of claims for damages for personal injuries to which careless conduct of others can in some way be associated. To persist in applying the tort liability concept of proximate cause to prosecutions for criminal homicide after the marked expansion of civil liability of defendants in tort actions for negligence would be to extend possible criminal liability to persons chargeable with unlawful or reckless conduct in circumstances not generally considered to present the likelihood of a resultant death.

Legal theory which makes guilt or innocence of criminal homicide depend upon such accidental and fortuitous circumstances as are now embraced by modern tort law's encompassing concept of proximate cause is too harsh to be just. Even if the tort liability concept of proximate cause were to be deemed applicable, defendant's conviction of involuntary manslaughter in the instant case could not be sustained under the evidence. The operative effect of a supervening cause would have to be taken into consideration. But, the trial judge refused the defendant's point for charge to such effect and erroneously instructed the jury that "negligence or want of care on the part of the deceased is no defense to the criminal responsibility of the defendant."

The Superior Court, in affirming defendant's conviction, approved the charge, despite a number of decisions in involuntary manslaughter cases holding that the conduct of the deceased victim must be considered in order to determine whether the defendant's reckless acts were the proximate (*i.e.*, sufficiently direct) cause of his death. The Superior Court did so on the ground that there can be more than one proximate cause of death. The point is irrelevant. Of course there can be more than one proximate cause of death just as there can also be more than one direct cause of death. For example, in the so-called "shield" cases where a felon interposes the person of an innocent victim between himself and a pursuing officer, if the officer should fire his gun at the felon to prevent his escape and fatally wound the person used as a shield, the different acts of the policeman and the felon would each be a direct cause of the victim's death.

If the tort liability concept of proximate cause were to be applied in a criminal homicide prosecution, then the conduct of the person whose death is the basis of the indictment would have to be considered, not to prove that it was merely an additional proximate cause of the death, but to determine, under fundamental and long recognized law, whether the subsequent wrongful act superseded the original conduct chargeable to the defendant. If it did in fact supervene, then the original act is so insulated from the ensuing death as not to be its proximate cause.

Under the uncontradicted evidence in this case, the conduct of the defendant was not the proximate cause of the decedent's death as a matter of law. In *Kline v. Moyer and Albert*, 1937, 325 Pa. 357, 364, 191 A. 43, 46, the rule is stated as follows: "Where a second actor has become aware of the existence of a potential danger created by the negligence of an original tortfeasor, and thereafter, by an independent act of negligence, brings about an accident, the first tortfeasor is relieved of liability, because the condition created by him was merely a circumstance of the accident and not its proximate cause." In the case before us, deceased was aware of the dangerous condition created by the defendant's reckless conduct in driving his automobile at an excessive rate of speed along the highway but, despite such knowledge, he recklessly chose to swerve his car to the left and into the path of an oncoming truck, thereby bringing about the head-on collision which caused his own death. In the instant case, the defendant's reckless conduct was not a sufficiently direct cause of the competing driver's death to make him criminally liable therefore.

The judgment of sentence is reversed and the defendant's motion in arrest of judgment granted.

EAGEN, JUSTICE (dissenting).

Defendant, at the time of the fatal accident, was engaged in an unlawful and reckless course of conduct. Racing an automobile at 90 miles per hour, trying to prevent another automobile going in the same direction from passing him, in a no-passing zone on a two-lane public highway, is certainly all of that. Admittedly, there can be more than one direct cause of an unlawful death. But, says the majority opinion, the defendant's recklessness was not a direct cause of the death. I cannot agree. If the defendant did not engage in the unlawful race and so operate his automobile in such a reckless manner, this accident would never have occurred. He helped create the dangerous event. He was a vital part of it. The victim's acts were a natural reaction to the stimulus of the situation. The race, the attempt to pass the other car and forge ahead, the reckless speed, all of these factors the defendant himself helped create. He was part and parcel of them. That the victim's response was normal under the circumstances, that his reaction should have been expected and was clearly foreseeable, is to me beyond argument. That the defendant's recklessness was a substantial factor is obvious. All of this, in my opinion, makes his unlawful conduct a direct cause of the resulting collision.

The majority opinion states, "Legal theory which makes guilt or innocence of criminal homicide depend upon such accidental and fortuitous circumstances as are now embraced by modern tort law's encompassing concept is too harsh to be just." If the resulting death had been dependent upon "accidental and fortuitous circumstances" or, "in circumstances not generally considered to present the likelihood of a resultant death," we would agree that the defendant is not criminally responsible. However, acts should be judged by their tendency under the known circumstances, not by the actual intent which accompanies their performance. Every day, we read that some teen-agers, or young adults, somewhere in this country, have been killed or have killed others, while racing their automobiles. Hair-raising, death-defying, law-breaking rides, which encompass "racing" are the rule rather than the exception, and endanger not only the participants, but every motorist and passenger on the road. To call such resulting accidents "accidental and fortuitous," or unlikely to result in death, is to ignore the cold and harsh reality of everyday occurrences. Root's actions were as direct a cause of Hall's death. Root's shield was his high speed and any approaching traffic in his quest to prevent Hall from passing, which he knew Hall would undertake to do, the first time he thought he had the least opportunity. While the victim's foolhardiness in this case contributed to his own death, he was not the only one responsible and it is not he alone with whom we are concerned. It is the people of the Commonwealth who are harmed by the kind of conduct the defendant pursued. Their interests must be kept in mind.

I, therefore, dissent and would accordingly affirm the judgment of conviction.

Point for Discussion

Death of a Bystander

Was *Root* correctly decided? Consider *Jacobs v. State*, 184 So.2d 711 (Fla.App. 1966), which involved similar facts, but in which the innocent driver of an oncoming vehicle was killed. Jacobs was convicted of manslaughter and the conviction was upheld on appeal: "The evidence shows that appellant, together with others, was engaged in what is commonly known as a 'drag race' of motor vehicles on a two-lane public highway. The race entailed the operation of three motor vehicles traveling in the same direction at excessive and unlawful rates of speed contrary to the laws of this state. While engaged in such unlawful activity one of the three vehicles actively participating in the race was negligently operated in such manner as to cause the death of the person who drove that vehicle, as well as another innocent party who had no connection with the race. The deaths which proximately resulted from the activities of the three persons engaged in the unlawful activity of drag racing made each of the active participants equally guilty of the criminal act which caused the death of the innocent party." Is the holding in *Jacobs* preferable to the holding in *Root*? Should it matter that an innocent person was killed in *Jacobs* rather than a participant in the race?

Take Note

As the cases suggest, courts frequently encounter "intervening causes" that can have a bearing on criminal responsibility. These intervening causes can be dependent (in the sense that they are a "response" to defendant's conduct (e.g., defendant slaps a horse which starts to run and eventually kills the victim) or independent in the sense that they are simply a "coincidence" (after the horse comes to a stop, a lightning storm breaks out and the victim is struck and killed by lightning).

Food for Thought

Defendant and Bobby Osborne engaged in a drag race. After the drag race ended and defendant had stopped at the side of the road, Osborne continued to drive extremely fast on the wrong side of the road. A mile or so down the road, Osborne ran head on into an oncoming car killing the driver. Is defendant the cause of the oncoming driver's death?

Hypo 1: *Another Drag Race*

Defendant and Alvarez participated in a drag race. Both drivers completed the race without incident. However, at the end, Alvarez made a 180 degree turn and headed back towards the starting line at a speed of approximately 123 m.p.h. Defendant followed at a speed of 98 m.p.h. Alvarez was not wearing a seat belt and subsequent investigation revealed that he had a blood alcohol level between .11 and .12. At some point, Alvarez crashed through a guard rail, was thrown from his car, and was killed when his vehicle landed on top of him. Defendant also crashed through the guard rail, but escaped uninjured. Should defendant be held criminally responsible for Alvarez's death? *Velazquez v. State*, 561 So.2d 347 (Fla.App. 1990).

Food for Thought

In *Root*, suppose that the court had held that defendant can be held criminally liable for manslaughter because he participated in a race during which an act of manslaughter occurred. If so, can spectators (who were lined up along the race route to cheer the participants) be said to have caused the death as well?

Hypo 2: *The Game of Chicken*

Defendant and deceased entered into a suicide pact which was supposed to be carried out by driving a car off a cliff. The cliff was on a car turnout on a curve overlooking a 300 to 350-foot precipice on a country road. The two proceeded up the hill past the cliff, turned around, and drove down around the curve and over the steep cliff at a speed in excess of 50 mph. No one saw brake lights flash. The impact of the crash killed deceased and caused severe injuries to defendant, resulting in the amputation of a foot. The State has charged defendant with the homicide of deceased. Did defendant cause deceased's death? *See Forden v. Joseph G.*, 667 P.2d 1176 (Cal., En Banc, 1983).

Hypo 3: *The Drug Addicts*

David Groleau, who was an alcoholic and who previously had used depressants such as Valium and Percocet, "had been drinking and doing pills" throughout the day. By early evening, Groleau was visibly inebriated. Defendant prepared one "bag" of heroin and injected the heroin into his own arm and exclaimed that the heroin was "very, very good" which meant that it was particularly potent. Defendant then gave another bag of heroin to Groleau who injected the heroin into his own arm. Groleau, who was approximately thirty to forty pounds heavier than defendant, injected the same amount of heroin as had defendant. Approximately fifteen seconds later, Groleau lost consciousness, collapsed onto the floor, and died. The evidence revealed that the level of heroin was "potentially life-threatening," and that Groleau would not have died but for the administration of the heroin. Was defendant's conduct the cause of Groleau's death? *See State v. Wassil*, 658 A.2d 548 (Conn. 1995); *Shirah v. State*, 555 So.2d 807 (Ala. Crim. App.1989); *People v. Cline*, 270 Cal. App. 2d 328 (1969); *Ureta v. Superior Court*, 199 Cal. App. 2d 672 (1962).

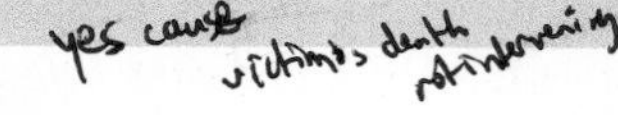

Food for Thought

In torts, an actor must take his victim as he finds him. Is the same thing true in the criminal law? For example, Joe Compton a hemophiliac, or "bleeder"—a hereditary condition of the blood that prevents coagulation and permits hemorrhages to continue unchecked. Defendant struck Compton on the jaw once with his fist. The injury would have caused only minor injuries to a normal person since it created only a slight laceration on the inside of the mouth. However, since defendant was a hemophiliac, the blow produced a hemorrhage lasting ten days and ending in death. Defendant swore that he was unaware that the deceased was a hemophiliac. Defendant argued that Gross' death was not caused by the blow, but by his disease. Given the victim's hemophilia, is defendant the cause of the death? *See State v. Frazier*, 98 S.W.2d 707 (1936); *Fine v. State*, 246 S.W.2d 70 (1952). Would you reach a different result if the victim, who had a heart condition, died as a result of excitement caused by a robbery? *See People v. Stamp*, 2 Cal. App. 3d 203 (1969).

Hypo 4: *The Cancer Patient*

The victim, who was a 70 year old rancher at the time of his death, was suffering from stomach cancer and receiving chemotherapy. Defendant came to the ranch and shot the victim, following which he was hospitalized for the abdominal wound. Although the chemotherapy had been effective in inhibiting the stomach cancer, it interfered with the healing of the abdominal wound and had to be discontinued. While the chemotherapy treatment was withheld, the cancer rebounded and rapidly grew, and the victim remained hospitalized until his death. Victim's death certificate listed the primary cause of death as tumor cachexia, a terminal state of cancer in which the body has a negative nitrogen balance, marked weight loss, propensity to infections, loss of strength, and a markedly diminished host resistance. The cancer had effectively overwhelmed the body's defenses. Was defendant the cause of the victim's death? *See In re Eliasen*, 668 P.2d 110 (Idaho 1983).

Hypo 5: *The Thieves and Their Victim*

Defendants robbed Stafford of his money and car, forced him to lower his trousers and take off his shoes, and then threw him out of a car onto the shoulder of a rural two-lane highway. His trousers were still around his ankles, his shirt was rolled up towards his chest, and he was shoeless. Defendants placed Stafford's shoes and jacket on the shoulder of the highway. Although Stafford's eyeglasses were in the vehicle, defendants (perhaps through inadvertence) did not give them to him. The temperature was near zero, visibility was occasionally obscured by heavy winds which intermittently blew previously fallen snow into the air and across the highway, and there was snow on both sides of the road. About an hour later, two cars approached from opposite directions. Immediately after passing the other car, a driver of one car saw Stafford sitting in the road in the middle of the northbound lane with his hands up in the air. The driver was travelling at 50 miles per hour, and he "didn't have time to react" before his vehicle struck Stafford. When the driver returned to try to offer assistance, the victim's trousers were down around his ankles and his shirt was up around his chest. Stafford was not wearing shoes or a jacket. At trial, the medical examiner testified that death had occurred fairly rapidly from massive head injuries. In addition, he found proof of a high degree of intoxication. Who is responsible for Stafford's death? The robbers? The passing driver? Both? *See People v. Kibbe*, 321 N.E.2d 773 (N.Y. 1974).

Hypo 6: *The Screaming Woman*

Defendant and Mary Berry got into a fight in a bar. Berry left the bar and got into a cab which she drove for a living. Defendant followed her, got into the driver's side, shoved Berry into the passenger's seat and drove away. Berry was hanging out of the passenger window, screaming "Help me, he's trying to kill me." Defendant was holding on to Berry, beating her and pulling her hair. Berry, by "fighting and kicking", managed to get one leg out of the passenger window even though defendant was "trying to pull her back in by her hair." Berry eventually fell out of the window, ran towards some oncoming cars, and finally managed to stop a station wagon. Berry grabbed the window of the station wagon, screaming "help me," and then fell beneath the wheels of the station wagon to her death. The driver of the station wagon, Vito Michielli, and his wife and two small children were driving home from a shopping trip when Berry and defendant approached his car forcing him to stop. The Michiellis' had reacted to Berry's pleas by locking all the doors and attempting to close the windows of the car. Indeed, Mr. Michielli had reached out of his window, pushed Berry away and sped off. Not until several days later, when a local newspaper reported the incident and Berry's tragic death, did Michielli realize that in leaving the scene his car had run over Berry. Who caused the death? *See Commonwealth v. Rementer*, 598 A.2d 1300 (Pa. Super. 1991).

Food for Thought

Eighteen-year-old Rachelle Cazin was pregnant with defendant's child. Cazin asked defendant to meet her in the woods near their home and to bring his gun. The couple met as planned and agreed to commit suicide together. Defendant testified Cazin put the gun in her mouth and he counted to three, but nothing happened. Defendant claims he then tried to talk Cazin out of shooting herself. As he walked away from her, he heard a gunshot. Bauer hid Cazin's body under a layer of brush, ran home, changed his clothes, unloaded the gun, threw the remaining shells outside and cleaned the gun. Did defendant cause Rachelle's death? *See State v. Bauer*, 471 N.W.2d 363 (Minn.App. 1991).

Hypo 7: *The Mother and the Abusive Lover*

Defendant, who had a daughter, moved in with Ed McCue who severely and brutally whipped the child. He would order the child to hold out her hand, and then he would slap her. Then he would say, "Where's your baby doll?" When the child reached for it, there would be a loud slap. A neighbor testified that his tone of voice was "crafty, nauseating." One night, McCue whipped the baby until 11:00pm. Defendant asked McCue to stop, but the whipping continued and he dragged "the baby up and down the hall beating her." Defendant pleaded with the neighbors not to call the police telling them that she loved "Eddie" and that they must have been imagining that the beatings were more severe than they actually were. Defendant explained that McCue was worried over some difficulty at work and was bothered by the heat. Later, McCue struck the child with blows which ripped the infant's liver and tore the mesentery, a fatty, vascular tissue supporting the colon. Hemorrhaging ensued and the baby began vomiting. Defendant took the baby to the doctor where she died. The child had multiple bruises from head to foot, including both arms, both legs, back, front and face. Defendant stated that she loved the child and was never unkind to her, and, if she had thought McCue's discipline of Terry too severe, she would have left him. Did defendant conduct cause the death? *See Palmer v. State*, 164 A.2d 467 (Md. 1960).

Hypo 8: *The Asphyxiated Widow*

Defendant beat and raped Elizabeth Winslow, an 85-year-old widow, for whom he had previously done yard work. She suffered a broken arm, a broken rib, bruises on her face, neck, arms, trunk and inner thighs, and lost her will to live. A day or so later, Mrs. Winslow was being served lunch. For approximately 20 minutes a nurse's aide was feeding her small portions of pureed food on a spoon, which Mrs. Winslow was accepting without choking or gagging in any way. She eventually spit out some vegetables, which the aide interpreted to mean that Mrs. Winslow did not want any more. The aide then noticed that Mrs. Winslow had stopped moving her mouth. The nurse's aide summoned the nurses who determined that Mrs. Winslow had died. The autopsy revealed that Mrs. Winslow died of asphyxiation, which resulted from six ounces of food being aspirated in her trachea. There were internal abdominal bruises around the colon and kidney, a broken rib, and facial bruises, but none of these injuries of themselves caused her death. However, the mechanics of clearing the trachea when food enters requires a sufficient volume of air to push the food out of the trachea and back into the mouth, thus preventing asphyxiation. The pain associated with a broken rib generally inhibits deep breathing which limits the amount of air available to the lungs. The volume of food lodged in Mrs. Winslow's trachea was very large and would have been difficult for a normal, healthy person to expel. Is defendant criminally responsible for Mrs. Winslow's death? *See People v. Brackett*, 510 N.E.2d 877 (Ill. 1987).

Hypo 9: *The Inmate*

As Charles Gardner, an inmate at the California Medical Facility, walked down a first-floor corridor, he was stabbed 11 times by defendant Menefield. Nevertheless, he was able to grab a knife that an assailant had left on the floor. In pursuit of defendant, Gardner staggered some distance up a flight of stairs to the second floor, where he plunged the knife into the chest of a prison guard, Officer Patch. Patch died within the hour at the prison clinic, Gardner shortly afterward. Is Menefield criminally responsible for Officer Patch's death? *See People v. Roberts*, 826 P.2d 274 (Cal. 1992).

Food for Thought

A fire erupted in a six-story warehouse operated by defendant Deitsch Textile Corporation in Brooklyn. While those who worked on the ground floor escaped to safety, two employees were trapped on the sixth floor. One was eventually rescued. The other, Nathaniel Logan, died. No cause for the fire was ever determined. On the day of the fire, a shipment of elastic material was delivered to the warehouse and employees were in the process of carrying it up to the sixth floor. Fire escapes were available, but they were blocked with bales of stored materials. Can it be said that the supervisors, who allowed the bales to be placed in front of the fire escapes, caused Logan's death? *See People v. Deitsch*, 97 A.D.2d 327, 470 N.Y.S.2d 158 (1983); *People v. Warner-Lambert Co.*, 51 N.Y.2d 295, 414 N.E.2d 660 (1980).

People v. McGee

31 Cal. 2d 229, 187 P.2d 706 (1947).

SCHAUER, JUSTICE.

Defendant and one Linck went to the club rooms of a fraternal organization in San Pedro, had two drinks at the bar, then entered the card room. Linck joined in a card game (with persons with whom defendant had no previous acquaintance) for 15 or 20 minutes. Defendant took Linck's place at the card table when Linck went to the bar, where he remained for about 15 minutes. Defendant then came from the card room and he and Linck went out of the club. They immediately returned to the card room because Linck believed he had left $40 on the card table. Linck asked, "Gentlemen, do you know what became of the money I left on the table?" One of the players pointed to defendant. Linck asked defendant, "Hank, did you take it?" or "Did you play?" Linck "understood him (defendant) to say yes" and Linck and defendant left the card room. As they walked through the bar, which was dimly lighted, defendant shot deceased in the abdomen. As a result of hemorrhage from the bullet wound deceased died the next day.

Defendant contends that the trial court erred by excluding evidence which would have tended to show that the proximate cause of Rypdahl's death was not the bullet wound but the manner in which the wound was treated. In 8 A.L.R. at page 516 the general rule as to criminal responsibility of one who wounds another, for the death of the victim, is stated as follows: "When a person inflicts a wound on another which is dangerous, or calculated to destroy life, the fact that the negligence, mistake, or lack of skill of an attending physician or surgeon contributes to the death affords no defense to a charge of homicide." Following this general rule it has been held that where the wound inflicted by the accused operates as a cause of death, the fact that the malpractice of attending surgeons may have had some causative influence will not relieve the accused from full responsibility for the ultimate result of his act. On the other hand, in qualification of the rule, it is said that "Where a person inflicts on another a wound not in itself calculated to produce death, and the injured person dies solely as a result of the improper treatment of the wound by an attending physician or surgeon, the fact that the death was caused by medical mistreatment is a good defense to a charge of homicide." On this subject it has been said to be "the proper", and probably generally accepted, view that mere negligence (in the treating of a wound) is no defense even though it is the sole cause of death because it is a foreseeable intervening cause. But death caused by grossly improper treatment is not the proximate consequence of the defendant's injury unless the injury is an actual contributing factor at the time of death, because such treatment is an unforeseeable intervening cause. The evidence as to the nature of the wound inflicted by defendant and the treatment thereof is as follows:

An autopsy was performed after the body had been embalmed. The autopsy surgeon testified that the bullet had grazed the liver, gone through the pancreas and spleen, and come to rest behind the upper pole of the left kidney; that there was "profuse hemorrhage throughout the course of the wound"; and that such hemorrhage was the immediate cause of death. In the opinion of the surgeon the gunshot wound was such that "If it was not controlled (by hemostasia, gauze packing, etc.) it would be only a matter of an hour, or an hour and a half, before there would be a profuse hemorrhage sufficient to cause death" and the anterior incision permitting such control was made "Within at least two hours after the wound." (the hospital records show that such incision was not made until some 12 hours after deceased was shot and 11 hours after his admission to the hospital.) The autopsy surgeon also found a posterior incision starting two inches to the left of the spine and following the course of the lower rib for 4 inches. The purpose and time of making this incision and the person by whom it was made, do not appear from the record.

The evidence disclosed the following situation: Defendant, without aiming and without intending to shoot Rypdahl, unlawfully, or "without due caution and circumspection," discharged a pistol which was pointed toward Rypdahl. The immediate result of this unlawful or incautious act was the wounding of Rypdahl. The direct result of the wound was "profuse hemorrhage" which would be "sufficient to cause death" if it was not promptly controlled. Having thus set in motion the events which culminated in Rypdahl's death, defendant departed. The surgeon in whose care Rypdahl was promptly placed neglected for more than ten hours, grossly contrary to good surgical practice, to control the hemorrhage. We assume further that Rypdahl's life might have been saved by prompt and proper surgical treatment. But defendant cannot complain because no force intervened to save him from the natural consequence of his criminal act. The factual situation is in legal effect the same, whether the victim of a wound bleeds to death because surgical attention is not available or because, although available, it is delayed by reason of the surgeon's gross neglect or incompetence. The delay in treatment is not in fact an intervening force; it cannot in law amount to a supervening cause.

For the reasons above stated the judgment and the order denying defendant's motion for new trial are affirmed. The attempted appeal from the order denying his motion in arrest of judgment is dismissed.

Hypo 1: *Negligent Medical Intervention*

Defendant stabbed Daniel Smith in the abdomen. Smith was rushed to the hospital. During the initial stages of the operation, the surgeons discovered that Smith also had an incarcerated hernia. After they had sutured the wounds and completed the stomach operation, the surgeons proceeded to correct the hernia. During this phase of the operation "the body was turning blue and there was no pulse, which means the person went into cardiac arrest." Smith then suffered a loss of oxygen to the brain and massive brain damage. He died a month later without ever regaining consciousness. At the time of death, the stomach wound had completely healed. Dr. Di Maio conceded that the chances were that, if the hernia operation had not been performed, the patient would have survived. Under the circumstances, should defendant's stab wound be regarded as the legal cause of death? *See People v. Stewart*, 40 N.Y.2d 692, 358 N.E.2d 487 (1976).

Food for Thought

The victim was stabbed in the abdomen by the defendant during a robbery. The stabbing necessitated an operation which resulted in complications including abdominal distention. As a result of the victim's post-operative condition, tubes were inserted through the victim's nostrils and into his stomach. The victim was disoriented, uncooperative and confused and pulled out the tubes on several occasions. Finally, he pulled out a tube, gagged and asphyxiated. Did defendant cause the victim's death? *See Commonwealth v. Cheeks*, 223 A.2d 291 (Pa. 1966); *United States v. Hamilton*, 182 F. Supp. 548 (D.D.C. 1960).

Hypo 2: *More on Negligent Medical Care*

Defendants were charged in the savage beating of Glen "Bear" Albea, a member of a drug ring headed by defendant Bowie in the Bronx. Essentially, defendant beat Albea with a baseball bat for 20–30 minutes, breaking several of his bones and splattering his blood at the scene. He later died at the hospital of complications stemming from the beating. Subsequent negligent treatment at the hospital may have contributed to Albea's death. When Albea developed malignant hyperthermia, a "possibly hereditary" reaction to anesthesia, his blood pressure dropped precipitously. Surgeons rushed to open his chest and perform cardiac massage. In doing so, they inadvertently punctured his lung, requiring three sutures to close the wound. Albea never recovered consciousness. The cause of death was septicemia, a bacterial infection resulting from "blunt force injuries of the head and extremities with surgical intervention." *See People v. Bowie*, 200 A.D.2d 511, 607 N.Y.S.2d 248 (1994).

Food for Thought

Defendant inflicted a mortal wound on Charles Cronkite. When Cronkite arrived at the hospital emergency room, he was comatose, but had some slight reaction to stimuli. Within minutes his condition deteriorated. He became totally unresponsive and remained so thereafter. He was placed on a respirator and various drug therapies were undertaken without result. On the following day, he was totally areflexic—completely unresponsive to all stimuli. His respiration and blood pressure were artificially supported. Two electroencephalograms (EEGs) were reported to be "flat." Dr. Meyer Rosenberg, chief of neuro-surgery at the hospital, pronounced Cronkite's condition to be cerebral death. Shortly thereafter the victim's mother signed a consent and Cronkite's kidneys and spleen were removed for donation. As Cronkite lay dying, his doctors decided to remove his kidneys and spleen for transplant and then disconnected his life support systems. Defendant contends that the doctor's actions were the cause of death and that he is not criminally responsible. Is defendant right? *See People v. Bonilla*, 95 A.D.2d 396, 467 N.Y.S.2d 599 (1983).

Hypo 3: *The Suicide Machine*

Marjorie Miller suffered from multiple sclerosis, and her condition had deteriorated to the point that she used a wheelchair and was confined to bed or to a wheelchair, did not have the use of her legs or her right arm, had only limited use of her left arm, and had problems talking and breathing. Miller contacted defendant, a champion of physician-assisted suicide, and he agreed to assist her in taking her life by hooking her up to his "suicide machine." The machine consisted of a needle to be inserted into a blood vessel that could convey various chemicals into the bloodstream. One of the chemicals was methohexital, a fast-acting barbiturate that quickly depresses respiration. A large dose can cause the recipient to stop breathing. After defendant inserted the needle into a vein in Ms. Miller's arm, he tied strings to two of her fingers. The strings were attached to clips on the tubing connected to the needle. Defendant instructed Ms. Miller how to pull the strings so as to allow the drugs to flow into her bloodstream. Ms. Miller followed defendant's instructions and died as a result of a lethal dose of methohexital. Is defendant criminally responsible for "causing" death when he provided deceased with the means by which she killed herself, but she performed the fatal final act? *See People v. Kevorkian*, 517 N.W.2d 293 (Mich. App. 1994).

Food for Thought

Defendant stabbed Amelia Robinson with a three-inch pocket knife following a fist fight on the victim's front porch. On arrival at the hospital, Robinson was found to be suffering from a stab wound to the upper abdomen and was in respiratory distress, with unstable vital signs and severe internal bleeding. On transfer to an operating table she suffered cardiac arrest attributable to an extreme loss of blood. Her left chest was opened, intravenous blood was supplied, and a heart massage was successful in re-establishing a heartbeat. Robinson languished for days when the surgical team and the I.C.U. physician decided that, despite all extraordinary measures, Robinson was beyond medical help and would surely die within three to five days. That evening, some 70 days after her initial wounding, she expired. Later, it was learned that a nurse stated "in sum and substance that she turned off the ventilator and the drips because somebody had to have the balls to do it." Does the nurse's action relieve defendant of liability? *See People v. Vaughn*, 152 Misc. 2d 731, 579 N.Y.S.2d 839 (1991).

Executive Summary

Proof of Causation. In order to convict a defendant of a "result" crime (*e.g.*, murder), the prosecution must show that defendant acted with the necessary *mens rea*, and committed any required acts or acted with any necessary attendant circumstances, but also that defendant caused the required result (the death of the victim).

Major Themes

a. Conduct Versus Result Crimes—Some crimes require only an *actus reus* committed with the required *mens rea*. Other crimes are "result" crimes which require that defendant "cause" some result. In some instances, it is not difficult to determine whether a defendant caused a particular result. In other instances, the "cause" of death may be less clear, as when "intervening factors" intrude between the act and the death.

b. Result Crimes and the Justifications for Punishment—In Chapter 1, we examined some of the justifications for imposing punishment under the criminal law—retribution, restraint, deterrence (both general and specific) and rehabilitation. The fact that defendant "caused" the prohibited result is a factor to be taken into account in deciding on the appropriate level of punishment. In other words, a defendant might be regarded as causing greater harm, and therefore as more deserving of punishment, when defendant actually commits murder (as opposed to attempting to commit murder).

"Year-and-a-Day" Rule. At common law, defendant's conduct could not be deemed to be the "cause" of a homicide unless the victim died within a year and a day following the defendant's acts. Even though defendant might not have been guilty of homicide, if the victim failed to die within a year-and-a-day, defendant might have been convicted of other crimes such as attempted murder, assault or battery.

MPC and Causation. The Model Penal Code provides that causation exists when conduct is the cause of a result, and either "it is an antecedent but for which the result in question would not have occurred," or "the relationship between the conduct and result satisfies any additional causal requirements imposed by the Code or by the law defining the offense." However, subject to some exceptions, when "purposely or knowingly causing a particular result is an element of an offense, the element is not established if the actual result is not within the purpose or the contemplation of the actor." Again, with exceptions, when "recklessly or negligently causing a particular result is an element of an offense, the element is not established if the actual result is not within the risk of which the actor is aware or, in the case of negligence." When "causing a particular result is a material element for which absolute liability is imposed by law, the element is not established unless the actual result is a probable consequence of the actor's conduct."

Actual Cause or Legal Cause. Even though a defendant may be the "actual cause" of a result (as exemplified by the "but for" test), courts also require proof that defendant was the "legal cause" of death. The concept of "legal cause" has been formulated in different ways, including "proximate cause."

Intervening Causes. Many jurisdictions distinguish between different types of "intervening causes." In general, an "independent intervening cause" breaks the chain of causation unless it was "foreseeable." A "dependent intervening cause" does not break the chain of causation unless it is regarded as "abnormal." Different jurisdictions also impose other limitations on whether an independent cause breaks the chain of causation.

MPC Approach to Intervening Causes. The Model Penal Code takes a similar approach, focusing on whether the result is "too remote or accidental in its occurrence to have a just bearing on the actor's liability or on the gravity of his offense." *See* MPC § 2.03(2)(b).

For More Information

- AMERICAN LAW INSTITUTE, MODEL PENAL CODE AND COMMENTARIES, Part I, § 2.03, Comments at 253–266 (1980).
- JOHN M. BURKOFF & RUSSELL L. WEAVER, INSIDE CRIMINAL LAW: WHAT MATTERS AND WHY 63–80 (2d ed. 2011).
- WAYNE R. LAFAVE, SUBSTANTIVE CRIMINAL LAW §§ 6.3–6.4 (6th ed. 2017).

Test Your Knowledge

To assess your understanding of the material in this chapter, click here to take a quiz.

Chapter 5

Complicity

A. Accomplice Liability

Whether they are referred to as accomplices, accessories, or aiders-and-abettors, every jurisdiction has statutory provisions that punish actors whose only relationship to a criminal offense is that they provided assistance to the principal offender.

Take Note

Take particular note of the different categories of "principals" and "accessories" that existed at common law (e.g., principals in the first degree, principals in the second degree, accessories before the fact, and accessories after the fact). Although most jurisdictions do not maintain all of these categories today, it is important to understand the historical distinctions, and the distinctions between the categories.

1. Principals & Accessories

a. Merger of Principals & Accessories

Standefer v. United States

447 U.S. 10 (1980).

Mr. Chief Justice Burger delivered the opinion of the Court.

At common law, the subject of principals and accessories was riddled with "intricate" distinctions. In felony cases, parties to a crime were divided into four distinct categories: (1) principals in the first degree who actually perpetrated the offense; (2) principals in the second degree who were actually or constructively present at the scene of the crime and aided or abetted its commission; (3) accessories before the fact who aided or abetted the crime, but were not present at its commission; and (4) accessories after the fact who rendered assistance after the crime was complete. By contrast, misdemeanor cases "did not admit of accessories [sic] either before or after the fact"; instead, all parties to a misdemeanor, whatever their roles, were principals.

Because at early common law all parties to a felony received the death penalty, certain procedural rules developed tending to shield accessories from punishment. Among them was the rule that an accessory could not be convicted without the prior conviction of the principal offender. Under this rule, the principal's flight, death, or acquittal barred prosecution of the accessory. If the principal were pardoned or his conviction reversed on appeal, the accessory's conviction could not stand. In every way "an accessory followed, like a shadow, his principal."

This procedural bar applied only to the prosecution of accessories in felony cases. In misdemeanor cases, where all participants were deemed principals, a prior acquittal of the actual perpetrator did not prevent the subsequent conviction of a person who rendered assistance. In felony cases a principal in the second degree could be convicted notwithstanding the prior acquittal of the first-degree principal. Not surprisingly, considerable effort was expended in defining the categories—in determining, for instance, when a person was "constructively present" so as to be a second-degree principal. In the process, justice all too frequently was defeated.

To overcome these judge-made rules, statutes were enacted in England and in the United States. In 1848 the Parliament enacted a statute providing that an accessory before the fact could be "indicted, tried, convicted, and punished in all respects like the Principal." As interpreted, the statute permitted an accessory to be convicted "although the principal be acquitted." Several state legislatures followed suit. In 1899, Congress joined this growing reform movement with the enactment of a general penal code for Alaska which abrogated the common-law distinctions and provided that "all persons concerned in the commission of a crime, whether it be felony or misdemeanor, and whether they directly commit the act constituting the crime or aid and abet in its commission, though not present, are principals, and to be tried and punished as such."

The enactment of 18 U.S.C. § 2 in 1909 was part and parcel of this same reform movement. The language of the statute, as enacted, unmistakably demonstrates the point: "Whoever directly commits any act constituting an offense defined in any law of the United States, or aids, abets, counsels, commands, induces, or procures its commission, is a principal." The statute "abolished the distinction between principals and accessories and made them all principals." Read against its common-law background, the provision evinces a clear intent to permit the conviction of accessories to federal criminal offenses despite the prior acquittal of the actual perpetrator of the offense. It gives general effect to what had always been the rule for second-decree principals and for all misdemeanants.

Food for Thought

As noted, the law continues to make distinctions between "principals" and "accessories after the fact." Why do you think that jurisdictions have maintained the "accessory after the fact" category when they have abolished the "principal in the second degree" and "accessory before the fact" categories?

With the enactment of that section, all participants in conduct violating a federal criminal statute are "principals." As such, they are punishable for their criminal conduct; the fate of other participants is irrelevant.

Points for Discussion

a. Merger

The merger of principals and accessories has occurred in all American jurisdictions. One significant exception, however, is for accessories after the fact. When an actor assists another *only* after the substantive criminal offense has taken place (e.g. harboring a fugitive after a bank robbery), that offense does *not* merge with the principal offense, bank robbery.

b. Acquittal of Principal

In *Standefer*, the Court concluded that an aider-and-abettor could be held culpable for a criminal offense (bribery) for which the principal had previously been acquitted. Does this make sense to you? *Standefer* dismissed concerns, observing that "while symmetry of results may be intellectually satisfying, it is not required."

Food for Thought

Is it fair to treat accomplices as if they had actually committed the criminal act in question themselves? Is a "getaway driver" just as culpable as a bank robber? How about the actor who simply arranges to provide the getaway car? Is the conduct of all accomplices (and principals) really equally blameworthy?

c. Significance of the Merger of Principals & Accessories

The merger of principals and accessories has created some significant procedural problems in criminal trials and criminal pretrial procedure. For example, what kind of notice (if any at all) must a defendant receive as to whether or not he or she is going to be tried as a principal and/or as an accessory? And when must or should that notice be received?

Baker v. Alaska

905 P.2d 479 (Alaska Ct. App. 1996).

MANNHEIMER, JUDGE.

Baker and two friends, John Stanfill and Jason Frazier, decided to get some free pizzas by telephoning a Pizza Hut restaurant, ordering pizzas for home delivery, and then robbing the delivery person when he came to deliver their order. Baker's first attack on his conviction concerns the issue of whether he acted as a principal or an accessory in this robbery.

Stanfill, testifying under a grant of immunity, admitted taking part in the robbery. He described the planning of the robbery and the role each person played in the crime. Stanfill phoned in the pizza order and told the restaurant to deliver the pizzas to a neighboring apartment building. The three friends then stationed themselves near the entrance to this building. Stanfill waited on the stairs, Frazier near the door, and Baker in the hallway. Stanfill and Frazier had bandannas over their faces for concealment; Baker wore a dark blue ski mask. The delivery person, James Seymour, arrived with the pizzas but was unable to find the person who had placed the order. As Seymour turned to leave, the three robbers made their move. Seymour testified he was struck by a man who emerged from beneath a set of stairs. He described his assailant as a light-complexioned black male wearing a one-holed dark blue ski mask and dark gloves. Seymour fell to the ground, dropping the pizzas. The man continued to hit Seymour. After the third blow, Seymour shouted to his assailant that he could take the pizzas. In a blur, Seymour saw someone kneel down, take the pizzas, and flee the building. Seymour was never able to positively identify the person who hit him.

Seymour's testimony that he was struck by a man who emerged from underneath the stairs, in combination with Stanfill's description of where each of the three men waited (Stanfill on the stairs, Frazier near the door, and Baker in the hallway), tended to identify Baker as the robber who struck Seymour—the robber whom Seymour saw emerge from "beneath the stairs". Moreover, when Stanfill was asked, "What happened right when the robbery took place?", Stanfill replied that he "saw the pizzas fall to the ground" and that he and Frazier grabbed the pizzas and ran. This response again raised the inference that Baker had been the one who physically accosted Seymour. However, Stanfill was never asked directly whether Baker was the one who hit Seymour.

Frazier, who testified as part of a plea bargain, also admitted taking part in the robbery. He recounted that it was Baker who first proposed the robbery and that it was Stanfill who left the apartment and placed the call to Pizza Hut. Frazier corroborated Stanfill's description of each man's location as they waited for the pizza delivery person to arrive. Like Stanfill, Frazier never directly testified that it was Baker who struck Seymour. Frazier did say that, as Seymour turned to leave the building with the undelivered pizzas, Frazier and Stanfill "grabbed the pizza, and we ran. Then all three of us ran back to Stanfill's apartment." Frazier stated that the three men set about eating the pizzas until Stanfill's mother returned home and told the men to leave.

Baker did not testify at trial, but his attorney suggested that Baker had not participated in the robbery. The defense attorney argued that Stanfill and Frazier might be lying about Baker's involvement in order to shield an unidentified friend and in order to obtain favorable treatment for their own crimes. Toward the end of Baker's trial, the question arose whether the jury should be instructed on accomplice liability. Included among the jury instructions was instruction number "9" relating to accomplice liability. The jurors were told that, if they found that one or more of the witnesses were accomplices to the crime under consideration, then they should view the testimony of these witnesses with distrust.

Baker's attorney voiced no objection when the trial judge declared his intention to give the jury this accomplice liability instruction. Nevertheless, Baker now argues on appeal that the jury's receipt of this instruction prejudiced the fairness of his trial. Baker points out that the accomplice liability instruction could play two roles during jury deliberations. First, the instruction informed the jury of the circumstances under which Stanfill and Frazier should be considered "accomplices", thus obliging the jury to view their testimony with distrust. Second, the instruction informed the jury of the circumstances under which Baker could be held accountable for Stanfill's and Frazier's conduct. To the extent that Instruction 9 filled the first of these roles, Baker contends that it was unnecessary. To the extent that Instruction 9 filled the second of these roles, Baker contends that it deprived him of a fair trial by allowing the jury to convict him of robbery under a complicity theory even after the prosecutor announced that the State viewed Baker as a "principal", not an "accomplice". Baker asserts that the fairness of his trial was prejudiced when the prosecutor, during final argument, suggested to the jury that Baker could be convicted of robbery even if the State failed to prove that Baker was the man who struck Seymour, so long as the State proved that Baker was one of the three robbers.

The common-law distinction between principals and accessories was abrogated in Alaska almost 100 years ago. At common law, a person who personally committed the *actus reus* of the crime was a "principal in the first degree". Any person who was present at the commission of the crime and who aided or abetted the commission of the crime was a "principal in the second degree". Anyone who aided or abetted the crime before it was committed and who was not present at the commission of the crime was an "accessory before the fact".

At common law, "the distinction between principals in the first degree and those in the second degree was one of fact rather than of legal consequence". A defendant who was indicted as a principal in the first degree could be convicted even though the proof established that he acted as a principal in the second degree, and vice-versa. It was not necessary for the indictment to disclose whether the defendant was a principal in one degree or the other. Conviction could be obtained although the proof established that the one charged as abettor was in fact the perpetrator, while the other was present aiding and abetting him.

However, the common law required that an indictment clearly specify whether a defendant acted as a principal or an accessory. A defendant might escape criminal liability altogether by creating a reasonable doubt as to whether he had been a principal or an accessory (i.e., whether he had been present at the commission of the crime or not). The statutory abrogation of the distinction between principals and accessories was intended to change this rule of pleading and to avoid this potential result.

Applying these common-law definitions to Baker's case, if Baker was one of the three men who waited in ambush for the pizza delivery person, then he was a principal in the robbery. If Baker either struck the delivery person or helped to carry away the pizzas, he was a principal in the first degree—since the *actus reus* of robbery requires both an assault and the taking (or attempted taking) of property. If Baker was present but only provided aid or encouragement to the enterprise, then he was a principal in the second degree. The common law saw no legal distinction here. A common-law indictment would not have needed to specify which of these roles Baker played. At trial, as long as the State established that Baker was present at the commission of the robbery and either personally performed some part of the *actus reus* or aided or abetted those who did, Baker could be convicted of the robbery.

For almost a century, Alaska law has recognized no distinction between principals and accessories—no distinction in the manner they are charged, tried, or punished. Both this court and the Alaska Supreme Court have repeatedly declared "that a defendant charged as a principal may be convicted as an accessory, and the converse is also true." When the Alaska Legislature revised the criminal code in 1980, it abandoned the labels "principal" and "accessory" in favor of a more straightforward approach. Former AS 12.15.010, the statute abrogating the distinction between principals and accessories, was repealed. In its place, AS 11.16.100 states the general rule of criminal liability without reference to the terms "principal" and "accessory": "A person is guilty of an offense if it is committed by the person's own conduct, or by the conduct of another for which the person is legally accountable under AS 11.16.110, or by both." The legislative commentary to this statute explains "AS 11.16.100 restates the basic principle of criminal law that criminal liability is based upon conduct. When liability exists, it is immaterial whether the elements of the crime are satisfied by the defendant's own behavior, or by the behavior of another person for which he is accountable, or by both."

Thus, while Alaska law no longer uses the terms "principal" and "accessory" to describe the theories under which a person may be held responsible for a crime, the revised criminal code was not intended to reintroduce the distinctions between principals and accessories before the fact. When an indictment alleges that the defendant personally committed the acts constituting the crime, the defendant is on notice that he or she may also be convicted under a theory of accomplice liability if the State establishes that the defendant is responsible for the acts of others under AS 11.16.110.

Baker nevertheless argues that once the prosecutor announced his theory of the case (that Baker was the one who struck the robbery victim), Baker was entitled to have his case submitted to the jury without reference to any theory of accomplice liability. Baker relies on *Michael v. State*, 805 P.2d 371 (Alaska 1991). In that case, defendant and his wife were indicted for assaulting their child. Because it was unclear which spouse actually attacked the child, Michael was indicted both as a principal and, alternatively, as an accessory. At trial, the State relied on yet another theory of culpability: that even though Michael did not strike the child and even though he neither aided nor abetted his wife's abuse of the child, [he could] be convicted of assault for failing to perform his parental duty to protect the child from the assaults of others. Michael objected that this theory of liability varied materially from the theories considered by the grand jury. The superior court overruled Michael's objection and, ultimately, convicted him. The supreme court overturned the conviction, ruling that, even though "Michael's failure to carry out his parental duty was clear from the grand jury evidence", "the fact remains that the grand jury made no such charge in the indictment." *Michael*'s indictment could not be construed to include this theory.

Baker's case presents no issue outside traditional notions of accomplice liability. Under either of the State's theories of this case—that is, whether Baker personally struck the pizza delivery man or was present only to help carry away the pizzas—Baker was a "principal" in the commission of the robbery. Even at common law, Baker would have no variance claim. He certainly has none now. We reject Baker's argument that the indictment failed to put him on notice that he might be convicted under the rules of accomplice liability codified in AS 11.16.110(2).

As a fall-back position, Baker asserts that he was misled when the prosecutor announced at trial that the State viewed Baker as a principal, not an "accomplice". There are two problems with this argument. First, Baker's trial attorney never suggested that he was surprised or prejudiced when the jury was asked to consider Baker's accomplice liability. Second, even under the State's primary theory of the crime, to evaluate Baker's guilt, the jury would necessarily have to receive instruction on the rules governing Baker's liability for Stanfill's and Frazier's acts of taking the property.

For these reasons, we hold that it was not error for the trial judge to instruct the jury on accomplice liability and it was not error for the prosecutor to argue that theory of liability to the jury.

The judgment of the superior court is AFFIRMED.

Points for Discussion

a. Distinguishing *Michael*

Do you think that the *Baker* Court did an adequate job of distinguishing the *Michael* decision in which the defendant was held not to have had sufficient notice of the theory under which he was going to be prosecuted? Why is this case different from the situation presented in *Michael*?

> **Food for Thought**
>
> Is it fair for a defendant who has been indicted as a principal to be convicted as an accessory? Is that what happened in this case? Was there fair notice to the defendant, Baker, that this might happen?

b. Prejudice to *Baker*

Baker held that "under either of the State's theories of this case—that is, whether Baker personally struck the pizza delivery man or was present only to help carry away the pizzas—Baker was a 'principal' in the commission of the robbery." If that is true, why wasn't Baker prejudiced when it was argued to the jury that he might be guilty as an *accessory*—not as a principal?

New Hampshire v. Sinbandith

143 N.H. 579, 729 A.2d 994 (1999).

BROCK, C.J.

Defendant, Bounleuth "Pheng" Sinbandith, was convicted after a jury trial in Superior Court (O'Neill, J.) on seven indictments relating to the sale of a controlled drug. We affirm.

Corporal Nightingale, an undercover narcotics detective, conducted an investigation in Laconia. In the course of that investigation, Nightingale made arrangements with the defendant for purchases of crack cocaine. On four occasions, Nightingale gave defendant a sum of money, and defendant drove to a separate location. On all but one of these occasions either Elizabeth Begin, defendant's girlfriend, or Velvet Weeks, another associate of defendant, accompanied defendant to the other location. Upon defendant's return, Weeks would hand Nightingale or another undercover officer a quantity of crack cocaine. On one occasion, defendant, apparently unable to acquire the cocaine, returned the money to Nightingale. A grand jury returned seven indictments against defendant. Three of the indictments (sale indictments) alleged that defendant "DID, IN CONCERT WITH AND AIDED BY ANOTHER, KNOWINGLY SELL OR DISPENSE A QUANTITY OF THE CONTROLLED DRUG, CRACK COCAINE." Each of these indictments contained a caption at the top corner of the page that read "ACCOMPLICE TO SALE OF A CONTROLLED DRUG."

Defendant argues that the trial court should have dismissed the sale indictments for failure to allege the proper *mens rea*. At the close of the State's case, defendant moved to dismiss the accomplice indictments, arguing that they were defective because they alleged that he had acted "knowingly" when accomplice liability requires the *mens rea* of "purposely." The State countered that the "in concert with and aided by another" language of the indictments charged defendant either as a principal or as an accomplice, and that "knowingly" was the proper *mens rea* to charge defendant as a principal. Conceding that he had notice that he was being charged as either a principal or an accomplice, defendant asserted that the State nevertheless was required to allege that he had acted purposely. The trial court denied the motion.

An indictment is constitutionally sufficient if it provides enough information to apprise defendant of the charges with adequate specificity to prepare a defense and to be protected against double jeopardy. To this end, the indictment must contain the elements of the offense and enough facts to notify defendant of the specific charges. An indictment that alleges principal liability without reference to accomplice liability sufficiently charges defendant as an accomplice. Neither defendant nor the State contests that an indictment charging defendant solely as an accomplice must allege the appropriate elements of the accomplice liability statute, including the proper *mens rea*. Defendant does not argue on appeal that "purposely" is the proper *mens rea*. Rather, acknowledging that the jury could have convicted him as an accomplice had the State charged him as a principal, he argues that the State chose to charge him as an accomplice, and as such was required to allege purposeful conduct.

We have consistently stated that language in an indictment alleging that a defendant acted "in concert with" another is sufficient to charge defendant both as a principal and as an accomplice. Thus, the indictments in this case provided sufficient notice to defendant that he was being charged as a principal. Indeed, defendant conceded that he had such notice. That they were captioned as accomplice charges does not alter the explicit language of the indictments that put defendant on notice that he could be convicted as either a principal or an accomplice. Having sufficiently charged defendant as a principal, the indictments provided defendant adequate notice to prepare a defense to principal or accomplice liability. Therefore, we affirm the trial court's denial of the motion to dismiss.

Affirmed.

Points for Discussion

a. Sinbandith as Accomplice

Sinbandith held that the defendant was charged *both* as a principal and an accomplice. If that was *not* the case—if Sinbandith had been charged *only* as an accomplice—what result should the court have reached?

b. Notice for Accomplice Charge

Do you think that the court was correct in concluding that the language "in concert with" gave defendant adequate notice that he was being charged as a principal when the indictment was captioned "ACCOMPLICE TO SALE OF A CONTROLLED DRUG"?

Hypo 1: *Scope of Accomplice Responsibility*

Defendant is charged with being an accomplice to murder. The evidence shows that the perpetrator used defendant's shotgun in committing the murder, and that defendant loaned him the shotgun just prior to the murder. Is defendant an accomplice to murder if defendant loaned the gun based on the perpetrator's assertion that he was going duck hunting? Suppose, instead, that defendant knew that the perpetrator was going to commit a murder?

Hypo 2: *Jury Instructions*

Ronald Soares and Hollie Suratt were each charged with a *separate* count of assault resulting from their *separate* altercations with a store detective and a store clerk, respectively, who observed them shoplifting. The trial court gave the jury an accomplice instruction as to each defendant, i.e. the jury was instructed that it could find that each defendant acted as an accomplice in the other defendant's assault. Since each charge involved different facts with different victims, was the giving of an accomplice instruction reversible error? *State v. Soares*, 72 Haw. 278, 815 P.2d 428 (1991).

---

2. The Act of Aiding or Encouraging

It is critically important—but often difficult to determine—just how much participatory or encouraging activity on the part of an alleged accomplice is necessary to establish the *actus reus* of aiding or encouraging a principal. It is clear that an individual's "mere presence" at the scene of a crime does not (in and of itself) suffice to make an actor an accomplice. The cases that follow explore what more is required.

Lane v. Texas

991 S.W.2d 904 (Tex. Ct. App. 1999).

PER CURIAM.

Appellant James William Lane was convicted of the offense of aggravated robbery of an elderly person. The issue is whether the trial court erred in refusing Lane's request to instruct the jury that a particular witness, Patricia R., was an accomplice as a matter of fact. Patricia and Kris Shank, who lived together, went to Lane's house. Lane quickly recruited Patricia, Shank and Anna Eason to rob 71-year-old Hillard Doss. Lane drove Shank and Eason to the scene of the robbery. Patricia was a passenger in Lane's truck. Lane and Patricia waited in the truck while Shank and Eason went to commit the crime. At first the pair returned to the truck without having carried out the plan, but after encouragement from Lane, they went back to Doss's home, again gained entrance, committed the robbery, and returned to Lane's truck for their get-a-way.

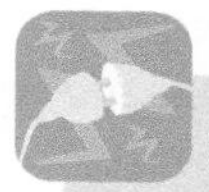

Make the Connection

Just as the *actus reus* requirement is important with regard to other crimes, it is equally important with regard to the crime of complicity. However, with complicity, the focus is a bit different. Whereas burglary focuses on whether defendant broke and entered the dwelling of another with the intent to commit a felony, complicity focuses on whether defendant provided aid, encouragement or assistance to someone who committed the burglary crime.

At trial, both Patricia and Eason testified against Lane. Shank's testimony from a prior hearing was also introduced against Lane. The jury was instructed that Shank and Eason were accomplices as a matter of law. Therefore, the only testimony linking Lane to the crime, except Patricia's, came from accomplices. Because a conviction cannot be had on uncorroborated accomplice testimony, and the only evidence corroborating Lane and Shank's testimony came from Patricia, the issue of whether she is an accomplice is crucial to the case. Were the jury to have found that Patricia was an accomplice, there would be no corroborating evidence upon which a conviction in this case could be upheld against a sufficiency challenge.

The court of criminal appeals set out the general requirements for a finding that a witness is an accomplice: "A person who is merely present at the scene of the offense is not an accomplice; an affirmative act or omission is required. An accomplice participates before, during, or after the commission of the crime—presence at the scene of the offense is not required—though one is not an accomplice for knowing about a crime and failing to disclose it, or even concealing it." We have also repeatedly stated that a person is an accomplice if he or she could be prosecuted for the same offense as the defendant, or a lesser included offense.

To make the determination, the entire record is examined for the issue of whether or not a particular witness is an accomplice. In doing so, we eliminate from our consideration evidence from the accomplice witness and examine the remaining evidence to ascertain if there is inculpatory evidence, that is, evidence of incriminating character, which tends to connect defendant with the commission of the offense. An accomplice witness charge is required if raised by the evidence.

Patricia was present when Lane told Shank and Eason that he knew of an old man who carried lots of money in cash. Patricia was present when Lane, Shank and Eason planned the crime. Patricia was a passenger in Lane's truck as he drove Shank and Eason to the scene of the crime and let them out of the truck to commit the crime. Patricia remained present in the truck when Shank and Eason returned the first time without committing the robbery, traveled back to Lane's residence, and were there encouraged by Lane to begin anew and carry out the robbery plan. Patricia was a passenger in the truck when Lane again drove Shank and Eason to the crime scene. Patricia was present when the pair returned to the truck after committing the robbery, and accompanied the trio back to Lane's residence. At the residence, she was present when the other three divided up the cash taken from Doss. She also saw Shank toss his dirty clothing into the bathtub.

Taking these facts as a whole and measuring them against the criteria espoused by the court of criminal appeals, we do not believe that an issue as to whether Patricia was an accomplice was raised by the evidence. Patricia was present during the entire series of events that night and knew full well what the other three actors were doing. However, Patricia committed no affirmative act in furtherance of the crime. Further, her omission of not stopping the crime and not alerting anyone about the crime was not an omission that our laws have criminalized so that she would become an accomplice by omission. In sum, we disagree with Lane's characterization of the facts. There was simply no accomplice witness fact issue raised for the jury to decide. We therefore hold that the trial judge did not err in denying Lane's request for an instruction on Patricia's status as an accomplice.

The judgment of the trial court is *affirmed*.

Points for Discussion

a. Model Penal Code

Consider the MPC's provisions relating to accomplice liability:

§ 2.06. Liability for Conduct of Another; Complicity.

(1) A person is guilty of an offense if it is committed by his own conduct or by the conduct of another person for which he is legally accountable, or both.

(2) A person is legally accountable for the conduct of another person when:

(a) acting with the kind of culpability that is sufficient for the commission of the offense, he causes an innocent or irresponsible person to engage in such conduct; or

(b) he is made accountable for the conduct of such other person by the Code or by the law defining the offense; or

(c) he is an accomplice of such other person in the commission of the offense.

(3) A person is an accomplice of another person in the commission of an offense if:

(a) with the purpose of promoting or facilitating the commission of the offense, he

(i) solicits such other person to commit it, or

(ii) aids or agrees or attempts to aid such other person in planning or committing it, or

(iii) having a legal duty to prevent the commission of the offense, fails to make proper effort so to do; or

(b) his conduct is expressly declared by law to establish his complicity.

(4) When causing a particular result is an element of an offense, an accomplice in the conduct causing such result is an accomplice in the commission of that offense if he acts with the kind of culpability, if any, with respect to that result that is sufficient for the commission of the offense.

(5) A person who is legally incapable of committing a particular offense himself may be guilty thereof if it is committed by the conduct of another person for which he is legally accountable, unless such liability is inconsistent with the purpose of the provision establishing his incapacity.

(6) Unless otherwise provided by the Code or by the law defining the offense, a person is not an accomplice in an offense committed by another person if:

(a) he is a victim of that offense; or

(b) the offense is so defined that his conduct is inevitably incident to its commission; or

(c) he terminates his complicity prior to the commission of the offense and

(i) wholly deprives it of effectiveness in the commission of the offense; or

(ii) gives timely warning to the law enforcement authorities or otherwise makes proper effort to prevent the commission of the offense.

(7) An accomplice may be convicted on proof of the commission of the offense and of his complicity therein, though the person claimed to have committed the offense has not been prosecuted or convicted or has been convicted of a different offense or degree of offense or has an immunity to prosecution or conviction or has been acquitted.

Food for Thought

Why do you suppose that Texas follows the rule that "a conviction cannot be based on uncorroborated accomplice testimony"? Does that rule make sense? What if there are no eyewitnesses? Does that mean that there can be no conviction?

b. Mere Presence

Do you agree that there is no evidence that Patricia did *anything* other than be present as the robbery took place? Does it matter that the court acknowledged that Lane "recruited" Patricia to participate in the robbery and that she "went along for the ride?"

c. Convicted Accomplice

Do you think that it made any difference that the court was deciding Patricia's accomplice status only to determine whether her testimony was admissible to uphold Lane's conviction? If Patricia had been charged and convicted as an accomplice, do you think that the appellate court would have upheld her conviction?

Hypo 1: *The Judge and the Seducer*

Ross seduced Annie Skelton, a sister of the Skelton brothers (Robert, John, James and Walter), as well as of Judge Tally's wife. When the Skeltons and Tally learned about the seduction from letters written by Ross to Annie, the Skelton brothers immediately decided to kill Ross. In an effort to escape, Ross left town in a hack headed for Stevenson (18 miles away), intending to catch a train to Chattanooga. The Skelton brothers set off in pursuit of Ross and eventually succeeded in killing him. When the Skelton brothers left, Judge Tally knew that they intended to kill Ross. Under which of the following factual scenarios is Judge Tally guilty of complicity? A) He silently wishes and hopes that the Skelton brothers kill Ross, but does nothing to help. B) He tells friends that he hopes that the Skelton brothers kill Ross. C) He pays for the rental of a horse on which one of the Skelton brothers rode. D) He spends several hours at the telegraph office in order to prevent others from sending a telegraph to warn Ross. E) He actually prevents Ross's brother from sending a telegram warning Ross that the Skelton brothers are pursuing him. F) He sends a telegram to friends in Stevenson asking them to make sure that Ross is not warned that the Skeltons are in pursuit. *See State ex rel. Martin v. Tally*, 102 Ala. 25, 15 So. 722 (1894).

Hypo 2: *Accomplice Liability and Ineffective Assistance*

In the prior Hypo, for any acts which you deem sufficient to impose accomplice liability on Judge Tally, does it matter whether the acts actually helped the Skelton brothers bring about Ross's death? For example, suppose that: A) Judge Tally spent several hours at the telegraph office (in an effort to prevent anyone from sending a telegram to warn Ross), but no one tried to send a telegram; B) Although Judge Tally sent a telegram to friends urging them to make sure that Ross was not warned about the Skelton brothers, Ross's friends tried to warn him.

Food for Thought

Defendant's boyfriend brutally shook her 3-month old son for three minutes thereby causing the boy's death. During the shaking, defendant stood by doing nothing. In regard to defendant's liability: A) Is she an accomplice to manslaughter (defined as a "recklessly" committed homicide)? B) Might she be responsible for the death on a non-accomplice theory? *See State v. Walden*, 306 N.C. 466, 293 S.E.2d 780 (1982).

Hypo 3: *The Security Guard*

Defendant shot at his girlfriend and then threw the gun away near his apartment complex. Later, he returned to retrieve the gun, but could not find it. He blamed a security guard for taking it. Defendant told two of his friends, Richardson and Waller, while he was visiting Richardson's apartment in the same complex, that he was angry at the security guard for taking his gun, and that he was "going to kill his ass." Defendant asked them to go with him to shoot the guard, but both declined. In fact, Richardson tried to talk defendant out of shooting the guard. Defendant then left Richardson's apartment while Richardson and Waller remained. Later, they heard shots fired outside. Defendant then returned to the apartment, holding a rifle, which was smoking. Defendant said, "I got him." Defendant was charged with first-degree murder for shooting the security guard to death. Were Richardson and Waller defendant's accomplices? *California v. Hypolite*, 2005 WL 758440 (Cal.App. 2 Dist. 2005).

New Hampshire v. Merritt

143 N.H. 714, 738 A.2d 343 (1999).

BRODERICK, J.

Defendant Kevin Merritt and his girlfriend, Kelly Higgins, had been living together for eighteen months. Higgins was in dire financial straits and did not have any source of income. On December 18, 1995, they went shopping and Higgins made numerous, expensive purchases with credit cards belonging to Frances Driscoll and Marjorie Dannis. That afternoon, Driscoll noticed that her purse, which contained her Jordan Marsh and Visa credit cards, was missing. Driscoll was the only person authorized to use the cards. Afterwards, Higgins used Driscoll's Jordan Marsh card to buy jewelry at a store in the Fox Run Mall. Several days later, a sales clerk gave a written statement to the police that "on 12/18, in the fine jewelry department in Jordan Marsh, Higgins was accompanied by defendant and made a purchase using a credit card" belonging to Driscoll. There was no other evidence concerning the jewelry purchase.

Around 3:17 p.m. after defendant tried on clothes at American Eagle Outfitters in the mall, Higgins purchased men's pants and shirts with Driscoll's Visa card. The sales clerk testified that defendant "was standing right next to Higgins" while the sale was taking place and that defendant basically "did all the talking." Later that afternoon, defendant and Higgins looked at a men's gold bracelet at Hannoush Jewelers in the mall. The sales clerk testified that she had "a long conversation" with defendant about the bracelet and that they "went back and forth" over the price for twenty-five minutes. Defendant successfully negotiated a lower price, and Higgins bought the bracelet with the Visa card. Subsequently, Higgins and defendant patronized Whitehall Jewelers and said they were interested in buying defendant a gold bracelet. The sales clerk testified that she interacted principally with defendant and that he was interested in negotiating a lower price. The clerk obtained the manager's approval to reduce the price, which made defendant "very, very excited." He shook her hand "for helping him pick out such a real nice piece that he was very anxious to have." At 3:52 p.m., Higgins bought the bracelet with Driscoll's Visa card. Defendant and Higgins then proceeded to Prelude Jewelers in downtown Portsmouth. The store owner testified that defendant and Higgins had been in the store previously and admired a women's diamond ring. During the December 18 visit, the owner heard defendant tell Higgins he wanted to buy her the ring but that he would need to use her credit card. At 4:53 p.m., Higgins again used Driscoll's Visa card and purchased the ring.

Around 5:30 p.m., a short distance from Prelude Jewelers, a man stole Marjorie Dannis' purse from her car. Her purse contained her Visa and Mastercard, which only she was authorized to use. At 7:30 p.m., a male matching defendant's description tried on a pair of men's work boots at J.C. Penney in the Fox Run Mall, and the woman with him purchased them with Dannis' Mastercard. At 7:44 p.m., defendant and Higgins purchased a men's diamond ring from the store's jewelry department, with Higgins using Dannis' Mastercard. The sales clerk spoke mainly with defendant. When the sale was completed, the clerk gave defendant, who identified himself as "Kevin Johnson," a diamond certificate. At trial, the clerk explained that the individual named in the certificate was entitled to free diamond cleanings and to trade the diamond for one of greater value in the future. When Dannis' purse was later recovered at a gas station in Portsmouth, it contained a diamond certificate and part of a receipt.

Based on this evidence, defendant was indicted on four charges of fraudulent use of credit cards, alleging that he acted in concert with Higgins: the first count was for the Jordan Marsh jewelry; the second count was for the purchases at American Eagle, Hannoush Jewelers, and Whitehall Jewelers; the third count related to the ring purchased at Prelude Jewelers; and the fourth count identified the ring bought at J.C. Penney. The jury found defendant guilty on all four counts, and this appeal followed.

The indictments alleged that defendant "acted in concert" with Higgins in the fraudulent use of the Driscoll and Dannis credit cards. The trial court instructed the jury that "acting in concert" meant accomplice liability. Under our Criminal Code, a person may be legally accountable for the conduct of another person if "he is an accomplice of such other person in the commission of an offense." A person is an accomplice if, "with the purpose of promoting or facilitating the commission of an offense, he aids or agrees or attempts to aid such other person in planning or committing it."

In reviewing the sufficiency of the evidence, "we must determine whether, based upon all the evidence and all reasonable inferences from it, when considered in a light most favorable to the State, any rational trier of fact could have found beyond a reasonable doubt that the defendant was a voluntary and active participant" in each of the fraudulent credit card transactions.

Defendant contends that no rational jury could have found him guilty as an accomplice for the Jordan Marsh jewelry purchase because he was merely present in the store and did not take affirmative steps to satisfy the *actus reus* requirement. We agree. The crime of accomplice liability necessitates "some active participation by the accomplice." Mere presence at the scene of a crime is insufficient. Defendant's presence, however, can be sufficient if it was intended to, and does, aid the primary actor. Thus, defendant's presence may constitute aiding and abetting when it is shown to encourage the perpetrator or facilitate the perpetrator's unlawful deed. Moreover, the circumstances surrounding defendant's presence at the scene may warrant a jury inference beyond a reasonable doubt that he sought to make the crime succeed.

The State relies on *State v. Laudarowicz*, 142 N.H. 1, 694 A.2d 980 (1997), to argue that defendant's act of accompanying Higgins to Jordan Marsh, given the relationship between the two, was sufficient to constitute "encouragement" and trigger accomplice liability. *Laudarowicz*, however, is inapplicable because defendant in that case conceded that he aided the principal and challenged only the evidence of his intent. Moreover, we relied upon substantial evidence other than defendant's presence at the scene to support his convictions. Here, there is no evidence that defendant did anything other than accompany Higgins to the Jordan Marsh store. The record does not indicate where defendant was when the jewelry was purchased, nor does it reflect that he did or said anything which could be construed as aiding Higgins.

The State also relies on evidence of defendant's other conduct on the day in question to support the inference that he engaged in similar conduct at Jordan Marsh. Assuming that defendant's subsequent conduct might be relevant to his intent, we conclude that the State failed to present sufficient facts to satisfy the *actus reus* element of accomplice liability. Accordingly, we reverse defendant's conviction with respect to count one. Defendant next contends that no rational jury could have found him guilty as an accomplice for the remaining transactions because he did not participate in them. He asserts no *actus reus* was proven. We disagree.

With respect to *actus reus*, the jury could have found that defendant aided Higgins in these other transactions. In each transaction, defendant dominated the exchange with the sales clerk, especially at the moment the sale was completed. Moreover, defendant selected, or assisted Higgins in selecting, the merchandise that was ultimately purchased. Although the evidence shows that defendant did not present the cards or sign any of the credit card slips, we are satisfied that the jury could have found he aided Higgins in committing fraud by picking out the merchandise and distracting the sales clerks from closely examining the credit cards while the merchandise was being purchased. Furthermore, we conclude that a rational jury could have reasonably decided, viewing the totality of the evidence in the State's favor, that all rational inferences other than guilt had been excluded beyond a reasonable doubt. Defendant and Higgins had a relationship and were living together. Moreover, the credit cards were used six times in six stores, over a period of about five and a quarter-hours, for merchandise totaling over $2,600. In addition, jewelry and clothes purchased fit the defendant or were items defendant expressed an intent to give to Higgins. Finally, the defendant gave a false name on the diamond certificate that accompanied.

Food for Thought

Do you agree that there is no evidence of an accomplice *actus reus* sufficient to tie Merritt to the Jordan Marsh episode? Isn't the evidence clear (or, put another way, couldn't a reasonable jury find from the evidence) that Merritt and Higgins were on a shopping spree with stolen credit cards?

Affirmed in part; reversed in part; remanded.

Point for Discussion

Lack of Knowledge

With respect to the other transactions, would Merritt be guilty if he simply did not know that Higgins was using stolen credit cards? Is there any evidence at all that he did know? Does it matter in this analysis that Merritt and Higgins were living together?

Make the Connection

Related to the crime of complicity is the crime of conspiracy. In general, conspiracy involves an agreement between two or more persons (although an actual agreement between the two may not be required) to commit an unlawful act or a lawful act by unlawful means. One who is complicit in a crime may have explicitly or implicitly engaged in a conspiracy to commit that crime, and the prosecution could have argued that Merritt and Higgins were involved in a conspiracy to commit the crime. However, we will examine the requirements of conspiracy in Chapter 7.

Food for Thought

Washington Tazwell and Wilson Kealey were convicted of the burglary of a store with intent to steal, and Zeke Hall was charged as an accessory before the fact. The evidence shows that Hall provided Tazwell and Kealey with burglary tools before they went to the store, but that the two found more convenient and more suitable tools when they arrived. As a result, they did not use Hall's tools. Is Hall nonetheless an accomplice to the burglary? *State v. Tazwell,* 30 La. Ann. 884 (1878).

Hypo 1: *Intoxicated Driver and Borrowed Car*

Defendant allowed his friend to borrow his car, even though he knew the friend was legally intoxicated. An hour later, while defendant was sound asleep in his bed, the friend caused an accident that resulted in the death of a passenger in another car. Consider whether defendant is an accomplice to the crime of: a) Murder (defined as a purposeful or knowing homicide); or b) Manslaughter (defined as a reckless or negligent homicide). See *People v. Marshall*, 362 Mich. 170, 106 N.W.2d 842 (1961).

Hypo 2: *Narcotics Information*

An undercover police officer told defendant that he was interested in buying "hash." In an effort to be helpful, defendant told the officer that a man by the name of Craig "deals heavily in narcotics." Defendant gave the officer Craig's address and told the officer to go to that address. The officer succeeded in purchasing narcotics from Craig who was arrested and charged with narcotics trafficking. Can defendant be convicted of complicity in the offense? Would it make any difference regarding defendant's criminal liability whether: a) Defendant was working with the seller and receiving a kickback on all sales? b) Defendant was simply trying to help the buyer find what he wanted? *See State v. Gordon*, 32 N.Y.2d 62, 295 N.E.2d 777, 343 N.Y.S.2d 103 (N.Y. App.1973).

Food for Thought

A foreign national, a famous saxophonist, was given permission to enter the United States on condition that he take no employment, paid or unpaid. In violation of the condition, the saxophonist performs for compensation at a local night club. Which of the following have committed the *actus reus* of accomplice liability (assuming, of course, that they have the necessary *mens rea*): a) Customers who go to the club, pay the admission price, and clap between sets; b) A magazine owner and editor who attends the concert as a spectator, having paid for his ticket, who does not clap, but does not protest. Afterwards he publishes in his magazine a most laudatory description, fully illustrated, of the concert. *See Wilcox v. Jeffrey* [1951] 1 All E.R. 464.

Hypo 3: *Accomplices to Rape*

You are an assistant district attorney, and police officers have reported to you that a victim, Jane Roe, was raped in a pool hall by two men: John Smith and Joe Doe. While the rapes were taking place, three other individuals were present: a bartender, Jerry Ames, and two individuals drinking at the bar, Bob Baker and Cathy Cox. Ames watched the rapes take place and yelled at the rapists to "stop," but when they did not listen to him, he did nothing to stop them nor did he call the police. Baker watched the rapes and yelled at Smith and Doe to encourage them to commit the assaults. Cox watched the rapes and said nothing. Should Ames, Baker and Cox be charged as accomplices in the rape? Why?

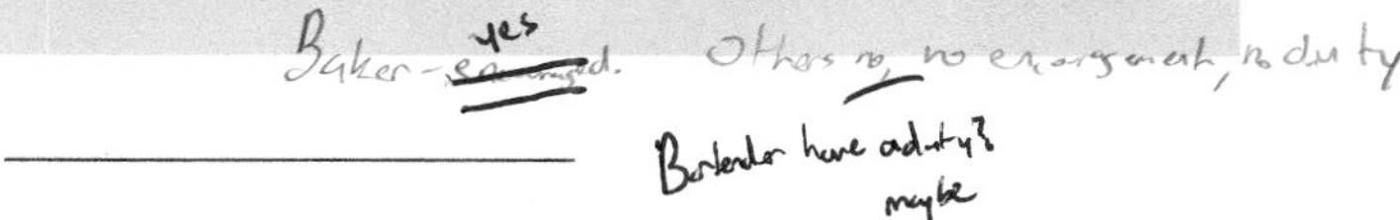

3. Intent to Promote or Facilitate a Crime

The *mens rea* of accomplice liability is often described as having two separate (and independent) components: (1) the intent to assist a principal actor in committing the target act; and (2) the intent that the principal actually commit that act. In most jurisdictions, this intent can be (and often is) implied from a person's actions.

Hawaii v. Soares

72 Haw. 278, 815 P.2d 428 (1991).

LUM, CHIEF JUSTICE.

Holiday Mart store detective Mitchell Tam observed appellants [Ronald Soares and Hollie Suratt] placing several cartons of cigarettes into a shopping cart. Tam then saw Soares place the cigarettes into a large handbag. Appellants left the store, with Suratt carrying the bag, without paying for the cigarettes. Outside the store, Tam approached appellants, identified himself, showed his badge, and told appellants that they were under citizen's arrest for shoplifting. As Soares turned towards him, Tam grabbed Soares. During their struggle, the back of Soares' head hit Tam in the mouth causing Tam to release Soares. Soares then fled. While struggling with Soares, Tam instructed Conway Marks, a Holiday Mart clerk who was assisting Tam, to stop Suratt from leaving the area. Marks blocked Suratt's escape by standing directly in front of her path. After unsuccessfully attempting to push Marks out of her way, Suratt tricked Marks into looking the other direction and then fled with the bag.

We conclude that the court's accomplice jury instruction was a misstatement of Hawaii law. The accomplice instruction provided: All persons who are present and participate in the commission of a crime are responsible for the acts of each other done or made in furtherance of the crime. It is not necessary to prove that each one committed all of the acts of the crime. Each person who does one act which is an ingredient of the crime or immediately connected with it is as guilty as if he or she committed the whole crime with his or her own hands.

Food for Thought

What acts, if any, gave rise to an implication of criminal intent in these circumstances?

Section 702–222 requires that to be guilty as an accomplice, a person must act with the intent of promoting or facilitating the commission of the crime. The court's accomplice instruction clearly does not contain such a *mens rea* element. The court's instruction implies that a person merely needs to be present and participate in an act of the crime to be guilty as an accomplice. Under the court's accomplice instruction, the State is relieved from its burden of proving that appellants acted with the requisite intent.

Accordingly, appellants' convictions are reversed and the cases are remanded for new trials.

Point for Discussion

Proper Instruction

If the jury had been properly instructed on intent, what do you think the result would have been in the prior case?

Hypo 1: *The Burglary*

David Vaillancourt and a friend, Richard Burhoe, were seen standing on the front porch of a home, ringing the doorbell and conversing with one another for ten minutes. When there was no answer, the pair walked around the side of the house where Burhoe allegedly attempted to break into a basement window. Tipped off by a suspicious neighbor, the police arrived and arrested Vaillancourt and Burhoe as they were fleeing the scene. Burhoe is charged with attempted burglary. If you are the prosecutor, what kind of proof would you use to show that Vaillancourt was an accomplice? *See New Hampshire v. Vaillancourt*, 122 N.H. 1153, 453 A.2d 1327 (1982).

Hypo 2: *The Mother and the Murdering Husband*

Carol Hoffman, was murdered by her husband David because she refused to have sexual relations with him. While he was choking her, he began to believe he was "doing the right thing" and that, to get "the evil out of her," he had to dismember her body. After Carol was dead, David did the dismembering in the bathtub. Is David's mother an accomplice if: A) She had strained relations with Carol and told friends that she hated her. On the morning of the murder, David told his mother that he was going to "put her to sleep" and then he would then have to dispose of the body. The mother replied that it would "be for the best." (David later testified that his mother thought that he was "kidding."); B) During the murder, the mother was asleep. However, when the mother woke up, she was adamant about shielding her granddaughter (the couple's older daughter) from witnessing the dismembering should she awake and try to use the bathroom. As a result, the mother decided to lie on a couch near the bathroom and keep watch for the granddaughter; C) Suppose that, instead of trying to protect the daughter against the trauma of witnessing the dismemberment, the mother was trying to protect her son from detection by preventing the daughter from becoming a witness to the crime. D) More generally, what kinds of proof might suffice to implicate the mother as an accomplice? What kinds of proof might tend to exonerate her from accomplice liability? *See State v. Ulvinen*, 313 N.W.2d 425 (Minn. 1981).

Hypo 3: *The Murdered Father and Husband*

Defendant Virginia's husband, Joe Davis, died of a shotgun wound outside his home. W. Day, defendant's acquaintance, committed the crime, and defendant was charged with complicity. The evidence showed that defendant had repeatedly expressed a desire to have her husband killed (claiming that he beat her), and that she had offered Day money to do the killing. Defendant's daughter, Angel, who was sexually involved with Day, independently asked Day to kill Davis because he was sexually assaulting her. When asked why he killed Davis, Day said: "Well, some of me wants to say about what he done to Angel, but I can't say that was the only reason. I don't believe if Virginia and them wouldn't have kept pressuring me about killing Joe or having someone kill Joe, I don't think I would have done it." An inmate at the jail testified that he asked defendant whether Virginia had anything to do with the killing of her husband. Day said, "No. She didn't have anything to do with it." On these facts, is defendant guilty as an accomplice? *State v. Davis*, 319 N.C. 620, 356 S.E.2d 340 (1987).

Food for Thought

Reconsider the case of the famous saxophonist who was given permission to enter the United States on condition that he take no employment, paid or unpaid. In violation of the condition, the saxophonist performs for compensation at a local night club. If the state wants to charge customers with "complicity" in the immigration violation, what will it need to show in terms of their *mens rea*? Does it seem fair or appropriate to impose accomplice liability on customers and spectators? Is the customer's participation a necessary predicate to the event? In a similar vein, although cock fighting is illegal (because it is deemed to be cruel to the animals who are bloodied and injured by the fights), some individuals still stage cock fights. Are they likely to do so without the customer base that pays for the tickets and, in regard to cockfighting, engages in illegal betting? *See Wilcox v. Jeffrey* [1951] 1 All E.R. 464.

Hypo 4: *The Housekeeper*

Gudelia Ramirez was found in a residence with a large amount of heroin when police arrived to execute a lawful search warrant for evidence related to a heroin-distribution operation. The State's evidence showed that, although Ramirez was not a "member" of the operation, she was aware of its existence, and she cooked and cleaned for the group that ran it. She was cooking dinner in the kitchen when heroin was cut and packaged on the kitchen table. However, her wages were those of a housekeeper and a cook. Under these circumstances: a) is there sufficient evidence to establish her culpability as an accomplice to the crime of possession of heroin? b) What if, instead of paying Ramirez an hourly rate, she is paid a percentage of the profits? *See Washington v. Amezola*, 49 Wash. App. 78, 741 P.2d 1024 (1987).

New York v. Kaplan

76 N.Y.2d 140, 556 N.E.2d 415, 556 N.Y.S.2d 976 (1990).

TITONE, JUDGE.

Defendant Murray Kaplan was convicted of first degree criminal sale of a controlled substance because of his involvement in a narcotics network which operated out of a garment business office located in the Empire State Building. His primary contention on appeal is that although the culpable state required for the commission of this crime is "knowledge," the trial court should have instructed the jury that defendant could not be held liable as an accomplice unless he acted with the specific intent to sell a controlled substance. We conclude that such an instruction is not required and that the conviction should be affirmed.

From 1986 to 1987, the police investigated a cocaine ring which operated out of an office maintained by defendant's cousin, Mike Kaplan, in the Empire State Building. Detective Janis Grasso, posing as a drug courier for "Ronnie" from Atlantic City, engaged in a series of transactions, primarily with Mike Kaplan. The charges against defendant were based on his actions on October 15, 1986, when, pursuant to a prior phone call, Grasso went to Kaplan's office to purchase 10 ounces of cocaine and found Kaplan, Kaplan's brother and defendant present. After introducing Grasso to the other two men, Mike Kaplan told defendant "to take care of the young lady." Defendant got off the couch, walked to a file cabinet in the room, removed a manila envelope from it, and placed it on the desk in front of Grasso. She took out $15,000 in prerecorded buy money and placed it on the table. Defendant picked up the money, took it over to the table and began counting it. At the same time, Grasso opened the manila envelope, took out a zip-lock plastic bag, and placed the drugs into her purse remarking that "it looks nice."

Defendant was subsequently charged with, *inter alia*, criminal sale of a controlled substance. Before the case was submitted to the jury, defense counsel asked the court to instruct the jurors that in order to convict defendant as an accomplice they must find that he had "specific intent" to sell a controlled substance, and that he had to "share the intent or purpose of the principal actors." The court denied defendant's request, noting that the mental culpability required for criminal sale was not "intent" but "knowledge" and, further, that the standard charge for accomplice liability requires proof that the defendant "intentionally aided" the other participants. Following the court's charge, which tracked the language of the applicable statutes, the jury found defendant guilty of criminal sale. The Appellate Division affirmed defendant's conviction.

Penal Law § 20.00 provides that a person may be held criminally liable as an accomplice when he performs certain acts and does so "with the mental culpability required for the commission" of the substantive crime. Despite this language, defendant argues that even though the substantive crime with which he was charged—criminal sale of a controlled substance—requires only knowledge,[3] the statute should be construed to require proof of a more exacting *mens rea*, namely specific intent to sell.

Under section 2 of the former Penal Law, a person could be convicted as a principal if he "aided and abetted in the commission of a crime". The former Penal Law, however, did not specifically state what type of acts were required for conviction. Consequently, in order to prevent the imposition of criminal liability for the principal's crime on someone who may have been merely present, the courts required proof that the aider or abetter "shared the intent or purpose of the principal actor."

Defendant's argument is that this "shared intent or purpose" test required proof that he acted with the specific intent to sell cocaine. However, any lack of clarity that previously existed under section 2 of the former Penal Law was eliminated by the adoption of section 20.00 of the revised Penal Law, which specifies that an accomplice must have acted with the "mental culpability required for the commission" of the particular crime. Further, we have already construed section 20.00 as not requiring specific intent within the meaning of Penal Law § 15.05(1) when the substantive crime does not involve such intent. Finally, the "shared intent or purpose" language from our earlier cases cannot be read for the proposition, advanced by defendant, that a specific wish to commit the principal's substantive crime is required in all circumstances, including those involving substantive crimes with mental states other than that defined in Penal Law § 15.05(1). Indeed, the "shared intent or purpose" test set forth in the case law merely establishes that acts undertaken in relative innocence and without a conscious design to advance the principal's crime will not support a conviction for accomplice liability. The same conclusion, however, is implicit in the specific requirement in Penal Law § 20.00

---

3 Penal Law § 220.43 provides, in pertinent part, that "a person is guilty of criminal sale of a controlled substance in the first degree when he knowingly and unlawfully sells". A person acts knowingly "when he is aware that his conduct is of such nature or that such circumstance exists". In contrast, a person acts intentionally "when his conscious objective is to cause such result or to engage in such conduct."

that the accomplice "solicit, request, command, importune, or intentionally aid" the principal, since all of the delineated acts import goal-directed conduct.

The distinction made here is a subtle, but important, one. It is well illustrated by our holding in *People v. Flayhart*, 72 N.Y.2d 737, 536 N.Y.S.2d 727, 533 N.E.2d 657, in which we concluded that the defendants could be guilty as accomplices to the crime of criminally negligent homicide under Penal Law § 125.10, even though neither defendant had the victim's death as a "conscious object". This result flowed naturally from the fact that both defendants could be found to have "failed to perceive a substantial and unjustifiable risk" of death—the "mental culpability required for the crime"—and that both engaged in deliberate conduct to advance the common enterprise, i.e., the egregious neglect of the victim.

For the same reasons, we reject defendant's argument that the crime of which he was convicted under the court's charge is indistinguishable from second degree criminal facilitation. A person is guilty of second degree criminal facilitation when "believing it probable that he is rendering aid to a person who intends to commit a class A felony, he engages in conduct which provides such person with means or opportunity for the commission thereof and which in fact aids such person to commit such class A felony". This statute was enacted to provide an additional tool in the prosecutorial arsenal for situations where the "facilitator" knowingly aided the commission of a crime but did not possess the mental culpability required for commission of the substantive crime. Additionally an "accomplice" and a "facilitator" are distinguishable in that the accomplice must have intentionally aided the principal in bringing forth a result, while the facilitator need only have provided assistance "believing it probable" that he was rendering aid.

Practice Pointer

In determining whether an individual is complicit in a crime, the prosecution sometimes will be able to obtain direct evidence of the individual's intent through, for example, a confession. More commonly, an individual's intent will be inferred from his or her conduct.

In defendant's case there was sufficient evidence for the jury to find that, knowing the substance in question was cocaine, defendant intentionally aided Mike Kaplan by delivering it to Detective Grasso. After being asked by Mike Kaplan to "take care of" Detective Grasso, defendant immediately went to a file cabinet drawer, retrieved a package containing cocaine, and gave the package to Grasso in exchange for money which defendant immediately began to count. That defendant neither negotiated nor arranged the transactions does not affect his liability as an accomplice, and the court was not required to include specific intent to sell as an element in its charge on accessorial liability. The elements were adequately conveyed when the court told the jury that it must find both that defendant acted with the specific intent required for the substantive offense, i.e., knowledge that the substance was cocaine, and that he "intentionally aided" the sale.

Order *affirmed.*

Point for Discussion

Specific Intent

If the court had ruled differently—if it had held that a specific intent to sell a controlled substance was required in order to support a conviction—was there sufficient evidence on the record to support a jury verdict based upon accomplice culpability? What was that evidence?

Food for Thought

Do you agree with the court that accomplice liability and criminal facilitation are distinguishable? How are they distinguishable?

Hypo 1: *The Execution*

Following an all-night dance at which a good deal of whisky was consumed, Rowe and Colvard got into an argument which continued for some time. Twice, Rowe raised his rifle, aimed it at Colvard, and then lowered it. The third time that Rowe raised the rifle, he fired it, killing Colvard. Consider the following facts and decide whether Hicks was complicit in the murder: A) Hicks sat and silently watched the entire series of events; B) Each time Rowe raised the rifle, Hicks laughed; C) Each time Rowe raised the rifle, Hicks not only laughed, but also yelled "Take off your hat and die like a man"; D) Prior to the killing, Hicks yelled to Rowe: "Go ahead and shoot him." *See Hicks v. United States*, 150 U.S. 442 (1893).

Hypo 2: *The Contrived Burglary*

Hayes agreed with Hill to burglarize a store. Hayes raised a store window and helped Hill slide through it. Hill then handed Hayes a 45-pound piece of meat through the window. Both men were captured within a matter of minutes. Hill was not arrested because he was the brother of the store's owner. The facts showed that Hayes had originally proposed the burglary. When Hill agreed to commit the crime, he had no intent to actually burgle the store, but simply wanted to trap Hayes. To this end, Hill alerted his brother, the store's owner, about the plan. Police were waiting to apprehend Hayes, and Hill knew that they were there when he entered the store. Can Hayes be an accomplice to the crime of burglary if Hill had absolutely no intention of actually burglarizing the store and in fact acted with the knowledge and consent of the store owner? *See State v. Hayes*, 105 Mo. 76, 16 S.W. 514 (1891).

Hypo 3: *More on Contrived Burglaries*

Wilson and Pierce agreed to burglarize a drugstore. Pierce helped Wilson enter the store. While Wilson was inside stealing cash, Pierce called the police. Pierce then helped the police track Wilson down. Pierce later testified that the sole reason for his participation in the burglary was to get even with Wilson, and to arrange for the police to "catch Wilson in the act." Can Wilson be convicted of burglary? Can Pierce be convicted as an accomplice? *See Wilson v. People*, 103 Colo. 441, 87 P.2d 5 (1939). Suppose that Wilson told Pierce that he planned to burglarize a store and asked Pierce for help. Pierce responded by giving Wilson a list of tools that would be needed, and by helping Wilson plan the crime. However, before the plan could be executed, Pierce told the police who were lying in wait when Wilson arrived. Wilson is charged with attempted burglary. Can Pierce be convicted as an accomplice?

Hypo 4: *Bystander or Accomplice?*

Corbin and Mitchell are charged with robbing Roosevelt in order to steal his paycheck. Corbin and Mitchell were to be paid $10 for their efforts. Mitchell claimed that he was just a bystander and that he did not (and never did) have any intention of robbing Roosevelt. However, following the attack, when Corbin dumped Roosevelt by the side of the road, Mitchell drove the car and stopped at Corbin's request to dump Roosevelt's body out. However, he did plead with Corbin not to kill Roosevelt. Afterwards, Corbin and Mitchell went off to a bar to drink. When they were apprehended a few hours later, they had spent $10 on drinks. Was Mitchell complicit in the robbery? *See State v. Corbin*, 186 S.W.2d 469 (Mo. 1945).

Food for Thought

In a "red-light district," a drug store regularly sells condoms. Known prostitutes frequently purchase condoms from the store, and some have negotiated bulk discounts. The store's owner is aware that the prostitutes are using the condoms in their trade. If prostitution is illegal in the jurisdiction, is the store owner an accomplice to prostitution? Could Planned Parenthood be convicted as an accomplice if it were distributing condoms to prostitutes to protect them against STDs?

Pennsylvania v. Potts

388 Pa. Super. 593, 566 A.2d 287 (1989).

BECK, JUDGE:

This is a direct appeal by Ernest Potts from a judgment of sentence of life imprisonment for the offense of murder of the first degree. Potts and David Owens met and drove in a car together to the residence of Michael Cunerd to inquire into an alleged burglary of Potts' apartment during which two pounds of marijuana, various articles of jewelry, and $400.00 in cash had been stolen. Potts testified that subsequent to the alleged burglary, Owens told him that Cunerd was the person who had burglarized his apartment. Potts and Owens successfully accosted Cunerd on a street corner near his residence. Potts exited his car and told Cunerd that he wanted to speak with him. Cunerd excused himself by claiming that he needed to first talk with a neighbor, but that he would return to speak with Potts subsequent to that conversation. Potts and Owens waited. When Cunerd returned, Potts asked him to get into his car and Cunerd obliged. A three-way conversation ensued during which Potts continually asked Cunerd if he had burglarized his apartment. Cunerd denied having committed the burglary, and Owens that Cunerd had committed the burglary. The three eventually reached a deserted area in southeastern Philadelphia known as the "Meadows". The conversation continued with Cunerd protesting his innocence and Owens periodically grabbing Cunerd's shoulders from behind and shaking him. Eventually, Potts ordered Cunerd from the car stating that he and Cunerd "were going to fight." Potts got out and confronted Cunerd. Ultimately, Potts pushed Cunerd onto the hood of the car. At this point, Owens exited the car. Cunerd jumped off the hood and ran with Owens in pursuit. Owens caught Cunerd within 100 yards and began to stab him in the back. When Cunerd had fallen, Owens pinned him with his knees and stabbed him more times. Potts contends that he watched the stabbing from a distance of approximately 30 feet. After the stabbing, Potts approached Owens and told him to "See if anything is in his pockets." Owens did so, and Potts claimed that he may have seen his wedding ring which was allegedly taken during the burglary. Owens also found a small spoon in the deceased's pocket which he placed in the deceased's mouth and thereafter kicked down his throat. At this point, Owens told him "Let's get the hell out of here. The _______ f_______ is dead." During this incident, Potts was armed with a pen-gun and Owens with a knife with a seven-inch blade. Potts contends that as he drove Owens advised that "If anything ever comes down on this, you don't know anything." Appellant contends that since his stated intention was to beat up the deceased, rather than to kill him, there was insufficient evidence to establish his intention to kill Cunerd, as required for conviction of murder of the first degree.

The Pennsylvania Crimes Code provides that for liability to attach for an offense, the offense must be committed by the person's own conduct or by the conduct of another person for which he is legally accountable, or both. A person is legally accountable for the conduct of another if "he is an accomplice of such other person in the commission of the offense." A person is an accomplice if "with the intent of promoting or facilitating the commission of the offense, he aids or agrees or attempts to aid such other person in planning or committing it."

Thus, to be convicted as an accomplice of the crime of murder of the first degree, a two-step analysis is required. The first step is to consider whether an accused possessed the requisite criminal intent. An accomplice's conduct need not result in the ultimate criminal offense. Rather, an accomplice is equally criminally liable for the acts of another if he acts "with the intent of promoting or facilitating the commission of an offense," and agrees or aids or attempts to aid such other person in either planning or committing the criminal offense. Thus in the instant case, because appellant has been convicted of murder of the first degree, the Commonwealth must have presented sufficient evidence to establish that he possessed the specific intent to facilitate the crime of murder. The next step is to examine the actions of the accused to determine whether such actions rise to the level of criminal activity, such that the accused has promoted or facilitated the commission of the crime, and, thus, may be held responsible as an accomplice to another's acts and the consequences of such acts. In order to establish the appellant's guilt on an accomplice theory, no agreement is required. Rather, the only requirement is that the accomplice have aided the principal. It is well settled that this requirement is satisfied by "the least degree of concert or collusion" between the accomplice and the principal.

In evaluating whether there was sufficient evidence to establish beyond a reasonable doubt that appellant possessed the intent to promote or facilitate Cunerd's death, the evidence presented and the inferences which follow from that evidence must be viewed in the light most favorable to the Commonwealth as the verdict winner below. From this record there was sufficient evidence for the fact finder to reject appellant's contention that he merely intended to beat up deceased, and to instead find that based upon appellant's actions, he intended to facilitate the killing of Cunerd. Appellant suggests that because he testified to wanting merely to beat Cunerd up and not to kill him, and since there was no evidence to the contrary, that the Commonwealth has failed to carry its burden of proving intent. However, the Commonwealth did offer contrary evidence through the testimony of William Dales, who testified that approximately two days prior to Cunerd's death, appellant told him that he was going to kill Cunerd. It is firmly established that where conflicting evidence is presented, it is the fact finder's duty to assess the credibility of the proponents of such evidence. It is clearly within the fact finder's province "to believe all, part, or none of the evidence presented." The jury thus was free to disbelieve that portion of appellant's confession which suggested that he only intended to hurt Cunerd and not to facilitate his death. Viewed in this light, and based upon the additional evidence adduced at trial regarding the events which occurred, the fact finder could have found beyond a reasonable doubt that appellant entertained the intent to promote or facilitate Cunerd's death.

We turn now to the second step of the analysis. The focus at this stage is whether appellant's conduct was sufficient to satisfy the mandates of accomplice liability delineated in the Crimes Code. It is clear that the jury could have found beyond a reasonable doubt that appellant promoted or facilitated Cunerd's death by aiding or agreeing or attempting to aid Owens in the killing and thus satisfied the "least degree of concert or collusion" standard. First, appellant admitted to knowing that earlier on the day of Cunerd's death, Owens had a knife with him. In addition, appellant admitted to carrying a pen-gun in his pocket and to driving the car to the "Meadows," which was described during the trial as a desolate, deserted area. Based upon the murky details presented regarding the actual stabbing, it was never proven who actually stabbed Cunerd. Even assuming that Owens stabbed Cunerd, the jury could still have found that appellant drove Cunerd to the deserted area and stood by and watched as Owens stabbed Cunerd twenty-nine times. In addition, appellant admitted that after the stabbing he suggested going through Cunerd's pockets to see if they contained any fruits from the burglary. This suggestion is clearly contrary to appellant's testimony that he feared Owens and was shocked by his killing of Cunerd.

The record discloses several contradictions between appellant's first statement to the police, his second statement to the police, and his testimony at trial. These contradictions could have persuaded the fact finder to disbelieve appellant when he contended that he only intended to beat up Cunerd and was surprised that Owens killed him. Instead, the fact finder may have believed that all of appellant's actions were in an effort to bring Cunerd to the "Meadows" so that Owens would kill him. Finally, appellant suggested that it was not until later that he realized that he had been set-up by Owens, and that it was probably Owens and Dales who had burglarized his apartment. This is inconsistent with appellant's statement to police that he may have seen his wedding ring which was stolen from his home pulled out of Cunerd's pocket when Owen's searched through it. If one of appellant's rings was in Cunerd's pocket, it does not make sense that appellant would believe that Cunerd was not involved in the burglary.

Based upon the evidence adduced at trial, Dales' testimony, and the inconsistencies contained in appellant's statements and trial testimony, there was clearly sufficient evidence, albeit circumstantial, to prove beyond a reasonable doubt that appellant facilitated or promoted Cunerd's death by providing aid to Owens in that effort.

Judgment of sentence affirmed.

Points for Discussion

a. Reconciling *Potts* & *Kaplan*

Potts concluded that to convict someone of murder as an accomplice in Pennsylvania, "the Commonwealth must have presented sufficient evidence to establish that defendant possessed the specific intent to facilitate the crime of murder." The *Kaplan* Court rejected the applicability of a "specific intent" requirement. Are these two decisions simply inconsistent with one another?

b. Conspiracy Liability

How, if at all, is accomplice liability in this case different from an actor's culpability as a co-conspirator? Could Potts and Owens have been convicted of conspiracy on these facts?

Food for Thought

Vicarious liability is unusual in the criminal law. As a general rule, an individual cannot be held liable for the conduct of another absent evidence of complicity. When vicarious liability can be imposed, criminal liability is imposed absent complicity. Why do legislatures and courts sometimes impose vicarious liability?

B. Vicarious Liability

Sometimes, an individual may be found guilty of criminal conduct based on the criminal actions of other persons, about which the individual may be unaware. This "vicarious liability" is most commonly employed against corporations and corporate agents. There are, however, limits to the scope of such culpability.

United States v. Park

421 U.S. 658 (1975).

MR. CHIEF JUSTICE BURGER delivered the opinion of the Court.

Acme Markets, Inc., is a national retail food chain with approximately 36,000 employees, 874 retail outlets, 12 general warehouses, and four special warehouses. Its headquarters, including the office of the president, respondent Park, who is chief executive officer of the corporation, are located in Philadelphia, Pa. In a five-count information filed in the United States District Court for the District of Maryland, the Government charged Acme and respondent with violations of the Federal Food, Drug and Cosmetic Act. Each count of the information alleged that the defendants had received food that had been shipped in interstate commerce and that, while the food was being held for sale in Acme's Baltimore warehouse following shipment in interstate commerce, they caused it to be held in a building accessible to rodents and to be exposed to contamination by rodents.

Acme pleaded guilty to each count of the information. Respondent pleaded not guilty. The evidence demonstrated that in April 1970 the Food and Drug Administration (FDA) advised respondent by letter of insanitary conditions in Acme's Philadelphia warehouse. In 1971 the FDA found that similar conditions existed in the firm's Baltimore warehouse. An FDA consumer safety officer testified concerning evidence of rodent infestation and other insanitary conditions discovered during a 12-day inspection of the Baltimore warehouse in November and December 1971. A second inspection of the warehouse had been conducted in March 1972. On that occasion the inspectors found that there had been improvement in the sanitary conditions, but that 'there was still evidence of rodent activity in the building and in the warehouses and we found some rodent-contaminated lots of food items.'

The Government also presented testimony by the Chief of Compliance of the FDA's Baltimore office, who informed respondent by letter of the conditions at the Baltimore warehouse after the first inspection.[4] There was testimony by Acme's Baltimore division vice president, who

4 The letter, dated January 27, 1972, included the following: "We note with much concern that the old and new warehouse areas used for food storage were actively and extensively inhabited by live rodents. Of even more concern

had responded to the letter on behalf of Acme and respondent and who described the steps taken to remedy the insanitary conditions discovered by both inspections. The Government's final witness, Acme's vice president for legal affairs and assistant secretary, identified respondent as the president and chief executive officer of the company and read a bylaw prescribing the duties of the chief executive officer. He testified that respondent functioned by delegating 'normal operating duties,' including sanitation, but that he retained 'certain things, which are the big, broad, principles of the operation of the company,' and had "the responsibility of seeing that they all work together.'

At the close of the Government's case in chief, respondent moved for a judgment of acquittal on the ground that 'the evidence in chief has shown that Mr. Park is not personally concerned in this Food and Drug violation.' The trial judge denied the motion, stating that *United States v. Dotterweich*, 320 U.S. 277 (1943), was controlling.

Respondent was the only defense witness. He testified that, although all of Acme's employees were in a sense under his general direction, the company had an 'organizational structure for responsibilities for certain functions' according to which different phases of its operation were 'assigned to individuals who, in turn, have staff and departments under them.' He identified those individuals responsible for sanitation, and related that upon receipt of the January 1972 FDA letter, he had conferred with the vice president for legal affairs, who informed him that the Baltimore division vice president 'was investigating the situation immediately and would be taking corrective action and would be preparing a summary of the corrective action to reply to the letter.' Respondent stated that he did not 'believe there was anything he could have done more constructively than what (he) found was being done.'

On cross-examination, respondent conceded that providing sanitary conditions for food offered for sale to the public was something that he was 'responsible for in the entire operation of the company,' and he stated that it was one of many phases of the company that he assigned to 'dependable subordinates.' Respondent was asked about and admitted receiving, the April 1970 letter addressed to him from the FDA regarding insanitary conditions at Acme's Philadelphia warehouse. In response to questions concerning the Philadelphia and Baltimore incidents, respondent admitted that the Baltimore problem indicated the system for handling sanitation 'wasn't working perfectly' and that as Acme's chief executive officer he was responsible for 'any result which occurs in our company.'

At the close of the evidence, respondent's renewed motion for a judgment of acquittal was denied. Respondent's counsel objected to the instructions on the ground that they failed fairly to reflect our decision in *United States v. Dotterweich* and to define "responsible relationship." The trial judge overruled the objection. The jury found respondent guilty on all counts of the information, and he was subsequently sentenced to pay a fine of $50 on each count. The

---

was the observation that such reprehensible conditions obviously existed for a prolonged period of time without any detection, or were completely ignored. We trust this letter will serve to direct your attention to the seriousness of the problem and formally advise you of the urgent need to initiate whatever measures are necessary to prevent recurrence and ensure compliance with the law."

Court of Appeals reversed the conviction and remanded for a new trial. That court viewed the Government as arguing 'that the conviction may be predicated solely upon a showing that respondent was the President of the offending corporation,' and it stated that as 'a general proposition, some act of commission or omission is an essential element of every crime.'

The question presented in *United States v. Dotterweich* was whether 'the manager of a corporation, as well as the corporation itself, may be prosecuted under the Federal Food, Drug, and Cosmetic Act of 1938 for the introduction of misbranded and adulterated articles into interstate commerce.' In *Dotterweich*, a jury had disagreed as to the corporation, a jobber purchasing drugs from manufacturers and shipping them in interstate commerce under its own label, but had convicted Dotterweich, the corporation's president and general manager. The Court of Appeals reversed the conviction on the ground that only the drug dealer, whether corporation or individual, was subject to the criminal provisions of the Act, and that where the dealer was a corporation, an individual connected therewith might be held personally only if he was operating the corporation 'as his 'alter ego." In reversing the judgment of the Court of Appeals and reinstating Dotterweich's conviction, this Court looked to the purposes of the Act and noted that they 'touch phases of the lives and health of the people which, in the circumstances of modern industrialism, are largely beyond self-protection.' It observed that the Act is of 'a now familiar type' which 'dispenses with the conventional requirement for criminal conduct—awareness of some wrongdoing. In the interest of the larger good it puts the burden of acting at hazard upon a person otherwise innocent but standing in responsible relation to a public danger.'

Central to the Court's conclusion that individuals other than proprietors are subject to the criminal provisions of the Act was the reality that 'the only way in which a corporation can act is through the individuals who act on its behalf. At the same time, the Court was aware of the concern which was the motivating factor in the Court of Appeals' decision, that literal enforcement 'might operate too harshly by sweeping within its condemnation any person however remotely entangled in the proscribed shipment.' A limiting principle, in the form of 'settled doctrines of criminal law' defining those who 'are responsible for the commission of a misdemeanor,' was available. In this context, the Court concluded, those doctrines dictated that the offense was committed 'by all who have. a responsible share in the furtherance of the transaction which the statute outlaws.'

The rule that corporate employees who have 'a responsible share in the furtherance of the transaction which the statute outlaws' are subject to the criminal provisions of the Act was not formulated in a vacuum. Cases under the Federal Food and Drugs Act of 1906 reflected the view both that knowledge or intent were not required to be proved in prosecutions under its criminal provisions, and that responsible corporate agents could be subjected to the liability thereby imposed. Moreover, the principle had been recognized that a corporate agent, through whose act, default, or omission the corporation committed a crime, was himself guilty individually of that crime. The principle had been applied whether or not the crime required 'consciousness of wrongdoing,' and it had been applied not only to those corporate agents who themselves committed the criminal act, but also to those who by virtue of their managerial positions or other similar relation to the actor could be deemed responsible for its commission.

In the latter class of cases, the liability of managerial officers did not depend on their knowledge of, or personal participation in, the act made criminal by the statute. Rather, where the statute under which they were prosecuted dispensed with 'consciousness of wrongdoing,' an omission or failure to act was deemed a sufficient basis for a responsible corporate agent's liability. It was enough in such cases that, by virtue of the relationship he bore to the corporation, the agent had the power to prevent the act complained of.

Thus *Dotterweich* and the cases which have followed reveal that in providing sanctions which reach and touch the individuals who execute the corporate mission—and this is by no means necessarily confined to a single corporate agent or employee—the Act imposes not only a positive duty to seek out and remedy violations when they occur but also, and primarily, a duty to implement measures that will insure that violations will not occur. The requirements of foresight and vigilance imposed on responsible corporate agents are beyond question demanding, and perhaps onerous, but they are no more stringent than the public has a right to expect of those who voluntarily assume positions of authority in business enterprises whose services and products affect the health and well-being of the public that supports them.

The Act does not, as we observed in *Dotterweich*, make criminal liability turn on 'awareness of some wrongdoing' or 'conscious fraud.' The duty imposed by Congress on responsible corporate agents is one that requires the highest standard of foresight and vigilance, but the Act, in its criminal aspect, does not require that which is objectively impossible. The theory upon which responsible corporate agents are held criminally accountable for 'causing' violations of the Act permits a claim that a defendant was 'powerless' to prevent or correct the violation to 'be raised defensively at a trial on the merits.' If such a claim is made, the defendant has the burden of coming forward with evidence, but this does not alter the Government's ultimate burden of proving beyond a reasonable doubt the defendant's guilt, including his power, in light of the duty imposed by the Act, to prevent or correct the prohibited condition.

We cannot agree that it was incumbent upon the District Court to instruct the jury that the Government had the burden of establishing 'wrongful action' in the sense in which the Court of Appeals used that phrase. The concept of a 'responsible relationship' to, or a 'responsible share' in, a violation of the Act indeed imports some measure of blameworthiness; but it is equally clear that the Government establishes a *prima facie* case when it introduces evidence sufficient to warrant a finding by the trier of the facts that the defendant had, by reason of his position in the corporation, responsibility and authority either to prevent in the first instance, or promptly to correct, the violation complained of, and that he failed to do so. The failure thus to fulfill the duty imposed by the interaction of the corporate agent's authority and the statute furnishes a sufficient causal link. The considerations which prompted the imposition of this duty, and the scope of the duty, provide the measure of culpability.

Turning to the jury charge in this case, it is arguable that isolated parts can be read as intimating that a finding of guilt could be predicated solely on respondent's corporate position.

But this is not the way we review jury instructions, because 'a single instruction to a jury may not be judged in artificial isolation, but must be viewed in the context of the overall charge.' Reading the entire charge satisfies us that the jury's attention was adequately focused on the issue of respondent's authority with respect to the conditions that formed the basis of the alleged violations. Viewed as a whole, the charge did not permit the jury to find guilt solely on the basis of respondent's position in the corporation; rather, it fairly advised the jury that to find guilt it must find respondent 'had a responsible relation to the situation,' and 'by virtue of his position [had] authority and responsibility' to deal with the situation. The situation referred to could only be 'food held in unsanitary conditions in a warehouse with the result that it consisted, in part, of filth or may have been contaminated with filth.'

Viewed as a whole and in the context of the trial, the charge was not misleading and contained an adequate statement of the law to guide the jury's determination. Although it would have been better to give an instruction more precisely relating the legal issue to the facts of the case, we cannot say that the failure to provide the amplification requested by respondent was an abuse of discretion

Reversed.

MR. JUSTICE STEWART, with whom MR. JUSTICE MARSHALL and MR. JUSTICE POWELL join, dissenting.

The Court holds that in order to sustain a conviction under § 301(k) of the Federal Food, Drug, and Cosmetic Act the prosecution must at least show that by reason of an individual's corporate position and responsibilities, he had a duty to use care to maintain the physical integrity of the corporation's food products. A jury may then draw the inference that when the food is found to be in such condition as to violate the statute's prohibitions, that condition was 'caused' by a breach of the standard of care imposed upon the responsible official. This is the language of negligence, and I agree with it.

To affirm this conviction, the Court must approve the instructions given to the members of the jury who were entrusted with determining whether the respondent was innocent or guilty. Those instructions did not conform to the standards that the Court sets out today. The trial judge instructed the jury to find Park guilty if it found beyond a reasonable doubt that Park 'had a responsible relation to the situation. The issue is whether the Defendant, John R. Park, by virtue of his position in the company, had a position of authority and responsibility in the situation out of which these charges arose.' Requiring, as it did, a verdict of guilty upon a finding of 'responsibility,' this instruction standing alone could have been construed as a direction to convict if the jury found Park 'responsible' for the condition in the sense that his position as chief executive officer gave him formal responsibility within the structure of the corporation. But the trial judge went on specifically to caution the jury not to attach such a meaning to his instruction, saying that 'the fact that the Defendant is president and is a chief executive officer of the Acme Markets does not require a finding of guilt.' 'Responsibility' as used by the trial judge therefore had whatever meaning the jury in its unguided discretion chose to give it. The instructions, therefore, expressed nothing more than a tautology. They told the jury: 'You must find the defendant guilty if you find that he is to be held accountable for this adulterated food.' In other words: 'You must find the defendant guilty if you conclude that he is guilty.' Before a person can be convicted of a criminal violation of this Act, a jury must find—and must be clearly instructed that it must find—evidence beyond a reasonable doubt that he engaged in wrongful conduct amounting at least to common-law negligence. There were no such instructions, and clearly, therefore, no such finding in this case. For these reasons, I cannot join the Court in affirming Park's criminal conviction.

Points for Discussion

a. Legislative Requirements

While the *Park* decision describes constitutional limits on the vicarious strict liability of corporate officers, a number of jurisdictions have legislated higher *mens rea* requirements by statute. *See, e.g.,* 18 Pa. C. S. § 307(e)(2) ("Whenever a duty to act is imposed by law upon a corporation or an unincorporated association, any agent of the corporation or association having primary responsibility for the discharge of the duty is legally accountable for a reckless omission to perform the required act to the same extent as if the duty were imposed by law directly upon himself.").

b. Model Penal Code

Consider the Model Penal Code's provisions relating to corporate liability:

§ 2.07. Liability of Corporations, Unincorporated Associations and Persons Acting, or Under a Duty to Act, in Their Behalf.

(1) A corporation may be convicted of the commission of an offense if:

(a) the offense is a violation or the offense is defined by a statute other than the Code in which a legislative purpose to impose liability on corporations plainly appears and the conduct is performed by an agent of the corporation acting in behalf of the corporation within the scope of his office or employment, except that if the law defining the offense designates the agents for whose conduct the corporation is accountable or the circumstances under which it is accountable, such provisions shall apply; or

(b) the offense consists of an omission to discharge a specific duty of affirmative performance imposed on corporations by law; or

(c) the commission of the offense was authorized, requested, commanded, performed or recklessly tolerated by the board of directors or by a high managerial agent acting in behalf of the corporation within the scope of his office or employment.

(2) When absolute liability is imposed for the commission of an offense, a legislative purpose to impose liability on a corporation shall be assumed, unless the contrary plainly appears.

(3) An unincorporated association may be convicted of the commission of an offense if:

(a) the offense is defined by a statute other than the Code that expressly provides for the liability of such an association and the conduct is performed by an agent of the association acting in behalf of the association within the scope of his office or employment, except that if the law defining the offense designates the agents for whose conduct the association is accountable or the circumstances under which it is accountable, such provisions shall apply; or

(b) the offense consists of an omission to discharge a specific duty of affirmative performance imposed on associations by law.

(4) As used in this Section:

(a) "corporation" does not include an entity organized as or by a governmental agency for the execution of a governmental program;

(b) "agent" means any director, officer, servant, employee or other person authorized to act in behalf of the corporation or association and, in the case of an unincorporated association, a member of such association;

(c) "high managerial agent" means an officer of a corporation or an unincorporated association, or, in the case of a partnership, a partner, or any other agent of a corporation or association having duties of such responsibility that his conduct may fairly be assumed to represent the policy of the corporation or association.

(5) In any prosecution of a corporation or an unincorporated association for the commission of an offense included within the terms of Subsection (1)(a) or Subsection (3)(a) of this Section, other than an offense for which absolute liability has been imposed, it shall be a defense if the defendant proves by a preponderance of evidence that the high managerial agent having supervisory responsibility over the subject matter of the offense employed due diligence to prevent its commission. This paragraph shall not apply if it is plainly inconsistent with the legislative purpose in defining the particular offense.

(a) A person is legally accountable for any conduct he performs or causes to be performed in the name of the corporation or an unincorporated association or in its behalf to the same extent as if it were performed in his own name or behalf.

(b) Whenever a duty to act is imposed by law upon a corporation or an unincorporated association, any agent of the corporation or association having primary responsibility for the discharge of the duty is legally accountable for a reckless omission to perform the required act to the same extent as if the duty were imposed by law directly upon himself.

Take Note

Note how the Model Penal Code permits the imposition of vicarious liability, not only on corporations, but also on various corporate employees who have responsibility for issues implicated by a statute.

(c) When a person is convicted of an offense by reason of his legal accountability for the conduct of a corporation or an unincorporated association, he is subject to the sentence authorized by law when a natural person is convicted of an offense of the grade and the degree involved.

Hypo 1: *The Coal Sample Switch*

Richard Schomaker, an attorney, entered into a business venture with Robert Todd, a client, and Stephen Levitt, to create a coal brokerage firm called American International Company ("AIC"), which contracted to supply West Penn Power Company with low-sulfur coal. The contract provided that, if the average sulfur content for any month's shipment exceeded a specified level, Utility Company could cancel the remainder of the contract and pay only half the $120,000-per-month contract price for the nonconforming shipment. To measure sulfur content, Utility Company accumulated samples of pulverized coal for each 10-day period, stored them in a shed, and subsequently tested them before making payment. AIC's first twenty days of shipment drastically exceeded the specified sulfur level. Schomaker met several times with Todd and Levitt to discuss the problem. Soon thereafter, Todd and Levitt went to Utility Company's shed and replaced the last 10-day sample from their company with a similar quantity of extra-low sulfur coal. Although Todd told Schomaker about the sample switch the following day, there was a dispute as to whether Schomaker actually believed Todd. In any event, Schomaker did not notify the Utility Company. As a result of the switch, the month's sulfur content was within specified levels, and a few weeks later, Schomaker accepted Utility Company's full payment of $120,000 on behalf of AIC. If Schomaker is charged with theft, what would the government need to show in order to gain a conviction? *See Commonwealth v. Schomaker*, 501 Pa. 404, 461 A.2d 1220 (1983).

Hypo 2: *Ford Motor Co. and the Exploding Gas Tank*

At one point, the Ford Motor Company (Ford) manufactured the "Pinto," a compact car. The Pinto suffered from a major gas tank defect that could cause the vehicle to explode when it was hit from behind, and lots of people were killed or seriously injured as a result of this defect. There is evidence suggesting that Ford's officers were aware of the problem, and could have remedied the problem rather cheaply, but chose not to spend the money. What would it take to impose criminal liability on Ford or its officers for the deaths or injuries? If you are the prosecutor in the case, what types of proof might you offer against the officers?

Food for Thought

Assume that the *Park* facts occurred in Pennsylvania, where 18 Pa. C. S. § 307(e)(2) applies, as described in point a. *supra*, and assume further that the defendant in *Park* was convicted at trial in a Pennsylvania trial court under a Pennsylvania law similar to the federal Food, Drug and Cosmetic Act. On appeal, how will the defense counsel argue that the conviction was not lawful under § 307(e)(2)? How will the prosecutor respond?

South Dakota v. Hy Vee Food Stores, Inc.

533 N.W.2d 147 (S.D. 1995).

KONENKAMP, JUSTICE.

A corporation appeals its misdemeanor conviction for selling an alcoholic beverage to a person under age twenty-one. We affirm.

As part of an undercover sting operation Sioux Falls police sent a nineteen-year-old college student into a Hy Vee grocery store to attempt to purchase liquor. Wearing a college sweatshirt and football jacket, the police infiltrator carried a bottle of whiskey to the checkout counter. Too young to sell liquor herself the cashier asked an older employee to scan the item. The cashier then took the purchase money and rang up the sale. Neither employee asked for identification to verify the purchaser's age. Based upon the actions of these two employees, Hy Vee Food Stores, Inc. was charged with and found guilty in magistrate court of selling an alcoholic beverage to a person under twenty-one. The magistrate imposed a $200 fine. Neither employee was charged with committing a crime. Hy Vee appealed to circuit court seeking to have the statute declared unconstitutional. The circuit court upheld the conviction. Hy Vee asserts that the individual employees committed the wrongful acts, not the corporation, and appeals.

Hy Vee concedes its employees sold alcohol to an underage person in violation of SDCL 35–4–78(1): "No licensee may sell any alcoholic beverage: (1) To any person under the age of twenty-one years. . . ." A violation of this section is a Class 1 misdemeanor punishable by one year in jail or a one thousand dollar fine, or both. Hy Vee avers that the imposition of criminal penalties on it for acts of its employees constitutes an impermissible infringement upon Hy Vee's substantive due process rights in violation of both Article VI of the South Dakota Constitution and the 14th Amendment of the United States Constitution. The question is whether criminal liability can be imposed against an alcoholic beverage corporate licensee for the unlawful acts of its employees?

All legislative enactments arrive before us with a presumption in favor of their constitutionality; Hy Vee bears the burden of proving beyond a reasonable doubt that the law is unconstitutional. Under this criterion we determine if the statute as applied to Hy Vee has "a real and substantial relation to the objects sought to be attained." "Whenever within the bounds of reasonable and legitimate construction, an act of the legislature can be construed so as not to violate the constitution, that construction should be adopted."

The law disfavors statutes which impose criminal liability without fault, much less those enactments which impose such liability vicariously. Yet states "have power to legislate against what are found to be injurious practices in their internal commercial and business affairs, so long as their laws do not run afoul of some specific federal constitutional prohibition." Hy

Vee notes certain "state supreme courts have directly addressed the constitutionality of similar statutes and have found them to be in violation of the liquor licensee's due process rights under the state and federal constitutions." *Commonwealth v. Koczwara*, 155 A.2d 825 (Pa. 1959), *cert. denied*, 363 U.S. 848 (1960); *Davis v. City of Peachtree City*, 304 S.E.2d 701 (Ga. 1983); *State v. Guminga*, 395 N.W.2d 344 (Minn. 1986). In *Koczwara*, an individual owner-licensee was fined $500 and sentenced to three months in jail for the actions of an employee who sold liquor to a minor. Holding that imprisonment under these facts deprives the defendant of due process, the Court made an observation germane to our case: "Were this the defendant's first violation of the Code, and the penalty solely a minor fine of from $100–$300, we would have no hesitation in upholding such a judgment. Defendant, by accepting a liquor license, must bear such a financial risk." The *Koczwara* court overturned the jail sentence, but upheld the $500 fine. In *Davis v. City of Peachtree City*, the court held that a violation of due process occurred when the president of a convenience store chain was fined $200 and given 60 days in jail with conditions for a suspended sentence when an employee sold wine to a minor. Georgia's Supreme Court held that imposing even a slight fine violates due process. After one of his employees sold an alcoholic beverage to a minor, the restaurant owner in *State v. Guminga* faced imprisonment and a fine under Minnesota law. The Court declared that criminal penalties based upon vicarious liability under Minnesota law violated Guminga's due process rights: "Even if there is no prison sentence imposed, under the new statutory guidelines, a gross misdemeanor conviction will affect his criminal history score were he to be convicted of a felony in the future only civil penalties would be constitutional."

We begin our analysis with the rather mundane observation that a corporation cannot act but through its agents. Well settled is the basic principle that criminal liability for certain offenses may be imputed to corporate defendants for the unlawful acts of its employees, provided that the conduct is within the scope of the employee's authority whether actual or apparent. *Koczwara*, *Guminga*, and *Davis* involved individuals subjected to vicarious liability for illegal liquor sales. We must leave for some future time whether those precedents will guide us when an individual licensee comes before us to constitutionally challenge a conviction for the acts of an employee. Almost six decades ago this Court sustained vicarious criminal liability against a licensee for an employee's illegal sale to a minor, but the constitutional issues raised now were not dealt with then. Here, a corporate entity, not an individual, was charged with violating SDCL 35–4–78(1) and upon conviction only a fine was imposed. Pennsylvania's highest court in *Koczwara*, discerning the contrast, was "extremely careful to distinguish its facts from the question of corporate criminal liability." Corporations have been held criminally accountable in numerous circumstances involving a variety of crimes.

Hy Vee urges us to avert constitutional entanglement by reading into the statute a knowledge or *scienter* requirement and hold that a corporate superior must know that an employee is selling liquor to an underage person and either consent to or ratify the act. We decline to do so because "legislative acts which are essentially public welfare regulatory measures may omit the knowledge element without violating substantive due process guarantees." Where "penalties commonly are relatively small, and conviction does no grave damage to an offender's reputation" under such circumstances statutes dispensing with a *mens rea* component have been upheld.

Hy Vee asserts that criminal liability should not be imputed here because it adopted a firm, oft-reiterated policy that its employees, new and old, must not sell liquor to underage persons. Constitutional questions aside, the general rule is that merely stating or promulgating policies will not insulate a corporation from liability. Moreover, corporations may be held responsible for violations "even though its employees or agents acted contrary to express instructions when they violated the law, so long as they were acting for the benefit of the corporation and within the scope of their actual or apparent authority."

As the statute provides for a potential one-year jail sentence, Hy Vee argues that the enactment goes beyond being a mere regulatory measure with minor consequences for its violation. If the defendant was not a corporation, this argument might carry serious merit. In this case, a fine was all that could have been imposed; corporations cannot be imprisoned. We will not speculate over the law's applicability to persons not before us or assume that some future court will impose a jail sentence upon such persons. Hy Vee's maximum criminal exposure was a $1,000 fine.

South Dakota's alcoholic beverage laws manifest an unwavering public interest in prohibiting liquor sales to persons under twenty-one. The serious problems associated with youth who abuse alcohol justify stringent enforcement against those who dispense it. By establishing vicarious liability against a corporate alcoholic beverage licensee, our laws hold accountable the true beneficiary of illegal sales and encourage such licensees to exercise intensified supervision over employees delegated with liquor sale responsibilities. Thus, the challenged statute has a real and substantial relation to the objects sought to be attained.

Was Hy Vee's $200 fine a constitutionally permissible sanction under the circumstances? WAYNE R. LAFAVE & AUSTIN W. SCOTT, JR., HANDBOOK ON CRIMINAL LAW § 32, at 227 (1972), supports the view that: "Imposition of a fine is consistent with the rationale behind vicarious criminal liability. Vicarious liability is imposed because of the nature and inherent danger of certain business activities and the difficulties of establishing actual fault in the operation of such businesses. A fine, unlike imprisonment, is less personal and is more properly viewed as a penalty on the business enterprise.'

The magistrate's imposition of a $200 fine was consistent with the nature of regulatory offenses and did not offend Hy Vee's state and federal constitutional due process rights.

Affirmed.

AMUNDSON, JUSTICE (dissenting).

The fact that there may be serious problems in our society with abuse of alcohol by our youth does not warrant the imposition of a criminal conviction where there is no showing of knowledge or authorization of the crime by the employer/Hy Vee. Discussing vicarious liability in the criminal arena, the court in *Davis v. City of Peachtree City* stated:

> In balancing this burden against the public's interests, we find that a criminal conviction cannot be justified under the due process clauses of the Georgia or United States Constitutions, regardless of Peachtree City's admittedly legitimate

> interests of deterring employers from allowing their employees to break the law and of facilitating the enforcement of these laws. This is especially true, when, as here, there are other, less onerous alternatives which sufficiently promote these interests. The Model Penal Code recommends that civil violations providing civil penalties such as fines or revocation of licenses be used for offenses for which the individual was not morally blameworthy and does not deserve the social condemnation 'implicit in the concept "crime".' The availability of such sanctions renders the use of criminal sanctions in vicarious liability cases unjustifiable.

Similarly, commentators LaFave and Scott have written in opposition to criminal sanctions based on vicarious liability:

> It must be recognized that the imposition of criminal liability for faultless conduct is contrary to the basic Anglo-American premise of criminal justice that crime requires personal fault on the part of the accused. Perhaps the answer should be the same as the answer proposed in the case of strict-liability crimes: it is proper for the legislature to single out some special areas of human activity and impose vicarious liability on employers who are without fault, but the matter should not be called a 'crime' As the law now stands, however, in almost all jurisdictions imprisonment and the word 'criminal' may be visited upon perfectly innocent employers for the sins of their employees.

Adopting this vicarious liability/respondeat superior theory to brand a corporation/employer as a criminal, does not comport with the precept of criminal jurisprudence that guilt is personal and individual. Whether or not one should be so branded, should not rest on whether an employee commits a mistake in judgment. Even the court, which found Hy Vee guilty, understood the fact that employees can make mistakes and will intentionally violate the law notwithstanding the store policy on training and handling mistaken sale of alcohol to underage persons. In this case, as in others, there are appropriate mechanisms to civilly deal with liquor-sale violations if a license holder violates the law; namely, regulatory revocation or suspension of the license. I would reverse this conviction.

Food for Thought

Do you agree with the majority, or the dissent, in the *Hy Vee Food Stores* decision? If the dissenting position became the accepted law in South Dakota, wouldn't this create a deterrent *disincentive* for Hy Vee to adopt policies restricting the sale of alcohol to underage persons?

Iowa v. Casey's General Stores, Inc.

587 N.W.2d 599 (Iowa 1998).

TERNUS, JUSTICE.

This consolidated appeal involves simple misdemeanor convictions of two corporations whose employees sold alcoholic beverages to underage customers during a "sting" operation by the local police. The corporations argue they cannot be held criminally responsible for their employees' actions under the circumstances presented. We agree and so reverse their convictions and remand for dismissal of the criminal charges.

The factual predicate for the charges at issue here is undisputed. Both appellants, Casey's General Stores, Inc. and Hy-Vee, Inc., operate stores in Oskaloosa, Iowa. Cashiers in both stores sold alcoholic beverages to underage customers without requiring identification or attempting to ascertain the customer's age. These sales violated policies and procedures established by the corporations to prevent the sale of alcoholic beverages to minors. Both corporations were charged with the crime of selling alcoholic beverages to an underage person. These simple misdemeanor charges were tried to the court and both defendants were found guilty. Their convictions were affirmed on appeal to the district court. Casey's and Hy-Vee argue that there is no evidence that they, as corporate entities, engaged in culpable conduct. The State does not contest this assertion, but rather relies on the corporations' alleged vicarious responsibility for their employees' actions.

The claim in this appeal is based on the alleged insufficiency of the evidence to support the verdict. We review the record in the light most favorable to the State in assessing the sufficiency of the evidence. The determinative question is whether the statutes in question render corporate defendants criminally responsible for the actions of their employees in selling alcoholic beverages to a minor in contravention of company policies and procedures.

The primary rule of statutory interpretation is to give effect to the intention of the legislature. To ascertain that intent, we look to the language of the statute. We consider not only the commonly understood meaning of the words used in the statute, but also the context within which they appear. Finally, we construe statutes that relate to the same or a closely allied subject together so as to produce a harmonious and consistent body of legislation.

Section 123.47 prohibits the sale of alcohol to a minor: "A person shall not sell alcoholic liquor, wine, or beer to any person knowing or having reasonable cause to believe that person to be under the age of eighteen." Section 123.49(2)(h) contains a similar prohibition: "A person or club holding a liquor control license or retail wine or beer permit under this chapter, and the person's or club's agents or employees, shall not . . . . h. Sell, give, or otherwise supply any alcoholic beverage, wine, or beer to any person, knowing or failing to exercise reasonable care to ascertain whether the person is under legal age."

The State argues that the evidence supports the defendants' convictions for violating these statutes under the following rationale. The State points out that the statutory prohibitions apply to a "person," and that word is defined to include a corporation. Because a corporation can act only through an employee, the State reasons that the legislature must have contemplated criminal liability for corporations based on the acts of their employees. We find this analysis unpersuasive because these statutes do not impose vicarious liability.

Vicarious liability occurs when "one person is made liable, though without personal fault, for the bad conduct of someone else." This doctrine is contrary to the "basic premise of criminal justice that crime requires personal fault." As Professor LaFave explains in his treatise on criminal law, "It is a general principle of criminal law that one is not criminally liable for how someone else acts, unless of course he directs or encourages or aids the other so to act. Thus, unlike the case with torts, an employer is not generally liable for the criminal acts of his employee even though the latter does them in furtherance of his employer's business. In other words, with crimes defined in terms of harmful acts and bad thoughts, the defendant himself must personally engage in the acts and personally think the bad thoughts, unless, in the case of a statutory crime, the legislature has otherwise provided." Thus, if a statutory crime requires mental fault, "it is the rule that the employer must personally know or be willful or have the requisite intention before he will be liable for the criminal conduct of his employee."

We begin with an examination of the statutes to determine whether they require mental fault or whether they impose strict liability. Such an examination reveals that a *mens rea* element is included in both crimes. We had the opportunity to consider whether section 123.47 required mental fault in *Bauer v. Cole*, 467 N.W.2d 221 (Iowa 1991), a negligence case premised on a violation of section 123.47. In that case, the plaintiffs, an injured minor and his parents, sued the hosts of a New Year's Eve party for injuries sustained by the minor in an automobile accident. Plaintiffs alleged defendants had provided liquor to the minor driver causing his intoxication, which in turn caused the accident. Plaintiffs appealed from an adverse jury verdict, claiming error in the instruction submitting the plaintiffs' negligence claim based on section 123.47. In the challenged instruction, the trial court had required the plaintiffs to prove the defendants had knowingly supplied alcohol to the minor driver. The plaintiffs argued that knowledge was not an element of the offense. In ruling that the instruction was correct, this court held that section 123.47 requires proof of the defendants criminal intent: "We conclude that defendants' knowledge of the transaction must be shown to prove a criminal violation under section 123.47."

We think the same conclusion is appropriate with respect to section 123.49(2)(h). Section 123.49(2)(h) requires that the defendant sell the alcoholic beverage "knowing or failing to exercise reasonable care to ascertain whether the person is under legal age." Similarly, section 123.47 requires that the defendant "know or have reasonable cause to believe" that the person buying the alcoholic beverage is under the age of eighteen. The similar language of section 123.49(2)(h) calls for the same interpretation given to section 123.47 in *Bauer*, namely, that proof of the defendant's criminal intent is required for a criminal violation. Thus, a licensee or permittee cannot be held strictly criminally liable for the illegal sale of alcohol to a minor; there must be proof that the sale to a minor was made "with the knowledge, or by the direction, sanction, or approval of the defendant." Because sections 123.47 and 123.49(2)(h) specifically require fault, we will not read vicarious liability into these criminal statutes, but must first find a legislative expression of an intent to impose vicarious liability. Clearly, there is no expression of such an intent in the statutory language.

We now consider the State's contention that the defendants can be held vicariously liable for the conduct of their employees under section 703.5(1). Section 703.5 provides for the vicarious liability of a corporation in two different situations:

> A private corporation shall have the same level of culpability as an individual committing the crime when any of the following are true:
>
> 1. The conduct constituting the offense consists of an omission to discharge a specific duty or an affirmative performance imposed on the accused by the law.
>
> 2. The conduct or act constituting the offense is committed by an agent, officer, director, or employee of the accused while acting within the scope of the authority of the agent, officer, director or employee and in behalf of the accused and when said act or conduct is authorized, requested, or tolerated by the board of directors or by a high managerial agent . . . .

The first subsection of this statute addresses crimes of omission, ones in which the criminal statute imposes an obligation on the corporation to do something, as opposed to criminal statutes prohibiting certain conduct. The second subsection of the statute addresses criminal conduct that consists of the commission of a prohibited act. The State does not rely on section 703.5(2) to support the defendants' convictions. Indeed, there is no evidence that these sales of alcohol to minors were "authorized, requested, or tolerated" by the companies' boards of directors or any high managerial agents of the defendants. Therefore, we must focus on the requirements of section 703.5(1) and decide whether there is sufficient evidence of those requirements. To determine whether section 703.5(1) applies, we must identify the "conduct constituting the offense" and then consider whether that conduct constitutes "an omission to discharge a specific duty or an affirmative performance imposed on the accused by the law."

The State argues that the conduct constituting the offense is the failure to use reasonable care to ascertain the purchaser's age. But a defendant can be convicted of a violation of sections 123.47 and 123.49(2)(h) in the absence of such evidence, for example, where the defendant knew the purchaser was a minor. Thus, the requirement of reasonable care is merely a substitute for the *mens rea* or knowledge element of the crime. We think "the conduct constituting the offense," as contemplated by section 703.5(1), is not the *mens rea* element of the crime, but rather is the core conduct of selling alcohol to a minor.

We next consider whether this conduct is "an omission to discharge a specific duty or an affirmative performance imposed on the accused by law" within the meaning of section 703.5(1). The sale of alcohol to a minor is the commission of a prohibited act; it is not the omission of a specific duty or affirmative obligation. Therefore, section 703.5(1) does not apply. Sections 123.47 and 123.49(2)(h) do not impose vicarious liability on licensees and permittees for illegal sales made by their employees. Therefore, the criminal culpability of Casey's and Hy-Vee's employees does not provide a basis for the convictions of these corporations. In addition, the factual prerequisites of the statute providing for a corporation's vicarious liability, section 703.5, are not satisfied under the facts before us.

We conclude, therefore, that there is insufficient evidence to support a finding that the corporate defendants violated sections 123.47 and 123.49(2)(h). Accordingly, we reverse the defendants' convictions and remand for dismissal of the charges.

Executive Summary

The Nature of Accomplice Liability. Whether they are referred to as accomplices, accessories, or aiders-and-abettors, every jurisdiction has statutory provisions that punish actors whose only relationship to a criminal offense was the provision of assistance to the principal offender.

Common Law Classifications. At common law, the parties to a crime were divided into four distinct categories: (1) principals in the first degree (who actually perpetrated the crime); (2) principals in the second degree (who were actually or constructively present at the scene of the crime and aided or abetted its commission); (3) accessories before the fact (who aided or abetted the crime, but were not present at its commission); and (4) accessories after the fact (who rendered assistance after the crime was completed). In misdemeanor cases, all accomplices were treated as principals.

Common Law Oddities. In the early common law, all parties to a felony received the death penalty. An accessory to a felony could not be convicted without the prior conviction of the principal offender. As a result, if the principal fled, died or was acquitted, an accomplice could not be convicted. These rules did not apply to accomplices to misdemeanors. Modern rules overturn the common law conviction distinctions.

Merger. The merger of principals and accessories has occurred in all American jurisdictions so that there is only a single crime: complicity. One significant exception, however, is for accessories after the fact. When an actor assists another only after the substantive criminal offense has taken place (e.g. harboring a fugitive after a bank robbery), that offense does not merge with the principal offense, (e.g., bank robbery).

Major Themes

a. ***Actus Reus***—The modern crime of complicity applies to persons who aid in the commission of a crime, or who provide assistance after the crime is completed. In evaluating whether a person's conduct satisfies the *actus reus* element, courts usually require evidence of tangible assistance or active promotion that goes beyond mere encouragement.

b. ***Mens Rea***—The mental state for complicity is the purpose of promoting or facilitating the commission of the crime. Such purpose may be inferred from a person's conduct.

c. **Corporate Liability**—Although vicarious liability is disfavored, a corporation may be held liable for the unlawful acts of employees, with additional limitations often imposed by statute. A corporate officer may be held liable for such unlawful acts when serving in a managerial position with the power to correct the criminal conduct.

Model Penal Code. Under the Model Penal Code, a defendant is an accomplice to another person in the commission of an offense if either (a) with the purpose of promoting or facilitating the commission of the offense, he (i) solicits such other person to commit it, or (ii) aids or agrees or attempts to aid such other person in planning or committing it, or (iii) having a legal duty to prevent the commission of the offense, fails to make proper effort so to do; or (b) his conduct is expressly declared by law to establish his complicity. Special rules can apply to result crimes, to victims, and to those incapable of committing a crime.

Accomplice Liability and Conspiracy. Related to the crime of complicity is the crime of conspiracy. In general, conspiracy involves an agreement between two or more persons (although an actual agreement between the two may not be required) to commit an unlawful act or a lawful act by unlawful means. One who is complicit in a crime may have explicitly or implicitly engaged in a conspiracy to commit that crime.

***Mens Rea* of Complicity.** The *mens rea* of accomplice liability is often described in the case law as having two separate (and independent) components: (1) the intent to assist a principal actor in committing the target act; and (2) the intent that the principal actually commit that act. In most jurisdictions, this intent can be (and often is) inferred from a person's actions.

Vicarious Liability. Sometimes, an individual may be found guilty based on vicarious liability, in other words based on the criminal actions of other persons, about which the individual may be unaware. This liability is regarded as unusual and generally inappropriate in the criminal law, and is most commonly employed against corporations and corporate agents. A number of jurisdictions have legislated higher *mens rea* requirements for the imposition of such liability.

Model Penal Code and Corporate Liability. The Model Penal Code provides for the imposition of criminal liability on corporations, and some corporate officials, in limited situations.

For More Information

- AMERICAN LAW INSTITUTE, MODEL PENAL CODE AND COMMENTARIES, Part I, §§ 2.06–2.07, Comments at 295–348 (1980).
- JOHN M. BURKOFF & RUSSELL L. WEAVER, INSIDE CRIMINAL LAW: WHAT MATTERS AND WHY 81–98 (2d ed. 2011).
- WAYNE R. LAFAVE, CRIMINAL LAW §§ 13.1–13.6 (6th ed. 2017).

Test Your Knowledge

To assess your understanding of the material in this chapter, click here to take a quiz.

Chapter 6

Attempt

Although the criminal law does not punish people merely for "bad thoughts," the State does have an interest in intervening early before a suspect actually commits a crime and actually causes harm. The law of attempt plays this role in the law. The evidence required for an attempt conviction, both as to the *mens rea* and the *actus reus*, can vary from state to state.

Make the Connection

In the criminal law, various crimes are used to allow police to intervene early to prevent the commission of criminal acts. Included are crimes like attempt, conspiracy and solicitation. Solicitation was discussed in Chapter 4, in relation to the topic of complicity, and conspiracy will be discussed in Chapter 7.

A. *Mens Rea*

State v. Maestas

652 P.2d 903 (Utah 1982).

Hall, Chief Justice:

Defendant allegedly robbed a bank and attempted to escape in a black van. Sergeant Cecil Throckmorton of the Salt Lake City Police Department had stationed his car on an island in the center of the street and was standing beside the car awaiting defendant's approach. As defendant's van passed, Sergeant Throckmorton fired a shot in an unsuccessful attempt to disable it. As he drove away, defendant allegedly leaned out of the van window holding a 38-caliber revolver and fired it at the officer. Defendant drove several blocks further before crashing into a parked car, at which time he was apprehended by other police officers.

Defendant was found guilty of attempted first degree murder. The court granted defendant's motion to dismiss on the ground that "specific intent to kill could not properly be inferred from the evidence." U.C.A., 1953, 76–5–202(1) describes the elements of first degree murder:

> Criminal homicide constitutes murder in the first degree if the actor intentionally or knowingly causes the death of another under any of the following circumstances:
>
> * * *
>
> (d) The homicide was committed while the actor was engaged in the commission of, or an attempt to commit, or flight after committing or attempting to commit,

aggravated robbery, robbery, rape, forcible arson, aggravated burglary, burglary, aggravated kidnapping or kidnapping.

(e) The homicide was committed for the purpose of avoiding or preventing an arrest by a peace officer acting under color of legal authority or for the purpose of effecting an escape from lawful custody.

In order to find defendant guilty of attempted first degree murder, the jury was required to determine beyond a reasonable doubt that he "intentionally or knowingly" attempted to kill Sergeant Throckmorton under one of the circumstances listed above.

Defendant argues that the crime of attempted murder requires a stronger showing of intent than does the crime of murder itself. This theory derives from the common law rule that intent is a necessary element of every "attempt" crime even where the corresponding completed crime does not require intent. As an example, defendant cites cases which discuss the common law rule that there is no crime of "attempted felony murder" because of the fact that felony murder requires no specific intent to kill, while an "attempt" crime must always consist of an intent to commit the corresponding completed crime accompanied by a substantial step toward realization of that crime. Defendant then attempts to carry this rule one step further by asserting that the crime of attempted first degree murder with which he is charged requires a "specific intent" beyond that which would have been required in order to prove first degree murder itself if an actual death had occurred. Defendant does not argue that the evidence concerning intent would have failed to support a first degree murder conviction in the event of actual death, but rather that such evidence fell short of establishing the stronger "specific intent" allegedly required for the crime of attempted first degree murder.

The statute makes clear that regardless of any requirements which the common law may impose concerning "attempt" crimes, Utah law requires only "the kind of culpability otherwise required for the commission of the completed offense." Thus, there can be no difference between the intent required as an element of the crime of attempted first degree murder and that required for first degree murder itself.

Even if the common law rule of attempt governed this Court's interpretation of the elements of that crime, that rule would not require the result urged by defendant. That rule differentiates between the intent requirements for an attempted and a completed crime only where the completed crime may be committed without the intent to commit that crime in particular, as in the case of felony murder. Where an intent to commit the particular crime committed is an element of the completed crime, the same intent requirement applies to the corresponding "attempt" crime, even at common law. Thus, Utah's first degree murder statute, which does contain such an intent requirement, would not fall within the rule cited by defendant even under common law principles.

There was "substantial evidence" from which the jury could have concluded not only that defendant aimed and fired a revolver at Sergeant Throckmorton, but also that he did so "intentionally or knowingly." Because of the near impossibility of proving intent directly, Utah law clearly permits the inference of such intent from the actions of a defendant considered in light of surrounding circumstances.

Take Note

When an individual attempts to kill another person, but fails, it is impossible to charge the individual with murder. The required "result" of death is missing. It is common to charge the individual with attempted murder, as well as (possibly) other crimes such as aggravated assault or battery.

In order to determine defendant's intent, the jury might have considered further evidence concerning his conduct and the circumstances surrounding the alleged gunshot, including testimony that he had just committed a bank robbery, that he had attempted to avoid capture by throwing money out of the van window and that he had demonstrated an indifference to the safety of others by driving erratically and on the wrong side of the traffic divider in his efforts to elude pursuers. We therefore hold that substantial evidence supported the jury in finding that the state had established both the act and the intent components of attempted first degree murder by defendant.

Reversed.

Point for Discussion

The Model Penal Code

Consider the MPC's approach to defining the crime of Attempt:

§ 5.01. Criminal Attempt

(1) *Definition of Attempt.* A person is guilty of an attempt to commit a crime if, acting with the kind of culpability otherwise required for commission of the crime, he:

(a) purposely engages in conduct that would constitute the crime if the attendant circumstances were as he believes them to be; or

(b) when causing a particular result is an element of the crime, does or omits to do anything with the purpose of causing or with the belief that it will cause such result without further conduct on his part; or

(c) purposely does or omits to do anything that, under the circumstances as he believes them to be, is an act or omission constituting a substantial step in a course of conduct planned to culminate in his commission of the crime.

Food for Thought

In *Maestas*, suppose defendant testified that his intention was not to kill Officer Throckmorton, but simply to scare him. Defendant hoped that the shot would force the officer to duck and stop shooting at him. If you were the prosecutor, how would you rebut defendant's testimony? If the jury believed the defendant, should he be convicted of attempted murder? *See People v. Harris*, 72 Ill. 2d 16, 377 N.E.2d 28, 17 Ill. Dec. 838 (1978).

Hypo 1: *The Driver and the Failing Brakes*

The brakes on defendant's car were old and sometimes failed to work. Fully aware of this fact, and of the danger to others, defendant decides to drive to the grocery store. Defendant drives safely. A police officer, aware that defendant's brakes sometimes fail, charges defendant with attempted manslaughter. Given these facts, does defendant have the *mens rea* for this crime?

Hypo 2: *The Accidental Shooting*

Defendants entered a shoe store armed with handguns. One defendant ordered the owner to open the cash register. A second defendant jumped over the counter, and took the cash in the drawer. Defendants then ordered the owner to open a second register. Upon finding it empty, defendants demanded to know where the money could be found. When the owner said "that's all there is," one defendant stuck a gun in the owner's face and yelled, "I'm going to kill you." At that point, the store owner tried to escape. In doing so, he bumped into one of the defendants and a gun accidentally discharged. The store owner was hospitalized for five weeks from a gunshot wound to his stomach. Did the defendant who held the gun (that fired the shot) have the *mens rea* for the crime of attempted murder? How would you argue the case for the State? How might the defense respond? *See Bruce v. State*, 317 Md. 642, 566 A.2d 103 (Md. App.1989).

Hypo 3: *Love Rival*

In February, 2007, NASA Astronaut Lisa Marie Nowak was charged with attempted murder for an attack on another woman, an Air Force captain. The prosecution alleged that Nowak drove 900 miles from Houston to Florida, and that she carried a wig to disguise her appearance. She brought a steel mallet, a knife, pepper spray, rubber tubing, latex gloves and garbage bags with her. The prosecution also alleged that she wore a diaper during her drive so that she would not have to stop. Nowak claims that she did not intend to murder the captain, or even to hurt her, but only to talk to her and perhaps intimidate her. However, Nowak did approach the captain's car in a parking lot and a minor altercation ensued before Nowak drove off. If you are the prosecutor, how do you go about proving intent to murder?

Food for Thought

In Chapter 1, we examined the justifications for punishment—retribution, restraint, deterrence (both specific and general) and rehabilitation. What punishment is appropriate for a person who attempts to commit a crime (e.g., murder), but fails? When the defendant fails to "cause" the required result, should the punishment be the same as for the completed crime? Why or why not?

People v. Gibson

94 Cal. App. 2d 468, 210 P.2d 747 (1949).

MOORE, PRESIDING JUSTICE.

After midnight, appellant crossed an alley carrying a 14-foot wooden ladder which he placed horizontally by the fence in the rear of a department store. The darkness was marred only by street lights that reflected into the alley. Having deposited his burden, he stood erect, looked upward and walked along the edge of the building. Appellant then proceeded easterly for 120 feet when commanded to halt. As he stood in the beam of the officer's flashlight he stated that he was considering whether he could use the ladder at his home and that he might steal it. The officer noticed that appellant wore brown cotton gloves, placed him under arrest, directed him to the police station and returned to the scene where he found a burlap sack which contained various tools and burglars' equipment, including an eight pound sledge hammer, bits, braces, flashlights, gloves and 30 feet of quarter-inch, white rope ladder of about 15 steps. In appellant's pockets were two flashlights, wire cutters and a coil of small brown copper wire. At the station appellant said that he was fixing to commit a burglary. While he had not yet selected a building, "he said after I got on top I was going to see which was the most likely looking spot."

Two elements are essential to an attempted crime, namely, a specific intent and an ineffectual overt act directed at its consummation. Of course, the intent of any person at the time of his attempt to offend the state is a question of fact. It may be inferred from the circumstances in evidence. If a man traveled 25 miles from his home by the seashore to Burbank north of the Hollywood hills to find a store to burglarize and thereafter was detected by an officer at midnight bearing a ladder down a dark alley and placing it at the rear of a department store and if he is equipped with all the tools commonly used by burglars, there could be no doubt that he was attempting to commit a burglary. It could not reasonably be said that he was out to improve his health or the condition of the merchant on San Fernando Road. Even without his admissions, his criminal purpose was clearly evident. With such admissions in evidence his attempt to commit burglary was positively established.

Judgment *affirmed.*

Food for Thought

In the absence of direct and unequivocal evidence of intent, a court must infer defendant's intent from the circumstances. Note how the *Gibson* court puts together a series of objective facts to infer that defendant intended to commit a burglary. Would the same result have been reached if: a) These events had occurred during the middle of the day rather than at night? b) Defendant had not been in possession of burglar's tools?

Hypo: *Attempted Assault?*

Defendant was charged with attempt to commit assault with intent to rape. When Ms. Allen left the "Tiny Diner," she noticed defendant sitting in a truck. According to Allen, as she passed the truck, defendant said something unintelligible, and opened the door. He then followed her down the street until she stopped at a friend's house. By this time, defendant was within two or three feet of her. She waited ten minutes for appellant to pass. When she proceeded, defendant came toward her from behind a telephone pole. When a man unexpectedly emerged from a nearby house, defendant immediately turned and went back to his truck. Defendant gave a different version of the facts. He testified that, on the evening in question, he was carrying a load of junk-iron with a partner, and happened to stop near the diner. When the partner disappeared, defendant walked up the street to look for him. As he did, he saw Ms. Allen. He waited until she had gone, and then walked up the street. When he reached the telephone pole, he remained there for 25 or 30 minutes to see if his partner would arrive. He denied that he followed Allen or made any gesture toward molesting her. Under the circumstances, is there sufficient evidence to conclude that defendant had the *mens rea* for the crime of attempted assault with intent to commit rape? *See McQuirter v. State*, 36 Ala. App. 707, 63 So.2d 388 (1953).

B. *Actus Reus*

Even if defendant has the required *mens rea* for attempt, it may be difficult to prove the *actus reus*. Different jurisdictions define the *actus reus* using a variety of statutory and case law formulas.

Take Note

The *actus reus* for the crime of Attempt may be different than the *actus reus* for the completed crime. As you work through the following materials, be alert to the different ways in which the *actus reus* of Attempt might be formulated.

Commonwealth v. Peaslee

177 Mass. 267, 59 N.E. 55 (1901).

HOLMES, C.J.

Defendant was indicted for an attempt to burn a building and certain goods therein, with intent to injure the insurers of the same. The defense is that the overt acts alleged and proved do not amount to an offense.

Defendant constructed and arranged combustibles in the building in such a way that they were ready to be lighted, and if lighted would have set fire to the building and its contents. To be exact, the plan would have required a candle which was standing on a shelf six feet away to be placed on a piece of wood in a pan of turpentine and lighted. The defendant offered to pay a younger man to go to the building, seemingly some miles away, and carry out the plan. This was refused. Later the defendant and the young man drove towards the building, but when within a quarter of a mile the defendant said that he had changed his mind, and drove away. This is as near as he ever came to accomplishing what he had in contemplation.

The question is whether defendant's acts come near enough to the accomplishment of the substantive offense to be punishable. The statute does not punish every act done towards the commission of a crime, but only such acts done in an attempt to commit it. The most common types of an attempt are either an act which is intended to bring about the substantive crime, and which sets in motion natural forces that would bring it about in the expected course of events, but for the unforeseen interruption, as in this case, if the candle had been set in its place and lighted, but had been put out by the police, or an act which is intended to bring about the substantive crime, and would bring it about but for a mistake of judgment in a matter of nice estimate or experiment, as when a pistol is fired at a man, but misses him, or when one tries to pick a pocket which turns out to be empty. In either case the would-be criminal has done his last act.

New considerations come in when further acts on the part of the person who has taken the first steps are necessary before the substantive crime can come to pass. In this class of cases there is still a chance that the would-be criminal may change his mind. In strictness, such first steps cannot be described as an attempt, because that word suggests an act seemingly sufficient to accomplish the end, and has been supposed to have no other meaning. That an overt act, although coupled with an intent to commit the crime, commonly is not punishable if further acts are contemplated as needful, is expressed in the familiar rule that preparation is not an attempt. But some preparations may amount to an attempt. It is a question of degree. If the preparation comes very near to the accomplishment of the act, the intent to complete it renders the crime so probable that the act will be a misdemeanor, although there is still a *locus poenitentiae*, in the need of a further exertion of the will to complete the crime. The degree of proximity held sufficient may vary with circumstances, including, among other things, the apprehension which the particular crime is calculated to excite.

As a further illustration, when the servant of a contractor had delivered short rations by the help of a weight, which he had substituted for the true one, intending to steal the meat left over, it was held by four judges that he could be convicted of an attempt to steal. *Cheeseman's Case*, Leigh & C. 140, 10 Wkly. Rep. 255. So, lighting a match with intent to set fire to a haystack, although the prisoner desisted on discovering that he was watched. So, getting into a stall with a poisoned potato, intending to give it to a horse there, which the prisoner was prevented from doing by his arrest.

In this case, a majority of the court is of opinion that the exceptions must be sustained. A mere collection and preparation of materials in a room for the purpose of setting fire to them, unaccompanied by any present intent to set the fire, would be too remote. If the accused intended to rely upon his own hands to the end, he must be shown to have had a present intent to accomplish the crime without much delay, and to have had this intent at a time and place where he was able to carry it out. We are not aware of any carefully considered case that has gone further than this. The indictment would have been proved if, for instance, the evidence had been that the defendant had been frightened by the police as he was about to light the candle. On the other hand, if the offense is to be made out by showing a preparation of the room, and a solicitation of someone else to set the fire, which solicitation, if successful, would have been the defendant's last act, the solicitation must be alleged as one of the overt acts. If the indictment had been properly drawn, we have no question that the defendant might have been convicted.

Exceptions sustained.

Points for Discussion

a. Common Law Definitions

At common law, the *actus reus* of the crime of attempt was defined in many different ways. Consider the following common law tests as summarized by the drafters of the MPC:

(1) The "physical proximity" doctrine under which defendant must have committed an overt act that was proximate to the completed crime, or directly tending toward the completion of the crime, or amounting to the commencement of the consummation.

(2) The "dangerous proximity" doctrine under which the court considers the gravity and probability of the offense, and the nearness of the act to the crime.

(3) The "indispensable element" test (similar to the proximity tests) which emphasizes whether an indispensable aspect of the criminal endeavor remains over which the actor has not yet acquired control.

(4) The "probable desistance" test which focuses on whether, in the ordinary and natural course of events, without interruption from an outside source, defendant's conduct will result in the crime intended.

(5) The "abnormal step" approach under which the focus is on whether defendant's conduct has gone beyond the point where the normal citizen would think better of his conduct and desist.

(6) The "*res ipsa* loquitur" or unequivocality test under which the defendant's conduct manifests an intent to commit a crime.

See United States v. Mandujano, 499 F.2d 370, 376 (5th Cir. 1974).

b. Model Penal Code

Consider the MPC's definition of a "substantial step":

§ 5.01. Criminal Attempt.

* * *

(2) **Conduct That May Be Held Substantial Step Under Subsection (1)(c).** Conduct shall not be held to constitute a substantial step under Subsection (1)(c) of this Section unless it is strongly corroborative of the actor's criminal purpose. Without negativing the sufficiency of other conduct, the following, if strongly corroborative of the actor's criminal purpose, shall not be held insufficient as a matter of law:

(a) lying in wait, searching for or following the contemplated victim of the crime;

(b) enticing or seeking to entice the contemplated victim of the crime to go to the place contemplated for its commission;

(c) reconnoitering the place contemplated for the commission of the crime;

(d) unlawful entry of a structure, vehicle or enclosure in which it is contemplated that the crime will be committed;

(e) possession of materials to be employed in the commission of the crime, that are specially designed for such unlawful use or that can serve no lawful purpose of the actor under the circumstances;

(f) possession, collection or fabrication of materials to be employed in the commission of the crime, at or near the place contemplated for its commission, if such possession, collection or fabrication serves no lawful purpose of the actor under the circumstances;

(g) soliciting an innocent agent to engage in conduct constituting an element of the crime.

(3) **Conduct Designed to Aid Another in Commission of a Crime.** A person who engages in conduct designed to aid another to commit a crime that would establish his complicity under Section 2.06 if the crime were committed by such other person, is guilty of an attempt to commit the crime, although the crime is not committed or attempted by such other person.

Hypo 1: *More on* Peaslee

According to the *Peaslee* Court, what additional acts would have been required to convict that defendant of attempt? Would it have been enough if Peaslee had: A) Purchased materials needed to start a fire, arranged them in a combustible manner, struck the match, and set the candle afire; B) Agreed with another person that that person would set the candle afire? C) Made such an agreement with another person, who then set out for the building with the intention of setting fire to the materials? D) Made such an agreement with a person who actually entered the building and struck the match?

Food for Thought

Does solicitation to commit a crime constitute an attempt? In *Peaslee*, the defendant clearly solicited another person to help him commit the crime. Under the MPC's "substantial step" test, does the solicitation by itself (in other words, considered without reference to the other preparatory acts) constitute an attempt? Should it?

Hypo 2: *An Attempted Attack on the Capitol?*

Police receive information suggesting that a man is planning an attack on the U.S Capitol building and the Pentagon using remote-controlled aircraft armed with explosives. They receive this information from jihadi websites which indicate that the man is "evil," and that he is planning to conduct a "jihad" against the U.S. On those websites, the man indicates that he wants to strike a "psychological blow" against the "enemies of Allah" by striking at the Pentagon and the Capitol.

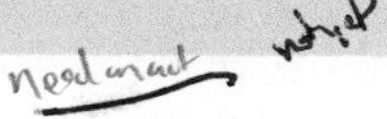

Food for Thought

In the prior Hypo, the evidence shows that the man ordered, and received, grenades, machine guns, and 24 pounds of C4 explosives. Did he commit a sufficient *actus reus* for the crime of attempt under the various tests set forth above? How would the *Peaslee* case have been resolved under the other common law tests, described in point a. supra? Under the MPC's "substantial step" test?

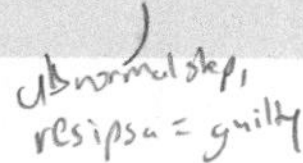

Hypo 3: Actus Reus *Scenarios*

Consider the following problems under the various common law tests, and the MPC's substantial step test, to decide whether the *actus reus* of attempt has been committed. As you think about how these tests apply, consider whether one test is preferable to the others. Is one test more consistent with justifications for punishment? Does a particular test encourage the police to intervene too early or too late?

a. *The Agreement.* Defendant agrees with another person to burn a building. The two do nothing more than agree to commit the crime and they take no further actions. Would any of the *actus reus* tests set forth above allow a conviction for attempted arson?

b. *Searching for the Intended Victim.* Carrying a firearm and ammunition, the Ortiz brothers leave their apartment in search of Jose Rodriguez. The Ortiz and Rodriguez families were feuding, and the Ortizes believed that Rodriguez had gone to their father's apartment with a gun. The Ortizes drove through Rodriguez's neighborhood six times hoping to find him. When they could not find him, the Ortizes drove to their father's apartment. As the vehicle arrived at the apartment building, the police stopped the brothers, who admitted that they wanted to "hurt" Rodriguez. What tests would allow conviction for attempted assault and battery with a dangerous weapon on Rodriguez? *See Commonwealth v. Ortiz*, 408 Mass. 463, 560 N.E.2d 698 (1990).

c. *Approaching the Intended Victim with a Loaded Weapon.* Defendant, who threatened to kill Delbert Jeans for annoying his wife, went to a field where Jeans was working. Carrying a rifle, defendant walked in a direct line toward Jeans who was 250 yards away. When defendant was 100 yards away, he stopped to load his rifle. At no time did he take aim. When Jeans saw defendant, Jeans fled. Defendant started to chase after Jeans, but another man stepped in and took the rifle from Jeans. Defendant was drunk and offered no resistance. The gun was loaded with a .22-caliber long, or high-speed, cartridge. What tests would allow conviction for attempted murder? *See People v. Miller*, 2 Cal. 2d 527, 42 P.2d 308 (1935).

d. *The Reverse Sting Operation.* The police conducted a "reverse sting operation," in which undercover police officers posed as drug sellers and actively solicited drug transactions. Joyce had twenty thousand dollars that he was interested in using to purchase cocaine. An informant took Joyce to a hotel room where an undercover officer (Jones) offered him a duct-tape wrapped package said to contain a kilogram of cocaine. Joyce refused to take it because he could not see the cocaine. Jones then unwrapped half of the package. Joyce again refused the package and asked Jones to completely open it. Jones refused unless Joyce produced the purchase price. Joyce refused and left. Did Joyce commit a sufficient "actus reus" for the crime of attempt under the various tests that you have studied?

People v. Rizzo

246 N.Y. 334, 158 N.E. 888 (1927).

CRANE, J.

Defendant has been convicted of an attempt to commit the crime of robbery in the first degree. There is no doubt that he had the intention to commit robbery, if he got the chance. An examination of the facts is necessary to determine whether his acts were in preparation to commit the crime if the opportunity offered, or constituted a crime in itself, known to our law as an attempt to commit robbery in the first degree. Defendant Rizzo, with three others, planned to rob Charles Rao of a pay roll which he was to carry from the bank for the United Lathing Company. Defendants, two of whom had firearms, started out in an automobile, looking for Rao. They went to the bank from which he was supposed to get the money and to various buildings being constructed by the United Lathing Company. At last they came to One Hundred and Eightieth Street and Morris Park Avenue. By this time, they were being watched and followed by two police officers. As Rizzo jumped out of the car and ran into the building, all four were arrested. The four men intended to rob the pay roll man, whoever he was. They were looking for him, but they had not seen or discovered him up to the time they were arrested.

Does this constitute the crime of an attempt to commit robbery in the first degree? The Penal Law, § 2, prescribes:" An act, done with intent to commit a crime, and tending but failing to effect its commission, is "an attempt to commit that crime."

The word "tending" is very indefinite. "Tending" means to exert activity in a particular direction. Any act in preparation to commit a crime may be said to have a tendency towards its accomplishment. The procuring of the automobile, searching the streets looking for the desired victim, were in reality acts tending toward the commission of the proposed crime. The law, however, had recognized that many acts in the way of preparation are too remote to constitute the crime of attempt. The line has been drawn between those acts which are remote and those which are proximate and near to the consummation. The law must be practical, and therefore considers those acts only as tending to the commission of the crime which are so near to its accomplishment that in all reasonable probability the crime itself would have been committed, but for timely interference. The cases which have been before the courts express this idea in different language, but the idea remains the same. The act or acts must come or advance very near to the accomplishment of the intended crime.

In *Hyde v. U.S.*, 225 U. S. 347, it was stated that the act amounts to an attempt when it is so near to the result that the danger of success is very great. "There must be dangerous proximity to success." Halsbury in his "Laws of England," says:" An act in order to be a criminal attempt must be immediately and not remotely connected with an directly tending to the commission of an offense."

The method of committing or attempting crime varies in each case, so that the difficulty, if any, is not with this rule of law regarding an attempt, which is well understood, but with its application to the facts. As I have said before, minds differ over proximity and the nearness of the approach.

How shall we apply this rule of immediate nearness to this case? To constitute the crime of robbery, the money must have been taken from Rao by means of force or violence, or through fear. The crime of attempt to commit robbery was committed, if these defendants did an act tending to the commission of this robbery. Did the acts above described come dangerously near to the taking of Rao's property? Did the acts come so near the commission of robbery that there was reasonable likelihood of its accomplishment but for the interference? These defendants had planned to commit a crime, and were looking around the city for an opportunity to commit it, but had planned to break into a building and were arrested while they were hunting about the streets for the building not knowing where it was. So here these defendants were not guilty of an attempt to commit robbery in the first degree when they had not found or reached the presence of the person they intended to rob.

For these reasons, the judgment of conviction of this defendant appellant must be reversed and a new trial granted.

Food for Thought

Did the Court reach the correct result in this case? If the court had applied the MPC's "substantial step" test, would there have been an "attempt?"

United States v. Jackson

560 F.2d 112 (2d Cir. 1977).

FREDERICK VAN PELT BRYAN, SENIOR DISTRICT JUDGE:

Vanessa Hodges wanted someone help her rob a Manufacturers Hanover branch in Brooklyn, and she invited Martin Allen to join her. Hodges proposed that the bank be robbed the next Monday at 7:30 A.M. They would enter with the bank manager, grab the weekend deposits, and leave. Allen agreed to rob the bank, and told her he had access to a car, two sawed-off shotguns, and a .38 caliber revolver.

The following Monday, June 14, Allen arrived at Longhorne's house about 7:30 A.M. in a car driven by appellant Robert Jackson. A suitcase in the back seat of the car contained a sawed-off shotgun, shells, materials intended as masks, and handcuffs to bind the bank manager. While Allen picked up Hodges, Jackson filled the car with gas. The trio then left for the bank.

When they arrived, it was almost 8:00 A.M. It was thus too late to effect the first step of the plan, viz., entering the bank as the manager opened the door. They rode around for a while, and then went to a restaurant to get something to eat and discuss their next move. After eating, the trio drove back to the bank. Allen and Hodges left the car and walked to the bank. They peered in and saw the bulky weekend deposits, but decided it was too risky to rob the bank without an extra man.

Consequently, Jackson, Hodges, and Allen drove to Coney Island in search of another accomplice. They found appellant William Scott, who promptly joined the team. Allen added to the arsenal another sawed-off shotgun, and the group drove back to the bank.

When they arrived again, Allen entered the bank to check the location of any surveillance cameras, while Jackson placed a piece of cardboard with a false license number over the authentic license plate of the car. Allen reported that a single surveillance camera was over the entrance door. After further discussion, Scott left the car and entered the bank. He came back and informed the group that the tellers were separating the weekend deposits and that a number of patrons were now in the bank. Hodges suggested that they reschedule for the following Monday, June 21. Accordingly, they left the vicinity of the bank and returned to Coney Island where, before splitting up, they purchased a pair of stockings for Hodges to wear over her head as a disguise and pairs of gloves for Hodges, Scott, and Allen to don before entering the bank.

Hodges was arrested on Friday, June 18, on an unrelated bank robbery charge, and immediately began cooperating with the Government. After relating the events on June 14, she told FBI agents that the robbery was now scheduled for June 21. At the request of the agents, Hodges called Allen on Saturday and asked if he were still planning to do the job. He said that he was ready. On Sunday she called him again. This time Allen said that he was not going to rob the bank because Hodges had been arrested and he feared that federal agents might be watching. Hodges nevertheless advised the agents that the robbery might still take place as planned.

On June 21, FBI agents took various surveilling positions in the area of the bank. At about 7:39 A.M., the agents observed a brown four-door Lincoln, with a New York license plate on the front and a cardboard facsimile of a license plate on the rear, moving in an easterly direction on Flushing Avenue past the bank. The front seat of the Lincoln was occupied by a black male driver and a black male passenger. The Lincoln circled the block and came to a stop at a fire hydrant situated at the side of the bank. A third black male, who appeared to have an eye deformity, got out of the passenger side rear door of the Lincoln, and stood on the sidewalk in the vicinity of the bank's entrance. He then walked south only to return a short time later with coffee. He stood again on the corner in front of the bank, drinking the coffee and looking around, before returning to the parked Lincoln.

The Lincoln pulled out, made a left turn onto Flushing, and proceeded one block to Waverly Avenue. It stopped, made a U-turn, and parked on the same side of the street as the bank entrance. After remaining parked for five minutes, it cruised past the bank again, made a right turn and headed south. It stopped halfway down the block and remained there for several minutes. During this time Jackson was seen working in the front of the car, which had its hood up. When the Lincoln was next sighted, its front license plate was missing. It began moving in the direction of the bank.

At some point, appellants detected the presence of the surveillance agents. The Lincoln accelerated and turned south. It was overtaken by FBI agents who ordered the appellants out of the car and arrested them. The agents found a black and red plaid suitcase in the rear of the car. The zipper of the suitcase was partially open and exposed two loaded sawed-off shotguns, a toy nickel-plated revolver, a pair of handcuffs, and masks. A New York license plate was seen lying on the front floor of the car. All of these items were seized.

In his memorandum of decision, Chief Judge Mishler applied the following two-tiered inquiry formulated in *United States v. Mandujano*, 499 F.2d 370, 376 (5th Cir. 1974), *cert. denied*, 419 U.S. 1114 (1975): "First, the defendant must have been acting with the kind of culpability otherwise required for the commission of the crime which he is charged with attempting. Second, the defendant must have engaged in conduct which constitutes a substantial step toward commission of the crime. A substantial step must be conduct strongly corroborative of the firmness of the defendant's criminal intent." He concluded that on June 14 and again on June 21, the defendants took substantial steps, strongly corroborative of the firmness of their criminal intent, toward commission of the crime of bank robbery and found the defendants guilty on each of the two attempt counts. These appeals followed.

Fed.R.Crim.P. 31(c) provides in pertinent part that a defendant may be found guilty of "an attempt to commit either the offense charged or an offense specifically makes attempted bank robbery an offense.

Appellant Scott argues that the very wording of 18 U.S.C. § 2113(a) precludes a finding that the actions charged in counts two and three reached the level of attempts. He contends that since the statute only mentions attempted taking and not attempted force, violence, or intimidation, it clearly contemplates that actual use of force, violence, or intimidation must precede an attempted taking in order to make out the offense of attempted bank robbery.

The court in *United States v. Stallworth*, 543 F.2d 1038 (2d Cir. 1976), faced a similar statutory construction argument. In response to the assertion that the defendants in that case could not be convicted of attempted bank robbery because they neither entered the bank nor brandished weapons, Chief Judge Kaufman stated:" We reject this wooden logic. Attempt is a subtle concept that requires a rational and logically sound definition, one that enables society to punish malefactors who have unequivocally set out upon a criminal course without requiring law enforcement officers to delay until innocent bystanders are imperiled."

We conclude that Scott's argument is foreclosed by this *Stallworth* holding, with which we are in entire accord.

Appellants Jackson and Allen seek to distinguish the instant case from *Stallworth.* They claim that while the conduct of the defendants in that case could properly support a finding of attempted bank robbery, this is not true in the case at bar. In *Stallworth*, the robbers pulled up directly in front of the bank and Sellers, armed with the sawed-off shotgun and positioned at an adjacent liquor store, started to approach the bank. Campbell said "let's go," and the occupants of the car reached for the doors. Immediately, FBI agents and New York City policemen who had staked out the parking lot and were monitoring the gang's conversations moved in and arrested the men.

Chief Judge Kaufman used the two-tiered inquiry of *Mandujano*, which "conforms closely to the sensible definition of an attempt proffered by the American Law Institute's Model Penal Code." The draftsmen of the Model Penal Code recognized the difficulty of arriving at a general standard for distinguishing acts of preparation from acts constituting an attempt. They found general agreement that when an actor committed the "last proximate act," *i.e.*, when he had done all that he believed necessary to effect a particular result which is an element of the offense, he committed an attempt. They also concluded, however, that while the last proximate act is sufficient to constitute an attempt, it is not necessary to such a finding. The problem then was to devise a standard more inclusive than one requiring the last proximate act before attempt liability would attach, but less inclusive than one which would make every act done with the intent to commit a crime criminal.

The draftsmen considered and rejected the common law approaches to distinguishing preparation from attempt. The formulation upon which the draftsmen ultimately agreed required, in addition to criminal purpose, that an act be a substantial step in a course of conduct designed to accomplish a criminal result, and that it be strongly corroborative of criminal purpose in order for it to constitute such a substantial step. The following differences between this test and previous approaches to the preparation-attempt problem were noted:

> First, this formulation shifts the emphasis from what remains to be done the chief concern of the proximity tests to what the actor has already done. The fact that further major steps must be taken before the crime can be completed does not preclude a finding that the steps already undertaken are substantial. It is expected, in the normal case, that this approach will broaden the scope of attempt liability. Second, although it is intended that the requirement of a substantial step will result in the imposition of attempt liability only in those instances in which some firmness of criminal purpose is shown, no finding is required as to whether the actor would probably have desisted prior to completing the crime. Potentially the probable desistance test could reach very early steps toward crime depending upon how one assesses the probabilities of desistance but since in practice this test follows closely the proximity approaches, rejection of probable desistance will not narrow the scope of attempt liability. Finally, the requirement of proving a substantial step generally will prove less of a hurdle for the prosecution than the *res*

ipsa loquitur approach, which requires that the actor's conduct must itself manifest the criminal purpose. The difference will be illustrated in connection with the present section's requirement of corroboration. Here it should be noted that, in the present formulation, the two purposes to be served by the *res ipsa loquitur* test are, to a large extent, treated separately. Firmness of criminal purpose is intended to be shown by requiring a substantial step, while problems of proof are dealt with by the requirement of corroboration (although, under the reasoning previously expressed, the latter will also tend to establish firmness of purpose).

Model Penal Code § 5.01, Comment at 47 (Tent. Draft No. 10, 1960).

The draftsmen concluded that, in addition to assuring firmness of criminal design, the requirement of a substantial step would preclude attempt liability, with its accompanying harsh penalties, for relatively remote preparatory acts. At the same time, however, by not requiring a "last proximate act" or one of its various analogues it would permit the apprehension of dangerous persons at an earlier stage than the other approaches without immunizing them from attempt liability.

Applying the *Mandujano* test, which in turn was derived in large part from the Model Penal Code's standard, Chief Judge Kaufman concluded that since the *Stallworth* appellants intended to execute a successful bank robbery and took substantial steps in furtherance of their plan that strongly corroborated their criminal intent, their attempted bank robbery convictions were proper.

As in *Stallworth*, the criminal intent of these appellants was beyond dispute. The question remaining then is the substantiality of the steps taken on the dates in question, and how strongly this corroborates the firmness of their obvious criminal intent. This is a matter of degree.

On two separate occasions, appellants reconnoitered the place contemplated for the commission of the crime and possessed the paraphernalia to be employed in the commission of the crime loaded sawed-off shotguns, extra shells, a toy revolver, handcuffs, and masks which was specially designed for such unlawful use and which could serve no lawful purpose under the circumstances. Under the Model Penal Code formulation, approved by the *Stallworth* court, either type of conduct, standing alone, was sufficient as a matter of law to constitute a "substantial step" if it strongly corroborated their criminal purpose. Here both types of conduct coincided on both June 14 and June 21, along with numerous other elements strongly corroborative of the firmness of appellants' criminal intent. The steps taken toward a successful bank robbery thus were not "insubstantial" as a matter of law, and Chief Judge Mishler found them "substantial" as

Take Note

In addition to the crime of attempt, most criminal codes also prohibit possession of burglar tools or other tools that might be used in the commission of a crime. For example, in *Moore v. State*, 197 Ga. App. 9, 397 S.E.2d 477 (1990), defendant was convicted of possession of tools for the commission of a crime.

a matter of fact. We are unwilling to substitute our assessment of the evidence for his, and thus affirm the convictions for attempted bank robbery on counts two and three.

The judgments of conviction are affirmed.

Hypo: *More* Actus Reus *Scenarios*

Consider the following problems. Decide whether the *actus reus* of attempt has been committed under the various common law tests, or under the MPC's substantial step test:

a. *The Men in the Weeds.* At 6:15 a.m., the police are informed that two armed men are hiding behind a service station. When a police officer arrives, he sees defendant crouched in the weeds in an empty lot 20 to 30 feet from the station. Defendant jumps up, climbs a fence, and runs down an adjoining street. He throws away a gun before he scales the fence. Minutes later, defendant is found hiding in the weeds behind a company some 200 feet from the service station. He has removed his shirt, and has a black nylon stocking with a knot in the end. Although defendant claims that he went to the gas station to buy cigarettes, he has no money. On these facts, can defendant be convicted of the crime of attempted robbery? How would you argue the case for the State? How might defendant respond? *See People v. Terrell*, 99 Ill. 2d 427, 459 N.E.2d 1337, 77 Ill. Dec. 88 (1984).

b. *The Illegal Abortion "Sting."* Defendant agrees to perform an illegal abortion for an undercover police officer who goes to defendant's apartment. She see a table with a sheet and cover; a large folding screen (for privacy); a chair at one end of the table; a stove with a covered pan on the burner that contains instruments commonly used in performing abortions; and various medicines, medical instruments and books. Defendant gives the officer two sedative pills which she pretends to swallow, and she pays him the agreed-upon price. Defendant then explains the operation, and tells the officer that he will have to examine her. The officer removes her shoes and suit jacket and unbuttons two buttons on her blouse when she reveals her true identity and arrests defendant. Did defendant commit the crime of attempted abortion? *See People v. Woods*, 24 Ill. 2d 154, 180 N.E.2d 475 (1962).

c. *Attempted Robbery?* Defendant hires a taxi cab and directs the driver to take him to Genesee Street to a jewelry store. The driver points out a jewelry store, but defendant tells him that it is a "low class" store. The driver then notices a police car and asks defendant if they should ask for directions. Defendant rejects this idea and then exits the taxi. The suspicious taxi driver notifies the police who quickly apprehend defendant. He admits that he intended to rob an unidentified jewelry store on Genesee Street. Although defendant did not know the name of the jewelry store, he did know what the building

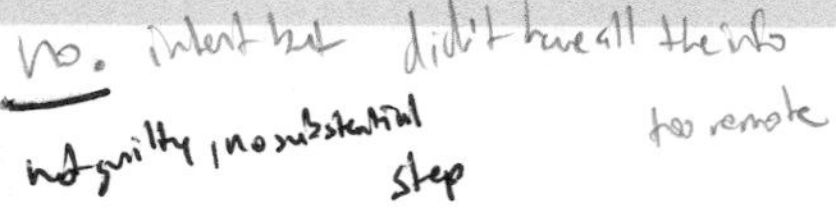

looked like. Has defendant committed the crime of attempted robbery of the jewelry store? *See People v. Smith*, 148 Ill. 2d 454, 593 N.E.2d 533, 170 Ill. Dec. 644 (1992).

d. *Attempted Burglary?* Defendant left his home at night and drove approximately twenty miles to a nearby city while being surreptitiously observed by several unmarked police cars. After driving slowly down several residential streets, he parks his car at an apartment complex and turns his lights off. Defendant exits the car and walks a short distance. When a police car appears, he crosses the street, and begins running behind a group of homes. Shortly thereafter, he is arrested. He is dressed in dark clothing, and is carrying a heavy-gauge screwdriver, a ten-inch pry bar, two flashlights, a knit cap, and a pair of gloves. The temperature is 70 degrees Fahrenheit. There was no evidence that any nearby house had been burglarized. Did defendant take a "substantial step" towards the commission of a burglary? *See Commonwealth v. Melnyczenko*, 422 Pa. Super. 363, 619 A.2d 719 (1992).

e. *Attempted Grand Larceny?* Defendant Mahboubian insured his collection of gold and silver Persian antiquities with Lloyd's of London for $18.5 million. He then traveled to New York where he rented a vault at a long-term storage facility, and arranged to have two men steal the art. Although they were expert burglars, when they tried to burglarize the facility, they were apprehended by police. Defendant Mahboubian was charged with staging the theft with the objective of recovering insurance proceeds (*i.e.*, attempted grand larceny). Did he commit the *actus reus* if he never submitted a false claim to his insurer? *See People v. Mahboubian*, 74 N.Y.2d 174, 543 N.E.2d 34, 544 N.Y.S.2d 769 (1989).

f. *Attempted Bank Robbery?* The police receive information that defendants plan to rob a bank and that one of them will be dressed as a woman. On the day of the robbery, defendants (two men and a third person appearing to be a woman) drive slowly past the bank, make a U-turn, drive past the bank again, and park by a nearby store. One defendant leaves the car, enters the store, and walks to a window which overlooks the bank. He stands there for several minutes, but does no shopping. The other two defendants exit the car and stand facing the bank. When a power outage hits the area, a bank teller locks the bank's door. All three defendants re-enter the car and start to drive away. A police officer stops the vehicle and finds a revolver in possession of one of the defendants and another revolver on the floor of the car. Did defendants commit the crime of attempted bank robbery? *See United States v. Buffington*, 815 F.2d 1292 (9th Cir. 1987).

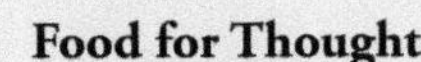

Food for Thought

Defendant, who had been diagnosed as HIV positive, was incarcerated in the county jail. Defendant knew that if he had sex with others, he risked infecting them with HIV. After his release, defendant committed a rape. If defendant failed to use a condom when he committed the rape, has he committed the actus reus of assault with intent to commit murder? *See Smallwood v. State*, 106 Md. App. 1, 661 A.2d 747 (1995).

g. *Attempted Gas Station Robbery?* Defendants go to a service station to purchase gas. After they make the purchase, they decide to rob the station with a shotgun. One defendant points the gun at the owner of the station and tells him that it is a "stick-up." The owner tries to talk them out of it, and they tell him they need more gas. The owner then offers to give them $2 worth of gas if they abandon the robbery. They agree, take the gas, and leave the station without robbing it. Is this attempted robbery? How would the case be resolved under the Model Penal Code? *See People v. Crary*, 265 Cal. App. 2d 534, 71 Cal. Rptr. 457 (1968).

h. *The "Bill Trap."* Defendants are found in a rented car with two loaded handguns, a roll of duct tape, a stun gun, and two pairs of latex surgical gloves. They are parked next to an ATM machine, and one defendant carries a stolen ATM card which he used to request a twenty-dollar withdrawal, but he did not remove the cash from the machine. By his failure to remove the cash, he created a "bill trap," so that the ATM shut itself down and sent a signal to summon a service technician. The "bill trap" procedure is familiar to defendants because they had worked for an ATM service company. The prosecution argues that defendants intentionally caused the bill trap to summon the ATM service technicians so that defendants could rob the technicians of the money in the ATM. Did defendants cross the line between preparation and attempt? *See United States v. Harper*, 33 F.3d 1143 (9th Cir. 1994).

i. *Attempted Murder?* Dillon, an undercover FBI agent, agrees to hire defendant to protect him during a pretended drug transaction in a motel room. After the transaction, Dillon claims that he was shortchanged by the buyer. At that point, defendant offers to kill the buyer for $10,000. Dillon and defendant agree to meet at a lounge near the motel. They decide that defendant should go to the lobby, call the buyer, and convince him to come down to the lobby where defendant would then shoot him. Defendant goes to the lobby with a loaded gun, but does not call the buyer's room. As defendant leaves the lobby, sheriff's deputies arrest him. Defendant contends that he was collecting evidence to build a case against Dillon. Did defendant commit attempted murder? *See State v. Pacheco*, 125 Wash. 2d 150, 882 P.2d 183 (En Banc 1994).

Take Note

With many crimes, if defendant commits both the *actus reus* and the *mens rea* of the crime, the crime is complete and chargeable. By contrast, since attempt can involve something less than the completed crime, abandonment of the criminal enterprise is still possible.

C. Abandonment

If a defendant has the necessary *mens rea* for attempt, and commits the *actus reus*, should it matter that defendant subsequently "abandons" the attempt?

State v. Workman

90 Wash. 2d 443, 584 P.2d 382 (En Banc 1978).

HOROWITZ, JUSTICE.

Defendants Lawrence Dean Workman and Steven Lynn Hughes spent the evening of July 22, 1976 drinking and dancing with their wives in State Line, Idaho. On the way home to Moses Lake, Washington after the taverns closed, defendants decided to commit a robbery. Taking the freeway exit for Spokane, they spotted the Fill-em' Fast Gas Station and chose it as their target. They parked their car in an alley behind the station. Leaving their wives asleep, they took a .22 caliber rifle from the trunk of the car and loaded it. They also took a gunny sack with holes punched in it for eyeholes, and a stocking cap, both intended for use as masks. Then they walked up the alley to a fence behind the station and waited. This was normally a busy time at the station. After about 15 minutes, they moved to a hiding place just behind the pay booth, where they waited again.

At about 2:30 a.m., when business at the station was slack, the attendant took a short walk to get some fresh air and saw defendants, unmasked, behind the pay booth. He returned to the booth and called the police. Defendant Workman later appeared at the window without a mask or gun and asked for a cigarette and match. The attendant refused, and Workman rejoined defendant Hughes. During this period, according to defendants' testimony, they were trying to summon the "courage" to commit the robbery and decide how to do it.

Sometime after the cigarette episode, an unmarked police car took up a position across the street from the station. The police officer could see both the defendants and a second police car which had turned into the alley behind the station. The first car then pulled into the station.

At that time, defendants, having decided not to go through with their plans, started walking away from the station. They testified at their trials that they had not seen the police before they decided to leave. They were stopped and arrested in the alley behind the station. Defendant Hughes was found to have the sawed-off rifle concealed under his clothes.

Defendants were each charged with attempted first degree robbery while armed with a deadly weapon. At their separate trials, each defendant was found guilty. At trial, defendants tried to show they abandoned their plan before the crime of attempt was committed. They proposed an instruction on abandonment derived essentially from a New York statute which sets up abandonment of criminal purpose as an affirmative defense to the crime of attempt. The trial courts both rejected the proposed instruction and gave an instruction properly based on our attempt statute.

The instruction, given correctly, stated that a person is guilty of attempt if, with intent to commit a specific crime, he does any act which is a substantial step towards the commission of the crime. The instruction qualified the meaning of a "substantial step" by stating that the conduct must be more than mere preparation. Defendants contend, however, that the statutory language, "substantial step," is unconstitutionally vague unless further defined, that an instruction on abandonment is necessary in order to properly define it, and that without the requested instruction, they were precluded from arguing their theory of the case to the jury.

We disagree. The question of what constitutes a "substantial step" under the particular facts of the case is for the trier of fact. The instruction given informed the jury that mere preparation would not be sufficient, that something more must be present in order to constitute a substantial step. When preparation ends and an attempt begins, depends on the facts of the particular case. We cannot agree that the instruction given was unconstitutionally vague.

Furthermore, an instruction relating to abandonment is neither necessary, nor particularly helpful in defining the meaning of a substantial step. Once a substantial step has been taken, and the crime of attempt is accomplished, the crime cannot be abandoned. Defendants' attempt to show they abandoned their plan is thus relevant only if the abandonment occurred before a substantial step was taken. Through arguing their theory at trial, they could only have hoped to show they never took a substantial step toward the specific crime. Abandonment is not, however, a true defense to the crime of attempt under our statute that is, a showing of abandonment does not negate the State's allegation that a substantial step occurred. Thus, pursuing the theory of abandonment could only be a strategy for showing why a substantial step was never taken. Defendants could not thereby show whether such a step was taken. We therefore conclude an instruction on abandonment is not necessary as a matter of law to properly define a "substantial step."

It is so ordered.

Point for Discussion

Model Penal Code

The MPC takes the following position regarding abandonment:

§ 5.01 Criminal Attempt.

* * *

(4) **Renunciation of Criminal Purpose.** When the actor's conduct would otherwise constitute an attempt under Subsection (1)(b) or (1)(c) of this Section, it is an affirmative defense that he abandoned his effort to commit the crime or otherwise prevented its commission, under circumstances manifesting a complete and voluntary renunciation of his criminal purpose. The establishment of such defense does not, however, affect the liability of an accomplice who did not join in such abandonment or prevention.

Within the meaning of this Article, renunciation of criminal purpose is not voluntary if it is motivated, in whole or in part, by circumstances, not present or apparent at the inception of the actor's course of conduct, that increase the probability of detection or apprehension or that make more difficult the accomplishment of the criminal purpose. Renunciation is not complete if it is motivated by a decision to postpone the criminal conduct until a more advantageous time or to transfer the criminal effort to another but similar objective or victim.

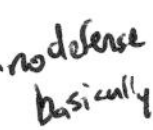

Food for Thought

Does *Workman*'s holding make sense? As the court recognizes, defendant committed a "substantial step" towards commission of the crime. Therefore, he was deserving of punishment, considering the justifications for punishment, i.e. deterrence, restraint, rehabilitation and retribution. On the other hand, should the law encourage renunciation? If defendant has already passed the point of no return, in the sense that he can be convicted of "attempt" but not the completed crime, would this fact reduce his incentive to desist?

Food for Thought

How would the *Workman* case be resolved under the MPC? Although he took a "substantial step," would the MPC permit him to assert the defense of renunciation? Moreover, is it clear that Workman's renunciation was "complete and voluntary" and unrelated to a fear of detection?

Hypo 1: *Attempted Escape?*

Shortly after midnight, a prison guard heard an alarm which indicated that someone was attempting to escape from a prison recreation area. Guards immediately check the prison population, but find no one missing. In the recreation area, they find that a piece of barbed wire has been cut, and they also find a prison laundry bag filled with civilian clothing. The next morning, without prompting, defendant voluntarily tells a guard that, "I was gonna make a break last night, but I changed my mind because I thought of my family, and I got scared of the consequences." Defendant testified that he was depressed because he had been denied a holiday furlough. Defendant is charged with attempted prison escape. On these facts, should defendant be convicted? Under the MPC, did he sufficiently renounce the attempt? What would you argue on defendant's behalf? How might the State respond? *See Commonwealth v. McCloskey*, 234 Pa. Super. 577, 341 A.2d 500 (1975).

Hypo 2: *Attempted Murder?*

Defendant went to the laundry of a hotel where his wife, from whom he was separated, was employed, and approached his wife. Defendant had been in the same laundry room the previous Saturday and had called her a "yellow-bellied son of a bitch" and had also said, "I'll give you just twenty-four hours to live." This time he told his wife: "This is it." She ran to an adjoining office where she tried to phone the police. Defendant followed her, took the phone, tore it loose from the wall and threw it at her. He missed. The wife then ran to another room where she did call the police. At this point, defendant retrieved a loaded 12-gauge shotgun from his car. His wife was still hiding in the room with the other phone. He returned to the laundry room with the gun positioned to shoot directly in front of him. As he entered, he said to two women there, "Don't move anyone or I'll shoot you." Shortly after that, defendant turned around and walked away. As he was leaving the building, he was apprehended by a police officer responding to the wife's phone call. Did defendant commit attempted murder? *See State v. Wilson*, 218 Or. 575, 346 P.2d 115 (1959).

Hypo 3: *Attempted Robbery?*

Defendant, who had been drinking very heavily, stopped at a store to buy a pack of cigarettes. Defendant approached the cashier and demanded money. The cashier thought defendant was joking until he demanded money again in a "firmer tone." The cashier then began fumbling with the one-dollar bills until defendant directed her to the "big bills." The cashier testified that defendant then said, "I won't do it to you; you're good-looking, but if you're here next time, it won't matter." Defendant's girlfriend then came in, put a hand on defendant's shoulder, and directed him out of the store. Did defendant "attempt" to rob the liquor store? *See People v. Kimball*, 109 Mich. App. 273, 311 N.W.2d 343 (1981).

Hypo 4: *Attempted Bank Robbery?*

While his wife was away, defendant rented an office directly over the vault of a bank. Defendant placed drilling tools, acetylene gas tanks, a blow torch, a blanket, and a linoleum rug in the office. Subsequently, defendant drilled two groups of holes in the floor above the vault. The holes did not go through the floor. He came back to the office several times to drill down, covering the holes with the linoleum rug. At some point, defendant's landlord became aware of his activities and notified the police. At trial, defendant testified that he had planned to rob the bank, but that he "began to realize that, even if I were to succeed, a fugitive life of living off of stolen money would not give me enjoyment of life. I still had not given up my plan however. I felt I had made a certain investment of time, money, effort and a certain psychological commitment to the concept. I came back several times thinking I might slowly drill down. When my wife came back, my life as bank robber seemed more and more absurd." Under the circumstances, should the defense of abandonment be available to defendant? *See People v. Staples*, 6 Cal. App. 3d 61, 85 Cal. Rptr. 589 (1970).

Hypo 5: *Attempted Arson?*

Lombardi, an undercover detective, arrested defendant for receiving stolen goods. A few days after defendant was released on bail, Lombardi saw a late-model car bearing a license plate assigned to defendant's automobile agency. The driver went down the street, turned left, came back on a perpendicular street, stopped directly across from Lombardi's residence, and extinguished its lights. Lombardi radioed for help. When the police arrived, the driver backed up, made a U-turn, and headed away. The police caught defendant, and a search revealed that the car contained a can of gasoline; a rag; matches; an aluminum baseball bat; and a note that read, "Hi, Sal, it's my turn." Defendant was charged with attempting knowingly and maliciously to dissuade a police officer from giving testimony. On these facts, is conviction appropriate? If an attempt occurred, did defendant "abandon" it? *See State v. Latraverse*, 443 A.2d 890 (R.I. 1982).

Food for Thought

Henley and her seven-year-old daughter lived in a trailer. Henley was alone and answered the door to find defendant asking directions. Then defendant pointed a handgun at her, ordered her into the house, told her to undress, and shoved her onto the couch. He also threatened to kill her. Henley described herself as frightened and crying. She attempted to escape from defendant and told him that her daughter would be home from school at any time. She testified: "I started crying and talking about my daughter, that I was all she had because her daddy was dead, and he said if I had a little girl he wouldn't do anything, for me just to go outside and turn my back." Defendant then departed. Did defendant abandon the attack? *See Ross v. State*, 601 So.2d 872 (Miss. 1992); *People v. McNeal*, 152 Mich. App. 404, 393 N.W.2d 907 (1986).

Hypo 6: *Attempted Purchase of Illegal Drugs?*

Defendant negotiated with Roger to purchase cocaine. Roger called defendant and asked, "are you ready?" Defendant replied "yes." Defendant called an associate, and told him that the man would be "coming over. Right now." Officers staked out defendant's apartment and saw a man pull up in a car, remove a plastic bag from the trunk, and enter the building. The handles of the bag were stretched, indicating that the contents were heavy. A half hour later, the man emerged from the building, carrying the same plastic bag which still appeared to be heavy. He placed the bag back in the trunk and drove off. The evidence showed that defendant intended to purchase the contents of the bag (cocaine), but declined to do so because of its inferior quality. On these facts, does the defense of abandonment apply? *See People v. Acosta*, 80 N.Y.2d 665, 609 N.E.2d 518, 593 N.Y.S.2d 978 (1993).

Hypo 7: *Attempted Sexual Assault?*

M.B. and J.G. skipped school and were drinking sodas outside a liquor store. Smith approached the boys, asked about their absence from school, and demanded identification. He had a gun and a badge, and he told the boys that he was a police officer. The boys started to walk back to school, but Smith told them he would drive them back. When the boys refused the ride, Smith threatened to use handcuffs to escort them to school. The boys then entered the car. Smith drove them to a wooded area, handcuffed M.B. to a tree, and ordered J.G. to exit the car. Then Smith held J.G.'s arm behind his back and shoved him into the woods. Smith commanded him to disrobe. When J.G. refused, Smith placed his gun to J.G.'s throat and again told him to remove his clothes. J.G. still refused. Smith was startled by the sound of a branch snapping, which was M.B. breaking free from the tree. Smith then took J.G. back to the car and released him. Meanwhile, M.B. ran to a nearby home and called the police. Was there abandonment? *See Smith v. State*, 636 N.E.2d 124 (Ind. 1994).

Food for Thought

Defendant and his uncle were drinking heavily and began quarreling. Defendant stabbed his uncle in the chest twice. The uncle then fled pursued by defendant. When the uncle collapsed a block away, defendant was remorseful and wept. Defendant dragged his uncle to his car, threw away the knife, "floored the accelerator," and sped towards the hospital. Examination by physicians at the hospital revealed that the uncle had suffered two deep stab wounds between his ribs and close to his heart which had penetrated and collapsed both lungs, but he survived. Should defendant be convicted of attempted murder? *See State v. Smith*, 409 N.E.2d 1199 (Ind. App.1980).

D. Impossibility

Suppose a defendant tries to commit a crime which turns out to be impossible to commit. Has the defendant committed attempt? Should defendant be punished?

Take Note

The crime of attempt is unique in that an individual may attempt to commit a crime under circumstances where it is impossible to actually complete the crime (e.g., an individual tries to murder someone who is already dead).

State v. Guffey

262 S.W.2d 152 (Mo. App.1953).

VANDEVENTER, PRESIDING JUDGE.

Appellants were convicted of violating Section 252.040, V.A.M.S. The information charges that defendants did "willfully and unlawfully hunt, pursue, and attempt to take, with the use of firearms, a deer during the prescribed closed season," contrary to the statute and the wild life code.

The State's evidence shows that Conservation agents procured the hide of a 2 1/2 year old doe which had been killed by an automobile. They had taken it to a taxidermist, who soaked it to soften it, stuffed it with excelsior and boards, inserted rods in the legs so it would stand upright and used the doe's skull in the head part of the hide so it would hold its former shape. For eyes, which had not been preserved, two small circular pieces of scotchlight reflector tape of a "white to amber color", had been placed over the eyeless sockets. The dummy was placed in a field about fifty yards from the north side of an old road so it could be seen by anyone coming along the road. Conservation agents, fully armed, concealed themselves in the brush and awaited the arrival of some citizen who might come that way, see the tempting bait and with visions of odoriferous venison cooking in pot or pan, decide not to wait until the 4th of December to replenish his larder.

A car was observed coming from the east at a speed of 10 or 15 miles per hour with two spotlights sweeping the countryside and piercing the darkness with their beams. As the car neared, one of the beams fell on the stuffed deer and someone in the car was heard to exclaim, "Wait, there stands one." The car stopped, a spotlight was trained upon the dummy deer. Immediately after the car stopped, there was a blast of a shotgun fired by a man on the right side of the front seat. The agents converged upon the Chevrolet and its occupants, seized the spotlights, a flashlight, the shotgun, an empty shell, and a loaded shell. Charges were filed against the two appellants.

It is argued that the evidence does not show the violation of any law; that though the mountain labored, it did not even bring forth a mouse. The State argues that the evidence does show that defendants did pursue a deer. The State then argues that one of the meanings of the word "pursue" is to "seek" and that the facts that defendants were going along the highway in an automobile with spotlights and a shotgun and did take a shot at the dummy deer proves that they did "seek" a deer, which being synonymous with "pursue" made them guilty of violating Section 252.040 and the regulations.

The State has wholly failed to make its case when it stands upon the proposition that defendants "pursued" a deer. In the first place there was no deer. The hide of a doe long since deceased, filled with boards, excelsior and rods with eyes made of a reflective scotch tape, was not a deer within the meaning of the statute and Section 33 of the "Wildlife Code of Missouri." The dummy, such as it was, was a stationary affair, it could not run, could not jump, it could not flee from the rifle slug of a hunter. It was not wild and it had no life.

Undoubtedly the words "pursued" as used in the statute and "pursue" as used in Section 33 of the Code means to follow with the intention of overtaking, or to chase. A deer's part in such a pursuit or chase is clearly described by the Scottish Bard, Sir Walter Scott, in "The Lady of the Lake, Canto First, The Chase."

The antler'd monarch of the waste Sprung from his heathery couch in haste

Then, as the headmost foes appear'd with one brave bound the copse he clear'd

And stretching forward free and far, sought the wild heaths of Uam-Var.

It is difficult for us to visualize the dummy with its tottering legs, synthetic eyes and vitals of shredded wood, springing from its couch, bounding a copse and "stretching forward free and far" seeking other fields. It could hardly stand alone and almost collapsed from loss of excelsior after it was shot.

Neither is the State's contention bolstered by the fact that the information contains the word "hunt" and "attempt to take." The State's evidence shows that one of the defendants did shoot the dummy but did they pursue, chase or follow a deer by shooting this stuffed defunct doe hide? It was not a deer. If the dummy had been actually taken, (it could not be pursued) defendants would not have committed any offense. It is no offense to attempt to do that which is not illegal. Neither is it a crime to attempt to do that which it is legally impossible to do. For instance, it is no crime to attempt to murder a corpse because it cannot be murdered.

If the State's evidence showed an attempt to take the dummy, it fell far short of proving an attempt to take a deer. We hold that the State wholly failed to make a case.

State v. Curtis

157 Vt. 629, 603 A.2d 356 (1992).

MORSE, JUSTICE.

Defendant shot a deer decoy and was convicted of attempting to take a wild deer out of season under 10 V.S.A. § 4745. His principal argument on appeal is that the defense of legal impossibility precludes a conviction under this statute and under Vermont's attempt statute.

A person is prohibited from taking "a wild deer except specified wild deer during the seasons provided by law." A person is guilty of attempting a crime by doing "an act toward its commission but by reason of being interrupted or prevented fails in the execution of the same." We have held that an "attempt consists not only of an intent to commit a particular crime, but some overt act designed to carry out such intent." Undoubtedly, defendant's behavior demonstrated an intent to take a wild deer out of season. He performed an overt act toward the commission of the intended crime. His conduct went as far as it could in achieving the goal of taking a wild deer out of season. Except for the fact that the "wild deer" in his sights was not real, he would be guilty of the crime prohibited by § 4745.

Defendant was "prevented" from shooting a wild deer because he was tricked into shooting a decoy. We see no meaningful distinction between the infeasible act of putting a bullet-proof protection on a live deer to prevent its demise and the use of a decoy to divert a hunter's attention from a live deer. Either way, live deer are given a measure of protection.

Defendant possessed the specific intent to take a wild deer out of season. Defendant's failure to actually take a live wild deer is of no consequence. This is not a case where defendant's conduct was equivocal. There was no testimony that defendant thought the decoy was not a live deer. Failure to find that defendant's actions amount to a crime would frustrate the goals underlying wildlife protection legislation. A contrary holding would oblige state and local officials to respond to illegal hunting by more cumbersome, dangerous, after-the-fact methods. Prosecution based on a fresh kill defeats the purpose of legislation drafted to preserve wildlife. The difficulties and risks associated with detecting poachers without the benefit of decoys are manifest. As stated by a game warden at trial, there is a serious concern for the safe detection of poachers, and the decoy system was established in response to those concerns.

Affirmed.

Point for Discussion

The *Jaffe* Rule

In *People v. Jaffe*, 185 N.Y. 497, 78 N.E. 169 (1906), defendant was charged with attempting to receive stolen property under a statute providing "that the accused shall have known to have been stolen or wrongfully appropriated in such a manner as to constitute larceny." When the property was sold to defendant, the police and the owner were acting in collaboration so that the goods were not actually stolen. The court reversed the conviction: "The defendant could not know that the property possessed the character of stolen property when it had not in fact been acquired by theft." The *Jaffe* rule was rejected in *People v. Rojas*, 55 Cal. 2d 252, 358 P.2d 921, 10 Cal. Rptr. 465 (1961): "The criminality of the attempt is not destroyed by the fact that the goods, having been recovered by the police had, unknown to defendants, lost their 'stolen' status." *See also People v. Rollino*, 37 Misc. 2d 14, 233 N.Y.S.2d 580 (1962).

Food for Thought

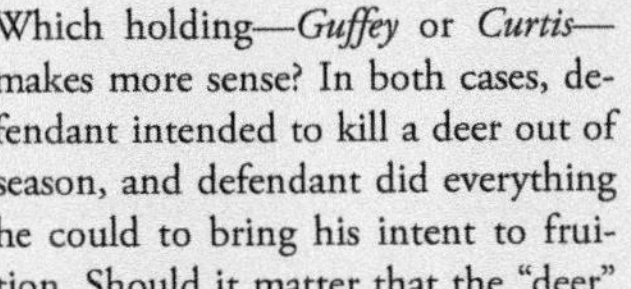

Which holding—*Guffey* or *Curtis*—makes more sense? In both cases, defendant intended to kill a deer out of season, and defendant did everything he could to bring his intent to fruition. Should it matter that the "deer" was a decoy rather than a real deer?

Hypo 1: *The Pickpocket*

Defendant was observed in a crowded market and was seen to thrust his hand into the pocket of a man. Defendant found the pocket empty and withdrew his hand without obtaining anything. A police officer arrested defendant and charged him with attempted theft. Given that the pocket was empty, can defendant be convicted of attempted theft? *See People v. Twiggs*, 223 Cal. App. 2d 455, 35 Cal. Rptr. 859 (1963); *People v. Moran*, 123 N.Y. 254, 25 N.E. 412 (1890).

Hypo 2: *The Fake Stash House*

The FBI establishes a fake "stash house" from which narcotics are supposedly stored and sold. Police undercover detectives agree with defendants to rob the stash house. When they arrive at the house, to execute the robbery, defendants are arrested. Given that the stash house was a fake, can defendants be convicted? *See United States v. Min*, 704 F.3d 314 (4th Cir.2013).

People v. Dlugash

41 N.Y.2d 725, 363 N.E.2d 1155, 395 N.Y.S.2d 419 (1977).

JASEN, JUDGE.

The issue is whether an individual's intentions and actions, though failing to achieve a manifest and malevolent criminal purpose, constitute a danger to organized society of sufficient magnitude to warrant the imposition of criminal sanctions. Difficulties in theoretical analysis and concomitant debate over very pragmatic questions of blameworthiness appear dramatically in reference to situations where the criminal attempt failed to achieve its purpose solely because the factual or legal context in which the individual acted was not as the actor supposed them to be. Phrased somewhat differently, the concern centers on whether an individual should be liable for an attempt to commit a crime when, unknown to him, it was impossible to successfully complete the crime attempted. For years, serious studies have been made on the subject in an effort to resolve the continuing controversy when, if at all, the impossibility of successfully completing the criminal act should preclude liability for even making the futile attempt. The 1967 revision of the Penal Law approached the impossibility defense to the inchoate crime of attempt in a novel fashion. The statute provides that, if a person engages in conduct which would otherwise constitute an attempt to commit a crime, "it is no defense to a prosecution for such attempt that the crime charged to have been attempted was, under the attendant circumstances, factually or legally impossible of commission, if such crime could have been committed had the attendant circumstances been as such person believed them to be." This appeal presents to us, for the first time, a case involving the application of the modern statute.

Defendant admitted that, on the night in question, he, Bush and Geller had been out drinking. Bush had been staying at Geller's apartment and during the evening, Geller several times demanded that Bush pay $100 towards the rent on the apartment. Bush told Geller that "you better shut up or you're going to get a bullet." All three returned to Geller's apartment at midnight and continued to drink. When Geller again pressed his demand for rent money, Bush drew his .38 caliber pistol, aimed it at Geller and fired three times. Geller fell to the floor. After the passage of a few minutes, perhaps two, perhaps as much as five, defendant walked over to the fallen Geller, drew his .25 caliber pistol, and fired approximately five shots in the victim's head and face. At the time defendant shot at Geller, Geller was not moving and his eyes were closed.

The jury found the defendant guilty of murder. All three medical expert witnesses testified that they could not, with any degree of medical certainty, state whether the victim had been alive at the time the latter shots were fired by the defendant. Thus, the People failed to prove beyond a reasonable doubt that the victim had been alive at the time he was shot by the defendant. Whatever else it may be, it is not murder to shoot a dead body. Man dies but once.

The most intriguing attempt cases are those where the attempt to commit a crime was unsuccessful due to mistakes of fact or law on the part of the would-be criminal. A general rule developed in most American jurisdictions that legal impossibility is a good defense but factual impossibility is not. An example is Francis Wharton's classic hypothetical involving Lady Eldon and her French lace. Lady Eldon, traveling in Europe, purchased a quantity of French lace at a high price, intending to smuggle it into England without payment of the duty. When discovered in a customs search, the lace turned out to be of English origin, of little value and not subject to duty. The traditional view is that Lady Eldon is not liable for an attempt to smuggle.

On the other hand, factual impossibility was no defense. For example, a man was held liable for attempted murder when he shot into the room in which his target usually slept and, fortuitously, the target was sleeping elsewhere in the house that night. Although one bullet struck the target's customary pillow, attainment of the criminal objective was factually impossible. *State v. Moretti*, 52 N.J. 182, 244 A.2d 499, presents a similar instance of factual impossibility. Defendant agreed to perform an abortion, then a criminal act, upon a female undercover police investigator who was not, in fact, pregnant. The court sustained the conviction, ruling that "when the consequences sought by a defendant are forbidden by the law as criminal, it is no defense that the defendant could not succeed in reaching his goal because of circumstances unknown to him."

The New York cases can be parsed out along similar lines. One of the leading cases on legal impossibility is *People v. Jaffe*, 185 N.Y. 497, 78 N.E. 169, in which we held that there was no liability for the attempted receipt of stolen property when the property received by defendant in the belief that it was stolen was, in fact under the control of the true owner. Similarly, in

People v. Teal, 196 N.Y. 372, 89 N.E. 1086, a conviction for attempted subornation of perjury was overturned on the theory that the testimony attempted to be suborned was irrelevant to the merits of the case. Since it was not subornation of perjury to solicit false, but irrelevant, testimony, "the person through whose procuration the testimony is given cannot be guilty of subornation of perjury and, by the same rule, an unsuccessful attempt to that which is not a crime when effectuated, cannot be held to be an attempt to commit the crime specified." Factual impossibility, however, was no defense. Thus, a man could be held for attempted grand larceny when he picked an empty pocket.

As can be seen, the distinction between "factual" and "legal" impossibility was a nice one indeed and the courts tended to place a greater value on legal form than on any substantive danger the defendant's actions posed for society. The approach of the draftsmen of the Model Penal Code was to eliminate the defense of impossibility in virtually all situations. Under the code provision, to constitute an attempt, it is still necessary that the result intended or desired by the actor constitute a crime. However, the code suggested a fundamental change to shift the locus of analysis to the actor's mental frame of reference and away from undue dependence upon external considerations. The basic premise of the code provision is that what was in the actor's own mind should be the standard for determining his dangerousness to society and, hence, his liability for attempted criminal conduct.

In the belief that neither of the two branches of the traditional impossibility arguments detracts from the offender's moral culpability, the Legislature substantially carried the code's treatment of impossibility into the 1967 revision of the Penal Law. Thus, a person is guilty of an attempt when, with intent to commit a crime, he engages in conduct which tends to effect the commission of such crime. It is no defense that, under the attendant circumstances, the crime was factually or legally impossible of commission, "if such crime could have been committed had the attendant circumstances been as such person believed them to be." Thus, if defendant believed the victim to be alive at the time of the shooting, it is no defense to the charge of attempted murder that the victim may have been dead.

Turning to the facts of the case before us, the jury could conclude that the defendant believed Geller to be alive at the time defendant fired shots into Geller's head. Defendant admitted firing five shots at a most vital part of the victim's anatomy from virtually point blank range. Although defendant contended that the victim had already been grievously wounded by another, the jury could conclude that the defendant's purpose and intention was to administer the coup de grace.

The jury convicted the defendant of murder. Necessarily, they found that defendant intended to kill a live human being. Subsumed within this finding is the conclusion that defendant acted in the belief that Geller was alive. Thus, there is no need for additional fact findings by a jury. Although it was not established beyond a reasonable doubt that Geller was, in fact, alive, such is no defense to attempted murder since a murder would have been committed "had the attendant circumstances been as (defendant) believed them to be." The jury necessarily found that defendant believed Geller to be alive when defendant shot at him.

The order of the Appellate Division should be modified and the case remitted to the Appellate Division for its review of the facts and for further proceedings with respect to the sentence in the event that the facts are found favorably to the People.

Food for Thought

Over the years, commentators have offered numerous variations on the Lady Eldon hypothetical (referred to in the *Dlugash* case). Before you examine those hypotheticals, consider whether the facts stated in the case involve "legal impossibility" or "factual impossibility." The court offers the hypothetical as an example of "legal impossibility." Do you agree that the case should be characterized in that way?

Hypo 1: *The Ticket Scalper*

Defendant wants to scalp his tickets to the Louisville-Kentucky basketball game outside the Yum Arena in Louisville, Kentucky. Fearing that it is illegal to scalp tickets (in fact, it is not illegal), defendant is extremely furtive as he approaches prospective purchasers. An undercover detective, who happens to notice defendant's unusual behavior, approaches defendant to ask about the tickets. Realizing that defendant believes that it is illegal to scalp tickets, the officer charges defendant with attempted scalping. Can he be convicted?

Hypo 2: *HIV and Attempted Murder*

Defendant was an HIV positive inmate. On several occasions, he had threatened to kill corrections officers by biting or spitting at them. One day, he bit an officer's hand, causing puncture wounds of the skin during a struggle which he had precipitated. Defendant was charged with attempted murder. At trial, defendant claims that his bite could not transmit HIV. If defendant's claim is correct, can he be convicted of attempted murder? Would it matter whether he knew that a bite could not transmit HIV? *See State v. Smith*, 262 N.J. Super. 487, 621 A.2d 493 (1993).

Hypo 3: *Attempted Drug Distribution*

Defendant was convicted of attempting to distribute the drug phenyl-2-propanone (P-2-P). Both methamphetamine and P-2-P are non-narcotic controlled substances. P-2-P has no use other than in the manufacture of methamphetamine. An undercover police officer agreed to buy six pints of P-2-P from defendant at $1,250 per pint and then arrested defendant at the time of sale. After chemical testing, it was determined that the liquid was not P-2-P. Under these circumstances was conviction appropriate? *See United States v. Everett*, 700 F.2d 900 (3d Cir. 1983); *United States v. Oviedo*, 525 F.2d 881 (5th Cir. 1976).

Hypo 4: *Attempted Murder?*

McKinley, a gasoline station employee, was at the cashier's window when defendant gave him $4 for gasoline. After defendant pumped gasoline worth $3.99, he insisted that he had given McKinley "five dollars." McKinley denied he had been given that much money and both men began yelling. Defendant fired three shots at McKinley. Since McKinley was protected by bullet-proof glass, the bullets marred the glass but did not penetrate it. Defendant claims that he cannot be convicted of attempted murder because the glass made murder impossible. Is he right? *See People v. Valdez*, 175 Cal. App. 3d 103, 220 Cal. Rptr. 538 (1985).

Hypo 5: *Attempted Theft?*

An undercover officer called on defendant (a doctor) and told him that his sister was in failing health. In fact, the officer had no sister. Defendant told the officer to write her name on a piece of paper, and the officer wrote a fictitious name. Defendant placed the paper on what appeared to be an electrical instrument and rubbed it. He then told the officer that his sister was suffering from sarcoma, a blood clot on the brain, had beef worms, and was anemic. When the officer offered to bring his sister to see defendant, the doctor replied that it was unnecessary. The doctor claimed that he had cured patients he had never seen. Defendant offered to provide prospective "treatments" to the sister for a fee of $65 a month for twelve months. The officer gave a down payment of $25 in marked bills. The officer then arrested defendant. The instrument on which defendant placed the handwriting and which he had rubbed for the apparent purpose of diagnosing the supposed sister's ailments was found on investigation not to be wired to any electric current. Can the doctor be convicted of attempting to obtain money by false pretenses when the prosecutor was not deceived as to the legitimacy of the treatment? *See Harwei, Inc. v. State*, 459 N.E.2d 52 (Ind. App.1984); *Commonwealth v. Johnson*, 312 Pa. 140, 167 A. 344 (1933).

Food for Thought

Defendant paid a $100 finder's fee to an undercover officer to procure a young girl for sexual intercourse. He chose a young girl, represented to be five or six years of age, from a collection of photographs supplied by the officer. He prepared for sexual intercourse with the young girl by arranging for a motel room and purchasing Vaseline to use as a lubricant. Defendant was arrested and charged with attempted sexual assault. Does it matter that the undercover officer did not have a young girl available to have sexual intercourse with defendant? *See Van Bell v. State*, 105 Nev. 352, 775 P.2d 1273 (1989).

Hypo 6: *Attempted Possession of Narcotics?*

Defendant proposed to a police deputy, a member of the narcotics detail, that the deputy supply him with heroin. The deputy reported the conversation to the police chief and was instructed to go along with defendant. So the deputy asked defendant, "Were you serious about what we were talking about the other day?" Defendant said, "Yes." A day later, the deputy told defendant that he "had the stuff." The deputy gave defendant a package containing white powder. Defendant put the package in his pocket. When defendant opened his safe to get the money, the deputy arrested him. The package did not contain heroin, but only talcum powder. Can defendant be convicted of attempted possession of narcotics? *See United States v. McDowell*, 714 F.2d 106 (11th Cir. 1983); *People v. Siu*, 126 Cal. App. 2d 41, 271 P.2d 575 (1954).

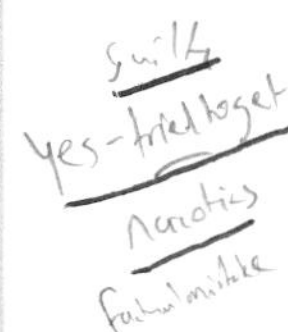

Food for Thought

Father Philip Berrigan and Sister Elizabeth McAlister were convicted of attempting to violate 18 U.S.C. § 1791 for sending seven letters out of a federal prison "without the knowledge and consent of the warden." The evidence shows that defendants did send the letters. However, the warden knew that they were trying to send the letters and allowed the letters to pass out of the institution. Given the warden's knowledge, can defendants be convicted? *See United States v. Berrigan*, 482 F.2d 171 (3d Cir. 1973).

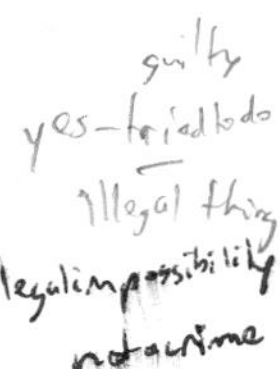

Hypo 7: *Attempted Rape?*

Defendant is charged with attempted rape. Defendant was out on a bar hopping spree with friends when a woman collapsed in his arms while the two of them were dancing. Defendant offered to take her home and placed her in his car. Believing that she was drunk and unconscious, defendant had sexual intercourse with her. It was later determined that she was dead and that she died when she collapsed on the dance floor. Can defendant be convicted of attempted rape? *See United States v. Thomas*, 32 C.M.R. 278, 13 USCMA 278 (1962).

Food for Thought

A labor union owned fourteen acres of land on which the union planned to develop a recreational facility for its members. The union began to dig a lake on the property, but stopped at the request of the County Commission. Believing that a county permit was required, a union official tried to bribe a county commissioner. As it turned out, no permit was required. Can defendant be convicted of attempted bribery? *See Nell v. State*, 277 So.2d 1 (Fla. 1973).

Hypo 8: *More on Attempted Bribery*

In an attempt to evade induction into the U.S. armed forces, defendant tried to bribe an induction official. The officer refused. After consulting with his superiors, who wanted to catch defendant, the official returned to defendant and offered to take the bribe. Defendant agreed that $450.00 was a fair price and paid it. Shortly afterwards, defendant was arrested. It was later shown that the official had nothing to do with the actual physical examination, and could not make any recommendation as to whether a prospective inductee should be accepted or rejected for military service. Under the circumstances, can defendant be convicted of attempted bribery, given the fact that the official could not prevent defendant's induction into the armed forces, and did not intend to do so? *See Hurley v. United States*, 192 F.2d 297 (4th Cir. 1951).

Food for Thought

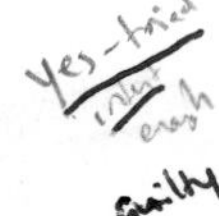

Defendant points a gun at his wife's head and pulls the trigger. Defendant incorrectly believes that the gun is loaded. Can defendant be convicted of attempted murder? *See State v. Damms*, 9 Wis. 2d 183, 100 N.W.2d 592 (1960).

Executive Summary

Theory of Attempt Law. Although the criminal law does not punish people merely for "bad thoughts," the State does have an interest in intervening early before a suspect goes so far as to commit a crime. The goal is to prevent defendant from actually causing harm. The law of attempt plays this role in the law. The evidence required for an attempt conviction, both as to the *mens rea* and the *actus reus*, can vary from state to state.

Relationship to Other Crimes. The crimes of solicitation and conspiracy also allow the police to intervene early to prevent the commission of criminal acts. Solicitation was discussed in Chapter 4, in relation to the topic of complicity, and conspiracy will be discussed in Chapter 7.

MPC Definition of *Mens Rea*. The Model Penal Code defines the crime of attempt as occurring when an individual, acting with the kind of culpability otherwise required for commission of the crime, does any of three things: (a) purposely engages in conduct that would constitute the crime if the attendant circumstances were as he believes them to be; or (b) when causing a particular result is an element of the crime, does or omits to do anything with the purpose of causing or with the belief that it will cause such result without further conduct on his part; or (c) purposely does or omits to do anything that, under the circumstances as he believes them to be, is an act or omission constituting a substantial step in a course of conduct planned to culminate in his commission of the crime.

Major Themes

a. Influence of the MPC—The MPC's influence led to the simplification and expansion of the attempt crime in most states. That crime, now recognizes attempt liability for the conduct of taking a "substantial step" toward the commission of a crime, when that step is strongly corroborative of criminal purpose. Other popular MPC reforms include elimination of the impossibility defense and imposition of strict limitations on the abandonment defense.

b. Traditional Approaches—Some states continue to rely on one of the various common law formulas for the *actus reus* of attempt, which require that a person's conduct must go beyond mere preparation and must come within a close degree of proximity to the completion of the crime. Although these formulas may be more difficult to apply than the "substantial step" test, they usually require evidence of conduct that supplies more unequivocal proof of the required *mens rea* of criminal purpose.

***Actus Reus* Requirement of Attempt.** Even if a defendant has the required *mens rea* for an attempt, the defendant must commit the *actus reus*. At common law, the *actus reus* of the crime of attempt was defined in many different ways, and included the following tests: (1) The "physical proximity" doctrine under which defendant must have committed an overt act that was proximate to the completed crime, or directly tending toward the completion of the crime, or amounting to the commencement of the consummation; (2) The "dangerous proximity" doctrine under which the court considers the gravity and probability of the offense, and the nearness of the act to the crime; (3) The "indispensable element" test (similar to the proximity tests) which emphasizes whether an indispensable aspect of the criminal endeavor remains, over which the actor has not yet acquired control; (4) The "probable desistance" test which focuses on whether, in the ordinary and natural course of events, without interruption from an outside source, defendant's conduct will result in the crime intended; (5) The "abnormal step" approach under which the focus is on whether defendant's conduct has gone beyond the point where the ordinary person would think better of his or her conduct and desist; (6) The "*res ipsa loquitur*" or unequivocality test under which the defendant's conduct must manifest an intent to commit a crime.

MPC Definition of *Actus Reus*. The Model Penal Code defines the crime of attempt as requiring a "substantial step" toward commission of the crime. Various acts can constitute a substantial step, if they are "strongly corroborative of the actor's criminal purpose, including: (a) lying in wait, searching for or following the contemplated victim of the crime; (b) enticing or seeking to entice the contemplated victim of the crime to go to the place contemplated for its commission; (c) reconnoitering the place contemplated for the commission of the crime;

(d) unlawful entry of a structure, vehicle or enclosure in which it is contemplated that the crime will be committed; (e) possession of materials to be employed in the commission of the crime, that are specially designed for such unlawful use or that can serve no lawful purpose of the actor under the circumstances; (f) possession, collection or fabrication of materials to be employed in the commission of the crime, at or near the place contemplated for its commission, if such possession, collection or fabrication serves no lawful purpose of the actor under the circumstances; (g) soliciting an innocent agent to engage in conduct constituting an element of the crime."

Attempt and Abandonment. With many crimes, if defendant commits both the *actus reus* and the *mens rea* of the crime, the crime is complete and chargeable. By contrast, since attempt can involve something less than the completed crime, abandonment of the criminal enterprise is still possible. The Model Penal Code recognizes the defense of abandonment under certain circumstances.

Impossibility. The crime of Attempt is somewhat unique in that an individual may attempt to commit a crime under circumstances where it is impossible to actually complete the crime (e.g., an individual tries to murder someone who is already dead). The courts, and criminal statutes, recognize the defense of impossibility in some circumstances (although defendant may be guilty of some other crime).

For More Information

- AMERICAN LAW INSTITUTE, MODEL PENAL CODE AND COMMENTARIES, Part II, §§ 5.01–5.02, Comments at 295–385 (1980).
- JOHN M. BURKOFF & RUSSELL L. WEAVER, INSIDE CRIMINAL LAW: WHAT MATTERS AND WHY 99–116 (2d ed. 2011).
- WAYNE R. LAFAVE, CRIMINAL LAW §§ 11.2–11.5 (5th ed. 2010).

Test Your Knowledge

To assess your understanding of the material in this chapter, click here to take a quiz.

Chapter 7

Conspiracy

Conspiracy statutes respond to the special danger to society posed by group criminal activity. It is more likely, in theory at least, that a group will succeed in its criminal endeavors than will an individual, acting alone. As a result, most (but not all) crimes codes contain a "general" conspiracy offense, a statute that prohibits individuals from agreeing with someone else to commit another criminal offense. A few jurisdictions, however, do not criminalize conspiracies, and some states limit the criminal conspiracy offense to agreements to commit only particular, serious crimes.

Given the increasingly widespread increase in conspiracy prosecutions over the last few decades in some jurisdictions, and given the fact that some conspiracy offenses overlap with the coverage of other inchoate and substantive offenses, and given the fact that most jurisdictions no longer even require an actual agreement between two or more individuals to make out a conspiracy, some commentators have argued that the crime of conspiracy no longer serves a useful or sensible function. See, e.g., Philip E. Johnson, *The Unnecessary Crime of Conspiracy*, 61 Cal. L. Rev. 1137 (1973); Neal Kumar Katyal, *Conspiracy Theory*, 112 Yale. L.J. 1307 (2003); *David Cole & James X. Dempsey, Civil Liberties and the Terrorism Prevention Paradigm: The Guilt By Association Critique: Sacrificing Civil Liberties in the Name of National Security*, 101 Mich. L. Rev. 1408, 1452 (2003); Paul Marcus, *Criminal Conspiracy Law: Time to Turn Back From an Ever Expanding, Ever More Troubling Area*, 1 Wm. & Mary Bill of Rts. J. 1 (1992); Steven R. Morrison, *Conspiracy Law's Threat to Free Speech*, 15 U. Pa. J. Const. L. 865 (2013); Martin H. Redish & Michael J. T. Downey, *Criminal Conspiracy As Free Expression*, 76 Alb. L. Rev. 697 (2012–2013); Laurent Sacharoff, *Conspiracy as Contract*, 50 U.C. Davis L. Rev. 405 (2016).

Food for Thought

As you review the cases and materials that follow, you should ask yourself whether there still is an appropriate place for the offense of conspiracy in our criminal justice system. Is it really necessary? Desirable?

A. Unilateral-Bilateral Jurisdictions

Food for Thought

Does it make sense to criminalize *one person's* actions as a conspiracy when the original rationale for the conspiracy offense was to respond to the special danger to society posed by *group* criminal activity?

At common law, a conspiracy consisted of an agreement between two or more persons to commit, by concerted action, an unlawful act or a lawful act by unlawful means (the "bilateral" approach, i.e. two or more persons must be in actual agreement). Today, in contrast, most jurisdictions follow the approach of the Model Penal Code, and focus on the act of a single individual who is or believes that he or she is agreeing with another person to commit a criminal act (the "unilateral" approach, i.e. one person who is or believes that he or she is agreeing with someone else).

This "unilateral" or "bilateral" distinction is very important. Given the extensive use of undercover agents by law enforcement agencies, the trend toward adoption of a unilateral—broader and more inclusive—conspiracy offense has resulted in harsher punishment for many defendants who are accused and convicted of conspiracy in addition to other inchoate and/or substantive offenses.

Take Note

In a unilateral jurisdiction, a person agreeing only with an undercover officer to commit a crime has committed the offense of conspiracy. In a bilateral jurisdiction, no conspiracy has been committed (because there are not two or more persons in actual agreement. The undercover officer's agreement is feigned.

State v. Huff

319 Wis. 2d 258, 769 N.W.2d 154 (Ct. App. 2009).

FINE, J.

Garrett L. Huff appeals the judgment convicting him after a jury trial of three counts of conspiracy to commit election bribery in violation of WIS. STAT. §§ 12.11(1m)(a)1 (election bribery) and 156 939.31 (conspiracy). He claims that because the persons with whom he was found to have conspired were undercover law-enforcement officers ineligible to vote in the election involved, it was impossible for him to have committed the crimes. We affirm.

Huff was convicted of conspiring to violate WIS. STAT. § 12.11(1m)(a)1. This statute provides:

> Any person who does any of the following violates this chapter:
>
> (a) Offers, gives, lends or promises to give or lend, or endeavors to procure, anything of value, or any office or employment or any privilege or immunity to, or for, any elector, or to or for any other person, in order to induce any elector to:
>
> 1. Go to or refrain from going to the polls.

" 'Anything of value' " is defined to "include any amount of money, or any object which has utility independent of any political message it contains and the value of which exceeds $1." Sec. 12.11(1).

This case arose out of a re-call election in the Sixth Aldermanic District in Milwaukee that was held on April 3, 2007. Qualified electors were able to vote before April 3rd by going to the Milwaukee City Hall. A Milwaukee election official testified that a flyer bearing the disclaimer that it was "paid for and authorized by citizens to re-elect Mike McGee, Jr," the Sixth District incumbent, invited people to attend an "election party" that promised "Free! Food/Drinks" and explained that to be admitted a person "must show vote sticker at door." The election official testified that he was concerned that the flyer was promoting a potential violation of the election law, and that as a result, he contacted the City Attorney. This set the stage for the undercover operations by Milwaukee police officers Wardell Dodds and Dwayne Barnes, and Willie Brantley, a special agent with the Wisconsin Department of Justice. The jury's verdicts found Huff guilty of conspiring with Dodds to violate WIS. STAT. § 12.11(1m)(a)1 on March 15, 2007, and of conspiring with Brantley and Barnes to violate § 12.11(1m)(a)1 on March 27, 2007.

Dodds testified that he went with Barnes to the "election party" at a store in Milwaukee on March 15, 2007. He testified that he met with Huff who told him that he would "take me downtown to vote and that he was working for the Mike McGee, Junior, campaign, that he was taking people downtown to City Hall to vote for Mike McGee." Dodds related that Huff drove him to City Hall and that when they arrived Huff told him to " 'go up to the fifth floor and vote,' " and that Huff also told him: " 'They'll give you something after you vote.' " Dodds testified that Huff paid him five dollars "on the return from City Hall," after Dodds showed Huff an "I voted" sticker. Dodds also testified that when they returned to the store Huff told him that if he, Dodds, knew of "anyone else that want[s] to vote in the election, the ballot, to tell them to come see Mr. Huff. Everyone come see Mr. Huff regarding transportation and getting paid to go vote." Dodds did not live in the Sixth Aldermanic District and could not have legally voted.

Brantley testified that he went to the "election party" store with Barnes on March 27th. According to Brantley's testimony, Barnes told Huff that Brantley was there to vote, and Brantley agreed that he would "if my change was right, indicating that I was going to get paid for the services of voting." Brantley told the jury that he got into a car with Huff who indicated in response to Brantley's question whether "my change was going to be right," that Huff "would take care of me when we got back," by paying him five dollars after they returned to the store.

Huff drove Brantley to City Hall and, Brantley testified, told him to go to the place where he could vote. According to Brantley, when he returned to the car, he showed Huff his "I voted" sticker and "the registration papers." Brantley told the jury that Huff gave him five dollars after they returned to the store. Brantley also did not live in the Sixth Aldermanic District and could not, therefore, legally vote in the re-call election.

Brantley also related Huff's interactions with Barnes, telling the jury that Barnes told Huff that he wanted, as phrased by Brantley, "to get paid for bringing people down for voting." Brantley testified that he saw Huff give Barnes five dollars.

Barnes testified that he went to the "election party" store on both March 15th and March 27th. He reiterated Brantley's testimony that he, Barnes, told Huff that he wanted to be paid for bringing people to the store so they could vote and that Huff then paid him five dollars. Barnes wanted to stay at the store and not vote so his cover story was that he "was on probation for a felony and could not vote."

Huff did not call any witnesses and rested his defense after the State presented its evidence.

Huff contends that because none of the law-enforcement officers pretending to be electors with whom he was convicted of conspiring to violate WIS. STAT. § 12.11(1m)(a)1 could lawfully vote in the April 3, 2007, special election in the Sixth Aldermanic District, they were not bona fide electors, and, accordingly, the conspiracy was a legal impossibility. We disagree.

As material here, WIS. STAT. § 939.31 provides:

> whoever, with intent that a crime be committed, agrees or combines with another for the purpose of committing that crime may, if one or more of the parties to the conspiracy does an act to effect its object, be fined or imprisoned or both not to exceed the maximum provided for the completed crime.

This makes unlawful both unilateral and bilateral conspiracies. *State v. Sample*, 215 Wis. 2d 487, 489, 502, 573 N.W.2d 187, 188, 193–194 (1998). *Sample* explained the difference between the two concepts:

> Under a unilateral formulation, the crime of conspiracy is committed when a person agrees to proceed in a prohibited manner." The unilateral approach assesses the subjective, individual behavior of a defendant in determining guilt. Under the unilateral approach, criminal conspiracy will lie even where one of two alleged "co-conspirators" is, unknown to the defendant, an undercover police agent or a police informant who merely feigns participation in the conspiracy. "The immateriality of co-conspirators' legal status to defendant's criminal liability is implicit in the unilateral approach." "Under a bilateral formulation, the crime of conspiracy is committed when two or more persons agree to proceed in [a prohibited] manner."

Thus, under a unilateral conspiracy a person who intends to accomplish the objects of the conspiracy is guilty even though "the other members of the conspiracy never intended that a crime be committed." For example, a person would be guilty of unlawfully conspiring to kill a business associate by hiring an undercover law-enforcement officer to commit the murder even though the officer had no intention to fulfill the contract. This same logic applies to the next step: that is, where the fulfillment of the conspiracy is not only highly unlikely, as in *Sample*, a reverse delivery-of-narcotics sting involving a jail inmate and an undercover officer, or our murder-for-hire hypothetical, but is legally impossible, as is the case here.

Make the Connection

Isn't a unilateral approach to conspiracy law simply an application of the modern rule that impossibility is not a defense when inchoate offenses are charged?

Indeed, although there is no published Wisconsin authority dealing with the legally-impossible situation, the law elsewhere is consistent with our next-logical-step conclusion, as revealed by a recent analysis and survey by *United States v. Fiander*, 547 F.3d 1036, 1042–1043 (9th Cir. 2008):

> "It is elementary that a conspiracy may exist and be punished whether or not the substantive crime ensues, for the conspiracy is a distinct evil, dangerous to the public, and so punishable in itself." Thus, we have held that a conspiracy conviction may be sustained even where the goal of the conspiracy is impossible. Our sister circuits are in accord.

As *Sample* recognizes, "under the inchoate crime of conspiracy, by definition ***no substantive crime is ever needed***. Wisconsin Stat. § 939.31 focuses on the subjective behavior of the individual defendant."

Take Note

Federal conspiracy law is actually bilateral, not unilateral like Wisconsin's statute. As a result, if the *Huff* facts were established in a federal prosecution, no conspiracy would exist as there would not have been two or more actual co-conspirators. However, the point that *Fiander* is being cited for here is nonetheless accurate: co-conspirators can be found to be guilty of a conspiracy even if their criminal object is impossible to achieve. And that is true in a unilateral or a bilateral jurisdiction.

Huff argues, however, that *State v. Crowley*, 41 Wis. 271 (1876), stands for the proposition that "impossibility" is "a defense to the crime of conspiracy." He is wrong. *Crowley* concerned a plan by the defendants to cheat Daniel Burke by purporting to sell Burke counterfeit money that turned out to be merely a box of sawdust. According to *Crowley*, "Burke purchased the counterfeit money for the purpose and with the intention of uttering and passing it as good money." Burke was arrested by a constable, also a defendant in the case, whom he and another of the defendants bribed. After an extensive analysis of conflicting case law from other jurisdictions, Crowley held that the conspiracy charging a plan to cheat Burke would not lie because Burke was not an innocent victim, noting: "Neither the law nor public policy designs the protection of rogues in their dealings with each other, or to insure fair dealing and truthfulness, as between each other, in their dishonest practices." *Crowley* has nothing to do with an alleged impossibility being a defense to a unilateral conspiracy.

Judgment affirmed and cause remanded with directions.

State v. Mendoza

889 A.2d 153 (R.I. 2005).

CHIEF JUSTICE WILLIAMS, for the Court.

At about 9:30 p.m. on March 18, 1998, undercover Detectives Angelo A'Vant (Det. A'vant) and Fabio Zuena (Det. Zuena) of the Providence Police Department were patrolling the area of Public and Broad Streets in Providence in response to numerous complaints of drug activity. While creeping along in an unmarked vehicle, the detectives were approached by Robert Clement (Clement), who asked if the officers were looking for "rock," or crack cocaine. The detectives responded in the affirmative, and Clement told the pair to follow him to Daboll Street, approximately one block from their present location.

When the detectives arrived at Daboll Street a short time later, Clement again approached the vehicle and beckoned Det. A'Vant to follow him. Detective A'Vant complied, and Det. Zuena remained in the vehicle. Clement led Det. A'Vant a few houses over to 55 Daboll Street, and into an unattached garage toward the rear of the property. Here, Det. A'Vant handed Clement a marked $20 bill, presumably as prepayment for the crack cocaine. Clement then rang a doorbell inside the garage, and a few moments later defendant and a second man emerged from the rear of the Daboll Street dwelling.

The defendant immediately began berating Clement for bringing a stranger to the property. Clement attempted to assuage the defendant's ire by handing him the $20 bill, which defendant snatched from Clement's hand. The defendant and Clement then entered the dwelling through the rear door.

Detective A'Vant testified that no more than a minute later defendant and Clement reemerged from the same door. The defendant apparently still was expressing his dissatisfaction with Clement's decision to bring a stranger by the house when Det. A'Vant saw defendant hand Clement a clear bag. The substance in the bag later tested positive for crack cocaine. Clement and Det. A'Vant then walked together back to the unmarked vehicle a few houses away. After the two got into the car, Clement handed the clear bag to Det. A'Vant and the two detectives identified themselves as police officers, placing Clement under arrest.

A short time later, Detectives A'Vant and Zuena returned to 55 Daboll Street with at least two other officers from their unit to arrest defendant. At the police station, the detectives searched defendant and uncovered three bags of marijuana on his person.

The defendant was charged by criminal information with delivery of a controlled substance in violation of G.L.1956 § 21–28–4.01(A)(2)(a), conspiracy to violate the Rhode Island Controlled Substances Act in violation of § 21–28–4.08, possession of marijuana in violation of § 21–28–4.01(C)(1)(b), and resisting arrest in violation of G.L.1956 § 12–7–10. After a jury trial, defendant was found guilty on all four counts.

The defendant argues that the trial justice erred in denying his motion for acquittal on the conspiracy count. Defendant argues that "Wharton's Rule" precludes application of the crime of conspiracy to the behavior charged in his criminal information. Defendant urges that Wharton's Rule precludes his conspiracy conviction, although he points us to no binding precedent to support such a contention. Section 21–28–4.08 makes it a criminal violation to conspire "to violate any provision" of the Rhode Island Uniform Controlled Substances Act. Rhode Island subscribes to the common law formulation of conspiracy, requiring "a combination of two or more persons to commit an unlawful act or to perform a lawful act for an unlawful purpose."

Wharton's Rule is a logical limitation to the prosecution of conspiracy. It provides that "an agreement between two persons to commit an offense does not constitute conspiracy when the target offense is so defined that it can be committed only by the participation of two persons." This precept speaks of congruence: when a statutory crime requires coalescent conduct, a conspiracy charge is redundant since it requires proof of no additional element than that required by the underlying offense, because agreement is implicit upon proof of the target crime. However, the United States Supreme Court has made clear that "the broadly formulated Wharton's Rule does not rest on principles of double jeopardy. Instead, it has current vitality only as a judicial presumption, to be applied in the absence of legislative intent to the contrary."

While the traditional Wharton's Rule offenses were limited to "dueling, bigamy, adultery, and incest, the buying and selling of contraband goods" has been added to the list. Indeed, one commentator has aptly explained that "when the sale of some commodity, such as illegal drugs, is the substantive crime, the sale agreement itself cannot be the conspiracy, for it has no separate criminal object." The presence of a third conspirator to a crime requiring only two participants for its commission, however, transforms the conspiratorial agreement into an offense distinct from any agreement implicit in the target crime, thereby rendering Wharton's Rule inapplicable.

We think defendant confounds the facts of his own conviction. It is clear from defendant's brief that he is under the impression he was charged with conspiring with *Clement* to deliver cocaine to *Clement*. Had this been the case, perhaps the conspiracy count would not lie; we are not called upon to decide this issue, however, and we decline to adopt Wharton's Rule.

Take Note

Note that the court has not decided whether or not to actually adopt Wharton's Rule in these circumstances. Should it? Or is the whole concept of Wharton's Rule simply outdated?

However, viewed in a light most favorable to the state, the state's evidence demonstrated that defendant was charged with conspiring with Clement to deliver cocaine to *Det. A'Vant*, and therefore the conspiratorial agreement was a wholly distinct and chargeable offense along with the substantive delivery count. Detective A'Vant's presence in the delivery scheme

Food for Thought

Would the result in this case have been different if Rhode Island was a unilateral conspiracy jurisdiction?

implicated more persons than necessary to effect the delivery charge, thereby precluding application of Wharton's Rule.[7]

Therefore, we hold the trial justice did not err in denying defendant's motion for acquittal.

For the reasons stated herein, we affirm the judgment of the Superior Court. The record shall be remanded to the Superior Court.

Points for Discussion

a. New Legislation

If you were enacting a conspiracy law today, in a jurisdiction which did not already have one, would you make it unilateral or bilateral? Why did you choose the approach that you chose?

b. Coverage

Is it really necessary—or even desirable—to punish individuals who have actually acted alone more harshly, just as if they were not acting alone?

c. Use of Undercover Agents

Assuming that your answer to the question above is "yes"—*yes*, it is either necessary or desirable to punish individuals who have acted alone more harshly in these circumstances—does that conclusion give the government the opportunity through the use of undercover agents to essentially "entrap" people into engaging in conspiracies, people who otherwise might not be so inclined?

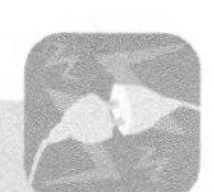

Make the Connection

Entrapment is a complete defense to criminal charges. Some jurisdictions use an "objective" entrapment test which focuses upon the question how outrageous the police conduct was in encouraging or assisting the accused criminal conduct. Other jurisdictions (including the federal) use a "subjective" entrapment test focusing instead on the question whether or not the accused was predisposed to commit the crime in question.

---

7 The defendant suggests that Det. A'Vant could not have been considered a legitimate party to the charged conspiracy under Rhode Island law. We assume this is a reference to Rhode Island's common law, bilateral formulation of conspiracy, requiring the participation of at least two parties, each with the capacity for culpability. Because there were two conspirators apart from Det. A'Vant in this case-defendant and Clement-our bilateral conspiracy requirement does not preclude defendant's prosecution.

B. *Mens Rea*

The *mens rea* of conspiracy is often described in the case law as having two separate (and independent) components: (1) the intent to agree with another person to commit a criminal act; and (2) the intent to commit the criminal act itself.

Palmer v. Colorado

964 P.2d 524 (Colo. 1998).

JUSTICE BENDER delivered the Opinion of the Court.

The defendant, Aaron Palmer, was convicted of multiple felonies for having fired gunshots at several victims. The district court sentenced Palmer to the Department of Corrections for a substantial period of time and imposed a concurrent term for the single count of conspiracy to commit reckless manslaughter that is at issue here. On appeal, Palmer argued that conspiracy to commit reckless manslaughter is not a legally cognizable crime in Colorado. Noting that conspiracy is a crime requiring a specific intention to achieve the forbidden result and that reckless manslaughter is a crime requiring recklessness with respect to the result, Palmer argued that it is logically impossible to specifically intend that an unintended death occur.

Food for Thought

Palmer was convicted of multiple felonies, *including but not limited to* this conspiracy offense, and his sentence for conspiracy was to run concurrently with the sentences for the other felonies, which were not being appealed. Accordingly, what was the value to him of bringing this appeal? Even if he was successful—as he was—the concurrent sentence for the other felonies was still in place. That being the case, what was the value of this appeal to Palmer? Was there any value?

The court of appeals determined that conspiracy does not require that the conspirator intend to cause a particular result but merely requires that the conspirator know that he or she and another are engaging in criminal conduct. Since it is possible to know that an agreement to engage in conduct creates a substantial and unjustifiable risk of death, and to disregard that risk, the court of appeals concluded that conspiracy to commit reckless manslaughter is a legally cognizable crime.

Conspiracy is a substantive "offense." Thus, the phrase "with the intent" as it appears in the conspiracy statute refers to and relies on the statutory definition of these words for its meaning: the defendant must have the "conscious objective to cause the specific result proscribed by the statute defining the offense." Since the culpable mental state for the crime of conspiracy is "with intent," conspiracy is a specific intent crime.

The crime of conspiracy requires two mental states. First, the defendant must possess the specific intent to agree to commit a particular crime. Second, the defendant must possess the specific intent to cause the result of the crime that is the subject of the agreement. Specific intent is an integral part of the crime and "must be established with the same certainty as any other material element of the crime."

By contrast, a criminal attempt requires that the accused act with the kind of culpability otherwise required for the commission of the underlying offense. If the underlying offense is a specific intent crime, then the culpable mental state for the crime of attempt will be "intentionally;" if the underlying offense is a general intent crime, then the culpable mental state will be "knowingly." Thus, unlike conspiracy, punishment for attempt "is not confined to actors whose conscious purpose is to perform the proscribed acts or to achieve the proscribed results." Instead, it is enough that the accused knowingly engages in the risk producing conduct that could lead to the result. It is possible to be convicted of attempt without the specific intent to obtain the forbidden result.

Unlike attempt and conspiracy, complicity is not a separate and distinct crime under the Colorado Criminal Code. It is not a violation of, or conduct defined by, a statute for which a fine or imprisonment may be imposed. Rather, complicity is a legal theory in which a person who aids, abets, or advises another who commits an offense is liable for that offense as a principal. The complicity statute creates criminal liability only if the defendant acts "with the intent" to promote or facilitate the offense. Unlike conspiracy, however, complicity is not a substantive offense, and therefore the word "intent" in the complicity statute does not mean specific intent but rather retains its plain and ordinary meaning.

Take Note

Conspiracy, attempt and complicity are entirely separate and distinct criminal offenses. As a result, a conspiracy conviction does not merge with a conviction for the crime which was the object of the conspiracy, i.e. a defendant can be convicted of and sentenced for both. However, in many jurisdictions, by statute, convictions for multiple inchoate offenses, e.g. conspiracy and attempt, arising out of the same criminal conduct do merge.

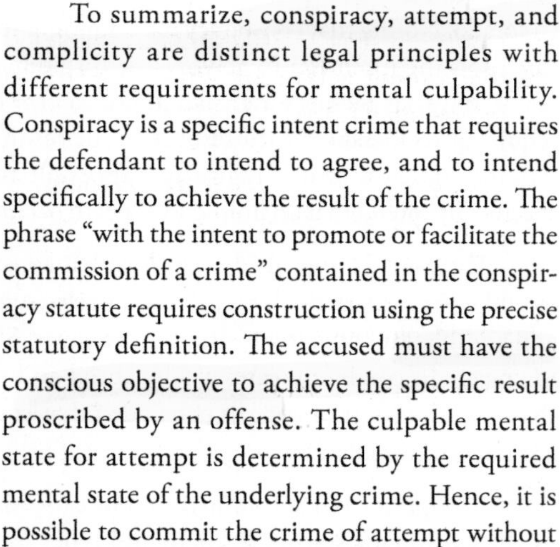

To summarize, conspiracy, attempt, and complicity are distinct legal principles with different requirements for mental culpability. Conspiracy is a specific intent crime that requires the defendant to intend to agree, and to intend specifically to achieve the result of the crime. The phrase "with the intent to promote or facilitate the commission of a crime" contained in the conspiracy statute requires construction using the precise statutory definition. The accused must have the conscious objective to achieve the specific result proscribed by an offense. The culpable mental state for attempt is determined by the required mental state of the underlying crime. Hence, it is possible to commit the crime of attempt without possessing a specific intent, provided that the underlying crime does not require a specific intent. Complicity is a legal theory rather than a crime; the phrase "with the intent to promote or facilitate the commission of the offense" contained in the complicity statute retains its ordinary meaning and usage and does not require specific intent as defined by the General Assembly. With these principles in mind, we turn to the issue of whether conspiracy to commit reckless manslaughter is a cognizable crime.

The People argue that the crime of conspiracy to commit reckless manslaughter, if recognized, would not require the defendant to specifically intend the death of the victim, and therefore such an offense would not be a logical impossibility. We disagree. Although a superficial reading of the conspiracy statute might support the People's argument, it is necessary to analyze the statute together with the legislative definition of specific intent and with our prior case law interpreting the crime of conspiracy in Colorado. In doing so, we reach the conclusion that a crime of conspiracy to commit reckless manslaughter would indeed pose a legal and logical conflict that is irreconcilable. Thus, we hold that conspiracy to commit reckless manslaughter is not a cognizable crime.

A person commits reckless manslaughter if "he recklessly causes the death of another person." Reckless manslaughter does not require the specific intent to cause the death of another. Rather, it requires that a person knowingly engage in risk producing acts or conduct that create a substantial and unjustifiable risk of causing a death. "One may be guilty of attempting to commit a crime of recklessness if it is shown that he was merely reckless toward the possibility that his conduct might have a certain consequence."

The culpable mental states for conspiracy and for reckless manslaughter are legally and logically inconsistent. The crime of conspiracy to commit reckless manslaughter would require that the defendant have the specific intent to commit reckless manslaughter. Crimes of recklessness are, by definition, crimes that are committed unintentionally, but with a conscious disregard for a substantial and unjustifiable risk that a result will occur. Thus, the state of mind required for reckless manslaughter is irreconcilable with the specific intent required for conspiracy. Logic dictates that one cannot agree in advance to accomplish an unintended result. Thus, we hold that conspiracy to commit reckless manslaughter is not a cognizable offense in Colorado.

Food for Thought

In some jurisdictions, attempt is a specific intent crime. Where that is true, would that change this analysis? How? *See, e.g., Commonwealth v. Griffin*, 310 Pa. Super. 39, 456 A.2d 171, 177 (1983): "Murder of the second or third degree occurs where the killing of the victim is the unintentional result of a criminal act. Thus, an attempt to commit second or third degree murder would seem to require proof that a defendant intended to perpetrate an unintentional killing—which is logically impossible. While a person who only intends to commit a felony may be guilty of second degree murder if a killing results, and a person who only intends to inflict bodily harm may be guilty of third degree murder if a killing results; it does not follow that those persons would be guilty of attempted murder if a killing did not occur. They would not be guilty of attempted murder because they did not intend to commit murder—they only intended to commit a felony or to commit bodily harm."

In *People v. Thomas*, 729 P.2d 972, 975 (Colo. 1986), the petitioner argued that the crime of attempted reckless manslaughter was a legal impossibility. We noted that the culpable mental state for attempted reckless manslaughter is the mental state required for the commission of the underlying offense, reckless manslaughter, and that attempt liability focuses on conduct rather than results. Reckless manslaughter requires the conscious disregard of a substantial and unjustifiable risk that death will occur. Thus, we held, the culpable mental state for attempted reckless manslaughter is that the accused knowingly engage in conduct while consciously disregarding a substantial and unjustifiable risk of death. Even though death is an element of reckless manslaughter, one may commit the crime of attempted reckless manslaughter without intending that death occur. Since attempt requires the same mental culpability as the underlying crime, we held that there is no inconsistency between the mental culpability requirement for attempt and that for the underlying crime, reckless manslaughter.

Here, however, the culpability requirement for conspiracy and that for the crime of reckless manslaughter conflict. Conspiracy is always a specific intent crime, and conspiracy liability focuses on specifically intended results rather than on conduct. Unlike attempted reckless manslaughter, conspiracy to commit reckless manslaughter would require the accused to possess the specific intent to achieve an unintentional death, which we conclude is a legal and logical impossibility.

In summary, we hold that conspiracy to commit reckless manslaughter is not a cognizable crime under Colorado law. Accordingly, we reverse the judgment of the court of appeals on this issue only and remand the case with instructions to vacate the judgment of conviction for the crime of conspiracy to commit reckless manslaughter.

Points for Discussion

a. Other Conspiracies?

Even though the Colorado Supreme Court held that Palmer cannot be convicted of the crime of conspiracy to commit manslaughter, did he conspire to commit any other crime? If so, what crime?

b. Conspiracies to Commit Negligent Crimes

In Colorado, after the decision in *Palmer*, can a defendant be found guilty of conspiracy to commit an offense which has the *mens rea* element of criminal negligence? Why or why not?

United States v. Hassoun

2007 WL 4180844 (S.D.Fla. 2007).

MARCIA G. COOKE, DISTRICT JUDGE.

Following a four-month jury trial, on August 16, 2007, defendants Adham Amin Hassoun, Jose Padilla and Kifah Wael Jayyousi were convicted of the three counts charged in the Fifth Superseding Indictment. Count One charged the defendants with violating 18 U.S.C. § 956(a)(1), conspiring to commit acts of murder, kidnaping or maiming outside of the United States, while committing one or more overt acts in furtherance thereof within the United States. Count Two charged the defendants with violating 18 U.S.C. § 371, conspiring to violate section 2339A (i.e., conspiring to provide material support to terrorists). Count Three charged the defendants with violating 18 U.S.C. § 2339A, providing material support or resources, or concealing the nature thereof, all while knowing or intending that they be used in preparation for, or in carrying out a violation of section 956 (i.e., a conspiracy to murder, kidnap or maim on foreign soil).

Defendants assert that the evidence at trial was insufficient to prove their intent, while in the United States, to murder, kidnap, or maim persons overseas. The arguments defendants offer to support these claims are unpersuasive and the defendants' Motions for Judgment of Acquittal are denied.

Hassoun claims that the government did not adduce sufficient evidence at trial to find beyond a reasonable doubt that he harbored the specific intent to commit any of the three objects of the conspiracy to murder, kidnap or maim. Consequently, Hassoun asserts that no reasonable jury could have found, beyond a reasonable doubt, that he possessed the requisite specific intent "which was the essential underpinning of the government's entire case." Hassoun correctly recites the well-established legal principle that a "conspiracy to commit a particular substantive offense cannot exist without at least the degree of criminal intent necessary for the substantive offense itself." Thus, to find Hassoun guilty of Count One, the jury needed to find that Hassoun had the specific intent to murder, kidnap or maim. When viewing the evidence in the light most favorable to the government, a reasonable jury could have found that Hassoun harbored the specific intent to murder, kidnap or maim.

The jury was entitled to consider the evidence, and decide whether Hassoun's actions were driven by the sole desire to provide humanitarian support or the violent intent to murder, maim or kidnap. The government's evidence indicated that Hassoun distinguished between jihad which he defined as "battle for the sake of Allah" and da'wa, which he defined as building schools and teaching people. Moreover, the government presented evidence indicating that Hassoun was committed to a violent form of jihad—which he frequently referred to using the code word "tourism"—and viewed it as paramount to providing humanitarian support.[12]

It was not unreasonable for the jury to weigh the evidence and conclude that Hassoun adopted a violent concept of jihad. The government also presented evidence indicating that code

---

12 After explaining to his co-conspirators that their roles in the conspiracy were akin to links in a chain, where "one completes the other," Hassoun explained:

> As to the other issues the Calling [missionary work] the people who work in the Calling, God bless, there are so many of them. But the people who work in "tourism," they are just few, you can count them on your fingers. So let those people who work in the Calling, let them work in the Calling do their books, newsletters, and matters it's not a problem, as long as they work on it. But with regard to the field of "tourism," let us work on it this is a very important issue because very few work in "tourism" very few.

This discussion evidences that Hassoun appreciated the significance of both "tourism"—defined as jihad—and humanitarian aid. However, he felt it his duty—along with his co-conspirators—to furnish the latter form of support.

words such as 'football,'[13] 'zucchini,'[14] and 'eggplant'[15] used by Hassoun were intended to cover up his participation in illicit violent activities. See, e.g., GX 28T/ 28TR (discussing the "first area"—identified as Afghanistan—and how there are "football courts"[17] ready for whomever wants to train for the game); GX 86T/86TR (inquiring whether the brothers bought "the zucchini and such"); GX 92T/92TR (discussing equipping an al Qaeda affiliate in Lebanon with funds to purchase "zucchini" and "eggplant" for future violent battles).[18]

Telephone conversations where Hassoun used this language could reasonably suggest that Hassoun actively sent money, recruits, and equipment overseas for use in future violent jihad conflicts. Hassoun's monetary contributions for 'tourism' must be viewed in the same light. When considered in conjunction with the other evidence at trial, these contributions could reasonably be viewed as Hassoun's attempts to equip mujahideen fighters with munitions for future battles. This support for violent jihadist activities—which had as an expected consequence, murder, kidnaping and maiming—was entitled to the jury's consideration when deciding Hassoun's specific intent.

Furthermore, with regard to having the intent to murder specifically, the jury was allowed to consider a variety of factors indicative of malice aforethought and premeditation. When drawing inferences in favor of the government, the jury was allowed to consider the lengthy time frame of the conspiracy, and how defendants observed and were informed of how their material support in America generated actual violence in various overseas locations. Furthermore, Hassoun's continued planning and involvement in these activities even after he observed the consequences of his actions is indicative of his premeditation and malice aforethought. Hassoun received news-report and first hand accounts of the jihad theaters to which he contributed, and could have disavowed the violence or extricated himself from the conspiracy if the violence did not comport with his intent. Hassoun never did this. Nor did he merely acquiesce in the violence perpetrated in these jihad areas. Rather, Hassoun continued to promote the violence in these regions and support the violence with money, equipment and recruits.

Accordingly, the government provided sufficient evidence that Hassoun harbored the requisite specific intent for Count One.

---

13 See Tr. (interpreting "football" as a code word for jihad).

14 See Tr. (defining "zucchini" as weapons and noting that support cells and radical Islamist groups commonly use this terminology).

15 Dr. Rohan Gunaratna defined "eggplant" as a rocket propelled grenade launcher ("RPG") and explained that he is familiar with this term being used in this regard through his research and study. Dr. Gunaratna added that an RPG is a standup weapon used by militant and terrorist organizations to conduct attacks. He additionally noted that, the weapon is intended to fire at and destroy its target, be it infrastructure, a vehicle or people.

17 See Tr. 6/28/07 (noting that "football courts" was a code expression for training camps intended to "train people to conduct attacks").

18 Hassoun also discussed the status of screws—referring to bullets during this call. Kassem Daher informed Hassoun that there were a million "screws" in Lebanon that "slipped through [their] hands because there's no money." After Hassoun affirms that he understood what Daher's reference to one-million screws meant, Daher adds that "the dogs the ones who are with the party of the devil" came and took the screws.

In his Motion for Judgment of Acquittal Padilla asserts that the government did not adduce sufficient evidence at trial for a reasonable jury to find, beyond a reasonable doubt, that Padilla engaged in a conspiracy to murder, kidnap, or maim while physically within the United States. Padilla correctly argues that the mere presence of a defendant with alleged conspirators is insufficient to support a conviction. However, the evidence at trial, when viewed most favorably to the government, does not merely show Padilla's presence among and association with his co-conspirators. Rather, the calls, testimony, and the fruit of defendants' effort—Padilla attending an al Qaeda training camp, evinced by his training camp application—prove that Padilla was an integral part of defendants' conspiratorial agreement. Specifically, the evidence demonstrated Padilla's complicity in a "specific plan to engage in violent jihad which had as a necessary consequence murder, kidnaping, and maiming."[26]

Take Note

The *mens rea* of conspiracy is not established simply by showing that an accused person was *merely present* while others were conspiring or that the accused *merely knew* that someone else intended to commit a crime.

Padilla actively participated in planning the defendants' scheme. He discussed his intentions to train and fight with his co-conspirators, he boarded a plane fully intending to train for and fight in violent jihad abroad, and he ultimately attended an al Qaeda training camp in Afghanistan. Furthermore, Padilla even criticized and instructed his co-conspirators about how jihad should be discussed and the attributes necessary to participate in jihad. Padilla's status as one of the conspiracy's mujahideen recruits further embroiled him in the conspiracy's web by making him an instrument of the scheme itself. Padilla's involvement in the defendants' agreement went well beyond mere presence. Padilla voluntarily participated in planning aspects of the conspiracy, participated in the accomplishment of its goals, and took steps to ensure that these goals were effectuated while in the United States. Accordingly, the jury were entitled to conclude that Padilla engaged in a conspiracy to murder, kidnap, or maim and provided or concealed material support to a section 956 conspiracy to murder, kidnap, or maim, both while physically within the United States.

Jayyousi's general assertion that "a reasonable jury could not have returned a verdict of guilty, based solely upon the evidence presented at trial" does not reflect the evidence presented at trial. The government's evidence documented Jayyousi's participation in the conspiracy and furtherance of its goals. Similarly to Hassoun, the government adduced evidence indicating that Jayyousi subscribed to a violent form of jihad. The government also provided significant evidence indicating Jayyousi's complicity in the conspiratorial scheme, including participa-

---

26 The government's evidence did not document Padilla's mere presence, passive acquiescence or knowledge of the conspiratorial scheme. Rather, the evidence proffered by the government indicated that Padilla pro-actively made himself a party to the conspiracy by agreeing to further its objectives and taking steps to ensure that these objectives were met. The government presented substantial evidence that Padilla was actively involved in planning and furthering the goals of the conspiracy.

FYI

In subsequent proceedings, the Eleventh Circuit Court of Appeals ruled that the three counts filed against the three petitioners in *Hassoun* did not charge "the same offense" in violation of their rights against double jeopardy, noting that "it bears repeating that double jeopardy is not implicated simply because a factual situation might exist where a defendant could commit one act that satisfies the elements of two distinct offenses." *United States v. Hassoun*, 476 F.3d 1181, 1188–89 (11th Cir. 2007).

tion in phone calls discussing funding violent jihad, utilizing code words to cover up illicit activity and recruiting mujahideen.

Furthermore, the government provided evidence documenting Jayyousi's efforts to secure communications equipment and to fund the travels of mujahideen recruits destined for training in Afghanistan or fighting in Chechnya. This evidence documented Jayyousi's ongoing, methodical and calculated complicity in the object of the conspiracy. Accordingly, the jury were entitled to conclude that Jayyousi engaged in a conspiracy to murder, kidnap, or maim and provided or concealed material support to a section 956 conspiracy to murder, kidnap, or maim, both while physically within the United States.

For all the foregoing reasons, and based upon the record at trial and the entirety of evidence presented by the government in this case, the defendants are not entitled to judgments of acquittal on any of the three counts in the Indictment.

Point for Discussion

Charging Conspiracy vs. Substantive Offenses

The federal district court in *Hassoun* noted that "Hassoun correctly recites the well-established legal principle that a 'conspiracy to commit a particular substantive offense cannot exist without at least the degree of criminal intent necessary for the substantive offense itself.' "

Since that is the case, with respect to the first charged conspiracy—conspiring to commit acts of murder, kidnaping or maiming outside of the United States, while committing one or more overt acts in furtherance thereof within the United States—why do you think that the prosecution did not simply charge and try these three co-defendants with the substantive offenses themselves (or, at least, attempts to commit these substantive offenses) rather than simply conspiracy to commit these offenses?

Practice Pointer

Some criminal offenses are simply easier to prove than other criminal offenses, even though both offenses are based upon the same conduct. Conspiracy is often easier to prove than attempt, for example, because there is no hearsay exception applicable to attempt prosecutions, and because an overt act (where proof of one is required) is much easier to prove than a substantial step.

With respect to the second charged conspiracy—conspiring to provide material support to terrorists—why do you think that the prosecution did charge these co-defendants both with conspiracy and the substantive offense itself?

United States v. Blankenship

970 F.2d 283 (7th Cir. 1992).

EASTERBROOK, CIRCUIT JUDGE.

Courts do not enforce bargains among the producers of illegal drugs, or between these producers and their customers. Extra-judicial remedies tend to be violent, which makes drug running a crime of the young and vigorous. Substitutes for both legal processes and brutality are possible, however; family ties may suffice. Nancy Nietupski, a grandmother in her early 60s, ran a methamphetamine ring through her extended family. She started on the west coast, working with her nephew William Zahm. Later she moved to her sister's farm in Illinois. While sister Violet Blankenship supplied a base of operations, nephew Robert Blankenship helped distribute the drug and collect debts.

Nietupski initially bought methamphetamine from outside sources. When these proved unreliable, Zahm helped her enter the manufacturing end of the business. "Cooking" methamphetamine is messy, and there is a risk of explosion when volatile chemicals such as acetone reach high temperatures. Nietupski and Zahm moved their laboratory frequently, to reduce the risk of detection. In February 1989 Zahm leased from Thomas Lawrence a house trailer in which to set up shop for a day. Nietupski told Lawrence what Zahm planned to make and offered $1,000 or one ounce of methamphetamine; Lawrence preferred the cash and took $100 as a down payment. He covered the floor of the trailer with plastic for protection. Zahm postponed the operation when he could not find a heating control. A few days later Lawrence got cold feet, telling Marvin Bland (one of Nietupski's assistants) that he wanted the chemicals and equipment removed. Bland complied.

> **Go Online**
>
> The "cooking" of methamphetamine ("meth") in clandestine laboratories is increasingly a problem in the United States. *See, e.g.,* http://www.fas.org/irp/agency/doj/dea/product/meth/threat.htm.

Zahm soon joined William Worker to set up a new methamphetamine ring. Agents of the DEA infiltrated the Zahm-Worker clique. Zahm cut his losses by turning against his aunt, whose operations collapsed. Eighteen persons from the Nietupski ring were indicted. Robert Blankenship, Thomas Lawrence, and six others were in one group, all charged in a single count with conspiring to manufacture and distribute methamphetamine. Of the six, three pleaded guilty and three were acquitted. Blankenship and Lawrence, convicted by the jury, received identical sentences of 120 months' imprisonment plus five years' supervised release.

Conspiracy is agreement to violate the law. Unless Lawrence willingly joined the Nietupski venture, he did not commit the crime of conspiracy. What evidence was there that Lawrence knew, let alone joined? Nietupski and Zahm told Lawrence what they planned to do in his trailer; Zahm and Lawrence sampled some of the product scraped off the apparatus; for $1,000 he furnished the space, covered the floor with plastic, supplied refreshments, and let Zahm take a shower to wash some acid off his legs. If providing assistance to a criminal organization were the same thing as conspiracy, then Lawrence would be guilty. Yet there is a difference between supplying goods to a syndicate and joining it, just as there is a difference between selling goods and being an employee of the buyer. Cargill sells malt and barley to Anheuser Busch, knowing that they will be made into beer, without being part of Busch; by parallel reasoning, someone who sells sugar to a bootlegger knowing the use that will be made of that staple is not thereby a conspirator, *United States v. Falcone*, 311 U.S. 205 (1940), and someone who buys one load of marijuana has not conspired with the sellers, *United States v. Baker*, 905 F.2d 1100, 1106–07 (7th Cir.1990).

Food for Thought

Judge Easterbrook opines that a finding of conspiratorial intent in situations such as those described in *Blankenship* would lead to an undesirable "parade of horribles": "Companies that sold cellular phones to teenage punks who have no use for them other than to set up drug deals would be in trouble, and many legitimate businesses would be required to monitor their customers' activities." Is this really such an undesirable result? Why or why not?

Falcone illustrates the doctrine that "mere" sellers and buyers are not automatically conspirators. If it were otherwise, companies that sold cellular phones to teenage punks who have no use for them other than to set up drug deals would be in trouble, and many legitimate businesses would be required to monitor their customers' activities.

Yet this does not get us very far, for no rule says that a supplier cannot join a conspiracy through which the product is put to an unlawful end. *Direct Sales Co. v. United States*, 319 U.S. 703 (1943), makes that point in holding that the jury may infer that a pharmaceutical house selling huge quantities of morphine to a physician over a seven-year span conspired with the physician to distribute the drug illegally.

Where does the "mere" sale end, the conspiracy begin? One may draw a line, as *Falcone* and *Direct Sales* did, between knowledge of other persons' crimes and intent to join them, but this restates the elements of the offense without telling us when an inference of intent to join is permissible. Selling a camera to a spy does not make one a traitor—but selling camera and film, developing the prints, enlarging the detail in the critical areas, and collecting half of the payment for the secret information would assuredly land one in prison. Stating polar cases is easy, but locating the line of demarcation is hard. Courts have a tendency in these situations to draw up a list of relevant factors, without describing necessary or sufficient conditions. Lists have burgeoned since *Falcone*.

When writing for the court of appeals in *Falcone*, Learned Hand concluded that a supplier joins a venture only if his fortunes rise or fall with the venture's, so that he gains by its success. On this view the sale of a staple commodity such as sugar or telephone service does not enlist the seller in the criminal venture; in a competitive market the vendor could sell to someone else at the market price, and the buyer could turn to other sources. Anonymous transactions are the norm in markets and do not create criminal liability; when the seller has knowledge but the terms remain the same, there is no reason to infer participation in the enterprise any more than in the Cargill-Busch case we have given.

Trailers do not rent for $1,000 per week—not in legitimate markets, anyway. By charging a premium price, Lawrence seemingly threw in his lot with the Nietupski operation and may be convicted under Judge Hand's approach. Yet the price cannot be the end of things. What does the $1,000 represent: a piece of the action, or only a premium for the risks? Lawrence bore two. One was that the chemicals would damage his trailer. Although he took precautions by spreading plastic on the floor, an explosion would have spattered chemicals on the walls and ceiling. Lawrence would have charged for taking this risk even if the manufacture of methamphetamine were entirely legal. The other risk was the hazard of criminal liability, a cost of doing business. One who covers his own costs and no more does not share in the venture's success. Using a price calculated by reference to the risk of criminal conviction as support for that conviction would be circular. Reduce the risk of conviction, and you reduce the price. Either way, the price responds to the legal system rather than to the potential profits of the Nietupski gang and does not establish a desire to promote its success. Repeat business, as in *Direct Sales*, might show such a desire, but Lawrence did not carry through with the initial transaction and never realized even the $1,000.

Other cases from this court speak reverentially of Judge Hand but actually ask a different, and more functional, question. It is whether the imposition of liability on transactions of the class depicted by the case would deter crime without adding unduly to the costs of legitimate transactions.

If the product is itself contraband—for example, the methamphetamine Nietupski bought in California early on—the analysis differs but the result is the same: an isolated sale is not the same thing as enlisting in the venture. A sale of methamphetamine is a substantive crime. Because the substance is illegal, the seller knows that the buyer will put the drug to an illegal use, yet this does not make the sale a second, inchoate offense. To treat it as a second crime of aiding and abetting (or conspiring with) the buyer is to multiply the criminal punishment and so distort the penalty system the legislature adopted—for what is the point of setting at five years the maximum penalty for selling a given quantity of methamphetamine if every sale violates a second law and doubles the penalty?

Food for Thought

Doesn't this observation beg the question? If Congress wanted to legislate that particular conduct violated more than one criminal statute, it would have the power to provide just that. Or would it?

Some states have statutes forbidding "criminal facilitation," an apt description of Lawrence's acts. Lawrence agreed to facilitate the manufacture of methamphetamine, but the United States Code lacks a facilitation statute. It does forbid aiding and abetting substantive offenses.

Neither *Direct Sales* nor any of this court's cases permits a supplier to a criminal organization to be sentenced for all of that organization's sins when he facilitated only one. If the United States Code contained a facilitation statute along the lines of New York's, Lawrence

> **FYI**
>
> *See, e.g.*, N.Y. Penal Law § 115.05 ("A person is guilty of criminal facilitation in the second degree when, believing it probable that he is rendering aid to a person who intends to commit a class A felony, he engages in conduct which provides such person with means or opportunity for the commission thereof and which in fact aids such person to commit such class A felony.").

would receive a sentence proportioned to his own iniquity rather than that of Nietupski and her henchmen. So too if the Code penalized abetting criminal attempts. But it does not, and if the only options are conspiracy, with full responsibility for all of the venture's other crimes, and no crime, then no crime comes much closer to describing Lawrence's responsibility.

Let us be clear: Lawrence knew what Zahm wanted to do in the trailer, but there is a gulf between knowledge and conspiracy. There is no evidence that Lawrence recognized, let alone that he joined and promoted, the full scope of the Nietupski organization's activities. He may have joined, or abetted, a more limited agreement to manufacture a quantity of methamphetamine, but he was not charged with that offense. Lawrence facilitated an attempted crime, and probably conspired to do this, but he did not subscribe to the broader agreement on which his conviction depends.

The judgment is reversed.

Point for Discussion

Knowledge vs. Intent

Should exceptions exist to the proposition that "knowledge is not intent?" What if someone knows that an actor is about to kill his or her spouse? Wouldn't silence be the same as a tacit agreement to assist in the homicide, i.e. assistance by not creating any impediments to the performance of the criminal act?

> ## Hypo 1: *Taking Messages*
>
> Louis Lauria operated a telephone-answering service which supplied its services to a number of prostitutes. Lauria knew that some of his customers were prostitutes—he used the services of one of them who received 500 calls a month—and he assured them of the utmost confidentiality in message-taking. When three of these prostitutes were arrested, Lauria was indicted along with the three for conspiracy to commit prostitution. Is he guilty of this charge? *People v. Lauria*, 251 Cal. App. 2d 471, 59 Cal. Rptr. 628 (1967).

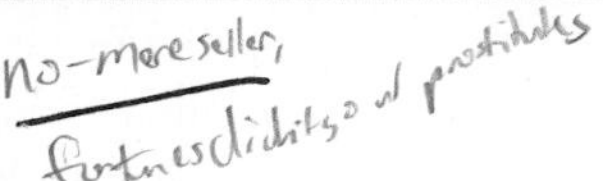

Hypo 2: *Perks for Prostitutes*

In Hypo 1, would or should the result be different if Lauria charged the prostitutes double the fees he charged his other customers? And would it or should it matter whether he provides a special paging service for an additional fee to his prostitute customers that he does not offer to his other customers?

Hypo 3: *Condom Sales*

Suppose that John Johnson, who owns a local pharmacy, sells condoms—*lots* of condoms, but at their normal retail price—to a known prostitute. Assuming that Johnson knows that she is using most or all of the condoms in her professional calling, is he a co-conspirator with her?

Hypo 4: *Unwitting Co-Conspirator*

Defendant Martínez concedes that he knew that he was doing something illegal when he was paid $1,000 for picking up packages for some friends, packages that turned out to contain cocaine. But Martínez claims that he did not know precisely what he was hired to pick up, i.e. that the transaction was actually part of a narcotics deal. Hence, he argues, he could not be convicted of conspiracy to engage in narcotics trafficking. If he's telling the truth, is this and should this be a good defense to a conspiracy charge? *United States v. Martínez-Lantigua,* 857 F.3d 453 (1st Cir. 2017).

C. *Actus Reus*: Agreement

Most conspiratorial agreements are clandestine. They are neither made in front of witnesses nor recorded on video or audio surveillance. Moreover, in the absence of a plea agreement, it is not in the self interest of individual coconspirators to testify to the existence of such incriminating matters. As a result, the *actus reus* element of conspiracy—the conspiratorial "agreement"—often is established only inferentially and/or circumstantially.

In large part due to the inferential and circumstantial nature of the proof, there is an abiding concern, particularly in large conspiracy trials, that some individuals who were not actually part of the conspiracy under scrutiny will be swept into the conspiratorial "net" simply because they have associated previously with one or more of the coconspirators, however innocently. As you read these decisions, you should bear in mind this concern. Short of eliminating the conspiracy offense, how can it be alleviated?

State v. Papillon

173 N.H. 13, 236 A.3d 839 (N.H. 2020).

HANTZ MARCONI, J.

Following a jury trial in Superior Court, the defendant, Paulson Papillon, was convicted of conspiracy to commit murder. On appeal, he argues that the trial court erred by finding the evidence sufficient to support his convictions. We affirm.

The jury could have found the following facts. During the latter half of 2015, the defendant and his associates, Adrien Stillwell, Nathaniel Smith, and Michael Younge, sold drugs in and around Manchester. The four men shared access to at least two apartment buildings, called "trap houses," from which they furthered their operation. The victim, M.P., regularly purchased drugs from the defendant, Stillwell, Smith, and Younge. On October 21, 2015, a confidential informant and M.P. each purchased drugs from the defendant at a Manchester hotel. That same day, the defendant was arrested and jailed after the hotel was searched, and the defendant came to believe that M.P. was the "snitch" responsible for his arrest.

The defendant was released on bail on October 26, and over the next several days, he urged Stillwell, Smith, and Younge to kill M.P. for his suspected role in the defendant's arrest. The day after the defendant was released, he paid to bail Smith out of jail so that Smith could help Stillwell and Younge murder M.P. The defendant continued to raise the topic of killing M.P. with his associates, offering them money and drugs to do so and emphasizing that it needed to happen "before he had court."

On October 31, Halloween, the defendant, Stillwell, Smith, and Younge met at one of the trap houses. The defendant once again pressed the three men to kill M.P., saying it should happen that night. To facilitate this plan, the defendant provided a gun—a .357—and Halloween costumes, which he intended Stillwell, Smith, and Younge to wear as disguises. Deciding against the costumes, Stillwell, Smith, and Younge left to find and kill M.P. Stillwell and Smith were both armed—Stillwell with the .357 that the defendant had provided. Meanwhile, the defendant went to a casino in Connecticut so that its security cameras could prove he was in another state when M.P. died. However, Stillwell, Smith, and Younge decided "it wasn't a good opportunity" to kill M.P. after they saw him in his residence that night.

The defendant was upset when he discovered that M.P. was still alive after Halloween. He reiterated that he "needed it done" before he had to appear in court and said if Stillwell, Smith, and Younge "couldn't do it," he would have someone else kill M.P. On both November 2 and 3, cell phone contact among the four men rose to an unusual level. At approximately 6:00 p.m. on November 3, Stillwell called and sent a text message to the defendant. Shortly after 6:00

p.m., Stillwell—armed again with the .357—and Smith met Younge at a convenience store near M.P.'s apartment building where they were captured on the store's security cameras. At approximately 6:17 p.m., they started walking up the street towards M.P.'s residence to make another attempt on his life. This time, Stillwell, Smith, and Younge found M.P. outside his apartment building. When M.P. began to walk away, Stillwell ran after him, firing the .357 six times. M.P. was shot twice and died at approximately 6:20 p.m. The defendant "made sure he wasn't there" when M.P. was killed, having had an acquaintance drive him to Massachusetts earlier that day.

After fleeing the scene, Stillwell and Younge returned to the apartment where they had met the defendant on Halloween and asked the woman who lived there, A.D., if the defendant "was back yet." Within minutes of the shooting, cell phone records showed that Stillwell had called the defendant twice and had exchanged text messages with the defendant. The defendant told A.D. to try calling M.P., feigning the need to set up a delivery for some drugs that she owed M.P. At approximately 8:00 p.m., the defendant, who by that time had returned to the trap house, sent Smith a text message that there was a large quantity of drugs waiting for him there. Smith arrived shortly thereafter.

The defendant met with Stillwell, Smith, and Younge in A.D.'s bathroom in an attempt to avoid being overheard, and his associates recounted how M.P. was killed. The defendant was happy to hear that M.P. was dead, started handing out drugs and money to his three associates, and said that they could "get back to business" now that the suspected informant was dead. However, the defendant became upset when Younge told him that the convenience store's security camera would have them on video before the murder, and the four of them discussed going to Connecticut the next day "to get out of town."

On November 4, the defendant, Stillwell, and Younge drove to Connecticut in a rented car. Along the way, Younge discarded the clothes he had worn the day before, and Stillwell and Younge discarded their cell phones. The defendant paid for Stillwell's and Younge's expenses at a casino and strip club in Connecticut. After a few days, the defendant returned to New Hampshire once he believed the investigation into M.P.'s death had cooled off. While another associate was driving the defendant around Manchester, the defendant said, "There's where I killed my f**king rat."

On November 9, the defendant was arrested on charges unrelated to M.P.'s murder. Stillwell and Smith had also been incarcerated in November on charges unrelated to M.P.'s murder, and Younge turned himself in on November 19 after his photograph was released in connection with M.P.'s death. The defendant was frustrated and nervous because he thought Stillwell, Smith, and/or Younge would implicate him in M.P.'s murder. The defendant told his sister that he wanted to send money to Stillwell and had her deliver drugs to Younge before Younge was arrested, but ultimately, the defendant wanted to bail himself and his associates out of jail in order to kill them before they could tell the police about his involvement in M.P.'s death.

Following a jury trial, the defendant was convicted of conspiracy to commit murder. This appeal followed. The defendant argues that the evidence was insufficient to support his conviction. To prevail upon his challenges to the sufficiency of the evidence, the defendant must prove that no rational trier of fact, viewing all of the evidence and all reasonable inferences from it in the light most favorable to the State, could have found guilt beyond a reasonable doubt.

RSA 629:3, I, provides:

> A person is guilty of conspiracy if, with a purpose that a crime defined by statute be committed, he agrees with one or more persons to commit or cause the commission of such crime, and an overt act is committed by one of the conspirators in furtherance of the conspiracy.

Conspiracy punishes the agreement to commit or cause the commission of a crime. A tacit understanding between the parties to cooperate in an illegal course of conduct will warrant a conviction for conspiracy, so long as one of the co-conspirators commits an overt act in furtherance thereof. Here, the State charged the defendant with conspiring to commit first degree murder.

The defendant argues that there was insufficient evidence of an agreement to cause M.P.'s death to support his conviction for conspiracy because "[t]here was no meeting of the minds to kill [M.P.] on November 3, 2015." This argument misconstrues the State's burden in proving the defendant's guilt.

As an initial matter, the State was not required to prove that an agreement to commit murder occurred on the same day that said murder was in fact committed because conspiracy is an inchoate crime that does not require the commission of the substantive offense that is the object of the conspiracy. Furthermore, the defendant's indictment did not allege that the defendant participated in an agreement to murder M.P. on November 3. The defendant's indictment for conspiracy to commit murder alleged in pertinent part:

> [O]n or between October 8, 2015, and November 3, 2015, . . . with the purpose that the crime of murder be committed, a crime defined by RSA 630, Paulson Papillon agreed with Michael Younge, Adrien Stillwell, [and/or] Nathaniel Smith . . . to cause the death of [M.P.], and that one or more of the co-conspirators committed one or more of the following overt acts in furtherance of the conspiracy: [alleging nineteen distinct overt acts.]

Thus, even assuming that no rational jury could have found that a "meeting of the minds" occurred on November 3, the defendant's argument is unavailing.

The defendant also attempts to import the contractual principles of "offer" and "reject[ion]" into the agreement element of the conspiracy statute, arguing that the evidence as to that element was insufficient because Stillwell, Smith, and Younge "expressly rejected the means and mode that [the defendant] proposed to carry out his intended plot"—namely, killing M.P. on Halloween while wearing costumes that the defendant had provided. This argument

> **Food for Thought**
>
> Is a "tacit understanding" really enough to establish an "agreement?" Shouldn't an agreement be express in order to meet the *actus reus* element? Or not?

presumes that the jury was compelled to adopt the defendant's characterization of Stillwell, Smith, and Younge's behavior. It was not.

There was sufficient evidence from which a jury could have found that the defendant had, at a minimum, a "tacit understanding" with Stillwell, Smith, and Younge to cause M.P.'s death as alleged in the indictment. At trial, the State presented evidence that, after the defendant was released on bail on October 26, the defendant had several conversations with Stillwell, Smith, and Younge regarding his desire to have M.P. killed and his willingness to work toward that end. The State presented evidence that the defendant urged Stillwell, Smith, and Younge to kill M.P., promised them money and drugs, and pushed them to kill M.P. on Halloween. After the aborted Halloween attempt, the defendant reiterated his need to have M.P. killed, and cell phone records showed that the defendant was in contact with his associates shortly before and after M.P. was shot on November 3. There was evidence that Stillwell and Younge took steps to report M.P.'s death to the defendant, that the defendant rewarded his associates with drugs and money the night of the murder, and that he had A.D. confirm that M.P. was dead. The State presented evidence that the defendant took steps to establish alibis for himself and attempted to cover up his involvement in the murder by taking Stillwell and Younge to Connecticut, coordinating with his sister while he was in prison to deliver drugs to Younge and money to Stillwell, and even planning to kill his co-conspirators to keep them quiet. The jury also heard witness testimony that, after M.P.'s killing, the defendant told an associate, "There's where I killed my f**king rat," and told L.M. in prison that he, the defendant, "had to have it done" because M.P. was going to inform on him "for some drugs."

Viewing this evidence in the light most favorable to the State, we hold that a rational trier of fact could have found beyond a reasonable doubt that there was an agreement between the defendant and Younge, Stillwell, and/or Smith to purposely cause the death of M.P. We accordingly uphold the defendant's conviction for conspiracy to commit murder.

Affirmed.

State v. Rosado

2009 WL 3086436 (Conn. Super. Ct. 2009).

JON C. BLUE, JUDGE of the Superior Court.

On a late summer afternoon in 2006, the young life of Aaron McCrae ended in a hail of bullets near the train station in New Haven. Two and a half years later, Geraldo Rosado, the defendant herein, was tried for being a member of the conspiracy that plotted McCrae's death. Examined in the light most favorable to the State, the evidence establishes the following facts. In the early morning hours of September 17, 2006, a man with the street name of "Carlito" was killed in the area of the Church Street South housing project near the train station in New Haven known as the "jungle." "Carlito's" associates blamed McCrae (who had the street name "A-Love") for the killing.

A man with the descriptive street name of "Primo" called a meeting to place a bounty on McCrae. The only evidentiary description of this meeting is contained in a tape-recorded statement that the defendant gave to the police on December 16, 2006. According to the defendant:

> We went to the jungle. Primo put a hit out to kill A-Love. He gave the two guns to Luis Santana and showed him fifteen thousand that once he do what he had to do he'll get the money and from there we went up chilled for a little bit. Went up the hill, they got a call that A-Love was out there and me, this other kid name Juan Nunez, known as Bebe, went up the hill. Louis Santana was in the alleyway, then from there he ran across the street and shot A-Love.

The evidence shows that McCrae was shot in the back by seven to nine bullets (the fragmentation of some bullets makes the exact count uncertain) fired by two different handguns. Two shots resulted in lethal wounds. McCrae died within moments.

The crime occurred on a warm, sunny afternoon in a public area. Within moments, a crowd of approximately 150 people had gathered. In spite of the fact that many people must have seen the shooting, no one came forward. A 911 caller reported that McCrae was shot by "two Spanish guys." The defendant, as mentioned, told the police that McCrae was shot by Luis Santana. No other description of the crime is in evidence.

According to the defendant's December 16, 2006 statement, after the shooting, "We ran up Carlisle and went straight to Bebe house, known as Juan Nunez." The defendant said that he was on the porch when Santana and Nunez went upstairs. Nunez told him that, "He put the guns away for Luis Santana." A few days later, when the guns were recovered at Nunez's residence, Santana called the defendant and told him "they caught his guns."

DNA mixtures of at least three individuals were recovered from the grips of each gun. The defendant could not be eliminated as a possible contributor with respect to either weapon. Subsequently, on two occasions prior to his December 16, 2006 statement, the defendant falsely told the police that he had not been at the scene of the killing.

Defendant was arrested and subsequently convicted for conspiracy to murder McRae. The question presented by the motion now before the court is whether the evidence is sufficient to sustain the defendant's conviction of conspiracy to commit murder.

The standard of review to be employed by the court in reviewing a sufficiency of the evidence claim following a jury verdict finding the defendant guilty of the crime of conspiracy is well settled:

> We apply a two part test. First, we construe the evidence in the light most favorable to sustaining the verdict. Second, we determine whether upon the facts so construed and the inferences reasonably drawn therefrom the jury reasonably could have

concluded that the cumulative force of the evidence established guilt beyond a reasonable doubt.

To establish the crime of conspiracy the state must show that there was an agreement between two or more persons to engage in conduct constituting a crime and that the agreement was followed by an overt act in furtherance of the conspiracy by any one of the conspirators. The state must also show intent on the part of the accused that conduct constituting a crime be performed. The existence of a formal agreement between the parties need not be proved; it is sufficient to show that they are knowingly engaged in a mutual plan to do a forbidden act.

While the state must prove an agreement the existence of a formal agreement between the coconspirators need not be proved because it is only in rare instances that conspiracy may be established by proof of an express agreement to unite to accomplish an unlawful purpose. The requisite agreement or confederation may be inferred from proof of the separate acts of the individuals accused as coconspirators and from the circumstances surrounding the commission of these acts. Further, conspiracy can seldom be proved by direct evidence. It may be inferred from the activities of the accused persons.

The sufficiency of the evidence issue presented here focuses on the element of agreement. Conn. Gen.Stat. § 53a–48(a) provides that, "A person is guilty of conspiracy when, with intent that conduct constituting a crime be performed, he *agrees* with one or more persons to engage in the performance of such conduct, and any one of them commits an overt act in pursuance of such conspiracy." Agreement is an element of the crime that must be proven beyond a reasonable doubt, and the jury in this case was instructed accordingly.[5]

FYI

Often coconspirators have multiple criminal objectives, raising questions about how many conspiracies exist. That question can be answered simply. If coconspirators make a single agreement to accomplish a number of criminal objectives, there is a single conspiracy. If, in contrast, coconspirators make two agreements, each to accomplish one or more criminal objectives, there are two conspiracies. And so on. *See, e.g., Braverman v. United States*, 317 U.S. 49 (1942). Since the *actus reus* of the conspiracy crime is the agreement not the criminal objective, there are as many conspiracies as there are agreements.

5 With respect to the element of agreement, the jury was instructed that:

The first element that the State must prove beyond a reasonable doubt is that the defendant made an agreement with one or more persons. It is not necessary for the State to prove that there was a formal or express agreement between them. It is sufficient to show that the parties knowingly engaged in a mutual plan to do a criminal act. Conspiracies are often formed in secret. But an agreement, just like any other fact, may be proven by circumstantial evidence. It is not necessary to establish that the persons making the agreement signed papers, shook hands, or uttered the words, "We have an agreement." Rather, a conspiracy can be inferred from the conduct of the persons involved.

A mere knowledge, acquiescence, or approval of the object of the agreement without cooperation or an agreement to cooperate is not, however, sufficient to make someone a party to a conspiracy to commit the criminal act. Mere presence at the scene of the crime, even when coupled with knowledge of the crime, is insufficient to establish a conspiracy.

The defendant's December 16, 2006 statement firmly establishes the existence of a conspiracy to murder McCrae. Whether the defendant joined with at least one other person in an agreement to commit the murder is an issue of fact. There was no direct evidence that the defendant joined in an agreement. The evidence was, instead, circumstantial. There is, however, nothing wrong with this latter manner of proof. "Because of the secret nature of conspiracies, a conviction usually is based on circumstantial evidence. Consequently, it is not necessary to establish that the defendant and his coconspirators signed papers, shook hands, or uttered the words we have an agreement. The requisite agreement or confederation may be inferred from proof of the separate acts of the individuals accused as coconspirators and from the circumstances surrounding the commission of these acts."

Circumstantial evidence is sometimes more reliable than direct evidence. "A fact positively sworn to by a single eyewitness of blemished character, is not so satisfactorily proved, as is a fact which is the necessary consequence of a chain of other facts sworn to by many witnesses of undoubted credibility." Conspiracy jurisprudence recognizes this well-known fact. At the same time, however, our jurisprudence also recognizes that, "Mere presence at the scene of the crime, even coupled with knowledge of the crime, is not sufficient to establish guilt of a conspiracy." The purpose of this rule is to require that a defendant cannot be convicted of conspiracy without evidence that he "was more than a mere bystander."

Rosado views the "mere presence" rule as his safe harbor in this case, but, on this evidence, it is not. The evidence establishes much more than Rosado's "mere presence at the scene of the crime." He was, of course, present at the scene of the crime-he claims to have personally witnessed McCrae's execution-but he was present at a great many other places as well. By his own admission, he was present when "Primo" put a bounty on McCrae and gave two guns to Luis Santana. He was present at the scene of the crime, along with Juan Nunez. He subsequently ran-with Nunez-to Nunez's house on Carlisle Street. Nunez's house is the same place to which Santana ran after the shooting and the location at which the murder weapons were subsequently discovered. After the murder weapons were discovered, Santana called Rosado and informed him of this fact. In addition to these facts-all admitted by Rosado-DNA evidence indicates a probability (although not a certainty) that Rosado at some point touched the grip of each of the murder weapons. Rosado also made false statements to the police concerning his whereabouts at the time of the killing.

This scenario involves much more than mere presence at the scene of the crime. It is, instead, an intricate web of circumstantial evidence. Rosado's statement puts him not just at the scene of the crime but at each of three locations associated with the murder-the bounty meeting

---

In order to convict a person of conspiracy, the State need not show that the person had direct communication with all other conspirators. It is not necessary that each conspirator be acquainted with all others or even know their names. It is sufficient that he has come to an understanding with at least one of the others and has come to such understanding with that person to further a criminal purpose. It is also not essential that he know the complete plan of the conspiracy in all of its details. It is enough if he knows that a conspiracy exists or that he is creating one and that he is joining with at least one other person in an agreement to commit a crime, in this case the crime of murder.

with "Primo," the murder scene itself, and Nunez's house. In addition, the same statement shows that Rosado had at least some involvement with at least three different conspirators-"Primo," Nunez, and Santana-and the involvement with Santana was on multiple locations. DNA evidence shows a probability that Rosado touched each of the murder weapons. Finally, Rosado made false statements to the police.

Could all of this be a coincidence? The jury was surely entitled to infer that it was not. It might have been a coincidence that Rosado was present at the bounty meeting with "Primo," it might have been a coincidence that he was present at the murder scene, and it might have been a coincidence that he was present at Nunez's house, but the likelihood that all of these personal appearances were coincidental quite safely approaches zero.

A series of decisions of the United States Court of Appeals for the Second Circuit recognizes the common sense decision between mere presence at the scene of the crime, on the one hand, and the more extensive involvement in a series of events that can safely underpin a finding of conspiracy, on the other. That court has long recognized that, "Mere presence at the scene of the crime, even when coupled with knowledge that at that moment a crime is being committed, is insufficient to prove membership in a conspiracy." *United States v. Johnson*, 513 F.2d 819, 823–24 (2d Cir. 1975).

Johnson is a much-cited case applying this rule. Johnson accompanied a boyhood friend in an automobile trip from New Hampshire to Montreal to buy a motorcycle. Unhappily for Johnson, his friend did not restrict his Canadian purchases to motorcycles. One night, while Johnson was asleep, his friend left their motel room to purchase drugs and secreted them behind a door panel in the car. The drugs were discovered by Customs authorities when the two friends returned to the United States, and Johnson was eventually arrested for conspiracy to import the drugs. On appeal, the Second Circuit vacated the conviction, holding this to be a case of "mere presence." Although Johnson had unwisely told the Customs authorities that he was hitchhiking, the Court explained that, "Falsehoods told by a defendant in the hope of extricating himself from suspicious circumstances are insufficient proof on which to convict where other evidence of guilt is weak and the evidence before the court is as hospitable to an interpretation consistent with the defendant's innocence as it is to the Government's theory of guilt."

The Second Circuit has subsequently explained that *Johnson* does not apply to cases involving multiple appearances by a defendant at a variety of places associated with the crime. *United States v. Pedroza*, 750 F.2d 187 (2d Cir. 1984), *cert. denied*, 479 U.S. 842 (1986), is instructive. Pedroza was convicted of membership in a conspiracy to kidnap. The evidence showed that Pedroza was present at the purchase of the van later used in the abduction. Although Pedroza did not participate in the abduction itself, he arrived at the house to which the victim had been taken. He was then present at a number of locations to which the victim was subsequently taken. *Johnson* did not save Pedroza on appeal following his conviction. The Court explained that, while Johnson's presence in his friend's automobile "could have resulted from happenstance," here there was "nothing in the record to suggest that [Pedroza] may have had any purpose in these timely appearances other than to further the goals of the conspiracy."

The dividing line between "mere presence at the scene of the crime," on the one hand, and a series of "timely appearances," must be located by judgment rather than mathematics in any given case. But the common-sense standard articulated by Ian Fleming's memorable villain, Auric Goldfinger, is helpful in this regard. "Mr. Bond, they have a saying in Chicago: 'Once is happenstance. Twice is coincidence. The third time it's enemy action.' " Ian Fleming, Goldfinger 204 (1959).

See It

If you haven't seen the James Bond movie, Goldfinger, you really should watch it. But only after you have finished your Criminal Law homework. See http://www.imdb.com/title/tt0058150/.

There was plenty of "enemy action" here. The totality of the evidence-including Rosado's many "timely appearances" at places closely associated with the crime-was sufficient to allow the jury to find that Rosado agreed with one or more of the other conspirators to take part in that action.

The evidence presented was, as mentioned, less than overwhelming on this issue. Different people, hearing and assessing the same evidence, might draw different inferences and come to different factual conclusions. But hearing and assessing the evidence, drawing inferences, and coming to factual conclusions was the job of the jury-a jury chosen by the defendant as well as by the State.

The motion for judgment of acquittal is denied.

Hypo 1: *Scalping Tickets*

A & B are scalping tickets to a University of Louisville basketball game in Freedom Hall, Louisville, Kentucky. In Kentucky, scalping is illegal. Before the police arrested A & B, they observed them holding up tickets (suggesting that the tickets were for sale), talking with potential customers, and eventually selling tickets above face value. In addition, from time-to-time, A & B conversed with each other and were observed passing something between one another. Is there sufficient evidence of conspiracy to scalp tickets to convict A & B?

Hypo 2: *Making Change*

In Hypo 1, assume that C is A's friend. While he is scalping tickets, she sits off to the side, smoking a cigarette. Once, police observed her getting coffee for A. In addition, during one sale, when A did not have exact change, C provided it to him. Is there sufficient evidence to convict C of conspiracy to scalp? Would it make any difference if A kept giving C all of the ticket sale proceeds to put in her purse?

Hypo 3: *The Lookout*

Luis Mercado was seen leaning out a third-floor window and observing three different crack cocaine sales (all to undercover police officers) made on three different occasions by Alex Colon. According to the government, Mercado was operating as a "lookout" for Colon. When the apartment was searched, no drugs were found on Mercado, but officers found 23.7 grams of cocaine sitting out in the open on a tabletop, as well as two plastic packets each containing 20 vials of crack cocaine, numerous clear plastic vials, caps, and packets, and a spoon and a razor, each containing white residue (which turned out to be cocaine). Is there sufficient evidence on this record to convict Mercado of conspiring with Colon to engage in the criminal sale of narcotics? *Commonwealth v. Mercado*, 420 Pa. Super. 588, 617 A.2d 342 (1992).

Hypo 4: *Cocaine Buddies*

Would the result in Hypo 3 be any different, do you think, if Mercado and Colon were frequently seen together, and Colon was not viewed looking out the window, but was instead simply found using cocaine in the apartment when the apartment was searched, i.e. could he be convicted of conspiracy in those circumstances? *See, e.g., Commonwealth v. Rodgers*, 410 Pa. Super. 341, 599 A.2d 1329 (1991).

Points for Discussion

a. Co-Conspirator Hearsay Exception

In establishing the existence of a conspiratorial agreement in court, prosecutors may use testimony by one coconspirator about what another coconspirator said, even though such testimony is ordinarily inadmissible as hearsay. The "coconspirator hearsay exception," is justified on the ground that coconspirators are acting as agents of one another. Under that exception, declarations made by one coconspirator during and in furtherance of the conspiracy are admissible in court, assuming that there has been a substantial and independent showing that a conspiracy existed and that the individuals in question were a part of that conspiracy.

b. Wheels & Chains

Some courts have used such metaphors as "wheels" and "chains" to describe the operation of common types of conspiratorial arrangements.

A "chain" conspiracy is a single conspiracy where individual members (the "links") interact only with the next link in the chain and may not know any of the other links farther up or down the chain. Narcotics importation and distribution schemes are common examples of chain conspiracies.

A "wheel" conspiracy, in contrast, involves separate chain conspiracies ("the spokes") linked to each other through a common individual ("the hub"). *See, e.g., Kotteakos v. United States*, 328 U.S. 750 (1946) (no wheel conspiracy where spokes not connected, e.g. through knowledge by the separate conspirators of the existence of other conspirators or conspiracies).

c. Scouts & Steerers

Law enforcement agents seeking to eradicate illegal narcotics sales in particular neighborhoods generally hope to arrest not only the street salespersons themselves, but also the various "scouts," "runners," "lookouts," and other individuals who are paid to support the narcotics sales operation by watching for police presence and/or steering potential customers to the sales force.

If you were an Assistant District Attorney assigned to support a joint state-federal law enforcement Task Force that had such a mission, how might you explain to the Task Force officers when precisely such "scouts" or "steerers" might be deemed to be coconspirators with the actual salespersons—and when they may not. What conduct or statements should the officers be looking for (or waiting for) in order to make a lawful arrest for conspiracy?

D. Overt Act

Most (but not all) jurisdictions with general conspiracy statutes require as an element of the offense proof of an "overt act" on the part of one of the coconspirators in order to establish the existence of a conspiracy. It does not usually take much, however, to establish the existence of an overt act. Even a relatively insignificant action on the part of one of the coconspirators will generally suffice.

State v. Garcia

376 P.3d 94 (Kan. 2016).

PER CURIAM.

In 2013, the KBI began working with a confidential informant who had been helping the Garden City Police Department and the Finney County Sheriff's Office. When this informant came forward with knowledge of a drug dealer in Dodge City, Kansas, the information was passed along to the KBI. The informant told the KBI that he could buy drugs from Garcia, his dealer. According to the informant, he had recently bought drugs from Garcia. By contacting locals, checking water records, reviewing past investigations, and using information provided by the informant, the KBI was able to find where Garcia lived. Because Garcia's location had been determined, the plan was to set up a drug deal by phone and then execute a search warrant without ever purchasing any drugs.

Instead of calling Garcia, the informant called Garcia's girlfriend, Mickashell Knapp, because an arrangement had been made that he should call Knapp if Garcia was unavailable. The phone call was made from a KBI special agent's phone in the late afternoon of August 13, 2013; Knapp answered. The informant asked for an ounce of methamphetamine, but Knapp replied that she could only get a half an ounce, or about 14 grams. The informant agreed to that amount, and the buy was scheduled for later that evening. Knapp said she could also get some cocaine. When the informant asked about Garcia, Knapp said he was dealing with some problems, and the informant understood that he was trying to stay clean or out of trouble.

The KBI applied for a search warrant and set up surveillance on the house where Garcia was staying. Surveillance units observed a black car pull into the driveway. A male and a female, later identified as Garcia and Knapp, got out of the car. Law enforcement officers then swarmed the house.

As the officers approached the house, several people, including Knapp, were outside, but Garcia was seen entering the house. Everyone had stopped when it was clear that law enforcement officers were pulling up, but Garcia continued into the house. After arresting Knapp, officers knocked on the front door and announced their presence. Garcia was told to come out and was seen coming from the area near the bedroom in the northeast part of the house. As he was being placed under arrest, Garcia said that he no longer lived at the house and that he had moved out or was moving out.

Law enforcement officers then began searching the house. A glass tray, snort tube, digital scale, and black box were found in the northeast bedroom. The glass tray, which had a white powdery substance on it, and the snort tube were found in plain view on a TV stand. The digital scale was also in plain view and was found to the right of the glass tray. A KBI special agent testified that a snort tube is a tube used to snort drugs. The same special agent testified that a digital scale can be evidence of drug distribution. The snort tube was tested, and traces of methadone and oxycodone were found. Methamphetamine, cocaine, and a synthetic cannabinoid, known as K2 or spice, were detected on the digital scale.

Inside the black box, which was found near the rest of the items, was a plastic bag with a crystalline substance and a prescription bottle. Garcia's name was on the prescription, and a white powdery substance was found inside the bottle. The crystalline substance in the plastic bag weighed 18.24 grams and tested positive for methamphetamine and cocaine. The white powdery substance found in the pill bottle weighed 1.48 grams and also tested positive for methamphetamine and cocaine.

As a result of the fruits from the search warrant and the investigation that followed, the State charged Garcia with possession of methamphetamine with intent to distribute within 1,000 feet of school property; conspiracy to distribute at least 3.5 grams of methamphetamine within 1,000 feet of school property; possession of cocaine with intent to distribute within 1,000 feet of school property; distribution of a naphthoylindole-based controlled substance of less than 3.5 grams within 1,000 feet of school property; conspiracy to distribute cocaine of less than 3.5 grams within 1,000 feet of school property; unlawful use of a communication facility; distributing or possessing methamphetamine without a tax stamp; distributing or possessing cocaine without a tax stamp; and two counts of possession of drug paraphernalia. The State later dismissed the distribution of a naphthoylindole-based controlled substance charge.

The jury found Garcia guilty on all counts, except for unlawful use of a communication device. Garcia timely appeals.

Did the State Present Sufficient Evidence to Support Garcia's Convictions of Conspiracy to Distribute?

Garcia claims that his conspiracy to distribute convictions were not supported by sufficient evidence. When the sufficiency of the evidence is challenged in a criminal case, we review "all the evidence in a light most favorable to the prosecution, and must be convinced a rational factfinder could have found the defendant guilty beyond a reasonable doubt." We also will not reweigh the evidence or the credibility of witnesses. Only in rare cases where the testimony is so incredible that no reasonable factfinder could find guilt beyond a reasonable doubt will a guilty verdict be reversed. To support a conspiracy conviction, the prosecution must present evidence that the defendant agreed with another person to commit or assist in committing a crime and that the defendant or the coconspirator committed an overt act to further the conspiracy. See K.S.A.2015 Supp. 21–5302(a).

> "An overt act which completes the crime of conspiracy is something apart from the conspiracy. It is an act to effect the object of the conspiracy but it need be neither a criminal act, nor the crime that is the object of the conspiracy. However, it must accompany or follow agreement and must be done in furtherance of the object of the agreement."
>
> "Conversations among co-conspirators in forming and planning the conspiracy are not overt acts." The prosecution must show that " 'defendant took a step beyond the mere preparation so that some appreciable fragment of the crime was committed.' "

In this case, the State presented sufficient evidence to prove both elements. First, the evidence showed that Garcia entered into an agreement with Knapp to sell or assist in the sale of drugs. The informant testified that Garcia was his dealer and that an arrangement had been made that if Garcia was not available, was not around, or was indisposed, the informant could deal with Knapp. When asked how recently that arrangement had been made, the informant said Garcia told him to deal with Knapp 2 or 3 weeks before the search warrant was executed. In her KBI interview, Knapp also stated that she had dealt for Garcia while he was in jail. She was also able to provide specific details about the deal with the informant. Although Knapp denied it at trial, she said that Garcia had been with her and told her what to say when she spoke with the informant on the phone and sent the text to the KBI special agent's phone. As it was for the jury to determine whether Knapp had been truthful during the interview or at trial, we cannot say as a matter of law that there was not sufficient evidence to support an agreement between Garcia and Knapp.

The State also presented evidence of an overt act: the use of a phone to arrange a time and place to sell drugs. Garcia notes the evidence did not show that he spoke with the informant on the phone and that he was acquitted on a separate charge of using a communication device in a drug transaction. But the overt act does not have to be committed by the defendant in order to convict the defendant of conspiracy—evidence that the defendant's coconspirator committed the overt act is also sufficient. In this case, Garcia's coconspirator was Knapp. And the evidence in support of her using a telephone to arrange a time and place to sell drugs to the informant is overwhelming. In fact, Garcia does not dispute that Knapp used a cell phone to arrange a deal with the informant. Instead, Garcia argues that State failed to present sufficient evidence of an agreement between him and Knapp. But as we have already explained above, the State presented sufficient evidence to establish this agreement.

In conclusion, the State presented evidence that when viewed in its most favorable light was sufficient to show that Garcia and Knapp had an agreement that Knapp would help Garcia sell drugs when Garcia was unavailable. The State also presented evidence showing that Knapp committed the overt act of using a telephone to arrange a time and place to sell drugs, in furtherance of their conspiracy. Thus, a rational factfinder could have found Garcia guilty beyond a reasonable doubt of conspiracy to distribute.

Food for Thought

Since conversations between co-conspirators are not enough to establish an overt act, do you think that it makes sense that a simple telephone conversation between one of the co-conspirators and a third party can be enough to establish an overt act?

Affirmed.

State v. Cottrell

310 Kan. 150, 445 P.3d 1132 (2019).

The opinion of the court was delivered by STEGALL, J.:

Ronald Cottrell sold prescription narcotics to an undercover detective in a QuikTrip parking lot in Sedgwick County. A jury convicted him of distributing of a controlled substance and conspiring to distribute a controlled substance. On appeal, he claims the conspiracy jury instruction, which alleged five overt acts in furtherance of the conspiracy, presented either a multiple acts or alternative means problem. We affirm.

On June 5, 2013, Eduardo Padron, an undercover detective with the Wichita Police Department, set up a controlled drug buy from Jennifer Curtis based on a tip that she was selling prescription drugs illegally. Padron texted Curtis and asked "what kind of pills" she sold. Curtis responded, "Ok well my father is the one with the product id have to get ahold of him what ya need he has everything." Pardon requested 8 oxycodone pills and 20 hydrocodone pills, which are prescription narcotics. Before long, Curtis texted back, "He's got yours ready when you are[.]" They decided to meet at a QuikTrip later that day, around 5 p.m.

Undercover officers conducted surveillance of the QuikTrip before Padron arrived. One officer observed several people lingering outside the QuikTrip who appeared to be watching for law enforcement, and two of them spoke with Curtis. The officer described this as "counter surveillance" activity. When Padron arrived, he parked his unmarked car in a parking lot next to the QuikTrip. The car was equipped with an interior video camera.

Padron notified Curtis of his location, but she did not approach his vehicle. Instead, she stayed near the QuikTrip and texted Padron, "Still waitin on mah pops." About 20 minutes later, a blue pickup truck arrived and parked between Padron's car and the QuikTrip. Curtis walked over to the truck and contacted the driver. As she stood beside the truck, she called Padron and asked him to relocate to the post office. Padron refused to do so, and in the background of the call, he heard a male voice say "Fuck it, let's just do it here."

At this point, Cottrell exited the driver's side of the truck, walked over to Padron's vehicle, and entered the passenger side. Inside Patron's vehicle, Cottrell exchanged a pill bottle for $350 cash. Padron's video camera captured the exchange, which lasted about 30 seconds. The video was played for the jury, but only the audio recording is included on the record on appeal. The audio is fuzzy at times, but it is clear that Cottrell introduced himself as "Randy"; said he did not usually meet people; called Curtis his "daughter"; and described the bottle as an "8 and 20." Then Cottrell returned to his truck, spoke with Curtis for a little while, and drove away. A forensic scientist later testified that the pill bottle contained 20 hydrocodone pills and 8 oxycodone pills.

About a week later, Padron texted Curtis about buying more oxycodone. Curtis replied, "[L]emme get with my pops how many u need?" Padron requested 10 pills. He also asked Curtis to let him know when she had the pills in her possession. But Curtis hesitated and explained, "My dad wont lemme that cuz its his business I just bring in the clientel I handle customers only no money no merch." Eventually, the second sale fell through because Curtis stopped responding to Padron's texts.

The State charged Cottrell with distribution of hydrocodone, distribution of oxycodone, and conspiracy to distribute a controlled substance. At trial, the State called three witnesses: Padron, a surveillance officer, and the forensic scientist who identified the drugs. The defense called Cottrell as its only witness. He insisted that he did not know what was inside the bottle and that he blindly followed Curtis' directions because he needed the money. He explained that Curtis and his son were dating before his son's death, and after his death, Cottrell loaned her money to pay the bills. He testified that Curtis told him to come to QuikTrip to pick up the money she owed him; when he arrived, she told him to exchange the pill bottle for the money; and he naïvely complied to get his repayment.

Defense counsel asked why Cottrell called the bottle "8 and 20" in his conversation with Padron. Cottrell explained that he learned the phrase from Curtis—when he asked her what the bottle was, she said it was "8 and 20." Cottrell claimed he did not know what this meant, but he exchanged the bottle anyway because, in his words, he "got mad and thought in the split second and went, fuck it, you know."

Go Online

To view a list of current street names for opiates, https://www.michaelshouse.com/opiate-addiction/street-names-for-opiates/.

The charging document and the conspiracy jury instruction alleged the same five overt acts committed in furtherance of the conspiracy to distribute a controlled substance:

1. JENNIFER M. CURTIS responded to Officer Padron's text inquiry with details on prices and where to go to conclude the sale of hydrocodone and oxycodone.

2. JENNIFER M. CURTIS contacted RONALD D. COTTRELL, JR., with the sales order she obtained from Officer Padrone [sic] and had, RONALD D. COTTRELL, JR., appear at the designated time and place with the pills Officer Padron ordered.

3. RONALD D. COTTRELL, JR., went to the transaction site which JENNIFER M. CURTIS had brokered between Officer Padron and RONALD D. COTTRELL, JR.

4. JENNIFER M. CURTIS waited by RONALD D. COTTRELL, JR.'s vehicle while he went to Officer Padron's vehicle and conducted the exchange brokered by JENNIFER M. CURTIS.

5. JENNIFER M. CURTIS met with RONALD D. COTTRELL, JR. at his vehicle after the brokered transaction with Officer Padron was completed.

In the end, the jury found Cottrell guilty. The Sedgwick County District Court sentenced Cottrell to a total of 68 months' imprisonment with 36 months' postrelease supervision.

On appeal, Cottrell argues: (1) The district court erred when it failed to give a unanimity instruction because the State alleged multiple overt acts in furtherance of the conspiracy; and (2) alternatively, the overt acts alleged were alternative means to commit the crime of conspiracy, and the State failed to produce sufficient evidence to support each one.

The Court of Appeals affirmed, holding that no unanimity instruction was required because the allegation of several overt acts in furtherance of one conspiracy does not present a multiple acts case. Similarly, the panel held that alleged overt acts committed in furtherance of one conspiracy are not alternative means requiring jury unanimity.

Cottrell claims this is a multiple acts case because the State alleged several overt acts in furtherance of the conspiracy, as reflected in the jury instruction, and thus a unanimity instruction was required to ensure the jury agreed about which overt act supported the crime. The State argues there is no multiple acts problem because it presented evidence of only one conspiracy—to sell the "8 and 20" drugs to Padron—and the overt acts supporting that conspiracy are not separate crimes.

When several acts are alleged, any of which could constitute the crime charged, the court is presented with a multiple acts case. In a multiple acts case, the jury must be unanimous as to which act or incident constitutes the crime. To ensure jury unanimity in multiple acts cases, courts require that either the State elect the particular criminal act upon which it will rely for conviction or that the district court instruct the jury that all jurors must agree that the same underlying criminal act has been proved beyond a reasonable doubt. Here, the State did not elect which overt act to rely on. So if Cottrell is correct that alleging several overt acts creates a multiple acts problem, then a unanimity instruction was required.

But the threshold question is whether this is a multiple acts case. To this end, we must determine whether jurors heard evidence of multiple acts, each of which could have supported conviction on a charged crime. More precisely, we must determine whether a jury instruction alleging several overt acts in furtherance of a conspiracy creates a multiple acts problem and thus requires a unanimity instruction.

"Multiple acts" are legally and factually separate incidents that independently satisfy the elements of the charged offense. The charged offense at issue is conspiracy. K.S.A. 2012 Supp. 21–5302(a) states:

> A conspiracy is an agreement with another person to commit a crime or to assist in committing a crime. No person may be convicted of a conspiracy unless an overt act in furtherance of such conspiracy is alleged and proved to have been committed by such person or by a co-conspirator.

Thus, conspiracy contains two elements: (1) An agreement between two or more persons to commit or assist in committing a crime and (2) the commission by one or more of the conspirators of an overt act in furtherance of the object of the conspiracy.

Food for Thought

If Cottrell had been charged with five counts of distribution of controlled substances based upon each of five acts alleged and if the jury found that the Government established each of those acts beyond a reasonable doubt, could he be convicted of all five narcotics counts? If so, and if the jury found each of these five overt acts established beyond a reasonable doubt, then why can he be convicted of only one conspiracy?

1 agreement

As the Court of Appeals aptly said, "In a conspiracy case, it is the agreement that is the crux of the offense." Indeed, a single conspiracy can last for years, with many of its substantive offenses being completed during that time but only the single agreement may be punished.

Put simply, a single conspiracy consists of one agreement, and a defendant may only be convicted of conspiracy if the State alleges and proves that the defendant or a co-conspirator committed an overt act in furtherance of that agreement. There may be one or many overt acts committed in furtherance of a single conspiracy. But a multiple acts problem requires evidence of separate incidents that independently satisfy the elements of the charged offense. For conspiracy, that means multiple acts require multiple agreements. Or, to state the same principle in reverse, no matter how many overt acts the State proved in this case, Cottrell could only ever be convicted of one conspiracy.

The State presented arguments and evidence about one agreement between Cottrell and Curtis: to illegally sell hydrocodone and oxycodone to Padron on June 5, 2013. The jury instruction on conspiracy listed that same agreement. Thus, we agree with the Court of Appeals when it held:

> [A] single agreement to commit several crimes constitutes one conspiracy. By the same reasoning, multiple agreements to commit separate crimes constitute multiple conspiracies. Here, there was only one conspiracy alleged: the distribution of controlled substances. Because none of the overt acts charged in furtherance of that conspiracy are factually and legally sufficient to constitute a crime in and of themselves, there is no risk here that the jury could have found multiple conspiracies. . . . Because the facts of this case support only one conspiracy to distribute controlled substances, a multiple acts instruction would not have been proper.

Are the overt acts listed in the jury instruction alternative means for the crime of conspiracy? Alternative means issues arise when the statute and any instructions that incorporate it list distinct alternatives for a material element of the crime. In recent years, we clarified that alternative means are legislatively determined, distinct, material elements of a crime, as opposed to legislative descriptions of the material elements or of the factual circumstances that would prove the crime. For example, the inherently dangerous felonies that support the charge of felony murder are alternative means.

But we held the plain language of the conspiracy statute does not set forth alternative means for committing an overt act. Thus, the Cottrell panel was correct on this point. Even so, this case presents a question that we have not yet addressed: whether a jury instruction that lists more than one overt act in furtherance of a conspiracy creates an alternative means problem. Today, we must determine whether the instruction here creates alternative means for the overt act in furtherance of the conspiracy, even though the conspiracy statute does not.

Recent caselaw distinguishes alternative means—which arise when a statute's plain language lists distinct alternatives for a material element of the crime—and mere descriptions of a material element or factual circumstance. Indeed, descriptions of material elements are secondary matters—options within a means—that do not, even if included in a jury instruction, raise a sufficiency issue that requires a court to examine whether the option is supported by evidence.

We affirm that only the language of a statute can create alternative means for a crime. If the statute lists "alternative, distinct, material elements" of a crime, then it creates alternative means. But a jury instruction that lists descriptions of how a material element might be satisfied does not, on its own, create alternative means. To hold otherwise would permit a jury instruction to override legislative intent and effectively revise the criminal code.

Thus, we affirm that the conspiracy statute does not set forth alternative means for committing an overt act. We also hold that a jury instruction listing more than one overt act in furtherance of a conspiracy does not create alternative means. Instead, such an instruction merely describes the factual scenarios that could prove the material element of an overt act.

Affirmed.

Points for Discussion

a. Venue

Venue for a conspiracy trial is typically deemed to be appropriate in any jurisdiction in which an overt act took place, even if that jurisdiction is not the jurisdiction in which most of the conspiratorial acts took place.

b. How Much Is Enough for an Overt Act?

In 2006, federal authorities charged seven men with plotting to blow up the Sears Tower in Chicago. The prosecution claimed that the men adhered to a militant (but vague) form of Islamic ideology, and had attempted to make contact with al Qaeda. The men provided a supposed al Qaeda representative (actually, an undercover federal officer) with a list of needed supplies (e.g., uniforms, boots, machine guns, radios and vehicles), and claimed that their objective was to wage jihad and to "kill all the devils we can" in a 9/11-style mission. In fact, no member of the group ever really made contact with al Qaeda at all, although the men did manage to obtain some boots and uniforms. Eventually, the plot just "petered out." Did these men commit the crime of conspiracy? Did they commit a sufficient overt act?

E. Renunciation or Withdrawal

Unlike acts leading to the commission of completed criminal offenses, acts leading toward the commission of inchoate offenses (like conspiracy, solicitation and attempt) may, in some jurisdictions, under the proper circumstances, be "taken back" by appropriate acts of withdrawal, contrition, and assistance of law enforcement efforts to prevent whatever criminal enterprise may be ongoing.

Gurwell v. Texas

2008 WL 3867637 (Tex. Ct. App.-Dallas 2008).

Opinion by JUSTICE LAGARDE.

Appellant was charged with online solicitation of a minor with intent to engage in sexual contact. He pleaded not guilty before a jury. The jury found appellant guilty and assessed his punishment at ten years' imprisonment. In his sole issue, appellant contends the trial court erred by denying his requested jury instruction on the defense of renunciation. We affirm the trial court's judgment as modified.

The events giving rise to this charge began in August 2006 when appellant contacted a girl named "Emma" through her MySpace and Yahoo! Accounts. Appellant concedes he believed Emma was a fourteen-year-old girl. Emma was actually a persona created by Collin County Sheriff's deputy Scotty Morrison. Appellant and Emma chatted via an instant messenger system. Appellant used the screen name "rygee253" and Emma used the screen name "tennisgirl0893." Over time, the chatting escalated into explicit sexual conversation. The online chat log was admitted into evidence at trial as State's Exhibit no. 1. Eventually "rygee253" and "tennisgirl0893" agreed to meet at a nearby park. When appellant went to the park, he was arrested. Upon being arrested, appellant said he was sorry and that he never intended to have sex with Emma.

Appellant asserts the trial court erred by denying his requested instruction on the renunciation defense. Appellant specifically points to the following portion of the chat log as evidence he renounced his intent that the minor engage in sex:

> rygee253 (8/31/2006 8:38:39 AM): lets meet and see where we go from there
>
> tennisgirl0893 (8/31/2006 8:39:06 AM): that's fine
>
> tennisgirl0893 (8/31/2006 8:39:06 AM): u don't wanna go back to ur hse
>
> rygee253 (8/31/2006 8:39:13AM): i mean lets just start out by meeting and see where it goes

Appellant argues the above evidence shows he renounced his intent that the minor engage in sex. He contends further that, pursuant to section 15.04 of the penal code, he was entitled to an instruction on the defense of renunciation.

The State responds that appellant was not entitled to a jury instruction on renunciation because the defense is only available for offenses under Chapter 15 of the Penal Code. Chapter 15 specifically concerns preparatory offenses, includ-

Practice Pointer

Note that renunciation would have been a tenable (if unsuccessful, see below) defense if Gurwell had been charged with conspiracy instead of or in addition to this substantive offense. You should recognize that prosecutors often do—or should—consider all of the potential defenses that exist to the specific charges they are considering bringing against a defendant. As demonstrated in this case, those potential defenses vary with the nature and type of charge being prosecuted.

ing criminal conspiracy, criminal solicitation, and criminal solicitation of a minor. Appellant was charged with online solicitation of a minor under Chapter 33, which provides its own list of defenses. The State further argues that even if the renunciation defense applies, appellant did not meet the requisites of renunciation because any claimed renunciation was not complete and voluntary and appellant did not take any affirmative acts to renounce the offense.

The appellant was not charged with a preparatory offense under chapter 15; he was charged with a completed offense under chapter 33 of the penal code. Thus, the renunciation defense in section 15.04 did not apply.

> **FYI**
>
> Model Penal Code § 5.03(6) provides that "it is an affirmative defense that the actor, after conspiring to commit a crime, thwarted the success of the conspiracy, under circumstances manifesting a complete and voluntary renunciation of his criminal purpose."

Moreover, even if the renunciation defense did apply, it was not raised by the evidence. The portion of the chat log upon which appellant relies does not raise renunciation because it was not complete and voluntary, nor did appellant take any affirmative acts to renounce the offense. Although it is true appellant appears in the chat log to be cautious and concerned about being caught, there is nothing in the chat log reflecting appellant's voluntary "repentance or change of heart."

Furthermore, other portions of the log show appellant's intent was to have sexual intercourse with tennisgirl0893:

> tennisgirl0893 (8/30/2006 6:33:22 PM): parents are gone
>
> tennisgirl0893 (8/30/2006 6:33:30 PM): kara and i may go get something with her boyfriend
>
> tennisgirl0893 (8/30/2006 6:33:39 PM): she spose to be callin me
>
> rygee253 (8/30/2006 6:33:51 PM): are you hanging out with your friend?
>
> rygee253 (8/30/2006 6:33:55 PM): or waiting to?
>
> tennisgirl 0893 (8/30/2006 6:34:01PM): when she calls
>
> tennisgirl0893 (8/30/2006 6:34:06 PM): im going over there
>
> rygee253 (8/30/2006 6:34:10PM): ahh
>
> rygee253 (8/30/2006 6:34:27 PM): this is a prime time to lose your virginity then.

Thus, the offense was complete well before appellant claims he renounced the offense.

Moreover, the court's charge gave the jury the option of finding appellant guilty of the lesser-included offense of online solicitation of a minor without the intent to engage in sexual

> **Food for Thought**
>
> But what if Gurwell had been charged with a conspiracy offense rather than a substantive offense? Would the conspiracy offense then have been "complete" at this point? *Could* it have been renounced thereafter?

contact, sexual intercourse, or deviate sexual intercourse with another. The jury rejected that option, finding instead, the defendant guilty of online solicitation of a minor as charged in the indictment.

Having reviewed the record under the appropriate standard, we conclude the trial court did not err by denying appellant's requested jury instruction on the renunciation defense. We resolve appellant's sole issue against him.

New Jersey v. Hughes

215 N.J. Super. 295, 521 A.2d 1295 (App.Div. 1986).

ANTELL, P.J.A.D.

At approximately 7:00 p.m. September 28, 1982 the cashier at the office of the Courier Post in Cherry Hill was robbed at gun point of a large amount of cash by two men. In connection therewith defendant was indicted for robbery, possession of a weapon for an unlawful purpose, and conspiracy to rob. After a trial by jury he was convicted of conspiracy and a jury disagreement was recorded as to the other two charges.

On this appeal defendant first argues that the trial court erred in failing to instruct the jury as to the defense of "renunciation of purpose" as an affirmative defense to the charge of conspiracy.

The evidence upon which defendant rests his claim to the defense of renunciation is found in the testimony of defendant himself and the testimony of Detective Beverly of the City of Camden Police Department. According to defendant, during the period of approximately one month before the robbery he had been approached on a number of occasions by Tyrone Wolley who solicited him to take part in robbing the Courier Post. On each occasion defendant rejected the invitation and answered Wolley that he was not interested in doing armed robberies. Approximately one or two weeks before the Courier Post robbery actually occurred, defendant visited Detective Beverly and told him of Wolley's solicitations. He did not, however, suggest that he had agreed to join the enterprise and, in fact, said that he told Wolley he would not do so. His purpose, he said, in giving Detective Beverly the information was to enable the police to investigate the matter.

The defense of renunciation to a charge of conspiracy is found, N.J.S.A. 2C:5–2e:

> Renunciation of purpose. It is an affirmative defense which the actor must prove by a

> Non constat
> jus civile
> a posteriori
>
> **It's Latin to Me**
>
> Where a renunciation defense exists in the law, it is often justified by the belief that would-be criminals should have a *locus poenitentiae*. Locus poenitentiae means "a point at which it is not too late for one to change one's legal position; the possibility of withdrawing from a contemplated course of action, esp. a wrong, before being committed to it."

> preponderance of the evidence that he, after conspiring to commit a crime, informed the authority of the existence of the conspiracy and his participation therein, and thwarted or caused to be thwarted the commission of any offense in furtherance of the conspiracy, under circumstances manifesting a complete and voluntary renunciation of criminal purpose.

It is evident that the basic condition of the defense finds no support in the evidence. The statute presupposes an acknowledgment by the actor that he actually conspired to commit a crime and its benefits are conferred only where he informs police authority of the conspiracy's existence "and his participation therein." Where the elements of the defense have been shown by a preponderance of the evidence one can be said to have "renounced" the conspiracy. Renunciation, after all, posits prior participation, and defendant could not renounce a conspiracy he had not joined. The defense was not available to defendant for the reason that, as he testified, he had steadfastly refused to support the criminal undertaking. His testimony to this effect as well as Detective Beverly's was relevant, not to whether he had renounced the conspiracy, but only to whether he had ever joined it in the first place. Once this issue was resolved against defendant there was nothing else in the record to support a finding of renunciation.

Food for Thought

If Hughes could not renounce the conspiracy because he claimed that he was not a part of it, how could he be convicted of conspiracy in the first place? If the jury did not believe Hughes' claim that he was not a party to the conspiracy, why wasn't he entitled to a renunciation instruction?

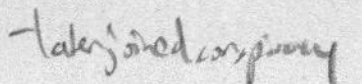

Affirmed.

Hypo: *Conspiracy or Duress*

Quinton Alston attempted to hijack a truck by pointing a gun at the driver (actually, it was a BB gun wrapped in a towel). When apprehended, he claimed that he was forced to participate in the hijacking by Bernard Short who told Alston that he would harm Alston's family if Alston didn't assist in the crime. Alston claims that he told the driver that he was being threatened and that the driver should go and call the police. (The driver denies this.) Alston has been charged, *inter alia*, with conspiracy to commit carjacking. Is Alston entitled to a renunciation instruction? *State v. Alston*, 311 N.J. Super. 113, 709 A.2d 310 (App.Div. 1998).

F. Merger

Since the *actus reus* of conspiracy (a conspiratorial agreement) is different from the *actus reus* of the target crime itself, e.g. the illegal sale of narcotics, the rule in most (but not all) jurisdictions is that a conviction for conspiracy to commit a crime does *not* merge with a conviction for that crime itself for purposes of sentencing, i.e. the accused can be sentenced for *both* crimes.

State v. Hardison

99 N.J. 379, 492 A.2d 1009 (1985).

O'HERN, J.

This appeal concerns the circumstances under which a conviction for a criminal conspiracy and a completed offense that was an object of the conspiracy will merge. Specifically, the appeal concerns N.J.S.A. 2C:1–8a(2), which provides that a defendant may not be convicted of more than one offense if "one offense consists only of a conspiracy or other form of preparation to commit the other." We hold that if the conspiracy proven has criminal objectives other than the substantive offense proven, the offenses will not merge. In this case the conviction does not establish that the conspiracy embraced criminal objectives in addition to the offense proven. Hence, we affirm the judgment below that merged the conviction of conspiracy with the completed offense.

The case arises from two incidents, commencing on the evening of November 19, 1980. At approximately 11:30 p.m., four men entered the Lincoln Café in New Brunswick. After about twenty minutes, when the crowd had thinned out, one of the defendants pulled out a gun, pointed the gun at the bartender and forced him to lie face down behind the bar. Two of the men herded the two remaining patrons, a man and a woman, into the bathroom. The four cleaned out the cash register, and took the bartender's watch and the woman's purse. All three victims were then locked in the men's room with a cigarette machine in front of the door. The four fled.

Within minutes the bartender pushed the door open and alerted the New Brunswick police. They came immediately to the scene, gathered information, and obtained identification of the defendants. The police learned that the four men had fled in a red and white Cadillac.

Before they were able to return to the New Brunswick stationhouse, the police heard on the radio that a robbery had taken place at the Edison Motor Lodge, north of New Brunswick on Route 1. Edison officers on patrol had spotted a suspicious car traveling on Route 1 with its lights off. They began to follow the car. They soon heard on the police radio that a robbery had taken place at the Edison Motor Lodge. They learned as well that a red and white Cadillac had been involved in a robbery in New Brunswick. Other police joined the chase. A high-speed pursuit took place up Route 1 and onto the Garden State Parkway. The chase ended when the car ran into a cement divider at Parkway Exit 131 in Clark Township.

At the Edison Motor Lodge, the night manager reported that two men had come into the premises and asked about the price of a room. They went out, came back in with a gun, and robbed him at gunpoint of the motel's property. One of the defendants threatened to kill him; the other brutally assaulted him with brass knuckles, shattering his teeth.

Hardison and Jackson were found within close proximity of the car that had crashed in Clark Township. They were taken to the Clark police station. The woman's purse was retrieved from the car as was a key to the Edison motel room. New Brunswick police took the three witnesses from the Lincoln Café to the Clark police station where they were shown Hardison and Jackson alone with a group of police officers. They identified Hardison and Jackson as being involved in the Lincoln Café robbery, although neither was identified as the gunman. The night manager at the Edison motel was shown the defendants later. He identified them as his assailants. Two other suspects were soon apprehended.

The four were charged with conspiracy to commit robbery, four counts of robbery of the three people in the tavern and the night manager at the motel, possession of a gun for an unlawful purpose, aggravated assault of the night manager; and Hardison was charged with possession of brass knuckles for an unlawful purpose. The trial of two co-defendants was severed. Hardison and Jackson went to trial together.

The jury acquitted these two defendants of the robbery of the Lincoln Café, but convicted them on all other charges. Each was sentenced to an aggregate term of twenty years with five years of parole ineligibility. Separate and consecutive sentences were imposed on the conspiracy and robbery counts. On appeal, the Appellate Division, in two separate opinions, affirmed on all issues but merger, concluding that because the illegal agreement included robbery and the jury found defendants guilty of the motel robbery within the ambit of the conspiracy, the convictions for both the conspiracy and the robbery were barred. We granted the State's petition for certification, limited solely to the issue of whether the conviction for conspiracy to commit robbery should have merged with that of armed robbery. We now affirm.

Food for Thought

Does the fact that the jury acquitted the defendants of the Lincoln Café robbery mean necessarily that the jury believed that they had not agreed to rob the Lincoln Café?

The law of conspiracy serves two independent values. First is the protection of society from the danger of concerted criminal activity. The second aspect is that conspiracy is an inchoate crime. "This is to say, that, although the law generally makes criminal only antisocial conduct, at some point in the continuum between preparation and consummation, the likelihood of a commission of an act is sufficiently great and the criminal intent sufficiently well formed to justify the intervention of the criminal law." Thus, the law of conspiracy identifies the agreement to engage in a criminal venture as an event of sufficient threat to social order, therefore permitting the imposition of criminal sanctions for the agreement alone, regardless of whether the crime agreed upon actually is committed.

In New Jersey, as elsewhere, the law traditionally considered conspiracy and the completed substantive offense to be separate crimes. Accordingly, the conspiracy to commit an offense and the subsequent commission of that crime normally did not merge.

The reason for the rule was the common law's deep distrust for criminal combinations. The group activity was seen as posing a "greater potential threat" to the public than individual crime.

> For two or more to confederate and combine together to commit or cause to be committed a breach of the criminal laws is an offense of the gravest character, sometimes quite outweighing, in injury to the public, the mere commission of the contemplated crime.

Deeply rooted in the fear of criminal political conspiracy, the substantive crime of conspiracy became superimposed on offenses having no such political motivation. The crime took on a life of its own. At common law, and under some statutes, the combination could be a criminal conspiracy even if it contemplated only acts that were not crimes at all when perpetrated by an individual, or by many acting severally, or could result in a conspirator being found guilty not only of the conspiracy but of a completed offense even when the accused did not participate in the substantive offense.

In addition to its substantive overlay, the crime had distinct procedural advantages including the ability to use the statements of a co-conspirator made during and in furtherance of a conspiracy, the ability to try co-conspirators jointly, flexibility in the selection and place of trial, and finally, the ability to establish the existence of such an agreement through circumstantial evidence.

In this setting, there was perceived a danger of punishment for mere criminal intent with juries unable to separate individual guilt from guilt by association. The drafters of the American Law Institute's 1962 Model Penal Code undertook the "difficult task of achieving an appropriate balance between the desire to afford adequate opportunity for early law enforcement efforts and the obligation to safeguard" individual rights.

The drafters of the New Jersey Criminal Code substantially adopted the approach of the Model Penal Code. They undertook, in the words of the drafters, to "meet or mitigate these objections and then go on to develop a basic framework for the development of a law of conspiracy." Our Code recognizes the dual conception of the offense (1) to reach further back into preparatory criminal conduct than attempt, and nip the crime before its inception, and (2) to provide additional means of facilitating prosecutions, striking against the special dangers of group criminal activity. It balances it with fairness thus:

> The Code embraces this conception in some part but rejects it in another. When a conspiracy is declared criminal because its object is a crime, we think it is entirely meaningless to say that the preliminary combination is more dangerous than the

> forbidden consummation; the measure of its danger is the risk of such a culmination. On the other hand, the combination may and often does have criminal objectives that transcend any particular offenses that have been committed in pursuance of its goals.

The Code's resolution then is to permit cumulative sentences when the combination has criminal objectives beyond any particular offense committed in pursuance of its goals. The Code takes the view that in this sense conspiracy is similar to attempt, which is a lesser-included offense of the completed offense. A conviction of the completed offense will adequately deal with the conduct. The Code's drafters were equally explicit that "this is not true, however, where the conspiracy has as its objective engaging in a course of criminal conduct since that involves a distinct danger in addition to that involved in the actual commission of any specific offense." The Code recognizes the grave dangers that organized criminal activity poses to society. Therefore, the limitation of the Code is confined to the situation in which the completed offense was the sole criminal objective of the conspiracy. "There may be conviction of both a conspiracy and a completed offense committed pursuant to that conspiracy if the prosecution shows that the objective of the conspiracy was the commission of additional offenses."

Turning to the record before us, we must determine whether the judgment of conviction establishes that the conspiracy had additional criminal objectives other than the completed offense. For purposes of analysis, we shall view the indictment as charging two robberies-one at the Lincoln Café and another at the Edison Motor Lodge-and a conspiracy. The jury acquitted the defendants of the incident at the Lincoln Café, but convicted them of robbery and assault at the Motor Lodge and of conspiracy. The question comes down to this: Does the jury verdict establish that Hardison and Jackson conspired to commit the Lincoln Café Robbery?

The State contends that it does, arguing that there was evidence from which the jury could have inferred that the four defendants traveled from Paterson to New Brunswick for the purpose of committing the crime; and that although they were not the triggermen at the café, they were part of the conspiracy. The State points to one aspect of the charge that suggested that unless there was a knowing agreement between the parties to participate in both robberies, the jury should acquit them on the charge of conspiracy. Yet, other provisions of the charge specifically authorize the jury to find the defendants guilty of conspiracy even if it embraced only the incident at the Edison Motor Lodge. In part, the court charged the jury:

> If, however, you found that these defendants did not enter a conspiracy or agreement to commit a crime of robbery at the Lincoln Café, you may then consider whether or not subsequent to that they formed a conspiracy or agreement to commit a crime at the motel.
>
> If there was one overall conspiracy that covered both robberies, then you may find them guilty.
>
> If you found that they formed a conspiracy or agreement to rob only the motel, you may still find them guilty if you are satisfied as to each and all elements of the crime beyond a reasonable doubt.

Of particular significance too is the fact that although conspiracy was the first offense charged in the indictment, it was not the first offense considered by the jury. The court opened its charge by reading the indictment and stated:

> First it simply says that on the day in question these four gentlemen got together and conspired or agreed with one another to commit the crime of robbery later that day.

The court did not address the substance of the offense further at that time, and, after charging generally with respect to the burden of proof, demeanor, identification, reasonable doubt, and circumstantial evidence, addressed the substantive offenses before turning to the liability of the defendants as conspirators or accomplices. It explained generally robbery, theft, and aggravated assault. The court concluded by stating:

> The last charge that I am going to charge you about, but which is the first charge in the indictment, is called conspiracy, and then that is that these persons agreed to commit a criminal act.

It then discussed the substance of the offense. The defense strategy at trial had focused upon the fact that Hardison and Jackson were the unwitting companions of the real perpetrators in the Lincoln Café incident; that they had been with them but had no intent to rob. The witnesses at the café did not identify Hardison or Jackson as the triggermen. It was the night manager of the Edison Motor Lodge who positively identified Hardison and Jackson as his assailants, describing Jackson as the gunman and Hardison as the one who had struck him with the brass knuckles.

The jury was given nineteen questions to answer dealing with the various counts. Basically, the jury was asked: did the defendants commit robbery of the bartender and the patron at the Lincoln Café; did they commit robbery or assault of the night manager of the Edison Motor Lodge; did they possess a weapon? Finally they were asked to answer a last question "as to the charge of conspiracy to commit robbery," did they find the defendants not guilty or guilty?

Of course, we will not look behind a guilty verdict if there is legally sufficient evidence to sustain it, but in determining the basis of a jury verdict, courts may consider "the manner in which the case was sent to the jury." In this case, the manner is suggestive that the jury's finding of conspiracy did not embrace the Lincoln Café robbery.

First, the jury asked to be recharged only on the question of accomplice liability. It was specifically charged again:

> A person is legally accountable for the conduct of another, if he is an accomplice of such another person in the commission of a crime or he is engaged in a conspiracy with such other person.
>
> Now, how do we know what is an accomplice? Conspiracy you're going to have to decide. A person is an accomplice of another in a commission of an offense if, with the purpose of promoting or facilitating the offense, he aids, agrees or attempts to aid such another person in the planning or committing of it.

The jury rendered its verdict, not by reference to the counts of the indictment, but by reference to the questions put to them. The jury was polled as to each of the questions. As to the questions of the robbery of the bartender and the patrons at the Lincoln Café, the verdict was "not guilty." Had they conspired to commit that offense, the charge on accomplice liability would have suggested a verdict of guilt. As to the questions concerning the robbery and aggravated assault of the night manager and the unlawful use of a weapon, the verdict was guilty. The next question as to each was:

Take Note

Note that the court supported its decision about the basis of the jury's verdict in part upon "the manner in which the case was sent to the jury." A small change in how the charges were presented or considered by the jury might have resulted in a different result. Both the prosecutor and defense counsel should bear this in mind in any case where a conspiracy is charged with multiple criminal objectives.

THE COURT: As to the charge of conspiracy to commit robbery, how do you find the defendant?

THE FOREMAN: We find the defendant guilty.

Based upon this record, we cannot conclude that the judgments establish that the preparatory conduct proven had other or further criminal objectives than the completed robbery. Hence, pursuant to the provisions of N.J.S.A. 2C:1–8a(2), the Appellate Division correctly ordered that the convictions should be merged.

It may be that in another case the proofs will be susceptible to a contrary conclusion. In this case, since we are satisfied that the conviction did not establish such multiple purposes, the judgment of the Appellate Division is affirmed.

Point for Discussion

Multiple Inchoate Offenses

In some jurisdictions, there are statutory provisions mandating that multiple inchoate offenses aimed at the same target offense merge into one another for purposes of sentencing. *See, e.g.,* 18 Pa. C. S. § 906 (1986) ("A person may not be convicted of more than one of the inchoate crimes of criminal attempt, criminal solicitation or criminal conspiracy for conduct designed to commit or to culminate in the commission of the same crime."). Does this approach make sense since each separate inchoate offense is based upon proof of a different *actus reus*?

Compare that Pennsylvania approach (which was taken from the Model Penal Code) to the approach taken by jurisdictions like Maryland, where the Court of Appeals has concluded that the offenses of *conspiracy* to commit armed robbery and *attempted* armed robbery, two inchoate offenses aimed at the same result, do *not* merge, holding that "the attempt to complete the elements of a crime is separate and distinct from the group planning of the crime itself." *Carroll v. State*, 428 Md. 679, 699, 53 A.3d 1159, 1170 (2012).

Which rule of law makes more sense to you? Why?

Hypo: *Murder and Conspiracy*

Defendant Jones planned with his codefendants, Craft and Moore, to rob Haywood. The three obtained a gun, waited outside the lounge Haywood frequented until he exited, followed him to a hotel, and waited again for him to emerge. After several hours of stalking him, they then followed Haywood to his home. One of Haywood's neighbors testified that she heard gunfire and looked out her window to see Jones walk from Haywood's car to an older two-door gray Chevrolet, while the victim's car slowly moved forward to rest against a tree. Haywood was found slumped over the steering wheel of his car, dead from multiple gunshot wounds. Jones was convicted of attempted armed robbery, conspiracy to commit armed robbery, and murder. Should any or all of these offenses merge with one another? What do you think? *People v. Jones,* 234 Ill. App. 3d 1082, 176 Ill. Dec. 382, 601 N.E.2d 1080 (1992).

G. Culpability of Co-Conspirators

To what extent should a conspirator be deemed culpable for the criminal acts of his or her other co-conspirators? Consider the following leading case.

Pinkerton v. United States

328 U.S. 640 (1946).

MR. JUSTICE DOUGLAS delivered the opinion of the Court.

Walter and Daniel Pinkerton are brothers who live a short distance from each other on Daniel's farm. They were indicted for violations of the Internal Revenue Code. The indictment contained ten substantive counts and one conspiracy count. The jury found Walter guilty on nine of the substantive counts and on the conspiracy count. It found Daniel guilty on six of the substantive counts and on the conspiracy count. Walter was fined $500 and sentenced generally on the substantive counts to imprisonment for thirty months. On the conspiracy count he was given a two year sentence to run concurrently with the other sentence. Daniel was fined $1,000 and sentenced generally on the substantive counts to imprisonment for thirty months. On the conspiracy count he was fined $500 and given a two year sentence to run concurrently with the other sentence. The judgments of conviction were affirmed by the Circuit Court of Appeals.

A single conspiracy was charged and proved. Some of the overt acts charged in the conspiracy count were the same acts charged in the substantive counts. Each of the substantive offenses found was committed pursuant to the conspiracy. Petitioners therefore contend that the substantive counts became merged in the conspiracy count, and that only a single sentence not exceeding the maximum two-year penalty provided by the conspiracy statute could be imposed. They rely on *Braverman v. United States*, 317 U.S. 49 (1942).

In the *Braverman* case the indictment charged no substantive offense. Each of the several counts charged a conspiracy to violate a different statute. But only one conspiracy was proved. We held that a single conspiracy, charged under the general conspiracy statute, however diverse its objects may be, violates but a single statute and no penalty greater than the maximum provided for one conspiracy may be imposed. That case is not apposite here. For the offenses charged and proved were not only a conspiracy but substantive offenses as well.

Nor can we accept the proposition that the substantive offenses were merged in the conspiracy. There are, of course, instances where a conspiracy charge may not be added to the substantive charge. One is where the agreement of two persons is necessary for the completion of the substantive crime and there is no ingredient in the conspiracy which is not present in the completed crime. Another is where the definition of the substantive offense excludes from punishment for conspiracy one who voluntarily participates in another's crime. But those exceptions are of a limited character. The common law rule that the substantive offense, if a felony, was merged in the conspiracy, has little vitality in this country. It has been long and consistently recognized by the Court that the commission of the substantive offense and a conspiracy to commit it are separate and distinct offenses. The power of Congress to separate the two and to affix to each a different penalty is well established. A conviction for the conspiracy may be had though the substantive offense was completed. And the plea of double jeopardy is no defense to a conviction for both offenses. It is only an identity of offenses which is fatal. A conspiracy is a partnership in crime. It has ingredients, as well as implications, distinct from the completion of the unlawful project. As stated in *United States v. Rabinowich*, 238 U.S. 78, 88 (1915):

> 'For two or more to confederate and combine together to commit or cause to be committed a breach of the criminal laws is an offense of the gravest character, sometimes quite outweighing, in injury to the public, the mere commission of the contemplated crime. It involves deliberate plotting to subvert the laws, educating and preparing the conspirators for further and habitual criminal practices. And it is characterized by secrecy, rendering it difficult of detection, requiring more time for its discovery, and adding to the importance of punishing it when discovered.'

Take Note

Remember that the *actus reus* of conspiracy is not the overt act, if one is required as an element of the crime. It is, instead, the conspiratorial agreement.

Moreover, it is not material that overt acts charged in the conspiracy counts were also charged and proved as substantive offenses. As stated in *Sneed v. United States*, 298 F. 911 (5th Cir. 1924), 'If the overt act be the offense which was the object of the conspiracy, and is also punished, there is not a double punishment of it.' The agreement to do an unlawful act is even then distinct from the doing of the act.

It is contended that there was insufficient evidence to implicate Daniel in the conspiracy. But we think there was enough evidence for submission of the issue to the jury.

There is, however, no evidence to show that Daniel participated directly in the commission of the substantive offenses on which his conviction has been sustained, although there was evidence to show that these substantive offenses were in fact committed by Walter in furtherance of the unlawful agreement or conspiracy existing between the brothers. The question was submitted to the jury on the theory that each petitioner could be found guilty of the substantive offenses, if it was found at the time those offenses were committed petitioners were parties to an unlawful conspiracy and the substantive offenses charged were in fact committed in furtherance of it.

Daniel relies on *United States v. Sall*, 116 F.2d 745 (3rd Cir. 1940). That case held that participation in the conspiracy was not itself enough to sustain a conviction for the substantive offense even though it was committed in furtherance of the conspiracy. The court held that, in addition to evidence that the offense was in fact committed in furtherance of the conspiracy, evidence of direct participation in the commission of the substantive offense or other evidence from which participation might fairly be inferred was necessary.

We take a different view. We have here a continuous conspiracy. There is here no evidence of the affirmative action on the part of Daniel which is necessary to establish his withdrawal from it. *Hyde v. United States*, 225 U.S. 347, 369 (1912). As stated in that case, 'having joined in an unlawful scheme, having constituted agents for its performance, scheme and agency to be continuous until full fruition be secured, until he does some act to disavow or defeat the purpose he is in no situation to claim the delay of the law. As the offense has not been terminated or accomplished, he is still offending. And we think, consciously offending,—offending as certainly, as we have said, as at the first moment of his confederation, and consciously through every moment of its existence.' And so long as the partnership in crime continues, the partners act for each other in carrying it forward. It is settled that 'an overt act of one partner may be the act of all without any new agreement specifically directed to that act.' Motive or intent may be proved by the acts or declarations of some of the conspirators in furtherance of the common objective. A scheme to use the mails to defraud, which is joined in by more than one person, is a conspiracy. Yet all members are responsible, though only one did the mailing. The governing principle is the same when the substantive offense is committed by one of the conspirators in furtherance of the unlawful project. The criminal intent to do the act is established by the formation of the conspiracy. Each conspirator instigated the commission of the crime. The unlawful agreement contemplated precisely what was done. It was formed for the purpose. The act done was in execution of the enterprise. The rule which holds responsible one who counsels, procures, or commands another to commit a crime is founded on the same principle. That principle is recognized in the law of conspiracy when the overt act of one partner in crime is attributable to all. An overt act is an essential ingredient of the crime of conspiracy. If that can be supplied by the act of one conspirator, we fail to see why the same or other acts in furtherance of the conspiracy are likewise not attributable to the others for the purpose of holding them responsible for the substantive offense.

A different case would arise if the substantive offense committed by one of the conspirators was not in fact done in furtherance of the conspiracy, did not fall within the scope of the unlawful project, or was merely a part of the ramifications of the plan which could not be reasonably foreseen as a necessary or natural consequence of the unlawful agreement. But as we read this record, that is not this case.

Affirmed.

MR. JUSTICE RUTLEDGE, dissenting in part.

The judgment concerning Daniel Pinkerton should be reversed. In my opinion it is without precedent here and is a dangerous precedent to establish.

Daniel and Walter, who were brothers living near each other, were charged in several counts with substantive offenses, and then a conspiracy count was added naming those offenses as overt acts. The proof showed that Walter alone committed the substantive crimes. There was none to establish that Daniel participated in them, aided and abetted Walter in committing them, or knew that he had done so. Daniel in fact was in the penitentiary, under sentence for other crimes, when some of Walter's crimes were done.

There was evidence, however, to show that over several years Daniel and Walter had confederated to commit similar crimes concerned with unlawful possession, transportation, and dealing in whiskey, in fraud of the federal revenues. On this evidence both were convicted of conspiracy. Walter also was convicted on the substantive counts on the proof of his committing the crimes charged. Then, on that evidence without more than the proof of Daniel's criminal agreement with Walter and the latter's overt acts, which were also the substantive offenses charged, the court told the jury they could find Daniel guilty of those substantive offenses. They did so.

I think this ruling violates both the letter and the spirit of what Congress did when it separately defined the three classes of crime, namely, (1) completed substantive offenses; (2) aiding, abetting or counseling another to commit them; and (3) conspiracy to commit them. Not only does this ignore the distinctions Congress has prescribed shall be observed. It either convicts one man for another's crime or punishes the man convicted twice for the same offense.

Daniel has been held guilty of the substantive crimes committed only by Walter on proof that he did no more than conspire with him to commit offenses of the same general character. There was no evidence that he counseled, advised or had knowledge of those particular acts or offenses. There was, therefore, none that he aided, abetted or took part in them. There was only evidence sufficient to show that he had agreed with Walter at some past time to engage in such transactions generally. As to Daniel this was only evidence of conspiracy, not of substantive crime.

Food for Thought

Is Justice Rutledge's description of the majority's "theory" correct? Or is the majority holding more limited and, if so, how?

The court's theory seems to be that Daniel and Walter became general partners in crime by virtue of their agreement and because of that agreement without more on his part Daniel became criminally responsible as a principal for everything Walter did thereafter in the nature of a criminal offense of the general sort the agreement contemplated, so long as there was not clear evidence that Daniel had withdrawn from or revoked the agreement.

Whether or not his commitment to the penitentiary had that effect, the result is a vicarious criminal responsibility as broad as, or broader than, the vicarious civil liability of a partner for acts done by a co-partner in the course of the firm's business.

Such analogies from private commercial law and the law of torts are dangerous, in my judgment, for transfer to the criminal field. Guilt there with us remains personal, not vicarious, for the more serious offenses. It should be kept so. The effect of Daniel's conviction in this case, to repeat, is either to attribute to him Walter's guilt or to punish him twice for the same offense, namely, agreeing with Walter to engage in crime. Without the agreement Daniel was guilty of no crime on this record. With it and no more, so far as his own conduct is concerned, he was guilty of two.

Hypo 1: *Bank Robbers*

A organizes a conspiracy to rob banks. B & C are included in the conspiracy, but they never meet and they rob different banks (with A). They do, however, know about the existence of each other. Is B responsible for crimes committed by C and vice-versa? Would your answer change if C never robbed a bank herself? Would it matter if A, B and C actually shared ideas and strategies about how to rob banks?

Hypo 2: *The Murdered Bank Teller*

X conspires with Y to rob a bank. Y is designated to "do the job" itself. X provides support and assistance before the fact. During the robbery, Y kills a bank teller. Can X be convicted of murder? Would it make a difference in your analysis if X and Y agreed that no guns were to be used, but where Y (without X's knowledge) did use a gun . . . and ended up killing someone in the course of the robbery?

Everritt v. Georgia

277 Ga. 457, 588 S.E.2d 691 (2003).

THOMPSON, JUSTICE.

Defendant Raymond F. Everritt, John Henry McDuffie and James Wallace Weeks were indicted for the murder with malice aforethought of Roosevelt Cox. McDuffie died one month before the case was to be tried; Weeks admitted his complicity in the murder and testified at trial against Everritt, who appeals from his conviction and enumerates error upon the denial of his motion for a directed verdict of acquittal. To address this enumeration, we must answer this question: Can one who enters a successful conspiracy to commit arson be held criminally responsible for the murder of one co-conspirator by another, when the murder was committed months after the arson in order to keep the conspiracy secret?

Viewing the evidence in a light to uphold the verdict, as we are bound to do, we find the following: Everritt owned and operated a service station in Shellman, Georgia. Because he was experiencing financial problems, Everritt hired James McDuffie to burn down the station, which was insured. Everritt was to pay McDuffie $5,000 for his services out of the insurance proceeds.

McDuffie tried to burn down the station with a Molotov cocktail in June of 1992. He recruited his teenage grandson, Jamie Weeks, to help him in that attempt, but they failed—the incendiary device hit the side of the building, missing the window. Soon thereafter, McDuffie asked Cox, who worked for McDuffie, to help him burn the station. He agreed to pay Cox $1,500. Two weeks after the first, failed attempt, McDuffie and Cox burned down the station with an accelerant.

At first, Everritt's insurance company declined to pay on the policy because of the suspicious circumstances surrounding the fire. Everritt hired an attorney to press his insurance claim. But payment was not forthcoming and, as time went by, Cox remained unpaid. Cox told friends that Everritt owed him $1,500 for burning down the station; and he began to complain that he had not yet been paid by either McDuffie or Everritt. McDuffie was worried because Cox would not keep quiet. In September of 1992, he lured Cox into his shop and killed him with an axe. That day, Everritt called his attorney's office more than three times. He also called his wife, who worked at a bank which had loaned him money.

Jamie Weeks helped McDuffie dispose of Cox's body, which was discovered by hunters on September 27, 1992. Thereafter, in March of 1993, Everritt's insurance claim was settled for $123,065. Nearly nine years later Everritt, McDuffie, and Weeks were charged with the murder of Cox.

Jamie Weeks, who was 26 years old at the time of trial, testified that shortly after the murder, Everritt gave McDuffie a set of tires to conceal the fact that McDuffie used his truck to transport the victim's body. He also testified that Everritt later warned Weeks to keep his mouth shut.

Everritt asserts the evidence is insufficient to enable a rational trier of fact to find him guilty beyond a reasonable doubt of the malice murder of Roosevelt Cox. In this regard, defendant posits that the evidence fails to demonstrate that he conspired with McDuffie to kill Cox. The State counters that the evidence suffices to show a conspiracy between Everritt and McDuffie to kill Cox; that, even if it does not, it proves that Everritt, McDuffie, and Cox conspired to burn down Everritt's place of business and that McDuffie murdered Cox in furtherance of that conspiracy.

As to the State's first argument, we agree with Everritt that the evidence fails to show a conspiracy to murder Cox. Although the existence of a conspiracy can be shown by circumstantial evidence, there was absolutely no evidence tying Everritt to a conspiracy to commit murder. That Everritt placed calls to his attorney and bank on the day of the murder proves nothing one way or the other. And the fact that Everritt gave McDuffie a set of tires after the murder only shows that he was a party to the murder after the fact.

Food for Thought

What if Everritt's attorney revealed that when Everritt called him the day of Cox's murder, he inquired about his culpability for Cox's murder by McDuffie. Would that additional fact suffice to establish Everritt's culpability for Cox's death as a co-conspirator?

With respect to the State's second argument, we agree that the evidence was sufficient to demonstrate that Everritt entered a conspiracy to commit arson with McDuffie and Cox. But that does not end our inquiry; it merely begs the question: Having entered into a conspiracy with McDuffie and Cox to commit arson, is Everritt responsible for the murder of Cox by McDuffie? The State asserts that he is because McDuffie killed Cox to further concealment of the conspiracy. We cannot accept this assertion.

> A criminal conspiracy is a partnership in crime, and there is in each conspiracy a joint or mutual agency for the prosecution of a common plan. Thus, if two or more persons enter into a conspiracy, any act done by any of them pursuant to the agreement is, in contemplation of law, the act of each of them and they are jointly responsible therefor. This means that everything said, written, or done by any of the conspirators in execution or furtherance of the common purpose is deemed to have been said, done, or written by each of them. And this joint responsibility extends not only to what is done by any of the conspirators pursuant to the original agreement but also to collateral acts incident to and growing out of the original purpose.

Burke v. State, 234 Ga. 512, 514, 216 S.E.2d 812 (1975). However, a defendant can be held criminally responsible for such collateral acts only if it can be said that they are a natural and probable consequence of the conspiracy.

The State argues that Cox's murder was necessary to conceal the conspiracy to commit arson and that, therefore, Everritt should be deemed responsible. This argument misses the mark because the question is not just one of necessity, but of "reasonable foreseeability." See *Pinkerton v. United States*, 328 U.S. 640, 647–648, 66 S.Ct. 1180, 90 L.Ed. 1489 (1946). Under

Food for Thought

Do you agree with the Georgia Supreme Court that Everritt was not responsible for the death of Cox? Would it make any difference in your analysis if the prosecution could have shown that Everritt knew that McDuffie wanted to kill Cox and Everritt did nothing about that information, e.g. he didn't report it to the police?

the facts of this case, it cannot be said that the murder of Cox could be reasonably foreseen as a necessary, probable consequence of the conspiracy to commit arson. Simply put, a conspiracy to commit arson, without more, does not naturally, necessarily, and probably result in the murder of one co-conspirator by another.

The evidence was insufficient to enable a rational trier of fact to find Everritt guilty beyond a reasonable doubt of the malice murder of Roosevelt Cox. It follows that the trial court erred in denying Everritt's motion for a directed verdict of acquittal.

Judgment reversed.

Snowden v. United States

52 A.3d 858 (D.C. 2012).

RUIZ, SENIOR JUDGE.

Appellant was convicted in Superior Court of several offenses related to an armed robbery of a group of individuals: one count of conspiracy to commit armed robbery, one count of armed robbery, four counts of assault with intent to rob while armed (AWIRWA), one count of aggravated assault while armed (AAWA), and two counts of possession of a firearm during a crime of violence (PFCV).

The charges against appellant stemmed from a robbery and shooting on the evening of May 2, 2008, on the 4900 block of Jay Street, Northeast. That evening Lorenzo Ross ("Lorenzo"), his father, Lorenzo Ross, Sr., and his cousins, Derrick Ross, DeAngelo Martino, and Martin Scales, were "hanging by the dumpster in the parking lot" of Lorenzo's apartment complex, celebrating Lorenzo Ross, Sr.'s recent release from prison. At some point during the celebration, Lorenzo saw a girl he knew from the complex, Shaelin Rush, and he left the group to talk with her privately. While Lorenzo and Shaelin were talking, they saw a group of five "boys" in the vicinity. Lorenzo saw Shaelin approach the boys, hug them, and then go inside a nearby apartment building. Lorenzo recognized one of the boys as appellant because he was standing "right underneath" a lamp post. Lorenzo knew appellant because they rode the bus together to school every day, and that appellant went by the name of "Snoop."

Lorenzo testified that after Shaelin went inside, he saw appellant put on a black ski mask and heard him say to the other boys, "y'all ready, let's go." As the group of boys began to move toward Lorenzo's father and cousins, Lorenzo started toward the dumpster to warn his family that he had a "bad feeling" about the boys. Just as Lorenzo got to the dumpster, however, appellant came around the corner with a gun. As appellant rounded the corner and approached the group, Scales was on a cellular phone walking away from the group and, unknowingly, toward appellant. Lorenzo testified that upon rounding the corner appellant said, "give that shit up." Scales testified that appellant said, "you know what it is, let me get that." A second gunman walked behind the group and positioned himself "to the point where if Lorenzo and his group wanted to run he had a perfect angle to shoot them." The second gunman, who had a bandana covering his face and wielded a "big handgun" similar to an Uzi, was aiming the gun at the group, "moving" the gun between "different people."

Appellant ordered Scales to "get on the gate," and then "patted Scales's pockets." Scales responded by giving appellant $20 that he had in his front pocket. Appellant poked the gun into Scales's side, attempted to search Scales's other pockets and "take him down to the dumpsters so he could do a thorough search." Scales reacted by grabbing the gun and trying "to get the gun away from appellant or to get away from him." Scales "was swinging at appellant trying to hit him with everything he had, hoping appellant would drop the gun." Scales shouted for the rest of his group to flee; as Lorenzo and the others ran, the second gunman did not attempt to stop them. Scales and appellant fell to the ground fighting and the gun fired. Lorenzo testified that after he heard the gun discharge, he looked back and saw "them still fighting, wrestling." Scales tussled with appellant for "a long time," while the second gunman stood about twenty feet away with his gun directed toward Scales. Appellant eventually wrestled free of Scales and took off running with his gun.

After appellant fled, the second gunman kept his gun trained on Scales. Scales raised his arms in submission and told the gunman "you got all of the money that I have." From the porch of a nearby house, Lanette Ross (Lorenzo's mother) and her sister said, "call the police," and yelled at the gunman, "don't shoot him." The gunman paused, raised and lowered his gun three times, and then shot Scales in the right-side of his abdomen.

The jury found appellant guilty of conspiracy to commit armed robbery; AAWA and armed robbery, as to Scales; four counts of AWIRWA, as to Lorenzo, Lorenzo Ross, Sr., Derrick Ross, and Martino; and seven counts of PFCV—one for each of the seven armed predicate offenses.

There was no evidence that appellant shot Scales; indeed, the evidence showed that appellant had fled with the $20 before the second gunman fired the shot. The government's theory of Scales's liability for AAWA was that the shooting was in furtherance of the conspiracy of which appellant was a part. In *Pinkerton v. United States*, 328 U.S. 640 (1946), the Supreme Court held that a defendant may be liable for the acts of his co-conspirator. Appellant argues that his conviction of AAWA must be vacated "because the evidence was insufficient to prove beyond a reasonable doubt that the aggravated assault of Mr. Scales by the second gunman was (1) in furtherance of the conspiracy or (2) a reasonably foreseeable consequence of it." Rather, he argues, what the evidence supports is that the shooting of Scales was a "random act of violence" by the second gunman for which appellant is not criminally responsible. We conclude that the evidence sufficed to permit the jury to find appellant guilty of AAWA under a *Pinkerton* theory of co-conspirator liability.

Appellant contends that there was no evidence that the second gunman's shooting of Scales was necessary to accomplish the objective of the conspiracy—robbery—as appellant had seized the money and run away with it, thus completing the robbery, by the time the shooting occurred. The government counters that the shooting was in furtherance of the conspiracy because it "occurred before all the culprits had escaped and it advanced the conspiracy's goals by assisting the escape and asportation of proceeds, protecting the robbers from Scales, punishing Scales' resistance, and discouraging Scales and others from reporting the offense or testifying against the robbers."

We have not previously considered whether a shooting by one co-conspirator that takes place after another co-conspirator has fled may be deemed to be "in furtherance of" the conspiracy for purposes of co-conspirator liability.

Insofar as the objective of appellant and his co-conspirators was to rob Scales, their goal was not completed until they had successfully made off with the fruits of their criminal endeavor. Although *Pinkerton* co-conspirator liability and accomplice liability are "distinct legal theories that require proof of different elements," we see no meaningful distinction between these theories of liability for the purpose of assessing whether the evidence supports that another's actions were committed "in furtherance of" a criminal enterprise. A shooting by a co-conspirator that is similarly causally linked to completion of the object of the conspiracy is properly charged against other co-conspirators under a theory of conspiracy liability.

Take Note

The abandonment of a conspiracy by all co-conspirators is generally presumed if none of the co-conspirators commits an overt act within the statute of limitations period. But, in the absence of a co-conspirator's prior, lawful act of renunciation or withdrawal, a conspiracy is deemed to continue even if only a single co-conspirator acts as part of the conspiracy within the limitations period.

Viewing the evidence presented in appellant's trial in the light most favorable to the government, we conclude that it was sufficient to support a determination that the shooting was in furtherance of the conspiracy to commit armed robbery. As noted, the second gunman shot Scales as appellant was fleeing with the money he had taken from Scales. Because the shooting guaranteed a clean escape for the assailants with the proceeds of their crime, the shooting aided in the successful completion of their criminal endeavor. Even if the second gunman appeared to hesitate, it was not a disconnected act, as the shooting occurred at the scene of the robbery and only about fifteen seconds after appellant had broken free from Scales, such that the jury could reasonably find that the shooting and the robbery were "one continuous and unbroken chain of events," rather than a "random act of violence," as appellant contends.

Appellant also argues that the shooting was not a reasonably foreseeable consequence of the robbery because the objective of the conspiracy had already been completed and there

Food for Thought

Is this decision consistent with the preceding *Everritt* decision? In *Everritt*, the Georgia court held that the murder of Cox *was not* reasonably foreseeable. In *Snowden*, the D.C. court held that the shooting of Scales *was* reasonably foreseeable. Can you make a good argument that both courts were correct in reaching these conclusions?

was "some appreciable interval of time" between the robbery and the shooting. We disagree. As the government points out, a shooting is quite naturally a reasonably foreseeable consequence of an armed robbery. A defendant who conspires to commit an armed robbery should anticipate that a shooting may occur during the commission of the robbery and is held accountable if a shooting does, in fact, occur. Appellant himself used a weapon to confront Scales and take his money. As we have discussed, the robbery was progressing even as appellant was fleeing the scene because the asportation of the proceeds was continuing at that time. Moreover, appellant's argument about the timing of the shooting (that "some appreciable interval of time" elapsed between the time appellant took the money from Scales and the shooting) is irrelevant because our proper focus is on whether a shooting is reasonably foreseeable at any point during the commission of the armed robbery. His argument is also factually inaccurate. Once Scales decided to fight back, appellant's ability to keep the cash could not be assured until he was able to break free and run away. The shooting took place only fifteen seconds later. Because appellant and at least one of his co-conspirators brought weapons to the scene of the robbery and both employed those weapons to effectuate the robbery, the jury could properly conclude that the shooting of Scales so soon after appellant fled was a reasonably foreseeable consequence of their conspiracy to commit armed robbery.

For the foregoing reasons, appellant's convictions are hereby Affirmed.

Executive Summary

Bilateral vs. Unilateral Conspiracies. In bilateral conspiracy jurisdictions, two or more persons must conspire for a conspiracy to exist. In unilateral jurisdictions, an accused can be found guilty of conspiracy if the accused believes that there he or she has agreed to commit a crime with another, whether or not that is true.

Mens Rea. The *mens rea* of conspiracy is the intent to agree with another person to commit a crime and the intent to commit that crime. There is no conspiracy to commit a crime with a *mens rea* of recklessness or negligence. And the mere knowledge that someone else intends to commit a crime is not enough to make a person a conspirator.

Actus Reus. The *actus reus* of conspiracy is an agreement with another person to commit a criminal act. A single conspiracy can have multiple criminal objectives. The number of conspiracies that exist is determined by the number of conspiratorial agreements not by the number of criminal objectives.

Major Themes

a. Controversial Crime—Most (but not all) jurisdictions include a conspiracy offense in their crimes code. Many jurisdictions do not, however, believing that the conduct covered by that offense is adequately criminalized by other substantive or inchoate offenses. And some commentators have argued that conspiracy no longer serves a useful or sensible function and that the conspiratorial "net" extends too broadly to individuals who were not significantly involved in the supposed criminal enterprise.

b. Change in Conspiracy Approach—The traditional "bilateral" conspiracy crime was aimed at responding to the supposed special danger to society posed by actual group criminal activity; the modern "unilateral" approach, in contrast, criminalizes the actions of a single individual who is or simply believes that he or she is agreeing with another person to commit a criminal act.

Overt Act. Some conspiracy statutes also require proof of an overt act undertaken by one of the co-conspirators in furtherance of the conspiracy. This overt act is separate from the *actus reus* of the conspiratorial offense.

Renunciation or Withdrawal. Some jurisdictions allow for a renunciation or withdrawal defense to the crime of conspiracy if the accused's actions are voluntary and complete and he or she provides assistance in preventing the crime.

Merger. Unless the law expressly provides otherwise, conspiracy convictions do not merge with convictions for crimes which were an object of the conspiracy unless the criminal objectives went beyond any particular offense actually committed in pursuance of the conspiratorial goals.

Culpability of Co-Conspirators. Many jurisdictions follow the federal criminal law approach which provides that a conspirator is deemed culpable for the reasonably foreseeable criminal acts of his or her co-conspirators undertaken in furtherance of the conspiracy.

For More Information

- American Law Institute, Model Penal Code and Commentaries, Part I, § 5.03 (1980).
- John M. Burkoff & Russell L. Weaver, Inside Criminal Law: What Matters and Why 117–134 (2d ed. 2011).
- R. Michael Cassidy & Gregory I. Massing, *The Model Penal Code's Wrong Turn: Renunciation as a Defense to Criminal Conspiracy*, 64 Fla. L. Rev. 353 (2012).
- Mitchell McBride, *Federal Criminal Conspiracy*, 57 Am. Crim. L. Rev. 759 (2020).
- Paul Marcus, Prosecution and Defense of Criminal Conspiracy Cases (1978).
- Allen Page, *The Problems With Alleging Federal Government Conspiracies Under 42 U.S.C. § 1985(3)*, 68 Emory L. J. 563 (2019).
- Laura Waters, *Federal Criminal Conspiracy*, 49 Am. Crim. L. Rev. 739 (2012).

Test Your Knowledge

To assess your understanding of the material in this chapter, click here to take a quiz.

Chapter 8

Homicide

Homicide, the most serious of all criminal offenses, involves the killing of a human being by another human being. In some jurisdictions, moreover, statutory enactments have extended homicide culpability to an actor's unlawful acts causing the death of a fetus.

By the late Common Law period in England, homicide consisted generally of only two constituent offenses, murder and manslaughter, the former crime distinguished from the latter by the presence of "malice aforethought." Despite the terminology, the crime of murder did not actually require either "malice" or "forethought." "Malice aforethought" was a term of art which referred to a homicide committed in any one of four ways: with the intent to cause death or serious bodily injury; with the knowledge that the action will cause death or serious bodily injury; when the killing occurred during the commission of a felony; or when the perpetrator intended to oppose, by force, an officer or justice of the peace in the performance of his or her duties.

Today, the various Crimes Code provisions relating to homicide found in federal law and in each of the fifty states (and the District of Columbia) are far more nuanced, often more complicated and, candidly, more idiosyncratic. Accordingly, the way in which homicide offenses are classified in this Chapter should be viewed simply as a typical—but not a universal—American homicide taxonomy. Do not assume that any particular jurisdiction follows this approach precisely.

FYI

In 2018, the estimated number of murders in the United States was 16,214. This was a 6.2% decrease from 2017, a 14.5% increase from 2014, and a 5.3% increase from 2009. There were 5.0 murders per 100,000 people in 2018. The murder rate in 2018 was down from the rates in 2017 (6.8 percent) and 2009 (1.2 percent). However, the murder rate climbed 11.6 percent when compared with the 2014 rate. Of the murders in the United States, 46.2% were reported in the South, 22.0% were reported in the Midwest, 19.9% were reported in the West, and 11.9% were reported in the Northeast. FBI, Uniform Crime Reporting Program, 2018 Crime in the United States, Murder, https://ucr.fbi.gov/crime-in-the-u.s/2018/crime-in-the-u.s.-2018/topic-pages/murder.

A. Intentional Killings

In general, and typically, each jurisdiction's homicide provisions can be divided into two distinct categories: intentional and unintentional killings. The most serious form of homicide is an intentional killing.

1. Murder by Degrees

In most states, the crime of murder is divided into degrees. Homicides committed with the specific intention to kill usually are treated as first-degree murders. Consider, for example, California Penal Code § 189, which provides as follows:

§ 189. Murder; degrees

(a) All murder that is perpetrated by means of a destructive device or explosive, a weapon of mass destruction, knowing use of ammunition designed primarily to penetrate metal or armor, poison, lying in wait, torture, or by any other kind of willful, deliberate, and premeditated killing, or that is committed in the perpetration of, or attempt to perpetrate, arson, rape, carjacking, robbery, burglary, mayhem, kidnapping, train wrecking, . . . or murder that is perpetrated by means of discharging a firearm from a motor vehicle, intentionally at another person outside of the vehicle with the intent to inflict death, is murder of the first degree.

(b) All other kinds of murders are of the second degree.

[(d)] To prove the killing was "deliberate and premeditated," it is not necessary to prove the defendant maturely and meaningfully reflected upon the gravity of the defendant's act.

Like California, many states that divide the crime of murder into degrees specifically provide that a "willful," "deliberate" and "premeditated" homicide constitutes first-degree murder. In some of these states, courts have held that "no time is too short" for a wicked person to premeditate and deliberate upon his or her intention to kill. In other states, in contrast, premeditation and deliberation are not established unless it is shown that a cognizable period of reflection has occurred. Are these positions irreconcilable? Which positions most appropriately reflects first-degree murder's status as the most heinous of homicide offenses?

State v. Ramirez

190 Ariz. 65, 945 P.2d 376 (Ct.App. 1997).

NOYES, PRESIDING JUDGE.

A young man named David knocked on the door of Appellant's girlfriend's townhouse. Appellant opened the door and greeted David with an aggressive handshake, as if trying to overpower him. The two struggled for a moment, then quit. As they walked into the house,

Appellant pressed a gun into David's ribs and said, "I could have took you out already." Nothing more happened between them.

About a month later, Appellant walked out of the townhouse and saw David's brother walking towards him. David and his brother looked alike. Appellant went up to the brother and shook hands with him, and greeted him, and then, for no apparent reason, pulled out a gun and shot him three times, killing him. Appellant paused between the second and third shots. There were several witnesses. As Appellant walked away, he pointed the gun at a girl and said, "Later, Vicki." Appellant said to one witness: "He started it. He deserves it." (The victim had done nothing.) Appellant said to another witness: "He showed me a gun. I gave him a bullet." (The victim had no gun.) By some accounts, Appellant appeared to be under the influence of alcohol and methamphetamine at the time. By all accounts, it was a senseless killing. Whether it was also a premeditated killing was the only contested issue in the trial.

The jury found Appellant guilty of first degree murder. Appellant claims that the jury instruction on premeditation "lessened the State's burden of proving premeditation." The statutory definition of premeditation provides:

> "Premeditation" means that the defendant acts with either the intention or the knowledge that he will kill another human being, when such intention or knowledge precedes the killing by a length of time to permit reflection. An act is not done with premeditation if it is the instant effect of a sudden quarrel or heat of passion.

In *Moore v. State*, 65 Ariz. 70, 75, 174 P.2d 282, 285 (1946), it was stated that, "deliberation and premeditation may be as instantaneous as successive thoughts of the mind."

Food for Thought

Does this make sense? How can someone premeditate and deliberate "instantaneously"? Isn't that a contradiction in terms?

Moore also cautioned that, "While the jury may be told that the brain can function rapidly they must not be misled into thinking that an act can at the same time be impulsive, unstudied and premeditated." The jury was so misled in Appellant's case. The court's instruction, as misargued by the State, essentially told the jury that an act could be both impulsive and premeditated.

The instruction given in Appellant's case was as follows:

> "Premeditation" means the defendant's knowledge that he will kill another person existed before the killing long enough to permit reflection. However, the time for reflection must be longer than the time required merely to form the knowledge that conduct will cause death. It may be as instantaneous as successive thoughts in the mind, and it may be proven by circumstantial evidence.
>
> It is this period of reflection, regardless of its length, which distinguishes first degree murder from second degree murder.

This instruction contains two ambiguities which turned into errors when the State misargued the law. First, by failing to be clear that premeditation requires actual reflection, the instruction allowed the State to argue that premeditation is just a period of time. Second, because the instruction commented that this period of time can be "instantaneous as successive thoughts in the mind" but provided no balancing language to the effect that an act cannot be both impulsive and premeditated, it allowed the State to argue, in effect, that premeditation is just an instant of time. The instruction says it can be as instantaneous as two thoughts in the mind.

The State argues that the instruction and the prosecutor were correct in Appellant's case; that premeditation is, in fact, a period of time rather than actual reflection. The State argues that actual reflection was not required after the 1978 enactment of A.R.S. section 13–1101(1).

Practice Pointer

How does a prosecutor in Arizona prove premeditation after this decision? Obviously, the lapse of time can still be a factor, but the court indicates that it is not a controlling factor. What other evidence could the prosecutor have introduced that would have tended to show that Ramirez *actually* reflected?

Defining premeditation as a length of time (which can be instantaneous as successive thoughts in the mind) obliterates any meaningful difference between first and second degree murder—other than the penalties. The legislature has not merged these two offenses; it has prescribed different elements and different penalties for them. The minimum sentence for first degree murder is life in prison with possible release in twenty-five years; the maximum is the death penalty. The minimum sentence for second degree murder is ten years in prison; the maximum is twenty-two years. This significant difference in penalty ranges strongly suggests that the legislature intended there to be an equally significant difference between first and second degree murder; something with more relevance to criminal responsibility than an instant of time.

In Appellant's case, the only difference between first and second degree murder was the element of premeditation. In this case, as in most, after defendant formed the knowledge that he would kill he could not possibly pull the gun, and aim it, and pull the trigger faster than he could form a successive thought in his mind. Therefore, if the State's argument prevails, any murder is premeditated unless defendant acted faster than he could have a second thought. In real life, of course, many persons act without thinking twice, even when they have time to do so. But the State's definition of premeditation would include those unreflecting killers in the first degree murder category, along with those who actually reflected before acting. We conclude that the first degree murder statute has never been aimed at those who had time to reflect but did not; it has always has been aimed at those who actually reflected—and then murdered.

If the difference between first and second degree murder is to be maintained, premeditation has to be understood as reflection. It is fair to talk of the period of time in which reflection might occur; but it is not fair to define reflection as the period of time in which it might occur. To have meaning, the element of premeditation must describe something that defendant actually does. Just as murder requires actual killing, premeditation requires actual reflection. Premeditation can, of course, be proven by circumstantial evidence; like knowledge or intention, it rarely can be proven by any other means. The more time defendant has to reflect, the stronger the inference that he actually did reflect. This is what the statute is getting at—that actual reflection can be inferred from the length of time to permit reflection. That is the way it has always been and nothing we say here changes that. What we reject, however, is the notion that premeditation is just an instant of time.

Food for Thought

The majority notes that "appellant claimed that he acted impulsively, without premeditation. Substantial evidence supports this claim." Given Appellant's history of "bad blood" with the victim, to what evidence was Judge Noyes referring? If it is conceded that the majority is correct that there was *both* evidence of impulsiveness and evidence supporting premeditation, why did the majority not simply defer to the jury's fact-finding?

Because of the premeditation instruction and argument in Appellant's case, however, the verdict merely establishes that an instant of time existed between Appellant's knowledge and his action. The verdict does not establish actual premeditation. Appellant claimed that he acted impulsively, without premeditation. Substantial evidence supports this claim. At sentencing, the trial court stated that defendant "impulsively and for no reason pulled out a gun and shot this person." If a properly-instructed jury viewed the evidence as the trial court did, it might have a reasonable doubt about premeditation; it might convict on second degree murder. On the other hand, if a properly-instructed jury viewed the evidence as our dissenting colleague does, it might convict on first degree murder.

We conclude that the jury instruction on premeditation, as argued by the State, obliterated the distinction between first and second degree murder. Because substantial evidence supports both Appellant's argument for second degree murder and the State's argument for first degree murder, we cannot say beyond a reasonable doubt that the error in the premeditation instruction did not contribute significantly to the first degree murder verdict.

Reversed and remanded for new trial.

RYAN, JUDGE, dissenting.

I disagree with the majority. This disagreement stems from A.R.S section 13–1101(1)'s clarity: "premeditation" is intent or knowledge of killing which precedes the killing "by a length of time to permit reflection." Under this language no actual reflection is required, and the jury decides the factual question of whether adequate time for reflection existed. Except for rare cases, reflection can be proven only by the passage of time. The legislature clearly decided not to require the state to prove actual reflection. Instead, it determined that an objective standard of proof of a passage of some period of time would be adequate. Such a determination is a legitimate legislative prerogative. Further, if the legislature had intended that actual reflection be an element of first-degree murder, it could have readily said so. I appreciate the majority's concern that, under the present statutory definition of premeditation, the line between first and second-degree murder is not entirely clear. While I share the majority's concern, the answer more appropriately rests with the legislature.

Food for Thought

If dissenting Judge Ryan was a legislator and not an appellate judge, how should he have worded a proposed (post-*Ramirez*) amendment to Arizona law which would have had the effect of codifying the views he expressed in his dissenting opinion?

Here's a big hint. The position that Judge Ryan took in his dissenting opinion was in fact subsequently enacted into law. See discussion of this course of events in *State v. Zamora*, 204 Ariz. 313, 63 P.3d 1050 (Ariz.App. 2003): "Prior to the 1998 amendment to § 13–1101(1), Division One of this court held that premeditation required actual reflection. *State v. Ramirez*, 190 Ariz. 65, 70, 945 P.2d 376, 381 (App. 1997). Division Two of this court disagreed, concluding that premeditation does not require actual reflection. *State v. Haley*, 194 Ariz. 123, 125–26, 978 P.2d 100, 102–03 (App. 1998) (interpreting the version of § 13–1101(1) in effect prior to the 1998 amendment). The legislature then amended the definition of premeditation in 1998 by adding the words 'Proof of actual reflection is not required.' 1998 Ariz. Sess. Laws, ch. 289 § 6. These additional words make it clear that the State need not prove actual reflection. Instead, the State need only prove that the defendant's intent to kill or knowledge that he or she will kill another person preceded the killing 'by any length of time to permit reflection.' "

State v. Hope

2019 -Ohio- 2174, 137 N.E.3d 549 (Ct. App. 11th Dist 2019).

MARY JANE TRAPP, J.

Appellant, Shawn Hope a.k.a. Shawn Johnson ("Mr. Hope"), appeals his conviction for aggravated murder following a jury trial in the Trumbull County Court of Common Pleas. We find the evidence was sufficient to support Mr. Hope's conviction for aggravated murder.

On December 1, 2016, Mr. Hope was playing cards with Alicia Binion, Tabitha Powell, and John Paul Kellar at a house located at 2313 Stephens Avenue, NW in Warren, Ohio. Ms. Binion resided at the house with Mr. Kellar, whom she described as her cousin, and Ms. Powell, who was engaged to Mr. Kellar. Ms. Binion was acquainted with Mr. Hope because she had been a drug user and purchased drugs from him.

At some point, Mr. Hope made advances toward Ms. Powell and Ms. Binion, and he and Mr. Kellar began arguing. The argument lasted only a few minutes and was resolved. Ms. Binion eventually asked Mr. Hope to leave the residence, which he did.

The following day, Ms. Binion, Ms. Powell, and Mr. Kellar were at the Stephens Avenue residence. Ms. Powell was in the back bedroom with Mr. Kellar rubbing his feet. Ms. Binion was getting ready to leave the residence to obtain money for the purchase of drugs.

At approximately 6:30 p.m., Mr. Hope knocked on the door. Ms. Binion did not want to answer the door, but Mr. Kellar told her to do so. After Ms. Binion answered the door, Mr. Hope came inside and asked where Mr. Kellar and Ms. Powell were located. He began walking toward the back bedroom. Mr. Kellar walked out into the hallway to meet him. Mr. Hope had his hands in his coat pockets. Suddenly, Mr. Hope removed a gun from his coat pocket and shot Mr. Kellar twice in the chest area at close range. Mr. Hope then said, "Who's the bitch now?" and kicked Mr. Kellar. According to the coroner's report, Mr. Kellar died from multiple gunshot wounds.

The Trumbull County Grand Jury indicted Mr. Hope on two counts of aggravated murder, each with a firearm specification. Mr. Hope pleaded not guilty, and after a number of continuances to permit additional discovery, the case proceeded to a jury trial. The jury found Mr. Hope guilty, but trial court determined Counts 1 and 2 merged for purposes of sentencing and sentenced Mr. Hope to 25 years to life on Count 2.

Mr. Hope claims the state failed to produce sufficient evidence to sustain his convictions for aggravated murder. Mr. Hope argues the state did not produce sufficient evidence of prior calculation and design. A sufficiency challenge requires this court to review the record to determine whether the state presented evidence on each of the elements of the offense. This test involves a question of law and does not permit us to weigh the evidence.

To convict Mr. Hope of aggravated murder, the state was required to prove beyond a reasonable doubt that Mr. Hope did purposely, and with prior calculation and design, cause the death of Mr. Kellar. Mr. Hope argues the state did not produce sufficient evidence of the element of prior calculation and design to support his conviction for aggravated murder.

Under prior Ohio law, "murder in the first degree" required proof of "deliberate and premeditated malice." Under this standard, "a killing could be premeditated even though conceived and executed on the spur of the moment. The only requirement was that the malicious purpose be formed before the homicidal act, however short in time."

Effective January 1, 1974, the General Assembly reclassified first-degree murder as "aggravated murder" and substituted a requirement of "prior calculation and design" in place of "deliberate and premeditated malice." According to the Supreme Court of Ohio, "prior calculation and design" is a more stringent element. The General Assembly's apparent intention was to require more than a few moments of deliberation and to require a scheme designed to implement the calculated decision to kill.

The phrase "prior calculation and design" is not defined in the Revised Code. By its own terms, the phrase suggests advance reasoning to formulate the purpose to kill. Evidence of an act committed on the spur of the moment or after momentary consideration is not evidence of a premeditated decision or a studied consideration of the method and the means to cause a death. There is also no bright-line test to determine whether prior calculation and design are present. Rather, each case must be decided on a case-by-case basis.

The Supreme Court of Ohio has held that where evidence adduced at trial reveals the presence of sufficient time and opportunity for the planning of an act of homicide to constitute prior calculation, and the circumstances surrounding the homicide show a scheme designed to implement the calculated decision to kill, a finding by the trier of fact of prior calculation and design is justified.

The Supreme Court of Ohio has also considered three factors in determining whether a defendant acted with prior calculation and design: (1) Did the accused and victim know each other, and if so, was that relationship strained? (2) Did the accused give thought or preparation to choosing the murder weapon or murder site? and (3) Was the act drawn out or an almost instantaneous eruption of events?

Food for Thought

Would Arizona's use of this Ohio "prior calculation and design" test and these three determining factors have changed the result in the preceding *Ramirez* case? Would Arizona's approach have changed the result in this case? How different are these two approaches in actual application?

Mr. Hope argues that the consideration of these three factors does not support a finding of prior calculation in design. We disagree.

With respect to the first factor, Mr. Hope claims the relationship between Mr. Kellar and himself was not strained. In support, Mr. Hope cites the testimony of Ms. Powell describing the night before the shooting. According to the testimony, Mr. Kellar and Mr. Hope had argued but stopped after a few minutes and began joking with each other.

Mr. Hope fails to acknowledge the testimony regarding the shooting itself, which indicated Mr. Hope arrived unexpectedly and uninvited at the Stephens Avenue residence, almost immediately shot Mr. Kellar twice in the chest area at close range, said "Who's the bitch now?," and kicked Mr. Kellar. These actions created a strong inference Mr. Hope was harboring some type of grudge against Mr. Kellar from the night before or from another event, which is evidence of a strained relationship.

With respect to the second factor, Mr. Hope argues there was no evidence presented that demonstrated he "had picked the house for the killing or a gun for any specific purpose."

The testimony establishes Mr. Hope apparently armed himself and, uninvited and unannounced, went to the Stephens Avenue residence where he knew Mr. Kellar lived. Upon entering the house, he immediately proceeded toward the room where he knew Mr. Kellar was present. He then shot Mr. Kellar prior to any conversation taking place between the two men. When a person takes a gun to a place where he knows the victim frequents, this creates a reasonable inference that a person carried the gun with an intention to use it. In this case, it is difficult to infer anything from the evidence other than Mr. Hope armed himself and arrived at the house specifically to commit murder.

With respect to the third factor, Mr. Hope argues that since "the killing happened almost instantaneously" after he entered the house, he did not act with prior calculation and design.

This evidence actually supports an opposite inference. The killing itself may have been an "almost instantaneous eruption" after Mr. Hope

Food for Thought

Does this "inference of prior calculation and design" from "sufficient time and opportunity for planning" mean that proof of *actual* prior thought and planning is unnecessary?

entered the residence. However, the events between Mr. Hope and Mr. Kellar began at least as early as the previous evening. After Mr. Hope left the house the night before, the testimony establishes no one had any contact with him until he appeared at the house the next evening. The presence of sufficient time and opportunity for the planning of a murder between these events creates a reasonable inference of prior calculation and design.

When this evidence is taken together and viewed in a light most favorable to the state, a rational trier-of-fact could reasonably conclude Mr. Hope acted with prior calculation and design. Based on the foregoing, the judgment of the Trumbull County Court of Common Pleas is affirmed.

Points for Discussion

a. Model Penal Code

The Model Penal Code does not divide the crime of murder into degrees. Instead, it treats "purposeful" or "knowing" homicides as murder, as well as unpremeditated murder (which is discussed in greater detail in Part B.1, *infra*):

§ 210.2. Murder.

(1) Except as provided in Section 210.3(1)(b), criminal homicide constitutes murder when:

(a) it is committed purposely or knowingly; or

(b) it is committed recklessly under circumstances manifesting extreme indifference to the value of human life. Such recklessness and indifference are presumed if the actor is engaged or is an accomplice in the commission of, or an attempt to commit, or flight after committing or attempting to commit robbery, rape or deviate sexual intercourse by force or threat of force, arson, burglary, kidnapping or felonious escape.

(2) Murder is a felony of the first degree but a person convicted of murder may be sentenced to death, as provided in Section 210.6.

b. Capital Punishment

In many jurisdictions, first-degree murder can be punished by imposition of the death penalty, a sentence that is not available for conviction of any lesser degrees of murder or other homicide offenses. *See* Chapter 14, Section B (Capital Punishment).

As you review the cases in this Chapter on Homicide, you might consider whether—in your view—the aggravating factor of premeditation—the specific intention to kill—*should be* the dispositive factor in determining whether or not a convicted killer might be executed. Indeed, does it make sense to aggravate a conviction from second degree murder to first degree murder based *solely* on the factor of premeditation? What is the logic behind the focus on this factor to the exclusion of other facts, e.g. the brutality of the killing?

Is the focus on premeditation as such a significant aggravating factor justified by any of the classic justifications for punishment: retribution, restraint, deterrence, or rehabilitation? *See* Chapter 1. Is someone who commits a premeditated murder necessarily more deserving of punishment than someone who commits an unpremeditated, but nonetheless intentional murder?

For example, a man's wife is dying from cancer and she is in great pain. She begs him to help her end her life by providing her with poison. At first, he refuses. Repeatedly. But, eventually, after much soul searching, he decides that the loving thing to do is to provide his much-beloved spouse with the poison she wants in order to end her suffering. He does; he helps her drink it; and she dies. Was there *premeditation* on these sketchy facts? Is husband deserving of greater punishment than a person who *impulsively* beats a child or an elderly victim to death, i.e. without premeditation? Does it make sense that only the former actor may face the death penalty as a result of his actions? Why?

c. Deterrence & Premeditation

Consider the issue of deterrence. Do you think that someone who reflects before committing a crime is more amenable to deterrence? If so, does that fact provide a reason for punishing premeditated homicides more severely?

Is the possibility of punishment likely to deter the anguished spouse of a suffering cancer patient who euthanizes his or spouse out of love? *See* discussion in the preceding section. Does a deterrence rationale provide sufficient—or any—justification to treat that spouse more severely than an accused person who brutally but impulsively beat an old woman or child to death?

d. Role of the Legislature

Consider how the Ohio legislature changed its murder statute to make it more difficult for the Government to establish the highest degree. Was this change effective in your view?

Do you think that the action of the Arizona legislature, amending the statute after the decision in *Ramirez* to provide that "proof of actual reflection is not required" was a good change in the law? If so, how so? If not, why not? *See* discussion in the final Food for Thought box in *Ramirez.*

Do you like or prefer the provision in the California Penal Code, set out *supra*, which provides that premeditation need not be "mature" and "meaningful?" What purpose does the premeditation requirement serve if it does not involve "mature" and "meaningful" premeditation?

Hypo 1: *Perils of Criminal Defense*

Defendant became upset with his defense counsel after a jury found him guilty of the charged offenses and, while the prosecutor was making his sentencing arguments to the court, defendant abruptly struck his attorney on the side of the head with his fist with such force that counsel was immediately knocked unconscious and fell to the floor. Defendant continued to punch and kick him until being tackled by sheriff's deputies. After he was subdued, defendant also attempted to bite his then-unconscious attorney as the two men lay on the courtroom floor. The audio recording device used by the court reporter captured several statements defendant made during and immediately after the incident, including the following:

> "I would try to kill. I hope he's dead! I tried to kill him, he tried, he just took my life. I hope you die m---- f-----! I told you you was f------ with the wrong one! Oh jack ass leg [sic] lawyer. They found me guilty. I hope you die George! You took my life, I'm gonna to take yours. I hope the bastard die. You done f----- the last n---- you gonna f--- in your lifetime."

Counsel was badly injured and had to be hospitalized in intensive care. Was this act premeditated sufficiently to support conviction of defendant for attempted murder? (Does this case give you any second thoughts about a career as criminal defense counsel?) *See State v. Forrest*, 609 S.E.2d 241 (N.C. Ct. App. 2005).

Hypo 2: *Homicidal Dream*

Defendant forcibly entered a mobile home while the residents were asleep. He removed his clothes, pulled four large steak knives from a knife block, walked to the bedroom where the residents were sleeping, and stabbed both of them in the chest. He then fled, leaving his clothing behind, and took refuge in his own nearby trailer. One victim died. The other called the police who found evidence linking defendant to the scene, including his wallet and the keys to his car and trailer house, all of which he had left behind in the kitchen when he fled the murder scene naked. When the police awakened defendant, he agreed to accompany them to the police station. On the way to the station, he told them that he knew why they wanted to talk with him. He said he had had a dream in which he "knifed" a couple of people and he was afraid they were dead. Defendant asked the police if this incident really happened. When told that it had, he started to cry. He said he had spent the evening drinking and that he did not remember everything that happened. He did remember entering the trailer, grabbing knives, entering a bedroom, and making a swinging motion at two people. He also remembered running naked back to his trailer. He previously had fantasized about killing people whom he did not know, "like a spy" would do. Also, months before the killing, defendant had wondered aloud in the presence of friends what it would be like to kill someone and had asked them if they ever had thought about killing anyone. Was this killing "premeditated?" *See State v. Netland*, 535 N.W.2d 328 (Minn. 1995).

Hypo 3: *Deadly Meeting*

Defendant James Wear arranged to meet an acquaintance, Ryan Rossknecht, and went to the meeting with a friend, Brandon Lowell. Wear apparently intended to buy or steal a gun from Rossknecht and possibly to supply him with heroin. The evidence suggested that an argument arose during the meeting, and Rossknecht, who had two guns with him, shot Lowell once with one of them. Wear, who was unarmed, then seized that gun, shot Rossknecht twice with it, and fled with the other gun. Lowell and Rossknecht died of their injuries. Was Wear's act of shooting Rossknecht "premeditated?" *See People v. Wear*, 44 Cal.App.5th 1007, 258 Cal.Rptr.3d 213 (2020).

Hypo 4: *Gun by the Bed*

Defendant's wife was diagnosed as having a schizoid personality. She complained of nervousness and told her doctor "I feel like hurting my children." She sometimes engaged in sadistic "discipline" of their children. When defendant husband was selected to attend an electronics school in another city for a few days, his wife greeted the news with a violent argument. Prior to his scheduled departure, he placed a loaded .22 caliber pistol on the window sill at the head of their bed so that his wife would feel safe while he was away. That same evening, a violent argument ensued and continued until four o'clock in the morning. The couple went to bed, but continued to argue. Wife kept yelling at defendant. He testified that he started to think about the children, "seeing my older son's feet what happened to them. I could see the bruises on him and Michael's chin was split open, four stitches. I didn't know what to do. I wanted to help my boys. Sometime in there she called me some kind of name. I kept thinking of this. During this time I either thought or felt—I thought of the gun, just thought of the gun. I am not sure whether I felt my hand move toward the gun—I saw my hand move, the next thing—the only thing I can recollect after that is right after the shots or right during the shots I saw the gun in my hand just pointed at my wife's head. She was still lying on her back—I mean her side. I could smell the gunpowder and I could hear something—it sounded like running water. I didn't know what it was at first, didn't realize what I'd done at first. Then I smelled it. I smelled blood before." On cross-examination, defendant estimated that five minutes elapsed between his wife's last remark and the shooting. Did defendant premeditate? *See Commonwealth v. Carroll*, 412 Pa. 525, 194 A.2d 911 (1963).

Hypo 5: *Shooting While High on Meth*

Crystal Brady, Andrea Larez, Kaprice Conde, and Julian Tafoya had been up for five days partying. They got into a car and began cruising around Roswell, New Mexico, where they lived, listening to loud music, smoking meth and marijuana, and drinking alcohol. Brady was driving the car, which belonged to Larez. The car had a standard transmission, which was unfamiliar to Brady, and at one point the occupants heard a loud sound, and the car stalled out. Right after the car stalled, Tafoya shot Larez repeatedly in the back of the head. Conde and Brady both testified that there was a sudden gunshot followed by more shots. A police officer in the area described the gunfire as multiple shots in fairly rapid succession, possibly with a short pause between the fourth and fifth shot. After the first shot, Brady observed that Larez had been shot and appeared to have died instantly from the wound. When asked what Brady was thinking after she saw that Larez had been shot, she testified that "she didn't think—it was all so sudden." Brady further testified that upon seeing that Larez had been shot, she turned toward the back of the car screaming and saw Tafoya's face. She did not remember him saying anything, but added that "he looked like a scared little punk," and that she thought he was really high. After being shot, Brady was able to exit the car and crawl away for help. Was Tafoya's killing of Larez "premeditated?" *See State v. Tafoya*, 285 P.3d 604, 2012–NMSC–030 (N.M. 2012).

State v. Davis

905 S.W.2d 921 (Mo. Ct. App. 1995).

CHARLES B. BLACKMAR, SENIOR JUDGE.

On the evening of Wednesday, December 2, 1992, Luther Blackwell, Demetrius Tabbs and the defendant were drinking copiously of beer intermingled with gin. Tabbs drove them in his newly acquired car to the central west end of St. Louis. During the ride one of the others told Tabbs that they were going to "jack" somebody. When the car reached the vicinity of Euclid and Maryland Plaza the group spied a couple on foot who turned out to be Natalie Hasty and Kevin Young. The defendant and Blackwell left the car and Tabbs drove one block west to Kings Highway. Tabbs testified that the defendant customarily carried a gun, which he concealed in the small of his back. He did not see him with the gun on this occasion, but did see the defendant reach for the small of his back as he left the car.

Hasty and Young were unloading groceries from their car in the parking lot at the rear of an apartment on Maryland Plaza. Blackwell approached Hasty, flourished a knife, and demanded her purse. He then grabbed the purse and she tried to hold on to it. At the same time the defendant headed toward Young. Just as soon as Hasty saw the person later identified as the defendant, she noticed that he was carrying a handgun. Hasty heard the sound of chains rattling and assumed that the defendant and Young were wrestling. The defendant said, "I want your money. Give me your wallet." She then heard three shots. While she was thus distracted Blackwell escaped with her purse. She then went to Young, who was lying on the ground. He and the defendant moved as much as 30 feet during the struggle. Young was mortally wounded and died before arriving at the hospital.

Food for Thought

Is the fact that Davis "formed a deliberate purpose of using the gun" the same thing as having a deliberate purpose to kill? Does the former lead ineluctably to the latter? Does this make a difference? What do you think?

Blackwell admitted the robbery, identifying the defendant as his companion. He testified for the state after a plea bargain. Tabbs also was apprehended at his home and testified for the state.

The defendant first argues that the evidence does not establish the element of deliberation which is essential to a first degree murder conviction. Hasty testified, however, that the defendant was carrying a handgun as he and Blackwell approached her and Young in the parking lot. The jury could have concluded that the defendant had formed a deliberate purpose of using the gun during his criminal enterprise if necessary to accomplish his ends.

Blackwell testified, furthermore, as follows:

> And when I snatched her purse, I seen a black male dude. I mean a black male jump up out of the car and wrestle with Reginald the defendant. And when he wrestled with Reginald, Reginald pulled the gun on him and shot him.

The defendant therefore made a decision to use the weapon he was carrying when he was confronted by his intended robbery victim. This demonstrates deliberation.

Food for Thought

If these facts establish "deliberation," what is impulsive conduct in Missouri, i.e. how do you distinguish first-degree murder from second-degree murder in that state? Would the result in this case have been different, in your view, if Missouri had been using Ohio's test for proof of aggravated murder?

The deliberation essential to a conviction of first degree murder need only be momentary. Perhaps the instruction language, "cool reflection" might be applied by some jurors in a manner more favorable to the defendant than the law strictly requires. The required reflection need be only momentary to establish deliberation.

Affirmed.

Hypo 1: *Boy at the Bridge*

A man crossing a bridge sees a young boy standing at the bridge railing and, for no apparent reason, pushes him into the water and the child drowns. Is this premeditated murder? Should it be? Does it make any difference if the boy struggles to resist the push and it takes a minute or two of fighting before the man is able to push him off the bridge? Does it make any difference if the man recognized the boy as his newspaper delivery person and had been angry at him for months because the morning paper was often thrown into the bushes and that he pushed him to teach him a lesson?

Hypo 2: *Firing at Police*

Uniformed police officers were executing a no-knock search warrant at Paul Lyons' apartment. The officers yelled "Police search" outside the apartment and, at the very same moment, broke down the front door with a battering ram. Lyons fired at the entering officers, killing one of them only a few feet inside his apartment. Is Lyons guilty of premeditated murder? *See State v. Lyons*, 340 N.C. 646, 459 S.E.2d 770 (1995).

Hypo 3: *Sixty Wounds*

Defendant, killed the ten-year-old daughter, Victoria, of the woman with whom he was living. The arresting officer found Victoria's body on the floor near her bed. He also found defendant's blood-spotted shorts on a chair in the living room, and a knife and defendant's socks, with blood encrusted on the soles, in the master bedroom. The victim's torn and bloodstained dress had been ripped from her, her clothes were found in various rooms of the house, there were bloody footprints matching the size of the victim's feet leading from the master bedroom to Victoria's room, and there was blood in almost every room of the house, including the kitchen, the floor of which appeared to have been mopped. Over 60 wounds were found on Victoria's body. Several of the wounds, including one extending from her rectum through her vagina, were post mortem. No evidence of sperm was found in the victim, on her underwear, or on the bed next to which she was found. Was there sufficient evidence on these facts of premeditation sufficient to establish premeditated murder? *See People v. Anderson*, 70 Cal. 2d 15, 447 P.2d 942, 73 Cal. Rptr. 550 (1968).

2. Voluntary Manslaughter

The offense of voluntary manslaughter is also an intentional killing, but it is an intentional killing which has been mitigated from murder to manslaughter due to the presence of adequate and sufficient provocation or other appropriate sorts of excuses for engaging in a killing act. Or, to put it another way, voluntary manslaughter is an intentional murder which includes additional circumstances that serve to negative the requisite element of malice needed to establish murder.

Given its mitigating status, voluntary manslaughter is usually not charged by the prosecution, but rather it is raised as a defense by the accused, i.e. "I killed the victim but the killing was the result of circumstances which mitigate the severity of the offense from murder to manslaughter." In most (but not all) jurisdictions, there are two distinct types of voluntary manslaughter: (1) provocation or "heat of passion" defenses; and (2) imperfect defenses.

a. Provocation or Heat of Passion Defense

One justification for mitigating an intentional homicide to manslaughter is when the defendant acted as a result of adequate "provocation" or in the "heat of passion."

Massachusetts v. Hinds

457 Mass. 83, 927 N.E.2d 1009 (2010).

GANTS, J.

On October 16, 1998, the defendant, in the kitchen of his mother's home, shot his sister, Patricia Melo, in the head, then walked outside and shot and killed his half-brother, Joseph Warren Beranger (Warren), and his sister-in-law, Mary Beranger (Mary). A jury convicted the defendant of the premeditated murder in the first degree of Warren, of murder in the second degree of Mary, of armed assault with intent to murder Melo, and of the assault and battery of Melo by means of a dangerous weapon.

The defendant appeals from his convictions. He argues that the judge erred in refusing to instruct the jury on voluntary manslaughter. We conclude that the evidence did not permit the jury to find the defendant guilty of voluntary manslaughter with respect to the killing of either Warren or Mary, and that the judge did not err in refusing to give such an instruction.

The evidence, viewed in the light most favorable to the Commonwealth, showed that the defendant lived with his eighty-seven year old mother, Mary Hinds (mother), at the two-family house she owned at 207 Charles Street (rear) in Cambridge. In March, 1998, the mother broke her hip and the defendant asked Melo if their mother could stay with her, because he was going to have heart bypass surgery. Their mother remained at Melo's house in Revere until October 8, 1998. On October 1, Warren and Mary arrived from California to stay at Melo's house for a few days before visiting Warren's relatives in Canada. On October 3, Warren, Mary, and Melo went to the mother's house to retrieve the mother's telephone and some of her clothes.

They did not have a key to the mother's first-floor apartment, and no one was home, so Warren opened the door by "picking" the lock.

That evening, Warren sent an e-mail to the defendant, stating:

> "Since you refused Ma's admission to her own home and have taken it upon yourself not to allow her access to her possessions at her convenience i.e. cordless phone and clothing, and since I have 'durable power of attorney,' I am exercising my rights of 'durable power of attorney,' I am putting the house up for sale in one week's time. Since she does not have access to her own home at her convenience, [there's] no need to have the house."
>
> Warren wrote that the defendant would have a right of first refusal to purchase the property.

On October 4, at approximately 11 A.M., the defendant spoke with a Cambridge police officer and reported that Warren had attempted to break into his mother's apartment. On October 7, after discussing the matter with a Cambridge police detective, the defendant applied for and obtained a temporary protective order which ordered Warren not to abuse or contact the defendant, to stay at least one hundred yards away from him, and to stay away from their mother's residence at 207 Charles Street. On October 8, while Melo was at work, the defendant, with his brother Charles, took their mother out to lunch and brought her back to her own house, where she remained until the killings on October 16.

On the morning of October 16, Warren, Mary, and Melo went together to the Cambridge Division of the District Court Department to attend the hearing to determine whether the temporary protective order would become permanent. At the hearing, Warren was represented by counsel; the defendant appeared *pro se*. The defendant told the judge, "My mother made a statement to the whole family, 'As long she [sic] has that house and she's alive, I have a home,' and Warren was trying to sell the home over her head." The judge replied, "You have to be in fear of imminent physical harm, not just imminent sale of real estate," and ordered the protective order dismissed.

It's Latin to Me

Shortened from *in propria persona*, *pro se* means "in his own person," i.e. to represent oneself (without an attorney).

After the hearing, Warren, Mary, and Melo stood on the corner one block away from the mother's house, waiting for the police to arrive to assist them in entering the house so they could bring the mother to Melo's house. After Warren twice telephoned the police and no police officer arrived, Melo decided to go into the house alone and pick up her mother; Warren and Mary waited at the corner. The defendant, who had returned earlier to his mother's house after the hearing, went outside to his automobile to find cigarettes he kept in the trunk. He observed Warren and Mary at the corner, saw his gun in the trunk, concealed the gun in a briefcase that was also in the trunk, and returned to the house carrying the briefcase.

When Melo arrived at the house, the defendant was in the doorway and asked her what she was doing there. She said she was there to see her mother, and he allowed her inside. When she spoke with her mother in the kitchen, the mother asked her, "What are you doing with Warren?" Melo replied, in an apparent reference to the defendant, "Well, you don't know what your golden boy did, do you?" Melo explained that she had been at the court house because of the protective order. The mother said that the defendant's former wife had told her that the defendant got a protective order because Warren had hit him. Melo said, "I was there; nothing happened." The defendant said, "Oh, yeah?" pulled a gun from his sweater vest, and shot her in the head from six to seven feet away. When she tried to move, he told her, "Stay down or I'll shoot you again."

The defendant then left the house, walked to the corner, and fired two shots at Mary, striking her twice in the head. He then shot Warren in the head and back. Mary died that day; Warren died from his gunshot wounds on October 23.

After shooting Warren and Mary, the defendant walked past Kevin Christie, who had been delivering a package and heard the gunshots. After Christie spoke to the defendant, the defendant replied, "They'll probably fry my ass now." Christie told him, "No, you could say self-defense." The defendant said, "Yeah, right," and "kind of chuckled" as he walked past Christie.

The defendant returned to the house, telephoned the 911 police emergency line, and told the dispatcher he had just killed his brother and sister-in-law, and shot his sister. When asked if they were injured, he replied, "I hope they're dead." While on the telephone with the dispatcher, the defendant said to Melo, "I wish I could have killed you, Patty." He said he would be standing outside in front of the house waiting for a police officer.

The defendant claims on appeal that an instruction on voluntary manslaughter, based on both reasonable provocation and excessive use of force in self-defense, was warranted by the evidence, and that the judge erred in refusing the defendant's request for such an instruction.[11] We conclude that a verdict of voluntary manslaughter was not supported by the evidence at trial, and that the judge correctly declined to give such an instruction.

In deciding whether a defendant is entitled to a voluntary manslaughter instruction based on either reasonable provocation or excessive use of force in self-defense, we view the evidence in the light most favorable to the defendant. Under that view of the evidence, which is based in large part on the defendant's testimony, the defendant had long feared Warren. Warren had attempted to break into the house the defendant shared with his mother on October 3, and threatened the defendant's life during their telephone call later that evening. The defendant had obtained a protective order against Warren because he feared for his life, and after the

---

11 In his final instructions, the judge told the jury they could consider reasonable provocation, but only as to the charge of armed assault with intent to murder. The judge said that for the Commonwealth to prove armed assault with intent to murder, it had to prove beyond a reasonable doubt the absence of the mitigating circumstance of provocation, "meaning that the defendant faced circumstances which would, in an ordinary person, produce such a state of anger, fright, or passion as to eclipse the person's capacity for restraint."

protective order had been dismissed and the defendant had returned home, he remained in fear and told his mother, "They can come in and get you; that they can come in and kill me if they want." At the time of the killings, the defendant was "kind of disoriented"; he believed that Warren, Mary, and Melo were there to take his mother from the house against her will, and that he had "no idea" what Warren would do to him.

The defendant tried to block Melo's entry into the house, but she knocked the defendant down by hitting the door as he tried to close it. When the defendant stood up and went into the kitchen, Melo was there standing "nose to nose" with the mother, pointing her finger at her, using profanity, and screaming that she had "started all this" and "was going to a nursing home." The mother, who was seated in a rocking chair, lost color in her face and was holding her chest and struggling to breathe. The defendant yelled to Melo to "knock it off." Melo would not stop screaming, and the defendant, who then had the gun in his hand, shot her. He turned to the mother and told her that he would protect her from harm.

With the gun still in his hand, he went outside to the corner to "talk some sense into" Warren and Mary, asking them, "Why are you guys fuckin' Ma and I around like this? Why don't you just leave us alone and go away?" Mary then put both hands on her pocketbook, as if she were trying to open it, and he told her to take her hands away from the pocketbook. When she failed to do so, he told her again, and the gun "went off." Warren then pushed his coat back with his right hand, and the defendant thought that Warren had a gun in his belt or back pocket. He told Warren to move his hand away, but Warren reached his hand to his back again. The defendant thought that Warren was reaching for a gun when he fired.

In *Commonwealth v. Acevedo*, 446 Mass. 435, 443, 845 N.E.2d 274 (2006), we defined the mitigating circumstance of reasonable provocation:

> "Voluntary manslaughter is an unlawful killing 'arising not from malice, but "from sudden passion induced by reasonable provocation, sudden combat, or excessive force in self-defense." ' Reasonable provocation is provocation that 'would have been likely to produce in an ordinary person such a state of passion, anger, fear, fright, or nervous excitement as would eclipse his capacity for reflection or restraint.' A jury instruction on reasonable provocation is warranted 'if there is evidence of provocation deemed adequate in law to cause the accused to lose his self-control in the heat of passion, and if the killing followed the provocation before sufficient time had elapsed for the accused's temper to cool.' The defendant's actions must be 'both objectively and subjectively reasonable. That is, the jury must be able to infer that a reasonable person would have become sufficiently provoked and would not have "cooled off" by the time of the homicide, and that in fact a defendant was provoked and did not cool off.' "

At trial, defense counsel argued that the defendant was provoked by Melo yelling obscenities at the mother. While Melo's purported conduct may warrant an instruction regarding reasonable provocation with respect to the charge of armed assault with intent to murder, it cannot support a voluntary manslaughter instruction because the "provocation must come from the victim," in this case either Mary or Warren. There was no evidence that the defendant had been provoked by Mary. Even assuming that the evidence at trial was sufficient to support the inference that the defendant was provoked by Warren, and had not cooled off by the time he shot him, the only conduct that arguably could have provoked a reasonable person was Warren's purported death threat on October 3, and a reasonable person would have cooled off in the thirteen days that had elapsed before the defendant shot and killed Warren.

Food for Thought

Do you agree? Would a reasonable person really have cooled off from a death threat after 13 days? Was that threat 13 days before really Warren's last provocative act directed at Hinds?

We decline the defendant's invitation to interpret reasonable provocation as the subjective experience of provocation by a person whose anxiety has resulted in paranoia.

The excessive use of force in self-defense is a separate mitigating circumstance that may justify a conviction of voluntary manslaughter.

The defendant, however, is not entitled to an instruction on the excessive use of force in self-defense where there is no evidence that, at a minimum, the defendant was entitled to use some force in self-defense. Here, there was no evidence of reasonable grounds to believe that the defendant was being attacked or about to be attacked and that his personal safety was in immediate danger when he confronted Mary and Warren; the only evidence was that they were waiting outside for Melo and the mother so they could drive to Melo's home together. Nor would a reasonable person have understood their purported hand movements to suggest that they were reaching for a gun to shoot the defendant. The defendant shot Mary first, and there was no evidence that Mary possessed a gun or opened her pocketbook. There was evidence that Warren owned a firearm, but not that he brought the firearm with him to Massachusetts or to the court house that morning. Nor is there any evidence that the defendant attempted to retreat or avoid using physical force before shooting Mary and Warren. He chose to leave his mother's home and confront them on the street corner with gun in hand after he had shot his sister; he did not seek to avoid them.

Take Note

This is not the law in every jurisdiction. Quite often, for example, an actor's use of deadly force in response to another person's *excessive* use of deadly force directed at him or her is treated as a complete—not a mitigating—defense (self defense).

Because the defendant was not entitled to use any degree of force in self-defense in confronting Mary and Warren, he did not deserve a voluntary manslaughter instruction regarding the excessive use of force in self-defense. The judge did not err in refusing to provide the jury with such an instruction.

Judgments affirmed.

Point for Discussion

Model Penal Code

The Model Penal Code also contains a "heat of passion" provision (although it does not refer to the provision in that way and does not limit the application to "passion" situations). Section 210.3, manslaughter, provides as follows: "Criminal homicide constitutes manslaughter when a homicide which would otherwise be murder is committed under the influence of extreme mental or emotional disturbance for which there is reasonable explanation or excuse. The reasonableness of such explanation or excuse shall be determined from the viewpoint of a person in the actor's situation under the circumstances as he believes them to be." Is this a better approach to this issue than that taken in *Hinds*?

Suprenant v. State

925 N.E.2d 1280 (Ind. Ct. App. 2010).

BAILEY, JUDGE.

Jack Edwin Suprenant, Jr. ("Suprenant") appeals his conviction and sixty-year sentence for Murder, a felony. We affirm.

Suprenant, Kerry Bruckman, and Bruckman's three children (two of which [*sic*] were fathered by Suprenant) lived together in Gary, Indiana. On September 16, 2006, after the couple had argued for several days, in part over Bruckman's involvement with a mutual friend, Bruckman stated her intention to leave Suprenant and began gathering her clothes. Suprenant tried to persuade Bruckman to stay; when his efforts failed, Suprenant stabbed Bruckman repeatedly. Bruckman's screams caused the children to run into their mother's bedroom, where they witnessed some of the attack. Suprenant chased the children back to their bedrooms and continued his attack on Bruckman. Ultimately, Suprenant inflicted sixty-one wounds (including forty-nine stab wounds) upon Bruckman and she died.

Suprenant was tried before a jury on the charge of Murder. He was convicted and sentenced to sixty years imprisonment. He now appeals.

Indiana's Voluntary Manslaughter statute provides:

(a) A person who knowingly or intentionally:

(1) kills another human being; or

(2) kills a fetus that has attained viability;

while acting under sudden heat commits voluntary manslaughter, a Class B felony. However, the offense is a Class A felony if it is committed by means of a deadly weapon.

(b) The existence of sudden heat is a mitigating factor that reduces what otherwise would be murder under section 1(1) of this chapter to voluntary manslaughter.

The statute specifies that sudden heat is a mitigating factor to Murder, as opposed to an element of Voluntary Manslaughter. Although Voluntary Manslaughter is a lesser-included offense of Murder, it is an atypical example of a lesser-included offense. Sudden heat must be separately proved and, therefore, if there is no serious evidentiary dispute over sudden heat, it is error for a trial court to instruct a jury on voluntary manslaughter in addition to murder.

"Sudden heat" is characterized as anger, rage, resentment, or terror sufficient to obscure the reason of an ordinary person, preventing deliberation and premeditation, excluding malice, and rendering a person incapable of cool reflection. Anger alone is not sufficient to support an instruction on sudden heat. Nor will words alone "constitute sufficient provocation to warrant a jury instruction on voluntary manslaughter," and this is "especially true" when the words at issue are not intentionally designed to provoke the defendant, such as fighting words.

Food for Thought

Is this a sensible rule, that words alone do not suffice to establish provocation for mitigation purposes? *Should* this be the rule? Are words and actions inevitably that different?

In addition to the requirement of something more than "mere words," the provocation must be "sufficient to obscure the reason of an ordinary man," an objective as opposed to subjective standard. Finally, Voluntary Manslaughter involves an "impetus to kill" which arises "suddenly."

The trial court refused to instruct the jury on Voluntary Manslaughter, concluding that Bruckman's words to Suprenant were insufficient provocation for sudden heat. Where the trial court rejects a Voluntary Manslaughter instruction based on a lack of evidence of sudden heat, we review the trial court's decision for an abuse of discretion.

The parties agree that the record discloses evidence that Suprenant became enraged; they disagree as to the existence of a serious evidentiary dispute such that the jury could conclude that the lesser offense was committed but the greater was not. In arguing that sufficient evidence existed to support the giving of a Voluntary Manslaughter instruction, Suprenant claims that he "lost it" when Bruckman failed to deny that she had been unfaithful to him and was gathering things to move out of the residence with their children. He argues that the act of gathering belongings went beyond mere words. In response, the State points to the legal insufficiency of mere words and also to evidence that shows deliberation and cool reflection inconsistent with sudden heat.

Perigo v. State, 541 N.E.2d 936, 938 (Ind.1989) involved the killing of a woman and her fetus after she admitted to the defendant that "their relationship was finished," she had engaged in sexual intercourse with another man, and did not know by whom she was pregnant. The defendant had unsuccessfully argued to the trial court that confessions of illicit sex are sufficient provocation for a Voluntary Manslaughter verdict. On appeal, the Court reiterated the principle that "words alone are not sufficient provocation to reduce murder to manslaughter", but nonetheless recognized, "[i]n some circumstances, words may be combined with actions engendering sufficient provocation to reduce an offense from murder to manslaughter."

Subsequently, the Court has recognized that discovery of alleged infidelity can "introduce the element of sudden heat." *Evans v. State,* 727 N.E.2d 1072, 1077 (Ind.2000). In *Evans,* the defendant had witnessed his recent girlfriend having sexual intercourse with another man, placing "sudden heat" in issue; yet the State had negated the presence of sudden heat by showing that the defendant had, after witnessing the tryst, gone downstairs, armed himself with knives, cut the telephone line, gone back upstairs, stood outside the bedroom for over a minute, and then struggled with and killed the man. *See also Ford v. State,* 704 N.E.2d 457, 460 (Ind.1998) (observing that there was substantial evidence that a husband was not acting under sudden heat when, three days after discovering his wife's affair, he took a pistol and shot her twice at close range); *Horan v. State,* 682 N.E.2d 502, 507 (Ind.1997) (there was no serious evidentiary dispute as to whether husband was acting in sudden heat when he beat his wife's lover to death after an earlier confrontation and beating).

Here, the alleged provocation was comprised of words ending a relationship accompanied by preparations to leave. Although there was some non-verbal action by the victim, we do not find that the lawful conduct of gathering ones belongings goes so far beyond "mere words" as to constitute "sudden heat" justifying a Voluntary Manslaughter instruction.

Furthermore, the record is replete with evidence that the impetus to kill did not "suddenly" arise in response to a contemporaneous event. The couple had been arguing at length. Earlier on the day of Bruckman's death, Suprenant had told his mother that Bruckman planned to leave and take the children. During that conversation, he was alternately calm and angry. He had also told his father of Bruckman's alleged infidelity.

Food for Thought

Do you agree? Do you think that a reasonable person in Suprenant's situation at the moment he began stabbing Bruckman would be capable of "cool reflection"? Is that the moment the court should look to, namely when he *began* to stab her?

Most compelling, Suprenant stopped his attack on Bruckman when confronted by the children, forced each of them into their rooms, and returned to resume stabbing his victim. [When] Suprenant's screaming children confronted him, he had ample time to reflect upon the heinousness of his actions and seek help for the children's mother. He chose not to do so. We find no abuse of discretion in the trial court's rejection of a Voluntary Manslaughter instruction.

Affirmed.

Points for Discussion

a. Proving Lack of Provocation

As a matter of due process, the prosecution has the burden of proving the existence of all of the elements of a crime beyond a reasonable doubt. *In re Winship*, 397 U.S. 358, 90 S.Ct. 1068, 25 L.Ed.2d 368 (1970). As a result, because the traditional provocation defense to a murder charge has been viewed as serving to negative the element of malice aforethought that is requisite for a murder conviction (thus mitigating the offense to voluntary manslaughter), in jurisdictions that use this traditional defense, the Supreme Court has held that—when provocation is offered as a (mitigating) defense—the burden of proof is upon the prosecution to prove beyond a reasonable doubt that the defendant was not provoked. *Mullaney v. Wilbur*, 421 U.S. 684, 95 S.Ct. 1881, 44 L.Ed.2d 508 (1975).

b. Extreme Emotional Disturbance

In jurisdictions where a version of the provocation defense has been enacted in such a way that it does *not* serve to mitigate a finding of malice necessary to establish murder, the burden of proof of establishing provocation may be placed upon the defendant. *Patterson v. New York*, 432 U.S. 197, 97 S.Ct. 2319, 53 L.Ed.2d 281 (1977) (upholding a New York "extreme emotional disturbance" mitigating defense which placed the burden of proof on the defendant where that defense served to mitigate second-degree murder which did not have malice aforethought as an element).

Hypo 1: *Provocation Without Passion*

Alice learns that her husband is having an adulterous relationship with Lorena. A reasonable person would have been outraged by the news, but Alice was not outraged. However, because she hates Lorena, Alice used the news as an opportunity to kill her. Is Alice entitled to a mitigation of her crime to manslaughter?

Hypo 2: *Mistaken Passion*

Bob tells Randy that he has been having an adulterous relationship with Randy's wife. Although Randy believes Bob, it was not true. There was no such adulterous relationship. In a fit of anger resulting from this communication, however, Randy kills Bob. Is Randy entitled to mitigation to manslaughter?

Hypo 3: *Relevance of Defendant's Characteristics*

Defendant, a man with only one leg, was standing next to a park bench on crutches. The victim, just prior to the killing, maliciously knocked one of defendant's crutches out from under him. In a fit of responsive anger, defendant stabbed the victim with a knife, killing him. Were the victim's actions sufficient to constitute adequate provocation? Should the judge/jury apply a reasonable person standard, in determining whether the provocation was sufficient, or should it apply a "reasonable one-legged man on crutches" standard? *See Rex v. Raney* [1942] 29 Crim. App. 14.

Hypo 4: *Reasonable Impotent?*

Bedder, who was sexually impotent, tried in vain to have sex with a prostitute. She jeered at him and attempted to get away. Defendant tried to prevent her from leaving, but she slapped him in the face and punched him in the stomach. At this point, defendant took out a knife and stabbed the prostitute to her to death. Is Bedder entitled to a voluntary manslaughter instruction if he is tried for murder? *See Bedder v. DPP*, [1954] 2 All E.R. 801, [1954] 1 W.L.R. 1119, 38 Cr.App. 133.

Hypo 5: *Cultural Provocation Defense?*

Oscar Trejo was quarreling with his cousin Ricardo Acosta. Both were intoxicated. After some friendly insults, Rosales insulted Trejo's mother by referring to her as a prostitute. Trejo broke a beer bottle on the sidewalk and threatened to "stick" Rosales unless Rosales stopped making such insults. When Rosales again called Trejo the "son of [a] whore mother," Trejo stabbed Rosales in the neck with the broken bottle. Rosales bled to death before he reached a hospital. At his trial for murder, Trejo's defense was that, although he killed his cousin, he was guilty of voluntary manslaughter, not murder. He argued that Rosales's insults aroused a heat of passion in him that negated the malice necessary for second degree murder. He presented expert evidence that an accusation of prostitution by one's own mother in Trejo's Mexican culture was likely to result in violence. He also tried to argue that references to Trejo's mother as a prostitute were especially inflammatory because certain members of his family had been prostitutes. The trial judge did not permit him to make the latter argument, holding that it was irrelevant to a provocation defense. Did the trial judge err? *See People v. Trejo*, 2008 WL 2132367 (Cal.App. 2 Dist. 2008), *cert. denied*, 556 U.S. 1108, 129 S.Ct. 1589, 173 L.Ed.2d 682 (2009).

Hypo 6: *The Klansman*

During the Summer of 2005, a former Klu Klux Klan member, Edgar Ray Killen, was convicted of killing three civil rights workers in 1964. The evidence showed that the victims were brutally beaten and shot, and that their bodies were buried in an earthen dam. The case was complicated by the age of the evidence, fading witness recollections, and by the fact that no witness was able to positively place Killen at the scene of the crime. The trial ended with a conviction of manslaughter as a lesser included offense of murder, rather than murder itself. Given the nature of the killings, how do you explain a conviction for manslaughter instead of murder? *See Killen v. State*, 958 So.2d 172 (Miss. 2007).

---

b. Imperfect Defense

An "imperfect defense" arises when a defendant commits an intentional murder, but does so under circumstances in which he or she honestly believes—unreasonably—fit within the parameters of a legal defense, usually self-defense. Most, but not all, jurisdictions recognize the existence of imperfect defenses. In those that do, when a complete defense is imperfectly established, i.e. every element is met except reasonableness, the crime is mitigated from murder to voluntary manslaughter.

State v. Ordway

261 Kan. 776, 934 P.2d 94 (1997).

ALLEGRUCCI, JUSTICE:

At the Kansas home of Clarence and Betty Ordway, the police found Clarence's deceased body. He died as a result of a shotgun wound to the back that caused extensive damage to his left lung and heart. There was no evidence of defensive injuries to his hands or feet. A few days later, New York police found defendant Kim Ordway, Clarence and Betty's son, sitting in his parent's car. A loaded shotgun was found on the front passenger seat, and a serrated kitchen knife was found under the driver's seat of the car. Clarence Ordway's wallet and two rings were found in a backpack in the back seat. Betty Ordway's body, wrapped in a tarp and a blanket, was found in the trunk. She had also died as a result of shotgun wounds in her right chest and one entry wound in her back, which caused damage to her lungs, heart, liver, ribs, vertebrae, and aorta. In addition, she had bruises, lacerations, abrasions, and fractures caused by impact with a blunt object. There were bruising and swelling around the left eyebrow; five lacerations on her head; bruising, swelling, and abrasion of the left forearm; and broken bones in both forearms. The pathologist's opinion was that the injuries to her forearms were defensive wounds.

The jury was instructed on the elements of first-and second-degree murder with respect to each count. Defendant's counsel requested that the jury be instructed on voluntary manslaughter, and the district court refused. Ordway contends that a voluntary manslaughter instruction was required because the evidence showed that he killed his parents without malice and for the purpose of preventing them from harming his children.

Voluntary manslaughter is defined in K.S.A. 21–3403: "Voluntary manslaughter is the intentional killing of a human being committed: (a) Upon a sudden quarrel or in the heat of passion; or (b) upon an unreasonable but honest belief that circumstances existed that justified deadly force." K.S.A. 21–3211 provides: "A person is justified in the use of force against an aggressor when and to the extent it appears to him and he reasonably believes that such conduct is necessary to defend himself or another against such aggressor's imminent use of unlawful force."

Ordway argues that a voluntary manslaughter instruction should have been given because the evidence showed that he killed his parents upon an unreasonable but honest belief that circumstances existed that justified the use of deadly force against them in the defense of his children. There was evidence to the effect that it appeared to Ordway that his use of force against his parents was necessary to defend his children from unlawful force being used against them by his parents. There is no evidence or even contention that his belief was reasonable.

K.S.A. 21–3403(b) defines voluntary manslaughter as an intentional killing upon an unreasonable but honest belief that circumstances existed that justified deadly force under 21–3211. K.S.A. 21–3211 provides that the circumstances justify the use of force when a defendant reasonably believes that its use is necessary to defend others. When the two statutes are read together, the unreasonable belief element of 21–3403 must be reconciled with the reasonable belief element of 21–3211. It seems that this may be accomplished by a plain reading. That is, if the reasonable belief that force was necessary, which is the substance of 21–3211, is substituted for the defense-of-self-or-others as designated in 21–3403(b), the latter provides that voluntary manslaughter is an intentional killing upon a defendant's unreasonable but honest belief that he or she reasonably believed the use of force was necessary to defend others. In other words, the 21–3211 reasonableness of the belief that deadly force was justified is irrelevant because the 21–3403(b) belief is unreasonable. Although Ordway could not qualify for acquittal under the perfect defense of defense of self or others under 21–3211, the reasonableness element of 21–3211 should not prevent a trial court's giving an instruction on the lesser included offense of voluntary manslaughter.

With regard to a defense-of-others instruction, this court has stated that the evidence must support affirmative findings by a rational factfinder to the subjective question whether defendant honestly believed his action was necessary to defend others as well as to the objective question whether his belief was reasonable. In a case such as the present one, however, where the defendant is seeking an instruction on the lesser included offense of voluntary manslaughter rather than asserting the affirmative defense of defense of others, the objective component of defense of others should be immaterial. Both elements in the offense of voluntary manslaughter as defined in 21–3403(b) are subjective. The defendant's belief must be sincerely held, and it must be unreasonable. For this reason, the "objective elements" of 21–3211—an aggressor, imminence, and unlawful force—would not come in for consideration.

Legislative history of K.S.A. 21–3403 shows that the definition of voluntary manslaughter was expanded by the addition of subsection (b) in 1992. Until then, the statute defined voluntary manslaughter as an intentional killing upon a sudden quarrel or in the heat of passion. Notes on proposed criminal code revisions were attached to the minutes of the Senate Judiciary Committee from March 22, 1992, which contained the following comments about subsection (b) of 21–3403:

> "(b) 'Imperfect right to self-defense' manslaughter
>
> "This new subsection covers intentional killings that result from an unreasonable but honest belief that deadly force was justified in self-defense. In essence, the defendant meets the subjective, but not the objective, test for self-defense. This so-called 'imperfect right to self-defense' is recognized in various forms. Kansas apparently recognizes it for unintentional killings under involuntary manslaughter. The Model Penal Code also follows this approach. Some states, e.g. Illinois, recognize this partial defense for intentional killings.
>
> "Applying this partial defense to intentional killings is simply a recognition of the practical realities of plea bargaining and jury verdicts. Often it is unjust to prosecute and convict such killers of murder and it is equally unjust to acquit them. This new subsection provides a middle category that is theoretically sound and legitimizes the realities of plea bargaining and jury verdicts."

There is no express indication in the note to 21–3403(b) that there was any contemplation that the subsection's unreasonable belief might be based on psychotic delusions (or some other form of mental illness). Nor does examination of the Kansas case law cited in the note indicate that application of subsection (b) to cases where a homicide defendant denied criminal responsibility due to mental illness was envisioned.

Food for Thought

If Ordway, instead of being psychotic and delusional, had instead stupidly misinterpreted his parents' actions and honestly (but stupidly) believed that these actions were aimed at harming his children, would he be entitled to acquittal on both charges of murder due to the existence of an imperfect defense?

In Illinois, the offense known as second-degree murder includes the elements of Kansas' voluntary manslaughter offense. The Illinois intermediate appellate court considered the "unreasonable but honest belief" mitigation provision of the statute in *People v. Aliwoli*, 238 Ill. App. 3d 602, 179 Ill. Dec. 515, 606 N.E.2d 347 (1992). The defendant in that case was charged with attempted first-degree murder of three police officers when he shot and wounded them trying to avoid being stopped for a traffic violation. Defense counsel asserted an insanity defense, but defendant testified that he acted in self-defense. The appellate court affirmed the trial court's refusing to give an instruction on second-degree murder for several reasons. One reason was that the court found "no evidence of mitigation in the case at bar that justifies the giving of the instruction even if the crime of attempted second degree murder existed in Illinois. Defendant failed to validly prove a sudden and intense passion or that he was seriously provoked by the officers' routine stop for passing a school bus. The evidence adduced at trial was that defendant was either insane or that he had a longstanding mental illness, neither of which is a mitigating factor under the statute. An unproved insanity defense was not intended to be a mitigating factor in the crime of second degree murder. The predatory conduct of the defendant in searching out his victims would negate the notion of self-defense."

We conclude that K.S.A. 21–3403(b) has no application where a defendant raises the defense of insanity, and more specifically, the "unreasonable but honest belief" necessary to support the "imperfect right to self-defense manslaughter" cannot be based upon a psychotic delusion.

Affirmed.

Hypo 1: *When Defense Available?*

A victim was found brutally murdered and forensic evidence showed that she had been sexually assaulted before her death. Witnesses saw her leave a bar with defendant the night before. Defendant admitted that he drove her home. Supposedly, as she left his car, she took a steak knife from her purse and held it at her side. Defendant claimed that he was scared, although the victim did not actually threaten him with the knife, but mentioned something about her "old man" being around. Defendant claimed he then "kicked" her from his car when she stated that she wanted to "hurt somebody." On these facts, does defendant have a right to an imperfect self-defense instruction when faced with a first-degree murder charge? *See People v. Stitely*, 35 Cal. 4th 514, 108 P.3d 182, 26 Cal. Rptr. 3d 1, *cert. denied*, 546 U.S. 865, 126 S.Ct. 164, 163 L.Ed.2d 151 (2005).

Hypo 2: *Imperfect Battered Spouse Defense?*

Defendant Karla Porter contracted with a third-party to kill her abusive husband. Convicted of first degree murder, she claims on appeal that because she believed she was in imminent danger from her husband even though she felt no such fear on the day of the murder, she was entitled to an imperfect self-defense jury instruction at trial. Does this argument make sense? *See Porter v. State*, 455 Md. 220, 166 A.3d 1044 (2017).

B. Unintentional Killings

The typical set of unintentional killings found in an American jurisdiction's crimes code consists of second-degree murder, felony-murder, and involuntary or reckless manslaughter.

Again, as mentioned previously, it is important to be aware that there is great variability in each state's homicide provisions. In some states, for example, the residual category of murder (sometimes called second-degree or, in some states, third-degree murder) is treated as the equivalent of an intentional killing, albeit as a lesser included offense of first-degree murder. In some states, there is no felony-murder offense at all. And in some states, there are additional homicide offenses which are deemed to be equivalent or less serious in moral culpability to involuntary manslaughter, e.g. negligent homicide or homicide by vehicle.

1. Unpremeditated Murder

At common law, as previously noted, the crime of murder involved a homicide committed with "malice aforethought." Malice could be express or implied. When implied, often these crimes involved unintentional killings that were committed by someone whose conduct manifested gross recklessness or an extreme indifference to the value of human life.

This type of murder is called different things in different jurisdictions. Most often, it is deemed "second-degree murder." In common law terms, it is referred to as "depraved heart murder"; in Model Penal Code terms, § 210.2, the crime is reckless murder committed "under circumstances manifesting extreme indifference to the value of human life." Sometimes, it is simply denominated "murder" (implying the absence of premeditation or the specific intent to kill found in "first-degree" or "premeditated" murder definitions).

State v. Burley

137 N.H. 286, 627 A.2d 98 (1993).

BATCHELDER, JUSTICE.

On January 7, 1989, the defendant was at home with his ex-wife, Debbie Glines, with whom he had reconciled. He drank at least six beers between noon and 6:00 p.m. At approximately 6:30 p.m., he telephoned 911 requesting an ambulance for a gunshot wound. The police and ambulance crews arrived to find Ms. Glines lying on the kitchen floor with a gunshot wound on the right side of her head, from which she eventually died.

The defendant told the officers on the scene that he had been cleaning a .22 caliber semi-automatic handgun when it accidentally discharged. At the station the defendant explained that he had been keeping the handgun and a .22 caliber rifle for a friend. He stated that he retrieved the gun and a loaded clip of ammunition from a closet, placed them on tables in the living room, went to the kitchen for a beer, and took a cotton swab from the bathroom to clean the gun, which he admitted he had cleaned two weeks before. He loaded the gun, knowing he had made it ready to fire, before getting the beer. After watching television for twenty minutes, he picked up the gun and went to sit on the living room floor at the entryway to the kitchen. He knew that his ex-wife was in the kitchen. The gun went off, he stated, as he was cleaning excess oil from it, with the gun in his left hand and a finger in the trigger housing. He acknowledged familiarity with the operation of a .45 caliber semi-automatic, which is functionally similar to a .22.

A search of the defendant's apartment revealed two spent bullet casings in a garbage bag. No cotton swabs were found in the living room or kitchen. The defendant agreed to re-enact the shooting at his apartment. Although at first stating that he did not know what had happened to the empty casing, when the officers told him it had been found in the trash, he admitted that he must have thrown it away. He admitted that he had occasionally "dry-fired" the gun by aiming the unloaded weapon at articles around the room. He was unable to tell the officers where they might find the clip to the .22, which they had been unsuccessful in locating.

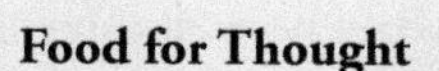

Food for Thought

Would it have made a difference which version of his story the jury believed? How so?

Several days later the defendant returned to the police station after locating the clip. It had apparently been in his jacket pocket and had fallen out at his mother's house later on the night of the shooting. At that time, he admitted, after being told of a bullet found lodged in his wall, that the second shell found in the trash came from his having fired the rifle in the apartment two days before shooting his ex-wife. He had been "joking around with it and it discharged." Ultimately, the defendant admitted he had not been cleaning the handgun when he shot his ex-wife, although he denied he had been dry-firing it. He stated that he "was fooling around with it on the floor and it went off." In all, he gave the police three different versions of how he had been holding the gun that night.

The defendant was tried on the charge of second degree murder. He requested and was granted a lesser included offense instruction for manslaughter and for negligent homicide.

The indictment charged that the "defendant committed the crime of second degree murder by causing the death of his wife under circumstances manifesting an extreme indifference to the value of human life, by shooting her in the head with a pistol." The defendant argues that, as extreme indifference represents a greater degree of culpability than recklessness, additional factual allegations must appear in the indictment. The indictment informed the defendant that he was charged with recklessly, under circumstances manifesting extreme indifference to the value of human life, causing his ex-wife's death on a specific date by shooting her in the head. This was constitutionally sufficient.

Food for Thought

What is the difference between acting "recklessly" or acting with "extreme indifference to the value of human life"? Is there a difference?

The defendant next argues that the evidence was insufficient to prove the element of extreme indifference. We will uphold the verdict unless, viewing the evidence and all reasonable inferences in the light most favorable to the State, no reasonable trier of fact could have found guilt beyond a reasonable doubt. In a prosecution for second degree murder charging extreme indifference to the value of human life, "the existence and extent of disregard manifested" are for the jury to determine on the facts of the case.

The evidence here showed, *inter alia*, that the defendant was familiar with the operation of a semi-automatic handgun, that he knew he had loaded the .22, and that he knew his ex-wife was in the next room. He had been drinking beer all afternoon and his blood alcohol content nearly five hours after the shooting was .15. At the time of the shooting, he was sitting with his elbows resting on raised knees with the barrel of a gun he knew to be loaded pointing into the kitchen where his ex-wife was located. The gun was cocked and ready to fire, and the defendant's finger was in the trigger housing. A firearms expert testified that due to its safety features the gun could not have fired without simultaneously gripping the safety on the back of the handle and squeezing the trigger. The defendant, who had told the police he knew not to point a gun at anyone, finally admitted that he had been "fooling around" with it after consistently lying by saying he had been cleaning it. On all the evidence the jury was warranted in finding that the defendant's conduct occurred under circumstances manifesting extreme indifference to the value of human life and in thereby finding him guilty of second degree murder.

Affirmed.

Hypo 1: *Russian Roulette*

Three teenage boys are playing Russian Roulette. They insert a single bullet in a gun that can be loaded with six bullets. One boy spins the cylinder, places the gun to another boy's head, and pulls the trigger. The gun discharges, killing the boy. The remaining two boys, who never intended to kill their friend, are horrified. Is it possible to say that they have committed murder in the "purposeful" or "knowing" sense? Have they committed reckless murder as in *Burley*? Argue the case for the prosecution. How might the defense respond? What facts makes this a "murder case?" Is it the way the gun was loaded? The way the "game" was played? Something else? *See Commonwealth v. Malone*, 354 Pa. 180, 47 A.2d 445, 447 (1946).

Hypo 2: *Shooting to Scare*

Burkman had a stormy relationship with the victim, Kathryn Burns. On the day in question, Burkman argued with her about whether she was having an affair with a co-worker. At some point, Burkman retrieved a gun from the linen closet and threw it on the bed in front of Burns who picked up the gun, looked at it, and pulled back the hammer. Burkman asked her why she pulled the hammer back—did she want to kill herself? Burns simply shrugged. Burkman then waved the gun in front of her face and yelled at her that she should kill herself. Intending to scare Burns, Burkman aimed the gun at a pillow behind her and fired. The bullet accidentally struck and killed her. Is Burkman guilty of murder? *See Cook v. Maryland*, 118 Md. App. 404, 702 A.2d 971 (Ct. Spec. App. 1997).

Hypo 3: *Swerving as Killing*

Johnson went to a birthday party at a friend's house. Rogers, another guest, argued with Johnson all evening. After midnight, the two threatened to attack each other with weapons, but both ultimately decided to desist. As Johnson got in his truck to leave, Rogers banged on the window and broke off the radio antenna. Johnson reacted by shifting into reverse and squealing his tires as he backed-up for approximately fifteen feet, then shifted into drive and drove towards Rogers as if he was going to hit him. He had no intention of hitting Rogers, but simply wanted to scare him. Johnson planned to swerve to the right at the last minute, but unfortunately, at the same moment he swerved right, Rogers tried to evade the truck by diving to his left (Johnson's right). As a result, Johnson's truck ran over Rogers, killing him. Would it be more appropriate to convict Johnson of voluntary manslaughter or murder? Or nothing at all? Why? *Cf. State v. Powell*, 872 P.2d 1027 (Utah 1994).

Hypo 4: *Homicidal Child Neglect*

The police, investigating allegations of child abuse, found Malone sitting with five of her children in the living room of her house. In a second floor bedroom, they found her seven-month-old twin daughters dead from starvation. The facts revealed that Malone was a cocaine addict who neglected her children. Neither the prosecution nor the defense denies that she neglected a "duty" to her children. The only question was whether she committed the crime of manslaughter or reckless murder. Is your answer to this question affected by the fact that Malone's drug addiction rendered her unaware of her children's needs and therefore of the risk of death? *See Commonwealth v. Miller*, 426 Pa. Super. 410, 627 A.2d 741 (1993).

Hypo 5: *Speeding Through Red Light*

Believing that she has committed a theft, a police officer pulls over a driver on a city street. As the officer approaches the vehicle, the driver drives off at a very high rate of speed, and attempts to go through a red light without stopping. Unfortunately, she does not make it, and smashes into another car, killing an 11-year old girl. Did the driver commit murder? Why? Why not?

Hypo 6: *High Speed Chase*

Defendant Jason McKinley was found guilty of second degree murder due to the fact that he had run a red light while being chased by a police car for speeding, smashing head on into another car at between 93 and 100 miles per hour, killing the driver. McKinley argues that while he was "admittedly reckless," the evidence did not support a murder conviction, only an involuntary manslaughter conviction. Is he right? *See McKinley v. State*, 945 A.2d 1158 (Del. 2008).

---

2. Felony-Murder

At common law, one of the ways in which murder could be established was to demonstrate that the accused committed a homicide in the process of committing or attempting to commit a felonious act. Today, most (but not all) jurisdictions continue to recognize felony-murder as a distinct homicide offense, either as a separate component of first-degree murder, or as an entirely distinct crime.

Although felony-murder can be proved by establishing an unintended killing in the course of the commission of certain specified felonies, in another sense, felony-murder is actually an intentional killing in which the intent to kill is imputed (or "transferred") from the accused's intent to commit the dangerous felony at issue.

State v. Blair

348 Or. 72, 228 P.3d 564 (2010).

DE MUNIZ, C.J.

Defendant petitions for review from a Court of Appeals opinion affirming his conviction for, among other crimes, felony murder. The Court of Appeals concluded that the felony murder statute, ORS 163.115(1)(b), does not require that the state allege and prove that a defendant acted with a culpable mental state in causing the victim's death; rather, the defendant's commission or attempted commission of the underlying felony establishes, as a matter of law, the requisite mens rea with respect to the victim's death. We allowed defendant's petition for review. As explained below, we agree with the Court of Appeals and the trial court, and therefore, affirm.

The facts are undisputed. Defendant broke into the victim's home, stole several marijuana plants and household items, and attempted to rape and sexually abuse the victim. The next day, the victim's son found her body on the floor next to her bed, with a bed sheet tied around one of her legs and also loosely tied to a bedpost. The cause of the victim's death was chronic obstructive pulmonary disease (COPD) due to emphysema. The victim suffered from acute COPD, which was exacerbated critically by defendant's burglary, attempted rape, and attempted sexual abuse.

Before trial, defendant demurred to the felony murder count in the indictment. Defendant argued that the demurrer should be sustained, because the felony murder count did not allege that defendant had caused the death of the victim with a culpable mental state and therefore did not allege facts "constituting an offense."

What's That?

A *demurrer* in this setting is an objection that admits *arguendo* the prosecutor's alleged facts, but argues that they are sufficient in and of themselves as a matter of law to support a prosecution.

Defendant argued that, because felony murder is a form of criminal homicide, the state was required to allege in the indictment one of the mental states described in ORS 163.005(1): that is, it was required to allege that defendant had killed the victim "intentionally, knowingly, recklessly or with criminal negligence." The trial court overruled the demurrer. During the trial, defendant submitted proposed jury instructions that would have required the state to prove beyond a reasonable doubt that defendant had caused the victim's death "knowingly, recklessly, or with criminal negligence" as one of the elements of felony murder. The trial court refused to give those requested instructions. A jury subsequently convicted defendant of felony murder, among other crimes. On the felony murder conviction, the trial court imposed a life sentence with the possibility of parole after 25 years.

Defendant appealed, and the Court of Appeals affirmed. We allowed defendant's petition for review to determine whether the definition of criminal homicide in ORS 163.005(1) applies to felony murder, as codified in ORS 163.115(1)(b), in such a way that felony murder in Oregon requires the state to allege and prove that a defendant acted with a mental state in causing the victim's death distinct from any mental state required to prove the underlying felony. In doing so, our task is to "ascertain and declare what is, in terms or in substance, contained therein, not to insert what has been omitted, or to omit what has been inserted; and where there are several provisions or particulars such construction is, if possible, to be adopted as will give effect to all." We interpret the statutory text in context, and then, to the extent we find it helpful, we consider the legislative history proffered by the parties. In this case, the context that we consider along with the text includes the law as it existed before the adoption of the 1971 criminal code.

ORS 163.005 provides, in part:

"(1) A person commits criminal homicide if, without justification or excuse, the person intentionally, knowingly, recklessly or with criminal negligence causes the death of another human being.

"(2) 'Criminal homicide' is murder, manslaughter, criminally negligent homicide or aggravated vehicular homicide."

The felony murder statute, ORS 163.115, provides, in part:

"(1) Except as provided in ORS 163.118 and 163.125, criminal homicide constitutes murder: . . . (b) When it is committed by a person, acting either alone or with one or more persons, who commits or attempts to commit any of the following crimes and in the course of and in furtherance of the crime the person is committing or attempting to commit, or during the immediate flight therefrom, the person, or another participant if there be any, causes the death of a person other than one of the participants: . . . (C) Burglary in the first degree."

As defendant reads the above statutes, because felony murder is a type of criminal homicide-and, under ORS 163.005(1), a person commits criminal homicide only if the person intentionally, knowingly, recklessly, or with criminal negligence causes the death of another-felony murder requires that, in causing the death, the defendant acted with a *mens rea* of at least criminal negligence. The state responds that ORS 163.005(1) does not provide the exclusive definition of criminal homicide because ORS 163.005(2) provides a further definition of criminal homicide and, under defendant's reading, subsection (2) would be rendered superfluous. Moreover, the state argues, under ORS 163.005(2), "criminal homicide" includes "murder." Accordingly, all the subspecies of murder listed in ORS 163.115(1) constitute "criminal homicide," regardless of whether the specific subspecies requires that a defendant act with a culpable mental state in causing the victim's death. The state asserts that nothing in ORS 163.005(1) prevents the *mens rea* required to prove the underlying felony from being imputed to the person who causes the death of a victim for purposes of ORS 163.115(1)(b). With those competing arguments in mind, we turn to an examination of the pertinent statutes.

The legislature adopted ORS 163.005 and ORS 163.115 in 1971 as part of an overall revision of the criminal code. "Criminal homicide" was a new offense created during the 1971 revision and thus had no preexisting history in Oregon law. On the other hand, the felony murder rule was first codified in Oregon in 1864 as part of both the first- and second-degree murder statutes. The relevant portions of the first- and second-degree felony murder statutes remained substantially unchanged until the criminal code revisions in 1971, and this court has consistently incorporated an "implied malice" rule into felony murder, that is, felony murder contains no distinct or independent mens rea requirement in relation to the cause of death of the victim.

Thus, when the legislature adopted ORS 163.005 and ORS 163.115 in 1971, the felony murder rule, as construed and applied by this court, long had operated to impose responsibility for homicides that occur during the commission or attempted commission of a felony, without the separate and additional requirement that the defendant acted with a mens rea in causing the death of another person. In addition, since 1971, this court has continued to treat felony murder as requiring no distinct or independent mens rea with respect to the cause of the victim's death.

Nothing in ORS 163.115 or any related statutes indicates that the legislature intended to change that long-standing rule. To the contrary, other aspects of the statutory scheme demonstrate that the legislature intended to retain the felony murder rule in its traditional form. For example, ORS 163.115(1)(b) provides that criminal homicide constitutes murder by a person when it is committed by that person "*or another participant if there be any.*" Under that provision, a defendant may be criminally liable for felony murder even if an accomplice causes the death of the victim. Another subsection in the same statute, ORS 163.115(3), provides for a limited affirmative defense to felony murder if a defendant

> "(a) Was not the only participant in the underlying crime;
>
> "(b) Did not commit the homicidal act or in any way solicit, request, command, importune, cause or aid in the commission thereof;
>
> "(c) Was not armed with a dangerous or deadly weapon;
>
> "(d) Had no reasonable ground to believe that any other participant was armed with a dangerous or deadly weapon; and
>
> "(e) Had no reasonable ground to believe that any other participant intended to engage in conduct likely to result in death."

Under defendant's interpretation of the felony murder statute, ORS 163.115(3) would be rendered unnecessary, in contravention of the statutory construction directive set out in ORS 174.010.

Take Note

Similarly, in many felony-murder jurisdictions, an accomplice has an affirmative defense to felony murder when the killing act of his or her accomplice was not reasonably foreseeable and where he or she was not armed with a deadly weapon and did not know that the shooter was armed.

Moreover, ORS 163.115(1)(a) provides that criminal homicide constitutes murder when it is "committed *intentionally.*" (Emphasis added.) Under a parallel reading of ORS 163.115(1)(a) and (b), the fact that the legislature included a mental state in paragraph (1)(a) but not (1)(b) supports the interpretation that the legislature intended that the mental state required for the underlying felony in paragraph (1)(b) to be imputed as a matter of law to the cause of the death of the victim.

Food for Thought

Should the Oregon legislature have made such a change? Is it *fair* to imply *mens rea,* particularly where the convicted accused could face life in prison as a result? Why discard the traditional rule requiring proof of a *mens rea* (for serious offenses, at least) to reflect our common law notions of appropriate blameworthiness?

Finally, nothing in the 1971 legislative history suggests that the legislature intended to change the longstanding rule regarding implied malice; in fact, much the legislative history suggests that the legislature intended to adhere to it.

Taken together, the context, including this court's case law and the legislative history, compel the conclusion that the legislature intended to continue the implied malice rule. Accordingly, we conclude that, (1) under ORS 163.005(1), "criminal homicide" requires that a defendant act with a culpable *mens rea* with respect to causing the victim's death; (2) under ORS 163.005(2), "criminal homicide" includes "murder," and (3) under ORS 163.115(1)(b), requisite culpable *mens rea* is established, as a matter of law, by the defendant's commission or attempted commission of the predicate felony. Thus, the trial court properly overruled defendant's demurrer and properly refused to give defendant's requested jury instruction. The Court of Appeals correctly affirmed the trial court's rulings.

The decision of the Court of Appeals and the judgment of the circuit court are affirmed.

Points for Discussion

a. Model Penal Code

Although the Model Penal Code nominally rejects the felony-murder rule, it does contain the following provision concerning homicides that occur in the course of the commission of seven specified felonies:

> **§ 210.2. Murder.**
>
> (1) Except as provided in Section 210.3(1)(b), criminal homicide constitutes murder when . . . it is committed recklessly under circumstances manifesting extreme indifference to the value of human life. Such recklessness and indifference are presumed if the actor is engaged or is an accomplice in the commission of, or an attempt to commit, or flight after committing or attempting to commit robbery, rape or deviate sexual intercourse by force or threat of force, arson, burglary, kidnapping or felonious escape.

b. Independent Felony Required

In many jurisdictions, the triggering felony for felony murder cannot be an offense that is inherent in the act of killing itself, like assault or battery or discharging a firearm. In other words, the triggering felony must be independent of the killing itself. *See, e.g., Griggs v. State*, 304 Ga. 806, 822 S.E.2d 246 (2018).

c. Triggering Felonies

Some states do not enumerate an exclusive list of triggering felonies for application of the felony-murder rule (or to establish murder, as in the MPC), but instead apply the rule to in any situation where the facts are deemed sufficiently dangerous to human life to justify application of the doctrine. Using this latter approach, would a defendant be guilty of felony murder where he and three of his friends chased their victim, tripped and kicked him, and dropped a boulder on his head, thus committing an aggravated assault that resulted in the victim's unintended death? Or would the defendant only be guilty of reckless or negligent homicide? *See Roary v. State*, 385 Md. 217, 867 A.2d 1095 (2005).

Does it make sense to apply the felony-murder doctrine to *all* felonies? For example, under federal law, it is a felony to file a false tax return. On the way to the post office to file a fraudulent return, A's brakes fail without warning and despite regular and diligent maintenance. Unable to stop, A hits and kills a pedestrian. Should this be treated as felony murder?

d. Acquittal of Underlying Felony

In Pennsylvania, as in many other states, a defendant may only be convicted of felony murder if the victim's death occurred during the commission of or an attempt to commit (or flight after committing or attempting to commit) enumerated, serious felonies, which include in Pennsylvania, "robbery, rape, or deviate sexual intercourse by force or threat of force, arson, burglary or kidnapping." Pa. Cons. Stat. § 2502(b) & (d). If a defendant is charged with *both* robbery and felony murder based upon the death of a frightened robbery victim from a heart attack, should a felony-murder conviction stand if the jury finds the defendant innocent of the robbery? Should a robbery verdict stand if the jury finds the defendant innocent of felony-murder during the commission of the robbery?

e. Misdemeanor Manslaughter

At common law, a misdemeanor-manslaughter rule also existed, imputing the offense of manslaughter to actors who committed an unlawful act not amounting to a felony which nonetheless resulted in the death of a victim. This rule was rejected by the draftsmen of the Model Penal Code as "objectionable on the same ground as the felony-murder rule." It has also been abolished in most states. Moreover, in those states that still retain a version of the rule, either by common law or by statute, typically the unlawful act needs to be "*malum in se*" (inherently wrong and immoral in nature in contrast to "*malum prohibitum*" offenses that are wrong simply because a legislature says so) in order to suffice to establish manslaughter. Do you think there is a place in modern American penal codes for some version of this common-law rule?

f. *Faulkner's* Logic

Is the felony murder doctrine consistent with *Regina v. Faulkner* (in Chapter 3 on *Mens Rea*), in which a sailor went down in the hold of a ship to steal some rum and accidentally burned the ship? The English court concluded that Faulkner could not be convicted of "maliciously" burning a ship. If A intends to rob a convenience store and a customer is accidentally killed when B drops his gun, is it fair or appropriate to convict A of murder? Is a murder conviction consistent with the justifications for punishment?

Hypo 1: *Bombing Buildings*

Would an individual who placed and exploded a bomb in a building which she believed was unoccupied, but which resulted in the unintended death of someone who was (unbeknownst to the bomber) trespassing in that building, be guilty of felony murder? Why or why not? How about second-degree (reckless) murder?

Hypo 2: *Guns for Intimidation*

A & B decide to rob a convenience store. Both are carrying guns, but they explicitly agree that neither is to shoot anyone else. The weapons are being carried simply for the purpose of intimidation. Consider the following scenarios and decide whether A is guilty of felony murder if the following events occur during the robbery:

a. becomes enraged at a recalcitrant clerk and kills him in cold blood;

b. accidentally drops his gun, and it discharges killing a customer;

c. the clerk pulls out a weapon and shoots and kills B;

d. as A & B are trying to escape, a police officer arrives and shoots and kills B; and

e. on the way to commit the robbery, A fails to see a red light and smashes into another car and kills a passenger.

People v. Portillo

107 Cal. App. 4th 834, 132 Cal. Rptr. 2d 435 (2003).

HUFFMAN, ACTING P. J.

A jury convicted Coby J. Portillo of first degree murder, forcible rape, and forcible sodomy. The trial court sentenced Portillo to life in prison without the possibility of parole, plus a consecutive one year for the deadly weapon use enhancement.

Portillo appeals, contending the trial court prejudicially erred in expanding the scope of felony-murder sex offenses to include a homicide that occurred after the sex offenses were complete, but before the defendant reached a place of temporary safety. We affirm.

During the summer of 2000, Portillo was a petty officer in the United States Navy stationed aboard the U.S.S. Ogden in San Diego. Due to the stress level aboard the ship, Portillo often talked with other seamen and petty officers about picking up a prostitute, raping her and then killing her. On August 25, 2000, Portillo said that when he killed a prostitute he would put her body in a seabag, which is a round, green duffel bag issued to Navy personnel. None of the other men reported his statements because they thought he was joking.

On August 27, 2000, Portillo, who lived with his wife off base in an apartment, called a professional escort service that provides strippers and nude entertainers, after he had taken his wife to work. Using a different name, he requested an "Asian girl," and offered to pay cash. The receptionist described the availability of a petite Asian escort who used the name "Monica." In agreement, Portillo gave the receptionist his telephone number and the apartment number of his neighbor who lived directly below him.

Monica, a 36-year-old licensed escort and mother of two whose real name was Natividad W. (Nancy), was given the assignment by the agency in response to Portillo's call. Less than five feet tall, Nancy was "security conscious," carried a stun gun, and was known to strictly follow the agency's procedures of collecting money up front and phoning in to verify receiving the funds before rendering any services. In over 100 calls for the agency, Nancy had never failed to phone in at the start of any service. When the receptionist gave Nancy the assignment, she gave her the address Portillo had given the agency and reminded her to call the office upon her arrival to the appointment.

When Nancy arrived at the given address around 2:00 p.m., the man answering the door told her he was not the person she was looking for. Shortly after she walked away, he heard muffled voices upstairs and "a loud thumping sound like somebody running across the floor."

Nancy never called into the agency that day and Portillo failed to pick up his wife from work at 3:15 p.m. as arranged. A coworker drove his wife home and she obtained a key from the apartment manager to enter their apartment around 6:30 p.m. When his wife entered the apartment, she saw blood on the floor near what appeared to be Portillo's seabag, an unknown pair of women's sandals in the hallway, a purse and cloth bag which did not belong to her near the dining room table, and a hammer with blood-like stains on it. She called 911.

When San Diego deputy sheriffs arrived, they found Nancy's body covered by two seabags, secured the area, and waited for homicide detectives. The subsequent investigation revealed that inside the seabag near Nancy's head were her pants with a broken zipper and torn underwear. Her bra was found pulled down underneath her breasts and her sweater pulled up, exposing them. An autopsy revealed she had sustained five blows to her head consistent with being hit by a hammer, and suffered broken bone and cartilage in her neck, petechiae hemorrhages in her eyes and eyelids, which are the "hallmarks of strangulation," two black eyes, bruises and lacerations on her lip, an abrasion on her left elbow, and blunt force injuries in her vaginal area and bruising around her anus. The medical examiner opined the cause of death was manual strangulation and multiple blunt force head injuries.

Further testing revealed that Nancy's blood was on Portillo's shorts, his carpet and the hammer in his apartment. Tests also showed that Portillo's DNA was in scrapings and clippings from her fingernails and his sperm was inside her vagina and around her anus.

Portillo was brought to trial for Nancy's rape, sodomy and murder, and the above evidence was presented in the prosecution case. The gist of Portillo's defense was that the sex with Nancy was consensual and her killing was committed in self-defense. According to Portillo, after Nancy orally copulated him and had both vaginal and anal intercourse with him, he stopped any sexual activity when she complained it hurt. When he told her he did not have the money to pay her, she became angry and attacked him. In the process, she tore the underwear she was putting on. As they exchanged punches, Nancy threatened to kill him.

When Portillo pushed her to the ground, she reached for an object from her bag and lunged at him. Thinking the object was a knife, Portillo grabbed a heavy hammer out of a box and "hit her like four, five times, just boom, real quick in the head." As she fell, she grabbed him and he fell on top of her with his hand on her neck, dropping the hammer on the floor nearby. He held her down as she started kicking and swinging at him. When she picked up the hammer to swing at him, he took it and threw it behind him. Nancy then "just like stopped." She was nonresponsive and not breathing.

The jury did not believe Portillo's version of the events the day Nancy was murdered.

During jury instruction discussions, Portillo asserted there was insufficient evidence for the court to give felony-murder instructions as an alternate theory for first degree murder because they contemplated a continuous action, which he argued was not present in this case due to the completion of the underlying rape and sodomy offenses. The court overruled the objection, finding there was a sufficient evidentiary basis for such instruction.

When the court instructed the jury on felony murder, it told the jurors that in order to find Portillo guilty under such theory, they had to find beyond a reasonable doubt he committed the murder "in the course of" rape or sodomy. During deliberations, the jury sent the court the following note: "We have a question about the terms 'commission' and 'in the course of' rape and sodomy. We were wondering about time frame, etc. [¶] legal definition of commission of rape as it is different from course of the rape. [¶] does the victim need to die while there is penetration or can the victim die after the crime[?] [¶] As to felony murder 1." Over defense counsel's objection the court then sent the following response to the jury: "'In the commission of' is synonymous with 'in the course of'. [¶] For the purposes of determining whether an unlawful killing has occurred during the commission or attempted commission of a forcible rape or sodomy by use of force, the commission of said crime (forcible rape or sodomy by use of force) is not confined to a fixed place or a limited period of time. Such crime is still in progress while a perpetrator is fleeing in an attempt to escape or to avoid detection. The crime is complete when the perpetrator has reached a place of temporary safety. [¶] The unlawful killing need not be simultaneous with the act of forcible penetration. However, it must be proven beyond any reasonable doubt that the unlawful killing occurred during the commission or attempted commission of a forcible rape or sodomy by use of force (as defined above), and that the death of the victim did not precede the commission or attempted commission of a forcible rape or sodomy by use of force."

Food for Thought

Do you think that there was sufficient evidence presented for the jury to return a first-degree murder verdict *without* considering the felony-murder doctrine?

On appeal, Portillo contends the trial court prejudicially erred in essentially expanding the scope of felony-murder sex offenses to include a homicide that occurred after the sex offenses were complete, but before the defendant reached a place of temporary safety. He argues that the portion of the court's instruction telling the jury the underlying crimes of rape and sodomy continue for felony-murder purposes while the perpetrator attempts to escape or to avoid detection was wrong because the so-called "escape rule" only applies to theft offenses. We disagree.

The felony-murder doctrine eliminates the requirements of malice and premeditation for first degree murder and provides that a killing is still murder of the first degree, whether intentional or unintentional, if it is committed in the perpetration of, or the attempt to perpetrate, certain serious felonies, including rape and sodomy as charged in this case. Such alternative theory to premeditated murder was adopted for the protection of the community and its residents, not for the benefit of the lawbreaker and was not intended to relieve the wrongdoer from any probable consequences of his act by placing a limitation upon the *res gestae* which is unreasonable or unnatural. Based on such intent and purpose, the established law of this state has never required proof of a strict causal relationship between the felony and the homicide. Thus it has been held that the homicide is committed in the perpetration of the felony if the killing and felony are parts of one continuous transaction.

It's Latin to Me

Res gestae means "the events at issue, or other events contemporaneous with them."

Moreover, because flight following a felony has also been considered as part of the same transaction, it has generally been held that a felony continues for purposes of the felony-murder rule until the criminal has reached a place of temporary safety.

Even though we have found no reported felony-murder decision which has specifically applied the so-called escape rule to crimes other than robbery and burglary, we believe, as the trial court here did, that the felony-murder law supports the court's answer given the jury in this case which essentially encompassed the "one continuous transaction" test for the felony sex offenses as the basis for the felony-murder theory as well as the language of the escape rule. As given, the instruction left open for the jury the question as to whether Portillo had reached a place of temporary safety cutting off felony-murder liability after raping and sodomizing his victim before killing her. Although it may appear illogical to attach such flight or escape language to a crime that is itself considered complete upon penetration, we do not believe the use of such escape principles are unreasonable or unnaturally extend the felony-murder rule beyond its established application of the "one continuous transaction" analysis used to define such theory based on underlying sexual offenses.

Food for Thought

Do you agree? Hadn't Portillo, who was already in his own apartment after he raped his victim, reached "a place of temporary safety"?

Moreover, even if the court's answer to the jury here were arguably an extension beyond the usual felony-murder rule via the so-called escape rule as contended by Portillo, we would find no prejudicial error. Because the evidence fully supported the giving of the felony-murder instructions based upon the underlying crimes of rape and sodomy, the inclusion of language of the escape rule in the court's answer to the jury inquiry clarifying those instructions reasonably defined the outer limits of the "continuous-transaction" theory.

In sum, we conclude the trial court's answer to the jury question on the theory of felony murder based on rape and sodomy was legally proper.

The judgment is affirmed.

Hypo: *Next Day Chase*

Suppose that the police are looking for A, a robbery suspect, the robbery having occurred the previous day. Suddenly a police officer sees A's car on the highway, and during the high-speed car chase that follows, A runs into and kills, B, a pedestrian. Is A guilty of felony murder under the California approach described in *Portillo*? If these events occurred in Pennsylvania with a felony murder statute as described in Point for Discussion d., *supra*, would that make a difference in your analysis?

---

3. Involuntary Manslaughter

The crime of involuntary manslaughter is, as the name implies, an unintentional killing. It is distinguished from unintentional murder, however, by the absence of the element of malice.

The *mens rea* showing actually required to establish the existence of involuntary manslaughter varies widely by jurisdiction. In most jurisdictions, involuntary manslaughter is established when it is proved that the accused has acted with gross negligence (sometimes, in circular fashion, deemed "criminal negligence"), resulting in someone's death. In other jurisdictions (and the Model Penal Code), however, involuntary manslaughter is not established absent the higher showing of recklessness; rarely, a lesser showing of ordinary negligence (sometimes, again, in circular fashion, called "civil negligence") is all that is required to establish this offense.

Noakes v. Virginia

280 Va. 338, 699 S.E.2d 284 (2010).

Opinion by JUSTICE CYNTHIA D. KINSER.

In this appeal, a defendant challenges the sufficiency of the evidence to support her conviction for involuntary manslaughter, specifically contesting the findings that she was criminally negligent and that her acts were a proximate cause of a toddler's death. Because there is sufficient evidence to support both findings, we will affirm the judgment of conviction.

The relevant facts are undisputed. The defendant, Elizabeth Pollard Noakes, provided child care services in her home, and on the day in question, October 18, 2006, had in her care Noah Alexander Colassaco, a fifteen-month-old child, and two other children. Noakes had been caring for Noah for approximately three weeks and, throughout that time, had experienced difficulty in getting Noah to lie down and sleep during "nap time." Instead, he usually would stand in the crib and cry. Noakes had tried "traditional means" to help Noah sleep, which included "rocking him to sleep" and "patting his back," without success.

Around noon on the day in question, Noakes put Noah and another toddler she was caring for in their cribs for an afternoon nap. The cribs were located in an upstairs, "loft" bedroom that was partially visible from Noakes' bedroom. The cribs, however, were not visible from Noakes' bedroom. Noah's crib, as viewed from the loft's entrance, was positioned lengthwise against the back wall of the room, in the far right corner. The rectangular crib was abutted on the right by one wall, on the rear with another, and on the left by another crib, with only the front, lengthwise portion unobstructed. A third crib, in which Noakes placed the other toddler that day, was positioned a few feet from Noah's crib, nearer the entrance of the loft and also on the right wall. When Noakes left the loft, Noah was standing "facing the front of the crib" and crying.

At approximately 12:30 p.m., Noakes returned to the loft to "check on" Noah, who was still standing in the crib and crying. Knowing that when Noah stood in his crib, his chin was above the crib's sides, and also that Noah would fall asleep if he were lying or sitting in the crib instead of standing, Noakes decided to place a make-shift covering over the crib to prevent Noah from standing. After removing Noah from his crib, Noakes placed a thirty-three and one-quarter pound, collapsed "dog crate," which ran the length of the crib but was substantially narrower, on top of the crib. Noakes reasoned that the crate's weight would prevent Noah from standing up in the crib.

Noakes tested the stability of her contraption by shaking the crib with the crate on top to determine if the crate could fall into the crib and injure Noah. Satisfied that the crate could not fall into the crib, Noakes removed the crate, put Noah back into the crib, and placed a fabric-covered piece of approximately one-inch thick cardboard on top of the crib. The cardboard was added, in part, to cushion the force of any impact between Noah's head and the crate if Noah attempted to stand. Although the cardboard would cover the entirety of the crib's top, Noakes positioned it so the cardboard extended out over the front of the crib, where Noah often stood, thus leaving a small "gap" in the rear between the crib's side and the cardboard. Noakes then placed the dog crate on top of the cardboard, towards the front side of the crib, where it covered a little more than one-half of the crib's width. Noakes examined the covering to ensure that Noah would not be able to reach into the dog crate and injure his fingers.

With Noah in his now-covered crib, Noakes remained in the loft for a short while to determine if the enclosure was causing any distress to Noah and if he was attempting to stand up in the crib despite the covering. Observing no problems, Noakes left the loft. Sometime before 1:00 p.m., Noakes, however, heard a noise from the loft and returned to find Noah sitting in his crib but not sleeping, with his face pressed against crib's front, mesh side. Concluding that Noah would not fall asleep if he were able to look for her, Noakes placed a toy in front of the crib to obstruct Noah's view "so that he would not be looking for Noakes but would just get bored and go to sleep."

Noakes again left the loft at about 1:00 p.m. and did not return until 3:15 p.m., when she came to wake the other toddler from his nap. Noakes testified, however, that she monitored the toddlers audibly from her bedroom during that time and heard no noise from either of them. Noakes testified that when she returned to wake the other child, she did not look at Noah's crib, which was several feet to the left of the other crib, but "within her peripheral vision of the room." She believed, however, that Noah was asleep since she did not hear any sounds from him when she awakened the other toddler.

Shortly after 4:00 p.m., Noakes returned to the loft to wake Noah and found him unconscious. He was standing with his chin resting on the side of the crib, one or both of his hands gripping the crib's side, and his head and neck wedged between the cardboard and the crib. His lips were blue and his skin was cold to Noakes' touch. Noakes surmised that Noah had attempted to stand, had pushed up against the cardboard causing the dog crate to slide a few inches thereby creating a space between the covering on top of the crib and the crib's wall. Noah then had moved his head toward the crib's center, where he normally stood, trapping himself in a space between the side of the crib and the cardboard, which was held in place by the weight of the dog crate. Despite Noakes' efforts to revive Noah and the intervention of emergency medical personnel, Noah was pronounced dead at Noakes' home.

Noakes was subsequently convicted in a bench trial in the Circuit Court of the County of Chesterfield of involuntary manslaughter. The trial court sentenced Noakes to five years of incarceration, with four years suspended on the condition that she "be of good behavior upon her release from confinement" for a period of twenty years.

Take Note

Note that the court of appeals found that Noakes acted recklessly. Was that the correct *mens rea* element to be satisfied to establish involuntary manslaughter?

On appeal to the Court of Appeals of Virginia, a divided panel affirmed the trial court's judgment. Upon rehearing en banc, the Court of Appeals found that the "trial court could reasonably have concluded that Noakes recklessly disregarded Noah's safety by proceeding with her plan to prevent Noah from standing up by placing the dog crate on his crib." Noakes now appeals to this Court. In a single assignment of error, she asserts the evidence was insufficient as a matter of law to sustain her conviction, claiming that "her acts did not rise to the level of criminal negligence nor could she have anticipated the unforeseeable acts that would be performed by the child while inside the crib."

When the sufficiency of the evidence is challenged on appeal, we review the evidence in the light most favorable to the Commonwealth, the prevailing party in the trial court and accord the Commonwealth the benefit of all reasonable inferences deducible from the evidence. We give the trial court's judgment sitting as the factfinder the same weight as a jury verdict, and we will affirm that judgment unless it is plainly wrong or without evidence to support it.

We have defined the common law crime of involuntary manslaughter as the killing of one accidentally, contrary to the intention of the parties, in the prosecution of some unlawful, but not felonious, act; or in the improper performance of a lawful act. To convict a person for involuntary manslaughter caused by the improper performance of a lawful act, the Commonwealth must show that the improper performance of the lawful act amounted to an unlawful performance of such lawful act, not merely a negligent performance; that is, the lawful act must have been done in a way so grossly negligent and culpable as to indicate an indifference to consequences or an absence of decent regard for human life. The accidental killing must be the proximate result of a lawful act performed in a manner so gross, wanton, and culpable as to show a reckless disregard of human life.

In this context, the terms "gross, wanton, and culpable" describe conduct. The word "gross" means "aggravated or increased negligence" while the word "culpable" means "deserving of blame or censure." Gross negligence amounts to criminal negligence when acts of a wanton or willful character, committed or omitted, show a reckless or indifferent disregard of the rights of others, under circumstances reasonably calculated to produce injury, or which make it not improbable that injury will be occasioned, and the offender knows, or is charged with the knowledge of, the probable result of his or her acts. While the improper performance of a lawful act must be so gross and culpable as to indicate a callous disregard of human life, it need not be so gross as to raise the presumption of malice.

In determining whether conduct rises to the level of criminal negligence, an objective standard applies, and criminal negligence may be found to exist when the defendant either knew or should have known the probable results of his/her acts. Thus, the Commonwealth did not need to prove that Noakes actually knew or intended that her conduct would cause, or would likely cause, Noah's death, but rather that Noakes should have known her acts created a substantial risk of harm to Noah.

Noakes concedes on brief "that it is not necessary for a defendant to foresee the specific manner in which injury occurred." Noakes, nevertheless, argues that in evaluating the foreseeability of death or serious injury to Noah, attention must be given to the measures she "took to insure that death or serious injury would not occur." Noakes points to her purpose for covering the crib-"to assist the child in sleeping"-and the "painstaking lengths [taken by her] to anticipate possible dangers and prevent them," as well her "regular" returns "to the adjoining bedroom so that she could monitor the child as she did housework." Noakes claims, "each of these measures reduced the probability of harm to the child to the point that no reasonably intelligent person, using an objective standard, could be charged with the knowledge that the child probably would be harmed by the object." In summary, Noakes claims that "it was her inability to predict any and all possible dangers that failed her."

Upon review of the evidence, we conclude that Noakes' conduct in placing cardboard and a thirty-three and one-quarter pound, collapsed dog crate atop Noah's crib and failing to visually check on him for about three hours was wanton and willful, showing a reckless or indifferent disregard of Noah's rights, under circumstances that made it not improbable that injury would be occasioned, and Noakes is charged with the knowledge of the probable result of her acts. Noakes knew that Noah would attempt to stand in his crib and also that when doing so, Noah's head and chin rose above the height of the crib's sides. While she obviously took steps to prevent the crate's falling upon Noah and his reaching into the crate, Noakes should have known that a toddler, used to standing but constrained against his will, might attempt to free himself, thereby dislodging the makeshift covering and sustaining serious injury. The measures that Noakes undertook to prevent the crate from falling upon Noah demonstrate her actual knowledge of the inherent danger of the contraption she placed atop the crib. And, because Noakes knew that she had placed Noah in an inherently dangerous situation that could cause serious injury, she certainly should not have left Noah unattended for approximately three hours.

Food for Thought

Do you agree? Should Noakes have known that? Or does it only seem that way after the fact, after this tragic event occurred?

In sum, we agree with the Court of Appeals' conclusion:

> The act of attempting to limit Noah's ability to stand in his crib was not inherently unlawful; however, a rational factfinder could indeed determine that the placing of a thirty-three-pound dog crate on Noah's crib, combined with Noakes' inattentiveness in the face of this experimental and dangerous set-up and with Noah's conceded determination to stand up in his crib, constituted reckless and unlawful conduct in utter disregard of Noah's safety.

Affirmed.

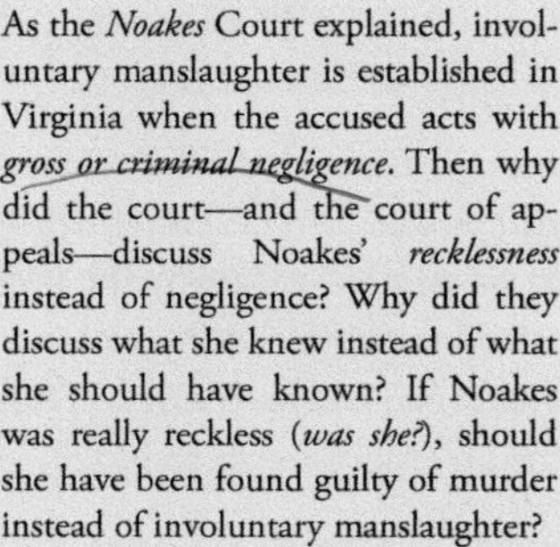

Food for Thought

As the *Noakes* Court explained, involuntary manslaughter is established in Virginia when the accused acts with *gross or criminal negligence*. Then why did the court—and the court of appeals—discuss Noakes' *recklessness* instead of negligence? Why did they discuss what she knew instead of what she should have known? If Noakes was really reckless (*was she?*), should she have been found guilty of murder instead of involuntary manslaughter?

Hypo: *Defense of Accident*

In *Glenn v. Commonwealth*, 2020 WL 2027767 (Va. Ct. App. 2020), defendant Glenn claimed that he shot and killed his thirteen-year old son by accident. The Commonwealth claimed that he had acted intentionally, and charged him with murder. The jury came back with a verdict of involuntary manslaughter. Glenn appealed, claiming that the trial court had erred in failing to give the following instruction that his counsel had requested:

> Where the defense is that the killing was an accident, the defense is not required to prove this fact. The burden is on the Commonwealth to prove beyond a reasonable doubt that the killing was not accidental. If after considering all the evidence you have a reasonable doubt whether the killing was accidental or intentional, then you shall find Glenn not guilty.

Did the trial court err by rejecting this instruction? Should Glenn's conviction of involuntary manslaughter be reversed and a new trial ordered as a result? What do you think? Who should bear the burden of proving or disproving the existence of an accident, the Government or the defense? Can a killing be both accidental and involuntary manslaughter at the very same time?

State v. Brooks

163 Vt. 245, 658 A.2d 22 (1995).

ALLEN, CHIEF JUSTICE.

Defendant purchased a home that was equipped with a driveway heater. Hot water, heated by gas in the unit's boiler, flowed through a system of pipes beneath the driveway to melt snow and ice. Exhaust fumes from the system were supposed to exit through a vent located on the backside of the garage. Defendant turned on the driveway heater before running an errand. While he was gone, another occupant, Jill McDermott, and her infant became ill from noxious fumes that had emanated from the garage. When defendant returned home, McDermott asked him to take her and the baby to the hospital. Defendant took them to the emergency room where they were examined and released.

Defendant thought the fumes were caused by a plumbing problem and called C & L Plumbing and Heating. C & L sent an employee to inspect the heater who determined that a dislodged flap was preventing proper exhaust. He explained the malfunction to defendant and told him that repairs should be made and safety features added. A Vermont Gas Systems (VGS) employee also examined the system. Both servicemen decided the gas should remain off until repairs were made. The VGS employee told McDermott the system was not safe to operate and that she was lucky to be alive, "because it was carbon monoxide." McDermott relayed these comments to defendant. That night, the owner of C & L called defendant and told him that the heater had been improperly installed. A VGS supervisor also called and explained the dangers of the condition and agreed that it should be repaired.

In May 1988, defendant hired a real estate agent to sell his home. Defendant did not mention the heater's history to the agent. Instead, defendant instructed the agent to turn the heater on, then off, when demonstrating it to prospective buyers. The heater was a highlighted feature in agent's marketing materials. In July 1988, the agent showed the house to Linda Cifarelli. The agent explained and demonstrated the driveway heating system by turning it on for approximately five minutes. During their second showing, defendant, who was present to answer questions, explained and demonstrated the driveway heater again, but did not mention its prior problem or faulty condition. Cifarelli purchased the house. During a professional home inspection, defendant demonstrated the heater, but did not explain how it worked or mention its history. At the closing, defendant insisted that the Cifarellis return to the house with him for a more detailed showing because "he knew things the inspector wouldn't know." Defendant showed Linda Cifarelli and her parents the central vacuum system, the drainage system, and the driveway heater. When showing the heater, he told them it was not necessary to run it for more than two hours.

On the evening of December 9, 1988, Linda Cifarelli and her husband, John, turned on the driveway heater because it was snowing. They put their two young daughters to bed upstairs and followed shortly after. A house guest, Andrew Csermak, stayed awake to watch television. After a while, Csermak became dizzy and nauseous, and eventually vomited. Csermak cracked a window and fell asleep on the downstairs couch. When Csermak awoke at noon, he was concerned because the Cifarellis were not yet awake. He went upstairs and discovered that only the infant daughter was still breathing. Csermak called 911.

Upon arrival, the police and firemen discovered the bodies of John and Linda Cifarelli and their four year old daughter. The police also found the garage door dripping with condensation and the driveway heater running. Autopsies revealed that Linda and John Cifarelli and their daughter died of carbon monoxide poisoning.

Take Note

Note that, unlike the previous *Noakes* decision from Virginia, conviction for involuntary manslaughter in Vermont requires a showing of recklessness, not gross negligence. Would Noakes have been convicted under the Vermont standard? Would Brooks have been convicted under the Virginia standard?

Defendant was convicted of involuntary manslaughter by reckless endangerment. Because the underlying unlawful act charged was reckless endangerment, defendant's conviction could only be sustained upon finding reckless intent. Defendant argues that the instruction defining recklessness was flawed because it incorporated both the criminal negligence and recklessness standards but did not distinguish between the two. Defendant maintains that while recklessness requires an actual awareness of the risk and of the resulting harm, criminal negligence requires a less stringent showing that the actor should have known of the risk and harm. According to defendant, the failure to distinguish between the two levels of intent amounted to plain error, because the jury could have convicted him if it found only that he should have known either that the heater was not repaired, or that the heater posed a risk.

We have endorsed the Model Penal Code's definition of recklessness, MPC § 2.02(2)(c), which explains:

> A person acts recklessly with respect to a material element of an offense when he consciously disregards a substantial and unjustifiable risk that the material element exists or will result from his conduct. The risk must be of such a nature and degree that, considering the nature and purpose of the actor's conduct and the circumstances known to him, its disregard involves a gross deviation from the standard of conduct that a law-abiding person would observe in the actor's situation.

In contrast, criminal negligence occurs when the actor should be aware that a substantial and unjustifiable risk exists or will result from his conduct. Disregarding the risk amounts to a gross deviation from the standard of care that a reasonable person would observe in the actor's situation.

Contrary to defendant's suggestion, both recklessness and criminal negligence require an objective view of the risk; the difference is one of degree. The more critical distinction between recklessness and criminal negligence is the actor's subjective awareness of the risk. Recklessness requires a conscious disregard of the risk. In contrast, criminal negligence results when an actor is unaware of the risk which the actor should have perceived.

The court properly instructed the jury to objectively assess the risk and to determine whether defendant consciously disregarded that risk. For further clarification, it referred the jury to the reckless endangerment instruction, which expressly required a finding that defendant "actually knew from the circumstances then existing that the heater had not properly been repaired." If there was any flaw in the instruction, it stemmed from the court's use of the term "reasonable-person" instead of "law-abiding person" when describing the standard for objectively assessing the nature of the risk. This does not amount to plain error.

Defendant challenges the court's denial of his motion for acquittal, claiming there was insufficient evidence to convict on the essential elements of recklessness and a legal duty. We consider whether the evidence, taken in a light most favorable to the State and excluding modifying evidence, is sufficient to fairly and reasonably support a finding of guilt beyond a reasonable doubt. Defendant contends that proof of both recklessness and the existence of a legal duty hinged on finding that he actually knew the driveway heater had not been repaired. Defendant argues that there was insufficient evidence to prove beyond a reasonable doubt that he knew the driveway heating unit had not been repaired. We disagree.

Defendant knew the heater was malfunctioning and emitting fumes when he took McDermott and her infant child to the hospital in November 1987. Representatives from C & L and VGS testified that they explained the exhaust problem to defendant and told him that the system was dangerous and needed repairs. Although there was conflicting testimony about who was responsible for the repairs, resolving this confusion was less important than determining when, and if, defendant thought the repairs were completed.

Defendant's position was that he thought the heater was fixed by VGS shortly after, if not immediately following, the November 1987 accident. Other witnesses, however, testified to conversations with defendant about repairing the heater which refute defendant's position. The C & L employee, Linden, testified that one month after the accident, defendant told him the heater was still unrepaired. Linden then told defendant he was "playing Russian roulette." Defendant suggests that he construed Linden's conversation with him to mean that Linden had fixed the problem. Linden testified, however, that a reasonable person would not have thought the problem was fixed. In sum, there was sufficient evidence fairly and reasonably supporting a finding that defendant actually knew the heater had not been repaired when he sold his home to the Cifarellis. With this critical finding and other supporting evidence, the jury could reasonably conclude that defendant had the requisite reckless intent. There was sufficient evidence to support a finding that defendant's failure to disclose the existence of the malfunctioning heater before selling his home amounted to a conscious disregard of a substantial and unjustifiable risk.

There was also sufficient evidence that defendant breached his legal duty to disclose the heater's defect. Where material facts are accessible to the vendor only, and he knows them not to be within the reach of the diligent attention, observation and judgment of the purchaser, the vendor of real estate is bound to disclose such facts. Defendant knew that the heater could emit noxious fumes into the home, if unattended, and that it was unrepaired when his home was on the market. Defendant also accompanied both Linda Cifarelli and the home inspector on their tours of the home. In each instance, he demonstrated the heater, but did not mention its history. The jury could reasonably conclude that defendant knew that the Cifarellis, despite two walk-throughs and a home inspection, were unaware of the heater's dangerous condition. Thus, there was sufficient evidence upon which the jury could find that defendant failed to disclose a material defect when he had a duty to disclose them.

Defendant also argues that the scope of involuntary manslaughter predicated on reckless endangerment is prone to arbitrary and discriminatory enforcement. Although we cannot specify every set of facts which constitute reckless conduct, the recklessness standard is sufficiently precise to prevent it from being arbitrarily applied. The scope of conduct which may be deemed reckless is sufficiently narrowed by the requirement that the risk, when objectively viewed, amounts to a gross deviation from the standard of conduct that a law-abiding person would observe in the actor's situation. The statute is not unconstitutionally vague.

Affirmed.

Point for Discussion

Model Penal Code

The Model Penal Code contains the following provisions defining manslaughter and negligent homicide. Note the difference in the applicable *mens rea* elements:

§ 210.3. Manslaughter.

(1) Criminal homicide constitutes manslaughter when:

(a) it is committed recklessly; or

(b) a homicide which would otherwise be murder is committed under the influence of extreme mental or emotional disturbance for which there is reasonable explanation or excuse. The reasonableness of such explanation or excuse shall be determined from the viewpoint of a person in the actor's situation under the circumstances as he believes them to be.

(2) Manslaughter is a felony of the second degree.

§ 210.4. Negligent Homicide.

(1) Criminal homicide constitutes negligent homicide when it is committed negligently.

(2) Negligent homicide is a felony of the third degree.

Hypo: *Horsing Around*

A horse escaped from a fenced enclosure at the Sea Horse Ranch. The fence was weather-worn, rotting, and dilapidated. The horse strayed onto an adjacent coastal highway, and while running free after dark one evening, collided with a car, killing the passenger when the impact of the collision crushed the roof of the passenger compartment. Assuming that the owners knew of the dilapidated condition of the fence and that horses had escaped from there previously (eight horses were found wandering free on the road that night), could they be prosecuted successfully for involuntary manslaughter? How about negligent homicide under the Model Penal Code formulation above? *See Sea Horse Ranch, Inc. v. Superior Court*, 24 Cal. App. 4th 446, 30 Cal. Rptr. 2d 681 (1994).

State v. Powell

336 N.C. 762, 446 S.E.2d 26 (1994).

FRYE, JUSTICE.

Hoke Lane Prevette, a five-foot, one and one-half inch, ninety-four pound jogger, was attacked by defendant's dogs and died as a result of multiple dog bites. The dogs were away from defendant's property and had been loose earlier that day.

Defendant owned two Rottweilers, "Bruno" and "Woody." Each dog was a little over one year old. Bruno weighed eighty pounds and Woody weighed one hundred pounds. At approximately 9:00 p.m., Hoke Prevette, who was five-foot, one and one-half inches tall and weighed ninety-four pounds, left his home to go jogging. At about 11:00 p.m., James Fainter and his wife returned [home,] discovered Prevette's body in their front yard, and notified the police. Prevette did not have a pulse. Dr. John Butts, Chief Medical Examiner for the State of North Carolina, concluded that Prevette died as the result of multiple dog bites. Prevette's external injuries included shallow scrapes, deeper puncture wounds that extended down into tissue, evulsing skin, and skin torn away creating large holes in some places. His internal injuries included broken ribs on the left side and collapsed lungs. The cause of death was determined to be collapsed lungs, loss of blood, and choking.

David Moore, who lived nearby, testified that he saw defendant's dogs when he arrived home at about 9:30 p.m. One of the dogs growled but both dogs relented when Moore stamped his foot. Another neighbor [encountered] two Rottweilers he recognized as defendant's dogs earlier that evening when he drove his sister and sister-in-law home. He held the dogs at bay while the women entered the house.

After the discovery of Prevette's body, Police Officer Jason Swaim went to defendant's house to investigate a report that defendant's dogs had been out that evening. When Swaim advised defendant that he wanted to see his dogs, defendant responded, "Oh my God, what have they done now?" Defendant admitted that his dogs had been out twice that day and that he picked the dogs up in his automobile at approximately 9:00 p.m. at the intersection of Cascade Avenue and Dinmont Street.

Robert Neill of the State Bureau of Investigation Crime Laboratory testified that six hairs removed from Prevette's clothing were canine; however, he could not match the hairs to a particular dog. An SBI forensic serologist found human blood on Woody's collar, on a sample of Woody's hair, on the dog dish, on a portion of the wall from defendant's home, and on defendant's car seat. A forensic odontologist testified that dental impressions taken from Bruno and Woody were compatible with some of the lacerations in the wounds pictured in scale photographs of Prevette's body.

Several witnesses testified to seeing Bruno and Woody running loose in the neighborhood prior to 20 October 1989 and to their aggressive behavior. Defendant's former girlfriend testified that defendant abused the dogs by kicking and hitting them. Animal Psychologist Donna Brown testified regarding an evaluation for aggressive propensities that she performed on Bruno and Woody in November 1989. She videotaped her testing and showed the videotape to the jury. Dr. Brown concluded that both dogs showed dominance and predatory aggression. She opined that an attack on a person would be consistent with her observations of Bruno's and Woody's behavior.

Animal Behavioralist Peter Borthelt testified for the defense that, although he had not evaluated the dogs, he had reviewed Dr. Brown's videotape and her results which he found to be ambiguous. He testified that aggressiveness was only one possible interpretation of the dogs' behavior and that some of it could be labeled "play."

Defendant presented several witnesses who testified that Bruno and Woody were friendly and playful and responded to his commands to get down or sit. Other defense witnesses testified that the dogs were not aggressive when they were loose in the neighborhood. Powell was convicted of involuntary manslaughter.

Defendant contends that there was insufficient evidence to establish the essential elements of involuntary manslaughter; thus, the trial court erred in denying his motion to dismiss at the close of all the evidence. Involuntary manslaughter is the unlawful killing of a human being without malice, without premeditation and deliberation, and without intention to kill or inflict serious bodily injury. Involuntary manslaughter may also be defined as the unintentional killing of a human being without malice, proximately caused by (1) an unlawful act not amounting to a felony nor naturally dangerous to human life, or (2) a culpably negligent act or omission. An intentional, willful or wanton violation of a statute or ordinance, designed for the protection of human life or limb, which proximately results in injury or death, is culpable negligence. A death which is proximately caused by culpable negligence is involuntary manslaughter.

Take Note

Note that, similar to the *Noakes* decision from Virginia but unlike the *Brooks* decision from Vermont, conviction for involuntary manslaughter in North Carolina requires a showing of culpable negligence, not recklessness. Would Powell have been convicted under the Vermont recklessness standard?

At the time of the attack on Prevette, a Winston-Salem ordinance provided:

> No dog shall be left unattended outdoors unless it is restrained and restricted to the owner's property by a tether, rope, chain, fence or other device. Fencing, as required herein, shall be adequate in height, construction and placement to keep resident dogs on the lot, and keep other dogs and children from accessing the lot. One (1) or more secured gates to the lot shall be provided.

A safety statute or ordinance is one designed for the protection of life or limb and which imposes a duty upon members of society to uphold that protection. According to the Court of Appeals and the State, this section of the Winston-Salem Code "was designed to protect both the persons of Winston-Salem and their property, and thus is a safety ordinance." Defendant contends that the ordinance is merely a nuisance law "designed to prevent roaming dogs from trespassing, damaging property, leaving waste in neighbors' yards and interfering with traffic."

After a careful reading of the ordinance, we conclude that it is designed to protect persons as well as property. Although it is silent as to its purpose, a logical reading of the ordinance leads us to conclude that it promotes the safety of persons as well as property. It is without question that the ordinance has the effect of protecting property from damage by roaming dogs. However, the life and limb of pedestrians, joggers, and the public at large are protected by this ordinance as well. The ordinance protects people generally by confining the dogs to the owner's property while providing, in some cases, an adequate fence to keep animals and children from accessing the lot and being exposed to the dogs. The fact that the ordinance serves a dual purpose does not make it any less a safety ordinance.

The evidence that defendant intentionally, willfully, or wantonly violated the safety ordinance was aptly set out by the Court of Appeals.

> Bruno and Woody had been picked up by animal control officers on at least three occasions prior to the fatal attack. The dogs had been taken by animal control officers to the animal shelter as recently as August, 1989, two months prior to the death of Prevette. Defendant admitted that his dogs had been out twice on the day of Prevette's death. On one occasion in July, 1989, after the dogs escaped by digging out from underneath the fence, defendant simply covered the escape hole with a cooler after returning the dogs to the fence. Defendant's next-door neighbor testified that the dogs were allowed to run loose "on a regular basis," day and night, and

that defendant would often "just open the door and let the dogs out." Defendant's ex-girlfriend testified that defendant let the dogs run free both day and night.

The trial judge instructed the jury that "the violation of a statute or ordinance governing the care of dogs which results in injury or death will constitute culpable negligence if the violation is willful, wanton, or intentional." Viewed in the light most favorable to the State, as we must on a motion to dismiss, we find that the State presented sufficient evidence that defendant intentionally, willfully, or wantonly violated the ordinance.

The decision of the Court of Appeals is affirmed.

Hypo: *Spousal Psychosis*

Andrea Yates was convicted of murder for drowning her five children. The evidence revealed that, following her second pregnancy and with every pregnancy thereafter, she suffered post-partum psychosis. At the time of the murders, she claimed that she believed that the only way to get her children to heaven (and thereby escape the devil), was to kill them. Suppose that Andrea's husband, Rusty, was aware that she suffered post-partum psychosis after each pregnancy, but continued having children with her. Suppose further that, at the time of the killings, it was clear that she was suffering mental problems in conjunction with post-partum psychosis following the birth of her fifth child. Nevertheless, each morning, Rusty went to work and left Andrea alone with their children. Rusty's mother came to help Andrea later in the day, but there was a two-hour gap during which Andrea was alone with the children. If the preceding suppositions are treated as fact, did Rusty commit either involuntary manslaughter or negligent homicide (as defined by the MPC)?

See It

See Rusty Yates tell "his side" of the story on CBS' 60 Minutes television show aired December 9, 2001, at http://www.youtube.com/watch?v=S3xN__s2-KQ. Do his comments in this interview make you feel more or less strongly about his potential culpability for the death of his children? How would you have responded to these comments if you were a prosecutor in this jurisdiction?

People v. McCoy

223 Mich.App. 500, 566 N.W.2d 667 (1997).

PER CURIAM.

Defendant appeals as of right his jury trial convictions of involuntary manslaughter, felonious driving, and leaving the scene of an accident. Defendant was sentenced as a third-offense habitual offender to concurrent terms of twelve to thirty years' imprisonment for the manslaughter conviction, three to ten years' imprisonment for the felonious driving conviction, and one to four years' imprisonment for the conviction of leaving the scene of an accident. We affirm.

Defendant's first claim on appeal is that the prosecution presented insufficient evidence of gross negligence to support his convictions of manslaughter and felonious driving. We disagree.

In reviewing claims of insufficiency of the evidence to sustain a verdict, this Court views the evidence in the light most favorable to the prosecution to determine if a rational factfinder could find the essential elements of the crime proved beyond a reasonable doubt. An unlawful act, committed with the intent to injure or in a grossly negligent manner, that proximately causes death is involuntary manslaughter. As with involuntary manslaughter, a conviction of felonious driving requires proof of gross negligence. The Court in *People v. Datema*, 448 Mich. 585, 604, 533 N.W.2d 272 (1995), explained the distinction between criminal intent, negligence, and gross negligence:

> The legally significant mental states should be viewed as lying on a continuum: criminal intention anchors one end of the spectrum and negligence anchors the other. Intention, as explained by Professor Hall, "emphasizes that the actor seeks the proscribed harm not in the sense that he desires it, but in the sense that he has chosen it, he has decided to bring it into being." Negligence, lying at the opposite end of the spectrum, "implies inadvertence, i.e., that the defendant was completely unaware of the dangerousness of this behavior although actually it was unreasonably increasing the risk of occurrence of an injury."
>
> Criminal negligence, also referred to as gross negligence, lies within the extremes of intention and negligence. As with intention, the actor realizes the risk of his behavior and consciously decides to create that risk. As with negligence, however, the actor does not seek to cause harm, but is simply recklessly or wantonly indifferent to the results.

Food for Thought

Is this definition of "criminal negligence" the same as the Model Penal Code definition? Is it the same definition the courts used in the previous *Noakes* and *Powell* decisions? Would a change in the way that "criminal negligence" is defined make a difference in outcome in any of these cases?

Here, two sisters were standing on the yellow line in the middle of Greenfield Road waiting for traffic to clear when they were struck from behind by a van driven by defendant. One of the sisters was killed, and the other was injured. The accident occurred at approximately 3:00 p.m. on February 3, 1995, as the deceased was on her way home from school. The sole witness to the accident testified that the van was traveling at a speed of approximately fifty to fifty-five miles an hour when it struck the two sisters. The posted speed limit was thirty-five miles an hour. Defendant argues that this evidence was insufficient to show that he was driving in a grossly negligent manner at the time that he struck the decedent.

In order to show gross negligence, the following elements must be established:

(1) Knowledge of a situation requiring the exercise of ordinary care and diligence to avert injury to another.

(2) Ability to avoid the resulting harm by ordinary care and diligence in the use of the means at hand.

(3) The omission to use such care and diligence to avert the threatened danger when to the ordinary mind it must be apparent that the result is likely to prove disastrous to another.

Here, there is no question that a jury could properly infer that defendant knew that the act of driving requires the exercise of ordinary care and diligence to avert injury to others. Similarly, there is no question that a jury could properly infer under these facts that defendant had the ability to avoid the harm that occurred by exercising ordinary care and diligence, but failed to do so. Accordingly, the only question is whether to the ordinary mind it must have been apparent that the result was likely to prove disastrous to another.

Food for Thought

Why not? Why isn't speeding enough to demonstrate gross negligence? Does this make sense?

A violation of the speed limit, by itself, is not adequate to establish the element of gross negligence. However, under certain circumstances, a violation of the speed limit can be gross negligence. A jury could properly determine that traveling at a speed of one hundred miles an hour through a residential neighborhood is gross negligence. Similarly, given the right conditions, it is possible to drive in a grossly negligent manner even in the absence of exceeding the speed limit (e.g., in heavy traffic, on slick roads, or in fog). Accordingly, the appropriate consideration is not whether defendant was exceeding the speed limit, but rather, whether defendant acted with gross negligence under the totality of the circumstances, including defendant's actual speed and the posted speed limit. This is a question that ordinarily is for the jury.

Viewing the evidence in a light most favorable to the prosecution, a jury could reasonably find that at the time his van struck the two sisters, defendant was traveling at a speed of fifty-five miles an hour in a thirty-five miles an hour zone during heavy traffic conditions. This speed was "a lot faster than the rest of traffic," and significantly faster than the average speed on that stretch of road of forty to forty-five miles an hour. Finally, the two sisters had been standing stationary at the same location for several seconds. The fact that defendant did not slow down or swerve in an attempt to avoid striking them suggests that he was traveling at a reckless speed. A reasonable jury could find that defendant was grossly negligent.

This conclusion is strengthened by the testimony concerning defendant's conduct immediately following the accident. Defendant approached the next light at a speed of fifty miles an hour. Defendant slowed down to a speed of twenty-five miles an hour to make a left turn onto Puritan against a red light. He nearly hit several cars in the process. Defendant continued on Puritan, weaving in and out of traffic, and forcing a vehicle in the oncoming lane off the road. The van then turned left, tires squealing, nearly hitting a grandmother and her grandchildren. It is true that evidence of immoderate speed at points remote from the scene of the accident is incompetent to establish immoderate speed at the accident scene itself. Here, however, the facts that subsequent observations took place in the immediate vicinity of the accident, and that defendant's speed did not change between the time of the accident and the time that he approached the first intersection, would allow a reasonable jury to conclude that defendant engaged in a single, continuous pattern of grossly negligent driving. Accordingly, the trial court did not err in denying defendant's motion for a directed verdict.

Affirmed.

Point for Discussion

Vehicular Homicide Offenses

In a number of jurisdictions, separate vehicular homicide offenses exist (distinct from involuntary manslaughter and other homicide offenses) which apply to deaths resulting from negligent operation of a motor vehicle. Typically, these specific forms of negligent homicide statutes provide for lower levels of punishment than involuntary manslaughter statutes, and are established by a lower level of intentionality. The appropriate *mens rea* for such an offense is, of course, dictated by the legislature.

Why do you suppose jurisdictions might prefer to enact *separate* criminal offenses to apply to vehicular homicide? Why not cover this activity under the standard involuntary manslaughter offense or under a *general* negligent homicide statute?

Hypo 1: *Deadly Texting*

Defendant was texting while driving down a city street. Her speed was at or near the speed limit, but because she was not paying sufficient attention, she ran off the road, killing a pedestrian. Is she guilty of involuntary manslaughter or negligent homicide? Or might she be guilty of murder instead?

Hypo 2: *Death by Skidding*

Defendant is driving on very icy streets going the speed limit (35 mph). When the car in front of him stops unexpectedly, he slams on his brakes but is unable to stop because of the ice. His car veers onto the sidewalk killing a pedestrian. Is he guilty of involuntary manslaughter or negligent homicide?

Executive Summary

Murder. All murder requires a showing of malice. Premeditated murder, sometimes termed murder in the first degree, is an intentional killing that also requires proof of premeditated, willful and deliberate conduct on the part of the accused.

Major Themes

a. Change from Common Law—At common law, the presence or absence of "malice aforethought" was the distinguishing factor between murder (requiring malice) and manslaughter (no malice). That distinction tends to remain true today. But a number of additional, statutory homicide offenses also exist in every jurisdiction, criminalizing both intentional and unintentional killings. Unintentional killings are typically treated as less heinous homicide crimes and are punished less severely; intentional killings are typically treated and punished as the most culpable kinds of homicides.

b. Nature of Homicide Offenses—All homicide offenses require proof of a killing act (*actus reus*) committed by the accused which caused the death of a human being. The key distinction between the various homicide crimes is the different *mens rea* required to establish each separate statutory offense. Typically, the more difficult the *mens rea* is to prove, the more serious the homicide offense.

Malice. Malice is wickedness of disposition, hardness of heart, wanton conduct, cruelty, recklessness of consequences, and/or a mind without regard to social duty. It is the distinguishing factor between murder and manslaughter in most jurisdictions. It may be proved expressly or it may usually be implied from the defendant's killing act committed with gross recklessness or from his or her actions establishing extreme indifference to the value of human life.

Premeditation and Deliberation. Some jurisdictions require proof of sustained and meaningful deliberation to establish this element, while others require proof only of momentary reflection. In the latter jurisdictions, "no time is too short" for an accused murderer to have been able to premeditate and deliberate sufficiently to justify conviction for first degree murder.

Voluntary Manslaughter. Voluntary manslaughter is mitigated murder. The mitigation usually arises because the defendant was found to have been reasonably provoked and to have acted in the heat of passion, or because the defendant honestly believed he or she needed to kill for protection purposes, but that belief was objectively unreasonable.

Felony Murder. Most jurisdictions have enacted a separate felony murder offense, transferring the necessary intent for murder from the accused person's commission of a specified, triggering felony.

Involuntary Manslaughter. Involuntary manslaughter is an unintentional killing committed without malice. Most jurisdictions use a gross (criminal) negligence *mens rea* as an element of this offense, but others use the *mens rea* element of recklessness instead.

Negligent Homicide. In some jurisdictions where involuntary manslaughter requires proof of recklessness, there is a lesser offense of negligent homicide which applies to criminally negligent killings.

For More Information

- AMERICAN LAW INSTITUTE, MODEL PENAL CODE AND COMMENTARIES, Part II, Article 210 (1980).
- Guyora Binder, *The Culpability of Felony Murder*, 83 NOTRE DAME L. REV. 965 (2008).
- Michal Buchhandler-Raphael, *Loss of Self-Control, Dual-Process Theories, and Provocation*, 88 FORDHAM L.REV. 1815 (2020).
- JOHN M. BURKOFF & RUSSELL L. WEAVER, INSIDE CRIMINAL LAW: WHAT MATTERS AND WHY 135–152 (2d ed. 2011).
- David Crump, *"Murder Pennsylvania Style": Comparing Traditional American Homicide Law to the Statutes of Model Penal Code Jurisdictions*, 109 W. VA. L. REV. 257 (2007).
- Joshua Dressler, *Rethinking Heat of Passion: A Defense in Search of a Rationale*, 73 J. CRIM. L. & CRIMINOLOGY 421 (1982).
- Joshua Dressler, *Why Keep the Provocation Defense?: Some Reflections on a Difficult Subject*, 86 MINN. L. REV. 959 (2002).
- Reid Fontaine, *Adequate (Non)Provocation and Heat of Passion as Excuse Not Justification*, 43 U. MICH. J.L. REFORM 27 (2009).
- Caroline Forell, *Domestic Homicides: The Continuing Search for Justice*, 25 AM. U. J. GENDER SOC. POL'Y & L. 1 (2017).
- Richard Holton & Stephen Shute, *Self-Control in the Modern Provocation Defense*, 27 OXFORD J. LEGAL STUD. 49 (2007).
- Kyron Huigens, *Provocation at Face Value*, 95 MARQ. L. REV. 409 (2012).
- Victoria F. Nourse, *Passion's Progress: Modern Law Reform and the Provocation Defense*, 106 YALE L.J. 1331 (1997).
- 3 JAMES STEPHEN, A HISTORY OF THE CRIMINAL LAW IN ENGLAND (1883).
- James J. Tomkovicz, *The Endurance of the Felony Murder Rule: A Study of the Forces that Shape Our Criminal Law*, 51 WASH. & LEE L. REV. 1429 (1994).

Test Your Knowledge

To assess your understanding of the material in this chapter, click here to take a quiz.

Chapter 9

Assault & Battery

Early state criminal codes often did not define the elements of the crimes of "battery" or "assault" because judges were expected to use English precedents to identify and interpret these elements. These precedents recognized two definitions of the battery crime and one definition of the assault crime. Over time, the elements of these definitions were codified in most states, but even today, some codes leave the terms "battery" and "assault" undefined.

The common law battery crimes were broadly defined under English law. One type required proof that the defendant's conduct caused "bodily injury" to the victim, and the other type required proof of an "offensive touching" of the victim. By contrast, the only type of "assault" crime under English law was the attempt to commit a battery, and it was defined narrowly to cover only defendants who had the actual ability to commit a battery and came very close to doing so. Over time, many state courts and legislatures decided to recognize a second type of "frightening" assault crime, requiring evidence that the defendant engaged in frightening conduct with the intent to cause the victim to fear bodily injury. Most states also require the result element of a frightened victim.

Today the bodily injury type of battery crime, and both types of assault crimes, are defined by statute in most states. The offensive touching battery crime has been preserved by only a minority of states, either through codification or through precedents interpreting the undefined term "battery" in a statute.

The MPC drafters endorsed the trend toward abandoning the offensive-touching battery crime by leaving this crime out of the MPC. They also followed the longstanding tradition established by state legislatures for distinguishing between "aggravated" and "simple" categories of battery and assault crimes. However, the MPC drafters used the name "Assault" for all versions of these crimes. In order to avoid confusion, the term "battery" will be used in this chapter as the name for *any* crime that derives from one of the two types of common law battery. The term "assault" will be used only for crimes that derive either from the attempted battery assault crime or the frightening assault crime.

In this chapter, the evolution of the elements of common law battery and assault will be studied, as the foundation for understanding the origins of such modern offenses as reckless endangerment, exposure to HIV, stalking, and domestic violence crimes.

A. Battery

1. Bodily Injury Battery

The *Gordon* case illustrates the broad scope of the definition of the element of "bodily injury" that is commonly used in state codes and case law.

State v. Gordon

560 N.W.2d 4 (Iowa 1997).

LAVARATO, JUSTICE.

A jury convicted [Gordon] of [the battery crime of] causing bodily injury, a serious misdemeanor. In his appeal, Gordon challenges [a jury] instruction defining bodily injury[.] [We] conclude the instruction was reversible error. We reverse and remand for a new trial[.]

[On] October 3, 1995, Gordon was in the home of Mary Johnston in Prairie City. Several other people were present, including Jeremiah Fry. Apparently unprovoked, Gordon stood up from where he was seated, spun around, and kicked Fry in the chest. As he kicked Fry, Gordon said, "Die pale-face pumpkin head." The kick left a red mark to the right of Fry's sternum. Two witnesses saw the incident, but neither saw whether Gordon's foot made contact with Fry's chest. A short time later, a Prairie City police officer saw Fry, interviewed him, and saw a heel imprint on Fry's shirt. When Fry raised his shirt, the officer saw what he described as a "reddening" on Fry's chest[.]

[After] all of the evidence was in, the State asked the court to instruct the jury that "marks" constitute an injury for purposes of [battery]. Defense counsel objected and suggested a definition of bodily injury taken from the Model Penal Code and adopted in *State v. McKee*, 312 N.W.2d 907, 913 (Iowa 1981). Defense counsel argued that no case had recognized a red mark as a bodily injury. This prompted [a] *colloquy* between the court and defense counsel.

What's That?

This *colloquy* was a conversation on the record, between the court and counsel, that occurred outside of the presence of the jury.

[The court asked counsel, "Are you going to argue to the jury that a red mark on the skin is not a bodily injury?" Counsel replied, "I may." The court responded, "All right. Then I'll tell the jury that a red mark on the skin is a bodily injury because they have a right to know that, and if there's a dispute, then I'll clear it up."]

Over defense counsel's objection, the court instructed the jury as follows:

A "bodily" injury means a bodily or physical pain, illness, or any impairment of physical condition. A red mark or bruise on the skin would constitute an impairment of physical condition, and therefore an injury.

Practice Pointer

The defense counsel in Gordon had a duty to object to the "red mark" instruction because it dictated conviction. But raising and preserving that objection required persistence, given the trial judge's determination to prevent defense counsel from arguing that the evidence of bodily injury was insufficient.

The jury convicted Gordon of [battery] and the court sentenced Gordon to one year in jail, suspended all but ninety days of the sentence, put him on supervised probation for one year, and fined him $200[.] . . .

[In] *McKee*, we adopted the Model Penal Code's definition of bodily injury [as] "physical pain, illness, or any impairment of physical condition." [In] adopting this definition[,] we explained[:]

> Bodily injury ordinarily "refers only to injury to the body, or to sickness or disease contracted by the injured as a result of injury." [BLACK'S LAW DICTIONARY 159 (5th ed. 1979).] Injury includes "an act that damages, harms, or hurts: an unjust or undeserved infliction of suffering or harm[.]" [WEBSTER'S THIRD NEW INTERNATIONAL DICTIONARY 1164 (1976).] Thus the ordinary dictionary definition of bodily injury coincides with the Model Penal Code definition of the term[.]

[We] have no quarrel, therefore, with the district court's definition of bodily injury in so far as it coincides with the Model Penal Code. We agree, however, with Gordon that the court went too far when it instructed the jury that "[a] red mark or bruise on the skin would constitute an impairment of physical condition, and therefore an injury."

Neither the Model Penal Code nor the Iowa Code defines impairment of physical condition. [Therefore,] [i]n *McKee* we also defined impairment[:]

> An impairment, according to common usage, includes any deviation from normal health. The term means: "To weaken, to make worse, to lessen in power, diminish, or relax, or otherwise affect in any injurious manner. [BLACK'S LAW DICTIONARY 677 (5th ed. 1979).]

There was no direct evidence that Fry suffered any deviation from normal health because of the blow. Nor did he testify that he had any pain or illness because of the blow. Those were fact questions peculiarly within the jury's common experience and for them to decide.

Food for Thought

What are the possible reasons why the *Gordon* prosecutor apparently failed to put the victim on the stand to testify about his experience of being kicked by the defendant?

In a recent case we observed that "welts, bruises, or similar markings are not physical injuries *per se* but may be and frequently are evidence from which the existence of a physical injury can be found." *Hildreth v. Iowa Dep't of Human Servs.*, 550 N.W.2d 157, 160 (Iowa 1996). Although the observation was made in a different context, [we] think it fits here. The red mark or bruise on Fry's chest was not a physical impairment *per se* but only evidence of such impairment.

Had the district court merely given the definition of a bodily injury and stopped, the jury could have found the red mark or bruise was not a bodily injury. The court's gratuitous addition was especially prejudicial to Gordon because [the] only direct evidence of injury was that Fry had suffered a "reddening" on his chest.

What's That?

A *directed verdict* occurs when a trial judge takes a case from the jury because only one reasonable verdict may be reached on the evidence. Such a ruling may be granted in favor of a defendant in a criminal case, but not in favor of the State.

In effect, the district court *directed a verdict* in favor of the State on bodily injury, a critical element of the offense. In doing so the court invaded the province of the jury and committed error[.] [Because] the error here was prejudicial, we reverse and remand for a new trial.

Reversed and Remanded.

Points for Discussion

a. *Actus Reus* & *Mens Rea* of Bodily Injury Battery

The same mental state of criminal negligence was used for both types of common law battery crimes—bodily injury battery and offensive touching battery. For the bodily injury crime, the MPC uses "recklessness", while saving the "negligence" mental state for the crime of causing bodily injury with a deadly weapon. The *Gordon* defendant made no argument on appeal concerning his mental state. Assuming that the *Gordon* prosecutor charged the defendant with "recklessly" causing a bodily injury to Fry by kicking him in the chest, could defense counsel have made any arguments to the jury to raise a reasonable doubt about the recklessness mental state?

The broad scope of the term "bodily injury" at common law is reflected in the similar Model Penal Code definition that was borrowed and adopted by the Iowa Supreme Court in the *McKee* case relied upon in *Gordon*, namely, "physical pain, illness, or any impairment of physical condition." The injury could be a minor one, as long as the victim experienced temporarily some "deviation from normal health." What are the policy reasons that may explain the unwillingness of courts and legislatures to define "bodily injury" more narrowly, especially in the majority of states that have abolished the "offensive touching" battery crime?

The *Gordon* Court did not need to address the question whether the prosecution produced sufficient evidence of "bodily injury" at the first trial, because of the trial judge's unusual blunder in giving an erroneous jury instruction. The *Gordon* Court observed hypothetically that a properly instructed jury might have acquitted the defendant because of insufficient evidence of "bodily injury." The following problems focus on the evidence needed for a bodily injury battery conviction.

Hypo 1: *New Evidence*

Assume that the prosecutor is preparing for the new trial of the *Gordon* defendant. The prosecutor is concerned about the challenge of persuading the jury to convict and the appellate court to affirm the conviction. What witnesses should the prosecutor use at the new trial, and what testimony should be elicited from them, in order to provide sufficient evidence of "bodily injury" of the victim? Explain.

Hypo 2: *When Impairment "Includes" Pain*

Bea is convicted for committing a bodily injury type of battery crime against Jane in Missouri under a "domestic battery" statute that applies to "a person who purposely or knowingly touches an individual who is or who was a spouse of the other person in a rude, insolent, or angry manner that results in bodily injury to the person touched," with bodily injury being defined by that statute "as any impairment of physical condition, including physical pain." Bea and Jane are ex-spouses. During a quarrel, Bea repeatedly poked Jane hard in the forehead, and Jane later testified that it felt as though someone was sticking a knife in her head. The language of the Missouri statute differs from the two typical definitions of bodily injury used in other states. Some state codes define bodily injury as "pain, illness, or an impairment of physical condition," which state courts interpret as meaning "any pain is bodily injury" so that "no particular level of pain (in degree or duration) is required to rise to the level of impairment of physical condition." However, other state codes define bodily injury as "an impairment of physical condition or substantial pain," which state courts interpret as meaning "only substantial pain is bodily injury," so that "pain must cross some threshold of severity in order to constitute bodily injury," which threshold "may be determined by the factfinder at trial."

When Bea appealed her conviction, the intermediate appellate court reversed on the theory that since the Missouri statute does not state expressly that "any pain is bodily injury," it should be interpreted like the statutes that require "substantial" pain. The intermediate appellate court also held that "pain is not substantial unless it is comparable or worse than the pain suffered by victims in prior Missouri prosecutions that produced convictions." What reasoning can the Missouri Supreme Court use to reject these interpretations and affirm Bea's conviction on the theory that the Missouri statute means that "any pain is bodily injury"?

b. Aggravated vs. Simple Battery

The crime of battery was only a misdemeanor under the English common law, and the corresponding felony crime was mayhem, which was defined narrowly to punish those who caused bodily injuries that affected a victim's ability to fight in battle. As the mayhem crime became obsolete in America, state legislatures replaced it with felony crime definitions of "aggravated" battery (an American invention) and changed the name of the English common law crime to "simple" battery. Today the "simple battery" crime in most state codes resembles the English misdemeanor crime of bodily injury battery, whereas "aggravated battery" is likely to include a variety of definitions with more serious penalties than simple battery. Many state statutes define aggravated battery to include these extra elements (as well as others): 1) the result of "serious bodily injury" instead of mere "bodily injury"; 2) the use of a "deadly or dangerous weapon"; 3) the mental state for a violent felony crime, such as the intent to kill or the intent to rob; or 4) the fact that the victim was a member of a specified class, such as law enforcement officers.

c. Model Penal Code Approach

The MPC drafters followed the tradition of using the serious injury and deadly weapon elements to make distinctions between aggravated and simple crimes, but rejected the use of the other types of elements. They defined the MPC versions of battery and assault using the MPC mental states, and they did not use any status-of-victim elements for their aggravated crimes, thereby treating all victims equally. See Model Penal Code § 211.1, Comment 2 at 185 (1980). However, many state statutes continue to use the four traditional elements to define the aggravated versions of battery and assault crimes today, and many state codes use a wide variety of other elements.

Hypo: *MPC Choices*

There are four different crimes in Model Penal Code § 211.1 that are derived from the common law crime of bodily injury battery. The provisions labeled here as (1) and (2) are the equivalent of simple battery, whereas (3) and (4) are the equivalent of aggravated battery:

(1) purposely, knowingly or recklessly causes *bodily injury* to another; or

(2) negligently causes *bodily injury* to another with a *deadly weapon*;

(3) causes *serious bodily injury* to another purposely, knowingly or recklessly under circumstances manifesting extreme indifference to the value of human life;

(4) purposely or knowingly causes *bodily injury* to another with a *deadly weapon*.

Identify any variations of bodily injury battery that you notice are missing from this list, and consider the reasons that the MPC drafters may have rejected them. Then explain whether the defendants in *Adams* and *Gordon* could be convicted using any of these MPC crimes.

d. Rare Consent Defense

Consent is rarely a defense to crimes that result in bodily injury, and one reason is because "society has an interest in punishing [such crimes] as breaches of the public peace and order so that an individual cannot consent to a wrong that is committed against the public peace." *State v. Shelley*, 85 Wash. App. 24, 29, 929 P.2d 489, 491–492 (1997). Another reason is that consent cannot be a defense to activities that are "against public policy"; thus, "a child cannot consent to hazing [and] a gang member cannot consent to an initiation beating." *State v. Hiott*, 97 Wash. App. 825, 828, 987 P.2d 135, 136–137 (1999). However, some states have codified MPC § 211(2)(b) that recognizes the consent defense when "the conduct and the injury are reasonably foreseeable hazards of joint participation in a lawful athletic contest or competitive sport." The *Hiott* Court emphasized that the consent defense must be limited to games that are "accepted by society as lawful athletic contests" or "competitive sports," which games "carry with them generally accepted rules, at least some of which are intended to prevent or minimize injuries", and which "commonly prescribe the use of protective devices or clothing to prevent injuries."

---

2. Offensive Touching Battery

It is useful to focus on the differences between the elements of the two common law battery crimes, in order to understand the reasons that most states now punish only the more serious type, which is bodily injury battery.

The *Adams* case illustrates the decision of one state court to expand the scope of offensive touching battery through judicial interpretation of its original common law elements. The *Adams* majority opinion and the *Adams* dissent implicitly disagree about the meaning of the *legality principle*, in the context of interpreting a common law battery crime that is not defined by statute. The *Adams* dissent reflects the view that legislatures, not courts, should invent new crimes such as "laser battery." The *Adams* majority assumes that the court has the authority to rely on the common law tradition of reasoning by analogy to expand an old legal concept to fit a new harm like an offensive touching with an "intangible substance."

> **What's That?**
>
> The *legality principle* is associated with the maxim, *nulla poena sine lege*, or "No punishment without law." In this instance, "law" means legislation that defines all crimes and provides fair notice of their meaning.

Adams v. Commonwealth

33 Va. App. 463, 534 S.E.2d 347 (2000).

[Before] WILLIS, LEMONS and FRANK, JJ.

FRANK, JUDGE.

[On] appeal, [Adams] contends the evidence was insufficient to prove: (1) a touching and (2) that he had the requisite intent to commit the offense [of battery]. We disagree and affirm the conviction.

I. BACKGROUND

[On] September 22, 1998, while on duty at the Gloucester County High School, Sergeant Steven Giles of the Gloucester County Sheriff's Department was struck in his right eye by a laser light owned by [Adams], who was a twelfth-grade student at the school. Giles had been talking with another [sheriff's officer] and the school nurse when he felt a "stinging sensation" in his eye. [The other officer] told Giles that [Adams] had "just lit [him] up," as there was "a red dot" on him.

Giles approached [Adams] and asked what he had. [Adams] said, "It can't hurt you," and handed over the laser light, which was attached to his key chain. Giles gave the laser light to the assistant principal and told [Adams] he could retrieve it later.

Giles said he "felt a burning sensation" in his eye and "saw red" before looking away, but he did not know how long the laser had been pointed at him. Giles had his eye checked the next morning by a local doctor who found "heavy irritation" but no other injury.

[The other officer] testified that [Adams] was approximately 150 feet from Giles and the laser light had "jump[ed] all around his upper torso and head." [The other officer] did not "actually see the thing strike [Giles'] eye," but he saw Giles flinch when he was hit. [Two students] testified that they did not see the laser strike Giles in the face or eyes. They also said they had not been hurt when similarly hit in the eye with a laser light.

[Adams] testified that he purchased the laser light for six dollars at a convenience store two days before the offense. He said it had no warning on it regarding use and that he had not been hurt when hit in the eye by the light. [Adams] denied hitting Giles in the face or eye and claimed he had not intended to strike Giles with the light but, instead, was "just goofing off" to get [the] attention [of the other officer] by waving the laser around. [Adams] had a friendly relationship with [the other officer.] [Adams], however, did not get along well with Sergeant Giles. He stated that Giles had previously given him a hard time. . . .

[After a bench trial, the trial judge convicted Adams of the crime of "[battery] against another [person,] knowing or having reason to know that such other person is a law-enforcement officer . . . engaged in the performance of his public duties." Conviction for this felony requires that a person "shall be sentenced to a *mandatory, minimum* term of six months in jail." VA. CODE ANN. § 18.2–57(C).]

II. ANALYSIS

In reviewing the sufficiency of the evidence on appeal, "[we] may not disturb the trial court's judgment unless it is 'plainly wrong or without evidence to support it.'" *Barlow v. Commonwealth*, 26 Va. App. 421, 429, 494 S.E.2d 901 (1998). . . . ["]Battery is [the] least touching of another's person[,] willfully or in anger, whether by the party's own hand, or by some means set in motion by him." *Seegars v. Commonwealth*, 18 Va. App. 641, 644, 445 S.E.2d 720, 722 (1994).

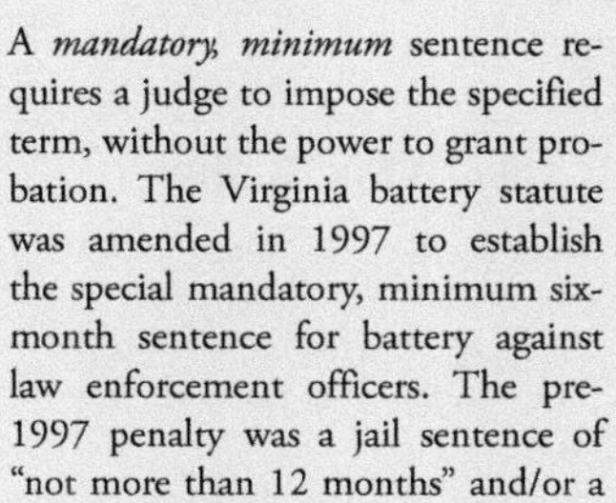

What's That?

A *mandatory, minimum* sentence requires a judge to impose the specified term, without the power to grant probation. The Virginia battery statute was amended in 1997 to establish the special mandatory, minimum six-month sentence for battery against law enforcement officers. The pre-1997 penalty was a jail sentence of "not more than 12 months" and/or a fine of not more than $2,500.

A battery is an unlawful touching of another. It is not necessary that the touching result in injury to the person. Whether a touching is a battery depends on the intent of the actor, not on the force applied. See *Wood v. Commonwealth*, 149 Va. 401, 140 S.E. 114, 115 (1927). . . .

A. Touching

Practice Pointer

When the "*assault and battery*" catchphrase appears in a statute, in charging documents, or in an opinion, the crime presented to the jury is likely to be battery, as in *Adams*. The prosecutor will choose the theory of the case that will dictate the elements of the crime to be proved at trial.

Adams contends that shining the laser on Sergeant Giles was insufficient to constitute a touching for the purposes of *assault and battery*. Touch is defined as to be in contact or to cause to be in contact. *See Merriam-Webster's Desk Dictionary* 573 (1995).

In Virginia, it is abundantly clear that a perpetrator need not inflict a physical injury to commit a battery. *See, e.g., Lynch v. Commonwealth*, 131 Va. 762, 765, 109 S.E. 427 (1921). The cases that guide our analysis, however, have not addressed circumstances where contact with the corporeal person was accomplished by directing a beam of light at the victim. Because substances such as light or sound become elusive when considered in terms of battery, contact by means of such substances must be examined further in determining whether a touching has occurred. Such a test is necessary due to the intangible nature of those substances and the need to limit application of such a principle (touching by intangible substances) to reasonable cases. Because the underlying concerns of battery law are breach of the peace and sacredness of the person, the dignity of the victim is implicated and the reasonableness and offensiveness of the contact must be considered. Otherwise, criminal convictions could result from the routine and insignificant exposure to concentrated energy that inevitably results from living in populated society.

Accordingly, we hold that for purposes of determining whether a battery has occurred, contact by an intangible substance such as light must be considered in terms of its effect on the victim. There need be no actual injury for a touching to have occurred. However, to prove a touching, the evidence must prove that the substance made objectively offensive or forcible contact with the victim's person resulting in some manifestation of a physical consequence or corporeal hurt. . . .

Food for Thought

What are the possible reasons why the *Adams* prosecutor did not charge the defendant with bodily injury battery as in *Gordon*?

[Adams], by aiming the laser at the officers, effected a contact that caused bodily harm to Sergeant Giles. [Adams] argued there was no touching because the laser has no mass and, therefore, cannot physically touch Sergeant Giles. This argument is misplaced. The laser, directed by [Adams], came into contact with Sergeant Giles' eye and, as a result, there was an unlawful touching.

B. Intent

Proving intent by direct evidence often is impossible. Like any other element of a crime, it may be proved by circumstantial evidence, as long as such evidence excludes all reasonable hypotheses of innocence flowing from it. Circumstantial evidence of intent may include the conduct and statements of the alleged offender, and "[t]he finder of fact may infer that [he] intends the natural and probable consequences of his acts." *Campbell v. Commonwealth*, 12 Va. App. 476, 484, 405 S.E.2d 1, 4 (1991) (en banc).

The trial court, sitting as the fact finder, was entitled to reject [the] testimony [of Adams] that he was "just goofing off" to attract [the] attention of [the officer standing next to Giles]. The court specifically found that [Adams] intended to hit Giles with the laser and that [a] battery occurred. That decision is not plainly wrong or without supporting evidence and must be upheld on appeal.

For the reasons stated, we affirm the judgment of the trial court.

LEMONS, JUDGE, dissenting.

Food for Thought

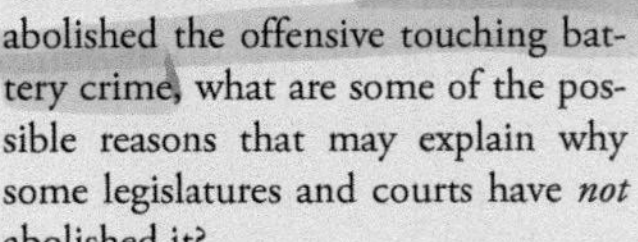

Given the fact that most states have abolished the offensive touching battery crime, what are some of the possible reasons that may explain why some legislatures and courts have ***not*** abolished it?

[Whether] a touching is a battery depends upon the intent of the actor, not upon the force applied. Here, the evidence does not support beyond a reasonable doubt that Adams had the intent to offensively touch Sergeant Giles. In order to have such intent, Adams would have to know or be reasonably charged with knowledge that a six-dollar novelty item attached to his key chain had the potential for offensive touching. It is not within common knowledge that such a device has such capacity. There is no evidence that Adams had specific knowledge of such capacity. That Adams had a bad relationship with Giles may explain his motive, but it does not prove intent to offensively touch. A finder of fact may infer that an actor intends the natural and probable consequences of his acts. In the absence of common knowledge of the capacity of this device, no inference may be drawn. Without inference or specific knowledge, there is no proof that Adams intended to offensively touch Giles.

Additionally, the majority redefines "touching" for the purpose of common law battery. Although the reasoning is logical, it is unwise, because the unintended consequences may reach too far. Will the next prosecution for battery be based upon failure to dim high beams in traffic, flash photography too close to the subject, high intensity flashlight beams or sonic waves from a teenager's car stereo? Rather than stretch the boundaries of the common law understanding of what is necessary for a "touching" to occur, criminalizing conduct that involves intangible objects put in motion should be left to specific legislative action rather than generalized redefinition that may sweep into the ambit of criminal behavior conduct that is not intended. *See, e.g.*, 720 Ill. Comp. Stat. 5/2–10.2, 2–10.3, 5/12–2, 12–4 (West 2000) (shining or flashing a laser gunsight near or on a person constitutes aggravated assault or aggravated battery); 720 Ill. Comp. Stat. 5/24.6/20 (West 2000) (aiming a laser pointer at a police officer is a misdemeanor); Wash. Rev. Code § 9A–49.020 (1999) (felony to discharge a laser beam at various peace officers or pilots, bus drivers or transit operators in the commission of their respective duties).

I respectfully dissent.

Points for Discussion

a. *Actus Reus* for Offensive Touching Battery

The *Adams* majority opinion relies on state precedents in criminal cases that quote approvingly from Blackstone's broad definition of the battery tort:

> The least touching of another's person wilfully, or in anger, is a battery; for the law cannot draw the line between different degrees of violence, and therefore totally prohibits the first and lowest stage of it: every man's person being sacred, and no other having a right to meddle with it, in any the slightest manner.

3 WILLIAM BLACKSTONE, COMMENTARIES ON THE LAWS OF ENGLAND *120. The *Adams* majority also echoes Blackstone's thinking in reasoning that "the underlying concerns of battery law" include "the sacredness" and "dignity" of the victim, as well as the need to deter breaches of the peace.

Implicitly, the *Adams* majority finds these policy concerns to be so strong that they require the judicial expansion of the *actus reus* element of "battery" to include offensive touching by "intangible substances." More specifically, the *Adams* majority endorses the need for a battery conviction when "the evidence prove[s] that [an intangible] substance made objectively offensive or forcible contact with the victim's person resulting in some manifestation of a physical consequence or corporeal hurt."

Should other state courts adopt the *Adams* majority's definition of battery? Does the *Adams* majority's definition of battery encompass even "offensive contacts" that are trivial or harmless? Assume, for example, that the laser beam had touched Sergeant Giles on the back of his hand, without causing pain, irritation, or even a red mark on his skin. Would this touching satisfy the *Adams* Court's definition of battery? How will a judge or jury draw the line between "offensive" touchings with intangible substances and inoffensive touching after *Adams*?

b. *Mens Rea* for Offensive Touching Battery

The *mens rea* element required for the offensive touching battery by the *Adams* Court is described as "the intent to touch offensively," but common law authorities and most states recognize that mere criminal negligence is sufficient for any type of battery conviction.

The contrasting opinions in *Adams* illustrate how the "intent to touch offensively" is an ambiguous concept. It is useful to compare the mental state analysis offered by Judge Frank and Judge Lemons with the four MPC mental states. This comparison makes it more obvious that the *Adams* majority does *not* require evidence of recklessness: that the defendant consciously disregarded the substantial risk that his conduct of "waving around the laser" would cause the result of an "offensive touching." What evidence of a criminal negligence mental state would Judge Lemons require, and what policy reasons support his view?

c. Enactment of Laser Battery Statute

After *Adams* was decided, the Virginia legislature did not modify the statute used to convict the defendant in *Adams*. Instead, the legislature enacted a new statute with the title, Pointing Laser at Law Enforcement Officer Unlawful, Va. Code Ann. §18.2–57.01 (2000), which provides:

> If any person, knowing or having reason to know another person is a law enforcement officer . . . in the performance of his public duties as such, intentionally projects at such other person a beam or a point of light from a laser, a laser gun sight, or any device that simulates a laser, shall be guilty of a Class 2 misdemeanor [for which the penalty is *up to* six months in jail and a fine of up to $1,000].

It appears that redundant criminal liability now exists for the conduct of people like the *Adams* defendant. A prosecutor may choose to charge such people either with the "Pointing Laser" crime or with the battery crime defined by the *Adams* Court. The latter crime carries the mandatory minimum penalty of six months, whereas the statutory crime allows for jail terms of less than six months, as well as sentences of probation or suspended sentences. The consequences of the legislature's decision to codify a laser battery crime without dealing with the *Adams* battery definition are explored in the following hypothetical.

Hypo: *After* Adams

Assume that the facts of *Adams* arise in another Virginia case in 2001 and that defendant Sarah is prosecuted.

a. *Laser Pointing Crime*. Assume that Sarah was convicted under the "Pointing Laser" crime that was enacted in 2000. On appeal, how will defense counsel argue that there is insufficient evidence of all the elements of this crime? What counter-arguments will the prosecutor make in reply?

b. *Overrule* Adams. Assume that Sarah was convicted instead under the "battery" crime used to convict the *Adams* defendant. Her defense counsel argues that the Virginia Supreme Court should overrule the Adams interpretation of the "battery" statute because the enactment of the "Pointing Laser" statute demonstrates the legislature's intent to supersede the judge-made "intangible substance" touching crime recognized in *Adams*. What arguments will defense counsel make to support this position, and what counter-arguments will the prosecutor make in reply?

d. New Crimes for Harms to Law Enforcement Officers

When a legislature fails to enact new crimes to define newly-recognized harms that pose a danger other than "bodily injury" to law enforcement officers, then a prosecutor must rely on the old common law crime of "offensive touching" battery if that crime continues to be recognized in state precedents. For example, Virginia prosecutors relied on that crime to convict a defendant who spat on an officer during an arrest, and to convict a defendant who left a deputy's hand covered in blood during a handshake. *See Gilbert v. Commonwealth*, 45 Va. App. 67, 608 S.E.2d 509 (2005); *Harman v. Commonwealth*, 2009 WL 362126 (Va. App.) (Feb. 17, 2009).

A more tailored way to punish such conduct is illustrated by the Indiana legislature's enactment of the crime of "battery by body waste" to cover persons who "knowingly or intentionally in a rude, insolent, or angry manner plac[e] blood or another body fluid or waste on a law enforcement officer . . . identified as such and while engaged in the performance of official duties." A higher penalty is imposed if the defendant "knew or recklessly failed to know that [he or she] was infected with: (a) hepatitis B; (b) HIV; or (c) tuberculosis." *See Newman v. State*, 677 N.E.2d 590 (Ind. App. 1997). How many policy decisions about the elements of a body-waste type of battery crime are reflected in this Indiana statute?

Take Note

The American Association of Prosecuting Attorneys has sponsored a fact sheet for law enforcement professionals entitled, "Spit Does Not Transmit." It states that there is no documented case of HIV transmission caused by spitting, and that biting is not an established route of HIV transmission. *See* http://www.hivlawandpolicy.org/resources/view/834.

As of 2012, there were HIV-specific laws in thirteen states that punished the conduct of spitting or biting. Most of the prosecutions for these HIV-specific charges have been brought when a defendant spits at or bites a police officer or corrections personnel. However, "there are no known cases of a law enforcement officer getting infected with HIV in the line of duty through these kinds of events." Nor are there any documented cases of HIV transmission "caused by contact with vomit, urine, or feces." *See* http://www.hivlawandpolicy.org/resources/view/834.

---

3. Exposure to Life-Threatening Disease

The common law extended the bodily injury battery crime to acts that indirectly inflict physical harm, such as causing a victim to ingest poison or to become infected with a sexually-transmitted disease, such as syphilis. See *State v. Lankford*, 29 Del. 594, 102 A. 63 (1917). As of 2019, 34 state codes included provisions that establish criminal liability for conduct that creates a risk of exposure or transmission of HIV or the AIDS virus. In 2014, the Civil Rights Division of the Department of Justice issued this recommendation concerning "HIV-specific state laws that criminalize engaging in certain behaviors before disclosing known HIV-positive status":

> Most of these laws do not account for actual scientifically-supported level of risk by type of activities engaged in or risk reduction measures undertaken. As a result, many of these state laws criminalize behaviors that the CDC regards as posing either no or negligible risk for HIV transmission even in the absence of risk reduction measures. The majority were passed before the development of antiretroviral therapy ("ART"), which the CDC acknowledges can reduce the risk of HIV transmission by up to 96%. Most of these laws do not, therefore, account for the use of ART, condoms, or pre-exposure prophylaxis. [The DOJ] encourages states to use scientific findings to, "re-examine [these] laws, assess the laws' alignment with current evidence regarding HIV transmission risk, and consider whether the laws are the best vehicle to achieve their intended purposes."

Dept. of Justice, Civil Rights Division, Best Practices Guide to Reform HIV-Specific Criminal Laws to Align with Scientifically-Supported Factors (2014), https://www.hivlawandpolicy.org/sites/default/files/DOJ-HIV-Criminal-Law-Best-Practices-Guide.pdf.

The Center for Disease Control and Prevention issued a report in 2019, indicating that since 2014, "at least five states have modernized their HIV criminal laws. Changes include removing HIV prevention issues from the criminal code and including them under disease control regulations, requiring intent to transmit, actual HIV transmission, or providing defenses for taking measures to prevent transmission such as viral suppression, condom use, and partner PrEP use." Center for Disease Control and Prevention, HIV and STD Criminal Laws, https://www.cdc.gov/hiv/policies/law/states/exposure.html. As of 2019, the CDCP found that HIV-related criminal laws fall into these categories:

1. HIV-specific criminal laws criminalize behaviors that can potentially expose another to HIV.
2. STD/communicable/infectious disease criminal laws criminalize behaviors that can potentially expose another to STD/communicable/infectious diseases. This might include HIV.
3. Sentence enhancement laws specific to HIV are laws that do not criminalize behavior but increase the sentence when a person commits certain crimes while infected with HIV.
4. Sentence enhancement laws specific to STD are laws that do not criminalize behavior but increase the sentence when a person commits certain crimes while infected with an STD. This might include HIV.

The next case provides one example of a legislative decision to enact a statute tailored specifically to sexual acts by persons who know that they are infected with a life-threatening communicable disease.

State v. Richardson

289 Kan. 118, 209 P.3d 696 (2009).

The opinion of the court was delivered by JOHNSON, J.

[Richardson] appeals his convictions and sentences for two counts of exposing another to a life-threatening communicable disease. [He first] claims that the statute defining the crime is unconstitutionally *vague* [and also claims] that the district court erred in failing to treat K.S.A. 21–3435 as a specific intent crime[.]

What's That?

A criminal statute is ***void for vagueness*** under the Due Process Clause when its language is so indefinite that a reasonable person cannot ascertain its meaning, and when such vagueness creates a danger of arbitrary enforcement of the law. When a statute is *substantially* vague and cannot be narrowly construed to eliminate its vagueness, the statute will be invalidated.

For more than a decade, Richardson has known that he is infected with [HIV]. . . . [The] State charged Richardson with violating K.S.A. 21–3435 for having sexual intercourse with M.K. and E.Z. [Richardson] waived his right to a jury trial and proceeded to a bench trial, which included the parties' *stipulations* that Richardson knew he was infected with HIV; that he engaged in sexual intercourse with [M.K. on] October 17, 2005, and [with E.Z.] between October 1 [and] 30, 2005[.] Other than the parties' stipulations, the evidence submitted during Richardson's bench trial consisted entirely of the testimony of two medical doctors[.] [Their testimony concerned the circumstances when HIV may be transmitted.]

What's That?

A *stipulation* concerning the facts may be agreed upon by the defendant and the prosecutor, and entered into evidence.

Richardson defended on the basis that the State had failed to establish that HIV is always a life-threatening disease; that he had actually exposed the victims to the disease because of the lack of evidence that bodily fluids were exchanged during intercourse; [and that] he had the specific intent to expose his sexual partners to HIV. The District Court found Richardson guilty on both counts and sentenced him to consecutive prison terms[.]

[We first consider] whether K.S.A. 21–3435 is a specific intent crime. The district court did not specifically say that it was interpreting [the statute] as only requiring a general criminal intent. However, Richardson insists that the district court must have applied that interpretation because it found Richardson guilty without the State presenting any evidence of a specific intent to expose the victims to HIV. The State counters that, despite the language of the applicable statute, the legislature intended to create a general intent crime. . . .

Food for Thought

How is it possible that the defendant's sexual activities and HIV status came to the attention of the prosecutor? What are the reasons that may make it difficult to prosecute the exposure crime?

[In] relevant part, the statute provides:

"(a) It is unlawful for an individual who knows oneself to be infected with a life threatening communicable disease knowingly:

(1) To engage in sexual intercourse or *sodomy* with another individual with the intent to expose that individual to that life threatening communicable disease."

What's That?

The Kansas statute defined *sodomy* as the oral contact or oral penetration of female genitalia, oral contact of male genitalia, oral or anal copulation, or anal penetration of a male or female by any body part or object. *See* K.S.A. § 21–3501(2).

[The] statute requires the defendant to "knowingly" engage in that prohibited conduct. Therefore, [the] crime-defining statute does not criminalize reckless conduct. Just as clearly, [the statute] "identifies or requires a further particular intent which must accompany the prohibited acts," *i.e.*, the intent to expose the sex partner to the life-threatening communicable disease. See [*State v.*] *Cantrell*, 234 Kan. 426, 673 P.2d 1147 [(1983)].

The State acknowledges that, on its face, [the statute] purports to be a specific intent crime. However, the State does not acknowledge that this State's appellate courts have consistently interpreted statutes that define a crime by using the phrase "with intent to" as requiring a specific intent element.

Instead, without proffering any authority, the State contends that giving effect to the statute's plain specific intent language would actually thwart the legislature's intended purpose of preventing the intentional exposure of others to HIV. The State argues that any act of sexual intercourse or sodomy by an HIV positive person, even utilizing a condom, creates some element of risk that the virus will be transmitted to the sex partner, so that total abstinence is the only means by which an infected person may avoid exposing another to HIV. Accordingly, the State suggests that the specific intent to expose another to HIV is inherently included in the defendant's general intent to engage in sexual intercourse.

Under the State's interpretation, a person infected with HIV must be totally abstinent or risk being prosecuted for a felony each and every time he or she engages in sexual intercourse or sodomy, regardless of whether the act is between two consenting (perhaps married) adults with full knowledge of the virus and utilizing prophylactic measures. We disagree.

[The] State's public policy arguments cannot be reconciled with the plain language of [the statute] and we find that the statute creates a specific intent crime. The State was required to prove that Richardson, knowing he was infected with HIV[,] engaged in sexual intercourse with M.K. and E.Z. with the specific intent to expose them to HIV.

[Second,] a claim that a statute is void for vagueness necessarily requires a court to interpret the language of the statute in question to determine whether it gives adequate warning as to the prescribed conduct. . . . [Moreover,] the need for clarity of definition and the prevention of arbitrary and discriminatory enforcement is heightened for criminal statutes because criminal violations result in the loss of liberty[.]

Richardson [argues] that the term "expose" [in the "intent to expose" element] is [unconstitutionally vague] as to the conduct which is prohibited. He suggests that it could mean engaging in conduct which might present any risk of transmission of HIV or it could mean that the prohibited conduct must involve causing bodily fluids to actually come into contact with the other person. He also suggests that a person infected with HIV must speculate on what viral load level might be sufficient to trigger a criminally prohibited exposure[.]

The flaw in those arguments is that the statute does not define the prohibited conduct as exposing another to the life-threatening disease, but rather it criminalizes sexual intercourse or sodomy with the *specific intent* to expose the sex partner to the known life-threatening communicable disease. One need not ruminate on exactly how the act must be performed to meet the legal definition of "expose" or even know that a transmittal of the disease is possible. It is enough that the defendant intended to expose his or her sex partner to the disease. That state of mind is certainly a matter well within the common understanding of a defendant. . . .

[Richardson] also complains that [the statute] does not specifically define the term "life threatening." Ironically, however, he states in his brief that "[t]he common sense definition of the term 'life threatening' is 'something that poses a threat to life.'" We wholeheartedly agree with that assessment and believe that it effectively refutes the [vagueness argument]. A person of ordinary intelligence would understand what the statute means by the term "life threatening."

Moreover, Richardson's example that such common diseases as influenza can be threatening does not support his argument. If, during a swine flue pandemic, a person knowingly has sexual intercourse or sodomy with another with the intent to expose the sex partner to the life-threatening influenza, then the offender has subjected himself or herself to prosecution under [the statute]. [The] prosecutor's burden may be more difficult to carry. Nevertheless, that does not make the fact that influenza may be a life-threatening communicable disease any less amenable to common understanding. . . . [The] statute is not unconstitutionally vague.

[Third,] Richardson argues that the evidence was insufficient to support his convictions because the State presented no evidence on the requisite element of specific intent[.] . . . [The State argues that the mere fact that Richardson engaged in sexual intercourse while knowing that he was infected with HIV was enough to prove that he intended to expose M.K. and E.Z. to the virus. According to the State, "there is no conceivable means by which the State could prove, apart from the act of sexual intercourse itself, that an HIV positive individual who knowingly engages in sexual intercourse with another acts with 'intent to expose' the other to the virus." We disagree. Prosecutors are routinely called upon to prove a defendant's specific intent in committing a prohibited act and normally must carry that burden with circumstantial evidence. Here the State simply made no attempt to prove the requisite circumstances.

Food for Thought

The *Richardson* prosecutor and Judge Johnson have different ideas about what the "intent to expose" means and how its existence may be inferred from a defendant's conduct, omissions, and statements. How are their differences illustrated in Judge Johnson's reasoning?

Interestingly, at the preliminary hearing, the State presented evidence that M.K. and E.Z did not know that Richardson had HIV when they had sex with him; that Richardson did not use a condom; and that Richardson had falsely represented to E.Z. that he was free from sexually transmitted diseases. These are prime examples of proven circumstances that could support an inference that Richardson intended to expose M.K. and E.Z. to HIV. Inexplicably the State chose not to present any of this information at trial, and those facts were not included in the parties' stipulation. . . .

[In] conclusion, the record reveals that, at trial, the State failed to prove circumstances from which a rational factfinder could reasonably infer that the defendant had the specific intent to expose either M.K. or E.Z. to HIV. Instead, the State has asked us to infer or presume the requisite circumstantial evidence of specific intent from other circumstances or inferences. Such a presumption upon a presumption is insufficient to carry the State's burden. Accordingly, we find the evidence was insufficient to support the convictions and reverse[.]

Points for Discussion

a. Intent to Expose vs. Act of Exposure

After the discovery of AIDS in 1981, it was evident that the act of intentionally exposing a person to the HIV infection could be punished using common law battery statutes that prohibit the reckless causing of serious bodily harm. The Kansas statute in *Richardson* illustrates the benefits of enacting a new crime for which *actus reus* and *mens rea* elements may be selected carefully so that ambiguity may be avoided. For example, the elements of the Kansas statute reflect these four policy decisions concerning the scope of criminal liability: 1) a defendant must *know* of his or her own infected condition; 2) a defendant may be infected with *any* "life threatening communicable disease"; 3) a defendant must engage *knowingly* in specifically defined sexual acts; and 4) a defendant must have the "intent to expose" the sexual partner to the disease. Notably, the statute does *not* define the crime by requiring an act of "*exposure*" of a sexual partner to infection, but instead requires that particular sexual acts must occur.

The only statutory interpretation question at trial in *Richardson* concerned the meaning of the "intent to expose", and the prosecutor convinced the trial judge that this mental state element could be equated with the "general intent to engage in sexual intercourse." Therefore, the *Richardson* Court reversed the conviction for two reasons: 1) the trial judge was wrong and the prosecutor was required to prove the defendant's specific intent to expose his sexual partners to his HIV infection; and 2) no evidence was introduced by the prosecutor at trial to attempt to prove that required mental state, and so a new trial was required. The *Richardson* opinion provides examples of evidence from the preliminary hearing that could be introduced at the new trial to show the defendant's "intent to expose." What are these examples? Will this evidence be sufficient to convict the defendant of the "intent to expose" both E.Z. and M.K. to his HIV infection? What kind of additional evidence would be useful for this purpose?

New criminal statutes are sometimes challenged on vagueness grounds, but it may be difficult to persuade a court that any vagueness is so "substantial" as to require the invalidation of the statute. Thus, *Richardson* provides a typical example of an unsuccessful challenge. However, the court's analysis provides a reminder that a legislature often can avoid vagueness problems by narrow drafting. How does the statute's use of the "intent-to-expose" element but *not* an "*exposure*" element influence the *Richardson* Court's reasoning on the vagueness issue?

b. Comparing Exposure Statutes

The "exposure" element has been used in other state codes. For example, the definition of aggravated battery in a Washington statute was amended in 1997 to add the italicized language:

> [a] person is guilty of [battery] in the first degree if he or she, with intent to inflict great bodily harm[,] administers, *exposes, or transmits* to or causes to be taken by another, poison, *the human immunodeficiency virus,* or any other destructive or noxious substance.

See REV. CODE WASH. 9A.36.011(1)(B). This statute has been interpreted by state courts as implicitly including the "intent to expose," and the undefined term "expose" has been interpreted as follows: 1) "exposure occurs with any sexual activity that involves vaginal, oral or anal exchange of bodily fluids as occurs during unprotected sex"; and 2) "every incidence of sexual activity would be a period of exposure, although not every exposure would necessarily transmit HIV."

Another example of a statute that uses the "exposure" element is the Tennessee statute that provides as follows:

> A person commits the offense of criminal exposure of another to HIV when, knowing that he or she is infected with HIV, such person knowingly engages in intimate contact with another person. The term intimate contact means the exposure of the body of one person to a bodily fluid of another person in any manner that presents a significant risk of HIV transmission.

The following hypotheticals present comparisons between the Washington and Tennessee statutes. Hypo 1 raises questions concerning the options for defining the mental state and consent defense for the HIV crime and Hypo 2 addresses the issue of exposure to COVID19.

Hypo 1: *HIV Statutes*

These hypotheticals focus on arguments that may be made for choosing particular elements to define the HIV exposure crime.

a. *Conduct Element.* If a defendant is convicted based on the same evidence that was available to the *Richardson* prosecutor concerning victim E.Z., would it be more difficult for the prosecutor to persuade the appellate court to affirm a conviction under the Washington statute or under the Tennessee statute? Explain. *Compare State v. Whitfield*, 132 Wash. App. 878, 134 P.3d 1203 (2006); *State v. Bonds*, 189 S.W.3d 249 (Tenn. 2006).

b. *Mental State Element.* Most statutes require the prosecutor to prove that the defendant knows of his or her HIV-positive status. Consider the implications of a statute that used the recklessly mental state for this element. What are the pros and cons of using "recklessly" instead of "knowingly"?

Hypo 2: *Exposure to COVID19*

What pro and con arguments can be made as to whether state legislatures should amend their criminal codes to enact new provisions that apply to "exposure to COVID19"? If such measures are enacted, what elements should be used to define this exposure crime?

Should some exclusions be specified in these statutes? If Congress decides to criminalize exposure to COVID19 based on the requisite federal policy interests, what federal definition should be used? In the absence of new statutes explicitly identifying exposure "to COVID19," if state prosecutors decide to bring charges based on existing state exposure statutes that do not mention this disease, what problems may they encounter?

c. Criticism of Exposure Statutes

During the decade between 1987 and 1995, the number of AIDS deaths rose from approximately 13,000 per year to 41,000 per year. By 1997, after treatment by the anti-HIV drug "cocktail" became available, the number of deaths fell to approximately 16,000. One example of the attitude of legislatures toward AIDS in 1990 is illustrated by the Ryan White Comprehensive AIDS Resources Emergency (CARE) Act, which included a requirement for every state to certify that state criminal prosecutions could be brought against "any HIV-infected individual who knowingly exposed another person to HIV." In addition to the HIV-specific exposure laws, non-specific laws also have been used in 28 states to prosecute the non-disclosure of HIV-positive status when engaging in sexual activity, needle-sharing, sex work, exposure to bodily fluids, or donation of blood, organs or semen. See Map: HIV Criminalization in the United States, The Center for HIV Law & Policy, https://www.hivlawandpolicy.org/resources/map-hiv-criminalization-united-states-center-hiv-law-and-policy-updated-july-2020 (updated July 2020).

In 2010, with more than one million people living with HIV, the White House announcement of a new National HIV/AIDS Strategy was accompanied by the statement that the "continued existence and enforcement" of HIV transmission laws runs "counter to scientific evidence about routes of HIV transmission and may undermine the public health goals of promoting HIV screening and treatment." This finding was cited in federal legislation introduced in 2013 "to modernize laws, and eliminate discrimination, with respect to people living with HIV/AIDS." *See* https://www.congress.gov/bill/113th-congress/house-bill/1843/text. Also in 2013, the President's Advisory Council on HIV/AIDS (PACHA) adopted a resolution that HIV-specific criminal laws should be eliminated, and that the Departments of Justice and Health and Human Services should offer incentives so that state government officials can accomplish this goal. *See* https://www.hivlawandpolicy.org/sites/default/files/PACHA_Criminalization_Resolution%20Final%20012513.pdf.

Food for Thought

What problems with the enforcement of HIV-exposure crimes could have persuaded the Obama administration to call for the elimination of these laws?

For examples of criticisms of HIV-exposure statute presented to PACHA in October 2012, see Center for HIV Law & Policy, Positive Justice Project Proposed Resolution Submitted to President's Advisory Council on AIDS (PACHA) on Ending Federal and State HIV-Specific Criminal Laws, http://www.hivlawandpolicy.org/resources/pjp-proposed-resolution-submitted-president%E2%80%99s-advisory-council-hivaids-pacha-ending.

In 2017, some members of PACHA resigned in protest of President Trump's HIV-related policies and the remaining members were dismissed by the President. PACHA reconvened in 2019 after the appointment of new members.

B. Assault

1. Attempted Battery Assault

Under English law, assault was the name given to the attempted battery crime. The strict proof requirements of this crime inspired state courts to recognize the frightening assault crime, drawing from elements of the same assault tort.

The *Yslas* case illustrates the concept of an "offer of violence" that establishes the *actus reus* of the attempt to commit battery that made an assault "complete." The *Henson* case explores the reasons for the development of the trend in favor of replacing the attempted battery requirement of "actual ability" with "apparent ability" to commit battery.

People v. Yslas

27 Cal. 630 (1865).

The testimony for the prosecution showed that the defendant entered the house of the [victim] and called for liquor, and was refused. He insisted, and it was given to him, when he called on the [victim] to drink, and upon her declining to do so, [he threw] the tumbler on the floor, threatened to kill her, and seized a hatchet and started towards her, having it raised in a threatening attitude. The [victim], when the defendant had approached within seven or eight feet of her, fled through the door into an adjoining room, and locked the door after her. The defendant then went up to the door and struck it with his hatchet[.]

[By] SANDERSON, C.J.

Practice Pointer

In 1865 a California lawyer had to obtain the facts of the case from the summary of the arguments that preceded the opinion in the state court reports.

The defendant was indicted for an assault with the intent to commit murder, tried, and convicted as charged.

[The] instructions asked for [by] the defendant were properly refused[.] The common law definition of an assault is substantially the same as that [intended] in our statute. The vice in [the defendant's proposed] instructions [is] found in the idea which they countenance that there may be an intermediate point between the commencement and the end of an assault where if the assailant is interrupted either by the escape of the party assailed or the interference of bystanders, the offense is thereby made incomplete.

In order to commit an assault there must be something more than a mere menace. There must be violence begun to be executed. But where there is a clear intent to commit violence accompanied by acts which if not interrupted will be followed by personal injury, the violence is commenced and the assault is complete. [It] is not indispensable to the commission of an assault that the assailant should be at any time within striking distance. If he is advancing with intent to strike his [victim] and come sufficiently near to induce a [person] of ordinary firmness to believe, in view of all the circumstances, that he will instantly receive a blow unless he strike in self-defense or retreat, the assault is complete. In such a case the attempt has been made coupled with a present ability to commit a violent injury within the meaning of the statute. It cannot be said that the ability to do the act threatened is wanting because the act was in some manner prevented. In the present case the defendant was guilty of an assault if he advanced on the [victim] in such a manner as to threaten immediate violence, notwithstanding she succeeded in making her escape without injury.

> **FYI**
>
> The *Yslas* opinion paraphrased portions of an 1856 American treatise on Criminal Law, called Bishop's Commentaries, and relied on the two cases from the Court of King's Bench that comprised Bishop's authorities.

Judgment affirmed.

Points for Discussion

a. No Requirement of Victim Awareness

The *Yslas* opinion illustrates only one case law example of an "attempted battery assault" crime, in which a court focuses on the question whether the defendant came "sufficiently near" to a victim who fled from the assault. But the English common law's version of the attempted battery crime was not limited to the *Yslas* scenario in which the victim was aware of the defendant's approach. What changes could be made in the *Yslas* facts to illustrate an "attempted battery assault" crime in which the victim was not aware of the defendant's conduct? How would a court determine whether the defendant in that example came "sufficiently near" to achieving the result of a battery, without the victim's reaction to use as a reference point? Why would the defendant in that example be viewed as deserving of conviction for the same crime as the *Yslas* defendant?

b. Actual Ability to Achieve the Result of a Battery

Note that there was no necessity for the *Yslas* Court to discuss the common law requirement for the prosecutor to show that the defendant possessed the "actual ability" to commit battery. It was obvious that the hatchet used by the *Yslas* defendant provided him with that "actual ability." But what if the defendant had seized an unloaded revolver and pointed it the victim while using the same language and engaging in the same conduct? In that scenario, the *Yslas* Court would have been required to address the issue of "actual ability" confronted in the next case.

Commonwealth v. Henson

357 Mass. 686, 259 N.E.2d 769 (1970).

QUIRICO, JUSTICE.

[This is an appeal from conviction for the crime of assault by means of a dangerous weapon, to wit, a revolver.] The only issue before us is whether there was error in denying a motion by the defendant for a directed verdict.

The evidence would permit the jury to find the following facts. On December 24, 1968, Theodore Finochio, an off-duty police officer[,] was at a gasoline station in Boston. He was not in uniform, but he had his service revolver in a holster under his coat. Another man and woman also were in the station at that time. The defendant and a female companion entered the station and the female [companion] used profane language. Finochio asked the defendant to keep [his companion] quiet. The defendant reached in his pocket, pulled out a revolver, aimed it at Finochio's stomach and said[,] "Why should I?" Finochio put up his hands and said[,] "No reason at all." He described his state of mind at that time by saying[,] "I thought I was done for." The defendant then turned to go out of the station, holding the revolver at his side. Finochio took out his revolver, pointed it at the defendant and said, "Hold it there, buddy, I am a police officer." The defendant [turned] and fired two shots at Finochio at a distance of about five feet. They exchanged further shots in that chase which lasted about twenty to thirty seconds until the defendant was captured, subdued and handcuffed, and his revolver taken from his hand. The defendant fired a total of five or more shots, and Finochio fired six, one of which struck the defendant. Finochio was not struck by any projectile, and he received no injuries or powder burns in the incident. No projectiles were recovered at the scene. The defendant had taken the revolver from his female companion before going to the gasoline station. Before the shooting he noticed that it was loaded. [He had examined the shells and recognized them as blanks.]

> **FYI**
>
> The revolver used by the defendant in *Henson* was manufactured with a plug in the barrel, and it was designed for firing .22 caliber "acorn blanks," which are shells without a bullet or projectile.

On this evidence the jury could find that the defendant . . . intended to create, and did create, the impression on the persons present that he had a loaded revolver which was capable of shooting Finochio, and that until the defendant's running gun battle with Finochio was over and he was subdued, no one present except the defendant knew that [his] revolver was loaded with blanks. Finally, [the jury] could find that all persons present, except the defendant, reasonably believed that the defendant's revolver was loaded with live bullets which he was firing at Finochio.

Despite this factual situation, the defendant contends that [his] conduct could not [constitute] the aggravated offence of assault by means of a dangerous weapon since the shells in the revolver at the time were blanks. [Basically,] he argues that because the revolver was not loaded with live ammunition, he did not have the ability to accomplish a battery by means of the revolver, and thus cannot be convicted of assault by means of the revolver. . . .

[But] the defendant's secret intent not to shoot Finochio based on his undisclosed inability to do so with the blank shells is not material. The defendant's acts, judged without the benefit of his secret knowledge that he was firing blanks, constituted a reasonably obvious case of an assault by means of a loaded revolver, involving a violent breach of the public order and setting in motion the normal reaction thereto by Finochio. The issue before us is[,] [S]hould the defendant now be allowed to avoid criminal responsibility for his conduct on the ground that he had only blank shells in his [revolver]?

[An] examination of decisions on this question in other jurisdictions shows a considerable conflict of authority, but it may be accurate to state that a majority [have] concluded that the crime of aggravated assault by means of a firearm [is] not made out by evidence of the pointing of an unloaded firearm. *See* Annotation, 79 A.L.R.2d 1412. That [conclusion] applies whether the case is one where it was established that the firearm was not loaded at the time of the alleged assault, or one where was there was no proof that the firearm was loaded[.]

[In *Commonwealth v. White*, 110 Mass. 407, 409 (1872), a conviction for simple assault was upheld because, "It is not the secret intent of the assaulting party, nor the undisclosed fact of his ability or inability to commit a battery, that is material; but what his conduct and the attending circumstances denote at the time to the [victim] assaulted. . . . It is the outward demonstration that constitutes the mischief which is punished as a breach of the peace."]

[This reasoning] applies with even greater force to a case of apparent ability to accomplish a battery attempted or threatened by means of a firearm. The threat to the public peace and order is greater, and natural reactions thereto by the intended victim and others may be more sudden and violent than in cases where no weapon is involved. There is no reason why the rule of apparent ability should not apply to charges of aggravated assaults by means of weapons[.] Thus, the mere fact that a firearm brandished by an assailant is known by him to be unloaded, or to be loaded with blank cartridges, does not entitle him to an acquittal on a charge of assault by means of a dangerous weapon.

Points for Discussion

a. *Actus Reus* & *Mens Rea* of Attempted Battery Assault

The *Yslas* opinion illustrates the difficulty of determining "how close" a defendant must come to committing a battery, in order to be guilty of the attempted battery crime known as assault. Common law authorities distinguished between the phase of "violence menaced", which was not close enough to the completion of a battery to be punishable, and the phase of "violence begun to be executed," which *did* qualify as assault.

The defense counsel in *Yslas* argued that a more concrete rule of thumb should be provided to the jury, namely, that no assault occurred if the defendant did not raise the hatchet while in striking distance. In rejecting that rule, the *Yslas* Court adopted a pragmatic perspective and refused to make fine distinctions regarding predictions as to whether a battery was about to occur. Moreover, the prosecutor had strong "proximity" evidence that satisfied every test mentioned by the court for defining the *actus reus* of attempted battery.

Although the "fight or flight" reaction of a reasonable victim is one test for defining proximity evidence, the crime of attempted battery assault requires neither the result of the victim's fear of bodily injury nor the intent to create such fear. Instead, the crime requires the intent to achieve the result of a battery, and acts that came "sufficiently near" to that result. If the victim in *Yslas* had never noticed the defendant creeping up behind her back, with his hatchet raised in the air, the jury could have convicted him of assault. The crime of attempted battery assault was, like battery, concerned with deterring breaches of the peace, and so an insensible victim was no obstacle to prosecution. If the defendant had never seized the hatchet, and merely frightened the victim with threats to kill and glances toward the hatchet, the *Yslas* Court would not have affirmed his conviction. Acts that fell short of an "offer of violence" did not fall into the attempted battery assault category.

The momentum for the judicial recognition of the frightening assault crime was fueled by the restrictions of attempted battery assault, which also required "a present ability to commit a violent injury." As the MPC Commentaries observed, this element "imported into the offense an even stricter notion of proximity to the completed act than characterized the law of criminal attempt." Model Penal Code § 211.1, Comment 1 at 177 (1980). Even acts that qualified as an "offer of violence," coupled with the intent to achieve the result of a battery, would not fit into the attempted battery assault category when guns were raised instead of hatchets, and those guns were unloaded.

The Model Penal Code drafters chose to redefine the attempted battery type of assault in accordance with the *actus reus* and *mens rea* requirements used for any attempt crime in the MPC. Thus, the term "attempt" incorporates these two elements within it: 1) the mental state of an affirmative "desire to cause the result" of either bodily injury or serious bodily injury; and 2) an act of preparation that takes a "substantial step in a course of conduct planned to culminate in [the] commission of the crime." *See* Model Penal Code § 5.01, Comment 2 at 301 (1980); Model Penal Code § 5.01(1)(c).

b. Actual or Apparent Ability to Commit Battery

In reflecting upon the significance of the landmark Massachusetts decision in *Commonwealth v. White*, the *Henson* Court characterized the *White* holding as the "modern rule" of assault, and quoted this description of *White*'s implications, which serves equally well to describe *Henson*'s ruling:

> Where an assault may be committed[,] [t]here must be some power, actual or apparent, for doing bodily harm, but apparent power is sufficient[.] Hence in jurisdictions giving full scope to the modern rule of criminal assault, this offense may be committed where the battery itself is actually impossible, if it reasonably seems possible either to the assailant or to his victim[,] [assuming that] the assailant could place the [victim] in apprehension of an immediate battery by means that appeared to be effective although the assailant himself knew otherwise. [In these] jurisdictions [it] is possible to commit [assault] by pointing an unloaded weapon at another within normal range.

Henson, 259 N.E.2d at 774 (quoting ROLLIN M. PERKINS, CRIMINAL LAW 91–93 (1957)).

Consider the possible reasons that led the majority of state courts and legislatures, at the time of the *Henson* decision, to retain the common law requirement of "actual ability" for attempted battery assault. Would the widespread recognition of the frightening assault crime make it more or less likely for courts to abandon the "actual ability" requirement and endorse the "apparent ability" requirement instead?

One important aspect of a court's decision to endorse the "apparent ability" concept is the impact of this decision on the mental state definition for the attempted battery crime. For example, a person like the *Henson* defendant, who knows that his weapon lacks the "present ability" to cause bodily injury, does not possess the necessary "intent to accomplish a battery." How does the *Henson* Court describe the defendant's mental state? Why does the court find this mental state to be the equivalent of the intent to accomplish battery?

Hypo 1: *MPC Choices*

There are three different assault crimes in Model Penal Code § 211.1 that are derived from the common law crime of attempted battery assault. The provision labeled here as (1) defines simple assault, whereas provisions (2) and (3) define aggravated assault:

(1) attempts to cause bodily injury to another;

(2) attempts to cause serious bodily injury to another; or

(3) attempts to cause bodily injury to another with a deadly weapon.

Identify any variations of attempted battery assault that you notice are missing from this list, and consider the reasons that the MPC drafters may have rejected them. Then explain whether the defendants in *Yslas* and *Henson* could be convicted using any of these three MPC definitions of assault.

Hypo 2: *Pick Up Your Own Mail*

Hal was delivering the mail on his "walking delivery route" as an employee of the U. S. Postal Service. He was still about a block away when from the corner store when the storeowner, Zeke, started shouting his usual demands for Hal to hurry up and bring Zeke his mail, which shouting included a variety of swear words and highly insulting language. Hal stuck to his normal walking pace and remained calm as he crossed the street and arrived in front of the store. Hal had quietly resolved to show Zeke that his daily insults would have consequences. Hal was well trained in the recommended Postal Service protocols that mail delivery personnel can use to avoid challenges to their authority or well-being. One approved tactic is to inform a troublemaker, "that you will have to pick up your own mail at the post office and that your mail delivery will be restored only when you are prepared to respect the people who deliver it." So Hal paused a few feet from Zeke, stood his ground, and recited that message to Zeke. Hal's speech enraged Zeke, who lunged forward, grabbed Hal by his shirt collar, pulled Hal forward so that he and Zeke were almost touching noses, and yelled epithets in Hal's face. Then when Hal took a step back, Zeke let him go. But Hal was taking no chances. He ran as fast as he could to the police station around the corner. After hearing about Zeke's conduct, a police officer arrested Zeke and charged him with "simple assault," the elements of which are not defined in the state criminal code, which provides that: "Any person who commits a simple assault shall be guilty of a misdemeanor." If state court precedents interpret "assault" to mean the "attempted battery" version of assault, can Zeke be convicted?

---

2. Frightening Assault

The following case illustrates how statutes that punished only "assault" came to be interpreted by nineteenth century state court judges to include both the original attempted battery crime and a tort type of frightening assault crime. Yet the tort model was only a starting point for judges engaged in the task of defining the elements of the frightening assault crime. That task proved to be a difficult one, and modern cases can provide the occasion for judicial disputes about whether particular elements should be required, and why legislative definitions are preferable.

Carter v. Commonwealth

42 Va. App. 681, 594 S.E.2d 284 (2004) (en banc).

JEAN HARRISON CLEMENTS, JUDGE:

[On] December 29, 1998, around 11:00 p.m., Officer B.N. O'Donnell of the City of Charlottesville Police Department observed a speeding car and, activating his vehicle's overhead flashing blue emergency lights, initiated a traffic stop. O'Donnell, who was on routine patrol at the time in a high crime area of the city, was driving a marked police vehicle and wearing his police uniform and badge. After the car pulled over, O'Donnell shone his vehicle's "take down" lights and spotlight onto the car and approached on foot. [Take-down lights supply high intensity white lighting directed toward the front of the patrol car.]

Two people were inside the car, the driver and Carter, who was seated in the front passenger seat. O'Donnell initiated a conversation with the driver, asking for his driver's license and registration and informing him why he had been stopped. The driver responded to O'Donnell in a "hostile" tone of voice. While conversing with the driver, O'Donnell used his flashlight to conduct a "plain view search" of the car to make sure there were no visible weapons or drugs in it. O'Donnell noticed that Carter had his right hand out of sight "down by his right leg." Carter then suddenly brought his right hand up and across his body. Extending the index finger on his right hand straight out and the thumb straight up, he pointed his index finger at the officer and said, "Pow." Thinking Carter "had a weapon and was going to shoot" him, O'Donnell "began to move backwards" and went for his weapon. A "split second" later, O'Donnell realized "it was only [Carter's] finger." O'Donnell testified: "The first thing I thought was that I was going to get shot. [It's] a terrifying experience, and if I could have gotten my weapon, I would have shot him. [O'Donnell testified that Carter then "started laughing."] [O'Donnell] asked Carter "if he thought it was funny," and Carter responded, "Yes, I think it is funny."

[Initially, O'Donnell did not arrest Carter because O'Donnell did not know whether he could charge Carter with any crime. A few days later, O'Donnell obtained a warrant for Carter's arrest for assaulting a police officer under VA. CODE ANN. § 18.2–57(C), which provides that "any person [who] commits an assault . . . against . . . a law-enforcement officer . . . engaged in the performance of his public duties as such . . . shall be guilty of a Class 6 felony."]

Take Note

The *Carter* defendant was sentenced by the trial judge to three years in prison, with two years and six months suspended. He was convicted of a crime that carried a mandatory minimum penalty of six months in jail, like the crime in *Adams*.

On appeal, Carter asserts the Commonwealth failed to prove his conduct constituted an assault of a law-enforcement officer because [in pointing his finger,] he did not have the present ability to inflict harm on the officer. [The] Commonwealth contends that, under long-established Virginia case law, a defendant need not have had the present ability to inflict harm at the time of the offense to be guilty of assault. It is enough [that] the defendant's conduct created in the mind of the victim a reasonable fear of apprehension of bodily harm[,] [and] the trial court properly found the evidence sufficient[.]

[At] common law, the term "assault" originally had two distinct meanings, one when used in the context of criminal law and another when used in the context of torts law. A criminal assault was "an attempt to commit a battery." Under this definition of assault, it did not matter "whether the victim was put in fear or was even aware of the assault." ROGER D. GROOT, *CRIMINAL OFFENSES AND DEFENSES IN VIRGINIA* 48 (2004). It mattered only that the accused had the specific intent and present ability to commit the battery and "performed some direct [act] towards its commission."

Conversely, a tortious assault was an overt intentional act that placed another in reasonable apprehension of immediate bodily harm. [Additionally,] absent an intention to batter, there must have been "an actual intention to cause apprehension[,] [which must have been] one which normally [would] be aroused in the mind of a reasonable person." [W. PAGE KEETON et al, *KEETON & PROSSER ON THE LAW OF TORTS* § 10 (5th ed. 1984).] In time, however, the tort type of assault [became] recognized, "in addition to (not as an alternative to) the attempted-battery type of assault." [WAYNE R. LAFAVE, *CRIMINAL LAW* § 7.16, at 746 (3d ed. 2000).] In Virginia, our Supreme Court has long recognized the existence of both concepts of assault in the criminal-law context. [*See*] *Berkeley v. Commonwealth*, 88 Va. 1017, 14 S.E. 916 (1892)[.]

[Although the phrase] "coupled with a present ability" [appeared] in the common law definition of assault in *Harper v. Commonwealth*, 196 Va. 723, 733, 85 S.E.2d 249, 255 (1955), [that definition] was not intended to be an all-inclusive definition of assault in Virginia[.] [*Harper* was] a case requiring determination of whether an attempted-battery type of criminal assault occurred.

[For] these reasons, we hold that one need not, in cases such as this [one], have a present ability to inflict imminent bodily harm at the time of the alleged offense to be guilty of assault. It is enough that one's conduct created at the time of the alleged offense a reasonable apprehension of bodily harm in the mind of the victim. Thus, an apparent present ability to inflict imminent bodily harm is sufficient to support a conviction for assault.

In this case, the trial court found that Carter's "act of pointing what the officer believed at the time to be a weapon at him" did, "in fact, place Officer O'Donnell in reasonable apprehension or fear." The evidence in the record abundantly supports this finding, and the finding is not plainly wrong. [That] the officer's terror was brief does not alter the fact, as found by the trial court, that the officer believed for a moment that Carter had the intention and present ability to kill him. Moreover, under the circumstances surrounding the incident, we cannot say, as a matter of law, that such a belief was unreasonable. Thus, although Carter did not have a weapon, the trial court could properly conclude from the evidence presented that Carter had an apparent present ability to inflict imminent bodily harm and that his conduct placed Officer O'Donnell in reasonable apprehension of such harm." [Accordingly,] we affirm Carter's conviction.

Affirmed.

BENTON, J., with whom FITZPATRICK, C.M., joins, dissenting.

The common law definition of "assault" [did] not encompass this type of intentional conduct, which is intended to startle but is performed without a present ability to produce the end if carried out. Because of the definitional limitations of this common law rule, other states have addressed this type of conduct by statutory enactments. "[M]ost modern codes either include physical menacing in the crime of assault or else create a separate crime of 'menacing' or 'threatening' covering such conduct." WAYNE R. LAFAVE, *Criminal Law* § 16.3(b), at 825 n.21 (4th ed. 2003). When legislatures statutorily define a crime in this manner "[f]or this type of assault, a present ability to inflict injury is clearly unnecessary." *Id.*

For these reasons, I disagree with the majority opinion's holding that a conviction for criminal assault can be sustained [even] though the evidence failed to prove the accused had a present ability to harm the officer. I would hold that Carter committed an "act accompanied with circumstances denoting an intention" to menace but it was not "coupled with a present ability . . . to use actual violence" or "calculated to produce the end if carried into execution." *See, e.g., People v. Vaiza*, 244 Cal. App. 2d 121, 52 Cal. Rptr. 733 (1966) (holding that "[i]f a person threatens to shoot another with . . . a chocolate candy pistol, there is no ability to commit . . . any injury with it on the person of another"); *Johnson v. State,* 158 Ga. App. 432, 280 S.E.2d 856, 857 (1981) (holding that the evidence failed to establish "the present ability to inflict a violent injury" where the evidence proved the accused shook his finger while making a threat at persons in a car).

FYI

The Virginia Supreme Court affirmed the En Banc Majority's decision unanimously. *See Carter v. Commonwealth,* 269 Va. 44, 606 S.E.2d 839 (2005).

[Accordingly,] I would reverse the conviction for assault.

Hypo: *MPC Choice*

There is only one assault crime in Model Penal Code § 211.1 that is derived from the crime of frightening assault. There is no aggravated MPC version of the crime, and the crime of "simple assault" establishes liability for:

(1) attempts by physical menace to put another in fear of imminent serious bodily injury.

Recall that the MPC defines the mental state of an "attempt" as "the desire to cause the result" and defines the conduct as an act of preparation that takes a "substantial step in a course of conduct planned to culminate in [the] commission of a crime."

Now identify the possible elements of the frightening assault crime that you notice are missing from the MPC definition, and consider the possible reasons that the MPC drafters may have rejected them. Then explain whether the defendant in *Carter* could be convicted under this MPC definition of assault.

MPC doesn't include result of fear

Points for Discussion

a. Attempt Crime or Result Crime

By the time the Model Penal Code was proposed, most state courts had given judicial recognition to the frightening assault crime, and had articulated the definition of its elements in precedents interpreting the undefined statutory term "assault" in state criminal codes. For some courts, the elements of the attempted battery assault crime provided a model that could be mimicked by defining the elements of the frightening assault crime to require: 1) a menacing threat of injury, or "conduct as could induce in a victim a well-founded apprehension of peril" of such injury; 2) the actual or apparent ability to injure the victim; and 3) the intent to frighten the victim. The *Carter* case illustrates a debate over the definition of the second element.

When state courts used the "attempt crime" model as the template for the elements of the frightening assault crime, there was no reason to require the result element that the victim was frightened. Necessarily, an "attempt crime" is not a "result crime." The MPC drafters approved of the element choices made by courts that adopted the "attempt crime" model for defining frightening assault. For example, the mental state element is the affirmative "desire to cause the result" of putting a victim in fear, which resembles the "intent to frighten." *Compare* Model Penal Code §5.01. Similarly, the MPC conduct element of "physical menace" resembles the case law element of "menacing threat of injury." Moreover, the MPC implicitly creates liability for defendants who have the *apparent* ability to carry out their threats of "physical menace," which rule is endorsed in the case law definitions of the frightening assault crime.

However, most state courts adopted a definition of frightening assault that is based on the "result model," not on the "attempt model." As *Carter* explains, tort law was the source from which judges borrowed the policy justification for expanding criminal assault liability. The tort of assault covered civil defendants whose threats of bodily harm were accompanied with the intent to frighten rather than the intent to injure. These defendants could not be prosecuted criminally for attempted battery assault, and judges invoked the existence of tort liability as a reason for expanding the assault crime to encompass their behavior, which "is so likely to result in a breach of the peace that it should be a punishable offense." For those judges who preferred to define the frightening assault crime with the same elements as the corresponding tort, only the "result model" could accomplish that goal, because the tort of frightening assault did not exist in the absence of a victim who suffered fear. By contrast, the "attempt model" appealed to judges who did not view the suffering of a frightened victim as the *sine qua non* of the criminal harm to be punished with the frightening assault crime.

The limits of the "result model" for the frightening assault crime may be circumvented if the prosecutor can charge the attempted battery assault crime instead. For example, in *United States v. Bell*, 505 F.2d 539 (7th Cir. 1974), the defendant was convicted of "assault" based on his conduct toward a victim who suffered from a mental condition that made her unable to comprehend what was going on around her. The "assault" statute did not define the elements of the crime. According to case law, the frightening assault crime required "an act putting another in reasonable apprehension of bodily harm." Therefore, given the victim's lack of capacity to be frightened by the defendant's conduct, the court upheld the conviction on the theory that the defendant committed attempted battery assault, which may be committed upon a victim without his or her knowledge.

The usefulness of the frightening assault crime is illustrated by the court's analysis in *Robinson v. United States*, 506 A.2d 572 (D.C. App. 1986), where the defendant pointed a gun at a police officer and then put the gun down as ordered. He was charged with "assault" under a statute that did not define the elements of the crime, and the court observed that it was fortunate that the trial judge instructed the jury using case law definitions that covered both types of assault crime. The defendant could not have been convicted of attempted battery assault in the absence of demanding "proximity" evidence that he either fired the gun at the officer or attempted to fire it. However, the evidence was sufficient to show a frightening assault because the act of pointing the gun constituted a menacing threat and the "intent to frighten" the officer could be inferred from that conduct. The result of a frightened victim was not required by case law, and so the court ignored the defendant's argument that the victim's training as a police officer "might have made him resistant to such threats of danger," because the officer's reaction to the defendant's frightening conduct was irrelevant.

Two limitations upon the frightening assault crime may be found in case law and codes. The first is the exclusion of merely verbal threats, unless accompanied by some show of physical force, which is described in the MPC as "physical menace." A second typical limit is the requirement noted in *Carter*, that such conduct must be of the kind to cause "reasonable" apprehension, and in states where actual fear is required it must be "reasonable." The MPC does not use the term "reasonable." A third limit is codified in only a few states, which is the MPC requirement that the attempt must be to put another in "fear of imminent *serious* bodily injury." Most state codes extend the crime to include "fear of immediate bodily injury."

b. Proof Requirements

In a state where the "attempt model" of the elements is used, the mental state will be the "purpose" or "intent" to accomplish the result, namely, the result of causing apprehension of bodily injury. In a state where the "result model" of the elements is used, the same mental state will be required, presumably because it was borrowed from the assault tort mental state of the intent to frighten. Thus, the mental states of recklessly or negligently causing another person to be frightened will not establish the frightening assault crime.

What implicit policy reasons may explain Justice Benton's disagreement, as expressed in his dissenting opinion, with the majority opinion in *Carter*? Does Justice Benton's dissent in *Carter* implicitly echo any of the concerns of the dissent by Justice Lemons in *Adams*?

Hypo 1: *Hiding a Gun*

In the early morning hours of October, on an isolated stretch of Interstate 89 near St. Albans, Vermont, the defendant Riley stopped his car in the breakdown lane of the highway. He was seated in the driver's seat with the interior car light on when a state trooper pulled up behind him and approached his vehicle. Riley rolled down his window to talk to the trooper. When the trooper asked Riley if he needed assistance, Riley replied that he had stopped because he had a cramp in his leg, which he was massaging during the conversation. From his position outside the driver's door, the trooper noticed that a handgun was on the passenger's seat beside Riley, with its barrel pointed toward the passenger door. So the trooper opened the driver's door and ordered Riley to get out of the car. Riley hesitated at first, and then the trooper saw Riley reach over to the gun and brush it off the seat so that it fell on the car floor in front of the passenger's seat. When he saw what Riley was doing, the trooper drew his own weapon and told Riley to "hold it right there." While Riley was brushing the gun off the seat, he responded, "Everything is cool, don't shoot." Then Riley got out of the car.

The trooper arrested Riley for assault. It turned out that the gun did not have a firing pin and therefore could not have caused harm to the trooper. At Riley's trial, the trooper testified that he had been frightened by Riley's conduct. Assume that Riley was convicted for the frightening assault crime as defined in MPC § 211.1(1). On appeal, what arguments could be made by the defense counsel and prosecutor concerning the sufficiency of evidence of each element of the crime? If the scenario in this case had occurred in Virginia, what arguments could be made about the sufficiency of the evidence of each element of the frightening assault crime as defined by the *Carter* majority? As defined by the *Carter* dissent? *Compare State v. Riley*, 141 Vt. 29, 442 A.2d 1297 (1982).

guilty vs. NO mens rea of trying to frighten

hard case for prosecutor

Hypo 2: *Running to the Police Station*

Consider the facts in the prior Hypo, "You Can Pick Up Your Mail," which appears in the Points for Discussion that follow the *Henson* case. Recall how Zeke was enraged by the declaration of Hal, the postal worker, when Hal told Zeke to pick up his own mail. That is when Zeke lunged forward, grabbed Hal by his shirt collar, pulled Hal forward so that he and Zeke were almost touching noses, and then yelled epithets in Hal's face. Then when Hal took a step back, Zeke let him go. Taking no chances, Hal ran as fast as he could to the police station around the corner and reported Zeke's conduct to a police officer. Assume that this time, when Zeke was charged with "simple assault," the prosecutor argued that state court precedents interpreted the term "assault" to include the "frightening assault" crime. Can Zeke be convicted of this version of assault as defined in *Carter*?

c. Aggravated vs. Simple Assault

Just as the English misdemeanor battery crime evolved into the state crimes of simple battery and aggravated battery, so did the original English assault crime of attempted battery evolve into simple and aggravated forms, as did the tort type of frightening assault crime that was recognized by many state courts, starting in the nineteenth century. The *Yslas* statute provides an example of an aggravated type of attempted battery assault that includes the extra element of an intent to kill. The attempted battery assault crime in the *Henson* statute is categorized as aggravated because of the extra element of using a dangerous weapon. The assault crime in *Carter* is an aggravated type because of the extra element of a law enforcement officer victim. For an example of a wide variety of elements that can be used in an aggravated assault statute, see the Illinois statute, 720 ILCS 5/10–5.5, at http://www.ilga.gov/legislation/ilcs/fulltext.asp?DocName=072000050K12-2.

Hypo: *Lying in Wait*

When Sergeant Judy arrived at Tad's home in Gallup, New Mexico, with a warrant to arrest him for possession of an illegal handgun, Tad ran out the back door and down the street. Then with Judy chasing him on foot, Tad ran around the front end of a house trailer that was 20 feet long. Instead of following him, Judy stopped to listen for any indication that Tad was still running. When she heard no footsteps, Judy assumed that Tad might be lying in wait for her on the other side of the trailer. So Judy went the other way and tiptoed around the back end of the trailer. She carefully peered around the corner and saw that Tad was, indeed, facing toward the front end of the trailer with the gun in his right hand, extended forward and pointing toward the space where he expected Judy to appear. Therefore, Judy trained her gun on Tad and approached him quietly from behind. Then she shouted, "Drop the gun, now!" and Tad dropped his gun immediately. Tad was arrested and charged with the crime of "aggravated assault with a firearm on a law enforcement officer." The New Mexico statute that defines Tad's crime does not specify the elements of "assault," and the statute was enacted in 1912 when New Mexico became a state. Tad's defense counsel filed a pre-trial motion to dismiss the charge on the grounds that Tad "did not have the present ability to commit an injury," because Tad's gun did not have a bullet in the firing chamber when he dropped it. However, the gun was loaded and all Tad needed to do was to pull back a slide mechanism, in order to "chamber" the bullet so he could shoot it. Also, Tad had already taken off the safety catch when he was pointing the gun at the space where he expected Judy to appear, while he was lying in wait.

You are the assistant prosecutor in Tad's case, and you recognize that the term "assault" in the statute can be interpreted in two different ways. First, what are the elements of each type of assault crime that is encompassed in the statute? Second, for each type of assault crime, explain how the facts provide sufficient evidence of all the elements of that crime. Third, assuming that defense counsel argues that there is insufficient evidence for particular element(s), explain why the defense argument(s) are unpersuasive. *Compare People v. Chance*, 44 Cal. 4th 1164, 189 P.3d 971, 81 Cal. Rptr. 3d 723 (2008).

C. Modern Crimes Beyond Assault & Battery

1. Reckless Endangerment

The MPC drafters proposed the creation of the new crime of "recklessly endangering another person," in order to fill liability gaps that existed because of the limitations of the battery and assault crimes. The drafters recognized that many states had enacted crimes for particular types of endangerment, and they proposed instead to "replace the haphazard coverage of prior law with one comprehensive provision" to reach "any kind of [reckless] conduct" that places other people in danger. Model Penal Code § 211.2, Comment 1 at 196 (1980). This crime is defined as follows:

> A person commits a misdemeanor if he recklessly engages in conduct which places or may place another person in danger of death or serious bodily injury. Recklessness and danger shall be *presumed* where a person knowingly points a firearm at or in the direction of another, whether or not the actor believes the firearm to be loaded.

More specifically, the presumption means that jurors may be instructed that "they may regard knowingly pointing a firearm at another as sufficient evidence of the dangerousness of the actor's conduct and of his recklessness with respect to risk of death or serious bodily injury." Model Penal Code § 211.2, Comment 3 at 204 (1980).

Although the reckless endangerment crime has been enacted in many states, some courts have interpreted its scope in restrictive ways. Moreover, in the decades since the MPC was proposed, courts have recognized that the MPC definition of the crime was not drafted with particular kinds of modern dangers in mind.

Hypo 1: *Cocaine During Pregnancy*

Assume that when baby Ron is born in the county hospital, he has cocaine in his bloodstream. His mother Regina admits that she used cocaine during her pregnancy. The prosecutor charges her with the crime of reckless endangerment as defined in MPC § 211.2. Regina is convicted. On appeal, her defense counsel argues that the crime of reckless endangerment was not intended to encompass the conduct of a mother in using cocaine during her pregnancy. What arguments can be made in favor of this position? Can the prosecutor make any counter-arguments in reply? *Compare Kilmon v. State*, 394 Md. 168, 905 A.2d 306 (2006); *Whitner v. State*, 328 S.C. 1, 492 S.E.2d 777 (1997).

Hypo 2: *Freedom Tower Revisited*

Just before the construction of the new Freedom Tower building is finished, four men decide to perform BASE jumping from the roof of the Tower, which is 1,776 feet in height. They climb through a hole in the perimeter security fence at midnight and enter through the front door, which is open because the security guards are taking a break. They climb the stairs to the top floor which has been completed except for the glass in the windows. The men are wearing jumpsuits and helmets. They find their skydiving equipment and parachutes, which were stashed by one of the men who has special access. Then they emerge on the roof and spend several hours planning their jump, which occurs at 3:00 am. They land safely but their images are captured on a security camera across the street from the Tower, and they are seen by the owner of a bagel shop who is baking at an early hour. Each of the men has extensive skydiving and BASE jumping experience. They choose the night for their jump based on the lack of significant wind and the bright moonlight. They wear video cameras on their helmets and record their jumps. The recordings show that the streets are not entirely empty—there are a few cars moving about.

The men jump off the Tower one at a time and their jumps take about two minutes. Three land in the street, some blocks away from the Tower, and one lands further away in Battery Park. When the men are caught, they are charged with Reckless Endangerment, defined in the New York criminal code as follows: "It shall be unlawful to recklessly engage in conduct which creates a substantial risk of serious physical injury to another person." Serious physical injury is defined as including "protracted impairment of health" and "recklessly" has the same definition that is used in the Model Penal Code. On the facts, what arguments can be made by the prosecutor and defense counsel as to whether the men should be convicted of the Reckless Endangerment crime?

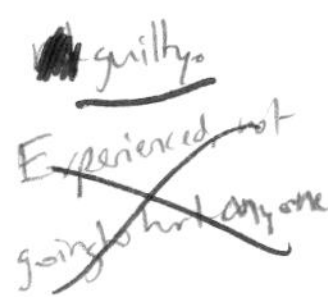

2. Stalking

The first stalking statute was enacted in 1990 and today the stalking crime is included in all state codes and in the federal code. The *Simone* case illustrates the difficulties involved in defining the elements of the crime, in obtaining evidence for conviction, and in ensuring the enforcement of stalking laws generally.

State v. Simone

152 N.H. 755, 887 A.2d 135 (2005).

DALIANIS, J.

[In] 2001, Coral Olson was employed by the U.S. Census Bureau as a field service representative. Olson traveled door-to-door to conduct census surveys. She would then re-contact the same respondents by telephone and by personal visit until she had obtained sufficient survey information. In January 2001, Olson went to the [Simone's] home to conduct a census survey. Olson gave [Simone] her business card with her home phone number, and conducted several follow-up telephone calls and one follow-up personal visit to complete the census survey. After [Simone] completed his census survey, however, he continued to call Olson. The defendant told Olson that he was interested in her; Olson responded that she was married and not interested in him. Nevertheless [he] persisted in calling her. [She] did not initiate any of these personal telephone calls. [She] told him not to contact her. If she did not answer the telephone, [Simone] would call repeatedly and leave messages each time until she finally answered. . . .

In August 2001, Olson contacted the Temple Police Department[,] met with Officer Steven Duval [and] expressed her desire that [Simone] cease contact. On August 18, 2001, Officer Duval spoke with [Simone] about the situation. Nonetheless, [Simone] continued to pursue Olson [and so] Olson obtained a protective order prohibiting [Simone] from contacting her. Notwithstanding the protective order, [Simone] continued to call her. Olson testified that between the fall of 2001 and June 2003, [Simone] placed more unwanted calls to her than she could estimate [and] also sent [her] packages, which she did not open. As a result, Olson frequently contacted the Temple police.

Food for Thought

Why would it have been useful for Olson to have the assistance of an attorney when seeking the protective order at a judicial hearing? Consider the information that Olson would need to know in order to obtain the order, and what would happen if the defendant had an attorney and Olson did not.

On June 11, 2003, [Simone] called Olson [and] she again told [him] not to contact her [but] he called back and left [three] lengthy messages on Olson's answering machine. [In his first message, he said,] "that he had a lot of anger towards [her]." [In his second message, he] admitted that he had previously misrepresented himself to Olson's husband in order to obtain personal information about her and about her marriage. [Then he] said, "I don't care if the police come and arrest me. I don't care if I go to court. And I don't care if I get seven years or 70 years. This means so much to me to tell you that I'm terribly sorry and remorseful and I don't care if I rot in hell. And I know I will die in, in jail[.]" [In his third message, he said:]

> [I] honestly don't care and I've made the decision now. I know this is very severe and even stupid of me to call you, but I basically don't care because I, I consider on August the 13th of 2001 when you broke up with me, that my life had changed drastically. It's not gotten any better and I realize that was like, you know, that was like the nail in the coffin for me. I, I'm already dead and jail is just a place to finalize that act.

[Simone's message also said that even though] he "was terribly, terribly sorry over the bad things that he did[,] it was worth rotting in jail for, and [he] would do it again in a heartbeat." He said that "he had a lot of demons inside" but that . . . [he] "never entertained the thoughts of hurting [Olson]." He also admitted that he was stopped [by the police] while traveling to her home late at night.

> **Food for Thought**
>
> What are the possible reasons why Officer Duval apparently never arrested Simone before June 24, 2003, either for violating the protective order or for committing the crime of stalking?

After listening to these messages, Olson called the police department and Officer Duval came to her home. Olson received another call from [Simone] just as Officer Duval arrived. Officer Duval took the telephone and spoke with [Simone] for about 20 minutes [and then Simone] called again and left a fourth message . . . . [stating] that he would be "prosecuted and face a felony charge" and [that] he would pray for Olson every night. Officer Duval left [and] returned [30 minutes later] to respond to a 911 call made by Olson. . . .

Olson arrived home on June 17, 2003 to find twenty new messages [left by Simone during a two-hour period] on her answering machine. [In his messages, Simone said that] he was "sorry it had come to this"[,] . . . implored Olson "not to return the things that are coming in the mail [and said] that he was sorry that he did not have her anymore [and] that he lost everything that he loved. . . . [In sixteen of the calls, Simone repeatedly asked Olson if she was present in her home and begged her to answer the telephone.] [Olson] immediately called the police department and Officer Duval came to her home. [On June 18,] Olson called Officer Duval to report that she had received two packages from [Simone]. On June 24, Olson reported to Officer Duval that she had received yet another package and a letter from [Simone, who] continued to call . . . .

In October 2003, a [county grand jury] indicted [Simone] on one count of stalking under [a New Hampshire statute] which criminalizes "knowingly . . . engag[ing] in a course of conduct targeted at a specific person which would cause a reasonable person to fear for his or her personal safety ... and the person is actually placed in such fear." [On] appeal, [Simone] argues [that] the State failed to present sufficient evidence to support the jury's verdict [that]

his conduct: (1) would cause a reasonable person to fear for his or her personal safety; and (2) actually placed Olson in fear for her personal safety[.] . . .

[Simone] argues that we must interpret the phrase, "fear for his or her personal safety," as used in the stalking statute, to require a fear of physical violence. We need not reach [this] argument, however, because even if [this is so,] the evidence was sufficient to [satisfy the elements of the statute].

[Simone] contends that his conduct would not cause a reasonable person to fear physical violence because he never assaulted Olson or explicitly threatened her with violence, and he "mostly apologized and expressed his continuing love" in his repeated telephone calls to her. We disagree. . . . [A] reasonable person could view [Simone's] unrelenting telephone calls and gifts to Olson, especially in light of [Simone's] emotional instability, as evidence that [he] was obsessed with Olson and posed a threat of physical violence to her. [He told Olson that he had "serious personal problems" and felt suicidal and out of control.] [Simone] and Olson never had a personal relationship. . . . [In light of all the evidence,] we conclude that there was sufficient evidence to prove beyond a reasonable doubt that [Simone's] conduct would cause a reasonable person to fear for his or her personal safety.

Next, [Simone] argues the State failed to prove that his conduct caused Olson actually to fear for her personal safety. At trial, the State asked Olson about the impact of [Simone's] conduct upon her. Olson answered, "I live in fear every day. I don't know—I don't know what's going to happen next, or what [the defendant is] going to do." Both Olson and Officer Duval testified that Olson frequently contacted the police between August 2001 and June 2003 as a result of [Simone's] conduct. [The] trial court twice noted that Olson's testimony and demeanor on the witness stand . . . gave rise to a reasonable inference that Olson actually feared the defendant. [In light of all the evidence, we conclude] that there was sufficient evidence beyond a reasonable doubt that [Simone's] conduct actually caused Olson to fear for her personal safety. Accordingly, the jury properly convicted the defendant of stalking . . . .

Points for Discussion

a. Original Elements of Stalking Crime

The first stalking statute was enacted in California in 1990 after five women were murdered by their stalkers. The goal of stalking statutes is to address the harmful features of stalking behavior that are not addressed by assault and related crimes. Such crimes are concerned with single incidents whereas a stalking statute focuses on repeated behavior that causes fear of bodily injury, in the absence of oral or written threats and where evidence of the intention to cause fear may be lacking. In theory, a stalking statute makes it possible for police to intervene before a stalker takes violent action, and imposes more serious penalties that may serve as a greater deterrent to stalking behavior. Legislatures have continued to amend their stalking statutes in order to take account of criticisms and enforcement problems with the earliest versions of these laws.

In 1993, the National Institute of Justice developed a "Model Anti-Stalking Code" which has been influential in some states. There are several points of consensus displayed by most stalking statutes, but a variety of legislative preferences are exhibited with regard to particular elements. The typical stalking statute will require that the defendant's "course of conduct" must be "directed at a specific person," and must be "repeated" at least twice. Some statutes require that the conduct must create actual fear in the victim, and some statutes require that the conduct would cause fear in a reasonable person. Other statutes follow the approach in the New Hampshire statute in *Simone*, which requires both of the latter elements. Like the Model Code and most statutes, the *Simone* statute applies to conduct that causes the victim either to fear for her own physical safety or for the physical safety of an immediate family member.

One influential aspect of the 1993 Model Code is the conduct element, which is defined so as to create two independent bases for prosecution. One type of prohibited conduct is the act of maintaining "a visual or physical proximity to a person," and most state statutes now include the acts of following a person or placing a person under surveillance. The second type of prohibited conduct is the conveyance of "threats" that may be oral, written, or implied by conduct.

Most states followed the broad approach of the Model Code in not providing specific examples of acts that qualify as part of a "course of conduct." But some statutes include such examples, while noting that a "course of conduct" may "include but not be limited to" such acts. The *Simone* statute uses a list that includes these and other examples: 1) appearing in close proximity to or entering the victim's (or immediate family member's) residence, place of employment, school, or other place where the person may be found; 2) causing damage to the victim's (or immediate family member's) residence or property; and 3) any act of communication by any method of transmission (including electronic transmission) after being notified that the victim does not desire further communication. Why would a legislature choose to include such a list? What additional examples would be useful to include?

b. Modern Trends

In 2007, the National Center for Victims of Crime proposed revisions for the Model Code based on empirical research about stalking behavior and victim experiences, which research revealed the need for broader definitions of the crime, especially given the many ways in which "affordable technology has fundamentally and profoundly changed the way stalkers monitor and initiate contact with their victims." The new proposed definition of stalking applies to:

> Any person who purposefully engages in a course of conduct directed at a specific person and knows or should know that the course of conduct would cause a reasonable person to: (a) fear for his or her safety or the safety of a third person; or (b) suffer other emotional distress.

Note that the updated definition does not require the "actual fear" element, in accordance with the judgment of 14 states in 2007. This definition also makes it unnecessary to show, as required by the *Simone* statute, that the victim suffered "fear for her safety," because proof of the alternate element of "emotional distress" is sufficient. In 2007, "roughly half the states include[d] 'emotional distress' or something similar in their stalking laws." The latter concept is defined as "significant mental suffering or distress that may, but does not necessarily, require medical or other professional treatment or counseling." A "reasonable person" is defined as a "reasonable person in the victim's circumstances." The term "course of conduct" has been expanded to include "two or more acts, including, but not limited to," the following:

> acts in which the stalker directly, indirectly, or through third parties, through any action, method, device, or means, follows, monitors, observes, surveils, threatens, or communicates to or about a person, or interferes with a person's property.

Take Note

According to the Supplemental Victim Survey of the Bureau of Justice Statistics, "nearly 7 in 10 stalking victims knew their offender in some capacity." *See* www.bjs.gov/content/pub/pdf/svus_rev.pdf.

Finally, unlike the 1993 Model Code, the 2007 Code includes an illustrative, non-exhaustive, list of 19 examples of stalking behaviors that all state laws should cover. Here are a few examples of the technology-related behaviors: 1) using the internet or a computer "to steal a victim's identity or to interfere with a victim's credit;" 2) using surveillance either in person, or "through technology," or "through third parties"; 3) "posting pictures of a victim on the internet," or "disseminating embarrassing or inaccurate information about a victim"; 4) "impersonating a victim through technology or other means"; and 5) sending "flowers, cards, or e-mail messages to a victim's home or workplace." *See* National Center for the Victims of Crime, The Model Stalking Code Revisited: Responding to the New Realities of Stalking (2007), https://members.victimsofcrime.org/docs/default-source/src/model-stalking-code.pdf?sfvrsn=12.

From a prosecutor's point of view, what are the potential effects of each of the changes in the 2007 model definition of the elements of the stalking crime? How are the experiences of stalking victims, like Coral Olson in the *Simone* case, reflected in each of the changes? Assuming that a state legislature enacts the proposed 2007 definition of the stalking crime, what barriers to effective enforcement of the crime may remain?

c. Enforcement of Stalking Laws

The *Simone* case illustrates how a variety of factors may impede the enforcement of the stalking laws. Notably, the problem of enforcement in *Simone* cannot be attributed to a lack of legislation. First, each of the defendant's telephone calls and deliveries of packages to the victim could have been prosecuted under the state statute defining the crime of "harassment." Second, each time the defendant engaged in two of these communications, they could have been prosecuted as a "course of conduct" under the stalking statute, because that term is defined as including two or more acts "over a period of time, however brief," which evidence "a continuity of purpose." Third, after the victim in *Simone* obtained the protective order that prohibited the defendant from contacting her, the defendant could have been prosecuted under the stalking statute for each time that he recklessly engaged in a single act that violated the order. *See* N.H. REV. STAT. §§ 633:3–a, 644:4 (West 2006). Yet the *Simone* opinion describes a prosecution for a single count of stalking that began with an indictment obtained more than two years after the victim first contacted the police department, seeking assistance in putting an end to the communications from the defendant.

In retrospect, one factor that may have delayed the stalking prosecution was the need for evidence that the defendant's conduct would cause a "reasonable person" to fear for his or her physical safety. What evidence did the *Simone* Court rely on to support its conclusions that there was sufficient fear of each kind to justify conviction? Aside from concern about the adequacy of the fear evidence, what other factors could explain the delay in prosecution?

The following hypotheticals provide the opportunity for making arguments about the interpretation of "fear for personal safety," which is used in most stalking statutes, and about the need for legislatures to redefine and expand this concept.

Hypo 1: *Gym Class*

Kia was married when she sought counseling from Joe, a counselor employed by her church in Nashua, New Hampshire. After some months, their relationship became "intimate." Kia recognized that it was "unhealthy" and told other church members, so Joe was fired by church officials, who told him to cut off contact with Kia. During the year that followed, Kia obtained a divorce, met and dated a new acquaintance, and then remarried. Six months later, when Kia was driving to her husband's office with her four-year-old daughter in the car, she realized that Joe was following her in his car. She pulled over and when Joe approached the vehicle to talk to her, she spoke to him through a crack in the window. When Joe asked for her address so that he could send her a "wedding card," Kia refused to give it to him and told him to stop all contact with her. Joe agreed. The next week, Joe started showing up at the gym where Kia exercised, and he began to attend the weekly yoga class that she attended. Kia was "very alarmed" by Joe's presence in the class, and she tried to ignore it for two weeks. Once when Joe tried to talk to her during the class, Kia told him to stop all contact with her. Again, Joe agreed. But he kept attending the yoga class. Finally, Kia stopped going because Joe's presence in the class "felt so threatening."

One month later, Joe started calling Kia's house. When Kia or her husband would answer the phone, Joe would hang up without saying anything. Then after a few weeks, Joe called and told Kia's husband that he (Joe) "had some unfinished business with her." At this point, Kia and her husband called the police, and Joe was arrested for the stalking crime. Assume that the stalking statute in *Simone* applies to this case. How will the prosecutor argue at trial that the evidence shows that all the elements of the statute are satisfied? If the New Hampshire legislature enacted the updated 2007 model definition of the stalking crime, and if that statute applied to this case, what difference would that make? *Compare Sparks v. Deveny*, 189 P.3d 1268 (Ore. App. 2008).

Hypo 2: *Separate Occasions*

When Sue was jogging on the shoulder of a road that ran along Lake Samish in Bellingham, a white van drove up behind her, and Len was driving. As he drove along next to her, he shouted out of the window and asked her for directions to a particular address. Sue told him that she had never heard of the place. Len drove off but a few minutes later, he circled back and again shouted out to Sue, asking her for "directions to the freeway." This time Sue pretended that she didn't hear him and then Len drove away. A few minutes later, Len's van approached her from the opposite direction, pulled a U-turn, and parked next to Sue. Len asked her, "Do you need a ride?" Sue said, "No." Then Len asked her, "Do you need money?" Sue said, "No." Then Sue started jogging again and Len drove off. Sue was now "really scared" of Len, so when two bicyclists came along, Sue asked them if she could borrow a cell phone to call the police. Len was arrested and charged with stalking.

The prosecutor argues that the Washington statute applies to Len because his course of conduct was "repeatedly following" Sue. The term "following" is defined in the statute as "deliberately maintaining visual or physical proximity to a specific person over a period of time"; the term "repeatedly" is defined as "on two or more separate occasions." The term "occasion" is not defined, however. Len's defense counsel argues that: 1) Len did not follow Sue on "separate occasions" because his interactions with Sue were merely a series of "microevents" in the larger scheme of a single "occasion"; and 2) the term "occasion" should be defined as "events occurring at least over a substantial period of time," which did not occur in Len's case. In reply, the prosecutor argues that Len followed Sue "repeatedly" because each interaction with Sue constituted one "distinct, individual, non-continuous occurrence or incident," and thus, a "separate occasion" under the statute. How should the court rule? *Compare State v. Kintz*, 169 Wash. 2d 537, 238 P.3d 470 (2010).

Hypo 3: *Time Gap Between Acts*

The typical stalking statute requires two "repeated" acts directed against a particular victim in order to constitute a "course of conduct," and state legislatures take different approaches concerning the time period during which the two acts must occur. Assume that the Indiana statute is silent on this issue and that a prosecutor must advise the Indiana Supreme Court how to interpret that silence. One option is to assume that the Indiana legislature intended for the court to pick a fixed time period, like the express one-year limit in the Arkansas statute or the express five-year limit in the Minnesota statute. A second option is illustrated by the Ohio statute, which gives courts the discretion to decide whether the two acts are "closely related in time" on a case-by-case basis. A third option is illustrated by the Wisconsin statute that requires that the two acts must "show the defendant's continuity of purpose" over the period of time during which the two acts occur, "in light of the totality of all the evidence in a given case."

The Indiana prosecutor hopes to persuade the Indiana Supreme Court to choose an interpretation that will serve the purposes of the stalking crime and also justify the affirmance of Dirk's stalking conviction. Dirk's first act of stalking was a telephone call to the victim that occurred a few days before his two-year term of imprisonment began. His second act of stalking was a telephone call to the victim that was placed a few days after he was released from prison. Notably, Dirk's defense counsel simply argues that the more-than-two-year time gap between Dirk's the two calls was "too long."

Assume that Dirk's prison sentence was imposed for his conviction for "criminal voyeurism" committed against the same victim who received his calls. What arguments can the prosecutor make to criticize the Arkansas, Minnesota, and Ohio statutes, while defending the value of choosing the Wisconsin approach as an appropriate interpretation of the silent Indiana statute? Assuming that this approach is adopted by the Court, how can the prosecutor show that the facts of Dirk's case fit the Wisconsin formula so that his stalking conviction may be affirmed?

---

3. Domestic Violence

There are many crimes that may be committed during the course of abusive behavior by a person who fits a modern definition of a "family or household member of the victim," which could include "a spouse, a person living as a spouse, or a former spouse" or other relationships. These crimes include murder or manslaughter, negligent homicide, rape or sexual assault, assault and battery (possibly with a dangerous weapon), burglary or breaking and entering, criminal trespass, disorderly conduct, disturbing the peace, willful and malicious destruction of property, harassment (including harassing phone calls), violation of a restraining order, intimidation of a witness, and a variety of attempt crimes. *See* ELIZABETH M. SCHNEIDER *ET AL*, DOMESTIC VIOLENCE AND THE LAW: THEORY AND PRACTICE, 275–276 (2d ed. 2008).

In 1977 the California legislature enacted the felony crime of "domestic violence" to cover "the infliction of injury on [the] spouse, cohabitee or parent of a child" of the defendant. Many state codes now include such crimes and define them in a variety of ways. For example, the Vermont legislature enacted a Domestic Assault statute in 1993 with three degrees of the crime. The lowest degree of the crime imposes a maximum punishment of one year in jail for attempting to cause or recklessly causing bodily injury to a family or household member, or for willfully causing such a victim to fear imminent serious bodily injury. The aggravated second degree crime allows for a five-year prison sentence for committing a second domestic assault offense or for committing a first offense that violates a restraining order issued by the criminal court. The aggravated first degree crime applies when a person commits domestic assault while armed with a deadly weapon, or after having been convicted of this crime, or attempts to cause or recklessly causes serious bodily injury to the victim. *See* 33 Vt. Stat. Ann. 13 §§ 1042, 1043, 1044 (1993).

When Congress enacted the Violent Crime Control and Law Enforcement Act of 1994, this statute included the Violence Against Women Act of 1994 (VAWA), which "federalized the enforcement of restraining orders by requiring that states provide full faith and credit to orders issued by sister states [and] also criminalized interstate violations of restraining orders." *See* Schneider at 355. The VAWA also made "interstate domestic violence" a federal crime that encompasses all "intimate partners", and interstate stalking was added to the list of crimes in this provision in 1996. The statutory definition of interstate domestic violence in 18 U.S.C. § 2261 provides as follows:

> (1) Crossing a State line—A person who travels across a State line [with] the intent to injure, harass, or intimidate that person's spouse or intimate partner, and who, in the course of or as a result of such travel, intentionally commits a crime of violence and thereby causes bodily injury to such spouse or intimate partner, shall be punished [as provided].
>
> (2) Causing the crossing of a State line—A person who causes a spouse or intimate partner to cross a State line [by] force, coercion, duress, or fraud and, in the course or as a result of that conduct, intentionally commits a crime of violence and thereby causes bodily injury to the person's spouse or intimate partner, shall be punished [as provided].

The penalty for the § 2261 crime depends on the injuries to the victim. A sentence of life or any term of years may be imposed if the victim dies; a maximum sentence of 20 years is allowed if the victim suffers permanent disfigurement or life-threatening bodily injury. A maximum sentence of 10 years applies if a dangerous weapon is used or if the victim suffers serious bodily injury. Otherwise, the maximum sentence is five years. *See* Michelle Easterling, *For Better or Worse: The Federalization of Domestic Violence*, 98 W. Va. L. Rev. 933 (1996).

Hypo: *Policies and Impact*

Describe the various policy reasons that may explain why state legislatures have enacted "domestic assault" crimes like those in Vermont, and the impact that such crimes could have on the criminal justice system.

4. Civil Rights

Some criminal civil rights laws serve to punish bodily injury battery crimes (and attempted battery crimes) that are motivated by the victim's identity. For example, the Matthew Shepard and James Byrd, Jr., Hate Crimes Prevention Act of 2009, 18 U.S.C. § 249, applies to a person who "willfully causes bodily injury [or death] to any person," or who "attempts to cause bodily injury" "through the use of fire, a firearm, a dangerous weapon, or an explosive or incendiary device," either (1) "because of the actual or perceived race, color, religion, or national origin of any person"; or (2) "because of the actual or perceived religion, national origin, gender, sexual orientation, gender identity, or disability of any person" when the crime affected interstate and foreign commerce.

Although this statute does not apply to identity-motivated threats of injury, such acts may be prosecuted under other federal criminal laws, such as the Civil Rights Act of 1968, 18 U.S.C. § 249, or the federal statute that punishes the interstate communication of threats. *See* http://www.justice.gov/crt/about/crm/matthewshepard.php. Almost all state criminal codes include hate crime laws that apply to identity-motivated acts of violence or frightening crimes.

Executive Summary

Offensive Touching Battery. This common law crime required the *actus reus* of offensive touching and the *mens rea* of criminal negligence. The MPC and most states have abolished this crime. Some legislatures have enacted "laser battery" statutes to extend the common law crime to cover touchings with the intangible substance of a laser.

Bodily Injury Battery. This common law crime required the *actus reus* of causing bodily injury and the *mens rea* of criminal negligence. The MPC and many states use the MPC mental states for this crime, along with broad definitions of bodily injury.

Exposure to Life-Threatening Disease. Many states have enacted statutes to define this crime, some of which are focused specifically on intentional exposure to the HIV infection. Some states have amended their battery statutes to achieve the same purpose.

Attempted Battery Assault. This common law crime required the *actus reus* of an attempt, meaning "coming close" to the completion of the battery crime, by such means as "an offer of violence." The *mens rea* for attempt is the intent to achieve the result of the completed crime, and typically this is the intent to commit bodily injury battery. Courts are divided regarding the requirement of the actual ability to commit a battery.

Frightening Assault. This crime was adopted originally through judicial recognition by state courts. The elements of this crime resemble those of assault in tort law, including the *actus reus* of frightening conduct and the *mens rea* of the intent to put the victim in fear of receiving bodily injury. Most states also require the result element of a frightened victim.

Major Themes

a. **Battery**—Today most states codes and courts recognize the validity of the common law bodily injury battery crime, whereas the offensive touching crime is recognized only by a minority. Both types of battery are treated as simple battery, and most states use additional elements to punish aggravated battery. The need for a crime to punish the intentional exposure to HIV has inspired the enactment of new statutory provisions as well as amendments to expand battery crimes to cover this conduct.

b. **Assault**—The crime of assault has expanded over time. The common law provided only for the crime of attempted battery assault, which has been expanded in some states to cover defendants who lack the actual ability but have the apparent ability to commit a battery. The trend toward expansion was also expressed through the judicial recognition of the frightening assault crime. Legislatures have recognized the need for enacting new assault-like crimes, including reckless endangerment, stalking, and domestic violence crimes.

Reckless Endangerment. This crime was proposed in the MPC and is used in many states. The *actus reus* is conduct that may place another person in danger of serious bodily injury and the *mens rea* is recklessness.

Stalking. This crime has been enacted in many states since 1990. A typical modern statute includes the elements of recklessly engaging in a course of conduct, targeted at a specific person, which would cause a reasonable person to fear for his or her personal safety or to suffer emotional distress.

Domestic Violence. This crime has been enacted in many states since 1977, and its names include "domestic assault," "domestic battery," and "domestic violence." A typical statute includes the elements of causing specified harms, such as those prescribed in battery and assault statutes, against a family or household member.

Civil Rights. Both federal and state hate-crime laws punish the commission of bodily injury batteries (and attempted batteries) motivated by the "actual or perceived" identity of the victim.

For More Information

- American Law Institute, Model Penal Code and Commentaries, Part II, § 211.1, Comments at 172–204 (1980).
- John M. Burkoff & Russell L. Weaver, Inside Criminal Law: What Matters and Why 153–166 (2d ed. 2011).
- Wayne R. LaFave, Criminal Law §§ 16.1–16.3 (5th ed. 2010).

Test Your Knowledge

To assess your understanding of the material in this chapter, click here to take a quiz.

Chapter 10

Rape & Sexual Assault

The common law crime of rape was a capital offense and it was defined as an act of genital penetration through sexual intercourse, by a man with a woman not his wife, through the use of force or by threat of force, without the consent of the victim. This definition was reflected in the case law and statutes of most states until the 1970s. Courts required a prosecutor to prove that the victim resisted the defendant "to the utmost" and reported the crime promptly. Corroborating evidence was required to support the victim's testimony, and jurors were instructed in the words of Lord Hale that they should give special scrutiny to the victim's testimony because rape "is an accusation easily to be made and hard to be proved, and harder to be defended by the party accused." Evidence of the victim's sexual reputation and prior sexual experiences could be offered by the defendant to show that her "lack of chastity" demonstrated that she was more likely to fabricate a claim of rape or to consent to forcible sex.

In 1975 the Michigan legislature enacted the first "rape reform" statute and thereby launched a widespread movement for statutory change in the definitions of the elements of rape crimes and the evidentiary rules governing rape trials. The new statutes typically redefined the rape crime as gender neutral, and expanded the scope of the crime to include acts of sexual penetration by fingers or objects, and to encompass oral or anal sexual conduct. Some statutes eliminated the "resistance" and "lack of consent" elements and allowed conviction when sexual intercourse was accomplished by "fear" in lieu of "force" or "threat of force." Courts and legislatures abolished the utmost resistance requirement, the corroboration requirement, the prompt report requirement, and the Lord Hale instruction. Even the marital rape exemption was abandoned or limited. Many states enacted new crimes to allow convictions for lesser degrees of rape, thus expanding the scope of criminal sexual conduct. States also adopted "rape shield" provisions in evidence codes which

Take Note

The FBI did not update the definition of the rape crime until 2012 for purposes of the Uniform Crime Report (UCR) data gathered from state and local police departments. The prior definition was based on the common law elements of rape from the pre-reform era. Therefore, none of the reported rape crimes that fit the broader definitions used in post-reform statutes and case law could be counted as rape crimes in the FBI's UCR data. The revised definition still requires lack of consent, which a majority of state statutes no longer require. But it is gender neutral and it does encompass sexual acts other than intercourse. *See* http://www.fbi.gov/news/pressrel/press-releases/attorney-general-eric-holder-announces-revisions-to-the-uniform-crime-reports-definition-of-rape.

regulate the admissibility of evidence of the victim's prior sexual conduct. The large variety of statutory changes required courts to revise their interpretations of rape crime elements and defenses, to design new jury instructions, and to modify "sufficiency of the evidence" standards for conviction. Many legislatures changed the name of the "rape" crime to "sexual assault" and these terms will be used synonymously in this chapter where appropriate.

As new elements were added to the emerging rape definitions in statutes, courts took on the task of redefining the concepts of force, threat, fear, resistance, and consent. Their decisions often evidenced sharp disagreements and the subsequent codifications of contested holdings have provided a continuing supply of controversies. The social and legal definitions of rape have evolved over time and they remain contested.

Over 40 years after the "rape reform" era began, the "Me Too" movement on social media led to more widespread awareness of the frequency of sexual violence and sexual harassment against women and of the causes for women's long enduring silence about these experiences. Whether this movement marked the beginning of another "rape reform era"—in terms of changes in the criminal law and its enforcement by legislature, judges, jurors, prosecutors, and police—remains to be seen.

A. Forcible Rape

The two most important elements for the common law crime of forcible rape were "force" and "lack of consent." While it is useful to study these elements separately, it is important to understand the historical connections between them that continue to influence modern judicial interpretations of their meaning. Some modern statutes define these elements as separate and independent requirements for conviction, whereas other statutes treat them as being intertwined, as when the term "force" is described as "force used to overcome the victim's will." Today most statutes define rape with reference to "force," "threat of force," and "fear," rather than "lack of consent." Even statutes that rely on "lack of consent" as the key element of rape may define that term so as to equate it with "force" or "compulsion."

The common law definition of rape did not include an explicit *mens rea*, and rape was viewed as a general intent crime. A prosecutor was required to prove that a defendant engaged intentionally in sexual intercourse, and intended to use force or threat of force to accomplish that act. But a prosecutor did not need to prove that a defendant intended to engage in nonconsensual intercourse.

---

1. Force, Threat, or Fear

During the pre-reform era, courts looked to the victim to supply evidence of the defendant's use of unlawful "force," as illustrated by the "utmost resistance" requirement. The function of this extreme type of resistance evidence was to persuade judges that a defendant's use of "force" was sufficiently harmful to justify conviction, and that a victim's claim of rape was credible. Without such proof of resistance, judges could view the use of "force" to accomplish sexual intercourse as an ambiguous event that could be characterized as "seduction" rather than "rape."

Over time, some courts replaced the "utmost resistance" requirement with that of "sufficient" resistance under the circumstances, depending on the character of the "force" or "threat of force" used by the defendant. As judges began to recognize that a threat of violence could explain a victim's submission to sexual intercourse without resistance, the "force" and "threat" concepts began to expand. Ultimately, statutes and judicial decisions came to endorse the view that a defendant's provocation of a victim's "reasonable fear" could justify conviction in the absence of a victim's physical resistance. In this way, "fear" caused by an implicit threat came to serve as a substitute for actual "force" or an explicit "threat of force." However, during the pre-reform era, courts and legislatures usually required fear of imminent death or serious bodily injury.

At the outset of the rape reform era, some judges began to question the need for any type of resistance requirement on policy grounds, arguing that women should not be forced to risk death or injury in order to provide the prosecutor with evidence that a rape occurred. Courts began to accept proof of verbal resistance as a substitute for physical resistance, and to look more closely at a defendant's actions, rather than a victim's actions, in assessing the existence of "force" and "fear." Legislatures began to enact new statutes that codified "fear" as a prohibited means for accomplishing rape, and some statutes required only fear of "immediate and unlawful bodily injury." Such reform statutes, like that in the *Iniguez* case, required courts to rethink their prior interpretations of the evolving elements of the rape crime.

People v. Iniguez

7 Cal. 4th 847, 872 P.2d 1183, 30 Cal. Rptr. 2d 258 (1994) (In Bank).

ARABIAN, J.

[The] Court of Appeal reversed the defendant's conviction for rape on the grounds that the evidence of force or fear of immediate and unlawful bodily injury was insufficient. We granted review to determine whether there was sufficient evidence to support the verdict, and to delineate the relationship between evidence of fear and the requirement under Penal Code [§] 261(a)(2) that the sexual intercourse be "accomplished against a person's will" in a case where lack of consent is not disputed. We reverse the Court of Appeal.

On June 15, 1990, the eve of her wedding, at approximately 8:30 p.m., 22 year-old Mercy P. arrived at the home of Sandra S., a close family friend [who] was to stand in at the wedding the next day for Mercy's mother[.] Mercy was planning to spend the night at [Sandra's] home [and Mercy] met defendant, Sandra's fiancé, for the first time that evening. Defendant was scheduled to stand in for Mercy's father during the wedding. Mercy noticed that defendant was somewhat "tipsy" when he arrived. He had consumed a couple of beers and a pint of Southern Comfort[.] Mercy, Sandra, and defendant celebrated Mercy's impending wedding by having dinner and drinking some wine. There was no flirtation or any remarks of a sexual nature between defendant and Mercy at any time during the evening. Around 11:30 p.m., Mercy went to bed in the living room. She slept on top of her sleeping bag. She was wearing pants with an attached skirt, and a shirt. She fell asleep at approximately midnight.

Mercy was awakened between 1:00 and 2:00 a.m. when she heard some movements behind her. She was lying on her stomach, and saw defendant, who was naked, approach her from behind. Without saying anything, defendant pulled down her pants, fondled her buttocks, and inserted his penis inside her. Mercy weighed 105 pounds. Defendant weighed approximately 205 pounds[.] Less than a minute later, defendant ejaculated, got off her, and walked back to the bedroom[.]

Officer Fragoso, who interviewed Mercy several days after the attack, testified that she told him she had not resisted defendant's sexual assault because, "She said she knew that the man had been drinking. She hadn't met him before; he was a complete stranger to her. When she realized what was going on, she said she panicked, she froze. She was afraid that if she said or did anything, his reaction could be of a violent nature. So she decided just to lay still, wait until it was over with and then get out of the house as quickly as she could and get to her [fiancé] *and tell him what happened*."

Mercy immediately telephoned her fiancé Gary and left a message for him. She then telephoned her best friend Pam, who testified that Mercy was so distraught she was barely comprehensible. Mercy asked Pam to pick her up, grabbed her purse and shoes, and ran out of the apartment. Mercy hid in the bushes outside [for] approximately half an hour while waiting for Pam because she was terrified defendant would look for her.

Pam arrived about 30 minutes later, and drove Mercy to Pam's house. Mercy sat on Pam's kitchen floor, her back to the wall, and asked Pam, "Do I look like the word 'rape' [is] written on [my] face?" Mercy wanted to take a shower because she "felt dirty," but was dissuaded by Pam. Pam telephoned Gary, who called the police. Gary and his best man then drove Mercy to the hospital, where a "rape examination" was performed. [Blood and semen were found in Mercy's vagina and on her underpants.]

The following day, Mercy and Gary married[.] Neither Sandra nor defendant participated in the wedding. [The defendant] was arrested the same day. When asked by the arresting officer if he had had sexual intercourse with Mercy, defendant replied, "I guess I did, yes."

Dr. Charles Nelson, a psychologist, testified as an expert on "rape trauma syndrome." He stated that victims respond in a variety of ways to the trauma of being raped. Some try to flee, and others are paralyzed by fear. This latter response he termed "frozen fright."

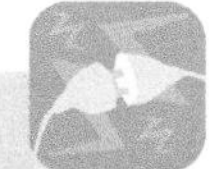

Make the Connection

The permissible scope of expert testimony on rape trauma syndrome is examined in *State v. Kinney* in section E of this chapter.

Defendant conceded at trial that the sexual intercourse was nonconsensual. However, defense counsel argued that the element of force or fear was absent. "So if he was doing anything, it's not force or fear[.] It's a situation where it looks to him like he can get away with it and a situation where his judgment [has] flown out the window[.] He keeps doing it, probably without giving much thought to it, but certainly there is nothing there to indicate using fear ever entered his mind. What he was doing was taking advantage, in a drunken way, of a situation where somebody appeared to be out of it."

Practice Pointer

Notwithstanding defense counsel's argument, the defendant would be guilty of rape under the California statute if he engaged in sexual intercourse with a person whom he knows is "unconscious of the act" because the person is asleep.

[Rape is defined under Penal Code § 261(a)(2) as "an act of sexual intercourse accomplished with a person not the spouse of the perpetrator, [w]here it is accomplished against a person's will by means of force, violence, or fear of immediate and unlawful bodily injury on the person of another."] [The trial] court [also] instructed in relevant part[,] "Verbal threats are not critical to a finding of fear of unlawful injury, threats can be implied from the circumstances or inferred from the assailant's conduct. A victim may entertain a reasonable fear even where the assailant does not threaten by words or deed." The jury found defendant guilty of rape. He was sentenced to state prison [for] six years.

The Court of Appeal reversed, concluding that there was insufficient evidence that the act of sexual intercourse was accomplished by means of force or fear of immediate and unlawful bodily injury. On the issue of fear, the court stated: "While the [defendant] was admittedly much larger than the small victim, he did nothing to suggest that he intended to injure her. No coarse or sexually suggestive conversation had taken place. Nothing of an abusive or threatening nature had occurred. The victim was sleeping in her aunt's house, in which screams presumably would have raised the aunt and interrupted the intercourse. Although the assailant was a stranger to the victim, she knew nothing about him which would suggest that he was violent. [The] event of intercourse [was] singularly unusual in terms of its ease of facilitation, causing no struggle, no injury, no abrasions or other marks, and lasting, as the victim testified, 'maybe a minute.'" . . .

The test on appeal for determining if substantial evidence supports a conviction is whether "a reasonable trier of fact could have found the prosecution sustained its burden of proving the defendant guilty beyond a reasonable doubt." In making this determination, we "'must view the evidence in a light most favorable to [the State] and presume in support of the judgment the existence of every fact the trier could reasonably deduce from the evidence.'" [*People v. Johnson*, 26 Cal. 3d 557, 576 (1980).]

Prior to 1980, section 261 "defined rape as an act of sexual intercourse under circumstances where the person resists, but where 'resistance is overcome by force or violence' or where 'a person is prevented from resisting by threats of great and immediate bodily harm, accompanied by apparent power of execution[.]'" *People v. Barnes*, 42 Cal. 3d 284, 292 (1986). Under the former law, a person was required to either resist or be prevented from resisting because of threats. *Id.* at 295.

Section 261 was amended in 1980 to eliminate both the resistance requirement and the requirement that the threat of immediate bodily harm be accompanied by an apparent power to inflict the harm. As the legislative history explains, "threat is eliminated and the victim need only fear harm. The standard for injury is reduced from great and immediate bodily harm to immediate and unlawful bodily injury."

In discussing the significance of the 1980 amendments in *Barnes*, we noted that "studies have demonstrated that while some women respond to sexual assault with active resistance, others 'freeze,'" and "become helpless from panic and numbing fear." *Barnes*, *supra*, 42 Cal.3d at 299. In response to this information, "For the first time, the Legislature has assigned the decision as to whether a sexual assault should be resisted to the realm of personal choice." "By removing resistance as a prerequisite to a rape conviction, the Legislature has brought the law of rape into conformity with other crimes such as robbery, kidnapping and assault, which require force, fear, and nonconsent to convict. In these crimes, the law does not expect falsity from the complainant who alleges their commission and thus demand resistance as a corroboration and predicate to conviction." *Id.* at 301.

[The] deletion of the resistance language from section 261 by the 1980 amendments thus effected a change in the purpose of evidence of fear of immediate and unlawful injury. Prior to 1980, evidence of fear was directly linked to resistance; the prosecution was required to demonstrate that a person's *resistance* had been overcome by force, or that a person was prevented from resisting by threats of great and immediate bodily harm. As a result of the amendments, evidence of fear is now directly linked to the overbearing of a victim's will; the prosecution is required to demonstrate that the act of sexual intercourse was accomplished against the person's *will* by means of force, violence, or fear of immediate and unlawful bodily injury.

In *Barnes*, [we] addressed the question of the role of force or fear of immediate and unlawful bodily injury in the absence of a resistance requirement. We stated that "[a]lthough resistance is no longer the touchstone of the element of force, the reviewing court still looks to the circumstances of the case, including the presence of verbal or nonverbal threats, or the kind of force that might reasonably induce fear in the mind of the victim, to ascertain sufficiency of the evidence of a conviction under § 261(2)." "Additionally, the [victim's] conduct must be measured against the degree of force manifested or in light of whether her fears were genuine and reasonably grounded." "In some circumstances, even a [victim's] unreasonable fear of immediate and unlawful bodily injury may suffice to sustain a conviction under § 261(2) if the accused knowingly takes advantage of that fear in order to accomplish sexual intercourse." [*Id.* at 304.]

Thus, the element of fear of immediate and unlawful bodily injury has two components, one subjective and one objective. The subjective component asks whether a victim genuinely entertained a fear of immediate and unlawful bodily injury sufficient to induce her to submit to sexual intercourse against her will. In order to satisfy this component, the extent or seriousness of the injury feared is immaterial.

In addition, the prosecution must satisfy the objective component, which asks whether the victim's fear was reasonable under the circumstances, or, if unreasonable, whether the perpetrator knew of the victim's subjective fear and took advantage of it. The particular means by which fear is imparted is not an element of rape.

Applying these principles, we conclude that the evidence that the sexual intercourse was accomplished against Mercy's will by means of fear of immediate and unlawful bodily injury was sufficient to support the verdict in this case. First, there was substantial evidence that Mercy genuinely feared immediate and unlawful bodily injury. Mercy testified that she froze because she was afraid, and the investigating police officer testified that she told him she did not move because she feared defendant would do something violent.

The Court of Appeal stated, however, "But most importantly, the victim was unable to articulate an experience of fear of immediate and unlawful bodily injury." This statement ignores the officer's testimony as to Mercy's state of mind. Moreover, even absent the officer's testimony, the prosecution was not required to elicit from Mercy testimony regarding what precisely she feared. "Fear" may be inferred from the circumstances despite even superficially *contrary* testimony of the victim. See *People v. Renteria*, 61 Cal.2d 497, 499 (1964); *People v. Borra*, 123 Cal. App. 482, 484–85 (1932) [robbery cases]. In addition, immediately after the attack, Mercy was so distraught her friend Pam could barely understand her. Mercy hid in the bushes outside the house waiting for Pam to pick her up because she was terrified defendant would find her; she subsequently asked Pam if the word "rape" was written on her forehead, and had to be dissuaded from bathing prior to going to the hospital.

Second, there was substantial evidence that Mercy's fear of immediate and unlawful bodily injury was reasonable. The Court of Appeal's statements[—]that defendant "did nothing to suggest that he intended to injure" Mercy, and that "[a]lthough the assailant was a stranger to the victim, she knew nothing about him which would suggest that he was violent"[—] ignor[e] the import of the undisputed facts. Defendant, who weighed twice as much as Mercy, accosted her while she slept in the home of a close friend, thus violating the victim's enhanced level of security and privacy.

Defendant, who was naked, then removed Mercy's pants, fondled her buttocks, and inserted his penis into her vagina for approximately one minute, without warning, without her consent, and without a reasonable belief of consent. Any man or woman awakening to find himself or herself in this situation could reasonably react with fear of immediate and unlawful bodily injury. Sudden, unconsented-to groping, disrobing, and ensuing sexual intercourse while one appears to lie sleeping is an appalling and intolerable invasion of one's personal autonomy that, in and of itself, would reasonably cause one to react with fear.

The Court of Appeal's suggestion that Mercy could have stopped the sexual assault by screaming and thus eliciting Sandra S.'s help, disregards both the Legislature's 1980 elimination of the resistance requirement and our express language in *Barnes* upholding that amendment. It effectively guarantees an attacker freedom to intimidate his victim and exploit any resulting reasonable fear so long as she neither struggles nor cries out. Moreover, it is sheer speculation that Mercy's assailant would have responded to screams by desisting the attack, and not by causing her further injury or death.

Food for Thought

What unstated policy concerns may help to explain the *Iniguez* Court's unwillingness to endorse the perspectives of the Court of Appeal?

The jury could reasonably have concluded that under the totality of the circumstances, this scenario, instigated and choreographed by defendant, created a situation in which Mercy genuinely and reasonably responded with fear of immediate and unlawful bodily injury, and that such fear allowed him to accomplish sexual intercourse with Mercy against her will.

The judgment of the Court of Appeal is reversed, and the case is remanded to that court for further proceedings consistent with this opinion.

Points for Discussion

a. Reasons for Rape Law Reforms

The 1980 reform statute in *Iniguez* is one example of a nationwide pattern of legislative action that emerged after the enactment of the 1975 Michigan reform statute. The 1980 Revised Comments to the republished Model Penal Code of 1962 explain some of the reasons that rape law reforms were viewed as necessary:

> [T]here is reason to suppose that rape is the most dramatically under-reported of all violent crimes and that the incidence of rape far exceeds the number of reported crimes. This assumption certainly seems plausible in light of the ordeal that a rape victim may face upon public disclosure of the event.
>
> There are at least two other factors that may contribute to the present sense [that rape law revision is necessary]. The first is that the probability of apprehension of a suspect is not good even when the police are called. Among the factors that contribute to this result are conclusions by the police that the rape complaint is unfounded and the relatively high frequency of cases where the offender and the victim are strangers and where there is consequent difficulty in identifying the offender. Second, arrest for rape is unlikely to result in conviction. Contributing factors to this result include the unwitting destruction of evidence by victims, special evidentiary rules relating to rape, and the difficulty of tying the offender to the crime by evidence other than the testimony of a victim who, because of

the emotions surrounding the event and testimony about it, may prove especially vulnerable to disbelief.

Cumulatively, these bits of data suggest that the criminal justice system actually identifies and punishes a small fraction of the total population of rape offenders. [Rape law reform] has also been a special target of feminist reform. There have been accusations that the law of rape reflects sexist assumptions about appropriate behavior of men and women, as well [as] insensitivity to the plight of rape victims.

Model Penal Code § 213.1, Comment (3), at 283–286 (1980). For a study of the history of the enactment and impact of the Michigan rape reform statute, see JEANNE C. MARSH, ALISON GEIST & NATHAN CAPLAN, RAPE AND THE LIMITS OF LAW REFORM (1982).

b. Studies of Jury Attitudes

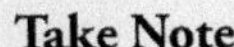

One source reports that roughly 66% of sexual assault victims know their assailants, that men make up about 10% of all victims of sexual assault, that 54% of sexual assaults are not reported to the police; and that 44% of sexual assault victims are under age 18 and 80% are under age 30. *See* Rape Abuse & Incest National Network (RAINN), www.rain.org/statistics. Some other sources report different data.

One famous study of criminal jury trials was published in 1966, four years after the publication of the Model Penal Code. This study described additional reasons to explain why juries failed to convict in rape cases. The goal of the study was to determine whether juries view evidence differently from judges in criminal cases generally. The authors used questionnaires to survey trial judges in 3,500 criminal cases during 1954–55 and 1958; the judges were asked to describe the jury verdicts in these cases and to explain whether they agreed with these verdicts. The study revealed a high rate of disagreement between judges and juries with regard to 106 cases of forcible rape, with the jury almost always acquitting or convicting on a lesser charge when the judges would have convicted on the major charge. The study concluded that the juries were redefining the rape crime using "notions of assumption of risk." According to the explanations provided for the jury verdicts by the judges in the survey, jurors would scrutinize the conduct of the victim "harshly" and treat the defendant leniently when there were "suggestions of contributory behavior" by the victim, even in cases where the defendant engaged in "brutal" physical violence against the victim. *See* HARRY KALVEN, JR. & HANS ZEISEL, THE AMERICAN JURY 249–54 (1966).

A smaller study of sexual assault trials was undertaken in Indianapolis between 1978 and 1980, with the goal of determining how gender-role behavior by women victims may affect jury verdicts in rape cases. The study relied on observers who witnessed 38 rape trials and collected detailed information about the testimony of witnesses, including the characteristics and behavior of defendants and victims. The authors also conducted post-trial interviews with 331 jurors (70%), and obtained data about their reactions to the victims and defendants. These criteria were used as definitions of non-traditional gender role behavior: 1) drinking or using drugs, at the time of the alleged crime or generally; 2) being sexually active with any non-marital partners; 3) having non-marital children; and 4) having a reputation as a person who "parties" or stays out late. Based on the courtroom data of the observers, at least one of the behaviors on this list was attributed to 58% of the victims.

The Indianapolis study found that in cases where the defendant argued either that the victim consented or that no sexual intercourse occurred, the jurors were less likely to believe the defendant was guilty if the victim was sexually active, drank or used drugs, or was acquainted with the defendant (even if only briefly). The juror interviews included comments from many jurors that women "ask" to be raped based on their clothing and behavior; another common attitude was the idea that an unwilling woman cannot be raped. The interview comments also indicated that many jurors drew conclusions about a victim's "carelessness" that were linked to her shared responsibility for the sexual assault. The authors of the study concluded that the jurors used the evidence of non-traditional gender role behavior to make judgments both about the credibility and the moral character of victims, which judgments were directly linked to their decisions concerning her consent. *See* GARY D. LAFREE, RAPE AND CRIMINAL JUSTICE: THE SOCIAL CONSTRUCTION OF SEXUAL ASSAULT 154–55, 201, 217–18, 225–27 (1989).

Courts have noted the persistence of false and biased juror perceptions of rape complainants, some which are described in *Commonwealth v. King*, 445 Mass. 217, 238–39, 834 N.E.2d 1175, 1194–95 (2005), as follows:

> [T]he research and scholarship of which we are aware suggests that damaging stereotypes persist. Some jurors may continue to believe incorrectly that "real" victims will *promptly* disclose a sexual attack. Some jurors may continue to harbor prejudicial misperceptions about the nature of rape and rape allegations, including that complainants who wear revealing clothing, consume drugs or alcohol, or have unorthodox or promiscuous lifestyles cannot be "real" victims of rape; that forced sex by a spouse or a past partner does not constitute "real" rape; and that false accusations of sexual assault are more frequent than those of other violent crimes.

The sources cited in the *King* opinion included "empirical research on juries' decision-making behavior in rape cases," which revealed that jurors "may rely on rape 'scripts' which they bring with them into the jury room," and that jurors "come to the rape judgment situation with preconceptions and attitudes that lead them to entertain particular stories about what may have happened [and] these stories are then used to arrive at a legal decision or verdict." *Id.* at 239 n.20, 834 N.E.2d at 1195 n.20.

The persistent problem of skepticism regarding the credibility of rape victims has provoked a variety of legal changes in the "rape reform" era. In the wake of the "Me Too" movement, it might be expected that if accusations of sexual assault are "being taken more seriously" by the public as a whole, then "sexual assault laws [might] have the enforcement mechanism that they were previously lacking." Michael Conklin, *#metoo Effects on Juror Decision Making*, 11 CAL. L. REV. ONLINE 179 (2020). Surveys of "mock jurors" in 2010 and 2019 cast doubt upon the thesis that public attitudes have changed in this way. These surveys asked whether the respondents would find the defendant guilty or not guilty in a "sexual assault" case summary, and also asked them to identify the percentage (on a scale of zero to 100) of their level of certainty about the guilt of the defendant. "The primary result of comparing the pre- and post-#MeToo surveys [was] the drastic reduction in willingness to convict, despite similar predictions of guilt." *Id.* at 187.

The MPC § 213.1(a) defines rape as follows: "A male who has sexual intercourse with a female not his wife is guilty if he compels her to submit by force or by threat of imminent death, serious bodily injury, extreme pain or kidnapping, to be inflicted on anyone."

c. Model Penal Code Proposals

The American Law Institute published the final draft of the MPC in 1962, and the drafters did much of their work on prior drafts during the 1950s. Their proposals reflect the law and legal thinking of their times. The MPC definition of rape is not gender neutral, and the MPC also retains the marital rape exemption, the corroboration requirement, and a version of the Lord Hale instruction. *See* Model Penal Code §§ 213.6(2), (4) & (5). The MPC included no proposal for a "rape shield" evidence rule, which first appeared in the 1975 Michigan reform statute. The MPC applies to compulsion to submit to sexual intercourse "by force or by threat of imminent death, serious bodily injury, extreme pain or kidnapping." The term compulsion "plainly implies nonconsent," and the absence of a resistance element does not mean that "inquiry into the level of resistance by the victim cannot or should not be made." Model Penal Code § 213.1, Comment (4)(a), at 306–307 (1980). Notably, the 1980 Commentary criticized the 1975 Michigan reform statute as an "unacceptable" "overreaction" to the concerns of reformers. In hindsight, however, the Michigan statute provided a more enduring legacy than the 1962 MPC rape definition, because the MPC drafters did not anticipate the imminent widespread abandonment or modification of the various common law concepts and evidence rules embedded in their definition of rape. *Compare id.*, Comment (3)(b)(ii), at 288–89 (1980).

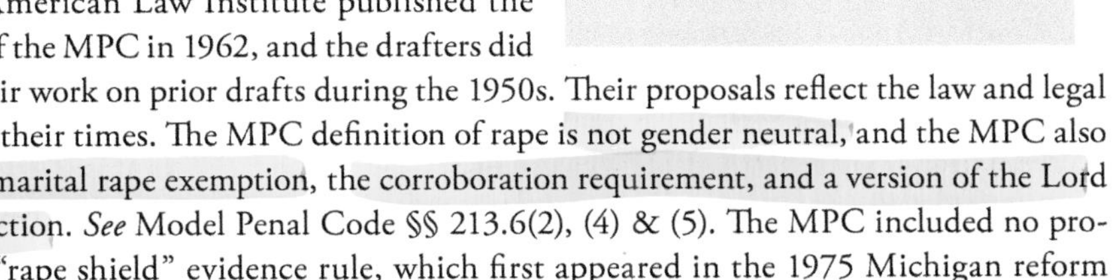

Food for Thought

The MPC definition of rape reflected at least three aspects of the typical state statute of its era. It included a "marital rape exemption," and it focused exclusively on the act of sexual intercourse, committed by a male defendant with a female victim. What new cases of rape prosecution became possible when each of these limitations was abandoned during the post-1975 era?

Since 2012, the American Law Institute has been embarked upon a project to re-examine and update the 1962 MPC provisions on Rape, entitled Model Penal Code: Sexual Assault and Related Offenses. For the prospectus, see https://jpp.whs.mil/Public/docs/04-Meetings/sub-20150409/09_Prospectus_for_Revision_MPC213.pdf. Approved and rejected proposals are described at https://www.ali.org/projects/show/sexual-assault-and-related-offenses/.

d. Opposing Perspectives in *Iniguez*

The California Supreme Court's *Iniguez* opinion is a study in contrast with the Court of Appeal's unpublished decision described in the latter opinion. What are the most significant differences between them? One difference is the perspective of each court concerning the jury's fact-finding authority in rape cases. A second difference concerns the nature of the evidence of the victim's fear required for conviction. The Court of Appeal implicitly expected the prosecutor to provide: 1) evidence of express statements by the victim concerning her "fear of immediate and unlawful bodily injury"; 2) evidence based on more than inferences about her non-specific fear that could be drawn from the victim's conduct and statements after the sexual act occurred; and 3) evidence of the defendant's propensity for violence that could justify the victim's fear of immediate bodily injury.

These expectations are illustrated by two comments in the Court of Appeal's unpublished opinion that were not quoted by the *Iniguez* Court. First, in describing the victim's testimony, the Court of Appeal acknowledged that "the victim was filled with fear—as would be any person subjected to an unwanted intrusion into a private bodily cavity in the middle of the night," but then noted that, "[t] here was essentially no evidence, however, of anticipation or consideration by the victim of danger of bodily injury." Second, in describing defendant's conduct, the Court of Appeal opined that "there is nothing to suggest" that the defendant's "drunk and silent, apparently cautious but successful effort to penetrate the victim's vagina signaled the likelihood of any other kind of assault."

What are the arguments about statutory interpretation and sufficiency of evidence that are used by the *Iniguez* Court to justify the affirmance of the conviction? What reasoning does the Court rely on to rebut the perspectives of the Court of Appeal? If the *Iniguez* Court had adopted the reasoning of the Court of Appeal and reversed the conviction, what would have been the potential effects of such a decision on lower courts, prosecutors, and defense counsel in future rape prosecutions? How are contrasting attitudes toward rape victims expressed in the reasoning of the Court of Appeal and the California Supreme Court in *Iniguez*?

Hypo: *Questions from the Bench*

An unrepresented female plaintiff in a civil action sought a restraining order against her ex-partner, who was represented by counsel. Her testimony described the ex-partner's threats to burn down her house and to kill her, and also included the following statements: "He forced me to have sex with him, after he grabbed at my clothes and pulled down my pants. I repeatedly told him to stop and I tried to push him off me, but he is bigger and stronger and he was holding me down tightly with his hands and body weight." The trial judge then asked the victim these questions: "Do you know how to stop somebody from having intercourse with you?" "Did you block your body parts? Close your legs? Call the police? Try to run away?" The victim answered Yes to each question. If believed, her testimony was sufficient to find that the crime of sexual assault occurred (since no resistance was required) and to issue the restraining order. The trial judge denied the restraining order based on his finding that the victim was not credible and that "she didn't have an answer" when asked "whether she tried to do anything to stop the sexual assault." If the victim obtains pro bono counsel at this stage of the proceeding, what strategies may counsel choose to pursue? *See In the Matter of Russo*, 231 A.3d 563 (N.J. 2020).

e. Definitions of Force

The *Iniguez* Court did not address the sufficiency of the evidence of the "force" element because there was sufficient evidence of the "fear" element. Even though the element of "force" may operate in a variety of ways, statutes that use this element typically do not specify the nature or amount of the force required. Notably, in "almost half the states, sexual penetration is not a crime unless there is both nonconsent and some sort of force." Stephen J. Schulhofer, *Reforming the Law of Rape*, 35 L. & INEQUALITY 335, 343 (2017). Here are three different case law definitions of "force," which illustrate a wide range of meanings for this ambiguous concept.

i. Force as Threat That Overcomes Will to Resist

The term "force" has been defined as including threats that create fear. When the element of "force" appears in a rape statute, then "[f]orce is an essential element of the crime [but] no particular amount of force, either actual or constructive, is required to constitute rape. [Force] may exist without violence. If the acts and threats of the defendant were reasonably calculated to create in the mind of the victim—having regard to the circumstances in which she was placed—a real apprehension, due to fear, of imminent bodily harm, serious enough to impair or overcome her will to resist, then such acts and threats are the equivalent of force." *State v. Baby*, 404 Md. 220, 260, 946 A.2d 463, 486–87 (2008) (relying on *Hazel v. State*, 221 Md. 464, 469, 157 A.2d 922, 925 (1960)).

ii. Force as Psychological Pressure

The term "force" has been defined to include the imposition of psychological pressure. Where the statutory definition of "force" includes an act that "coerces the victim to submit by threatening to use force or violence on the victim," then "force" may include a threat that "may be implied as well as express," and "force" may "consist of the imposition of psychological pressure upon a person who, under all of the circumstances, is vulnerable and susceptible to such pressure." *State v. DiPetrillo*, 922 A.2d 124, 134 (R.I. 2007).

iii. Force as the Act of Penetration

One broad definition of "force" equates it with the type of force required for a battery. Where the crime of sexual assault is defined by statute as the commission of "an act of sexual penetration with another person [where] the actor uses physical force," the term "physical force" should be interpreted as "any amount of force" that results in "offensive touching." The term "physical force" should *not* be interpreted as requiring "the application of some amount of force in addition to the act of penetration," or as "force used to overcome lack of consent." *State of New Jersey in the Interest of M.T.S.*, 129 N.J. 422, 443, 609 A.2d 1266, 1277 (1992).

f. Removal of Force Element

One study sought to determine whether the removal of the force element from a rape statute may have a practical impact. This study compared statistics for the rape reporting rate in two states—one state legislature had removed the force element and the other state legislature had retained the force element. Admittedly, this comparison was difficult to perform because "rape statistics available to researchers are notoriously untrustworthy," and because "there are a wide variety of estimations of how many rapes go unreported." Peter Landsman, *Does Removing the Force Element Matter?: An Empirical Comparison of Rape Statistics in Massachusetts and Colorado*, 21 Wm. & Mary J. Women & L. 767, 774–775 (2015). The study concluded that although "[t]here are compelling reasons to believe the removal of the force requirement from Colorado's sexual assault statute may have affected its rape reporting rate and its fluctuation from the rates of Massachusetts and the United States," it is "impossible to prove without better statistics about actual rapes, arrest rates through the decades, conviction rates, and a comparison with the rape rates of other jurisdictions without force requirements." *Id.* at 789.

The following hypotheticals present the opportunity to apply the analysis of the "fear" element in the *Iniguez* opinion to different facts, and to compare the applications of different interpretations of the ambiguous "force" element to the same facts.

Hypo 1: *Taking Car Keys*

Pat met Rusk at a bar where she went with a woman friend after a high school reunion. Pat testified that she told Rusk that she was a single mother and had to be home soon to take care of her child. Rusk asked her for a ride home and she agreed, telling him it was "just a ride." When they arrived at his rooming house, Pat parked but did not turn off the ignition. Rusk asked her to come up to his room and she refused. Rusk then took the car keys out of the ignition, walked over to Pat's side of the car, opened the door and said, "Now will you come up?" Pat was stranded in an unfamiliar neighborhood, and so she followed Rusk up to his room. She begged Rusk to return her keys and to let her leave his room. He kept saying, "No." Pat was scared because of what he said and because of the look in his eyes. She asked him, "If I do what you want, will you let me go without killing me?" She started to cry and he put his hands on her throat. Pat described this act as a "light choking" but acknowledged that it could have been a "heavy caress." Pat asked Rusk, "If I do what you want, will you let me go?" Rusk said, "Yes," and sexual intercourse followed. Pat got dressed, left the rooming house, and then reported the rape to the police. *Compare Rusk v. State*, 43 Md. App. 476, 406 A.2d 624 (1979) *rev'd*, *State v. Rusk*, 289 Md. 230, 424 A.2d 720 (1981).

a. *Fear Theory.* Is there sufficient evidence to convict Rusk using the "fear" element in the *Iniguez* statute?

b. *Force Theory.* Is there sufficient evidence to convict Rusk using any of the three definitions of "force" described in point d. *supra*?

Hypo 2: *Dorm Room*

Berkowitz and Kia are college sophomores. Berkowitz was in his dorm room when Kia came looking for his roommate. He invited her to "hang out for a while" and offered to give her a back rub. She declined the back rub but sat down on his floor. Berkowitz moved down to the floor and "kind of pushed" Kia with his body, straddled her and kissed her. Kia could not move because his weight was over her body. She said she had to go and meet her boyfriend and Berkowitz lifted up her shirt and bra and fondled her. Kia said, "No." He undid his pants while she said, "No." When Berkowitz tried to put his penis in her mouth, she said, "No, I gotta go, let me go." Berkowitz got up and locked the door so that people outside could not enter but a person inside could leave. When Kia rose to her feet, Berkowitz put Kia down on the bed, straddled her and removed her sweatpants and underwear. Kia could not move because Berkowitz was on top of her. Berkowitz put his penis in her vagina, and she muttered, "No, no, no" because, as she testified later, "It was just so scary." After 30 seconds, Berkowitz pulled out his penis, ejaculated on Kia's stomach, and got off her. She got up, dressed quickly, grabbed her books, and ran downstairs to her boyfriend. Kia was crying and her boyfriend called the police to report the rape. *Compare Commonwealth v. Berkowitz*, 415 Pa. Super. 505, 522–523, 609 A.2d 1338, 1346–1347 (1992), *aff'd*, 537 Pa. 143, 641 A.2d 1161 (1994).

a. *Fear Theory.* Is there sufficient evidence to convict Berkowitz using the "fear" element in the *Iniguez* statute?

b. *Force Theory.* Is there sufficient evidence to convict Berkowitz using any of the three definitions of "force" described in point d. *supra*?

---

2. Lack of Consent

The importance of a victim's "lack of consent" casts a long shadow over modern rape law. At common law, defendants could attempt to raise a reasonable doubt about the "lack of consent" element by arguing that a victim's consent could be inferred from submission or lack of resistance. Some drafters of rape reform statutes singled out this element for elimination in the hope of making it easier to obtain convictions, by making it unnecessary to prove lack of consent beyond a reasonable doubt.

Almost half the states continue to use the "lack of consent" element in rape statutes. Some of these states use this element exclusively, but more states use it together with the "force, threat, or fear" elements. When the "lack of consent" element does not appear in a statute, this does not mean that consent is irrelevant to conviction. For example, the element of "force" or "compulsion" may be interpreted as incorporating the "lack of consent" concept into the meaning of that term.

Points for Discussion

a. Reforms Regarding Lack of Consent Element

The original functions of the "lack of consent" element in common law definitions of rape are summarized in *State of New Jersey in the Interest of M.T.S.*, 129 N.J. 422, 432–39, 609 A.2d 1266, 1271–74 (1992):

> Under traditional rape law[,] the state had to show both that force had been used and that the penetration had been against the woman's will. Force was identified and determined not as an independent factor but in relation to the response of the victim, which in turn implicated the victim's own state of mind[.] Although the terms "non-consent" and "against her will" were often treated as equivalent under the traditional definition of rape, both formulations squarely placed on the victim the burden of proof and of action. Effectively, a woman who was above the age of consent had [to] actively and affirmatively withdraw that consent for the intercourse to be against her will[.]
>
> The presence or absence of consent often turned on credibility[.] According to the oft quoted Lord Hale, to be deemed a credible witness, a woman had to be of good fame, disclose the injury immediately, suffer signs of injury, and cry out for help. Courts and commentators historically distrusted the testimony of victims, "assuming that women lie about their lack of consent for various reasons: to blackmail men, to explain the discovery of a consensual affair, or because of psychological illness." [Note, 56 GEO. WASH. L. REV. 399, 403 (1988).] Evidence of resistance was viewed as a solution to the credibility problem; it was the "outward manifestation of nonconsent, [a] device for determining whether a woman actually gave consent." [Note, 18 STAN. L. REV. 680, 689 (1966).]
>
> [To] refute the misguided belief that rape was not real unless the victim fought back, reformers emphasized empirical research indicating that women who resisted forcible intercourse often suffered far more serious injury as a result. [Reformers also] emphasized that rape had its legal origins in laws designed to protect the property rights of men to their wives and daughters. [They] argued that vestiges of the old law remained, particularly in the understanding of rape as a crime against the purity or chastity of a woman. The burden of protecting that chastity fell on the woman, with the state offering its protection only after the woman demonstrated that she had resisted sufficiently[.]
>
> Critics of rape law agreed that the focus of the crime should be shifted from the victim's behavior to the defendant's [conduct]. [There] were, however, differences over the best way to redefine the crime. Some reformers advocated a standard that [did not use the "force, threat or fear" elements and instead] defined rape as unconsented-to sexual intercourse; others urged the elimination of any reference to

consent from the definition of rape. Nonetheless, all proponents of reform shared a central premise: that the burden of showing non-consent should not fall on the victim of the crime. In dealing with the problem of consent the reform goal was not so much to purge the entire concept of consent from the law as to eliminate the burden that had been placed on victims to prove they had not consented.

b. Current Frontier of Reform

One scholar has summarized the trend in favor of criminalizing non-consensual sex without force and the current debates about non-consent as follows: "In a majority of states, it is finally true that non-consent alone suffices," but "[t]hat leaves two important issues" where "the trend is not clear and where reform still faces formidable opposition. First, What is the minimum requirement? [That is,] what counts as consent? And second, when that minimum requirement is met, [what] circumstances nullify that apparent consent? When does yes not mean yes? These are the places where the key battles for reform are now being fought." Stephen J. Schulhofer, *Reforming the Law of Rape*, 35 L. & INEQUALITY 335, 343 (2017).

c. Definitions of Lack of Consent

During the reform era, some legislatures and courts adopted definitions of lack of consent that made it easier for prosecutors to obtain convictions in cases where the evidence showed verbal resistance by the victim or passive submission as in *Iniguez*. In the pre-reform era, defense counsel could attempt to raise a reasonable doubt about the "lack of consent" element by arguing that consent was implied by the victim's ultimate submission and failure to demonstrate sufficient resistance. But when "consent" was redefined to require evidence of "affirmative agreement," for example, the prosecutor could show "lack of consent" by pointing to an absence of "agreement evidence," and defense counsel presumably would need some agreement evidence to raise a reasonable doubt about the lack of consent element.

Food for Thought

Assume that the victim testifies that she offered verbal resistance to the defendant's sexual advances by saying "No" repeatedly. During closing argument, the defense counsel says, "In our culture, 'no' does not always mean 'no' with regard to sexual conduct—sometimes 'no' means 'maybe,' or even 'yes.'" May the prosecutor object to this argument? Would the trial judge approve the defendant's request for a jury instruction that uses the same language?

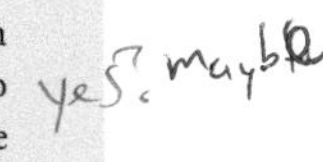

Here are three different definitions of "lack of consent" that illustrate the modern range of its meanings.

i. Lack of Consent as Resistance

One statute defines the lack of consent element as including: "a) the victim expressed a lack of consent through words; or b) the victim expressed a lack of consent through conduct." The statute also provides: "c) the victim need only resist, either verbally or physically, so as to make the victim's refusal to consent genuine and real and so as to reasonably make known to the actor the victim's refusal to consent; and d) a victim need not resist verbally or physically where it would be useless or futile to do so." *See* Neb. Rev. Stat. § 28–318 (1995).

ii. Lack of Consent as Manifested Unwillingness

The lack of consent element has been defined by one court as communication from the victim to the defendant, in which "the victim must manifest her unwillingness objectively." "If [the] victim objectively communicates lack of consent and the defendant subjectively fails to receive the message, he is guilty. The appropriate inquiry is whether a reasonable person in the circumstances would have understood that the victim did not consent." *State v. Ayer*, 136 N.H. 191, 195–96, 612 A.2d 923, 926 (1992).

iii. Lack of Consent as Absence of Affirmative Agreement

The lack of consent element may be defined through definitions of "consent," as in a statute that defines this term as "words or overt actions" "indicating freely given agreement to have sexual intercourse." *See* Wisc. Stat. Ann. § 940.225(3) (1979). This definition "demonstrates that failure to resist is not consent." *State v. Lederer*, 99 Wis. 2d 430, 299 N.W.2d 457 (Ct. App. 1980). Compare STEPHEN J. SCHULHOFER, UNWANTED SEX: THE CULTURE OF INTIMIDATION AND THE FAILURE OF LAW 271 (1998). Another court's interpretation of "freely given agreement" is that "permission to engage in sexual penetration must be affirmative and it must be given freely, but that permission may be inferred either from acts or statements reasonably viewed in light of the surrounding circumstances. Persons need not, of course, expressly announce their consent to engage in intercourse for there to be affirmative permission. Permission . . . can be and indeed often is indicated through physical actions rather than words. Permission is demonstrated when the evidence, in whatever form, is sufficient to demonstrate that a reasonable person would have believed that the [victim] had affirmatively and freely given authorization to the act." *State of New Jersey in the Interest of M.T.S.*, 129 N.J. 422, 432–39, 609 A.2d 1266, 1271–74 (1992).

Practice Pointer

Even when the lack of consent element is defined as the "absence of affirmative and freely-given agreement," the defendant will be acquitted if the defense counsel can create a reasonable doubt about that "absence" in the minds of jurors. In order to rebut that doubt, prosecutors will rely on evidence of a victim's verbal and physical resistance, if available. Thus, even in states where the resistance requirement has been eliminated, resistance evidence remains important.

d. Uses of Resistance Evidence

During the pre-reform era, courts recognized that resistance evidence could serve as "force" or "fear" elements as well as the "lack of consent" element. In the modern era, some judges have objected this idea. For example, in *State v. Borthwick*, 255 Kan. 899, 880 P.2d 1261 (1994), the court was unanimous in ruling that the victim's testimony concerning her verbal and physical resistance provided sufficient evidence of the element of lack of consent. This evidence included the victim's testimony that she tried to keep her legs together and said "stop" repeatedly. The *Borthwick* majority also relied on this evidence, as well as other testimony of the victim, to affirm the reasonableness of the jury's finding that the victim was "overcome by force or fear." But the *Borthwick* dissenters argued that the "lack of consent" evidence could not be used in this way. What reasons may explain the conflicting views on this point?

e. Withdrawal of Consent

The following hypothetical presents the opportunity to consider the reasons why most courts hold that the withdrawal of a victim's consent after the commencement of sexual intercourse may lead to conviction for the rape crime.

Hypo 1: *Withdrawal of Consent*

Assume that after initially consenting to sexual intercourse, a person withdraws her consent after penetration. The defendant is convicted of rape under the *Iniguez* statute. The appellate court reverses the conviction, relying on the following reasoning: "If a female withdraws consent during the act of intercourse and the male forcibly continues the act without interruption, the female may certainly feel outrage because the male ignored her wishes. However, the sense of outrage to her person and feelings could hardly be of the same magnitude as that resulting from an initial nonconsensual violation." What arguments can the state supreme court use to rebut this reasoning, and to support the holding that the defendant's continuation of sexual intercourse should constitute rape? *Compare People v. Vela*, 172 Cal. App. 3d 237, 218 Cal. Rptr. 161 (1985), *disapproved in In re John Z.*, 29 Cal. 4th 756, 128 Cal. Rptr. 2d 783, 60 P.3d 183 (2003).

Hypo 2: *"Stealthing"*

Assume that a woman initially consents to engage in sexual intercourse with a male sexual partner who agrees to wear a condom, so that the woman will be protected from the risks of pregnancy and the transmission of sexually transmitted diseases. However, at some point during the act of sexual intercourse, the sexual partner knowingly removes the condom without the woman's knowledge or consent. Should this act be a crime? If so, how should it be defined and what punishment should be prescribed? Should the act be defined as a tort instead? See Alexandra Brodsky, *"Rape-Adjacent": Imagining Legal Responses to Nonconsensual Condom Removal*, 32 COLUM. J. GENDER & L. 183 (2017).

---

3. Consent as an Affirmative Defense

When the legislature removes the lack of consent element from a modern rape statute, a court may decide that this policy decision was not intended to preclude judicial recognition of the defendant's ability to raise "consent" as an affirmative defense. The *Koperski* opinion describes the reasons why courts recognize that defense, and thereby establish the opportunity for acquittal that exists when a defendant can supply sufficient evidence of a victim's "consent."

State v. Koperski

254 Neb. 624, 578 N.W.2d 837 (1998).

GERRARD, JUSTICE.

David Koperski was convicted by a jury of first degree sexual assault and sentenced [to] 4 years probation and 60 days in jail. The [court of appeals] affirmed the district court's judgment. [We] reverse [and] remand this [case] to the district court for a new trial. . . .

> **Food for Thought**
>
> The first degree rape statute was amended *after* the events in *Koperski* to apply to "any person who subjects another person to sexual penetration (a) without consent of the victim" and the term "without consent" was defined as existing when, *inter alia*, "the victim was compelled to submit due to the use of force or threat of force or coercion." Does this later amendment of the statute shed any light on the reasoning in *Koperski*?

At the close of the evidence, Koperski's counsel asked the trial court to instruct the jury with respect to the issue of consent. The trial court refused because [under the statute] the lack of consent was not an element to be proved by the State. The court thought that allowing each side an opportunity to argue the issue of consent would be adequate[.] . . .

[Koperski] was charged under § 28–319(1)(a), which provides: "(1) Any person who subjects another person to sexual penetration and (a) overcomes the victim by force, threat of force, express or implied, [or] coercion . . . is guilty of sexual assault in the first degree." Noticeably absent from the statutory text is the word "consent." . . . [The] trial court is required to give an instruction where there is any evidence, which could be believed by the trier of fact, in support of a legally cognizable theory of defense[.]

Accordingly, the issues before this court are whether consent is a defense to a charge of first degree sexual assault[,] and if so, whether any evidence was adduced in support of a legally cognizable theory of defense regarding consent. If such evidence was adduced, then the jury instructions given must . . . adequately cover [the] theory [of] defense[.] . . .

Although lack of consent is not an element of § 28–319(1)(a), it can hardly be said that consent is not an issue in regard to a charge of first degree sexual assault. Generally, the law may only proscribe nonconsensual sexual conduct, in other words, sexual conduct which is forced upon a person by another without the consent of such person, or where one person is incapable of consenting, or where, although there is consent, such consent is invalid due to, for example, the victim's minority or diminished mental capacity. However, it is evident that consent may well be an issue in a prosecution for first degree sexual assault even though lack of consent is not an express, substantive element of the crime. . . .

It is true that consent is not a statutorily defined affirmative defense[.] Nonetheless, consent can operate as a defense to a charge of first degree sexual assault under § 28–319(1)(a) [because] [c]onsent may operate as a failure of proof in regard to the essential element of the use of force, or in regard to the essential element that the victim must be overcome[.] Accordingly, we conclude that consent may be a defense to a charge of first degree sexual assault[.] The next step in our inquiry is to determine whether any evidence was adduced [in] support of [the] consent theory of defense. . . .

[Because] consensual sexual intercourse is not a harm proscribed by legislative enactment, if, by examining the facts and circumstances of the accused's conduct, it is objectively reasonable to conclude that the alleged victim consented to sexual penetration, then the accused should be free from criminal culpability. The [court] reached a similar conclusion in *State v. Smith*, 210 Conn. 132, 554 A.2d 713 (1989). Like § 28–319(1)(a), the Connecticut statute . . . did not expressly make lack of consent an element of the crime of first degree sexual assault. Nevertheless, the court held that consent was a defense because it negated the statutory element of force. The court went on to explain how the defense of consent operates:

> While the word "consent" is commonly regarded as referring to the state of mind of the complainant in a sexual assault case, it cannot be viewed as a wholly subjective concept. Although the actual state of mind of the actor in a criminal case may in many instances be the issue upon which culpability depends, a defendant is not chargeable with knowledge of the internal workings of the minds of others except to the extent that he should reasonably have gained such knowledge from his observations of their [conduct]. [W]hether a complainant has consented to intercourse depends upon her manifestations of such consent as reasonably construed. . . .

[In] this regard, we agree with the reasoning of the Connecticut [court]. Accordingly, for criminal prosecutions brought under § 28–319(1)(a), we hold that the trial court must instruct the jury on the defense of consent when evidence is produced which, under all of the circumstances, could reasonably be viewed by the jury as an indication of affirmative and freely given consent to sexual penetration by the alleged victim. The focus remains on the accused's conduct in determining whether or not the accused has overcome the alleged victim, resulting in sexual penetration against his or her will[.] [Because] enough evidence had been produced in support of [Koperski's] theory of defense [based on his testimony], we determine that the issue of consent should have been submitted to the jury. . . .

Food for Thought

Some state statutes expressly define the requirements for an affirmative defense of consent to a prosecution for a rape crime. What are the benefits of legislative definitions, compared to judicial definitions such as those described in *Koperski*?

[In] refusing Koperski's proffered jury instructions regarding consent, the trial court expressed the view that making consent a separate element or aspect of the case was confusing. Instead of an instruction regarding Koperski's theory of defense, the trial court thought it sufficient to simply not prohibit Koperski from arguing the issue of consent in his closing statement to the jury. Contrary to the trial court's intuition, failing to instruct the jury regarding Koperski's consent theory of defense was in fact a source of confusion as evidenced by the jury's question to the court during deliberations asking whether it could even consider the issue of consent[.] . . .

We cannot agree with the State than an instruction regarding the substantive elements of the offense subsumes an instruction regarding Koperski's consent theory of defense. An instruction regarding [those] elements alone fails to apprise the jury that an alleged victim's consent must be affirmatively and freely given, that such consent may be manifested by words or conduct, and that from the facts and circumstances in regard to the accused's conduct, it must be objectively reasonable to conclude that consent was given by the alleged victim. Thus, we determine that the trial court erred in not submitting the issue of consent to the jury and that such error was prejudicial to Koperski[.]

Reversed and remanded with directions.

Points for Discussion

a. Recognition of the Consent Defense

The *Koperski* decision illustrates how the goal of reformers "was not so much to purge the entire concept of consent from the law as to eliminate the burden that had been placed on victims to prove they had not consented," as noted earlier in the excerpt from the *M.T.S.* opinion. The *Koperski* Court assumed that the Nebraska legislature, in removing the lack of consent element from the statute, only sought to achieve this limited goal. There would seem to be no danger that the statute would punish consensual sexual conduct, given the fact that criminal liability is limited to a person who "overcomes the victim by force, [or] threat of force, express or implied, [or by] coercion." Yet the court reasoned that the concept of "consent" cannot be disentangled from these other elements and made irrelevant to conviction, even after the removal of the "lack of consent" element. One telltale indication of this linkage is expressed in the amended rape statute, enacted after the events in *Koperski*, in which the legislature restored the "lack of consent" element and defined it as the equivalent of compelling the victim to "submit due to the use of force or threat of force or coercion," among other definitions.

The impact of any court's recognition of the consent defense will depend, of course, on the definition of "consent." The *Smith* case, relied on by the *Koperski* Court, notes only that a finding of consent will depend upon the victim's "manifestations of such consent as reasonably construed." By contrast, the *Koperski* definition refers to "affirmatively and freely given consent." Why does this difference matter?

Finally, like other courts that recognize the affirmative defense of consent, the *Koperski* Court required that "it must be objectively reasonable" for the defendant "to conclude that consent was given by [the] victim." The defendant's proposed jury instruction echoed this requirement in requiring "a reasonable and good faith belief" in consent. This concept should not be confused with the "reasonable *mistake of fact* as to consent," which concept is explored in the next topic in this chapter. The function of the *Koperski* holding is to allow the "affirmative defense of consent" to be raised when the rape statute includes *no* reference to a "lack of consent" element. By contrast, the function of the "reasonable mistake of fact defense" is to attach the *de facto* mental state of "negligence" to the element of the "lack of consent," when that element is required either by statute or by case law.

b. Consent Evidence Needed for Acquittal

The *Koperski* Court observed that the trial judge was obliged to give an instruction for a cognizable defense when there is "*any* evidence" in support that "could be believed by the trier of fact." The facts set forth in the following two Hypos provide the summaries of the testimony of the defendant and victim in *Koperski*, upon which the court relied in ruling that the defendant had satisfied the burden of producing "enough" evidence to obtain an instruction on the consent defense. However, the court did not describe the defendant's burden of persuasion that would be required to obtain an acquittal based on the consent defense.

When an affirmative defense does not negate an element of a crime, as was true in *Koperski*, the burden of persuasion may be placed upon the defendant. So the *Koperski* defendant presumably could be required to prove "consent" by at least a preponderance of the evidence (51%) to obtain an acquittal at his new trial. Then the prosecutor would argue that the jurors should convict the defendant if they viewed the evidence concerning "consent" as 50/50 at best, assuming that all the elements of the crime had been proved beyond a reasonable doubt.

---

4. *Mens Rea* & Mistake of Fact

a. General Intent

At common law, rape was a "general intent" crime, which meant that courts required a prosecutor to prove only that the defendant intentionally engaged in the prohibited conduct of sexual intercourse. There was no need for proof of the defendant's mental state concerning the element of "lack of consent." This view was consistent with the common law assumption that each crime has essentially one mental state, which contrasts with the modern view that a particular mental state must be identified for every element of a crime. Statutes that codified the elements of the common law rape crime typically made no mention of mental state. This silence was interpreted by courts as evidence that legislatures did not intend to require any proof of mental state, aside from the same "general intent" required by the common law. As long as this status quo prevailed, the defense of "mistake of fact as to consent" was not relevant to the rape crime, for the recognition of such a defense would have required the existence of a mental state that may be negated by the mistake.

b. Recognition of Mistake of Fact Defense

The first case to establish a different approach to the mental state for rape was *People v. Mayberry*, 15 Cal. 3d 143, 125 Cal. Rptr. 745, 542 P.2d 1337 (1975), which was decided the same year that the first rape reform statute was enacted in Michigan. However, the *Mayberry* rule did not reflect the emerging "reform" policies of the new era. On the contrary, the *Mayberry* rule created a new *mens rea* defense to the rape crime.

The rape crime in *Mayberry* was defined in the pre-1980 statute described in *Iniguez*, which covered cases where the victim "resists, but her resistance is overcome by force or violence," or where the victim "is prevented from resisting by threats of great and immediate bodily harm, accompanied by apparent power of execution." The prosecutor was required to show that the victim's resistance demonstrated her lack of consent. So the "resistance" element operated as the equivalent of a "lack of consent" element, according to case law.

The victim testified in *Mayberry* that the defendant was stranger who grabbed her on the street, kicked her, struck her with a bottle, and shouted obscenities at her. She evaded him and entered a grocery store, where he followed her and threatened her. When she refused to accompany him outside, he threatened her again. She did not see any security guard and she was afraid, so she accompanied him outside the store. When he demanded sex, she rebuffed him and he ordered her to come with him. When she refused, he struck her in the chest, knocked her down, and threatened to knock out her teeth if she did not come with him. She told him to leave her alone, and he seized her wrist. She tried to "buy time" by saying that she wanted to get cigarettes, but he held her arm while taking her to a nearby store to buy them. She was afraid and felt "completely beaten," and so she did not seek help from the store clerk. Once outside again, she sat on the curb, smoked a cigarette, and talked to the defendant, thinking that she might be able to escape if she could "put on an act" and "fool" him. But after "she tried to talk him out of it," he became angry and ordered her to get up, seized her elbow, and led her several blocks to his apartment. She noticed no one on the street, and she was afraid of him, so she did not resist. After they entered the apartment, the defendant barricaded the door behind her. She had an arthritic leg and could not run away. She tried but failed "to persuade him to change his mind," and without her consent, he engaged in acts of sexual intercourse. He struck her during this sexual assault and "she did not physically resist his advances" because of her fear.

The victim also testified that the defendant's brother arrived after the assault and seized her when she tried to leave. He threw her against the wall, struck her face, and attempted to strangle her. The defendant then pushed her towards the door, and the victim broke free and left. She went to her own apartment and reported the events to the manager, who summoned the police. Two witnesses testified as to the bruises on the victim's arms, and her bruised and swollen face and eye. The defendant testified that he never threatened the victim, that she never protested and that she went to his home willingly and agreed to the sexual acts. His brother, a co-defendant, testified that he found the defendant and the victim in bed and never touched the victim. *Id.* at 1340–41.

The *Mayberry* Court held that the trial judge erred in refusing the defendant's request for an instruction on "a mistake of fact as to consent." The court reasoned broadly that the mistake of fact defense should be recognized for rape because of the existence of two statutes that prescribed general rules for the entire criminal code: 1) that "in every crime . . . there must exist a union, or joint operation of act and intent, or criminal negligence," which "intent" means a "wrongful intent"; and 2) that a person is incapable of committing a crime who commits an act under a mistake of fact disproving any criminal intent. According to the court, the potential life sentence for rape made it "extremely unlikely that the Legislature intended to exclude the rape crime from the requirement of "wrongful intent." Therefore, if the victim did not consent but the defendant made a good faith, reasonable mistake about that "fact," then he could not possess the wrongful intent about consent that should be required for a rape conviction.

However, the *Mayberry* Court limited the circumstances in which the mistake of fact jury instruction would be available, in observing that two aspects of the trial record justified the mistake instruction. First, the defendant's own testimony "could be viewed" as demonstrating his reasonable and good faith mistaken belief in the victim's consent. Second, the victim's testimony was "equivocal." The court explained this characterization as follows: "Although she did not want the defendant to think she was consenting, her 'act' and admitted failure physically to resist him after the initial encounter or to attempt to escape or obtain help might have misled him as to whether she was consenting." *Id.* at 1344–46.

The court's judicial recognition of the defendant's right to a mistake of fact instruction imposed a new burden on the prosecutor at the new trial in *Mayberry*. When a defense *does* seek to negate an element of a crime, such as the mental state of "wrongful intent," the burden of persuasion may *not* be placed upon the defendant. Therefore, it would be the prosecutor's burden to prove beyond a reasonable doubt that the *Mayberry* defendant did *not* have a good faith, reasonable mistaken belief in consent. He would obtain an acquittal if he raised a reasonable doubt as to whether he had such a belief. In effect, the *Mayberry* Court redefined the rape crime to require proof of the common law mental state of "criminal negligence" concerning the "lack of consent" element.

c. Refusal to Recognize Mistake of Fact Defense

When the "lack of consent" element is removed from a reform statute defining the rape crime, a court may decide to reject a defendant's argument that the *Mayberry* "mistake of fact as to consent" defense should be given judicial recognition. For example, the Nebraska Supreme Court was willing to recognize the "affirmative defense of consent," but not the "mistake of fact as to consent" defense in *State v. Koperski*, 254 Neb. 624, 578 N.W.2d 837, 845 (1998). The court reasoned as follows:

> The purpose of the 1975 revision of Nebraska's former rape [statute] was to make our law, with respect to sexual assault, gender neutral and treat the offense as one involving assaultive conduct, not sexual activity. Thus, [the new statute] sought to

> shift the focus of the inquiry away from an examination of what the victim did or should have done and instead concentrate on the conduct of the assailant.
>
> In that regard, this court, as well as the courts of other jurisdictions construing similar legislative enactments, have removed or limited the many evidentiary impediments made applicable to the former crime of rape which distinguished it from other assaultive offenses. For example, courts and legislatures have either abandoned or severely limited the requirement of corroboration of a victim's testimony, the requirement that the victim must offer palpable resistance, the requirement of prompt reporting, the spousal exemption, and evidence of a victim's prior sexual conduct. *State of New Jersey in the Interest of M.T.S.*, 129 N.J. 422, 432–39, 609 A.2d 1266, 1271–74 (1992).
>
> The common thread running through each of these abrogated impediments to proof is that, formerly, each was thought to be an essential evidentiary precaution so as to test whether the victim had consented to sexual penetration. Moreover, each, in effect, served to protect an accused's subjective belief that the victim had consented to sexual penetration, even when such belief was predicated on a mistake of fact whether reasonable or not. Abrogation of these impediments to proof necessarily means that an accused's subjective or mistaken belief as to a victim's consent is a harm which the 1975 legislative enactment sought to preclude.
>
> [The defendant] argues that an accused's subjective belief that consent has been given to sexual penetration should act as a complete defense to [first degree sexual assault] if, and only if, this subjective belief is also objectively reasonable. However, no statutory authority exists for [this proposition]. If the element of the accused's subjective belief as to the alleged victim's state of mind is to be established as a defense to the crime of first degree sexual assault, then it should be done by our Legislature which has the power to define crimes and offenses.

A minority of states do not recognize the "mistake of fact as to consent" defense. Like the *Koperski* Court, some courts have decided that it is up to the legislature to create such a defense by statute, and some courts have decided not to recognize the defense because of the language of the state rape statutes. *See, e.g., Commonwealth v. Lopez*, 433 Mass. 722, 745 N.E.2d 961 (2001). What policy arguments may be used by courts taking these positions? What policy arguments support the recognition of the mistake defense?

Points for Discussion

a. Comparing *Mayberry* & *Iniguez*

Almost twenty years passed after the *Mayberry* decision before the same court decided *Iniguez*. There are striking differences in the opinions with regard to the judicial understanding of the evidence of a victim's fear and lack of resistance. If the California Supreme Court had decided not to address the *Mayberry* issue until after *Iniguez* was decided in 1994, the prosecutor could have argued that the proposed "mistake of fact as to consent" defense was inconsistent with many changes in rape law during the reform era. The fact that the *Mayberry* case was decided in 1975, at the very beginning of the rape reform era, may explain why the court viewed the defense of "mistake of fact" as requiring universal applicability to all crimes. This position was supported by the MPC, which also required the mental state of recklessness for the "compulsion" or nonconsent element.

The prosecutor in *Mayberry* tried but failed to persuade the court that, in effect, the rape crime is different, and so the mistake of fact defense "should be rejected as against the law and public policy." For example, the prosecutor argued that by requiring proof beyond a reasonable doubt that a defendant made an "unreasonable" or negligent mistake about consent, the court achieved the same result as the reinstatement of the "utmost resistance" requirement. But the *Mayberry* Court rejected the argument that the recognition of the mistake of fact defense would require "greater resistance by the victim to assure there is no misunderstanding as to consent and that such resistance could result in harm to the victim." The court simply noted that acceptance of such an argument would "result in effective nullification" of the general "intent" and "mistake of fact" provisions in the penal code, and that the State's argument "invoked a policy consideration for the legislature." How could a prosecutor in 1994 have drawn upon the reasoning of *Iniguez* to argue that the legislative goals underlying the 1980 rape reform statute did not support the continued recognition of the "mistake of fact as to consent" defense?

b. Limitations on Mistake Instruction

The mistake of fact defense is now recognized in a majority of states, usually based on legislation rather than judicial recognition. But courts in these states have established a variety of limitations upon the right to obtain a jury instruction on the mistake of fact defense. Some courts require that a defendant must testify, and some will not allow an instruction where there is evidence of force or of actual consent. In some states, there is a heightened evidence requirement for the defendant's burden of production. For example, the California Supreme Court decided after *Mayberry* that "some evidence" of the defense was not enough, and that a trial court must give a requested instruction "only when the defense is supported" by "substantial evidence." *People v. Flannel*, 25 Cal.3d 668, 684–85, 160 Cal.Rptr. 84, 603 P.2d 1 (1979).

Some courts follow *Mayberry* in requiring evidence that the victim's conduct as to consent was "equivocal," and this concept was given further elaboration in *People v. Williams*, 4 Cal. 4th 354, 841 P.2d 961, 966, 14 Cal. Rptr. 2d 441 (1992) (In Bank). The *Williams* Court affirmed the trial court's rejection of the defendant's request for a *Mayberry* instruction, reasoning that, "[A] mistake of fact occurs when one perceives facts differently from how they actually exist. [Here] the testimony [of the defendant], if believed, established actual consent[.] [The] testimony [of the victim], if believed, would preclude any

Food for Thought

Under the *Williams* standard for determining whether a *Mayberry* instruction should be given, would a trial judge find that the victim's conduct was sufficiently "equivocal" to grant the *Mayberry* defendant an instruction today?

probably not

reasonable belief of consent. These wholly divergent accounts create no middle ground from which [the defendant] could argue he reasonably misinterpreted [the victim's] conduct. There was no substantial evidence of equivocal conduct warranting an instruction as to reasonable and good faith, but mistaken, belief of consent to intercourse."

The following hypothetical provides an opportunity to consider the implications of the *Mayberry* and *Williams* decisions.

Hypo 1: *Ignoring Protests*

Morgan and his friend Mack went drinking together one night in Chicago to celebrate their retirement from the military. They encountered Joe, who had been their commanding officer in Iraq. Joe proposed that the men should go to his house and have sex with his wife. He told them that she liked to engage in rough sex with multiple partners simultaneously, and that she was a masochist who would scream in protest and fight them back while enjoying their forcible sexual conduct. The men did not know that Joe wanted to get revenge against his wife by persuading the men to rape her, and that everything Joe told them about her was a lie. Joe gave them a key to Joe's house, and the two men went there and had sexual intercourse with Joe's wife. They held her down and ignored all of her loud and continuous verbal objections and her unsuccessful attempts at physical resistance.

Assume that Morgan and Mack are charged under an Illinois statute that includes the "lack of consent" element as well as the other elements in the *Iniguez* statute. Each defendant requests a jury instruction on "mistake of fact as to consent," but their requests are denied by the trial judge and the men are convicted. On appeal, explain the arguments that their defense counsel will make to support these positions: 1) that the defendants were entitled to the mistake of fact instruction under *Mayberry* and *Williams*; 2) that there was insufficient evidence for conviction because the evidence established a reasonable doubt as to whether the men had the mental state required for the "lack of consent" element under *Mayberry*; and 3) that in the alternative, the court should interpret the legislature's silence concerning mental state as to the "lack of consent" element in the Illinois statute to require that the prosecutor must prove "recklessness" as to that element. What counter-arguments will the prosecutor make concerning these three issues? *Compare Regina v. Morgan*, 2 All. E.R. 347 (H.L. 1975).

Hypo 2: *Rape Myths*

Scholars have noted that, "Rape myths vary among societies and cultures," "consistently following a patten whereby they blame the victim for their rape, express a disbelief in claims of rape, exonerate the perpetrator, and [imply] that only certain types of women are raped." The same scholars observed that "rape myths, like all myths, are designed to serve up psychological comfort, not hard facts," because believing "that rape victims are innocent and not deserving of their fate is incongruous with the general belief in a just world." Thus, "in order to avoid cognitive dissonance, rape myths serve to protect" that belief. What rape myths can be identified as influencing the pre-reform legal doctrines and the later reforms concerning the forcible rape crime? In addition to the avoidance of cognitive dissonance, what other factors may explain the persistence of rape myths? What additional legal reforms could be adopted to decrease their influence? *See* Kate Harding, ASKING FOR IT: THE ALARMING RISE OF RAPE CULTURE—AND WHAT WE CAN DO ABOUT IT at 22 (2015) citing Amy Grubb & Emily Turner, *Attribution of Blame in Rape Cases: A Review of the Impact of Rape Myth Acceptance, Gender Role Conformity and Substance Use on Victim Blaming*, 17 AGGRESSION AND VIOLENT BEHAVIOR 443–453 (2012).

---

5. Marital Rape Exemption

Today all the states have abolished the marital rape exemption, but some allow lesser punishment for spousal rape. The earliest justifications for the exemption included the idea that wives had no legal identity that was independent from their husbands, and that consent to matrimony operated to establish a wife's consent to intercourse with her husband in all circumstances. Even before the rape reform era, however, these justifications had become outmoded, and courts endorsed additional rationales to explain the need for the marital rape exemption. What rationales could have been used for this purpose, and why would judicial support for those rationales lose ground during the rape reform era?

The MPC drafters proposed that the marital rape exemption should be retained and should be extended to apply to unmarried persons living together as spouses. *See* Model Penal Code 213.1, Comment (8)(c), at 345–346 (1980). The reasons for the MPC position are as follows:

> [In] the case of intercourse coerced by force or threat of physical harm [the] law already authorizes a penalty for assault. [The] issue is whether the still more drastic sanctions of rape should apply. The answer depends on whether the injury caused by forcible intercourse by a husband is equivalent to that inflicted by someone else. The gravity of the crime of forcible rape derives not merely from its violent character but also from its achievement of a particularly degrading kind of unwanted intimacy. Where the attacker stands in an ongoing relation of sexual intimacy, that evil, as distinct from the force used to compel submission, may well be thought qualitatively different. [That], in any event, is the conclusion long endorsed by the law of rape and carried forward in the Model Penal Code provision.

During the early years of the rape reform era, when 40 states still retained some form of the marital rape exemption, one court famously invalidated it on Equal Protection grounds as gender-based discrimination in *People v. Liberta*, 64 N.Y.2d 152, 166–167, 474 N.E.2d 567, 575, 485 N.Y.S.2d 207, 215 (1984). The *Liberta* Court criticized the MPC defense of the exemption as follows:

> The fact that rape statutes exist [is] a recognition that the harm caused by a forcible rape is different, and more severe, than the harm caused by an ordinary assault. [There] is no evidence to support the argument that marital rape has less severe consequences than other rape. On the contrary, numerous studies have shown that marital rape is frequently quite violent and generally has *more* severe, traumatic effects on the victim than other rape. [We] agree with the other courts which have analyzed the [marital rape] exemption, which have been unable to find any present justification for it.

Food for Thought

What reasons may explain the retention of the marital rape exemption in some states for the simple rape crime, usually defined so as to require lack of consent but not the use of force or threat of force?

Some other courts have followed *Liberta*'s approach and invalidated the marital rape exemption. But usually the abolition of the exemption has occurred through legislation rather than through judicial decisions. *See* WAYNE R. LAFAVE, CRIMINAL LAW § 17.4(d).

---

6. Death Penalty for Rape

In the 1960s, civil rights litigation was undertaken in a number of states in order to challenge the constitutionality of the death penalty for rape on Equal Protection grounds. *See* MICHAEL MELTSNER, CRUEL AND UNUSUAL: THE SUPREME COURT AND CAPITAL PUNISHMENT, 73–105 (1973). This litigation relied on empirical evidence concerning race discrimination. *See* Model Penal Code § 213.1, Comment (3)(a), at 281–282 n. 27 (1980). The MPC Commentary summarized the history of race discrimination and the rape crime as follows:

> White [men's sexual] imposition upon black women may have been common in the old South. It is the reverse case that tended to dominate the public mind and that assumed a distinctive role in the regional consciousness. [This] reaction also explains the disproportionate tendency of Southern and Border states to punish rape as a capital offense. In 1925, the following states authorized the death penalty for rape: Alabama, Arkansas, Delaware, Florida, Georgia, Kentucky, Louisiana, Maryland, Mississippi, Missouri, Nevada, North Carolina, Oklahoma, South Carolina, Tennessee, Texas, Virginia, West Virginia. There has also been a long history in those jurisdictions of a *de jure* or *de facto* limitation of the death penalty for rape to black offenders. The Georgia Penal Code of 1811 set the penalty for rape at 16 years imprisonment, but the Code applied only to free whites. Blacks

were subject to punishment of death under Georgia [statutes]. Even [after] *de jure* discrimination in rape penalties was [abolished], blacks continued to be subject disproportionately to the death penalty for rape. [The Wolfgang and Reidel study published in 1973 showed that] in a 20-year period in 11 southern states, seven times as many blacks were sentenced to death as [whites]. [The Justice Department statistics of 1971 showed that] 89.9 per cent of those executed for rape since 1930 have been non-white, almost double the percentage of blacks among those persons executed for [murder].

The Equal Protection litigation of the 1960s was followed by the Supreme Court's invalidation of death penalty statutes under the Eighth Amendment in *Furman v. Georgia*, 408 U.S. 238 (1972). At the time, statutes in 17 jurisdictions allowed capital punishment for rape. After *Furman*, 35 states enacted new capital homicide statues, but only six Southern states enacted new capital rape statutes. In *Gregg v. Georgia*, 428 U.S. 153, 179 (1976), the Court validated the post-*Furman* homicide statutes with procedural safeguards that complied with the Eighth Amendment's prohibition on "arbitrary" capital sentencing procedures. But in *Coker v. Georgia*, 433 U.S. 584 (1977), the Court invalidated a death sentence for rape on Eighth Amendment grounds, without reference to the pre-*Furman* Equal Protection challenges or the empirical evidence of race discrimination. The *Coker* defendant received a death sentence for the rape of an "adult" woman, and the Court limited its holding to this crime. But the Court also reasoned more broadly that rape cannot be compared to murder "in terms of moral depravity and of the injury to the person and to the public," and concluded that it is "disproportionate" and "excessive" to impose the death penalty, "which 'is unique in its severity and irrevocability,' [upon] the rapist who, as such, does not take human life." *Id.* at 598.

In *Kennedy v. Louisiana*, 554 U.S. 407 (2008), the Court addressed the issue left open in *Coker* and held that the death penalty is "disproportionate" and "excessive" for the crime of child rape. The Court's narrow reasoning emphasized that the Eighth Amendment's "evolving standards of decency" required this determination, as evidenced by the consensus of 44 state legislatures and Congress, which did not make child rape a capital crime as of 2008. More broadly, the *Kennedy* Court expanded upon *Coker*'s logic, and ruled that any "nonhomicide crimes against individual persons" cannot be punished with the severe and irrevocable penalty of death, because such crimes "cannot be compared" in their "severity and irrevocability" with "intentional first degree murder." *Id.* at 2660.

B. Rape by Deception

When state courts encountered the idea of "rape by deception" in the nineteenth century, this occurred in cases where prosecutors sought to persuade judges to adopt the fiction that the common law element of "force" could be interpreted to include a defendant's misrepresentations or "fraud" upon the victim. Modern courts have hesitated to go beyond the nineteenth century solutions to the problem of fraud, in the absence of a statute that expressly prohibits sex acts "accomplished by fraud."

Suliveres v. Commonwealth

449 Mass. 112, 865 N.E.2d 1086 (2007).

COWIN, J.

In *Commonwealth v. Goldenberg*, 338 Mass. 377, 155 N.E.2d 187 (1959), we concluded that it is not rape when consent to sexual intercourse is obtained through fraud or deceit[.] In the present case, the Commonwealth asks us to overrule the *Goldenberg* decision and hold that misrepresentations can in fact substitute for the requisite force. Because the *Goldenberg* case has been the law for nearly one-half century, during which the legislature has had ample opportunity to change the statute and has not done so, we decline to overrule our decision in *Goldenberg*.

[The] crime of rape is defined in G.L. c. 265, § 22(b): "Whoever has sexual intercourse or unnatural sexual intercourse with a person and compels such person to submit by force and against his will, or compels such person to submit by threat of bodily injury, shall be punished. . . ." This definition has changed over time, but the requirement that the act be "by force and against [the] will" of the victim has remained constant for two hundred years. We have said that "by force" and "against [the] will" are "two separate elements each of which must independently be satisfied." *Commonwealth v. Lopez*, 433 Mass. 722, 745 N.E.2d 961 (2001).

The *Goldenberg* case involved a woman who had gone to the defendant, a physiotherapist, to procure an abortion. The defendant told her that, as part of the procedure, he "had to have intercourse" with her and that it would "help it some way." He then proceeded to have intercourse with her. We noted that "it could not be found beyond a reasonable doubt that the intercourse was without her consent," and that the evidence "negatived the use of force." Thus, the only way the defendant could have been convicted was if his fraudulent representation that the intercourse was medically necessary could both invalidate the consent and supply the requisite "force." We concluded, however, that "[f]raud cannot be allowed to supply the place of the force which the statute makes mandatory," and cited with approval [a] case, *Don Moran v. People*, 25 Mich. 356 (1872), which on "facts strikingly similar" had found no rape to have been committed.

We turn now to the facts of the present case. On the night in question, the defendant had sexual intercourse with the [victim] by impersonating her longtime boy friend, his brother. [She testified that] while she was asleep alone in the bedroom she shared with her boy friend, the defendant entered the room, and she awoke. In the dark room, [she] assumed that the defendant was her boy friend returning home from work, and addressed him by her boy friend's name. [The defendant] got into the bed and had intercourse with her. [She] was "not fully awake" at the time of the penetration. During the intercourse, she believed that the man was her boy friend, and had she known it was the defendant, she "would have never consented."

The defendant was indicted for rape and tried before a jury[.] At trial, the main issue was whether the complainant knew at the time the identity of the person with whom she was having sex. The defense was that the sex was fully consensual. The defendant told an investigating police officer that the [victim] had come to him while he was asleep in another room and had invited him to her bedroom to have sex with her. The [prosecutor] argued that the defendant had procured the [victim's] consent to sex fraudulently by impersonating her boy friend. [The trial judge denied the defendant's motion for a required finding of not guilty. When the jury could not reach a verdict, the trial judge declared a *mistrial*. The defendant then moved to dismiss the indictment, and when this motion was denied, this appeal followed.]

What's That?

A mistrial occurs when the trial judge orders that the trial must end without a determination on the merits. This may occur when the jury is not able to agree on the verdict, or when a procedural error occurs. Usually a mistrial does not pose an impediment to the commencement of a new trial before another jury.

Taking the evidence in the light most favorable to the Commonwealth, we assume that the defendant fraudulently induced the complainant to have intercourse. However, [the] rule of *Goldenberg* is that intercourse where consent is achieved by fraud does not constitute rape. That rule compels the conclusion that there was no evidence of rape in this case, and we decline to overrule the *Goldenberg* decision.

[The] crime of rape is defined by statute as nonconsensual intercourse achieved "by force." The Commonwealth [contends] that the defendant's fraud should be allowed to satisfy the requirement of force. In requesting that we overrule the *Goldenberg* case, the Commonwealth asks us to read "force" out of the statute in cases involving misrepresentation as to identity. Yet we have never suggested that force is not an element of the crime[.] Because "[n]o portion of the statutory language may be deemed superfluous," we are not free, any more than we were in the *Goldenberg* case, to adopt the Commonwealth's proposed interpretation.

FYI

In describing the *Goldenberg* rule as "consistent with the law in a majority of other jurisdictions, the court cited five English cases decided between 1822 and 1868, six American cases decided between 1857 and 1926, and two American cases from the 1990s.

We assume that, when it enacts legislation, the Legislature is not only aware of existing statutes, but is also aware of the prior state of the law as explicated by the decisions of this court. Thus, we find it significant that the Legislature has not seen fit to overrule the *Goldenberg* decision in forty-eight years, during which the rape statute was amended three times, [and] scholarship and attitudes regarding rape changed considerably[.] The Legislature is free to amend the rape statute or create a new substantive offense to encompass the conduct at issue, as many other States have done. However, where the Legislature has chosen not to do so, "[i]t is not for this court [to] rewrite the clear intention expressed by the statute." *Commonwealth v. Leno*, 415 Mass. 835, 841, 616 N.E.2d 453 (1993).

[The] Commonwealth attempts to distinguish the *Goldenberg* decision on the ground that it involved "fraud in the inducement" while the present case is one of "fraud in the factum." We find this argument unpersuasive[.] The term "fraud in the factum" typically refers to "the rare case when there has been fraud as to the essential nature of [a legal] instrument or an essential element of it." *Federico v. Brockton Credit Union*, 39 Mass. App. Ct. 57, 63, 653 N.E.2d 607 (1995). "Fraud in the inducement," by contrast, occurs "when a misrepresentation leads another to enter into a transaction with a false impression of the risks, duties, or obligations involved," but there is no fraud as to the essential nature of the transaction. In the context of rape, by analogy, "fraud in the factum" must mean that the victim is defrauded as to the nature of the act performed, rather than the reason for doing it. *Compare Boro v. Superior Court,* 163 Cal. App. 3d 1224, 1228, 210 Cal. Rptr. 122 (1985) ([upholding conviction and finding] fraud in factum where victim consents to doctor's penetration of her with medical instrument but he then penetrates her with his penis), with *State v. Bolsinger*, 709 N.W.2d 560, 564 (Iowa 2006) ([reversing conviction and finding only] fraud in inducement where defendant touched victims' genitals on pretext of medical examination [for reason of sexual gratification]). In the present case, there is no claim that the [victim] did not know she was consenting to a sex act; rather, just as in the *Goldenberg* case, her consent was induced by fraud as to the circumstances surrounding the act. Thus, the present case involves "fraud in the inducement," as did *Goldenberg*, and is squarely controlled by that decision.

Take Note

The prosecutor's alternate argument on appeal was that the victim was not "fully awake," and therefore not sufficiently conscious to consent. The court rejected this argument based on the record, which showed that the victim "had intelligible and appropriate conversation" with the defendant prior to the intercourse.

Fraudulently obtaining consent to sexual intercourse does not constitute rape as defined in our statute. Accordingly, the defendant's motion for a required finding of not guilty should have been granted[.]

Points to Remember

a. *Suliveres* in Retrospect

After 30 years of rape law reforms produced by courts through judicial redefinitions of statutory terms such as "force," "resistance" and "lack of consent," why does the harm to the victims in *Suliveres* and *Goldenberg* still not qualify as "rape"? The *Suliveres* Court relied unquestioningly on the 1959 *Goldenberg* decision and on the 1872 precedent on which *Goldenberg* relied. The *Suliveres* Court also endorsed the nineteenth century doctrine that equated the rare "fraud in the factum" scenario with forcible rape, but excluded the more common "fraud in the inducement" scenarios from the crime. Not surprisingly, in the pre-reform era, the MPC drafters were unwilling to criminalize the "fraud in the inducement" scenario, although they defined the "fraud in the factum" scenario as rape MPC § 213.1. It is more surprising to find that modern cases like *Suliveres* continue to validate this old distinction. What unstated policy reasons may possibly explain the reluctance of courts to expand the scope of the rape by fraud crime, as requested by the prosecutor in *Suliveres*?

The *Suliveres* ruling did not allude to the fact that the victim's consent was based on a unique type of fraud that involved "mistaken identity." Even some nineteenth century courts treated this type of case as "fraud in the factum" when a defendant pretended to be the woman's husband. The MPC proposal to codify this crime has been endorsed in some modern statutes. For example, the Louisiana crime of simple rape codifies the "mistaken identity" fraud category as follows: "[w]hen the female victim submits under the belief that the person committing the act is her husband and such belief is intentionally induced by any artifice, pretense, or concealment practiced by the offender." *See* La. Rev. Stat. § 14–43–A(3) (2007). What arguments could have been made by the *Suliveres* prosecutor that "fraud in the factum" should include a defendant's deception of a victim who consents to sexual intercourse only because of a reasonable belief in the mistaken identity of a "boy friend" instead of a husband? Why would those arguments have been unlikely to persuade the court?

> **FYI**
>
> The MPC § 213.1(2)(c) defines rape as follows: "A male who has sexual intercourse with a female not his wife is guilty if he knows that she is unaware that a sexual act is being committed upon her."

b. Statutory Definitions of Deception

The *Suliveres* Court noted that other state legislatures have defined "fraud" as a basis for sexual assault crimes. These statutes take different approaches to defining the scope of the fraud concept. For example, the Michigan sexual conduct crime includes sexual penetration of another "through concealment," and the Tennessee rape crime applying to sexual penetration "accomplished by fraud." In 2002, the California rape definition was amended so as to blur the distinction between the fraud distinctions approved by the Massachusetts court in *Suliveres*, by including sexual penetration when the victim "is unconscious of the nature of the act," when the victim is "not aware, knowing, perceiving, or cognizant of the essential characteristics of the act due to the perpetrator's fraudulent representation that the sexual penetration served a professional purpose when it served no professional purpose." *Compare* Mich. Comp. Laws Ann. § 750.520b (2007); Tenn. Code Ann. § 39–13–503 (2006); Cal. Pen. Code § 289(d)(4) (2002).

The following hypothetical provides the opportunity to consider the implicit policy concerns of courts that are hesitant to expand "force" to include "fraud" in the absence of legislative action.

Hypo 1: *Force as Fraud*

The *Suliveres* decision appears to illustrate the inherent limitations of statutory interpretation as a vehicle for rape reform. Explain the unstated policy reasons that may explain the reluctance of the *Suliveres* Court to expand the definition of "force" to encompass "fraud." What are the benefits of using legislation to define the elements of any "rape by deception" crime, rather than relying on the judicial recognition of "force" as "fraud"? Would the *Suliveres* Court have reached the same decision if the facts involved a defendant who hypnotized his clients so that he was able to rape them without them either resisting or remembering what had happened to them?

Hypo 2: *Criminalizing Deception Scenarios*

One scholar has suggested that three "obvious candidates" for a legislature to punish selectively as specific forms of rape by deception are cases featuring deception that is "also coercive," deception that "amounts to a breach of trust by a person in a position of authority," and deception that "causes significant harm in addition to the infringement of the victim's autonomy." What examples of conduct might fall into each of these categories? What do these three categories share in common that justify criminal punishment? *See* Luis E. Chiesa, *Solving the Riddle of Rape-by-Deception*, 35 YALE L. & POL'Y REV. 407 (2017).

C. Rape of Drugged or Intoxicated Victim

At common law, the crime of rape included the act of sexual intercourse with a sleeping, unconscious, or drugged woman, because such victims are incapable of giving consent or resisting unwanted sexual acts. Most state codes include a definition of rape that either requires the defendant to administer drugs to the victim or requires that the victim should be in an impaired state because of drugs when the rape occurred. For example, the California rape statute applies where sexual intercourse occurs and "where a person is prevented from resisting by any intoxicating or anaesthetic substance, or any controlled substance, and this condition was known, or reasonably should have been known by the accused" or "where a person is unconscious or asleep [and this is known by the accused]." *See* Cal. Pen. Code § 261(a)(3) (2002). It is also common for rape statutes to apply where a victim is incapable of giving consent because of physical or mental helplessness.

Some drugs can cause a victim to become unconscious and then, after a rape occurs, to have amnesia about what happened before the victim became unconscious. These circumstances may make it difficult for a prosecutor to obtain sufficient evidence for a rape conviction. However, in *Sera v. Norris*, 400 F.3d 538 (8th Cir. 2005), the victim could not testify that an act of sexual intercourse occurred, but the court upheld the defendant's convictions for multiple rapes of the victim based on unusual circumstantial evidence. The defendant was found to be in possession of a bottle of Rohypnol in his suitcase, "a so-called 'date rape drug'" that can cause "hypnosis, total muscle relaxation, and loss of memory" in the form of "anterograde amnesia." A person who has taken the drug "can be talking and functioning yet still not be able to remember what is happening" and alcohol magnifies the effects of the drug, causing a deeper state of unconsciousness. The victim testified that she took three trips with the defendant, and that he gave her two alcoholic drinks during each trip, just before she lost her memory of what happened next. There was sufficient evidence for a jury to find that the defendant raped the victim after putting Rohypnol in her drinks during each of the three trips, based on the similarity of her symptoms, the defendant's access to the drug, and a videotape which showed the defendant raping the unconscious victim during the first trip.

FYI

The MPC § 213.1(b) defines rape as follows: "A male who has sexual intercourse with a female not his wife is guilty if he has substantially impaired her power to appraise or control her conduct by administering or employing without her knowledge drugs, intoxicants or other means for the purpose of preventing resistance." Section (c) of this provision provides that such "[a] male . . . is guilty if the female is unconscious."

Take Note

In 2012, two male high school students were convicted of rape in a case where they performed sex acts upon a 16-year-old female student who had no memory of this event. The evidence included text messages by the defendants, as well as photographs and videos of the victim (some of which showed her to be unconscious), which were taken by witnesses and displayed on social media websites. The media coverage of the trial received public criticism for bias. *See* http://www.nytimes.com/2012/12/17/sports/high-school-football-rape-case-unfolds-online-and-divides-steubenville-ohio.html?pagewanted=all&_r=0.

Even though a victim was not unconscious, the prosecutor may seek to prove that the victim was "sufficiently" impaired to lack "the capacity" for consent. Assume, for example, that the legislature decides to define rape to include "an act of sexual penetration accomplished with any person" when "the victim is incapable of giving consent because of any intoxicating agent." Notice that this statute does not require the prosecutor to prove the element of the victim's "lack of consent." Also, the statute implicitly provides that the affirmative defense of consent is not available when the victim is "incapable of giving consent" for the reason described. Notably, the prosecution must show, beyond a reasonable doubt, that the victim did lack "the capacity to consent" because of the consumption of alcohol, for example. Then defense counsel presumably would attempt to raise a reasonable doubt about this element. One important question is whether the prosecutor also should be required to prove that the defendant possessed a particular mental state regarding the victim's lack of capacity to consent due to intoxication. The following hypothetical raises this question.

Hypo: *Intoxicated Victim*

Inga went to a bar on Hilton Head Island at 9:00 p.m. with her friend Abby to celebrate Abby's birthday. By midnight, Inga had consumed four beers and several shots of hard liquor. Then Abby's boyfriend Al arrived at the bar, accompanied by his friend Derk, whom Inga did not know. The four agreed to go to Al's house, where Inga consumed two more beers. Abby and Al noticed that Inga seemed incoherent when she lay down on the living room couch around 1:00 a.m., which is when Abby and Al retired for the night. At the time, Derk was lying down on the floor. Inga testified that she does not remember what happened from the time that she arrived at Al's house until the time when she noticed that she was lying on the floor with Derk on top of her, engaging in sexual intercourse. Inga pushed Derk off and screamed for Abby and Al, who took Inga to the hospital. The police arrested Derk for rape. Derk testified at his trial that, "I don't know how intoxicated Inga was that night. I only saw her drink two beers at Al's house. Then after Abby and Al went to bed, Inga rolled off the couch and found me on the floor. She said that she wanted to have sex, and so we did."

The trial judge must decide between two competing jury instructions. Assume that the relevant definition of rape in South Carolina is "an act of sexual penetration accomplished with any person" when "the victim is incapable of giving consent because of any intoxicating agent." The prosecutor argues that this instruction should be given:

> Consent is not a defense to the crime of rape defined as sexual penetration where the victim is incapable of giving consent because of intoxication. In determining whether the victim was incapable of giving consent because of intoxication, *you must consider all the circumstances in determining whether the victim's intoxication rendered her unable to exercise reasonable judgment.*

FYI

The revised FBI definition of rape "includes instances in which the victim is incapable of giving consent because of temporary or permanent mental or physical incapacity, including due to the influence of drugs or alcohol[.]" See http://www.fbi.gov/news/pressrel/press-releases/attorney-general-eric-holder-announces-revisions-to-the-uniform-crime-reports-definition-of-rape.

The defense counsel argues that this instruction should be given:

> Consent is not a defense to the crime of rape defined as sexual penetration where the victim is incapable of giving consent because of intoxication, if the victim was incapable of giving consent because intoxication rendered her unable to

exercise reasonable judgment, *and if the Defendant knew that the victim was unable to exercise reasonable judgment because of her intoxication.*

What arguments will be made by each side to support these competing instructions? How should the court rule, in light of all the rape reform policies that are illustrated in the cases in this chapter? *Compare State v. Jones*, 804 N.W.2d 409 (S.D. 2011).

D. Statutory Rape

When the American common law absorbed the English statutory crime of sexual intercourse with a female under the age of 10, the term "statutory rape" became the name of the crime. Consent was no defense because a child victim was presumed to be incapable of consent. Mistake as to the victim's age was no defense because strict liability was allowed for this key element of the crime. By the 1950s, most statutes had raised the age of the victim to 16 or 17, or even to 18 in a few states. This development was troubling for judges who did not want to impose harsh penalties for the crime of consensual sex *between* underage teenagers, especially when only boys were subject to prosecution. By 1980 the crime covered only victims under 16 in most states. During the rape reform era, most states adopted gender-neutral statutory rape provisions. Yet these legislative strategies did not relieve courts from resolving difficult questions concerning the scope of the crime, as illustrated in the statutory interpretation problem confronted by the court in the following case.

In re G.T.

170 Vt. 507, 758 A.2d 301 (2000).

DOOLEY, J.

G.T. appeals from a family court order adjudicating him to be a delinquent child because he is guilty of statutory rape, that is, he engaged in a sexual act with a person under the age of sixteen years in violation of 13 V.S.A. § 3252(a)(3). At the time of the alleged offense, G.T. was fourteen years of age [and the victim was a twelve-year-old girl]. He contends that, as a person within the protection of the statutory rape statute, he cannot be charged with violation the statute. We agree and reverse.

The trial court's findings are not contested on appeal. G.T. lived across the street from M.N. [and] [t]he two had been friends, but had never had sexual contact with each other prior to the incident in question. One night in October 1995, while G.T. and M.N. were watching a television movie in M.N.'s house, G.T. began kissing M.N. on the mouth. G.T. then pulled M.N.'s legs out straight, pulled her shorts down, pulled his pants down, and got on top of her. He continued kissing her with his hands on her shoulders. M.N., who had never previously had intercourse, felt what she believed was G.T.'s penis in her vagina. G.T. asked if it hurt, but did not stop when M.N. said it hurt. Although she was not afraid of him, M.N. was not sure what G.T. would have done if she had pushed him off of her.

What's That?

A delinquent child is a child between the ages of ten and sixteen who has committed a delinquent act, which is defined as "an act designated a crime" under state law. Even though G.T. could not receive the adult penalty of up to 20 years in prison for statutory rape, he could be placed in a "treatment, rehabilitative, or educational institution or facility" and his "adjudication of delinquency" would become part of his record "available to the court in a future sentencing proceeding."

G.T.'s actions were interrupted when M.N.'s mother and boyfriend unexpectedly returned to the house. They saw G.T. scramble up off M.N., but did not observe sexual contact. They ordered G.T. out of the house. M.N. began crying and ran upstairs. She revealed to her mother what had occurred.

On these facts, the State alleged that G.T. had committed statutory rape and, therefore, had engaged in a *delinquent act*. Based upon the above facts, the family court adjudicated G.T. a *delinquent child*, and this appeal followed[.] The question we must address is whether the family court properly found that G.T. committed a crime, specifically the crime of statutory rape.

The crime of statutory rape is defined in § 3252(a)(3) as follows: (a) A person who engages in a sexual act with another person and . . . (3) The other person is under the age of 16, except where the persons are married to each other and the sexual act is consensual[.] [A sexual act is defined as "any intrusion, however, slight, by any part of a person's body or any object into the genital or anal opening of another."] G.T. argues that the juxtaposition of the word "person" in the two parts of the statute shows that the Legislature intended that the perpetrator be a person of sixteen years of age or older. Although G.T. recognizes that the plain meaning of the term might not contain that limitation, he argues that the context does not require such a limitation.

Take Note

The court cited a state health department report from 1997 which noted that "among students in the eleventh grade, the year in which they generally turn sixteen, fifty-six percent of males and fifty percent of females report having had sexual intercourse."

G.T. also stresses [that] statutory rape is a strict liability offense, for which the only elements are the age of the "victim" and the presence of a sexual act. Thus, under the State's theory, both G.T. and M.N. have necessarily committed the crime, and all consensual sexual activity between teenagers is a felony for both participants. Given the prevalence of such activity, and the potential sentence of twenty years in jail, G.T. argues that such a construction creates absurd, irrational or unjust results[.] . . .

[We] find [two] reasons [to] question the apparent plain meaning of § 3252(a)(3) in this case. . . . [First,] [u]nder the State's theory in this case, if two persons under sixteen years of age commit consensual, mutual sexual acts with each other, they are both guilty of statutory rape. Thus, under the child abuse reporting laws, any of the *listed professionals* [in 33 V.S.A. § 4913(a)] who learn [of] acts [including statutory rape] must report them to the [Department of Social and Rehabilitation Services (SRS) within 24 hours] or risk prosecution. SRS must notify each child's parents and list both children in the child abuse registry as victims and perpetrators. We [have previously] noted the irony of maintaining confidential the fact and detail of a juvenile delinquency adjudication, while placing and disseminating information about the same juvenile in the child abuse registry. Here the tension goes beyond irony. We seriously doubt that the Legislature intended to label a juvenile under sixteen years who engages in a sexual act a child abuser for life[.] . . .

What's That?

The listed professionals in the child abuse reporting laws include a "health care provider, school teacher, librarian, principal, or guidance counselor; mental health professional; day care worker; social worker; police or probation officer; or camp owner, administrator or counselor, among others[.]"

The second reason is that the State's construction of § 3252(a)(3) involves a breadth of prosecutorial discretion that raises serious concerns about whether the resulting prosecutions are consistent with equal protection of the law. In this case, the prosecutor was candid that he believed G.T. had violated [the forcible rape statute, § 3252(a)(1), which applies to:] "(a) A person who engages in a sexual act: (A) Without the consent of the other person; or (B) By threatening or coercing the other person." [The prosecutor] chose to charge the case under [the statutory rape statute, § 3252(a)(3)] because it creates a strict liability offense which is easy to prove. Because sexual conduct is private, prosecution necessarily arises from complaints. [The] Windham County State's Attorney's office receives numerous complaints to prosecute teenagers under [the statutory rape crime, § 3252(a)(3)], usually from parents, but does so only when there is evidence of coercion or a lack of true consent. Thus, the prosecutor's office brings delinquency proceedings only when it believes the juvenile [violated the forcible rape statute], but it never charges the juvenile [with that more serious crime]. Thus, the prosecutor determines what crime the juvenile has committed, but charges in such a way as to ensure that the juvenile never has the opportunity to show that he or she did not commit the crime found by the prosecutor[.]

Practice Pointer

During the oral argument of an appeal, an attorney may refer to facts that are thereby "added to the record," even though the facts are not set forth in the briefs before argument. Here the facts about the "numerous complaints" and prosecutor's charging policy were "added at argument" and quoted in the opinion.

Although we have only a limited record here, we note that the selective enforcement of the underlying statute has the hallmarks that other courts have relied upon to find discriminatory prosecution[.] We are not, however, suggesting that we should impose limits on prosecutorial discretion; we are questioning instead a statutory interpretation that necessarily results in this kind of enforcement administration. It is one thing to give discretion in enforcing a legislatively defined crime; it is quite another to give to prosecutors the power to define the crime[.] . . .

We return to the statutory construction question before us. We have expressed the plain meaning rule as a presumption, recognizing that in some circumstances the literal meaning of the words employed cannot prevail. We are faced with [a] unique confluence [of] factors that weigh heavily against the plain meaning rule[.] . . . [In] order to make § 3252(a)(3) consistent with the child abuse reporting statute [and] to avoid the real possibility of discriminatory enforcement[,] we construe subsection (a)(3) as inapplicable in cases where the alleged perpetrator is also a victim under the age of consent [which is 16]. . . .

Reversed.

Food for Thought

Assume that the prosecutor had decided to charge G.T. with the forcible rape crime under § 3252(a)(1), which applies to a person who compels another person to participate in a sexual act either without the consent of the other person or by threatening or coercing the other person. Based on the facts of G.T.'s case, would it have been easy for a prosecutor to prove the elements of the forcible rape crime beyond a reasonable doubt?

JOHNSON, J., dissenting.

[Under] the majority's holding, a fifteen-year-old minor cannot be found delinquent for the statutory rape of, say, a nine-or ten-year-old minor. The majority [assumes] that this will not impose any great burden on prosecutors because they can always seek an adjudication of delinquency based on an allegation of forcible rape[.] [The] majority fails to acknowledge that there will be instances, not unlike the present case, where the coercion is subtle and results from the different age, mental capacity, or maturity of the participants engaged in the conduct. [There] will be [cases] in which forcible rape will be difficult to prove. . . .

[The] majority's concern regarding the breadth of prosecutorial discretion is speculative in nature. There is not the slightest indication that any abuse of that discretion occurred in this case or is occurring generally. [Under] the facts of this case, [the] prosecutor acted properly in filing a petition of delinquency alleging statutory rape against only G.T. and not M.N. As the trial court stated, even though the difference between the two juveniles in this case was only two years, those two years between twelve and fourteen often encompass significant differences in psychological growth, cognitive skills, and sexuality. . . .

Our duty [is] to give effect to the intent of the Legislature. That intent is clear in this case. [Indeed,] Vermont "has long recognized an obligation to protect its children from others *and from themselves*." [*State v.*] *Barlow*, 160 Vt. [527,] 528, 630 A.2d [1299,] 1301 (1993) (emphasis added). The salutary purposes of the statutory rape law identified by this Court [in prior cases]—reducing teen-age pregnancy, preventing venereal disease and damage to reproductive organs, and protecting minors who may be unable to give considered consent or who may have a heightened vulnerability to physical and psychological harm—are furthered regardless of the age of the alleged perpetrator. *See id.*, 160 Vt. at 530, 630 A.2d at 1300–1301 (recognizing that minors often lack experience, perspective, and judgment to avoid choices that could be detrimental to themselves and others).

I am authorized to say that Justice Gibson joins in this dissent.

Points for Discussion

a. Evolution of "Romeo and Juliet" Statutes

During the rape reform era, states adopted "age gap" provisions conferring immunity from prosecution for statutory rape where both "victims" and "defendants" are teenagers. These provisions resemble the MPC proposal of a four-year-age-gap immunity, which was "chosen to reflect the prevailing pattern of secondary education" so that "felony sanctions for mutually consensual behavior" would not apply to school "romancers." *See* Model Penal Code § 213.3(1)(a), Comment (2), at 386. These age-gap immunity provisions are sometimes called "Romeo and Juliet" statutes. In a few states, age-gap statutes that are not gender neutral have been challenged on equal protection grounds. *See, e.g., State v. Limon*, 280 Kan. 275, 122 P.3d 22 (2005) (invalidating opposite-sex clause in Romeo and Juliet statute).

b. Reasonable Mistake of Fact as to Age

State courts continue to debate the question whether to recognize the "mistake of fact as to age" defense for statutory rape. The common law definition of the crime treated the age element as having a strict liability mental state. The trend toward recognizing the mistake of fact defense began with *People v. Hernandez*, 61 Cal. 2d 529, 39 Cal. Rptr. 361, 393 P.2d 673 (1964), which precedent was relied on in *Mayberry* when the same court recognized the "mistake of fact as to consent" defense to forcible rape. However, the trend developed slowly, and it has taken over 40 years for one third of the states to endorse the defense of mistake of fact as to age.

Like the *Mayberry* mistake defense, courts usually require the mistake about age to be reasonable, thereby requiring a mental state of negligence for the age element. Only a few states require recklessness. In defending a strict liability interpretation for statutes that apply only to younger victims, such as those under age 14, some courts have emphasized the need to protect from them the severe physical and psychological consequences of sexual acts. *See, e.g., People v. Douglas*, 381 Ill. App.3d 1067, 886 N.E.2d 1232 (2008); WAYNE R. LAFAVE, CRIMINAL LAW, § 17.4(c) (5th ed. 2010).

Some state legislatures have not enacted changes in their statutes to reflect the adoption of the *Hernandez* rule, the Model Penal Code approach, or other express provisions regarding the "mistake of fact as to age" defense. If a statute is ambiguous or silent on this issue, how should a court interpret the statute?

c. Possible Legislative Responses to *In re G.T.*

Both opinions in *In re G.T.* provide a glimpse of how statutory rape statutes have changed during the rape reform era. The majority's holding is consistent with the legislative trend toward revising the common law version of statutory rape to cover only "predator" scenarios where the defendant is significantly older than the victim when both are teenagers. But the dissent's concerns reveal how controversial it is for courts to adopt statutory interpretations that limit either the scope of liability for statutory rape or the scope of prosecutorial discretion. Both opinions also reveal how the Vermont legislature could address the problems in the statute by amending the Vermont rape laws. For example, the dissenters argue that the plain-meaning interpretation of the statutory rape provision is necessary because there will be cases involving teenagers "in which forcible rape will be difficult to prove." What legislation could provide an alternate solution to this problem? What are the pros and cons of amending the statute to expressly codify either the majority's holding or the dissent's plain-meaning interpretation?

Take Note

In 2008, a 47-year old male teacher was charged with three counts of "sex without consent" with a 14-year-old female student. After the student committed suicide in 2010, the defendant pled guilty to one count and his prosecution was deferred. In 2013, when the prosecution was revived, the judge sentenced the defendant to 15 years but suspended the sentence except for 31 days. The judge said that the victim "was older than her chronological age" and "as much in control of the situation as the defendant." *See* https://www.theguardian.com/commentisfree/2013/sep/03/painful-lesson-cherice-moralez-rape.

Hypo: *Amended Statute*

The Vermont legislature enacted the "Sexual Violence Prevention Act" in 2006, which amended the statutory rape definition by adding a new immunity section. That statute provides in § 3252(c): "No person shall engage in a sexual act with a child who is under the age of 16, except: (1) where the persons are married to each other and the sexual act is consensual; or (2) *where the person is less than 19 years old, the child is at least 15 years old, and the sexual act is consensual.*" The Vermont legislature also added a third definition of the forcible rape crime in § 3252, which is that "No person shall engage in a sexual act with another person and compel the other person to participate in a sexual act by placing the other person in fear that any person will suffer imminent bodily injury." Explain the various policy judgments that are expressed in these two legislative responses to the *In re G.T.* decision. Then explain what would happen if the defendant G.T. were prosecuted under the 2006 statute.

E. Internet Crimes

Modern sexual assault statutes include enactments that seek to protect victims, including minors, from dangers related to sexual activity that is facilitated by internet communications.

One example is provided by a statute enacted by the New Hampshire legislature in 1998, which defines the prohibited "use of computer services" crime as follows: "No person shall knowingly utilize a computer on-line service, internet service, or local bulletin board service to solicit, lure, or entice a child [defined as a person under age 18] to commit acts described in any offense under [a provision that includes a long list of sex crimes]." The legislative history indicates that the "overarching purpose" of the enactment of the statute was to "deter sexual offenses against juveniles." New Hampshire precedents have construed the term "utilize" to establish criminal liability for defendants who "enlist computer technology" in some way other than communicating with a victim. Such defendants have included a stepfather who used a laptop computer to show his stepdaughter a pornographic video during a weekend visit in order to "lure or entice" her into the future commission of a sexual act, which was an enumerated crime. Another enumerated crime is the solicitation of sex acts, which means that prohibited communications under the "uses of computer services" statute may include emails and Facebook messages sent to victims by defendants. The legislative history of the New Hampshire statute illustrates the traditional purposes of such enactments, which include the need for new and broader statutes to "deter sexual offenses against juveniles" and to "assist law enforcement in the protection of [juveniles] from the types of dangers presented by the computer and the internet."

Hypo: *Arranging a Rendezvous*

Assume that an eighteen-year-old male student sends Facebook messages to a fifteen-year-old female student at the same residential prep school. These messages offer to meet the female in a "hidden location" on campus where sexual activity may ensue. Later the male student is charged with a variety of sexual offenses, including the "use of computer services" crime, which is a felony. Notably, the jury acquits the male student of the Misdemeanor Sexual Assault crime of "sexual penetration" committed upon a child "who is over 13 years of age and under 16 years of age" when "the age difference between the perpetrator and the child is 4 years or less." However, the defense counsel for the male student conceded that the 18-year-old defendant's electronic communications did "solicit" the "child" victim "to commit" the sexual penetration acts that are on the prohibited list of offenses in the computer crime statute. When the jury convicts the defendant of the computer crime, the accompanying penalties include the defendant's registration as a sex offender. His defense counsel concedes on appeal that the literal meaning of the text of the computer statute is clear, and that on the facts, the defendant is guilty of the computer crime.

Even so, the defense counsel argues that if the literal meaning of the statute is applied by the court, then there will be "absurd results," and therefore, the statute should not be enforced against the defendant and his conviction should be reversed. More specifically, defense counsel argues that: 1) the legislature was primarily concerned with the use of the computer and the internet by "adult pedophile strangers," not students attending the same school; and

2) no conviction would have occurred if the defendant had solicited the same sex acts with the victim in a note or conversation, so it is absurd to convict the defendant based on his use of emails and Facebook messages. What arguments can the prosecutor make to rebut these "absurd results" arguments?

F. Sex Trafficking

A federal statute, 18 U.S.C. § 1591(a), punishes several crimes, including the crime known to law enforcement officials as "sex trafficking of a minor." This crime takes its name from the "minors clause" in the last two lines of the statutory text, which provides as follows:

> Whoever knowingly—
>
> (1) In or affecting interstate or foreign commerce, or within the special maritime and territorial jurisdiction of the United States, recruits, harbors, transports, provides, or maintains by any means a person [a victim]; or
>
> (2) Benefits, financially or by receiving anything of value, from participation in a venture which has engaged in an act described in violation of paragraph (1),
>
> *knowing, or in reckless disregard* of the fact, that means of force, threats of force, fraud, coercion, or any combination of such means will be used to cause the person [the victim] to engage in a commercial sex act, or that the person [the victim] has not attained the age of 18 years and will be caused to engage in a commercial sex act, shall be punished.

Ever since the enactment of the statute in 2012, one issue has arisen repeatedly in federal prosecutions for "sex trafficking of minors" under § 1591(a), which is the question whether the Government is required to prove that a defendant actually knew that the victim was under the age of 18. The following Hypo addresses this question.

Hypo: *Reckless Disregard or Knowledge?*

Assume that Ed is convicted of the federal crime of "sex trafficking of a minor" under 18 U.S.C. § 1591(a), and that the minor in this case is 17 years old. At Ed's trial, the judge instructed the jurors that they could convict Ed based upon proof that he acted *either knowingly OR in reckless disregard* of the victim's age. On appeal, Ed's defense counsel argues that the jury should have been instructed that proof of Ed's actual knowledge of the victim's age was required for conviction. The defense argument is based on the following logic: 1) that "knowingly" modifies the phrase "that the person has not attained the age of 18 years" ("the minors clause"); 2) that "or in reckless disregard" only applies to the "force clause" that follows it ("means of force, threats of force, fraud, coercion" and so on);

and 3) that any ambiguity must be resolved in the defendant Ed's favor under the rule of lenity. The Government's position is that the trial judge's instruction was correct because: 1) a "natural reading" of the statute allows the finding of either "force" or the victim's age to be based on the defendant's knowledge OR reckless disregard; 2) the structure of the text and other linguistic aspects support that reading; and 3) there are policy reasons why Congress would have chosen not to require knowledge and to require only reckless disregard. Therefore, the statute is sufficiently clear to make it inappropriate for the court to consider the rule of lenity. What reasoning can be used by the federal circuit court to choose the Government's interpretation?

G. Evidence Rules for Rape Prosecutions

1. Rape Trauma Syndrome Evidence

During the 1980s, prosecutors started to use the testimony of expert witnesses concerning "rape trauma syndrome." This evidence is widely used in rape trials today, and its relevance is based on its potential usefulness to explain post-rape victim behavior that may seem otherwise inexplicable to jurors. However, courts continue to confront the need to identify limits on expert testimony, in order to avoid the presentation of unreliable evidence and the danger that jurors will abandon their fact-finding responsibility by deferring to expert testimony. The *Kinney* case requires the court to articulate such limitations on expert testimony.

State v. Kinney

171 Vt. 239, 762 A.2d 833 (2000).

DOOLEY, J.

[The defendant was convicted of aggravated sexual assault. On appeal he argued that the trial court erred in admitting expert testimony about rape trauma syndrome. The defendant and the victim told conflicting stories at trial. The defendant testified that the victim consented at every turn—she allowed him to carry her to his car, traveled to a party with him and his friends, then traveled to his parents' house with him, went into his bedroom, got into bed, and had consensual sex. The victim testified that the defendant carried her to his car over her protests, dragged her to the house party, took her to his parents' home with the promise of driving her home from there, then took her to his own room and raped her. Afterwards she fell asleep, and when she woke up in the morning she asked again to be taken home, and he arranged for a ride.]

What's That?

An offer of proof is a procedure that occurs outside the presence of the jury, so that the trial judge can determine the admissibility of evidence. Here the prosecutor would have provided the judge with a description of Dr. Tyler's testimony, explained the purpose of the evidence, and provided legal arguments to support its admissibility.

[The] State called Dr. Jan Tyler to testify about rape trauma syndrome and the characteristics and conduct of rape victims. The admissibility of this testimony was first contested in pretrial proceedings when the State made an *offer of proof* indicating Dr. Tyler would testify about rape trauma syndrome and "the behavioral patterns of victims of sexual assault." The State noted that the expert witness would have no contact with the victim and would not offer an opinion on whether the victim was raped by defendant. [Defense counsel objected generally to the reliability and relevancy of Dr. Tyler's testimony and contended that it would impermissibly bolster the credibility of the victim. The trial court rejected the challenge and Dr. Tyler was allowed to testify. Defense counsel raised no objection to any specific part of Dr. Tyler's testimony when it was being given.]

Dr. Tyler testified that rape trauma syndrome is associated with post-traumatic stress disorder—that is, it is a set of behaviors and symptoms experienced by victims of trauma. She explained that victims of severe trauma commonly experience symptoms such as nightmares, anxiety, and fear as a result of the trauma. Victims of rape, in particular, may experience symptoms such as difficulty in interpersonal relationships, guilt, shame, and sexual dysfunction.

Dr. Tyler also testified that studies have shown that victims of rape are more likely to resist their attacker by making verbal protests than by struggling or screaming, and that victims are less likely to resist if force is used or threatened. Furthermore, she said that it is not unusual for victims to delay in reporting a rape, especially if the attacker is an acquaintance, and that a rape victim may be more likely to report to a friend first, rather than to someone with whom she is having an intimate relationship. This delay in reporting is related to the feelings of guilt and shame experienced due to the trauma of the rape. Dr. Tyler then testified to statistics regarding the rate of false reporting of rape. Finally, she testified that, although she had no statistics, she thought it would not be unusual for a victim of rape to fall asleep immediately after the assault, due to the physical exertion and psychological responses to the trauma such as denial and withdrawal. . . .

[We] acknowledge that we have never explicitly ruled upon the admissibility of evidence of rape trauma syndrome and the common behavior of adult rape victims[.] [The trial court] could find the evidence admissible because its reliability equals that of other technical evidence we have given trial courts the discretion to admit and the evaluation of other courts allowing admission of the evidence is complete and persuasive[.]

Food for Thought

For what purpose could a prosecutor use an expert witness like Dr. Tyler to testify about the ways that rape victims describe their experience to others, during the first few days after the sexual conduct occurs and then later, during the ensuing weeks and months?

We concur with the trial court that expert evidence of rape trauma syndrome and the associated typical behavior [of] rape victims is admissible to assist the jury in evaluating the evidence, and frequently to respond to defense claims that the victim's behavior after the alleged rape was inconsistent with the claim that the rape occurred. [T]he jury may be at a loss to understand the behavior of a rape victim. For example, the defense made much of the fact that defendant's parents were close by when the sexual contact took place but heard no signs of a struggle, that the victim appeared to be sleeping peacefully in defendant's bed the next morning, and that she failed to immediately tell her boyfriend she had been raped. Dr. Tyler's testimony explained why a rape victim might exhibit these behaviors.

For the purpose the evidence was used here, it is sufficiently reliable to be admitted. Rape trauma syndrome is professionally recognized as a type of post-traumatic stress disorder, and the behavioral characteristics of rape victims has been the subject of numerous professional studies. As the trial court noted in this case, Dr. Tyler was prepared to address some of the studies that formed the bases for her opinions if the defendant raised them in cross-examination.

We note that the evidence here was of a type that the danger of improper usage or excessive prejudice was at a minimum. The expert never interviewed the victim and offered no opinion whether the victim suffered from rape trauma syndrome or exhibited any of the behavior of a rape victim. Thus, there was little risk that Dr. Tyler would be seen [by the jury] as a truth detector.

We do not, however, have the same view of the expert's testimony about the incidence of false reporting by rape victims. The prosecutor asked Dr. Tyler whether "there are any data on the issue of false reporting that you are aware of?" She answered:

> False reporting, the percentages are very low. About two percent. That's about the same as any other crime that's committed. In other words, the number of people who would report a burglary that didn't happen is about the same as people who would report a rape, with one difference. The statistics for the rape include those reports that are made and then either withdrawn by the victim for whatever reason, either they were false or there's a fear of going through the legal system, or they're being pressured by other persons. Those also include reports that the police will not arrest on because they don't feel they have enough evidence. And they also include those that don't get to trial because the prosecutor feels it's not a winnable case. So when you get down to literal false reporting of this really never happened, it's very small.

In short, Dr. Tyler testified that at least 98% of the rapes reported actually occurred.

In *State v. Percy*, 146 Vt. [475,] 484, 507 A.2d [955,] 960 [(1986)], a rape case in which defendant claimed amnesia caused by insanity and consent of the victim, three psychiatrists testified for the State that rapists typically claim consent or amnesia. We reversed defendant's conviction in part because of the admission of this testimony. We concluded that explanations or excuses offered by other rapists were not relevant, and, in any event, the prejudicial effect of the testimony outweighed the probative value because the jury could have convicted defendant because "he fit the mold" and not because of the evidence in the case.

Similarly, in [*State v.*] *Catsam*, 148 Vt. [366,] 371, 534 A.2d [184,] 188 [(1987)], we found inadmissible an expert's opinion that child victims of sexual abuse do not make up stories of the abuse. As in this case, the evidence was offered as part of the expert's explanation of the typical behavior of victims. We concluded that the expert testimony was tantamount to an expert opinion that the victim was telling the truth and that it invaded the proper role of the jury.

Dr. Tyler's testimony on the rate of false reporting clearly went over the line as explained in *Percy* and *Catsam*. The jury could infer from her testimony that scientific studies have shown that almost no woman falsely claims to have been raped and convict defendant on that basis. . . . [However, the defense counsel's failure to object to this testimony meant that the defendant could not obtain a reversal of the conviction unless the admission of the expert's objectionable testimony was "plain error." A finding of "plain error" occurs "only in exceptional circumstances where the failure to recognize [the error] would result in a miscarriage of justice."]

[*State v. Weeks*, 160 Vt. 393 (1993), is] one case in which we did find plain error. In that case, the expert testified to the general behavior of sexual abuse victims and then went into the behavior of the victim in the criminal case before the court. We described his testimony as follows:

> [H]is testimony is a richly detailed roadmap of how he elicited and came to believe the [child victim's] allegations of abuse. From the outset, the jury knew, not only that he had personally examined the victim, but that he had tested her perceptions and credibility, and, that based on his conclusions, he reported the abuse and defendant as the perpetrator to the [state human services department]. He not only vouched for the victim's credibility but staked his professional reputation on it. When [he] was finished testifying, no one could reasonably doubt that he had given his unqualified endorsement to the [child victim's] believability.

This case exhibits none of the hallmarks of *Weeks*. Dr. Tyler never testified about the story or credibility of the victim because she had never interviewed, or even met, the victim. Her testimony was entirely theoretical[.] Further, defense counsel was able to reduce the prejudicial effect of the testimony of the low incidence of false reporting by cross-examination. Finally, the prosecutor did not highlight this testimony in closing argument.

We cannot conclude that failure to exclude the inadmissible expert testimony caused a miscarriage of justice in this case. Accordingly, we find no plain error[.]

Affirmed.

Points for Discussion

a. Truth Detectors

There are several limitations upon the use of expert testimony that are described approvingly in *Kinney*. How do they serve the goal of reducing the danger that the jurors will defer to the expert to such a degree that they will abandon their fact-finding role and treat the expert as the "truth detector"? Even though the prosecutor in *Kinney* was careful to abide by most of those limitations, the prosecutor did fail to stop the expert witness from making inadmissible statements that could have drawn an objection from defense counsel and caused the trial judge to declare a mistrial. What are the key factors that explain why the *Kinney* Court does not find the inadmissible statements to be "bad enough" to constitute "plain error" and require a new trial for the defendant?

b. "Syndrome" Evidence

State evidence codes allow expert testimony to be admissible on any subject "sufficiently beyond common experience that the opinion of an expert would assist the trier of fact." This evidence rule may be used by courts to justify the admission of expert testimony concerning the behavior of rape victims, both to dispel common misconceptions about how they behave and to allow the prosecutor to rehabilitate a rape victim's credibility if defense counsel argues that the victim's conduct is inconsistent with the claim of rape. As the *Kinney* Court explains, such testimony may not be used by a prosecutor to prove the elements of the crime. The purpose of the expert's testimony is to provide information about the potential effects of trauma that may be experienced by victims generally, so that informed jurors may evaluate the victim's behavior based on that information. Given the fact that the purpose of expert testimony is *not* to provide a diagnosis of the victim, some courts have recognized that the admissibility of such testimony "does not depend on a showing based on a recognized 'syndrome.'" *See People v. Brown*, 33 Cal. 4th 892, 905–06, 16 Cal.Rptr.3d 447, 94 P.3d 574 (2004).

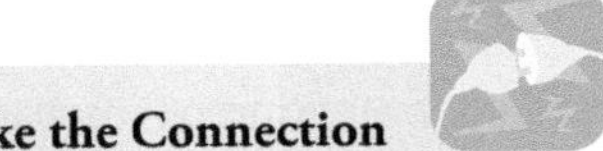

Make the Connection

The role of expert testimony to describe "the experience and effects of battering" (formerly called "battered women's syndrome" testimony), to support a defendant's plea of self-defense, is presented in Chapter 12 on Justification Defenses.

Hypo: *Expert Witness*

Assume you are a prosecutor in Vermont who is preparing an expert witness who will testify about rape trauma syndrome. Explain to your expert what kinds of testimony may be presented and what testimony must be avoided according to *Kinney*. Now assume you are a defense counsel in Vermont who is preparing to cross-examine an expert witness who will testify about rape trauma syndrome. What questions will you ask in order to attempt to cast doubt on the testimony? What testimony will provoke you to object?

---

2. Rape Shield Laws

The first rape shield statute was part of the 1975 Michigan rape reform statute; within three years of its enactment, 30 states had adopted such laws and Congress adopted Federal Rule 412. All states now use some type of rape shield law, and many of them based on the Michigan model. Rape shield laws eliminate the common law presumption that a victim's prior sexual conduct is relevant to prove her lack of credibility and willingness to consent to forcible sex. The opposite presumption, that such evidence is not generally relevant in a rape trial, is expressed in rape shield laws, either through a statutory list of exclusions and exceptions or through the delegation of case-by-case determinations of relevancy to the discretion of trial judges. Both types of rape shield laws require that even non-excluded evidence will not be admissible unless its probative value outweighs its potential prejudicial effect. When defendants challenge the exclusion of rape-shield evidence as a violation of their Sixth Amendment rights to fair trial and confrontation of witnesses, courts will apply specific interpretations of these rights that have been established in the rape-shield context. The complexity and variety of state and federal rape shield rules has spawned a constant stream of litigation and continuing legislative change.

a. Goals of Rape Shield Laws

The main goal of rape shield laws is "to prevent a sexual assault trial from degenerating into an attack upon the [victim's] reputation rather than focusing on the relevant legal issues[.]" *Commonwealth v. Jones*, 826 A.2d 900 (Pa. Super. 2003). In *State v. Sheline*, 955 S.W.2d 42, 44–45 (Tenn. 1997), the court summarized the relevant policy concerns as follows:

> Rape shield laws were adopted in response to anachronistic and sexist views that a woman who had sexual relations in the past was more likely to have consented to sexual relations with a specific criminal defendant. Those attitudes resulted in two rape trials at the same time—the trial of the defendant and the trial of the rape victim based on her past sexual conduct. It has been said that the victim of a sexual assault is assaulted twice—once by the criminal justice system. The protections in rape shield laws recognized that intrusions into the irrelevant sexual history of a victim were not only prejudicial and embarrassing but also a practical barrier to many victims reporting sexual crimes.

FYI

In an Article 32 proceeding in the military, which helps "to determine whether cases are sent to courts-martial," no rape shield law prevents defense counsel from cross-examining a soldier-victim in a sexual assault case. *See* http://www.nytimes.com/2013/09/21/us/intrusive-grilling-in-rape-case-raises-alarm-on-military-hearings.html?pagewanted=all. According to one 2017 report, "overall prosecution rates of military sexual assault cases remain flat," and "six out of 10 survivors report[ed] that they had been retaliated against." See http://thehill.com/policy/defense/349672-dem-senator-military-sexual-assault-as-pervasive-as-ever.

The presumption that sexual history evidence will cause the jury to be unfairly prejudiced against the victim and the prosecution derives from the experience of prosecutors in the pre-reform era. Studies of rape reforms report judges, prosecutors, and defense attorneys typically view rape shield laws as the reform with the most significant impact, in terms of enhancing the prosecutor's opportunity to obtain rape convictions. *See, e.g.*, JEANNE C. MARSH, ALISON GEIST, & NATHAN CAPLAN, RAPE AND THE LIMITS OF LAW REFORM. 59–65 (1982); CASSIA SPOHN & JULIE HORNEY, RAPE LAW REFORM: A GRASSROOTS REVOLUTION AND ITS IMPACT (1992).

b. Exclusions & Exceptions

The "exclusions and exceptions" model of rape shield laws is illustrated by Federal Rule of Evidence 412. The Rule defines "generally inadmissible evidence" to include: (1) evidence offered to prove that any alleged victim engaged in any sexual behavior; and (2) evidence offered to prove any alleged victim's sexual disposition. The Rule also provides for these exceptions: A) a "specific instance of sexual behavior" by the victim to prove that a person other than the accused was the source of semen, injury, or other physical evidence; B) a "specific instance of sexual behavior" by the victim with respect to the person accused of the sexual misconduct, offered by the accused to prove consent or by the prosecution; C) evidence the exclusion of which would violate the constitutional rights of the defendant. Almost half the states use a similar model, but a substantial minority use a case-by-case approach that requires trial judges to weigh the probative value of the evidence against the prejudicial impact of the evidence on the jury.

c. Prior Sexual Conduct

In 1994, the term "prior sexual conduct" in Federal Rule 412 was amended to replace the word "conduct" with "behavior." According to the Advisory Committee Notes, "prior sexual behavior" of the victim "connotes all activities that involve actual physical conduct" and "the word 'behavior' should be construed to include activities of the mind, such as fantasies or dreams." In arguing that the term "prior sexual conduct" in a statute should be interpreted to emulate the federal definition of "prior sexual behavior," one judge reasoned as follows:

> As recently as 1970, *Wigmore on Evidence* suggested that every woman who claimed she had been raped should be subjected to a psychological evaluation. The reason for this claim was, "The unchaste (let us call it) mentality finds incidental but direct expression in the narration of imaginary sex incidents of which the narrator is the heroine or victim." [This] language suggests the attitude that some women accuse men of rape because they have conflated sexual fantasy with criminal violence.
>
> The Rape Shield Statute represents an express rejection of such attitudes. We now recognize the scarring effects of sexual assault, and the burden placed on victims by testifying about such a deeply personal invasion. [E]vidence of past sexual acts with others has little probative value of whether a victim consented to have sex with a defendant in the present [and] this lack of probative force extends to evidence about a victim's sexual fantasies. Requiring a victim to testify about sexual fantasies can be as intrusive as testifying about prior sexual acts.

People v. Garcia, 179 P.3d 250, 261 (Colo. App. 2007) (Bernard, J., specially concurring). However, the *Garcia* majority rejected this argument because "[the] fantasy could be established without revealing whether the victim had ever acted it out" and so inquiry into such statements would not subject the victim "to a fishing expedition into her past sexual conduct." State courts remain divided as to whether prior sexual "conduct" or "behavior" should include oral or written statements about previous sexual activity, sexual thoughts or sexual fantasies.

d. Sixth Amendment Challenges

In *Michigan v. Lucas*, 500 U.S. 145 (1991), the Court determined that case-by-case determinations are required to decide whether the exclusion of evidence under a rape shield statute violates the Sixth Amendment right to confrontation. For example, Federal Rule 412 requires a defendant to give notice 15 days before trial regarding rape-shield-related evidence that the defendant will seek to introduce at trial. In *LaJoie v. Thompson*, 217 F.3d 663 (9th Cir. 2000), the court exercised the discretion allowed by *Lucas* and held on the facts that the trial judge violated the Sixth Amendment by excluding evidence submitted after the deadline that was otherwise admissible under the rape shield statute. Some courts use a five-factor test to determine whether evidence that violates a rape shield law should be admissible under the Sixth Amendment: 1) whether there is a clear showing that the complainant committed the prior acts; 2) whether the circumstances of the prior acts closely resemble those of the present case; 3) whether the prior acts are clearly relevant to a material issue, such as identity, intent, or bias; 4) whether the evidence is necessary to the defendant's case; 5) whether the probative value of the evidence outweighs its prejudicial effect. *See, e.g., State v. Harris*, 272 Wis. 2d 80, 680 N.W.2d 737 (2004).

Hypo: *Self-Representation*

Assume that a 58-year-old defendant is charged with sexual assault upon a 15-year-old female victim based on evidence that includes her statements and the results of a medical examination. The defendant was granted the right to proceed *pro se* based on his timely request and he was subsequently released on bail. One condition of bail was that he should have no contact with the victim. When the victim reported that he called her multiple times and phone records corroborated this fact, the defendant's bail was revoked. At trial, the defendant asked to cross-examine the victim personally in exercising his right to self-representation. When the trial court denied his request, the defendant argued that this decision violated his Sixth Amendment right to confrontation. Did the trial judge violate either of the defendant's Sixth Amendment rights? If the defendant is prohibited from conducting the cross-examination, who will perform this task? *See Commonwealth v. Tight*, 224 A.3d 1268 (Pa. 2020).

Executive Summary

Force, Threat, or Fear. Modern statutes and decisions recognize that force or threat of force are unnecessary for conviction, because rape may be committed when accomplished by conduct creating fear of bodily injury when there is evidence that the victim's fear is genuine and reasonable.

Lack of Consent. When lack of consent is an element of rape, modern courts recognize that it may be expressed through the victim's words or conduct, and that evidence of verbal resistance may be sufficient. Where consent is defined as freely given and affirmative agreement, the absence of such agreement is evidence of lack of consent.

Affirmative Defense of Consent. Even when the lack of consent element is not present in a rape statute, courts may recognize the affirmative defense of consent. The defendant must have a reasonable belief in such consent and may bear the burden of persuasion because this affirmative defense does not negate an element of the crime.

***Mens Rea* and Mistake of Fact.** When lack of consent is an element of the rape crime, the "mistake of fact as to consent" defense may be recognized in statute or case law. Courts require the defendant's mistake to be reasonable and based on good faith, which means that the mental state of negligence is required for the lack of consent element. The prosecution bears the burden of persuasion and must rebut the mistake defense beyond a reasonable doubt because this defense seeks to negate an element of the crime.

Major Themes

a. Common Law Rape Crime—Before the rape reform era, most state codes and case law used definitions of rape that included the conduct of sexual intercourse by genital penetration by a man with a woman not his wife, through the use of force or by threat of force, without the consent of the victim. The victim's "utmost resistance" to this act was required. It was difficult to obtain convictions because of special evidence rules, jury attitudes toward victims and defendants, and appellate court reversals of convictions based on sufficiency-of-the-evidence formulas that reflected lack of deference to jury fact-finding concerning the credibility of victims and defendants.

b. Rape Reforms—The rape reform era began in 1975 with the enactment of the Michigan rape statute. In the ensuing decades, there were widespread changes in the law of rape, including the relabeling of the crime as sexual assault, the redefinition of the elements of the forcible rape crime, the enactment of crimes involving additional types of sexual conduct, the enactment of gender neutral statutes, the abolition of the marital rape exemption, and the abandonment of special evidence rules that created barriers to conviction. Appellate courts began to defer to jury fact-finding on credibility issues, and to affirm convictions in cases that could not have been prosecuted in the pre-reform era.

Rape by Deception. Some states have enacted statutory definitions of this crime. But courts continue to define it narrowly to include only cases where the defendant's "fraud" caused the victim to be ignorant of the fact that the defendant performed sexual intercourse upon the victim.

Rape of Drugged or Intoxicated Victim. Both the common law and modern statutes define rape to include sexual intercourse with a sleeping, unconscious, or drugged victim, who necessarily lacks the capacity to consent. A defendant can be convicted when he administered drugs to an unknowing victim that caused the lack of capacity to consent.

Statutory Rape. Most states use gender neutral statutes with age-gap provisions to confer immunity on teenagers who are close in age and engage in consensual sex. Some states recognize the "mistake of fact as to age" defense.

Rape Trauma Syndrome. An expert witness may provide testimony to describe the behavior of rape victims in order to dispel the misconceptions of jurors about such behavior, and in order to rehabilitate a rape victim's credibility when defense counsel argues that the victim's behavior is not consistent with the claim of rape.

Rape Shield Laws. These laws create general prohibitions on the admission of evidence regarding prior sexual conduct of the victim in rape prosecutions, with exceptions made for particular types of evidence that is deemed to be probative concerning the elements of the crime.

For More Information

- American Law Institute, Model Penal Code and Commentaries, Part II, §§ 221.0–221.1, 222.1, 223.0–223.7, Comments at 60–84, 96–121, 122–255 (1980).
- John M. Burkoff & Russell L. Weaver, Inside Criminal Law: What Matters and Why 167–184 (2d ed. 2011).
- Wayne R. LaFave, Criminal Law § 17.1–17.5 (5th ed. 2010).

Test Your Knowledge

To assess your understanding of the material in this chapter, click here to take a quiz.

Chapter 11

Property Crimes

The roots of the modern law of property crimes lie in the fifteenth century when English judges invented the crimes of larceny and larceny by trick. Although the judges were willing to use legal fictions to expand the original larceny crime to some degree, it required legislation by Parliament to create the crimes of embezzlement and false pretenses in the late eighteenth century. These four crimes were codified only by name in early state criminal codes and their elements were defined by precedents. The same was true for other English property crimes, including receiving stolen property, robbery, and burglary. Today most states use some version of the Model Penal Code (MPC) provisions on theft crimes, which are widely regarded as one of the most significant and successful MPC reforms. Yet some state codes retain the definitions of common law property crimes, and some codes blend these old definitions together with MPC elements.

The broad goals of the MPC drafters mirror those of the English judges whose opinions helped to expand the scope of larceny to encompass new harms that came to be recognized by society. The most significant revisions of the common law crimes occurred in the MPC's merger of larceny, larceny by trick, and embezzlement into the new crime of "theft by unlawful taking or disposition," and in the revision of the false pretenses crime into the new crime of "theft by deception." These innovative crimes abandoned many of the common law elements that had become anachronistic technicalities, thereby both simplifying and broadening the modern definitions of "theft." The same goals also characterize the MPC's expanded versions of the crimes of receiving stolen goods and robbery, and the MPC version of burglary crime is exceptional in embodying the goal of staying closer to the original common law definition.

In this chapter, the evolution of the elements of the seven most important common law property crimes will be studied in order to show how the original definitions influenced the elements of their modern descendants. In addition, the modern crime of carjacking will be examined as an illustration of the evolution of the robbery crime. The chapter begins with two cases involving the federal crime of interstate transportation of stolen property in order to illustrate the difficulties inherent in defining the taking of "property" that may be subject to a criminal prosecution.

A. Property Subject to Theft

Definitions of "property" that is subject to theft have changed over time as new forms of property have been recognized by legislatures and courts. Yet the unpredictable evolution of technology has created an endless stream of issues for courts charged with the task of interpreting the meaning of "property" in particular statutory contexts. The *Farraj* and *Aleynikov* cases illustrate how it is necessary for courts to interpret legislative intent when determining whether to apply the term "goods" to intangible property, such as a stolen document sent via email or stolen computer source code.

United States v. Farraj

142 F. Supp. 2d 484 (S.D.N.Y. 2001).

MARRERO, DISTRICT JUDGE.

[Said Farraj is charged with crimes including one count of] interstate transportation of stolen property in violation of 18 U.S.C. § 2314[.] [He] now moves [to] dismiss [the count charging this crime] on the ground that the allegedly stolen property does not fall within the scope of § 2314[.] For the reasons discussed below, the [motion is] denied.

In [the] summer of 2000, Said Farraj was a paralegal with the [Manhattan] law firm of Orrick, Harrington & Sutcliffe LLP. At the time, Orrick represented plaintiffs in a *class action tobacco case*[.] [*See Falise v. American Tobacco Co.*, 94 F. Supp. 2d 316 (E.D.N.Y. 2000).] In preparation for the *Falise* trial, the attorneys and paralegals at Orrick created a trial plan ["Trial Plan"], "exceed[ing] 400 pages and includ[ing], among other things, trial strategy, deposition excerpts and summaries, and references to anticipated trial exhibits." Only Orrick employees assigned to *Falise* were permitted access to the Trial Plan. [Farraj was included among such employees].

What's That?

Class action tort suits were brought by plaintiff smokers against tobacco companies, after the FDA obtained evidence in the early 1990s that company executives knew for years that nicotine in cigarettes was habit-forming, while publicly denying such knowledge.

The Government charges that [Farraj], using the moniker "FlyGuyNYt," e-mailed an 80-page excerpt of the Trial Plan [on June 17, 2000] to the *Falise* defendants' attorneys [located in five states] and offered to sell them the entire Plan. An FBI agent posing as one of the *Falise* defendants' attorneys negotiated with [Farraj] via email and ultimately agreed to purchase the Trial Plan for $2 million. On July 21, 2000, [the defendant's brother] met with a second undercover FBI agent at a McDonald's restaurant in lower Manhattan to receive payment. [The brother] was arrested then and gave a statement to the FBI implicating [the defendant].

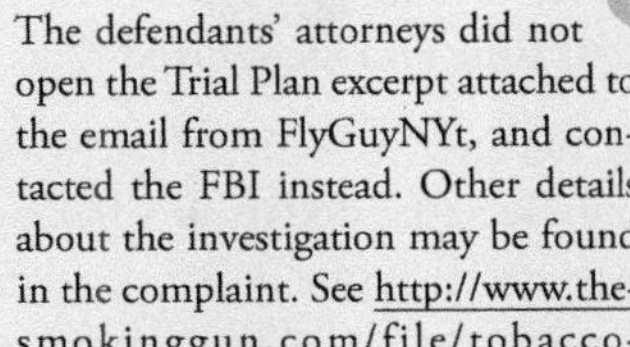

The defendants' attorneys did not open the Trial Plan excerpt attached to the email from FlyGuyNYt, and contacted the FBI instead. Other details about the investigation may be found in the complaint. See http://www.thesmokinggun.com/file/tobacco-scheme-goes-smoke-0.

The Government charges [that] by e-mailing the Trial Plan excerpt across state lines, [Farraj] violated [the National Stolen Property Act], which provides [that] "[w]hoever transports, transmits, or transfers in interstate or foreign commerce any goods, wares, merchandise, securities, or money, of the value of $5,000 or more, knowing the same to have been stolen, converted, or taken by fraud . . . shall be fined under this title or imprisoned [up to ten years]." [Farraj] moves to dismiss, arguing that § 2314 applies only to the physical asportation of tangible goods or currency, not to "information" stored and transmitted electronically, such as the Trial Plan excerpt e-mailed here. Neither the Supreme Court nor the Second Circuit has addressed this question directly, and this appears to be an issue of first impression in this District.

[The] Second Circuit has held that the phrase "goods, wares, or merchandise" is "a general and comprehensive designation of such personal property or chattels as are ordinarily a subject of commerce." *In re Vericker*, 446 F.2d 244, 248 (2d Cir. 1971) (Friendly, J.). The Second Circuit has at times determined that [paper] documents fall outside the scope of § 2314. At other times, however, the Second Circuit and other courts have held that documents may be considered "goods, wares, [or] merchandise" under § 2314. *See, e.g., United States v. Greenwald*, 479 F.2d 320 (6th Cir. 1973) (documents containing secret chemical formulae); *United States v. Bottone*, 365 F.2d 389 (2d Cir. 1966) (drug manufacturing processes); *United States v. Seagraves*, 265 F.2d 876 (3d Cir. 1966) (geophysical maps).

The FBI documents at issue in *Vericker* detailed the criminal activity of certain individuals. Judge Friendly reasoned that the FBI documents were not "goods, wares, [or] merchandise" within the meaning of [§ 2314] because the substance contained in the documents was not ordinarily the subject of commerce. The Trial Plan at issue here, however, [was] the work product of a business relationship between client and attorney, and may thus be viewed as an ordinary subject of commerce, created for a commercial purpose and carrying inherent commercial value at least as to the persons directly interested in the matter.

[Farraj] argues that even if trial plans generally may be viewed as goods under § 2314, he is accused of transmitting an "intangible," an electronic form of the document, and therefore that it was not a good, but merely "information."

The text of § 2314 makes no distinction between tangible and intangible property, or between electronic and other manner of transfer across state lines. Indeed, in 1988, Congress amended § 2314 to include the term[s] "transmits" [or "transfers"] to reflect its agreement with the Second Circuit and other courts which had held that § 2314 applied to money wire transfers, where the only interstate transportation took place electronically and where there was no transportation of any physical item. *See* Anti-Drug Abuse Act of 1988, § 7507(a), 134

Cong. Reg. S17367, S17370 (statement of Sen. Biden) (citing *United States v. Gilboe*, 684 F.2d 235 (2d Cir. 1982)[.]) In *Gilboe*, the Second Circuit addressed the issue of electronic transfer for the first time and recognized that

> the manner in which funds were moved does not affect the ability to obtain tangible paper dollars or a bank check from the receiving account. . . . Indeed, we suspect that actual dollars rarely move between banks, particularly in international transactions. . . . The primary element of this offense, transportation, "does not require proof that any specific means of transporting were used."

684 F.2d at 238 (quoting *Pereira v. United States*, 347 U.S. 1, 9, 74 S. Ct. 358, 98 L.Ed. 435 (1954)).

The Second Circuit has also held that § 2314 was violated when the defendants stole documents containing some drug manufacturing process, copied and returned them, and then sent the copies abroad. The court noted that it did not matter that the item stolen was not the same as that transported. Rather, as observed by Judge Friendly [in *Bottone*, 365 F.2d at 394]:

> where the physical form of the stolen goods is secondary in every respect to the matter recorded in them, the transformation of the information in the stolen papers into a tangible object never possessed by the original owner should be deemed immaterial. It would offend common sense to hold that these defendants fall outside the statute simply because, in efforts to avoid detection, their confederates were at pains to restore the original papers to [the employer] and transport only copies or notes[.]

Relying in part on the Second Circuit's decisions in *Gilboe* and *Bottone*, the court in *United States v. Riggs*, 739 F. Supp. 414 (N.D.Ill. 1990), held that the defendant violated § 2314 when he downloaded a text file containing proprietary information onto a home computer [and] transferred it over a computer network to his co-defendant in another state, who then uploaded it onto a computer bulletin board. The court reasoned that just because the defendant stored the information on a computer, rather than printing it on paper, his acts were not removed from the purview of the statute:

> [I]n the instant case, if the information in [the] text file had been affixed to a floppy disk, or printed out on a computer printer, then [the defendant's] transfer of that information across state lines would clearly constitute the transfer of "goods, wares, or merchandise" within the meaning of § 2314. This court sees no reason to hold differently simply because [the defendant] stored the information inside a computer instead of printing it out on paper. In either case, the information is in a transferable, accessible, even salable form.

Take Note

For information about the *Farraj* defendant's subsequent guilty plea and sentence, see the DOJ report at http://www.justice.gov/archive/criminal/cybercrime/press-releases/2002/farrajSentence.htm.

Id. at 421. The court noted that "[r]eading a tangibility requirement into the definition of 'goods, wares, or merchandise' might unduly restrict the scope of § 2314, especially in this modern technological age," and recognized that although not tangible in a conventional sense, the stolen property was physically stored on a computer hard drive and could be viewed and printed out with the push of a button. *See id.* at 422[.]

[Weighing] the scant authority at hand, the Court is persuaded that the view most closely analogous to Second Circuit doctrine is that which holds that the transfer of electronic documents via the internet across state lines does fall within the purview of § 2314. The indictment is therefore upheld and the motion to dismiss [the count charged under § 2314] is denied.

Points for Discussion

a. Common Law Limitations on "Property"

In the fifteenth century, English judges took on the task of defining the elements of the earliest property crime, which they called "larceny." Their view was that only "tangible" personal property ("personalty") needed to be protected by the criminal law, such as livestock, harvested crops, and weapons of war. This is why they defined the larceny crime to punish the act of "taking and carrying away" such property. The judges did not define larceny to cover the taking of property that they viewed as having little or no value, such as wild and domesticated animals. They also decided that land ("realty") could "safely be excluded" from the larceny crime because it was "immovable," "fairly indestructible," and difficult to take and carry away. The judges also excluded things attached to land, such as growing crops and "fixtures." *See* Model Penal Code § 223.2, Comment 3, at 166–167 (1980). During the ensuing centuries, Parliament enacted statutes that defined specific types of "property" as being subject to larceny prosecutions. Some of these things had been excluded by earlier judicial decisions, whereas other things represented new forms of wealth. The early American state larceny statutes imitated the English statutes, and preserved the tradition of creating miscellaneous collections of "property" examples.

b. Updating "Property" Definitions

When a statutory definition of "property" consists of an exclusive list of examples, it is necessary for the legislature to keep adding examples to protect new forms of property. Here is an example of an evolving list in a Massachusetts statute (Mass. Gen. Laws. Ann. Ch. 266, § 30(2)):

> The term "property" . . . shall include money, personal chattels, a bank note, bond, promissory note, bill of exchange or other bill, order or certificate, a book of accounts for or concerning money or goods due or to become due or to be delivered, a deed or writing containing a conveyance of land, any valuable contract in force, a receipt, release or defeasance, a writ, process, certificate of title or duplicate certificate [issued under ch. 185], a public record, anything which is of the realty

or is annexed thereto, a security deposit received [pursuant to § 15B, ch. 196], electronically processed or stored data, either tangible or intangible, data while in transit, telecommunications services, and any domesticated animal, including dogs, or a beast or bird which is ordinarily kept in confinement.

Two of these statutory examples of "property"—"domesticated animals" and "anything which is of the realty or is annexed thereto"—are derived from an earlier Massachusetts statute that expanded the English judge-made definition of "property." Yet it was not until 1987 that the legislature amended the statute to add the phrase "including dogs." Before 1987, the statute only described the "beast or bird" category. More predictably, the terms "electronically processed or stored data" were added in 1983 and "telecommunications services" was added in 1995.

Whenever a court identifies a gap in a statutory list of property examples, it is traditional for the court to dismiss a prosecution involving the omitted type of property and declare that the legislature should decide whether or not to amend the statute to fill that gap. Note that a court identified the "release of the right to money" as not covered by the Massachusetts statute in *Commonwealth v. Mills*, 51 Mass. App. Ct. 366, 371–372, 745 N.E.2d 981, 987 (2001). But the legislature has not yet amended the statute to add that type of property.

The National Stolen Property Act (NSPA) in *Farraj* describes an exclusive list of property examples: "goods, wares, merchandise, securities, or money." One solution for the statutory interpretation problem in *Farraj* was for the trial judge to dismiss the prosecution and declare that Congress should decide whether to amend the statute to add the words, "tangible or intangible," before the term "goods." What reasons may explain why other courts might prefer to adopt this solution instead of endorsing the *Farraj* interpretation of the statute?

c. Model Penal Code Approach

The MPC defines "property" in § 223.0(6) as "anything of value." This phrase is followed by a list of illustrative (not exclusive) examples, in order to make it clear that particular types of property, which were excluded under English law, qualify as a thing of value. This illustrative list includes: real estate, tangible and intangible personal property, contract rights, choses-in-action and other interests in or claims to wealth, admission or transportation tickets, captured or domestic animals, food and drink, [and] electric or other power." Note that in 1962, the term "intangible personal property" meant a legally enforceable property right, which might or might not be expressed in a document. The term "thing of value" had been used in some federal and state statutes that recognized a broad definition of property in the pre-MPC era. What does the absence of this term in the NSPA suggest regarding the likely Congressional intent concerning its application to the *Farraj* defendant's conduct?

FYI

The MPC defines the term "property" broadly as "anything of value," in order to insure it will "include anything that is part of one person's wealth that another person can appropriate." Model Penal Code § 223.2, Comment 3, at 167 (1980).

d. Intangible Information as "Goods"

The National Stolen Property Act was enacted in 1934 as an "extension of the National Motor Vehicle Theft Act," which was enacted in 1919. That earlier statute "was an attempt to supplement the efforts of the States to combat automobile thefts," "[p]articularly in areas close to state lines, [where] state law enforcement authorities were seriously hampered by car thieves' ability to transport stolen vehicles beyond the jurisdiction in which the theft occurred." *Dowling v. United States*, 473 U.S. 207, 218–219 (1986). The NSPA does not define the terms "goods," "wares," "merchandise," or "money," but the statute does use a list of more than 25 exclusive examples to define the term "security." The *Farraj* case did not make new law in holding that a paper copy of the Trial Plan would qualify as "ordinarily the subject of commerce." This is because other federal precedents recognized that stolen documents containing confidential business information may qualify as "goods," as long as "a market, legal or otherwise, exists" for that information. But the *Farraj* case did make new law in holding that the NSPA could be applied to intangible information.

How does the trial judge in *Farraj* use the existing federal precedents and the legislative history of the 1988 amendment to support the expansion of the term "goods" to include information conveyed in an electronic format? Does the opinion indicate that there are any limits to the use of the NSPA statute to punish interstate transmission of e-information, as long as it carries "inherent commercial value"? For example, does a violation of the NSPA occur when "a crook in Chicago" provides a telephone tip "to one in San Francisco," which consists of the information that "by posing as a police officer, [the Chicago crook has] learned the Wells Fargo bank in San Francisco is poorly protected and so can be knocked off easily?" *See United States v. Stafford*, 136 F.3d 1109, 1113–1114 (7th Cir. 1998). What reasons may explain why virtually no other federal court after *Farraj* approved the extension of the NSPA to stolen intangible information? When the S.D.N.Y. U.S. Attorney's Office brought a NSPA prosecution in 2009 based on the *Farraj* theory, the *Aleynikov* decision was the result.

e. Computer Crimes

The *Farraj* defendant faced an additional charge under the federal Computer Fraud and Abuse Act (CFAA), 18 U.S.C. § 1030(a). There are seven CFAA crimes, and ultimately the defendant pled guilty to one of them, "unauthorized computer access" under § 1030(a)(3). Since the enactment of CFAA in 1984, "Congress has steadily increased the breadth of the coverage" of this statute, which "in practical terms, [now] protects all computers that are used in interstate communication." *See* A. HUGH SCOTT, COMPUTER AND INTELLECTUAL PROPERTY CRIME: FEDERAL AND STATE LAW 4–3, 4–4 (Cumulative Supplement) (2006).

United States v. Aleynikov

676 F.3d 71 (2d Cir. 2012).

Before JACOBS, CHIEF JUDGE, CALABRESI and POOLER, CIRCUIT JUDGES.

JACOBS, CHIEF JUDGE:

Sergey Aleynikov was convicted [of] stealing and transferring some of the proprietary computer source code used in his employer's high frequency trading system, in violation of the National Stolen Property Act, 18 U.S.C. § 2314 (the "NSPA")[.] On appeal, Aleynikov argues [that] his conduct did not constitute an offense [because] the source code was not a "stolen" "good" within the meaning of the NSPA[.] We agree, and reverse the judgment of the district court.

> **FYI**
>
> Immediately after hearing oral argument, the Second Circuit issued an order reversing the conviction in *Aleynikov*, and the opinion followed two months later. *See* https://en.wikipedia.org/wiki/Sergey_Aleynikov.

Sergey Aleynikov, a computer programmer, was employed by Goldman Sachs & Co. ("Goldman") from May 2007 through June 2009, developing computer source code for the comp any's proprietary high-frequency trading ("HFT") system. An HFT system is a mechanism for making large volumes of trades in securities and commodities based on trading decisions effected in fractions of a second. Trades are executed on the basis of algorithms that incorporate rapid market developments and data from past trades. The computer programs used to operate Goldman's HFT system are of three kinds: [1] market connectivity programs that process real-time market data and execute trades; [2] programs that use algorithms to determine which trades to make; and [3] infrastructure programs that facilitate the flow of information throughout the trading system and monitor the system's performance. Aleynikov's work focused on developing code [for] infrastructure programs[.] High frequency trading is a competitive business that depends in large part on the speed with which information can be processed to seize fleeting market opportunities. Goldman closely guards the secrecy of each component of the system, and does not license the system to anyone. Goldman's confidentiality policies bound Aleynikov to keep in strict confidence all the firm's proprietary information, including any intellectual property created by Aleynikov. He was barred as well from taking it or using it when his employment ended.

By 2009, Aleynikov was earning $400,000, the highest-paid of the twenty-five programmers in his group. In April 2009, he accepted an offer to become an Executive Vice President at Teza Technologies LLC, a Chicago-based startup that was looking to develop its own HFT system. Aleynikov was hired, at over $1 million a year, to develop the market connectivity and infrastructure components of Teza's HFT system. Teza's founder [emailed] Aleynikov [in] late May, conveying his expectation that they would develop a functional trading system within six months. It usually takes years for a team of programmers to develop an HFT system from scratch.

Aleynikov's last day at Goldman was June 5, 2009. At approximately 5:20 p.m., just before his going-away party, Aleynikov encrypted and uploaded to a server in Germany more than 500,000 lines of source code for Goldman's HFT system, including code for a substantial part of the infrastructure, and some of the algorithms and market data connectivity programs. [Most of the uploaded files contained Goldman's proprietary code and some files also included open source software.] Some of the code pertained to programs that could operate independently of the rest of the Goldman system and could be integrated into a competitor's system. After uploading the source code, Aleynikov deleted the encryption program as well as the history of his computer commands. When he returned to his home in New Jersey, Aleynikov downloaded the source code from the server in Germany to his home computer, and copied some of the files to other computer devices he owned.

On July 2, 2009, Aleynikov flew from New Jersey to Chicago to attend meetings at Teza. He brought with him a flash drive and a laptop containing portions of the Goldman source code. When Aleynikov flew back the following day, he was arrested by the FBI at Newark Liberty International Airport.

[Aleynikov] moved to dismiss the indictment for failure to state an offense. The district court denied Aleynikov's motion. [737 F. Supp. 2d 173, 186–190 (S.D.N.Y. 2010).] [First, the] court held that the source code for Goldman's HFT system constitute[d] "goods" that were "stolen" within the meaning of the NSPA because, [it] "contains highly confidential trade secrets related to the Trading System" that "would be valuable for any firm seeking to launch, or enhance, a high-frequency trading business." [Thus, the source code qualified as property that is "ordinarily a subject of commerce." Second, the court rejected Aleynikov's argument that the NSPA does not apply to "intangible intellectual property." The intangible source code was "in human-readable format," and Aleynikov conceded that a printout of the code would constitute "goods." The court observed that the electronic version of the source code was "much more commercially valuable than a hard copy," and then relied on *Farraj*'s reasoning in holding that anyone who "transmits" or "transfers" stolen property violates § 2314, "even if the mode of such transmission or transfer is not physical."]

Food for Thought

Under 18 U.S.C. § 1030(a)(3), the crime of "unauthorized computer access" applies to anyone who "intentionally accesses a computer without authorization or exceeds authorized access, and thereby obtains . . . information from any protected computer if the conduct involved an interstate or foreign communication." Did Aleynikov commit this crime?

The jury convicted Aleynikov[.] He was sentenced to 97 months of imprisonment followed by a three-year term of supervised release, and was ordered to pay a $12,500 fine[.] Aleynikov appealed his conviction and sentence, arguing [that] the district court erred in denying his motion to dismiss the indictment[.] [He served one year in prison pending appeal.]

The decisive question is whether the source code that Aleynikov uploaded to a server in Germany, then downloaded to his computer devices in New Jersey, and later transferred to Illinois, constituted stolen "goods," "wares," or "merchandise" within the meaning of the

NSPA. Based on the substantial weight of the case law, as well as the ordinary meaning of the words, we conclude that it did not.

We first considered the applicability of the NSPA to the theft of intellectual property in *United States v. Bottone,* 365 F.2d 389 (2d Cir. 1966) (Friendly, J.), in which photocopied documents outlining manufacturing procedures for certain pharmaceuticals were transported across state lines. Since the actual processes themselves (as opposed to photocopies) were never transported across state lines, the "serious question" (we explained) was whether "the papers showing [the] processes that were transported in interstate or foreign commerce were 'goods' which had been 'stolen, converted or taken by fraud' in view of the lack of proof that any of the physical materials so transported came from [the manufacturer's] possession." We held that the NSPA was violated there, observing that what was "stolen and transported" was, ultimately, "tangible goods," notwithstanding the "clever intermediate transcription [and] use of a photocopy machine." However, we suggested that a different result would obtain if there was no physical taking of tangible property whatsoever: "To be sure, where no tangible objects were ever taken or transported, a court would be hard pressed to conclude that 'goods' had been stolen and transported within the meaning of 2314." Hence, we observed, "the statute would presumably not extend to the case where a carefully guarded secret formula was memorized, carried away in the recesses of a thievish mind and placed in writing only after a boundary had been crossed." *Bottone* itself thus treats its holding as the furthest limit of a statute that is not endlessly elastic: Some tangible property must be taken from the owner for there to be deemed a "good" that is "stolen" for purposes of the NSPA.

[T]he Seventh Circuit has held that numerical "Comdata codes" used by truckers to access money transfers at truck stops constitute intangible property the theft of which is not a violation of the NSPA. *United States v. Stafford,* 136 F.3d 1109 (7th Cir. 1998) [(where the defendant was assumed to have transmitted the stolen codes to a confederate during an interstate telephone conversation)]. The court reasoned that the codes themselves were not "goods, wares, or merchandise," but rather "information"; that the defendant had not been charged with transporting pieces of paper containing the codes; and that the only conduct charged was "transferring the codes themselves, which are simply sequences of digits."

FYI

In Judge Friendly's hypothetical scenario, the person who memorizes a "carefully guarded secret formula," in the "recesses of a thievish mind," bears a strong resemblance to the character named Mr. Memory, who is unmasked as a spy during the climax of Alfred Hitchcock's 1935 film, The Thirty-Nine Steps.

The First Circuit has also concluded that the NSPA does not criminalize the theft of intangible things: The NSPA "does not apply to purely 'intangible information,' the theft of which is punishable under copyright law and other intellectual property statutes" but "*does apply* when there has been 'some tangible item taken, however insignificant or valueless it may be, absent the intangible component.'" *United States v. Martin,* 228 F.3d 1, 14–15 (1st Cir. 2000).

The Government argues that a tangibility requirement ignores a 1988 amendment, which added the words "transmit[ ]" and "transfer[ ]" to the terms: "transport[ ], transmit[ ], or transfer[ ]." The Government contends that the added words reflect an intent to cover generally transfers and transmissions of non-physical forms of stolen property. The evident purpose of the amendment, however, was to clarify that the statute applied to non-physical electronic transfers of *money*. Money, though it can be intangible, is specifically enumerated in § 2314 as a thing apart and distinct from "goods," "wares," or "merchandise." The addition to the possible means of transport does not bespeak an intent to alter or expand the ordinary meaning of "goods," "wares," or "merchandise" and therefore does not obviate the Government's need to identify a predicate good, ware, merchandise, security, or money that has been stolen.

By uploading Goldman's proprietary source code to a computer server in Germany, Aleynikov stole purely intangible property embodied in a purely intangible format. There was no allegation that he physically seized anything tangible from Goldman, such as a compact disc or thumb drive containing source code, so we need not decide whether that would suffice as a physical theft. Aleynikov later transported portions of the source code to Chicago, on his laptop and flash drive. However, there is no violation of the statute unless the good is transported with knowledge that "the same" has been stolen; the statute therefore presupposes that the thing stolen was a good [at] *the time of the theft.* [The] later storage of intangible property on a tangible medium does not transform the intangible property into a stolen good.

[There] is no doubt that in virtually every case involving proprietary computer code worth stealing, the value of the intangible code will vastly exceed the value of any physical item on which it might be stored. But [we] decline to stretch or update statutory words of plain and ordinary meaning in order to better accommodate the digital age.

Take Note

Six months after his release, Aleynikov was charged with state crimes by the Manhattan state prosecutor, who offered to allow Aleynikov to plead guilty to those crimes without serving any prison time. Aleynikov rejected this plea offer. *See* https://en.wikipedia.org/wiki/Sergey_Aleynikov.

For the foregoing reasons, the judgment of the district court is reversed.

Points for Discussion

a. Additional Facts

Aleynikov did not testify at his trial, and his interview with Michael Lewis was published after the reversal of Aleynikov's federal convictions. It describes how Aleynikov sought permission from his boss to release open source software "back into open source" on the Web, after making "very slight" modifications that were "of general rather than financial use." His boss refused this request and instructed Aleynikov to treat everything on Goldman Sachs's servers as its property, including material transferred from open source. So when Aleynikov sent himself the source code on his last day on the job, "he knew that Goldman wouldn't be happy about it." But when he was arrested one month later, "he was genuinely bewildered." When an FBI agent explained that the crime was "stealing computer code owned by Goldman," Aleynikov talked openly with the agent because he thought that what he had done was "trivial," and that "the matter would be quickly cleared up."

During his two years at Goldman, Aleynikov "had sent himself files nearly every week," and "[n]o one had ever said a word." During his last six weeks on the job, he had "mailed himself source code that he was working on" four times. He told an FBI agent that his reason for doing so was because "he hoped to disentangle" the open source code that he had modified from Goldman's proprietary code, "in case he needed to remind himself how he had done what he had done with the open-source code, in the event he might need to do it again." Lewis explained the logic behind this explanation:

Practice Pointer

The F.B.I.'s investigation before Aleynikov's arrest "consisted of trusting Goldman's explanation" of the content and value of the downloaded source code. After five hours of explaining his actions to the arresting agent, Aleynikov signed a statement, "scarred by phrases crossed-out and re-written by the agent." It would be presented to the jury "as the work of a thief who was being cautious, even tricky, with his words." *See* http://online.wsj.com/public/resources/documents/021110aleynikovindictment.pdf.

> As Goldman hadn't permitted him to release his debugged or improved code back to the public—possibly in violation of the original free licenses, which often stated that improvements must be publicly shared—the only way to get his hands on these was to take the Goldman code. That he had taken, in the bargain, some code that wasn't open source, which happened to be contained in the same files as the open-source code, [was not surprising]. [It] was a quick and efficient [way] to collect the open-source code, even if the open-source code was the only part that interested him. [His] interest was confined to the open-source code because that was the general-purpose code that might be re-purposed later. The Goldman proprietary code was written specifically for Goldman's platform; it would have been of little use in any new system he wished to build.

Several other aspects of the interview shed light on the nature of Aleynikov's conduct and mental state. For example, during the month after Aleynikov left Goldman, "he barely touched the code he had taken." According to programmers consulted by Lewis, this was not surprising because programmers want to save their code "to remember what they worked on," but typically "it has very little relevance to what they will build next." When Teza's founder was subpoenaed as a witness by the prosecution, he testified that "Goldman's code was of no use whatsoever in the system he'd hired [Aleynikov] to build," and that "he wanted to build Teza's system from scratch." Moreover, according to Lewis, the new system "was likely to be written in a different computer language than the Goldman code." Finally, when Aleynikov deleted his "bash history" after uploading the source code on his last day at Goldman, this was an action that he performed regularly each time he accessed a computer, just as "he had always done since he first started programming computers." If he failed to delete his "bash history," his password would remain visible on the computer and unauthorized persons could obtain access to the system. *See* Michael Lewis, *Did Goldman Sachs Overstep in Criminally Charging Its Ex-Programmer?* Vanity Fair 314 (September 2013).

b. Considering *Aleynikov*

Assume that one of the Second Circuit judges in *Aleynikov* had doubts about the persuasiveness of the court's reasoning, though not about the result in the case. Why might this judge find the court's analysis of the applicability of the *Bottone* reasoning to be problematic? Why might this judge regard the meaning of the 1988 amendment as ambiguous at best, especially given the grammatical construction chosen for that amendment? Why might this judge have concerns about the implications of the First Circuit's reasoning that the NSPA should apply in a case "when there has been 'some tangible item taken, however insignificant or valueless it may be, absent the intangible component' "? Assume that this judge would have preferred to justify the reversal of the conviction on the basis of reasoning that was not used by the Second Circuit. What arguments based on precedents, statutory text, legislative history, and policy, could have been used in such an opinion?

Hypo: *DEA Database*

Zoe is a DEA agent who is approached by Max, a drug smuggler, who wants to find out whether any of his four drug suppliers are DEA informants. Max offers to pay Zoe $10,000 per name checked for the information he seeks. Zoe uses the computer in her DEA office to click on the links that give her access to a database with the names of DEA informants. She learns that none of Max's suppliers are informants, and Max pays her $40,000 for this information. When the DEA learns about Zoe's conduct, she is convicted of the federal crime of "unauthorized sale of *government property*" under 18 U.S.C. § 641, which applies to anyone who "without authority, sells any *record, voucher, money* or *thing of value* of the United States or of any department or agency thereof[.]" On appeal, defense counsel argues that the language of § 641 does not apply to Zoe's conduct. What reasoning will the court use to reject that argument and affirm the conviction? *Compare United States v. Girard*, 601 F.2d 69 (2d Cir. 1979).

B. Larceny & Embezzlement (Theft by Unlawful Taking or Disposition)

Many modern theft statutes emulate the MPC's merger of the crimes of larceny and embezzlement in the Theft by Unlawful Taking or Disposition crime. An understanding of the reasons that underlie this merger may be obtained from the cases that illustrate the anachronistic distinctions between these crimes, which are still used in some state codes, and which depend upon the meaning of the complex and fictionalized concept of a "trespassory taking from possession."

---

1. Larceny

The original crime of larceny required a "trespassory taking" of property from the "possession" of the owner, without the consent of the owner. There was also an "asportation" requirement, which meant that the property was supposed to be "carried away." Even a small movement could satisfy this element. The crime required the "intent to steal," meaning an intent to deprive the owner permanently of the property. The federal criminal code and some state codes continue to use this definition, but most states have replaced it with some version of the MPC crime of Theft by Unlawful Taking or Disposition. The *Mafnas* case illustrates how some courts must rely on 500-year-old larceny fictions invented by English judges in order to interpret the scope of a modern federal statute.

United States v. Mafnas

701 F.2d 83 (9th Cir. 1983).

Before ELY, and KENNEDY, CIRCUIT JUDGES, and NIELSEN, DISTRICT JUDGE.

PER CURIAM:

Food for Thought

What words in the text of the federal statute in *Mafnas* served as a signal to the federal court that Congress intended to codify the elements of the common law larceny crime, rather than enacting an entirely new crime? What other words in the text are not elements of the common law crime? Why do these words play no role in the court's reasoning?

Appellant (Mafnas) was convicted in the U.S. District Court of Guam of stealing money from two federally insured banks in violation of 18 U.S.C. § 2113(b) which [applies to] "[whoever] take[s] [and carries away,] with intent to steal [or purloin, any property or] money belonging to . . . any bank[.]"

Mafnas was employed by the Guam Armored Car Service (Service), which was hired by the Bank of Hawaii and the Bank of America to deliver bags of money. On three occasions Mafnas opened the bags and removed money. As a result he was convicted of three counts of stealing money from the banks.

This Circuit has held that § 2113(b) applies only to common law larceny which requires a trespassory taking. *Bennett v. United States*, 399 F.2d 740 (9th Cir. 1968). Mafnas argues his taking was embezzlement rather than larceny as he had lawful possession of the bags, with the consent of the banks, when he took the money. [If Mafnas is correct, his conviction must be reversed, and then presumably he may be indicted for committing the embezzlement crime.]

This problem arose centuries ago, and common law has evolved to handle it. The law distinguishes between possession and custody. [As explained in 3 WHARTON'S CRIMINAL LAW 353 (1980):]

> Ordinarily, . . . if a person receives property for a limited or temporary purpose, he is only acquiring custody. Thus, if a person receives property from the owner with instructions to deliver it to the owner's house, he is only acquiring custody; therefore, his subsequent decision to keep the property for himself would constitute larceny.

The District Court concluded that Mafnas was given temporary custody only, to deliver the money bags to their various destinations. The later decision to take the money was larceny, because it was beyond the consent of the owner, who retained constructive possession until the custodian's task was completed. This rationale was used in *United States v. Pruitt*, 446 F.2d 513, 515 (6th Cir. 1971). There, Pruitt was employed by a bank as a messenger. He devised a plan with another person to stage a fake robbery and split the money which Pruitt was delivering for the bank. The Sixth Circuit found that Pruitt had mere custody for the purpose of delivering the money, and that his wrongful conversion constituted larceny.

What's That?

Personalty is personal property. It includes anything that is not "real" property, which term refers to things that are fixed or immovable, such as land and buildings.

Mafnas distinguishes *Pruitt* because the common law sometimes differentiates between employees, who generally obtain custody only, and others[,] who acquire [lawful] possession. Although not spelled out, Mafnas essentially claims that he was a bailee, and that the contract between the banks and Service resulted in Service having lawful possession, and not mere custody over the bags. ["]A bailment situation is said to arise where an owner, while retaining title, delivers *personalty* to another for some particular purpose upon an express or implied contract.["] [*See Lionberger v. United States*, 371 F.2d 831, 840 (Ct.Cl. 1967).]

The common law also found an answer to this situation[:]

> [When] the bailee-carrier was given possession of a bale, but not its contents[,] [and] pilfered the entire bale, he was not guilty of larceny; but when he broke open the bale and took a portion or all of the contents, he was guilty of larceny because his taking was trespassory and it was from the constructive possession of another.

3 WHARTON'S CRIMINAL LAW 353–354. Either way, Mafnas has committed the common law crime of larceny, replete with trespassory taking.

Mafnas also cannot profit from an argument that any theft on his part was from [the] Service and not from the banks. Case law is clear that since what was taken was property belonging to the banks, it was property or money "in the care, custody, control, management, or possession of any bank" within the meaning of 18 U.S.C. § 2113(b), notwithstanding the fact that it may have been in the possession of an armored car service serving as a bailee for hire. *See United States v. Jakalski*, 237 F.2d 503 (7th Cir. 1956).

Therefore, his conviction is affirmed.

Points for Discussion

a. Origins of Trespass Element in Larceny

In the fifteenth century and earlier, the meaning of a "taking" as an element of the judge-made crime of larceny "had no artificial meaning." As one scholar explains:

> Trespass as an essential element of larceny simply meant taking a chattel from one who had possession of it. [Anglo-Saxon] and early Norman economic conditions limited both the objects and the methods of theft. Movable property consisted of cattle, farm products, and furniture. [Since] theft of cattle by armed bands was by far the most important crime against property, it requires no stretch of imagination to see what was meant by "trespass" in the early law.

JEROME HALL, THEFT, LAW AND SOCIETY 6 (2d ed. 1952). When the judicial definition of larceny expanded, on a case-by-case basis, to cover any "trespassory" taking from the owner's "constructive possession," the common law meaning of this element of larceny became highly fictionalized.

b. Taking & "Carrying Away"

By the time Blackstone described the asportation or "carrying away" element of larceny in the 1783 edition of his treatise, its meaning had become fictionalized, as evidenced by these examples of sufficient proof of asportation: 1) if a person "leads another man's horse out of a close and is apprehended in the fact"; 2) if a guest, "stealing goods out of an inn, removes them from his chamber"; 3) if a thief, "intending to steal plate, takes it out of a chest and lays it down upon the floor, but is surprised before he can make his escape with it." 4 WILLIAM BLACKSTONE, COMMENTARIES ON THE LAWS OF ENGLAND, *200.Ultimately, American courts held that a "slight movement" was held to be sufficient to show asportation.

c. "Trespassory Taking from Possession"

The original scenario for larceny was the stealth crime of taking a horse away from the owner's barn. In this case, the owner's rightful possession of the horse was obvious, and the trespass was synonymous with the act of taking without the consent of the owner. But in situations in which property came into the hands of the thief through some action of the owner, the English judges invented the concept of mere "custody" to describe the thief's relationship to the property. Such "custody" meant, first, that the property remained in the "constructive possession" of the rightful owner, and second, that when the thief absconded with the property, that act constituted a "trespassory taking" from the "possession" of the owner.

One obstacle that confronted the English judges was that a contract of bailment created lawful possession of goods in the "bailee," who held the bailor-owner's property for some purpose, such as transportation and delivery, and who typically received compensation for carrying out that purpose. Therefore, the judges created two larceny rules to deal with thieving bailees. When goods were shipped together in bulk without being packaged, taking any part of the shipment constituted the trespassory taking of "breaking bulk." When goods were shipped in packaging, the package was the "bale", and opening the packaging to remove the contents constituted the trespassory taking of "breaking bale." Taking an entire bale without breaking it open would not constitute larceny. These larceny fictions emerged from the *Carrier's Case* (1473), where the defendant was hired to deliver bales but never did so, breaking open the bales instead, and taking the contents. He was guilty of larceny because the owner was deemed to have retained lawful possession of the contents inside the bale. *See generally* WAYNE R. LAFAVE, CRIMINAL LAW §§ 19.2, 19.8, 974–976, 1026 (5th ed. 2010).

How does the *Mafnas* Court apply these larceny fictions to the facts of *Mafnas*? What reasons may explain the failure of the English judges to abandon the "trespassory taking" requirement entirely, and their preference for stretching its meaning through a variety of larceny fictions instead? What reasons may explain the failure of Congress to replace the larceny crime in the *Mafnas* statute with a modern definition of the crime?

d. Larceny by Trick

The crime of larceny by trick enabled prosecutors to convict defendants who "trespassed against possession" by telling lies to obtain possession of property, instead of taking it by stealth. The crime is illustrated by the English decision in *Pear's Case* (1779), where the defendant hired a horse with the understanding that the horse would be returned to the owner. But the defendant actually intended to sell the horse at the time of the hire and he sold the horse and kept the proceeds. The defendant was not a servant, employee, bailee or other agent, and so he claimed that he had obtained temporary lawful possession of the horse. But the English judges decided to call this conduct "larceny," based on the reasoning that the defendant's false promise to return the horse was a "trick" that could be treated as a "trespass," thus making the defendant's conduct a "taking from the owner's possession." Given the fact that the owner's act of parting with possession was based on fraud, this act could not create lawful possession in the thief.

The larceny by trick crime requires proof of all the elements of larceny, as well as the trick element of false representation, which can be a false promise about the future or a false statement about past or present facts. The element of "conversion" of the property also is necessary for a conviction for larceny by trick, and the owner must be tricked into parting with possession of property, not into parting with title. Like the larceny crime, larceny by trick is a crime designed to protect actual or constructive possession of property.

e. Gaps in the Larceny Rules

The willingness of English judges to construct larceny fictions had two important limits, which explains why Parliament enacted statutes to define the crimes of embezzlement and false pretenses. The scenario that required the enactment of the embezzlement crime was the decision in *Bazeley's Case* (1799), where property was transmitted from a third party to the master's servant, with instructions to deliver it to the master. The English judges held that no larceny occurred when the servant misappropriated the property by converting it for his own benefit. In their view, the servant had acquired lawful "possession" of the property from the third party, and could not be guilty of a "trespassory taking" from the possession of the master.

Similarly, the English judges were not willing to expand larceny by trick to encompass the case where a thief obtained *title* to property by means of false statements. They limited the scope of the larceny by trick crime to a scenario where the owner's apparent passing of possession was nullified because of the trick, so that possession remained with the owner, as occurs in all larceny fictions. In their view, this fiction could not be maintained when the owner passed title because of the trick. Therefore, the judges interpreted Parliament's "false pretenses" crime as covering this liability gap. Notably, the MPC Commentaries attribute the reluctance of English judges to expand the larceny fictions to a "combination of circumstances," with the "most direct influence" being "a revulsion against capital punishment, which was the penalty for all theft offenses except petty larceny during much of the 18th century." *See* Model Penal Code § 223.2, Comment (1)(a), at 128–129 (1980).

The following hypothetical illustrates the use of the larceny crime in the shoplifting context.

Hypo: *Leaving Store*

A security officer in a J.C. Penney's store was behind an observation window when he saw Ellis concealing sportswear items under her clothing and in her purse. The officer, who was holding his walkie-talkie radio transmitter, followed her out of the store. When Ellis was 10 feet outside the store, she turned around and saw the officer directly approaching her, radio in hand. Ellis then ran back into the store and threw the sportswear items under a rack displaying other clothing. Does this evidence prove all the elements of larceny? *Compare State v. Ellis*, 618 So.2d 616 (La. App. 1993).

2. Embezzlement

The crime of embezzlement was established by the inventive action of Parliament in 1799 when English judges refused to stretch the larceny crime to cover the conduct of embezzlers. Early American statutes followed Parliament's example in limiting the categories of entrusted persons whose conduct was subject to prosecution for embezzlement. Later statutes expanded the concept of entrustment to cover a wide variety of defendants. The traditional elements of embezzlement include the fraudulent conversion of the property of another by an entrusted person in lawful possession who had the intent to convert the property for his or her own use. These elements are simplified in the modern MPC crime of Theft by Unlawful Taking or Disposition, which applies to a person who "unlawfully takes or *exercises unlawful control over*" property, and who has either the "purpose to deprive" or the purpose "to benefit himself or another not entitled thereto." The *Batin* case illustrates how it may be difficult for a prosecutor to persuade a court that an employee was entrusted with the kind of "constructive possession" of property that makes an embezzlement conviction possible.

Batin v. State

118 Nev. 61, 38 P.3d 880 (2002) (en banc).

LEAVITT, J.:

Appellant Marlon Javar Batin was convicted [of] embezzlement for stealing money from his employer, [the] Nugget Hotel and Casino. [W]e now conclude that Batin did not commit embezzlement as a matter of law because there was no evidence presented of the entrustment element of that crime. [We] reverse the judgment of conviction.

In 1993, Batin moved [to Nevada] from the Philippines and began working as a dishwasher at the Nugget. After several years at the Nugget, Batin became a slot mechanic. Batin's job duties [included] fixing jammed coins and refilling the "hopper." Warren Reid Anderson, Batin's supervisor, explained [in his testimony] that the "hopper" is the part of the slot machine that pays the coins back, and is separate from the "bill validator" component of the slot machine where the paper currency is kept. Anderson further testified that Batin had no duties with respect to the paper currency in the bill validator, except to safeguard the funds, and that the cash in the bill validator "wasn't to be touched." Likewise, Anderson testified that if a customer had a problem with a machine that required a cash refund, "it would require supervisory backup in order to take any money out of a slot machine and pass it back to a customer." Batin also testified about his job duties as a slot mechanic. Like Anderson, Batin testified that he was prohibited from handling the paper currency inside the bill validator.

As a slot mechanic, Batin was given an "SDS" card that was used to both access the inside of the slot machine and identify him as the employee that was opening the slot machine door. The computerized SDS system is physically connected to each slot machine and counts the paper currency placed into each machine's bill validator. The SDS actually records the different denominations of bills and runs numerous reports concerning the currency. The SDS also registers every time that the slot machine door is open or closed. If the power is turned off to a particular slot machine, the SDS system will only record the opening and closing of the door; it cannot track what happens inside the machine.

Lori Barrington, soft count supervisor, explained that after the money is counted by SDS, it is then counted three more times by a minimum of three Nugget employees. Barrington further testified that there was not much variance between the amount of money SDS recorded that the casino was supposed to have and the amount of money the casino actually had. In fact, out of 1100 slot machines, there were perhaps three errors per month totaling approximately $100.00 in variance.

In March and early June 1999, however, there were larger discrepancies discovered between the amount of money that the SDS recorded had been put into the slot machines and the amount of money the slot machine actually contained. Kathleen Plamabeck, the Nugget's Internal Auditor, testified to several shortages from four different slot machines, totaling approximately $40,000.00.

In reviewing the SDS reports, Plambeck testified that she found a pattern of conduct. Namely, prior to the time that a shortage had been detected on a slot machine, Batin inserted his SDS card into the slot machine, opened the door, turned off the power, and thereafter closed the door on the machine. Plambeck found this pattern of conduct unusual because it was not necessary to turn off the slot machine for most repairs, and no one other than Batin had been turning off the power on the slot machines with the shortages. Batin testified at trial, however, that he turned off the power on the slot machines so that he would not be electrocuted and that he had always turned off the power prior to working on the slot machines.

James Carlisle, an agent with the Nevada Gaming Control Board, investigated Batin and discovered that he gambled regularly at three local casinos, and that he lost tens of thousands of dollars. When Carlisle questioned Batin about how he was able to afford to gamble such large sums of money, Batin could not or did not answer. At trial, however, Batin testified that he was able to afford to gamble large sums of money because he won often.

Food for Thought

The *Batin* Court observed in a footnote that the evidence at trial would have supported a conviction for larceny, and that the prosecutor may retry the defendant on that charge. Why are the elements of larceny satisfied on the facts?

Although Batin adamantly denied taking the money, Batin was arrested and charged [with] embezzlement. The information alleged that Batin had been entrusted with money by his employer and converted the money for a purpose other than that for which it was entrusted. After a jury trial, Batin was convicted [of] embezzlement.

Batin contends that his [conviction] for embezzlement should be reversed because there was insufficient evidence of an essential element of the crime. We agree.

[To] prove that a defendant committed the crime of embezzlement, the State must demonstrate [that] the defendant was a "*person with whom any money, property or effects ha[d] been deposited or entrusted*," and that the defendant "use[d] or appropriate[d] the money, property, or effects . . . in any manner or for any other purpose than that for which [it was] deposited or entrusted." [Nev. Rev. Stat. § 205.300(1).]

The key distinguishing element of the crime of embezzlement is the element of entrustment. In order to be guilty of embezzlement, a defendant must have been entrusted with lawful possession of the property prior to its conversion. For purposes of proving embezzlement, the lawful possession need not be actual; rather, the State may show that a defendant had constructive possession of the property converted. This court has defined constructive possession as " 'both the power and the intention at a given time to exercise dominion or control over a thing, either directly or through another person or persons.' " [*Palmer v. State*, 112 Nev. 763, 768, 920 P.2d 112, 115 (1996) (quoting *Black's Law Dictionary* 1163 (6th ed. 1990)).]

In proving constructive possession, a showing that a defendant was given mere access to the property converted is insufficient. Often, an individual is entrusted with access to a particular place or thing without being given dominion and control over the property therein. This is particularly true in instances, like the present one, where the individual is expressly told that he is not allowed to touch the property in the place to which access is granted.

[Here] the record reveals that Batin was not entrusted with lawful possession, constructive or otherwise, of the currency he allegedly took from the bill validators. In fact, both Batin and his supervisor testified that Batin had no job duties whatsoever involving this currency and that it "wasn't to be touched." Further, Batin had absolutely no power to exercise control over this currency, as Batin was required to contact his supervisor for any job task involving possession of the currency inside the bill validator, such as a cash refund to a customer. [We] cannot say that an individual exercises control over property when he is prohibited from touching it.

In light of the foregoing, we are compelled to reverse Batin's conviction. The State failed to prove the entrustment element of the crime of embezzlement beyond a reasonable doubt[.]

Take Note

The *Batin* Court's analysis relied on state court precedents from Arizona, Kansas, Louisiana, Minnesota, and the federal Fifth and Eighth Circuits, as well as Nevada precedents going back to 1893.

MAUPIN, C.J., with whom BECKER, J., agrees, dissenting.

In viewing the evidence in a light most favorable to the State, we conclude that there is ample evidence to support the jury's verdict that Batin had constructive possession of the paper currency inside the bill validator. The State proffered evidence that Batin's employer entrusted him with an SDS card, which allowed Batin to access the bill validator inside the slot machine where the currency was kept. Moreover, Batin's job, as prescribed by his employer, included safeguarding the funds contained inside the bill validator when he made a slot machine repair and when supervising non-employee slot machine repairmen. In safeguarding the currency inside the bill validator, Batin was entrusted with dominion and control over that currency in a manner sufficient to support the jury's finding that Batin had constructive possession over the funds that he converted.

Accordingly, because we conclude that there was sufficient evidence of the crime of embezzlement, we would affirm the judgment of conviction.

Points for Discussion

a. Charging the Wrong Crime

It may be difficult for a prosecutor to charge a defendant with the "right" property crime without knowing how an appellate court will define embezzlement and larceny in the context of particular facts. After several years of litigation, the *Batin* prosecutor learned that larceny, not embezzlement, was the right crime to charge in the *Batin* case. What are the reasons that explain why defense counsel argue on appeal that their clients were convicted of the wrong theft crime, even when counsel recognize that these clients could be charged and convicted later for the right theft crime?

b. Entrustment Proof

The *Batin* prosecutor lost because of a failure of proof concerning the "entrustment" of the defendant's by his employer with the "possession" of the paper currency in the form of "control" over it. As the court explained, "We cannot say that an individual exercises control over property when he is prohibited from touching it." At the charging stage of a case, however, it may be difficult for a prosecutor to anticipate what the testimony of all the witnesses will show at trial. Assuming that the *Batin* prosecutor could have predicted the court's ruling, what different testimony and documentary evidence would have been necessary for the prosecutor to present at trial, in order to persuade the state supreme court to affirm a conviction for embezzlement?

c. Entrustment Defined

The concept of "constructive possession" of property by an "entrusted" employee is a legal fiction, and so it is not surprising to discover that the inherent ambiguity of this concept led to disagreement about its meaning in *Batin*. What are the two key aspects of the defendant's job duties that led the *Batin* dissenters to conclude that his relationship to the paper currency demonstrated "dominion and control" over it? What are the possible reasons that may explain their willingness to be less demanding regarding "entrustment" evidence than the *Batin* majority?

Hypo 1: *Lottery Tickets*

The Tiger Mart store in Reno has a contract with the Nevada State Lottery Commission (NSLC) that allows the store to dispense lottery tickets from the special "lottery terminal" machine that is located inside the store within easy reach of the store employee who works at the cash register. The lottery terminal is a touchscreen machine that is "networked" to the Nevada State Lottery (NSL) but not "networked" to the cash register in the Tiger Mart store. Each morning when the Tiger Mart store opens for business, the store manager Mara must "activate" the lottery terminal by using the NSL password that is provided by Tiger Mart only to store managers like Mara. Then once it is activated, the lottery terminal does not require any sort of password to operate it. The cashier is trained to collect payments first from customers who want to buy lottery tickets, and then to put the payments in the cash register drawer before using the touchscreen on the lottery terminal to print out the tickets and deliver them to the customers.

When Masood, the vice-president of Tiger Mart, discovered unexplained shortages of $25,000 in the cash register during 2016, he suspected that the deli assistant Dee was printing and taking—but not paying for—lottery tickets that she obtained from the lottery terminal in the store. Dee was charged with embezzlement based on the evidence of the videotape from a camera inside the store. At her trial, when Masood was asked whether a "deli assistant" like Dee was "supposed to be operating the lottery terminal," he testified, "Not as far as I know." However, Masood did not work in the store himself. As the store manager, Mara was Dee's direct supervisor. Mara testified that she had trained Dee and all the other employees so that they could take over the cash register whenever the cashier needed to take a break. As part of that training, Mara showed all the employees, including Dee, how to print lottery tickets from the lottery terminal (after Mara activated it every morning), so that they could sell tickets to customers whenever they had to take over for the cashier. The videotape showed that during brief periods when Dee was working at the cash register and no customers were present, Dee would use the lottery terminal to print lottery tickets, which she then pocketed. The same video evidence showed that Dee failed to pay for those tickets. Other evidence showed that Dee had redeemed some winning lottery tickets through the mail, and that these winning tickets had been printed at the lottery terminal in the Tiger Mart store in Reno.

Assume that after Dee's conviction for embezzlement, her defense counsel argues on appeal that Dee's conviction must be reversed under *Batin* because two elements of embezzlement are missing—the entrustment requirement and the requirement that Dee was entrusted with "lawful possession." Explain the arguments that the prosecutor will make to rebut these two arguments and distinguish *Batin*?

Hypo 2: *Locked File Cabinet*

Ann was charged and convicted of the crime of embezzlement as defined in *Batin*. On appeal, her defense counsel argues that the element of "entrustment" was not proved but concedes that all the other elements of the crime were satisfied on the facts. Ann worked for the accounting department of Ace Conditioning Experts (ACE), which "department" consisted of Ann and her co-worker Sal. Rick was the office manager for ACE and he supervised the work that Ann and Sal did. Rick's husband Zeb was the owner and chief operating officer of ACE. Ann was responsible for performing these six tasks to assist Rick in the accounting department: 1) performing data entry activities; 2) printing checks for payroll and accounts payable; 3) preparing cash receipts; 4) writing up and making bank deposits; 5) cashing petty cash checks for the company; and 6) filing items in the locked personnel filing cabinet. Whenever Ann would print checks, she would then take them to Rick for his signature, since only Rick and Zeb were authorized to sign checks for ACE.

Rick kept a locked file cabinet in the accounting department, which contained employee files, titles, records, and payroll materials. Only Rick and Sal had keys to the file cabinet. Ann did not have a key. However, as part of her duties, Ann had to file copies of checks and letters to employees in the file cabinet. On these occasions, Ann would ask Rick for the key to unlock the cabinet, and Rick always gave Ann his key whenever she asked for it. When Rick and Zeke took an out of town trip together, Rick would leave pre-signed but otherwise blank checks with Sal and instruct Sal to keep the checks safe. Sal chose to store the pre-signed checks in the locked file cabinet.

The prosecutor charged Ann with the embezzlement crime based on her conduct in taking two of the pre-signed blank checks, filling out each check for a large amount and including the name of a payee, and then enlisting the help of accomplices to cash the two checks. Ann was able to obtain the two pre-signed blank checks from the locked file cabinet because she asked Rick for the key and he gave it to her. At Ann's trial, Zeb testified that he had no idea where the pre-signed blank checks were kept because that was an issue for Rick to decide. Rick testified that he knew that Sal kept the pre-signed checks in the locked file cabinet. Rick also testified that he assumed that if Ann needed one of the pre-signed checks, then she would tell Sal, who would fetch the check from the file cabinet so that Ann could perform one of her assigned tasks. Rick also testified that Ann had access to ACE's bank account in order to perform her tasks, and Rick confirmed that one of Ann's tasks was filing items in the locked file cabinet. But Rick also noted that Ann "was not supposed to have access" to the pre-signed blank checks.

What arguments will Ann's counsel make to support the defense position that there was insufficient evidence to establish the entrustment element of embezzlement, given the lack of evidence that Ann was in lawful possession of the pre-signed blank checks when she converted them to her own use? Can the defense counsel make analogies to the facts of *Batin* here?

d. MPC Fusion of Larceny & Embezzlement Crimes

Take Note

The MPC redefined the *larceny* crime as the conduct of "a person who unlawfully *takes* . . . movable property of another with purpose to deprive him thereof," and the *embezzlement* crime as the conduct of a person who "unlawfully . . . *exercises unlawful control* over, movable property of another with purpose to deprive him thereof." See Model Penal Code § 223.2(1).

The MPC drafters proposed that a single crime, Theft by Unlawful Taking or Disposition (TUTD) under § 223.2(1), should be created to replace the English common law crimes of larceny, larceny by trick, and embezzlement. This MPC crime applies to "movable" property, namely "anything of value," the location of which can be moved. The use of new vocabulary, both for the name of the crime and for its elements, signaled the intent of the MPC drafters to abandon the legal fictions and technical distinctions that characterized the old common law crimes. The MPC crime is a much simpler and broader version of its predecessors.

The MPC Commentary for the TUTD crime explains the meaning and purpose of each element. First, the term "unlawfully" is a substitute for the "without consent" element of larceny and embezzlement. Second, the term "takes" is a substitute for the larceny elements of "takes and carries away" (or "caption and asportation"). Thus, the term "unlawfully takes" applies to any "assumption of physical possession or control without consent or authority," which "includes the typical common law category of larceny." Third, the alternative conduct element, namely "exercises unlawful control over," was "designed to cover the typical embezzlement situation." The "twofold" inquiry regarding this element is, "whether the actor had control of the property, no matter how he got it, and whether the actor's acquisition or use of the property was authorized." This element is satisfied "at the moment" the actor "begins to use [the property] in a manner beyond his authority." *See* Model Penal Code Comments § 223.2, Comments 1, 2, at 163–166 (1980).

The "property of another" element in the TUTD crime is broadly defined under § 223.0(7) to include "property in which any person other than the actor has an interest which the actor is not privileged to infringe, regardless of the fact that the actor also has an interest in the property." Similarly, the "purpose to deprive" element is defined broadly under § 223.0(1) to encompass any of these four mental states:

(1) the purpose to withhold property of another permanently; or

(2) the purpose to deprive for so extended a period as to appropriate a major portion of its economic value; or

(3) the purpose to deprive with intent to restore only upon payment of reward or other compensation; or

(4) the purpose to dispose of the property so as to make it unlikely that the owner will recover it.

The MPC drafters designed an additional provision in § 223.2(2) that applies the TUTD crime to a person who "unlawfully transfers immovable property of another or any interest therein with purpose to benefit himself or another not entitled to." The goal of this provision is to make it clear that "a trustee, guardian, or other person empowered to dispose of 'immovable' property of others subjects himself to theft liability if he misappropriates the property." *See* Model Penal Code § 223.2, Comment 5, at 172 (1980).

C. False Pretenses (Theft by Deception)

After English judges expanded the larceny concept to include "larceny by trick," they refused to expand this crime to cover defendants who used deception to obtain title to property, and Parliament's "false pretenses" crime was used to fill that liability gap. Many legislatures enacted this crime in early state criminal codes. The *Traster* case illustrates key distinction between the false pretenses crime and larceny by trick.

People v. Traster

111 Cal. App. 4th 1377, 4 Cal. Rptr. 3d 680 (2003).

JOHNSON, J.

> **FYI**
>
> A few months after leaving the law firm, Traster went to work for a company in the nearby city of Compton, where he used a similar scam to obtain company checks for $132,000 to pay for software licenses. The company found him out, fired him, reported him to the police, won a civil judgment against him, and placed a lien on his house. His prior attempted fraud against the law firm was discovered during the police investigation of the fraud committed in Compton. He was tried on false pretenses charges for both crimes, and in affirming both convictions, the *Traster* Court held that the second fraud was larceny by trick.

[Traster] had a computer consulting business he called Pen, Paper, and Mouse Ink. In July 1997 the Long Beach law firm of Demler, Armstrong and Rowland hired [Traster] as its first computer administrator. His initial duties included converting the firm from the word processing system WordPerfect 5.1 to Windows and Microsoft Word. His responsibilities also included training on Microsoft Word as well as assisting the 35 attorneys and 35 staff persons with computer problems.

In April 1999, [Traster] met with [Ms.] Stevens, the law firm's administrator. He informed her the law firm was not in legal compliance because it did not have Microsoft licenses for all its computers. [Traster] explained he had done some research on the Internet and discovered he could acquire the necessary Microsoft licenses at a large discount from Billpoint Company. [Traster] stated it would cost $37,290.94 to acquire licenses for the firm's 65 computers.

Neither Ms. Stevens [nor] anyone else supervising [Traster] had any special knowledge about computers. Ms. Stevens said she would present [Traster's] proposal to the firm's partners for decision. [Traster] filled out a purchase order form for $37,290.94 for the purchase of 65 licenses for Microsoft Office and Windows 98 software.

On April 27, 1999, the partners approved the expenditure to acquire the necessary Microsoft licenses. They gave [Traster] the partnership's credit card to buy the licenses from Billpoint Company, the vendor [Traster] named on the purchase order.

[Traster] resigned from his position a few days later on May 3, 1999. Before he left Ms. Stevens asked [Traster] whether the Microsoft licenses had been received, and if so, where he had placed them. [Traster] said the licenses were in a locked filing cabinet in the paralegal office. [This was not true because no licenses for the firm had been obtained. When Ms. Stevens could not find the licenses, she reported this to a law firm partner, Mr. Wade.]

The next morning, Mr. Wade and Ms. Stevens called the Billpoint Company [and discovered that] Billpoint was not a vendor of any product, was not a software company, and did not sell software licenses. [In fact,] Billpoint was primarily a credit card processing company for E-Bay [and for] other Internet transactions[,] [and] functioned solely as a clearing house between buyers and sellers. . . .

[The] senior fraud investigator [at] Billpoint explained that [Traster] had established a seller's account with Billpoint [in] the name of his consulting firm, Pen, Paper and Mouse Ink, at his residence address. . . . [Then] on April 27, 1999, [he] charged two amounts totaling $37,290.94 to the law firm's credit card to purchase some "bundled software licenses" from his company Pen, Paper and Mouse Ink. The transactions were posted to Billpoint the next day [and] the law firm's credit card account was debited accordingly[.] However, Mr. Wade cancelled the transaction with Billpoint and the credit card company both verbally and in writing before [Traster's] company's account could be credited.

The debit to the law firm's credit card account was reversed within the month. However, the law firm's credit line was reduced by this [debited] amount between April 28, 1999, and May 24, 1999. The law firm ultimately purchased the Microsoft licenses it needed for $20,000.00. [Traster was charged with the crime of theft by false pretenses and convicted. He appeals from the judgment of conviction.]

[To] establish the crime of theft by false pretenses the prosecution was required to prove: [that] *"[t]he theft was accomplished in that the alleged victi[m] parted with . . . money or property intending to transfer ownership thereof."* The presence or absence of evidence of [this] element of transferring "ownership" or "title" distinguishes the crime of theft by false pretenses from the crime of [larceny] by trick[.] . . .

[If] the defendant obtains possession of property for a specific or special purpose, the owner does not relinquish title and the crime committed is larceny by trick. On the other hand, it is theft by false pretenses if the owner of the property gives the property to the defendant[,] intending the defendant [to] become the unconditional and unrestricted owner.

A noted treatise writer explains the difference between the two crimes when the property at issue, as in this case, is cash. "In most cases one who hands over money to another never expects to get that very money back; and so it might be thought that in most cases of money obtained by fraud the wrongdoer obtains title, making his crime false pretenses rather than larceny by trick. [But] [i]t is generally held that where the victim hands money to the wrongdoer with the understanding that the latter is to spend it only for a particular purpose[,] title does not pass to the wrongdoer; he has only a power to pass title by spending it for the specified purpose[.]" [2 LaFave & Scott, Substantive Criminal Law § 8.7, at 396 (1986).] The law is the same in California[.]

[The] evidence in the present case established that the [victim] provided [Traster with] funds, or access to funds, [for] the express purpose of purchasing Microsoft licenses, and for no other reason. No [law firm] representative . . . suggested [Traster] received the funds unconditionally to use as he wished. [The firm] did not intend to pass title to the money until or unless it was spent [for] the Microsoft licenses, and then only to the ultimate vendor or supplier of the Microsoft licenses. [Because] the evidence established [that Traster] never acquired title to the money, the [crime] in this case [is] more appropriately characterized as larceny by trick than as theft by false pretenses. Accordingly, [Traster] was convicted [under] an erroneous theory[.]

[In California,] these two offenses [have] been consolidated into the single crime of theft, but their elements have not been changed thereby[.] Thus, the error in this case is merely a technical one in which the jury was instructed on a particular theory of theft which turned out to be the wrong one. [In these circumstances, [the instruction on false pretenses was] harmless [and the next question to be addressed is whether the evidence is sufficient to sustain a conviction of larceny by trick.]

[Traster] made false representations to the law firm [that] induced the law firm to provide him use of the partnership's credit card. [The] only step remaining to complete the crime of [larceny by trick] was his actual receipt of the money. However, [the] evidence established [that] neither [Traster] nor his company ever gained possession of the money. [The] law firm upon discovery of [Traster's] deceit then cancelled the transaction [and] Billpoint credited the law firm's account for the [debited sum] within the month. Because there was no evidence [Traster] ever obtained possession or control of the firm's money, a [larceny by trick crime] was not completed. Accordingly, [Traster] can only be guilty of an attempt to commit the crime of larceny by trick[.]

The judgment of conviction is modified [to] reflect a conviction of attempted [larceny by trick]. The cause is remanded for the trial court to exercise its discretion in resentencing [Traster] in accordance with the modified judgment of conviction.

Points for Discussion

a. Theft by Deception

In theory, the broad language of the MPC Theft by Unlawful Taking or Disposition crime—unlawfully takes or unlawfully exercises control over property—could encompass the crime of false pretenses as well as larceny and embezzlement. But the MPC drafters decided to propose a separate Theft by Deception crime in order to specify the many types of deceptive behavior that qualify for liability, some of which were excluded from the scope of the false pretenses crime.

The Theft by Deception crime applies to a person who "purposely obtains property of another by deception," and the definition of the word "obtain" is "to bring about a transfer or purported transfer of a legal interest in the property." This means that Theft by Deception is *not* intended to cover the larceny by trick crime, which is covered instead by the Theft by Unlawful Taking crime. *See* Model Penal Code § 223.3, Comment 2, at 182 (1980).

Many states have revised their statutes to replace the larceny, larceny by trick, embezzlement, and false pretenses crimes with some version of the pair of MPC offenses, Theft by Unlawful Taking or Disposition and Theft by Deception. The *Traster* case illustrates the alternative approach of combining several common law crimes into a new "single crime of theft," while preserving their original names and elements.

b. Consolidation

The MPC drafters proposed the reform of "consolidation" in order to eliminate the need to reverse convictions for the wrong theft crime, as long as the evidence supported conviction for another theft crime. Many state legislatures have enacted some version of the MPC provision that allows a group of particular theft crimes to be consolidated. These crimes are enumerated in a consolidation statute in order to provide fair notice to defendants. As described more specifically in Model Penal Code § 223.1(1):

> An accusation of theft may be supported by evidence that it was committed in any manner that would be theft [under § 223], notwithstanding the specification of a different manner in the indictment or information, subject only to the power of the [trial court] to ensure fair trial by granting . . . appropriate relief where the conduct of the defense would be prejudiced by lack of fair notice or by surprise.

The *Traster* case illustrates the usefulness of a consolidation statute that included the crimes of larceny, larceny by trick, embezzlement, and false pretenses. Based on this statute, the *Traster* Court had the authority to affirm the defendant's conviction for the wrong crime of false pretenses because there was sufficient evidence to support a conviction for attempted larceny by trick. Then the court modified the judgment to reflect a conviction for the right crime. The *Batin* prosecutor failed for unknown reasons to rely on the Nevada consolidation statute when charging the defendant with embezzlement, and therefore, the Nevada Supreme

Court was required to reverse the conviction instead of modifying the judgment to reflect a conviction for larceny.

Both *Traster* and *Batin* also illustrate the reasons for widespread enactment of consolidation statutes that typically encompass at least the four crimes included in the California consolidation statute in *Traster*. These crimes typically impose similar penalties, and the crimes are mutually exclusive. The distinctions among these crimes are based on highly technical rules and legal fictions, and it may be impossible for a prosecutor to determine which crime fits the defendant's conduct until all the evidence is presented at trial.

Hypo 1: *Switching Tags*

A security guard saw Finch take the $100 price tag off a dress and switch that tag with the $50 sale price tag from a different dress. The guard informed Gary, the cashier, that a customer fitting Finch's description had switched price tags on a dress, and that Gary should charge her the erroneous sale price when the dress was presented for purchase. After Gary followed this instruction, the guard followed Finch out of the store and arrested her. If Finch is convicted for false pretenses, why might the appellate court reverse this conviction? By contrast, why might the appellate court affirm Finch's conviction for false pretenses if the guard only told Gary to "watch out for a customer" fitting Finch's description "who may do something suspicious," and if Gary testified that he did not know whether the price tag on the dress was the right price or not, and so he just charged that sale price. *Compare State v. Finch*, 223 Kan. 398, 573 P.2d 1048 (1978); *People v. Lorenzo*, 64 Cal. App. 3d Supp. 43, 135 Cal. Rptr. 337 (1976).

Hypo 2: *Influence of MPC and Common Law*

Based on the text of each of the following statutes, identify and explain the influence of the common law and the MPC upon each:

New York Penal Code § 155.05: Larceny Defined:

1. A person steals property and commits larceny when, with intent to deprive another of property or to appropriate the same to himself or to a third person, he wrongfully takes, obtains or withholds such property from an owner thereof.

2. Larceny includes a wrongful taking, obtaining or withholding of another's property, with the intent prescribed in [§ 1.], committed in any of the following ways:

(a) By conduct heretofore defined or known as common law larceny by trespassory taking, common law larceny by trick, embezzlement, or obtaining property by false pretenses[.]

California Penal Code, § 484–502.9:

(a) Every person who shall feloniously steal, take, carry, lead, or drive away the personal property of another, or who shall fraudulently appropriate property which has been entrusted to him or her, or who shall knowingly and designedly, by any false or fraudulent representation or pretense, defraud any other person of money, labor or real or personal property, or who causes or procures others to report falsely of his or her wealth or mercantile character and by thus imposing upon any person, obtains credit and thereby fraudulently gets or obtains possession of money, or property or obtains the labor or service of another, is guilty of theft.

D. Receiving Stolen Property

In late seventeenth century England, a person who received stolen goods could be prosecuted only as an accessory after the fact to the theft crime committed by the thief, and only if the thief was convicted first. Not until the early nineteenth century was the conduct of "receiving stolen goods" recognized by Parliament as a separate and independent crime. State codes originally defined the crime to cover defendants who "receive" property, "knowing" the property is "stolen," with the "intent to deprive the owner." Modern statutes typically use some expanded version of these elements for the crime of "Receiving Stolen Property" (RSP). The *McCoy* case illustrates the consensus that the "receiving" element should be equated with "possession" of the stolen property, while revealing the difficulties of identifying the earmarks of possession in the context of prosecutions for receiving stolen automobiles.

State v. McCoy

116 N.J. 293, 561 A.2d 582 (1989).

POLLOCK, J.

The sole issue on this appeal is whether defendant provided an adequate basis for a plea of guilty of receiving stolen property in violation of *N.J.S.A.* [§] 2C:20–7. The Appellate Division found that the basis was inadequate[,] reversed [the] defendant's conviction and remanded the matter to the Law Division [the trial court]. Although we disagree with the reasoning of the Appellate Division, we affirm the judgment of remand.

On December [10,] 1985, defendant [was] arrested for [the] offense of receiving a stolen automobile. Following his indictment, he pled guilty pursuant to a *plea agreement*. Thereafter,

What's That?

A *plea agreement* is an agreement whereby a defendant pleads guilty in exchange for some benefit offered by the prosecutor, such as dropping some charges, accepting a plea to a lesser offense, making a sentencing recommendation for a lesser penalty, or some combination of these benefits.

in providing a factual basis for his plea, defendant described the events of December 10th:

THE DEFENDANT: I was walking down the street and my friend came around the corner. Keith Martin came around the corner in the car and he called me over there to him. So I came to the car. I was getting ready to enter the car. I put my hands on the car. As soon as I put my hands on the car, the cop told me freeze, so I ran.

THE COURT: Okay. [Mr.] McCoy, did you have any reason to believe that the car was or might be stolen?

THE DEFENDANT: Yes, I did.

THE COURT: Did you think the car was or was likely to be stolen?

THE DEFENDANT: Yes.

THE COURT: He says he wasn't in the car.

[THE ASSISTANT PROSECUTOR]: Were you about to get into the car, Mr. McCoy?

THE DEFENDANT: Yes, I was.

[THE DEFENDANT'S ATTORNEY]: What were you about to get into the car for?

THE DEFENDANT: I was going to ride around in it.

[THE DEFENDANT'S ATTORNEY]: Knowing that the car was stolen?

THE DEFENDANT: Yes.

The trial court ascertained that defendant's plea was knowing and voluntary and that defendant knew and understood his rights. Before sentencing, defendant moved to withdraw his plea, but the trial court concluded that the plea was supported by an adequate factual basis[.]

Food for Thought

What information is the trial judge attempting to elicit from the defendant during the guilty plea hearing? Why are the defense counsel and prosecutor asking the defendant these particular questions?

Defendant appealed his conviction on the grounds that there was an insufficient factual basis to support the plea[.] The Appellate Division [concluded] that the facts were insufficient to establish that defendant had "received" the stolen automobile. [*See* 222 N.J. Super. 626, 631, 537 A.2d 787 (1988).] In reaching this decision, the [court] observed that under [§] 2C:20–7 receipt equates with possession[,] [and] that "possession" is defined as " 'intentional control and dominion' " [under our precedents]. [T]he court concluded that there was no evidence that defendant intended to control the vehicle, or that he and the driver were on a joint or common mission, or that defendant was in a position to assert control or dominion over the driver of the vehicle[.] The court recognized, however, that defendant's conduct could subject him to a charge of attempted receipt of stolen property[.]

Defendant was charged under N.J.S.A. [§] 2C:20–7a, which provides:

> A person is guilty of theft if he knowingly receives or brings into this State movable property of another knowing that it has been stolen, or believing that it is probably stolen[.] "Receiving" means acquiring possession, control or title, or lending on the security of the property.

"Possession" is defined in N.J.S.A. [§] 2C:2–1c as "an act, within the meaning of this section, if the possessor knowingly procured or received the thing possessed or was aware of his control thereof for a sufficient period to have been able to terminate his possession."

The key elements of the offense are knowing that the property is stolen and possession. When entering his plea, the defendant explicitly stated that he knew the automobile was stolen. Hence, our attention shifts to the question of possession[.]

Possession [can] be actual or constructive. Here, for example, the driver was in actual possession of the stolen automobile. As we have previously stated, however, "[p]hysical or manual control of the proscribed item is not required as long as there is an intention to exercise control over it manifested in circumstances where it is reasonable to infer that the capacity to do so exists." *Brown, supra*, 80 N.J. at 597, 404 A.2d 1111[.] [Moreover,] possession may be exercised jointly by two or more persons at the same time. Consequently, the question in the present case becomes whether defendant's relationship to the car was sufficient to permit a finding that he shared possession with the driver. . . .

[A] defendant's mere presence in or near a stolen vehicle will not create an inference of possession if there is no other evidence to establish a connection between the defendant and the vehicle. Consequently, an innocent passenger who does not know that the car is stolen does not have sufficient possession to sustain a conviction for receiving stolen property. *State v. Serrano*, 53 N.J. 356, 359, 251 A.2d 97 (1969). In *Serrano*, the only evidence was that the defendant was a passenger and that he fled from the automobile when stopped by the police[.] Other jurisdictions have similarly decided that a mere passenger is not in possession of a car.

A defendant's words or conduct, as well as other evidence, may sufficiently substantiate his or her relationship to the stolen property to support an inference of possession. Thus, when police observed the defendant unloading beer from a stolen truck and defendant fled when approached by the police, the evidence was sufficient for the jury to infer that the defendant had the requisite intention and control to be in constructive possession of the truck. *State v. Bozeyowski*, 77 N.J. Super. 49, 57–58, 185 A.2d 393 (App. Div. 1962). Similarly, in *State v. Alexander*, 215 N.J. Super. 523, 529, 522 A.2d 464 (App. Div. 1987), the defendant was riding in a stolen vehicle within six hours after its theft, lived in close proximity to the place of the theft, and gave the police false information. This evidence was sufficient for the jury to infer that the defendant constructively possessed the automobile[.] *See also People v. Murphy*, 126 Misc. 2d 1023, 484 N.Y.S.2d 411 (Sup. Ct. 1984) (defendant-passenger in possession where he witnessed theft by friend, accepted invitation from him to ride in the car, rode in car for five hours, and got in and out of the auto at various points).

Food for Thought

What possible reasons may explain why the New Jersey Supreme Court chose to establish its four-factor formula to describe the positive requirements for affirming an RSP conviction, instead of endorsing the App. Div. court's analysis?

[We] conclude that an inference of possession may arise from a passenger's presence in a stolen automobile when that presence is coupled with additional evidence that the passenger knew the driver, knew that the vehicle was stolen, and intended to use the vehicle for his or her own benefit and enjoyment. [A] jury [might infer] that the passenger had both the intention and the capacity to control the stolen vehicle. A jury might infer that such a passenger could exert control over the vehicle, an inference that would support a finding of constructive possession. Although a jury might reject the inference in a contested case, the facts would be sufficient to support a plea of guilty to possession of a stolen automobile.

[When] a defendant is outside the car, proof of his or her possession is more problematic. Here, for example, the defendant was arrested before he entered the stolen automobile. The facts reveal nothing more than that he had placed his hands on the automobile with the intent "to ride around in it," knowing the driver, and knowing that the automobile was stolen. We believe that those facts are insufficient to support an inference that at the time of his arrest defendant could have exercised dominion and control over the automobile. In brief, the evidence was insufficient to support a conviction for receipt of a stolen automobile. Consequently, defendant must be allowed to withdraw his plea.

At oral argument, however, the State argued that "what we have is enough to show that defendant attempted to possess the car[.]" . . . [But] [w]hen defendant entered his plea [to the crime of receipt of stolen property,] no one thought he was pleading to the offense of an *attempted* receipt of stolen property. Consequently, the trial court did not explain that offense to him, and defendant did not plead to it. In that context, we cannot transmute defendant's plea to the receipt of stolen property to one for the *attempt* to receive that property. Should defendant elect to plead guilty to either receipt or the attempted receipt of stolen property, the court must establish anew a sufficient factual basis for the offense.

The judgment of the Appellate Division is affirmed, and the matter is remanded to the Law Division to allow defendant to withdraw his plea.

Points for Discussion

a. Elements of Receiving Stolen Property

Originally the crime of receiving stolen property applied to property that was stolen through larceny. But gradually it came to apply to the receipt of goods stolen by any means of theft, and most modern statutes use that broad definition, even when the larceny term "stolen" appears in the title of the crime. Most states also have abandoned the common law element that required the goods to be "stolen," so that it is possible to prosecute defendants who have been caught in a sting operation, even when the goods may have lost their stolen character. *See* Model Penal Code § 223.6, Comments 4(b), 4(c), at 239–240 (1980).

Most states use the MPC mental state that allows conviction upon proof that the defendant believed the property probably was stolen. Even in states where the mental state element is knowledge that property was stolen, the consensus in case law is that proof of positive knowledge is not required. Evidence of suspicious circumstances or suspicious comments and behavior by the defendant may supply the necessary inference of knowledge. Most states also require that a defendant possess the "intent to deprive the owner" of the property, whereas the MPC requires that the prosecutor prove only that the defendant did not possess the intent to restore the property. *See* Model Penal Code § 223.6, Comment 4(a), at 237 (1980).

b. Receiving as Possesssion

The concept of "possession" is vital for the definition of the crime of receiving stolen property because courts and legislatures equate that concept with the element of "receiving." Like the *McCoy* Court, other courts agree that "mere presence near the stolen property, or access to the location where the stolen property is found is not sufficient evidence of possession, standing alone, to sustain a conviction for receiving stolen property." Other courts also have looked to the same earmarks of possession recognized in the precedents cited in *McCoy*.

The statutory definition of "possession" in *McCoy* is described as satisfied by evidence that the defendant "was *aware* of his control" over the thing possessed. The *Brown* definition of possession is satisfied when "there is an *intention* to exercise control" as well as the implicit capacity to do so. Do these definitions suggest that "possession" is essentially a state of mind? If so, it may be difficult for a prosecutor to obtain direct evidence of a defendant's state of mind in order to establish the necessary "awareness" or "intention." Therefore, the *McCoy* Court's task is to identify the circumstantial evidence that will justify a jury's finding of the defendant's possessory state of mind. The *McCoy* opinion implicitly recognizes the danger that an overbroad definition of "possession" may lead to unfair convictions. Does the court's four-factor test minimize that danger?

The following hypothetical illustrates the difficulties involved in obtaining sufficient evidence to prove beyond a reasonable doubt that a defendant possessed the requisite knowledge that a car was stolen. In this case, the defendant is not charged with the RSP crime, but with the lesser crime of "unauthorized use of a vehicle" (UUV), which does not require proof of the element of "receiving" ("possession"), but instead requires proof of "presence inside the car" and knowledge that the car was stolen.

Hypo: *Knowing That Vehicle Is Stolen*

The owner of a Ford Taurus reported it stolen from the parking lot in front of her apartment building. The next evening, Officer Williams was on foot patrol when he spotted the stolen Taurus, which was parked a few blocks from the apartment, with four individuals inside. Officer Williams was wearing a vest with the word "Police" in large letters, and as he approached the Taurus, the four individuals jumped out and all of them started to run away. D.P. is a thirteen-year-old passenger who was sitting in the back seat of the Taurus. Officer Williams caught D.P. some 30 feet from the Taurus and arrested him for the crime of "unauthorized use of a vehicle" (UUV). This crime applies to a person who "is present in a vehicle" "with knowledge that the vehicle is stolen or being operated without the owner's consent." In juvenile court proceedings, D.P. was adjudicated a delinquent based on the judge's finding that he had committed the UUV crime. The evidence included a photograph of the steering column of the Taurus, which showed that the ignition had been completely removed so that the car could be driven without a key. However, this photo was taken by a crime scene technician who was sitting in the front seat of the Taurus. Officer Williams testified that he found no other visible damage to the Taurus, and D.P. did not testify. On appeal, D.P.'s counsel argues that there was insufficient evidence to show that D.P. had the required mental state of "knowledge." What reasons could a court use to reverse the adjudication of delinquency on this grounds? *Compare In re D.P.*, 996 A.2d 1286 (D.C. Ct. App. 2010).

just a passenger, no proof he knew it was stolen

E. Robbery & Carjacking

Robbery is the oldest common law property crime and predates larceny. The MPC Commentary describes robbery as "the theft of property under circumstances calculated to terrorize the victim." *See* Model Penal Code § 222.1, Comment 1, at 96 (1980). The earliest version of the robbery crime required a taking of property by means of actual physical violence committed upon the person. Later it was expanded to punish a taking by the "constructive violence" of putting the victim in fear. Initially, this fear included either fear of bodily injury or fear of violence to "habitation or property." *See* WAYNE R. LAFAVE, CRIMINAL LAW, § 20.3, at 1046, n.1 (5th ed. 2010). Later this element evolved into fear of violence to the victim, and the robbery crime took on its familiar English common law form, which required all the same elements as larceny, plus two additional elements: 1) the taking of property "from the person or presence of the victim"; 2) by means of force or by putting the victim in fear of violence.

In the early 1990s, Congress and many state legislatures decided to enact "carjacking" statutes in order to punish one type of robbery with more severe penalties, namely the violent taking of an automobile. Some carjacking statutes, including the federal statute in *Lake*, were modeled on the elements of the common law robbery crime, and therefore included the requirement that the car must be taken "from the person or presence of the victim." The *Lake* case illustrates how courts have sought to achieve the purposes of both the robbery and the carjacking crime by using an expansive definition of "presence."

United States v. Lake

150 F.3d 269 (3d Cir. 1998).

ALITO, CIRCUIT JUDGE

[Lake] was convicted under 18 U.S.C. § 924(c)(1) of using or carrying a firearm during and in relation to a crime of violence, namely, a carjacking [under] 18 U.S.C. § 2119[.] Lake challenges his conviction on [the] grounds [that] he did not take the motor vehicle in question "from the person or presence" of the victim. We reject this [argument,] and we therefore affirm.

The events that led to Lake's prosecution occurred at Little Magen's Bay in St. Thomas, United States Virgin Islands. The road to the beach at Little Magen's Bay ends at the top of a hill [where a parking area is located]. There is a steep path bordered by vegetation and rocks that leads from the [parking area] down to the beach, and the [parking area] cannot be seen from the beach.

On the day in question, Lake hitchhiked to Little Magen's Bay and encountered Milton Clarke, who was sitting on the beach reading a newspaper. Lake asked whether Clarke owned a white car parked up on the road [at the parking area]. Clarke said that he did, and Lake initially walked away. However, Lake returned a few moments later and asked to borrow the car. When Clarke refused, Lake stated that it was an emergency. Clarke again refused and Lake walked off. When Lake returned yet again, Clarke said: ["L]isten, think about it. If I walked up to you and asked you, can I borrow your car[,] [a]re you going to lend it to me? Of course not. So why don't you leave me the hell alone. I'm here to have a nice time. Just chill. Go someplace else.["]

Lake walked off and sat on a rock, while Clarke anxiously watched him out of the corner of his eye, but Lake soon returned with the same request. When Clarke swore again, Lake asked if he could have a drink from Clarke's cooler. Clarke said: "[D]on't you get it? Leave me alone." Lake then lifted up his shirt, showed Clarke the handle of a gun, and said: "[Y]ou know what that is?" Clarke stood up and started backing away, but Lake pulled the gun from his waist band, put it against Clarke's face, and demanded the car keys. Clarke said that he did not have the keys and started walking toward the water with Lake following. Clarke waded into waist-deep water, and Lake walked out onto a promontory overlooking the water.

While Clarke was in the water, his friend, Pamela Croaker, appeared on the beach. Clarke shouted a warning, prompting Lake to approach Croaker. Lake demanded that Croaker surrender her car keys, and Croaker said: "I don't even know you. Why would I give you the keys to the car?" Lake then grabbed the keys, and the two wrestled for possession of the keys. [Lake placed the gun close to her head and again told her to surrender the keys.] [Croaker] surrendered the keys but asked to keep her house keys. Lake went up the steep path to the parking area where Croaker had parked her car out of sight of the beach. Lake then drove away in Croaker's car after leaving her house keys on the hood of Clarke's car. [B]oth Croaker and Clarke followed [Lake] up the path, but when they arrived [at the parking area], [Lake] was driving away. [Later] that day, the police apprehended Lake in the stolen car[.] The gun was never recovered. . . .

[Under] the carjacking statute, the prosecution must prove that the defendant (1) "with intent to cause death or serious bodily harm" (2) took a motor vehicle (3) that had been "transported, shipped, or received in interstate or foreign commerce" (4) "from the person or presence of another" (5) "by force and violence or by intimidation." . . . [Lake] maintains [that] he took [Croaker's] keys, not her car, from her person or presence and that the car was not in Croaker's presence when he took it because she could not see or touch the car at that moment.

The carjacking statute's requirement that the vehicle be taken "from the person or presence of the victim" "tracks the language used in other federal robbery statutes," such as 18 U.S.C. §§ 2111, 2113, and 2118. [H.R.Rep. No. 102–851(I), at 5 (1992).] Under these statutes, "property is in the presence of a person if it is 'so within his reach, observation or control, that he could if not overcome by violence or prevented by fear, retain his possession of it.'" *United States v. Burns*, 701 F.2d 840, 843 (9th Cir. 1983). *See also* LaFave & Scott, Substantive Criminal Law § 8.11 at 443 (1986) ("'Presence' in this connection is not so much a matter of eyesight as it is one of proximity and control[.]")

Here [Lake] took Croaker's car keys at gunpoint on the beach and then ran up the path and drove away in her car. Croaker pursued Lake but did not reach the parking area in time to stop him. Applying the definition of "presence" [used in *Burns*,] we conclude that a rational jury could have found that Croaker could have prevented the taking of her car if she had not been fearful that Lake would shoot or otherwise harm her. Croaker testified that the sight of Lake's gun caused her great fear. She stated that when she first saw the gun she "felt like [she] was going [to] faint." Although Croaker did not say in so many words that she hesitated for some time before pursuing Lake up the path, the sequence of events laid out in her testimony supports the inference that this is what occurred. Croaker stated that at the point when she surrendered the keys, Clarke "was struggling back through the water to come back," but that she did not start to run up the path until Clarke emerged from the water[.] Clarke testified that, when Lake ran up the path, Croaker was "pulling herself together[,]" that he "caught up to [Croaker] at the bottom of the paved driveway" and that the two of them proceeded up the path together. They reached the parking area in time for Croaker to see Lake driving away in her car but not in time to stop him. Both Croaker and Clarke stated that at this point they were very scared. Based on this testimony, a rational jury could infer that Croaker hesitated before pursuing Lake due to fear and that if she had not hesitated she could have reached the parking area in time to prevent Lake from taking her car without employing further force, violence, or intimidation. We do not suggest this inference was compelled, but because such an inference was rational, we hold that the evidence was sufficient. . . .

In sum, we hold that the evidence was sufficient to establish all of the elements of the carjacking statute[.]

For these reasons, we affirm the judgment of the district court.

BECKER, CHIEF JUDGE, dissenting.

When the defendant took the car keys from his victim, Pamela Croaker, Ms. Croaker's car was, in city terms, a block away, up the hill, out of sight. Under these circumstances, I would join an opinion upholding Lake's conviction for "keyjacking," or for both key robbery [and key] larceny. I cannot, however, agree that he is guilty of carjacking. The majority draws upon federal robbery statutes to explicate how the vehicle (as opposed to its keys) may be considered to have been taken from the "person or presence of the victim." Disciples of the jurisprudence of pure reason may, in analytic terms, find this approach convincing. As I will explain[,] I do not. At all events, my polestar is the plain meaning of words, and in my lexicon, Ms. Croaker's car cannot fairly be said to have been taken from her person or presence, hence I respectfully dissent.

Food for Thought

What scenarios would not qualify for carjacking liability under Chief Judge Becker's narrow definition of the "purpose or presence" element, but would qualify for liability under the *Lake* majority's definition?

The robbery statutes upon which the carjacking statute is based do not themselves define the phrase "from the person or presence of the victim." Webster's New International Dictionary defines presence as "the vicinity of, or area immediately near one." However, rather than relying on the plain meaning, the majority turns to a construction of the phrase "person or presence" adopted by the Ninth Circuit in *United States v. Burns*, 701 F.2d 840 (9th Cir. 1983), where, in construing a federal robbery statute, that court reasoned that "property is in the presence of a person if it is 'so within his reach, inspection, observation or control, that he could if not overcome by violence or prevented by fear, retain his possession of it.'" Based on this definition, the majority concludes that a rational jury "could infer that Croaker hesitated before pursuing Lake due to fear and that if she had not hesitated she could have reached the parking area in time to prevent Lake from taking her car without employing further force, violence, or intimidation." This proves too much. If it is true that had Croaker not hesitated out of fear she could have followed Lake up the steep path leading from the secluded beach to the road, then it is equally true (barring physical limitations) that she could have followed him up that path and then halfway across St. Thomas. The fact that Croaker's car was nearby is thus not relevant; if she could have followed Lake up the hill, she could have followed him anywhere. I am aware, of course, that the craft of judging requires line-drawing, but I simply do not see how that endeavor can be principled when it is predicated on open-ended definitions of key statutory terms, especially where those terms admit of plain meaning.

Points for Discussion

a. Elements of Carjacking

In 1991, the conduct that became known as "carjacking" attracted public attention when one victim died after being dragged for two miles during a violent seizure of a car in Maryland. This event inspired the widespread enactment of carjacking statutes, including the federal Anti Car Theft Act of 1992 and similar state statutes, even though the conduct of carjackers was covered by the robbery crime. The federal statute was amended in 1994 to require "the intent to cause death or serious bodily harm." State statutes exhibit a variety of mental state choices.

Even when a legislature borrows the elements of a state's common law robbery statute in order to define the carjacking crime, it is common for a legislature to add extra elements to a carjacking statute. For example, a California carjacking statute applies to cases where the defendant has only the intent to "temporarily deprive" the person in possession of a motor vehicle, and to cases where the defendant takes the motor vehicle from the "person or presence" of a passenger who is *not* in possession of it, including children. Moreover, a court will interpret the elements of a carjacking crime based on policy concerns relating to the unique dangers to which carjacking victims are subjected. For example, carjacking victims may be run over, abducted in their vehicles, driven at high speeds by captors who are chased by police, and killed or injured in car crashes. *See People v. Lopez*, 31 Cal. 4th 1051, 79 P.3d 548, 6 Cal. Rptr. 3d 432 (2003).

By the time that carjacking statutes were enacted, however, most states no longer defined robbery using all the elements of larceny plus the elements of a forcible taking from the "person or presence" of the victim. Instead, most states endorsed the MPC view that the "person or presence" element is unnecessary in a modern robbery statute. A typical modern robbery crime only requires the defendant to intentionally threaten the victim with bodily harm during the course of committing a theft. *Compare* Model Penal Code § 222.1, Comment (3)(d), at 112 (1980). This is why many state carjacking statutes do not reflect the borrowing of all the common law elements of robbery. For example, the Maryland statute requires only the intent to do the prohibited act of "obtaining unauthorized possession" of a motor vehicle "from another individual in actual possession" by "putting that individual in fear" through "intimidation"[.]" *See Harris v. State*, 353 Md. 596, 728 A.2d 180 (1999). What are the possible reasons that most state codes today do not include the "person or presence" element in the robbery crime? Do those reasons apply equally well to the carjacking crime?

b. Defining Presence

The *Lake* majority takes a conventional approach to the interpretation of the federal carjacking statute by identifying the federal robbery statutes as the source of the "person or presence" element, and relying on robbery precedents to interpret the meaning of that element. The *Lake* dissent rejects this approach and prefers to rely on the dictionary meaning of "presence." Similarly, each opinion goes in opposite directions in explaining why the defendant's conduct does or does not fit the harm that Congress intended to punish in the carjacking statute.

Why is the dissent's argument about the applicability of the dictionary definition of "presence" unpersuasive in light of the language of the carjacking statute and its legislative history? Although the *Burns* interpretation of the term "presence" may be "open-ended" to some degree, is the dissent correct to say that the *Lake* majority's reasoning would require the affirmance of the conviction if the victim's car had been located "halfway across St. Thomas"? Should the carjacking crime apply to a case in which the defendant, after robbing a bank, tied up the bank manager in her office, ordered her (at gunpoint) to turn over her car keys and reveal the location of her car, and then used the bank manager's car to flee the scene? *Compare United States v. Moore*, 198 F.3d 793 (10th Cir. 1999).

Hypo 1 and Hypo 2 address the circumstances that may qualify for a robbery conviction. Hypo 3 relates to a carjacking scenario.

Hypo 1: *Physically Restrained*

Deb had no idea that her classmate Sara needed money to support her heroin habit. Nor did Deb realize that Sara was armed with a concealed revolver while they were having lunch together. When the conversation turned to the subject of firearms, Deb showed Sara the Heckler and Koch 9mm pistol that she had inherited from her grandmother. Sara recognized that this pistol was worth $900 and asked Deb whether she could examine it. Then Sara pocketed the valuable gun while pointing her own revolver at Deb, saying, "Look. Just stay in your chair. Don't move. I don't want to blow you away, but I will if I have to." Then Sara jumped up and ran out the front door of Deb's house. Deb ignored Sara's order and chased her out the door and across the front yard. Then Deb tackled Sara, knocking the revolver out of Sara's hand and the pistol out of Sara's pocket. Sara was arrested and charged under a federal statute defining robbery as "the taking or the attempt to take anything of value from another by force, violence, or intimidation."

Sara pleaded guilty to the robbery crime because she had no defense. During Sara's sentencing, the federal district court judge added two years to her robbery sentence based on a federal statute that authorizes this extra two-year penalty when during a robbery, "any person was *physically restrained* to facilitate commission of the offense or to facilitate escape." The judge interpreted this provision broadly, as do four federal circuit courts, to include "a situation in which an armed defendant uses some coercive action to restrict a person's ability to act," including the scenario in which a defendant like Sara "simply points a gun at the victim, orders the victim not to move, and does not otherwise immobilize the victim."

On appeal, Sara's defense counsel argues that the federal circuit court, which has taken no position yet on the meaning of "physically restrained" in the robbery statute, should adopt the narrow interpretation of four other federal circuits. These courts rely on legislative history indicating that Congress was most concerned with cases in which a robber used "*forcible* restraint of a victim," "such as the restraint of being tied, bound, or locked up." Therefore, these four circuits equate "*physical* restraint" with "depriving a victim of the freedom of physical *movement*" through "physical coercion. They reject the use of the extra penalty in cases where mere "*psychological* coercion" is used. What are the pro and con arguments for these two competing interpretations of "physically restrained"?

Hypo 2: *Handing over the Cashier's Drawer*

When Bob was charged with robbery, Tina testified at his trial, stating that, "I got robbed." When asked for details, Tina testified that Bob walked into the Jiffy Lube Automobile Service Center at 3:00 pm and approached Tina, who was working as the cashier. Tina did not know Bob and she assumed that he was a customer with a question. Bob walked up to the Tina, stood in front of the cash register counter, and then uttered three words without making any gestures: "Don't say anything." Then Tina decided that she had better hand over the cash register drawer to Bob. He walked away with the drawer, which was full of cash, and he left the store. When Tina was asked by the prosecutor whether she believed that Bob had a weapon, she testified that, "I wasn't taking any chances." When asked to describe Bob's appearance, Tina stated that, "He had a tear drop tattoo under one eye." When asked what this tattoo meant to her, Tina testified that, "One of my friends got the same tattoo when one of his relatives died. But I've heard that sometimes people get that tattoo in prison." Bob was convicted of robbery and sentenced to 15 years. If Bob had been convicted of larceny instead, the maximum sentence would have been two years. Assume that the only issue raised by Bob's defense counsel on appeal is whether the evidence showed that Bob's conduct satisfied the required elements of robbery because he "took property *either* by means of force *or* by putting the other person in fear of violence." What pro and con arguments will be made by the prosecutor and defense regarding the evidence that Bob took the cash drawer from Tina "by means of force"? What arguments will be made regarding the evidence he took the cash drawer "by putting Tina in fear of violence"?

Hypo 3: *During the Course of the Carjacking*

Ed was installing drywall in a home that was undergoing renovations. He parked his truck in the driveway. At 5:00 pm, even though all the other construction workers had gone home, Ed decided to work longer. Then Ed heard a voice and saw Mel walking toward him with a gun pointed in Ed's direction. When Mel told Ed, "Don't look at me," Ed looked at the ground and stood motionless. Mel reached into Ed's pockets and removed Ed's cell phone, wallet, and the keys to Ed's truck. Mel told Ed, "Don't follow me," and Ed did not look up until he heard Mel's footsteps fading away. When Ed saw that Mel was gone, Ed went to the front window of the house and saw Mel driving away in Ed's truck. Two days later, Mel was driving the truck when he failed to stop at a stop sign. Officer Juana was following Mel and tried to pull him over; instead, he led her on a high speed chase until he was forced to stop when several police cars converged on the scene. When Ed later retrieved his truck from the police impound lot, the gas tank was nearly empty but there was no damage to the truck. Ed found his wallet and cell phone in the glove compartment, and nothing had been taken from the wallet.

The Chief Prosecutor wants to know whether Mel can be convicted of carjacking under a 2006 statute that defines the crime as follows: "The taking of a motor vehicle from the person or custody of another, with the intent to either permanently or temporarily deprive that person of the motor vehicle; when in the course of the taking there is use of force, violence, or putting in fear. An Act shall be deemed to be 'in the course of the taking' if such act [that is, the use of force, violence, or fear] occurs either prior to, contemporaneous with, or subsequent to the taking of the property, and if such act and the act of taking constitute a continuous series of acts or events." Explain the reasons that can be used by the Chief to convict Mel under this statute.

F. Burglary

The crime of common law burglary required the breaking and entering of a dwelling at night time with the intent to commit a felony therein. That felony crime might be theft in many cases, but burglary encompassed the intent to commit any felony. Modern burglary statutes have broadened the crime to cover daytime intrusions into structures or vehicles. The *T.J.E.* case illustrates how a court may decide to interpret a modern burglary statute narrowly, in order to make it inapplicable to mere shoplifters. The subsequent redefinitions of burglary by the state legislature, which implicitly rejected the *T.J.E.* interpretation, reveal how difficult it may be to achieve the same result in other ways.

In the Matter of T.J.E.

426 N.W.2d 23 (S.D. 1988).

WUEST, CHIEF JUSTICE.

What's That?

When the state's attorney files a delinquency petition, the juvenile court judge in South Dakota makes the decision whether to find that a child has committed an act that would be a crime if committed by an adult. If the child is adjudicated a *juvenile delinquent* after an adjudicatory hearing," then after a "dispositional hearing" to determine punishment, the judge will issue a decree of disposition describing the outcome, including the sentence. See https://www.sdlawhelp.org/node/63/juvenile-delinquency-supervision

T.J.E. appeals her adjudication and disposition as a *juvenile delinquent*. We reverse.

T.J.E., age 11, entered a retail store during business hours with her aunt. While in the store, T.J.E. took and ate a piece of candy from a display and left with her aunt without paying for the candy. T.J.E. was stopped outside of the store by the manager and ultimately admitted to him that she had eaten a piece of candy without paying for it. [Her aunt offered to pay for it but the manager called the police.]

[The] State subsequently filed a petition in the circuit court alleging T.J.E. to be a delinquent child [because she allegedly committed] second degree burglary. After an adjudicatory hearing the circuit court sustained the allegations of second degree burglary.

We find that the evidence presented by [the] state during T.J.E.'s adjudicatory hearing was insufficient to sustain the allegations in its petition [that] T.J.E. committed the offense of second degree burglary in violation of SDCL [§] 22–32–3: ["] Any person who *enters* or *remains* in an occupied structure with intent to commit any crime therein[.]"

[First,] [w]e find no proof in the record that at the time T.J.E. entered the store with her aunt she had the intent to commit a crime inside. We decline to interpret the impulsive act of this 11 year old child in taking candy after entering the store as evincing an intent *at the time of her entry* to commit theft. This clearly distinguishes this case from our affirmance of a burglary conviction in *State v. Shult*, 380 N.W.2d 352 (S.D. 1986), where the defendant took an item of merchandise [a frozen pizza] from a convenience store [at a time when it was open to the public]. In *Shult* there was an admission by him that at the time he entered the store he had the specific intent to commit theft therein. There is no such evidence in the present case.

[Second,] [t]he circuit court [found] that T.J.E. *remained* in the store with the intent to commit theft, thereby committing second degree burglary by *remaining* in an occupied structure with the intent to commit a crime therein. A literal reading of the word "remains" in the statute would support this finding and would end the need for further inquiry. However, where the literal meaning of a statute leads to absurd or unreasonable conclusions, ambiguity exists. To interpret the word "remains" in [§] 22–32–3 to hold [that] a person commits second degree burglary whenever he is present in an occupied structure with the intent to commit a crime therein would make every shoplifter a burglar. It would make the commission of any crime indoors, no matter how severe, subject to a felony burglary charge. We do not believe the legislature intended such absurd results when it amended the burglary statutes in 1976.

Because the history of our state burglary statutes makes reference to the state of California, we have previously looked to that state for guidance in interpretation of our own burglary provisions[.] The statute defining the offense of burglary in California, unlike [§] 22–32–3, does not contain the word "remains." Nevertheless, the [S]upreme [C]ourt of [California] has discussed the type of presence in a building or structure necessary for commission of burglary. [That] court has interpreted the law of burglary in that state as retaining the principle that burglary must be committed by a person who has no right to be in the building or structure burglarized. [*People v.*] *Gauze*, 125 Cal. Rptr. [773,] 775, 542 P.2d [1365,] 1367 [(1975)].

To read the word "remains" in [§ 22–32–3] to mean that a person can commit burglary when he is lawfully present in an occupied structure . . . contravenes the principle [that] burglary must be committed by a person who has no right to be in the structure. However, if we were to read the word "remains" as it is qualified in the statutes of eleven other states to mean that a person can commit second degree burglary when he is *unlawfully* present or present *without authority* in an occupied structure, [then this interpretation] would avoid the possibility for absurdity and retain the principle that burglary must be committed by a person with no right to be in the structure. . . .

[Where] a person enters a business place open to the general public with the intent to commit a crime therein, he enters without invitation and is not one of the public invited or entitled to enter the structure. *People v. Barry*, 94 Cal. 481, 29 P. 1026, 1027 (1892). Relying on this premise, the California Supreme Court has reasoned that holding such a person subject to prosecution for burglary does not reflect abandonment of the principle that burglary must be committed by a person who has no right to be in the structure. We find this reasoning persuasive[.]

[We] conclude, therefore, that the word "remains" in the second degree burglary statute means to *unlawfully* remain in a structure. Therefore, second degree burglary was not committed in this case where T.J.E. entered an occupied structure and *after* entry, while *lawfully* remaining in the structure, formed the intent to commit an offense therein[.]

We find that state failed to establish that T.J.E. either entered or *unlawfully* remained in an occupied structure with the intent to commit a crime therein. Therefore, the evidence was insufficient to sustain the allegations in [the] state's delinquency petition. Accordingly, we reverse the circuit court's adjudication and disposition of T.J.E. as a juvenile delinquent.

Food for Thought

If the South Dakota legislature decides to amend the burglary statute in order to prevent a prosecutor from charging any shoplifter with burglary, should the legislature codify the *T.J.E.* holding? What other amendments of the burglary statute would achieve this result?

HENDERSON, JUSTICE (specially concurring).

Take Note

Justice Henderson's *Shult* dissent criticized the broad scope of the 1976 burglary statute because it would apply to anyone who enters a friend's house with the intent to smoke marijuana, and anyone who enters a tavern with the intent to bounce a check. *See* 380 N.W.2d at 357.

[Under § 22–30A–17,] [p]etty theft of less than $100 is [a] Class 2 misdemeanor [punishable by no more than 30 days jail and/or a fine of no more than $100]. Here, obviously, the shoplifting is a petty theft offense[.]

[If] an eleven year old takes a chocolate Easter egg, a few days before Easter, and without paying for it, eats it, and walks out of the store, has he/she committed second-degree burglary under the statutes of South Dakota? [The shoplifting charge] was not considered by the State. [Instead,] the State and trial court seized upon, and employed, a second-degree burglary charge. [The] preposterous result witnessed in Tripp County by the prosecution of this little girl, was a type of horror/nonsensical situation envisioned in my dissent [in] *Schult*[,] 380 N.W.2d at 358:

> "This second-degree burglary statute has a sweep whereby any and all crimes in occupied structures are amalgamated together by the same punishment depending upon the whim of the prosecutor. Prosecutors must have some channels of discretion and restraint."

[The] prosecutor [here] chose to prosecute under a felony, the child having eaten a chocolate Easter egg, rather than prosecuting for a Class 2 misdemeanor[.] No child should suffer such an adjudication upon his/her record for second-degree burglary by virtue of snitching a chocolate Easter egg and eating it without paying for it; nor, for that matter, be put under the mandate of a court with five conditions which govern the child's conduct for a period of three months. [The] child was determined, as a matter of law, to be a burglar. [The] penalty [for an adult defendant] for second-degree burglary in South Dakota is a maximum sentence of 15 years and a $15,000 fine. [The] adjudication [of delinquency] afflicts a harm upon the child which is needless and disproportionate to the act[.] For a child to go through this type of proceeding and counseling and trips to a court services officer, can be humiliating, degrading, and self-defeating. In common language, a little girl should not have been treated this way. This was a de minimis act. This case should not have reached the circuit court and Supreme Court levels. It could have been treated in an informal setting.

This prosecution creates [an] opportunity of political advantage for the prosecutor to be known as a tough prosecutor to enhance his image of convictions in the community. [But] [h]ow harmful is it to society to remove a candy chocolate egg from a store? . . .

FYI

Tripp County is a rural county of 1,617 square miles on the border between South Dakota and Nebraska. Twenty percent of the population is below the poverty line. Half the population lives in Winner, a town of 2,900 people, where T.J.E. was adjudicated a delinquent. There is no intermediate state appellate court, and the South Dakota Supreme Court is one hundred miles away in the city of Pierre.

[T.J.E.] should have, initially, been treated as a possible shoplifter with store manager and parent(s) having a conference[.] Prosecutors should use a prosecutorial function to a better advantage than displayed here. [T.J.E's] adult relative offered to pay for the chocolate egg which T.J.E. consumed before the forces of the law were set in motion. It is difficult not to scoff at this type of justice and not to feel sorry for the little girl and her aunt who were caught up in the capricious law enforcement on a given day in Tripp County. Law, in the end, does have to make sense.

Points for Discussion

a. Who Is a Burglar?

The starting point for the *T.J.E.* Court's analysis is the observation that the burglary crime is meant to punish people who have "no right to be in the building or structure burglarized." The need for identifying this class of appropriate defendants is a result of the 1976 repeal of the longstanding statutory definition of burglary, rooted in the 1862 Dakota Territory Statute: "If a person break and enter the dwelling house of another in the night time, with intent to commit larceny, he shall be deemed guilty of burglary[.]" The "distinctive situation" for which this crime "was originally devised" was the "invasion of premises under circumstances that are likely to terrorize occupants." *See* Model Penal Code § 222.1, Comment (2), at 67 (1980). Proof of the breaking and entering elements usually supplied evidence of the *mens rea*, namely the intent at the time of entry to commit the requisite crime inside the dwelling. In the absence of a violent type of entry to confirm the defendant's criminal purpose for entry, the defendant was *not* a burglar and would be prosecuted instead for trespass or whatever crimes were committed inside the dwelling, such as larceny or attempted larceny.

By contrast, the broad scope of the new 1976 burglary definition in the *T.J.E.* statute requires only the act of entering *or* remaining in an occupied structure, and a literal reading implies that the timing of the formation of the requisite "intent to commit a crime therein" is irrelevant. Therefore, this statute creates two distinct problems. First, it makes it possible for a prosecutor to charge all shoplifters with burglary. Second, it provides no means for limiting the status of "burglar" to the category of target defendants who "have no right to be in the building or structure burglarized."

The task of the *T.J.E.* Court is to remedy both of these problems, through the strategy of first declaring the 1976 statute to be "ambiguous" because of the "absurd" breadth of its literal interpretation, and then finding a narrowing construction that will provide a workable formula to answer the question, Who is a burglar? As it turns out, this task implicitly requires the court to answer the more specific question, Who is a *mere* shoplifter and *not* a burglar?

It is evident that the *T.J.E.* Court views the candy-eating juvenile as an impulsive shoplifter who does *not* belong in the burglary category. How does the court's narrowing interpretation of the word "remains" to mean "unlawfully remains" allow the juvenile defendant to escape liability for burglary? Note that the *T.J.E.* Court refers approvingly to the burglary conviction of the *Shult* defendant, who was caught taking a frozen pizza from a convenience store and later admitted to the police that he intended to take it when he entered the store. Why is the *Shult* defendant both a shoplifter *and* a burglar under the *T.J.E.* Court's reasoning? Would it be possible to interpret the "unlawfully-remains" concept so as to treat the *Shult* defendant as being *merely* a shoplifter and not a burglar?

b. Limiting the Expansion of Burglary

The MPC drafters viewed modern burglary statutes as too broad, recognizing that "a greatly expanded burglary statute authorizes the prosecutor and the courts to treat as burglary behavior that is distinguishable from theft [only] on purely artificial grounds." This is why the MPC burglary definition preserves the common law requirement that the *mens rea* must coincide with the act of *entry*: "A person is guilty of burglary if he enters a building or occupied structure . . . with purpose to commit a crime therein." The definition of "occupied" structure is limited to any "place adapted for overnight accommodation of persons, or for carrying on business therein, whether or not a person is actually present." *See* Model Penal Code §§ 221.0, 221.1. This restriction preserves the common law's concern with the protection of places where people might normally be present, and excludes many of the places covered by modern burglary statutes, such as aircraft, watercraft, land vehicles, and buildings of any kind. *See* Model Penal Code § 221.1, Comment 3, at 72. Although some states emulate these limitations, most state codes continue to rely on elements that resemble the contemporary statutes described in the *T.J.E.* opinion.

c. Legislative Exemptions

The problems addressed by the *T.J.E.* Court are solved in the MPC burglary definition by including two exemptions used in many states. A burglary does not occur either when "the premises are at the time [of the entry] open to the public" *or* when the defendant "is licensed or privileged to enter." The second exemption is meant to cover cases where a person's "ownership or employment interest in the premises warrant his entry" or "where there are other circumstances where a privilege to enter should be inferred." *See* Model Penal Code § 221.1, Comment 3, at 68.

d. Responses to *T.J.E.* Decision

In response to the *T.J.E.* decision, the South Dakota legislature enacted similar amendments to the definitions of second degree burglary (for occupied structures) and third degree burglary (for unoccupied structures) in 1989. The revised version of the second degree burglary statute applied to:

> Any person who enters an occupied structure with intent to commit any crime other than the act of *shoplifting*[,] or [who] remains in an occupied structure after forming the intent to commit any crime other than *shoplifting*[.]

Note that the shoplifting statute applied at the time to "any person who takes merchandise displayed for sale in a store without the consent of the owner and with the intention of converting it to the person's use without paying the purchase price for the merchandise." *See* SDCL § 22–30A.–19.1.

Even though the 1989 statute did not codify the *T.J.E.* interpretation of the 1976 statute, the South Dakota Supreme Court continued to require this interpretation until 2006. Then the court reversed its position, and overruled *T.J.E.* on the theory that the legislature's failure to codify the *T.J.E.* holding in the 1989 statute constituted an implicit rejection of it. *See State v. Burdick*, 712 N.W.2d 5 (S.D. 2006). By this time, however, the South Dakota legislature had amended the burglary statutes again in 2005. A few years later, the court ruled that the legislature's failure to codify the *T.J.E.* holding in the 2005 statute implied the intent to reject that holding again. *See State v. Miranda*, 776 N.W.2d 77 (S.D. 2009). The amended 2005 statute is still in force, and the second degree burglary statute now emulates the exemptions in the MPC, because it applies to:

> Any person who enters or remains in an occupied structure with intent to commit any crime, unless the premises are, at the time, open to the public or the person is licensed or privileged to enter or remain[.]

The following hypotheticals illustrate the difficulties of solving the problems encountered in *T.J.E.*, and of interpreting the term "structure" in a burglary statute.

Hypo 1: *Who Is a Burglar?*

Millie is a truck driver who delivers milk to stores on her route. She has keys that allow her to enter each store through the back door so that she can put the milk containers into the refrigerators located in the storeroom areas. One evening at midnight, Millie is putting away the milk at a store in Bismarck, South Dakota, when she happens to notice that the refrigerator contains two six-packs of her favorite root beer. So she takes one of the six-packs with her when she drives away. A few minutes later, Rick emerges from the restroom inside the store. Rick had entered the store at 10:55 p.m. and purchased a candy bar. Then he went to the restroom. The clerk locked up the store at 11:00 p.m. and failed to notice that Rick never left the restroom. Rick peeks into the refrigerator, notices the remaining six-pack of root beer, picks it up, and leaves the store with it. The next morning, Palmer arrives at the store after it opens, picks up a carton of eggs, and pays for it at the cash register. As he walks toward the exit door, Palmer notices a display of root beer for sale inside the store. He picks up one can of root beer and palms it, dropping it into his pocket as he leaves. Are any of these three people guilty of burglary? Explain whether the prosecutor can obtain convictions against Millie, Rick, and Palmer, under each of these statutes: 1) the 1976 burglary statute as construed in the *T.J.E.* opinion; 2) the amended 1989 burglary statute; 3) the amended 2005 burglary statute. *Compare State v. Burdick*, 712 N.W.2d 5 (S.D. 2006); *State v. Miranda*, 776 N.W.2d 77 (S.D. 2009).

Hypo 2: *The Greenleaf Deli*

The Greenleaf Deli in Manhattan is located on the ground floor of a seven-story building, with six floors of residential apartments above it. The basement of the Deli, where merchandise was stored, is only accessible through two cellar doors located on the public sidewalk adjacent to the Deli. There is no access from the basement to any part of the residential units of the building, or to the Deli itself. The apartment residents do not have access to the basement. Only Deli employees are permitted to enter the basement. One busy evening at the Deli, the doors to the basement were left open for a short time. There is a 24/7 surveillance camera in the basement which was connected to a monitor inside the deli store. This camera made it possible for one of the Deli employees to see Joseph come down the basement stairs and walk around inside the basement, shining a flashlight to look at things. The employee quickly ran outside, locked the cellar doors, trapped Joseph in the basement, and called the police. When they arrived, they asked Joseph to climb out of the basement and then they arrested him.

It is clear that Joseph could be convicted for third degree burglary under the New York statute that applies to a person who "knowingly enters or remains unlawfully in a *building* with intent to commit a crime therein." What is unclear under state court precedents is whether Joseph could be convicted of second degree burglary, which requires an entry into a "dwelling" defined as a "building occupied by a person lodging therein." Even though the Deli basement itself is not a "dwelling" in that sense, the Deli is part of a building that contains six floors of residential apartments. The relevant precedents hold that "a burglary committed in *any part* of a building that contains a dwelling is the burglary *of* a dwelling." The one case law exception to this rule applies when "the crime is committed in a place so remote and inaccessible from the living quarters that the special dangers inherent in the burglary of a dwelling do not exist." Should Joseph be convicted of second degree burglary or only third degree burglary? See *People v. Joseph*, 28 N.Y.3d 1003, 64 N.E.3d 957 (2016).

Hypo 3: *Freedom Tower*

The New York City Council enacted a misdemeanor ordinance in 2008 that prohibits the following conduct, in order to punish and deter certain types of BASE jumping: "It shall be unlawful to (i) jump or attempt to jump from a structure, or (ii) climb or attempt to climb up, down or around the exterior of a structure, or suspend or attempt to suspend oneself from the exterior of a structure or on a device attached to one or more structures." The term "structure" shall mean "any building, monument, statue, crane, bridge, sign, tower or other object, or any combination thereof, exceeding fifty feet in height." Just before the construction of the new Freedom Tower building is finished, four men decide to perform BASE jumping from the roof of the Tower, which is 1,776 feet in height. They climb through a hole in the perimeter security fence at midnight and enter through the front door, which is open because the security guards are taking a break. They climb the stairs to the top floor which has been completed except for the glass in the windows. The men are wearing jumpsuits and helmets and they put on their skydiving equipment and parachutes. Then they emerge on the roof and spend several hours planning the jump, which occurs at 3:00 am. They land safely but their images are captured on a security camera across the street from the Tower, and they are seen by the owner of a bagel shop who is baking at an early hour.

The four defendants are charged with the Jumping from a Structure misdemeanor crime as well as the felony burglary crime defined as follows: "It shall be unlawful to knowingly enter or remain unlawfully in a building with intent to commit a crime therein." "In addition to its ordinary meaning, a building includes any structure, vehicle or watercraft used for overnight lodging of persons, or used by persons for carrying on business therein." "A person enters or remains 'unlawfully' in a building when he is not licensed or privileged to do so. A person who, regardless of his intent, enters or remains in a building which are at the time is open to the public does so with license and privilege." Assume that defense counsel do not contest the defendants' guilt regarding the Jumping crime but argue that the burglary charge should be dismissed because "jumping from the roof of the building is not a crime that is committed 'therein' or 'inside' the building, but rather, on top of, or on the exterior of the building." How will the prosecutor rebut this argument? On the facts, should the jury convict of burglary?

Executive Summary

Property Subject to Theft. Modern statutes often follow the approach of the MPC in defining property as "anything of value," but more limited definitions may be used to serve a particular purpose.

Larceny. This crime was designed by English judges and requires a trespassory taking and carrying away of property from the possession of another, without consent, with the intent to steal, which means the intent to deprive the owner permanently of the property.

Larceny by Trick. This version of larceny applies where the trespassory taking occurs by means of false representations that lead the owner to pass only possession of the property, not title. Both the larceny and larceny by trick crimes were redefined in the Model Penal Code as Theft by Unlawful Taking or Disposition.

Major Themes

a. **Influence of MPC**—The MPC has had a major influence on theft law and most states have enacted versions of the simplified MPC elements of the old common law crimes.

b. ***Mens Rea* & *Actus Reus***—Virtually all definitions of theft crimes require specific intent, such as the intent or purpose to deprive another of his or her property. The concept of possession is a key element of defining the *actus reus* for all theft crimes except burglary.

Embezzlement. This crime was designed by Parliament and requires the fraudulent conversion of the property of another by an entrusted person in lawful possession who has the intent to steal and the intent to convert the property to his or her own benefit. The embezzlement crime was redefined in the Model Penal Code as Theft by Unlawful Taking or Disposition.

False Pretenses. This crime was designed by Parliament and requires the owner to pass title to property through reliance on false representations. The False Pretenses crime was redefined in the Model Penal Code as Theft by Deception.

Receiving Stolen Property. This crime was designed by Parliament and requires the act of receiving property which is stolen, knowing that it is stolen, with the intent to deprive the owner of it. The Model Penal Code expanded the mental state of this crime to include the belief that the property probably was stolen.

Robbery & Carjacking. This crime was designed by English judges and requires all the elements of larceny, plus two more, namely taking from the person or presence of the victim, by means of force or putting in fear of violence. The federal carjacking statute uses robbery elements plus the intent to cause serious bodily harm. The Model Penal Code eliminated the element of "person or presence" from the robbery crime, and expanded robbery to include an intentional threat to cause bodily harm on the victim, during the course of committing a theft.

Burglary. This crime was designed by English judges and requires the breaking and entering of a dwelling at night time with the intent to commit a felony therein. Modern burglary statutes have expanded the crime to include the act of entering or remaining in an occupied structure with the intent to commit a crime at the time of entry.

For More Information

- American Law Institute, Model Penal Code and Commentaries, Part II, §§ 221.0–221.1, 222.1, 223.0–223.7, Comments at 60–84, 96–121, 122–255 (1980).
- John M. Burkoff & Russell L. Weaver, Inside Criminal Law: What Matters and Why 185–202 (2d ed. 2011).
- Jerome Hall, Theft, Law and Society (2d ed.) (1952).
- Wayne R. LaFave, Criminal Law §§ 19.1–21.1 (5th ed. 2010).

Test Your Knowledge

To assess your understanding of the material in this chapter, click here to take a quiz.

Chapter 12

Justification Defenses

The defenses that are commonly known as "justification" defenses include self-defense, defense of others, defense of property and of dwelling, the law enforcement defense, and the necessity or choice of evils defense. Each defense has a different common law history, but most of these defenses share a special concern with the use of deadly force which a defendant seeks to justify on the basis of a belief in some perceived danger. Most of the limitations on these defenses, which are imposed by statutes and case law, concern the meaning of the requirements as "necessity," "imminence," and the "reasonableness" of the defendant's belief in the latter conditions.

A. Self-Defense

The English common law interpretation of self-defense allowed a person to use deadly force against an aggressor who threatened deadly force, as long as the defensive use of such force was necessary because of the imminent threat of death or great bodily harm that was posed by the aggressor's conduct. What was essential, however, was not the factual reality of these conditions, but the requirement of a reasonable belief in the imminence and deadly character of the threat, and in the necessity of using deadly force for self-protection from that threat. Modern statutory definitions of self-defense usually reflect some versions of these elements.

FYI

The MPC § 3.04(2)(b) states that the use of deadly force is not justifiable unless a person believes that such force is necessary for self-protection against death or serious bodily injury. A person also must believe that such force is immediately necessary for that purpose against the use of unlawful force by another person on the present occasion under MPC § 3.04(1).

1. Necessity & Duty to Retreat

The English common law required a reasonable belief in the necessity of using deadly force in self-defense, and one hallmark of this necessity was the defender's compliance with the duty to retreat before resorting to deadly force. The state courts recognized this requirement until the 1870s, when one court declared that a "true man" should not be "obliged to fly" from an attacker, but should be able to stand his ground without retreating, in order to use deadly force in self-defense. The *Brown* case illustrates the influence of "no duty to retreat" rule some 50 years later in federal court, by which time this position had gained the support of many state courts.

Brown v. United States

256 U.S. 335 (1921).

MR. JUSTICE HOLMES delivered the opinion of the Court.

The petitioner was convicted of murder in the second degree committed upon one Hermis at a place in Texas within the exclusive jurisdiction of the United States, and the judgment was affirmed by the Circuit Court of Appeals[.] A writ of certiorari was granted by this Court[.] . . .

[One] question [that is raised] concerns the instructions at the trial. There had been trouble between Hermis and the defendant for a long time. There was evidence that Hermis had twice assaulted the defendant with a knife and had made threats communicated to the defendant that the next time, one of them would go off in a black box. On the day in question the defendant [was on federal property,] superintending excavation work for a post office [in Beeville, Texas]. In view of Hermis's threats[,] [the defendant] had taken a pistol with him and had laid it in his coat upon a dump. Hermis was driven up by a witness, in a cart to be loaded, and the defendant said that certain earth was not to be removed, whereupon Hermis came toward him, the defendant says, with a knife. The defendant retreated some twenty or twenty-five feet to where his coat was and got his pistol. Hermis was striking at him and the defendant fired four shots and killed [Hermis]. The judge instructed the jury among other things that "it is necessary to remember, in considering the question of self defence, that the party assaulted is always under the obligation to retreat so long as retreat is open to him, provided that he can do so without subjecting himself to the danger of death or great bodily harm." The instruction was reinforced by the further intimation that unless "retreat would have appeared to a man of reasonable prudence, in the position of the defendant, as involving danger of death or serious bodily harm[,]" the defendant was not entitled to stand his ground. An instruction to the effect that if the defendant had reasonable grounds of apprehension that he was in danger of losing his life or of suffering serious bodily harm from Hermis he was not bound to retreat was refused. So the question is brought out with sufficient clearness whether the formula laid down by the Court and often repeated by the ancient law is adequate to the protection of the defendant's rights.

[Concrete] cases or illustrations stated in the early law in conditions very different from the present[,] like the reference to retreat in Coke['s] [Third Institute (1669)], have had a tendency to ossify into specific rules without much regard for reason. Rationally the failure to retreat is a circumstance to be considered with all the others in order to determine whether the defendant went farther than he was justified in doing[,] not a categorical proof of guilt. The law has grown, and even if historical mistakes have contributed to its growth it has tended in the direction of rules consistent with human nature. Many respectable writers agree that if a man reasonably believes that he is in immediate danger of death or grievous bodily harm from his assailant he may stand his ground and that if he kills him he has not [exceeded] the bounds of lawful self defence[.] Detached reflection cannot be demanded in the presence of an uplifted knife. Therefore in this Court, at least, it is not a condition of immunity that one in that situation should pause to consider whether a reasonable man might not think it possible to fly with safety or to disable his assailant rather than to kill him[.] The law of Texas very strongly adopts these views as is shown by many cases[.]

[There] was evidence that the last shot was fired after Hermis was down. The jury might not believe the defendant's testimony that it was an accidental discharge[.] [But even] if the last shot was intentional and may seem to have been unnecessary[,] the defendant would not necessarily lose his immunity if it followed close upon the others while the heat of the conflict was on, and if the defendant believed that he was fighting for his life.

The Government presents a different case. It denies that Hermis had a knife and even that Brown was acting in self defence. Notwithstanding the repeated threats of Hermis and intimations that one of the two would die at the next encounter, which seem hardly to be denied, of course it was possible for the jury to find that Brown had not sufficient reason to think that his life was in danger at that time, that he exceeded the limits of reasonable self defence or even that he was the attacking party. But upon the hypothesis to which the evidence gave much color, that Hermis began the attack, the instruction [on the duty to retreat] was wrong.

Judgment reversed.

Points for Discussion

a. Rejection of the Duty to Retreat

Soon after the Ohio Supreme Court opined in 1876 that a "true man" should not be bound by the duty to retreat, the Indiana Supreme Court endorsed this position in 1877, reasoning that the right of self-defense is "founded on the law of nature[,] and is not, nor can be, superseded by any law of society." The court declared that, "[T]he tendency of the American mind seems to be very strongly against the enforcement of any rule which requires a person to flee when assailed[.]" The Texas Supreme Court decided in 1885 that although the common law required "the assailed party to 'retreat to the wall' ", it was unnecessary to maintain that doctrine because the Texas Penal Code had abandoned it. Therefore, defendants should have the right to obtain a jury instruction that there was no duty to retreat required to invoke the defense of self-defense. One scholar describes the spread of the "no duty to retreat" doctrine as "[f]ollowing the westward movement of settlers from the Appalachians to the Pacific Coast," and notes that the rule "became so deeply entrenched" in Texas "as to be referred to by legal scholars generally as the 'Texas rule.' " *See* RICHARD MAXWELL BROWN, NO DUTY TO RETREAT: VIOLENCE AND VALUES IN AMERICAN HISTORY AND SOCIETY 8, 26 (1991).

b. Preservation of the Duty to Retreat

> **FYI**
>
> The MPC § 3.04(2)(b)(ii)(A) defines the duty to retreat as follows: "The use of deadly force is not justifiable if . . . the person knows that [he or she] can avoid the necessity of using such force with complete safety by retreating . . . except that the person is not obliged to retreat from his dwelling or place of work, unless [he or she] was the initial aggressor[.]

The MPC Commentary observes that Justice Holmes does not advocate that a rigid "no duty to retreat" rule should be adopted as a rule for the federal criminal law. Instead, he advances "what seems to be a median position," which is expressed in his statement that, "rationally the failure to retreat is a circumstance to be considered with all the others in order to determine whether the defendant went farther than he was justified in doing[,] not a categorical proof of guilt." This Commentary also describes the duty to retreat rule as a "logical derivative of the underlying justifying principle of self-defense: belief in the necessity of the protective action." The MPC position is that the duty to retreat only arises when a person needs to use deadly force, "and even then retreat is only a requisite if the actor knows that [he or she] can avoid the need to use such force *with complete safety* by retreating." This standard is supported by the assumption that "it is to be expected that all doubts will be resolved in the actor's favor, and that such moral claim as there is to standing one's ground can easily be recognized in the doubtful cases." The MPC drafters placed "a high value on the preservation of life." Therefore, they were not willing to recognize the "moral claim to exoneration" of an actor who "kills when [he or she] clearly need not do so" for self-protection—"when, in other words, [the actor] knows that he can avoid the need to kill at no risk to [self]." *See* Model Penal Code § 3.04, Comment (4)(c), at 52–55. Today many states endorse some version of the duty to retreat.

c. Defense of Others

The elements of the "defense of others" are similar to the elements of self-defense. One important requirement for the defense of others is that a person must reasonably believe that the other person is being subjected to an unlawful use of force. Only if such force is deadly may a person resort to deadly force in an attempt to defend the other. If it turns out that, unbeknownst to the rescuer, the force used against the other person was lawful, as when an undercover officer uses force to arrest the other person, the older view was that the defense of others would be unavailable because the other had no right to defend himself or herself. However, this "alter ego" rule is not endorsed in more recent statutes and case law, which protect a defender who reasonably believes that the other is being unlawfully attacked.

d. Original Castle Doctrine

The English common law's commitment to the duty to retreat was limited to the sphere of public spaces and did not apply to a defendant's dwelling. Instead, judges viewed a person's home as that person's "castle," where retreat was never required before resorting to the use of deadly force in self-defense. Some state courts applied this "no duty to retreat in the castle" doctrine to cases involving the use of deadly force against intruders or cohabitants of the dwelling. Other state courts, however, limited this doctrine to invocations of the right to self-defense against an intruder, and rejected the right of cohabitants to invoke the castle doctrine against each other.

e. Aggressor Rule

An aggressor is a person who cannot invoke self-defense at common law because the aggressor was the first person to threaten the use of deadly force. The defender who responds to an aggressor justifiably with deadly force is the person who is entitled to claim self-defense. However, an aggressor who threatens non-deadly force may become a person who is then threatened unjustifiably with deadly force in response. In this case, the aggressor will be entitled to claim self-defense when responding in kind with deadly force. Notably, an aggressor who is the first to threaten deadly force, and thereby loses the right to self-defense, will be able to regain that right as long as the aggressor takes steps to make it clear to the defender that the aggressor is withdrawing from conflict in good faith.

FYI

The MPC § 3.04(2)(b)(i) defines an aggressor who loses the right to use deadly force self-defense as a person, who "with the purpose of causing death or serious bodily injury, provoked the use of force against [himself or herself] in the same encounter." The right to self-defense may be regained "by so far breaking off the struggle that any renewal by the other party can be viewed as a distinct engagement." Model Penal Code § 3.04, Comment 4(b), at 52.

What are the differences between the duty to retreat instruction rejected by Justice Holmes and the MPC definition of the duty to retreat? How would the MPC drafters explain why the MPC definition is preferable to the "median position" taken by Holmes? How would the defendant in *Brown* argue for self-defense under the MPC version of the duty to retreat?

These hypotheticals offer the opportunity to consider the connection between the aggressor rule and the duty to retreat doctrine. The facts in the second hypothetical are similar to those in a famous case in which a jury acquitted a defendant of attempted murder based on his claim of self-defense. *See People v. Goetz*, 68 N.Y.2d 96, 497 N.E.2d 41, 506 N.Y.S.2d 18 (1986).

Hypo 1: *Broken Bottle*

Ron pulls into a gas station in the heart of Los Angeles. While he is pumping gas, he is approached by an impoverished man wearing very old and dirty clothes, who is begging for money. The man says, very politely, "Gee mister, is there any chance that you could spare some money for some food. If so, I'd really appreciate it. Thank you." However, the man is carrying a broken whiskey bottle in his hand and the bottle is pointed toward Ron. Can Ron respond by using deadly force? If California law imposes the duty to retreat, as long as such retreat can occur in complete safety, does Ron have the duty to retreat? If so, what must Ron do on these facts?

Hypo 2: *"Give Me Five Dollars"*

Assume that Goetz is a passenger on the downtown IRT express subway train in New York City. He is carrying a loaded .38 caliber pistol inside his coat, in violation of the prohibition against possession of unlicensed weapons. Goetz had been mugged on a prior occasion on the streets of the city, and this is why he carries the pistol. When Goetz enters the subway car, he notices four noisy and boisterous youths, who are sitting together at one end of the car. The other 20 passengers are sitting at the other end of the car. Two of the youths are carrying screwdrivers inside their coats so that they can break into video game coin boxes. But Goetz cannot see the screwdrivers. Goetz sits down near the four youths. Two of the youths stand up and approach Goetz, and one youth asks for five dollars. Goetz asks him to repeat his question. This time the youth says, "Give me five dollars."

a. *Shooting at Youths.* Assume that the sound of shots rings out in the subway car. Goetz has taken aim at each of the four youths and fired a shot at each one. Goetz is charged with attempted murder. How can his defense counsel argue self-defense?

b. *Backs Turned.* Assume that before Goetz fired any shots, he said, "I have no money." Then the two youths turned their backs to Goetz and moved a few feet away from him, which is as far as they could move because they were at the end of the car already. If Goetz takes aim at each youth and fires at their backs, how can his defense counsel argue for self-defense if Goetz is charged with attempted murder?

c. *Flashing Gun.* Assume that instead of firing any shots, Goetz shows the handle of the gun to the four youths, and that he "flashes" it in a threatening manner that suggests he will use it if he is not left alone. Assume that one of the youths does have a gun concealed in his jacket, and that in response to Goetz's "flashing" of the gun, the youth pulls out his weapon and points it at Goetz. If Goetz draws and fires at this youth, how can his defense counsel argue self-defense in a trial for attempted murder?

Hypo 3: *The Death of Trayvon Martin*

Zimmerman was charged with second degree murder but did not testify at his trial. Assume that when the jury heard his recorded statements to police, the following details emerged. Zimmerman, age 28, acknowledged that he had been following Martin, age 17, as Martin walked through a housing complex on his way to a condo where he was staying as a guest. Zimmerman was a neighborhood watch volunteer at the complex. He did not recognize Martin and thought he might be a burglar. While Zimmerman was in his car and on the phone with a police dispatcher to report Martin's presence, Martin circled the car, reached for his waistband, and then walked off. Zimmerman got out of his car and walked in the same direction as Martin, in order to look at a street sign to relay the street name to the dispatcher. The dispatcher told Zimmerman to wait for the police and not approach Martin.

When he was on his way back to his car, Martin appeared out of nowhere and asked Zimmerman, "Do you have a problem?" Zimmerman answered "No," and Martin said, "You do now," attacking Zimmerman as he tried to use his cell phone to call 911. Martin knocked him to the ground with a punch. Martin also screamed, "You're going to die tonight," and put his hand over Zimmerman's nose and mouth so that he could not breathe. Martin was on top of Zimmerman, pummeling him and slamming his head repeatedly into the pavement, so that it felt like Zimmerman's "head was going to explode." When Zimmerman felt Martin's hand "go down" his side, Zimmerman thought Martin was reaching for Zimmerman's gun. So Zimmerman grabbed it, pulled it out, and shot Martin. During the struggle, Zimmerman said that he repeatedly screamed for help, and witnesses saw Martin on top of Zimmerman. The police also noticed that Zimmerman had a broken nose and injuries on the back of his head.

Take Note

The media coverage of the Florida prosecution of George Zimmerman—for fatally shooting the unarmed Trayvon Martin—transfixed the nation in 2012 and 2013. After Zimmerman's acquittal based on self-defense, there were widespread protests. For the jury instructions in the Zimmerman case, see https://www.npr.org/sections/thetwo-way/2013/07/12/201410108/read-instructions-for-the-jury-in-trial-of-george-zimmerman. For a transcript of his statements to police, see https://famous-trials.com/zimmerman1/2298-zimmermancourtdox and https://archive.org/stream/326700-full-transcript-zimmerman/326700-full-transcript-zimmerman_djvu.txt.

If these facts are believed by the jury, is there sufficient evidence to show by a preponderance that Zimmerman established these common law elements of self-defense: 1) that he had a reasonable belief that Martin posed an imminent threat of great bodily harm or death; and 2) that he had a reasonable belief that it was necessary to use deadly force in order to avoid that threat? Could the prosecutor have persuaded a reasonable jury, beyond a reasonable doubt, that the evidence did not support Zimmerman's self-defense claim? Or at least that Zimmerman's beliefs in imminence and necessity were unreasonable so that a reckless manslaughter conviction was appropriate? If Florida law required a duty to retreat as defined in the MPC, would Zimmerman have lost the right to self-defense on these facts because of his failure to retreat? *See* http://www.nytimes.com/2012/06/22/us/documents-tell-zimmermans-side-in-martin-shooting.html?ref=us.

---

2. Reasonable Belief & Imperfect Self-Defense

The common law required a reasonable belief in the elements of self-defense. But the Model Penal Code drafters describe this defense as applying to any person who "believes" in the existence of the relevant elements, in order to make it clear that an objectively "reasonable" belief is unnecessary. Most states use a hybrid standard like that described in the *Marr* case that follows. This case reveals how difficult it may be to define such a standard, where the jury's decision to characterize the defendant's belief in the need to use deadly force as reasonable or unreasonable will have the consequence of producing different homicide verdicts.

State v. Marr

362 Md. 467, 765 A.2d 645 (2001).

WILNER, JUDGE:

Respondent, Nathaniel Marr, was convicted [of] the first degree premeditated murder of Arthur Carroll [and other crimes], for which he was given substantial consecutive sentences. The killing [occurred] on the evening of December 2, 1998, when Marr and a confederate, Curtis Alston, approached the rear of a waiting taxicab and opened fire on Carroll, who was about to enter the cab. Carroll was killed[.]

That Marr shot Carroll [was] never in dispute[.] The shooting of Carroll stemmed from an incident that occurred three days earlier, on November 29, when Carroll [and] Kevin Jackson went to Marr's home with the intent to rob him. Marr was not at home, but the [men] came upon Marr's cousin, Ronald Muse, with whom Marr lived. In the course of searching for drugs and money, one or [both men] shot and killed Muse. Marr later went looking for Carroll and Jackson, allegedly to inquire about their involvement in the killing of Muse. On December 2, he caught up with Carroll[.]

[Marr's] defense [was] self-defense. That defense [came] through statements he gave to the police upon his arrest, as Marr did not testify. In his first statement, which was an oral one, he said nothing about self-defense. He told the officer that, believing that Carroll was responsible for his cousin's death, he and Alston went to Carroll's home, in a stolen van, "to talk to him about that," that Marr was armed with [a] semi-automatic machine pistol, and that, when he saw Carroll come out of his home and approach a waiting cab, he fired; one of the shots, he acknowledged, went into the cab. In an ensuing written statement, he claimed that he was both enraged and terrified when he learned about the earlier episode and that he went to see Carroll "to see what his feelings were and to see if things could be resolved, and if he would confess to the murder of my cousin." He and Alston were armed, he said, "for our protection." Just as they arrived, Carroll was about to enter a cab, and, apparently startled to see them, he "grabbed at his waist as if to draw a weapon." In fear of their lives, he and Alston opened fire.

In response to this evidence, [the trial court] instructed the jury on the defenses of "perfect" and "imperfect" self-defense, using the language suggested in [the *pattern* jury instructions published by the state bar association]. [However,] Marr asked for two additional instructions, as follows:

> In determining whether the defendant's conduct was reasonable under the circumstances, you should judge his conduct by the facts as you believe they appeared to him.
>
> A belief which may be unreasonable to a calm mind may be actually and reasonably held under the circumstances as they appeared to the defendant at the time of the incident.

What's That?

Pattern jury instructions are based on statements of legal rules that appear in the holdings and reasoning of cases in a particular jurisdiction. They are composed and published in order to enable trial judges to take a consistent approach to making jury instruction choices and to avoid making errors in describing the current law to juries. However, the parties may request instructions that do not appear in pattern instructions, and such requests are granted when appropriate.

[The] trial court refused to give the additional instructions[.] Marr appealed from the ensuing convictions[,] claiming, among other things, error in that refusal. [T]he Court of Special Appeals [held] that the refusal *did* constitute reversible error. We granted the State's petition for *certiorari* to determine whether the Court of Special Appeals erred in that judgment[.] . . .

Maryland recognizes two varieties of self-defense—the traditional one, which we have sometimes termed "perfect" or "complete" self-defense, and a lesser form, sometimes called "imperfect" or "partial" self-defense. Although "perfect" self-defense is universally recognized in the United States, not all of our courts recognize the lesser variety as a separately defined defense, and there is no universal agreement on the precise elements of either variety. . . .

We defined the defenses of "perfect" and "imperfect" self-defense, and the relationship between them, in [prior cases] and noted that "perfect" or traditional self-defense, is a complete defense to a charge of criminal homicide—murder or manslaughter—and, if credited by the trier of fact, results in an acquittal. The elements, or requirements, of that defense [are]:

> "(1) The accused must have had reasonable grounds to believe himself in apparent imminent or immediate danger of death or serious bodily harm from his assailant or potential assailant;
>
> (2) The accused must have in fact believed himself in this danger;
>
> (3) The accused claiming the right of self-defense must not have been the aggressor or provoked the conflict; and
>
> (4) The force used must have not been unreasonable and excessive, that is, the force must not have been more force than the exigency demanded."

[W]e first adopted the concept of "imperfect" self-defense [in *State v. Faulkner*, 301 Md. 482, 483 A.2d 759 (1984)]. The prospect of "imperfect" self-defense arises when the actual, subjective belief on the part of the accused that he/she is in apparent imminent danger of death or serious bodily harm from the assailant, requiring the use of deadly force, is not an objectively reasonable belief. What may be unreasonable is the perception of imminent danger or the belief that the force employed is necessary to meet the danger, or both. . . .

Unlike its "perfect" cousin, "imperfect" self-defense, if credited, does not result in an acquittal, but merely serves to negate the element of malice required for a conviction of murder and thus reduces the offense to manslaughter. . . . Some courts [have] applied the doctrine only where "perfect" self-defense would apply but for the fact that the defendant initiated the confrontation at the non-deadly level. Other courts found "imperfect" self-defense applicable when the defendant committed the killing because of an honest, though unreasonable belief of the imminence of death or serious bodily harm, and still others applied it when the defendant satisfied all other aspects of "perfect" self-defense but used unreasonable force in defending himself. [Our precedents recognize] the middle approach [as] the most appropriate, declaring as persuasive the reasoning given in *People v. Flannel*, 25 Cal. 3d 668, 160 Cal. Rptr. 84, 603 P.2d 1, 7 (1979):

> "[T]he state has no legitimate interest in obtaining a conviction of murder when, by virtue of defendant's unreasonable belief, the jury entertains a reasonable doubt whether defendant harbored malice. Likewise, a defendant has no legitimate interest in complete exculpation when acting outside the range of reasonable behavior[.]"

[The] jury was told that Marr should be acquitted, on a theory of [perfect] self-defense, if the jury found that (1) he was not the aggressor or, if the initial aggressor, did not raise the fight to the deadly force level, (2) he "actually believed" that he was in immediate and imminent danger of death or serious bodily harm, (3) his belief "was reasonable," and (4) he used no more force than was reasonably necessary. The court instructed further that, even if the jury was unable to find each of those four elements, it could find that Marr acted in "partial self-defense" if he "actually believed he was in immediate and imminent danger of death or serious bodily harm, even though a reasonable person would not have so believed," and, if it found that to be the case, the crime would be manslaughter rather than murder.

The two additional instructions requested by Marr were necessarily premised on the assumption that he actually believed that he was in imminent danger of death or serious bodily harm from Carroll and that the deadly force he employed was a necessary response to that threat, and they sought to focus the jury's attention on the reasonableness of those subjective beliefs. Those instructions thus related to the defense of "perfect," rather than "imperfect," self-defense. They would have the jury determine the reasonableness of the defendant's belief as to either of those elements by looking at things solely through his eyes and mind-state, regardless of how someone else, including the imaginary reasonable person, would have viewed the situation.

Marr urges that this concept or standard is required in a self-defense analysis[.] . . . [But] we have never held that the bare statement that "the necessity for the defendant's resorting to [a theory of self-defense] should be judged by the facts as they appeared to him, whatever they truly were," devoid of its evidentiary context, was required as an instruction to the jury. The problem with the statement is that it is too broad and therefore could be misleading. We do not disavow the notion that, as part of a self-defense analysis, the trier of fact must look at the circumstances as they appeared to the defendant, for that is important in understanding the defendant's explanation for his or her conduct. It provides the necessary underpinning for the defendant's subjective beliefs that (1) he/she was in imminent danger, and (2) the force used was necessary. When judging the reasonableness of the defendant's conduct, however, that notion has some limits. Our jurisprudence [is] consistent with an objective, rather than a subjective, standard of reasonableness. . . . [Our precedents require] that, not only must the defendant subjectively believe that his actions were necessary "but objectively, that a reasonable man would so consider them."

[The] instructions requested here, unshorn of context, could create a real danger of blurring the distinction we have carefully crafted between "perfect" and "imperfect" self-defense and allow a jury to find a defendant's belief, either of imminent death or serious harm or of the need to use deadly force, to be reasonable when the cognitive perception leading to that belief is wholly unreasonable. The effect of that would be to apply "perfect" self-defense and acquit the defendant, when only "imperfect" self-defense, warranting a reduction of the crime to manslaughter, is appropriate[.]

Points for Discussion

a. Comparing Mistake & Imperfect Self-Defense

The problem addressed in *Marr* is the need to limit the benefit of acquittal to deserving defendants with worthy self-defense claims, while according some benefit to defendants with less worthy self-defense claims and implicitly greater culpability. The MPC drafters preferred to conceive of these less deserving defendants as people who had made a "mistake" about the necessity for using deadly force. Although they may have "believed" in this need, if they were reckless or negligent in forming that belief under the circumstances, then they could be convicted of recklessness or negligence crimes, as the case may be. But they could not be convicted of crimes with purposely or knowingly mental states, because an honest, good faith, subjective yet mistaken belief in self-defense will disable a prosecutor from proving such mental states. By contrast, the *Marr* Court represents the common law approach to these less deserving defendants, which holds that the jury could find their belief to be too "unreasonable" for "perfect" self-defense, but still allow them access to the benefit of "imperfect" self-defense that would produce a verdict of guilty for lesser crimes, such as the voluntary manslaughter crime.

Why does the *Marr* Court find the defendant's proposed jury instructions to be an inaccurate statement of the law? If the instructions had been given at trial, what impact could they have had on the jury? Why did the jury convict the defendant of murder and reject his plea of self-defense as defined by the pattern instruction?

b. Objections to the Subjective Standard

Courts have criticized the MPC's reliance on a subjective standard that is expressed through conferring the right to self-defense on any person who "believes" in the existence of the relevant elements of the defense. For example, in the *Goetz* case from which Hypo 2 after *Brown* is derived, the New York Court of Appeals reasoned that interpreting the statutory definition of self-defense "to require only that the defendant's belief was 'reasonable to *him*' " would be to allow "the defendant's own perceptions" to "completely exonerate him from any criminal liability." In the court's view, "[t]o completely exonerate such an individual, no matter how aberrational or bizarre his thought patterns, would allow citizens to set their own standards for the permissible use of force."

c. Measuring Reasonableness

By contrast, the *Goetz* Court's endorsement of the so-called hybrid standard used by the *Marr* Court may help to explain the continued adherence of a majority of states to the requirement of an objectively "reasonable" belief in all the elements of self-defense. The measure of such "reasonableness," according to the *Goetz* Court, should take into account "the 'circumstances' facing a defendant [in] his 'situation.' " These circumstances include "the physical movements of the potential assailant," "any relevant knowledge the defendant had about that person," "the physical attributes of all persons involved, including the defendant," and "any prior experiences" the defendant had which could provide a "reasonable basis" for the belief that a threat of deadly force was to be expected from the potential assailant, and that the use of deadly force was needed for self-protection.

The following hypothetical presents the opportunity to compare the operation of the MPC and common law approaches to the beliefs that are required for self-defense.

Hypo 1: *Sensitive to Threats*

Assume that Jack has been an inmate at a state prison in Illinois for several decades. Now he is an old man, and the day comes when he is finally released from prison. His prison experience has made him very sensitive to potential threats when others get close to him. So when Jack is standing at a bus stop outside the prison walls, Jack notices immediately when the man standing next to him reaches into a raincoat pocket. Jack's perception at that moment is that the man intends to kill Jack with a weapon that is concealed in the pocket. As it happens, Jack managed to leave the prison with a homemade knife or "shiv" concealed in his sock. So just as the man pulls his hand out of the pocket, Jack reaches down quickly, pulls out the shiv, and stabs the man in the chest. The man dies and Jack is charged with murder. Assume that self-defense is defined in Illinois using the MPC provision, and so Jack must *believe* that deadly force is *necessary* for self-protection against death or serious bodily injury, and *also* must *believe* that such force is *immediately* necessary for that purpose against the use of unlawful force by another person *on the present occasion*. How can Jack's defense counsel argue for acquittal based on "perfect" self-defense? How can the prosecutor argue that Jack must be convicted of murder or manslaughter?

Hypo 2: *The Death of Tamir Rice*

One scholar has summarized the facts as follows regarding the killing of Tamir Rice: "At approximately 3:20 PM on November 22, 2014, an individual in Cleveland, Ohio called 911 to report that there was a "guy with a pistol" in the park by the West Boulevard Rapid Transit Station, pointing it at people. At 3:26 PM, the 911 dispatcher requested an available unit to respond to a Code 1 at the Cudell Recreation Center. Officers Frank Garmback and Timothy Loehmann advised the dispatcher that they were able to respond. The two officers were in a fully marked patrol car and both officers were in uniform. Officer Garmback drove the patrol car, and Officer Loehmann was in the front passenger seat. The 911 dispatcher told the officers: "[I]t's at Cudell Rec Center, 1910 West Boulevard, 1-9-1-0 West Boulevard . . . [The caller] said in the park by the youth center there's a black male sitting on a swing. He's wearing a camouflage hat, a gray jacket with black sleeves. He keeps pulling a gun out of his pants and pointing it at people." The 911 dispatcher did not tell the officers that the caller had also said the gun was "probably fake" and the suspect was "probably a juvenile." The officers arrived at the scene at approximately 3:30 PM. At that time, Tamir Rice, a twelve-year-old African American male, was sitting by himself at a gazebo. According to surveillance video, at 3:30:13 PM, Rice stood up and took three or four steps in the direction of the approaching police car. His hands were out of his pocket and midway between his waist and chest. As the patrol car came to a stop near the gazebo, Rice's hands dropped to his waistband area. At 3:30:23 PM, Officer Loehmann opened the passenger door of the patrol car, firing his gun twice at Rice. After

Rice fell to the ground, Officer Loehmann moved rapidly around the back of the patrol car to a position behind the rear of the patrol car on the driver's side with his weapon drawn and aimed in Rice's direction. At about the same time, Officer Garmback got out of the patrol car with his weapon drawn and moved around the front of the patrol car to a position near the front-right bumper. Both officers arrived at their positions of cover at 3:30:32 PM. "The surveillance video shows that the critical events took place in less than ten seconds." *See* Cynthia Lee, *Reforming the Law on the Police Use of Deadly Force: De-Escalation, Pre-Seizure Conduct, and Imperfect Self-Defense*, 2018 U. ILLINOIS L. REV. 629, 675–676 (2018).

The question raised by Professor Lee is whether a jury might conclude that the facts in this case satisfy the "imperfect self-defense" standard, "under which would a defendant charged with murder can be found not guilty of murder but convicted of voluntary manslaughter if he honestly but unreasonably believed in the need to act in self-defense or used force that was disproportionate to the force threatened and thus unreasonable." In assessing whether the officer's beliefs were reasonable or unreasonable regarding the necessity for using deadly force, Professor Lee proposes that the jury "must consider": "1. Whether the deceased or injured person was, or appeared to be, in possession of a deadly weapon or an object that could be used as a deadly weapon and refused to comply with an order to drop the object or any other order reasonably related to officer or public safety prior to being shot; 2. Whether the officer engaged in de-escalation measures, such as taking cover, waiting for backup, trying to calm the deceased or injured person, and/or using less lethal types of force prior to the use of the force in question, if such measures were feasible; and 3. Any preseizure conduct by the officer that increased the risk of a deadly confrontation." *Id.* at 664–665, 674. Based on an application of Professor Lee's three criteria, were the officers who killed Tamir Rice reasonable or unreasonable in their beliefs regarding the necessity for using deadly force—and why?

---

3. Battered Defendants

In the early 1980s, defense counsel began to seek admission of expert testimony concerning the battering experiences of defendants who killed their batterers and were charged with murder or manslaughter crimes. These defense counsel also requested jury instructions on self-defense that allowed a jury to consider how the battering experience could inform the reasonableness of a battered defendant's belief in the necessity of using deadly force for self-protection against the imminent threat of death or great bodily harm posed by a batterer. For the first decade of the era when battered defendants came to the attention of the courts, it was difficult to achieve either of these goals. The following case illustrates the responses of one court that ultimately became the norm in the case law of many states.

Bechtel v. State

840 P.2d 1 (Okla. Crim. App. 1992).

JOHNSON, JUDGE:

[Donna Lee Brechtel was convicted of first degree murder for the killing of her husband, Ken Brechtel, and sentenced by the jury to life imprisonment. On appeal she argued that the trial judge erred in refusing to allow expert testimony on the battered women syndrome. The court concluded that the trial court's failure to allow this testimony amounted to reversible error requiring a new trial.]

The following facts are primarily from the testimony of the Appellant[.] Although there was great conflict between her testimony and that as presented by the State, [we] are presenting her testimony to show facts necessary to meet the first prong of our guidelines under the Battered Woman Syndrome.

> **Take Note**
>
> During the pre-Bechtel era, many battered women defendants were convicted and sentenced to prison without jury consideration of the history of their battering by their intimate partner. Some states have enacted laws that allow courts to reconsider the judgments in some of these cases. For an example of a case seeking this remedy under the California statute, see https://www.pbs.org/newshour/show/crime-after-crime-examines-battered-woman-s-struggle-to-leave-prison.

[Appellant married the victim, Ken Brechtel, on August 25, 1982.] She recalled that the first incidence of violence perpetrated by the victim upon her was on July 4, 1982, when around midnight, he began crying about his deceased son and, in a drunken rage, grabbed her by the head and threw her into the windshield of his boat. As she tried to get to the telephone, he started to throw canned goods out of the closet at her. She left but was caught and put in a car by Ken; while they were stopped at a stop sign, she jumped out of the car. Mr. Bechtel came around the side of the car, threw her back in, and told her not to ever do that again. Inside the car, he grabbed her head by the hair and slammed her into the window and again, told her not to get out of the car. When they arrived at her home, Appellant jumped out of the car, ran into her house and locked the doors. When Ken Bechtel threatened to kick the "m . . . f . . ." door in, Appellant responded by telling him that she had guns in her home. Mr. Bechtel eventually left. This was the first of approximately 23 battering incidents leading to the fatal shooting on September 23, 1984.

Testimony at trial revealed that the deceased committed the batterings when intoxicated and without provocation. The batterings consisted of the deceased grabbing Appellant by either her ears or hair and pounding her head on the ground, wall, door, cabinet or other available object. During many of the episodes he would sob profusely and ramble about his deceased son who was born retarded. During all of the episodes, the deceased threatened or otherwise intimidated Appellant.

On three occasions, Appellant was treated in the Emergency Room. On each of the occasions, the deceased provided the information as to the cause of the injury. On one occasion, Appellant was treated for neck injury and provided with a neck collar. On the other occasions, she was treated for cuts to her hand and feet. On five occasions, Appellant sought police help. Each time the police arrived at her home, the deceased was made to leave. On one occasion, Appellant stopped at the scene of an accident and asked the policeman at the scene to remove the deceased who, in a drunken rage, was kicking the windshield and beating on the dashboard. The deceased was removed and taken to the residence and was there when Appellant arrived. Appellant was subsequently beaten by the deceased.

On several occasions, Appellant was able to escape her residence and stay overnight at various hotels. Appellant related the incidents to some of her close friends and the deceased's family. However, though some of the abuse occurred on business trips, she never told the deceased's business associates. Appellant also sought help from the deceased's family as to his alcohol problem. She made inquiries of several treatment facilities and made appointments for the deceased, who promised after later incidents to undergo treatment, but never did.

On September 23, 1984, the day of his death, the deceased returned home unexpectedly at approximately 5:30 a.m. from a hunting trip, highly intoxicated. He awakened Appellant and ordered her to get out of the bed so they could have a drink. He ordered her out on the patio where the deceased related to her and her friend, Billy Bender, who was visiting from out of state, that he had been picked up for driving under the influence by the Nichols Hills Police. Ken Bechtel continued to drink coffee with liquor. He became angry when Appellant kept turning down the jukebox whenever he would turn it up.

After about three or four hours, Appellant decided to go back to bed. Once in her bedroom, she could hear Mr. Bechtel crying. She became afraid. Aware that Ms. Bender might be in difficulty, she went to the doors of the patio to try to get Ms. Bender's attention. Finally, Ms. Bender came inside to get some cigarettes. When she tried to return to the patio, Appellant admonished her not to go back but to leave Mr. Bechtel alone to sleep it off and for her to go to bed immediately. The next thing Appellant remembered was hearing the night table drawer opening and seeing the deceased with the .25 gun in his hand. He told Appellant that she would not need that G. D. gun anymore.

As he walked towards the door leading to the backyard, Appellant jumped up and ran to the closet where she frantically looked for her purse and keys. After retrieving her purse, she turned to go to the kitchen when a naked Ken Bechtel pulled her by the hair and threw her back on the bed. He was rambling and crying about his son Kenny and questioning her about why she was not at home when he tried to call her earlier. He held his arm against her throat. Appellant raised her leg to free herself when they both fell onto the floor. The deceased threatened to "f--k you and kill your ass." He began pounding her head into the floor. He picked her up by the head and pulled her back on the bed. He pulled her gown off and rammed his fingers into her vagina. He then climbed on top of her, held her down by placing his knees on her arms and banged her head against the headboard. He ejaculated on her face and stomach, after which he slumped on top of her. She eased from under him and went to the bathroom to wash herself.

While in the bathroom, the deceased came up behind her, grabbed the back of her head, threw her down on the floor, bit her on the left breast and finally lay his head on her lower body. During this time, Appellant tried to calm him down by repeating it's okay, it's all right. Then the telephone rang. It was a friend inquiring about his luggage. During this time, Appellant vomited. As she was trying to put on some clothes, Ken returned, accusing her of taking the friend's luggage and betting that she thought it was her "G.D." kids. He put her arm behind her back and his arm against her throat and forced her back onto the bed. At this point his eyes were glazed over and he was crying and rambling as he continued to beat her head against the headboard. He slumped on top of her.

Appellant tried to get from under him, but he would mumble whenever she made an effort. Finally, she eased herself from under him. As she sat on her knees on the floor beside the bed, she lit a cigarette, held it in one hand and her head with the other hand. As she got ready to smoke the cigarette, she heard a gurgling sound, looked up and saw the contorted look and glazed eyes of the deceased with his arms raised. Appellant reached for the gun under the bed and shot the deceased as she tried to get up and run.

Appellant defended this case on the theory of self-defense. In Oklahoma, self-defense is the subject of statutory and case law. The relevant portions of [the self-defense statute provide]:

> Homicide is also justifiable when committed by any person . . . in the lawful defense of such person . . . when there is a reasonable ground to apprehend a design to commit a felony, or to do some great personal injury, and imminent danger of such design being accomplished[.]

This Court has held that the bare belief that one is about to suffer death or great personal injury will not, in itself, justify taking the life of his adversary. There must exist *reasonable* grounds for such belief at the time of the killing. Further, the right to take another's life in self-defense is not to be tested by the honesty or good faith of the defendant's belief in the necessity of the killing, but by the fact whether he had *reasonable* grounds for such belief. Fear alone never justifies one person to take the life of another. Such fear must have been induced by some overt act, gesture or word spoken by the deceased at the time the homicide occurred which would form a *reasonable* ground for the belief that the accused is about to suffer death or great bodily harm.

For the purposes of deciding this appeal, we analyze two of the requirements of self-defense: (1) *reasonableness* and (2) *imminence.* These two requirements, as applied to this case, can be understood only within the framework of the Battered Woman Syndrome.

1. Admissibility of Testimony as It Relates to the Battered Woman Syndrome

On appeal, Appellant contends that the trial court erred in refusing to allow expert testimony on the battered woman syndrome as such testimony would aid the trier of fact in assessing how her experiences as a battered woman affected her state of mind at the time of the killing. This, she argues, goes to the *reasonableness* of her belief that she was in *imminent* danger. We agree.

An offer of proof concerning the admissibility of testimony on the Battered Woman Syndrome was made in-camera where the trial judge heard testimony from Dr. Lenore Walker, a licensed, practicing psychologist and diplomate in clinical psychology who pioneered the research on the Battered Woman Syndrome, and the State's witness, Dr. Herbert C. Modlin, a licensed, practicing psychiatrist. Dr. Walker discussed the methodology used by her in diagnosing such syndrome and related that this is taught in the graduate schools and accepted in the entire scientific community of research. On refusing to allow the testimony, the trial judge offered [these] reasons: 1) The lack of general acceptance of the theory in the psychological community based on the fact that the syndrome is not listed in the *Diagnostic and Statistical Manual of Mental Disorders-3-R* (DMS-3R), a publication of the American Psychiatric Association; and 2) The testimony did not appear to be necessary or helpful to the jury since the jury was capable of making a decision based on all of the evidence.

We find no support for the trial court's first reason. The relevant scientific community in this case is the psychological community and not the psychiatric community. Moreover, both experts acknowledged that the syndrome is considered a sub-category of Post-traumatic Stress Disorder, which is generally accepted and is listed in the DSM-3R. Based upon our independent review of the available sources on the subject, we believe that the syndrome is a mixture of both psychological and physiological symptoms but is not a mental disease in the context of insanity. Further, we believe that because psychologists see more battered women than psychiatrists, the psychological community has had the opportunity to be and, indeed, have been more responsive to the problems or symptoms experienced by those suffering from the syndrome.

Other courts have accepted the syndrome as a scientifically recognized theory. To date, thirty-one (31) states and the District of Columbia allow the use of expert testimony on the subject. Five (5) states acknowledged its validity, but held the testimony inadmissible based on the facts of the particular case. In addition, hundreds of books, articles and commentaries have been written and numerous studies have been done on the subject. Based on the aforesaid, we find that the Battered Woman Syndrome is a substantially scientifically accepted theory.

We next address the trial court's ruling that expert testimony does not appear to be necessary or helpful to the jury since Appellant's testimony [describes] numerous drunken assaults and threats, including the vicious assault and threat to kill her on the night of the homicide, [which] are, in the trial court's opinion, "easily within the common understanding of all the jurors and easily come within the legal definition of self-defense. The jury may consider all the rest of the evidence offered and yet to be offered in conjunction with the Defendant's statement of the incident, and they can make the decision." We do not agree, especially in light of the two inquiries submitted by the jury during its deliberation. These inquiries demonstrate the lack of common understanding of the elements of self-defense, particularly where the defendant is a battered woman.

FYI

Instead of using the term "battered women's syndrome," today a court would be more likely to refer to "intimate partner battering and its effects." *See* Points for Discussion after *Brechtel.*

Expert testimony in Oklahoma is admissible if it will assist the trier of fact in search of the truth and augment the normal experience of the juror by helping him or her draw proper conclusions concerning particular behavior of a victim in a particular circumstance or circumstances. [The evidence rule in 12 O.S.1981 § 2702] provides: "If scientific, technical or *other specialized knowledge* will assist the trier of fact to understand the evidence or to determine a fact in issue, a witness qualified as an expert by knowledge, skill, experience, training or education may testify in the form of an opinion or otherwise." (Emphasis added).

Appellant argues that expert testimony regarding the syndrome is admissible to help the jury understand the battered woman, and, why Appellant acted out of a reasonable belief that she was in imminent danger when considering the issue of self-defense. We agree.

While the Court does not, as a matter of law, adopt the definition of a "Battered Woman", it was first defined by Dr. Lenore Walker in her book, *THE BATTERED WOMAN SYNDROME* (1979), as follows:

> The battered woman is a woman who is repeatedly subjected to any forceful, physical or psychological behavior by a man in order to coerce her to do something he wants her to do without any concern for her rights. Battered women include wives or women in any form of intimate relationship with men. Furthermore, in order to be classified as a battered woman, the couple must go through the battering cycle at least twice. Any woman may find herself in an abusive relationship with a man once. If it occurs a second time, and she remains in the situation, she is defined as a battered woman. *Id.* at XV.

Misconceptions regarding battered women abound, making it more likely than not that the average juror will draw from his or her own experience or common myths, which may lead to a wholly incorrect conclusion. Thus, we believe that expert testimony on the syndrome is necessary to counter these misconceptions. . . .

Food for Thought

Critics have pointed out a variety of flaws in Dr. Walker's 1979 definition of a "battered woman." How is it underinclusive? What other shortcomings does it have?

We believe that the Battered Woman Syndrome has gained substantial scientific acceptance and will aid the trier of fact in determining facts in issue, i.e., *reasonableness* and *imminence* (discussed below), when testimony on the same is offered in cases of self-defense[.] Thus, we conclude that the trial court erred in not allowing testimony on the syndrome. We find the trial court's failure to allow said testimony amounts to reversible error requiring a new trial.

2. Reasonableness and the Battered Woman Syndrome

The key to the defense of self-defense is reasonableness. A defendant must show that she had a *reasonable* belief as to the *imminence* of great bodily harm or death and as to the force necessary to compel it. Several of the psychological symptoms that develop in one suffering from the syndrome are particularly relevant to the standard of *reasonableness* in self-defense. One such symptom is a greater sensitivity to danger which has come about because of the intimacy and history of the relationship. Dr. Walker, in her offer of proof below, explained that the abuse occurs in a cycle (The Cycle Theory), which consists of three phases. The first phase is the "tension-building" period. The second stage is the "acute-explosion" period, where the abuse takes place. The third stage is the "loving, contrition" period.

It is during the tension-building period that the battered woman develops a heightened sensitivity to any kinds of cues of distress. Thus, because of her intimate knowledge of her batterer, the battered woman perceives danger faster and more accurately as she is more acutely aware that a new or escalated violent episode is about to occur.

> What is or is not an overt demonstration of violence varies with the circumstances. Under some circumstances a slight movement may justify instant action because of reasonable apprehension of danger, under other circumstances this would not be so. And it is for the jury, and not for the judge passing upon the weight and effect of the evidence, to determine how this may be.

Indeed, considering her particular circumstances, the battered woman's perception of the situation and her belief as to the *imminence* of great bodily harm or death may be deemed *reasonable.*

During the loving, contrition period, the abuser makes amends by being loving, making promises to change and avowing that the abuse will never happen again. It is during this stage that the battered woman is being positively reinforced by her abuser. In most battering cases, this period is of the longest duration. The cultural characteristics of women influence the battered woman's belief that if she could only do something to help her abuser, then the bad part of him will go away. Thus, the battered woman learns to develop coping skills rather than escape skills and develops a "psychological paralysis" and "learned helplessness."

Thus, Dr. Walker's testimony as to how Appellant's particular experiences as a battered woman suffering from the Battered Woman Syndrome affected her perceptions of danger, its imminence, what actions were necessary to protect herself and the reasonableness of those perceptions are relevant and necessary to prove Appellant's defense of self-defense. However, it now becomes necessary to determine the standard of reasonableness against which the finder of fact must measure the accused's belief.

Standards of reasonableness has been traditionally characterized as either "objective" or "subjective." Under the objective standard of reasonableness, the trier of fact is required to view the circumstances, surrounding the accused at the time of the use of force, from the standpoint of hypothetical reasonable person. Under the subjective standard of reasonableness, the fact finder is required to determine whether the circumstances, surrounding the accused at the time of the use of force, are sufficient to induce in the accused an honest and reasonable belief that he/she must use force to defend himself/herself against imminent harm.

Oklahoma's standard of reasonableness may be gleaned from past decisions of this Court and is set forth in [jury instruction 743], which reads as follows:

> A person is justified in using deadly force in self-defense if that person reasonably believed that use of deadly force was necessary to protect herself from imminent danger of death or great bodily harm. Self-defense is a defense although the danger to life or personal security may not have been real, if a reasonable person, in the circumstances and from the viewpoint of the defendant, would reasonably have believed that she was in imminent danger of death or great bodily harm.

The aforesaid instruction was given in this case. While the instruction explicitly states that the fact finder should assume the viewpoint and circumstances of the defendant in assessing the reasonableness of his or her belief, i.e. subjective, it also requires the defendant's viewpoint to be that of a reasonable person, in similar circumstances and with the same perceptions, i.e., objective. Thus, Oklahoma's standard is a hybrid, combining both the objective and subjective standards[.] . . .

However, in light of the jury's inquiry and our decision today to allow testimony on the Battered Woman Syndrome in appropriate cases, we deem it necessary to modify [jury instruction] 743 by striking the words "reasonably" and "reasonable" from such instruction. We hereby adopt a new [743A] instruction that will be given in all Battered Woman Syndrome cases. Such modified instruction shall read as follows:

> A person is justified in using deadly force in self-defense if that person believed that use of deadly force was necessary to protect herself from imminent danger of death or great bodily harm. Self-defense is a defense although the danger to life or personal security may not have been real, if a person, in the circumstances and from the viewpoint of the defendant, would reasonably have believed that she was in imminent danger of death or great bodily harm.

3. *Imminence and the Battered Woman Syndrome*

In addition to the reasonableness standard, Oklahoma's law of self-defense also imposes the temporal requirement of *imminence*. The think-

Take Note

The *Bechtel* Court noted that the legislature recently had enacted a new evidence statute and opined that the statute was not inconsistent with the court's analysis. The statute provided that, "In an action in a court of this state, if a party offers evidence of domestic abuse, testimony of an expert witness concerning the effects of such domestic abuse on the beliefs, behavior and perception of the person being abused shall be admissible as evidence." *See* 22 Okl. Stat. Ann. § 40.7 (1992).

ing is that it is unreasonable to be provoked to the point of killing well after the provocative or assertive conduct has occurred.

Furthermore, the syndrome has been analogized to the classic hostage situation in that the battered woman lives under long-term, life-threatening conditions in constant fear of another eruption of violence. *See* W. LaFave & A. Scott, Criminal Law 458 (2d ed. 1986), and P. Robinson, 2 Criminal Law Defenses (1984). Robinson gives the example where the captor tells the hostage that he intends to kill him in three days. If on the first day, the hostage sees an opportunity to kill the captor and avoid the threat of his own death, a literal application of the requirement that the threat be "imminent" would prevent the hostage from using deadly force until the captor is standing over him with a knife. For the battered woman, if there is no escape or sense of safety, then the next attack, which could be fatal or cause serious bodily harm, is imminent. Based on the traditionally accepted definition of imminent and its functional derivatives, a battered woman, to whom the threat of serious bodily harm or death is always imminent, would be precluded from asserting the defense of self-defense.

Under our "hybrid" reasonableness standard, the meaning of *imminent* must necessarily envelope the battered woman's perceptions based on all the facts and circumstances of his or her relationship with the victim. In *Women's Self-Defense Cases: Theory and Practice* (1981), Elizabeth Bochnak writes:

> The battered woman learns to recognize the small signs that precede periods of escalated violence. She learns to distinguish subtle changes in tone of voice, facial expression, and levels of danger. She is in a position to know, perhaps with greater certainty than someone attacked by a stranger, that the batterer's threat is real and will be acted upon.

Thus, according to the author, an abused woman may kill her mate during the period of threat that precedes a violent incident, right before the violence escalates to the more dangerous levels of an acute battering episode. Or, she may take action against him during a lull in an assaultive incident, or after it has culminated, in an effort to prevent a recurrence of the violence. And so, the issue is not whether the danger was in *fact* imminent, but whether, given the circumstances as she perceived them, the defendant's *belief was reasonable that the danger was imminent.*

Practice Pointer

For an example of material intended to educate judges on the role of experts in cases involving intimate partner violence, see The Jurist: eNews for Pennsylvania Judges About Domestic Violence Jurisprudence, *Expert Testimony: Expanding Its Role in Domestic Violence Civil Cases* (December 2016), https://us6.campaign-archive.com/?u=58bd1722d2d1aa95cf893c7d1&id=cb7bf65549&e=[UNIQID]

Because there is the presumption in *imminence* that the defender may find an alternative to the use of deadly force, we find it necessary to address the duty to retreat, which duty is implicit in said presumption. Additionally, Appellant complained that the trial court refused to give her requested instructions on "no duty to retreat" but gave instead [the pattern instruction 748]. [That instruction provides: "A person who was not the aggressor or who did not provoke another with intent to cause an altercation has no duty to retreat, but may stand firm and use the right of self-defense."] [We] find that [the instruction given by the trial judge] adequately states the law in Oklahoma and the trial court did not err in refusing to give Appellant's requested instruction[.]

For the foregoing reasons, this case is Reversed and Remanded for a new trial, consistent with this opinion.

PARKS, J., concurring in result:

I find that evidence concerning Battered Woman Syndrome was relevant to the jury's assessment of appellant's theory of the case—self defense. While I conclude that the syndrome should have been presented to the jury in this case, I disagree with the majority's decision to radically overhaul the laws pertaining to self defense. The facts asserted by appellant, that the victim made a threatening movement and she shot him, constitute classic self defense and do not necessitate the sweeping changes imposed by the majority. Our inquiry should be limited to an assessment of the syndrome's reliability and its relevance to the facts presented. . . .

Currently, the jury is asked to view the circumstances as they appeared to the defendant and then is asked to determine whether a reasonable person, caught in the dynamics of those identical circumstances, would respond as the defendant did. I find that the syndrome should have been admitted as it sheds light on the circumstances surrounding the altercation *as they appeared to the appellant*. The facts before us require us to decide nothing more. . . .

LUMPKIN, VICE-PRESIDING JUDGE, dissenting:

[Appellant's] evidence does not reveal the "Battered Woman Syndrome" was implicated on the night of September 23, 1984. The facts related by Appellant only raise a case of traditional self defense based on the right of self defense to resist any attempt to murder or commit a felony upon her, or the imminent threat as perceived by Appellant due to the victim's threats and actions committed that night. The "Cycle Theory" is not relevant based on the evidence. However, I recognize evidence regarding the victim's past trait of character for violence [is] relevant [and admissible] as it goes to Appellant's perception as a reasonable person regarding the imminence of danger of death or great bodily harm. The admissibility of this evidence does not require the adoption of the "Battered Woman Syndrome". . . .

[The] Court seems to disregard the evidence of the case in a reaching attempt to adopt a syndrome which is not applicable to the facts and does not comport with the requirements of being generally accepted in the scientific/medical community. While I agree that evidence of the Post-traumatic Stress Disorder, which is accepted as a standard for diagnosis in the medical community, would be relevant evidence in a proper case to provide a jury with the medical and psychological diagnostic criteria required to determine the reasonableness of a defendant's actions, it is not relevant here. The appropriate resolution of the ills of society should be left to the Legislative and Executive branches of our government. This Court should restrict itself to the application of the law to the facts presented in the record. I therefore must dissent [from] the Court's actions in this case.

Points for Discussion

a. Evidence of Battering "Effects" & "Experiences"

The *Bechtel* opinion illustrates the controversies that occupied the attention of courts in self-defense cases with battered defendants during the first fifteen years after the publication of Lenore Walker's study in 1979. That era was followed by a period of revisionism, illustrated by the California legislature's enactment in 2004 of a statute that deleted all statutory references to "Battered Women's Syndrome" and replaced them with references to "intimate partner battering and its effects." Similarly, it is common for courts today to avoid references to the "syndrome" and to make references instead to "expert testimony on domestic violence," for example. In a recent case in which the prosecutor sought to introduce expert testimony about battering when prosecuting the batterer, the evidence was deemed admissible even though the battering episode that led to the criminal charges was the first episode of physical violence in the relationship between the battered victim and the defendant. *See People v. Brown*, 33 Cal. 4th 892, 16 Cal. Rptr. 3d 447, 94 P.3d 574 (Cal. 2004).

Food for Thought

Is it possible that the abandonment of the "syndrome" label will make it easier for expert witnesses to present useful information about battering "effects and experiences" to juries in a way that will influence the outcomes of cases in which battered defendants plead self-defense when charged with killing their intimate partners who batter them?

The national aspect of this trend is illustrated by the 1996 report prepared by the U.S. Department of Justice, the National Institute of Justice, the U.S. Department of Health and Human Services, and the National Institute of Mental Health. That report stated that the "strong consensus among researchers," as well as judges and attorneys, "is that the term 'battered women syndrome' does not reflect the scientific knowledge now available regarding battering and its effects, implies a psychological impairment, and suggests a single pattern of response to battering." This finding is described in the amicus brief in *Brown* that was filed on behalf of the California Alliance Against Domestic Violence, which summarizes the flaws of the syndrome concept. For example, the term "battered women syndrome" ignores the 8% of men who are estimated to be victims of domestic violence in their lifetimes, and it erroneously implies "that all victims of domestic violence experience one common set of effects from battering." The responses of victims are "not limited to PTSD," and the "syndrome" concept creates a "misleading checklist of elements" that are assumed erroneously to define the status and experience of a battered person. Moreover, the "syndrome" term is harmful to victims and misleading to juries because "it implies that the victim suffers from a psychological impairment or pathology," and "sends a message that the victim is passive or helpless in the face of abuse."

Why does the *Bechtel* Court conclude that the syndrome evidence provided by the expert witness should have been admitted at trial? What function will this evidence serve at the new trial? How will the court's modification of the jury instruction affect the arguments of counsel at the new trial? How has the *Bechtel* opinion altered the law on self-defense and why?

b. Retreat from Batterer's Castle

The trial judge in *Bechtel* rejected the defendant's proposed instruction on the duty to retreat, which read as follows: "If [the defendant] actually believed and had reasonable grounds to believe that she was in imminent danger of death or serious bodily harm and that deadly force was necessary to repel such danger, she was not required to retreat or consider whether she could retreat safely. No woman is required to leave her home to avoid an attack, even if the attacker is another member of the same household. A woman is entitled to stand her ground and use such force as is reasonably necessary under the circumstances to protect herself from serious bodily harm." The *Bechtel* Court approved the trial judge's instruction, which contained no reference to retreat from a batterer in the home, as an accurate statement of the law, and thereby ignored the value of informing jurors of the more particular right of a battered cohabitant wife to stand her ground when attacked by a battering cohabitant husband.

However, the *Bechtel* defendant's proposed jury instruction foreshadowed the increasing judicial approval during the 1990s of the "no duty to retreat from an attacking cohabitant in the castle" rule. This development may be attributed to the increased familiarity of appellate court judges with expert witness testimony concerning domestic violence, and their increased sensitivity to the impact of the older rules in some states that limited the protection of the castle doctrine to the inhabitants of the castle who need to use deadly force in self-defense against intruders. *Compare Weiand v. State*, 732 So.2d 1044 (Fla. 1999) (overruling *State v. Bobbitt*, 415 So.2d 724 (Fla. 1982)).

The following hypothetical provides the opportunity to consider the difficulties involved in obtaining a jury instruction on self-defense in a case where a battered defendant kills a sleeping spouse or partner.

Hypo: *New Trial*

Assume that you are the defense counsel in the *Bechtel* case, and that the "syndrome" evidence excluded by the trial judge will be admitted at the new trial. As you prepare for trial, consider these questions:

a. *Using MPC Elements.* On the facts, assume that the trial judge grants the defendant's request for an instruction on self-defense, and assume that the MPC definition of self-defense in § 3.04(1) and (2) (b) will be used at the new trial. What arguments will you make to the jury as to the defendant's beliefs in the required elements of self-defense?

b. *Sleeping Batterer.* Assume that the evidence at the new trial differs in one key respect from the evidence at the first trial. The defendant testifies that at the end of the final encounter, when she looked up, she did not see the "contorted look and glazed eyes" of her husband with his arms raised. Instead, she saw that he had fallen asleep. Then she reached for the gun under the bed and shot him, and then she got up and ran. What arguments will the prosecutor make to attempt to persuade the trial judge to deny the defendant's request for a self-defense instruction on these facts? What counter-arguments will you make in reply as defense counsel?

B. Defense of Dwelling

Assuming that the requirements for self-defense cannot be met, when can a person use deadly force in relation to property, and more specifically, in relation to a dwelling? In the case of defense of property that is not a dwelling, even if a person reasonably believes that there is a threat of trespass or theft, this would not justify the use of deadly force. In the case of defense of a dwelling against entry by an intruder, statutes and courts allow the use of deadly force but place limitations upon that use. The most demanding limitations require that the defending person must reasonably believe that an intruder posed "a substantial danger of serious bodily harm" to the defending person or others, or that the intruder actually "threatened deadly force" against the defending person. But some courts and statutes impose less stringent conditions, requiring only that the defending person reasonably believes that the intruder will commit a felony or seek to harm a person in the dwelling. During recent decades, legislatures have enacted new defense-of-dwelling statutes that establish even more generous rights to use deadly force, as illustrated by the *Anderson* case that follows.

FYI

The MPC § 3.06(3)(d)(ii) defines the right to use deadly force for protection of property to require that a person must believe that "the person against whom the force is used is attempting to commit . . . arson, burglary, robbery or other felonious theft or property destruction" and either (A) "has employed or threatened deadly force against or in [his or her] presence" or (B) "the use of force other than deadly force to prevent the commission of the crime would expose the actor or another in [his or her] presence to substantial danger of serious bodily injury."

State v. Anderson

972 P.2d 32 (Okla. Crim. App. 1998).

LUMPKIN, JUDGE:

[Defendant-Appellee Anderson was charged with first degree murder and with the lesser crime of shooting with intent to kill. He requested a jury instruction on the affirmative defense established by state statute that allows an "occupant" of a dwelling to use deadly force against a person who has made an unlawful entry, when the occupant reasonably believes the other person might use physical force against any occupant. The State argued that the defendant did not qualify for the defense because he was only an invited guest, and did not reside in the dwelling. The trial court rejected the State's argument and granted the defendant's request for the jury instruction. The State objected and reserved, as a question of law, the issue of "whether the term 'occupant' [in the statute] can include people other than the home owner or continuous resident of the premises." The jury returned verdicts of not guilty. The State appealed on the reserved question of law.]

What's That?

Although the State may not appeal a verdict of acquittal because that procedure would violate the constitutional protection against double jeopardy, a state appeal on a reserved question of law does not cause such a violation. By establishing the "reserved question of law" procedure, a state allows for greater judicial attention to the resolution of important legal issues that otherwise would be unreviewable because of the fortuity of an acquittal.

Initially, we note that a *state appeal* on a reserved question of law does not address any part of the trial or proceedings except the precise legal issue reserved[.] Therefore, the only facts from Appellee's trial that now concern us are that he was an invited guest in the home of Joe Alvey and Chris Wilson; that the victims, Joe Younger and Chris Harris, forcibly broke into Alvey and Wilson's home, and that Appellee shot the victims.

Whether the term "occupant" as used in § 1289.25 includes people other than the home owner or continuous resident of the premises presents an issue of first impression for this Court. As we answer this question, we must keep in mind the fundamental rule of statutory construction—to ascertain and give effect to the intention of the Legislature as expressed in the statute. To ascertain the intention of the Legislature in the enactment of a statute, the court may look to each part of the same, to other statutes upon the same or relative subjects, to the evils and mischiefs to be remedied, and to the natural or absurd consequences of any particular interpretation. A statute should be given a construction according to the fair import of its words taken in their usual sense, in connection with the context, and with reference to the purpose of the provision. It is the text of the statute which gives notice to the citizen of the prohibited conduct subject to prosecution and the scope of conduct which is allowable to defend against prohibited conduct committed against a person. Therefore, the text of the statute should guide this Court's interpretation of it.

[The statute here, § 1289.25,] also known as the "Make My Day" Law, provides:

A. The Legislature hereby recognizes that the citizens of the State of Oklahoma have a right to expect absolute safety within their own homes.

B. *Any occupant* of a dwelling is justified in using any degree of physical force, including but not limited to deadly force, against another person who has made an unlawful entry into that dwelling, and when *the occupant* has a reasonable belief that such other person might use any physical force, no matter how slight, against *any occupant* of the dwelling.

C. *Any occupant* of a dwelling using physical force, including but not limited to deadly force, pursuant to the provisions of subsection B of this section, shall have an affirmative defense in any criminal prosecution for an offense arising from the *reasonable use of such force* and shall be immune from any civil liability for injuries or death resulting from the reasonable use of such force.

D. The provisions of this section and the provisions of the Oklahoma Self-Defense Act, Sections 1 through 25 of this act, shall not be construed to require any person using a pistol pursuant to the provisions of this section to be licensed in any manner (emphasis added).

FYI

The phrase, "Go ahead, make my day," entered the public vocabulary after it was uttered by the actor Clint Eastwood when he played the character Harry Callahan in the 1983 film, "Sudden Impact." Callahan utters the line while pointing a gun at man who is threatening to shoot another person, and so in context it means, "I'd be happy to shoot you dead." *See* http://www.youtube.com/watch?v=3ishbTwXf1g.

This statute does not contain a list of definitions. Lacking a specific statutory definition, we must look to the common ordinary meaning of the term "occupant." *Webster's II* defines "occupant" as "1. One that occupies a place or position, esp. a resident. 2. One who is the first to take possession of previously unowned land or premises." *Webster's II New Riverside University Dictionary* (1984). The State argues that under these definitions, and those of "occupancy" and "occupy," § 1289.25 refers only to a person who has a possessory or privacy interest in the premises. While we find these definitions instructive, we do not find they answer the questions before us.

Looking to other statutory uses of the term "occupant," we do not find a requirement for a possessory or privacy interest. *See* 21 O.S.1991 § 1171 (peeping tom is any person who loiters in the vicinity of a private dwelling with the intent to gaze upon occupants therein in a clandestine manner); 21 O.S.1991 § 1438(B) (malicious mischief is the breaking and entering of a dwelling without permission of the owner or occupant thereof); 21 O.S.1991 §§ 10–111; 11–507; 11–705; 11–1110 (references to occupants of vehicles.) The use of the term "occupied" similarly implies no possessory interest. *See* 21 O.S.1991 § 1401 (first degree arson committed by willful burning of any building or structure, inhabited or occupied by one or more persons).

Appellant directs us to the Colorado "Make My Day" law [enacted in 1986], after which § 1289.25 was patterned. Much of the Oklahoma statute is the same as the Colorado law, including the preamble and the use of the term "occupant." Appellant cites to several cases in which the Colorado courts had held the term "occupant" is synonymous with "homeowner." However, a review of those cases reveals the Colorado courts have not been presented with the question we now have before us and therefore have not addressed whether "occupant" includes a visitor to the home. Likewise, other jurisdictions cited to us by Appellant have not addressed the question before us. Appellant is correct in noting these jurisdictions permit the homeowner to use deadly force within his own residence, but the issue of whether a visitor is similarly permitted to use deadly force is not addressed.

While dictionary definitions, statutory references and case law from Oklahoma and other jurisdictions are helpful in our analysis, the interpretation of the Legislature's intent in § 1289.25 is ultimately based upon the words in the statute itself. Reading the statute in its entirety, we find it a study in contradiction or compromise. The preamble seems to clearly set forth the intent of the law—"that the citizens of the State of Oklahoma have a right to expect absolute safety within their own homes." However, the terms "resident," "homeowner" or other such restrictive terms were not used in the remainder of the statute. Likewise, the all encompassing term "any person" was not used. Therefore, we are left with the term "occupant," a term with no specific statutory definition. That term is used three times in subsection B. It is the third use of the term "occupant" which leads us to the conclusion that the law was intended to protect anyone legally inside the dwelling, and not just the legal residents of the dwelling. Reading the statute in that manner, any person legally in the dwelling is justified in using any degree of physical force, including but not limited to deadly force, against another person who has made an unlawful entry into that dwelling, and when the person legally inside the dwelling has a reasonable belief that such other person might use any physical force, no matter how slight, against any person legally in the dwelling. To read it in any other manner would permit only residents or homeowners to protect only other residents or homeowners. Invited guests or employees would be left to fend for themselves. This type of application would lead to many absurd results and is not supported by any statements of legislative intent. There are many fact situations which illustrate this point, but we will look at just two.

The baby-sitter comes to the homeowner's residence to watch the children while the parents (the homeowners) are away. If someone breaks into the house making an unlawful entry, is the babysitter allowed to protect herself and the children in her care? Under the State's interpretation of the statute, the baby-sitter would not be able to use any physical force, including deadly force, against the intruder because she was not the homeowner or resident. We do not believe the Legislature intended to exclude someone in that position from using physical or deadly force to protect him or herself and those in his or her charge. Another scenario involves that of the invited guest. An unlawful entry is made into the home, the homeowners or residents are either away from the house or unable to defend themselves and only the invited guest is able to muster a defense. Is the invited guest allowed to use any physical force, including deadly force, against the intruder? We think so. Under the State's interpretation of the statute, the invited guest would not be able to so defend him or herself. While these are just two of many situations which could arise, they adequately illustrate the practical application of the statute. These situations also point out how our interpretation of the statute is consistent with the other laws on self-defense and defense of another.

The Oklahoma statutes addressing self-defense, defense of others, defense of habitation, and defense of property are numerous and often confusing and inconsistent. However, one common aspect is shared. Exoneration is dependent on facts which an innocent defender may not know or be able to know until it is too late, and legal conclusions about those facts which the lay person cannot be expected to make, particularly when one is facing an attacker or unknown intruder. For example, under 21 O.S.1991 § 733(1) and (2), if the attacker's intent is felonious or there is reasonable grounds to fear great personal injury, the innocent persons inside the dwelling have a right to use deadly force. Under 21 O.S.1991 § 643(3) force may be used by a party about to be injured in order to prevent the commission of an offense, but the amount of force is limited to that sufficient to prevent such offense. Whether the intruder intends a felony or not may depend on facts that the victim may not know until it is too late. Under § 1289.25, the person inside the dwelling does not have to determine the intruder's intentions. An unlawful entry and the reasonable belief that the intruder might use any physical force is sufficient to permit the person inside the dwelling to use any physical force, including deadly force, against the person making the unlawful entry. Under § 1289.25, persons legally inside a dwelling have the right to expect safety and freedom from unlawful intrusion. With the enactment of § 1289.25 it appears the Legislature was trying to create a place of absolute safety and freedom—the home, whether it be your own home or one in which you are legally present.

The State's argument that including visitors in the term "occupant" will result in some sort of carnage is groundless. The statute has been on the books for approximately a decade without incident. It contains sufficient safeguards to prevent abuse. Under [section (B) of] the statute, if the occupant does not "reasonably believe" that the intruder intends to use force, then he or she is not justified in using deadly force. This statute merely tells those who would break into other people's homes that they do so at their own risk. When one is going about his or her business, in the safety of a dwelling, and is suddenly surprised by an intruder breaking into the dwelling, we find the Legislature intended to give the benefit of the doubt to the law-abiding occupant rather than the law breaking intruder. When one intrudes into a dwelling that is not his, the extent of his wrongdoing should not depend on the legal relationship between the dwelling and those lawfully inside it. When one intrudes into the dwelling of another, the harm is the violation of the sanctity of the dwelling itself, not merely to a particular person's property interest. An invited guest in a dwelling has just a much right to expect safety therein as the owner.

Granted, as with many of our laws, this statute applies to the "good guys" as well as the "bad guys." While the persons legally inside the residence may be engaged in illegal activity, or may have occupations which are illegal, if they are legally inside the residence and an intruder illegally enters the dwelling, they are entitled to use any physical force, including deadly force, against the intruder. Whether the use of this force exonerates them from the result of the use of that force, *i.e.*, murder, shooting with intent to kill, etc. would be for a jury to decide under the appropriate instructions.

Therefore, we find the Legislature intended for the term "occupant" as used in § 1289.25 to include visitors, *i.e.* persons legally inside the dwelling.

In its second proposition of error, the State contends that [the applicable jury instruction, OUJI-CR (2nd) 8–15], omits the element of requiring the force used against the intruder to be reasonable. The uniform instruction reads as follows:

Food for Thought

The original version of the Oklahoma Make My Day law was vetoed by the governor, on the grounds that existing law provided sufficient protection for homeowners, and because he viewed the expansion of an affirmative justifiable homicide defense as preferable to immunity from criminal prosecution. He signed the law when it was amended to establish an affirmative defense. See Donna Smith, Recent Development: *Oklahoma's "Make My Day" Law* 23 TULSA L.J. 533 (1988).

> A/An resident/tenant/occupant of a house/apartment/dwelling is justified in using physical force, including deadly force, against another person who has unlawfully entered the house/apartment/dwelling if the resident/tenant/occupant reasonably believes that the other person might use any physical force, no matter how slight, against any resident/tenant/occupant of the house/apartment/dwelling.

The instruction given in the present case was this instruction *verbatim*, with the trial court using the term "occupant" instead of resident or tenant and the term "dwelling" instead of house or apartment. The State seeks to amend the instruction to include an additional requirement that the use of force by the occupant must be reasonable under the circumstances. In support of its argument, the State relies on subsection C of § 1289.25, [which makes reference to the "reasonable use" of force].

We reject the State's argument and find [jury instruction] 8–15 is an appropriate statement of the law. The uniform instruction is taken directly from subsection B of the statute. When the statute is read as a whole and in its entirety, the only "reasonableness" test set forth is that the occupant "reasonably believes" the intruder might use any force. The statute does not state [that] the use of the force must be reasonable under the circumstances. To the contrary, it appears the intent of § 1289.25 of was to remove any "reasonable under the circumstances" test and permit the force used against the intruder based solely upon the occupant's belief that the intruder might use any force against the occupant. The Legislature specifically did not limit the amount of force the occupant could use against the intruder. The reference in subsection C to reasonable force does not create a "reasonable under the circumstances" test. It merely describes when an accused may claim the defense set out in subsection B. The use of the word "reasonable" in

Take Note

In 2006, the Oklahoma legislature amended the *Anderson* statute so as to replace it with a statute that appears to be identical to the 2005 Florida "Stand Your Ground" Law. The Oklahoma legislature also renamed its statute the "Stand Your Ground" Law.

subsection C corresponds to the use of the term "reasonably" in subsection B. The only "reasonableness" prerequisite to claiming the affirmative defense set forth in § 1289.25 is set out in subsection B, *i.e.*, that the occupant reasonably believes the intruder might use some force, however slight, against the occupant. Accordingly, we find [jury instruction] 8–15 is a correct statement of the law as set forth in § 1289.25 and that no additional requirement of "reasonableness" need be included in the instruction.

CHAPEL, P.J., dissenting [joined by LANE, J. and JOHNSON, J.]:

I dissent. Title 21 O.S.1991 § 1289.25, often referred to as the "Make My Day" Law, provides in Subsection A that it is intended to protect citizens "within their own home." I would therefore limit the application of the Act. In view of Subsection A, I am of the opinion that the word "occupant" which appears in Subsections B and C refers only to residents of a dwelling and no others.

The following hypothetical provides the opportunity to consider the competing policy arguments at stake in the expansion of the right to use deadly force beyond the traditional boundaries of the requirements for defense of dwelling.

Hypo: Anderson *Dissent*

How do the elements of the Oklahoma law in *Anderson* compare to the elements of the MPC definition for the defense of property? What other arguments could have been made in the dissenting opinion in *Anderson* to respond to the arguments of the *Anderson* majority? What other pro and con arguments can be made about the policy concerns that underlie the statutory interpretation question in *Anderson*?

C. Expanding the Right to Use Deadly Force

The "Make My Day" laws of the 1980s and 1990s can be viewed as the "first wave" of statutes that expanded the common law requirements for the "defense of dwelling." The "second wave" of such statutes include the new "castle" laws related to dwellings, the expanded version of such laws that extends to vehicles ("shoot the carjacker" laws), and finally, the "stand your ground" laws. All of these laws expand the right to use deadly force, and in each state where they have been enacted, the legislative history typically shows that the National Rifle Association drafted and lobbied for these statutes.

Points for Discussion

a. Modern "Castle" Laws

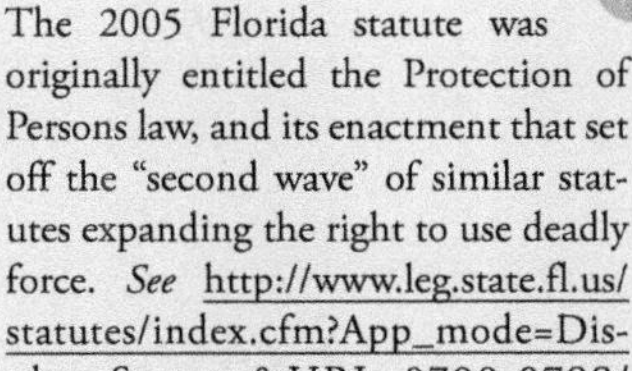

The 2005 Florida statute was originally entitled the Protection of Persons law, and its enactment that set off the "second wave" of similar statutes expanding the right to use deadly force. *See* http://www.leg.state.fl.us/statutes/index.cfm?App_mode=Display_Statute&URL=0700-0799/0776/Sections/0776.013.html.

The common law "castle doctrine" held that there was no "duty to retreat" inside one's dwelling when relying upon the affirmative defense of self-defense. That defense was limited as described in topic A in this chapter, *supra*. The modern "castle" laws, however, do not require a defendant who uses deadly force inside a dwelling against an intruder to satisfy the traditional self-defense requirements (or the common law "defense of dwelling" requirements). The first castle law was enacted in Florida in 2005. As of 2020, such laws have been enacted in at least 25 states. A "castle" law authorizes the use of deadly force when a dwelling occupant has "reason to believe" that an unlawful and forcible entry is occurring. The occupant is presumed to have the reasonable fear of imminent peril of great bodily harm or death that would be needed to raise the affirmative defense of self-defense at trial. The intruder is presumed to be entering with the intent to commit an unlawful act involving force or violence. The law confers immunity from prosecution and civil liability, and the occupant who uses deadly force may not be arrested unless "there is probable cause that the force that was used was unlawful." Finally, a court must award "reasonable attorneys fees, court costs, compensation for loss of income, and all expenses incurred by the defendant of any civil action if the court finds that the defendant is immune from prosecution." *See* Fla. Stat. Ann. § 776.013 (2005).

b. "Shoot the Intruder" Laws

Take Note

In the wake of the shooting of Trayvon Martin, public debate has focused on the question whether legislatures should abandon or modify the "no duty to retreat" rule, in those states where it is either incorporated into traditional self-defense doctrine or enforced through the immunity provisions of new "stand your ground" laws. The debate has only intensified since George Zimmerman was acquitted and at least one juror has described the "no-duty-to-retreat" rule in Florida as "a key factor in the jury's verdict." For one study criticizing the rule, see https://s3.amazonaws.com/s3.mayorsagainstillegalguns.org/images/ShootFirst_v4.pdf.

An example of this type of law is the Louisiana statute enacted in 1998, which allows deadly force to be used against a person who is attempting to make an unlawful entry into a vehicle. A person who is lawfully inside a vehicle may kill the person seeking entry unlawfully, based on a reasonable belief that deadly force is necessary "to prevent the entry or to compel the intruder to leave." *See generally* Stuart P. Green, *Castles and Carjackers: Proportionality and the Use of Deadly Force in Defense of Vehicles and Dwellings*, 1999 U. Ill. L. Rev. 1. According to Green, the enactment of the Louisiana law was inspired by two carjacking crimes, both of which would have justified the use of deadly force by the victims under existing self-defense law. The influence of the 1998 Louisiana law can be seen in the provision allowing the use of deadly force against "vehicle intruders" by vehicle occupants under the 2005 Florida law. They benefit from the same entitlement to use deadly force as home occupants who exercise their rights under the "castle law" provisions.

Hypo: *Road Rage*

Assume that when one driver almost collides with another car, the driver of the other car chases the first driver in a road rage event, until finally the two cars stop side by side at a stop light. The driver who was being chased gets out of his car and approaches the open front passenger window of the other car, where no passenger is sitting. The seated driver pulls a gun and shoots the driver standing at the front passenger window, who later dies. The seated driver is charged with murder and testifies that was afraid for his life because the first driver "made an aggressive move and lunged with his hands and upper body through the front passenger window." What evidence will the prosecutor need to persuade the jury and later the appellate court that the defendant was not entitled to use deadly force to "compel" the other driver to leave the car by shooting him dead? *See State v. Gasser*, 275 So.3d 976 (La. App. 2019).

c. "Stand Your Ground" Laws

The statutes of 25 states provide that there is "no duty to retreat from an attacker in any place in which one is lawfully present." "[A]t least ten of those states" use the language that one may "stand his or her ground." Laws in at least 23 states provide civil immunity for those who act in self-defense under certain circumstances. *See* National Conference of State Legislatures, *Self-Defense and "Stand Your Ground"*, May 26, 2020, https://www.ncsl.org/research/civil-and-criminal-justice/self-defense-and-stand-your-ground.aspx.

The term "stand your ground law" sometimes may be used to refer to the much older "no-duty-to-retreat" doctrine discussed in *Brown*, which is also codified in some state statutes that define the elements of self-defense. However, the term "stand your ground law" has now become associated with a law that incorporates all the facets of the expanded right to use deadly force established in the 2005 Florida statute. The "castle" and "carjacker" facets of that law do not create immunities for a defendant like George Zimmerman (whose actions are summarized in Hypo 3 after the *Brown* opinion, "The Death of Trayvon Martin") because he was not using deadly force against an intruder into a dwelling or a vehicle. But he could have qualified for the immunity from prosecution and civil liability established in the "stand your ground" provision of the 2005 Florida statute. However, if he had chosen to exercise his right to a pre-trial hearing under that law, where the trial judge would determine whether he acted unlawfully or whether he was entitled to immunity from prosecution and civil liability, then presumably it would have been necessary for him to testify at that hearing. By waiving the right to raise the immunity claim, Zimmerman was able to remain silent at his trial while advancing a traditional self-defense claim through the evidence of his statements to police and his other public interviews covered by the media. *See* http://www.cnn.com/2013/04/30/justice/florida-zimmerman-defense.

The jury instructions in the *Zimmerman* prosecution defined the scope of the "no duty to retreat" rule in a self-defense case as follows:

> "A person who is not engaged in an unlawful activity and who is attacked in any other place where he or she has a right to be has no duty to retreat and has the right to stand his or her ground and meet force with force, including deadly force if he or she reasonably believes it is necessary to do so to prevent death or great bodily harm to himself or herself or another or to prevent the commission of a forcible felony."

Hypo 1: *Stand Your Ground Laws and the MPC*

What are the pro and con arguments concerning the enactment of the MPC rule that imposes a duty to retreat outside of one's dwelling (but only when it is possible to retreat in "complete safety") upon a person who otherwise qualifies for the traditional requirements of self-defense? What are the pro and con arguments concerning the enactment of a law that reflects all the elements of the 2005 Florida statute?

Hypo 2: *Dispute over Parking Space*

What basis for invoking the "stand your ground" provision of Florida law did the defense have in the scenario that is summarized in the following news report? Why was that invocation unsuccessful? Here is the report: "Drejka, 49, shot [and killed] McGlockton in July 2018 after McGlockton shoved Drejka to the ground following a dispute over a handicap-accessible parking space. Drejka claimed self-defense under Florida's "stand your ground" law[.] The Pinellas County sheriff's decision to not press charges provoked an angry response by the black community in Florida and beyond [and a] month after the shooting, the state attorney's office brought a charge of manslaughter. [T]he confrontation between Drejka and McGlockton was captured on a convenience store surveillance video. In the video, Drejka can be seen arguing with McGlockton's girlfriend, [who was] sitting inside McGlockton's car, which [was] parked in the handicap-accessible space. McGlockton was inside the store at the time with his 5-year-old son. Witnesses say another patron mentioned an argument outside and McGlockton left.

The video shows McGlockton opening the [store] door, spotting Drejka and shoving him to the ground. Drejka immediately pulled out a handgun. A slow-motion version of the video shows McGlockton backing up and starting to turn away. That's when Drejka shot him [and killed him]." *See* Alex Pickett, *Shooter in Florida 'Stand Your Ground' Case Gets 20 Years,* COURTHOUSE NEWS SERVICE, Oct. 10, 2019, https://www.courthousenews.com/shooter-in-florida-stand-your-ground-case-gets-20-years/.

D. Law Enforcement Defense

The law enforcement defense may be invoked by law enforcement officers in a variety of contexts. An officer may invoke the right to use deadly force to make an arrest, although the Supreme Court has held that under the Fourth Amendment, "[w]here the suspect poses no immediate threat to the officer and no threat to others, the harm resulting from failing to apprehend him does not justify the use of deadly force to do so." *Tennessee v. Garner*, 471 U.S. 1 (1985). In *Graham v. Connor*, 490 U.S. 386 (1989), the Court held that the police use of deadly force is not "excessive" when it is "objectively reasonable" under the Fourth Amendment. This standard focuses on the perspective of the "reasonable police officer" on the scene and under the circumstances. The Court observed that although the standard "is not capable of precise definition or mechanical application," its "proper application requires careful attention" to such factors as "the severity of the crime at issue, whether the suspect poses an immediate threat to the safety of the officer or others, and whether he is actively resisting arrest or attempting to evade arrest by flight." In *Scott v. Harris*, 550 U.S. 372 (2007), for example, the Court upheld the reasonableness of the police use of force in the form of a high speed car chase of a suspect that led to a crash in which the suspect suffered injuries that made him a quadriplegic. The Court reasoned that the extremely reckless driving of the suspect created a deadly threat to the public, including police officers and motorists, and so the harm of failing to apprehend him did justify the dangerous pursuit.

On May 25, 2020, Derek Chauvin, a white police officer in Minneapolis, killed George Floyd, a Black man, by kneeling on his neck for more than eight minutes while detaining him. Two other officers had responded to "a report that a possible counterfeit $20 bill had been passed at a grocery store. George Floyd was parked nearby. He was removed from his car at the point of an officer's gun, handcuffed, put face-down on the pavement, and ultimately "pinned down by three different officers" while Chauvin kneeled on Floyd's neck. Floyd died at the scene as a result of "cardiopulmonary arrest complicating law enforcement subdual, restraint, and neck compression." He was heard to say to the officers, "I can't breathe" and "Please" several times. Derek Chauvin was charged with second-degree murder and the other three officers were charged with aiding and abetting murder. *See* Doha Madani, *3 More Minneapolis officers charged in George Floyd's Death, Derek Chauvin Charges Elevated*, NBC News, June 3, 2020, https://www.nbcnews.com/news/us-news/3-more-minneapolis-officers-charged-george-floyd-death-derek-chauvin-n1222796.

The brutality of George Floyd's death at the hands of the police led to world-wide protests led by the Black Lives Matter movement and allies, including protests in over 2,000 cities in all 50 states and 60 countries, beginning on May 26 and continuing into the summer, with an estimated 15 to 26 million people participating as of early July. *See* https://en.wikipedia.org/wiki/List_of_George_Floyd_protests_in_the_United_States. The death of George Floyd brought renewed national attention to the death of Breonna Taylor, who was shot eight times in her Louisville home on March 13, 2020, when police officers executed a no-knock warrant. On June 17, 2020, Rayshard Brooks, a Black man, was shot in the back by Garrett Rolfe, a white police officer, in Atlanta, who was subsequently charged with felony murder. The protests against police violence grew to include these victims as well as others and the calls of protesters for "defunding the police" led to steps being taken in some cities toward that goal. Meanwhile, media reports emphasized the disproportionate killings of Black Americans, who comprise "28% of those killed by police since 2013 despite being only 13% of the population." Mapping Police Violence, https://mappingpoliceviolence.org/.

The protests against police violence have drawn new attention to how rarely criminal prosecutions have been brought against police officers for their use of deadly force to kill on duty. Thus, the right of police officers to invoke the "law enforcement defense" should be understood as operating in the context of these rare prosecutions. According to one report, there were 110 officers "charged with murder or manslaughter in an on-duty shooting" between 2005 and 2020, while roughly 1,000 people were fatally shot by police annually during that period. Of those 110 officers, "42 officers were convicted, 50 were not, and 18 cases are still pending." Amelia Thomson-DeVeaux, Nathaniel Rakich, and Likhitha Butchireddygari, *Why It's So Rare For Police Officers To Face Legal Consequences*, FIVETHIRTYEIGHT, ABC NEWS, June 4, 2020, https://fivethirtyeight.com/features/why-its-still-so-rare-for-police-officers-to-face-legal-consequences-for-misconduct/; see also Osagie K. Obasogie, *The Bad-Apple Myth of Policing*, THE ATLANTIC, Aug. 2, 2019, https://www.theatlantic.com/politics/archive/2019/08/how-courts-judge-police-use-force/594832/.

E. Necessity or Choice of Evils Defense

The necessity defense is presented in Chapter One through the study of the *Dudley & Stephens* case, and although the facts of that case are extraordinary, the difficulty encountered by the defendants in proposing the defense is typical. The *Crawford* case that follows, therefore, represents an atypical example of a defendant who not only persuaded an appellate court that he was entitled to a necessity defense instruction, but also presented facts that should make it possible for a jury to acquit him on the basis of the necessity defense.

State v. Crawford

308 Md. 683, 521 A.2d 1193 (1987).

COLE, JUDGE.

[The defendant Leonard Crawford was charged with assault and with illegal possession of a handgun in violation of a state statute, Art. 27, § 36(b), that established "a blanket rule that prohibits any person from carrying, whether open or concealed, any handgun."]

At the close of the evidence, defense counsel requested that the trial judge instruct the jury as to the availability of the defense of necessity to the charge of unlawful possession of a handgun. The trial judge refused to give the instruction, finding that there was no exception for necessity provided in Art. 27, § 36B(b) [the handgun statute]. The jury found Crawford not guilty of assault, but guilty of unlawful possession of a handgun. The Court of Special Appeals reversed, finding that the trial court erred in not giving a necessity instruction. [We] granted certiorari to consider the important question presented.

We begin our analysis by reviewing the defense of necessity. [Recently we examined this] defense and found that it arises when an individual is faced with a choice of two evils, and one is the commission of an illegal act. [The] justification for the necessity defense is not that a person faced with a choice of two evils lacks the *mens rea* for the crime in question, but that the law promotes the achievement of higher values at the expense of lower ones and that " 'sometimes the greater good for society will be accomplished by violating the literal language of the criminal law.' " W. LAFAVE & A. SCOTT, JR., CRIMINAL LAW § 50 (1972).

With this rationale in mind, we must examine the class of crimes for which the defense of necessity is available. The Court of Special Appeals has previously stated that the defense of necessity is available to all crimes except the killing of an innocent person. While we agree with [the] conclusion that the defense has a broad application, we also recognize that the legislature is empowered to eliminate the necessity defense for any crime. Accordingly, we must determine whether the General Assembly, by enacting § 36B(b), intended to eliminate the defense of necessity to a charge of unlawful possession of a handgun.

A review of § 36B(b)'s history is essential. Prior to the section's enactment, prohibitions on the possession of a handgun were controlled by § 36 [of the 1957 Code]. [Subsection 36(a) of that Code] prohibited any person from carrying a weapon, including a pistol, concealed on his person or openly with the intent to injure. [Subsection 36(b)] created an exception from the prohibition for officers of the government and persons carrying weapons "as a reasonable precaution against apprehended danger."

In 1972, the General Assembly enacted strong handgun control legislation. The impetus for the reform was the legislature's recognition that there had been a dramatic increase in the number of crimes perpetrated with handguns and a concommitant increase in the number of deaths and injuries caused by persons carrying handguns on the streets[.] As part of the more stringent regulation [in § 36B], the legislature [enacted] a blanket rule that prohibits any person from carrying, whether open or concealed, any handgun in § 36B(b). Subsection 36B(c) of [that statute] specifically sets forth the exceptions to subsection § 36B(b). Individuals who may lawfully carry handguns include law enforcement personnel, persons with permits, persons transporting handguns for legitimate purposes, and persons on their own property. Conspicuously absent from subsection § 36B(c) is an exception for carrying a handgun "as a reasonable precaution against apprehended danger." The legislature did not carry over this exception from [the old statute] and instead created § 36E, which requires any person wishing to carry a handgun to apply for a permit from the Superintendent of the Maryland State Police. A permit will be issued when there is a "good and substantial reason," including when it "is necessary as a reasonable precaution against apprehended danger."

FYI

The MPC term for the necessity defense is the choice of evils defense in MPC § 3.02(1), which applies where a person believes conduct is necessary to avoid a harm or evil to self or to another, provided that: (a) the harm or evil is greater than the one sought to be prevented by the law defining the crime; (b) the law does not provide exceptions or defenses dealing with the specific situation; and (c) a legislative purpose to exclude the claimed justification does not otherwise plainly appear.

The MPC § 3.02(2) provides that if recklessness or negligence is sufficient to establish guilt, then the choice of evils defense is unavailable if a person was reckless or negligent in bringing about the situation or in appraising the necessity for the conduct taken to avoid the harm or evil.

It is clear that the 1972 handgun control legislation is designed to discourage and punish the possession of handguns on the streets and public ways. The legislature determined that if a citizen is apprehensive of impending danger, his recourse is not to immediately arm himself, but instead to seek help from the State—by applying for a permit to carry a gun or, of course, by contacting the police for protection. Thus, by controlling the number of handguns in the public, and not permitting citizens to carry guns when there is time for alternative, safe action, the legislature sought to "preserve the peace and tranquility of the State and to protect the rights and liberties of its citizens." *Id.*

As we see it, the 1972 handgun control legislation does not address the unexpected and sudden circumstance when an individual is threatened with present, impending danger to his life or limb and as a consequence has no time to seek other protection. Furthermore, we cannot accept the contention that, in such circumstances, the General Assembly intended that the individual should succumb to his attacker and possibly forfeit his life rather than take possession of a handgun and act in self-defense. We find it entirely reasonable and consistent with § 36B's legislative purpose to conclude that when an individual finds himself in sudden, imminent danger of loss of life or serious bodily harm, or reasonably believes himself or others to be in such danger, and without preconceived design on his part a handgun comes into his possession, he may temporarily possess the weapon for a period no longer than the necessity or apparent necessity requires him to use it in self-defense. We therefore hold that necessity may be a defense to the charge of unlawful possession of a handgun.

A number of jurisdictions support our point of view. [In] *United States v. Gant*, 691 F.2d 1159 (5th Cir. 1982), two undercover police officers entered the front room of a store owned by the defendant, a convicted felon. The police officers offered to sell Gant a .45 caliber machine gun. After Gant refused the offer, he went into the storage room to confer with one of his employees. Gant had been robbed a few weeks earlier and suspected that another robbery was in the making. He and his employee decided to evict the two men, and his employee suggested that Gant take the gun kept in the desk. Gant took the suggestion, and when he returned to the front room, with the butt of the gun sticking out of his pants pocket, he was arrested for unlawful possession of a firearm. The trial court found that Gant had not acted under necessity and was thus guilty.

On appeal, the Fifth Circuit affirmed the lower court's decision and applied a four-part test to determine the validity of a necessity defense to the charge of unlawful possession of a handgun:

> [D]efendant must show (1) that defendant was under an unlawful and "present, imminent, and impending [threat] of such a nature as to induce a well-grounded apprehension of death or serious bodily injury," (2) that defendant had not "recklessly or negligently placed himself in a situation in which it was probable that he would be [forced to choose the criminal conduct]," (3) that defendant had no "reasonable, legal alternative to violating the law, 'a choice both to refuse to do the criminal act and also avoid the threatened harm,' " and (4) "that a direct causal relationship may be reasonably anticipated between the [criminal] action and the avoidance of the [threatened] harm." (brackets in original).

The *Gant* court found that the defendant did not satisfy the third and fourth elements. The court noted that Gant had a legal alternative to taking possession of the gun—he could have called the police. Moreover, although Gant's possession of the gun made a robbery attempt less attractive, the court found that it did not eliminate the danger. [*Id.* at] 1164–65.

The California Supreme Court has also devised a four-part test for the defense of necessity to illegal possession of a handgun. In *People v. King*, 22 Cal. 3d 12, 148 Cal. Rptr. 409, 582 P.2d 1000 (1978), the defendant, a convicted felon, was a guest at a party when a violent altercation broke out between the guests and a group of party crashers who had attempted to break down the front door. King was handed a gun by someone in the apartment, and he used it to defend himself and the others in the apartment. King was later charged with unlawful possession of a handgun. The trial court refused to give a self-defense instruction to the jury and King was convicted.

The California Supreme Court reversed the trial court and held that a citizen may legally possess a firearm for self-defense when: (1) the defendant "is in imminent peril of great bodily harm or reasonably believes himself or others to be in such danger," (2) "without preconceived design on his part a firearm is made available to him," (3) his temporary possession only persists until the necessity or apparent necessity dissipates, and (4) "no other alternative means of avoiding the danger are available." *Id.* at 24. The court found that the defendant had a reasonable fear of imminent bodily harm and only used the gun, which he received without preconceived design, for a short period of time. The court therefore reversed the trial court on its refusal to give the defendant's requested instruction.

We find these cases instructive and hold that necessity is a valid defense to the crime of unlawful possession of a handgun when five elements are present: (1) the defendant must be in present, imminent, and impending peril of death or serious bodily injury, or reasonably believe himself or others to be in such danger; (2) the defendant must not have intentionally or recklessly placed himself in a situation in which it was probable that he would be forced to choose the criminal conduct; (3) the defendant must not have any reasonable, legal alternative to possessing the handgun; (4) the handgun must be made available to the defendant without preconceived design, and (5) the defendant must give up possession of the handgun as soon as the necessity or apparent necessity ends. We emphasize that if the threatened harm is property damage or future personal injury, the defense of necessity will not be viable; nor can the defense be asserted if the compulsion to possess the handgun arose directly from the defendant's own misconduct.

Based on Crawford's testimony, he satisfies each element of the test. First, after being attacked and shot, Crawford wrestled the gun away from one of his assailants, and in so doing fell out of his second story apartment window. Crawford landed next to the gun. He heard footsteps coming from around the corner and picked up the gun to defend himself if the person or persons who had assaulted him in his apartment were pursuing him. Thus, Crawford had a reasonable belief that imminent peril was at hand. Second, Crawford did not intentionally or recklessly place himself in the predicament; he was attacked in his own apartment. Third, Crawford was wounded and dazed. Crawford had no opportunity to contact the police to seek protection, and neither retreating nor trying to talk to his assailants was a reasonable, legal alternative. Fourth, Crawford's possession of the handgun was merely fortuitous. The handgun was originally possessed by Crawford's assailant and only became available to him after he disarmed the assailant. Thus, Crawford had no preconceived design to gain possession of the handgun before being attacked. Fifth, after grabbing the handgun, Crawford crawled and staggered away from his apartment in an effort to reach safety, but his assailants continued to follow and shoot him. He surrendered the handgun when a police officer stood beside him so that he could see the officer's pants leg and thus be sure he was out of danger. Thus, if the jury believed Crawford's testimony on each of these points, a defense of necessity would have barred conviction. . . .

Lastly, we believe that common sense supports our decision[.] . . . [We] think it is common sense that the legislature could not have intended that a man, who has been attacked and shot and lies injured after falling from a window, cannot pick up a handgun that, as luck would have it, falls next to him when he hears what he believes are his aggressors in hot pursuit. It is utter folly to talk of requiring a man to get a permit to carry a handgun when threatened with death or serious bodily harm under such circumstances. Thus, we find that the trial court erred in failing to instruct the jury on the availability of the necessity defense, because if Crawford's version of the story is believed, his possession of the handgun was not unlawful.

Judgment of the Court of Special Appeals affirmed.

Points for Discussion

a. Factor Tests for Necessity

By contrast with the MPC's all-purpose definition of necessity, the *Crawford* opinion illustrates the appeal of "factor tests" that may be created by courts to define specialized parameters for necessity defense claims that fall into particular categories. For example, one such category is that of prisoner escape cases, and courts continue to debate whether one of the required factors for such cases should be an attempt to surrender to the authorities after the escape from dangerous prison conditions has been accomplished. *See, e.g., People v. Lovercamp*, 43 Cal. App. 3d 823, 118 Cal. Rptr. 110 (1975) (requiring this factor); *Spakes v. State*, 913 S.W.2d 597 (Tex. Crim. App. 1996) (en banc) (not requiring this factor). The popularity of "factor tests" suggests that courts may be willing to treat the necessity defense as an opportunity to construct policy-based criteria for the enforcement of particular laws.

How does the *Crawford* Court's factor test compare to those designed by the Fifth Circuit and the California Supreme Court for necessity defense claims by defendants charged with illegal gun possession? What policy reasons may explain the court's reliance on each factor in the test endorsed in *Crawford*?

b. Rarely Successful Defense

Although it is the rare defendant who succeeds in obtaining a necessity instruction, there are a wide variety of circumstances in which defendants seek to raise the necessity defense. Courts traditionally reject requested instructions on necessity when sought by defendants who commit acts of civil disobedience that violate trespass laws during political protests, who violate drunk driving laws in order to achieve particular purposes, and who violate "contraband" laws concerning the regulation of drugs and weapons.

Even when defendants do not obtain jury instructions, however, a necessity defense may have an impact on the outcome of a case. For example, three defendants were charged with trespassing for "locking themselves inside a natural gas pipeline" for 16 hours to protest "the federal government's decision to allow the pipeline [to] be installed near Indian Point nuclear power plant." Their defense counsel argued that they "were trying to prevent a greater harm" from the pipeline, and therefore, their actions were analogous to those of people "who burn down property to prevent a forest fire from spreading," or "those who break into an occupied building to place a call that saves someone's life." The trial judge rejected the necessity defense, finding that the defendants "had failed to exhaust every avenue of protest available," such as writing letters of protest or attempting to "intervene in the regulatory protest." However, the judge imposed no punishment on the defendants, even though the prosecutor requested that they should be sentenced to "300 hours of community service." *See* Thomas C. Zambito, *Algonquin pipeline protesters guilty of trespassing, but judge spares them punishment*, Rockland/Westchester Journal News, Jan. 8, 2019, https://sape2016.org/2019/02/24/algonquin-pipeline-protesters-guilty-of-trespassing-but-judge-spares-them-punishment-january-2019/.

Similarly, when 13 "climate activists" were arrested for trespassing and disturbing the peace when protesting the West Roxbury pipeline, the prosecutor reduced the charges to "civil infractions." Although the protesters reportedly were disappointed at the loss of the opportunity to present their necessity defense to a jury, they celebrated the fact that the trial judge acquitted them of the "civil infractions" after hearing each protester testify about why "the threat of climate change necessitated their civil disobedience." See Lorraine Chow, *Boston Judge Acquits 13 Pipeline Protesters in Groundbreaking Decision*, ECOWATCH, March 28, 2018, https://www.ecowatch.com/pipeline-protestors-acquitted-boston-2554052139.html.

The *Crawford* case illustrates how the door of the necessity defense remains open for some defendants, even if the opening is necessarily narrow because of judicial recognition of the need to enforce the legislature's definitions of the criminal law.

The following hypotheticals provide an opportunity to examine the application of the MPC requirements for the choice of evils defense.

Hypo: *MPC Elements*

Each of these defendants seeks an instruction on the choice of evils defense. You are the law clerk to a trial judge who asks for your advice as to whether the instruction should be granted. Examine the elements of the MPC requirements in § 3.02(1) and (2), and identify any weaknesses that you see in each defendant's claim to invoke the choice of evils defense.

a. *Killing Pedestrian.* Dan is driving at 70 mph in a 35 mph zone in a residential area. Unexpectedly, a group of children walk across the sidewalk in front of Dan's car. Making a quick calculation of "evils," Dan swerves on to the sidewalk, figuring that it is better to damage property or to injure a single pedestrian than to run down a group of children. Unfortunately, Dan does kill a pedestrian who happens to be walking on the sidewalk in Dan's path. Dan is charged with involuntary manslaughter and seeks a choice of evils instruction.

b. *Cabin in Woods.* Sarah has been hiking alone in the back woods of Wyoming for several weeks in December. The weather is 20 degrees below zero and Sarah has been lost for several days. She is starving because she didn't bring enough food, and the snow is deep in the woods. Sarah is extremely debilitated physically, and has almost given up hope of survival. Suddenly, she comes upon a cabin in the woods, which is off the beaten path. She breaks into the cabin, starts a fire in the fireplace, and eats the food that she finds in the pantry. Sara is charged with trespass, burglary, and theft of the food and the wood for the fire. She seeks a choice of evils instruction.

c. *Medicinal Marijuana.* Jane has suffered from muscular dystrophy for five years. The doctors have given her a diagnosis of less than six months to live. She suffers from excruciating pain and her prescribed medications do very little to relieve this pain.

Jane learns from internet sources that smoking marijuana may relieve her pain. When she tries smoking it, she discovers that her pain is greatly reduced. Jane asks her doctors to prescribe marijuana for her as a medical treatment, and they tell her that they cannot do this because it would be illegal under state law. Jane continues to buy marijuana from illegal sources and she keeps smoking it to relieve her pain. She is caught and charged with possession of marijuana. She seeks a choice of evils instruction.

Executive Summary

Self-Defense. This defense requires a person to have a reasonable belief that the use of deadly force is necessary in order to avoid the imminent threat of deadly force from another person. An aggressor who is the first to use deadly force against another person will lose the right of self-defense unless the aggressor withdraws from the conflict. Most states require the duty to retreat in public spaces, and the castle doctrine protects a person from the need to retreat in his or her dwelling from an intruder—and sometimes from a cohabitant.

Major Themes

a. Influence of the MPC—The MPC made a significant contribution in clarifying the elements of the justification defenses and in influencing the codification of those elements. The MPC endorsed some rules that continue to attract support from a majority of states, such as the duty to retreat.

b. Modern Expansion of Defenses—There has been notable legislative expansion of the right to use deadly force in situations where self-defense would not be justified, specifically concerning the right to use such force against intruders into a dwelling or a vehicle. The use of expert testimony concerning the effects of battering has become a widespread norm for trials of battered criminal defendants, and self-defense claims by such defendants continues to test the limitations imposed by the traditional requirements of self-defense.

Imperfect Self-Defense. Some courts define this defense as being applicable to a case where a defendant is unreasonable in his or her perception of imminent danger, or in his or her belief that deadly force is necessary to respond to the danger, or both.

Defense of Dwelling. This defense traditionally required a reasonable belief that an intruder threatened harm to the occupants of a dwelling, but new statutory rights to use deadly force have modified or eliminated this requirement.

Necessity or Choice of Evils. The all-purpose MPC definition of this defense requires that a person must believe that the violation of a law is required in order to avoid a greater evil, assuming that the evil avoided is greater than the one sought to be prevented by the enforcement of the law. Courts sometimes rely on "factor tests" to delineate the scope of a necessity defense for a particular category of recurring claims.

For More Information

- AMERICAN LAW INSTITUTE, MODEL PENAL CODE AND COMMENTARIES, Part II, §§ 221.0–221.1, 222.1, 223.0–223.7, Comments at 60–84, 96–121, 122–255 (1980).
- JOHN M. BURKOFF & RUSSELL L. WEAVER, INSIDE CRIMINAL LAW: WHAT MATTERS AND WHY 205–224 (2d ed. 2011).
- WAYNE R. LAFAVE, CRIMINAL LAW § 17.1–17.5 (5th ed. 2010).

Test Your Knowledge

To assess your understanding of the material in this chapter, click here to take a quiz.

CHAPTER 13

Excuses

Like justification defenses, excuses are general defenses applicable to all offenses and available even though the person satisfies the offense's elements. However, excuse defenses concentrate on the person's lack of subjective blameworthiness, while justification defenses focus on the person's conduct. Excuses admit that the act may cause or threaten a harm the criminal law normally disallows, but excuse the person because his characteristics or situation suggest that he does not merit criminal liability.

A. Duress

The defense of duress arises when an individual is faced with a threat of death or serious bodily injury, and chooses to commit a crime rather than suffer the threatened consequences. *See United States v. Contento-Pachon*, 723 F.2d 691 (9th Cir. 1984). In general, the individual must have a reasonable belief that the threat is serious, and there must be no reasonable means of escape.

Make the Connection

Criminal liability arises in part from the choice a person makes to engage in conduct that constitutes a criminal harm. Without sufficient capacity to choose, blame is improper. An excuse defense represents a legal conclusion that even though a person's conduct is wrong, liability is inappropriate because some characteristic of the person or his situation vitiates the person's blameworthiness.

Although it may be theoretically possible for a defendant to assert that he is innocent of the underlying offense, and that he committed it because of duress, there is a logical inconsistency between the two positions. The defense of duress assumes that defendant committed the crime, and that the ordinary requirements for conviction are present, but allows defendant to argue that the commission should be excused because of the duress. *See Dixon v. United States*, 548 U.S. 1 (2006); *United States v. Bailey*, 444 U.S. 394 (1980).

United States v. Contento-Pachon

723 F.2d 691 (9th Cir. 1984).

BOOCHEVER, CIRCUIT JUDGE.

This case presents an appeal from a conviction for unlawful possession with intent to distribute a narcotic controlled substance in violation of 21 U.S.C. § 841(a)(1) (1976). At trial, defendant attempted to offer evidence of duress and necessity defenses. The district court excluded this evidence on the ground that it was insufficient to support the defenses. We reverse because there was sufficient evidence of duress to present a triable issue of fact.

Take Note

There is significant overlap between the defense of duress and the defense of necessity in the sense that the individual may sometimes be choosing to commit a crime involving a lesser evil in order to avoid a greater evil. However, the defense of duress is premised on the idea that criminal actions are excusable for defendants who are threatened with force (death or serious bodily injury) that a reasonable person would not have been able to resist (and, of course, the other requirements for the defense must be satisfied as well).

Defendant-appellant, Juan Manuel Contento-Pachon, is a native of Bogota, Colombia and was employed there as a taxicab driver. He asserts that one of his passengers, Jorge, offered him a job as the driver of a privately-owned car. Contento-Pachon expressed an interest in the job and agreed to meet Jorge and the owner of the car the next day. Instead of a driving job, Jorge proposed that Contento-Pachon swallow cocaine-filled balloons and transport them to the United States. Contento-Pachon agreed to consider the proposition. He was told not to mention the proposition to anyone, otherwise he would "get into serious trouble." Contento-Pachon testified that he did not contact the police because he believes that the Bogota police are corrupt and that they are paid off by drug traffickers.

Approximately one week later, Contento-Pachon told Jorge that he would not carry the cocaine. In response, Jorge mentioned facts about Contento-Pachon's personal life, including private details which Contento-Pachon had never mentioned to Jorge. Jorge told Contento-Pachon that his failure to cooperate would result in the death of his wife and three year-old child. The following day the pair met again. Contento-Pachon's life and the lives of his family were again threatened. At this point, Contento-Pachon agreed to take the cocaine into the United States. The pair met two more times. At the last meeting, Contento-Pachon swallowed 129 balloons of cocaine. He was informed that he would be watched at all times during the trip, and that if he failed to follow Jorge's instruction he and his family would be killed.

After leaving Bogota, Contento-Pachon's plane landed in Panama. Contento-Pachon asserts that he did not notify the authorities there because he felt that the Panamanian police were as corrupt as those in Bogota. Also, he felt that any such action on his part would place his family in jeopardy. When he arrived at the customs inspection point in Los Angeles, Contento-Pachon consented to have his stomach x-rayed. The x-rays revealed a foreign substance which was later determined to be cocaine. At Contento-Pachon's trial, the government moved to exclude the defenses of duress and necessity. The motion was granted. We reverse.

There are three elements of the duress defense: (1) an immediate threat of death or serious bodily injury, (2) a well-grounded fear that the threat will be carried out, and (3) no reasonable opportunity to escape the threatened harm. *United States v. Shapiro,* 669 F.2d 593 (9th Cir. 1982). Sometimes a fourth element is required: the defendant must submit to proper authorities after attaining a position of safety. *United States v. Peltier,* 693 F.2d 96 (9th Cir. 1982) (per curiam). If the evidence is insufficient as a matter of law to support a duress defense, the trial court should exclude that evidence.

The trial court found Contento-Pachon's offer of proof insufficient to support a duress defense because he failed to offer proof of two elements: immediacy and inescapability. We examine the elements of duress.

Immediacy: The element of immediacy requires that there be some evidence that the threat of injury was present, immediate, or impending. "A veiled threat of future unspecified harm" will not satisfy this requirement. *Rhode Island Recreation Center v. Aetna Casualty and Surety Co.,* 177 F.2d 603 (1st Cir. 1949). The district court found that the initial threats were not immediate because "they were conditioned on defendant's failure to cooperate in the future and did not place defendant and his family in immediate danger." Evidence indicated that the defendant was dealing with a man who was deeply involved in the exportation of illegal substances. Large sums of money were at stake and, consequently, Contento-Pachon had reason to believe that Jorge would carry out his threats. Jorge had gone to the trouble to discover that Contento-Pachon was married, that he had a child, the names of his wife and child, and the location of his residence. These were not vague threats of possible future harm. According to defendant, if he had refused to cooperate, the consequences would have been immediate and harsh. Contento-Pachon contends that he was being watched by one of Jorge's accomplices at all times during the airplane trip. As a consequence, the force of the threats continued to restrain him. Contento-Pachon's contention that he was operating under the threat of immediate harm was supported by sufficient evidence to present a triable issue of fact.

Escapability: Defendant must show that he had no reasonable opportunity to escape. *See United States v. Gordon,* 526 F.2d 406 (9th Cir. 1975). The district court found that because Contento-Pachon was not physically restrained prior to the time he swallowed the balloons, he could have sought help from the police or fled. Contento-Pachon explained that he did not report the threats because he feared that the police were corrupt. The trier of fact should decide whether one in Contento-Pachon's position might believe that some of the Bogota police were paid informants for drug traffickers and that reporting the matter to the police did not represent a reasonable opportunity of escape. If he chose not to go to the police, Contento-Pachon's alternative was to flee. The opportunity to escape must be reasonable. To flee, Contento-Pachon, along with his wife and three year-old child, would have been forced to pack his possessions, leave his job, and travel to a place beyond the reaches of the drug traffickers. A juror might find that this was not a reasonable avenue of escape. Thus, Contento-Pachon presented a triable issue on the element of escapability.

Surrender to Authorities: The government argues that the defense also requires that a defendant offer evidence that he intended to turn himself in to the authorities upon reaching a position of safety. Although it has not been expressly limited, this fourth element seems to be required only in prison escape cases. *United States v. Peltier,* 693 F.2d 96 (9th Cir. 1982) (per curiam); *United States v. Michelson,* 559 F.2d 567 (9th Cir. 1977). Under other circumstances, the defense has been defined to include only three elements. *United States v. Shapiro,* 669 F.2d 593 (9th Cir. 1982) (sale of drugs); *United States v. Atencio,* 586 F.2d 744 (9th Cir. 1978) (per curiam) (failure to appear for trial); and *United States v. Wood,* 566 F.2d 1108 (9th Cir. 1977) (per curiam) (carrying a knife in a federal prison). The Supreme Court in *United States v. Bailey,* 444 U.S. 394, 413 (1980), noted that "escape from federal custody is a continuing offense and an escapee can be held liable for failure to return to custody as well as for his initial departure." This factor would not be present in most crimes other than escape.

In cases not involving escape from prison there seems little difference between the third basic requirement that there be no reasonable opportunity to escape the threatened harm and the obligation to turn oneself in to authorities on reaching a point of safety. Once a defendant has reached a position where he can safely turn himself in to the authorities he will likewise have a reasonable opportunity to escape the threatened harm. That is true in this case. Contento-Pachon claims that he was being watched at all times. According to him, at the first opportunity to cooperate with authorities without alerting the observer, he consented to the x-ray. We hold that a defendant who has acted under a well-grounded fear of immediate harm with no opportunity to escape may assert the duress defense, if there is a triable issue of fact whether he took the opportunity to escape the threatened harm by submitting to authorities at the first reasonable opportunity.

The defense of necessity is available when a person is faced with a choice of two evils and must then decide whether to commit a crime or an alternative act that constitutes a greater evil. *United States v. Richardson,* 588 F.2d 1235 (9th Cir. 1978), *cert. denied,* 441 U.S. 931 (1979). Contento-Pachon has attempted to justify his violation of 21 U.S.C. § 841(a)(1) by showing that the alternative, the death of his family, was a greater evil. Traditionally, in order for the necessity defense to apply, the coercion must have had its source in the physical forces of nature. The duress defense was applicable when the defendant's acts were coerced by a human force. W. LaFave & A. Scott, Handbook on Criminal Law § 50 at 383 (1972). This distinction served to separate the two similar defenses. But modern courts have tended to blur the distinction between duress and necessity.

It has been suggested that, "the major difference between duress and necessity is that the former negates the existence of the requisite *mens rea* for the crime in question, whereas under the latter theory there is no *actus reus.*" *United States v. Micklus,* 581 F.2d 612, 615 (7th Cir. 1978). The theory of necessity is that the defendant's free will was properly exercised to achieve the greater good and not that his free will was overcome by an outside force as with duress.

The defense of necessity is usually invoked when the defendant acted in the interest of the general welfare. For example, defendants have asserted the defense as a justification for (1) bringing laetrile into the United States for the treatment of cancer patients, *Richardson,* 588

F.2d at 1239; (2) unlawfully entering a naval base to protest the Trident missile system, *United States v. May*, 622 F.2d 1000 (9th Cir.), *cert. denied*, 449 U.S. 984 (1980); (3) burning Selective Service System records to protest United States military action, *United States v. Simpson*, 460 F.2d 515 (9th Cir. 1972). Contento-Pachon's acts were allegedly coerced by human, not physical forces. In addition, he did not act to promote the general welfare. Therefore, the necessity defense was not available to him. Contento-Pachon mischaracterized evidence of duress as evidence of necessity. The district court correctly disallowed his use of the necessity defense.

Contento-Pachon presented credible evidence that he acted under an immediate and well-grounded threat of serious bodily injury, with no opportunity to escape. Because the trier of fact should have been allowed to consider the credibility of the proffered evidence, we reverse. The district court correctly excluded Contento-Pachon's necessity defense.

REVERSED and REMANDED.

COYLE, DISTRICT JUDGE (dissenting in part and concurring in part):

The trial court found that defendant's offer of proof was insufficient to support a defense of duress. The government argues that this holding should be affirmed and I agree. In granting the government's motion *in limine* excluding the defense of duress, the trial court specifically found Contento-Pachon had failed to present sufficient evidence to establish the necessary elements of immediacy and inescapability. The district court concluded that defendant "could have sought help from the police or fled. No such efforts were attempted by defendant." Courts have indicated that the element of immediacy is of crucial importance. *See, e.g., United States v. Atencio*, 586 F.2d 744 (9th Cir. 1978); *United States v. Patrick*, 542 F.2d 381 (7th Cir. 1976). The trial court found that the threats made against the defendant and his family lacked the requisite element of immediacy. Defendant was outside the presence of the drug dealers on numerous occasions for varying lengths of time. There is no evidence that his family was ever directly threatened or even had knowledge of the threats allegedly directed against the defendant. Moreover, the trial court found that defendant and his family enjoyed an adequate and reasonable opportunity to avoid or escape the threats of the drug dealers in the weeks before his flight. Defendant and his family were not physically restrained or prevented from seeking help. They could have sought assistance from the authorities or have fled. Duress is permitted as a defense only when a criminal act was committed because there was no other opportunity to avoid the threatened danger. *United States v. Hernandez*, 608 F.2d 741 (9th Cir. 1979).

Take Note

At common law, defendant bore the burden of proof when the defense of duress was raised. *See Patterson v. New York*, 432 U.S. 197 (1977). In *Dixon v. United States*, 548 U.S. 1 (2006), the Court held that a state could continue to allocate the burden of proof to the defendant, and require proof by a preponderance of the evidence.

Point for Discussion

Model Penal Code

Consider the MPC's approach to the defense of duress:

§ 2.09. Duress.

(1) It is an affirmative defense that the actor engaged in the conduct charged to constitute an offense because he was coerced to do so by the use of, or a threat to use, unlawful force against his person or the person of another, which a person of reasonable firmness in his situation would have been unable to resist.

(2) The defense provided by this Section is unavailable if the actor recklessly placed himself in a situation in which it was probable that he would be subjected to duress. The defense is also unavailable if he was negligent in placing himself in such a situation, whenever negligence suffices to establish culpability for the offense charged.

(3) It is not a defense that a woman acted on the command of her husband, unless she acted under such coercion as would establish a defense under this Section. [The presumption that a woman, acting in the presence of her husband, is coerced is abolished.

(4) When the conduct of the actor would otherwise be justifiable under Section 3.02, choice of evils, this Section does not preclude such defense.

> **FYI**
>
> Since the defense of duress applies only to threats of death or serious bodily injury, it is not available to a defendant who is threatened with nothing more than damage to his reputation.

Hypo 1: *The Bank Robbery*

Defendant Anguish, who was charged with robbery, admitted that he committed the crime, but claimed that he acted under duress. The evidence showed that Anguish stole a van from a child care center, drove to a bank where he threatened to blow up the bank unless they gave him money, and escaped with $15,000. Anguish learned that a Federal Bureau of Investigation agent was having an extra-marital affair, and that the FBI agent and his lover had conspired to kill the lover's husband. After defendant confronted the FBI agent with his knowledge, his house was burglarized and he began receiving threatening telephone calls. He reported these incidents to the police and the FBI, but neither took any action. Subsequently, but prior to the robbery, two men accosted him, put a gun to his head, and told him to rob a bank. The men told him that if he did not, he and his family would be harmed. The men showed defendant a copy of a picture of his wife and daughter. In order to facilitate the robbery, defendant decided to steal the van. Was the threat sufficiently imminent? Was defendant required to go to the police rather than comply with the threat? Can the defense also be used to excuse the theft of the van? *See Anguish v. State*, 991 S.W.2d 883 (Tex. App. 1999).

Food for Thought

Does the MPC require that the threat be imminent or immediate? How would the prior Hypo be resolved under the MPC?

Hypo 2: *Duress and the Timid Individual*

Suppose that defendant is a particularly timid individual, and his timidity makes him unusually susceptible to coercion. Defendant is charged with committing a robbery, but claims that he acted under duress. Defendant's offer of proof included a letter from a psychologist, who declared defendant was "submissive, and readily influenced by a forceful or coercive significant other." At trial, defendant testified that his co-conspirator (Reniff) had stated that he would shoot defendant if he did not carry out the robbery. It is not clear whether the threat was believable. However, defendant claims that he should be allowed to assert the defense because of his nature. Should a timid individual be able to claim the defense of duress when an ordinary person would not be able to do so? How would the MPC provision answer this question? *See State v. VanNatta*, 149 Or. App. 587, 945 P.2d 1062 (1997).

Hypo 3: *Duress and the Crime of Murder*

Jonathan, with a cocked gun pointed at his head, is ordered by his arch-enemy to kill another person "or die." The other person is lying helpless on the floor, and Jonathan takes a knife (given to him by the threatener) and slits the victim's throat. Should the defense of duress apply to an intentional murder? Can the law hope to deter Jonathan from committing a murder under such circumstances? *See United States v. LaFleur*, 971 F.2d 200 (9th Cir. 1992). Since the threatener provided Jonathan with a knife, did he have a sufficient and adequate means of escape so that the defense should not apply? How would this problem be resolved under the MPC?

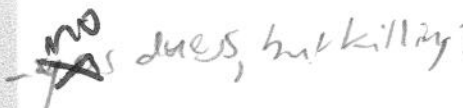

Food for Thought

Delbert is forced to participate in a bank robbery (by wearing a mask and acting like he is holding a gun) by a man who threatens to shoot him if he does not. During the robbery, the threatener shoots and kills a bank guard. At his trial, Delbert offer proof of duress, but the state objects that the defense cannot be invoked as a defense to murder. Should felony murder be handled differently (in terms of whether the defense applies) than an intentional murder? *See State v. Hunter*, 241 Kan. 629, 740 P.2d 559 (1987).

Hypo 4: *Duress and the Battered Woman*

Michelle Marenghi was charged with illegally distributing cocaine, but claims that she acted under duress. She offers proof showing that she was physically, mentally, and emotionally abused by her boyfriend, Freddie "Pit Bull" Long, who was arrested with Marenghi, and with whom it is alleged that she conspired to possess and sell crack cocaine. Defendant's proof would show that battered women develop certain "survival skills," such as "hyper alertness" to their abuser, at the expense of "escape skills." As a result, when the abuser orders the battered woman to commit a crime, the woman will do it even if not explicitly threatened with death or serious bodily injury. Should Marenghi be allowed to introduce her evidence regarding battered woman's syndrome? Under the MPC, might a battered woman be allowed to avail herself of the defense? *See United States v. Marenghi*, 893 F. Supp. 85 (D.Me. 1995); *United States v. Willis*, 38 F.3d 170 (5th Cir. 1994).

Food for Thought

Rios, who said offensive things in a bar, was chased to his car by an angry mob. Rios managed to get into the car and lock the doors, but some members of the mob began beating on his car. In fear for his life, Rios starts the car and begins inching forward. When the police arrive, they realize that Rios is legally drunk and charge him with driving under the influence. Can Rios assert the defense of duress to the offense of driving under the influence? *See State v. Rios*, 127 N.M. 334, 980 P.2d 1068 (Ct. App. 1999).

Hypo 5: *The Reckless Defendant*

Is the defense of duress available to a defendant who has acted recklessly? Defendant voluntarily joined a criminal organization that sold illegal drugs, and stupidly borrowed money from the organization. When he was unable to repay the money, members of the organization "roughed" defendant up and demanded that he transport drugs on their behalf "or else." On one of his runs, defendant is apprehended and charged with illegal possession of drugs. Defendant asserts that he agreed to transport the drugs only under threat of death or serious bodily injury. Can defendant avail himself of the defense? What result under the MPC? *See Williams v. State*, 101 Md. App. 408, 646 A.2d 1101 (1994).

B. Insanity

There is little justification for punishing those who commit crimes while insane. As the Second Circuit stated in *United States v. Freeman*, 357 F.2d 606, 615 (2d Cir. 1966):

> Those who are substantially unable to restrain their conduct are, by definition, undeterrable and their "punishment" is no example for others. Indeed, those who are unaware of or do not appreciate the nature and quality of their actions can hardly be expected rationally to weigh the consequences of their conduct. Finally, what segment of society can feel its desire for retribution satisfied when it wreaks vengeance upon the incompetent? Although an understandable emotion, a need for retribution can never be permitted in a civilized society to degenerate into a sadistic form of revenge.

1. *M'Naghten* & Irresistible Impulse Tests

Although there is general agreement that the insane should not be held criminally responsible for their conduct, few agree about how to define insanity. For many years, U.S. courts applied the insanity test articulated by the House of Lords in the nineteenth century in *M'Naghten's Case*.

M'Naghten's Case

10 Cl. & F. 200, 8 Eng. Rep. 718 (House of Lords 1843).

LORD CHIEF JUSTICE TINDAL:

[Daniel M'Naghten shot at Sir Robert Peel's carriage intending to kill Peel. M'Naghten actually shot Edward Drummond, Peel's private secretary, who was the only person inside the carriage. At his trial, M'Naghten claimed that he killed Drummond under the influence of insane delusions, and the jury found him not guilty by reason of insanity. Because the verdict was unpopular, the House of Lords debated the decision and appended conclusions to the case report.]

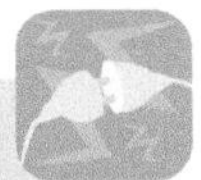

Make the Connection

Note how the court refers to the justifications for punishment that you studied in Chapter 1, and suggests that there may be little justification for punishing someone who commits a criminal act while insane.

The first question proposed by your Lordships is this: "What is the law respecting alleged crimes committed by persons afflicted with insane delusion in respect of one or more particular subjects or personas, for instance, where at the time of commission of the alleged crime the accused knew he was acting contrary to law, but did the act complained of with a view, under the influence of insane delusion, of redressing or revenging some supposed grievance or injury, or of producing some supposed public benefit?"

In answer to which question, assuming that your Lordships' inquiries are confined to those persons who labour under such partial delusions only, and are not in other respects insane, we are of opinion that, notwithstanding the party accused did the act complained of with a view, under the influence of redressing or revenging some supposed grievance or injury, or of producing some public benefit, he is nevertheless punishable according to the nature of the crime committed, if he knew at the time of committing such crime that he was acting contrary to law; by which expression we understand your Lordships to mean the law of the land.

Your Lordships are pleased to inquire of us, secondly, "What are the proper questions to be submitted to the jury, where a person alleged to be afflicted with insane delusion respecting one or more subjects or persons, is charged with the commission of a crime (murder, for example), and insanity is set up as a defence?" And, thirdly, "In what terms ought the question to be left to the jury as to the prisoner's state of mind at the time when the act was committed?" As these two questions appear to be more conveniently answered together, we have to submit our opinion to be, that the jurors ought to be told in all cases that every man is to be presumed to be sane, and to possess a sufficient degree of reason to be responsible for his crimes, until the contrary be proved to their satisfaction; and that to establish a defence on the ground of insanity, it must be clearly proved that, at the time of the committing of the act, the party accused was labouring under such a defect of reason, from disease of the mind, as not to know the nature and quality of the act he was doing; or, if he did know it, that he did not know he was doing what was wrong. The mode of putting the latter part of the question to the jury on these occasions has generally been, whether the accused at the time of doing the act knew the difference between right and wrong. If the accused was conscious that the act was one which he ought not to do, and if that act was at the same time contrary to the law of the land, he is punishable; and the usual course therefore has been to leave the question to the jury, whether the accused had a sufficient degree of reason to know that he was doing an act that was wrong.

The fourth question which your Lordships have proposed to us is this:—"If a person under an insane delusion as to existing facts, commits an offence in consequence thereof, is he thereby excused? To which question the answer must of course depend on the nature of the delusion: but, making the same assumption, namely, that he labours under such partial delusion only, and is not in other respects insane, he must be considered in the same situation as to responsibility as if the facts with respect to which the delusion exists were real. For example, if under the influence of his delusion, he supposes another man to be in the act of attempting to take his life, and he kills that man, as he supposes, in self-defense, he would be exempt from punishment. If his delusion was that the deceased has inflicted a serious injury to his character and fortune, and he killed him in revenge for such supposed injury, he would be liable to punishment.

The question lastly proposed by your Lordships is—"Can a medical man conversant with the disease of insanity, who never saw the prisoner previously to the trial, but who was present during the whole trial and the examination of all the witnesses, be asked his opinion as to the state of the prisoner's mind at the time of the commission of the alleged crime, or his opinion whether the prisoner was conscious at the time of doing the act that he was acting contrary to law, or whether he was labouring under any and what delusion at the time? In answer thereto, we state to your Lordships, that we think the medical man, under the circumstances supposed, cannot in strictness be asked his opinion in the terms above stated, because each of those questions involves the determination of the truth of the facts deposed to, which it is for the jury to decide, and the questions are not mere questions upon a matter of science, in which case such evidence is admissible. But where the facts are admitted or not disputed, and the question becomes substantially one of science only, it may be convenient to allow the question to be put in that general form, though the same cannot be insisted on as a matter of right.

Points for Discussion

a. *M'Naghten* & Insane Delusions

Because of the House of Lords' answer to the fourth question, some jurisdictions interpreted *M'Naghten* to apply to insane delusions only when "the imaginary state of facts would, if real, justify or excuse the act." These jurisdictions held that defendant "must be considered in the same situation as to responsibility as if the facts with respect to which the delusion exists were real." *See Parsons v. State*, 81 Ala. 577, 2 So. 854 (1887).

Food for Thought

Under the interpretation of *M'Naghten* described in point a., *supra*, suppose that defendant shoots his neighbor in New York City. At the time, defendant believed that it was bear season, that he was hunting bears, and that his neighbor was a bear. Under *M'Naghten*, can defendant be convicted of murder? Can defendant be convicted of hunting bears out of season or without a license?*

b. Irresistible Impulse Test

Some jurisdictions supplemented the *M'Naghten* test with the "irresistible impulse" test which provided that, even if defendant knew the difference between right and wrong and knew that his act was wrong, defendant cannot be convicted if he acted under an "irresistible impulse." *Parsons v. State*, 81 Ala. 577, 2 So. 854 (1887), is the leading case: "We think it sufficient if the insane delusion so subverts his will as to destroy his free agency by rendering him powerless to resist by reason of the duress of the disease."

Hypo 1: *Making Grapefruit Juice*

Defendant squeezes Johnson's head until Johnson dies. At trial, the evidence shows that defendant was so mentally ill that he perceived that Johnson was a grapefruit rather than a person. In squeezing Johnson's head, defendant believed that he was creating grapefruit juice. Under *M'Naghten*, is defendant insane?

Hypo 2: *"Legal Wrong" or "Moral Wrong"?*

Defendant, a patient at a state mental hospital, strangled his wife while he was out of the hospital on a one-day pass. A clinical psychologist testified that defendant suffered from classic paranoid schizophrenia. A delusional product of this illness was his belief that the marriage vow "till death do us part" bestows on a marital partner a God-given right to kill the other partner who has violated or is inclined to violate the marital vows. Because the vows reflect the direct wishes of God, the killing is done with complete moral and criminal impunity and is not wrongful because it is sanctified by the will and desire of God. Under the *M'Naghten* test, is defendant insane? In considering *M'Naghten*, and its requirement that defendant know that what he did was "wrong," is the court referring to "legal wrong" or "moral wrong"? Does the distinction matter in this case? How would you argue the case for the defendant? How might the State respond? *See People v. Skinner*, 39 Cal. 3d 765, 704 P.2d 752, 217 Cal. Rptr. 685 (1985).

Take Note

Bear in mind that some defendants will not have sufficient capacity to form the necessary *mens rea* for the crime. As a result, insanity is not needed as a defense, and defendant cannot be convicted, because the required elements of the crime are not present.

Clark v. Arizona

548 U.S. 735 (2006).

JUSTICE SOUTER delivered the opinion of the Court.

The case presents two questions: whether due process prohibits Arizona's use of an insanity test stated solely in terms of the capacity to tell whether an act charged as a crime was right or wrong; and whether Arizona violates due process in restricting consideration of defense evidence of mental illness and incapacity to its bearing on a claim of insanity, thus eliminating its significance directly on the issue of the mental element of the crime charged (known in legal shorthand as the mens rea, or guilty mind). We hold that there is no violation of due process in either instance.

Officer Jeffrey Moritz of the Flagstaff Police responded to complaints that a pickup truck with loud music blaring was circling a residential block. The officer pulled Clark over. Less than a minute later, Clark shot the officer, who died. Clark was charged with first-degree murder for intentionally or knowingly killing a law enforcement officer in the line of duty. At trial, Clark did not contest the shooting and death, but relied on his undisputed paranoid schizophrenia at the time of the incident in denying that he had the specific intent to shoot a law enforcement officer or knowledge that he was doing so, as required by the statute. Accordingly, the prosecutor offered circumstantial evidence that Clark knew Officer Moritz was a law enforcement officer[, and] that Clark had intentionally lured an officer to the scene to kill him, having told people before the incident that he wanted to shoot police officers.

In defense, Clark claimed mental illness, which he sought to introduce for two purposes. First, he raised the affirmative defense of insanity, putting the burden on himself to prove by clear and convincing evidence, that "at the time of the commission of the criminal act he was afflicted with a mental disease or defect of such severity that he did not know the criminal act was wrong." Second, he aimed to rebut the prosecution's evidence of the requisite *mens rea*, that he had acted intentionally or knowingly to kill a law enforcement officer. The trial court ruled that Clark could not rely on evidence bearing on insanity to dispute the *mens rea*. The court cited *State* v. *Mott*, 187 Ariz. 536, 931 P.2d 1046 (en banc) (1997), which "refused to allow psychiatric testimony to negate specific intent," and held that "Arizona does not allow evidence of a defendant's mental disorder short of insanity to negate the *mens rea* element of a crime."

As to insanity, Clark presented testimony from classmates, school officials, and family describing his increasingly bizarre behavior over the year before the shooting. Witnesses testified that paranoid delusions led Clark to rig a fishing line with beads and wind chimes at home to alert him to intrusion by invaders, and to keep a bird in his automobile to warn of airborne poison. There was lay and expert testimony that Clark thought Flagstaff was populated with "aliens" (some impersonating government agents), the "aliens" were trying to kill him, and bullets were the only way to stop them. A psychiatrist testified that Clark was suffering from paranoid schizophrenia with delusions about "aliens" when he killed Officer Moritz, and he concluded that Clark was incapable of luring the officer or understanding right from wrong and that he was thus insane at the time of the killing. In rebuttal, a psychiatrist for the State gave his opinion that Clark's paranoid schizophrenia did not keep him from appreciating the wrongfulness of his conduct, as shown by his actions before and after the shooting (such as circling the residential block with music blaring as if to lure the police to intervene, evading the police after the shooting, and hiding the gun). The judge then issued a special verdict of first-degree murder, expressly finding that Clark shot and caused the death of Officer Moritz beyond a reasonable doubt and that Clark had not shown that he was insane at the time. The judge noted that though Clark was indisputably afflicted with paranoid schizophrenia at the time of the shooting, the mental illness "did not distort his perception of reality so severely that he did not know his actions were wrong." For this conclusion, the judge expressly relied on "the facts of the crime, the evaluations of the experts, Clark's actions and behavior both before and after the shooting, and the observations of those that knew Clark." The sentence was life imprisonment without the possibility of release for 25 years. The Court of Appeals affirmed the conviction and the Supreme Court of Arizona denied review. We affirm.

Clark says that Arizona's definition of insanity, being only a fragment of the Victorian standard from which it derives, violates due process. *M'Naghten's Case*, 10 Cl. & Fin. 200, 8 Eng. Rep. 718 (1843). When the Arizona Legislature first codified an insanity rule, it adopted the full *M'Naghten* test. In 1993, the legislature dropped the cognitive incapacity part, leaving only moral incapacity as the nub of the stated definition. Under current Arizona law, a defendant will not be adjudged insane unless he demonstrates that "at the time of the commission of the criminal act he was afflicted with a mental disease or defect of such severity that he did not know the criminal act was wrong."

Clark challenges the 1993 amendment excising the express reference to the cognitive incapacity element. He argues that elimination of the *M'Naghten* reference to nature and quality "offends a principle of justice so rooted in the traditions and conscience of our people as to be ranked as fundamental," *Patterson* v. *New York,* 432 U. S. 197, 202 (1977). History shows no deference to *M'Naghten* that could elevate its formula to the level of fundamental principle, so as to limit the traditional recognition of a State's capacity to define crimes and defenses. Even a cursory examination of the traditional Anglo-American approaches to insanity reveals significant differences, with four traditional strains variously combined to yield a diversity of standards. The main variants are the cognitive incapacity, the moral incapacity, the volitional incapacity, and the product-of-mental-illness tests. The first two emanate from alternatives stated in the *M'Naghten* rule. The volitional incapacity or irresistible-impulse test, which surfaced over two centuries ago (first in England, then in this country), asks whether a person was so lacking in volition due to a mental defect or illness that he could not have controlled his actions. The product-of-mental-illness test was used as early as 1870, and simply asks whether a person's action was a product of a mental disease or defect.

Seventeen States and the Federal Government have adopted a recognizable version of the *M'Naghten* test with both its cognitive incapacity and moral incapacity components. One State has adopted only *M'Naghten*'s cognitive incapacity test, and 10 (including Arizona) have adopted the moral incapacity test alone. Fourteen jurisdictions, inspired by the Model Penal Code, have in place an amalgam of the volitional incapacity test and some variant of the moral incapacity test, satisfaction of either (generally by showing a defendant's substantial lack of capacity) being enough to excuse. Three States combine a full *M'Naghten* test with a volitional incapacity formula. New Hampshire alone stands by the product-of-mental-illness test. The alternatives are multiplied further by variations in the prescribed insanity verdict: a significant number of these jurisdictions supplement the traditional "not guilty by reason of insanity" verdict with an alternative of "guilty but mentally ill." Finally, four States have no affirmative insanity defense, though one provides for a "guilty and mentally ill" verdict. These four, like a number of others that recognize an affirmative insanity defense, allow consideration of evidence of mental illness directly on the element of *mens rea* defining the offense.

With this varied background, it is clear that no particular formulation has evolved into a baseline for due process, and that the insanity rule, like the conceptualization of criminal offenses, is substantially open to state choice. Indeed, the legitimacy of such choice is the more obvious when one considers the interplay of legal concepts of mental illness or deficiency required for an insanity defense, with the medical concepts of mental abnormality that influence the expert opinion testimony by psychologists and psychiatrists commonly introduced to support or contest insanity claims. For medical definitions devised to justify treatment, like legal ones devised to excuse from conventional criminal responsibility, are subject to flux and disagreement. There being such fodder for reasonable debate about what the cognate legal and medical tests should be, due process imposes no single canonical formulation of legal insanity.

Though Clark is correct that the application of the moral incapacity test (telling right from wrong) does not necessarily require evaluation of a defendant's cognitive capacity to appreciate the nature and quality of the acts charged against him, his argument fails to recognize that cognitive incapacity is itself enough to demonstrate moral incapacity. Cognitive incapacity, in other words, is a sufficient condition for establishing a defense of insanity, albeit not a necessary one. As a defendant can therefore make out moral incapacity by demonstrating cognitive incapacity, evidence bearing on whether the defendant knew the nature and quality of his actions is both relevant and admissible. In practical terms, if a defendant did not know what he was doing when he acted, he could not have known that he was performing the wrongful act charged as a crime. We are satisfied that neither in theory nor in practice did Arizona's 1993 abridgment of the insanity formulation deprive Clark of due process.

Clark's second claim of a due process violation challenges the rule adopted by *Mott*. This case ruled on the admissibility of testimony from a psychologist offered to show that the defendant suffered from battered women's syndrome and therefore lacked the capacity to form the *mens rea* of the crime charged. The state court held that testimony of a professional psychologist or psychiatrist about a defendant's mental incapacity owing to mental disease or defect was admissible, and could be considered, only for its bearing on an insanity defense; such evidence could not be considered on the element of *mens rea*, that is, what the State must show about a defendant's mental state (such as intent or understanding) when he performed the act charged against him.

Understanding Clark's claim requires attention to the categories of evidence with a potential bearing on *mens rea*. First, there is "observation evidence" in the everyday sense, testimony from those who observed what Clark did and heard what he said; this category would also include testimony that an expert witness might give about Clark's tendency to think in a certain way and his behavioral characteristics. This evidence may support a professional diagnosis of mental disease and in any event is the kind of evidence that can be relevant to show what in fact was on Clark's mind when he fired the gun. Observation evidence in the record covers Clark's behavior at home and with friends, his expressions of belief around the time of the killing that "aliens" were inhabiting the bodies of local people (including government agents), his driving around the neighborhood before the police arrived, and so on. Observation evidence can be presented by either lay or expert witnesses.

Second, there is "mental-disease evidence" in the form of opinion testimony that Clark suffered from a mental disease with features described by the witness. This evidence characteristically but not always comes from professional psychologists or psychiatrists who testify as expert witnesses and base their opinions in part on examination of a defendant, usually conducted after the events in question. The thrust of this evidence was that, based on factual reports, professional observations, and tests, Clark was psychotic at the time in question, with a condition that fell within the category of schizophrenia.

Third, there is evidence we will refer to as "capacity evidence" about a defendant's capacity for cognition and moral judgment (and ultimately his capacity to form *mens rea*). This, too, is opinion evidence. Here, this testimony came from the same experts and concentrated on those specific details of the mental condition that make the difference between sanity and insanity under the Arizona definition. In their respective testimony on these details the experts disagreed: the defense expert gave his opinion that the symptoms or effects of the disease in Clark's case included inability to appreciate the nature of his action and to tell that it was wrong, whereas the State's psychiatrist was of the view that Clark was a schizophrenic who was still sufficiently able to appreciate the reality of shooting the officer and to know that it was wrong to do that.

Mott itself imposed no restriction on considering evidence of the first sort, the observation evidence. We read the *Mott* restriction to apply, rather, to evidence addressing the two issues in testimony that characteristically comes only from psychologists or psychiatrists qualified to give opinions as expert witnesses: mental-disease evidence (whether at the time of the crime a defendant suffered from a mental disease or defect, such as schizophrenia) and capacity evidence (whether the disease or defect left him incapable of performing or experiencing a mental process defined as necessary for sanity such as appreciating the nature and quality of his act and knowing that it was wrong). *Mott* was careful to distinguish this kind of opinion evidence from observation evidence generally and even from observation evidence that an expert witness might offer, such as descriptions of a defendant's tendency to think in a certain way or his behavioral characteristics; the Arizona court made clear that this sort of testimony was perfectly admissible to rebut the prosecution's evidence of *mens rea*. Only opinion testimony going to mental defect or disease, and its effect on the cognitive or moral capacities on which sanity depends under the Arizona rule, is restricted.

The trial court seems to have applied the *Mott* restriction to all evidence offered by Clark for the purpose of showing his inability to form the required *mens rea*. Thus, the trial court's restriction may have covered not only mental-disease and capacity evidence as just defined, but also observation evidence offered by lay (and expert) witnesses who described Clark's unusual behavior. Clark's objection to the application of the *Mott* rule does not, however, turn on the distinction between lay and expert witnesses or the kinds of testimony they were competent to present. [The Court agrees] that Clark's general attack on the *Mott* rule covers its application in confining consideration of capacity evidence to the insanity defense. The only issue before us is the challenge to *Mott* on due process grounds, comprising objections to limits on the use of mental-disease and capacity evidence. We consider the claim "Arizona's prohibition of 'diminished capacity' evidence by criminal defendants violates" due process.

Clark claims a right to require the fact finder case to consider testimony about his mental illness and his incapacity directly, when weighing the persuasiveness of evidence tending to show *mens rea*, which the prosecution has the burden to prove. The right to introduce relevant evidence can be curtailed if there is a good reason for doing that. *Holmes v. South Carolina*, 547 U. S. 319 (2006). If evidence may be kept out entirely, its consideration may be subject to limitation, which Arizona claims the power to impose. State law says that evidence of mental disease and incapacity may be introduced and considered, and if sufficiently forceful to satisfy the defendant's burden of proof under the insanity rule it will displace the presumption of sanity and excuse from criminal responsibility. But mental-disease and capacity evidence may be considered only for its bearing on the insanity defense, and it will avail a defendant only if it is persuasive enough to satisfy the defendant's burden as defined by the terms of that defense. The mental-disease and capacity evidence is thus being channeled or restricted to one issue and given effect only if the defendant carries the burden to convince the fact finder of insanity; the evidence is not being excluded entirely, and the question is whether reasons for requiring it to be channeled and restricted are good enough to satisfy the standard of fundamental fairness that due process requires. We think they are.

The first reason supporting the *Mott* rule is Arizona's authority to define its presumption of sanity (or capacity or responsibility) by choosing an insanity definition, and by placing the burden of persuasion on defendants who claim incapacity as an excuse from customary criminal responsibility. But if a State is to have this authority, it must be able to deny a defendant the opportunity to displace the presumption of sanity more easily when addressing a different issue in the course of the criminal trial. Yet, just such an opportunity would be available if expert testimony of mental disease and incapacity could be considered for whatever a fact finder might think it was worth on the issue of *mens rea*. A State is of course free to accept such a possibility. After all, it is free to define the insanity defense by treating the presumption of sanity as a bursting bubble, whose disappearance shifts the burden to the prosecution to prove sanity whenever a defendant presents any credible evidence of mental disease or incapacity. In States with this kind of insanity rule, the legislature may well be willing to allow such evidence to be considered on the *mens rea* element for whatever the fact finder thinks it is worth. What counts for due process, however, is simply that a State that wishes to avoid a second avenue for exploring capacity, less stringent for a defendant, has a good reason for confining the consideration of evidence of mental disease and incapacity to the insanity defense. Arizona's *Mott* rule reflects such a choice.

An insanity rule gives a defendant already found guilty the opportunity to excuse his conduct by showing he was insane when he acted, that is, that he did not have the mental capacity for conventional guilt and criminal responsibility. But, if the same evidence that affirmatively shows he was not guilty by reason of insanity (or "guilty except insane") under Arizona law also shows it was at least doubtful that he could form *mens rea*, then he should not be found guilty in the first place; it thus violates due process when the State impedes him from using mental-disease and capacity evidence directly to rebut the prosecution's evidence that he did form *mens rea*.

Are there, then, characteristics of mental-disease and capacity evidence giving rise to risks that may reasonably be hedged by channeling the consideration of such evidence to the insanity issue on which, in States like Arizona, a defendant has the burden of persuasion? We think there are: in the controversial character of some categories of mental disease, in the potential of mental-disease evidence to mislead, and in the danger of according greater certainty to capacity evidence than experts claim for it. To begin with, the diagnosis may mask vigorous debate within the profession about the very contours of the mental disease itself. See, *e.g.*, American Psychiatric Association, Diagnostic and Statistical Manual of Mental Disorders xxxiii (4th ed. text rev. 2000) (hereinafter DSM-IV-TR). Members of this Court have previously recognized that the end of such debate is not imminent. The consequence of this professional ferment is a general caution in treating psychological classifications as predicates for excusing otherwise criminal conduct. Next, there is the potential of mental-disease evidence to mislead jurors (when they are the fact finders) through the power of this kind of evidence to suggest that a defendant suffering from a recognized mental disease lacks cognitive, moral, volitional, or other capacity, when that may not be a sound conclusion at all. Even when a category of mental disease is broadly accepted and the assignment of a defendant's behavior to that category is uncontroversial, the classification may suggest something very significant about a defendant's capacity, when in fact the classification tells us little or nothing about the ability of the defendant to form *mens rea* or to exercise the cognitive, moral, or volitional capacities that define legal sanity. The limits of the utility of a professional disease diagnosis are evident in the dispute between the two testifying experts in this case; they agree that Clark was schizophrenic, but they come to opposite conclusions on whether the mental disease left him bereft of cognitive or moral capacity. Evidence of mental disease, then, can easily mislead; it is very easy to slide from evidence that an individual with a professionally recognized mental disease is very different, into doubting that he has the capacity to form *mens rea*, whereas that doubt may not be justified. Of course, in the cases mentioned, in which the categorization is doubtful or the category of mental disease is itself subject to controversy, the risks are even greater that opinions about mental disease may confuse a jury into thinking the opinions show more than they do. Because allowing mental-disease evidence on *mens rea* can thus easily mislead, it is not unreasonable to address that tendency by confining consideration of this kind of evidence to insanity, on which a defendant may be assigned the burden of persuasion.

There are particular risks inherent in the opinions of the experts who supplement the mental-disease classifications with opinions on incapacity: on whether the mental disease rendered a particular defendant incapable of the cognition necessary for moral judgment or *mens rea* or otherwise incapable of understanding the wrongfulness of the conduct charged. Unlike observational evidence bearing on *mens rea*, capacity evidence consists of judgment, and judgment fraught with multiple perils: a defendant's state of mind at the crucial moment can be elusive no matter how conscientious the enquiry, and the law's categories that set the terms of the capacity judgment are not the categories of psychology that govern the expert's professional thinking. Even when an expert is confident that his understanding of the mind is reliable, judgment addressing the basic categories of capacity requires a leap from the concepts of psychology, which are devised for thinking about treatment, to the concepts of legal sanity, which are devised for thinking about criminal responsibility. In sum, these empirical and conceptual problems add up to a real risk that an expert's judgment in giving capacity evidence will come with an apparent authority that psychologists and psychiatrists do not claim to have. This risk, like the difficulty in assessing the significance of mental-disease evidence, supports the State's decision to channel such expert testimony to consideration on the insanity defense, on which the party seeking the benefit of this evidence has the burden of persuasion. It bears repeating that not every State will find it worthwhile to make the judgment Arizona has made, and the choices the States do make about dealing with the risks posed by mental-disease and capacity evidence will reflect their varying assessments about the presumption of sanity as expressed in choices of insanity rules. The point here simply is that Arizona has sensible reasons to assign the risks as it has done by channeling the evidence.

Arizona's rule serves to preserve the State's chosen standard for recognizing insanity as a defense and to avoid confusion and misunderstanding on the part of jurors. For these reasons, there is no violation of due process under *Chambers* and its progeny, and no cause to claim that channeling evidence on mental disease and capacity offends any "principle of justice so rooted in the traditions and conscience of our people as to be ranked as fundamental," *Patterson*, 432 U. S, at 202.

The judgment of the Court of Appeals of Arizona is, accordingly, affirmed.

It is so ordered.

JUSTICE KENNEDY, with whom JUSTICE STEVENS and JUSTICE GINSBURG join, dissenting.

The central theory of Clark's defense was that his schizophrenia made him delusional. He lived in a universe where the delusions were so dominant, the theory was, that he had no intent to shoot a police officer or knowledge he was doing so. It is one thing to say he acted with intent or knowledge to pull the trigger. It is quite another to say he pulled the trigger to kill someone he knew to be a human being and a police officer. If the trier of fact were to find Clark's evidence sufficient to discount the case made by the State, which has the burden to prove knowledge or intent as an element of the offense, Clark would not be guilty of first-degree murder under Arizona law.

The trial court's exclusion was all the more severe because it barred from consideration on the issue of *mens rea* all this evidence, from any source, thus preventing Clark from showing he did not commit the crime as defined by Arizona law. Arizona's rule is problematic because it excludes evidence no matter how credible and material it may be in disproving an element of the offense. The Court's cases have noted the potential arbitrariness of *per se* exclusions and, on this rationale, have invalidated various state prohibitions. If the rule does not substantially burden the defense, then it is likely permissible. Where, however, the burden is substantial, the State must present a valid reason for its *per se* evidentiary rule.

In the instant case Arizona's proposed reasons are insufficient to support its categorical exclusion. While the State contends that testimony regarding mental illness may be too incredible or speculative for the jury to consider, this does not explain why the exclusion applies in all cases to all evidence of mental illness. "A State's legitimate interest in barring unreliable evidence does not extend to *per se* exclusions that may be reliable in an individual case." States have discretion to bar unreliable or speculative testimony and to adopt rules to ensure the reliability of expert testimony. Arizona has done so, and there is no reason to believe its rules are insufficient to avoid speculative evidence of mental illness. The risk of jury confusion also fails to justify the rule. The State defends its rule as a means to avoid the complexities of determining how and to what degree a mental illness affects a person's mental state. The difficulty of resolving a factual issue, though, does not present a sufficient reason to take evidence away from the jury when it is crucial for the defense. Even were the risk of jury confusion real enough to justify excluding evidence in most cases, this would provide little basis for prohibiting all evidence of mental illness without any inquiry into its likely effect on the jury or its role in deciding the linchpin issue of knowledge and intent. Indeed, Arizona has a rule in place to serve this very purpose.

Even assuming the reliability and jury-confusion justifications were persuasive in some cases, they would not suffice here. It does not overcome the constitutional objection to say that an evidentiary rule that is reasonable on its face can be applied to bar significant defense evidence without any rational basis for doing so. The reliability rationale has minimal applicability here. Many mental diseases are difficult to define and the subject of great debate. Schizophrenia, however, is a well-documented mental illness, and no one seriously disputes either its definition or its most prominent clinical manifestations. The State's own expert conceded that Clark had paranoid schizophrenia and was actively psychotic at the time of the killing. The jury-confusion rationale, if applicable, is the result of the Court's own insistence on conflating the insanity defense and the question of intent. Considered on its own terms, the issue of intent and knowledge is a straightforward factual question. A trier of fact is quite capable of weighing defense testimony and then determining whether the accused did or did not intend to kill or knowingly kill a human being who was a police officer. The issue can be difficult to decide in particular instances, but no more so than many matters juries must confront.

The Court says mental-illness evidence "can easily mislead." and may "tell us little or nothing about the ability of the defendant to form *mens rea.*" These generalities do not, however, show how relevant or misleading the evidence in this case would be. Evidence of Clark's mental illness bears directly on *mens rea*, for it suggests Clark may not have known he was killing a human being. While the Court discusses at length the likelihood of misjudgment from placing too much emphasis on evidence of mental illness, it ignores the risk of misjudging an innocent man guilty from refusing to consider this highly relevant evidence at all. This testimony was relevant to determining whether Clark knew he was killing a human being.

The fact that mental-illness evidence may be considered in deciding criminal responsibility does not compensate for its exclusion from consideration on the *mens rea* elements of the crime. While 13 States still impose significant restrictions on the use of mental-illness evidence to negate *mens rea*, a substantial majority of the States allow it. The fact that a reasonable number of States restrict this evidence weighs into the analysis, but applying the rule as a *per se* bar, as Arizona does, is so plainly unreasonable that it cannot be sustained. While defining mental illness is a difficult matter, the State seems to exclude the evidence one would think most reliable by allowing unexplained and uncategorized tendencies to be introduced while excluding relatively well-understood psychiatric testimony regarding well-documented mental illnesses. It is unclear what would have happened in this case had the defendant wanted to testify that he thought Officer Moritz was an alien. If disallowed, it would be tantamount to barring Clark from testifying on his behalf to explain his own actions. If allowed, Arizona's rule would simply prohibit the corroboration necessary to make sense of Clark's explanation. In sum, the rule forces the jury to decide guilt in a fictional world with undefined and unexplained behaviors but without mental illness. This rule has no rational justification and imposes a significant burden upon a straightforward defense: He did not commit the crime with which he was charged.

Take Note

Insanity can be relevant at three different points in the criminal process. First, as in *M'Naghten*, individuals who commit criminal acts while insane cannot be convicted of those acts. Second, defendants who are insane at the time of their trials cannot be tried, and will be committed until they are sane enough to proceed. The defendant must "have sufficient present ability to consult with his lawyer with a reasonable degree of rational understanding—and have a rational as well as factual understanding of the proceedings against him." *Dusky v. United States*, 362 U.S. 402 (1960). Finally, defendants sentenced to capital punishment cannot be executed until they regain their sanity. See *Ford v. Wainwright*, 477 U.S. 399 (1986); *Panetti v. Quarterman*, 551 U.S. 930 (2007).

Points for Discussion

a. Indefinite Commitment

In *Jackson v. Indiana*, 406 U.S. 715 (1972), defendant was unable to understand the nature of the charges against him or to participate in his defense, and the court ordered him committed until he "is sane." Jackson's counsel claimed that the commitment amounted to a "life sentence" without conviction. The Court agreed, noting that Jackson was subjected "to a more lenient commitment standard and to a more stringent standard of release" which condemned him "in effect to permanent institutionalization without the showing required for commitment or the opportunity for release." The Court found violations of equal protection and due process. In such circumstances, the state must pursue commitment under ordinary commitment standards.

b. Pleading Insanity

In order to invoke the sanity issue, defendant must plead the defense. Consider the requirements of the Federal Rules of Criminal Procedure:

Rule 12.2. Notice of Insanity Defense; Mental Condition

(a) Notice of an Insanity Defense. A defendant who intends to assert a defense of insanity at the time of the alleged offense must so notify an attorney for the government in writing within the time provided for filing a pretrial motion, or at any later time the court sets, and file a copy of the notice with the clerk. A defendant who fails to do so cannot rely on an insanity defense. The court may, for good cause, allow the defendant to file the notice late, grant additional trial-preparation time, or make other appropriate orders.

(b) Notice of Expert Evidence of a Mental Condition. If a defendant intends to introduce expert evidence relating to a mental disease or defect or any other mental condition of the defendant bearing on either (1) the issue of guilt or (2) the issue of punishment in a capital case, the defendant must—within the time provided for filing a pretrial motion or at any later time the court sets—notify an attorney for the government in writing of this intention and file a copy of the notice with the clerk. The court may, for good cause, allow the defendant to file the notice late, grant the parties additional trial-preparation time, or make other appropriate orders.

(c) Mental Examination.

(1) Authority to Order an Examination; Procedures.

(A) The court may order the defendant to submit to a competency examination under 18 U.S.C. § 4241.

(B) If the defendant provides notice under Rule 12.2(a), the court must, upon the government's motion, order the defendant to be examined under 18 U.S.C. § 4242. If the defendant provides notice under Rule 12.2(b) the court may, upon the government's motion, order the defendant to be examined under procedures ordered by the court.

(2) Disclosing Results and Reports of Capital Sentencing Examination. The results and reports of any examination conducted solely under Rule 12.2(c)(1) after notice under Rule 12.2(b)(2) must be sealed and must not be disclosed to any attorney for the government or the defendant unless the defendant is found guilty of one or more capital crimes and the defendant confirms an intent to offer during sentencing proceedings expert evidence on mental condition.

(3) Disclosing Results and Reports of the Defendant's Expert Examination. After disclosure under Rule 12.2(c)(2) of the results and reports of the government's examination, the defendant must disclose to the government the results and reports of any examination on mental condition conducted by the defendant's expert about which the defendant intends to introduce expert evidence.

(4) Inadmissibility of a Defendant's Statements. No statement made by a defendant in the course of any examination conducted under this rule (whether conducted with or without the defendant's consent), no testimony by the expert based on the statement, and no other fruits of the statement may be admitted into evidence against the defendant in any criminal proceeding except on an issue regarding mental condition on which the defendant:

(A) has introduced evidence of incompetency or evidence requiring notice under Rule 12.2(a) or (b)(1), or

(B) has introduced expert evidence in a capital sentencing proceeding requiring notice under Rule 12.2(b)(2).

(d) Failure to Comply.

(1) Failure to Give Notice or to Submit to Examination. The court may exclude any expert evidence from the defendant on the issue of the defendant's mental disease, mental defect, or any other mental condition bearing on the defendant's guilt or the issue of punishment in a capital case if the defendant fails to:

(A) give notice under Rule 12.2(b); or

(B) submit to an examination when ordered under Rule 12.2(c).

(2) Failure to Disclose. The court may exclude any expert evidence for which the defendant has failed to comply with the disclosure requirement of Rule 12.2(c)(3).

(e) Inadmissibility of Withdrawn Intention. Evidence of an intention as to which notice was given under Rule 12.2(a) or (b), later withdrawn, is not, in any civil or criminal proceeding, admissible against the person who gave notice of the intention.

Hypo: *Rule 12.2*

Consider F.R. Crim. Pro. Rule 12.2 and answer the following questions: A) Does Rule 12.2 cover only the insanity defense, or is it broader? B) Why does the defendant have the burden of notifying the prosecutor about the intent to rely on an insanity defense prior to trial? What is the nature of the required disclosure? C) Do the notice of insanity rules present Fifth Amendment privilege against self-incrimination problems? D) Does the defendant have a reciprocal right to discovery from the prosecution? E) Is there any harm or advantage to the defendant of making the required disclosures under the rule?

c. Imposing the Defense

In *State v. Jones*, 99 Wash. 2d 735, 664 P.2d 1216 (En Banc 1983), the court held that an insanity plea could be imposed over the defendant's objection. However, in *Frendak v. United States*, 408 A.2d 364 (D.C. App. 1979), when the court also imposed an insanity plea over the defendant's objection, it was held that "the trial judge may not force an insanity defense on a defendant found competent to stand trial if the individual intelligently and voluntarily decides to forego that defense":

> A defendant may fear that an insanity acquittal will lead to confinement in a men-

FYI

In *United States v. Winn*, 577 F.2d 86 (9th Cir. 1978), defendant failed to raise the insanity issue, and the court concluded that the trial court was not required to instruct the jury on that issue. "The Government must bear the burden of proving sanity beyond a reasonable doubt." "Rule 12.2 is designed to insure that the government has ample opportunity to investigate the facts of an issue critical to the determination of guilt or innocence." *Cf. Williams v. Florida*, 399 U.S. 78 (1970).

FYI

The federal government and the states can require a defendant to give notice of an intent to rely on an alibi defense, including the insanity defense, and can also require defendant to provide the names and addresses of witnesses on which he will rely. *See Williams v. Florida*, 399 U.S. 78, 100 (1970). If the defense provides this information, then it has a reciprocal right to receive similar information regarding the state's rebuttal witnesses. *See Wardius v. Oregon*, 412 U.S. 470 (1973). The defendant can then be subjected to examination by a court-appointed psychiatrist.

tal institution for a period longer than the potential jail sentence. Second, defendant may object to the quality of treatment or the type of confinement to which he may be subject in an institution for the mentally ill. Third, a defendant may choose to avoid the stigma of insanity. Fourth, in some states, an adjudication of insanity may affect a person's legal rights, for example, the right to vote or serve on a federal jury, and may even restrict his or her ability to obtain a driver's license. Finally, a defendant may oppose the imposition of an insanity defense because he or she views the crime as a political or religious protest which a finding of insanity would denigrate. In any event, a defendant may forego the defense because of a feeling that he or she is not insane, or that raising the defense would be equivalent to an admission of guilt. These reasons substantially outweigh the goal of ensuring that some abstract concept of justice is satisfied by protecting one who may be morally blameless from a conviction and punishment which he or she might choose to accept. Because the defendant must bear the ultimate consequences of any decision, if a defendant has acted intelligently and voluntarily, a trial court must defer to his or her decision to waive the insanity defense.

The court held that "the trial court still must have the discretion to raise an insanity defense, *sua sponte*, when a defendant does not have the capacity to reject the defense." When a defendant refuses to plead insanity, and the judge interposes the defense against his wishes, defendant is not automatically committed under federal law. *Lynch v. Overholser*, 369 U.S. 705 (1962).

d. Drugs & Competency

In *Sell v. United States*, 539 U.S. 166 (2003), the Court held that the Constitution allows the government to administer antipsychotic drugs involuntarily to a mentally ill criminal defendant—in order to render that defendant competent to stand trial for serious, but nonviolent, crimes—in limited circumstances. Relying on its prior decisions in *Washington v. Harper*, 494 U.S. 210 (1990), and *Riggins v. Nevada*, 504 U.S. 127 (1992), the Court stated that "the Constitution permits the Government involuntarily to administer antipsychotic drugs to a mentally ill defendant facing serious criminal charges in order to render that defendant competent to stand trial, but only if the treatment is medically appropriate, is substantially unlikely to have side effects that may undermine the fairness of the trial, and, taking account of less intrusive alternatives, is necessary significantly to further important governmental trial-related interests." The Court emphasized the important governmental interest in bringing a defendant charged with a serious crime to trial. However, the Court held that, "In order to make this evaluation, the court should focus upon such questions as: Why is it medically appropriate forcibly to administer antipsychotic drugs to an individual who (1) is *not* dangerous *and* (2) *is* competent to make up his own mind about treatment? Can bringing such an individual to trial *alone* justify administration of a drug that may have adverse side effects, including side effects that may to some extent impair a defense at trial? Courts must also consider whether a particular drug will tend to sedate a defendant, interfere with communication with counsel, prevent rapid reaction to trial developments, or diminish the ability to express emotions are matters important in determining the permissibility of medication to restore competence, but not necessarily relevant when dangerousness is primarily at issue. We cannot tell whether the side effects of antipsychotic medication were likely to undermine the fairness of a trial in Sell's case."

Take Note

In the wake of the verdict in the John Hinckley case (he was accused of attempting to assassinate President Ronald Reagan, but was found not guilty by reason of insanity), some jurisdictions moved to abolish the insanity defense. In *State v. Korell*, 213 Mont. 316, 690 P.2d 992 (1984), the court considered a Montana statute which abolished the not guilty by reason of insanity plea, but allowed evidence of mental illness or insanity to be admitted on the question of whether defendant was fit to proceed to trial, whether defendant had the *mens rea* required for the crime, and during the sentencing phase. The court upheld the law rejecting arguments that abolition of the insanity defense violates the Eighth Amendment's prohibition of cruel and unusual punishment.

e. Self-Representation

In *Indiana v. Edwards*, 554 U.S. 164 (2008), the Court held that a State may deny the right of self-representation to a defendant "who is found mentally competent to stand trial if represented by counsel but not mentally competent to conduct that trial" *pro se* because the defendant suffers from "severe mental illness." The Court reasoned that mental illness "is not a unitary concept" and that an individual may be "able to work with counsel at trial" but "unable to carry out the basic tasks needed to present his own defense without the help of counsel." The Court relied on an *amicus* brief from the American Psychiatric Association in support of this reasoning, and also emphasized that "proceedings must "appear fair to all who observe them."

Hypo 1: *God's Representative*

Defendant entered a church with a shotgun and tried to kill a minister. At the time, defendant suffered from paranoid schizophrenia, which caused him to hear voices. Defendant had a feeling of being God or a representative of God, who was present at the Last Supper, and who had at various times been threatened or attacked by others who did not give him credit for his rightful position. At the time of the shooting, defendant felt that he was being "threatened" and he responded violently in order to protect himself. Defendant believed that his actions were totally justified, "sensing" that other persons were in his body displacing him. Defendant found the situation intolerable and felt that he had to defend himself from what he described as "salvation level attacks." In shooting the minister, defendant believed that he rightfully deserved money and respect from the church that he was not getting. Therefore, defendant needed to eliminate this "sermon giver" (the minister) so that he could arrange for another who would respond and give defendant the money to which he was entitled. Was defendant insane under the *M'Naghten* test? *See State v. Boan*, 235 Kan. 800, 686 P.2d 160 (1984).

Hypo 2: *Satan's Agent*

Defendant stabbed his stepmother more than 70 times, leaving the knife sticking out of her heart. He left her body in the bathtub, making no attempt to conceal it. Later that day, a police officer saw him downtown wearing a pair of women's stretch pants, a woman's housecoat, a shirt and no shoes. Defendant suffered from paranoid schizophrenia. He understood that, as a mechanical thing, he killed his stepmother and he knew it was against the laws of the state. However, at the time, he was preoccupied with the delusional belief that his stepmother was an agent of Satan who was persecuting him, as were others like Yasser Arafat and the Ayatollah Khomeini. He believed he was directed by God to kill Satan's angel and that he was obeying God's higher directive or law. He believed himself to be a messiah and compared himself with Jesus Christ. He felt God had directed him to send his stepmother from this life to another. He had no remorse over the killing, felt that it was justified by God, and believed that he was merely doing a service. "He felt he would generally be protected from any difficulties" because "God would not allow it to happen." Was defendant insane under *M'Naghten*? *See State v. Cameron*, 100 Wash. 2d 520, 674 P.2d 650 (En Banc 1983).

Hypo 3: *Oustographs*

Defendant first received psychiatric treatment at age seven after being suspended from school for "viciously beating" other children. At age sixteen, he refused to go to school, stayed in bed all day, and was out all night. He refused to bathe. When spoken to, he would laugh hysterically. Defendant carried a bag around with him that he said "kept him company." He complained that the television talked back at him. At first defendant insisted there was nothing wrong with him, but he eventually agreed to psychiatric treatment. During this period he was heavily medicated and "was like a zombie." Because the medication made defendant drowsy, he stopped taking it and refused to visit the out-patient clinic. As an adult, defendant went to an FBI office and told an agent that people were sending messages to his brain "directing" him. Defendant said that there was a machine called an "oustograph" that could detect these matters. The FBI agent thought that defendant "had mental problems," and urged him to go to a psychiatric hospital for help. Later, defendant was charged with murdering a police officer. At the time of his arrest, the officers found a note that contained a meaningless string of words and phrases, including reference to an "oustograph." Defendant was "agitated" and "mumbled" continually to himself. A court psychiatrist diagnosed him as paranoid schizophrenia, a condition characterized by irrational thinking, inappropriate feelings, an overly suspicious nature, hostility, and delusions of grandeur and persecution. He was prone to delusions of persecution, and suffered from auditory hallucinations. When arrested, defendant spoke only in "gibberish" and claimed that he was speaking "Chinese" (a Chinese-speaking staff member disagreed). Under medication, Green's gibberish gave way to coherence and there was a lessening of inappropriate laughter and his tendency to talk to the ceiling. Does the evidence establish insanity under *M'Naghten*? *See State v. Green*, 643 S.W.2d 902 (Tenn. Crim. App. 1982).

Hypo 4: *Religious Beliefs and Murder*

While defendant and his wife were honeymooning in Canada, he was deported to the U.S. following a brawl. When his wife arrived two days later, he immediately "felt" that she had been unfaithful. Defendant took his wife to a motel, beat her unconscious, and inflicted fatal stab wounds. Then, using an ax, he decapitated her with such force that he cut the concrete floor. Defendant tried to conceal his actions by placing her body parts in a blanket. He then borrowed a bucket and sponge, and cleaned the room of blood and fingerprints. Before leaving, he chatted with the motel manager over a beer. He left the motel and drove to a remote area 25 miles away where he hid the body parts. He picked up two hitchhikers 200 miles farther away, told them of his crime, and enlisted their aid in disposing of his wife's car in a river. Although he confessed to murder, he claimed that he followed the Moscovite religious faith, and that a Moscovite is required to kill his wife if she commits adultery. Defendant had a history of mental problems, for which he had been hospitalized. Was defendant insane under *M'Naghten*? What relevance do you attach to the fact that defendant cleaned the room and concealed the body parts? *See State v. Crenshaw*, 98 Wash. 2d 789, 659 P.2d 488 (En Banc 1983).

Hypo 5: *Evil Spirits*

Near midnight, defendant sat in the kitchen reading his Bible. Later, he went to the bedroom where his wife was sleeping and stabbed her in the back. When his wife awoke, defendant told her that she had been stabbed by an intruder. Defendant told the police that he had gone to the grocery store, that he returned to hear the front door slam, and that he found his wife bleeding from a wound in her back. Several weeks later, defendant's wife found letters which stated that, "our marriage was severed when I put the knife in your back," and that, "I have gone to be with Jehovah in heaven for three and one-half days." Defendant's wife confronted him by telephone, and he stated that God told him to stab her in order to sever the marriage bond. Defendant was charged with attempted premeditated murder. At trial, a psychiatrist (Dr. Seig) stated that defendant had a plan, inspired by his relationship to God, to establish a multi-million dollar sports complex. This facility would enable him to achieve his goal of teaching people the path to perfection. On the night of the stabbing, defendant was discouraged by inner "evil spirits" who questioned his wife's lack of encouragement and support. Dr. Seig diagnosed defendant as suffering either from an organic delusional disorder or paranoid schizophrenia. Either diagnosis would account for defendant's delusional belief that he had a privileged relationship and communication with God. Dr. Seig found that defendant was operating under this delusional system when he stabbed his wife, that these delusions caused him to believe that his act was morally justified, but that he was aware that the stabbing was contrary to law. Dr. Miller testified that defendant suffered from a psychotic delusion that it was his divine mission to kill his wife and that he was morally justified in stabbing her because God had told him to do so. Dr. Miller testified that defendant's mental illness made it impossible for him to distinguish right from wrong even though defendant was aware that such conduct was legally wrong. Dr. Kaplan testified that defendant was suffering from paranoid schizophrenia and was laboring under the paranoid delusion that his wife stood in the way of his divine mission of completing the large sports complex, that defendant believed that the stabbing was the right thing to do, and that defendant, as a result of his mental illness, was unable to distinguish right from wrong with respect to the stabbing. Two other psychiatrists, Dr. Heron and Dr. Sundell, offered the opinion that defendant was suffering from paranoid schizophrenia and a paranoid delusion about God. These conditions so affected his cognitive ability as to render him incapable of distinguishing right from wrong as normal people would be able to do in accordance with societal standards of morality. Was defendant insane under *M'Naghten*? *See People v. Serravo*, 823 P.2d 128 (Colo. 1992).

Hypo 6: *The Astronaut*

In 2007, NASA Astronaut Lisa Nowak was charged with attempted murder for an attack on another woman, an Air Force captain. The prosecution alleged that Nowak drove 900 miles from Houston to Florida, and that she carried a wig to disguise her appearance. She also had a steel mallet, a knife, pepper spray, rubber tubing, latex gloves and garbage bags. The prosecution alleged that she wore a diaper during her drive so that she would not have to take rest breaks. News reports suggested that Nowak was under a great deal of stress, attempting to manage her career, her marriage, her children, and may have suffered from severe sleep deprivation. However, she had been successful enough to participate in a space mission even though a neighbor reported hearing an altercation inside Nowak's home that involved the throwing of dishes. Was Nowak "insane" under *M'Naghten*?

Food for Thought

A love-sick driver is absolutely distraught over the fact that the object of her affections has spurned her sexual advances. As a result, she decides to commit suicide by crashing her vehicle into another vehicle. The driver does a "countdown" to the crash in text messages sent to the person who spurned her affections. In the crash, the driver crosses the center line and runs head-on into an oncoming vehicle. The driver of the other vehicle is killed and a passenger is seriously injured. Was the love-sick driver "insane" under *M'Naghten*?

2. Other Tests

Because of dissatisfaction with the *M'Naghten* and irresistible impulse tests, the courts and the American Law Institute developed alternative tests.

United States v. Freeman

357 F.2d 606 (2d Cir. 1966).

KAUFMAN, CIRCUIT JUDGE:

[Charles Freeman was found guilty on two counts of selling narcotics. Freeman's defense was that, at the time of the alleged sale of narcotics, he did not possess sufficient capacity and will to be held responsible for the criminality of his acts. In rejecting this contention, the District Court relied upon the *M'Naghten* rules.]

The bulk of the evidence directly relating to the issue of criminal responsibility took the form of expert psychiatric testimony of witnesses called by both the government and the defense. Freeman's expert witness at trial was Dr. Herman Denber, Associate Professor of Clinical Psychiatry at New York Medical College and Director of Psychiatric Research at Manhattan State Hospital. Dr. Denber [testified] that Freeman was not only a narcotics addict, but also a confirmed alcoholic. The doctor noted that Freeman's body had become accustomed to the consumption of large amounts of heroin over a fourteen-year period, and that the defendant was in the habit of drinking one or two bottles of wine daily to increase the potency of the narcotics. In addition, Freeman regularly imbibed six to nine "shots" of whiskey each day.

Dr. Denber testified that Freeman displayed no depth or variation in his emotional reactions, spoke in a flat monotone and paused for excessively long periods before responding to questions. As a result of taking impure narcotics for so long a time, Freeman suffered from frequent episodes of toxic psychosis leading to a clouding of the sensorium (inability to know what one is doing or where one is) as well as delusions, hallucinations, epileptic convulsions and, at times, amnesia. Moreover, Freeman had suffered "knock-outs" on three occasions while engaging in prize fighting, and that had led to a general vagueness about details. Finally, Freeman had experienced "innumerable brain traumata" which produced such organic and structural changes as destroyed brain tissue.

Restricted to stating a conclusory opinion under *M'Naghten*, Dr. Denber initially averred that Freeman was incapable of knowing right from wrong, even under a strict interpretation of that limited test. However, upon amplifying this conclusion, he acknowledged that Freeman had an awareness of what he was doing on the nights in the sense that he possessed cognition that he was selling heroin. Also, Freeman was not in "such a state of toxicity that he did not remember the dates. It is my feeling that as far as the social implications or the nature or meaning of what this meant to him at that moment he was not aware of it."

The government called Dr. Robert Carson, Clinical Instructor in Psychiatry at Cornell University. Dr. Carson testified that Freeman was able to distinguish between right and wrong within the meaning of the *M'Naghten* test despite his heavy use of narcotics and alcohol. He noted that Freeman possessed the capacity to enter into purposeful activity such as the sale of narcotics, and he expressed the opinion that defendant had been aware of the wrongfulness of his acts. Dr. Carson pointed to the fact that Freeman had been sufficiently fearful of being apprehended that he suggested that the transfer of narcotics take place in the privacy of the men's room of Marvin's Bar. Dr. Carson acknowledged that Freeman had "some limitations" on his ability to distinguish right from wrong, but not to the degree required by the *M'Naghten* test.

We are concerned with whether the Court should have applied a test less rigid than *M'Naghten*, so that the essential examination and psychiatric testimony could have been directed towards Freeman's capacity to exercise will or appreciate the wrongfulness of his conduct, rather than being confined to the relatively narrow inquiry required by *M'Naghten*.

M'Naghten and its antecedents can be seen as examples of the law's conscientious efforts to place in a separate category, people who cannot be justly held "responsible" for their acts. By modern scientific standards the language of these early tests is primitive. In the 18th Century, psychiatry had hardly become a profession, let alone a science. Thus, these tests and their progeny were evolved at a time when psychiatry was literally in the Dark Ages.

In the pre-*M'Naghten* period, the concepts of phrenology and monomania were being developed and had significant influence on the right and wrong test. Phrenologists believed that the human brain was divided into thirty-five separate areas, each with its own peculiar mental function. The sixth area, was designated "destructiveness." It was located, we are told, above the ear because this was the widest part of the skull of carnivorous animals. Monomania, on the other hand, was a state of mind in which one insane idea predominated while the rest of the thinking processes remained normal.

Of course, both phrenology and monomania are rejected today as meaningless medical concepts since the human personality is viewed as a fully integrated system. But, by an accident of history, the rule of *M'Naghten's* case froze these concepts into the common law just at a time when they were becoming obsolete. M'Naghten's exculpation from criminal responsibility was most significant for several reasons. His defense counsel had relied in part upon Dr. Isaac Ray's historic work, MEDICAL JURISPRUDENCE OF INSANITY which had been published in 1838. This book contained many enlightened views on the subject of criminal responsibility in general and on the weaknesses of the right and wrong test in particular. Thus, for example, the jury was told that the human mind is not compartmentalized and that a defect in one aspect of the personality could spill over and affect other areas. As Chief Judge Biggs tells us in his Isaac Ray lectures compiled in THE GUILTY MIND, the court was so impressed with this and other medical evidence of M'Naghten's incompetency that Lord Chief Justice Tindal practically directed a verdict for the accused.

For these reasons, *M'Naghten's* case could have been the turning point for a new approach to more modern methods of determining criminal responsibility. But the Queen's ire was raised by the acquittal and she was prompted to intervene. Mid-19th Century England was in a state of social upheaval and there had been three attempts on the life of the Queen and one on the Prince Consort. Queen Victoria was so concerned about M'Naghten's acquittal that she summoned the House of Lords to "take the opinion of the Judges on the law governing such cases." Consequently, the fifteen judges of the common law courts were called into extraordinary session under a not too subtle atmosphere of pressure to answer five prolix and obtuse questions on the status of criminal responsibility in England. Significantly, it was Lord Chief Justice Tindal who responded for fourteen of the fifteen judges, and thus articulated what has come to be known as the *M'Naghten* Rules or *M'Naghten* test. Rather than relying on Dr. Ray's monumental work which had impressed him at M'Naghten's trial, Tindal, with the Queen's breath upon him, reaffirmed the right-wrong test despite its 16th Century roots and the fact that it echoed such uninformed concepts as phrenology and monomania. Dr. Ray's insights were lost to the common law for over one hundred years except in the small state of New Hampshire.

The principal objection to *M'Naghten* is that it has several serious deficiencies which stem from its narrow scope. Because *M'Naghten* focuses only on the cognitive aspect of the personality, *i.e.*, the ability to know right from wrong, we are told by eminent medical scholars that it does not permit the jury to identify those who can distinguish between good and evil but who cannot control their behavior. The result is that instead of being treated at appropriate mental institutions for a sufficiently long period to bring about a cure or sufficient improvement so that the accused may return with relative safety to himself and the community, he is ordinarily sentenced to a prison term as if criminally responsible and then released as a potential recidivist with society at his mercy. To the extent that these individuals continue to be released from prison because of the narrow scope of *M'Naghten*, that test poses a serious danger to society's welfare.

Similarly, *M'Naghten's* single track emphasis on the cognitive aspect of the personality recognizes no degrees of incapacity. Either the defendant knows right from wrong or he does not and that is the only choice the jury is given. But such a test is grossly unrealistic; our mental institutions, as any qualified psychiatrist will attest, are filled with people who to some extent can differentiate between right and wrong, but lack the capacity to control their acts to a substantial degree.

A further fatal defect of the *M'Naghten* Rules stems from the unrealistically tight shackles which they place upon expert psychiatric testimony. When the law limits a testifying psychiatrist to stating his opinion whether the accused is capable of knowing right from wrong, the expert is thereby compelled to test guilt or innocence by a concept which bears little relationship to reality. He is required thus to consider one aspect of the mind as a "logic-tight compartment in which the delusion holds sway leaving the balance of the mind intact."

Prominent psychiatrists have expressed their frustration when confronted with such requirements. Edward de Grazia has asked, "How does one translate 'psychosis' or 'psychopathy' or 'dementia praecox' or even 'sociopathy' or 'mental disorder' or 'neurotic character disorder' or 'mental illness' into a psychiatric judgment of whether the accused knew 'right' from 'wrong.' " Dr. Lawrence Kolb, Director of the New York Psychiatric Institute, professor and Chairman of the Department of Psychiatry at Columbia University and Director of the Psychiatric Service at Presbyterian Hospital, declared that "answers supplied by a psychiatrist in regard to questions of rightness or wrongness of an act or 'knowing' its nature constitute a professional perjury."

Psychiatrists are not alone in their recognition of the unreality of *M'Naghten*. As long ago as 1930, Mr. Justice Cardozo observed that "everyone contends that the present definition of insanity has little relation to the truths of mental life." Mr. Justice Frankfurter, as a witness before the Royal Commission on Capital Punishment, declared with his usual fervor: "I do not see why the rules of law should be arrested at the state of psychological knowledge of the time when they were formulated. I think the *M'Naghten* Rules are in large measure shams. That is a very strong word, but I think the *M'Naghten* Rules are very difficult for conscientious people and not difficult enough for people who say, 'We'll just juggle them.' "

At bottom, the determination whether a man is or is not held responsible for his conduct is not a medical but a legal, social or moral judgment. It is the psychiatrist who informs as to the mental state of the accused—his characteristics, his potentialities, his capabilities. But once this information is disclosed, it is society as a whole, represented by judge or jury, which decides whether a man with the characteristics described should or should not be held accountable for his acts. It cannot be presumed that juries will check their common sense at the courtroom door. As Professor Wechsler has rightly commented, "It's not to be expected that juries will lightly accept the proposition that one who seemingly knew in a true sense did not know. One would expect jury skepticism and the system is the healthier for that jury skepticism."

The true vice of *M'Naghten* is that the ultimate deciders—the judge or the jury—will be deprived of information vital to their final judgment. A test which depends vitally on notions already discredited when *M'Naghten* was adopted can no longer be blandly accepted as representing the "moral sense of the community." To continue to apply such medically discarded concepts would be to follow a negative approach which is the result of a holdover of long outmoded attitudes rather than a policy decision grounded in reason or science.

Efforts to supplement or replace the *M'Naghten* Rules with a more meaningful and workable test have persisted for generations, with varying degrees of success. Perhaps the first to receive judicial approval, however, was more an added fillip to *M'Naghten* than a true substitute: the doctrine which permits acquittal on grounds of lack of responsibility when a defendant is found to have been driven by an "irresistible impulse" to commit his offense. We find the "irresistible impulse" test to be inherently inadequate and unsatisfactory. Psychiatrists have long questioned whether "irresistible impulses" actually exist; the more basic legal objection to the term "irresistible impulse" is that it is too narrow and carries the misleading implication that a crime impulsively committed must have been perpetrated in a sudden and explosive fit. The "irresistible impulse" test is unduly restrictive because it excludes the far more numerous instances of crimes committed after excessive brooding and melancholy by one who is unable to resist sustained psychic compulsion or to make any real attempt to control his conduct. In seeking one isolated and indefinite cause for every act, the test is unhappily evocative of the notions which underlay *M'Naghten*—unfortunate assumptions that the problem can be viewed in black and white absolutes and in crystal-clear causative terms.

With the exception of New Hampshire, American courts waited until 1954 and Judge Bazelon's opinion for the District of Columbia Circuit in *Durham v. United States*, for legal recognition that disease or defect of the mind may impair the whole mind and not a subdivided portion of it. The *Durham* court swept away the intellectual debris of a century and articulated a test which was as simple in its formulation as its sources were complex. A defendant is not criminally responsible, wrote Judge Bazelon, "if his unlawful act was the product of mental disease or mental defect." The advantages of *Durham* were apparent and its arrival was widely hailed. The new test entirely eliminated the "right-wrong" dichotomy, and hence interred the overriding emphasis on the cognitive element of the personality which had for so long plagued *M'Naghten*. The fetters upon expert testimony were removed and psychiatrists were permitted and indeed encouraged to provide all relevant medical information for the common sense application of judge or jury. Finally, *Durham* ended to a large degree the "professional perjury" decried by psychiatrists and made inevitable by *M'Naghten*. Sympathetic to the plight of a defendant who was not, in fairness, responsible for his conduct, psychiatrists had found it necessary to testify that the accused did not know his act was "wrong" even when the defendant's words belied this conclusion. In its frank and express recognition that criminality resulting from mental disease or defect should not bring forth penal sanctions, *Durham* brought an end to this all too-frequent practice of "winking" at legal requirements, a practice which had contributed little to the self-respect and integrity of either medicine or the law.

Many students of the law recognized that the new rule, despite its many advantages, also possessed serious deficiencies. It has been suggested, for example, that *Durham's* insistence that an offense be the "product" of a mental disease or defect raised near-impossible problems of causation, closely resembling those encountered by the *M'Naghten* and irresistible impulse tests. The most significant criticism of *Durham*, however, is that it fails to give the fact-finder any standard by which to measure the competency of the accused. As a result, psychiatrists when testifying that a defendant suffered from a "mental disease or defect" in effect usurped the jury's function. This problem was strikingly illustrated in 1957, when a staff conference at Washington's St. Elizabeth's Hospital reversed its previous determination and reclassified "psychopathic personality" as a "mental disease." Because this single hospital provides most of the psychiatric witnesses in the District of Columbia courts, juries were abruptly informed that certain defendants who had previously been considered responsible were now to be acquitted. It seems clear that a test which permits all to stand or fall upon the labels or classifications employed by testifying psychiatrists hardly affords the court the opportunity to perform its function of rendering an independent legal and social judgment.[51]

In 1953, a year before *Durham*, the American Law Institute commenced an exhaustive study of criminal conduct including the problem of criminal responsibility. Gradually and painstakingly a new definition of criminal responsibility began taking shape as Section 4.01 of the Model Penal Code was evolved. Section 4.01 provides that "A person is not responsible for criminal conduct if at the time of such conduct as a result of mental disease or defect he lacks substantial capacity either to appreciate the wrongfulness of his conduct or to conform his conduct to the requirements of law."[52] We believe this test to be the soundest yet formulated and we accordingly adopt it as the standard of criminal responsibility in the Courts of this Circuit. The Model Penal Code formulation views the mind as a unified entity and recognizes that mental disease or defect may impair its functioning in numerous ways. The rule, moreover, reflects awareness that from the perspective of psychiatry absolutes are ephemeral and gradations are inevitable. By employing the telling word "substantial" to modify "incapacity," the rule emphasizes that "any" incapacity is not sufficient to justify avoidance of criminal responsibility but that "total" incapacity is also unnecessary. The choice of the word "appreciate," rather than "know" in the first branch of the test also is significant; mere intellectual awareness that conduct is wrongful, when divorced from appreciation or understanding of the moral or legal import of behavior, can have little significance.

While permitting the utilization of meaningful psychiatric testimony,[53] the American Law Institute formulation, is free of many of the defects which accompanied *Durham*. Although it eschews rigid classification, the Section is couched in sufficiently precise terms to provide the jury with a workable standard when the judge charges in terms comprehensible to laymen. Expert testimony, in short, will be admissible whenever

FYI

In some jurisdictions, a bifurcated trial procedure is used. Defendant is first tried for the underlying crime. If convicted, a separate trial on the question of insanity is held.

51 To correct the deficiencies of Durham, the Washington, D.C. Court of Appeals amplified its definition of mental disorder for the purpose of making "it very clear that neither the court nor the jury is bound by ad hoc definitions or conclusions as to what experts state is a disease or defect." The Court redefined mental disease and defect to include "any abnormal condition of the mind which substantially affects mental or emotional processes and substantially impairs behavior controls." McDonald v. United States, 312 F.2d 847, 851 (D.C. Cir. 1962). It thus adopted a formulation which closely approximates the recommendation of the American Law Institute in its Model Penal Code.

52 American Law Institute, Model Penal Code (final draft) (1962). We have adopted the word "wrongfulness" in Section 4.01 as the American Law Institute's suggested alternative to "criminality" because we wish to include the case where the perpetrator appreciates that his conduct is criminal, but, because of a delusion, believes it to be morally justified.

53 While the Model Penal Code permits, and, indeed, encourages the production of full psychiatric data and information at trial, such testimony can have weight only if the underlying examination of the defendant was thorough. In most instances, one hour of psychiatric examination of the defendant in the House of Detention in preparation for trial is not an adequate substitute for a complete psychiatric and neurological work-up of the defendant in a hospital under the care and guidance of a staff of experts.

relevant but always as expert testimony—and not as moral or legal pronouncement. Relieved of their burden of divining precise causal relationships, the judge or jury can concentrate upon the ultimate decisions which are properly theirs, fully informed as to the facts.

Under the American Law Institute formulation, an inquiry based on meaningful psychological concepts can be pursued. The most modern psychiatric insights will be available, but, even more importantly, the legal focus will be sharper and clearer. The twin branches of the test, significantly phrased in the alternative, will remove from the pale of criminal sanctions precisely those who are in no meaningful sense responsible for their actions.

We believe that the American Law Institute test—which makes no pretension at being the ultimate in faultless definition—is an infinite improvement over the *M'Naghten* Rules, even when those Rules are supplemented by the "irresistible impulse" doctrine. All legal definitions involve elements of abstraction and approximation which are difficult to apply in marginal cases. The impossibility of guaranteeing that a new rule will always be infallible cannot justify continued adherence to an outmoded standard, sorely at variance with enlightened medical and legal scholarship.

The genius of the common law has been its responsiveness to changing times, its ability to reflect developing moral and social values. Drawing upon the past, the law must serve—and traditionally has served—the needs of the present. In the past century, psychiatry has evolved from tentative, hesitant gropings in the dark of human ignorance to a recognized and important branch of modern medicine. The outrage of a frightened Queen has for too long caused us to forego the expert guidance that modern psychiatry is able to provide.

Since Freeman's responsibility was determined under the rigid standards of the *M'Naghten* Rules, we are compelled to reverse his conviction and remand the case for a new trial in which the criteria employed will be those provided by Section 4.01 of the Model Penal Code. And lest our opinion be misunderstood or distorted, some additional discussion is in order. First, we wish to make it absolutely clear that mere recidivism or narcotics addiction will not of themselves justify acquittal under the American Law Institute standards which we adopt today. Indeed, the second clause of Section 4.01 explicitly states that "the terms 'mental disease or defect' do not include an abnormality manifested only by repeated criminal or otherwise anti-social conduct." We approve and adopt this important caveat. There may be instances where recidivists will not be criminally responsible, but this will be for determination in each individual case depending upon other evidence of mental disease augmenting mere recidivism with the ultimate determination dependent upon the proper application of the standards we have adopted. But, we stress, repeated criminality cannot be the sole ground for a finding of mental disorder. Nor may narcotics addiction without more be the sole evidence of abnormality under the American Law Institute test. We have observed that the defense of lack of responsibility is essentially an acknowledgment on the part of society that because of mental disease or defect certain classes of wrongdoers are not properly the subjects of criminal punishment. In light of the severe penalties imposed by Congress for the possession and sale of narcotics, it would be unwise at this stage of medical knowledge, for a court to conclude that those addicted to narcotics should be, for that reason alone, immune from criminal sanctions.

Secondly, there is no question but that the security of the community must be the paramount interest. It would be obviously intolerable if those suffering from a mental disease or defect of such a nature as to relieve them from criminal responsibility were to be set free to continue to pose a threat to life and property. We suggest that those adjudged criminally irresponsible promptly be turned over to state officials for commitment pursuant to state procedures.

Reversed and remanded.

Points for Discussion

a. Evaluation by State Psychiatrists

In *State v. Richardson*, 276 Or. 325, 555 P.2d 202 (In Banc 1976), the court held that "when a defendant pleads not guilty by reason of insanity the state is entitled to a mental examination," and the privilege against self-incrimination does not protect a defendant against that examination: "if he refuses, his affirmative defense of mental defect will be stricken." However, in *Motes v. State*, 256 Ga. 831, 353 S.E.2d 348 (1987), the court held that defendant was not required to submit to an examination if he proceeds without an expert: "If the defendant wants to introduce expert testimony, then the state must be allowed the same privilege and the defendant must cooperate."

b. Consequences of NGI Verdict

In *State v. Karstetter*, 110 Ariz. 539, 521 P.2d 626 (In Banc 1974), defendant was convicted of murder after the prosecutor stated in closing argument that the court appointed psychologist did not recommend hospitalization and psychiatric care. The court concluded that the prosecutor did not commit reversible error even though a majority of the states preclude the jury from receiving this information. See *Erdman v. State*, 315 Md. 46, 553 A.2d 244, 249–50 (1989). However, in *Shannon v. United States*, 512 U.S. 573 (1994), the Court held that a federal district court is not required to inform the jury of the consequences of rendering a "not guilty by reason of insanity" (NGI) verdict: "The principle that juries are not to consider the consequences of their verdicts is a reflection of the basic division of labor in our legal system between judge and jury. The jury's function is to find the facts and to decide whether, on those facts, the defendant is guilty of the crime charged. The judge, by contrast, imposes sentence on the defendant after the jury has arrived at a guilty verdict. Information regarding the consequences of a verdict is therefore irrelevant to the jury's task. Moreover, providing jurors sentencing information invites them to ponder matters that are not within their province, distracts them from their fact-finding responsibilities, and creates a strong possibility of confusion. An instruction of some form may be necessary under certain limited circumstances. If, for example, a witness or prosecutor states in the presence of the jury that a particular defendant would 'go free' if found NGI, it may be necessary for the district court to intervene with an instruction to counter such a misstatement."

Take Note

In *Ake v. Oklahoma*, 470 U.S. 68 (1985), the Court held that: "when a defendant has made a preliminary showing that his sanity at the time of the offense is likely to be a significant factor at trial, the Constitution requires that a State provide access to a psychiatrist's assistance on this issue if the defendant cannot otherwise afford one." As the Court noted: "Without the assistance of a psychiatrist to conduct a professional examination on issues relevant to the defense, to help determine whether the insanity defense is viable, to present testimony, and to assist in preparing the cross-examination of a State's psychiatric witnesses, the risk of an inaccurate resolution of sanity issues is extremely high. With such assistance, the defendant is fairly able to present at least enough information to the jury, in a meaningful manner, as to permit it to make a sensible determination." Most requests for psychiatric assistance turn on whether defendant has made "a preliminary showing that his sanity at the time of the offense was likely to be a significant factor at trial." *See State v. Gambrell*, 318 N.C. 249, 347 S.E.2d 390 (1986). Even when the state must pay for a psychiatrist, "the Constitution does not give an indigent defendant the right to choose his own psychiatrist or even to receive funds to hire a private psychiatric expert. The appointment of State-employed psychiatrists may fulfill the state's constitutional obligation. Their employment by the state, we are satisfied, creates no conflict of interest which would disable them from fulfilling the constitutional requirements." *Id.*

In *Cordova v. People*, 817 P.2d 66 (Colo. 1991), the trial court overruled defendant's request for an informational instruction advising the jury of the consequences of a NGI verdict (that defendant would be committed). The court reversed: "In light of the manifest risk of the jury's mistaken belief that a verdict of not guilty by reason of impaired mental condition might result in the defendant's return to the community—a risk which the defendant's requested instruction was calculated to negate—the fairness of the trial was detrimentally affected by the trial court's erroneous ruling on the defendant's request for the informational instruction." See also *State v. Shickles*, 760 P.2d 291 (Utah 1988); *State v. Hamann*, 285 N.W.2d 180 (Iowa 1979).

c. Jury's Awareness of Drugs

FYI

It is constitutionally permissible for the state to treat insanity as an affirmative defense and to saddle defendant with the burden of proof "beyond a reasonable doubt." *See Leland v. Oregon*, 343 U.S. 790 (1952). Regardless, the state has the obligation to prove all elements of the criminal offense beyond a reasonable doubt including showing that defendant was capable of forming, and did in fact form, the required *mens rea*. *See Rivera v. Delaware*, 429 U.S. 877 (1976).

In *In re Pray*, 133 Vt. 253, 336 A.2d 174 (1975), defendant, while in state custody for trial purposes, was given thorazine four times a day, and tofranil and phenobarbital twice a day, and an occasional dosage of chlorohydrate. Absent the medicine, he was not competent to stand trial. With the medicine, he was quiet, tractable, rational, well oriented, answered questions clearly, cooperatively, and knew what was going on. He showed no effects of the depression on which his insanity defense was based. The Court reversed his conviction: "At the very least, the jury should have been informed that he was under heavy, sedative medication, that his behavior in their presence was strongly conditioned by drugs administered to him at the direction of the State, and that his defense of insanity was to be applied to a basic behavior pattern that was not the one they were observing. In fact, it may well have been necessary, in view of the critical nature of the issue, to expose the jury to the undrugged, unsedated Gary Pray, insofar as safety and trial progress might permit. A life sentence ought not to rest on the shaky premise that an undisclosed behavioral alteration, brought about by the State, did not affect the jury's resolution of the issue of insanity. The matter must be retried."

d. Bifurcation of Guilt & Sanity

In some states, the insanity issue is bifurcated from guilt issues. In *Vardas v. Estelle*, 715 F.2d 206 (5th Cir. 1983), defendant claimed that his due process rights were violated by the established Texas procedure which allowed the issue of sanity to be tried contemporaneously with the issue of guilt or innocence. Defendant claimed that he should have been granted a separate trial on the issue of insanity. The court rejected the argument. In *United States v. Bennett*, 460 F.2d 872 (D.C.Cir. 1972), defendant argued that:

> his entire defense was prejudiced by the intermingling at trial of his insanity defense and his defense on the merits. The prejudice, he asserts, was of two types. First, he argues that the introduction of evidence on the merits prejudiced his insanity defense because the jury was exposed to the "unpleasant details" of the "shocking sexual assault on a 13-year-old boy." Second, his defense was prejudiced by the introduction of evidence, ostensibly relevant only to the issue of sanity, which was tantamount to a confession of guilt by appellant. The evidence was to the effect that Bennett's sanity was evidenced by his "very good recollection of the events of the alleged events. He recalls minutely what happened prior to the offense, of the alleged offense, and following it. He expressed his own version of the story, his feeling about it.'" Although the court held that: "Bifurcation lies in the first instance within the 'sound discretion' of the trial court", it concluded that bifurcation is required when necessary to avoid prejudice.

Take Note

In *Jones v. State*, 289 So.2d 725 (Fla. 1974), defendant offered the testimony of two psychiatrists and a psychologist based on a history testified to by them. The State objected to the testimony on the basis that defendant had not testified as to the history. The court concluded that a "qualified expert may testify to his opinion concerning the defendant's mental condition based either upon (1) personal examination of the defendant made by the witness, or (2) the testimony in the case, if he has been in court and heard it all. (3) He may also give his opinion upon hypothetical questions propounded by counsel." "It is not necessary that the expert state the detailed circumstances of the examination before giving his finding. The facts and symptoms which he observed, and on which he bases his opinion, may be brought out on cross-examination. The court below should have allowed the psychiatrists to testify as to their opinions without relating what the defendant told concerning the alleged facts of the case. Unless a person is a raving maniac or complete imbecile, a jury can hardly be deemed competent to reach a satisfactory decision on the question of his mental condition without the aid of expert witnesses."

e. Guilty but Mentally Ill

John Hinckley attempted to assassinate President Ronald Reagan outside a hotel in Washington, D.C., and was acquitted on the grounds of insanity. *See United States v. Hinckley*, 525 F. Supp. 1342 (D.D.C. 1981), *aff'd*, 672 F.2d 115 (D.C.Cir. 1982). The verdict provoked a strong adverse public reaction. Following the Hinckley verdict, a number of states made it more difficult to assert the insanity defense and others abolished the defense altogether. The verdict also led to creation of the so-called "guilty but mentally ill" verdict. Essentially, under this approach, defendant is convicted of the crime but declared to be mentally ill. In theory, this verdict requires the state to determine whether psychiatric treatment is necessary or warranted, and (hopefully) to provide treatment. At the end of the sentence, defendant must be released—unless the state is able to satisfy the standards for commitment. Led also to 18 U.S.C. § 20(a).

Take Note

In addition to the insanity defense, a defendant might also raise a "diminished capacity" defense. This defense questions whether defendant had the capacity to form the *mens rea* of the crime. In *United States v. Brawner*, 471 F.2d 969, 153 U.S. App. D.C. 1 (D.C.Cir. 1972), the court summarized this defense: "Expert testimony as to a defendant's abnormal mental condition may be received and considered, as tending to show that defendant did not have the specific mental state required for a particular crime or degree of crime-even though he was aware that his act was wrongful and was able to control it, and hence was not entitled to complete exoneration."

f. Lay Witnesses

In *United States v. Milne*, 487 F.2d 1232 (5th Cir. 1973), defendant sought to offer the testimony of three lay witnesses who described their interactions with defendant, his heavy drug use and his bizarre behavior. All of the witnesses had known defendant for a year or more and had seen him nearly every day. The court overruled the trial court's decision to exclude the evidence: "The lay opinion of a witness who is sufficiently acquainted with the person involved and has observed his conduct is admissible as to the sanity of such individual." "Insanity is a variance from usual or normal conduct. For that reason, a lay witness should be required to testify as to unusual, abnormal or bizarre conduct before being permitted to express an opinion as to insanity. The trial judge must exercise a sound discretion in concluding whether or not a particular witness is qualified."

g. *Yates* Case

In 2006, the murder conviction of Andrea Yates was reversed on appeal because of false testimony given by the State's expert witness at trial. Yates is a woman who murdered her five children in 2001 by drowning them in a bathtub. *See* Deborah W. Denno, *Who Is Andrea Yates? A Short Story About Insanity*, 10 DUKE J. GENDER L. & POLICY 1–139 (2003). On July 26, 2006 at her retrial, Andrea Yates was acquitted by reason of insanity under the *M'Naghten* test, based on evidence of her post-partum depression and psychosis. Under Texas law, she was required to be institutionalized until a court found that she was no longer deemed to be a threat to herself or to others. She was sent to a prison-like maximum security facility and she was later moved to a low security mental hospital.

Hypo 1: *The MPC Test*

Reconsider the three hypotheticals after the *M'Naghten* case. Under the MPC test, how would the answers to the questions in those hypotheticals change, in terms of rhetoric or result?

Food for Thought

How does an attorney go about proving that a client was insane at the time of the alleged offense? In other words, what types of evidence might be offered in support of a plea of insanity?

Hypo 2: *Multiple Personalities*

Defendant was charged with kidnapping a baby. She suffered from multiple personality disorder resulting from childhood physical and sexual abuse and two rapes. At the time of the kidnapping, defendant wanted to convince a former boyfriend that she was pregnant with his child. She had photographs made which made her appear pregnant. Later, she abducted a baby from a hospital nursery. One of defendant's alter personalities, "Rina," perhaps with another alter personality, "Bridget," controlled defendant's conduct at the time of the kidnapping. Her host or dominant personality, "Gidget," did not consciously participate in the abduction. Psychiatric experts could not establish that the alter personality in control at the time of the offense ("Rina") was legally insane, *i.e.*, "unable to appreciate the nature and quality or the wrongfulness of [defendant's] acts." The experts also testified that "each of the personalities taken alone knew, or were very capable of knowing, what she was doing and of making moral judgments." Under the circumstances, was defendant insane and not criminally responsible for the abduction? *See United States v. Denny-Shaffer*, 2 F.3d 999 (10th Cir. 1993); *see also State v. Wheaton*, 121 Wash. 2d 347, 850 P.2d 507 (En Banc 1993).

Food for Thought

Defendant, who possessed an extra male (Y) chromosome, was charged with attempted murder. Studies have shown that males who possess this extra Y chromosome, referred to as "47 XYY individuals" exhibit aggressive behavior as a result of this chromosomal abnormality. However, not all XYY individuals are by nature involuntarily aggressive. Some XYY individuals have not exhibited such behavior. Given this evidence, is defendant insane under the *M'Naghten* or MPC tests? *See People v. Tanner*, 13 Cal. App. 3d 596, 91 Cal. Rptr. 656 (1970).

Hypo 3: *Pathological Gambling Disorder*

A jewelry store manager was indicted for stealing jewelry from his employer. Defendant contends that a compulsion to gamble rendered him unable to resist becoming a thief and stealing to support his habit. The American Psychiatric Association's Diagnostic and Statistical Manual of Mental Disorders § 312.31 (3d ed. 1980) contains the following description of pathological gambling:

> The essential features are a chronic and progressive failure to resist impulses to gamble and gambling behavior that compromises, disrupts, or damages personal, family, or vocational pursuits. The gambling preoccupation, urge, and activity increase during periods of stress. As the gambling increases, the individual is usually forced to lie in order to obtain money and to continue gambling, but hides the extent of the gambling. There is no serious attempt to budget or save money. When borrowing resources are strained, antisocial behavior in order to obtain money for more gambling is likely. Any criminal behavior—*e.g.*, forgery, embezzlement, or fraud—is typically nonviolent. There is a conscious intent to return or repay the money.

Was defendant "insane" under the MPC test? *See United States v. Runnells*, 985 F.2d 554 (4th Cir. 1993); *United States v. Gould*, 741 F.2d 45 (4th Cir. 1984); *United States v. Torniero*, 735 F.2d 725 (2d Cir. 1984); *United States v. Lewellyn*, 723 F.2d 615 (8th Cir. 1983).

Food for Thought

At the time he committed a double homicide, defendant believed he was in a combat situation during the Vietnam War. Psychiatric evidence revealed that defendant was suffering a dissociative flashback episode related to his Vietnam experience. He perceived himself as searching for a suspected enemy, such as Viet Cong guerrillas, rather than robbing a tavern. Is defendant insane under the *M'Naghten* or MPC tests? *See State v. Coogan*, 154 Wis. 2d 387, 453 N.W.2d 186 (Ct.App. 1990).

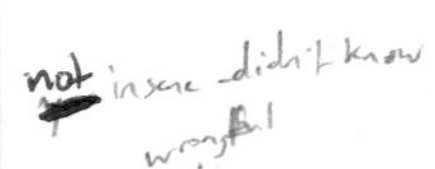

Hypo 4: *More on PTSD*

Defendant was suffering from PTSD at the time of a homicide. A psychologist testified that children who grow up in war-torn and other violent areas can suffer PTSD. Defendant offered seventeen examples of violent events during her childhood that allegedly caused the onset of PTSD. These included the fact that: defendant saw a friend shoot his gun in a drug house and was terrified; a man pulled a gun on defendant and her mother, and defendant stepped into the path of the gun; gang members shot at a friend while in defendant's presence; defendant's sister's boyfriend, a father-figure to defendant, was shot and paralyzed; defendant was robbed of her coat at gunpoint; defendant's cousin was killed in a drive-by shooting; defendant's uncle, a close friend, was shot and killed; defendant was robbed of jewelry at gunpoint; defendant was tied up and raped when she was fourteen years old; defendant's cousin was shot in a street fight and lost the use of her arm; defendant stepped in front of a man with a gun to protect her aunt; defendant was severely beaten and robbed by a group of girls; defendant's mother shot a man, in front of defendant, because he was molesting defendant while giving her a bath; defendant was regularly beaten by her mother and father; defendant's father shot at her mother "because there was too much salt in the gravy"; and defendant, from age four to six, saw her mother and father "regularly dine with loaded revolvers at their sides during family dinners" to protect them from the violent outbursts of the other. Defendant argues that she was unable to appreciate the wrongfulness of her conduct or conform her conduct to the requirements of law. Can defendant argue that she was insane under the MPC test?" *See State v. Morgan*, 195 Wis. 2d 388, 536 N.W.2d 425 (1995).

Hypo 5: *Traumatic Neurosis*

Defendant was a married policeman with three sons and a daughter. He seemed to be a well-adjusted, happy, family man when his wife and infant daughter were brutally killed in an unprovoked attack by a drunken neighbor. Two years later, one day before defendant was to remarry, defendant robbed a bank. Defendant was found to be suffering from "traumatic neurosis" or "dissociative reaction", characterized by moods of depression and severe feelings of guilt, induced by the traumatic effect of the death of his wife and child and by his belief that he was responsible for their deaths because he was not home. He had an unconscious desire to be punished by society to expiate his guilt feelings. The defense claimed that his mind was so destroyed or impaired that he was unable to resist the impulse to rob the bank. Defendant was not psychotic, but he had been despondent, seemed to be lost in thought, and did not respond to questions directed to him. On one occasion, prior to the crime, defendant repeatedly beat the steering wheel of a police car while at the same time saying the name of his murdered wife. Defendant's present wife testified that on two occasions defendant suddenly, and for no apparent reason, lapsed into crying spells and talked about committing suicide. During one such period, he pointed a gun at himself and the police took him to the station. After he returned home, defendant appeared jovial and acted as if nothing had happened. After his child and his first wife died, defendant expressed a desire to commit suicide because he no longer had a reason for living. However, a police lieutenant testified that defendant's police work, as evidenced by his efficiency rating and his written duty reports was, if anything, more effective than his service prior to the death of his wife. Was defendant insane under *M'Naghten* or the MPC test at the time of the robbery? *See United States v. Pollard*, 171 F. Supp. 474 (E.D.Mich. 1959).

Hypo 6: *Murder by Burning*

Defendant was charged with the murder of his wife. The marriage was never happy, and defendant became increasingly violent. One day, defendant went to a police station and told them that he had burned his wife. Defendant was very upset and agitated, pacing back and forth, sometimes refusing to answer questions. At one point he said, "Help her!" As they talked, the officers detected the smell of gasoline and noticed that defendant's facial and neck hair were singed. Defendant eventually told the officers that his wife was in a wildlife refuge, and they transported him to the scene to help find the body. Defendant shouted at the officers to hurry and to go faster, saying that his wife was hurt. The officers found the wife's badly burnt body and a dented gas can in the middle of a dirt road at the refuge. Medical testimony revealed that defendant suffered from chronic and sub-chronic undifferentiated schizophrenia. However, the State's expert witnesses testified that defendant understood that he was burning his wife and that he knew it was wrong. Under the MPC test, was defendant insane? *See State v. Provost*, 490 N.W.2d 93 (Minn. 1992).

Food for Thought

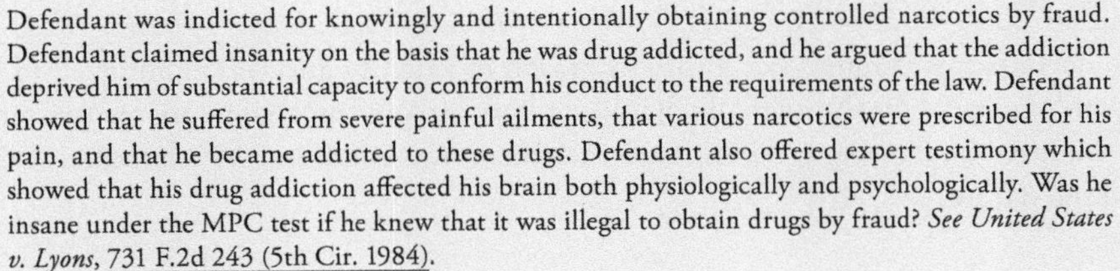

Defendant was indicted for knowingly and intentionally obtaining controlled narcotics by fraud. Defendant claimed insanity on the basis that he was drug addicted, and he argued that the addiction deprived him of substantial capacity to conform his conduct to the requirements of the law. Defendant showed that he suffered from severe painful ailments, that various narcotics were prescribed for his pain, and that he became addicted to these drugs. Defendant also offered expert testimony which showed that his drug addiction affected his brain both physiologically and psychologically. Was he insane under the MPC test if he knew that it was illegal to obtain drugs by fraud? *See United States v. Lyons*, 731 F.2d 243 (5th Cir. 1984).

Hypo 7: *Battered Woman Syndrome*

Defendant was charged with murdering her husband. During the marriage, defendant had been subjected to physical abuse. After defendant gave birth to a daughter, her husband became involved with another woman and moved to Florida. On one of his return trips, he went to defendant's place of employment where he brandished a pocket knife and tried to choke her. Later, at her apartment, he pressed defendant to move with him to Florida. Defendant refused. He then took a weapon from his travel bag and threatened to use it if she thwarted him. After he fell asleep on a couch in the living room, defendant took the gun intending to end her own life. Deciding that suicide would be no solution, she returned to the living room to put the weapon back in the suitcase. But when her eyes fell upon her sleeping husband, she raised the weapon and fired until it was empty. Under the circumstances, can defendant establish the defense of insanity under

M'Naghten or the MPC test? Is there such a thing as "temporary insanity?" Did defendant suffer from it? *See State v. Guido*, 40 N.J. 191, 191 A.2d 45 (1963); *see also State v. Myers*, 239 N.J. Super. 158, 570 A.2d 1260 (1990).

Food for Thought

A mother called 911 just after midnight and stated that "I've just killed my boys" and that God ordered her to do it. When police officers arrived at the scene, they found a six-year-old and eight-year-old in the front yard with their skulls smashed. They also found a 14-month-old baby alive in his crib with a fractured skull. The evidence revealed that the mother had suffered from delusional psychotic disorder and had been through three major psychotic episodes over the prior three years. Does the fact that the mother was sufficiently "aware" of reality to contact police after the killings suggest that she was not insane?

3. Effect of Insanity Acquittal

What happens to a defendant who is acquitted by reason of insanity? In some jurisdictions, the defendant is automatically committed to an insane asylum. In most jurisdictions, the decision to commit is discretionary. At the federal level, someone who is acquitted may be held for up to 40 days. 18 U.S.C. § 4243. In *In re Rosenfield*, 157 F. Supp. 18 (D.D.C. 1957), defendant was found not guilty by reason of insanity and was committed to Saint Elizabeth's Hospital for the mentally ill under a statute requiring mandatory commitment of those acquitted on insanity grounds. Later, defendant was conditionally released. The Court upheld the statute.

Jones v. United States

463 U.S. 354 (1983).

JUSTICE POWELL delivered the opinion of the Court.

The question is whether petitioner, who was committed to a mental hospital upon being acquitted of a criminal offense by reason of insanity, must be released because he has been hospitalized for a period longer than he might have served in prison had he been convicted.

In the District of Columbia a criminal defendant who successfully invokes the insanity defense is committed to a mental hospital. The statute provides several ways of obtaining release. Within 50 days of commitment the acquittee is entitled to a judicial hearing to determine his eligibility for release, at which he has the burden of proving by a preponderance of the evidence that he is no longer mentally ill or dangerous. If he fails to meet this burden, the committed acquittee subsequently may be released, with court approval, upon certification of his recovery by the hospital chief of service. Alternatively, the acquittee is entitled to a judicial hearing every six months at which he may establish by a preponderance of the evidence that he is entitled to release.

Independent of its provision for the commitment of insanity acquittees, the District of Columbia also has adopted a civil-commitment procedure, under which an individual may be committed upon clear and convincing proof by the Government that he is mentally ill and likely to injure himself or others. The individual may demand a jury in the civil-commitment proceeding. Once committed, a patient may be released at any time upon certification of recovery by the hospital chief of service. Alternatively, the patient is entitled after the first 90 days, and subsequently at 6-month intervals, to request a judicial hearing at which he may gain his release by proving by a preponderance of the evidence that he is no longer mentally ill or dangerous.

Petitioner was arrested for attempting to steal a jacket from a department store and charged with attempted petit larceny, a misdemeanor punishable by a maximum prison sentence of one year. The court ordered petitioner committed to St. Elizabeth's, a public hospital for the mentally ill, for a determination of his competency to stand trial. A hospital psychologist submitted a report to the court stating that petitioner was competent to stand trial, that petitioner suffered from "Schizophrenia, paranoid type," and that petitioner's alleged offense was "the product of his mental disease." Petitioner subsequently pleaded not guilty by reason of insanity. The Government did not contest the plea. The court found petitioner not guilty by reason of insanity and committed him to St. Elizabeth's pursuant to § 24–301(d)(1).

On May 25, 1976, the court held the 50-day hearing required by § 24–301(d)(2)(A). A psychologist from St. Elizabeth's testified that, in the opinion of the staff, petitioner continued to suffer from paranoid schizophrenia and that "because his illness is still quite active, he is still a danger to himself and to others." Petitioner's counsel presented no evidence. The court then found that "defendant-patient is mentally ill and as a result of his mental illness, at this time, he constitutes a danger to himself or others." Petitioner was returned to St. Elizabeth's. Petitioner obtained new counsel and a second release hearing was held on February 22, 1977. By that date, petitioner had been hospitalized for more than one year, the maximum period he could have spent in prison if he had been convicted. On that basis, he demanded that he be released unconditionally or recommitted pursuant to the civil-commitment standards in § 21–545(b), including a jury trial and proof by clear and convincing evidence of his mental illness and dangerousness. The Superior Court denied petitioner's request for a civil-commitment hearing, reaffirmed the findings made at the May 25, 1976, hearing, and continued petitioner's commitment to St. Elizabeth's. The District of Columbia Court of Appeals affirmed the judgment. We granted certiorari and affirm.

It is clear that "commitment for any purpose constitutes a significant deprivation of liberty that requires due process protection." A State must have "a constitutionally adequate purpose for the confinement." Congress has determined that a criminal defendant found not guilty by reason of insanity in the District of Columbia should be committed indefinitely to a mental institution for treatment and the protection of society. Petitioner does not contest the Government's authority to commit a mentally ill and dangerous person indefinitely to a mental institution, but rather contends that "the petitioner's trial was not a constitutionally adequate hearing to justify an indefinite commitment."

Petitioner's argument rests principally on *Addington v. Texas*, 441 U.S. 418 (1979), in which the Court held that the Due Process Clause requires the Government in a civil-commitment proceeding to demonstrate by clear and convincing evidence that the individual is mentally ill and dangerous. Petitioner contends that these due process standards were not met in his case because the judgment of not guilty by reason of insanity did not constitute a finding of present mental illness and dangerousness and because it was established only by a preponderance of the evidence. Petitioner concludes that the Government's only conceivably legitimate justification for automatic commitment is to ensure that insanity acquittees do not escape confinement entirely, and that this interest can justify commitment at most for a period equal to the maximum prison sentence the acquittee could have received if convicted. Because petitioner has been hospitalized for longer than the one year he might have served in prison, he asserts that he should be released unconditionally or recommitted under the District's civil-commitment procedures.

A verdict of not guilty by reason of insanity establishes two facts: (I) defendant committed an act that constitutes a criminal offense, and (ii) he committed the act because of mental illness. Congress has determined that these findings constitute an adequate basis for hospitalizing the acquittee as a dangerous and mentally ill person. We cannot say that it was unreasonable and therefore unconstitutional for Congress to make this determination. The fact that a person has been found, beyond a reasonable doubt, to have committed a criminal act certainly indicates dangerousness. Indeed, this concrete evidence generally may be at least as persuasive as any predictions about dangerousness that might be made in a civil-commitment proceeding. We do not agree with petitioner's suggestion that the requisite dangerousness is not established by proof that a person committed a non-violent crime against property. This Court never has held that "violence," however that term might be defined, is a prerequisite for a constitutional commitment. Nor can we say that it was unreasonable for Congress to determine that the insanity acquittal supports an inference of continuing mental illness. It comports with common sense to conclude that someone whose mental illness was sufficient to lead him to commit a criminal act is likely to remain ill and in need of treatment. The precise evidentiary force of the insanity acquittal, of course, may vary from case to case, but the Due Process Clause does not require Congress to make classifications that fit every individual with the same degree of relevance. Because a hearing is provided within 50 days of the commitment, there is assurance that every acquittee has prompt opportunity to obtain release if he has recovered.

Petitioner also argues that, whatever the evidentiary value of the insanity acquittal, the Government lacks a legitimate reason for committing insanity acquittees automatically because it can introduce the insanity acquittal as evidence in a subsequent civil proceeding. This argument fails to consider the Government's strong interest in avoiding the need to conduct a *de novo* commitment hearing following every insanity acquittal—a hearing at which a jury trial may be demanded, and at which the Government bears the burden of proof by clear and convincing evidence. Instead of focusing on the critical question whether the acquittee has recovered, the new proceeding likely would have to relitigate much of the criminal trial. These problems accent the Government's important interest in automatic commitment. We therefore conclude that a finding of not guilty by reason of insanity is a sufficient foundation for commitment of an insanity acquittee for the purposes of treatment and the protection of society.

Petitioner contends that his indefinite commitment is unconstitutional because the proof of his insanity was based only on a preponderance of the evidence, as compared to *Addington's* civil-commitment requirement of proof by clear and convincing evidence. Petitioner ignores important differences between the class of potential civil-commitment candidates and the class of insanity acquittees that justify differing standards of proof. The *Addington* Court expressed particular concern that members of the public could be confined on the basis of "some abnormal behavior which might be perceived by some as symptomatic of a mental or emotional disorder, but which is in fact within a range of conduct that is generally acceptable." In view of this concern, the Court deemed it inappropriate to ask the individual "to share equally with society the risk of error." But since automatic commitment under § 24–301(d) (1) follows only if the acquittee himself advances insanity as a defense and proves that his criminal act was a product of his mental illness, there is good reason for diminished concern as to the risk of error. The proof that he committed a criminal act as a result of mental illness eliminates the risk that he is being committed for mere "idiosyncratic behavior." A criminal act by definition is not "within a range of conduct that is generally acceptable." We conclude that concerns critical to our decision in *Addington* are diminished or absent in the case of insanity acquittees. Accordingly, there is no reason for adopting the same standard of proof in both cases. "Due process is flexible and calls for such procedural protections as the particular situation demands." The preponderance of the evidence standard comports with due process for commitment of insanity acquittees.[17]

The remaining question is whether petitioner nonetheless is entitled to his release because he has been hospitalized for a period longer than he could have been incarcerated if convicted. The Due Process Clause "requires that the nature and duration of commitment bear some reasonable relation to the purpose for which the individual is committed." The purpose of commitment following an insanity acquittal, like that of civil commitment, is to treat the individual's mental illness and protect him and society from his potential dangerousness. The committed acquittee is entitled to release when he has recovered his sanity or is no longer dangerous. Because it is impossible to predict how long it will take for any given individual to recover—or indeed whether he ever will recover—Congress has chosen, as it has with respect to civil commitment, to leave the length of commitment indeterminate, subject to periodic review of the patient's suitability for release. In light of the congressional purposes underlying commitment of insanity acquittees, we think petitioner clearly errs in contending that an acquittee's hypothetical maximum sentence provides the constitutional limit for his commitment. A particular sentence of incarceration is chosen to reflect society's view of the proper response to commission of a particular criminal offense, based on a variety of considerations such as retribution, deterrence, and rehabilitation. The State may punish a person convicted of a crime

17 A defendant could be required to prove his insanity by a higher standard than a preponderance of the evidence.

even if satisfied that he is unlikely to commit further crimes. Different considerations underlie commitment of an insanity acquittee. As he was not convicted, he may not be punished. His confinement rests on his continuing illness and dangerousness. Thus, under the District of Columbia statute, no matter how serious the act committed by the acquittee, he may be released within 50 days of his acquittal if he has recovered. In contrast, one who committed a less serious act may be confined for a longer period if he remains ill and dangerous. There simply is no necessary correlation between severity of the offense and length of time necessary for recovery. The length of the acquittee's hypothetical criminal sentence therefore is irrelevant to the purposes of his commitment.

We hold that when a criminal defendant establishes by a preponderance of the evidence that he is not guilty of a crime by reason of insanity, the Constitution permits the Government, on the basis of the insanity judgment, to confine him to a mental institution until such time as he has regained his sanity or is no longer a danger to himself or society. This holding accords with the widely and reasonably held view that insanity acquittees constitute a special class that should be treated differently from other candidates for commitment. We have observed before that "when Congress undertakes to act in areas fraught with medical and scientific uncertainties, legislative options must be especially broad and courts should be cautious not to rewrite legislation." This admonition has particular force in the context of legislative efforts to deal with the special problems raised by the insanity defense.

The judgment of the District of Columbia Court of Appeals is

Affirmed.

JUSTICE BRENNAN, with whom JUSTICE MARSHALL and JUSTICE BLACKMUN join, dissenting.

The Government's interests in committing petitioner are the isolation, protection, and treatment of a person who may, through no fault of his own, cause harm to others or to himself. Whenever involuntary commitment is a possibility, the Government has a strong interest in accurate, efficient commitment decisions. Nevertheless, *Addington* held both that the Government's interest in accuracy was not impaired by a requirement that it bear the burden of persuasion by clear and convincing evidence, and that the individual's interests in liberty and autonomy required the Government to bear at least that burden. An acquittal by reason of insanity of a single, nonviolent misdemeanor is not a constitutionally adequate substitute for the due process protections of proof by clear and convincing evidence of present mental illness or dangerousness, with the Government bearing the burden of persuasion. I cannot agree that the Government should be excused from the burden that *Addington* held was required by due process.

JUSTICE STEVENS, dissenting.

A plea of guilty, may provide a sufficient basis for confinement for the period fixed by the legislature as punishment for the acknowledged conduct, provided of course that the acquittee is given a fair opportunity to prove that he has recovered from his illness. But surely if he is to be confined for a longer period, the State must shoulder the burden of proving by clear and convincing evidence that such additional confinement is appropriate.

Points for Discussion

a. Civil Commitment

In *Baxstrom v. Herold*, 383 U.S. 107 (1966), when petitioner's prison term ended, he was committed to a hospital for the criminally ill. The Court held that petitioner had not been committed pursuant to proper procedures: "Petitioner was denied equal protection by the statutory procedure under which a person may be civilly committed at the expiration of his penal sentence without the jury review available to all other persons civilly committed. Petitioner was further denied equal protection by his civil commitment to an institution maintained by the Department of Correction beyond the expiration of his prison term without a judicial determination that he is dangerously mentally ill."

Food for Thought

Prior to *Jones*, in order to civilly commit someone to a mental institution, the state was required to prove by clear and convincing evidence that he was presently mentally ill and dangerous to himself or to others. *Jones* suggests that such proof is not required when a defendant is found not guilty by reason of insanity. Was *Jones* correctly decided? *See State ex rel Collins v. Superior Court*, 150 Ariz. 295, 723 P.2d 644 (1986).

b. Medical Treatment

In *Rouse v. Cameron*, 373 F.2d 451, 125 U.S. App. D.C. 366 (D.C.Cir. 1966), defendant was acquitted on the grounds of insanity and confined to Saint Elizabeth's Hospital. When he received no psychiatric treatment, defendant sought habeas relief. The court held that defendant was entitled to treatment, but not necessarily to release: "The purpose of involuntary hospitalization is treatment, not punishment. Commitment rests upon the 'necessity for treatment of the mental condition which led to the acquittal by reason of insanity.' Absent treatment, the hospital is 'a penitentiary where one could be held indefinitely for no convicted offense even though the offense of which he was previously acquitted might not have been a serious felony or might have been a misdemeanor.' " The court's holding was based on a statute which provided that a "person hospitalized for a mental illness shall be entitled to medical and psychiatric care and treatment." Some studies show that most insanity acquittees spend more time in mental hospitals than they would have spent in prison had they been convicted of the crime of which they were acquitted.

C. Infancy & Mental Retardation

Mental capacity issues can arise when a child or a mentally retarded adult commits a crime. In such cases, there will be questions about whether the individual has the criminal capacity to be held responsible for the crime. Consider the following case.

In re Devon T.

85 Md. App. 674, 584 A.2d 1287 (1991).

MOYLAN, JUDGE.

In a world dizzy with change, it is reassuring to find Daniel M'Naghten alive and well in juvenile court. It was, of course, M'Naghten's bungled attempt to assassinate Prime Minister Sir Robert Peel, killing by mistake Sir Robert's private secretary Edward Drummond, that led to his prosecution for murder and the assertion of his now eponymic insanity defense. When the House of Lords placed its imprimatur upon the jury's acquittal by reason of insanity, "the *M'Naghten* test" was impressed indelibly upon the Common Law of Anglo-America. *Regina v. M'Naghten,* 10 Cl. and Fin. 200, 8 Eng. Rep. 718 (1843). The cognitive capacity to distinguish right from wrong in the language of *M'Naghten* was not a characteristic of the insanity defense exclusively. It has traditionally been the common denominator criterion for a whole family of defenses based upon mental incapacity—insanity, infancy, mental retardation, intoxication (at least of the involuntary variety). The cause of the mental incapacity might vary from one such defense to the next but the ultimate nature of the resulting incapacity was a constant. In any of its manifestations, criminal responsibility traditionally turned and largely still turns upon the difference between a mind *doli capax* (capable of malice or criminal intent) and a mind *doli incapax* (incapable of malice or criminal intent). Capability or capacity might be eroded in various ways but the ultimate quality of the required mental capacity itself was unchanging. Hence, we tentatively use the traditional *M'Naghten* test in our review of an adjudication of juvenile delinquency. For the moment, however, let Daniel M'Naghten retire to the wings as we bring onto the stage the contemporary players.

The juvenile appellant, Devon T., was charged with committing an act which, if committed by an adult, would have constituted the crime of possession of heroin with intent to distribute. The trial court concluded that Devon was delinquent. The case arose when Devon was directed to empty his pockets by the security guard at the Booker T. Washington Middle School, under the watchful eye of the Assistant Principal, the search produced a brown bag containing twenty zip-lock pink plastic bags that contained heroin. Devon contends that the State did not offer legally sufficient evidence to rebut his presumptive incapacity because of infancy. At the time of the offense, Devon was 13 years, 10 months, and 2 weeks of age.

The case law and the academic literature alike conceptualize the infancy defense as an instance of the broader phenomenon of a defense based upon lack of moral responsibility or capacity. The criminal law generally will only impose its retributive or deterrent sanctions upon those who are morally blameworthy—those who know they are doing wrong but nonetheless persist in their wrongdoing.

After several centuries of pondering the criminal capacity of children and experimenting with various cut-off ages, the Common Law settled upon its current resolution of the problem by late Tudor and early Stuart times. As explained by LAFAVE & SCOTT, CRIMINAL LAW, (2d ed. 1986), at 398, the resolution was fairly simple: "At common law, children under the age of seven are conclusively presumed to be without criminal capacity, those who have reached the age of fourteen are treated as fully responsible, while as to those between the ages of seven and fourteen there is a rebuttable presumption of criminal incapacity." The authors make clear that infancy was an instance of criminal capacity generally: "The early common law infancy defense was based upon an unwillingness to punish those thought to be incapable of forming criminal intent and not of an age where the threat of punishment could serve as a deterrent." *See also* Walkover, *The Infancy Defense in the New Juvenile Court*, 31 UCLA L. REV. 503, 507 (1984). In *Adams v. State*, 8 Md. App. 684, 262 A.2d 69 (1970), *cert. denied*, 400 U.S. 928 (1970), we recognized for the first time this venerable common law defense as part of the inherent law of Maryland.

With the creation shortly after the turn of the present century of juvenile courts in America, diverting many youthful offenders from criminal courts into equity and other civil courts, the question arose as to whether the infancy defense had any pertinence to a juvenile delinquency adjudication. Under the initially prevailing philosophy that the State was acting in delinquency cases as *parens patriae* (sovereign parent of the country), the State was perceived to be not the retributive punisher of the child for its misdeeds but the paternalistic guardian of the child for its own best interests. Under such a regime, the moral responsibility or blameworthiness of the child was of no consequence. Morally responsible or not, the child was in apparent need of the State's rehabilitative intervention and the delinquency adjudication was but the avenue for such intervention. This was the philosophy that persuaded this Court in *Matter of Davis* to forbear from extending the defense of infancy to juvenile court proceedings.

Over the course of the century, however, buffeted by unanticipated urban deterioration and staggering case loads, the reforming vision faded. Although continuing to stress rehabilitation over retribution more heavily than did the adult criminal courts, delinquency adjudications nonetheless took on, in practice if not in theory, many of the attributes of junior varsity criminal trials. The Supreme Court, in *In re Gault*, 387 U.S. 1 (1967), and *In re Winship*, 397 U.S. 358 (1970), acknowledged this slow but inexorable transformation of the juvenile court apparatus into one with increasingly penal overtones. It ultimately guaranteed, therefore, a juvenile charged with delinquency most of the due process protections afforded an adult charged with crime. *Mullaney v. Wilbur*, 421 U.S. 684 (1975), soon made explicit what was implicit in *Winship* that among the elements of a crime that the State is constitutionally obligated to prove beyond a reasonable doubt are mental elements as well as physical elements. A crime, by definition, consists of guilty mind as well as a guilty act—the *mens rea* as well as the *actus reus*. It follows ineluctably that if the State, when the issue is properly generated, is required to prove beyond a reasonable doubt the existence of a criminally responsible *mens rea* when proceeding against an adult, it cannot be relieved of that burden when proceeding in a quasi-penal fashion against a juvenile.

In terms of the applicability of the infancy defense to delinquency proceedings, the implications of the new dispensation are clear. A finding of delinquency, unlike other proceedings in a juvenile court, unmistakably connotes some degree of blameworthiness and unmistakably exposes the delinquent to, whatever the gloss, the possibility of unpleasant sanctions. Clearly, the juvenile would have as an available defense to the delinquency charge 1) the fact that he was too criminally insane to have known that what he did was wrong, 2) that he was too mentally retarded to have known that what he did was wrong, or 3) that he was too involuntarily intoxicated through no fault of his own to have known that what he did was wrong. It would be inconceivable that he could be found blameworthy and suffer sanctions, notwithstanding precisely the same lack of understanding and absence of moral accountability, simply because the cognitive defect was caused by infancy.

The infancy defense was not applied to all juvenile court proceedings but only to delinquency adjudications, where moral blameworthiness is an integral part of the wrongdoing. Where the conduct itself of the juvenile, irrespective of moral accountability, calls for some rehabilitative intervention on the part of the State, the State may still file a petition alleging a Child in Need of Supervision (CINS) or a Child in Need of Assistance (CINA). "As these proceedings are not necessarily based on the commission of acts constituting crimes, the infancy defense obviously has no relevance to them."

In a juvenile delinquency adjudication, however, the defense of infancy is now indisputably available in precisely the same manner as it is available in a criminal trial. The availability of such a defense raises several subsidiary questions. What precisely is the *probandum*—the quality of mind that has to be proved? To whom are allocated the burdens of proof (production and persuasion) with respect to that *probandum*? What are the standards or levels of proof necessary to carry those burdens? With respect to the allocation of both burdens, the answer is clear. Once the question of criminal incapacity because of infancy is legitimately in the case, the unequivocal command of the due process clause is that the burdens of proof (assuming the proper generation of the issue) are allocated to the State. *In re Winship*, 397 U.S. 358 (1970). It is equally clear, under *Winship*, that the State's constitutionally mandated standard of persuasion is that of beyond a reasonable doubt. Those questions do not concern us here. Our attention, rather, turns to the two remaining questions: 1) what precisely is that quality of mind that constitutes criminal capacity in an infant? and 2) was the State's evidence in this case legally sufficient to satisfy its burden of production that the infant here possessed such mental capacity?

Before the juvenile master, the appellant timely raised the infancy defense. One party or the other introduced the undisputed fact that at the time of the allegedly delinquent act, Devon was 13 years, 10 months, and 2 weeks of age. Thus, the issue of mental incapacity due to infancy was properly before the court.

On that issue, Devon initially had the benefit of presumptive incapacity. The presumption having been generated, the State had the burdens (of both production and persuasion) of rebutting that presumption. Assuming that it met its burden of production, an issue we shall turn to in the next section of this opinion, the State successfully carried its burden of persuasion. The fact finder was persuaded. Since the weighing of evidence (that admissible data which may persuade one fact finder not at all or only a little bit may persuade another fact finder a lot) is the exclusive prerogative of the fact finder, there is nothing before us with respect to the burden of persuasion. To overcome the presumption of incapacity, what precisely was that quality of Devon's mind as to which the State was required to produce legally sufficient evidence? It was required to produce evidence permitting the reasonable inference that Devon—the Ghost of *M'Naghten* speaks:—"at the time of doing the act knew the difference between right and wrong."

We resort to the analogy between this particular incapacity and other incapacities as a precedential "backup" because the Maryland case law bearing directly upon this particular instance of the larger phenomenon is so scant. The first of our analogues is incapacity due to involuntary intoxication. Although as a policy matter, general mental incapacity (even when, in fact, present) may never be predicated upon *voluntary* intoxication, involuntary intoxication may give rise to a defense of mental incapacity in much the same way that insanity traditionally did. The authorities generally analyzed the intoxication (provided it was involuntary) in terms of its corrosive effect upon the cognitive ability of the mind to discriminate between right and wrong.

The second of our analogues is incapacity due to mental retardation. The Common Law always treated mental retardation as a separate category of mental incapacity, although it analogized it to both infancy and lunacy as an effective cause of the inability to know right from wrong, to distinguish between good and evil. Maryland has recently merged two of these traditionally distinguishable incapacity defenses into one, broadening its test for "insanity" or "criminal responsibility" to include as an effective cause thereof not only "mental disorder" but also "mental retardation." Health-Gen. Art., § 12–108(a) (1982, 1990 Repl. Vol).

The third and final analogue is the thoroughly litigated defense of incapacity due to criminal insanity during the approximate century and a quarter when that defense was analyzed exclusively in terms of cognitive capacity under the *M'Naghten* test.

The analogy between incapacity due to infancy and incapacity due to insanity, mental retardation, or involuntary intoxication has lost some of its original symmetry to the extent that those latter incapacities have been broadened (directly or indirectly) to include a volitional as well as a cognitive component. The infancy defense retains its exclusive concern with the cognitive element.

When *Adams v. State* first incorporated the infancy defense into Maryland law, the opinion of Judge Morton made it very clear that the pivotal mental quality being examined was *M'Naghten*'s classic cognitive appreciation of the difference between right and wrong:

> "It was, therefore, incumbent upon the State to produce sufficient evidence to overcome the presumption that the appellant was *doli incapax,* an expression ordinarily employed by the text writers. The proof necessary to meet this burden has been variously phrased: It must be shown that the individual 'had discretion to judge between good and evil;' 'knew right from wrong;' had 'a guilty knowledge of wrong-doing;' was 'competent to know the nature and consequences of his conduct and to appreciate that it was wrong.' Perhaps the most modern definition of the test is simply that the surrounding circumstances must demonstrate, beyond a reasonable doubt, that the individual knew what he was doing and that it was wrong."

In *In re William A.*, 313 Md. 690, 548 A.2d 130 (1988), Judge Eldridge perceptively stressed that the critical mental faculty for rendering an infant morally responsible for his otherwise delinquent actions was that same cognitive or intellectual capacity that would enable an adult to entertain a criminal *mens rea:* "Maryland law defines a 'delinquent act' as 'an act which would be a crime if committed by an adult.' Most crimes require some *mens rea* characteristics; they are elements of the crimes. If, when one commits an act, the requisite *mens rea* for a crime does not exist, the act does not constitute a crime. The defense of infancy relates to the presence or absence of the *mens rea.* Consequently, the infancy defense relates to whether the act committed by a juvenile 'would be a crime if committed by an adult.' " In short, when Devon walked around the Booker T. Washington Middle School with twenty zip-lock bags of heroin, apparently for sale or other distribution, could Devon pass the *M'Naghten* test? Was there legally sufficient data before him to permit Judge Brown to infer that Devon knew the difference between right and wrong and knew, moreover, that what he was doing was wrong?

As we turn to the legal sufficiency of the evidence, it is important to know that the only mental quality we are probing is the cognitive capacity to distinguish right from wrong. Other aspects of Devon's mental and psychological make-up, such as his scholastic attainments, his I.Q., his social maturity, his societal adjustment, his basic personality, etc., might well require evidentiary input from psychologists, from parents, from teachers or other school authorities, etc. On knowledge of the difference between right and wrong, however, the general case law, as well as the inherent logic of the situation, has established that that particular psychic phenomenon may sometimes permissibly be inferred from the very circumstances of the criminal or delinquent act itself. Indeed, *Adams v. State* spoke of the fact that "the surrounding circumstances must demonstrate that the individual knew what he was doing and that it was wrong."

Before looking at the circumstances of the delinquent act in this case, a word is in order about the quantity of proof required. *In re William A.* quotes with approval from *Adams v. State*, 8 Md. App. at 688–689, 262 A.2d 69, in pointing out: "It is generally held that the presumption of *doli incapax* is 'extremely strong at the age of seven and diminishes gradually until it disappears entirely at the age of fourteen. ' Since the strength of the presumption of incapacity decreases with the increase in the years of the accused, the quantum of proof necessary to overcome the presumption would diminish in substantially the same ratio." *See also* R. BOYCE & R. PERKINS, CRIMINAL LAW, (3d ed. 1983), at 936.

That kind of a sliding standard of proof or inverse proportion is relatively rare in law. Because the weighing of evidence is in the *unfettered* discretion of the fact finder, that sliding standard of proof cannot, as a matter of pure logic, affect the literal issue of the legal sufficiency of the evidence, that is, the burden of production. It speaks volumes, however, about the burden of persuasion. It thereby casts at least reflected light on the issue before us, as it communicates a strong sense of precisely what it is that is being adjudicated. Some analysis may be helpful as to how a presumption "diminishes gradually until it disappears entirely," as to how "incapacity decreases" as age increases, and as to how "the quantum of proof diminishes in substantially the same ratio."

On the issue of Devon's knowledge of the difference between right and wrong, if all we knew were that Devon's age was at some indeterminate point between his seventh birthday and his fourteenth birthday, the State's case would be substantially weaker than it is now. The evidence before Judge Brown that Devon, at the time of the allegedly delinquent act, was 13 years, 10 months, and 2 weeks of age was substantial, although not quite sufficient, proof of his cognitive capacity.

The applicable common law on *doli incapax* with relation to the infancy defense establishes that on the day before their seventh birthday, no persons possess cognitive capacity. (0 per cent). It also establishes that on the day of their fourteenth birthday, all persons (at least as far as age is concerned) possess cognitive capacity. (100 per cent). On the time scale between the day of the seventh birthday and the day before the fourteenth birthday, the percentage of persons possessing such capacity steadily increases. The statistical probability is that on the day of the seventh birthday, at most a tiny fraction of one per cent will possess cognitive capacity. Conversely, on the day before the fourteenth birthday, only a tiny fraction of one per cent will lack such cognitive capacity. Assuming a steady rate of climb, the mid-point where fifty per cent of persons will lack cognitive capacity and fifty per cent will possess it would be at 10 years and 6 months of age. That is the scale on which we must place Devon.

We stress that the burden in that regard, notwithstanding the probabilities, was nonetheless on the State. The impact of the allocation of the burden of proof to the State is that the infant will enjoy the benefit of the doubt. The fact that the quantum of proof necessary to overcome presumptive incapacity diminishes in substantially the same ratio as the infant's age increases only serves to lessen the State's burden, not to eliminate it. The State's burden is still an affirmative one. It may not, therefore, passively rely upon the mere absence of evidence to the contrary.

We hold that the State successfully carried that burden. A minor factor, albeit of some weight, was that Devon was essentially at or near grade level in school. At the time of the offense, Devon was in middle school, embracing grades 6, 7, and 8. Devon had flunked the sixth grade twice, with truancy and lack of motivation as apparent causes. That fact nonetheless revealed that Devon had initially reached the sixth grade while still eleven years of age. That would tend to support his probable inclusion in the large majority of his age group rather than in a small and subnormal minority of it. The juvenile master was in a position to observe first-hand Devon's receiving of legal advice from his lawyer, his acknowledgment of his understanding of it, and his acting upon it. His lawyer explained that he had a right to remain silent and that the master would not infer guilt from his exercise of that right. He acknowledged understanding that right. His lawyer also advised him of his right to testify but informed him that both the assistant state's attorney and the judge might question him about the delinquent act. Devon indicated that he wished to remain silent and say nothing. Although reduced to relatively simple language, the exchange with respect to the risk of self-incrimination and the privilege against self-incrimination forms a predicate from which an observer might infer some knowledge on Devon's part of the significance of incrimination. The exchange, moreover, might have significance in two distinct evidentiary regards. It suggests that Devon's lawyer, who presumably had significant opportunity to talk to him before the hearing, concluded that

Devon understood the significance of criminality and incrimination. Under the classic case in all of the evidence textbooks of *Wright v. Tatham*, 5 Cl. & Fin. 670 (1838), this belief on the part of a close observer is relevant evidence for the proposition that the thing believed is true.

The significance of the colloquy in this case is far more direct. Here, the master was in a position to observe Devon closely throughout the exchange. It does require us to extrapolate that Devon's mental capacity on the day of the hearing, July 20, reflected his mental capacity two months earlier on May 25. That precise situation was before the Court in *Adams v. State*. The appellant Adams there was 13 years, 9 months, and 2 weeks old at the time of the alleged murder; one month younger than Devon here at the time of his alleged delinquency. Adams there, as Devon here, "did not testify in his own defense at the guilt or innocence stage of the trial." Adams nonetheless received legal advice from his lawyer under the watchful eye of the judge. We found that fact very significant in holding that the evidence there was legally sufficient to overcome the presumption of incapacity due to infancy.

8 Md.App. at 689, 262 A.2d 69. The transcript revealed a further exchange between the juvenile master and Devon, also not without significance. After Devon and his companion Edward had already been adjudicated delinquent and when no further risk of incrimination inhered, the master asked each of the two what, if anything, he would like to say and was met by "stonewalling." This inferable allegiance to the Underworld's "Code of Silence" suggests that Devon and Edward were no mere babies caught up in a web they did not comprehend. The permitted inference, rather, was that they were fully conscious of the ongoing war between lawful authority and those who flout it and had deliberately chosen to adhere to the latter camp.

We turn, most significantly, to the circumstances of the criminal act itself. We note the relevance of such circumstances to the issue at hand. R. PERKINS & R. BOYCE, CRIMINAL LAW, (3d ed. 1982), points out, at 938: "The prosecution, in brief, cannot obtain the conviction of such a person without showing that he had such maturity in fact as to have a guilty knowledge that he was doing wrong. Conduct of the defendant such as concealing himself or the evidence of his misdeed may be such under all the circumstances as to authorize a finding of such maturity." Just such a use of a secluded location or concealment was present in this case. The case broke when a grandmother, concerned enough to have had her own live-in grandson institutionalized, complained to the authorities at Booker T. Washington Middle School that several of her grandson's classmates were being truant on a regular basis and were using her home, while she was out working, as the "hide out" from which to sell drugs. Although the initial suspicion was directed toward Edward, it ultimately appeared that Edward and Devon were in the enterprise together. Children who are unaware that what they are doing is wrong have no need to hide out or to conceal their activities.

The most significant circumstance was the very nature of the criminal activity in which Devon engaged. It was not mere possession of heroin. It was possession of twenty packets of heroin with the intent to distribute. There were no needle marks or other indications of personal use on Devon's body. There is no evidence suggesting that this sixth grader, directly or indirectly, had the affluence to purchase drugs for himself in that amount. Indeed, he acknowledged that he had been selling drugs for two days when the current offense occurred. His motivation was "that he just wanted something to do."

The evidence indicated that Devon and Edward and several other students had been regularly using the absent grandmother's home as a base of operations for selling drugs. Devon and his companions were not innocent children unaware of the difference between games and crimes but "street wise" young delinquents knowingly involved in illicit activities. Realistically, one cannot engage in the business of selling drugs without some knowledge as to sources of supply, some pattern for receiving and passing on the money, some network of potential customers, and some *modus operandi* to avoid the eye of the police and of school authorities. It is almost inconceivable that such a crime could be engaged in without the drug pusher's being aware that it was against the law. That is, by definition, criminal capacity.

We hold that the surrounding circumstances here were legally sufficient to overcome the slight residual weight of the presumption of incapacity due to infancy.

Judgment affirmed; costs to be paid by appellant.

Executive Summary

Justification Versus Excuse. Like justification defenses, excuses are general defenses applicable to all offenses and available even though the person's conduct satisfies the elements of an offense. However, excuse defenses focus on the person's lack of subjective blameworthiness. Even though an act may cause or threaten a harm the criminal law normally would punish, an excuse defense applies when a person's characteristics or situation suggest that he or she does not merit criminal liability.

Defense of Duress. The defense of duress arises when an individual is faced with a threat of death or serious bodily injury, and chooses to commit a crime rather than suffer the threatened consequences. *See United States v. Contento-Pachon*, 723 F.2d 691 (9th Cir. 1984). In general, the individual must have a reasonable belief that the threat is serious, and there must be no reasonable means of escape. Duress is usually not a defense to

Major Themes

a. Duress—The duress defense recognizes the non-blameworthy character of a person's criminal act when that act is coerced by a threat of immediate serious bodily harm. The common law requires that an immediate and inescapable threat, typically of serious bodily harm, must have provided the source of the duress that led to the commission of the crime.

b. Insanity—Many states define legal insanity as a condition that exists when, because of a mental disease or defect, a person lacks the capacity to know that his conduct was wrong. Ever since the *M'Naghten* decision in 1847, there has been judicial and legislative debate over the question whether additional definitions of insanity are needed. Today a large minority of states define insanity to include a person who lacks the capacity to conform his or her conduct to the requirements of the law. An even larger minority of states make the defense available to a person who does not know the nature and quality of his or her conduct.

c. Infancy—Infancy can also be a defense to criminal conduct. Some courts apply the *M'Naghten* rule to determine whether a minor has sufficient mental capacity to be criminally responsible.

an intentional murder. However, the Model Penal Code permits the defense in any situation when an individual is faced with threat "which a person of reasonable firmness in his situation would have been unable to resist."

Insanity. There is little justification for punishing those who commit crimes while insane. As the court stated in *United States v. Freeman*, 357 F.2d 606, 615 (2d Cir. 1966): "Those who are substantially unable to restrain their conduct are, by definition, undeterrable and their 'punishment' is no example for others; those who are unaware of or do not appreciate the nature and quality of their actions can hardly be expected rationally to weigh the consequences of their conduct. Finally, what segment of society can feel its desire for retribution satisfied when it wreaks vengeance upon the incompetent? Although an understandable emotion, a need for retribution can never be permitted in a civilized society to degenerate into a sadistic form of revenge."

Test for Insanity. Although there is general agreement that the insane should not be held criminally responsible for their conduct, few agree about how to define insanity. For many years, U.S. courts applied the insanity test articulated by the English House of Lords in the nineteenth century in *M'Naghten's Case*. Because of dissatisfaction with the *M'Naghten* and irresistible impulse tests, the courts and the American Law Institute developed alternative tests. In *United States v. Freeman*, 357 F.2d 606 (2d Cir. 1966), the court applied a test focusing on whether the unlawful act "was the product of mental disease or mental defect." Section 4.01 of the Model Penal Code provides that "A person is not responsible for criminal conduct if at the time of such conduct as a result of mental disease or defect he lacks substantial capacity either to appreciate the wrongfulness of his conduct or to conform his conduct to the requirements of law."

Insanity and the Criminal Process. Insanity can be relevant at three different points in the criminal process. First, as in *M'Naghten*, individuals who commit criminal acts while insane cannot be convicted of those acts. Second, defendants who are insane at the time of their trials cannot be tried, and will be committed until they are sane enough to proceed: defendant must "have sufficient present ability to consult with his lawyer with a reasonable degree of rational understanding—and have a rational as well as factual understanding of the proceedings against him." *Dusky v. United States*, 362 U.S. 402 (1960). Finally, defendants sentenced to capital punishment cannot be executed until they regain their sanity. *See Ford v. Wainwright*, 477 U.S. 399 (1986).

Infancy and Capacity. The question, in some cases, is whether the age of a juvenile affects his capacity to commit a crime. At one point, the law relied on age-based assumptions regarding capacity. Later decisions applied the *M'Naghten* test. Some modern decisions rely on circumstantial factors which suggest that the defendant does, or does not, have capacity.

For More Information

- AMERICAN LAW INSTITUTE, MODEL PENAL CODE AND COMMENTARIES, Part I, § 2.09, Comments at 367–385; Part II, §§ 4.01–4.12, Comments at 163–282 (1980).
- JOHN M. BURKOFF & RUSSELL L. WEAVER, INSIDE CRIMINAL LAW: WHAT MATTERS AND WHY 225–238 (2d ed. 2011).
- LINCOLN CAPLAN, THE INSANITY DEFENSE AND THE TRIAL OF JOHN W. HINCKLEY, JR. (1984).
- WAYNE R. LAFAVE, CRIMINAL LAW §§ 8.1–8.4, 9.6–9.7 (7th ed. 2017).

Test Your Knowledge

To assess your understanding of the material in this chapter, click here to take a quiz.

Chapter 14

Sentencing

Every jurisdiction has its own sentencing provisions and its own sentencing procedures. As with the issues of whether and how to criminalize any particular conduct, the legislature in each jurisdiction has the power and the discretion essentially to enact whatever punishments for whatever criminal conduct it desires. In general, it can be said that crimes designated as felonies are more heinous and punished more severely—both in potential incarceration periods and/or fines—than those denominated misdemeanors. But even that basic rule of thumb is not always true. Again, what to punish and how much to punish it are decisions for the legislature, and there is a great deal of variation between different jurisdictions.

That said, however, there are some very limited but very important constitutional limits on this power, involving the Sixth and Eighth Amendments. Those limitations are the subject of this chapter.

> **FYI**
>
> The Sixth and Eighth Amendments to the United States Constitution (part of the Bill of Rights) provide as follows:
>
> Amendment VI
>
> In all criminal prosecutions, the accused shall enjoy the right to a speedy and public trial, by an impartial jury of the state and district wherein the crime shall have been committed, which district shall have been previously ascertained by law, and to be informed of the nature and cause of the accusation; to be confronted with the witnesses against him; to have compulsory process for obtaining witnesses in his favor, and to have the assistance of counsel for his defense.
>
> Amendment VIII
>
> Excessive bail shall not be required, nor excessive fines imposed, nor cruel and unusual punishments inflicted.

A. Judge vs. Jury

In recent years, the Supreme Court, interpreting the Sixth Amendment, has made it clear that sentencing judges may not engage in fact-finding relevant to an increase in sentencing where that is the province of the jury. When precisely is that the province of the jury? *Booker* is the leading case on that point.

United States v. Booker

543 U.S. 220 (2005).

JUSTICE STEVENS delivered the opinion of the Court in part.*

Hear It

You can listen to the oral argument in this case at http://www.oyez.org/cases/2000-2009/2004/2004_04_104/.

The question presented in each of these cases is whether an application of the Federal Sentencing Guidelines violated the Sixth Amendment. In each case, the courts below held that binding rules set forth in the Guidelines limited the severity of the sentence that the judge could lawfully impose on the defendant based on the facts found by the jury at his trial. We hold that both courts correctly concluded that the Sixth Amendment does apply to the Sentencing Guidelines. In a separate opinion authored by Justice BREYER, the Court concludes that in light of this holding, two provisions of the Sentencing Reform Act of 1984 (SRA) that have the effect of making the Guidelines mandatory must be invalidated in order to allow the statute to operate in a manner consistent with congressional intent.

Respondent Booker was charged with possession with intent to distribute at least 50 grams of cocaine base (crack). Having heard evidence that he had 92.5 grams in his duffel bag, the jury found him guilty of violating 21 U.S.C. § 841(a)(1). That statute prescribes a minimum sentence of 10 years in prison and a maximum sentence of life for that offense. § 841(b)(1)(A)(iii).

Based upon Booker's criminal history and the quantity of drugs found by the jury, the Sentencing Guidelines required the District Court Judge to select a "base" sentence of not less than 210 nor more than 262 months in prison. The judge, however, held a post-trial sentencing proceeding and concluded by a preponderance of the evidence that Booker had possessed an additional 566 grams of crack and that he was guilty of obstructing justice. Those findings mandated that the judge select a sentence between 360 months and life imprisonment; the judge imposed a sentence at the low end of the range. Thus, instead of the sentence of 21 years and 10 months that the judge could have imposed on the basis of the facts proved to the jury beyond a reasonable doubt, Booker received a 30-year sentence.

Respondent Fanfan was charged with conspiracy to distribute and to possess with intent to distribute at least 500 grams of cocaine in violation of 21 U.S.C. §§ 846, 841(a)(1), and 841(b)(1)(B)(ii). He was convicted by the jury after it answered "Yes" to the question "Was the amount of cocaine 500 or more grams?" Under the Guidelines, without additional findings of fact, the maximum sentence authorized by the jury verdict was imprisonment for 78 months. The trial judge conducted a sentencing hearing at which he found additional facts that, under the Guidelines, would have authorized a sentence in the 188-to-235-month range. Specifically, he found that respondent Fanfan was responsible for 2.5 kilograms of cocaine powder, and

---

* JUSTICE SCALIA, JUSTICE SOUTER, JUSTICE THOMAS, and JUSTICE GINSBURG join this opinion.

261.6 grams of crack. He also concluded that respondent had been an organizer, leader, manager, or supervisor in the criminal activity. Both findings were made by a preponderance of the evidence. Under the Guidelines, these additional findings would have required an enhanced sentence of 15 or 16 years instead of the 5 or 6 years authorized by the jury verdict alone. The judge followed the provisions of the Guidelines that did not implicate the Sixth Amendment by imposing a sentence on respondent based solely upon the jury verdict in this case.

It has been settled throughout our history that the Constitution protects every criminal defendant "against conviction except upon proof beyond a reasonable doubt of every fact necessary to constitute the crime with which he is charged." *In re Winship*, 397 U.S. 358, 364, 90 S.Ct. 1068, 25 L.Ed.2d 368 (1970). It is equally clear that the Constitution gives a criminal defendant the right to demand that a jury find him guilty of all the elements of the crime with which he is charged. These basic precepts, firmly rooted in the common law, have provided the basis for recent decisions interpreting modern criminal statutes and sentencing procedures.

Take Note

This is an important point, namely that the prosecution has the burden of proving every element of a charged criminal offense beyond a reasonable doubt.

In *Apprendi v. New Jersey*, 530 U.S. 466, 120 S.Ct. 2348, 147 L.Ed.2d 435 (2000), the defendant pleaded guilty to second-degree possession of a firearm for an unlawful purpose, which carried a prison term of 5-to-10 years. Thereafter, the trial court found that his conduct had violated New Jersey's "hate crime" law because it was racially motivated, and imposed a 12-year sentence. This Court set aside the enhanced sentence. We held: "Other than the fact of a prior conviction, any fact that increases the penalty for a crime beyond the prescribed statutory maximum must be submitted to a jury, and proved beyond a reasonable doubt."

The fact that New Jersey labeled the hate crime a "sentence enhancement" rather than a separate criminal act was irrelevant for constitutional purposes. As a matter of simple justice, it seemed obvious that the procedural safeguards designed to protect Apprendi from punishment for the possession of a firearm should apply equally to his violation of the hate crime statute. Merely using the label "sentence enhancement" to describe the latter did not provide a principled basis for treating the two crimes differently.

In *Blakely v. Washington*, 542 U.S. 296, 124 S.Ct. 2531, 159 L.Ed.2d 403 (2004), we dealt with a determinate sentencing scheme similar to the Federal Sentencing Guidelines. There the defendant pleaded guilty to kidnaping, a class B felony punishable by a term of not more than 10 years. Other provisions of Washington law, comparable to the Federal Sentencing Guidelines, mandated a "standard" sentence of 49-to-53 months, unless the judge found aggravating facts justifying an exceptional sentence. Although the prosecutor recommended a sentence in the standard range, the judge found that the defendant had acted with "deliberate cruelty" and sentenced him to 90 months.

The requirements of the Sixth Amendment were clear. The application of Washington's sentencing scheme violated the defendant's right to have the jury find the existence of "any particular fact" that the law makes essential to his punishment. That right is implicated whenever a judge seeks to impose a sentence that is not solely based on facts reflected in the jury verdict or admitted by the defendant. We rejected the State's argument that the jury verdict was sufficient to authorize a sentence within the general 10-year sentence for class B felonies, noting that under Washington law, the judge was required to find additional facts in order to impose the greater 90-month sentence. Our precedents, we explained, make clear that the "statutory maximum" for *Apprendi* purposes is the maximum sentence a judge may impose solely on the basis of the facts reflected in the jury verdict or admitted by the defendant. The determination that the defendant acted with deliberate cruelty, like the determination in *Apprendi* that the defendant acted with racial malice, increased the sentence that the defendant could have otherwise received. Since this fact was found by a judge using a preponderance of the evidence standard, the sentence violated Blakely's Sixth Amendment rights.

As the dissenting opinions in *Blakely* recognized, there is no distinction of constitutional significance between the Federal Sentencing Guidelines and the Washington procedures at issue in that case. This conclusion rests on the premise, common to both systems, that the relevant sentencing rules are mandatory and impose binding requirements on all sentencing judges.

If the Guidelines as currently written could be read as merely advisory provisions that recommended, rather than required, the selection of particular sentences in response to differing sets of facts, their use would not implicate the Sixth Amendment. We have never doubted the authority of a judge to exercise broad discretion in imposing a sentence within a statutory range. Indeed, everyone agrees that the constitutional issues presented by these cases would have been avoided entirely if Congress had omitted from the SRA the provisions that make the Guidelines binding on district judges. For when a trial judge exercises his discretion to select a specific sentence within a defined range, the defendant has no right to a jury determination of the facts that the judge deems relevant.

The Guidelines as written, however, are not advisory; they are mandatory and binding on all judges. The availability of a departure in specified circumstances does not avoid the constitutional issue, just as it did not in *Blakely* itself. The Guidelines permit departures from the prescribed sentencing range in cases in which the judge "finds that there exists an aggravating or mitigating circumstance of a kind, or to a degree, not adequately taken into consideration by the Sentencing Commission in formulating the guidelines that should result in a sentence different from that described." At first glance, one might believe that the ability of a district judge to depart from the Guidelines means that she is bound only by the statutory maximum. Were this the case, there would be no *Apprendi* problem. Importantly, however, departures are not available in every case, and in fact are unavailable in most. In most cases, as a matter of law, the Commission will have adequately taken all relevant factors into account, and no departure will be legally permissible. In those instances, the judge is bound to impose a sentence within the Guidelines range. It was for this reason that we rejected a similar argument in *Blakely*, holding that although the Washington statute allowed the judge to impose a sentence outside the sentencing range for "substantial and compelling reasons," that exception was not available for Blakely himself. The sentencing judge would have been reversed had he invoked the departure section to justify the sentence.

Booker's case illustrates the mandatory nature of the Guidelines. The jury convicted him of possessing at least 50 grams of crack in violation of 21 U.S.C. § 841(b)(1)(A)(iii) based on evidence that he had 92.5 grams of crack in his duffel bag. Under these facts, the Guidelines specified an offense level of 32, which, given the defendant's criminal history category, authorized a sentence of 210-to-262 months. Booker's is a run-of-the-mill drug case, and does not present any factors that were inadequately considered by the Commission. The sentencing judge would therefore have been reversed had he not imposed a sentence within the level 32 Guidelines range.

Booker's actual sentence, however, was 360 months, almost 10 years longer than the Guidelines range supported by the jury verdict alone. To reach this sentence, the judge found facts beyond those found by the jury: namely, that Booker possessed 566 grams of crack in addition to the 92.5 grams in his duffel bag. The jury never heard any evidence of the additional drug quantity, and the judge found it true by a preponderance of the evidence. Thus, just as in *Blakely*, "the jury's verdict alone does not authorize the sentence. The judge acquires that authority only upon finding some additional fact." There is no relevant distinction between the sentence imposed pursuant to the Washington statutes in *Blakely* and the sentences imposed pursuant to the Federal Sentencing Guidelines in these cases.

Traditional judicial authority [existed] to increase sentences to take account of any unusual blameworthiness in the manner employed in committing a crime, an authority that the Guidelines require to be exercised consistently throughout the system. This tradition, however, does not provide a sound guide to enforcement of the Sixth Amendment's guarantee of a jury trial in today's world.

Food for Thought

Why not? Why not simply let sentencing judges do what they traditionally did, i.e. use their discretion in sentencing to tailor a sentence to the particular defendant's situation and the circumstances of the case?

It is quite true that once determinate sentencing had fallen from favor, American judges commonly determined facts justifying a choice of a heavier sentence on account of the manner in which particular defendants acted. The effect of the increasing emphasis on facts that enhanced sentencing ranges, however, was to increase the judge's power and diminish that of the jury. It became the judge, not the jury, who determined the upper limits of sentencing, and the facts determined were not required to be raised before trial or proved by more than a preponderance.

As the enhancements became greater, the jury's finding of the underlying crime became less significant. And the enhancements became very serious indeed.

As it thus became clear that sentencing was no longer taking place in this tradition, the Court was faced with the issue of preserving an ancient guarantee under a new set of circumstances. The new sentencing practice forced the Court to address the question how the right of jury trial could be preserved, in a meaningful way guaranteeing that the jury would still stand between the individual and the power of the government under the new sentencing regime. And it is the new circumstances, not a tradition or practice that the new circumstances have superseded, that have led us to the answer developed in *Apprendi* and subsequent cases culminating with this one. It is an answer not motivated by Sixth Amendment formalism, but by the need to preserve Sixth Amendment substance.

Take Note

Note this consequence of the legislative trend to adopt determinate sentencing schemes. This is typically viewed as a move designed to alleviate the disparity in sentences in indeterminate sentencing regimes. Do you think that reducing the power of juries was also part of the legislative intent? Or was it unintended?

All of the foregoing supports our conclusion that our holding in *Blakely* applies to the Sentencing Guidelines. We recognize, as we did in *Apprendi*, and *Blakely*, that in some cases jury factfinding may impair the most expedient and efficient sentencing of defendants. But the interest in fairness and reliability protected by the right to a jury trial-a common-law right that defendants enjoyed for centuries and that is now enshrined in the Sixth Amendment-has always outweighed the interest in concluding trials swiftly. As Blackstone put it:

> "However convenient these new methods of trial may appear at first, (as doubtless all arbitrary powers, well executed, are the most convenient) yet let it be again remembered, that delays, and little inconveniences in the forms of justice, are the price that all free nations must pay for their liberty in more substantial matters; that these inroads upon this sacred bulwark of the nation are fundamentally opposite to the spirit of our constitution; and that, though begun in trifles, the precedent may gradually increase and spread, to the utter disuse of juries in questions of the most momentous concerns."

Accordingly, we reaffirm our holding in *Apprendi*: Any fact (other than a prior conviction) which is necessary to support a sentence exceeding the maximum authorized by the facts established by a plea of guilty or a jury verdict must be admitted by the defendant or proved to a jury beyond a reasonable doubt.

JUSTICE BREYER delivered the opinion of the Court in part.*

We answer the question of remedy by finding the provision of the federal sentencing statute that makes the Guidelines mandatory incompatible with today's constitutional holding. We conclude that this provision must be severed and excised, as must one other statutory section which depends upon the Guidelines' mandatory nature. So modified, the federal sentencing statute makes the Guidelines effectively advisory. It requires a sentencing court to

---

* THE CHIEF JUSTICE, JUSTICE O'CONNOR, JUSTICE KENNEDY, and JUSTICE GINSBURG join this opinion.

consider Guidelines ranges, but it permits the court to tailor the sentence in light of other statutory concerns as well.

Ours, of course, is not the last word: The ball now lies in Congress' court. The National Legislature is equipped to devise and install, long term, the sentencing system, compatible with the Constitution, that Congress judges best for the federal system of justice.

Food for Thought

Why are there two different opinions of the Court?

Points for Discussion

a. Guilty Pleas

Note that when the Booker Court, in the Stevens majority opinion, concluded that "any fact (other than a prior conviction) which is necessary to support a sentence exceeding the maximum authorized by the facts established by a plea of guilty or a jury verdict *must be admitted by the defendant* or proved to a jury beyond a reasonable doubt" (emphasis added), it anticipated that when a criminal defendant pleaded guilty—often as a result of a plea bargain—he or she would also have to admit every fact leading to a sentence above the statutory maximum in a guilty plea colloquy. Why would a defendant ever do that?

b. "Sentencing Factors"

The Court in *Booker* made it clear that trial judges continue to retain discretion to consider traditional sentencing factors in determining an appropriate sentence. But what is a "sentencing factor" and what is, instead, an element of the crime (whether explicitly or implicitly)?

The Supreme Court was faced with this very question in *United States v. O'Brien*, 560 U.S. 218, 130 S.Ct. 2169, 176 L.Ed.2d 979 (2010). In *O'Brien*, the Court had to interpret 18 U.S.C. § 924(c), which prohibits the use or carrying of a firearm in relation to a crime of violence or drug trafficking crime, or the possession of a firearm in furtherance of such crimes. A violation of that statute carries a mandatory minimum term of five years' imprisonment, but if the firearm is a "machinegun," the statute requires a 30-year mandatory minimum sentence. Whether a firearm was used, carried, or possessed was, the Government and the defendant conceded, an element of the crime. What was at issue was the question whether the fact that the firearm was a machinegun was an element to be proved to the jury beyond a reasonable doubt or a sentencing factor to be proved to the judge at sentencing.

The Court first elucidated the legal backdrop for resolution of this question as follows:

> Elements of a crime must be charged in an indictment and proved to a jury beyond a reasonable doubt. Sentencing factors, on the other hand, can be proved to a judge at sentencing by a preponderance of the evidence. But it is unconstitutional for a legislature to remove from the jury the assessment of facts that increase the pre-

scribed range of penalties to which a criminal defendant is exposed. In other words, while sentencing factors may guide or confine a judge's discretion in sentencing an offender "within the range prescribed by statute," judge-found sentencing factors cannot increase the maximum sentence a defendant might otherwise receive based purely on the facts found by the jury.

The *O'Brien* Court then assessed the applicable Congressional intent by looking in detail at five factors: (1) the language and structure of the statute; (2) tradition; (3) the risk of unfairness; (4) the severity of the sentence; and (5) the legislative history. After this review, the Court concluded that whether a firearm was a machinegun or not is an element of the crime, not a sentencing factor.

What does that holding mean for a U.S. Attorney's office today that wants to prosecute someone under 18 U.S.C. § 924(c)?

Hypo: *Exposing* Booker*'s Meaning*

Pennsylvania's indecent exposure statute, 18 Pa.C.S. § 3127, provides as follows:

(a) Offense defined.—A person commits indecent exposure if that person exposes his or her genitals in any public place or in any place where there are present other persons under circumstances in which he or she knows or should know that this conduct is likely to offend, affront or alarm.

(b) Grading.—If the person knows or should have known that any of the persons present are less than 16 years of age, indecent exposure under subsection (a) is a misdemeanor of the first degree. Otherwise, indecent exposure under subsection (a) is a misdemeanor of the second degree.

After *Booker*, can a judge make the finding at sentencing under § 3127(b) that the conduct occurred where "any of the persons present" were less than 16 years old? Or must the jury make that finding at the guilt phase in order to make the offense a misdemeanor of the first degree?

c. Fines

The Supreme Court has made it clear that the *Booker* analysis also applies to sentences of fines, as well as incarceration:

> The "core concern" is to reserve to the jury "the determination of facts that warrant punishment for a specific statutory offense." That concern applies whether the sentence is a criminal fine or imprisonment or death. Criminal fines, like these other forms of punishment, are penalties inflicted by the sovereign for the commission of offenses. Fines were by far the most common form of noncapital

> punishment in colonial America. They are frequently imposed today, especially upon organizational defendants who cannot be imprisoned. And the amount of a fine, like the maximum term of imprisonment or eligibility for the death penalty, is often calculated by reference to particular facts. Sometimes, as here, the fact is the duration of a statutory violation; under other statutes it is the amount of the defendant's gain or the victim's loss, or some other factor. In all such cases, requiring juries to find beyond a reasonable doubt facts that determine the fine's maximum amount is necessary to implement the "animating principle" that the preservation of the jury's historic role as a bulwark between the State and the accused at the trial for an alleged offense.

Southern Union Co. v. U.S., 567 U.S. 343, 349, 132 S. Ct. 2344, 2350–51, 183 L.Ed.2d 318 (2012).

d. Resentencing

The Federal Sentencing Guidelines also contained a provision prohibiting a federal district court, after a sentence had been reversed on appeal and remanded to the court for resentencing, from imposing a sentence outside the Guidelines range except upon a ground it had relied upon at the prior sentencing. This provision effectively precluded a sentencing judge from considering post-sentencing rehabilitation for purposes of imposing a non-Guidelines sentence. The Supreme Court subsequently ruled that provision unconstitutional under *Booker*, holding instead that "when a defendant's sentence has been set aside on appeal, a district court at resentencing may consider evidence of the defendant's post-sentencing rehabilitation and that such evidence may, in appropriate cases, support a downward variance from the now-advisory Federal Sentencing Guidelines range." *Pepper v. U.S.*, 562 U.S. 476, 481, 131 S. Ct. 1229, 1236, 179 L.Ed.2d 196 (2011).

e. Mandatory Minimum Sentences

The Supreme Court has ruled that "facts that increase a mandatory minimum sentence are elements and must be submitted to the jury and found beyond a reasonable doubt," overruling its earlier decision directly to the contrary. *Alleyne v. United States*, 570 U.S. 99, 133 S.Ct. 2151, 186 L.Ed.2d 314 (2013). In *Alleyne*, the sentencing range supported by the jury's verdict was five years' imprisonment to life. The sentencing court, however, imposed a 7-year mandatory minimum sentence based on its finding by a preponderance of evidence that the firearm used in the commission of the crime was "brandished." Because the finding of brandishing increased the penalty to which the defendant was subjected, it was held to be an element of the crime which had to be found by the jury beyond a reasonable doubt. Since the judge, rather than the jury, found brandishing, the defendant's Sixth Amendment rights were violated.

f. Aggravating Circumstances for Death Penalty

The Supreme Court has made clear that an advisory jury's *recommendation* to a sentencing judge that aggravating circumstances exist supporting imposition of the death penalty does not comport with the Sixth Amendment where the court still had to independently find and weigh the aggravating and mitigating circumstances before entering a sentence of life or death:

"The maximum punishment Timothy Hurst could have received without any judge-made findings was life in prison without parole. A judge increased Hurst's authorized punishment based on her own factfinding. We hold that Hurst's sentence violates the Sixth Amendment." *Hurst v. Florida*, 577 U.S. 92, 136 S.Ct. 616, 193 L.Ed.2d 504 (2016). However, the Supreme Court subsequently ruled, in a 5-to-4 decision, that where appropriate and permitted by state law, state appellate courts could reweigh aggravating and mitigating circumstances to affirm a prisoner's death sentence without violating the Sixth Amendment. *McKinney v. Arizona*, 140 S.Ct. 702, 206 L.Ed.2d 69 (2020).

g. Unanimous Juries

The Supreme Court has recently held that in all convictions in state and federal jury trials, the Sixth Amendment (through the Fourteenth Amendment in the case of state trials) requires jury unanimity. *Ramos v. Louisiana*, 140 S.Ct. 1390, 1395 (2020) ("A jury must reach a unanimous verdict in order to convict.").

B. Capital Punishment

In 2008, the Supreme Court found that "[t]hirty-seven jurisdictions—36 States plus the Federal Government—have the death penalty." *Kennedy v. Louisiana*, 554 U.S. 407, 128 S.Ct. 2641, 2653, 171 L.Ed.2d 525 (2008). Since 2008, five more states have abolished the death penalty: Maryland (2013); Connecticut (2012 & 2016); Illinois (2011); New Mexico (2009), and Washington (2018). (The Nebraska Legislature also abolished capital punishment in 2015, but it was reinstated by a statewide vote in 2016.)

FYI

It has been reported that, as of May 19, 2020, 1,518 convicted criminal defendants have been executed in the United States. The names, year of execution, race, age at death, gender, state of execution, race of victim, and other information relating to each of them can be found at: http://www.deathpenaltyinfo.org/executions.

The constitutionality of capital punishment was established in *Gregg v. Georgia*, 428 U.S. 153, 96 S.Ct. 2909, 49 L.Ed.2d 859 (1976). Justices Stewart, Powell, and Stevens concluded that it is not necessarily wrong for a legislature to conclude that the death penalty "serve[s] two principal social purposes: retribution and deterrence of capital crimes by prospective offenders." *Id.* at 182, 96 S.Ct. at 2929. Justice White, Chief Justice Burger, Justice Rehnquist, and Justice Blackmun concurred.

Food for Thought

Do you agree with the reasonableness of the penological justifications for capital punishment endorsed in *Gregg*: retribution and deterrence? As you read the decisional law on proportionality in the next section of this Chapter, you might ask yourself how and whether the recent decisions in that area of the law square with the *Gregg* plurality's reasoning from more than three decades ago.

California v. Brown

479 U.S. 538 (1987).

CHIEF JUSTICE REHNQUIST delivered the opinion of the Court.

The question presented for review in this case is whether an instruction informing jurors that they "must not be swayed by mere sentiment, conjecture, sympathy, passion, prejudice, public opinion or public feeling" during the penalty phase of a capital murder trial violates the Eighth and Fourteenth Amendments to the United States Constitution. We hold that it does not.

Respondent Albert Brown was found guilty by a jury of forcible rape and first-degree murder in the death of 15-year-old Susan J. At the penalty phase, the State presented evidence that respondent had raped another young girl some years prior to his attack on Susan J. Respondent presented the testimony of several family members, who recounted respondent's peaceful nature and expressed disbelief that respondent was capable of such a brutal crime. Respondent also presented the testimony of a psychiatrist, who stated that Brown killed his victim because of his shame and fear over sexual dysfunction. Brown himself testified, stating that he was ashamed of his prior criminal conduct and asking for mercy from the jury.

California Penal Code Ann. § 190.3 provides that capital defendants may introduce at the penalty phase any evidence "as to any matter relevant to mitigation including, but not limited to, the nature and circumstances of the present offense, and the defendant's character, background, history, mental condition and physical condition." The trial court instructed the jury to consider the aggravating and mitigating circumstances and to weigh them in determining the appropriate penalty. But the court cautioned the jury that it "must not be swayed by mere sentiment, conjecture, sympathy, passion, prejudice, public opinion or public feeling." Respondent was sentenced to death.

On automatic appeal, the Supreme Court of California reversed the sentence of death. Over two dissents on this point, the majority opinion found that the instruction at issue here violates the Federal Constitution: " 'federal constitutional law forbids an instruction which denies a capital defendant the right to have the jury consider any "sympathy factor" raised by the evidence when determining the appropriate penalty.' " We granted certiorari to resolve whether such an instruction violates the United States Constitution.

The Eighth Amendment jurisprudence of this Court establishes two separate prerequisites to a valid death sentence. First, sentencers may not be given unbridled discretion in determining the fates of those charged with capital offenses. The Constitution instead requires that death penalty statutes be structured so as to prevent the penalty from being administered in an arbitrary and unpredictable fashion. *Gregg v. Georgia*, 428 U.S. 153, 96 S.Ct. 2909, 49 L.Ed.2d 859 (1976); *Furman v. Georgia*, 408 U.S. 238, 92 S.Ct. 2726, 33 L.Ed.2d 346 (1972). Second, even though the sentencer's discretion must be restricted, the capital defendant generally must be allowed to introduce any relevant mitigating evidence regarding his character or record and any of the circumstances of the offense. Consideration of such evidence is a constitutionally indispensable part of the process of inflicting the penalty of death. The instruction given by the trial court in this case violates neither of these constitutional principles.

We think that the California Supreme Court improperly focused solely on the word "sympathy" to determine that the instruction interferes with the jury's consideration of mitigating evidence. The question, however, is not what the State Supreme Court declares the meaning of the charge to be, but rather what a reasonable juror could have understood the charge as meaning. To determine how a reasonable juror could interpret an instruction, we must focus initially on the specific language challenged. If the specific instruction fails constitutional muster, we then review the instructions as a whole to see if the entire charge delivered a correct interpretation of the law. In this case, we need not reach the second step of analysis because we hold that a reasonable juror would not interpret the challenged instruction in a manner that would render it unconstitutional.

The jury was told not to be swayed by "mere sentiment, conjecture, sympathy, passion, prejudice, public opinion or public feeling." Respondent does not contend, and the Supreme Court of California did not hold, that conjecture, passion, prejudice, public opinion, or public feeling should properly play any role in the jury's sentencing determination, even if such factors might weigh in the defendant's favor. Rather, respondent reads the instruction as if it solely cautioned the jury not to be swayed by "sympathy." Even if we were to agree that a rational juror could parse the instruction in such a hypertechnical manner, we would disagree with both respondent's interpretation of the instruction and his conclusion that the instruction is unconstitutional.

Food for Thought

What do you think? How would or should a reasonable juror react to this instruction? Is this much ado about nothing? Would an ordinary juror even recognize the potential conflict here?

By concentrating on the noun "sympathy," respondent ignores the crucial fact that the jury was instructed to avoid basing its decision on mere sympathy. Even a juror who insisted on focusing on this one phrase in the instruction would likely interpret the phrase as an admonition to ignore emotional responses that are not rooted in the aggravating and mitigating evidence introduced during the penalty phase. While strained in the abstract, respondent's interpretation is simply untenable when viewed in light of the surrounding circumstances. This instruction was given at the end of the penalty phase, only after respondent had produced 13 witnesses in his favor. Yet respondent's interpretation would have these two words transform three days of favorable testimony into a virtual charade. We think a reasonable juror would reject that interpretation, and instead understand the instruction not to rely on "mere sympathy" as a directive to ignore only the sort of sympathy that would be totally divorced from the evidence adduced during the penalty phase.

We also think it highly unlikely that any reasonable juror would almost perversely single out the word "sympathy" from the other nouns which accompany it in the instruction: conjecture, passion, prejudice, public opinion, and public feeling. Reading the instruction as a whole, as we must, it is no more than a catalog of the kind of factors that could improperly influence a juror's decision to vote for or against the death penalty. The doctrine of *noscitur a sociis* is based on common sense, and a rational juror could hardly hear this instruction without concluding that it was meant to confine the jury's deliberations to considerations arising from the evidence presented, both aggravating and mitigating.

It's Latin to Me

Noscitur a sociis is "[a] canon of construction holding that the meaning of an unclear word or phrase should be determined by the words immediately surrounding it."

An instruction prohibiting juries from basing their sentencing decisions on factors not presented at the trial, and irrelevant to the issues at the trial, does not violate the United States Constitution. It serves the useful purpose of confining the jury's imposition of the death sentence by cautioning it against reliance on extraneous emotional factors, which, we think, would be far more likely to turn the jury against a capital defendant than for him. And to the extent that the instruction helps to limit the jury's consideration to matters introduced in evidence before it, it fosters the Eighth Amendment's need for reliability in the determination that death is the appropriate punishment in a specific case. Indeed, by limiting the jury's sentencing considerations to record evidence, the State also ensures the availability of meaningful judicial review, another safeguard that improves the reliability of the sentencing process.

We hold that the instruction challenged in this case does not violate the provisions of the Eighth and Fourteenth Amendments to the United States Constitution.

JUSTICE O'CONNOR, concurring.

This case squarely presents the tension that has long existed between the two central principles of our Eighth Amendment jurisprudence. In *Gregg v. Georgia*, 428 U.S. 153, 189, 96 S.Ct. 2909, 2932, 49 L.Ed.2d 859 (1976), Justices Stewart, Powell, and Stevens concluded that "where discretion is afforded a sentencing body on a matter so grave as the determination of whether a human life should be taken or spared, that discretion must be suitably directed and limited so as to minimize the risk of wholly arbitrary and capricious action." In capital sentencing, therefore, discretion must be controlled by clear and objective standards so as to produce nondiscriminatory application. On the other hand, this Court has also held that a sentencing body must be able to consider any relevant mitigating evidence regarding the defendant's character or background, and the circumstances of the particular offense.

Food for Thought

Have we accomplished this goal? Are capital sentencing proceedings "controlled by clear and objective standards so as to produce nondiscriminatory application"? What do you think?

The issue in this case is whether an instruction designed to satisfy the principle that capital sentencing decisions must not be made on mere whim, but instead on clear and objective standards, violates the principle that the sentencing body is to consider any relevant mitigating evidence. In my view, evidence about the defendant's background and character is relevant because of the belief, long held by this society, that defendants who commit criminal acts that are attributable to a disadvantaged background, or to emotional and mental problems, may be less culpable than defendants who have no such excuse.

Because the individualized assessment of the appropriateness of the death penalty is a moral inquiry into the culpability of the defendant, and not an emotional response to the mitigating evidence, I agree with the Court that an instruction informing the jury that they "must not be swayed by mere sentiment, conjecture, sympathy, passion, prejudice, public opinion or public feeling" does not by itself violate the Eighth and Fourteenth Amendments to the United States Constitution. At the same time, the jury instructions-taken as a whole-must clearly inform the jury that they are to consider any relevant mitigating evidence about a defendant's background and character, or about the circumstances of the crime.

On remand, the California Supreme Court should determine whether the jury instructions, taken as a whole, and considered in combination with the prosecutor's closing argument, adequately informed the jury of its responsibility to consider all of the mitigating evidence introduced by the respondent.

JUSTICE BRENNAN, with whom JUSTICE MARSHALL joins, and with whom JUSTICE STEVENS joins in part, dissenting.

Adhering to my view that the death penalty is in all circumstances cruel and unusual punishment forbidden by the Eighth and Fourteenth Amendments, I dissent from the Court's opinion to the extent that it would result in the imposition of the death penalty upon respondent. *Gregg v. Georgia*, 428 U.S. 153, 227, 96 S.Ct. 2909, 2950, 49 L.Ed.2d 859 (1976). However, even if I believed that the death penalty could be imposed constitutionally under certain circumstances, I would affirm the California Supreme Court, for that court has reasonably interpreted the jury instruction at issue to divert the jury from its constitutional duty to consider all mitigating evidence introduced by a defendant at the sentencing phase of trial.

Food for Thought

Is taking this position at odds with the traditional judicial principle of *stare decisis*?

A sentencing instruction is invalid if it precludes the sentencer from "considering, as a mitigating factor, any aspect of a defendant's character or record that the defendant proffers as a basis for a sentence less than death." Furthermore, an instruction cannot stand if it leaves the jury unclear as to whether it may consider such evidence. "We may not speculate as to whether the sentencer actually considered all of the mitigating factors and found them insufficient to offset the aggravating circumstances," since our case law "requires us to remove any legitimate basis for finding ambiguity concerning the factors actually considered."

The issue in this case is whether a jury might reasonably interpret the California jury instruction in either of these two ways. The facial language of the instruction, the manner in which it has been construed in trials in California, and experience with other provisions of the state sentencing scheme all buttress California's interpretation of its own jury instruction.

In light of this evidence, there is simply no warrant for this Court to override the state court's assessment of how a jury in California might reasonably interpret the instruction before us.

The instruction at issue informed the jury: "You must not be swayed by mere sentiment, conjecture, sympathy, passion, prejudice, public opinion or public feeling." In forbidding the sentencer to take sympathy into account, this language on its face precludes precisely the response that a defendant's evidence of character and background is designed to elicit, thus effectively negating the intended effect of the Court's requirement that all mitigating evidence be considered.

The State acknowledges that sympathy for the defendant is appropriate, but contends that the antisympathy instruction simply prevents the jury from relying on "untethered sympathy" unrelated to the circumstances of the offense or the defendant. Yet, as the California court has noted on other occasions, the instruction gives no indication whatsoever that the jury is to distinguish between "tethered" and "untethered" sympathy. The Court nonetheless accepts the notion that a jury would interpret the instruction to require such a distinction. None of the reasons it offers for accepting this implausible construction are persuasive. The vast majority of jurors can be expected to interpret "sympathy" to mean "sympathy," not to engage in the tortuous reasoning process necessary to construe it as "untethered sympathy."

This Court has proclaimed that in capital cases the fundamental respect for humanity underlying the Eighth Amendment requires consideration of the character and record of the individual offender and the circumstances of the particular offense as a constitutionally indispensable part of the process of inflicting the penalty of death. Because of the qualitatively different nature of the death penalty, there is a corresponding difference in the need for reliability in the determination that death is the appropriate punishment in a specific case. Even construed in its most favorable light, the jury instruction at issue in this case did not come close to providing the requisite assurance that the jury in this case was fully aware of the scope of its sentencing duties. Since Brown's mitigating evidence was composed totally of information on his character and background intended to elicit sympathy, it is highly likely that the instruction eliminated his only hope of gaining mercy from the sentencer. Given our particular concern for the reliability of the procedures used to impose the death penalty, as well as the considerable support for the California court's interpretation, it is baffling that this Court strains to find a way to override the state court's construction of its own jury instruction. I cannot acquiesce in such a course of action, and therefore dissent.

JUSTICE BLACKMUN, with whom JUSTICE MARSHALL joins, dissenting.

The defense's goal in the penalty phase of a capital trial is, of course, to receive a life sentence. While the sentencer's decision to accord life to a defendant at times might be a rational or moral one, it also may arise from the defendant's appeal to the sentencer's sympathy or mercy, human qualities that are undeniably emotional in nature.

In a capital sentencing proceeding, the sentencer's discretion must be guided to avoid arbitrary or irrational decisions. When a jury serves as the sentencing authority, such guidance is provided, in part, through jury instructions. This Court, however, has recognized and even safeguarded the sentencer's power to exercise its mercy to spare the defendant's life.

The sentencer's ability to respond with mercy towards a defendant has always struck me as a particularly valuable aspect of the capital sentencing procedure. Long ago, when, in dissent, I expressed my fear of legislation that would make the death penalty mandatory, and thus remove all discretion from the sentencer, I observed that such legislation would be "regressive, for it would eliminate the element of mercy in the imposition of punishment." In my view, we adhere so strongly to our belief that sentencers should have the opportunity to spare a capital defendant's life on account of compassion for the individual because, recognizing that the capital sentencing decision must be made in the context of "contemporary values" we see in the sentencer's expression of mercy a distinctive feature of our society that we deeply value.

In the real world, as in this case, it perhaps is unlikely that one word in an instruction would cause a jury totally to disregard mitigating factors that the defendant has presented through specific testimony. When, however, a jury member is moved to be merciful to the defendant, an instruction telling the juror that he or she cannot be "swayed" by sympathy well may arrest or restrain this humane response, with truly fatal consequences for the defendant. This possibility I cannot accept, in light of the special role of mercy in capital sentencing and the stark finality of the death sentence.

Points for Discussion

a. Mandatory Death Sentences

As intimated in *Brown*, the Supreme Court has made it clear that jurisdictions may not enact capital sentencing schemes that make imposition of capital punishment mandatory, rather than based upon an individualized consideration of the convicted defendant. *See, e.g., Woodson v. North Carolina*, 428 U.S. 280, 305, 96 S.Ct. 2978, 2991, 49 L.Ed.2d 944 (1976) (plurality opinion) ("we conclude that the death sentences imposed upon the petitioners under North Carolina's mandatory death sentence statute violated the Eighth and Fourteenth Amendments and therefore must be set aside"); *Roberts v. Louisiana*, 428 U.S. 325, 333, 96 S.Ct. 3001, 3006, 49 L.Ed.2d 974 (1976) ("The constitutional vice of mandatory death sentence statutes lack of focus on the circumstances of the particular offense and the character and propensities of the offender is not resolved by Louisiana's limitation of first-degree murder to various categories of killings.").

b. Aggravating & Mitigating Circumstances

The Supreme Court has *not* required that capital-punishment jurisdictions use any particular, specific, prescribed capital-sentencing scheme. *See, e.g., Kansas v. Marsh*, 548 U.S. 163, 173–75, 126 S.Ct. 2516, 165 L.Ed.2d 429 (2006); *Franklin v. Lynaugh*, 487 U.S. 164, 178, 108 S.Ct. 2320, 101 L.Ed.2d 155 (1988) (plurality).

But the Supreme Court *has required* that a convicted defendant in a homicide case cannot be sentenced to death unless the sentencing jury (or judge in a bench trial) finds at least one 'aggravating circumstance' to exist beyond a reasonable doubt at either the guilt or penalty phase. *See, e.g., Tuilaepa v. California*, 512 U.S. 967, 971–72, 114 S.Ct. 2630, 129 L.Ed.2d 750 (1994) ("To render a defendant eligible for the death penalty in a homicide case, we have indicated that the trier of fact must convict the defendant of murder and find one 'aggravating circumstance' (or its equivalent) at either the guilt or penalty phase.").

FYI

As an example of statutory aggravating circumstances in a capital-punishment sentencing scheme, consider Alabama Code 1975 § 13A–5–49:

> Aggravating circumstances shall be any of the following:
>
> (1) The capital offense was committed by a person under sentence of imprisonment.
>
> (2) The defendant was previously convicted of another capital offense or a felony involving the use or threat of violence to the person.
>
> (3) The defendant knowingly created a great risk of death to many persons.
>
> (4) The capital offense was committed while the defendant was engaged or was an accomplice in the commission of, or an attempt to commit, or flight after committing, or attempting to commit, rape, robbery, burglary, or kidnapping.
>
> (5) The capital offense was committed for the purpose of avoiding or preventing a lawful arrest or effecting an escape from custody.
>
> (6) The capital offense was committed for pecuniary gain.
>
> (7) The capital offense was committed to disrupt or hinder the lawful exercise of any governmental function or the enforcement of laws.
>
> (8) The capital offense was especially heinous, atrocious, or cruel compared to other capital offenses.
>
> (9) The defendant intentionally caused the death of two or more persons by one act or pursuant to one scheme or course of conduct.
>
> (10) The capital offense was one of a series of intentional killings committed by the defendant.
>
> (11) The capital offense was committed when the victim was less than 14 years of age.
>
> (12) The capital offense was committed by the defendant in the presence of a child under the age of 14 years at the time of the offense, if the victim was the parent or legal guardian of the child. For the purposes of this subdivision, "in the presence of a child" means in the physical presence of a child or having knowledge that a child is present and may see or hear the act.
>
> (13) The victim of the capital offense was any police officer, sheriff, deputy, state trooper, federal law enforcement officer, or any other state or federal peace officer of any kind, or prison or jail guard, while the officer or guard was on duty, regardless of whether the defendant knew or should have known the victim was an officer or guard on duty, or because of some official or job-related act or performance of the officer or guard.
>
> (14) The victim of the capital offense was a first responder who was operating in an official capacity. For the purposes of this subdivision, first responder includes emergency medical services personnel licensed by the Alabama Department of Public Health, as well as firefighters and volunteer firefighters.

These aggravating circumstances (sometimes called "special circumstances") must be narrowly and precisely defined by statute. Moreover, they must not apply to every defendant convicted of a capital offense (otherwise there would be an unconstitutional mandatory death sentence, as discussed above), and they must not be unconstitutionally vague.

In contrast, as discussed in *Brown*, *all* relevant mitigating evidence of any kind—whether cumulative or not—may be introduced at a capital-sentencing hearing on the convicted defendant's behalf. *See also, e.g., Roper v. Simmons*, 543 U.S. 551, 568, 125 S.Ct. 1183, 161 L.Ed.2d 1 (2005) ("In any capital case a defendant has wide latitude to raise as a mitigating factor 'any aspect of [his or her] character or record and any of the circumstances of the offense that the defendant proffers as a basis for a sentence less than death.' "); *Johnson v. Texas*, 509 U.S. 350, 361–62, 113 S.Ct. 2658, 125 L.Ed.2d 290 (1993); *Lockett v. Ohio*, 438 U.S. 586, 604, 98 S.Ct. 2954, 57 L.Ed.2d 973 (1978) ("[W]e conclude that the Eighth and Fourteenth Amendments require that the sentencer, in all but the rarest kind of capital case, not be precluded from considering, as a mitigating factor, any aspect of a defendant's character or record and any of the circumstances of the offense that the defendant proffers as a basis for a sentence less than death.").

c. Discriminatory Application

Whether or not capital punishment is constitutional, there is significant public debate about whether it is applied in a racially discriminatory fashion. In *McCleskey v. Kemp*, 481 U.S. 279, 107 S.Ct. 1756, 95 L.Ed.2d 262 (1987), a 5-to-4 majority of the Court rejected a challenge to Georgia's capital punishment procedures as racially discriminatory. *See, e.g., id.* at 313, 107 S.Ct. at 1778 ("In light of the safeguards designed to minimize racial bias in the process, the fundamental value of jury trial in our criminal justice system, and the benefits that discretion provides to criminal defendants, we hold that [the study alleging racial disparity in capital sentences put forward by defendant McCleskey] does not demonstrate a constitutionally significant risk of racial bias affecting the Georgia capital sentencing process.").

> **FYI**
>
> The American Bar Association Death Penalty Due Process Review Project website contains a great deal of information about death penalty process assessment reports and capital punishment moratorium efforts underway in many states in the United States. See https://www.americanbar.org/groups/crsj/projects/death_penalty_due_process_review_project.html.

Based, however, on the belief that the death penalty is applied unfairly throughout the United States, the American Bar Association has, since 1997, called for "capital jurisdictions to impose a moratorium on all executions until they can (1) ensure that death penalty cases are administered fairly and impartially, in accordance with due process, and (2) minimize the risk that innocent persons may be executed." See American Bar Association Death Penalty Due Process Review Project, https://www.americanbar.org/groups/crsj/projects/death_penalty_due_process_review_project/.

d. Method of Execution

Some prisoners sentenced to death in Oklahoma filed an action in federal court contending that the method of execution used by the State violated the Eighth Amendment because it created an unacceptable risk of severe pain. They argued that midazolam, the first drug employed in the State's three-drug protocol, failed to render a person insensate to pain. The Supreme Court, in a 5-to-4 decision, disagreed, holding that "first, the prisoners failed to identify a known and available alternative method of execution that entails a lesser risk of pain, a requirement of all Eighth Amendment method-of-execution claims. Second, the District Court did not commit clear error when it found that the prisoners failed to establish that Oklahoma's use of a massive dose of midazolam in its execution protocol entails a substantial risk of severe pain." *Glossip v. Gross*, 576 U.S. 863, 135 S.Ct. 2726, 192 L.Ed.2d 761 (2015). Justice Sotomayor, dissenting with three other Justices, argued that the majority reached this result "by misconstruing and ignoring the record evidence regarding the constitutional insufficiency of midazolam as a sedative in a three-drug lethal injection cocktail, and by imposing a wholly unprecedented obligation on the condemned inmate to identify an available means for his or her own execution. The contortions necessary to save this particular lethal injection protocol are not worth the price."

The Supreme Court subsequently held, in a 5-to-4 opinion, that an inmate failed to offer evidence that his proposed alternative method of execution, which would use nitrogen hypoxia as a lethal gas, was feasible and readily implemented and that it would significantly reduce the allegedly substantial risk of severe pain. *Bucklew v. Precythe*, 139 S.Ct. 1112, 1126–27, 203 L.Ed.2d 521 (2019) ("When it comes to determining whether a punishment is unconstitutionally cruel because of the pain involved, the law has always asked whether the punishment 'superadds' pain well beyond what's needed to effectuate a death sentence. And answering that question has always involved a comparison with available alternatives, not some abstract exercise in 'categorical' classification.").

e. Psychological Impediments to Death Penalty

The Supreme Court has ruled that the Eighth Amendment prohibits the execution of a prisoner whose mental illness prevents him from rationally understanding why the State seeks to impose that punishment. But that does not mean that a prisoner may not be executed where a mental disorder has left him with dementia and without any memory of committing his crime "because a person lacking such a memory may still be able to form a rational understanding of the reasons for his death sentence." *Madison v. Alabama*, 139 S.Ct. 718, 722, 203 L.Ed.2d 103 (2019).

C. Proportionality

The Supreme Court has held that punishments for criminal offenses violate the Cruel and Unusual Punishments Clause of the Eighth Amendment when they are disproportionate to the proscribed crime. When exactly is that the case? The Court has given this question a lot of thought the last few years in a variety of different settings.

Graham v. Florida

560 U.S. 48 (2010).

JUSTICE KENNEDY delivered the opinion of the Court.

Hear It

You can listen to the oral argument in this case at http://oyez.org/cases/2000-2009/2009/2009_08_7412.

Petitioner is Terrance Jamar Graham. He was born on January 6, 1987. Graham's parents were addicted to crack cocaine, and their drug use persisted in his early years. Graham was diagnosed with attention deficit hyperactivity disorder in elementary school. He began drinking alcohol and using tobacco at age 9 and smoked marijuana at age 13.

In July 2003, when Graham was age 16, he and three other school-age youths attempted to rob a barbeque restaurant in Jacksonville, Florida. One youth, who worked at the restaurant, left the back door unlocked just before closing time. Graham and another youth, wearing masks, entered through the unlocked door. Graham's masked accomplice twice struck the restaurant manager in the back of the head with a metal bar. When the manager started yelling at the assailant and Graham, the two youths ran out and escaped in a car driven by the third accomplice. The restaurant manager required stitches for his head injury. No money was taken.

Graham was arrested for the robbery attempt. Under Florida law, it is within a prosecutor's discretion whether to charge 16- and 17-year-olds as adults or juveniles for most felony crimes. Graham's prosecutor elected to charge Graham as an adult. The charges against Graham were armed burglary with assault or battery, a first-degree felony carrying a maximum penalty of life imprisonment without the possibility of parole; and attempted armed-robbery, a second-degree felony carrying a maximum penalty of 15 years' imprisonment.

On December 18, 2003, Graham pleaded guilty to both charges under a plea agreement. Graham wrote a letter to the trial court. After reciting "this is my first and last time getting in trouble," he continued "I've decided to turn my life around." Graham said "I made a promise to God and myself that if I get a second chance, I'm going to do whatever it takes to get to the National Football League."

The trial court accepted the plea agreement. The court withheld adjudication of guilt as to both charges and sentenced Graham to concurrent 3-year terms of probation.

Less than 6 months later, on the night of December 2, 2004, Graham again was arrested. The State's case was as follows: Earlier that evening, Graham participated in a home invasion robbery. His two accomplices were Meigo Bailey and Kirkland Lawrence, both 20-year-old men. According to the State, at 7 p.m. that night, Graham, Bailey, and Lawrence knocked on the door of the home where Carlos Rodriguez lived. Graham, followed by Bailey and Lawrence, forcibly entered the home and held a pistol to Rodriguez's chest. For the next 30 minutes, the three held Rodriguez and another man, a friend of Rodriguez, at gunpoint while they ransacked the home searching for money. Before leaving, Graham and his accomplices barricaded Rodriguez and his friend inside a closet.

The State further alleged that Graham, Bailey, and Lawrence, later the same evening, attempted a second robbery, during which Bailey was shot. When detectives interviewed Graham, he denied involvement in the crimes. He said he encountered Bailey and Lawrence only after Bailey had been shot. One of the detectives told Graham that the victims of the home invasion had identified him. He asked Graham, "Aside from the two robberies tonight how many more were you involved in?" Graham responded, "Two to three before tonight." The night that Graham allegedly committed the robbery, he was 34 days short of his 18th birthday.

The trial court held hearings on Graham's probation violations about a year later, in December 2005 and January 2006. The judge who presided was not the same judge who had accepted Graham's guilty plea to the earlier offenses.

Graham maintained that he had no involvement in the home invasion robbery; but, even after the court underscored that the admission could expose him to a life sentence on the earlier charges, he admitted violating probation conditions by fleeing. The State presented evidence related to the home invasion, including testimony from the victims. The trial court noted that Graham, in admitting his attempt to avoid arrest, had acknowledged violating his probation. The court further found that Graham had violated his probation by committing a home invasion robbery, by possessing a firearm, and by associating with persons engaged in criminal activity.

The trial court held a sentencing hearing. Under Florida law the minimum sentence Graham could receive absent a downward departure by the judge was 5 years' imprisonment. The maximum was life imprisonment. Graham's attorney requested the minimum nondeparture sentence of 5 years. A presentence report prepared by the Florida Department of Corrections recommended that Graham receive an even lower sentence-at most 4 years' imprisonment. The State recommended that Graham receive 30 years on the armed burglary count and 15 years on the attempted armed robbery count.

After hearing Graham's testimony, the trial court explained the sentence it was about to pronounce:

> "Mr. Graham, as I look back on your case, yours is really candidly a sad situation. You had, as far as I can tell, you have quite a family structure. You had a lot of people who wanted to try and help you get your life turned around including the court system, and you had a judge who took the step to try and give you direction

> through his probation order to give you a chance to get back onto track. And at the time you seemed through your letters that that is exactly what you wanted to do. And I don't know why it is that you threw your life away. I don't know why.
>
> "But you did, and that is what is so sad about this today is that you have actually been given a chance to get through this, the original charge, which were very serious charges to begin with. The attempted robbery with a weapon was a very serious charge.
>
> "In a very short period of time you were back before the Court on a violation of this probation, and then here you are two years later standing before me, literally the-facing a life sentence as to-up to life as to count 1 and up to 15 years as to count 2.
>
> "And I don't understand why you would be given such a great opportunity to do something with your life and why you would throw it away. The only thing that I can rationalize is that you decided that this is how you were going to lead your life and that there is nothing that we can do for you. And as the state pointed out, that this is an escalating pattern of criminal conduct on your part and that we can't help you any further. We can't do anything to deter you. This is the way you are going to lead your life, and I don't know why you are going to. You've made that decision. I have no idea. But, evidently, that is what you decided to do.
>
> "So then it becomes a focus, if I can't do anything to help you, if I can't do anything to get you back on the right path, then I have to start focusing on the community and trying to protect the community from your actions. And, unfortunately, that is where we are today is I don't see where I can do anything to help you any further. You've evidently decided this is the direction you're going to take in life, and it's unfortunate that you made that choice.
>
> "I have reviewed the statute. I don't see where any further juvenile sanctions would be appropriate. I don't see where any youthful offender sanctions would be appropriate. Given your escalating pattern of criminal conduct, it is apparent to the Court that you have decided that this is the way you are going to live your life and that the only thing I can do now is to try and protect the community from your actions."

The trial court found Graham guilty of the earlier armed burglary and attempted armed robbery charges. It sentenced him to the maximum sentence authorized by law on each charge: life imprisonment for the armed burglary and 15 years for the attempted armed robbery. Because Florida has abolished its parole system, a life sentence gives a defendant no possibility of release unless he is granted executive clemency.

Graham challenged his sentence under the Eighth Amendment. The First District Court of Appeal of Florida affirmed, concluding that Graham's sentence was not grossly disproportionate to his crimes. The Florida Supreme Court denied review.

The Eighth Amendment states: "Excessive bail shall not be required, nor excessive fines imposed, nor cruel and unusual punishments inflicted." To determine whether a punishment is cruel and unusual, courts must look beyond historical conceptions to "the evolving standards of decency that mark the progress of a maturing society." This is because the standard of extreme cruelty is not merely descriptive, but necessarily embodies a moral judgment. The standard itself remains the same, but its applicability must change as the basic mores of society change.

The Cruel and Unusual Punishments Clause prohibits the imposition of inherently barbaric punishments under all circumstances. "Punishments of torture," for example, are forbidden. These cases underscore the essential principle that, under the Eighth Amendment, the State must respect the human attributes even of those who have committed serious crimes.

For the most part, however, the Court's precedents consider punishments challenged not as inherently barbaric but as disproportionate to the crime. The concept of proportionality is central to the Eighth Amendment. Embodied in the Constitution's ban on cruel and unusual punishments is the precept of justice that punishment for crime should be graduated and proportioned to the offense.

The Court's cases addressing the proportionality of sentences fall within two general classifications. The first involves challenges to the length of term-of-years sentences given all the circumstances in a particular case. The second comprises cases in which the Court implements the proportionality standard by certain categorical restrictions on the death penalty.

In the first classification the Court considers all of the circumstances of the case to determine whether the sentence is unconstitutionally excessive. Under this approach, the Court has held unconstitutional a life without parole sentence for the defendant's seventh nonviolent felony, the crime of passing a worthless check. *Solem v. Helm*, 463 U.S. 277, 103 S.Ct. 3001, 77 L.Ed.2d 637 (1983). In other cases, however, it has been difficult for the challenger to establish a lack of proportionality. A leading case is *Harmelin v. Michigan*, 501 U.S. 957, 111 S.Ct. 2680, 115 L.Ed.2d 836 (1991), in which the offender was sentenced under state law to life without parole for possessing a large quantity of cocaine. A closely divided Court upheld the sentence. The controlling opinion concluded that the Eighth Amendment contains a "narrow proportionality principle," that "does not require strict proportionality between crime and sentence" but rather "forbids only extreme sentences that are 'grossly disproportionate' to the crime." Again closely divided, the Court rejected a challenge to a sentence of 25 years to life for the theft of a few golf clubs under California's so-called three-strikes recidivist sentencing scheme. *Ewing v. California*, 538 U.S. 11, 123 S.Ct. 1179, 155 L.Ed.2d 108 (2003). The Court has also upheld a sentence of life with the possibility of parole for a defendant's third nonviolent felony, the crime of obtaining money by false pretenses, *Rummel v. Estelle*, 445 U.S. 263, 100 S.Ct. 1133, 63 L.Ed.2d 382 (1980), and a sentence of 40 years for possession of marijuana with intent to distribute and distribution of marijuana, *Hutto v. Davis*, 454 U.S. 370, 102 S.Ct. 703, 70 L.Ed.2d 556 (1982).

The controlling opinion in *Harmelin* explained its approach for determining whether a sentence for a term of years is grossly disproportionate for a particular defendant's crime. A court must begin by comparing the gravity of the offense and the severity of the sentence. "In the rare case in which this threshold comparison leads to an inference of gross disproportionality" the court should then compare the defendant's sentence with the sentences received by other offenders in the same jurisdiction and with the sentences imposed for the same crime in other jurisdictions. If this comparative analysis "validates an initial judgment that the sentence is grossly disproportionate," the sentence is cruel and unusual.

The second classification of cases has used categorical rules to define Eighth Amendment standards. The previous cases in this classification involved the death penalty. The classification in turn consists of two subsets, one considering the nature of the offense, the other considering the characteristics of the offender. With respect to the nature of the offense, the Court has concluded that capital punishment is impermissible for nonhomicide crimes against individuals. *Kennedy v. Louisiana*, 554 U.S. 407, 128 S.Ct. 2641, 171 L.Ed.2d 525 (2008). In cases turning on the characteristics of the offender, the Court has adopted categorical rules prohibiting the death penalty for defendants who committed their crimes before the age of 18, *Roper v. Simmons*, 543 U.S. 551, 125 S.Ct. 1183, 161 L.Ed.2d 1 (2005), or whose intellectual functioning is in a low range, *Atkins v. Virginia*, 536 U.S. 304, 122 S.Ct. 2242, 153 L.Ed.2d 335 (2002).

In the cases adopting categorical rules the Court has taken the following approach. The Court first considers "objective indicia of society's standards, as expressed in legislative enactments and state practice" to determine whether there is a national consensus against the sentencing practice at issue. Next, guided by "the standards elaborated by controlling precedents and by the Court's own understanding and interpretation of the Eighth Amendment's text, history, meaning, and purpose," the Court must determine in the exercise of its own independent judgment whether the punishment in question violates the Constitution.

The present case involves an issue the Court has not considered previously: a categorical challenge to a term-of-years sentence. The approach in cases such as *Harmelin* and *Ewing* is suited for considering a gross proportionality challenge to a particular defendant's sentence, but here a sentencing practice itself is in question. This case implicates a particular type of sentence as it applies to an entire class of offenders who have committed a range of crimes. As a result, a threshold comparison between the severity of the penalty and the gravity of the crime does not advance the analysis. Here, in addressing the question presented, the appropriate analysis is the one used in cases that involved the categorical approach, specifically *Atkins*, *Roper*, and *Kennedy*.

The analysis begins with objective indicia of national consensus. The clearest and most reliable objective evidence of contemporary values is the legislation enacted by the country's legislatures. Six jurisdictions do not allow life without parole sentences for any juvenile offenders. Seven jurisdictions permit life without parole for juvenile offenders, but only for homicide crimes. Thirty-seven States as well as the District of Columbia permit sentences of life without parole for a juvenile nonhomicide offender in some circumstances. Federal law also allows for the possibility of life without parole for offenders as young as 13. Relying on this metric, the State and its amici argue that there is no national consensus against the sentencing practice at issue.

This argument is incomplete and unavailing. There are measures of consensus other than legislation. Actual sentencing practices are an important part of the Court's inquiry into consensus. Here, an examination of actual sentencing practices in jurisdictions where the sentence in question is permitted by statute discloses a consensus against its use. Although these statutory schemes contain no explicit prohibition on sentences of life without parole for juvenile nonhomicide offenders, those sentences are most infrequent. According to a recent study, nationwide there are only 109 juvenile offenders serving sentences of life without parole for nonhomicide offenses.

The State contends that this study's tally is inaccurate because it does not count juvenile offenders who were convicted of both a homicide and a nonhomicide offense, even when the offender received a life without parole sentence for the nonhomicide. This distinction is unpersuasive. Juvenile offenders who committed both homicide and nonhomicide crimes present a different situation for a sentencing judge than juvenile offenders who committed no homicide. It is difficult to say that a defendant who receives a life sentence on a nonhomicide offense but who was at the same time convicted of homicide is not in some sense being punished in part for the homicide when the judge makes the sentencing determination. The instant case concerns only those juvenile offenders sentenced to life without parole solely for a nonhomicide offense.

Food for Thought

Are you comfortable with the Supreme Court doing—and then relying upon—its own independent non-legal research? Do you think it is fair that the Court's research findings were not subject to review or comment by the state of Florida?

Florida further criticizes this study because the authors were unable to obtain complete information on some States and because the study was not peer reviewed. The State does not, however, provide any data of its own. Although in the first instance it is for the litigants to provide data to aid the Court, we have been able to supplement the study's findings. The study's authors were not able to obtain a definitive tally for Nevada, Utah, or Virginia. Our research shows that Nevada has five juvenile nonhomicide offenders serving life without parole sentences, Utah has none, and Virginia has eight. Finally, since the study was completed, a defendant in Oklahoma has apparently been sentenced to life without parole for a rape and stabbing he committed at the age of 16.

Thus, adding the individuals counted by the study to those we have been able to locate independently, there are 123 juvenile nonhomicide offenders serving life without parole sentences. A significant majority of those, 77 in total, are serving sentences imposed in Florida. The other 46 are imprisoned in just 10 States-California, Delaware, Iowa, Louisiana, Mississippi, Nebraska, Nevada, Oklahoma, South Carolina, and Virginia. Thus, only 11 jurisdictions nationwide in fact impose life without parole sentences on juvenile nonhomicide offenders-and most of those do so quite rarely-while 26 States, the District of Columbia, and the Federal Government do not impose them despite apparent statutory authorization.

The numbers cited above reflect all current convicts in a jurisdiction's penal system, regardless of when they were convicted. It becomes all the more clear how rare these sentences are, even within the jurisdictions that do sometimes impose them, when one considers that a juvenile sentenced to life without parole is likely to live in prison for decades. Thus, these statistics likely reflect nearly all juvenile nonhomicide offenders who have received a life without parole sentence stretching back many years. The available data are sufficient to demonstrate how rarely these sentences are imposed even if there are isolated cases that have not been included in the presentations of the parties or the analysis of the Court.

The evidence of consensus is not undermined by the fact that many jurisdictions do not prohibit life without parole for juvenile nonhomicide offenders. The Court confronted a similar situation in *Thompson*, where a plurality concluded that the death penalty for offenders younger than 16 was unconstitutional. A number of States then allowed the juvenile death penalty if one considered the statutory scheme.

Many States have chosen to move away from juvenile court systems and to allow juveniles to be transferred to, or charged directly in, adult court under certain circumstances. Once in adult court, a juvenile offender may receive the same sentence as would be given to an adult offender, including a life without parole sentence. But the fact that transfer and direct charging laws make life without parole possible for some juvenile nonhomicide offenders does not justify a judgment that many States intended to subject such offenders to life without parole sentences.

For example, under Florida law a child of any age can be prosecuted as an adult for certain crimes and can be sentenced to life without parole. The State acknowledged at oral argument that even a 5-year-old, theoretically, could receive such a sentence under the letter of the law. All would concede this to be unrealistic, but the example underscores that the statutory eligibility of a juvenile offender for life without parole does not indicate that the penalty has been endorsed through deliberate, express, and full legislative consideration. Similarly, the many States that allow life without parole for juvenile nonhomicide offenders but do not impose the punishment should not be treated as if they have expressed the view that the sentence is appropriate. The sentencing practice now under consideration is exceedingly rare. And it is fair to say that a national consensus has developed against it.

Community consensus, while entitled to great weight, is not itself determinative of whether a punishment is cruel and unusual. In accordance with the constitutional design, the task of interpreting the Eighth Amendment remains our responsibility.

Roper established that because juveniles have lessened culpability they are less deserving of the most severe punishments. As compared to adults, juveniles have a lack of maturity and an underdeveloped sense of responsibility; they are more vulnerable or susceptible to negative influences and outside pressures, including peer pressure; and their characters are not as well formed. These salient characteristics mean that it is difficult even for expert psychologists to differentiate between the juvenile offender whose crime reflects unfortunate yet transient immaturity, and the rare juvenile offender whose crime reflects irreparable corruption. Accordingly, juvenile offenders cannot with reliability be classified among the worst offenders. A juvenile is not absolved of responsibility for his actions, but his transgression is not as morally reprehensible as that of an adult.

No recent data provide reason to reconsider the Court's observations in *Roper* about the nature of juveniles. As petitioner's amici point out, developments in psychology and brain science continue to show fundamental differences between juvenile and adult minds. For example, parts of the brain involved in behavior control continue to mature through late adolescence. Juveniles are more capable of change than are adults, and their actions are less likely to be evidence of irretrievably depraved character than are the actions of adults. It remains true that from a moral standpoint it would be misguided to equate the failings of a minor with those of an adult, for a greater possibility exists that a minor's character deficiencies will be reformed.

The Court has recognized that defendants who do not kill, intend to kill, or foresee that life will be taken are categorically less deserving of the most serious forms of punishment than are murderers. There is a line between homicide and other serious violent offenses against the individual. Serious nonhomicide crimes may be devastating in their harm but in terms of moral depravity and of the injury to the person and to the public, they cannot be compared to murder in their severity and irrevocability. This is because life is over for the victim of the murderer, but for the victim of even a very serious nonhomicide crime, life is not over and normally is not beyond repair. Although an offense like robbery or rape is a serious crime deserving serious punishment, it follows that, when compared to an adult murderer, a juvenile offender who did not kill or intend to kill has a twice diminished moral culpability. The age of the offender and the nature of the crime each bear on the analysis.

As for the punishment, life without parole is the second most severe penalty permitted by law. It is true that a death sentence is unique in its severity and irrevocability; yet life without parole sentences share some characteristics with death sentences that are shared by no other sentences. The State does not execute the offender sentenced to life without parole, but the sentence alters the offender's life by a forfeiture that is irrevocable. It deprives the convict of the most basic liberties without giving hope of restoration, except perhaps by executive clemency-the remote possibility of which does not mitigate the harshness of the sentence.

Life without parole is an especially harsh punishment for a juvenile. Under this sentence a juvenile offender will on average serve more years and a greater percentage of his life in prison than an adult offender. A 16-year-old and a 75-year-old each sentenced to life without parole receive the same punishment in name only. This reality cannot be ignored.

The penological justifications for the sentencing practice are also relevant to the analysis. Criminal punishment can have different goals, and choosing among them is within a legislature's discretion. It does not follow, however, that the purposes and effects of penal sanctions are irrelevant to the determination of Eighth Amendment restrictions. A sentence lacking any legitimate penological justification is by its nature disproportionate to the offense. With respect to life without parole for juvenile nonhomicide offenders, none of the goals of penal sanctions that have been recognized as legitimate—retribution, deterrence, incapacitation, and rehabilitation—provides an adequate justification.

Retribution is a legitimate reason to punish, but it cannot support the sentence at issue here. Society is entitled to impose severe sanctions on a juvenile nonhomicide offender to express its condemnation of the crime and to seek restoration of the moral imbalance caused by the offense. But the heart of the retribution rationale is that a criminal sentence must be directly related to the personal culpability of the criminal offender. And as *Roper* observed, "whether viewed as an attempt to express the community's moral outrage or as an attempt to right the balance for the wrong to the victim, the case for retribution is not as strong with a minor as with an adult." The case becomes even weaker with respect to a juvenile who did not commit homicide. *Roper* found that "retribution is not proportional if the law's most severe penalty is imposed" on the juvenile murderer. The considerations underlying that holding support as well the conclusion that retribution does not justify imposing the second most severe penalty on the less culpable juvenile nonhomicide offender.

Deterrence does not suffice to justify the sentence either. *Roper* noted that "the same characteristics that render juveniles less culpable than adults suggest that juveniles will be less susceptible to deterrence." Because juveniles' lack of maturity and underdeveloped sense of responsibility often result in impetuous and ill-considered actions and decisions, they are less likely to take a possible punishment into consideration when making decisions. This is particularly so when that punishment is rarely imposed. That the sentence deters in a few cases is perhaps plausible, but this argument does not overcome other objections. Even if the punishment has some connection to a valid penological goal, it must be shown that the punishment is not grossly disproportionate in light of the justification offered. Here, in light of juvenile nonhomicide offenders' diminished moral responsibility, any limited deterrent effect provided by life without parole is not enough to justify the sentence.

Food for Thought

Do you agree? Is a 16-year old *always* different from an 18-year old in this respect, i.e. whether the former is "incorrigible" is "questionable," but whether the latter is "incorrigible" is not?

Incapacitation, a third legitimate reason for imprisonment, does not justify the life without parole sentence in question here. Recidivism is a serious risk to public safety, and so incapacitation is an important goal. But while incapacitation may be a legitimate penological goal sufficient to justify life without parole in other contexts, it is inadequate to justify that punishment for juveniles who did not commit homicide. To justify life without parole on the assumption that the juvenile offender forever will be a danger to society requires the sentencer to make a judgment that the juvenile is incorrigible. The characteristics of juveniles make that judgment questionable. It is difficult even for expert psychologists to differentiate between the juvenile offender whose crime reflects unfortunate yet transient immaturity, and the rare juvenile offender whose crime reflects irreparable corruption.

Here one cannot dispute that this defendant posed an immediate risk, for he had committed, we can assume, serious crimes early in his term of supervised release and despite his own assurances of reform. Graham deserved to be separated from society for some time in order to prevent what the trial court described as an "escalating pattern of criminal conduct," but it does not follow that he would be a risk to society for the rest of his life. Incapacitation cannot override all other considerations, lest the Eighth Amendment's rule against disproportionate sentences be a nullity.

Finally there is rehabilitation, a penological goal that forms the basis of parole systems. The concept of rehabilitation is imprecise; and its utility and proper implementation are the subject of a substantial, dynamic field of inquiry and dialogue. It is for legislatures to determine what rehabilitative techniques are appropriate and effective.

A sentence of life imprisonment without parole, however, cannot be justified by the goal of rehabilitation. The penalty forswears altogether the rehabilitative ideal. By denying the defendant the right to reenter the community, the State makes an irrevocable judgment about that person's value and place in society. This judgment is not appropriate in light of a juvenile nonhomicide offender's capacity for change and limited moral culpability.

Food for Thought

As Justice Alito points out in dissent, the majority opinion only applies to a life sentence. A state may still—constitutionally—sentence a juvenile to any term of years, e.g. 40 years in prison. Can this result be justified by appropriate penological justifications? How about 60 years?

In sum, penological theory is not adequate to justify life without parole for juvenile nonhomicide offenders. This determination; the limited culpability of juvenile nonhomicide offenders; and the severity of life without parole sentences all lead to the conclusion that the sentencing practice under consideration is cruel and unusual. This Court now holds that for a juvenile offender who did not commit homicide the Eighth Amendment forbids the sentence of life without parole. This clear line is necessary to prevent the possibility that life without parole sentences will be imposed on juvenile nonhomicide offenders who are not sufficiently culpable to merit that punishment. Because the age of 18 is the point where society draws the line for many purposes between childhood and adulthood, those who were below that age when the offense was committed may not be sentenced to life without parole for a nonhomicide crime.

A State is not required to guarantee eventual freedom to a juvenile offender convicted of a nonhomicide crime. What the State must do, however, is give defendants like Graham some meaningful opportunity to obtain release based on demonstrated maturity and rehabilitation. It is for the State, in the first instance, to explore the means and mechanisms for compliance. It bears emphasis, however, that while the Eighth Amendment forbids a State from imposing a life without parole sentence on a juvenile nonhomicide offender, it does not require the State to release that offender during his natural life. Those who commit truly horrifying crimes as juveniles may turn out to be irredeemable, and thus deserving of incarceration for the duration of their lives. The Eighth Amendment does not foreclose the possibility that persons convicted of nonhomicide crimes committed before adulthood will remain behind bars for life. It does forbid States from making the judgment at the outset that those offenders never will be fit to reenter society.

There is support for our conclusion in the fact that, in continuing to impose life without parole sentences on juveniles who did not commit homicide, the United States adheres to a sentencing practice rejected the world over. This observation does not control our decision. The judgments of other nations and the international community are not dispositive as to the meaning of the Eighth Amendment. But the climate of international opinion concerning the acceptability of a particular punishment is also not irrelevant. The Court has looked beyond our Nation's borders for support for its independent conclusion that a particular punishment is cruel and unusual.

As petitioner contends and respondent does not contest, the United States is the only Nation that imposes life without parole sentences on juvenile nonhomicide offenders. We also note, as petitioner and his amici emphasize, that Article 37(a) of the United Nations Convention on the Rights of the Child, ratified by every nation except the United States and Somalia, prohibits the imposition of "life imprisonment without possibility of release for offences committed by persons below eighteen years of age." As we concluded in *Roper* with respect to the juvenile death penalty, "the United States now stands alone in a world that has turned its face against" life without parole for juvenile nonhomicide offenders.

The Constitution prohibits the imposition of a life without parole sentence on a juvenile offender who did not commit homicide. A State need not guarantee the offender eventual release, but if it imposes a sentence of life it must provide him or her with some realistic opportunity to obtain release before the end of that term. The judgment of the First District Court of Appeal of Florida is reversed, and the case is remanded for further proceedings not inconsistent with this opinion.

JUSTICE STEVENS, with whom JUSTICE GINSBURG and JUSTICE SOTOMAYOR join, concurring.

Evolving standards of decency have played a central role in our Eighth Amendment jurisprudence for at least a century. Society changes. Knowledge accumulates. We learn, sometimes, from our mistakes. Punishments that did not seem cruel and unusual at one time may, in the light of reason and experience, be found cruel and unusual at a later time; unless we are to abandon the moral commitment embodied in the Eighth Amendment, proportionality review must never become effectively obsolete.

While Justice Thomas would apparently not rule out a death sentence for a $50 theft by a 7-year-old, the Court wisely rejects his static approach to the law. Standards of decency have evolved since 1980. They will never stop doing so.

CHIEF JUSTICE ROBERTS, concurring in the judgment.

Terrance Graham committed serious offenses, for which he deserves serious punishment. But he was only 16 years old, and under our Court's precedents, his youth is one factor, among others, that should be considered in deciding whether his punishment was unconstitutionally excessive. In my view, Graham's age—together with the nature of his criminal activity and the unusual severity of his sentence—tips the constitutional balance. I thus concur in the Court's judgment that Graham's sentence of life without parole violated the Eighth Amendment.

I would not, however, reach the same conclusion in every case involving a juvenile offender. Some crimes are so heinous, and some juvenile offenders so highly culpable, that a sentence of life without parole may be entirely justified under the Constitution.

JUSTICE THOMAS, with whom JUSTICE SCALIA joins, and with whom JUSTICE ALITO joins in part, dissenting.

The Court holds today that it is "grossly disproportionate" and hence unconstitutional for any judge or jury to impose a sentence of life without parole on an offender less than 18 years old, unless he has committed a homicide. Although the text of the Constitution is silent regarding the permissibility of this sentencing practice, and although it would not have offended the standards that prevailed at the founding, the Court insists that the standards of American society have evolved such that the Constitution now requires its prohibition.

The Court does not conclude that life without parole itself is a cruel and unusual punishment. It instead rejects the judgments of those legislatures, judges, and juries regarding what the Court describes as the "moral" question of whether this sentence can ever be "proportionate" when applied to the category of offenders at issue here.

I am unwilling to assume that we, as members of this Court, are any more capable of making such moral judgments than our fellow citizens. Nothing in our training as judges qualifies us for that task, and nothing in Article III gives us that authority.

Until today, the Court has based its categorical proportionality rulings on the notion that the Constitution gives special protection to capital defendants because the death penalty is a uniquely severe punishment that must be reserved for only those who are "most deserving of execution." Of course, the Eighth Amendment itself makes no distinction between capital and noncapital sentencing, but the "bright line" the Court drew between the two penalties has for many years served as the principal justification for the Court's willingness to reject democratic choices regarding the death penalty.

Today's decision eviscerates that distinction. "Death is different" no longer. The Court now claims not only the power categorically to reserve the "most severe punishment" for those the Court thinks are " 'the most deserving of execution,' " but also to declare that "less culpable" persons are categorically exempt from the "second most severe penalty." No reliable limiting principle remains to prevent the Court from immunizing any class of offenders from the law's third, fourth, fifth, or fiftieth most severe penalties as well.

Lacking any plausible claim to consensus, the Court shifts to the heart of its argument: its "independent judgment" that this sentencing practice does not serve legitimate penological goals. The Court begins that analysis with the obligatory preamble that " 'the Eighth Amendment does not mandate adoption of any one penological theory,' " then promptly mandates the adoption of the theories the Court deems best.

The Court acknowledges that, at a minimum, the imposition of life-without-parole sentences on juvenile nonhomicide offenders serves two "legitimate" penological goals: incapacitation and deterrence. That should settle the matter, since the Court acknowledges that incapacitation is an "important" penological goal. Yet, the Court finds this goal "inadequate" to justify the life-without-parole sentences here. A similar fate befalls deterrence. The Court acknowledges that such sentences will deter future juvenile offenders, at least to some degree, but rejects that penological goal, not as illegitimate, but as insufficient.

Ultimately, however, the Court's "independent judgment" and the proportionality rule itself center on retribution—the notion that a criminal sentence should be proportioned to the personal culpability of the criminal offender. Our society tends to treat the average juvenile as less culpable than the average adult. But the question here does not involve the average juvenile. The question, instead, is whether the Constitution prohibits judges and juries from ever concluding that an offender under the age of 18 has demonstrated sufficient depravity and incorrigibility to warrant his permanent incarceration.

In holding that the Constitution imposes such a ban, the Court cites developments in psychology and brain science indicating that juvenile minds "continue to mature through late adolescence," and that juveniles are "more likely than adults to engage in risky behaviors." But even if such generalizations from social science were relevant to constitutional rulemaking, the Court misstates the data on which it relies.

The Court equates the propensity of a fairly substantial number of youths to engage in "risky" or antisocial behaviors with the propensity of a much smaller group to commit violent crimes. But research relied upon by the amici cited in the Court's opinion differentiates between adolescents for whom antisocial behavior is a fleeting symptom and those for whom it is a lifelong pattern. That research further suggests that the pattern of behavior in the latter group often sets in before 18. And, notably, it suggests that violence itself is evidence that an adolescent offender's antisocial behavior is not transient.

In sum, even if it were relevant, none of this psychological or sociological data is sufficient to support the Court's "moral" conclusion that youth defeats culpability in every case. The integrity of our criminal justice system depends on the ability of citizens to stand between the defendant and an outraged public and dispassionately determine his guilt and the proper amount of punishment based on the evidence presented. That process necessarily admits of human error. But so does the process of judging in which we engage. As between the two, I find far more "unacceptable" that this Court, swayed by studies reflecting the general tendencies of youth, decree that the people of this country are not fit to decide for themselves when the rare case requires different treatment.

JUSTICE ALITO, dissenting.

I write separately to note that the Court holds only that "for a juvenile offender who did not commit homicide the Eighth Amendment forbids the sentence of life without parole." Nothing in the Court's opinion affects the imposition of a sentence to a term of years without the possibility of parole. Indeed, petitioner conceded at oral argument that a sentence of as much as 40 years without the possibility of parole "probably" would be constitutional.

Points for Discussion

a. *Kennedy v. Louisiana*

The *Graham* Court referred extensively to its earlier decision in *Kennedy v. Louisiana*, 554 U.S. 407, 128 S.Ct. 2641, 171 L.Ed.2d 525 (2008). A 5-to-4 majority of the *Kennedy* Court held that the Eighth Amendment prohibits the death penalty for the rape of a child where the crime did not result, and was not intended to result, in the death of the victim. The majority noted, *inter alia*, that

> the evidence of a national consensus with respect to the death penalty for child rapists, as with respect to juveniles, mentally retarded offenders, and vicarious felony murderers, shows divided opinion but, on balance, an opinion against it. Thirty-seven jurisdictions—36 States plus the Federal Government—have the death penalty. Only six of those jurisdictions authorize the death penalty for rape of a child. Though our review of national consensus is not confined to tallying the number of States with applicable death penalty legislation, it is of significance that, in 45 jurisdictions, petitioner could not be executed for child rape of any kind. That number surpasses the 30 States in *Atkins* and *Roper* and the 42 States in *Enmund* that prohibited the death penalty under the circumstances those cases considered.

Do you think that the Supreme Court is relying too heavily upon current state statutes in deciding how the Eighth Amendment applies today? Justice Alito, in dissent in *Kennedy*, argued that the only reason there were only 6 states permitting the imposition of the death penalty for the rape of the child is that most state legislatures believed (correctly, as it turned out) that, based upon its prior precedents, the Supreme Court would strike down such a statute:

> When state lawmakers believe that their decision will prevail on the question whether to permit the death penalty for a particular crime or class of offender, the legislators' resolution of the issue can be interpreted as an expression of their own judgment, informed by whatever weight they attach to the values of their constituents. But when state legislators think that the enactment of a new death penalty law is likely to be futile, inaction cannot reasonably be interpreted as an expression of their understanding of prevailing societal values. In that atmosphere, legislative inaction is more likely to evidence acquiescence.

The majority disagreed with this reasoning. Their review of the extant case law—state and federal—led them to believe that "there is no clear indication that state legislatures have misinterpreted [prior precedents of the Supreme Court] to hold that the death penalty for child rape is unconstitutional. The small number of States that have enacted this penalty, then, is relevant to determining whether there is a consensus against capital punishment for this crime."

What do you think? Do you agree?

b. *Ewing v. California*

You should not get the impression that the Court is quick to find exceptionally harsh punishments to be unconstitutionally cruel and unusual. That is not the case. The *Graham* Court referred, for example, to its earlier decision in *Ewing v. California*, 538 U.S. 11, 123 S.Ct. 1179, 155 L.Ed.2d 108 (2003), albeit by distinguishing it. In *Ewing*, a 5-to-4 majority of the Court ruled that the Eighth Amendment did not prohibit the State of California from sentencing a repeat felon to a prison term of 25 years to life under the State's "Three Strikes and You're Out" law, even though the sentence-triggering criminal conduct consisted only of the theft of three golf clubs priced at a total of $1,197.

What's That?

A *three-strikes law* is slang for "[a] statute prescribing an enhanced sentence, esp. life imprisonment, for a repeat offender's third felony conviction."

Justice O'Connor, writing for the majority, observed that "throughout the States, legislatures enacting three strikes laws made a deliberate policy choice that individuals who have repeatedly engaged in serious or violent criminal behavior, and whose conduct has not been deterred by more conventional approaches to punishment, must be isolated from society in order to protect the public safety. Though three strikes laws may be relatively new, our tradition of deferring to state legislatures in making and implementing such important policy decisions is longstanding."

In this case, Justice O'Connor added:

> When the California Legislature enacted the three strikes law, it made a judgment that protecting the public safety requires incapacitating criminals who have already been convicted of at least one serious or violent crime. Nothing in the Eighth Amendment prohibits California from making that choice. To the contrary, our cases establish that "States have a valid interest in deterring and segregating habitual criminals." Recidivism has long been recognized as a legitimate basis for increased punishment. The State's interest in deterring crime also lends some support to the three strikes law. We have long viewed both incapacitation and deterrence as rationales for recidivism statutes.
>
> In weighing the gravity of Ewing's offense, we must place on the scales not only his current felony, but also his long history of felony recidivism. Any other approach would fail to accord proper deference to the policy judgments that find expression in the legislature's choice of sanctions. In imposing a three strikes sentence, the State's interest is not merely punishing the offense of conviction, or the "triggering" offense: "It is in addition the interest in dealing in a harsher manner with those who by repeated criminal acts have shown that they are simply incapable of conforming to the norms of society as established by its criminal law." To give full effect to the State's choice of this legitimate penological goal, our proportionality review of Ewing's sentence must take that goal into account.

Ewing's sentence is justified by the State's public-safety interest in incapacitating and deterring recidivist felons, and amply supported by his own long, serious criminal record.

The *Graham* majority held that "the approach in cases such as *Ewing* is suited for considering a gross proportionality challenge to a particular defendant's sentence, but here a sentencing practice itself is in question." If Ewing had challenged the practice of sentencing under three-strikes laws rather than the unfairness of his own sentence, do you think the result in that case would have been different?

c. Geriatric Release

The Supreme Court has found that Virginia's decision to review the sentences of minors previously sentenced to life imprisonment under a "geriatric release program," applying only after they are over 65 years old and using normal parole consideration factors for assessment for release, was a reasonable application of *Graham*, providing a meaningful opportunity to obtain release. *Virginia v. LeBlanc,* 137 S.Ct. 1726, 198 L.Ed.2d 186 (2017). What do you think? Is this too long to wait—until he or she is 65—for a first meaningful review of the appropriateness of a minor's life sentence?

Miller v. Alabama

567 U.S. 460 (2012).

JUSTICE KAGAN delivered the opinion of the Court.

Hear It

The oral argument in *Miller* is particularly interesting. You can listen to it here: http://www.oyez.org/cases/2010-2019/2011/2011_10_9646. If you had been listening to this argument when it was made, how accurately do you think you would have been able to predict the positions that were ultimately taken by each of the justices?

The two 14-year-old offenders in these cases were convicted of murder and sentenced to life imprisonment without the possibility of parole. In neither case did the sentencing authority have any discretion to impose a different punishment. State law mandated that each juvenile die in prison even if a judge or jury would have thought that his youth and its attendant characteristics, along with the nature of his crime, made a lesser sentence (for example, life with the possibility of parole) more appropriate. Such a scheme prevents those meting out punishment from considering a juvenile's "lessened culpability" and greater "capacity for change," *Graham v. Florida*, 560 U.S. 48, 130 S.Ct. 2011, 2026–2027, 2029–2030 (2010), and runs afoul of our cases' requirement of individualized sentencing for defendants facing the most serious penalties. We therefore hold that mandatory life without parole for those under the age of 18 at the time of their crimes violates the Eighth Amendment's prohibition on "cruel and unusual punishments."

The Eighth Amendment's prohibition of cruel and unusual punishment guarantees individuals the right not to be subjected to excessive sanctions. That right, we have explained, flows from the basic precept of justice that punishment for crime should be graduated and proportioned to both the offender and the offense. As we noted the last time we considered life-without-parole sentences imposed on juveniles, "the concept of proportionality is central to the Eighth Amendment." *Graham*, 130 S.Ct., at 2021. And we view that concept less through a historical prism than according to " 'the evolving standards of decency that mark the progress of a maturing society.' "

The cases before us implicate two strands of precedent reflecting our concern with proportionate punishment. The first has adopted categorical bans on sentencing practices based on mismatches between the culpability of a class of offenders and the severity of a penalty. So, for example, we have held that imposing the death penalty for nonhomicide crimes against individuals, or imposing it on mentally retarded defendants, violates the Eighth Amendment. Several of the cases in this group have specially focused on juvenile offenders, because of their lesser culpability. *Graham* further likened life without parole for juveniles to the death penalty itself, thereby evoking a second line of our precedents. In those cases, we have prohibited mandatory imposition of capital punishment, requiring that sentencing authorities consider the characteristics of a defendant and the details of his offense before sentencing him to death. Here, the confluence of these two lines of precedent leads to the conclusion that mandatory life-without-parole sentences for juveniles violate the Eighth Amendment.

Children are constitutionally different from adults for purposes of sentencing. Because juveniles have diminished culpability and greater prospects for reform, we explained, they are less deserving of the most severe punishments. There are three significant gaps between juveniles and adults. First, children have a lack of maturity and an underdeveloped sense of responsibility, leading to recklessness, impulsivity, and heedless risk-taking. Second, children are more vulnerable to negative influences and outside pressures, including from their family and peers; they have limited control over their own environment and lack the ability to extricate themselves from horrific, crime-producing settings. And third, a child's character is not as well formed as an adult's; his traits are less fixed and his actions less likely to be evidence of irretrievable depravity.

Our decisions in this regard rest not only on common sense—on what "any parent knows"—but on science and social science as well. In *Roper v. Simmons*, 543 U.S. 551, 570 (2005), we cited studies showing that " 'only a relatively small proportion of adolescents' " who engage in illegal activity " 'develop entrenched patterns of problem behavior.' " And in *Graham*, we noted that "developments in psychology and brain science continue to show fundamental differences between juvenile and adult minds"—for example, in "parts of the brain involved in behavior control." We reasoned that those findings—of transient rashness, proclivity for risk, and inability to assess consequences—both lessened a child's "moral culpability" and enhanced the prospect that, as the years go by and neurological development occurs, his " 'deficiencies will be reformed.' "

Food for Thought

Simply as a matter of separation of powers, is it really the Supreme Court's proper role to assess such behavioral issues in deciding whether a legislative judgment is unconstitutional? What do you think?

Roper and *Graham* emphasized that the distinctive attributes of youth diminish the penological justifications for imposing the harshest sentences on juvenile offenders, even when they commit terrible crimes. Because " 'the heart of the retribution rationale' " relates to an offender's blameworthiness, " 'the case for retribution is not as strong with a minor as with an adult.' " Nor can deterrence do the work in this context, because " 'the same characteristics that render juveniles less culpable than adults' "—their immaturity, recklessness, and impetuosity—make them less likely to consider potential punishment. Similarly, incapacitation could not support the life-without-parole sentence in *Graham*: Deciding that a "juvenile offender forever will be a danger to society" would require "making a judgment that [he] is incorrigible"—but " 'incorrigibility is inconsistent with youth.' " And for the same reason, rehabilitation could not justify that sentence. Life without parole "forswears altogether the rehabilitative ideal." It reflects "an irrevocable judgment about an offender's value and place in society," at odds with a child's capacity for change.

Graham concluded from this analysis that life-without-parole sentences, like capital punishment, may violate the Eighth Amendment when imposed on children. To be sure, *Graham*'s flat ban on life without parole applied only to nonhomicide crimes, and the Court took care to distinguish those offenses from murder, based on both moral culpability and consequential harm. But none of what it said about children—about their distinctive (and transitory) mental traits and environmental vulnerabilities—is crime-specific. Those features are evident in the same way, and to the same degree, when (as in both cases here) a botched robbery turns into a killing. So *Graham*'s reasoning implicates any life-without-parole sentence imposed on a juvenile, even as its categorical bar relates only to nonhomicide offenses.

Most fundamentally, *Graham* insists that youth matters in determining the appropriateness of a lifetime of incarceration without the possibility of parole. In the circumstances there, juvenile status precluded a life-without-parole sentence, even though an adult could receive it for a similar crime.

But the mandatory penalty schemes at issue here prevent the sentencer from taking account of these central considerations. By removing youth from the balance—by subjecting a juvenile to the same life-without-parole sentence applicable to an adult—these laws prohibit a sentencing authority from assessing whether the law's harshest term of imprisonment proportionately punishes a juvenile offender. That contravenes *Graham's* (and also *Roper's*) foundational principle: that imposition of a State's most severe penalties on juvenile offenders cannot proceed as though they were not children.

And *Graham* makes plain these mandatory schemes' defects in another way: by likening life-without-parole sentences imposed on juveniles to the death penalty itself. Life-without-parole terms, the Court wrote, "share some characteristics with death sentences that are shared by no other sentences." Imprisoning an offender until he dies alters the remainder of his life by a forfeiture that is irrevocable. And this lengthiest possible incarceration is an especially harsh punishment for a juvenile, because he will almost inevitably serve more years and a greater percentage of his life in prison than an adult offender. The penalty when imposed on a teenager, as compared with an older person, is therefore "the same . . . in name only." All of that suggested a distinctive set of legal rules: In part because we viewed this ultimate penalty for juveniles as akin to the death penalty, we treated it similarly to that most severe punishment. We imposed a categorical ban on the sentence's use, in a way unprecedented for a term of imprisonment. And the bar we adopted mirrored a proscription first established in the death penalty context—that the punishment cannot be imposed for any nonhomicide crimes against individuals.

That correspondence—*Graham*'s "treatment of juvenile life sentences as analogous to capital punishment"—makes relevant here a second line of our precedents, demanding individualized sentencing when imposing the death penalty. Of special pertinence here, we insisted in these rulings that a sentencer have the ability to consider the "mitigating qualities of youth." So *Graham* and *Roper* and our individualized sentencing cases alike teach that in imposing a State's harshest penalties, a sentencer misses too much if he treats every child as an adult. To recap: Mandatory life without parole for a juvenile precludes consideration of his chronological age and its hallmark features—among them, immaturity, impetuosity, and failure to appreciate risks and consequences. It prevents taking into account the family and home environment that surrounds him—and from which he cannot usually extricate himself—no matter how brutal or dysfunctional. It neglects the circumstances of the homicide offense, including the extent of his participation in the conduct and the way familial and peer pressures may have affected him. Indeed, it ignores that he might have been charged and convicted of a lesser offense if not for incompetencies associated with youth—for example, his inability to deal with police officers or prosecutors (including on a plea agreement) or his incapacity to assist his own attorneys. And finally, this mandatory punishment disregards the possibility of rehabilitation even when the circumstances most suggest it.

We therefore hold that the Eighth Amendment forbids a sentencing scheme that mandates life in prison without possibility of parole for juvenile offenders. By making youth (and all that accompanies it) irrelevant to imposition of that harshest prison sentence, such a scheme poses too great a risk of disproportionate punishment. Because that holding is sufficient to decide these cases, we do not consider Jackson's and Miller's alternative argument that the Eighth Amendment requires a categorical bar on life without parole for juveniles, or at least for those 14 and younger. But given all we have said in *Roper*, *Graham*, and this decision about children's diminished culpability and heightened capacity for change, we think appropriate occasions for sentencing juveniles to this harshest possible penalty will be uncommon. That is especially so because of the great difficulty we noted in *Roper* and *Graham* of distinguishing at this early age between the juvenile offender whose crime reflects unfortunate yet transient immaturity, and the rare juvenile offender whose crime reflects irreparable corruption. Although we do not foreclose a sentencer's ability to make that judgment in homicide cases, we require it to take into account how children are different, and how those differences counsel against irrevocably sentencing them to a lifetime in prison. We accordingly reverse the judgments of the Arkansas

Supreme Court and Alabama Court of Criminal Appeals and remand the cases for further proceedings not inconsistent with this opinion.

CHIEF JUSTICE ROBERTS, with whom JUSTICE SCALIA, JUSTICE THOMAS, and JUSTICE ALITO join, dissenting.

Determining the appropriate sentence for a teenager convicted of murder presents grave and challenging questions of morality and social policy. Our role, however, is to apply the law, not to answer such questions. The pertinent law here is the Eighth Amendment to the Constitution, which prohibits "cruel and unusual punishments." Today, the Court invokes that Amendment to ban a punishment that the Court does not itself characterize as unusual, and that could not plausibly be described as such. I therefore dissent.

The parties agree that nearly 2,500 prisoners are presently serving life sentences without the possibility of parole for murders they committed before the age of 18. The Court accepts that over 2,000 of those prisoners received that sentence because it was mandated by a legislature. And it recognizes that the Federal Government and most States impose such mandatory sentences. Put simply, if a 17-year-old is convicted of deliberately murdering an innocent victim, it is not "unusual" for the murderer to receive a mandatory sentence of life without parole. That reality should preclude finding that mandatory life imprisonment for juvenile killers violates the Eighth Amendment.

In any event, the Court's holding does not follow from *Roper* and *Graham*. Those cases undoubtedly stand for the proposition that teenagers are less mature, less responsible, and less fixed in their ways than adults—not that a Supreme Court case was needed to establish that. What they do not stand for, and do not even suggest, is that legislators—who also know that teenagers are different from adults—may not require life without parole for juveniles who commit the worst types of murder.

It is a great tragedy when a juvenile commits murder—most of all for the innocent victims. But also for the murderer, whose life has gone so wrong so early. And for society as well, which has lost one or more of its members to deliberate violence, and must harshly punish another. In recent years, our society has moved toward requiring that the murderer, his age notwithstanding, be imprisoned for the remainder of his life. Members of this Court may disagree with that choice. Perhaps science and policy suggest society should show greater mercy to young killers, giving them a greater chance to reform themselves at the risk that they will kill again. But that is not our decision to make. Neither the text of the Constitution nor our precedent prohibits legislatures from requiring that juvenile murderers be sentenced to life without parole. I respectfully dissent.

JUSTICE THOMAS, with whom JUSTICE SCALIA joins, dissenting.

Today's decision invalidates a constitutionally permissible sentencing system based on nothing more than the Court's belief that "its own sense of morality pre-empts that of the people and their representatives." Because nothing in the Constitution grants the Court the authority it exercises today, I respectfully dissent.

JUSTICE ALITO, with whom JUSTICE SCALIA joins, dissenting.

The Court now holds that Congress and the legislatures of the 50 States are prohibited by the Constitution from identifying any category of murderers under the age of 18 who must be sentenced to life imprisonment without parole. Even a 17 ½-year-old who sets off a bomb in a crowded mall or guns down a dozen students and teachers is a "child" and must be given a chance to persuade a judge to permit his release into society. Nothing in the Constitution supports this arrogation of legislative authority.

Food for Thought

Justices Thomas, Scalia, and Alito dissented in the *Graham* decision. Simply as a matter of *stare decisis*, shouldn't the majority's holding in *Graham* be controlling? Did the four dissenting justices in *Miller* actually accept *Graham* and seek to apply it? Or are they continuing to take issue with the *Graham* majority? What do you think?

What today's decision shows is that our Eighth Amendment cases are no longer tied to any objective indicia of society's standards. Our Eighth Amendment case law is now entirely inward looking. Future cases may extrapolate from today's holding, and this process may continue until the majority brings sentencing practices into line with whatever the majority views as truly evolved standards of decency. The Constitution does not authorize us to take the country on this journey.

Point for Discussion

Miller Retroactive

The Supreme Court subsequently ruled that the *Miller* decision conclusion that life sentences without the possibility of parole for juvenile offenders were unconstitutional was retroactive. *Montgomery v. Louisiana*, 136 S.Ct. 718, 193 L.Ed.2d 599 (2016). However, the majority noted that "giving *Miller* retroactive effect does not require States to relitigate sentences, let alone convictions, in every case where a juvenile offender received mandatory life without parole. A State may remedy a *Miller* violation by permitting juvenile homicide offenders to be considered for parole, rather than by resentencing them." What do you think? Should a simple parole hearing suffice to meet the constitutional concerns discussed by the majority in *Miller*? And consider once again the Supreme Court's acceptance of a "geriatric release" remedy in 2017, discussed above.

Major Themes

a. **Juries' Fact-Finding Critical**—Sentencing judges may not engage in fact-finding that supplants the role of the jury by establishing explicit or implicit elements of a crime leading to an increase in sentencing.

b. **Death Is Different**—Jurisdictions have the authority to use the death penalty as criminal punishment, and most have done so. But any capital-punishment sentencing scheme must define the necessary showing of aggravating circumstances narrowly and precisely, and permit the defendant's introduction of all forms of mitigating evidence.

c. **Cruel & Unusual Punishment Is About Proportionality**—Punishment is unconstitutional under the Eighth Amendment when it is viewed as barbaric since it is disproportionate to the crime.

Executive Summary

Sentencing Fact-Finding. Any fact (other than a prior conviction) which is necessary to support a sentence exceeding the maximum authorized by the facts established by a plea of guilty or a jury verdict must be admitted by the defendant or proved to a jury beyond a reasonable doubt.

Judges' Sentencing Discretion. Trial judges still retain their traditional discretion to consider sentencing factors in determining an appropriate sentence as long as they do not engage in fact-finding with respect to an element of the crime in jury trials.

Capital Punishment Permissible. The Supreme Court has concluded that jurisdictions may punish heinous homicidal acts by imposition of the death penalty. Legislatures may reasonably conclude that capital punishment is justified on the basis of retribution and/or deterrence. There is a recent trend, however, toward legislative repeal of state death penalty statutes.

Capital-Sentencing Proceedings. Sentences of death must be individualized; they cannot be mandatory. The sentencing jury (or judge in a bench trial) must find the existence of at least one aggravating circumstance that has been narrowly and precisely defined by statute. But all relevant mitigating evidence of any kind may be introduced at a capital-sentencing hearing on the convicted defendant's behalf.

Life Sentence Without Parole Unconstitutional for Juveniles. The Supreme Court has recently held that imposition of a life without parole sentence on a juvenile offender who did not commit homicide is unconstitutional under the Eighth Amendment.

Some Death Sentences Cruel & Unusual. The Supreme Court has concluded that capital punishment is categorically unconstitutional for: rape and other non-homicide crimes committed against individuals; crimes committed before the accused reached the age of 18; and for defendants whose intellectual functioning is in a low range.

For More Information

- AMERICAN BAR ASSOCIATION, CRIMINAL JUSTICE SECTION, CRIMINAL JUSTICE STANDARDS, SENTENCING (3d ed. 1993).
- Douglas A. Berman, *Balanced and Purposeful Departures: Fixing a Jurisprudence That Undermines the Federal Sentencing Guidelines*, 76 NOTRE DAME L. REV. 21 (2000).
- Stephen B. Bright, *Discrimination, Death and Denial: The Tolerance of Racial Discrimination in Infliction of the Death Penalty*, 35 SANTA CLARA L. REV. 433 (1995).
- Mark L. Earley, Sr., *A Pink Cadillac, an IQ OF 63, and a Fourteen-Year-Old From South Carolina: Why I Can No Longer Support the Death Penalty*, 49 U. RICH. L. REV. 811 (2015).
- MARVIN E. FRANKEL, CRIMINAL SENTENCES: LAW WITHOUT ORDER (1973).
- DAVID GARLAND, PECULIAR INSTITUTION: AMERICA'S DEATH PENALTY IN AN AGE OF ABOLITION (2010).

- Brandon Garrett & John Monahan, *Judging Risk*, 108 CAL. L. REV. 439 (2020).
- Nancy Gertner, *Women and Sentencing*, 57 AM CRIM. L. REV. 1401 (2020).
- Gross, O'Brien, Hu, & Kennedy, *Rate of False Conviction of Criminal Defendants Who Are Sentenced to Death*, 111 PROCEEDING OF THE NATIONAL ACADEMY OF SCIENCES 7230 (2014).
- Molly Treadway Johnson & Scott A. Gilbert, Fed. Judicial Ctr., THE U.S. SENTENCING GUIDELINES: RESULTS OF THE FEDERAL JUDICIAL CENTER'S 1996 SURVEY (1997).
- John S. Martin, Jr., *Why Mandatory Minimums Make No Sense*, 18 NOTRE DAME J.L. ETHICS & PUB. POL'Y 311 (2004).
- Kevin R. Reitz, *Sentencing Guidelines Systems and Sentencing Appeals: A Comparison of Federal and State Experiences*, 91 NW. U. L. REV. 1441, 1446 (1997).
- Jennifer Skeem, Nicholas Scurich & John Monahan, *Impact of Risk Assessment on Judges' Fairness in Sentencing Relatively Poor Defendants*, 44 LAW & HUM. BEHAVIOR 51 (2020).
- Brenda L. Tofte, *Booker at Seven: Looking Behind Sentencing Decisions: What Is Motivating Judges?*, 65 ARK. L. REV. 529 (2012).
- Jack B. Weinstein, *Every Day is a Good Day for a Judge to Lay Down His Professional Life for Justice*, 32 FORDHAM URB. L.J. 131 (2004).
- Ronald F. Wright, *Rules for Sentencing Revolutions*, 108 YALE L.J. 1355, 1379 (1999).
- DEBORAH YOUNG & PETER HOFFMAN, FEDERAL SENTENCING LAW & PRACTICE, 2013 ed. (West Criminal Practice Series).

Test Your Knowledge

To assess your understanding of the material in this chapter, click here to take a quiz.

Model Penal Code

American Law Institute Model Penal Code

O O O

(Official Draft, 1962)

PART I. GENERAL PROVISIONS

Article 1. Preliminary

SECTION 1.01. [*Omitted*]

SECTION 1.02. PURPOSES; PRINCIPLES OF CONSTRUCTION

(1) The general purposes of the provisions governing the definition of offenses are:

(a) to forbid and prevent conduct that unjustifiably and inexcusably inflicts or threatens substantial harm to individual or public interests;

(b) to subject to public control persons whose conduct indicates that they are disposed to commit crimes;

(c) to safeguard conduct that is without fault from condemnation as criminal;

(d) to give fair warning of the nature of the conduct declared to constitute an offense;

(e) to differentiate on reasonable grounds between serious and minor offenses.

(2) The general purposes of the provisions governing the sentencing and treatment of offenders are:

(a) to prevent the commission of offenses;

(b) to promote the correction and rehabilitation of offenders;

(c) to safeguard offenders against excessive, disproportionate or arbitrary punishment;

(d) to give fair warning of the nature of the sentences that may be imposed on conviction of an offense;

(e) to differentiate among offenders with a view to a just individualization in their treatment;

(f) to define, coordinate and harmonize the powers, duties and functions of the courts and of administrative officers and agencies responsible for dealing with offenders;

(g) to advance the use of generally accepted scientific methods and knowledge in the sentencing and treatment of offenders;

(h) to integrate responsibility for the administration of the correctional system in a State Department of Correction [or other single department or agency].

(3) The provisions of the Code shall be construed according to the fair import of their terms but when the language is susceptible of differing constructions it shall be interpreted to further the general purposes stated in this Section and the special purposes of the particular provision involved. The discretionary powers conferred by the Code shall be exercised in accordance with the criteria stated in the Code and, insofar as such criteria are not decisive, to further the general purposes stated in this Section.

SECTION 1.03. [*Omitted*]

SECTION 1.04. CLASSES OF CRIMES; VIOLATIONS

(1) An offense defined by this Code or by any other statute of this State, for which a sentence of [death or of] imprisonment is authorized, constitutes a crime. Crimes are classified as felonies, misdemeanors or petty misdemeanors.

(2) A crime is a felony if it is so designated in this Code or if persons convicted thereof may be sentenced [to death or] to imprisonment for a term that, apart from an extended term, is in excess of one year.

(3) A crime is a misdemeanor if it is so designated in the Code or in a statute other than this Code enacted subsequent thereto.

(4) A crime is a petty misdemeanor if it is so designated in this Code or in a statute other than this Code enacted subsequent thereto or if it is defined by a statute other than this Code that now provides that persons convicted thereof may be sentenced to imprisonment for a term of which the maximum is less than one year.

(5) An offense defined by this Code or by any other statute of this State constitutes a violation if it is so designated in this Code or in the law defining the offense or if no other

sentence than a fine, or fine and forfeiture or other civil penalty is authorized upon conviction or if it is defined by a statute other than this Code that now provides that the offense shall not constitute a crime. A violation does not constitute a crime and conviction of a violation shall not give rise to any disability or legal disadvantage based on conviction of a criminal offense.

(6) Any offense declared by law to constitute a crime, without specification of the grade thereof or of the sentence authorized upon conviction, is a misdemeanor.

(7) An offense defined by any statute of this State other than this Code shall be classified as provided in this Section and the sentence that may be imposed upon conviction thereof shall hereafter be governed by the Code.

SECTION 1.05. ALL OFFENSES DEFINED BY STATUTE; APPLICATION OF GENERAL PROVISIONS OF THE CODE

(1) No conduct constitutes an offense unless it is a crime or violation under this Code or another statute of the State.

(2) The provisions of Part I of the Code are applicable to offenses defined by other statutes, unless the Code otherwise provides.

(3) This Section does not affect the power of a court to punish for contempt or to employ any sanction authorized by law for the enforcement of an order or a civil judgment or decree.

SECTION 1.06. [*Omitted*]

SECTION 1.07. METHOD OF PROSECUTION WHEN CONDUCT CONSTITUTES MORE THAN ONE OFFENSE

(1) *Prosecution for Multiple Offenses; Limitation on Convictions.* When the same conduct of a defendant may establish the commission of more than one offense, the defendant may be prosecuted for each such offense. He may not, however, be convicted of more than one offense if:

(a) one offense is included in the other, as defined in Subsection (4) of this Section; or

(b) one offense consists only of a conspiracy or other form of preparation to commit the other; or

(c) inconsistent findings of fact are required to establish the commission of the offenses; or

(d) the offenses differ only in that one is defined to prohibit a designated kind of conduct generally and the other to prohibit a specific instance of such conduct; or

(e) the offense is defined as a continuing course of conduct and the defendant's course of conduct was uninterrupted, unless the law provides that specific periods of such conduct constitute separate offenses.

(2) *Limitation on Separate Trials for Multiple Offenses.* Except as provided in Subsection (3) of this Section, a defendant shall not be subject to separate trials for multiple offenses based on the same conduct or arising from the same criminal episode, if such offenses are known to the appropriate prosecuting officer at the time of the commencement of the first trial and are within the jurisdiction of a single court.

(3) *Authority of Court to Order Separate Trials.* When a defendant is charged with two or more offenses based on the same conduct or arising from the same criminal episode, the Court, on application of the prosecuting attorney or of the defendant, may order any such charge to be tried separately, if it is satisfied that justice so requires.

(4) *Conviction of Included Offense Permitted.* A defendant may be convicted of an offense included in an offense charged in the indictment [or the information]. An offense is so included when:

(a) it is established by proof of the same or less than all the facts required to establish the commission of the offense charged; or

(b) it consists of an attempt or solicitation to commit the offense charged or to commit an offense otherwise included therein; or

(c) it differs from the offense charged only in the respect that a less serious injury or risk of injury to the same person, property or public interest or a lesser kind of culpability suffices to establish its commission.

(5) *Submission of Included Offense to Jury.* The Court shall not be obligated to charge the jury with respect to an included offense unless there is a rational basis for a verdict acquitting the defendant of the offense charged and convicting him of the included offense.

SECTIONS 1.08.B1.11. [*Omitted*]

SECTION 1.12. PROOF BEYOND A REASONABLE DOUBT; AFFIRMATIVE DEFENSES; BURDEN OF PROVING FACT WHEN NOT AN ELEMENT OF AN OFFENSE; PRESUMPTIONS

(1) No person may be convicted of an offense unless each element of such offense is proved beyond a reasonable doubt. In the absence of such proof, the innocence of the defendant is assumed.

(2) Subsection (1) of the Section does not:

(a) require the disproof of an affirmative defense unless and until there is evidence supporting such defense; or

(b) apply to any defense which the Code or another statute plainly requires the defendant to prove by a preponderance of evidence.

(3) A ground of defense is affirmative, within the meaning of Subsection (2)(a) of the Section, when:

(a) it arises under a section of the Code that so provides; or

(b) it relates to an offense defined by a statute other than the Code and such statute so provides; or

(c) it involves a matter of excuse or justification peculiarly within the knowledge of the defendant on which he can fairly be required to adduce supporting evidence.

(4) When the application of the Code depends upon the finding of a fact which is not an element of an offense, unless the Code otherwise provides:

(a) the burden of proving the fact is on the prosecution or defendant, depending on whose interest or contention will be furthered if the finding should be made; and

(b) the fact must be proved to the satisfaction of the Court or jury, as the case may be.

(5) When the Code establishes a presumption with respect to any fact that is an element of an offense, it has the following consequences:

(a) when there is evidence of the facts that give rise to the presumption, the issue of the existence of the presumed fact must be submitted to the jury, unless the Court is satisfied that the evidence as a whole clearly negatives the presumed fact; and

(b) when the issue of the existence of the presumed fact is submitted to the jury, the Court shall charge that while the presumed fact must, on all the evidence, be proved beyond a reasonable doubt, the law declares that the jury may regard the facts giving rise to the presumption as sufficient evidence of the presumed fact.

(6) A presumption not established by the Code or inconsistent with it has the consequences otherwise accorded it by law.

Section 1.13. General Definitions

In this Code, unless a different meaning plainly is required:

(1) "statute" includes the Constitution and a local law or ordinance of a political subdivision of the State;

(2) "act" or "action" means a bodily movement whether voluntary or involuntary;

(3) "voluntary" has the meaning specified in Section 2.01;

(4) "omission" means a failure to act;

(5) "conduct" means an action or omission and its accompanying state of mind, or, where relevant, a series of acts and omissions;

(6) "actor" includes, where relevant, a person guilty of an omission;

(7) "acted" includes, where relevant, "omitted to act";

(8) "person," "he" and "actor" include any natural person and, where relevant, a corporation or an unincorporated association;

(9) "element of an offense" means (i) such conduct or (ii) such attendant circumstance or (iii) such a result of conduct as

(a) is included in the description of the forbidden conduct in the definition of the offense; or

(b) establishes the required kind of culpability; or

(c) negatives an excuse or justification for such conduct; or

(d) negatives a defense under the statute of limitations; or

(e) establishes jurisdiction or venue;

(10) "material element of an offense" means an element that does not relate exclusively to the statute of limitations, jurisdiction, venue or to any other matter similarly unconnected with (i) the harm or evil, incident to conduct, sought to be prevented by the law defining the offense, or (ii) the existence of a justification or excuse for such conduct;

(11) "purposely" has the meaning specified in Section 2.02 and equivalent terms such as "with purpose," "designed" or "with design" have the same meaning;

(12) "intentionally" or "with intent" means purposely;

(13) "knowingly" has the meaning specified in Section 2.02 and equivalent terms such as "knowing" or "with knowledge" have the same meaning;

(14) "recklessly" has the meaning specified in Section 2.02 and equivalent terms such as "recklessness" or "with recklessness" have the same meaning;

(15) "negligently" has the meaning specified in Section 2.02 and equivalent terms such as "negligence" or "with negligence" have the same meaning;

(16) "reasonably believes" or "reasonable belief" designates a belief which the actor is not reckless or negligent in holding.

Article 2. General Principles of Liability

SECTION 2.01. REQUIREMENT OF VOLUNTARY ACT; OMISSION AS BASIS OF LIABILITY; POSSESSION AS AN ACT

(1) A person is not guilty of an offense unless his liability is based on conduct which includes a voluntary act or the omission to perform an act of which he is physically capable.

(2) The following are not voluntary acts within the meaning of this Section:

(a) a reflex or convulsion;

(b) a bodily movement during unconsciousness or sleep;

(c) conduct during hypnosis or resulting from hypnotic suggestion;

(d) a bodily movement that otherwise is not a product of the effort or determination of the actor, either conscious or habitual.

(3) Liability for the commission of an offense may not be based on an omission unaccompanied by action unless:

(a) the omission is expressly made sufficient by the law defining the offense; or

(b) a duty to perform the omitted act is otherwise imposed by law.

(4) Possession is an act, within the meaning of this Section, if the possessor knowingly procured or received the thing possessed or was aware of his control thereof for a sufficient period to have been able to terminate his possession.

SECTION 2.02. GENERAL REQUIREMENTS OF CULPABILITY

(1) *Minimum Requirements of Culpability.* Except as provided in Section 2.05, a person is not guilty of an offense unless he acted purposely, knowingly, recklessly or negligently, as the law may require, with respect to each material element of the offense.

(2) Kinds of Culpability Defined.

(a) *Purposely.* A person acts purposely with respect to a material element of an offense when:

(i) if the element involves the nature of his conduct or a result thereof, it is his conscious object to engage in conduct of that nature or to cause such a result; and

(ii) if the element involves the attendant circumstances, he is aware of the existence of such circumstances or he believes or hopes that they exist.

(b) *Knowingly.* A person acts knowingly with respect to a material element of an offense when:

(i) if the element involves the nature of his conduct or the attendant circumstances, he is aware that his conduct is of that nature or that such circumstances exist; and

(ii) if the element involves a result of his conduct, he is aware that it is practically certain that his conduct will cause such a result.

(c) *Recklessly.* A person acts recklessly with respect to a material element of an offense when he consciously disregards a substantial and unjustifiable risk that the material element exists or will result from his conduct. The risk must be of such a nature and degree that, considering the nature and purpose of the actor's conduct and the circumstances known to him, its disregard involves a gross deviation from the standard of conduct that a law-abiding person would observe in the actor's situation.

(d) *Negligently.* A person acts negligently with respect to a material element of an offense when he should be aware of a substantial and unjustifiable risk that the material element exists or will result from his conduct. The risk must be of such a nature and degree that the actor's failure to perceive it, considering the nature and purpose of his conduct and the circumstances known to him, involves a gross deviation from the standard of care that a reasonable person would observe in the actor's situation.

(3) *Culpability Required Unless Otherwise Provided.* When the culpability sufficient to establish a material element of an offense is not prescribed by law, such element is established if a person acts purposely, knowingly or recklessly with respect thereto.

(4) *Prescribed Culpability Requirement Applies to All Material Elements.* When the law defining an offense prescribes the kind of culpability that is sufficient for the commission of an offense, without distinguishing among the material elements thereof, such provision shall apply to all the material elements of the offense, unless a contrary purpose plainly appears.

(5) *Substitutes for Negligence, Recklessness and Knowledge.* When the law provides that negligence suffices to establish an element of an offense, such element also is established if a person acts purposely, knowingly or recklessly. When recklessness suffices to establish an element, such element also is established if a person acts purposely or knowingly. When acting knowingly suffices to establish an element, such element also is established if a person acts purposely.

(6) *Requirement of Purpose Satisfied if Purpose Is Conditional.* When a particular purpose is an element of an offense, the element is established although such purpose is conditional, unless the condition negatives the harm or evil sought to be prevented by the law defining the offense.

(7) *Requirement of Knowledge Satisfied by Knowledge of High Probability.* When knowledge of the existence of a particular fact is an element of an offense, such knowledge is established if a person is aware of a high probability of its existence, unless he actually believes that it does not exist.

(8) *Requirement of Wilfulness Satisfied by Acting Knowingly.* A requirement that an offense be committed wilfully is satisfied if a person acts knowingly with respect to the material elements of the offense, unless a purpose to impose further requirements appears.

(9) *Culpability as to Illegality of Conduct.* Neither knowledge nor recklessness or negligence as to whether conduct constitutes an offense or as to the existence, meaning or application of the law determining the elements of an offense is an element of such offense, unless the definition of the offense or the Code so provides.

(10) *Culpability as Determinant of Grade of Offense.* When the grade or degree of an offense depends on whether the offense is committed purposely, knowingly, recklessly or negligently, its grade or degree shall be the lowest for which the determinative kind of culpability is established with respect to any material element of the offense.

Section 2.03. Causal Relationship Between Conduct and Result; Divergence Between Result Designed or Contemplated and Actual Result or Between Probable and Actual Result

(1) Conduct is the cause of a result when:

(a) it is an antecedent but for which the result in question would not have occurred; and

(b) the relationship between the conduct and result satisfies any additional causal requirements imposed by the Code or by the law defining the offense.

(2) When purposely or knowingly causing a particular result is an element of an offense, the element is not established if the actual result is not within the purpose or the contemplation of the actor unless:

(a) the actual result differs from that designed or contemplated, as the case may be, only in the respect that a different person or different property is injured or affected or that the injury or harm designed or contemplated would have been more serious or more extensive than that caused; or

(b) the actual result involves the same kind of injury or harm as that designed or contemplated and is not too remote or accidental in its occurrence to have a [just] bearing on the actor's liability or on the gravity of his offense.

(3) When recklessly or negligently causing a particular result is an element of an offense, the element is not established if the actual result is not within the risk of which the actor is aware or, in the case of negligence, of which he should be aware unless:

(a) the actual result differs from the probable result only in the respect that a different person or different property is injured or affected or that the probable injury or harm would have been more serious or more extensive than that caused; or

(b) the actual result involves the same kind of injury or harm as the probable result and is not too remote or accidental in its occurrence to have a [just] bearing on the actor's liability or on the gravity of his offense.

(4) When causing a particular result is a material element of an offense for which absolute liability is imposed by law, the element is not established unless the actual result is a probable consequence of the actor's conduct.

SECTION 2.04. IGNORANCE OR MISTAKE

(1) Ignorance or mistake as to a matter of fact or law is a defense if:

(a) the ignorance or mistake negatives the purpose, knowledge, belief, recklessness or negligence required to establish a material element of the offense; or

(b) the law provides that the state of mind established by such ignorance or mistake constitutes a defense.

(2) Although ignorance or mistake would otherwise afford a defense to the offense charged, the defense is not available if the defendant would be guilty of another offense had the situation been as he supposed. In such case, however, the ignorance or mistake of the defendant shall reduce the grade and degree of the offense of which he may be convicted to those of the offense of which he would be guilty had the situation been as he supposed.

(3) A belief that conduct does not legally constitute an offense is a defense to a prosecution for that offense based upon such conduct when:

(a) the statute or other enactment defining the offense is not known to the actor and has not been published or otherwise reasonably made available prior to the conduct alleged; or

(b) he acts in reasonable reliance upon an official statement of the law, afterward determined to be invalid or erroneous, contained in (i) a statute or other enactment; (ii) a judicial decision, opinion or judgment; (iii) an administrative order or grant of permission; or (iv) an official interpretation of the public officer or body charged by law with responsibility for the interpretation, administration or enforcement of the law defining the offense.

(4) The defendant must prove a defense arising under Subsection (3) of this Section by a preponderance of evidence.

Section 2.05. When Culpability Requirements Are Inapplicable to Violations and to Offenses Defined by Other Statutes; Effect of Absolute Liability in Reducing Grade of Offense to Violation

(1) The requirements of culpability prescribed by Sections 2.01 and 2.02 do not apply to:

(a) offenses which constitute violations, unless the requirement involved is included in the definition of the offense or the Court determines that its application is consistent with effective enforcement of the law defining the offense; or

(b) offenses defined by statutes other than the Code, insofar as a legislative purpose to impose absolute liability for such offenses or with respect to any material element thereof plainly appears.

(2) Notwithstanding any other provision of existing law and unless a subsequent statute otherwise provides:

(a) when absolute liability is imposed with respect to any material element of an offense defined by a statute other than the Code and a conviction is based upon such liability, the offense constitutes a violation; and

(b) although absolute liability is imposed by law with respect to one or more of the material elements of an offense defined by a statute other than the Code, the culpable commission of the offense may be charged and proved, in which event negligence with respect to such elements constitutes sufficient culpability and the classification of the offense and the sentence that may be imposed therefor upon conviction are determined by Section 1.04 and Article 6 of the Code.

Section 2.06. Liability for Conduct of Another; Complicity

(1) A person is guilty of an offense if it is committed by his own conduct or by the conduct of another person for which he is legally accountable, or both.

(2) A person is legally accountable for the conduct of another person when:

(a) acting with the kind of culpability that is sufficient for the commission of the offense, he causes an innocent or irresponsible person to engage in such conduct; or

(b) he is made accountable for the conduct of such other person by the Code or by the law defining the offense; or

(c) he is an accomplice of such other person in the commission of the offense.

(3) A person is an accomplice of another person in the commission of an offense if:

(a) with the purpose of promoting or facilitating the commission of the offense, he

(i) solicits such other person to commit it; or

(ii) aids or agrees or attempts to aid such other person in planning or committing it; or

(iii) having a legal duty to prevent the commission of the offense, fails to make proper effort so to do; or

(b) his conduct is expressly declared by law to establish his complicity.

(4) When causing a particular result is an element of an offense, an accomplice in the conduct causing such result is an accomplice in the commission of that offense, if he acts with the kind of culpability, if any, with respect to that result that is sufficient for the commission of the offense.

(5) A person who is legally incapable of committing a particular offense himself may be guilty thereof if it is committed by the conduct of another person for which he is legally accountable, unless such liability is inconsistent with the purpose of the provision establishing his incapacity.

(6) Unless otherwise provided by the Code or by the law defining the offense, a person is not an accomplice in an offense committed by another person if:

(a) he is a victim of that offense; or

(b) the offense is so defined that his conduct is inevitably incident to its commission; or

(c) he terminates his complicity prior to the commission of the offense and

(i) wholly deprives it of effectiveness in the commission of the offense; or

(ii) gives timely warning to the law enforcement authorities or otherwise makes proper effort to prevent the commission of the offense.

(7) An accomplice may be convicted on proof of the commission of the offense and of his complicity therein, though the person claimed to have committed the offense has not been prosecuted or convicted or has been convicted of a different offense or degree of offense or has an immunity to prosecution or conviction or has been acquitted.

Section 2.07. Liability of Corporations, Unincorporated Associations and Persons Acting, or Under a Duty to Act, in Their Behalf

(1) A corporation may be convicted of the commission of an offense if:

(a) the offense is a violation or the offense is defined by a statute other than the Code in which a legislative purpose to impose liability on corporations plainly appears and the conduct is performed by an agent of the corporation acting in behalf of the corporation within the scope of his office or employment, except that if the law defining the offense designates the agents for whose conduct the corporation is accountable or the circumstance under which it is accountable, such provisions shall apply; or

(b) the offense consists of an omission to discharge a specific duty of affirmative performance imposed on corporations by law; or

(c) the commission of the offense was authorized, requested, commanded, performed or recklessly tolerated by the board of directors or by a high managerial agent acting in behalf of the corporation within the scope of his office or employment.

(2) When absolute liability is imposed for the commission of an offense, a legislative purpose to impose liability on a corporation shall be assumed, unless the contrary plainly appears.

(3) An unincorporated association may be convicted of the commission of an offense if:

(a) the offense is defined by a statute other than the Code which expressly provides for the liability of such an association and the conduct is performed by an agent of the association acting in behalf of the association within the scope of his office or employment, except that if the law defining the offense designates the agents for whose conduct the association is accountable or the circumstances under which it is accountable, such provisions shall apply; or

(b) the offense consists of an omission to discharge a specific duty of affirmative performance imposed on associations by law.

(4) As used in the Section:

(a) "corporation" does not include an entity organized as or by a governmental agency for the execution of a governmental program;

(b) "agent" means any director, officer, servant, employee or other person authorized to act in behalf of the corporation or association and, in the case of an unincorporated association, a member of such association;

(c) "high managerial agent" means an officer of a corporation or an unincorporated association, or, in the case of a partnership, a partner, or any other agent of a corporation or association having duties of such responsibilities that his conduct may fairly be assumed to represent the policy of the corporation or association.

(5) In any prosecution of a corporation or an unincorporated association for the commission of an offense included within the terms of Subsection (1)(a) or Subsection (3)(a) of this Section, other than an offense for which absolute liability has been imposed, it shall be a defense if the defendant proves by a preponderance of evidence that the high managerial agent having supervisory responsibility over the subject matter of the offense employed due diligence to prevent its commission. This paragraph shall not apply if it is plainly inconsistent with the legislative purpose in defining the particular offense.

(6)(a) A person is legally accountable for any conduct he performs or causes to be performed in the name of the corporation or an unincorporated association or in its behalf to the same extent as if it were performed in his own name or behalf.

(b) Whenever a duty to act is imposed by law upon a corporation or an unincorporated association, any agent of the corporation or association having responsibility for the discharge of the duty is legally accountable for a reckless omission to perform the required act to the same extent as if the duty were imposed by law directly upon himself.

(c) When a person is convicted of an offense by reason of his legal accountability for the conduct of a corporation or an unincorporated association, he is subject to the sentence authorized by law when a natural person is convicted of an offense of the grade and the degree involved.

SECTION 2.08. INTOXICATION

(1) Except as provided in Subsection (4) of this Section, intoxication of the actor is not a defense unless it negatives an element of the offense.

(2) When recklessness establishes an element of the offense, if the actor, due to self-induced intoxication, is unaware of a risk of which he would have been aware had he been sober, such unawareness is immaterial.

(3) Intoxication does not, in itself, constitute mental disease within the meaning of Section 4.01.

(4) Intoxication that (a) is not self-induced or (b) is pathological is an affirmative defense if by reason of such intoxication the actor at the time of his conduct lacks substantial capacity either to appreciate its criminality [wrongfulness] or to conform his conduct to the requirements of law.

(5) *Definitions.* In this Section unless a different meaning plainly is required:

(a) "intoxication" means a disturbance of mental or physical capacities resulting from the introduction of substances into the body;

(b) "self-induced intoxication" means intoxication caused by substances which the actor knowingly introduces into his body, the tendency of which to cause intoxication he knows or ought to know, unless he introduces them pursuant to medical advice or under such circumstances as would afford a defense to a charge of crime;

(c) "pathological intoxication" means intoxication grossly excessive in degree, given the amount of the intoxicant, to which the actor does not know he is susceptible.

Section 2.09. Duress

(1) It is an affirmative defense that the actor engaged in the conduct charged to constitute an offense because he was coerced to do so by the use of, or a threat to use, unlawful force against his person or the person of another, that a person of reasonable firmness in his situation would have been unable to resist.

(2) The defense provided by this Section is unavailable if the actor recklessly placed himself in a situation in which it was probable that he would be subjected to duress. The defense is also unavailable if he was negligent in placing himself in such a situation, whenever negligence suffices to establish culpability for the offense charged.

(3) It is not a defense that a woman acted on the command of her husband, unless she acted under such coercion as would establish a defense under this Section. [The presumption that a woman acting in the presence of her husband is coerced is abolished.]

(4) When the conduct of the actor would otherwise be justifiable under Section 3.02, this Section does not preclude such defense.

Section 2.10. Military Orders

It is an affirmative defense that the actor, in engaging in the conduct charged to constitute an offense, does no more than execute an order of his superior in the armed services which he does not know to be unlawful.

Section 2.11. Consent

(1) *In General.* The consent of the victim to conduct charged to constitute an offense or to the result thereof is a defense if such consent negatives an element of the offense or precludes the infliction of the harm or evil sought to be prevented by the law defining the offense.

(2) *Consent to Bodily Harm.* When conduct is charged to constitute an offense because it causes or threatens bodily harm, consent to such conduct or to the infliction of such harm is a defense if:

(a) the bodily injury consented to or threatened by the conduct consented to is not serious; or

(b) the conduct and the injury are reasonably foreseeable hazards of joint participation in a lawful athletic contest or competitive sport or other concerted activity not forbidden by law; or

(c) the consent establishes a justification for the conduct under Article 3 of the Code.

(3) *Ineffective Consent.* Unless otherwise provided by the Code or by the law defining the offense, assent does not constitute consent if:

(a) it is given by a person who is legally incompetent to authorize the conduct charged to constitute the offense; or

(b) it is given by a person who by reason of youth, mental disease or defect or intoxication is manifestly unable or known by the actor to be unable to make a reasonable judgment as to the nature or harmfulness of the conduct charged to constitute the offense; or

(c) it is given by a person whose improvident consent is sought to be prevented by the law defining the offense; or

(d) it is induced by force, duress or deception of a kind sought to be prevented by the law defining the offense.

SECTION 2.12. DE MINIMIS INFRACTIONS

The Court shall dismiss a prosecution if, having regard to the nature of the conduct charged to constitute an offense and the nature of the attendant circumstances, it finds that the defendant's conduct:

(1) was within a customary license of tolerance, neither expressly negatived by the person whose interest was infringed nor inconsistent with the purpose of the law defining the offense; or

(2) did not actually cause or threaten the harm or evil sought to be prevented by the law defining the offense or did so only to an extent too trivial to warrant the condemnation of conviction; or

(3) presents such other extenuations that it cannot reasonably be regarded as envisaged by the legislature in forbidding the offense.

The Court shall not dismiss a prosecution under Subsection (3) of this Section without filing a written statement of its reasons.

SECTION 2.13. ENTRAPMENT

(1) A public law enforcement official or a person acting in cooperation with such an official perpetrates an entrapment if for the purpose of obtaining evidence of the commission of an offense, he induces or encourages another person to engage in conduct constituting such offense by either:

(a) making knowingly false representations designed to induce the belief that such conduct is not prohibited; or

(b) employing methods of persuasion or inducement that create a substantial risk that such an offense will be committed by persons other than those who are ready to commit it.

(2) Except as provided in Subsection (3) of this Section, a person prosecuted for an offense shall be acquitted if he proves by a preponderance of evidence that his conduct occurred in response to an entrapment. The issue of entrapment shall be tried by the Court in the absence of the jury.

(3) The defense afforded by this Section is unavailable when causing or threatening bodily injury is an element of the offense charged and the prosecution is based on conduct causing or threatening such injury to a person other than the person perpetrating the entrapment.

Article 3. General Principles of Justification

SECTION 3.01. JUSTIFICATION AN AFFIRMATIVE DEFENSE; CIVIL REMEDIES UNAFFECTED

(1) In any prosecution based on conduct that is justifiable under this Article, justification is an affirmative defense.

(2) The fact that conduct is justifiable under this Article does not abolish or impair any remedy for such conduct that is available in any civil action.

SECTION 3.02. JUSTIFICATION GENERALLY: CHOICE OF EVILS

(1) Conduct that the actor believes to be necessary to avoid a harm or evil to himself or to another is justifiable, provided that:

(a) the harm or evil sought to be avoided by such conduct is greater than that sought to be prevented by the law defining the offense charged; and

(b) neither the Code nor other law defining the offense provides exceptions or defenses dealing with the specific situation involved; and

(c) a legislative purpose to exclude the justification claimed does not otherwise plainly appear.

(2) When the actor was reckless or negligent in bringing about the situation requiring a choice of harms or evils or in appraising the necessity for his conduct, the justification afforded by this Section is unavailable in a prosecution for any offense for which recklessness or negligence, as the case may be, suffices to establish culpability.

SECTION 3.03. EXECUTION OF PUBLIC DUTY

(1) Except as provided in Subsection (2) of this Section, conduct is justifiable when it is required or authorized by:

(a) the law defining the duties or functions of a public officer or the assistance to be rendered to such officer in the performance of his duties; or

(b) the law governing the execution of legal process; or

(c) the judgment or order of a competent court or tribunal; or

(d) the law governing the armed services or the lawful conduct of war; or

(e) any other provision of law imposing a public duty.

(2) The other sections of this Article apply to:

(a) the use of force upon or toward the person of another for any of the purposes dealt with in such sections; and

(b) the use of deadly force for any purpose, unless the use of such force is otherwise expressly authorized by law or occurs in the lawful conduct of war.

(3) The justification afforded by Subsection (1) of this Section applies:

(a) when the actor believes his conduct to be required or authorized by the judgment or direction of a competent court or tribunal or in the lawful execution of legal process, notwithstanding lack of jurisdiction of the court or defect in the legal process; and

(b) when the actor believes his conduct to be required or authorized to assist a public officer in the performance of his duties, notwithstanding that the officer exceeded his legal authority.

SECTION 3.04. USE OF FORCE IN SELFBPROTECTION

(1) *Use of Force Justifiable for Protection of the Person.* Subject to the provisions of this Section and of Section 3.09, the use of force upon or toward another person is justifiable when the actor believes that such force is immediately necessary for the purpose of protecting himself against the use of unlawful force by such other person on the present occasion.

(2) Limitations on Justifying Necessity for Use of Force.

(a) The use of force is not justifiable under this Section:

(i) to resist an arrest that the actor knows is being made by a peace officer, although the arrest is unlawful; or

(ii) to resist force used by the occupier or possessor of property or by another person on his behalf, where the actor knows that the person using the force is doing so under a claim of right to protect the property, except that this limitation shall not apply if:

(1) the actor is a public officer acting in the performance of his duties or a person lawfully assisting him therein or a person making or assisting in a lawful arrest; or

(2) the actor has been unlawfully dispossessed of the property and is making a re-entry or recaption justified by Section 3.06; or

(3) the actor believes that such force is necessary to protect himself against death or serious bodily harm.

(b) The use of deadly force is not justifiable under this Section unless the actor believes that such force is necessary to protect himself against death, serious bodily harm, kidnapping or sexual intercourse compelled by force or threat; nor is it justifiable if:

(i) the actor, with the purpose of causing death or serious bodily injury, provoked the use of force against himself in the same encounter; or

(ii) the actor knows that he can avoid the necessity of using such force with complete safety by retreating or by surrendering possession of a thing to a person asserting a claim of right thereto or by complying with a demand that he abstain from any action that he has no duty to take, except that:

(1) the actor is not obliged to retreat from his dwelling or place of work, unless he was the initial aggressor or is assailed in his place of work by another person whose place of work the actor knows it to be; and

(2) a public officer justified in using force in the performance of his duties or a person justified in using force in his assistance or a person justified in using force in making an arrest or preventing an escape is not obliged to desist from efforts to perform such duty, effect such arrest or prevent such escape because of resistance or threatened resistance by or on behalf of the person against whom such action is directed.

(c) Except as required by paragraphs (a) and (b) of this Subsection, a person employing protective force may estimate the necessity thereof under the circumstances as he believes them to be when the force is used, without retreating, surrendering possession, doing any other act which he has no legal duty to do or abstaining from any lawful action.

(3) *Use of Confinement as Protective Force.* The justification afforded by this Section extends to the use of confinement as protective force only if the actor takes all reasonable measures to terminate the confinement as soon as he knows that he safely can, unless the person confined has been arrested on a charge of crime.

SECTION 3.05. USE OF FORCE FOR THE PROTECTION OF OTHER PERSONS

(1) Subject to the provisions of this Section and of Section 3.09, the use of force upon or toward the person of another is justifiable to protect a third person when:

(a) the actor would be justified under Section 3.04 in using such force to protect himself against the injury he believes to be threatened to the person whom he seeks to protect; and

(b) under the circumstances as the actor believes them to be, the person whom he seeks to protect would be justified in using such protective force; and

(c) the actor believes that his intervention is necessary for the protection of such other person.

(2) Notwithstanding Subsection (1) of this Section:

(a) when the actor would be obliged under Section 3.04 to retreat, to surrender the possession of a thing or to comply with a demand before using force in self-protection, he is not obliged to do so before using force for the protection of another person, unless he knows that he can thereby secure the complete safety of such other person; and

(b) when the person whom the actor seeks to protect would be obliged under Section 3.04 to retreat, to surrender the possession of a thing or to comply with a demand if he knew that he could obtain complete safety by so doing, the actor is obliged to try to cause him to do so before using force in his protection if the actor knows that he can obtain complete safety in that way; and

(c) neither the actor nor the person whom he seeks to protect is obliged to retreat when in the other's dwelling or place of work to any greater extent than in his own.

SECTION 3.06. USE OF FORCE FOR THE PROTECTION OF PROPERTY

(1) *Use of Force Justifiable for Protection of Property.* Subject to the provisions of this Section and of Section 3.09, the use of force upon or toward the person of another is justifiable when the actor believes that such force is immediately necessary:

(a) to prevent or terminate an unlawful entry or other trespass upon land or a trespass against or the unlawful carrying away of tangible, movable property, provided that such land or movable property is, or is believed by the actor to be, in his possession or in the possession of another person for whose protection he acts; or

(b) to effect an entry or re-entry upon land or to retake tangible movable property, provided that the actor believes that he or the person by whose authority he acts or a person from whom he or such other person derives title was unlawfully dispossessed of such land or movable property and is entitled to possession, and provided, further, that:

(i) the force is used immediately or on fresh pursuit after such dispossession; or

(ii) the actor believes that the person against whom he uses force has no claim of right to the possession of the property and, in the case of land, the circumstances, as the actor believes them to be, are of such urgency that it would be an exceptional hardship to postpone the entry or re-entry until a court order is obtained.

(2) *Meaning of Possession.* For the purposes of Subsection (1) of this Section:

(a) a person who has parted with the custody of property to another who refuses to restore it to him is no longer in possession, unless the property is movable and was and still is located on land in his possession;

(b) a person who has been dispossessed of land does not regain possession thereof merely by setting foot thereon;

(c) a person who has a license to use or occupy real property is deemed to be in possession thereof except against the licensor acting under claim of right.

(3) Limitations on Justifiable Use of Force.

(a) *Request to Desist.* The use of force is justifiable under this Section only if the actor first requests the person against whom such force is used to desist from his interference with the property, unless the actor believes that:

(i) such request would be useless; or

(ii) it would be dangerous to himself or another person to make the request; or

(iii) substantial harm will be done to the physical condition of the property which is sought to be protected before the request can effectively be made.

(b) *Exclusion of Trespasser.* The use of force to prevent or terminate a trespass is not justifiable under this Section if the actor knows that the exclusion of the trespasser will expose him to substantial danger of serious bodily harm.

(c) *Resistance of Lawful Re-entry or Recaption.* The use of force to prevent an entry or re-entry upon land or the recaption of movable property is not justifiable under this Section, although the actor believes that such re-entry or recaption is unlawful, if:

(i) the re-entry or recaption is made by or on behalf of a person who was actually dispossessed of the property; and

(ii) it is otherwise justifiable under paragraph (1)(b) of this Section.

(d) *Use of Deadly Force.* The use of deadly force is not justifiable under this Section unless the actor believes that:

(i) the person against whom the force is used is attempting to dispossess him of his dwelling otherwise than under a claim of right to its possession; or

(ii) the person against whom the force is used is attempting to commit or consummate arson, burglary, robbery or other felonious theft or property destruction and either:

(1) has employed or threatened deadly force against or in the presence of the actor; or

(2) the use of force other than deadly force to prevent the commission or the consummation of the crime would expose the actor or another in his presence to substantial danger of serious bodily harm.

(4) *Use of Confinement as Protective Force.* The justification afforded by this Section extends to the use of confinement as protective force only if the actor takes all reasonable measures to terminate the confinement as soon as he knows that he can do so with safety to the property, unless the person confined has been arrested on a charge of crime.

(5) *Use of Device to Protect Property.* The justification afforded by this section extends to the use of a device for the purpose of protecting property only if:

(a) the device is not designed to cause or known to create a substantial risk of causing death or serious bodily injury; and

(b) the use of the particular device to protect the property from entry or trespass is reasonable under the circumstances, as the actor believes them to be; and

(c) the device is one customarily used for such a purpose or reasonable care is taken to make known to probable intruders the fact that it is used.

(6) *Use of Force to Pass Wrongful Obstructor.* The use of force to pass a person whom the actor believes to be purposely or knowingly and unjustifiably obstructing the actor from going to a place to which he may lawfully go is justifiable, provided that:

(a) the actor believes that the person against whom he uses force has no claim of right to obstruct the actor; and

(b) the actor is not being obstructed from entry or movement on land which he knows to be in the possession or custody of the person obstructing him, or in the possession or custody of another person by whose authority the obstructor acts, unless the circumstances, as the actor believes them to be, are of such urgency that it would not be reasonable to postpone the entry or movement on such land until a court order is obtained; and

(c) the force used is not greater than would be justifiable if the person obstructing the actor were using force against him to prevent his passage.

Section 3.07. Use of Force in Law Enforcement

(1) *Use of Force Justifiable to Effect an Arrest.* Subject to the provisions of this Section and of Section 3.09, the use of force upon or toward the person of another is justifiable when the actor is making or assisting in making an arrest and the actor believes that such force is immediately necessary to effect a lawful arrest.

(2) Limitations on the Use of Force.

(a) The use of force is not justifiable under this Section unless:

(i) the actor makes known the purpose of the arrest or believes that it is otherwise known by or cannot reasonably be made known to the person to be arrested; and

(ii) when the arrest is made under a warrant, the warrant is valid or believed by the actor to be valid.

(b) The use of deadly force is not justifiable under this Section unless:

(i) the arrest is for a felony; and

(ii) the person effecting the arrest is authorized to act as a peace officer or is assisting a person whom he believes to be authorized to act as a peace officer; and

(iii) the actor believes that the force employed creates no substantial risk of injury to innocent persons; and

(iv) the actor believes that:

(1) the crime for which the arrest is made involved conduct including the use or threatened use of deadly force; or

(2) there is a substantial risk that the person to be arrested will cause death or serious bodily harm if his apprehension is delayed.

(3) *Use of Force to Prevent Escape From Custody.* The use of force to prevent the escape of an arrested person from custody is justifiable when the force could justifiably have been employed to effect the arrest under which the person is in custody, except that a guard or other person authorized to act as a peace officer is justified in using any force, including deadly force, that he believes to be immediately necessary to prevent the escape of a person from a jail, prison, or other institution for the detention of persons charged with or convicted of a crime.

(4) Use of Force by Private Person Assisting an Unlawful Arrest.

(a) A private person who is summoned by a peace officer to assist in effecting an unlawful arrest, is justified in using any force that he would be justified in using if the arrest were lawful, provided that he does not believe the arrest is unlawful.

(b) A private person who assists another private person in effecting an unlawful arrest, or who, not being summoned, assists a peace officer in effecting an unlawful arrest, is justified in using any force that he would be justified in using if the arrest were lawful, provided that (i) he believes the arrest is lawful, and (ii) the arrest would be lawful if the facts were as he believes them to be.

(5) Use of Force to Prevent Suicide or the Commission of a Crime.

(a) The use of force upon or toward the person of another is justifiable when the actor believes that such force is immediately necessary to prevent such other person from committing suicide, inflicting serious bodily injury upon himself, committing or consummating the commission of a crime involving or threatening bodily injury, damage to or loss of property or a breach of the peace, except that:

(i) any limitations imposed by the other provisions of this Article on the justifiable use of force in self-protection, for the protection of others, the protection of property, the effectuation of an arrest or the prevention of an escape from custody shall apply notwithstanding the criminality of the conduct against which such force is used; and

(ii) the use of deadly force is not in any event justifiable under this Subsection unless:

(1) the actor believes that there is a substantial risk that the person whom he seeks to prevent from committing a crime will cause death or serious bodily harm to another unless the commission or the consummation of the crime is prevented and that the use of such force presents no substantial risk of injury to innocent persons; or

(2) the actor believes that the use of such force is necessary to suppress a riot or mutiny after the rioters or mutineers have been ordered to disperse and warned, in any particular manner that the law may require, that such force will be used if they do not obey.

(b) The justification afforded by this Subsection extends to the use of confinement as preventive force only if the actor takes all reasonable measures to terminate the confinement as soon as he knows that he safely can, unless the person confined has been arrested on a charge of crime.

Section 3.08. Use of Force by Persons With Special Responsibility for Care, Discipline or Safety of Other

The use of force upon or toward the person of another is justifiable if:

(1) the actor is the parent or guardian or other person similarly responsible for the general care and supervision of a minor or a person acting at the request of such parent, guardian or other responsible person and:

(a) the force is used for the purpose of safeguarding or promoting the welfare of the minor, including the prevention or punishment of his misconduct; and

(b) the force used is not designed to cause or known to create a substantial risk of causing death, serious bodily injury, disfigurement, extreme pain or mental distress or gross degradation; or

(2) the actor is a teacher or a person otherwise entrusted with the care or supervision for a special purpose of a minor and:

(a) the actor believes that the force used is necessary to further such special purpose, including the maintenance of reasonable discipline in a school, class or other group, and that the use of such force is consistent with the welfare of the minor; and

(b) the degree of force, if it had been used by the parent or guardian of the minor, would not be unjustifiable under Subsection (1)(b) of this Section; or

(3) the actor is the guardian or other person similarly responsible for the general care and supervision of an incompetent person and:

(a) the force is used for the purpose of safeguarding or promoting the welfare of the incompetent person, including the prevention of his misconduct, or, when such incompetent person is in a hospital or other institution for his care and custody, for the maintenance of reasonable discipline in such institution; and

(b) the force used is not designed to cause or known to create a substantial risk of causing death, serious bodily harm, disfigurement, extreme or unnecessary pain, mental distress, or humiliation; or

(4) the actor is a doctor or other therapist or a person assisting him at his direction and:

(a) the force is used for the purpose of administering a recognized form of treatment which the actor believes to be adapted to promoting the physical or mental health of the patient; and

(b) the treatment is administered with the consent of the patient or, if the patient is a minor or an incompetent person, with the consent of his parent or guardian or other person legally competent to consent in his behalf, or the treatment is administered in an emergency when the actor believes that no one competent to consent can be consulted and that a reasonable person, wishing to safeguard the welfare of the patient, would consent; or

(5) the actor is a warden or other authorized official of a correctional institution and:

(a) he believes that the force used is necessary for the purpose of enforcing the lawful rules or procedures of the institution, unless his belief in the lawfulness of the rule or procedure sought to be enforced is erroneous and his error is due to ignorance or mistake as to the provisions of the Code, and other provision of the criminal law or the law governing the administration of the institution; and

(b) the nature or degree of force used is not forbidden by Article 303 or 304 of the Code; and

(c) if deadly force is used, its use is otherwise justifiable under this Article; or

(6) the actor is a person responsible for the safety of a vessel or an aircraft or a person acting at his direction and:

(a) he believes that the force used is necessary to prevent interference with a lawful order, unless his belief in the lawfulness of the order is erroneous and his error is due to ignorance or mistake as to the law defining his authority; and

(b) if deadly force is used, its use is otherwise justifiable under this Article; or

(7) the actor is a person who is authorized or required by law to maintain order or decorum in a vehicle, train or other carrier or in a place where others are assembled, and:

(a) he believes that the force used is necessary for such purpose; and

(b) the force is not designed to cause or known to create a substantial risk of causing death, bodily harm, or extreme mental distress.

Section 3.09. Mistake of Law as to Unlawfulness of Force or Legality of Arrest; Reckless or Negligent Use of Otherwise Justifiable Force; Reckless or Negligent Injury or Risk of Injury to Innocent Persons

(1) The justification afforded by Sections 3.04 to 3.07, inclusive, is unavailable when:

(a) the actor's belief in the unlawfulness of the force or conduct against which he employs protective force or his belief in the lawfulness of an arrest which he endeavors to effect by force is erroneous; and

(b) his error is due to ignorance or mistake as to the provisions of the Code, any other provision of the criminal law or the law governing the legality of an arrest or search.

(2) When the actor believes that the use of force upon or toward the person of another is necessary for any of the purposes for which such belief would establish a justification under Sections 3.03 to 3.08 but the actor is reckless or negligent in having such belief or in acquiring or failing to acquire any knowledge or belief which is material to the justifiability of his use of force, the justification afforded by those Sections is unavailable in a prosecution for an offense for which recklessness or negligence, as the case may be, suffices to establish culpability.

(3) When the actor is justified under Sections 3.03 to 3.08 in using force upon or toward the person of another but he recklessly or negligently injures or creates a risk of injury to innocent persons, the justification afforded by those Sections is unavailable in a prosecution for such recklessness or negligence towards innocent persons.

Section 3.10. Justification in Property Crimes

Conduct involving the appropriation, seizure or destruction of, damage to, intrusion on or interference with property is justifiable under circumstances that would establish a defense of privilege in a civil action based thereon unless:

(1) the Code or the law defining the offense deals with the specific situation involved; or

(2) a legislative purpose to exclude the justification claimed otherwise plainly appears.

Section 3.11. Definitions

In this Article, unless a different meaning plainly is required:

(1) "unlawful force" means force, including confinement, which is employed without the consent of the person against whom it is directed and the employment of which constitutes an offense or actionable tort or would constitute such offense or tort except for a defense (such as the absence of intent, negligence, or mental capacity; duress; youth; or diplomatic status) not amounting to a privilege to use the force. Assent constitutes consent, within the meaning of this Section, whether or not it otherwise is legally effective, except assent to the infliction of death or serious bodily harm.

(2) "deadly force" means force which the actor uses with the purpose of causing or which he knows to create a substantial risk of causing death or serious bodily injury. Purposely firing a firearm in the direction of another person or at a vehicle in which another person is believed to be constitutes deadly force. A threat to cause death or serious bodily injury, by the production of a weapon or otherwise, so long as the actor's purpose is limited to creating an apprehension that he will use deadly force if necessary, does not constitute deadly force.

(3) "dwelling" means any building or structure, though movable or temporary, or a portion thereof, that is for the time being the actor's home or place of lodging.

Article 4. Responsibility

SECTION 4.01. MENTAL DISEASE OR DEFECT EXCLUDING RESPONSIBILITY

(1) A person is not responsible for criminal conduct if at the time of such conduct as a result of mental disease or defect he lacks substantial capacity either to appreciate the criminality [wrongfulness] of his conduct or to conform his conduct to the requirements of law.

(2) As used in this Article, the terms "mental disease or defect" do not include an abnormality manifested only by repeated criminal or otherwise antisocial conduct.

SECTION 4.02. EVIDENCE OF MENTAL DISEASE OR DEFECT ADMISSIBLE WHEN RELEVANT TO ELEMENT OF THE OFFENSE; [MENTAL DISEASE OR DEFECT IMPAIRING CAPACITY AS GROUND FOR MITIGATION OF PUNISHMENT IN CAPITAL CASES]

(1) Evidence that the defendant suffered from a mental disease or defect is admissible whenever it is relevant to prove that the defendant did or did not have a state of mind which is an element of the offense.

[(2) Whenever the jury or the Court is authorized to determine or to recommend whether or not the defendant shall be sentenced to death or imprisonment upon conviction, evidence that the capacity of the defendant to appreciate the criminality [wrongfulness] of his conduct or to conform his conduct to the requirements of law was impaired as a result of mental disease or defect is admissible in favor of sentence of imprisonment.]

SECTION 4.03. MENTAL DISEASE OR DEFECT EXCLUDING RESPONSIBILITY IS AFFIRMATIVE DEFENSE; REQUIREMENT OF NOTICE; FORM OF VERDICT AND JUDGMENT WHEN FINDING OF IRRESPONSIBILITY IS MADE

(1) Mental disease or defect excluding responsibility is an affirmative defense.

(2) Evidence of mental disease or defect excluding responsibility is not admissible unless the defendant, at the time of entering his plea of not guilty or within ten days thereafter or at such later time as the Court may for good cause permit, files a written notice of his purpose to rely on such defense.

(3) When the defendant is acquitted on the ground of mental disease or defect excluding responsibility, the verdict and the judgment shall so state.

Section 4.04. Mental Disease or Defect Excluding Fitness to Proceed

No person who as a result of mental disease or defect lacks capacity to understand the proceedings against him or to assist in his defense shall be tried, convicted or sentenced for the commission of an offense so long as such incapacity endures.

Section 4.05. Psychiatric Examination of Defendant With Respect to Mental Disease or Defect

(1) Whenever the defendant has filed a notice of intention to rely on the defense of mental disease or defect excluding responsibility, or there is reason to doubt his fitness to proceed, or reason to believe that mental disease or defect of the defendant will otherwise become an issue in the cause, the Court shall appoint at least one qualified psychiatrist or shall request the Superintendent of the _______ Hospital to designate at least one qualified psychiatrist, which designation may be or include himself, to examine and report upon the mental condition of the defendant. The Court may order the defendant to be committed to a hospital or other suitable facility for the purpose of the examination for a period of not exceeding sixty days or such longer period as the Court determines to be necessary for the purpose and may direct that a qualified psychiatrist retained by the defendant be permitted to witness and participate in the examination.

(2) In such examination any method may be employed which is accepted by the medical profession for the examination of those alleged to be suffering from mental disease or defect.

(3) The report of the examination shall include the following: (a) a description of the nature of the examination; (b) a diagnosis of the mental condition of the defendant; (c) if the defendant suffers from a mental disease or defect, an opinion as to his capacity to understand the proceedings against him and to assist in his own defense; (d) when a notice of intention to rely on the defense of irresponsibility has been filed, an opinion as to the extent, if any, to which the capacity of the defendant to appreciate the criminality [wrongfulness] of his conduct or to conform his conduct to the requirements of law was impaired at the time of the criminal conduct charged; and (e) when directed by the Court, an opinion as to the capacity of the defendant to have a particular state of mind which is an element of the offense charged.

If the examination cannot be conducted by reason of the unwillingness of the defendant to participate therein, the report shall so state and shall include, if possible, an opinion as to whether such unwillingness of the defendant was the result of mental disease or defect.

The report of the examination shall be filed [in triplicate] with the clerk of the Court, who shall cause copies to be delivered to the district attorney and to counsel for the defendant.

SECTION 4.06. DETERMINATION OF FITNESS TO PROCEED; EFFECT OF FINDING OF UNFITNESS; PROCEEDINGS IF FITNESS IS REGAINED [; POSTCCOMMITMENT HEARING]

(1) When the defendant's fitness to proceed is drawn in question, the issue shall be determined by the Court. If neither the prosecuting attorney nor counsel for the defendant contests the finding of the report filed pursuant to Section 4.05, the Court may make the determination on the basis of such report. If the finding is contested, the Court shall hold a hearing on the issue. If the report is received in evidence upon such hearing, the party who contests the finding thereof shall have the right to summon and to cross-examine the psychiatrists who joined in the report and to offer evidence upon the issue.

(2) If the Court determines that the defendant lacks fitness to proceed, the proceeding against him shall be suspended, except as provided in Subsection (3) [Subsections (3) and (4)] of this Section, and the Court shall commit him to the custody of the Commissioner of Mental Hygiene [Public Health or Correction] to be placed in an appropriate institution of the Department of Mental Hygiene [Public Health or Correction] for so long as such unfitness shall endure. When the Court, on its own motion or upon the application of the Commissioner of Mental Hygiene [Public Health or Correction] or the prosecuting attorney, determines, after a hearing if a hearing is requested, that the defendant has regained fitness to proceed, the proceeding shall be resumed. If, however, the Court is of the view that so much time has elapsed since the commitment of the defendant that it would be unjust to resume the criminal proceeding, the Court may dismiss the charge and may order the defendant to be discharged or, subject to the law governing the civil commitment of persons suffering from mental disease or defect, order the defendant to be committed to an appropriate institution of the Department of Mental Hygiene [Public Health].

(3) The fact that the defendant is unfit to proceed does not preclude any legal objection to the prosecution that is susceptible of fair determination prior to trial and without the personal participation of the defendant.

[Alternative: (3) At any time within ninety days after commitment as provided in Subsection (2) of this Section, or at any later time with permission of the Court granted for good cause, the defendant or his counsel or the Commissioner of Mental Hygiene [Public Health or Correction] may apply for a special post-commitment hearing. If the application is made by or on behalf of a defendant not represented by counsel, he shall be afforded a reasonable opportunity to obtain counsel, and if he lacks funds to do so, counsel shall be assigned by the Court. The application shall be granted only if counsel for the defendant satisfies the Court by affidavit or otherwise that as an attorney he has reasonable grounds for a good faith belief that his client has, on the facts and the law, a defense to the charge other than mental disease or defect excluding responsibility.

[(4) If the motion for a special post-commitment hearing is granted, the hearing shall be by the Court without a jury. No evidence shall be offered at the hearing by either party on the issue of mental disease or defect as a defense to, or in mitigation of, the crime charged. After hearing, the Court may in an appropriate case quash the indictment or other charge, or find it to be defective or insufficient, or determine that it is not proved beyond a reasonable doubt by the evidence, or otherwise terminate the proceedings on the evidence or the law. In any such case, unless all defects in the proceedings are promptly cured, the Court shall terminate the commitment ordered under Subsection (2) of this Section and order the defendant to be discharged or, subject to the law governing the civil commitment of persons suffering from mental disease or defect, order the defendant to be committed to an appropriate institution of the Department of Mental Hygiene [Public Health].]

Section 4.07. Determination of Irresponsibility on Basis of Report; Access to Defendant by Psychiatrist of His Own Choice; Form of Expert Testimony When Issue of Responsibility Is Tried

(1) If the report filed pursuant to Section 4.05 finds that the defendant at the time of the criminal conduct charged suffered from a mental disease or defect which substantially impaired his capacity to appreciate the criminality [wrongfulness] of the conduct or to conform his conduct to the requirements of law, and the Court, after a hearing if a hearing is requested by the prosecuting attorney or the defendant, is satisfied that such impairment was sufficient to exclude responsibility, the Court on motion of the defendant shall enter judgement of acquittal on the ground of mental disease or defect excluding responsibility.

(2) When, notwithstanding the report filed pursuant to Section 4.05, the defendant wishes to be examined by a qualified psychiatrist or other expert of his own choice, such examiner shall be permitted to have reasonable access to the defendant for the purposes of such examination.

(3) Upon the trial, the psychiatrists who reported pursuant to Section 4.05 may be called as witnesses by the prosecution, the defendant or the Court. If the issue is being tried before a jury, the jury may be informed that the psychiatrists were designated by the Court or by the Superintendent of the _______ Hospital at the request of the Court, as the case may be. If called by the Court, the witness shall be subject to cross-examination by the prosecution and by the defendant. Both the prosecution and the defendant may summon any other qualified psychiatrist or other expert to testify, but no one who has not examined the defendant shall be competent to testify to an expert opinion with respect to the mental condition or responsibility of the defendant, as distinguished from the validity of the procedure followed by, or the general scientific propositions stated by, another witness.

(4) When a psychiatrist or other expert who has examined the defendant testifies concerning his mental condition, he shall be permitted to make a statement as to the nature of his examination, his diagnosis of the mental condition of the defendant at the time of the commission of the offense charged and his opinion as to the extent, if any, to which the capacity of the defendant to appreciate the criminality [wrongfulness] of his conduct or to conform his conduct to the requirements of law or to have a particular state of mind that is an element of the offense charged was impaired as a result of mental disease or defect at that time. He shall be permitted to make any explanation reasonably serving to clarify his diagnosis and opinion and may be cross-examined as to any matter bearing on his competency or credibility or the validity of his diagnosis or opinion.

Section 4.08. Legal Effect of Acquittal on the Ground of Mental Disease or Defect Excluding Responsibility; Commitment; Release or Discharge

(1) When a defendant is acquitted on the ground of mental disease or defect excluding responsibility, the Court shall order him to be committed to the custody of the Commissioner of Mental Hygiene [Public Health] to be placed in an appropriate institution for custody, care and treatment.

(2) If the Commissioner of Mental Hygiene [Public Health] is of the view that a person committed to his custody, pursuant to paragraph (1) of this Section, may be discharged or released on condition without danger to himself or to others, he shall make application for the discharge or release of such person in a report to the Court by which such person was committed and shall transmit a copy of such application and report to the prosecuting attorney of the county [parish] from which the defendant was committed. The Court shall thereupon appoint at least two qualified psychiatrists to examine such person and to report within sixty days, or such longer period as the Court determines to be necessary for the purpose, their opinion as to his mental condition. To facilitate such examination and the proceedings thereon, the Court may cause such person to be confined in any institution located near the place where the Court sits, which may hereafter be designated by the Commissioner of Mental Hygiene [Public Health] as suitable for the temporary detention of irresponsible persons.

(3) If the Court is satisfied by the report filed pursuant to paragraph (2) of this Section and such testimony of the reporting psychiatrists as the Court deems necessary that the committed person may be discharged or released on condition without danger to himself or others, the Court shall order his discharge or his release on such conditions as the Court determines to be necessary. If the Court is not so satisfied, it shall promptly order a hearing to determine whether such person may safely be discharged or released. Any such hearing shall be deemed a civil proceeding and the burden shall be upon the committed person to prove that he may safely be discharged or released. According to the determination of the Court upon the hearing, the committed person shall thereupon be discharged or released on such conditions as the Court determines to be necessary, or shall be recommitted to the custody of the Commissioner of Mental Hygiene [Public Health], subject to discharge or release only in accordance with the procedure prescribed above for a first hearing.

(4) If, within [five] years after the conditional release of a committed person, the Court shall determine, after hearing evidence, that the conditions of release have not been fulfilled and that for the safety of such person or for the safety of others his conditional release should be revoked, the Court shall forthwith order him to be recommitted to the Commissioner of Mental Hygiene [Public Health], subject to discharge or release only in accordance with the procedure prescribed above for a first hearing.

(5) A committed person may make application for his discharge or release to the Court by which he was committed, and the procedure to be followed upon such application shall be the same as that prescribed above in the case of an application by the Commissioner of Mental Hygiene [Public Health]. However, no such application by a committed person need be considered until he has been confined for a period of not less than [six months] from the

date of the order of commitment, and if the determination of the Court be adverse to the application, such person shall not be permitted to file a further application until [one year] has elapsed from the date of any preceding hearing on an application for his release or discharge.

SECTION 4.09. [*Omitted*]

SECTION 4.10. IMMATURITY EXCLUDING CRIMINAL CONVICTION; TRANSFER OF PROCEEDINGS TO JUVENILE COURT

(1) A person shall not be tried for or convicted of an offense if:

(a) at the time of the conduct charged to constitute the offense he was less than sixteen years of age[, in which case the Juvenile Court shall have exclusive jurisdiction*]; or

(b) at the time of the conduct charged to constitute the offense he was sixteen or seventeen years of age, unless:

(i) the Juvenile Court has no jurisdiction over him, or,

(ii) the Juvenile Court has entered an order waiving jurisdiction and consenting to the institution of criminal proceedings against him.

(2) No court shall have jurisdiction to try or convict a person of an offense if criminal proceedings against him are barred by Subsection (1) of this Section. When it appears that a person charged with the commission of an offense may be of such an age that criminal proceedings may be barred under Subsection (1) of this Section, the Court shall hold a hearing thereon, and the burden shall be on the prosecution to establish to the satisfaction of the Court that the criminal proceeding is not barred upon such grounds. If the Court determines that the proceeding is barred, custody of the person charged shall be surrendered to the Juvenile Court, and the case, including all papers and processes relating thereto, shall be transferred.

Article 5. Inchoate Crimes

SECTION 5.01. CRIMINAL ATTEMPT

(1) *Definition of Attempt.* A person is guilty of an attempt to commit a crime if, acting with the kind of culpability otherwise required for commission of the crime, he:

(a) purposely engages in conduct that would constitute the crime if the attendant circumstances were as he believes them to be; or

(b) when causing a particular result is an element of the crime, does or omits to do anything with the purpose of causing or with the belief that it will cause such result without further conduct on his part; or

* The bracketed words are unnecessary if the Juvenile Court Act so provides or is amended accordingly.

(c) purposely does or omits to do anything which, under the circumstances as he believes them to be, is an act or omission constituting a substantial step in a course of conduct planned to culminate in his commission of the crime.

(2) *Conduct That May Be Held Substantial Step Under Subsection (1)(c).* Conduct shall not be held to constitute a substantial step under Subsection (1)(c) of this Section unless it is strongly corroborative of the actor's criminal purpose. Without negativing the sufficiency of other conduct, the following, if strongly corroborative of the actor's criminal purpose, shall not be held insufficient as a matter of law:

(a) lying in wait, searching for or following the contemplated victim of the crime;

(b) enticing or seeking to entice the contemplated victim of the crime to go to the place contemplated for its commission;

(c) reconnoitering the place contemplated for the commission of the crime;

(d) unlawful entry of a structure, vehicle or enclosure in which it is contemplated that the crime will be committed;

(e) possession of materials to be employed in the commission of the crime, that are specially designed for such unlawful use or which can serve no lawful purpose of the actor under the circumstances;

(f) possession, collection or fabrication of materials to be employed in the commission of the crime, at or near the place contemplated for its commission, where such possession, collection or fabrication serves no lawful purpose of the actor under the circumstances;

(g) soliciting an innocent agent to engage in conduct constituting an element of the crime.

(3) *Conduct Designed to Aid Another in Commission of a Crime.* A person who engages in conduct designed to aid another to commit a crime that would establish his complicity under Section 2.06 if the crime were committed by such other person, is guilty of an attempt to commit the crime, although the crime is not committed or attempted by such other person.

(4) *Renunciation of Criminal Purpose.* When the actor's conduct would otherwise constitute an attempt under Subsection (1)(b) or (1)(c) of this Section, it is an affirmative defense that he abandoned his effort to commit the crime or otherwise prevented its commission, under circumstances manifesting a complete and voluntary renunciation of his criminal purpose. The establishment of such defense does not, however, affect the liability of an accomplice who did not join in such abandonment or prevention.

Within the meaning of this Article, renunciation of criminal purpose is not voluntary if it is motivated, in whole or in part, by circumstances, not present or apparent at the inception of the actor's course of conduct, that increase the probability of detection or apprehension or which make more difficult the accomplishment of the criminal purpose. Renunciation is not complete if it is motivated by a decision to postpone the criminal conduct until a more advantageous time or to transfer the criminal effort to another but similar objective or victim.

Section 5.02. Criminal Solicitation

(1) *Definition of Solicitation.* A person is guilty of solicitation to commit a crime if with the purpose of promoting or facilitating its commission he commands, encourages or requests another person to engage in specific conduct that would constitute such crime or an attempt to commit such crime or which would establish his complicity in its commission or attempted commission.

(2) *Uncommunicated Solicitation.* It is immaterial under Subsection (1) of this Section that the actor fails to communicate with the person he solicits to commit a crime if his conduct was designed to effect such communication.

(3) *Renunciation of Criminal Purpose.* It is an affirmative defense that the actor, after soliciting another person to commit a crime, persuaded him not to do so or otherwise prevented the commission of the crime, under circumstances manifesting a complete and voluntary renunciation of his criminal purpose.

Section 5.03. Criminal Conspiracy

(1) *Definition of Conspiracy.* A person is guilty of conspiracy with another person or persons to commit a crime if with the purpose of promoting or facilitating its commission he:

(a) agrees with such other person or persons that they or one or more of them will engage in conduct that constitutes such crime or an attempt or solicitation to commit such crime; or

(b) agrees to aid such other person or persons in the planning or commission of such crime or of an attempt or solicitation to commit such crime.

(2) *Scope of Conspiratorial Relationship.* If a person guilty of conspiracy, as defined by Subsection (1) of this Section, knows that a person with whom he conspires to commit a crime has conspired with another person or persons to commit the same crime, he is guilty of conspiring with such other person or persons, whether or not he knows their identity, to commit such crime.

(3) *Conspiracy With Multiple Criminal Objectives.* If a person conspires to commit a number of crimes, he is guilty of only one conspiracy so long as such multiple crimes are the object of the same agreement or continuous conspiratorial relationship.

(4) Joinder and Venue in Conspiracy Prosecutions.

(a) Subject to the provisions of paragraph (b) of this Subsection, two or more persons charged with criminal conspiracy may be prosecuted jointly if:

(i) they are charged with conspiring with one another; or

(ii) the conspiracies alleged, whether they have the same or different parties, are so related that they constitute different aspects of a scheme of organized criminal conduct.

(b) In any joint prosecution under paragraph (a) of this Subsection:

(i) no defendant shall be charged with a conspiracy in any county [parish or district] other than one in which he entered into such conspiracy or in which an overt act pursuant to such conspiracy was done by him or by a person with whom he conspired; and

(ii) neither the liability of any defendant nor the admissibility against him of evidence of acts or declarations of another shall be enlarged by such joinder; and

(iii) the Court shall order a severance or take a special verdict as to any defendant who so requests, if it deems it necessary or appropriate to promote the fair determination of his guilt or innocence, and shall take any other proper measures to protect the fairness of the trial.

(5) *Overt Act.* No person may be convicted of conspiracy to commit a crime other than a felony of the first or second degree, unless an overt act in pursuance of such conspiracy is alleged and proved to have been done by him or by a person with whom he conspired.

(6) *Renunciation of Criminal Purpose.* It is an affirmative defense that the actor, after conspiring to commit a crime, thwarted the success of the conspiracy, under circumstances manifesting a complete and voluntary renunciation of his criminal purpose.

(7) *Duration of Conspiracy.* For purposes of Section 1.06(4) [relating to periods of limitation for bringing prosecutionsCed.]:

(a) conspiracy is a continuing course of conduct that terminates when the crime or crimes that are its object are committed or the agreement that they be committed is abandoned by the defendant and by those with whom he conspired; and

(b) such abandonment is presumed if neither the defendant nor anyone with whom he conspired does any overt act in pursuance of the conspiracy during the applicable period of limitation; and

(c) if an individual abandons the agreement, the conspiracy is terminated as to him only if and when he advises those with whom he conspired of his abandonment or he informs the law enforcement authorities of the existence of the conspiracy and of his participation therein.

Section 5.04. Incapacity, Irresponsibility or Immunity of Party to Solicitation or Conspiracy

(1) Except as provided in Subsection (2) of this Section, it is immaterial to the liability of a person who solicits or conspires with another to commit a crime that:

(a) he or the person whom he solicits or with whom he conspires does not occupy a particular position or have a particular characteristic that is an element of such crime, if he believes that one of them does; or

(b) the person whom he solicits or with whom he conspires is irresponsible or has an immunity to prosecution or conviction for the commission of the crime.

(2) It is defense to a charge of solicitation or conspiracy to commit a crime that if the criminal object were achieved, the actor would not be guilty of a crime under the law defining the offense or as an accomplice under Section 2.06(5) or 2.06(6)(a) or (b).

Section 5.05. Grading of Criminal Attempt, Solicitation and Conspiracy; Mitigation in Cases of Lesser Danger; Multiple Convictions Barred

(1) *Grading.* Except as otherwise provided in this Section, attempt, solicitation and conspiracy are crimes of the same grade and degree as the most serious offense that is attempted or solicited or is an object of the conspiracy. An attempt, solicitation or conspiracy to commit a [capital crime or a] felony of the first degree is a felony of the second degree.

(2) *Mitigation.* If the particular conduct charged to constitute a criminal attempt, solicitation or conspiracy is so inherently unlikely to result or culminate in the commission of a crime that neither such conduct nor the actor presents a public danger warranting the grading of such offense under this Section, the Court shall exercise its power under Section 6.12 to enter judgment and impose sentence for a crime of lower grade or degree or, in extreme cases, may dismiss the prosecution.

(3) *Multiple Convictions.* A person may not be convicted of more than one offense defined by this Article for conduct designed to commit or to culminate in the commission of the same crime.

Section 5.06. Possessing Instruments of Crime; Weapons

(1) *Criminal Instruments Generally.* A person commits a misdemeanor if he possesses any instrument of crime with purpose to employ it criminally. “Instrument of crime” means:

(a) anything specially made or specially adapted for criminal use; or

(b) anything commonly used for criminal purposes and possessed by the actor under circumstances that do not negative unlawful purpose.

(2) *Presumption of Criminal Purpose From Possession of Weapon.* If a person possesses a firearm or other weapon on or about his person, in a vehicle occupied by him, or otherwise readily available for use, it is presumed that he had the purpose to employ it criminally, unless:

(a) the weapon is possessed in the actor's home or place of business;

(b) the actor is licensed or otherwise authorized by law to possess such weapon; or

(c) the weapon is of a type commonly used in lawful sport.

"Weapon" means anything readily capable of lethal use and possessed under circumstances not manifestly appropriate for lawful uses it may have; the term includes a firearm that is not loaded or lacks a clip or other component to render it immediately operable, and components that can readily be assembled into a weapon.

(3) *Presumptions as to Possession of Criminal Instruments in Automobiles.* If a weapon or other instrument of crime is found in an automobile, it is presumed to be in the possession of the occupant if there is but one. If there is more than one occupant, it shall be presumed to be in the possession of all, except under the following circumstances:

(a) it is found upon the person of one of the occupants;

(b) the automobile is not a stolen one and the weapon or instrument is found out of view in a glove compartment, car trunk, or other enclosed customary depository, in which case it is presumed to be in the possession of the occupant or occupants who own or have authority to operate the automobile;

(c) in the case of a taxicab, a weapon or instrument found in the passenger's portion of the vehicle shall be presumed to be in the possession of all the passengers, if there are any, and, if not, in the possession of the driver.

SECTION 5.07. [*Omitted*]

Article 6. Authorized Disposition of Offenders

SECTION 6.01. DEGREES OF FELONIES

(1) Felonies defined by this Code are classified, for the purpose of sentence, into three degrees, as follows:

(a) felonies of the first degree;

(b) felonies of the second degree;

(c) felonies of the third degree.

A felony is of the first or second degree when it is so designated by the Code. A crime declared to be a felony, without specification of degree, is of the third degree.

(2) Notwithstanding any other provision of law, a felony defined by any statute of this State other than this Code shall constitute, for the purpose of sentence, a felony of the third degree.

SECTION 6.02. [*Omitted*]

SECTION 6.03. FINES

A person who has been convicted of an offense may be sentenced to pay a fine not exceeding:

(1) $10,000, when the conviction is of a felony of the first or second degree;

(2) $5,000, when the conviction is of a felony of the third degree;

(3) $1,000, when the conviction is of a misdemeanor;

(4) $500, when the conviction is of a petty misdemeanor or a violation;

(5) any higher amount equal to double the pecuniary gain derived from the offense by the offender;

(6) any higher amount specifically authorized by statute.

SECTION 6.04. PENALTIES AGAINST CORPORATIONS AND UNINCORPORATED ASSOCIATIONS; FORFEITURE OF CORPORATE CHARTER OR REVOCATION OF CERTIFICATE AUTHORIZING FOREIGN CORPORATION TO DO BUSINESS IN THE STATE

(1) The Court may suspend the sentence of a corporation or an unincorporated association that has been convicted of an offense or may sentence it to pay a fine authorized by Section 6.03.

(2)(a) The [prosecuting attorney] is authorized to institute civil proceedings in the appropriate court of general jurisdiction to forfeit the charter of a corporation organized under the laws of this State or to revoke the certificate authorizing a foreign corporation to conduct business in this State. The Court may order the charter forfeited or the certificate revoked upon finding (i) that the board of directors or a high managerial agent acting in behalf of the corporation has, in conducting the corporation's affairs, purposely engaged in a persistent course of criminal conduct and (ii) that for the prevention of future criminal conduct of the same character, the public interest requires the charter of the corporation to be forfeited and the corporation to be dissolved or the certificate to be revoked.

(b) When a corporation is convicted of a crime or a high managerial agent of a corporation, as defined in Section 2.07, is convicted of a crime committed in the conduct of the affairs of the corporation, the Court, in sentencing the corporation or the agent, may direct the [prosecuting attorney] to institute proceedings authorized by paragraph (a) of this Subsection.

(c) The proceedings authorized by paragraph (a) of this Subsection shall be conducted in accordance with the procedures authorized by law for the involuntary dissolution of a corporation or the revocation of the certificate authorizing a foreign corporation to conduct business in this State. Such proceedings shall be deemed additional to any other proceedings authorized by law for the purpose of forfeiting the charter of a corporation or revoking the certificate of a foreign corporation.

SECTION 6.05. [*Omitted*]

SECTION 6.06. SENTENCE OF IMPRISONMENT FOR FELONY; ORDINARY TERMS

A person who has been convicted of a felony may be sentenced to imprisonment, as follows:

(1) in the case of a felony of the first degree, for a term the minimum of which shall be fixed by the Court at not less than one year nor more than ten years, and the maximum of which shall be life imprisonment;

(2) in the case of a felony of the second degree, for a term the minimum of which shall be fixed by the Court at not less than one year nor more than three years, and the maximum of which shall be ten years;

(3) in the case of a felony of the third degree, for a term the minimum of which shall be fixed by the Court at not less than one year nor more than two years, and the maximum of which shall be five years.

ALTERNATE SECTION 6.06. SENTENCE OF IMPRISONMENT FOR FELONY; ORDINARY TERMS

A person who has been convicted of a felony may be sentenced to imprisonment, as follows:

(1) in the case of a felony of the first degree, for a term the minimum of which shall be fixed by the Court at not less than one year nor more than ten years, and the maximum at not more than twenty years or at life imprisonment;

(2) in the case of a felony of the second degree, for a term the minimum of which shall be fixed by the Court at not less than one year nor more than three years, and the maximum at not more than ten years;

(3) in the case of a felony of the third degree, for a term the minimum of which shall be fixed by the Court at not less than one year nor more than two years, and the maximum at not more than five years.

No sentence shall be imposed under this Section of which the minimum is longer than one-half the maximum, or, when the maximum is life imprisonment, longer than ten years.

Section 6.07. [*Omitted*]

Section 6.08. Sentence of Imprisonment for Misdemeanors and Petty Misdemeanors; Ordinary Terms

A person who has been convicted of a misdemeanor or a petty misdemeanor may be sentenced to imprisonment for a definite term which shall be fixed by the Court and shall not exceed one year in the case of a misdemeanor or thirty days in the case of a petty misdemeanor.

Sections 6.09.B6.11. [*Omitted*]

Section 6.12. Reduction of Conviction by Court to Lesser Degree of Felony or to Misdemeanor

If, when a person has been convicted of a felony, the Court, having regard to the nature and circumstances of the crime and to the history and character of the defendant, is of the view that it would be unduly harsh to sentence the offender in accordance with the Code, the Court may enter judgment of conviction for a lesser degree of felony or for a misdemeanor and impose sentence accordingly.

Section 6.13. [*Omitted*]

Article 7. Authority of Court in Sentencing [*Omitted*]

PART II. DEFINITION OF SPECIFIC CRIMES

OFFENSES INVOLVING DANGER TO THE PERSON

Article 210. Criminal Homicide

Section 210.0. Definitions

In Articles 210B213, unless a different meaning plainly is required:

(1) "human being" means a person who has been born and is alive;

(2) "bodily injury" means physical pain, illness or any impairment of physical condition;

(3) "serious bodily injury" means bodily injury which creates a substantial risk of death or which causes serious, permanent disfigurement, or protracted loss or impairment of the function of any bodily member or organ;

(4) "deadly weapon" means any firearm or other weapon, device, instrument, material or substance, whether animate or inanimate, which in the manner it is used or is intended to be used is known to be capable of producing death or serious bodily injury.

SECTION 210.1. CRIMINAL HOMICIDE

(1) A person is guilty of criminal homicide if he purposely, knowingly, recklessly or negligently causes the death of another human being.

(2) Criminal homicide is murder, manslaughter or negligent homicide.

SECTION 210.2. MURDER

(1) Except as provided in Section 210.3(1)(b), criminal homicide constitutes murder when:

(a) it is committed purposely or knowingly; or

(b) it is committed recklessly under circumstances manifesting extreme indifference to the value of human life. Such recklessness and indifference are presumed if the actor is engaged or is an accomplice in the commission of, or an attempt to commit, or flight after committing or attempting to commit robbery, rape or deviate sexual intercourse by force or threat of force, arson, burglary, kidnapping or felonious escape.

(2) Murder is a felony of the first degree [but a person convicted of murder may be sentenced to death, as provided in Section 210.6].

SECTION 210.3. MANSLAUGHTER

(1) Criminal homicide constitutes manslaughter when:

(a) it is committed recklessly; or

(b) a homicide which would otherwise be murder is committed under the influence of extreme mental or emotional disturbance for which there is reasonable explanation or excuse. The reasonableness of such explanation or excuse shall be determined from the viewpoint of a person in the actor's situation under the circumstances as he believes them to be.

(2) Manslaughter is a felony of the second degree.

SECTION 210.4. NEGLIGENT HOMICIDE

(1) Criminal homicide constitutes negligent homicide when it is committed negligently.

(2) Negligent homicide is a felony of the third degree.

SECTION 210.5. CAUSING OR AIDING SUICIDE

(1) *Causing Suicide as Criminal Homicide.* A person may be convicted of criminal homicide for causing another to commit suicide only if he purposely causes such suicide by force, duress or deception.

(2) *Aiding or Soliciting Suicide as an Independent Offense.* A person who purposely aids or solicits another to commit suicide is guilty of a felony of the second degree if his conduct causes such suicide or an attempted suicide, and otherwise of a misdemeanor.

[SECTION 210.6. SENTENCE OF DEATH FOR MURDER; FURTHER PROCEEDINGS TO DETERMINE SENTENCE*]

(1) *Death Sentence Excluded.* When a defendant is found guilty of murder, the Court shall impose sentence for a felony of the first degree if it is satisfied that:

(a) none of the aggravating circumstances enumerated in Subsection (3) of this Section was established by the evidence at the trial or will be established if further proceedings are initiated under Subsection (2) of this Section; or

(b) substantial mitigating circumstances, established by the evidence at the trial, call for leniency; or

(c) the defendant, with the consent of the prosecuting attorney and the approval of the Court, pleaded guilty to murder as a felony of the first degree; or

(d) the defendant was under 18 years of age at the time of the commission of the crime; or

(e) the defendant's physical or mental condition calls for leniency; or

(f) although the evidence suffices to sustain the verdict, it does not foreclose all doubt respecting the defendant's guilt.

(2) *Determination by Court or by Court and Jury.* Unless the Court imposes sentence under Subsection (1) of this Section, it shall conduct a separate proceeding to determine whether the defendant should be sentenced for a felony of the first degree or sentenced to death. The proceeding shall be conducted before the Court alone if the defendant was convicted by a Court sitting without a jury or upon his plea of guilty or if the prosecuting attorney and the

* The Brackets indicate that the Institute took no position on the desirability of the death penalty.

defendant waive a jury with respect to sentence. In other cases it shall be conducted before the Court sitting with the jury which determined the defendant's guilt or, if the Court for good cause shown discharges that jury, with a new jury empanelled for the purpose.

In the proceeding, evidence may be presented as to any matter that the Court deems relevant to sentence, including but not limited to the nature and circumstances of the crime, the defendant's character, background, history, mental and physical condition and any of the aggravating or mitigating circumstances enumerated in Subsections (3) and (4) of this Section. Any such evidence, not legally privileged, which the Court deems to have probative force, may be received, regardless of its admissibility under the exclusionary rules of evidence, provided that the defendant's counsel is accorded a fair opportunity to rebut such evidence. The prosecuting attorney and the defendant or his counsel shall be permitted to present argument for or against sentence of death.

The determination whether sentence of death shall be imposed shall be in the discretion of the Court, except that when the proceeding is conducted before the Court sitting with a jury, the Court shall not impose sentence of death unless it submits to the jury the issue whether the defendant should be sentenced to death or to imprisonment and the jury returns a verdict that the sentence should be death. If the jury is unable to reach a unanimous verdict, the Court shall dismiss the jury and impose sentence for a felony of the first degree.

The Court, in exercising its discretion as to sentence, and the jury, in determining upon its verdict, shall take into account the aggravating and mitigating circumstances enumerated in Subsections (3) and (4) and any other facts that it deems relevant, but it shall not impose or recommend sentence of death unless it finds one of the aggravating circumstances enumerated in Subsection (3) and further finds that there are no mitigating circumstances sufficiently substantial to call for leniency. When the issue is submitted to the jury, the Court shall so instruct and also shall inform the jury of the nature of the sentence of imprisonment that may be imposed, including its implication with respect to possible release upon parole, if the jury verdict is against sentence of death.

Alternative formulation of Subsection (2):

(2) *Determination by Court.* Unless the Court imposes sentence under Subsection (1) of this Section, it shall conduct a separate proceeding to determine whether the defendant should be sentenced for a felony of the first degree or sentenced to death. In the proceeding, the Court, in accordance with Section 7.07 [relating to procedures on sentence], shall consider the report of the presentence investigation and, if a psychiatric examination has been ordered, the report of such examination. In addition, evidence may be presented as to any matter that the Court deems relevant to sentence, including but not limited to the nature and circumstances of the crime, the defendant's character, background, history, mental and physical condition and any of the aggravating or mitigating circumstances enumerated in Subsections (3) and (4) of this Section. Any such evidence, not legally privileged, which the Court deems to have probative force, may be received, regardless of its admissibility under the exclusionary rules of evidence, provided that the defendant's counsel is accorded a fair opportunity to rebut such evidence. The prosecuting attorney and the defendant or his counsel shall be permitted to present argument for or against sentence of death.

The determination whether sentence of death shall be imposed shall be in the discretion of the Court. In exercising such discretion, the Court shall take into account the aggravating and mitigating circumstances enumerated in Subsections (3) and (4) and any other facts that it deems relevant but shall not impose sentence of death unless it finds one of the aggravating circumstances enumerated in Subsection (3) and further finds that there are no mitigating circumstances sufficiently substantial to call for leniency.

(3) Aggravating Circumstances.

(a) The murder was committed by a convict under sentence of imprisonment.

(b) The defendant was previously convicted of another murder or of a felony involving the use or threat of violence to the person.

(c) At the time the murder was committed the defendant also committed another murder.

(d) The defendant knowingly created a great risk of death to many persons.

(e) The murder was committed while the defendant was engaged or was an accomplice in the commission of, or an attempt to commit, or flight after committing or attempting to commit robbery, rape or deviate sexual intercourse by force or threat of force, arson, burglary or kidnapping.

(f) The murder was committed for the purpose of avoiding or preventing a lawful arrest or effecting an escape from lawful custody.

(g) The murder was committed for pecuniary gain.

(h) The murder was especially heinous, atrocious or cruel, manifesting exceptional depravity.

(4) Mitigating Circumstances.

(a) The defendant has no significant history of prior criminal activity.

(b) The murder was committed while the defendant was under the influence of extreme mental or emotional disturbance.

(c) The victim was a participant in the defendant's homicidal conduct or consented to the homicidal act.

(d) The murder was committed under circumstances which the defendant believed to provide a moral justification or extenuation for his conduct.

(e) The defendant was an accomplice in a murder committed by another person and his participation in the homicidal act was relatively minor.

(f) The defendant acted under duress or under the domination of another person.

(g) At the time of the murder, the capacity of the defendant to appreciate the criminality [wrongfulness] of his conduct or to conform his conduct to the requirements of law was impaired as a result of mental disease or defect or intoxication.

(h) The youth of the defendant at the time of the crime.]

Article 211. Assault; Reckless Endangering; Threats

SECTION 211.0. DEFINITIONS

In this Article, the definitions given in Section 210.0 apply unless a different meaning plainly is required.

SECTION 211.1. ASSAULT

(1) *Simple Assault.* A person is guilty of assault if he:

(a) attempts to cause or purposely, knowingly or recklessly causes bodily injury to another; or

(b) negligently causes bodily injury to another with a deadly weapon; or

(c) attempts by physical menace to put another in fear of imminent serious bodily injury.

Simple assault is a misdemeanor unless committed in a fight or scuffle entered into by mutual consent, in which case it is a petty misdemeanor.

(2) *Aggravated Assault.* A person is guilty of aggravated assault if he:

(a) attempts to cause serious bodily injury to another, or causes such injury purposely, knowingly or recklessly under circumstances manifesting extreme indifference to the value of human life; or

(b) attempts to cause or purposely or knowingly causes bodily injury to another with a deadly weapon.

Aggravated assault under paragraph (a) is a felony of the second degree; aggravated assault under paragraph (b) is a felony of the third degree.

Section 211.2. Recklessly Endangering Another Person

A person commits a misdemeanor if he recklessly engages in conduct which places or may place another person in danger of death or serious bodily injury. Recklessness and danger shall be presumed where a person knowingly points a firearm at or in the direction of another, whether or not the actor believed the firearm to be loaded.

Section 211.3. Terroristic Threats

A person is guilty of a felony of the third degree if he threatens to commit any crime of violence with purpose to terrorize another or to cause evacuation of a building, place of assembly, or facility of public transportation, or otherwise to cause serious public inconvenience, or in reckless disregard of the risk of causing such terror or inconvenience.

Article 212. Kidnapping and Related Offenses; Coercion

Section 212.0. Definitions

In this Article, the definitions given in section 210.0 apply unless a different meaning plainly is required.

Section 212.1. Kidnapping

A person is guilty of kidnapping if he unlawfully removes another from his place of residence or business, or a substantial distance from the vicinity where he is found, or if he unlawfully confines another for a substantial period in a place of isolation, with any of the following purposes:

(a) to hold for ransom or reward, or as a shield or hostage; or

(b) to facilitate commission of any felony or flight thereafter; or

(c) to inflict bodily injury on or to terrorize the victim or another; or

(d) to interfere with the performance of any governmental or political function.

Kidnapping is a felony of the first degree unless the actor voluntarily releases the victim alive and in a safe place prior to trial, in which case it is a felony of the second degree. A removal or confinement is unlawful within the meaning of this Section if it is accomplished by force, threat or deception, or, in the case of a person who is under the age of 14 or incompetent, if it is accomplished without the consent of a parent, guardian or other person responsible for general supervision of his welfare.

Section 212.2. Felonious Restraint

A person commits a felony of the third degree if he knowingly:

(a) restrains another unlawfully in circumstances exposing him to risk of serious bodily injury; or

(b) holds another in a condition of involuntary servitude.

Section 212.3. False Imprisonment

A person commits a misdemeanor if he knowingly restrains another unlawfully so as to interfere substantially with his liberty.

Section 212.4. Interference With Custody

(1) *Custody of Children.* A person commits an offense if he knowingly or recklessly takes or entices any child under the age of 18 from the custody of its parent, guardian or other lawful custodian, when he has no privilege to do so. It is an affirmative defense that:

(a) the actor believed that his action was necessary to preserve the child from danger to its welfare; or

(b) the child, being at the time not less than 14 years old, was taken away at its own instigation without enticement and without purpose to commit a criminal offense with or against the child.

Proof that the child was below the critical age gives rise to a presumption that the actor knew the child's age or acted in reckless disregard thereof. The offense is a misdemeanor unless the actor, not being a parent or person in equivalent relation to the child, acted with knowledge that his conduct would cause serious alarm for the child's safety, or in reckless disregard of a likelihood of causing such alarm, in which case the offense is a felony of the third degree.

(2) *Custody of Committed Persons.* A person is guilty of a misdemeanor if he knowingly or recklessly takes or entices any committed person away from lawful custody when he is not privileged to do so. "Committed person" means, in addition to anyone committed under judicial warrant, any orphan, neglected or delinquent child, mentally defective or insane person, or other dependent or incompetent person entrusted to another's custody by or through a recognized social agency or otherwise by authority of law.

Section 212.5. Criminal Coercion

(1) *Offense Defined.* A person is guilty of criminal coercion if, with purpose unlawfully to restrict another's freedom of action to his detriment, he threatens to:

(a) commit any criminal offense; or

(b) accuse anyone of a criminal offense; or

(c) expose any secret tending to subject any person to hatred, contempt or ridicule, or to impair his credit or business repute; or

(d) take or withhold action as an official, or cause an official to take or withhold action.

It is an affirmative defense to prosecution based on paragraphs (b), (c) or (d) that the actor believed the accusation or secret to be true or the proposed official action justified and that his purpose was limited to compelling the other to behave in a way reasonably related to the circumstances which were the subject of the accusation, exposure or proposed official action, as by desisting from further misbehavior, making good a wrong done, refraining from taking any action or responsibility for which the actor believes the other disqualified.

(2) *Grading.* Criminal coercion is a misdemeanor unless the threat is to commit a felony or the actor's purpose is felonious, in which cases the offense is a felony of the third degree.

Article 213. Sexual Offenses

Section 213.0. Definitions

In this Article, unless a different meaning plainly is required:

(1) the definitions given in Section 210.0 apply;

(2) "Sexual intercourse" includes intercourse per os or per anum, with some penetration however slight; emission is not required;

(3) "Deviate sexual intercourse" means sexual intercourse per os or per anum between human beings who are not husband and wife, and any form of sexual intercourse with an animal.

Section 213.1. Rape and Related Offenses

(1) *Rape.* A male who has sexual intercourse with a female not his wife is guilty of rape if:

(a) he compels her to submit by force or by threat of imminent death, serious bodily injury, extreme pain or kidnapping, to be inflicted on anyone; or

(b) he has substantially impaired her power to appraise or control her conduct by administering or employing without her knowledge drugs, intoxicants or other means for the purpose of preventing resistance; or

(c) the female is unconscious; or

(d) the female is less than 10 years old.

Rape is a felony of the second degree unless (i) in the course thereof the actor inflicts serious bodily injury upon anyone, or (ii) the victim was not a voluntary social companion of the actor upon the occasion of the crime and had not previously permitted him sexual liberties, in which cases the offense is a felony of the first degree.

(2) *Gross Sexual Imposition.* A male who has sexual intercourse with a female not his wife commits a felony of the third degree if:

(a) he compels her to submit by any threat that would prevent resistance by a woman of ordinary resolution; or

(b) he knows that she suffers from a mental disease or defect which renders her incapable of appraising the nature of her conduct; or

(c) he knows that she is unaware that a sexual act is being committed upon her or that she submits because she mistakenly supposes that he is her husband.

SECTION 213.2. DEVIATE SEXUAL INTERCOURSE BY FORCE OR IMPOSITION

(1) *By Force or Its Equivalent.* A person who engages in deviate sexual intercourse with another person, or who causes another to engage in deviate sexual intercourse, commits a felony of the second degree if:

(a) he compels the other person to participate by force or by threat of imminent death, serious bodily injury, extreme pain or kidnapping, to be inflicted on anyone; or

(b) he has substantially impaired the other person's power to appraise or control his conduct, by administering or employing without the knowledge of the other person drugs, intoxicants or other means for the purpose of preventing resistance; or

(c) the other person is unconscious; or

(d) the other person is less than 10 years old.

(2) *By Other Imposition.* A person who engages in deviate sexual intercourse with another person, or who causes another to engage in deviate sexual intercourse, commits a felony of the third degree if:

(a) he compels the other person to participate by any threat that would prevent resistance by a person of ordinary resolution; or

(b) he knows that the other person suffers from a mental disease or defect which renders him incapable of appraising the nature of his conduct; or

(c) he knows that the other person submits because he is unaware that a sexual act is being committed upon him.

Section 213.3. Corruption of Minors and Seduction

(1) *Offense Defined.* A male who has sexual intercourse with a female not his wife, or any person who engages in deviate sexual intercourse or causes another to engage in deviate sexual intercourse, is guilty of an offense if:

(a) the other person is less than [16] years old and the actor is at least [four] years older than the other person; or

(b) the other person is less than 21 years old and the actor is his guardian or otherwise responsible for general supervision of his welfare; or

(c) the other person is in custody of law or detained in a hospital or other institution and the actor has supervisory or disciplinary authority over him; or

(d) the other person is a female who is induced to participate by a promise of marriage which the actor does not mean to perform.

(2) *Grading.* An offense under paragraph (a) of Subsection (1) is a felony of the third degree. Otherwise an offense under this section is a misdemeanor.

Section 213.4. Sexual Assault

A person who has sexual contact with another not his spouse, or causes such other to have sexual conduct with him, is guilty of sexual assault, a misdemeanor, if:

(1) he knows that the contact is offensive to the other person; or

(2) he knows that the other person suffers from a mental disease or defect which renders him or her incapable of appraising the nature of his or her conduct; or

(3) he knows that the other person is unaware that a sexual act is being committed; or

(4) the other person is less than 10 years old; or

(5) he has substantially impaired the other person's power to appraise or control his or her conduct, by administering or employing without the other's knowledge drugs, intoxicants or other means for the purpose of preventing resistance; or

(6) the other person is less than [16] years old and the actor is at least [four] years older than the other person; or

(7) the other person is less than 21 years old and the actor is his guardian or otherwise responsible for general supervision of his welfare; or

(8) the other person is in custody of law or detained in a hospital or other institution and the actor has supervisory or disciplinary authority over him.

Sexual contact is any touching of the sexual or other intimate parts of the person for the purpose of arousing or gratifying sexual desire.

SECTION 213.5. INDECENT EXPOSURE

A person commits a misdemeanor if, for the purpose of arousing or gratifying sexual desire of himself or of any person other than his spouse, he exposes his genitals under circumstances in which he knows his conduct is likely to cause affront or alarm.

SECTION 213.6. PROVISIONS GENERALLY APPLICABLE TO ARTICLE 213

(1) *Mistake as to Age.* Whenever in this Article the criminality of conduct depends on a child's being below the age of 10, it is no defense that the actor did not know the child's age, or reasonably believed the child to be older than 10. When criminality depends on the child's being below a critical age other than 10, it is a defense for the actor to prove by a preponderance of the evidence that he reasonably believed the child to be above the critical age.

(2) *Spouse Relationships.* Whenever in this Article the definition of an offense excludes conduct with a spouse, the exclusion shall be deemed to extend to persons living as man and wife, regardless of the legal status of their relationship. The exclusion shall be inoperative as respects spouses living apart under a decree of judicial separation. Where the definition of an offense excludes conduct with a spouse or conduct by a woman, this shall not preclude conviction of a spouse or woman as accomplice in a sexual act which he or she causes another person, not within the exclusion, to perform.

(3) *Sexually Promiscuous Complainants.* It is a defense to prosecution under Section 213.3, and paragraphs (6), (7) and (8) of Section 213.4 for the actor to prove by a preponderance of the evidence that the alleged victim had, prior to the time of the offense charged, engaged promiscuously in sexual relations with others.

(4) *Prompt Complaint.* No prosecution may be instituted or maintained under this Article unless the alleged offense was brought to the notice of public authority within [3] months of its occurrence or, where the alleged victim was less than [16] years old or otherwise incompetent to make complaint, within [3] months after a parent, guardian or other competent person specially interested in the victim learns of the offense.

(5) *Testimony of Complainants.* No person shall be convicted of any felony under this Article upon the uncorroborated testimony of the alleged victim. Corroboration may be circumstantial. In any prosecution before a jury for an offense under this Article, the jury shall be instructed to evaluate the testimony of a victim or complaining witness with special care in view of the emotional involvement of the witness and the difficulty of determining the truth with respect to alleged sexual activities carried out in private.

OFFENSES AGAINST PROPERTY

Article 220. Arson, Criminal Mischief, and Other Property Destruction

SECTION 220.1. ARSON AND RELATED OFFENSES

(1) *Arson.* A person is guilty of arson, a felony of the second degree, if he starts a fire or causes an explosion with the purpose of:

(a) destroying a building or occupied structure of another; or

(b) destroying or damaging any property, whether his own or another's, to collect insurance for such loss. It shall be an affirmative defense to prosecution under this paragraph that the actor's conduct did not recklessly endanger any building or occupied structure of another or place any other person in danger of death or bodily injury.

(2) *Reckless Burning or Exploding.* A person commits a felony of the third degree if he purposely starts a fire or causes an explosion, whether on his own property or another's, and thereby recklessly:

(a) places another person in danger of death or bodily injury; or

(b) place a building or occupied structure of another in danger of damage or destruction.

(3) *Failure to Control or Report Dangerous Fire.* A person who knows that a fire is endangering life or a substantial amount of property of another and fails to take reasonable measures to put out or control the fire, when he can do so without substantial risk to himself, or to give a prompt fire alarm, commits a misdemeanor if:

(a) he knows that he is under an official, contractual, or other legal duty to prevent or combat the fire; or

(b) the fire was started, albeit lawfully, by him or with his assent, or on property in his custody or control.

(4) *Definitions.* "Occupied structure" means any structure, vehicle or place adapted for overnight accommodation of persons, or for carrying on business therein, whether or not a person is actually present. Property is that of another, for the purposes of this section, if anyone other than the actor has a possessory or proprietary interest therein. If a building or structure is divided into separately occupied units, any unit not occupied by the actor is an occupied structure of another.

SECTION 220.2. CAUSING OR RISKING CATASTROPHE

(1) *Causing Catastrophe.* A person who causes a catastrophe by explosion, fire, flood, avalanche, collapse of building, release of poison gas, radioactive material or other harmful or destructive force or substance, or by any other means of causing potentially widespread injury or damage, commits a felony of the second degree if he does so purposely or knowingly, or a felony of the third degree if he does so recklessly.

(2) *Risking Catastrophe.* A person is guilty of a misdemeanor if he recklessly creates a risk of catastrophe in the employment of fire, explosives or other dangerous means listed in Subsection (1).

(3) *Failure to Prevent Catastrophe.* A person who knowingly or recklessly fails to take reasonable measures to prevent or mitigate a catastrophe commits a misdemeanor if:

(a) he knows that he is under an official, contractual or other legal duty to take such measures; or

(b) he did or assented to the act causing or threatening the catastrophe.

SECTION 220.3. CRIMINAL MISCHIEF

(1) *Offense Defined.* A person is guilty of criminal mischief if he:

(a) damages tangible property of another purposely, recklessly, or by negligence in the employment of fire, explosives, or other dangerous means listed in Section 220.2(1); or

(b) purposely or recklessly tampers with tangible property of another so as to endanger persons or property; or

(c) purposely or recklessly causes another to suffer pecuniary loss by deception or threat.

(2) *Grading.* Criminal mischief is a felony of the third degree if the actor purposely causes pecuniary loss in excess of $5,000 or a substantial interruption or impairment of public communication, transportation, supply of water, gas or power, or other public service. It is a misdemeanor if the actor purposely causes pecuniary loss in excess of $100, or a petty misdemeanor if he purposely or recklessly causes pecuniary loss in excess of $25. Otherwise criminal mischief is a violation.

Article 221. Burglary and Other Criminal Intrusion

SECTION 221.0. DEFINITIONS

In this Article, unless a different meaning plainly is required:

(1) "occupied structure" means any structure, vehicle or place adapted for overnight accommodation of persons, or for carrying on business therein, whether or not a person is actually present.

(2) "night" means the period between thirty minutes past sunset and thirty minutes before sunrise.

Section 221.1. Burglary

(1) *Burglary Defined.* A person is guilty of burglary if he enters a building or occupied structure, or separately secured or occupied portion thereof, with purpose to commit a crime therein, unless the premises are at the time open to the public or the actor is licensed or privileged to enter. It is an affirmative defense to prosecution for burglary that the building or structure was abandoned.

(2) *Grading.* Burglary is a felony of the second degree if it is perpetrated in the dwelling of another at night, or if, in the course of committing the offense, the actor:

(a) purposely, knowingly or recklessly inflicts or attempts to inflict bodily injury on anyone; or

(b) is armed with explosives or a deadly weapon.

Otherwise, burglary is a felony of the third degree. An act shall be deemed "in the course of committing" an offense if it occurs in an attempt to commit the offense or in flight after the attempt or commission.

(3) *Multiple Convictions.* A person may not be convicted both for burglary and for the offense which it was his purpose to commit after the burglarious entry or for an attempt to commit that offense, unless the additional offense constitutes a felony of the first or second degree.

Section 221.2. Criminal Trespass

(1) *Buildings and Occupied Structures.* A person commits an offense if, knowing that he is not licensed or privileged to do so, he enters or surreptitiously remains in any building or occupied structure, or separately secured or occupied portion thereof. An offense under this Subsection is a misdemeanor if it is committed in a dwelling at night. Otherwise it is a petty misdemeanor.

(2) *Defiant Trespasser.* A person commits an offense if, knowing that he is not licensed or privileged to do so, he enters or remains in any place as to which notice against trespass is given by:

(a) actual communication to the actor; or

(b) posting in a manner prescribed by law or reasonably likely to come to the attention of intruders; or

(c) fencing or other enclosure manifestly designed to exclude intruders.

An offense under this Subsection constitutes a petty misdemeanor if the offender defies an order to leave personally communicated to him by the owner of the premises or other authorized person. Otherwise it is a violation.

(3) *Defenses.* It is an affirmative defense to prosecution under this Section that:

(a) a building or occupied structure involved in an offense under Subsection (1) was abandoned; or

(b) the premises were at the time open to members of the public and the actor complied with all lawful conditions imposed on access to or remaining in the premises; or

(c) the actor reasonably believed that the owner of the premises, or other person empowered to license access thereto, would have licensed him to enter or remain.

Article 222. Robbery

SECTION 222.1. ROBBERY

(1) *Robbery Defined.* A person is guilty of robbery if, in the course of committing a theft, he:

(a) inflicts serious bodily injury upon another; or

(b) threatens another with or purposely puts him in fear of immediate serious bodily injury; or

(c) commits or threatens immediately to commit any felony of the first or second degree.

An act shall be deemed "in the course of committing a theft" if it occurs in an attempt to commit theft or in flight after the attempt or commission.

(2) *Grading.* Robbery is a felony of the second degree, except that it is a felony of the first degree if in the course of committing the theft the actor attempts to kill anyone, or purposely inflicts or attempts to inflict serious bodily injury.

Article 223. Theft and Related Offenses

Section 223.0. Definitions

In this Article, unless a different meaning plainly is required:

(1) "deprive" means: (a) to withhold property of another permanently or for so extended a period as to appropriate a major portion of its economic value, or with intent to restore only upon payment of reward or other compensation; or (b) to dispose of the property so as to make it unlikely that the owner will recover it.

(2) "financial institution" means a bank, insurance company, credit union, building and loan association, investment trust or other organization held out to the public as a place of deposit of funds or medium of savings or collective investment.

(3) "government" means the United States, any State, county, municipality, or other political unit, or any department, agency or subdivision of any of the foregoing, or any corporation or other association carrying out the functions of government.

(4) "movable property" means property the location of which can be changed, including things growing on, affixed to, or found in land, and documents although the rights represented thereby have no physical location. "Immovable property" is all other property.

(5) "obtain" means: (a) in relation to property, to bring about a transfer or purported transfer of a legal interest in the property, whether to the obtainer or another; or (b) in relation to labor or service, to secure performance thereof.

(6) "property" means anything of value, including real estate, tangible and intangible personal property, contract rights, choses-in-action and other interests in or claims to wealth, admission or transportation tickets, captured or domestic animals, food and drink, electric or other power.

(7) "property of another" includes property in which any person other than the actor has an interest which the actor is not privileged to infringe, regardless of the fact that the actor also has an interest in the property and regardless of the fact that the other person might be precluded from civil recovery because the property was used in an unlawful transaction or was subject to forfeiture as contraband. Property in possession of the actor shall not be deemed property of another who has only a security interest therein, even if legal title is in the creditor pursuant to a conditional sales contract or other security agreement.

Section 223.1. Consolidation of Theft Offenses; Grading; Provisions Applicable to Theft Generally

(1) *Consolidation of Theft Offenses.* Conduct denominated theft in this Article constitutes a single offense. An accusation of theft may be supported by evidence that it was committed in any manner that would be theft under this Article, notwithstanding the specification of a

different manner in the indictment or information, subject only to the power of the Court to ensure fair trial by granting a continuance or other appropriate relief where the conduct of the defense would be prejudiced by lack of fair notice or by surprise.

(2) *Grading of Theft Offenses.*

(a) Theft constitutes a felony of the third degree if the amount involved exceeds $500, or if the property stolen is a firearm, automobile, airplane, motorcycle, motorboat or other motor-propelled vehicle, or in the case of theft by receiving stolen property, if the receiver is in the business of buying or selling stolen property.

(b) Theft not within the preceding paragraph constitutes a misdemeanor, except that if the property was not taken from the person or by threat, or in breach of a fiduciary obligation, and the actor proves by a preponderance of the evidence that the amount involved was less than $50, the offense constitutes a petty misdemeanor.

(c) The amount involved in a theft shall be deemed to be the highest value, by any reasonable standard, of the property or services which the actor stole or attempted to steal. Amounts involved in thefts committed pursuant to one scheme or course of conduct, whether from the same person or several persons, may be aggregated in determining the grade of the offense.

(3) *Claim of Right.* It is an affirmative defense to prosecution for theft that the actor:

(a) was unaware that the property or service was that of another; or

(b) acted under an honest claim of right to the property or service involved or that he had a right to acquire or dispose of it as he did; or

(c) took property exposed for sale, intending to purchase and pay for it promptly, or reasonably believing that the owner, if present, would have consented.

(4) *Theft from Spouse.* It is no defense that theft was from the actor's spouse, except that misappropriation of household and personal effects, or other property normally accessible to both spouses, is theft only if it occurs after the parties have ceased living together.

SECTION 223.2. THEFT BY UNLAWFUL TAKING OR DISPOSITION

(1) *Movable Property.* A person is guilty of theft if he unlawfully takes, or exercises unlawful control over, movable property of another with purpose to deprive him thereof.

(2) *Immovable property.* A person is guilty of theft if he unlawfully transfers immovable property of another or any interest therein with purpose to benefit himself or another not entitled thereto.

Section 223.3. Theft by Deception

A person is guilty of theft if he purposely obtains property of another by deception. A person deceives if he purposely:

(1) creates or reinforces a false impression, including false impressions as to law, value, intention or other state of mind; but deception as to a person's intention to perform a promise shall not be inferred from the fact alone that he did not subsequently perform the promise; or

(2) prevents another from acquiring information which would affect his judgment of a transaction; or

(3) fails to correct a false impression which the deceiver previously created or reinforced, or which the deceiver knows to be influencing another to whom he stands in a fiduciary or confidential relationship; or

(4) fails to disclose a known lien, adverse claim or other legal impediment to the enjoyment of property which he transfers or encumbers in consideration for the property obtained, whether such impediment is or is not valid, or is or is not a matter of official record.

The term "deceive" does not, however, include falsity as to matters having no pecuniary significance, or puffing by statements unlikely to deceive ordinary persons in the group addressed.

Section 223.4. Theft by Extortion

A person is guilty of theft if he obtains property of another by threatening to:

(1) inflict bodily injury on anyone or commit any other criminal offense; or

(2) accuse anyone of a criminal offense; or

(3) expose any secret tending to subject any person to hatred, contempt or ridicule, or to impair his credit or business repute; or

(4) take or withhold action as an official, or cause an official to take or withhold action; or

(5) bring about or continue a strike, boycott or other collective unofficial action, if the property is not demanded or received for the benefit of the group in whose interest the actor purports to act; or

(6) testify or provide information or withhold testimony or information with respect to another's legal claim or defense; or

(7) inflict any other harm which would not benefit the actor.

It is an affirmative defense to prosecution based on paragraphs (2), (3) or (4) that the property obtained by threat of accusation, exposure, lawsuit or other invocation of official action was honestly claimed as restitution or indemnification for harm done in the circumstances to which such accusation, exposure, lawsuit or other official action relates, or as compensation for property or lawful services.

SECTION 223.5. THEFT OF PROPERTY LOST, MISLAID, OR DELIVERED BY MISTAKE

A person who comes into control of property of another that he knows to have been lost, mislaid, or delivered under a mistake as to the nature or amount of the property or the identity of the recipient is guilty of theft if, with purpose to deprive the owner thereof, he fails to take reasonable measures to restore the property to a person entitled to have it.

SECTION 223.6. RECEIVING STOLEN PROPERTY

(1) *Receiving.* A person is guilty of theft if he purposely receives, retains, or disposes of movable property of another knowing that it has been stolen, or believing that it has probably been stolen, unless the property is received, retained, or disposed with purpose to restore it to the owner. "Receiving" means acquiring possession, control or title, or lending on the security of the property.

(2) *Presumption of Knowledge.* The requisite knowledge or belief is presumed in the case of a dealer who:

(a) is found in possession or control of property stolen from two or more persons on separate occasions; or

(b) has received stolen property in another transaction within the year preceding the transaction charged; or

(c) being a dealer in property of the sort received, acquires it for a consideration which he knows is far below its reasonable value.

"Dealer" means a person in the business of buying or selling goods including a pawnbroker.

SECTION 223.7. THEFT OF SERVICES

(1) A person is guilty of theft if he purposely obtains services which he knows are available only for compensation, by deception or threat, or by false token or other means to avoid payment for the service. "Services" includes labor, professional services, transportation, telephone or other public service, accommodation in hotels, restaurants or elsewhere, admission to exhibitions, use of vehicles or other movable property. Where compensation for service is ordinarily paid immediately upon the rendering for such service, as is the case of hotels and restaurants, refusal to pay or absconding without payment or offer to pay gives rise to a presumption that the service was obtained by deception as to intention to pay.

(2) A person commits theft if, having control over the disposition of services of others, to which he is not entitled, he knowingly diverts such services to his own benefit or to the benefit of another not entitled thereto.

Section 223.8. [*Omitted*]

Section 223.9. Unauthorized Use of Automobiles and Other Vehicles

A person commits a misdemeanor if he operates another's automobile, airplane, motorcycle, motorboat, or other motor propelled vehicle without consent of the owner. It is an affirmative defense to prosecution under this Section that the actor reasonably believed that the owner would have consented to the operation had he known of it.

Article 224. Forgery and Fraudulent Practices

Section 224.0. Definitions

In this Article, the definitions given in Section 223.0 apply unless a different meaning plainly is required.

Section 224.1. Forgery

(1) *Definition.* A person is guilty of forgery if, with purpose to defraud or injure anyone, or with knowledge that he is facilitating a fraud or injury to be perpetrated by anyone, the actor:

(a) alters any writing of another without his authority; or

(b) makes, completes, executes, authenticates, issues or transfers any writing so that it purports to be the act of another who did not authorize that act, or to have been executed at a time or place or in a numbered sequence other than was in fact the case, or to be a copy of an original when no such original existed; or

(c) utters any writing which he knows to be forged in a manner specified in paragraphs (a) or (b).

"Writing" includes printing or any other method of recording information, money, coins, tokens, stamps, seals, credit cards, badges, trade-marks, and other symbols of value, right, privilege, or identification.

(2) *Grading.* Forgery is a felony of the second degree if the writing is or purports to be part of an issue of money, securities, postage or revenue stamps, or other instruments issued by the government, or part of an issue of stock, bonds or other instruments representing interests in or claims against any property or enterprise. Forgery is a felony of the third degree if the writing is or purports to be a will, deed, contract, release, commercial instrument, or other document evidencing, creating, transferring, altering, terminating, or otherwise affecting legal relations. Otherwise forgery is a misdemeanor.

SECTIONS 224.2.B224.4. [*Omitted*]

SECTION 224.5. BAD CHECKS

A person who issues or passes a check or similar sight order for the payment of money, knowing that it will not be honored by the drawee, commits a misdemeanor. For the purposes of this Section as well as in any prosecutions for theft committed by means of a bad check, an issuer is presumed to know that the check or order (other than a postdated check or order) would not be paid if:

(1) the issuer had no account with the drawee at the time the check or order was issued; or

(2) payment was refused by the drawee for lack of funds, upon presentation within 30 days after issue, and the issuer failed to make good within 10 days after receiving notice of that refusal.

SECTION 224.6. CREDIT CARDS

A person commits an offense if he uses a credit card for the purpose of obtaining property or services with knowledge that:

(1) the card is stolen or forged;

(2) the card has been revoked or cancelled; or

(3) for any other reason his use of the card is unauthorized by the issuer.

It is an affirmative defense to prosecution under paragraph (3) if the actor proves by a preponderance of the evidence that he had the purpose and ability to meet all obligations to the issuer arising out of his use of the card. "Credit card" means a writing, or other evidence of an undertaking to pay for property or services delivered or rendered to or upon the order of a designated person or bearer. An offense under this Section is a felony of the third degree if the value of the property or services secured or sought to be secured by means of the credit card exceeds $500; otherwise it is a misdemeanor.

SECTIONS 224.7.B224.14. [*Omitted*]

OFFENSES AGAINST THE FAMILY

Article 230. Offenses Against the Family

SECTION 230.1. BIGAMY AND POLYGAMY

(1) *Bigamy.* A married person is guilty of bigamy, a misdemeanor, if he contracts or purports to contract another marriage, unless at the time of the subsequent marriage:

(a) the actor believes that the prior spouse is dead; or

(b) the actor and the prior spouse have been living apart for five consecutive years throughout which the prior spouse was not known by the actor to be alive; or

(c) a Court has entered a judgment purporting to terminate or annul any prior disqualifying marriage, and the actor does not know that judgment to be invalid; or

(d) the actor reasonably believes that he is legally eligible to remarry.

(2) *Polygamy.* A person is guilty of polygamy, a felony of the third degree, if he marries or cohabits with more than one spouse at a time in purported exercise of the right of plural marriage. The offense is a continuing one until all cohabitation and claim of marriage with more than one spouse terminates. This section does not apply to parties to a polygamous marriage, lawful in the country of which they are residents or nationals, while they are in transit through or temporarily visiting this State.

(3) *Other Party to Bigamous or Polygamous Marriage.* A person is guilty of bigamy or polygamy, as the case may be, if he contracts or purports to contract marriage with another knowing that the other is thereby committing bigamy or polygamy.

Section 230.2. Incest

A person is guilty of incest, a felony of the third degree, if he knowingly marries or cohabits or has sexual intercourse with an ancestor or descendant, a brother or sister of the whole or half blood [or an uncle, aunt, nephew or niece of the whole blood]. "Cohabit" means to live together under the representation or appearance of being married. The relationships referred to herein include blood relationships without regard to legitimacy, and relationship of parent and child by adoption.

Section 230.3. [*Omitted*]

Section 230.4. Endangering Welfare of Children

A parent, guardian, or other person supervising the welfare of a child under 18 commits a misdemeanor if he knowingly endangers the child's welfare by violating a duty of care, protection or support.

Section 230.5. Persistent Non-support

A person commits a misdemeanor if he persistently fails to provide support which he can provide and which he knows he is legally obliged to provide to a spouse, child or other dependent.

OFFENSES AGAINST PUBLIC ADMINISTRATION

Article 240. Bribery and Corrupt Influence

SECTION 240.0. DEFINITIONS

In Articles 240B243, unless a different meaning plainly is required:

(1) "benefit" means gain or advantage, or anything regarded by the beneficiary as gain or advantage, including benefit to any other person or entity in whose welfare he is interested, but not an advantage promised generally to a group or class of voters as a consequence of public measures which a candidate engages to support or oppose;

(2) "government" includes any branch, subdivision or agency of the government of the State or any locality within it;

(3) "harm" means loss, disadvantage or injury, or anything so regarded by the person affected, including loss, disadvantage or injury to any other person or entity in whose welfare he is interested;

(4) "official proceeding" means a proceeding heard or which may be heard before any legislative, judicial, administrative or other governmental agency or official authorized to take evidence under oath, including any referee, hearing examiner, commissioner, notary or other person taking testimony or deposition in connection with any such proceeding;

(5) "party official" means a person who holds an elective or appointive post in a political party in the United States by virtue of which he directs or conducts, or participates in directing or conducting party affairs at any level of responsibility;

(6) "pecuniary benefit" is benefit in the form of money, property, commercial interests or anything else the primary significance of which is economic gain;

(7) "public servant" means any officer or employee of government, including legislators and judges, and any person participating as juror, advisor, consultant or otherwise, in performing a governmental function; but the term does not include witnesses;

(8) "administrative proceeding" means any proceeding, other than a judicial proceeding, the outcome of which is required to be based on a record or documentation prescribed by law, or in which law or regulation is particularized in application to individuals.

SECTION 240.1. BRIBERY IN OFFICIAL AND POLITICAL MATTERS

A person is guilty of bribery, a felony of the third degree, if he offers, confers or agrees to confer upon another, or solicits, accepts or agrees to accept from another:

(1) any pecuniary benefit as consideration for the recipient's decision, opinion, recommendation, vote or other exercise of discretion as a public servant, party official or voter; or

(2) any benefit as consideration for the recipient's decision, vote, recommendation or other exercise of official discretion in a judicial or administrative proceeding; or

(3) any benefit as consideration for a violation of a known legal duty as public servant or party official.

It is no defense to prosecution under this Section that a person whom the actor sought to influence was not qualified to act in the desired way whether because he had not yet assumed office, or lacked jurisdiction, or for any other reason.

SECTIONS 240.2.B240.7. [*Omitted*]

Article 241. Perjury and Other Falsification in Official Matters

SECTION 241.0. DEFINITIONS

In this Article, unless a different meaning plainly is required:

(1) the definitions give in Section 240.0 apply; and

(2) "statement" means any representation, but includes a representation of opinion, belief or other state of mind only if the representation clearly relates to state of mind apart from or in addition to any facts which are the subject of the representation.

SECTION 241.1. PERJURY

(1) *Offense Defined.* A person is guilty of perjury, a felony of the third degree, if in any official proceeding he makes a false statement under oath or equivalent affirmation, or swears or affirms the truth of a statement previously made, when the statement is material and he does not believe it to be true.

(2) *Materiality.* Falsification is material, regardless of the admissibility of the statement under rules of evidence, if it could have affected the course or outcome of the proceeding. It is no defense that the declarant mistakenly believed the falsification to be immaterial. Whether a falsification is material in a given factual situation is a question of law.

(3) *Irregularities No Defense.* It is not a defense to prosecution under this Section that the oath or affirmation was administered or taken in an irregular manner or that the declarant was not competent to make the statement. A document purporting to be made upon oath or affirmation at any time when the actor presents it as being so verified shall be deemed to have been duly sworn or affirmed.

(4) *Retraction.* No person shall be guilty of an offense under this Section if he retracted the falsification in the course of the proceeding in which it was made before it became manifest that the falsification was or would be exposed and before the falsification substantially affected the proceeding.

(5) *Inconsistent Statements.* When the defendant made inconsistent statements under oath or equivalent affirmation, both having been made within the period of the statute of limitations, the prosecution may proceed by setting forth the inconsistent statements in a single count alleging in the alternative that one or the other was false and not believed by the defendant. In such case it shall not be necessary for the prosecution to prove which statement was false but only that one or the other was false and not believed by the defendant to be true.

(6) *Corroboration.* No person shall be convicted of an offense under this Section where proof of falsity rests solely upon contradiction by testimony of a single person other than the defendant.

SECTIONS 241.2.B241.9. [*Omitted*]

Article 242. Obstructing Governmental Operations; Escapes

SECTIONS 242.0.B242.1. [*Omitted*]

SECTION 242.2. RESISTING ARREST OR OTHER LAW ENFORCEMENT

A person commits a misdemeanor if, for the purpose of preventing a public servant from effecting a lawful arrest or discharging any other duty, the person creates a substantial risk of bodily injury to the public servant or anyone else, or employs means justifying or requiring substantial force to overcome the resistance.

SECTION 242.3. HINDERING APPREHENSION OR PROSECUTION

A person commits an offense if, with purpose to hinder the apprehension, prosecution, conviction or punishment of another for crime, he:

(1) harbors or conceals the other; or

(2) provides or aids in providing a weapon, transportation, disguise or other means of avoiding apprehension or effecting escape; or

(3) conceals or destroys evidence of the crime, or tampers with a witness, informant, document or other source of information, regardless of its admissibility in evidence; or

(4) warns the other of impending discovery or apprehension, except that this paragraph does not apply to a warning given in connection with an effort to bring another into compliance with law; or

(5) volunteers false information to a law enforcement officer.

The offense is a felony of the third degree if the conduct which the actor knows has been charged or is liable to be charged against the person aided would constitute a felony of the first or second degree. Otherwise it is a misdemeanor.

Sections 242.4.B242.5. [*Omitted*]

Section 242.6. Escape

(1) *Escape.* A person commits an offense if he unlawfully removes himself from official detention or fails to return to official detention following temporary leave granted for a specific purpose or limited period. "Official detention" means arrest, detention in any facility for custody of persons under charge or conviction of crime or alleged or found to be delinquent, detention for extradition or deportation, or any other detention for law enforcement purposes; but "official detention" does not include supervision of probation or parole, or constraint incidental to release on bail.

(2) *Permitting or Facilitating Escape.* A public servant concerned in detention commits an offense if he knowingly or recklessly permits an escape. Any person who knowingly causes or facilitates an escape commits an offense.

(3) *Effect of Legal Irregularity in Detention.* Irregularity in bringing about or maintaining detention, or lack of jurisdiction of the committing or detaining authority, shall not be a defense to prosecution under this Section if the escape is from a prison or other custodial facility or from detention pursuant to commitment by official proceedings. In the case of other detention, irregularity or lack of jurisdiction shall be a defense only if:

(a) the escape involved no substantial risk of harm to the person or property of anyone other than the detainee; or

(b) the detaining authority did not act in good faith under color of law.

(4) *Grading of Offenses.* An offense under this Section is a felony of the third degree where:

(a) the actor was under arrest for or detained on a charge of felony or following conviction of crime; or

(b) the actor employs force, threat, deadly weapon or other dangerous instrumentality to effect the escape; or

(c) a public servant concerned in detention of persons convicted of crime purposely facilitates or permits an escape from a detention facility.

Otherwise an offense under this section is a misdemeanor.

Sections 242.7.B242.8. [*Omitted*]

Article 243. Abuse of Office [*Omitted*]

OFFENSES AGAINST PUBLIC ORDER AND DECENCY

Article 250. Riot, Disorderly Conduct, and Related Offenses

SECTION 250.1. Riot; Failure to Disperse

(1) *Riot.* A person is guilty of riot, a felony of the third degree, if he participates with [two] or more others in a course of disorderly conduct:

(a) with the purpose to commit or facilitate the commission of a felony or misdemeanor;

(b) with purpose to prevent or coerce official action; or

(c) when the actor or any other participant to the knowledge of the actor uses or plans to use a firearm or other deadly weapon.

(2) *Failure of Disorderly Persons to Disperse upon Official Order.* Where [three] or more persons are participating in a course of disorderly conduct likely to cause substantial harm or serious inconvenience, annoyance or alarm, a peace officer or other public servant engaged in executing or enforcing the law may order the participants and others in the immediate vicinity to disperse. A person who refuses or knowingly fails to obey such order commits a misdemeanor.

SECTION 250.2. DISORDERLY CONDUCT

(1) *Offense Defined.* A person is guilty of disorderly conduct if, with purpose to cause public inconvenience, annoyance or alarm, or recklessly creating a risk thereof, he:

(a) engages in fighting or threatening, or in violent or tumultuous behavior; or

(b) makes unreasonable noise or offensively coarse utterance, gesture or display, or addresses abusive language to any person present; or

(c) creates a hazardous or physically offensive condition by any act which serves no legitimate purpose of the actor.

"Public" means affecting or likely to affect persons in a place to which the public or a substantial group has access; among the places included are highways, transport facilities, schools, prisons, apartment houses, places of business or amusement, or any neighborhood.

(2) *Grading.* An offense under this section is a petty misdemeanor if the actor's purpose is

to cause substantial harm or serious inconvenience, or if he persists in disorderly conduct after reasonable warning or request to desist. Otherwise disorderly conduct is a violation.

SECTIONS 250.3.B250.4. [*Omitted*]

SECTION 250.5. PUBLIC DRUNKENNESS; DRUG INCAPACITATION

A person is guilty of an offense if he appears in any public place manifestly under the influence of alcohol, narcotics or other drug, not therapeutically administered, to the degree that he may endanger himself or other persons or property, or annoy persons in his vicinity. An offense under this Section constitutes a petty misdemeanor if the actor has been convicted hereunder twice before within a period of one year. Otherwise the offense constitutes a violation.

SECTION 250.6. LOITERING OR PROWLING

A person commits a violation if he loiters or prowls in a place, at a time, or in a manner not usual for law-abiding individuals under circumstances that warrant alarm for the safety of persons or property in the vicinity. Among the circumstances which may be considered in determining whether such alarm is warranted is the fact that the actor takes flight upon appearance of a peace officer, refuses to identify himself, or manifestly endeavors to conceal himself or any object. Unless flight by the actor or other circumstance makes it impracticable, a peace officer shall prior to any arrest for an offense under this Section afford the actor an opportunity to dispel any alarm which would otherwise be warranted, by requesting him to identify himself and explain his presence and conduct. No person shall be convicted of an offense under this Section if the peace officer did not comply with the preceding sentence, or if it appears at trial that the explanation given by the actor was true and, if believed by the peace officer at the time, would have dispelled the alarm.

SECTIONS 250.7.B250.12. [*Omitted*]

Article 251. Public Indecency

SECTION 251.1. OPEN LEWDNESS

A person commits a petty misdemeanor if he does any lewd act which he knows is likely to be observed by others who would be affronted or alarmed.

SECTION 251.2. PROSTITUTION AND RELATED OFFENSES

(1) *Prostitution.* A person is guilty of prostitution, a petty misdemeanor, if he or she:

(a) is an inmate of a house of prostitution or otherwise engages in sexual activity as a business; or

(b) loiters in or within view of any public place for the purpose of being hired to engage in sexual activity.

"Sexual activity" includes homosexual and other deviate sexual relations. A "house of prostitution" is any place where prostitution or promotion of prostitution is regularly carried on by one person under the control, management or supervision of another. An "inmate" is a person who engages in prostitution in or through the agency of a house of prostitution. "Public place" means any place to which the public or any substantial group thereof has access.

(2) *Promoting Prostitution.* A person who knowingly promotes prostitution of another commits a misdemeanor or felony as provided in Subsection (3). The following acts shall, without limitation of the foregoing, constitute promoting prostitution:

(a) owning, controlling, managing, supervising or otherwise keeping, alone or in association with others, a house of prostitution or a prostitution business; or

(b) procuring an inmate for a house of prostitution or a place in a house of prostitution for one who would be an inmate; or

(c) encouraging, inducing, or otherwise purposely causing another to become or remain a prostitute; or

(d) soliciting a person to patronize a prostitute; or

(e) procuring a prostitute for a patron; or

(f) transporting a person into or within this state with purpose to promote that person's engaging in prostitution, or procuring or paying for transportation with that purpose; or

(g) leasing or otherwise permitting a place controlled by the actor, alone or in association with others, to be regularly used for prostitution or the promotion of prostitution, or failure to make reasonable effort to abate such use by ejecting the tenant, notifying law enforcement authorities, or other legally available means; or

(h) soliciting, receiving, or agreeing to receive any benefit for doing or agreeing to do anything forbidden by this Subsection.

(3) *Grading of Offenses Under Subsection (2).* An offense under Subsection (2) constitutes a felony of the third degree if:

(a) the offense falls within paragraph (a), (b) or (c) of Subsection (2); or

(b) the actor compels another to engage in or promote prostitution; or

(c) the actor promotes prostitution of a child under 16, whether or not he is aware of the child's age; or

(d) the actor promotes prostitution of his wife, child, ward or any person for whose care, protection or support he is responsible.

Otherwise the offense is a misdemeanor.

(4) *Presumption From Living off Prostitutes.* A person, other than the prostitute or the prostitute's minor child or other legal dependent incapable of self-support, who is supported in whole or substantial part by the proceeds of prostitution is presumed to be knowingly promoting prostitution in violation of Subsection (2).

(5) *Patronizing Prostitutes.* A person commits a violation if he hires a prostitute to engage in sexual activity with him, or if he enters or remains in a house of prostitution for the purpose of engaging in sexual activity.

(6) *Evidence.* On the issue whether a place is a house of prostitution the following shall be admissible evidence: its general repute; the repute of the persons who reside in or frequent the place; the frequency, timing and duration of visits by non-residents. Testimony of a person against his spouse shall be admissible to prove offenses under this Section.

Section 251.3.B251.4. [*Omitted*]

PART III. TREATMENT AND CORRECTION [*Omitted*]

PART IV. ORGANIZATION OF CORRECTION [*Omitted*]

Index

References are to Pages